Preface

It only seems like two minutes ago I was taking over from my esteemed predecessor Terry Moore. When first commencing employment in the Magistrates' Courts Service (which is longer ago than I care to remember), I recall several members of the Bench going into court armed with their copy of A&B. In those days, the law was far less complex and the size of the book was markedly smaller. It was also possible for a magistrate, legal adviser and the practitioner to be a 'Jack of all trades', able to deal with a variety of work spanning several jurisdictions such as licensing, betting and gaming, family work, criminal, youth and others forms of civil work.

This is not the case now and the Family Justice Review, which has been spearheaded so ably by Mr Justice Ryder, is due to be published shortly. The changes to the family jurisdiction will be profound. There will be a unified court with the emphasis on specialisation for all including, it is anticipated, the magistracy. The Courts and Crime Bill, supplemented by a Children's Bill, revised secondary legislation and several Practice Directions are already on the drawing board. My advice to the proprietors has been that it is no longer feasible to maintain section D (Family Proceedings) in its present format.

After last year's respite Parliamentary activity has noticeably picked up again. New criminal legislation has come on to the statute book. Successive governments cannot resist the temptation to tinker with the statute book, aided and abetted by their advisers, who miss the point that what is being proposed has often been tried and tested before. Consider suspended custodial sentences. After the Criminal Justice Act 1991 (CJA 1991), such sentences could only be imposed if there were 'exceptional circumstances'. As a result suspended sentences fell into desuetude until a new sentencing regime was introduced by the CJA 2003. However, associated with the new community order regime, it is incumbent on the sentencer to attach at least one community requirement to the order. Now we have come full circle. The Legal Aid, Sentencing and Punishment of Offenders Act 2012 (LASPOA 2012) will confer a discretion to attach a community requirement.

Staying with the same theme and to emphasise my point, here is an extract from a recent judgment handed down by the President of the Queen's Bench Division:

'This is yet another case in which this court is compelled to warn of the dangers associated with the complexities of criminal justice legislation. In the present case that warning arises in two different respects. First, the complexities have caused difficulties for judges, court staff, prosecution and defence advocates and legal advisers, and defendants. Those difficulties could be very substantially reduced if the patchwork of criminal justice legislation were overhauled and replaced.' (*R v Iles* [2012] EWHC Crim 1610).

It is anticipated that various Parts of LASPOA 2012 will be brought into force towards the end of 2012. Section 60 makes subtle changes to compensation orders; s 174 of the CJA 2003 (reasons for sentence) is re-enacted in a simplified form, but only for adult offenders; s 62 requires courts to treat hostility towards another based on transgender identity as an aggravating factor. Section 63 makes a number of detailed changes to the duration of community orders and requirements. Again we have come full circle; courts will have power to deal with breach of a community order by means of a fine, without prejudice to the continuance of the order. Other changes include: crediting time served in custody on remand; early release; recall to custody; the creation of new offences, defence costs and diversion. In anticipation of those changes, several sections of Anthony & Berryman highlight the changes by referring the reader to the relevant section or schedule.

Before leaving the subject of LASPOA 2012, there are two other topics to mention, legal aid and bail. As far as the former is concerned, Part 1 of the Act will fundamentally alter the nature of the legal aid scheme in England and Wales. Instead of legal aid being available in all areas of law, unless there is a specific exemption, services will be available only for those areas of law expressly included in the statutory provisions. It is anticipated that the changes will take place on or after April 2013. Turning to the latter (bail), a number of procedural issues are affected by Part 3 of LASPOA 2012. The objective is to reduce the prison population. It gives me no pleasure to observe that the Bail Act 1976 was once a statute of great clarity, but with the proposed changes, obfuscation is the order of the day.

The legislature seeks to exercise a modicum of procedural 'control' by reference to rules and regulations. The Criminal Procedure Rules (CPR) is a case in point. Speaking as an editor it was, to say the least, irritating to have spent time updating the text by reference to the CPR (Amendment) Rules 2011, only for an elongated 2012 version to supplant them. The new rules come into force on 1 October 2012. The new rules do not affect any right or duty that existed under the CPR 2011. As a taster here are some of the changes:

'The numbering of the 2011 rules has been maintained. A new Part 19 is substituted for Parts 19 (bail) and 20 (custody time limits), and a new

Part 64 (appeal to the High Court by way of case stated) is also substituted. The changes in the two new parts are cosmetic, save that there is now a requirement that notice of an application to a magistrates' court to state a case must be given to the other party, who must be allowed an opportunity to make representations about it (r.64.1).

There are further amendments to the rules in Parts 2 (understanding and applying the rules), 4 (service of documents), 6 (investigation orders), 9 (allocation and sending for trial), 10 (committal for trial), 16 (reporting, etc, restrictions), 18 (warrants for arrest, detention or imprisonment), 27 (witness statements), 34 (hearsay evidence), 37 (trial and sentence in a magistrates' court), 41 (retrial following acquittal for serious offence), 42 (sentencing procedure in special cases), 50 (civil behaviour orders after verdict or finding), 52 (enforcement of fines and other orders for payment), 57 (Proceeds of Crime Act 2002: rules applicable to all proceedings), 58 (2002 Act: rules applicable only to confiscation proceedings) and 63 (appeal to the Crown Court). Amendments that merely consist of minor drafting improvements or consequential changes are not detailed further, but there are more substantial changes to note.'

The work of the Sentencing Council continues. Having assimilated into the 2012 edition a new format involving offences of violence (assaults), followed by burglary, changes to the Misuse of Drugs guidelines came into force during the Spring of 2012 followed by prosecutions relating to dangerous dogs (August 2012). The Council has just published a proposed timetable or workplan. Although the timeframe cannot be absolutely guaranteed the proposed publication dates are:

Sex offences – draft guideline for consultation by end of 2012, definitive guideline published by end of 2013, implementation early 2014.
Environmental offences – draft guideline for consultation early 2013, definitive guideline by end of 2013, implementation early 2014. (There is likely to be training required for the introduction of this guideline as it will set the approach to be taken to corporate fines to be replicated in other offence-specific guidelines involving corporate offending.)
Theft – draft guideline early 2013, definitive guideline by end of 2013, implementation early 2014.
Fraud – draft guideline summer 2013, definitive guideline early 2014, implementation summer 2014.
Robbery – draft guideline late 2013, definitive guideline summer 2014, implementation late 2014.
Youth court guidelines – research currently being conducted with magistrates, district judges and Crown Court judges into use of current guidance and the requirement for further guidance. Council will consider findings of the research in 2013.

In the 21st century the emphasis shifted towards putting the needs of the victim ahead of those of the accused or defendant. This is reflected in, for example, the Victims Surcharge. This was a flat rate charge which only applied to those offenders where a fine was imposed. One can well understand the logic in extending a surcharge to others forms of sentence. At para **B[33.4]**, for ease of reference, I have included a chart which sets out those changes which relate only to a magistrates' court. Purely an observation, but I cannot understand the thinking behind making surcharge orders for offenders sentenced in the Crown Court to lengthy custodial sentences or even life imprisonment. What seems to have been overlooked is that offenders sentenced to imprisonment can apply to the enforcing court to have their outstanding financial penalties lodged.

In last year's edition at para **A[41.3]**, I questioned the decision of the Court of Appeal in *R v Major* [2010] EWCA Crim 3016, where it was held, inter alia, that a restraining order was a civil order and the civil standard of proof applied. Twelve months on I see no need to adjust my stance. *R v Major* was wrongly decided and takes no account of binding precedent: *R (McCann) v Crown Court at Manchester* [2002] UKHL 39. It is interesting that in the recent decision: *Metropolitan Police Comr v Ebanks* [2012] All ER (D) 45 (Jul), DC, it was held that the standard of proof on an application for a risk of sexual harm order under the Sexual Offences Act 2003 s 123(4) was the criminal standard of proof. The sooner the Court of Appeal revisits its decision in *R v Major*, the better.

The law is as stated as 1 October 2012 unless otherwise indicated. As ever I have proof read the text in an effort to eradicate any substantive or typographical errors. Any errors are nonetheless solely attributable to me.

F G Davies

Deputy Justices' Clerk, Cambridgeshire, October 2012

Contents

Preface to the 2013 edition   **iii**

Table of statutes   **ix**

Table of statutory instruments   **xxix**

Table of cases   **xxxv**

A CRIMINAL OFFENCES DEALT WITH IN MAGISTRATES' COURTS   **1**

Index to criminal offences and table of maximum penalties   **2**

B SENTENCING (INCLUDING ENFORCEMENT OF FINES)   **437**

Index to sentencing   **438**

C ROAD TRAFFIC OFFENCES   **647**

Index and penalties for road traffic offences   **648**

Speed and distance chart   **657**

Braking and stopping distances   **658**

Endorsement and disqualification   **660**

D FAMILY PROCEEDINGS   **803**

Index to family proceedings   **804**

E THE YOUTH COURT   **911**

F LIQUOR LICENSING   **929**

G   BETTING AND GAMING LICENSING   941

H   COUNCIL TAX   945

I   COURT ROOM PROCEDURE   955

J   REMANDS IN CUSTODY AND BAIL   1013

K   JUSTICES IN THE CROWN COURT   1037

L   THE ROLE OF THE JUSTICES' CLERK   1045

M   APPLICATIONS TO A JUSTICE   1053

General index   1075

Table of Statutes

Paragraph references printed in **bold** type indicate where the Statute is set out in part or in full.

A

Access to Justice Act 1999
.... B 20.19; L 1.19
s 14 .... I 7.2
Sch 3 .... I 7.2
para 5(2)(d) .... I 7.7
Adoption Act 1976
.... D 19.6
s 18 .... D 18.3
Adoption and Children Act 2002
... D 18, D 18.1, D 18.35
s 1 .... D 18.6, D 18.17
(1) .... D 18.15
(2) ..... D 18.15, D 18.19
(3) .... D 18.18
(4) .... D 18.19
(6) .... D 18.18
8 .... D 18.4
19 .... D 18.2
21 .... D 18.3
22 ...... D 18.2, D 18.5, D 18.15
26 .... D 18.4, D 18.17
29(3)–(5) .... D 18.4
(3) .... D 18.30
(5) .... D 18.30
51(2) .... D 18.10
52 .... D 18.3, D 18.15
(1) .... D 18.16
54 .... D 18.39, D 18.40, D 18.44
56 .... D 18.39, D 18.40
57 .... D 18.39
58 .... D 18.39, D 18.41
59–79 .... D 18.39

Adoption and Children Act 2002 – *cont.*
s 60 .... D 18.44
61–65 .... D 18.39
83(1) .... D 18.30
84 .... D 18.30
109 .... D 18.18
115 .... D 18.33
122 .... D 18.6
Animal Welfare Act 2006
s 1 .... A 5.2
2 .... A 5.2
4(1) .... A 5.1, A 5.2
(2) .... A 5.1
5 .... A 5.2
6 .... A 5.2
8(1) .... A 5.1
9 .... A 5.1
(1) .... A 5.1
31(2) .... A 5.2
33, 34 .... A 5.4
37 .... A 5.4
43 .... A 5.4
Anti Social Behaviour Act 2003
Pt 1 (ss 1–11) .... I 7.1A
s 2 .... A 84.37
(3)(a), (b) .... A 26.12
(6) .... A 26.12
4 .... A 26.12
5(4), (5) .... A 26.12
6(1), (2) .... A 26.12
Pt 1A (ss 11A–11I)
.... A 26.12, A 84.37
s 11A (7)(a) .... A 84.37
20 .... A.1; B 37; D 17.5
26 .... B 37A.1

Anti Social Behaviour Act 2003 –
cont.
  s 40 ..... A 26.12, A 84.7, A
                84.37
Anti-terrorism, Crime and Secu-
    rity Act 2001
  s 108(1), (2) .... A 89.8

B

Bail Act 1976 ...... A 81.17; B
                16.7; J 1.6, J 1.2
  s 3AA .... J 1.65
  6 .... B 16.20
    (1), (2) .... A 10.1, 10.3
    (6) .... A 10.2
      (a), (b) .... J 1.91
  6A, 6B .... J 1.62
  6D .... J 1.62
  7 .... I 6.19
    (4), (5) .... J 1.92
    (5A) .... **J 1.92**
  Sch 1 .... J 1.26
  Pt I
    para 6 .... J 1.2
          6A .... J 1.62
Bail (Amendment) Act 1993
    .... J 1.76
Banking and Financial Dealings
    Act 1971..... B 54.3, B 55.3
Betting, Gaming and Lotteries
    Act 1963............. G 1.1
Birth and Deaths Registration
    Act 1953........... D 18.15
Bribery Act 2010
    .... A 89.4
  s 1 ... A 89.1, A 89.5, A 89.8
  2 ... A 89.1, A 89.8
    (2)–(8) .... A 89.6
  3 . A 89.5, A 89.6, A 97.10
    (3)–(5) .... A 89.8, A 97.9
  4 . A 89.5, A 89.6, A 97.10
  5 .... A 89.5
    (2), (3) .... A 97.10
  6, 7 .... A 89.1, A 89.7

C

Care Standards Act 2000
    .... B 17.10, B 50.17
Child Abduction Act 1984
    .... D 16.1, D 16.5
Child Maintenance and Other
    Payments Act 2008
    .... D 7.1, D 7.47
Children Act 1989
    ... B 20.24; D 1.1, D 1.2,
      D 1.10, D 1.18, D 2, D 2.7,
      D 3.1, D 4.4, D 5.7, D
      5.9,D 9.1, D 18.4, D 18.8,
      D 18.18, D 18.19, D
      18.34;L 1.6, L 1.19; M 1.4
  s 1 .... D 6.4
    (1) .... D 2.1, D 4.1
    (2) .... D 2.3
    (5) .... D 2.5, D 5.7
  2(1) .... D 3.3
  3(1) .... D 3.6
  4 ... D 3.3, D 3.7, D 3.8, D
                4.1
  5 .... D 3.21, D 4.1
  7 .... D 4.1
    (1) .... D 4.2
  Pt II (ss 8–16A) .... D 4.1
  8 ... D 2.4, D 3.3, D 4.3, D
      4.8, D 5, D 5.1, D 5.3, D
      5.8, D 5.16, D 5.17, D 5.28
  9 .... D 5.3, D 5.8
  10 .... D 5.3
    (a) .... D 4.9, D 6.2
  11 .... D 4.1
    (1) .... D 5.6
    (7)(b) .... D 5.20
    (8) .... D 5.16
  11A ..... D 5.17, D 5.19, D
                5.24
    (5) .... D 5.18
  11B ..... D 5.17, D 5.19, D
                5.20, D 5.24
  11C ..... D 5.17, D 5.20, D
                5.24
  11D .... D 5.17

Children Act 1989 – *cont.*
s 11E .... D 5.17, D 5.21
11F .... D 5.17
11G .... D 5.17
(3) .... D 5.21
11H .... D 5.17
(7) .... D 5.22
11I .... D 5.17, D 5.23
11J .... D 5.17
(3) .... D 5.24
(9) .... D 5.24
11K .... D 5.17
(1) .... D 5.23
11L .... D 5.17
11M, 11N . D 5.17, D 5.24
11O .... D 5.17, D 5.26
11P .... D 5.17
(1) .... D 5.23
12 .... D 5.2
14A .... D 18.33
(6)(b) .... D 18.33
(8), (9) .... D 18.33
14B–14G .... D 18.33
16 .... D 4.1, D 5.28
23(2)(a) .... B 50.16
25 .... E 3.7
31 .. D 6.2A, D 6.4, D 6.6,
D 9.18, D 18.3
(2) .... D 6.4, D 18.5
31A .... D 6.24
33(4) .... D 6.23
34 .... D 6.24
37 .... D 4.1, D 5.27
38 .... D 6.34
(6), (7) .... D 9.18
39 .... D 6.46
40 .... D 6.49
41 .... D 6.17, D 18.7
43 .... D 9.3
(11) .... D 9.7
44 .... D 9.10
(13) .... D 9.21
46 .... D 9, D 10.2
47 .... D 9.1
48 .... D 9.22
(3) .... D 9.21

Children Act 1989 – *cont.*
s 50 .... D 10
91(12) .... D 6.31
(15) .... D 6.48
94 .... D 6.48
Sch A1
Pt 2 .... D 5.24
Sch 1 .... D 4.1
Children Act 2004
s 58 .... A 15.16
Children and Adoption Act 2006
.... D 18.18
Children and Young Persons Act
1933..................... E 1
s 1 .... A 19.1
9 .... I 1B.7
33 .... B 32A.5
37 .... A 52.11, A 53.13
39 .... A 52.12, A 53.12; E
2.4; I 1B.7
30 .... E 2.4
49 .... B 32A.5
50 .... E 3.2
Children and Young Persons Act
1963..................... E 1
s 28 .... E 3.22
29 .... E 3.17A
Children and Young Persons Act
1969..................... E 1
s 12–12C .... B 38.2
23 . E 3.3, E 4.8; J 1.22A, J
1.32
25 .... E 3.7
Child Support Act 1991
s 20 .... D 1.18, D 1.19
33 .... D 7.47
39A .... D 7.47
Civil Evidence Act 1968
s 11, 12 .... D 3.21
Civil Evidence Act 1995
.... B 8.4A; H 4.1
s 2(1) .... B 55.1
Civil Partnership Act 2004
.... D 8.2

Clean Neighbourhoods and Environment Act 2005
   s 84 .... A 84.33
   Sch 1
      Para 4A .... A 84.33
Communications Act 2003
   s 126 .... A 39.3
    127 .... A 16.2
      (1) .... A 16.1
        (a) .... A 16.6
      (2) ...... A 16.1, A 16.7
    363(2), (3) .... A 61.1
Constitutional Reform Act 2005
   Sch 2
     Pt 1
      para 2(2).............. D 4.1
Contempt of Court Act 1981
     .... I 1B.8
   s 4(1), (2) .... I 1B.7
    9 .... I 1B.9
    11 .... I 1B.7
    12 .... I 3.3, I 3.4, I 3.5
     (5) .... I 3.16
Control of Pollution Act 1974
   s 62 .... A 74.2, A 74.6
Copyright, Designs and Patents Act 1988
   s 297(1) .... F 3.1
Coroners and Justice Act 2009
     .... I 6.13B; J 1.22A
   s 62 .... A 43.1, A 43.4
    63–69 .... A 43.4
   Pt 3, Ch 2 (ss 86–97)
     .... I 1B.7
   s 115 .... J 1.32
    122(2) .... I 4.4
Counter-Terrorism Act 2008
   s 41–45 .... B 52
   Sch 4 .... B 52
   Sch 5
      para 2(3) .... B 52
        7(1) .... B 52
        8 .... B 52
        15(2) .... B 52

Counter-Terrorism Act 2008 – cont.
     para 15(4)(a)
      .... B 52
Courts Act 1971
   s 52(3) .... M 3.2
Courts Act 2003
    . A 72.21; L 1.3, L 1.5, L 1.6
   s 29 .... L 1.6
    30(3) .... B 1A.1
    44 .... K 1.6
    46 .... B 1A.1
    49 .... D 1.5
    50 .... E 2.1
    51 .... A 9.4
     (3) .... A 9.6
    53 .... I 6.19
    57 .... A 9.1, A 47.5
    66 .... B 1.5
    95 .... B 33.18
    98 .... B 20.20A
   Sch 5 .... B 33.38
Courts and Legal Services Act 1990................... F 1.12
   s 56(2), (3) .... M 4.23
Crime and Disorder Act 1998
   s 1 .... B 8
    (1)(a) .... B 8.5
    (8) .... B 8.12
    (10) .... B 8.13
    1A .... B 8.9
    1C .... B 8.5, B 8.8
    2–4 .... B 8
    5(2)(b) .... A 18.19
    8 .... B 37A
    10 .... B 37A.8
     (1) .... A 18.21
     (2) .... A 18.23
     (3) .... A 18.24
    11 .... D 17A
    26A, 26B .... B 37A.1
    28 .... B 5.2B
     (1)(a) .... A 8.16, A 20.6
      (b) .... A 20.6
     (3)(b) .... A 8.16

Crime and Disorder Act 1998 –
cont.
s 28(4) .... A 8.17
29 .. A 8.2, A 8.31, A 15.2,
A 15.33, A 70.1 A 70.20;
B 5.2B
30 .... A 18.16; B 5.2B
31 .... A 20.2, A 21.3, A
21.4; B 5.2B
32 . A 41.2, A 41.4; B 5.2B
34 .... E 3.2
50 .... I 7.2
51 .... A 12.2, A 12.3, A
12.4, A 12.5, A 13.2, A
13.3, A 13.4; I 1B.11, I
4.1, I 4.8
51A(6) .... I 4.1
57 .... J 1.22A
66(4) .... B 31.2
89(2) .... B 8.13
135 .... B 8.5
Crime and Security Act 2010
s 24 .... I 7.1A
(10), (11) .... B 54.1
25 .... B 54.1; I 7.1A
(2), (3) .... B 55.1
26 .... B 54.1; I 7.1A
27 . B 54.2, B 54.3, B 55.1;
I 7.1A
28 .... B 55.1; I 7.1A
(9) .... B 55.3
29 .... B 55.1; I 7.1A
30 .. B 55.1, B 55.3; I 7.1A
Criminal Appeal Act 1968
s 9 .... A 46.5
Criminal Attempts Act 1981
s 9(1) .... A 63.1
Criminal Damage Act 1971
s 1 .... A 18.1
(2), (3) .... A 18.2
2(a) .... A 18A.1
3(a) .... A 18B.1
6 .... A 87.19
Criminal Defence Service Act
2006.... B 2.8; I 7.2; L 1.19

Criminal Justice Act 1925
.... I 1B.8
s 41 .... I 1B.8
Criminal Justice Act 1967
s 3 .... A 9.8
9 ..... B 5.55; I 6.13, I 6.17
10 .... I 6.13
91 .... A 28.2
Criminal Justice Act 1971
s 1 .... A 18.1
Criminal Justice Act 1972
s 24 .... C 6.2
Criminal Justice Act 1982
.... C 1.1
Criminal Justice Act 1988
.... A 11.4
s 39 .... A 15.1, A 15.33
40 .... I 5.7, I 5.8
41 .... I 5.7
Pt VI (ss 71–103)
.... B 19
s 139 .... A 11.1
139A .... A 11.1
160 .... A 43.1
160A .... A 43.4
Criminal Justice Act 1991
s 20A .... B 33.18
78 .... A 9.1
Sch 6 .... B 16.20
Criminal Justice Act 1993
.... B 2.10
Criminal Justice Act 2003
.... A.2.15, A 14.6, A
15.33, A 18.32, A 19.32, A
29.4; A 30.3, A 36.4, A
37.1, A 38.1, A 39.1, A
52.14, A 53.15, A 80.22; B
1A.3, B 2.1, B 3.1, B 5.4, B
5.23, B 5.33, B 5.61, B 53.3;
C 1.6; I 5; J 1.94; K 3.2; L
1.19
s 19 .... J 1.32
51, 52 .... J 1.22C
98 .... I 6.14
100 .... I 6.15
101(1)(d) .... I 6.14

Criminal Justice Act 2003 – *cont.*
s (g) .... I 6.14
114(2) .... I 6.16
142(1) .... C 16A.10
143 .... B 34.5
(2) ...... A 5.4; B 37.47
144 .... A 7.4, A 8.31, A
9.10, A 12.20, A 13.19, A
15.33, A 25.16, A 26.5, A
27.3, A27A.4, A 27B.4, A
70.20, A 72.8, A 72.8A
145, 146 .... B 5.2B
147 .... B 17.1
148 .... B 17.1
(1) .... B 33.16
(5) .... B 3.2
149 .... B 17.1
150 .... B 17.1
151 .... B 50.2
150A .... B 3.2
152 .... B 25.3
(2) ... B 17.48, B 33.16
153 .... B 37.6
(2) .... B 2.17
156 .... B 37.17
(4), (5) .... B 50.2
157 .... B 37.18
161(2) .... B 50.5
161A(1) .. B 18.1, B 20.1A,
B 33.4
164(1), (2) .... B 33.16
(4) .... B 33.16
(5) .... B 33.18
165(2) .... B 33.18
170(9) .... A 50.18
172 .... B 5.2
(1)(b) .... I 6.33
173(3), (4) .... B 17.2
174 .... A 7.4, A 8.31, A
9.10, A 12.20, A 13.19, A
15.33, A 25.16, A 26.5, A
27.3, A27A.4, A 27B.4, A
70.20, A 72.8, A 72.8A; B
5.53
(1) .... A 41.13

Criminal Justice Act 2003 – *cont.*
s 177 .. B 4.1, B 4.2, B 4.3, B
4.4, B 9.1, B 38.2
Ch 3 (ss 181–195)
.... B 26
s 181 .. B 25.6, B26.0, J 1.91
182–188 ..... B26.0; J 1.91
189(2) .... B 37.40
195 .... B 25.6, J 1.91
204(3) .... B 21.17
209 .... A 25.16, A 26.5, A
27.3, A27A.4, A 27B.4
224 .... A 7.4, A 8.31, A
12.20, A 13.19, A 15.33
A 70.20; B 16.5; E 3.18,
E 3.18A; I 4.1
225(3), (4) .... B 16.5
226(3) ... B 16.5; E 3.18, E
3.18A, E 3.18B
(4) .... B 16.5
227 .... B 16.5
228 .... B 16.5
(2) ... E 3.18A, E 3.18B
(3) .... E 3.18
229 ... A 12.20, A 13.19; B
16.5
230–236 .... B 16.5
240 .... A 7.4, A 8.31, A
9.10, A 12.20, A 13.19, A
15.33, A 25.16, A 26.5, A
27.3, A27A.4, A 27B.4, A
70.20, A 72.8, A 72.8A
(3), (4) .... B 2.20
(7) .... B 2.20
240ZA(3) .... B 2.20
240A ..... A 7.4, A 8.31, A
9.10, A 12.20, A 13.19,
A 15.33, A 25.16, A
26.5, A 27.3, A27A.4, A
27B.4, A 70.20, A 72.8,
A 72.8A
(3), (4) .... B 2.20
280(2) .... A 41.5
322 .... B 8.9
444(1A) .... D 17.5
Sch 3 .... E 3.18; I 4.1

Criminal Justice Act 2003 – *cont.*
Sch 8 .... A 17.1; B 17.17
  para 9(1)(c) .... A 17.3
Sch 10 .... B 26.0
Sch 11 .... B 26.0
Sch 12 .... A 17.1
  para 8 .... B 37.46
Sch 15 .... B 16.5
  Pt 1 .. A 2.1, A 7.1, A 8.1,
    A 8.2, A 12.1, A 13.1, A
    15.2, A 18.2, A 19.1, A
    21.4, A 41.1, A 41.2, A
    46.1, A 59.1, A 66.1, A
        67.1, A 70.2
  Pt 2 ... A 14.1, A 14.1A, A
    29.1, A 29.2, A 30.1, A
    43.1, A 44.1, A 52.1, A
       53.2, A 68.1
Sch 15A .... B 16.5
Sch 25 .... A 79.1
Sch 26 .... D 17.5; F 2.1
Sch 32
  para 106 .... B 38.2
Sch 34 .... B 37A, B 42.1
Sch 37
  Pt 4 .... J 1.94
  Pt 9 .... A 79.1
Criminal Justice and Court Services Act 2000
s 12 .... D19.6
Criminal Justice and Immigration Act 2008........ A 43.3
s 1(4)(a)–(c) .... B 50.6
21 .... B 2.20
38 .... A 17.3
52 .... J 1.6, J 1.26
53 .... B 16.2
54 .... I 6.19
63–66 .... A 14.1A
76(3)–(8) .... A 8.20
Pt 7 (ss 98–117) ...... B 51.1
s 98(1)(b) .... B 51.1
99(4) .... B 51.2
100, 101 .... B 51.3
102 .... B 51.4
103 .... B 51.5

Criminal Justice and Immigration
  Act 2008 – *cont.*
s 104 .... B 51.6
105, 106 .... B 51.7
107–112 .... B 51.4
113(8) .... B 51.8
119, 120 .... A 74.1
Sch 1
  Pt 1 .... B 50.3
  para.4................ B 50.4
  Pt 2
  para 6,.7............. B 50.4
    .8...... B 50.4, B 50.16
    9–15............. B 50.4
    16..... B 50.4, B 50.16
    17................ B 50.4
    18..... B 50.4, B 50.15
    19–25........... B 50.4
    26.. B 50.4, B 50.12, B
        50.13
  Pt 4
  para 32(2)........... B 50.23
Sch 2
  Pt 3
  para 11(7.)........... B 50.25
    12.............. B 50.23
  Pt 4
  para 13, 14........ B 50.23
Sch 12 .... J 1.26
  para 24 .... B 50.5
Sch 26
  para 40, 45 .... B 37.55
Criminal Justice and Police Act
  2001
s 39, 40 .... A 69.2
42A .... A 41.5
130 .... E 4.8
Criminal Justice and Public Order Act 1994....... A 53.14
s 25(3) .... J 1.32
34–37 .... I 6.2, I 6.22
38 .... I 6.2
51 .... A 69.2
  (1) .... A 69.1
  (2) .... A 69.2
  (7) .... A 69.7

Criminal Justice and Public Order
    Act 1994 – *cont.*
    s 166 .... A 34.4
    167 .... A 56.1
    (5) .... A 56.2
Criminal   Justice   (Inter-
    national   Co-operation)
    Act 1990
    s 15 .... B 33.85A
Criminal Law Act 1967
    s 3 .... A 8.20, A 18.19
Criminal Procedure and Investi-
    gations Act 1996
    s 6A(1) .... I 6.2
    6C .... I 6.2
    11(2)(f)(ii) .... I 6.2
Criminal Procedure (Insanity)
    Act 1964............ B 51.2
Crossbows Act 1987
    .... A 64.3
Customs and Excise Manage-
    ment Act 1979...... B 34.18
    s 1(1) .... M 2.27
    8(2) .... M 2.27
    102 ...... C 47.16, C 47.21
    161A .... M 2.27
    170 .... A 4.1, A 4.23, A
                        27B.1
    (1)(a) .... B 47.2
    (2) .... A 27B.4
    179 .... A 62.5

D

Dangerous Dogs Act 1991
    .... A 72.21
    s 1(2), (3) .... A 72.8A
    3 .... A 72.20
    (1) ..... A 72.1, A 72.5, A
        72.8, A 72.8A, A 72.10,
                        A 72.16
    (3) ..... A 72.4, A 72.6, A
        72.8A, A 72.10, A 72.16
    (a) .... A 72.8
    4(1)(a) .... A 72.8, A 72.8A

Dangerous Dogs Act 1991 – *cont.*
    s 4(1)(b) ... A 72.8, A 72.8A,
                        A 72.17
    (4)(b) .... A 72.8, A 72.8A
    (1A) .... A 72.15
    (a) .... A 72.10
    4A .... A 72.15
    (4), (5) .... A 72.8, A
            72.8A, A 72.10
    10(2) .... A 72.5
Dogs Act 1871 .... A 72.21
Dogs (Protection of Livestock)
    Act 1953
    s 1 .... A 73.1
    3 .... A 73.3
Domestic Proceedings and Mag-
    istrates Court Act 1978
    .... D 1.1, D 1.18
    s 2 .... D 7.1, D 7.16
    6 .... D 7.1, D 7.9
    7 .... D 7.1, D 7.16
Domestic Violence, Crime and
    Victims Act 2004
    s 1 .... D 8.19
    4 .... D 8.2
    10 .... A 15.1, E 3.18
    12 .... A 41.13
Drugs Act 2005 .... A 23.1, A
                        26.4A
    s 9(2) .... A 23.1
    10(2) .... A 23.2
    12 .... A 23.1

E

Education Act 1996
    .... D 17.1
    s 8 .... A 49.3
    434 .... A 49.3
    444(1) .. A 49.1, A 49.3, A
                        49.4
    (1A) .... A 49.2, A 49.4
    566 .... A 49.3
    576 .... A 49.3
Environmental Protection Act
    1990

Environmental Protection Act
  1990 – *cont.*
  s 79 .... A 84.7, A 84.19
     (10) .... A 84.2
     80(4) .... A 84.17
     (6) .... A 84.17
     82 .... A 84.7, A 84.19
     (2) .... A 84.31
     87 .... A 83.18
Extradition Act 2003
     .... I 7.4

F

Family Law Act 1986
     .... D 3.16
     Pt III (ss 55–63) ...... D 19.6
     s 55A .... D 3.19
Family Law Act 1996
     .... D 1.1, D 4.1
     s 33(6) .... D 8.25
     42A(1)–(3) . A 46.1; D 8.19
     45(1) .... D 8.19
     62 .... B 54.1
     Sch 10 .... D 7.16
Family Law Reform Act 1969
     Pt III (ss 20–25) ...... D 3.16
     s 43 .... D 19.6
Family Law Reform Act 1987
     .... D 3.8
Finance Act 2000
     s 144 .... A 42.1
Firearms Act 1968
     .. A 11.3, A 33.4; B 17.6,
          B 47.2
     s 1 .... A 76.1
     2(1) .... A 88.1
     (2) .... A 88.5
     5 .... E 3.18
     8–10 .... A 76.10
     11(1) .... A 76.10
     (2)–(5) .... A 76.10
     12 .... A 76.10
     13 .... A 76.10
     (2) .... A 76.6
     18 .... A 77.6

Firearms Act 1968 – *cont.*
     s 19 .... A 33.1, A 33.4
     20(1) .... A 77.1
     (2) .... A 77.2
     21(2) .... A 76.7
     (3) .... B 10.16
     22(4) .... A 71.1
     23 .... A 71A.1
     (2) .... A 71.6
     24ZA .... A 71A.1
     46 .... M 2.4, M 2.7
     51A ...... E 3.18, E 3.18A
     58(2) .... A 76.17
Firearms Amendment Act 1988
     s 15–18 .... A 76.10
     Schedule
          para 1 .... A 76.10
Football (Disorder) Act 2000
     .... B 41
Football (Offences) Act 1991
     .... B 41.4
     s 2 .... A 34.1
     3 .... A 34.2
     4 .... A 34.3
Football Spectators Act 1989
     .... I 7.1A; B 41.18
     Pt II (ss 14–22A)
          .... B 41.2
     s 14 .... B 41
     14A .... B 41.7, B 41.19
     (5A) .... B 41.32
     14B ...... B 41.33, B 41.34
     14D .... B 41.35
     21A .... B 41.33
     22 .... B 41
     Sch 1 .... B 41.4, B 41.32
Forgery and Counterfeiting Act
     1981................... A 78.6
     s 1 .... A 78.1
     3 .... A 78.2, A 78.8
     4 .... A 78.3
Fraud Act 2006 ..... A 39.3, A
                    54.2, A 55.2
     s 1(2)(a) .. A 36.1, A 36.6, A
                    36.8

Fraud Act 2006 – *cont.*
  s 1(2)(b) .. A 36.1, A 36.2, A
                              36.8
      (c) .. A 36.1, A 36.3, A
                              36.9
  2 .... A 36.6
   (5) .... A 36.7
  3 .... A 36.8
  4 .... A 36.9
  5 .... A 36.7
  6 .... A 38.1
  7 .... A 39.1, A 39.4
   (1)(a), (b) .... A 39.3
  8 .... A 38.3, A 39.4
  11 .... A 37.1
  31–35 .... A 55.3

G

Gambling Act 2005
          .... G 1.1, G 1.2
  Pt 7 (ss 140–149)
          .... G 1.3
  Pt 8 (ss 150–213)
          .... G 1.3
  s 202–205 .... K 1.8
  206 .... G 1.3, G 1.4; K 1.8
  207 .... G 1.3
   (3) .... G 1.4
  208 .... G 1.4
Game Act 1831 ...... A 86.31
  s 2 .... A 86.6
  30 .... A 86.1
  34 .... A 86.5
  35 .... A 86.8
  41 .... A 86.2
Game Laws Amendment Act
    1960
  s 4 .... A 86.32
Game Licences Act 1860
  s 4 .... A 86.23
  11 .... A 86.7

H

Hares Act 1848 ...... A 86.25

Health and Safety at Work Act
    1974
  s 2 . A 80.3, A 80.7, A 80.19
  3 . A 80.3, A 80.7, A 80.19
   (1) .... A 80.3
  4–6 .... A 80.3, A 80.7
  33 .... A 80.8
   (1A) .... A 80.3
   (2A) ..... A 80.1, A 80.2
  42 .... A 80.16
  Sch 3A .... A 80.4
Highway Act 1835
  s 72 .... C 1.6
Highways Act 1980
  s 137 .... A 85.1; C 36.1A, C
                              36.9
Human Rights Act 1998
      .... D 7.36; I 1.1; J 1.2
  s 2(1) .... L 1.6
  Sch 1
    art 2 .... I 1.5
    3 .... I 1.5
    4(1), (2) .... I 1.5
    5 .... I 1.5, I 1.7
    6 . I 1.5, I 1.6, I 1.8, IB
                              1
     (1) . IA 1, IA 3, IB 2, I
                              3 7
     (3)(b) .... A 89.8
    7 .... I 1.5
    8 .... I 1.5
    9 .... I 1.5
    10 .... I 1.5, I 1.7
    11 .... I 1.5
Hunting Act 2004
  s 1–5 .... A 86.1
  Sch 3 .... A 86.8

I

Identity Cards Act 2006
  s 25(1) .... A 32.2A
Identity Documents Act 2010
  s 4 .... A 32.2A
   (1) .... A 32.3

Identity Documents Act 2010 –
    cont.
    s 6(1) .... A 32.1, A 32.2A
Immigration Act 1971
    .... B 23.3
    s 3(6) .... A 81.17; B 23.1
    24 .... A 81.1
        (a), (aa) .... A 81.7
        (b) .... A 81.7
            (i) .... A 81.5
    25 .... A 81.2
    25A, 25B .... A 81.2
    26 .... A 81.3
        (1)(c), (d) .... A 81.6
    26A .... A 81.3
    28(1)(a) .... A 81.6
        (c) .... A 81.6
    28D(4) .... M 2.8
Immigration and Asylum Act
    1999
    s 7 .... A 81.7
    31(1) .... A 32.2A
Insolvency Act 1986
    .... B 33.31
Interpretation Act 1978
    s 5 .... A 41.13
    32 .... C 1.1
    Sch 1 .... A 41.2; C 1.1

                    J

Justices of the Peace Act 1361
    .... B 10.21
Justices of the Peace Act 1968
    s 1(7) .... B 10.21
Justices of the Peace Act 1997
    .... L 1.6

                    L

Legal Aid, Sentencing and Pun-
    ishment of Offenders Act
    2012
    Pt 1 (ss 1–43) .... I 7.1
    13–20 .... I 7.1
    38 .... I 7.1

Legal Aid, Sentencing and Punish-
    ment of Offenders Act 2012 –
    cont.
    s 67 .... A 17.3
    90–104 .... E 3.3
    108–118 .... B 16.20
    142 .... A 11.15
    148 .... A 8.19, A 8.20
Licensed Premises (Exclusion of
    Certain Persons) Act 1980
    .... B 32
Licensing Act 1872
    s 12 .... A 28.1
Licensing Act 2003
    .. A 28.7; B 32.1, B 47.2;
        F 1, F 1.1, F 1.2; K 1.8
    s 1 .... F 1.4
    7 .... F 1.15
    10 .... F 1.15
    11 .... F 1.3
    14 .... B 32.1
    29 .... F 1.15
    51 .... F 1.14
    111 .... F 1.2
    120 .... F 1.5
    128(1) .... F 3.1
    129 .... B 47; F 3.1
        (2), (3) .... B 47.1
    131(2)(a) .... F 3.1
    141 .... A 3.1, A 3.3
        (2) .... A 3.4
    146 .... A 3.2, A 3.3
    147 .... A 3.3
    147A .... F 2.7
    161 .... F 2, F 2.5
    162, 163 .... F 2
    164, 165 ...... F 2, F 2.4
    166 .... F 2, F 2.6; K 1.8
    167 .... F 2, F 2.5
    168 .... F 2
    169 .... F 2
    169A .... F 2, F 2.7
    170, 171 .... F 2
    181 .... F 1.11, F 1.16
        (2)(b) .... F 1.14
    182 .... F 1.15

Licensing Act 2003 – *cont.*
  Sch 4 .... B 47.1
  Sch 5 .... F 1.6
Limitation Act 1980
  s 9 .... D 7.47
Lotteries and Amusements Act
  1976.................... G 1.1

M

Magistrates' Courts Act 1980
  .... A 84.37; C 1.1
  s 2 .... I 4.5; K 1.6
  3 .... E 3.18
  3B .... E 3.18B
  3C .... E 3.18B
  4 .... I 4.1, I 5.4
  4A .... E 3.18B
  5 .... I 4.1
  5B–5E .... I 5.3
  6 .... E 3.18B; I 4.1
  (2) .... L 1.19
  7 .... I 4.1
  8 .... I 4.1
  8A, 8B .... I 6.13A
  11 .... I 6.19
  12 .... I 6.26
  17, 18 .... I 4.1
  19 .... I 4.1
  (3) .... I 4.2
  20–23 .... I 4.1
  24 ..... E 3.18; I 4.1; J 1.51
  25 .... B 1.5; I 4.1
  27A .... B 1A.1
  29(2) .... B 1.5
  32(9) .... C 1.1
  33 .... I 4.5
  42 .... J 1.94
  50 .... A 84.31
  51–57 .... B 10.21
  63 .... B 54.3, B 55.3
  (3) .... D 5.25
  64 .... A 26.17, A 84.31; B
    20.23; F 1.16; M 3.2
  (1) .... M 3.2
  65 .... D 1.1

Magistrates' Courts Act 1980 –
cont.
  s 65(1)(o) .... D 1.18, D 1.19
  (2) .... D 1.18, D 2.1
  69 .... D 1.7, D 1.8
  71 .... D 1.16
  (1) .... D 1.10
  82(4) .... B 33.76
  97 .... B 55.1
  101 .... A 61.5
  108 .. I 3.16, I 6.46; K 1.8,
    K 3.1
  111 .... D 1.19; I 6.47
  111A(3)(a) .... D 1.19
  115(3) .... B 10.21
  121 .... I 1B.1
  123(2) .... I 6.23
  125 .... I 6.2B
  127 .... A 5.2; I 6.23
  133 .... B 37.40
  135 .... B 24
  142 .... B 7.4; H 3.3
  (1) .... B 7.1
  (2) .... B 7.1, B 7.2
Maintenance Order 1958
  s 4(4) .... D 7.18
Marriage Act 1949
  s 3 .... D 1.1
Matrimonial Causes Act 1973
  .... D 19.6
Mental Capacity Act 2005
  .... D 19.1, D 19.5
  s 2(1) .... D 19.2
Mental Health Act 1983
  .... B 2.23, B 26.20, B
    37.18, B 48.7; I 6.37; M
    4.18, M 4.19
  s 12 .... B 17.10; J 1.62
  35 .... B 36.21
  37 .... B 35, 36, 36.2
  (2)(a) .. B 17.10, B 50.17
  38 .... B 36.21
  41 .... B 36.10
  54(2) ..... B 17.10, B 50.17
  (3)(a) .. B 17.10, B 50.17
  135 .... M 4.17

Misuse of Drugs Act 1971
.... A 22.1, A 25.10, A
    26.4A, A 38.3, A 39.4
s 3 .... A 27B.1, A 27B.4
    4(1) .... A 27A.1
    (2) .... B 47.2
    (a), (b) . A 27.1, A 27.3
    (3) ..... A 26.1, A 26.5, A
        26.4A; B 47.2
    5(2) ..... A 22.6, A 25.1, A
        25.16; J 1.32
    (3) ..... A 22.6, A 26.1, A
        26.5; B 47.2; J 1.32
    (4)(a), (b) .... A 25.8
    6(2) .... A 27.1, A 27.3
    8 .... A 27A.1, A 27A.4
    7 .... A 25.8, A 27.2
    23(4) .... M 2.4
    27 .... A 25.18
    28 .... A 26.4B, A 27.2
    (2), (3) .... A 25.8
    37(3) .... A 25.7, A 37.3
Mobile   Telephones   (Re-
    programming) Act 2002
s 2 .... A 39.3

N

National Assistance Act 1948
s 47 .... M 4.3
National   Assistance
    (Amendment) Act 1951
s 1 .... M 4.3
Nationality, Immigration and
    Asylum Act 2002
.... A 81.3
Night Poaching Act 1828
.... A 86.31
s 1 .... A 86.9, A 86.19
    2 .... A 86.9
    9 .... A 86.10
    13 .... A 86.17
Noise Act 1996 .... A 84.33

O

Obscene Publications Act 1959
s 3 .... M 2.4
Offences Against the Person Act
    1861
s 16 .... A 59.1, A 59.4
    18 .... B 51.1
    20 ...... A 70.1, A 70.2, A
        70.5, A 70.20; B 51.1
    38 .... A 7.1, A 7.4
    44 .... A 15.21
    47 .... A 8.1, A 8.31
Official Secrets Act 1920
.... I 1B.2

P

Police Act 1861
s 89 .... A 9.10
Police Act 1996
s 89 .... A 9.1
    (2) .... A 47.4
Police and Criminal Evidence
    Act 1984.............. M 3.1
s 2(3) .... A 9.8
    8 . M 2.5, M 2.10, M 2.17,
        M 2.20A
    (1)(a)–(d) .... M 2.7
    (5) .... M 2.8
    15(6)(b) .... M 2.9
    17 .... A 9.8
    22(2)–(4) .... A 87.3
    24(2) .... A 20.18
    (4) .... A 20.18
    (5)(e) .... A 20.18
    30A .... J 1.55
    30cB .... J 1.55
    47(1E) .... J 1.56
    63B .... A 24.1, A 27.1
Police and Justice Act 2006
s 34 .... B 25.6, J 1.91
    39 .... A 43.9

Police (Property) Act 1897
. A 87.8; B 20.31, B 34.5,
B 34.16
s 1 .... A 87.1
Police Reform Act 2002
s 46 .... A 9.3, A 47.10
Powers of Criminal Courts
(Sentencing) Act 2000
.... B 16.20, B 26.1
s 1A .... B 21
1B .... B 21
(2)(c) .... B 21.20
(3) .... B 21.20
1C .... B 21, B 21.1
1D .... B 21
(2)(b) .... B 21.21
1E .... B 21
1F .... B 21
3 ... A 17.5, B 4.4, B 11, B
21.21, B 26.33, B 36.10; I
4.5
(2) .... B 16.8
3A .... B 16.5
3C .... B 4.1
4 .. B 4.1, B 4.2, B 4.4, B 5,
B 16, B 16.2, B 16.10
6 ... B 4.2, B 16.10, B 31.7,
B 50.24
8 .... B 1.3, B 50.1
10 .... B 1.1
12 .... B 31
(6) .... B 10.21
(7) .... B 31.8
13(5) .... B 31.7
16 ...... B 42, B 42.1, B 48
17 .... B 4.3
51A .... B 16.5
60 .... B 9, B 9.1
69–72 .... B 7A.1
73 .... B 38
78 ...... A 36.4, A 37.1, A
38.1, A 39.1; B 37
91 .... B 2.20; E 3.18
(3) .... E 3.18B
96 .... B 26
100 .... B 25

Powers of Criminal Courts
(Sentencing) Act 2000 – cont.
s 110 ..... A 25.3, A 26.5, A
27.3, A 27A.4, A 27B.4
111 .... A 12.4, A 12.20
116 ... B 16.20, B 37.54, B
37.55
130 .... A 72.8, A 72.8A; B
18
(2A) .... B 18.1
(4) .... B 18.6
131, 132 .... B 18
133 .... B 18, B 18.6
134 .... B 18
135 .... B 33.93
136 .... B 18
137 .... B 18
(4) .... B 33.8
138 .... B 18
143 .... B 34
146 ... C 5.5, C 5.45, C 6.2
147 .... C 6.2
148 .... B 39
150 .... B 10.21, B 42.4
Sch 7 .... B 26
Prevention of Corruption Act
1906.................... A 89.4
Prevention of Corruption Act
1916.................... A 89.4
Prevention of Crime Act 1953
.... A 9.10, A 11.8
s 1 .... A 11.1
(4) .... A 11.5
Proceeds of Crime Act 2002
... B 33.36, B 34.2; I 6.8;
M 1.8, M 3.1
s 10 .... B 19
242(2)(b) .... M 3.2
294 .... M 3.2
298(2) .... F 1.6; M 3.2
299(2) .... M 3.2
329 .... A 40.11
Prosecution of Offences Act
1985
s 16 .... B 20.1
(1) .... A 84.31

Prosecution of Offences Act 1985
  – cont.
  s 17 .... B 20.1
     (2) .... B 20.4
     18 .... B 20.1
     19 .... B 20.1, I 6.12
     19A .... I 6.12
     19B ...... B 20.20A, I 6.12
     22 .... J 1.51
Protection from Harassment Act
     1997................. A 41.10
  s 1 .... A 43.4
     (3)(a) .... A 41.10
     1A .... A 41.7
     2 .. A 41.3, A 41.6, A 41.7,
                              A 41.13
     4 .. A 41.1, A 41.2, A 41.7,
        A 41.10, A 41.13, A 53.17
        (1) .... A 41.7
     5 .... A 53.17
        (1) .... A 41.13
        (4) .... A 46.5
        (5) .... A 46.1, A 46.3
        (6) .... A 46.3
     5A(1) .... A 41.13
Protection of Animals Act 1954
  s 1(1) .... A 5.4
Protection of Children Act 1978
  s 1 .... A 43.1
     (1)(b) .... A 43.6
     5 .... A 43.11
     7(4) .... A 43.3
        (4A) .... A 43.3
Public Order Act 1986
  s 2(1) .... A 67.1
     3 .... A 2.1
     4 .... I 6.19
        (1) .... A 21.1, A21.7
           (a) .... B 41.4
     4A .... A 21.2
        (2) .... A 21.9
     5 .. A 9.5, A 20.1, A 20.18;
                              B 41.4
  Pt III (ss 17–29) ...... B 41.4

Public Bodies Corrupt Practices
     Act 1889............. A 89.4
Public Passenger Vehicles Act
     1981
  Pt II (ss 6–29) .... A 56.2
  s 181 .... A 35.4

R

Refuse Disposal (Amenity) Act
     1978
  s 2(1)(a) .... A 83.2
     (b) .... A 83.10
Regulation of the Railways Act
     1889
  s 5(1) .... A 48.1
     (3)(a)–(c) .... A 48.3
Rehabilitation of Offenders Act
     1974
  s 7(5) .... B 10.21
Restriction of Offensive Weap-
     ons Act 1959........ A 11.4
Road Safety Act 2006
     ... C 1.6, C 25.5, C 46.1,
                              C 49.1
  s 3, 4 .... C 8.8
Road Traffic Act 1988
     .... B 34.17; C 5.49
  s 1 .... C 9.5
     1A .... C 16B.7
     2 .... C 16.1, C 25.16, C
                              46.16
     2A(3) .... C 16.8
     2B ... C 16A.1, C 16A.7, C
                              16A.10
     3 ...... C 16A.7, C 25.1, C
        25.16, C 46.1, C 46.16
     3A .... C 23.2, C 25.5
     3ZA .... C 25.5, C 46.2
     3ZB ..... C 9.5, C 16B.1, C
                              16B.6
     4 . B 41.7, B 47.2; C 22.10,
                              C 23.2
        (1) .... C 20.1, C 20.18
        (2) .... C 20.18, C 21.1

Road Traffic Act 1988 – *cont.*
s 5 ... B 41.7, B 47.2; C 23.2
  (1)(a) .... C 22.1, C 22.31
  (b) ... C 22.31, C 22.62
6 .... C 22.10, C 23.3
(4) .... C 24.1
7(6) ..... C 23.1, C 23.3, C
    23.6; I 6.23
7A .... C 23.1, C 23.5
14 .... C 48.1
15 .... C 48.1
  (2) .... C 48.9
16(4) .... C 35.1
20(8) .... C 49.4
24 .... C 22.31
34 .... C 10.1
  (1A) .... A 3.21
  (4) .... C 5.6
35(1) .... C 5.24
36 .... C 52.1
38(7) .... C 3.1
40A .... C 10.1
41A(b) ... C 9.1, C 50.1, C
    53.1
41B .... C 38.1
41C .... C 38A.1
42 . C 34.4, C 36.1, C 37.1
47 .... C 8.9
  (1) .... C 51.1
75(7)(c) .... C 8.21
87 .... C 18.1, C 18.2
  (1) .... C 16B.1
103 .... C 19.1
  (1)(b) .... C 16B.1
143 ..... C 8.9, C 16B.1, C
    33.1
164, 165 .... C 17.3
168 .... C 46.5
170(4) ...... C 31.1, C 32.1
  (7) .... C 31.16
172 .... C 8.9, C 8.21
  (2)(a) .... C 8.22
Sch 2
  Pt 1 .... C 10.1
Road Traffic Act 1991
  . B 34.17; C 16.1, C 49.4

Road Traffic Act 1991 – *cont.*
s 24 .... C 20.18
Road Traffic (Driver Licensing
  and Information Systems)
  Act 1989............ C 18.31
Road Traffic Offenders Act 1988
  .... C 5.32
s 2 .... C 49.3
20 .... C 49.4
24 .. C 16A.18, C 20.18, C
    25.17, C 46.17
34(4) .... C 23.10
34A .... C 22.56
35 .... C 5.20, C 5.37
36 .... C 5.38
  (4) .. C 16A.10, C 16B.6
Road Traffic Regulation Act
  1984.................. C 6.2
s 5 .... C 9.4
16 .... C 49.22
17 ...... C 49.1, C 49.2, C
    49.19
25(5) .... C 39.1, C 40.1
81 .... C 49.1, C 49.2, C
    49.10
82(1)(a) .... I 6.4
84 .... C 49.1, C 49.2, C
    49.22
85(1), (2) .... C 49.10
  (4) .... C 49.10
86 ...... C 49.1, C 49.2, C
    49.25
88 .... C 49.2, C 49.31
89 .... C 49.1, C 49.4

S

Safety of Sports Grounds Act
  1975.................. A 34.7
s 10 .... A 34.17
Serious Organised Crime and
  Police Act 2005.. A 41.5; M
    2.5
s 73, 74 . A 25.16, A 26.5, A
    27.3, A27A.4, A 27B.4,
    A 72.8, A 72.8A

Serious Organised Crime and Police Act 2005 – *cont.*
s 76(3) .... A 4.23
  110 .... A 20.18
  126 .... A 41.5
Sex Offenders Act 1997
  .... A 52.15; B 31.9
Sexual Offences Act 1985
s 1 .... A 82.3
  (1) .... A 82.1
  2(1) .... A 82.2
Sexual Offences Act 2003
  ...... A 14.6, A 52.15; B 26.10; E 3.18A
s 3 . A 53.1, A 53.16; B 47.2; E 3.18A, E 3.18B
  4 .... A 53.2, A 53.15
  5, 6 .... A 53.9
  7 ... A 52.1, A 52.5, A 53.9
  8 .... A 53.9; E 3.18
  9 .... A 52.1, A 52.5, A 52.14, A 53.7, A 53.9
  10–12 ...... A 53.7, A 53.9
  13 .... A 53.7, A 53.9, A 53.16; E 3.18A, E 3.18B
  14, 15 ...... A 53.7, A 53.9
  25, 26 ... E 3.18A, E 3.18B
  45 .... A 43.5
  48–50 ...... A 14.1, A 14.3
  51(1) .... A 14.3
  (2) .... A 14.4, A 44.3
  (3) .... A 14.5
  51A .... A 29.1
  52 .... A 29.1; B 47.2
  53 .... A 29.2; B 47.2
  53A .... A 29.2
  66 .... A 30.1; B 47.2
  67 .... B 47.2
  (1) .... A 68.1
  (2), (3) .... A 68.3
  68 .... A 68.4
  71 .... A 51.1, A 51.2
  74 .... A 68.4
  77 .... A 52.3
  79 .... A 68.4

Sexual Offences Act 2003 – *cont.*
Pt II (ss 80–136)
  .. A 52.15, A 52.16, A 53.17
s 80 .... A 14.6, A 30.3, A 43.9, A 52.14, A 52.15, A 53.15, A 68.5; C 68.23, C 68.24, C 69.33, C 69.34
  83(1) .... A 50.1
  84(1) .... A 50.1
  (4)(b) .... A 50.1
  85(1) .... A 50.1
  86(1) .... A 50.1
  87(4) .... A 50.1
  89(2)(b) .... A 50.1
  91(1) .... A 50.1
  95(1) .... A 50.1
  123(4) .... A 53.17
Pt IIA (ss 136A–136R)
  .... A 26.12
s 136B(7)(b) . B 53.1, B 53.2, B 53.4
  136C(3) .... B 53.3
  (a) .... B 53.1
  (d) .... B 53.2
  (4) .... B 53.3
  136D .... B 53.1
  136E(2) .... B 53.3
  (4) .... B 53.3
  136H–J .... B 53.4
  136K .... B 53.5
  136M .... B 53.6
  Sch 3 ..... A 14.6, A 30.3, A 43.9, A 52.14, A 52.15, A 53.15, A 53.16, A 68.5
Sexual Offences (Amendment) Act 1992............ A 53.11
Serious Crime Act 2007
  .... I 7.1A
Social Security Administration Act 1992
s 111A .... A 54.1, A 54.3, A 54.6
  (1A) ... A 54.3, A 54.5
  (1B–1G) .... A 54.3
  112 ..... A 54.3, A 54.4, A 54.6

Social Security Administration Act 1992 – *cont.*
s 112(1) .... A 54.1
(1A–1F) .... A 54.3
116(2) .... A 54.4

Sporting Events (Control of Alcohol etc) Act 1985
.... A 35.7
s 1 .... B 41.7
(2)–(4) .... A 35.1, A 35.2
1A .... A 35.4
2 .... B 41.4
(1), (2) .... A 35.1, A 35.2
2A .... A 35.9

State Pension Credit Act 2002
s 1(3)(a) .... I 7.2A

Statutory Declarations Act 1835
.... M 4.10

Street Offences Act 1959
s 1 .... A 82.2

Supreme Court Act 1981
s 29 .... I 6.48
31 .... I 6.48

T

Tax Credits Act 2002
s 35 .... A 54.3, A 55.1

Terrorism Act 2000
s 42 .... M 1.9
Sch 5 .... M 1.9
Sch 8 .... M 1.9

Theft Act 1968 ..... A 37.3, A 57.7, A 57.17; B 18.3
s 1 .... B 47.2
(1) .... A 57.1
3 .... A 21.6
6(1) .... A 57.32
9 ...... A 12.20, A 13.19; B 47.2
(1)(a) ...... A 12.1, A 13.1
(b) ..... A 12.1, A 13.1
12 .... C 1.6
(1) .... A 65.1

Theft Act 1968 – *cont.*
s 12(5) .... A 65.2
12A .... C 1.6
(1) .... A 66.1
(2)(a), (b) .... A 66.1, A 66.17
(c), (d) .... A 66.1, A 66.16
13 .... A 1.1; B 47.2
15, 15A .... A 22.1
17 .... A 31.1
22 ...... A 40.1, A 40.11; B 47.2
24 .... A 36.7
25 . A 38.3, A 58.1; B 47.2
26 .... M 2.4, M 2.21

Theft Act 1978 .... A 37.3
s 3 .... A 45.1, A 57.22

Trade Descriptions Act 1968
.... A 75.3
s 1 .... A 75.1

Trade Marks Act 1994
s 10–12 .... A 60.3
92 .... A 60.3
(1) .... B 47.2
(a)–(c) .... A 60.1
(2) .... B 47.2
(a)–(c) .... A 60.1
(3)(a), (b) .... A 60.1
(4) .... A 60.3
(5) .... A 60.3

Transport Act 1968
s 96 .... I 1B.11

Transport Act 1985
s 10 .... A 56.2

U

UK Borders Act 2007
s 32, 33 .... B 23.1

V

Vagrancy Act 1824
.... A 79.9
s 4 .... A 79.1

Vagrancy Act 1824 – *cont.*
  s 5 .... B 16.20
Value Added Tax Act 1983
  s 22 .... A 62
Value Added Tax Act 1994
  s 13(5) .... A 62.2
    35, 36 .... A 62.2
    39, 40 .... A 62.2
    72(1) .... A 62
Vehicle Excise and Registration
    Act 1994... B 18.1, B 20.1A
  s 29(3) .... C 47.2
    (3A) ..... C 47.1, C 47.2
    31A .... C 47.2
    31B .... C 47.25
    33 .... C 8.9
    42, 43 .... C 8.9
    44 .... A 64.1; C 47.32
  Sch 2 .... C 47.17
Violent Crime Reduction Act
    2006... A 11.10; B 41.33, B
                     41.37
  Pt 1, Ch 1 (ss 1–14)
    .... B 32A.1
  s 1, 2 .... B 32A.2
    3, 4 .... B 32A.1
    5 .... B 32A.3
    6–8 .... B 32.1

Violent Crime Reduction Act 2006
  – *cont.*
  s 9 .... B 32A.1, B 32A.4
    10 .... B 32A.6
    11 .... B 32A.5
    23 .... A 3.3
    29(3) ...... E 3.18, E 3.18A

W

Wild Mammals (Protection) Act
  1996................... A 17.6
Wireless Telegraphy Act 1949
  .... A 61.1
  s 8 .... A 61.1
    35 .... A 61.1

Y

Youth Justice and Criminal Evi-
    dence Act 1999..... J 1.22B
  s 16–19 .... A 52.10
    35 .... I 6.13B
    46 .... I 1B.7
    49 .... E 2.5
    53 .... A 52.7
    55 .... A 52.6
  Sch 1A .... I 6.13B

Table
of Statutory Instruments

Paragraph references printed in **bold** type indicate where the Statutory Instrument is set out in part or in full.

A

Access to Justice Act 1999
(Destination of Appeals)
(Family Proceedings) Order
2009, SI 2009/871
.... D 1.18, D 1.19

Adoption Agencies (Panel
and Consequential
Amendments) Regulations
2012, SI 2012/1410
.... D 18.5

Adoption Agencies Regulations
2005, SI 2005/389
.... D 18.5A

Allocation and Transfer of
Proceedings Order 2008, SI
2008/2836 .... D 1.4, D 4.1
art 15 .... D 20.1

C

Children (Allocation and
Proceedings) Order 1991, SI
1991/1677 .... D 18.14

Civil Procedure Rules 1998, SI
1998/3132
Pt 3 .... D 18.25
Pt 8 .... D 18.21
Pt 54 .... I 6.48

Consumer Protection from
Unfair Trading Regulations
2008, SI 2008/1277
reg 8(1) .... A 75.1
(2) .... A 75.4
9–12 ..... A 75.1, A 75.5
14, 15 .... A 75.3
16–18 .... A 75.5

Coroners and Justice Act 2009
(Commencement No. 3 and
Transitional Provision) Order
2010, SI 2010/145
.... J 1.32

Costs in Criminal Cases
(General) (Amendment)
Regulations 2012, SI
2012/1804 .... B 20.16

Costs in Criminal Cases
(General) Regulations 1986,
SI 1986/1335
Pt III (regs 4–13)
.... B 20.16
reg 20 .... B 20.16

Council Tax (Administration and
Enforcement) Regulations
1992, SI 1992/613
.... H 1.1
reg 36A .... B 7.5; H 3.3
47(2) .... H 6.3
(3) .... H 6.3

Council Tax (Administration and
Enforcement) Regulations
1992, SI 1992/613 – *cont.*
reg 52 .... H 6.2

Crime and Security Act 2010
(Domestic Violence: Pilot
Schemes) Order 2011, SI
2011/1440
art 2, 3 .... B 54.1, B 55.1

Criminal Defence Service
(Contribution Orders)
Regulations 2009, SI
2009/3328 .... I 7.2A

Criminal Defence Service
(Funding) Order 2007, SI
2007/1174
Sch 1 .... B 20.19
Sch 2 .... B 20.19

Criminal Defence Service
(General) (No. 2)
(Amendment) Regulations
2008, SI 2008/725
.... I 7.1A

Criminal Defence Service
(General) (No 2) Regulations
2001, SI 2001/1437
.... I 7.2, I 7.3
reg 3 .... I 7.1A
12(1) .... I 7.4

Criminal Defence Service
(General) (No 2)
(Amendment) Regulations
2011, SI 2011/1453
.... I 7.1A

Criminal Defence Service
(Interests of Justice)
Regulations 2009, SI
2009/2875 .... I 7.6

Criminal Defence Service
(Representation Orders:
Appeals etc.) (Amendment)
Regulations 2009, SI
2009/3329 .... I 7.9

Criminal Defence Service
(Representation Orders:
Appeals etc.) (Amendment)
Regulations 2010, SI
2010/1186 .... I 7.9

Criminal Justice Act 1988
(Offensive Weapons)
(Amendment) Order 1988, SI
1988/2019 .... A 11.3

Criminal Justice Act 2003
(Commencement No 8 and
Transitional and Saving
Provisions) Order 2005, SI
2005/950
art 2(1) .... B 37.55
Sch 1
para 42(1) .... B 37.55

Criminal Justice Act 2003
(Sentencing) (Transitory
Provisions) Order 2005, SI
2005/643
art 2(2)(b) .... B 37.40

Criminal Justice Act 2003
(Surcharge) Order 2012, SI
2012/1696 .... B 33.4

Criminal Justice and Immigration
Act 2008 (Commencement
No. 3 and Transitional
Provisions) Order 2008, SI
2008/2712 .... I 6.2

Criminal Procedure (Amendment
No 3) Rules 2007, SI
2007/3662 .... I 6.2

Criminal Procedure Rules 2005,
SI 2005/384
Pt 1 .... I 6.6
r 1.1 .... I 6.2
1.2(a)–(c) .... I 6.2
Pt 3
3.8(4) .... I 6.17
Pt 34 .... I 6.16
Pt 35 .... I 6.14, I 6.15

Criminal Procedure Rules 2005, SI
   2005/384 – *cont.*
   Pt 37
   r 37 .... I 1B.1
    37.9 .... I 6.27
Criminal Procedure Rules 2010,
   SI 2010/60 .... I 6.13A, I
              6.13B, I 6.21
   Pt 1 .... I 6.1
   Pt 3
   r 3.2 .... I 6.3, I 6.4
    3.3 .... I 6.1, I 6.4
    3.5 .... I 6.2
    3.10 .... I 6.2
   Pt 42
   r 42.3 ..... A 52.15, A 52.16
   Pt 50 .... A 41.13
   r 50.2 .. B 32A.1, B 37A.2, B
              41.18
Criminal Procedure Rules 2011,
   SI 2011/1709 .... I 6.23
   Pt 19
   r 19.25 .... J 1.81A
   Pt 21 .... I 6.9
   Pt 63 .... K 1.5
Criminal Procedure Rules 2011,
   SI 2012/1726 .... B 20.19
   Pt 19
   r 19.1 .... J 1.56
    19.25 .... J 1.63
   Pt 44 .... B 17.18
   Pt 50
   r 50.2 .... B 8.8
    50.3(2) .... B 8.8
    50.4 .... B 8.8
   Pt 76 ...... B 20.2, B 20.3, B
         20.4, B20.20, B20.20A

D

Dangerous Dogs Compensation
   and Exemption Schemes
   Order 1991, SI 1991/1744
   .... A 72.8A

F

Family Procedure (Adoption)
   Rules 2005, SI 2005/2795
   .... D 18.20
   r 1 .... D 18.22
    4 .... D 18.23
   Pt X (rr 97–105)
   .... D 18.25
Family Proceedings (Amendment)
   Rules 2009, SI 2009/636
   r 8.2A(4) .... D 1.18
Family Proceedings Courts
   (Children Act 1989) Rules
   1991, SI 1991/1395
   .... L 1.6
   r 20, 21 .... D 1.18
Family Proceedings Courts
   (Constitution of Committees
   and Right to Preside) Rules
   2007, SI 2007/1610
   .... D 1.5
Family Proceedings Courts
   (Matrimonial Proceedings
   etc) Rules 1991, SI
   1991/1991
   r 11, 12 .... D 1.18
Family Proceedings Rules 1991,
   SI 1999/1247
   r 2.57 .... D 19.6
    9.1 .... D 19.6
    9.2, 9.2A .... D 19.6
    9.5 .... D 19.6
Family Procedure Rules 2010, SI
   2010/2955
   Pt 1 .... D 1.20
   r 1.1 .... D 2.1
   Pt 2
   r 2.1(2)(a) .... D 2.1
   Pt 4 .... D 1.20
   Pt 15
   r 15.2 .... D 19.3
    15.3 .... D 19.4
    15.4(2), (3) .... D 19.3
    15.5(2) .... D 19.3

Family Procedure Rules 2010, SI
    2010/2955 – *cont.*
    r 15.5(3) ..... D 19.3, D 19.4
    15.6(2) .... D 19.3
    15.7 .... D 19.3
    PD 15A .. D 19.1, D 19.3, D
        19.5

    Pt 16
    r 16.2 .... D 20.1
    PD 16A
    Part 4
        7.1 .... D 20.1
        7.2(c) .... D 20.1
        7.3 .... D 20.1
        7.5 .... D 20.1

G

Gambling Act 2005
    (Commencement No 6 and
    Transitional Provisions)
    Order 2006, SI 2006/3272
        .... G 1.1

J

Justices' Clerks Rules 1999, SI
    1999/2784 .... L 1.6, L 1.18
Justices of the Peace (Training
    and
    Development Committee)
    Rules 2007, SI 2007/1609
        .... D 1.5; E 2.1

L

Licensing Act 2003 (Persistent
    Selling of Alcohol to
    Children) (Prescribed Form
    of Closure Notice)
    Regulations 2012, SI
    2012/963 .... F 2.7

Licensing Act 2003 (Premises
    licences and club premises
    certificates) (Amendment)
    Regulations 2012, SI
    2012/955 .... F 1.2
Litigants in Person (Costs and
    Expenses)
    (Magistrates' Courts) Order
    2001, SI 2001/3438
        .... B 20.1

M

Magistrates' Courts (Detention
    and Forfeiture of Cash)
    Rules 2002, SI 2002/2998
        .... M 3.2
Magistrates' Courts (Detention
    and Forfeiture of Cash)
    (Amendment) Rules 2012, SI
    2012/1275 .... M 3.2
Magistrates' Courts (Domestic
    Violence Protection Order
    Proceedings) Rules 2011, SI
    2011/1434 .... B 55.1
Magistrates' Courts (Drinking
    Banning Orders) Rules 2009,
    SI 2009/2937 ...... B 32A.1
Magistrates' Courts (Hearsay
    Evidence in Civil
    Proceedings) Rules 1999, SI
    1999/681 .... B 8.4A
    r 2–6 .... B 55.1
Magistrates' Courts (Parenting
    Orders) Rules 2004, SI
    2004/247 ... B 37, B 37A.1;
        A.8
Magistrates Courts Rules 1981,
    SI 1981/552
    r 14 .... F 1.13
    34 .... F 1.14

Motor Cycles (Protective
   Helmets) Regulations 1980,
   SI 1980/1279
   reg 4 .... C 35.1
Motor Vehicles (Driving
   Licences) Regulations 1987,
   SI 1987/1378 .... C 18.2
Motor Vehicles (Wearing of Seat
   Belts by Children in Front
   Seats) Regulations 1993, SI
   1993/31 .... C 48.10
Motor Vehicles (Wearing of Seat
   Belts) Regulations 1993, SI
   1993/176 ...... C 48.1, 48.3

P

"Pelican" Pedestrian Crossings
   Regulations and General
   Directions 1987, SI 1987/16
   reg 17 .... C 39.1
Policing and Crime Act 2009
   (Commencement No. 4)
   Order 2010, SI 2010/507
   .... A 82.2
Proceeds of Crime Act 2002
   (Recovery of Cash in
   Summary Proceedings:
   Minimum Amount) Order
   2006, SI 2006/1699
   .... M 3.2

R

Road Safety Act 2006
   (Commencement No 2)
   Order 2007, SI 2007/2472
   .... C 8.21, C 10.1
Road Safety Act 2006
   (Commencement No. 4)
   Order 2008, SI 2008/1918
   .... C 16A.1, C 16B.1
Road Vehicles (Construction and
   Use) Regulations 1986, SI
   1986/1078 ...... C 5.32, 6.2

Road Vehicles (Construction and
   Use) Regulations 1986, SI
   1986/1078 – *cont.*
   reg 18 .... C 9.1
         27 .... C 53.1
         29 .... C 50.1
         66 .... C 38.1
         75–79 .... C 38.2
         80 .... C 38.1
         103 .... C 36.1
         105 .... C 37.1
   Sch 8 .... C 38.2
Road Vehicles Lighting
   Regulations 1989, SI
   1989/1796
   reg 23(1) .... C 34.4
         24(1) .... C 34.4
         25(1) .... C 34.4
         27 .... C 34.4

S

Sexual Offences Act 2003
   (Amendment of Schedules 3
   and 5) Order 2007, SI
   2007/296 .... A 52.15, A
         53.16, A 53.17
Sexual Offences Act 2003
   (Notification Requirements)
   (England and Wales)
   Regulations 2012, SI
   2012/1876 .... A 52.15
Sexual Offences Act 2003 (Travel
   Notification Requirements)
   Regulations 2004, SI
   2004/1220 .... A 52.15

T

Traffic Signs Regulations and
   General Directions 2002, SI
   2002/3113
   reg 10 .... C 52.16
   Sch 17
   Item 10 .... C 49.10

V

Violent Crime Reduction Act
2006 (Commencement No 8)
Order 2010, SI 2010/469
.... B 32A.1
Violent Crime Reduction Act
2006 (Commencement No 9)
Order 2010, SI 2010/2541
.... B 32A.1

Y

Youth Courts (Constitution
of Committees and Right to
Preside) Rules 2007, SI
2007/1611 .... E 2.1

Z

"Zebra" Pedestrian Crossings
Regulations 1971, SI
1971/1524
reg 8 .... C 39.1
9 .... C 40.1
12 .... C 40.7
Zebra, Pelican and Puffin
Pedestrian Crossings
Regulations and General
Directions 1997, SI
1997/2400 .... C 6.2

Table of Cases

A

A (a child) (disclosure of child's existence to paternal grandparents), Re [2006] EWHC 3065 (Fam), [2007] 1 FLR 1223, [2006] All ER (D) 24 (Dec), sub nom Birmingham City Council v S [2007] Fam Law 300 .... D 6.5

AB (care proceedings: service on husband ignorant of child's existence), Re. See B (a child), Re

ADT v United Kingdom [2000] 2 FLR 697, [2000] Fam Law 797, [2000] Crim LR 1009, 9 BHRC 112, ECtHR .... A 15.11

Abdul v DPP [2011] EWHC 247 (Admin), 175 JP 190, [2011] Crim LR 553, 175 CL&J 127, [2011] All ER (D) 181 (Feb) ... A20.5

Akhurst v Enfield Magistrates' Court [2009] EWHC 806 (Admin), 173 JP 499, (2009) Times, 13 April, [2009] All ER (D) 126 (Mar) .... A 79.4

Aldis v DPP [2002] EWHC 403 (Admin), (2002) Times, 6 March, [2002] All ER (D) 128 (Feb) .... E 3.17A

Ali v DPP [2009] EWHC 3353 (Admin), 174 JP 149, [2009] All ER (D) 256 (Nov) .... A 9.7

Amendment No. 15 to the Consolidated Criminal Practice Direction (Treatment of Vulnerable Defendants, Binding Over Orders and Conditional Discharges, Settling the Indictment, Management of Cases to be heard in the Crown Court and Forms for Use in Criminal Proceedings) [2007] All ER (D) 520 (Mar) .... B 10.20

Angus v United Kingdom Border Agency [2011] EWHC 461 (Admin), [2011] All ER (D) 138 (Mar) .... M 3.2

Arrowsmith v Jenkins [1963] 2 QB 561, [1963] 2 All ER 210, [1963] 2 WLR 856, 61 LGR 312, 127 JP 289, 107 Sol Jo 215 .... C 36.2

Atkinson v DPP [2004] EWHC 1457 (Admin), [2004] 3 All ER 971, [2005] 1 WLR 96, 168 JP 472, [2004] All ER (D) 247 (Jun) .... A 5.2

A-G v Leveller Magazine Ltd [1979] AC 440, [1979] 1 All ER 745, [1979] 2 WLR 247, 68 Cr App Rep 342, 143 JP 260, 123 Sol Jo 129, HL .... I 1B.4

A-G's Reference (No 1 of 1999) [2000] 1 QB 365, [1999] 3 WLR 769, [1999] 2 Cr App Rep 418, 163 JP 769, CA .... A 69.6

A-G's Reference (No 4 of 2000) [2001] EWCA Crim 780 [2001] RTR 415, [2001] 2 Cr App Rep 417, [2001] Crim LR 578 .... C 16.5

A-G's Reference (No 64 of 2003) [2003] EWCA Crim 3514, [2004] 2 Cr App Rep (S) 106, [2004] Crim LR 241, (2003) Times, 1 December, [2003] All ER (D) 288 (Nov) ...... A 1.4, A 45.8

A-G's Reference (No 1 of 2004), R v Edwards [2004] EWCA Crim 1025, [2005] 4 All ER 457, [2004] 1 WLR 2111, [2004] 2 Cr App Rep 424, [2004] Crim LR 832, [2004] 20 LS Gaz R 34, (2004) Times, 30 April, 148 Sol Jo LB 568, [2004] BPIR 1073, [2004] All ER (D) 318 (Apr) .... A 69.7

A-G's Reference (No 1 of 2004), R v Edwards [2004] EWCA Crim 1332, [2004] All ER (D) 288 (May) .... I 1.8

A-G's Reference (No 2 of 2004) [2005] EWCA Crim 1415, [2006] 1 All ER 988, [2005] 1 WLR 3642, [2005] 2 Cr App Rep 527, [2006] Crim LR 148, (2005) Times, 22 June, 149 Sol Jo LB 712, [2005] All ER (D) 447 (May) .... A 25.8 A

B

B (procedure in family proceedings courts), Re [1992] 2 FCR 631, [1993] Fam Law 209, CA .... D 1.18

B (threshold criteria: agreed facts), Re [1999] 2 FCR 328, [1998] 2 FLR 968, CA .... D 6.6

B (a child) (parentage: knowledge of proceedings), Re [2003] EWCA Civ 1842, [2004] 1 FCR 473, [2003] All ER (D) 129 (Nov), sub nom AB (care proceedings: service on husband ignorant of child's existence), Re [2004] 1 FLR 527, [2004] Fam Law 178 .... D 6.3

B (a child) (serious injury: standard of proof), Re [2004] EWCA Civ 567, [2005] Fam 134, [2004] 3 WLR 753, [2004] 2 FCR 257, [2004] 2 FLR 263, [2004] Fam Law 565, [2004] NLJR 824, (2004) Times, 27 May, [2004] All ER (D) 197 (May); affd [2005] EWCA Civ 52, [2005] 3 All ER 550, [2005] 1 WLR 2398, [2005] 1 FCR 583, [2005] NLJR 325, (2005) Times, 31 March, 149 Sol Jo LB 266, [2005] All ER (D) 385 (Feb) .... D 6.7

B (a child), Re [2007] EWCA Civ 556, [2007] 2 FLR 979, [2007] Fam Law 798, 151 Sol Jo LB 673, [2007] All ER (D) 241 (May) .... D 9.18

B (children) (sexual abuse: standard of proof), Re [2008] UKHL 35, [2008] 4 All ER 1, [2008] 3 WLR 1, [2008] 2 FCR 339, [2008] 2 FLR 141, [2008] Fam Law 837, [2008] Fam Law 619, (2008) Times, 12 June, [2008] All ER (D) 134 (Jun) .... D 4.4, D 6.4

B v C [1995] 2 FCR 678, [1995] 1 FLR 467, [1995] Fam Law 243 .... D 7.20

B v Chief Constable of Avon and Somerset Constabulary [2001] 1 All ER 562, [2001] 1 WLR 340 .... A 52.16, A 53.17

B (a minor) v DPP [2000] 2 AC 428, [2000] 1 All ER 833, [2000] 2 WLR 452, [2000] 2 Cr App Rep 65, [2000] Crim LR 403, [2000] 11 LS Gaz R 36, 144 Sol Jo LB 108, HL .... A 52.5

Baker v Crown Prosecution Service [2009] EWHC 299 (Admin), 173 JP 215, [2009] All ER (D) 237 (Jan) .... A 9.8

Baker v Quantum Clothing Group [2011] UKSC 17, [2011] 4 All ER 223, [2011] 1 WLR 1003, [2011] ICR 523, [2011] 17 LS Gaz R 13, (2011) Times, 14 April, 155 Sol Jo (no 15) 38, [2011] All ER (D) 137 (Apr) .... A 80.19

Balshaw v Crown Prosecution Service [2009] EWCA Crim 470, [2009] 2 Cr App Rep 95, [2009] 2 Cr App Rep (S) 712, 173 JP 242, [2009] Crim LR 532, [2009] All ER (D) 184 (Mar) ...... B 20.8

Barnfather v Islington Education Authority [2003] EWHC 418 (Admin), [2003] 1 WLR 2318, [2003] ELR 263, [2003] All ER (D) 89 (Mar) .... A 49.3; D 17.4

Bates v DPP (1993) 157 JP 1004 .... A 72.7

Bayliss v DPP [2003] All ER (D) 71 (Feb) .... A 11.7

Beckford v R [1988] AC 130, [1987] 3 All ER 425, [1987] 3 WLR 611, 85 Cr App Rep 378, [1988] Crim LR 116, 131 Sol Jo 1122, [1987] LS Gaz R 2192, [1987] NLJ Rep 591, PC ..... A 8.18, A 8.19

Begum v West Midlands Police [2012] EWHC 2304 (Admin) .. M 3.2

Bennett v Brown (1980) 71 Cr App Rep 109 .... A 76.17

Bennett v Horseferry Road Magistrates Court. See R v Horseferry Road Magistrates, ex p Bennett

Bennett v Secretary of State for Work and Pensions [2012] EWHC 371 (Admin), 176 JP 181, [2012] All ER (D) 160 (Jan) .... A 54.4

Best v United Kingdom (2005) Times, 10 March .... B 33.50

Birmingham City Council v Dixon [2009] EWHC 761 (Admin), 173 JP 233, (2009) Times, 13 April .... B 8.5

Birmingham City Council v R (2006) Times, 29 December ... D 18.34

Birmingham City Council v S. See A (a child) (disclosure of child's existence to paternal grandparents), Re

Blackburn v Bowering [1994] 3 All ER 380, [1994] 1 WLR 1324, [1995] Crim LR 38, CA .... A 9.7

Blake v DPP [2002] EWHC 2014 (Admin), [2002] All ER (D) 125 (Sep) .... C 25.9

Bond v Chief Constable of Kent [1983] 1 All ER 456, [1983] 1 WLR 40, 76 Cr App Rep 56, 4 Cr App Rep (S) 324, 147 JP 107, [1983] Crim LR 166, 126 Sol Jo 707, [1983] LS Gaz R 29 .... B 18.2

Bonner v DPP [2004] EWHC 2415 (Admin), [2004] All ER (D) 74 (Oct) .... A 9.8

Booth v Crown Prosecution Service [2006] EWHC 192 (Admin), (2006) 170 JP 305, 170 JPN 513, [2006] All ER (D) 225 (Jan) .... A 18.31

Bradford Metropolitan District Council v Booth (2002), unreported .... F 1.16

Brants v DPP [2011] EWHC 754 (Admin), 175 JP 246, [2011] All ER (D) 92 (Mar) .... I 1B.11

Breckon v DPP [2007] EWHC 2013 (Admin), [2007] All ER (D) 135 (Aug) .... C 22.16

Briffet and Bradshaw v DPP [2001] EWHC Admin 841 (2001) 166 JP 66, sub nom Briffett v Crown Prosecution Service [2002] EMLR 203 .... A 52.12

Briscoe v Shattock [1999] 1 WLR 432, 163 JP 201, [1999] Crim LR 396 .... A 72.24

BBC Litigation Department, Re [2002] All ER (D) 69 (Apr), CA .... A 52.12

Brown v Stott [2001] 2 All ER 97, [2001] 2 WLR 817, [2001] RTR 121, 145 Sol Jo LB 100, PC .... C 8.22

C

C (a minor) (interim care order: residential assessment), Re [1997] AC 489, [1996] 4 All ER 871, [1996] 3 WLR 1098, 95 LGR 367, [1997] 1 FCR 149, [1997] 1 FLR 1, [1997] 01 LS Gaz R 32, [1996] NLJR 1777, 141 Sol Jo LB 12, HL .... D 9.18

C (a child), Re [2001] EWCA Civ 810 [2001] 3 FCR 381 ..... D 6.37

C (child) (contact order: fact finding hearing), Re [2009] EWCA Civ 994, [2010] 1 FLR 1728, [2010] Fam Law 586, [2009] All ER (D) 252 (Oct) .... D 4.4

C v C (non-molestation order: jurisdiction) [1998] Fam 70, [1998] 2 WLR 599, [1998] 1 FCR 11, [1998] 1 FLR 554, [1998] Fam Law 254, [1997] 47 LS Gaz R 30, 141 Sol Jo LB 236 .... D 8.1

C v Crown Prosecution Service [2008] EWHC 854 (Admin), 172 JP 273, (2008) Times, 20 February, [2008] All ER (D) 112 (Feb) .... A 52.12; I 1B.7

C v DPP [2001] EWHC Admin 453 [2002] 1 Cr App Rep (S) 189, [2001] Crim LR 671 .... B 25.8

C and V (minors) (parental responsibility and contact), Re [1998] 1 FCR 52, [1998] 1 FLR 392, [1998] Fam Law 10, CA .... D 4.4

CB and JB (minors) (care proceedings: case conduct), Re [1998] 2 FCR 313, [1998] 2 FLR 211, [1998] Fam Law 454 .... D 6.21

CE (a minor) (appointment of Guardian ad Litem), Re [1995] 1 FCR 387, [1995] 1 FLR 26, [1995] Fam Law 67 .... D 5.17

Calderdale Metropolitan Borough Council v S [2004] EWHC 2529 (Fam), [2005] 1 FLR 751, [2005] Fam Law 353, (2004) Times, 18 November, [2004] All ER (D) 346 (Nov) .... D 6.2A

Cambridge City Council v Alex Nestling Ltd [2006] EWHC 1374 (Admin), 170 JP 539, (2006) Times, 11 July, [2006] All ER (D) 252 (May) .... F 1.16

Cambridgeshire County Council v Associated Lead Mills Ltd [2005] EWHC 1627 (Admin), [2006] RTR 82, 169 JP 489, [2005] All ER (D) 318 (Jul) .... C 9.4

Carroll v DPP [2009] EWHC 554 (Admin), 173 JP 285, [2009] All ER (D) 35 (Mar) .... A 28.5

Carruthers v Hampshire Probation Service [2010] EWHC 1961 (Admin), 174 CL&J 510, (2010) Times, 26 August, [2010] All ER (D) 14 (Jul) .... B 2.20

Castle v DPP (1998) Times, 3 April .... A 33.8

Caurti v DPP [2001] EWHC Admin 867, [2002] Crim LR 131, [2001] All ER (D) 287 (Oct) .... A 41.7

Cawthorn v DPP [2000] RTR 45, sub nom Cawthorn v Newcastle upon Tyne Crown Court 164 JP 527 .... C 18.9

Chahal v DPP [2010] EWHC 439 (Admin), [2010] 2 Cr App Rep 33, [2010] All ER (D) 37 (Apr) .... A 11.14

Chambers and Edwards v DPP [1995] Crim LR 896 .... A 20.8

Chechi v Bashier [1999] 2 FCR 241, [1999] 2 FLR 489, [1999] Fam Law 528, 143 Sol Jo LB 113, CA .... D 8.3

Chief Constable of Avon and Somerset v Fleming [1987] 1 All ER 318, [1987] RTR 378, 84 Cr App Rep 345, [1987] Crim LR 277 .... C 9.7

Chief Constable of Cumbria Constabulary v Wright [2006] EWHC 3574 (Admin), [2007] 1 WLR 1407, [2006] All ER (D) 265 (Nov) .... A 26.12

Chief Constable of Merseyside Police v Harrison (Secretary of State for the Home Department intervening) [2006] EWHC 1106 (Admin), [2006] 3 WLR 171, 170 JP 523, (2006) Times, 14 April, 150 Sol Jo LB 469, [2006] All ER (D) 115 (Apr) ... A 26.12

Chief Constable of Merseyside Police v Owens [2012] EWHC 1515 (Admin), 176 CL&J 353, [2012] All ER (D) 03 (Jun) . A 87.3, A 87.7, B 34.5

Chief Constable of North Yorkshire Police v Saddington. See DPP v Saddington

Child Maintenance and Enforcement Commission v Mitchell [2010] EWCA Civ 333, [2010] 2 FCR 526, [2010] 2 FLR 622, [2010] Fam Law 696 , 174 CL&J 255, 154 Sol Jo (no 13) 28, [2010] All ER (D) 278 (Mar) .... D 7.47

Clark (Procurator Fiscal, Kirkcaldy) v Kelly [2003] UKPC D1, [2004] 1 AC 681, [2003] 1 All ER 1106, [2003] 2 WLR 1586, 2003n SCCR 194, 2003 SLT 308, 147 Sol Jo LB 234 .... L 1.17

Clarke v Kato [1998] 4 All ER 417, [1998] 1 WLR 1647, [1998] 43 LS Gaz R 31, [1998] NLJR 1640, 142 Sol Jo LB 278, sub nom Clarke v General Accident Fire and Life Assurance Corpn plc [1999] RTR 153, 163 JP 502, HL ...... C 18.16

Clayton v Clayton [2006] EWCA Civ 878, [2006] Fam 83, [2007] 1 All ER 1197, [2006] 3 WLR 599, [2006] 2 FCR 405, [2007] 1 FLR 11, [2006] Fam Law 926, [2006] NLJR 1101, (2006) Times, 4 July, 150 Sol Jo LB 890, [2007] EMLR 65, [2006] All ER (D) 301 (Jun) .... D 1.10

Clear v Smith [1981] 1 WLR 399, [1980] Crim LR 246, 125 Sol Jo 256 .... A 54.4

Cleveland Police v Haggas [2009] EWHC 3231 (Admin), [2010] 3 All ER 506, [2010] All ER (D) 119 (Jan) .... A 53.17

Collins v Wilcock [1984] 3 All ER 374, [1984] 1 WLR 1172, 79 Cr App Rep 229, 148 JP 692, [1984] Crim LR 481, 128 Sol Jo 660, [1984] LS Gaz R 2140 .... A 15.10

Condron v United Kingdom (Application 35718/97) (2000) 21 EHRR 1, [2000] Crim LR 679, 8 BHRC 290, ECtHR .... I 1A.3, I 6.22

Connell v DPP [2011] EWHC 158 (Admin), 175 JP 151, [2011] All ER (D) 155 (Jan) .... C 49.4

Cooke v DPP [2008] EWHC 2703 (Admin), 172 JP 596, [2008] All ER (D) 202 (Oct) .... B 8.5

Coombes v DPP [2006] EWHC 3263 (Admin), [2007] RTR 383, 171 JP 271, (2006) Times, 29 December, [2006] All ER (D) 296 (Dec) .... C 49.10

Cox v Riley (1986) 83 Cr App Rep 54, [1986] Crim LR 460 .... A 18.22

Crawley Borough Council v Attenborough [2006] EWHC 1278 (Admin), (2006) 170 JP 593, [2006] All ER (D) 104 (May) .... F 1.16

Cresswell v DPP. See Currie v DPP

Crown Prosecution Service v Humphries. See DPP v Humphries

Crown Prosecution Service v T. See DPP v T

Cumberbatch v Crown Prosecution Service [2009] EWHC 3353 (Admin), 174 JP 149, [2009] All ER (D) 256 (Nov) .... A 47.11

Cummings v DPP (1999) 143 Sol Jo LB 112, Times, 26 March .... A 72.7

Currie v DPP [2006] EWHC 3379 (Admin), [2006] All ER (D) 429 (Nov), sub nom Cresswell v DPP; Currie v DPP 171 JP 233, 151 Sol Jo LB 500 .... A 18.19

Customs and Excise Comrs v Brunt (1998) 163 JP 161 .... A 4.19

Customs and Excise Comrs v Newbury [2003] EWHC 702 (Admin), [2003] 2 All ER 964, [2003] 1 WLR 2131, [2003] 23 LS Gaz R 39 .... B 34.18

Cutter v Eagle Star Insurance Co Ltd [1998] 4 All ER 417, [1998] 1 WLR 1647, [1999] RTR 153, 163 JP 502, [1998] 43 LS Gaz R 31, [1998] NLJR 1640, 142 Sol Jo LB 278, HL .... C 9.10

D

D (a minor) (contact: interim order), Re [1995] 1 FCR 501, [1995] 1 FLR 495, [1995] Fam Law 239 .... D 6.37

D v DPP [2005] EWHC 967 (Admin), [2005] Crim LR 962, [2005] All ER (D) 260 (May) A8.7, A15.4, A70.5

D and R v DPP (1995) 160 LG Rev 481, 160 JP 275, sub nom D (a minor) v DPP 16 Cr App Rep (S) 1040, [1995] 3 FCR 725, [1995] 2 FLR 502, [1995] Fam Law 595, [1995] Crim LR 748, [1995] NLJR 560 .... B 33.10

Dannenberg v Secretary of State for the Home Department. See R v Secretary of State for the House Department ex p Dannenberg

Darroch v DPP (1990) 90 Cr App Rep 378, 154 JP 844, [1990] Crim LR 814 .... A 82.4

Davies v Health and Safety Executive. See R v Davies

Dehal v DPP [2005] EWHC 2154 (Admin), [2005] All ER (D) 152 (Sep), sub nom Dehal v Crown Prosecution Service 169 JP 581 .... A 21.5 A

Demetriou (Leon) v DPP (2012) 156 Sol Jo (no 18) 31, [2012] All ER (D) 165 (Apr) .... A 9.8

Dewar v DPP [2010] All ER (D) 83 (Jan), DC .... A 8.20

Dica, Re (5 May 2004, unreported), CA .... A 70.5

DPP v A [2000] All ER (D) 1247 .... A 70.5

DPP v Alderton [2003] EWHC 2917 (Admin), [2004] RTR 367, 147 Sol Jo LB 1398, [2003] All ER (D) 360 (Nov) .... C 18.8

DPP v Barker (2004) 168 JP 617, [2004] All ER (D) 246 (Oct), DC .... C 5.38

DPP v Baker (2004) 169 JP 140, [2004] All ER (D) 28 (Nov), DC .... A 41.7; C 19.7

DPP v Beaumont [2008] EWHC 523 (Admin), [2008] 1 WLR 2186, [2008] 2 Cr App Rep (S) 549, 172 JP 283, [2008] Crim LR 572, [2008] All ER (D) 36 (Mar) .... B 41.7

DPP v Bennett [1993] RTR 175, 157 JP 493, [1993] Crim LR 71 .... C 31.2

DPP v Bristow [1998] RTR 100, 161 JP 35 .... C 22.25

DPP v Broomfield [2002] EWHC 1962 (Admin), [2003] RTR 108, 166 JP 736 .... C 8.21

DPP v Butterworth [1995] 1 AC 381, [1994] 3 All ER 289, [1994] 3 WLR 538, [1994] RTR 330, 159 JP 33, [1995] Crim LR 71, [1994] NLJR 1043, HL .... I 6.23

DPP v Chippendale [2004] EWHC 464 (Admin), [2004] Crim LR 755, [2004] All ER (D) 308 (Jan) .... A 21.7

DPP v Collins [2006] UKHL 40, [2006] 4 All ER 602, [2006] 1 WLR 2223, [2007] 1 Cr App Rep 49, 170 JP 712, [2006] IP & T 875, [2006] NLJR 1212, 171 JPN 162, (2006) Times, 21 July, 150 Sol Jo LB 987, [2006] All ER (D) 249 (Jul) ... A 16.2, A 16.3, A 16.4, A 16.5, A 16.6

DPP v Cove [2008] EWHC 441 (Admin), [2008] All ER (D) 199 (Feb) .... C 22.25

DPP v Darwin [2007] EWHC (Admin) 337 .... C 23.3

DPP v Dunn (2008) 165 JP 130 .... A 41.7

DPP v Everest [2005] EWHC 1124 (Admin), 169 JP 345, [2005] All ER (D) 363 (May) .... I 6.23

DPP v Fearon [2010] EWHC 340 (Admin), [2010] 2 Cr App Rep 169, 174 JP 145, [2010] Crim LR 646, [2010] All ER (D) 32 (Mar) .... A 82.4

DPP v Gregson (1992) 96 Cr App Rep 240, 157 JP 201, [1992] 34 LS Gaz R 34, 136 Sol Jo LB 245 .... A 11.12

DPP v H [1997] 1 WLR 1406, [1998] RTR 200, [1997] 18 LS Gaz R 31, sub nom DPP v Harper 161 JP 697 .... C 20.3

DPP v Hall [2005] EWHC 2612 (Admin), [2006] 3 All ER 170, [2006] 1 WLR 1000, 170 JP 11, [2005] All ER (D) 37 (Oct) .. A 46.5

DPP v Hammerton [2009] EWHC 921 (Admin), [2009] 2 Cr App Rep 322 .... I 6.23

DPP v Hardy [2008] EWHC 2874 (Admin), 173 JP 10, [2008] All ER (D) 315 (Oct) .... A 41.7

DPP v Harper. See DPP v H

DPP v Hastings [1993] RTR 205, 158 JP 118 .... C 18.9

DPP v Hay [2005] EWHC 1395 (Admin), (2005) 169 JP 429, (2005) Times, 13 July, [2005] All ER (D) 90 (Jun) . C 18.17, C 32.18

DPP v Heritage [2002] EWHC 2139 (Admin), (2002) 166 JP 772 .... C 33.23A

DPP v Heywood [1998] RTR 1, DC .... C 23.3

DPP v Holden [2006] All ER (D) 363 (Feb) .... C 8.21

DPP v Howard [2008] All ER (D) 88 (Feb) .... A 20.6

DPP v Humphries [2000] RTR 52, sub nom Crown Prosecution Service v Humphries [2000] 2 Cr App Rep (S) 1, 164 JP 502 .... C 22.25

DPP v Janman [2004] EWHC 101 (Admin), [2004] Crim LR 478, [2004] All ER (D) 171 (Jan) .... C 21.4, C 22.64

DPP v K (a minor) [1990] 1 All ER 331, [1990] 1 WLR 1067, 91 Cr App Rep 23, 154 JP 192, [1990] Crim LR 321, 134 Sol Jo 636, [1989] NLJR 1455 .... A 8.8

DPP v Karamouzis [2006] EWHC 2634 (Admin), [2006] All ER (D) 109 (Oct) .... C 23.3

DPP v Kemsley [2004] EWHC 278 (Admin), [2004] All ER (D) 53 (Feb), sub nom Kemsley v DPP 169 JP 148 .... C 25.10

DPP v King [2008] EWHC 447 (Admin), 172 JP 401, [2008] All ER (D) 170 (Feb) .... A 66.5

DPP v M [1998] QB 913, [1997] 2 All ER 749, [1998] 2 WLR 604, [1997] 2 Cr App Rep 70, [1997] 2 FLR 804, [1998] Fam Law 11, 161 JP 491 .... A 52.7

DPP v M [2004] EWHC 1453 (Admin), [2004] 1 WLR 2758, 148
Sol Jo LB 660, [2004] All ER (D) 358 (May) .... A 18.17
DPP v McCarthy [1999] RTR 323, 163 JP 585 .... C 31.8
DPP v McFarlane [2002] EWHC 485 (Admin) [2002] All ER (D)
78 (Mar) .... A 21.10
DPP v Memery [2002] EWHC 1720 (Admin), [2003] RTR 249,
167 JP 238, (2002) Times, 9 July, [2002] All ER (D) 64 (Jul) C
22.23
DPP v Mills [1997] QB 300, [1996] 3 WLR 1093, [1997] 2 Cr App
Rep 6, 160 JP 377, [1996] Crim LR 746 .... A 69.4
DPP v Milton [2006] EWHC 242 (Admin), (2006) 170 JP 319, 170
JPN 533, 150 Sol Jo LB 166, [2006] All ER (D) 04 (Feb) ..... C 49.7
DPP v Noe [2000] RTR 351, [2000] 20 LS Gaz R 43 .... C 23.4
DPP v Oram [2005] EWHC 964 (Admin), [2005] All ER (D) 57
(May) .... C 22.24
DPP v P [2007] EWHC 946 (Admin), 171 JP 349, 171 JPN 659,
[2007] All ER (D) 244 (Apr) .... E 3.2, E 3.25
DPP v Parmenter [1992] 1 AC 699, sub nom R v Parmenter [1991]
2 All ER 225, [1991] 2 WLR 408, 92 Cr App Rep 68, 164, 154
JP 941, [1991] Crim LR 41, 134 Sol Jo 1368, [1990] NLJR
1231, CA; revsd sub nom DPP v Parmenter [1992] 1 AC 699,
[1991] 3 WLR 914, 94 Cr App Rep 193, 155 JP 935, sub nom R
v Parmenter [1991] 4 All ER 698, HL .... A 8.7
DPP v Patterson [2004] All ER (D) 239 (Oct), DC .... A 11.14
DPP v Revitt [2006] EWHC 2266 (Admin), [2006] 1 WLR 3172,
[2007] 1 Cr App Rep 266, 170 JP 729, [2007] Crim LR 238,
[2006] NLJR 1476, 171 JPN 251, (2006) Times, 14 September,
[2006] All ER (D) 34 (Sep) .... I 6.26
DPP v Richards [1988] QB 701, [1988] 3 All ER 406, [1988] 3
WLR 153, 88 Cr App Rep 97, 152 JP 333, 132 Sol Jo 623,
DC .... A 10.2
DPP v Robertson [2002] 15 LS Gaz R 33 .... C 22.10
DPP v S [2007] All ER (D) 148 (Dec), DC .... I 6.21
DPP v Saddington [2001] RTR 227, sub nom Chief Constable of
North Yorkshire Police v Saddington 165 JP 122, [2001] Crim
LR 41 .... C 9.7
DPP v Santra-Bermudez [2003] EWHC 2908 (Admin), (2003) 168
JP 373, [2004] Crim LR 471, [2003] All ER (D) 168 (Nov) .... A 8.8
DPP v Smith (Michael Ross) [2006] EWHC 94 (Admin), [2006]
2 All ER 16, [2006] 1 WLR 1571, (2006) Times, 19 January,
150 Sol Jo LB 130, [2006] All ER (D) 69 (Jan) .... A 8.9
DPP v Spriggs [1994] RTR 1, 157 JP 1143, [1993] Crim LR 622
.... A 65.4
DPP v Spurrier [2000] RTR 60, sub nom R v Crown Prosecution
Service, ex p Spurrier 164 JP 369 .... C 22.23

DPP v Stoke on Trent Magistrates' Court [2003] EWHC 1593 (Admin), [2003] 3 All ER 1086, [2004] 1 Cr App Rep 55, 167 JP 436, [2003] Crim LR 804, [2003] NLJR 1063 .... A 34.11

DPP v T [2006] EWHC 728 (Admin), [2006] 3 All ER 471, [2006] 3 FCR 184, [2006] All ER (D) 41 (Apr), sub nom Crown Prosecution Service v T 170 JP 470, (2006) Times, 13 April ... B 8.13

DPP v Taylor [1992] QB 645, [1992] 1 All ER 299, [1992] 2 WLR 460, 95 Cr App Rep 28, [1992] Fam Law 377, 155 JP 713, [1991] Crim LR 904 .... A 15.5

DPP v Teixeira (2001) 166 JP 1 .... C 22.23

DPP v Thornley [2006] EWHC 312 (Admin), [2006] 09 LS Gaz R 32, 170 JPN 656, [2006] All ER (D) 41 (Feb) .... C 49.4

DPP v Warren [1993] AC 319, [1992] 4 All ER 865, [1992] 3 WLR 884, [1993] RTR 58, 96 Cr App Rep 312, 157 JP 297, [1992] 45 LS Gaz R 26, [1992] NLJR 1684, HL .... C 23.6

DPP v Watkins [1989] QB 821, [1989] 1 All ER 1126, [1989] 2 WLR 966, [1989] RTR 324, 89 Cr App Rep 112, 154 JP 370, 133 Sol Jo 514, [1989] 19 LS Gaz R 45, [1989] NLJR 365 ... C 21.3

DPP v Woods [2002] EWHC 85 (Admin) [2002] All ER (D) 154 (Jan) .... A 8.16, A 15.7, A 18.18, A 20.7

Director of the Assets Recovery Agency v Green [2005] EWHC 3168 (Admin), (2006) Times, 27 February, [2005] All ER (D) 261 (Dec) .... M 3.2

Donnelly v Jackman [1970] 1 All ER 987, [1970] 1 WLR 562, 54 Cr App Rep 229, 134 JP 352, 114 Sol Jo 130 .... A 9.5

Dowler v Merseyrail [2009] EWHC 558 (Admin), 173 JP 332, [2009] All ER (D) 97 (May) .... B 20.18

Down Lisburn Health and Social Services Trust v H [2006] UKHL 36, [2007] 1 FLR 121, [2006] Fam Law 920, 150 Sol Jo LB 986 .... D 18.16

Dumble v Metropolitan Police Comr [2009] All ER (D) 66 (Feb) .... A 26.12

E

EH v Greenwich London Borough Council [2010] EWCA Civ 344, [2010] PTSR (CS) 23, [2010] 2 FCR 106, [2010] 2 FLR 661, [2010] Fam Law 577, [2010] 17 LS Gaz R 15, [2010] All ER (D) 30 (Apr) .... D 9.18

Evans v Barker [1971] RTR 453 .... C 36.4

F

F (children) (adoption: notice of hearing), Re [2006] EWCA Civ 1345, (2006) Times, 16 November, 150 Sol Jo LB 1394, [2006] All ER (D) 205 (Oct), sub nom F (adoption: natural parents), Re [2007] 1 FLR 363 .... D 18.3

F v Child Support Agency [1999] 2 FCR 385, [1999] 2 FLR 244, [1999] Fam Law 540 .... D 3.19

F and R (Section 8 order: grandparents' application), Re. See R (minors), Re,

Farley v Child Support Agency [2006] UKHL 31, [2006] 2 FCR 713, 150 Sol Jo LB 889, [2006] All ER (D) 318 (Jun), sub nom Farley v Secretary of State for Work and Pensions [2006] 3 All ER 935, [2006] 1 WLR 1817, (2006) Times, 29 June ... D 7.47

Felix v DPP [1998] Crim LR 657 .... A 83.21

Filmer v DPP [2006] EWHC 3450 (Admin), [2007] RTR 330, [2006] All ER (D) 08 (Nov) .... C 20.8

Flintshire County Council v Reynolds [2006] EWHC 195 (Admin), 170 JP 73, [2006] All ER (D) 130 (Jan) .... A 54.4

Foulkes v Chief Constable of Merseyside Police [1998] 3 All ER 705, [1999] 1 FCR 98, [1998] 2 FLR 798, [1998] Fam Law 661, [1998] All ER (D) 254, CA .... A 9.8

Francis v DPP [2004] EWHC 591 (Admin), (2004) 168 JP 492, [2004] All ER (D) 443 (Mar) .... C 8.21

G

G (minors), Re [1994] 1 FCR 37, [1993] 2 FLR 293, [1993] Fam Law 570, CA .... D 4.2

G (a minor) (parental responsibility order), Re [1994] 2 FCR 1037, [1994] 1 FLR 504, [1994] Fam Law 372, CA .... D 3.7

G (minors) (care proceedings: wasted costs) [2000] Fam 104, [1999] 4 All ER 371, [2000] 2 WLR 1007, [1999] 3 FCR 303, sub nom Re G, S and M (wasted costs) [2000] 1 FLR 52, [2000] Fam Law 24 .... D 5.6

G (care proceedings: joinder of father), Re [2004] EWHC 1474 (Fam), [2004] All ER (D) 163 (May) .... D 6.3

G (a child) (interim care order: residential assessment), Re [2005] UKHL 68, [2006] 1 AC 576, [2006] 1 All ER 706, [2005] 3 WLR 1166, [2005] 3 FCR 621, [2006] 1 FLR 601, [2006] Fam Law 91, (2005) Times, 25 November, 149 Sol Jo LB 1455, [2005] All ER (D) 321 (Nov) .... D 9.18

G (children) (care proceedings: adequacy of reasons), Re [2007] All ER (D) 210 (May) .... D 1.18

G v DPP [2004] EWHC 183 (Admin), (2004) 168 JP 313, 148 Sol Jo LB 149, [2004] All ER (D) 278 (Jan) .... A 15.7

G v F (non-molestation order: jurisdiction) [2000] Fam 186,
[2000] 3 WLR 1202, [2000] 2 FCR 638, [2000] 25 LS Gaz R 40,
sub nom G v G (non- molestation order: jurisdiction) [2000] 2
FLR 533, [2000] Fam Law 703 .... D 8.2
Glaser v United Kingdom [2000] 3 FCR 193, [2001] 1 FLR 153,
[2000] Fam Law 880, ECtHR .... D 4.4
Glenn & Co (Essex) Ltd v Revenue and Customs Comrs and East
Berkshire Magistrates' Court [2011] EWHC 2998 (Admin),
[2012] 1 Cr App Rep 291, 176 JP 65, [2012] Crim LR 464,
[2011] All ER (D) 149 (Nov) .... M 2.7
Godwin v DPP (1992) 96 Cr App Rep 244, 157 JP 197 .... A 11.9
Goodall v Jolly [1984] FLR 143, [1984] Fam Law 23, 147 JP
513 .... B 7.18
Gough v Chief Constable of the Derbyshire Constabulary [2001]
EWHC Admin 554, [2002] QB 459, [2001] 4 All ER 289,
[2001] 3 WLR 1392, [2001] 3 CMLR 613, [2001] 31 LS Gaz R
30, (2001) Times, 19 July, 145 Sol Jo LB 186, [2001] All ER (D)
169 (Jul); affd [2002] EWCA Civ 351, [2002] QB 1213, [2002]
2 All ER 985, [2002] 3 WLR 289, (2002) Times, 10 April,
[2002] All ER (D) 308 (Mar) .... B 41.22, B 41.33
Gough v Chief Constable of West Midland Police [2004] EWCA
Civ 206, 148 Sol Jo LB 298, [2004] All ER (D) 45 (Mar) .... A 87.17
Greener v DPP (1996) Times, 15 February .... A 72.4
Griffiths v DPP [2002] EWHC 792 (Admin), (2002) 166 JP 629,
[2002] All ER (D) 132 (Apr) .... C 22.30
Griffiths v DPP [2007] EWHC 619 (Admin), [2007] All ER (D)
356 (Mar) .... C 49.4
Gunnell v DPP [1993] Crim LR 619 .... C 18.8

H

H (minors) (access), Re [1992] 1 FCR 70, [1992] 1 FLR 148,
[1992] Fam Law 152, CA .... D 4.4
H (minors) (sexual abuse: standard of proof), Re [1996] AC 563,
[1996] 1 All ER 1, [1996] 2 WLR 8, [1996] 1 FCR 509, [1996]
1 FLR 80, [1996] Fam Law 74, 140 Sol Jo LB 24, HL .... D 6.6
H (care proceedings: intervener), Re [2000] 1 FLR 775 .... D 19.6
H (children: relocation), Re (2001) Times, 29 August, CA ...... D 5.2
H (children) (residence order), Re [2007] EWCA Civ 529, [2007] 2
FCR 621, [2007] All ER (D) 26 (May) .... D 4.6
H (a child) (abuse: oral evidence), Re [2011] EWCA Civ 741,
[2011] All ER (D) 84 (May) .... D 2.6
H (Children) [2012] All ER (D) 124 (Jun), CA .... D 1.8
H v Balham Youth Court [2003] EWHC 3267 (Admin), (2003)
168 JP 177, [2003] All ER (D) 173 (Dec) .... I 4.1A

H v Crown Prosecution Service [2010] EWHC 1374 (Admin), 174
CL&J 271, [2010] All ER (D) 56 (Apr) .... A 15.11

H v DPP [2005] EWHC 2459 (Admin), (2005) 170 JP 4,
[2005] All ER (D) 177 (Nov) .... A 28.4

H v Liverpool City Court [2001] Crim LR 897 .... A 66.11

H and A (paternity: blood tests), Re [2002] EWCA Civ 383, [2002]
2 FCR 469, [2002] 1 FLR 1145 .... D 3.19

Hackshaw v Hackshaw [1999] 3 FCR 451, [1999] 2 FLR 876,
[1999] Fam Law 697 .... D 7.18

Hallett v DPP [2011] EWHC 488 (Admin), [2011] All ER (D) 91
(Mar) .... C 20.8

Hallinan v DPP [1998] Crim LR 754 .... C 31.3

Hammond v DPP [2004] EWHC 69 (Admin), [2004] All ER (D)
50 (Jan) .... A 21.5

Hampshire Police Authority v Smith [2009] EWHC 174 (Admin),
173 JP 207, [2009] All ER (D) 117 (Feb) .... A 26.16

Harriott v DPP [2005] EWHC 965 (Admin), (2005) 170 JP 494,
[2005] All ER (D) 28 (May) .... A 11.8

Harris v DPP [1993] 1 All ER 562, [1993] 1 WLR 82, 96 Cr App
Rep 235, 157 JP 205, [1992] 32 LS Gaz R 35, 136 Sol Jo LB
228 .... A 11.9

Harrogate Borough Council v Barker (1995) 159 LG Rev 889, 159
JP 809, [1995] RVR 193 .... H 6.2

Harvey v DPP [2011] EWHC 3992 (Admin), 176 JP 265, [2012]
Crim LR 553, [2011] 47 LS Gaz R 20, [2011] All ER (D) 143
(Nov) .... A 20.8

Hashman and Harrup v United Kingdom (1999) 30 EHRR 241,
[2000] Crim LR 185, 8 BHRC 104, ECtHR .... B 10.6, B 10.21

Haw v City of Westminster Magistrates' Court [2007] EWHC
2960 (Admin), [2008] 2 All ER 326, [2008] 3 WLR 465, 172
JPN 309, 172 JP 122, [2007] All ER (D) 164 (Dec) .... I 3.16

Hayes v Chief Constable of Merseyside Police [2011] EWCA Civ
911, [2012] 1 WLR 517, [2011] 2 Cr App Rep 434, [2012] Crim
LR 35, (2011) Times, 19 August, [2011] All ER (D) 286 (Jul)
.... A20.18

Hayes v DPP [2004] EWHC 277 (Admin), [2004] All ER (D) 55
(Feb) .... C 8.22

Hayes v Willoughby [2011] EWCA Civ 1541, [2012] 1 WLR
1510, (2012) Times, 13 January, [2011] All ER (D) 144 (Dec)
.... A 41.10

Haystead v Chief Constable of Derbyshire [2000] 3 All ER 890,
[2000] 2 Cr App Rep 339, [2000] Crim LR 758, sub nom
Haystead v DPP 164 JP 396 .... A 15.6

Hertfordshire County Council v W [1992] 2 FCR 885, [1992] 39 LS Gaz R 33, 136 Sol Jo LB 259, sub nom W v Hertfordshire County Council [1993] 1 FLR 118, [1993] Fam Law 75 .... D 1.18

Hillingdon London Borough Council v H [1993] Fam 43, [1993] 1 All ER 198, [1992] 3 WLR 521, [1992] 2 FCR 299, [1992] 2 FLR 372, [1992] Fam Law 536 .... D 1.18

Hills v Chief Constable of Essex Police [2006] EWHC 2633 (Admin), 171 JP 14, [2006] All ER (D) 35 (Oct) .... B 8.5

Hinchley v Rankin [1961] 1 All ER 692, [1961] 1 WLR 421, 59 LGR 190, 125 JP 293, 105 Sol Jo 158, DC .... A 49.3

Hirst and Agu v Chief Constable of West Yorkshire (1986) 85 Cr App Rep 143, 151 JP 304, [1987] Crim LR 330 .... A 85.3

Hogan v DPP [2007] EWHC 978 (Admin), (2007) Times, 28 February, [2007] All ER (D) 253 (Feb) .... A 40.11

Hollis v Dudley Metropolitan Borough Council [1998] 1 All ER 759, [1999] 1 WLR 642, 30 HLR 902, [1998] 18 EG 133 ... A 84.31

Hooper v United Kingdom (App No 42317/98) (2004) Times, 19 November, [2004] All ER (D) 254 (Nov), ECtHR .... B 10.6

Hounslow London Borough Council v Thames Water Utilities Ltd [2004] All ER (D) 94 (Feb) .... A 84.9

Hughes v DPP [2012] EWHC 606 (Admin), [2012] All ER (D) 180 (Jan) .... A 21.7

I

I (care proceedings: HR Claims), Re (2004) 1 FLR 289 .... D 6.24

Idrees v DPP [2011] All ER (D) 156 (Feb) A36.6

Islington London Borough Council v TD [2011] EWHC 990 (Admin), [2011] All ER (D) 265 (Mar) A49.3

J

J (leave to issue application for residence order), Re [2003] 1 FLR 114, [2003] Fam Law 27, CA .... D 6.2

J (a child) (care proceedings: assessment), Re [2009] EWCA Civ 1210, [2010] Fam Law 131, [2010] 1 FLR 1290, [2010] All ER (D) 97 (Jan) .... D 9.18

JB v DPP [2012] EWHC 72 (Admin), [2012] 1 WLR 2357, [2012] 2 Cr App Rep 9, 176 JP 97, [2012] All ER (D) 120 (Jan) ...... B 8.13

Jaggard v Dickinson [1981] QB 527, [1980] 3 All ER 716, [1981] 2 WLR 118, 72 Cr App Rep 33, [1980] Crim LR 717, 124 Sol Jo 847 .... A 18.19

James v Birmingham City Council [2010] EWHC 282 (Admin),
174 JP 250, [2010] All ER (D) 218 (Feb) .... B 8.12
James v DPP [2012] EWHC 1317 (Admin), 176 JP 346, 176 CL&J
291, [2012] All ER (D) 150 (Apr) .... M 2.4
James and Chorley v DPP (1997) 163 JP 89, [1997] Crim LR
831 .... A 47.12
Johnson v RSPCA (2000) 164 JP 345, [2000] 20 LS Gaz R 42
.... K 3.1
Jones v Chief Constable of West Mercia Police Authority (2000)
165 JP 6 .... C 5.20
Jones v DPP [2004] EWHC 236 (Admin), [2004] RTR 331, 168 JP
393, [2004] Crim LR 667, [2004] All ER (D) 319 (Jan) .... C 8.21
Jones v DPP [2010] EWHC 523 (Admin), [2010] 3 All ER 1057,
174 JP 278, 174 CL&J 172, [2010] All ER (D) 230 (Feb) ..... A 20.6
Jones v DPP [2011] EWHC 50 (Admin), 175 JP 129 .... C 49.10
Jones v South East Surrey Local Justice Area [2010] EWHC 916
(Admin), 174 JP 342 .... I 6.13A
Joseph v DPP [2003] EWHC 3078 (Admin), [2004] RTR 341, 168
JP 575, [2004] 02 LS Gaz R 29, [2003] All ER (D) 326 (Nov)
.... C 23.6

K

K (procedure: family proceedings rules), Re [2004] EWCA Civ
1827, [2005] 1 FLR 764, [2005] Fam Law 275, sub nom K
(children: interim residence order), Re [2007] 2 FCR 631, 149
Sol Jo LB 29, [2004] All ER (D) 276 (Dec) .... D 4.6
K (adoption) (permission to advertise), Re [2007] EWHC 544
(Fam), [2007] 2 FLR 326, [2007] Fam Law 681, (2007) Times,
20 April, [2007] All ER (D) 310 (Mar) .... D 18.5A
K (a child) (care order), Re [2007] EWCA Civ 697, [2007] 2 FLR
1066, [2007] Fam Law 797, [2007] All ER (D) 93 (Jun) ...... D 9.18
KDT (a minor), Re [1994] 2 FCR 721, sub nom T (a minor), Re
[1994] 2 FLR 423, [1994] Fam Law 558, [1994] 21 LS Gaz R
40, CA .... D 6.24
Katsonis v Crown Prosecution Service [2011] EWHC 1860
(Admin), 175 JP 396, [2011] All ER (D) 16 (Jul) . A8.7, A15.4, A70.5
Keating v Knowsley Metropolitan Borough Council. See R (on the
application of K) v Knowsley Metropolitan Borough Council
Kelly v DPP [2002] All ER (D) 177 (Jun) .... A 41.7
Kemsley v DPP. See DPP v Kemsley
Kendall v South East Essex Magistrates Court [2008] EWHC 1848
(Admin), [2008] All ER (D) 356 (Jun) .... A 20.6
Kennet District Council v Young [1999] RTR 235, 163 JP 622,
163 JP 854 .... C 8.21

Khan v DPP. See R (on the application of Khan) v DPP
Kingsnorth v DPP [2003] All ER (D) 235 (Mar) .... C 19.6
Kirkup v DPP [2003] EWHC 2354 (Admin), (2003) 168 JP 255,
  [2004] Crim LR 230, [2003] All ER (D) 53 (Oct) .... C 23.4
Knight v DPP [2012] EWHC 605 (Admin), 176 JP 177 .... A 21.7

L

L (a child) (contact: domestic violence), Re [2001] Fam 260,
  [2000] 4 All ER 609, [2001] 2 WLR 339, [2000] 2 FCR 404,
  [2000] 2 FLR 334, [2000] Fam Law 603, 144 Sol Jo LB 222,
  [2000] All ER (D) 827, CA .... D 4.4
L (a child) (special guardianship order and ancillary orders), Re
  [2007] EWCA Civ 196, [2007] 1 FCR 804, [2007] 2 FLR 50,
  [2007] Fam Law 498, [2007] All ER (D) 208 (Mar), sub nom E
  (a child) (special guardianship order), Re (2007) Times,
  11 April .... D 18.37
L (children) (care order: residential assessment), Re [2007] EWCA
  Civ 213, [2007] 3 FCR 259, [2007] 1 FLR 1370, [2007] Fam
  Law 584, [2007] All ER (D) 246 (Mar) .... D 6.35, D 9.18
L (Children) (Occupation order: absence of domestic violence), Re
  [2012] EWCA Civ 721, [2012] All ER (D) 189 (Jun) .... D 8.25
L v Crown Prosecution Service [2007] EWHC 1843 (Admin),
  [2007] All ER (D) 224 (Jul) .... A 79.5
L v Crown Prosecution Service [2010] EWHC 341 (Admin), 174
  JP 209, [2010] All ER (D) 128 (Feb) .... A 72.4
L v DPP [2001] EWHC Admin 882 [2002] 2 All ER 854, [2002] 3
  WLR 863, [2002] 1 Cr App Rep 420, 166 JP 113, [2002] Crim
  LR 320 .... A 11.11
Lamont-Perkins v Royal Society for the Prevention of Cruelty to
  Animals [2012]EWHC 1002 (Admin), 176 JP 369,
  [2012] All ER (D) 149 (Apr) .... A 5.2
Lancashire County Council v A [2000] 2 AC 147, [2000] 2 All ER
  97, [2000] 2 WLR 590, [2000] 1 FCR 509, [2000] 1 FLR 583,
  [2000] 13 LS Gaz R 42, [2000] NLJR 429, HL .... D 6.7
Lau v DPP [2000] 1 FLR 799, [2000] Fam Law 610, [2000] Crim
  LR 580 .... A 41.7
Leary v Chief Constable of West Midlands Police [2012] EWHC
  639 (Admin), 176 CL&J 143, [2012] All ER (D) 137 (Feb) .. A 26.12
Leeds City Council v G [2007] EWHC 1612 (Admin), (2007)
  Times, 11 September, [2007] All ER (D) 114 (Jul) .... B 8.12
Leeson v DPP [2010] EWHC 994 (Admin), 174 JP 367, [2010]
  17 LS Gaz R 16, 174 CL&J 284, [2010] All ER (D) 84 (Apr)
  .... A 2.6
Levine v DPP (6 May 2010, unreported), QBD .... A 21.9

Lewis v DPP [2004] EWHC 3081 (Admin), [2005] All ER (D) 66 (Jan) .... C 20.7

Liverpool v DPP [2008] EWHC 2540 (Admin), [2008] All ER (D) 50 (Oct) .... A 21.6

Longstaff v DPP [2008] EWHC 303 (Admin), [2008] RTR 212, [2008] All ER (D) 276 (Jan) .... C 23.6

M

M (a minor) (care order: threshold conditions), Re [1994] 2 AC 424, [1994] 3 All ER 298, [1994] 3 WLR 558, 92 LGR 701, [1994] 2 FCR 871, [1994] 2 FLR 577, [1994] Fam Law 501, [1994] 37 LS Gaz R 50, 138 Sol Jo LB 168, HL .... D 6.5

M (a minor), Re [1995] Fam 108, [1995] 3 All ER 407, [1995] 2 WLR 302, [1995] 2 FCR 373, [1995] 1 FLR 418, 138 Sol Jo LB 241, CA .... E 3.7

M (residential assessment directions), Re [1998] 2 FLR 371, [1998] Fam Law 518 .... D 9.18

M (a child) (care proceedings: witness summons), Re [2007] EWCA Civ 9, [2007] 1 FCR 253, [2007] 1 FLR 1698, [2007] Fam Law 491, [2007] NLJR 142, [2007] All ER (D) 108 (Jan) .... D 6.5

M (a child) (care order), Re [2009] EWCA Civ 315, [2009] 2 FLR 950, [2009] Fam Law 570, [2009] All ER (D) 181 (Apr) ...... D 9.18

M (A Child), Re [2009] EWCA Civ 1486 .... D 6.24, D 6.35

M v DPP [2007] EWHC 1032 (Admin), 171 JP 457, [2007] All ER (D) 74 (Mar) .... B 8.4A

M-H (a child) (care order), Re [2006] EWCA Civ 1864, [2007] 3 FCR 319, [2007] 1 FLR 1715, [2007] Fam Law 487, [2007] All ER (D) 436 (Mar) .... D 6.24

MB v Switzerland (2001) 37 EHRR 1000, ECtHR .... J 1.2

McCaskill v DPP [2005] EWHC 3208 (Admin), (2005) 170 JP 301, 170 JPN 554, [2005] All ER (D) 292 (Dec) .... A 46.3

McConnell v Chief Constable of the Greater Manchester Police [1990] 1 All ER 423, [1990] 1 WLR 364, 91 Cr App Rep 88, 154 JP 325, 134 Sol Jo 457, CA .... A 9.8

McFarlane v McFarlane [2006] UKHL 24, [2006] 3 All ER 1, [2006] 2 WLR 1283, [2006] 2 FCR 213, [2006] 1 FLR 1186, [2006] Fam Law 629, [2006] NLJR 916, (2006) Times, 25 May, 150 Sol Jo LB 704, [2006] All ER (D) 343 (May) .... D 7.4

McKeon v DPP [2007] EWHC 3216 (Admin), [2008] RTR 165, [2007] All ER (D) 314 (Dec) .... C 23.4

McKerry v Teesdale and Wear Valley Justices (2000) 164 JP 355, [2000] Crim LR 594, [2000] COD 199, [2001] EMLR 127, sub nom McKerry v DPP [2000] 11 LS Gaz R 36, 144 Sol Jo LB 126, CA .... I 1A.2

McKoen v Ellis [1987] RTR 26, 151 JP 60, [1987] Crim LR 54 .... C 18.9

McMillan v Crown Prosecution Service [2008] EWHC 1457 (Admin), 172 JP 485, 172 JPN 646, 172 JPN 694, [2008] All ER (D) 142 (May) .... A 28.3

McNeil v DPP [2008] EWHC 1254 (Admin), [2008] All ER (D) 375 (Apr) .... C 23.6

Malcolm v DPP [2007] EWHC 363 (QB), [2007] 3 All ER 578, [2007] 1 WLR 1230, [2007] RTR 316, [2007] 2 Cr App Rep 1, 171 JP 293, (2007) Times, 4 April, [2007] All ER (D) 344 (Feb) .... I 6.1

Martin v DPP [2000] RTR 188, [2000] 2 Cr App Rep (S) 18, 164 JP 405, [2000] Crim LR 320 .... C 5.19

Martiner v DPP [2004] EWHC 2484 (Admin), [2004] All ER (D) 122 (Oct) .... C 23.3

May v DPP [2005] EWHC 1280 (Admin), [2005] All ER (D) 182 (Apr) .... C 16A.5, C 20.7, C 25.4

Mepstead v DPP (1995) 160 JP 475, [1996] Crim LR 111, [1996] COD 13 .... A 9.8

Metropolitan Police Comr v Ebanks [2012] All ER (D) 45 (Jul), DC .... A 53.17

Metropolitan Police Comr v Hooper [2005] EWHC 340 (Admin), [2005] 4 All ER 1095, [2005] 1 WLR 1995, 169 JP 409, (2005) Times, 3 March, [2005] All ER (D) 245 (Feb) .... A 26.12

Miller v DPP [2004] EWHC 595 (Admin), [2004] 17 LS Gaz R 30, [2004] All ER (D) 477 (Mar) .... C 5.24

Miller v Miller [2006] UKHL 24, [2006] 3 All ER 1, [2006] 2 WLR 1283, [2006] 2 FCR 213, [2006] 1 FLR 1186, [2006] Fam Law 629, [2006] NLJR 916, (2006) Times, 25 May, 150 Sol Jo LB 704, [2006] All ER (D) 343 (May) .... D 7.4

Mills v DPP [2008] EWHC 3304 (Admin), [2009] RTR 143, 173 JP 157, [2008] All ER (D) 39 (Dec) .... C 19.6

Milton v DPP [2007] EWHC 532 (Admin), [2007] All ER (D) 285 (Mar) .... C 16.8

Mohindra v DPP [2004] EWHC 490 (Admin), (2004) 168 JP 448, [2004] NLJR 468, [2004] All ER (D) 269 (Mar) .... C 8.22

Monks v Pilgrim [1979] Crim LR 595 .... A 61.4

Moran v DPP [2002] EWHC 89 (Admin) (2002) 166 JP 467 ... I 6.21

N

N v DPP [2011] EWHC 1807 (Admin), 175 JP 337, [2011] All ER (D) 04 (Jul) A11.13

Nedic v South Staffordshire Council [2005] EWHC 1481 (Admin), [2005] All ER (D) 182 (Jun) .... B 20.2

Neil v Ryan [1999] 1 FCR 241, [1998] 2 FLR 1068, [1998] Fam Law 728, CA .... D 8.20

Ng v DPP [2007] EWHC 36 (Admin), [2007] RTR 431, (2007) Times, 7 February, [2007] All ER (D) 214 (Jan) .... C 22.30

Nicholas v Chester Magistrates' Court [2009] EWHC 1504 (Admin) (11 June 2009) .... B 16.1, I 6.32

Nicholls v Brentwood Justices. See R v Brentwood Justices, ex p Nicholls

Norbert Dentressangle Continental Ltd v Wing (1998), unreported .... C 38.20

Norwood v United Kingdom (2004) 40 EHRR SE 111 .... A 16.6

O

O (a minor), Re [1992] 4 All ER 905, [1992] 1 WLR 912, [1992] 1 FCR 489, [1992] 2 FLR 7, [1992] Fam Law 487, [1992] 21 LS Gaz R 26 .... D 17.6

O (a child) (supervision order: future harm), Re [2001] EWCA Civ 16 [2001] 1 FCR 289, [2001] 1 FLR 923, [2001] Fam Law 336 .... D 6.6

O (minors) (care: preliminary hearing), Re [2003] UKHL 18, [2004] 1 AC 523, [2003] 2 All ER 305, [2003] 2 WLR 1075, [2003] 1 FCR 673, [2003] 23 LS Gaz R 36, sub nom Re O and N [2003] 1 FLR 1169 .... D 6.4

Oddy v Bug Bugs Ltd [2003] All ER (D) 156 (Nov) .... B 20.19

O'Halloran v United Kingdom (Application Nos 15809/02 and 25624/02) (2007) Times, 13 July, [2007] All ER (D) 07 (Jul), ECtHR .... C 8.22

O'Leary International Ltd v Chief Constable of North Wales Police [2012] EWHC 1516 (Admin), 176 JP 514, 176 CL&J 370, [2012] All ER (D) 27 (Jun) .... B 34.5

Osman v DPP (1999) 163 JP 725 .... A 9.5

Oxfordshire County Council v L (3 March 2010, unreported) .... A 49.3

Oxfordshire County Council v S (2005) FLR 426 .... D 1.18

P

P (parental dispute: judicial determination), Re [2002] EWCA Civ 1627, [2003] 1 FLR 286, [2003] Fam Law 80, [2002] All ER (D) 80 (Oct) .... D 4.4

P-B (a child) (placement order), Re [2006] EWCA Civ 1016, [2007] 3 FCR 308, [2007] 1 FLR 1106, [2006] All ER (D) 64 (Nov) .... D 18.5

P (a child) (care and placement order proceedings: mental capacity of parent), Re [2008] EWCA Civ 462, [2009] LGR 213, [2008] 3 FCR 243, [2008] 2 FLR 1516, [2008] Fam Law 835, (2008) Times, 10 June, 152 Sol Jo (no 21) 31, [2008] All ER (D) 102 (May) .... D 19.1, 19.3

Parry v DPP [2004] EWHC 3112 (Admin), [2004] All ER (D) 335 (Dec) .... A 18.17

Patel and a defendant's costs order, Re [2012] EWCA Crim 1508, [2012] All ER (D) 115 (Jul) .... B 20.17

Pattison v DPP [2005] EWHC 2938 (Admin), [2006] 2 All ER 317, [2005] All ER (D) 237 (Dec) .... C 19.6

Paul v DPP (1989) 90 Cr App Rep 173, [1989] Crim LR 660, sub nom Paul v Luton Justices, ex p Crown Prosecution Service 153 JP 512 .... A 82.8

Peake v DPP [2010] EWHC 286 (Admin), 174 JP 457, [2010] All ER (D) 223 (Feb) .... C 49.10

Percy v DPP [2001] EWHC Admin 1125, (2001) 166 JP 93, [2002] Crim LR 835, [2001] All ER (D) 387 (Dec) .... A 21.5

Plackett v DPP [2008] EWHC 1335 (Admin), 172 JP 455, [2008] All ER (D) 194 (May) .... C 23.6A

Planton v DPP [2001] EWHC Admin 450 (2001) 166 JP 324, [2001] 27 LS Gaz R 40 .... A 36.3; C 18.8

Plunkett v DPP [2004] EWHC 1937 (Admin), [2004] All ER (D) 82 (Jul) .... C 22.5

Polychronakis v Richards and Jerrom Ltd [1998] JPL 588, [1998] Env LR 347 .... A 84.17

Power-Hynes v Norwich Magistrates' Court [2009] EWHC 1512 (Admin), 173 JP 573, [2009] All ER (D) 277 (Jun) .... M 2.9

Practice Direction (19 January 2000, unreported) .... D 8.18

Practice Direction (magistrates' courts: contempt) [2001] 2 Cr App Rep 272 .... I 3.7

Practice Direction (criminal proceedings: victim personal statements) [2001] 4 All ER 640, [2001] 1 WLR 2038, [2002] 1 Cr App Rep 69, [2002] 1 Cr App Rep (S) 482, 165 JP 759, CA .... B 5.56

Practice Direction (Criminal: Consolidated) [2002] 3 All ER 90 .... A 10.2, B 5.55, I 6.22

Practice Direction (costs: criminal proceedings) [2004] 2 All ER 1070, [2004] 1 WLR 2657, [2004] 2 Cr App Rep 395, CA .. B 20.18

Practice Direction (bail: failure to surrender and trials in absence) (2004) Times, 26 January, CA .... J 1.83

Practice Direction (magistrates' courts: anti-social behaviour orders: composition of benches) (24 February 2006, unreported) .... B 8.4

Practice Direction: Allocation and Transfer of Proceedings (3 November 2008, unreported) .... D 1.4

Practice Direction: Residence and Contact Orders: Domestic Violence and Harm [2009] 2 FLR 1400, [2009] 1 FCR 223, [2009] All ER (D) 122 (Jan) .... D 4.4, D 6.4A

Practice Direction (Attendance of Media Representatives at Hearings in Family Proceedings) (20 April 2009, unreported) ... D 1.8

Practice Direction (Appeals) (Allocation to Judiciary) [2009] All ER (D) 128 (Apr) .... D 1.18

Practice Direction (Cost in Criminal Proceedings) (CLW/10/32/26) (30 July 2010, unreported) .... B 20.2A

Practice Note (McKenzie Friends: Civil and Family Courts) [2010] 1 WLR 1881 .... D 1.8

Pratt v DPP [2001] EWHC Admin 483, (2001) 165 JP 800 ... A 41.7

President's Practice Direction (Experts in Family Proceedings relating to Children) [2008] All ER (D) 18 (May) .... D 6.2A

Prosecution Appeal (No 32 of 2007), R v N Ltd [2008] EWCA Crim 1223, (2008) Times, 25 August, [2008] All ER (D) 112 (Jun) .... I 6.21

Pumbien v Vines [1996] RTR 37, [1996] Crim LR 124   . C 9.4, C 33.8, C 51.5

Pye v Leeds Youth Court [2006] EWHC 2527 (Admin), [2006] All ER (D) 16 (Oct) .... B 2.6, B 25.6

R

R (minors), Re [1995] 1 FCR 563, sub nom F and R (Section 8 order: grandparents' application), Re [1995] 1 FLR 524, [1995] Fam Law 235 .... D 4.9

R (a child) (special guardianship order), Re [2006] EWCA Civ 1748, [2007] Fam 41, [2007] 2 WLR 1130, [2007] 1 FCR 121, [2007] Fam Law 307, (2006) Times, 29 December, [2006] All ER (D) 299 (Dec) .... D 18.34

R v A [2007] EWCA Crim 1950, [2007] All ER (D) 127 (Jun) .... A 1.33

R v A Local Authority [2011] EWCA Civ 1451, [2012] 1 FLR 1302, [2012] Fam Law 265, 155 Sol Jo (no 47) 31, [2011] All ER (D) 30 (Dec) .... D 6.2A

R (on the application of Robinson) v Abergavenny Magistrates' Court [2007] All ER (D) 210 (Jul), DC .... I 6.4

R (on the application of Denny) v Acton Youth Court (2004) Independent, 24 May .... E 3.24

R v Akram [2002] All ER (D) 44 (Jun), CA .... A 3.17

R v Al-Daour (Tariq) [2011] EWCA Crim 2392 .... B 2.20

R (on the application of Harper) v Aldershot Magistrates' Court [2010] EWHC 1319 (Admin), 174 JP 410, 174 CL&J 383, [2010] All ER (D) 11 (Jun) .... I 1B.8

R v Allen [1985] 1 All ER 148, [1985] 1 WLR 50, 79 Cr App Rep 265, [1984] Crim LR 498, 128 Sol Jo 660, [1984] LS Gaz R 1994, CA; affd [1985] AC 1029, [1985] 2 All ER 641, [1985] 3 WLR 107, 81 Cr App Rep 200, 149 JP 587, [1985] Crim LR 739, 129 Sol Jo 447, [1985] LS Gaz R 2740, [1985] NLJ Rep 603, HL .... A 45.7

R v Allen and Lambert (1999) 163 JP 841, CA .... E 3.19

R v Amey [1983] 1 All ER 865, [1983] 1 WLR 345, [1983] RTR 192, 76 Cr App Rep 206, 4 Cr App Rep (S) 410, 147 JP 124, [1983] Crim LR 268, 127 Sol Jo 85, CA .... B 18.9

R v Angel [1998] 1 Cr App Rep (S) 347, CA .... A 81.16

R v Arbery [2008] EWCA Crim 702, 172 JP 291 .... B 41.7

R v Argent [1997] 2 Cr App Rep 27, 161 JP 190, [1997] Crim LR 346, CA .... I 6.22

R v Ashley [2003] EWCA Crim 2571, [2004] 1 WLR 2057, [2004] 1 Cr App Rep 299, 167 JP 548, [2004] Crim LR 297, [2003] All ER (D) 106 (Aug) .... J 1.92

R (on the application of Y) v Aylesbury Crown Court, Crown Prosecution Service and Newsquest Media Group Ltd [2012] EWHC 1140 (Admin), [2012] All ER (D) 89 (May) .... A 52.12

R v B [2000] Crim LR 870 .... B 25.7

R v Ball [2002] EWCA Crim 2777, [2003] 2 Cr App Rep (S) 92, [2003] Crim LR 122 .... B 34.9

R v Bannister [2009] EWCA Crim 1571, (2009) Times, 24 August, 153 Sol Jo (no 30) 30, [2009] All ER (D) 289 (Jul) .... C 16.8

R v Barber [2006] EWCA Crim 162, [2006] 2 Cr App Rep (S) 539, (2006) Times, 4 April, [2006] All ER (D) 240 (Feb) ... B 2.20, B 25.7

R v Barker [2010] EWCA Crim 4, [2011] Crim LR 233, (2010) Times, 5 February, [2010] All ER (D) 126 (Jan) A52.7

R (on the application of Ethos Recycling Ltd) v Barking and Dagenham Magistrates' Court [2009] EWHC 2885 (Admin), [2010] PTSR 787, 174 JP 25, 173 CL&J 766, (2010) Times, 2 February, [2009] All ER (D) 162 (Nov) .... A 84.2, A 84.8

R (on the application of P) v Barking Youth Court [2002] EWHC 734 (Admin), [2002] 2 Cr App Rep 294, 166 JP 641, [2002] All ER (D) 93 (Apr) .... E 3.25

R v Barnes [2004] EWCA Crim 3246, [2005] 2 All ER 113, [2005] 1 WLR 910, [2005] 1 Cr App Rep 507, [2005] Crim LR 381, (2005) Times, 10 January, [2004] All ER (D) 338 (Dec) ...... A 15.18

R v Barrick (1985) 81 Cr App Rep 78, 7 Cr App Rep (S) 142, 149 JP 705, [1985] Crim LR 602, 129 Sol Jo 416, [1985] LS Gaz R 3173, [1985] NLJ Rep 509, CA .... A 57.38

R (on the application of Spiteri) v Basildon Crown Court [2009] EWHC 665 (Admin), 173 JP 327, [2009] All ER (D) 197 (Mar) .... B 20.18

R v Bassett [2008] EWCA Crim 1174, 172 JP 491, (2008) Times, 18 June, [2008] All ER (D) 48 (Jun) .... A 68.5

R v Bebbington [2005] EWCA Crim 2395, [2006] 1 Cr App Rep (S) 690, 169 JP 621, [2006] Crim LR 160, (2005) Times, 24 October, [2005] All ER (D) 153 (Oct) .... B 8.5

R v Becouarn [2005] UKHL 55, [2005] 4 All ER 673, [2005] 1 WLR 2589, [2006] 1 Cr App Rep 19, [2006] Crim LR 373, [2005] NLJR 1416, (2005) Times, 1 August, [2005] All ER (D) 412 (Jul) .... I 6.22

R v Belmarsh Magistrates' Court, ex p Watts [1999] 2 Cr App Rep 188, DC .... I 4.8

R v Bentham [2005] UKHL 18, [2005] 2 All ER 65, [2005] 1 WLR 1057, 169 JP 181, [2005] Crim LR 648, [2005] NLJR 545, (2005) Times, 11 March, 149 Sol Jo LB 358, [2005] All ER (D) 161 (Mar) .... A 76.6

R v Bezzina [1994] 3 All ER 964, [1994] 1 WLR 1057, 158 JP 671, 138 Sol Jo LB 11, CA .... A 72.3

R v Bickerton [2007] EWCA Crim 2884, [2007] All ER (D) 230 (Nov) .... A 52.15

R v Bird [1985] 2 All ER 513, [1985] 1 WLR 816, 81 Cr App Rep 110, [1985] Crim LR 388, 129 Sol Jo 362, [1985] LS Gaz R 1709, CA .... A 8.18

R v Birmingham Justices, ex p F (1999) 164 JP 523, [2000] Crim LR 588 .... E 2.2

R (on the application of Blackwood) v Birmingham Magistrates Court [2006] EWHC 1800 (Admin), [2006] All ER (D) 324 (Jun) .... F 1.15

R (on the application of Mills) v Birmingham Magistrates' Court [2005] EWHC 2732 (Admin), (2005) 170 JP 237, 170 JPN 473, 170 JPN 457, [2005] All ER (D) 94 (Oct) .... B 8.5

R (on the application of Harrison) v Birmingham Magistrate's Court [2011] EWCA Civ 332, [2011] 14 LS Gaz R 21, [2011] All ER (D) 294 (Mar) .... M 3.2

R (on application of Johnson (Craig Matthew)) v Birmingham Magistrates' Court and Crown Prosecution Services [2012] EWHC 596 (Admin), 176 JP 298 .... B 19.1, B 33.76

R v Bishop [2004] EWCA Crim 2956, [2004] All ER (D) 116 (Dec) .... B 17.18

R (on the application of Crown Prosecution Service) v Blaydon
Youth Court [2004] EWHC 2296 (Admin), (2004) 168 JP 638,
[2005] Crim LR 495, [2004] All ER (D) 45 (Oct) . A 15.3, A 41.9, A
50.8
R v Bogdal [2008] EWCA Crim 1, 172 JP 178, 172 JPN 403, 152
Sol Jo (no 4) 30, [2008] All ER (D) 44 (Jan) .... A 72.5
R v Boggild [2011] EWCA Crim 1928, 175 CL&J 502, (2011)
Times, 05 September, [2011] All ER (D) 167 (Jul) .... B 41.18
R v Boness [2005] EWCA Crim 2395, [2006] 1 Cr App Rep (S)
690, 169 JP 621, [2006] Crim LR 160, (2005) Times,
24 October, [2005] All ER (D) 153 (Oct) .... B 8.5
R v Bore [2004] EWCA Crim 1452, (2004) 169 JP 245,
[2005] All ER (D) 12 (Feb) .... A A 75.7
R v Bouchereau: 30/77 [1978] QB 732, [1981] 2 All ER 924n,
[1978] 2 WLR 250, [1977] ECR 1999, [1977] 2 CMLR 800, 66
Cr App Rep 202, 122 Sol Jo 79, ECJ .... B 23.8
R v Bow [1977] RTR 6, 64 Cr App Rep 54, [1977] Crim LR 176,
CA .... A 65.4
R v Bradfield [2006] EWCA Crim 2917, [2006] All ER (D) 394
(Nov) .... A 46.5
R v Bradish [2004] EWCA Crim 1340, (2004) 148 Sol Jo LB 474,
[2004] All ER (D) 40 (Apr) .... A 77.6
R v Braxton [2004] EWCA Crim 1374, [2005] 1 Cr App Rep (S)
167 .... B 8.13
R v Brazil [2004] EWCA Crim 1975, [2004] All ER (D) 348
(Jun) .... B 18.5
R (on the application of Matara) v Brent Magistrates' Court
[2005] All ER (D) 263 (Jul), DC .... I 7.6
R v Brentwood Justices, ex p Nicholls [1990] 2 QB 598, [1990]
3 All ER 516, [1990] 3 WLR 534, 154 JP 487, [1990] Crim LR
736, [1990] 31 LS Gaz R 33, DC; revsd [1992] 1 AC 1, [1991] 3
WLR 201, 155 JP 753, [1992] Crim LR 52, 135 Sol Jo LB 70,
sub nom Nicholls v Brentwood Justices [1991] 3 All ER 359, 93
Cr App Rep 400, HL .... I 4.1
R v Brightling [1991] Crim LR 364 .... A 7.3
R v Bristol [2007] EWCA Crim 3214, 172 JP 161, 172 JPN 421,
[2007] All ER (D) 47 (Dec) .... A 9.8
R v Bristol City Council, ex p Everett [1999] 2 All ER 193, [1999]
1 WLR 1170, 31 HLR 1102, [1999] 3 PLR 14, [1999] NPC 28,
[1999] 13 LS Gaz R 31, [1999] NLJR 370, [1999] EGCS 33, 143
Sol Jo LB 104, [1999] BLGR 513, [1999] Env LR 587, [1999]
EHLR 265, CA .... A 84.2
R v Britton [2006] EWCA Crim 2875, [2007] 1 Cr App Rep (S)
754, [2006] All ER (D) 334 (Oct) .... E 3.17A
R v Brock (1991) 165 JP 331, CA .... A 27A.2, 27B.2

R (on the application of Harrington) v Bromley Magistrates Court [2007] EWHC 2896 (Admin), [2007] All ER (D) 199 (Nov) ... B 16.1

R (on the application of H) v Bromley Youth Court [2006] All ER (D) 266 (Oct), DC .... B 5.46

R v Brown [1985] Crim LR 212, CA .... A 12.7, A 13.6

R v Brown [1992] QB 491, [1992] 2 All ER 552, [1992] 2 WLR 441, 94 Cr App Rep 302, 156 JP 475, [1992] 15 LS Gaz R 31, [1992] NLJR 275, 136 Sol Jo LB 90, CA; affd [1994] 1 AC 212, [1993] 2 All ER 75, [1993] 2 WLR 556, 97 Cr App Rep 44, 157 JP 337, [1993] Crim LR 583, [1993] NLJR 399, HL .... A 15.11

R v Buckley (1994) 15 Cr App Rep (S) 695, [1994] Crim LR 387, CA .... C 5.9

R (on the application of G) v Burnley Magistrates' Court [2007] EWHC 1033 (Admin), 171 JP 445, [2007] All ER (D) 196 (Apr) .... E 3.18, E 3.18A

R v Burns [2012] EWCA Crim 192, [2012] 2 Cr App Rep (S) 384 .... A 14.6

R (on the application of DPP) v Bury Magistrates' Court [2007] All ER (D) 208 (Dec) .... B 20.19

R v Buxton [2010] EWCA Crim 2923, [2011] 1 WLR 857, [2011] Bus LR 448, [2011] 2 Cr App Rep (S) 121, [2011] Crim LR 332, (2011) Times, 21 February, [2010] All ER (D) 215 (Dec) A41.13

R v C [2007] EWCA Crim 1757, [2007] All ER (D) 342 (Jul) .... A 72.5

R v CS [2012] EWCA Crim 389, [2012] 1 Cr App Rep 429, 176 CL&J 157, (2012) Times, 08 May, [2012] All ER (D) 06 (Mar) .... D 16.5

R v Calderdale Magistrates' Court, ex p Donahue and Cutler [2001] Crim LR 141 .... I 6.9

R (on the application of the DPP) v Camberwell Youth Court [2005] UKHL 4, [2005] 1 All ER 999, [2005] 1 WLR 393, [2005] 2 Cr App Rep 1, [2005] 1 FCR 365, 169 JP 105, [2005] Crim LR 497, (2005) Times, 1 February, 149 Sol Jo LB 146, [2005] All ER (D) 259 (Jan) .... A 68.10; I 4.1A

R (on the application of D) v Camberwell Green Youth Court [2003] EWHC 227 (Admin), [2003] 2 Cr App Rep 257, 167 JP 210, [2003] Crim LR 659, [2003] All ER (D) 32 (Feb) .... A 52.10

R (on the application of M) v Camberwell Green Youth Court [2004] All ER (D) 95 (Dec), DC .... E 3.18

R v Camberwell Green Youth Court, ex p G [2005] UKHL 4, [2005] 1 All ER 999, [2005] 1 WLR 393, [2005] 2 Cr App Rep 1, [2005] 1 FCR 365, 169 JP 105, [2005] Crim LR 497, (2005) Times, 1 February, 149 Sol Jo LB 146, [2005] All ER (D) 259 (Jan) .... E 3.22

R (on the application of Middleton) v Cambridge Magistrates' Court [2012] EWHC 2122 (Admin), 176 JP 569, [2012] All ER (D) 35 (Jul) .... B 20.8

R v Campbell [2006] EWCA Crim 726, [2006] All ER (D) 137 (Mar) .... B 26.0

R v Campbell [2009] EWCA Crim 2459, [2010] 2 Cr App Rep (S) 175, 174 JP 73, [2010] Crim LR 241, [2009] All ER (D) 295 (Nov) .... C 16A.10

R v Cardiff Magistrates, ex p Czech [1999] 1 FCR 721, [1999] 1 FLR 95, [1998] Fam Law 658 .... D 7.46

R v Carmona [2006] EWCA Crim 508, [2006] 1 WLR 2264, [2006] 2 Cr App Rep (S) 662, (2006) Times, 13 April, [2006] All ER (D) 186 (Mar) .... B 23.8

R v Carr-Briant [1943] KB 607, [1943] 2 All ER 156, 41 LGR 183, 29 Cr App Rep 76, 107 JP 167, 112 LJKB 581, 169 LT 175, 59 TLR 300, CCA .... A 10.2

R v Cartwright [2010] EWCA Crim 2803, [2011] 2 Cr App Rep (S) 54, 175 JP 33 .... B 41.7

R v Celaire [2002] EWCA Crim 2487, [2003] 4 All ER 869, [2003] 1 Cr App Rep (S) 610, [2003] Crim LR 124, [2002] All ER (D) 365 (Oct) .... A 11.15

R v Central Criminal Court, ex p Bennett (1999) Times, 25 January .... J 1.53

R v Central Criminal Court, ex p Bright [2001] 2 All ER 244, [2001] 1 WLR 662, [2001] EMLR 79, [2000] All ER (D) 1042, DC .... M 2.7

R v Central Criminal Court, ex p Johnson [1999] 2 Cr App Rep 51 .... J 1.53

R v Chan-Fook [1994] 2 All ER 552, [1994] 1 WLR 689, 99 Cr App Rep 147, [1994] Crim LR 432, [1994] JPIL 332, CA ...... A 8.9

R v Chargot Ltd (t/a Contract Services) [2007] EWCA Crim 3032, [2008] 2 All ER 1077, [2008] ICR 517, [2007] All ER (D) 198 (Dec); affd [2008] UKHL 73, [2009] 2 All ER 645, [2009] 1 WLR 1, (2008) Times, 16 December, 153 Sol Jo (no 1) 32, [2008] All ER (D) 106 (Dec) .... A 80.19

R v Charles [2004] EWCA Crim 1977, [2005] 1 Cr App Rep (S) 253 .... A 76.19

R v Charles [2009] EWCA Crim 1570, [2010] 4 All ER 553, [2010] 1 Cr App Rep 38, 173 JP 481, [2010] Crim LR 303, (2009) Times, 25 August, [2009] All ER (D) 290 (Jul) .... B 8.13

R v Charlton (2000) 164 JP 685, CA .... B 25.4

R (on the application of the Royal Society for the Prevention of Cruelty to Animals) v Chester Crown Court [2006] EWHC 1273 (Admin), 170 JP 725, 171 JPN 179, [2006] All ER (D) 244 (May) .... A 5.4

R (on the application of Evans) v Chester Magistrates' Court [2004] All ER (D) 260 (Mar) .... I 7.8

R v Chichester Justices, ex p Crouch (1981) 146 JP 26 .... C 5.49

R (on the application of Shufflebottom) v Chief Constable of Greater Manchester [2003] EWHC 246 (Admin), (2003) 167 JP 153 .... A 72.21

R (on the application of Bates) v Chief Constable of the Avon and Somerset Police [2009] EWHC 942 (Admin), 173 JP 313, [2009] All ER (D) 59 (May) .... M 2.9

R (on the application of Laporte) v Chief Constable of the Gloucestershire Constabulary (Chief Constable of Thames Valley Police and Comr of Police of the Metropolis, interested parties) [2004] EWHC 253 (Admin), [2004] 2 All ER 874, [2004] NLJR 308, (2004) Times, 26 February, [2004] All ER (D) 313 (Feb); affd [2004] EWCA Civ 1639, [2005] QB 678, [2005] 1 All ER 473, [2005] 2 WLR 789, [2005] Crim LR 467, (2004) Times, 13 December, [2004] All ER (D) 118 (Dec) .... I 1.7

R v Chippenham Magistrates' Court, ex p Thompson (1995) 160 JP 207 .... B 36.1

R v Chopra [2006] EWCA Crim 2133, [2007] 1 Cr App Rep 225, [2006] All ER (D) 44 (Dec) .... I 6.14

R (on the application of Crown Prosecution Service) v Chorley Justices [2002] EWHC 2162 (Admin), (2002) 166 JP 764, sub nom R (on the application of DPP) v Chorley Justices [2002] 43 LS Gaz R 34 .... J 1.63

R v Chute [2003] EWCA Crim 177, [2003] 2 Cr App Rep (S) 445, [2003] Crim LR 295 .... A 7.22

R (on the application of the Crown Prosecution Service) v City of London Magistrates Court [2007] All ER (D) 302 (Jul), DC . B 7.1, B 33.85A

R (on the application of the Chief Constable of Greater Manchester Police) v City of Salford Magistrates' Court [2008] EWHC 1651 (Admin), 172 JP 497, 172 JPN 708, [2008] All ER (D) 272 (Jul) .... M 3.2

R (on the application of Hope and Glory Public House Ltd) v City of Westminster Magistrates' Court (Lord Mayor and Citizens of the City of Westminster, interested party) [2011] EWCA Civ 31, [2011] 3 All ER 579, [2011] PTSR 868, 175 JP 77, [2011] 18 EG 110, [2011] All ER (D) 206 (Jan) .... F 1.15

R (on the application of Williamson (Simon)) v City of Westminster Magistrates' Court, Crown Prosecution Service and Solicitor Rhys Maron [2012] EWHC 1444 (Admin), [2012] 2 Cr App Rep 299, [2012] All ER (D) 242 (May) .... B 7.2

R v Clancy [2012] EWCA Crim 8, [2012] 1 WLR 2536, [2012] 2 Cr App Rep 71, 176 JP 111, [2012] Crim LR 548, [2012] All ER (D) 97 (Jan) .... A 11.13

R v Clark [1998] 2 Cr App Rep 137, [1998] 2 Cr App Rep (S) 95, [1998] Crim LR 227, [1998] 02 LS Gaz R 22, (1997) Times, 4 December, 142 Sol Jo LB 27, CA .... A 57.38
R v Clarke [1997] 1 Cr App Rep (S) 323, CA .... A 76.20
R v Clarke [2000] 1 Cr App Rep (S) 224, CA .... J 1.91
R v Cliff [2004] EWCA Crim 3139, [2005] RTR 147, [2005] 2 Cr App Rep (S) 118, (2004) Times, 1 December, [2004] All ER (D) 400 (Nov) .... C 5.45
R v Clifton Steel Ltd [2007] EWCA Crim 1537, [2008] 1 Cr App Rep (S) 298, [2007] All ER (D) 108 (Jun) .... A 80.22
R v Cole [2007] EWCA Crim 1924, [2007] All ER (D) 472 (Jul) .... I 6.16
R v Collins [1973] QB 100, [1972] 2 All ER 1105, [1972] 3 WLR 243, 56 Cr App Rep 554, 136 JP 605, 116 Sol Jo 432, CA . A 12.17, A 13.17
R (on the application of Taylor) v Comr of the Metropolitan Police [2009] EWHC 264 (Admin), 173 JP 121, [2009] All ER (D) 156 (Jun) .... A 26.17
R v Condron [1997] 1 WLR 827, [1997] 1 Cr App Rep 185, 161 JP 1, [1997] Crim LR 215, CA .... I 6.22
R v Court [1989] AC 28, [1988] 2 All ER 221, [1988] 2 WLR 1071, 87 Cr App Rep 144, 152 JP 422, [1988] Crim LR 537, 132 Sol Jo 658, [1988] NLJR 128, HL .... A 53.5
R v Cousins [1982] QB 526, [1982] 2 All ER 115, [1982] 2 WLR 621, 74 Cr App Rep 363, 146 JP 264, [1982] Crim LR 444, 126 Sol Jo 154, CA .... A 59.3
R (on the application of McAuley (Clarke)) v Coventry Crown Court and Crown Prosecution Service [2012] EWHC 680 (Admin), [2012] 3 All ER 519, [2012] 1 WLR 2766, 176 JP 418, [2012] Crim LR 697, 176 CL&J 206, [2012] All ER (D) 144 (Mar) .... J 1.52
R (on the application of Khan) v Coventry Magistrates' Court [2011] EWCA Civ 751, [2011] All ER (D) 226 (Jun) .... F 1.14
R v Cowan [1996] QB 373, [1995] 4 All ER 939, [1995] 3 WLR 818, [1996] 1 Cr App Rep 1, 160 JP 165, [1996] Crim LR 409, [1995] 38 LS Gaz R 26, [1995] NLJR 1611, 139 Sol Jo LB 215, CA .... I 6.22
R v Cox (Jacqueline) (2004) Times, 20 February, CA .... A 72.9
R (on the application of DPP) v Crown Court at Blackfriars [2001] EWHC Admin 56 [2001] All ER (D) 205 .... J 1.52
R (on the application of M) v Crown Court at Inner London [2004] 1 FCR 178, [2003] 1 FLR 994 .... E 4.6
R v Crown Court at Knightsbridge, ex p Dunne [1993] 4 All ER 491, [1994] 1 WLR 296, 158 JP 213, [1993] Crim LR 853, [1993] NLJR 1479n .... A 72.20

R (on the application of Holland) v Crown Court at Leeds [2002] EWHC 1862 (Admin), [2003] Crim LR 272 .... J 1.52

R (on the application of Wardle) v Crown Court at Leeds [2001] UKHL 12, [2002] 1 AC 754, [2001] 2 All ER 1, [2001] 2 WLR 865, [2001] 2 Cr App Rep 301, 165 JP 465, [2001] 21 LS Gaz R 39, [2001] NLJR 386, 145 Sol Jo LB 117 .... J 1.54

R v Crown Court at Leeds, ex p Bagoutie (1999) Times, 31 May .... J 1.53

R v Crown Court at Lincoln, ex p Jude [1997] 3 All ER 737, [1998] 1 WLR 24, [1998] 1 Cr App Rep 130, 161 JP 589, 141 Sol Jo LB 138 .... B 10.6

R v Crown Court at Liverpool, ex p McCann [1995] RTR 23, [1995] Crim LR 425 .... I 7.1A

R (on the application of McCann) v Crown Court at Manchester [2001] 1 WLR 358, sub nom R v Crown Court at Manchester, ex p McCann 165 JP 225, [2001] 02 LS Gaz R 40, 144 Sol Jo LB 287; affd [2001] EWCA Civ 281 [2001] 4 All ER 264, [2001] 1 WLR 1084, 165 JP 545 .... B 8.4

R (on the application of McCann) v Crown Court at Manchester [2002] UKHL 39, [2003] 1 AC 787, [2002] 4 All ER 593, [2002] 3 WLR 1313, [2003] LGR 57, [2003] 1 Cr App Rep 419, 166 JP 657, [2003] Crim LR 269, [2003] HLR 189, (2002) Times, 21 October, 146 Sol Jo LB 239, [2002] All ER (D) 246 (Oct), 13 BHRC 482 .... A 41.13

R v Crown Court at Middlesex Guildhall, ex p Okoli (2000) 165 JP 144, [2000] Crim LR 921, 144 Sol Jo LB 228 .... J 1.76

R v Crown Court at St Albans, ex p O'Donovan [2000] 1 Cr App Rep (S) 344 .... C 22.24

R (on the application of Jeffrey) v Crown Court at Warwick [2002] EWHC 2469 (Admin), [2003] Crim LR 190 .... J 1.76

R (on the application of Smith) v Crown Court at Woolwich [2002] EWHC 995 (Admin) [2002] All ER (D) 05 (May) ...... J 1.53

R v Crown Prosecution Service [2010] EWHC 3593 (Admin) . A41.13

R v Crown Prosecution Service, ex p Spurrier. See DPP v Spurrier

R (on the application of Trinity Mirror plc) v Croydon Crown Court. See Trinity Mirror plc, Re

R (on the application of Desouza) v Croydon Magistrates' Court [2012] EWHC 1362 (Admin), 176 JP 624 .... A 84.31

R (on the application of the DPP) v Croydon Magistrates' Court [2001] EWHC Admin 552, [2001] All ER (D) 113 (Jul) .... I 6.9

R (on the application of DPP) v Croydon Youth Court (2000) 165 JP 181, 165 JPN 34 .... E 3.25

R v Cugullere [1961] 2 All ER 343, [1961] 1 WLR 858, 45 Cr App Rep 108, 125 JP 414, 105 Sol Jo 386, CCA .... A 11.7

R v Cunningham [1957] 2 QB 396, [1957] 2 All ER 412, [1957] 3
WLR 76, 41 Cr App Rep 155, 121 JP 451, 101 Sol Jo 503,
CCA .... A 15.4, A 70.5

R v Currie [2007] EWCA Crim 926, [2007] RTR 450, [2007] 2 Cr
App Rep 246, 151 Sol Jo LB 609, [2007] All ER (D) 233 (Apr)
.... C 49.3

R v Curtis [2010] EWCA Crim 123, [2010] 3 All ER 849, [2010]
1 Cr App Rep 457, [2010] Crim LR 638, 174 CL&J 156,
[2010] All ER (D) 94 (Feb) .... A 14.7

R v Czyzewski [2003] EWCA Crim 2139, [2004] 3 All ER 135,
[2004] 1 Cr App Rep (S) 289, 167 JP 409, (2003) Times, 25 July,
[2003] All ER (D) 276 (Jul) .... A 4.16

R v D (contempt of court: illegal photography) (2004) Times,
13 May .... I 3.4, I 3.15

R (on the application of Aldous) v Dartford Magistrates' Court
[2011] EWHC 1919 (Admin), [2011] All ER (D) 237 (Jul) ..... H 6.3

R v Daubney (2000) 164 JP 519, CA .... A 11.9

R v Davies [2002] EWCA Crim 2949, [2002] All ER (D) 275
(Dec), [2003] ICR 486, [2003] 09 LS Gaz R 27, [2003] JPN 42,
sub nom Davies v Health and Safety Executive [2003] IRLR 170,
147 Sol Jo LB 29 .... A 80.19

R v Davies [2010] EWCA Crim 1923, 174 CL&J 574,
[2010] All ER (D) 25 (Aug) .... A 72.15

R v Dealy [1995] 1 WLR 658, [1995] 2 Cr App Rep 398, [1995]
STC 217, [1994] 46 LS Gaz R 30, CA .... A 62.3

R v Debnath (2 December 2005, unreported) .... A 41.13

R v Densu [1998] 1 Cr App Rep 400, [1998] Crim LR 345, [1998]
02 LS Gaz R 22, 141 Sol Jo LB 250, CA .... A 11.14

R (on the application of Hussain) v Derby Magistrates' Court
[2001] EWHC Admin 507 [2001] 1 WLR 2454, [2002] 1 Cr
App Rep 37, 145 Sol Jo LB 168 .... J 1.92

R v Derwentside Magistrates' Court, ex p Swift [1997] RTR 89,
160 JP 468 .... C 19.6

R v DPP [2001] EWHC Admin 17, 165 JP 349, [2001] All ER (D)
120 (Jan) .... A 41.7

R (on the application of Khan) v DPP [2004] EWHC 2505
(Admin), sub nom Khan v DPP [2004] All ER (D) 134 (Oct) . C 22.25

R (on the application of Reda) v DPP [2011] EWHC 1550
(Admin), 175 JP 329, [2011] All ER (D) 167 (Jun) A9.5, A20.8

R (on the application of Traves) v DPP [2005] EWHC 1482
(Admin), 169 JP 421, sub nom Traves v DPP [2005] All ER (D)
381 (Jun) .... C 18.8, C 18.9

R (on the application of W) v DPP [2005] EWCA Civ 1333, (2005)
169 JP 435, sub nom W v DPP (2005) Times, 20 June,
[2005] All ER (D) 29 (Jun) .... B 8.13

R v DPP [2006] EWHC 1375 (Admin), 171 JPN 140,
[2006] All ER (D) 250 (May) .... A 20.3A
R v Divers [1999] 2 Cr App Rep (S) 421, [1999] Crim LR 843,
CA .... B 37.54
R v Docklands Estates Ltd (2000) 164 JP 505, [2000] 3 EGLR 17,
[2000] 45 EG 175, CA .... A 75.7
R v Doick [2004] EWCA Crim 139, [2004] 2 Cr App Rep (S)
203 .... C 5.45
R v Doncaster Justices, ex p Hannan (1998) 163 JP 182, [1998]
32 LS Gaz R 30, [1998] RVR 254, 142 Sol Jo LB 218 .... B 33.52; H
                                                                                    7.3
R (on the application of Blick) v Doncaster Magistrates' Court
[2008] EWHC 2698 (Admin), 172 JP 651, [2008] All ER (D) 51
(Oct) .... B 7.1
R (on the application of Culley) v Dorchester Crown Court [2007]
EWHC 109 (Admin), 171 JP 373, 171 JPN 706, [2007] All ER
(D) 295 (Jan) .... J 1.92
R v Dosanjh [1998] 3 All ER 618, [1999] 1 Cr App Rep 371,
[1999] 1 Cr App Rep (S) 107, [1998] Crim LR 593, [1998]
22 LS Gaz R 28, 142 Sol Jo LB 163, CA .... A 4.17
R v Doukas [1978] 1 All ER 1061, [1978] 1 WLR 372, 66 Cr App
Rep 228, [1978] Crim LR 177, 122 Sol Jo 30, CA .... A 36.9
R v Doyle [2012] EWCA Crim 995, 176 JP 337, 176 CL&J 322,
[2012] All ER (D) 130 (May) .... B 41.18
R (on the application of the DPP) v Dykes [2008] EWHC 2775
(Admin), (2009) 173 JP 88 .... A 20.6
R v EGS Ltd [2009] EWCA Crim 1942 .... A 80.19
R (on the application of Louis) v Ealing Magistrates' Court [2009]
EWHC 521 (Admin), 173 JP 248, [2009] All ER (D) 215 (Feb)
.... B 33.70
R v Ealing Magistrates' Court, ex p Burgess (1999) 165 JP 82,
[2000] Crim LR 855 .... I 6.19
R v Ealing Magistrates' Court, ex p Fanneran (1995) 160 JP 409, 8
Admin LR 351 .... A 72.10
R v Ealing Magistrates' Court, ex p Sahota (1997) 162 JP 73,
[1997] 45 LS Gaz R 29, 141 Sol Jo LB 251 .... B 7.1
R (on the application of Developing Retail Ltd) v East Hampshire
Magistrates' Court [2011] EWHC 618 (Admin), [2011] All ER
(D) 29 (Apr) .... F 1.15
R v Edmunds [2000] 2 Cr App Rep (S) 62, CA .... C 5.48
R v Edwards [2011] EWCA Crim 3028, [2012] Crim LR 563,
[2011] All ER (D) 108 (Nov) .... I 6.13A
R v Emery [2007] EWCA Crim 2469, [2007] All ER (D) 02
(Dec) .... A 53.17
R v Engen [2004] EWCA Crim 1536, [2004] All ER (D) 117
(Jun) .... B 33.22

R v Evans [2011] EWCA Crim 2842, [2012] 1 WLR 1192, [2012] 2 Cr App Rep 279, 176 JP 139, (2012) Times, 16 January .... A 10.2

R v Evesham Justices, ex p McDonagh [1988] QB 553, [1988] 1 All ER 371, [1988] 2 WLR 227, 87 Cr App Rep 28, 152 JP 65, [1988] Crim LR 181, 131 Sol Jo 1698, [1988] 2 LS Gaz R 36, [1987] NLJ Rep 757 .... I 1B.6

R v Eyck [2000] 3 All ER 569, [2000] 1 WLR 1389, [2000] 2 Cr App Rep 50, [2000] Crim LR 299, [2000] 05 LS Gaz R 34, 144 Sol Jo LB 59, CA .... A 81.8

R v F [2006] EWCA Crim 686, [2006] 3 All ER 562, 170 JPN 716, [2006] All ER (D) 410 (Mar) .... B 8.5

R v F [2011] EWCA Crim 726, [2011] 2 Cr App Rep 145, 175 CL&J 213, [2011] All ER (D) 275 (Mar) .... I 1B.11

R v F Howe & Son (Engineers) Ltd [1999] 2 All ER 249, [1999] 2 Cr App Rep (S) 37, [1999] IRLR 434, 163 JP 359, [1999] Crim LR 238, [1998] 46 LS Gaz R 34, CA .... A 80.22

R v Falmouth and Truro Port Health Authority, ex p South West Water Services [2001] QB 445, [2000] 3 All ER 306, [2000] All ER (D) 429, [2000] 3 WLR 1464, [2000] NPC 36, [2000] EGCS 50, [2000] EHLR 306, [2000] Env LR 658, CA

.... A 84.8

R (on the application of Gosport Borough Council) v Fareham Magistrates' Court [2006] EWHC 3047 (Admin), [2007] 1 WLR 634, 171 JP 102, 171 JPN 363, (2006) Times, 18 December, [2006] All ER (D) 267 (Nov) .... B 8.5

R v Faversham and Sittingbourne Magistrates' Court, ex p Ursell [1992] RA 99, 156 JP 765 .... H 7.1

R v Felixstowe, Ipswich and Woodbridge Magistrates' Court and Ipswich Borough Council, ex p Herridge [1993] RA 83, 158 JP 307 .... H 6.4

R v Feltham Justices, ex p Rees [2001] 2 Cr App Rep (S) 1, [2001] Crim LR 47 .... B 16.1

R v Finn [2012] EWCA Crim 881 .... B 37.50

R v Fitzgerald [2012] 3 Costs LR 437 .... B 20.19

R v Flack [2008] EWCA Crim 204, [2008] 2 Cr App Rep (S) 395 .... A 72.15

R v Flax Bourton Magistrates' Court, ex p Customs and Excise Comrs (1996) 160 JP 481, [1996] Crim LR 907 .... I 4.2

R (on the application of Gonzales) v Folkestone Magistrates' Court [2010] EWHC 3428 (Admin), 175 JP 453, [2010] All ER (D) 172 (Dec) A41.13

R v Francis [2006] EWCA Crim 3323, [2007] 1 WLR 1021, [2007] All ER (D) 179 (May) .... A 21.9

R v Freeman [1970] 2 All ER 413, [1970] 1 WLR 788, 54 Cr App Rep 251, 134 JP 462, 114 Sol Jo 336, CA .... A 33.9, A 76.7

R v G (Autrefois Acquit) [2001] EWCA Crim 1215 [2001] 1 WLR
1727, [2001] 2 Cr App Rep 615, 165 JP 513, 145 Sol Jo LB
126 .... A 15.31
R v G [2003] UKHL 50, [2004] 1 AC 1034, [2003] 4 All ER 765,
[2003] 3 WLR 1060, [2004] 1 Cr App Rep 237, 167 JP 621,
[2004] Crim LR 369, [2003] 43 LS Gaz R 31, [2004] 2 LRC
546, [2003] All ER (D) 257 (Oct) .... A 18.31
R v Galbraith [1981] 2 All ER 1060, [1981] 1 WLR 1039, 73 Cr
App Rep 124, 144 JP 406, [1981] Crim LR 648, 125 Sol Jo 442,
CA .... I 6.21
R v Ganley [2000] All ER (D) 594, [2001] 1 Cr App Rep (S) 60,
CA .... B 25.11
R v Ganyo (Molly and Prize) [2011] EWCA Crim 2491, [2012] 1
Cr App Rep (S) 650, 176 JP 396 .... B 18.6
R v Garcia (1987) 87 Cr App Rep 175, [1988] Crim LR 115,
CA .... A 78.9
R v Gedminintaite [2008] EWCA Crim 814, 172 JP 413 ...... A 72.3
R v Gent [2002] EWCA Crim 943 [2002] All ER (D) 46 (Apr)
.... A 76.18
R v Ghafoor [2002] EWCA Crim 1857, [2003] 1 Cr App Rep (S)
428, 166 JP 601, [2002] Crim LR 739 .... E 3.17A
R v Ghosh [1982] QB 1053, [1982] 2 All ER 689, [1982] 3 WLR
110, 75 Cr App Rep 154, 146 JP 376, [1982] Crim LR 608, 126
Sol Jo 429, CA .... A 36.7, A 45.5, A 57.6
R v Gillette (1999) Times, 3 December, CA .... B 26.18, B 37.16
R v Glidewell (1999) 163 JP 557, CA .... A 11.14
R (on the application of the Crown Prosecution Service) v
Gloucester Justices [2008] EWHC 1488 (Admin), 172 JP 506,
172 JPN 723, [2008] All ER (D) 197 (Jun) .... I 6.13A
R v Gloucester Magistrates' Court, ex p Chung (1988) 153 JP 75
.... C 16.19
R v Gough (2001) 165 JPN 895 .... I 6.22
R (on the application of A) v Governor of Huntercombe Young
Offender Institution [2006] EWHC 2544 (Admin), 171 JP 65,
171 JPN 345, [2006] All ER (D) 226 (Oct) .... B 25.7
R v Graham [2004] EWCA Crim 2755, [2005] 1 Cr App Rep (S)
640, [2004] All ER (D) 320 (Nov) .... A 54.5
R v Gravesend Justices, ex p Dexter [1977] Crim LR 298 .... B 7.3
R v Gravesend Magistrates' Court, ex p Baker (1997) 161 JP 765
.... I 7.7
R (on the application of AS) v Great Yarmouth Youth Court
[2011] EWHC 2059 (Admin) .... I 6.13B
R (on the application of B) v Greenwich Magistrates' Court [2008]
EWHC 2882 (Admin), 173 JP 52, [2009] HLR 425, (2008)
Times, 22 December, [2008] All ER (D) 70 (Nov) .... B 8.8

R (on the application of Pearson) v Greenwich Magistrates' Court
[2008] EWHC 300 (Admin), sub nom Pearson v Greenwich
Borough Council [2008] RVR 234, [2008] All ER (D) 256
(Jan) .... A 54.4
R (on the application of Thomas) v Greenwich Magistrates' Court
[2009] EWHC 1180 (Admin), 173 JP 345, [2009] All ER (D) 85
(May) .... J 1.92
R (on the application of C) v Grimsby and Cleethorpes
Magistrates' Court [2004] EWHC 2240 (Admin), 168 JP 569,
[2004] All ER (D) 494 (Jul) .... I 4.1A
R v Grout [2011] EWCA Crim 299, [2011] 1 Cr App Rep 472,
175 JP 209, [2011] Crim LR 584, [2011] All ER (D) 21 (Mar)
.... A53.9
R (on the application of Stokes) v Gwent Magistrates' Court
[2001] EWHC Admin 569 [2001] All ER (D) 125 (Jul), 165 JP
766 .... B 33.50
R v Gwynn [2002] EWCA Crim 2951, [2003] 2 Cr App Rep (S)
267, [2003] Crim LR 421, [2003] All ER (D) 318 (Dec) .... A 18.3
R v H [2005] EWCA Crim 732, [2005] 2 All ER 859, [2005] 1
WLR 2005, [2005] Crim LR 735, (2005) Times, 8 February,
[2005] All ER (D) 16 (Feb) .... A 53.5
R v H [2006] EWCA Crim 1470, [2006] All ER (D) 87 (Jun)
.... A 53.17
R v H [2010] EWCA Crim 1931, 174 CL&J 573, 154 Sol Jo (no
31) 28, [2010] All ER (D) 14 (Aug) .... A 8.10
R v Hackett [2011] EWCA Crim 380, [2011] 2 Cr App Rep 35,
[2011] All ER (D) 28 (Mar) .... I 6.22
R v Hall (1985) 81 Cr App Rep 260, [1985] Crim LR 377, 129 Sol
Jo 283, [1985] LS Gaz R 1485, [1985] NLJ Rep 604, CA ... A 40.10
R v Hall [2004] EWCA Crim 2671, [2005] 1 Cr App Rep (S) 671,
[2005] Crim LR 152, [2004] All ER (D) 377 (Nov) .... B 8.8
R v Hall-Chung [2002] EWCA Crim 3088, [2003] All ER (D) 113
(Feb) .... A 76.3
R v Hamidi [2010] EWCA Crim 66, [2010] Crim LR 578,
[2010] All ER (D) 33 (Feb) .... I 6.22
R v Hampshire [1996] QB 1, [1995] 2 All ER 1019, [1995] 3 WLR
260, [1995] 2 Cr App Rep 319, CA .... A 52.6
R v Hanson [2005] EWCA Crim 824, [2005] 1 WLR 3169, [2005]
2 Cr App Rep 299, 169 JP 250, (2005) Times, 24 March,
[2005] All ER (D) 380 (Mar) .... I 6.14
R v Haque [2011] EWCA Crim 1871, [2012] 1 Cr App Rep 48,
[2011] Crim LR 962, (2011) Times, 20 September, [2011] All ER
(D) 238 (Jul) A41.7
R v Harrison [2003] EWCA Crim 3514, [2004] 2 Cr App Rep (S)
106, [2004] Crim LR 241, (2003) Times, 1 December,
[2003] All ER (D) 288 (Nov) .... A 1.4

R (on the application of Martin) v Harrow Crown Court [2007]
EWHC 3193 (Admin), [2007] All ER (D) 106 (Dec) .... I 6.4
R v Havant Justices, ex p Palmer (1985) 149 JP 609, [1985] Crim
LR 658 .... I 3.5
R (on the application of the DPP) v Havering Magistrates' Court
[2001] 3 All ER 997, [2000] All ER (D) 2307, [2001] 1 WLR
805, [2001] 2 Cr App Rep 12, 165 JP 391 .... J 1.2
R v Haynes [2004] EWCA Crim 390, (2004) Times, 27 February,
[2004] All ER (D) 235 (Mar) .... A 72.17
R v Hayward [2001] EWCA Crim 168, [2001] QB 862, [2001] 3
WLR 125, [2001] 2 Cr App Rep 156, 165 JP 281, [2001]
09 LS Gaz R 38, 145 Sol Jo LB 53, [2001] All ER (D) 256 (Jan);
affd [2002] UKHL 5, [2003] 1 AC 1, [2002] 2 All ER 113,
[2002] 2 WLR 524, [2002] 2 Cr App Rep 128, 166 JP 333,
[2002] 13 LS Gaz R 26, 146 Sol Jo LB 61, [2002] 5 LRC 50,
[2002] All ER (D) 275 (Feb) .... I 6.19
R v Heard [2007] EWCA Crim 125, [2007] 3 All ER 306, [2007]
3 WLR 475, [2007] Crim LR 654, (2007) Times, 6 March,
[2007] All ER (D) 158 (Feb) .... A 53.4, A 53.6
R v Heathcote-Smith (Benjamin) [2011] EWCA Crim 2846, [2012]
2 Cr App Rep (S) 133, [2012] Crim LR 304 .... B 5.2
R v Hennigan [1971] 3 All ER 133, [1971] RTR 305, 55 Cr App
Rep 262, 135 JP 504, 115 Sol Jo 268, CA .... C 9.5
R (on the application of Jones) v HM Justices of the Peace [2008]
EWHC 2740 (Admin), [2008] All ER (D) 331 (Oct) .... B 7.5
R v Hichens [2011] EWCA Crim 1626, [2011] 2 Cr App Rep 370,
[2011] Crim LR 873, (2011) Times, 20 July, [2011] All ER (D)
81 (Jun) .... A 8.20
R (on the application of Cleary) v Highbury Corner
Magistrates' Court [2006] EWHC 1869 (Admin), (2006) Times,
12 September, 150 Sol Jo LB 1052, [2006] All ER (D) 376
(Jul) .... A 26.12
R (on the application of Raphael t/a Orleans) v Highbury Corner
Magistrates Court [2011] EWCA Civ 462, [2011] All ER (D)
224 (Apr) .... F 1.15
R (on the application of Turner) v Highbury Corner
Magistrates Court [2005] EWHC 2568 (Admin), [2006] 1 WLR
220, 170 JP 93, (2005) Times, 26 October, [2005] All ER (D)
105 (Oct) .... A 26.12, B 53.1
R v Highbury Corner Magistrates' Court, ex p Uchendu (1994)
158 LGR 481, [1994] RA 51, 158 JP 409 .... H 6.3
R v Hinks [2001] 2 AC 241, [2000] 4 All ER 833, [2000] 3 WLR
1590, [2001] 1 Cr App Rep 252, 165 JP 21, [2000] 43 LS Gaz R
37, 144 Sol Jo LB 265, HL .... A 57.8
R v Hodgson [2008] EWCA Crim 1180, [2008] All ER (D) 64
(Jun) .... A 68.5

R v Holland [2002] EWCA Crim 1585, [2003] 1 Cr App Rep (S) 288, [2002] All ER (D) 113 (Jun) .... A 72.17

R v Horseferry Road Magistrates' Court, ex p Bennett [1994] AC 42, [1993] 3 WLR 90, 98 Cr App Rep 114, 137 Sol Jo LB 159, sub nom Bennett v Horseferry Road Magistrates' Court [1993] 3 All ER 138, HL .... I 1B.10

R v Horseferry Road Metropolitan Stipendiary Magistrate, ex p Siadatan [1991] 1 QB 260, [1991] 1 All ER 324, [1990] 3 WLR 1006, 92 Cr App Rep 257, [1990] Crim LR 598, [1990] NLJR 704 .... A 21.6

R v Horsham Justices, ex p Farquharson [1982] QB 762, [1982] 2 All ER 269, [1982] 2 WLR 430, 76 Cr App Rep 87, 126 Sol Jo 98, CA .... I 1B.7

R v Horsham Justices, ex p Richards [1985] 2 All ER 1114, [1985] 1 WLR 986, 82 Cr App Rep 254, 7 Cr App Rep (S) 158, 149 JP 567, 129 Sol Jo 467, [1985] LS Gaz R 2499 .... B 18.5

R v Howard [2012] EWCA Crim 671, [2012] All ER (D) 43 (Apr) .... A 55.3

R v Howells [1999] 1 All ER 50, [1999] 1 WLR 307, [1999] 1 Cr App Rep 98, [1999] 1 Cr App Rep (S) 335, 162 JP 731, [1998] Crim LR 836, CA .... B 5.34

R v Howlett [1999] All ER (D) 777, CA .... A 4.17

R v Huddart [1999] Crim LR 568, CA .... A 72.2

R v Ingram (2004) Telegraph, 27 May, CA .... B 33.16

R (on the application of Brown) v Inner London Crown Court [2003] EWHC 3194 (Admin), [2003] All ER (D) 256 (Dec) . A 34.17; B 41.5

R v Iqbal [2011] 2 Cr App Rep 250, (2011) Times, 21 April, CA .... I 7.5B

R v Ireland [1998] AC 147, [1997] 4 All ER 225, [1997] 3 WLR 534, [1998] 1 Cr App Rep 177, [1998] 1 FLR 105, [1998] Fam Law 137, [1997] Crim LR 810, [1997] NLJR 1273, HL .... A 8.9

R v Isaac [2004] EWCA Crim 1082, 168 JP 417, [2004] All ER (D) 209 (Apr) .... A 60.3

R (on the application of Sandhu) v Isleworth Crown Court [2012] EWHC 1658 (Admin), 176 JP 537, 176 CL&J 339, [2012] All ER (D) 183 (May) .... A 72.15

R (on the application of Mohuddin Khan) v Isleworth Crown Court and Hillingdon London Borough of Council (Interested Party) [2011] EWHC 3164 (Admin), 176 JP 6 ..... A 84.8

R v JD (2000) 165 JP 1, CA .... B 25.4

R v Jayson [2002] EWCA Crim 683, [2003] 1 Cr App Rep 212 .... A 43.3

R v Jelk [2002] EWCA Crim 184 [2002] All ER (D) 200 (Jan) .... B 23.8

R v Johnson [1995] RTR 15, 158 JP 788, [1995] Crim LR 250, [1994] 13 LS Gaz R 35, CA .... A 64.3

R v Johnson [2006] EWCA Crim 2486, [2007] 1 All ER 1237, [2007] 1 WLR 585, [2007] 1 Cr App Rep (S) 674, 171 JP 172, [2007] Crim LR 177, 171 JPN 410, (2006) Times, 2 November, [2006] All ER (D) 257 (Oct) .... B 16.5; E 3.18

R v Johnstone [2003] UKHL 28, [2003] 3 All ER 884, [2003] 1 WLR 1736, [2003] 2 Cr App Rep 493, 167 JP 281, [2004] Crim LR 244, [2003] IP & T 901, [2003] 26 LS Gaz R 36, 147 Sol Jo LB 625, [2003] All ER (D) 323 (May) .... A 60.3; I 1.8

R v Jones [1995] QB 235, [1995] 3 All ER 139, [1995] 2 WLR 64, [1995] 1 Cr App Rep 262, 159 JP 94, [1995] Crim LR 416, [1994] 39 LS Gaz R 38, 138 Sol Jo LB 194, CA .... A 33.4

R v Jones [2002] UKHL 5, [2003] 1 AC 1, [2002] 2 All ER 113, [2002] 2 WLR 524, [2002] 2 Cr App Rep 128, 166 JP 333, [2002] 13 LS Gaz R 26, 146 Sol Jo LB 61 .... I 6.19

R v Jones [2006] UKHL 16, [2006] 2 All ER 741, [2006] 2 WLR 772, [2006] 15 LS Gaz R 20, [2006] NLJR 600, (2006) Times, 30 March, 150 Sol Jo LB 433, [2006] All ER (D) 419 (Mar) . A 18.19

R v Jordan [1998] Crim LR 353, CA .... A 17.3

R v K [2001] 1 Cr App Rep 493, [2001] Crim LR 134, CA; revsd sub nom R v K [2001] UKHL 41 [2002] 1 AC 462, [2001] 3 All ER 897, [2001] 3 WLR 471, [2002] 1 Cr App Rep 121, [2001] 3 FCR 115, [2001] 34 LS Gaz R 39, 145 Sol Jo LB 202 .... A 53.7

R v K [2011] EWCA Crim 1843, 175 JP 378, [2011] All ER (D) 230 (Jul) A41.13

R v Kefford [2002] EWCA Crim 519 [2002] Crim LR 432 .... B 37.6

R v Kelly [2001] EWCA Crim 1751, [2002] 1 Cr App Rep (S) 360, [2001] All ER (D) 195 (Jul) .... B 5.2B

R v Kelly [2001] RTR 45, CA .... A 18.3, A 66.2

R v Kelt [1977] 3 All ER 1099, [1977] 1 WLR 1365, 65 Cr App Rep 74, 142 JP 60, 121 Sol Jo 423, CA .... A 77.6

R v Keltbray Ltd [2001] 1 Cr App Rep (S) 132, [2000] All ER (D) 705, CA .... A 80.22

R v King [1993] RTR 245, 13 Cr App Rep (S) 668, CA .... C 5.9

R v Kingston-upon-Hull Stipendiary Magistrate, ex p Hartung [1981] RTR 262, 72 Cr App Rep 26, [1981] Crim LR 42 ..... B 34.8

R v Kluxen [2010] EWCA Crim 1081, [2010] Crim LR 657, 174 CL&J 380, (2010) Times, 23 June, [2010] All ER (D) 124 (May) .... B 23.1

R (on the application of K) v Knowsley Metropolitan Borough Council [2004] EWHC 1933 (Admin), 168 JP 461, sub nom Keating v Knowsley Metropolitan Borough Council [2004] All ER (D) 383 (Jul) .... B 8.7

R v Kolawole [2004] EWCA Crim 3047, [2005] 2 Cr App Rep (S) 71, (2004) Times, 16 November, 148 Sol Jo LB 1370, [2004] All ER (D) 439 (Nov) .... A 81.16

R v Konzani [2005] EWCA Crim 706, [2005] All ER (D) 292 (Mar) .... A 70.5

R v Kuxhaus. See R v Nazari

R v L [2007] EWCA Crim 764, [2007] All ER (D) 489 (Mar) .... I 6.1

R v LM [2002] EWCA Crim 3047, [2003] 2 Cr App Rep (S) 124, [2003] Crim LR 205, [2002] All ER (D) 35 (Dec) .... B 25.4

R v Lambert [2001] 1 All ER 1014, [2001] 2 WLR 211, [2001] 1 Cr App Rep 205, [2000] 35 LS Gaz R 36, 144 Sol Jo LB 226, CA; affd sub nom [2001] UKHL 37, [2002] 2 AC 545, [2001] 3 All ER 577, [2001] 3 WLR 206, [2001] 2 Cr App Rep 511, [2001] 31 LS Gaz R 29, 145 Sol Jo LB 174 .... A 25.10, A 26.4B

R v Land [1999] QB 65, [1998] 1 All ER 403, [1998] 3 WLR 322, [1998] 1 Cr App Rep 301, [1998] 1 FLR 438, [1998] Fam Law 133, [1998] Crim LR 70, [1997] 42 LS Gaz R 32, CA .... A 43.5

R v Lang [2005] EWCA Crim 2864, [2006] 2 All ER 410, [2006] 1 WLR 2509, [2006] Crim LR 174, (2005) Times, 10 November, 149 Sol Jo LB 1450, [2005] All ER (D) 54 (Nov) ...... B 16.5; E 3.18

R v Lavery [2008] EWCA Crim 2499, [2009] 3 All ER 295, 172 JP 561, 172 JPN 806, (2008) Times, 20 October, [2008] All ER (D) 227 (Oct) .... B 5.9

R v Law [2002] All ER (D) 40 (Jan), CA .... B 16.1

R (on the application of Child Support Agency) v Learad [2008] EWHC 2193 (Admin), [2009] 1 FLR 31, [2008] Fam Law 1086, [2008] Fam Law 949, 172 JP 547, 172 JPN 789, [2008] All ER (D) 218 (Jul) .... D 7.47

R v Lee (2001) 165 JP 634 .... A 7.3

R (on the application of Lee) v Leeds Crown Court [2006] EWHC 2550 (Admin), [2006] All ER (D) 18 (Oct) .... A 46.5

R (on the application of W) v Leeds Crown Court and Crown Prosecution Service [2011] EWHC 2326 (Admin), [2012] 1 Cr App Rep 162, 175 JP 467, [2012] Crim LR 160, [2011] All ER (D) 52 (Oct) .... B 1.5

R v Leeds Justices, ex p Kennett [1996] RVR 53 .... H 6.3

R (on the application of Grimshaw) v Leeds Magistrates' Court [2001] EWHC Admin 880 [2001] All ER (D) 350 (Oct) .... J 1.23

R (on the application of Kenny) v Leeds Magistrates' Court [2003] EWHC 2963 (Admin), [2004] 1 All ER 1333, 168 JP 125, [2003] All ER (D) 104 (Dec); affd sub nom R (on the application of M) v Secretary of State for Constitutional Affairs and Lord Chancellor [2004] EWCA Civ 312, [2004] 2 All ER 531, [2004] 1 WLR 2298, [2004] LGR 417, 168 JP 529, 148 Sol Jo LB 385, [2004] All ER (D) 345 (Mar) .... B 8.7

R v Leonard [2012] EWCA Crim 277, [2012] 2 Cr App Rep 138, 176 CL&J 466, [2012] All ER (D) 235 (Jul) .... A 43.3

R v Levesconte [2011] EWCA Crim 2754, [2012] 2 Cr App Rep (S) 80, 176 JP 204, [2012] Crim LR 236, [2011] 47 LS Gaz R 21, [2011] All ER (D) 183 (Nov) .... B 37.47

R (on the application of Lonergan) v Lewes Crown Court (Secretary of State for the Home Department, interested party) [2005] EWHC 457 (Admin), [2005] 2 All ER 362, [2005] 1 WLR 2570, 169 JP 324, (2005) Times, 25 April, [2005] All ER (D) 382 (Mar) .... B 8.5

R (on the application of A) v Lewisham Youth Court [2011] EWHC 1193 (Admin), 175 JP 321, [2011] All ER (D) 99 (May) .... J 1.32

R v Lima (James) [2010] EWCA Crim 284 .... B 8.4A

R (on the application of P) v Liverpool City Magistrates' Court [2006] EWHC 887 (Admin), 170 JP 453, [2006] All ER (D) 211 (Mar) .... D 17.5

R v Liverpool City Magistrates, ex p Quantrell [1999] 2 Cr App Rep 24, 163 JP 420, [1999] Crim LR 734 .... I 5.4

R v Liverpool City Justices, ex p McGhee (1993) 158 JP 275, [1993] Crim LR 609 .... I 7.7

R (on the application of GKR Law Solicitors) v Liverpool Magistrates Court [2008] EWHC 2974 (Admin), [2008] All ER (D) 315 (Nov) .... I 7.7

R v Longworth [2004] EWCA Crim 2145, [2005] 1 Cr App Rep (S) 419, (2004) Times, 17 August, [2004] All ER (D) 439 (Jul); revsd [2006] UKHL 1, [2006] 1 All ER 887, [2006] 1 WLR 313, [2006] 2 Cr App Rep (S) 401, (2006) Times, 1 February, 150 Sol Jo LB 132, [2006] All ER (D) 182 (Jan) .... A 43.12

R v Longworth (26 January 2006, unreported) .... A 53.16

R v MV [2010] EWCA Crim 2400, [2011] 1 Cr App Rep 432, [2010] All ER (D) 181 (Oct) A32.2A

R v Mabee [2007] EWCA Crim 3230, [2008] 2 Cr App Rep (S) 143 .... B 41.7

R v McCalla (1988) 87 Cr App Rep 372, 152 JP 481, CA .... A 11.7

R v McCreadie and Tume (1993) 157 JP 541 .... A 1.3

R v McGillivray [2005] EWCA Crim 604, [2005] 2 Cr App Rep (S) 366, [2005] Crim LR 484, [2005] All ER (D) 208 (Jan) .... B 5.2B

R v McGrath [2003] EWCA Crim 2062, (2003) 167 JP 554, [2004] Crim LR 142, [2003] All ER (D) 397 (Jun) .... A 12.5, A 13.4

R v McGrath [2005] EWCA Crim 353, [2005] 2 Cr App Rep (S) 525, [2005] NLJ 826, [2005] All ER (D) 81 (May) .... B 8.5

R v McHoul [2002] EWCA Crim 1918, [2003] 1 Cr App Rep (S) 382 .... B 16.1

R v Macrae (1993) 159 JP 359, [1994] Crim LR 363, CA ..... A 64.4

R v Mahmood [2007] EWCA Crim 13, [2007] All ER (D) 28
(May) .... A 69.4
R v Major [2010] EWCA Crim 3016, [2011] 1 Cr App Rep 322,
[2011] 2 Cr App Rep (S) 139, [2011] Crim LR 328, (2010)
Times, 14 December .... A41.13, A 53.17
R v Malvern Justices, ex p Evans [1988] QB 540, [1988] 1 All ER
371, [1988] 2 WLR 218, 87 Cr App Rep 19, 152 JP 74, [1988]
Crim LR 120, 131 Sol Jo 1698, [1988] 2 LS Gaz R 36, [1987]
NLJ Rep 757 .... I 1B.5
R (on the application of Coxon) v Manchester City
Magistrates Court [2010] EWHC 712 (Admin), 174 CL&J 221,
[2010] All ER (D) 123 (Mar) .... C 22.16
R (on the application of Manchester City Council) v Manchester
Magistrates' Court (2005) Times, 8 March, [2005] All ER (D)
103 (Feb) .... B 8.7
R v Mann (2000) 144 Sol Jo LB 150, CA .... A 41.13, A 46.3
R v Martindale [1986] 3 All ER 25, [1986] 1 WLR 1042, 84 Cr
App Rep 31, 150 JP 548, [1986] Crim LR 736, 130 Sol Jo 613,
[1986] LS Gaz R 2412, CA .... A 25.8
R v Matthews [2003] EWCA Crim 813, [2004] QB 690, [2003] 3
WLR 693, [2003] 2 Cr App Rep 302, 147 Sol Jo LB 383 . A 11.11, A
                                                                    11.13
R v Maxwell. See R v Williams
R (on the application of Tullet) v Medway Magistrates' Court
[2003] EWHC 2279 (Admin), (2003) 167 JP 541 .... E 3.18
R v Melton (Christopher Timothy) [2011] EWCA Crim 2846,
[2012] 2 Cr App Rep (S) 133, [2012] Crim LR 304 .... B 5.2
R v Miller [1954] 2 QB 282, [1954] 2 All ER 529, [1954] 2 WLR
138, 38 Cr App Rep 1, 118 JP 340, 98 Sol Jo 62 .... A 8.9
R v Miller (1993) 15 Cr App Rep (S) 505, [1994] Crim LR 231,
CA .... C 5.38
R v Miller [1999] 2 Cr App Rep (S) 392, [1999] Crim LR 590,
CA .... A 21.10
R v Miller [2010] EWCA Crim 809, [2011] 1 Cr App Rep (S) 7,
[2010] Crim LR 648 .... A12.4
R v Mills [1998] 2 Cr App Rep (S) 128, [1998] Crim LR 220,
CA .... E 3.18
R v Mills [2002] EWCA Crim 26 [2002] 2 Cr App Rep (S) 51,
[2002] Crim LR 331, 146 Sol Jo LB 29 .... B 37.6
R v Mitchell [2003] EWCA Crim 2188, [2004] RTR 224, [2004]
Crim LR 139, [2003] All ER (D) 99 (Aug) .... A 18.19
R v Mowatt [1968] 1 QB 421, [1967] 3 All ER 47, [1967] 3 WLR
1192, 51 Cr App Rep 402, 131 JP 463, 111 Sol Jo 716, CA .. A 70.5
R v Mughal (Wassem) [2011] EWCA Crim 2392 .... B 2.20
R v Muir (1986) 83 Cr App Rep 375, CA .... A 15.17

R v Myers [2007] EWCA Crim 599, [2007] RTR 425, [2007] 2 Cr App Rep 258, [2007] All ER (D) 241 (Feb) .... C 49.3

R v NW [2010] EWCA Crim 404, [2010] 2 Cr App Rep 54, [2010] Crim LR 723, (2010) Times, 29 April, [2010] All ER (D) 34 (Mar) .... A 67.4

R v Nazari [1988] QB 631, [1988] 2 WLR 1005, 87 LGR 193, 87 Cr App Rep 135, sub nom R v Kuxhaus [1988] 2 All ER 705, 56 P & CR 229, 152 JP 546, [1988] Crim LR 459, 132 Sol Jo 750, [1988] 13 LS Gaz R 33, CA .... B 23.24

R v Newcastle under Lyme Justices, ex p Massey [1995] 1 All ER 120, 158 JP 1037, [1994] NLJR 1444, sub nom R v Stoke-on-Trent Justices, ex p Knight [1994] 1 WLR 1684 .... H 7.4

R (on the application of Craik, Chief Constable of Northumbria Police) v Newcastle Upon Tyne Magistrates' Court (Price, interested party's) [2010] EWHC 935 (Admin), 174 CL&J 334, [2010] All ER (D) 223 (Apr) .... I 4.8

R v Nicholson [2006] EWCA Crim 1518, (2006) 170 JP 573, (2006) Times, 13 June, [2006] All ER (D) 218 (May) .... B 8.13

R v Nolan [2012] EWCA Crim 671, [2012] All ER (D) 43 (Apr) .... A 55.3

R v Norman [2007] EWCA Crim 624, [2007] All ER (D) 523 (Mar) .... B 34.17

R (on the application of Wood) v North Avon Magistrates' Court [2009] EWHC 3614 (Admin), 174 JP 157, [2009] All ER (D) 133 (Nov) .... M 2.6

R (on the application of Durham County Council) v North Durham Justices [2004] EWHC 1073 (Admin), (2004) 168 JP 269, [2004] All ER (D) 260 (Apr) .... I 6.19, I 6.48

R (on the application of Hale) v North Sefton Justices [2002] EWHC 257 (Admin) [2002] All ER (D) 10 (Jan) .... B 20.16

R v Northallerton Magistrates' Court, ex p Dove [2000] 1 Cr App Rep (S) 136, 163 JP 657, [1999] Crim LR 760 .... B 20.8

R (on the application of Trigger) v Northampton Magistrates' Court (Northamptonshire Probation Trust and Northamptonshire Crown Prosecution Service, Interested Parties) [2011] EWHC 149 (QB), (2011) 175 JP 101 .... B 7.2

R (on the application of the Crown Prosecution Service) v Norwich Magistrates' Court [2011] EWHC 82 (Admin), [2011] All ER (D) 249 (Apr) .... I 6.21

R v Norwich Magistrates' Court, ex p Elliott [2000] 1 Cr App Rep (S) 152 .... B 16.1

R v Norwood [2002] Crim LR 888 .... A 20.11

R (on the application of SR) v Nottingham Magistrates' Court [2001] EWHC Admin 802 (2001) 166 JP 132 .... E 3.17

R v Nottingham Magistrates' Court, ex p Fohmann (1986) 84 Cr App Rep 316, 151 JP 49 .... B 20.2

R v O [2010] EWCA Crim 2233, [2011] 2 All ER 656, 174 JP 529,
[2011] Crim LR 403, [2010] All ER (D) 71 (Dec) A31.3
R v O'Callaghan [2005] EWCA Crim 317, [2005] 2 Cr App Rep
(S) 514, [2005] Crim LR 486, [2005] All ER (D) 114 (Feb) ... B 5.2B
R v Odam [2008] EWCA Crim 1087 .... A 53.15, A 68.5
R v Oldham Justices, ex p Cawley [1997] QB 1, [1996] 1 All ER
464, [1996] 2 WLR 681, 160 JP 133 .... B 33.50, B 33.86
R v Olliver and Olliver (1989) 11 Cr App Rep (S) 10, 153 JP 369,
[1989] Crim LR 387, CA .... B 18.6
R v P [2006] All ER (D) 238 (Oct), CA .... A 43.6
R v P (10 May 2012, unreported), CA .... A 53.17
R v P & O Ferries (Irish Sea) Ltd [2004] EWCA Crim 3236, [2005]
2 Cr App Rep (S) 113, [2004] All ER (D) 380 (Nov) .... A 80.22
R v Page [2004] EWCA Crim 3358, (2004) Times, 23 December,
149 Sol Jo LB 26, [2004] All ER (D) 108 (Dec) .... A 57.38
R v Pakes [2010] EWCA Crim 2803, [2011] 2 Cr App Rep (S) 54,
175 JP 33 .... B 41.7
R v Panayi (No 2) [1989] 1 WLR 187, 88 Cr App Rep 267, [1989]
Crim LR 210, 132 Sol Jo 1697, CA .... A 4.4
R v Panton [2001] 19 LS Gaz R 36, CA .... A 26.4
R v Parkin [2004] EWCA Crim 287, [2004] 2 Cr App Rep (S) 343,
[2004] Crim LR 490, [2004] All ER (D) 32 (Feb) .... B 8.8
R v Parmenter. See DPP v Parmenter
R v Patel (1994) 16 Cr App Rep (S) 756, [1995] Crim LR 440,
CA .... C 5.5
R v Patrascu [2004] EWCA Crim 2417, [2004] 4 All ER 1066,
[2005] 1 Cr App Rep 577, 168 JP 589, [2005] Crim LR 593,
[2004] All ER (D) 167 (Oct) .... A 69.4
R v Pawlicki [1992] 3 All ER 902, [1992] 1 WLR 827, 95 Cr App
Rep 246, [1992] Crim LR 584, 30 LS Gaz R 32, [1992]
21 LS Gaz R 27, 136 Sol Jo LB 104, CA .... A 76.3
R v Peart [1970] 2 QB 672, [1970] 2 All ER 823, [1970] 3 WLR
63, 54 Cr App Rep 374, 114 Sol Jo 418, CA .... A 65.9
R v Penfold (1995) 16 Cr App Rep (S) 1016, [1995] Crim LR 666,
CA .... B 31.7
R v Penford [2007] EWCA Crim 1645, [2007] All ER (D) 179
(Jun) .... A 75.7
R v Plavecz (2002), unreported .... A 2.6
R (on the application of Sainsbury's Supermarkets Ltd) v Plymouth
Magistrates Court [2006] EWHC 1749 (Admin), [2006] All ER
(D) 137 (Jun) .... I 6.23
R (on the application of Williams) v Pontefract Magistrates' Court
[2002] All ER (D) 465 (May) .... H 4.2
R v Poulton [2002] EWCA Crim 2487, [2003] 4 All ER 869,
[2003] 1 Cr App Rep (S) 610, [2003] Crim LR 124,
[2002] All ER (D) 365 (Oct) .... A 11.15

R v Povey [2008] EWCA Crim 1261, [2008] All ER (D) 279 (May) .... A 11.15

R (on the application of DPP) v Prestatyn Magistrates' Court [2002] All ER (D) 421 (May) .... A 18.6

R (on the application of Langley) v Preston Crown Court [2008] EWHC 2623 (Admin), [2009] 3 All ER 1026, [2009] 1 WLR 1612, 172 JP 605, 172 JPN 845, [2008] All ER (D) 300 (Oct) .... B 8.12

R v Pritipal Singh [2011] EWCA Crim 1756 .... A 72.3

R v Quayle [2005] EWCA Crim 1415, [2006] 1 All ER 988, [2005] 1 WLR 3642, [2005] 2 Cr App Rep 527, [2006] Crim LR 148, (2005) Times, 22 June, 149 Sol Jo LB 712, [2005] All ER (D) 447 (May) .... A 25.8A

R v R [2007] EWCA Crim 1603, [2007] All ER (D) 335 (Jul) .... A 53.17

R v R (L) [2010] EWCA Crim 924, [2011] 1 WLR 359, [2010] 2 Cr App Rep 63, 174 JP 271, [2011] Crim LR 319, 174 CL&J 318, (2010) Times, 21 June, [2010] All ER (D) 202 (Apr) .... I 1B.11

R v Rana [2007] EWCA Crim 2261, [2007] All ER (D) 183 (Nov) .... I 6.22

R v Raphael [2008] EWCA Crim 1014, [2008] All ER (D) 159 (May) .... A 57.32

R (on the application of Nicolaou) v Redbridge Magistrates' Court and Crown Prosecution Service [2012] EWHC 1647 (Admin), [2012] 2 Cr App Rep 290, 176 JP 441, [2012] All ER (D) 131 (Jun) .... D 16.4

R v Richards [2004] EWCA Crim 192, [2004] 2 Cr App Rep (S) 264, 168 JP 249, [2004] All ER (D) 15 (Mar) .... A 75.7

R v Richards [2006] EWCA Crim 2519, [2007] 1 WLR 847, [2007] 1 Cr App Rep (S) 734, [2007] Crim LR 173, (2006) Times, 13 November, [2006] All ER (D) 338 (Oct) .... A 53.17

R v Richards (9 March 2010, unreported) .... D 8.19

R v Rivano (1993) 14 Cr App Rep (S) 578, 158 JP 288, CA .... C 5.9

R v Roberts [2003] EWCA Crim 2753, [2004] 1 WLR 181, 167 JP 675, [2004] Crim LR 141, [2003] 44 LS Gaz R 30, 147 Sol Jo LB 1238, [2003] All ER (D) 325 (Oct) .... A 11.8

R v Rogers [2007] UKHL 8, [2007] 2 AC 62, [2007] 2 All ER 433, [2007] 2 WLR 280, [2007] 2 Cr App Rep 99, (2007) Times, 1 March, [2007] All ER (D) 359 (Feb) ..... A 18.17, A 20.6, A 21.10

R v Rowe [2008] EWCA Crim 2712, 172 JP 585, 172 JPN 845, [2008] All ER (D) 17 (Nov) .... A 43.7

R v S (crime: delay in prosecution) [2006] EWCA Crim 756, (2006) 170 JP 434, (2006) Times, 29 March, [2006] All ER (D) 73 (Mar) .... I 1B.11

R v Saeed Ali [2011] EWCA Crim 2747, 176 JP 1 .... B 21.2

R v Salisbury and Tisbury and Mere Combined Juvenile Court, ex
p Ball [1986] 1 FLR 1, [1985] Fam Law 313, 149 JP 346 . A 87.20, B
20.31
R v Salisbury Magistrates' Court, ex p Gray [2000] 1 Cr App Rep
(S) 267, 163 JP 732 .... I 6.35
R v Sallis [2003] EWCA Crim 233, [2003] 2 Cr App Rep (S) 394,
167 JP 103, [2003] Crim LR 291, [2003] All ER (D) 275 (Jan)
.... B 16.8
R v Sanchez (1996) 160 JP 321, [1996] Crim LR 572, CA ...... A 2.6
R v Savage [1992] 1 AC 699, [1991] 2 All ER 220, [1991] 2 WLR
418n, 91 Cr App Rep 317, 154 JP 757, [1990] Crim LR 709,
CA; affd [1992] 1 AC 699, [1991] 4 All ER 698, [1991] 3 WLR
914, 94 Cr App Rep 193, 155 JP 935, HL .... A 8.7
R v Scott [2007] EWCA Crim 2757, 172 JP 149, 172 JPN 325,
[2007] All ER (D) 191 (Oct) .... J 1.85
R (on the application of M) v Secretary of State for Constitutional
Affairs and Lord Chancellor. See R (on the application of Kenny)
v Leeds Magistrates' Court
R (on the application of Adebowale) v Secretary of State for the
Department of Transport [2004] EWHC 1741 (Admin),
[2004] All ER (D) 335 (Jun) .... C 5.48
R v Secretary of State for the Home Department, ex p Dannenberg
[1984] QB 766, [1984] 2 All ER 481, [1984] 2 WLR 855,
[1984] 2 CMLR 456, [1984] Crim LR 362, 128 Sol Jo 349, sub
nom Dannenberg v Secretary of State for the Home Department
148 JP 321, [1984] Imm AR 33, CA .... B 23.21
R v Secretary of State for the Home Department, ex p Santillo:
131/79 [1981] QB 778, [1981] 2 All ER 897, [1981] 2 WLR
362, [1981] 1 CMLR 569, 73 Cr App Rep 71, 125 Sol Jo 100,
CA .... B 23.19
R v Sheffield City Justices, ex p Foster (1999) Times,
2 November .... B 7.2
R (on the application of Broadhurst) v Sheffield Justices (2000) 164
JP Jo 870 .... H 6.2
R (on the application of D) v Sheffield Youth Court [2008] EWHC
601 (Admin), [2008] All ER (D) 70 (Mar), DC .... B 7.3, B 7.4
R v Singh (Daljit) [1999] 1 Cr App Rep (S) 490, [1999] Crim LR
236, CA .... A 81.16
R v Skitt [2004] EWCA Crim 3141, [2005] 2 Cr App Rep (S) 122,
[2004] All ER (D) 401 (Nov) .... C 5.45
R v Smith (Andrew Benjamin) (2000) 164 JP 681, [2000] Crim LR
613, CA .... B 25.4
R v Smith [2002] EWCA Crim 683, [2003] 1 Cr App Rep 212
.... A 43.3, B 41.5

R v Smith [2011] EWCA Crim 66, [2011] 1 Cr App Rep 379, [2011] Crim LR 719, (2011) Times, 28 March, [2011] All ER (D) 105 (Jan) .... A 57.17

R (on the application of Smith) v Snaresbrook Crown Court [2008] EWHC 1282 (Admin), 172 JP 473, 172 JPN 675, [2008] All ER (D) 98 (Jun) .... A 26.12

R v Sofroniou [2003] EWCA Crim 3681, [2004] QB 1218, [2004] 3 WLR 161, [2004] 1 Cr App Rep 460, [2004] Crim LR 381, [2004] 06 LS Gaz R 31, (2004) Times, 5 January, [2003] All ER (D) 362 (Dec) .... A 37.3

R (on the application of Davies) v Solihull Justices [2008] EWHC 1157 (Admin), [2008] All ER (D) 310 (Apr) .... I 6.19

R (on the application of Drinkwater) v Solihull Magistrates Court and Crown Prosecution Service [2012] EWHC 765 (Admin), 176 JP 401, [2012] All ER (D) 206 (Mar) .... I 6.3

R (on the application of Howe) v South Durham Justices [2004] EWHC 362 (Admin), 168 JP 424, [2004] All ER (D) 226 (Feb) .... C 19.6

R v South Tameside Magistrates' Court, ex p Rowland [1983] 3 All ER 689, 148 JP 202 .... I 6.25

R v South Tyneside Justices, ex p Martin (1995) Independent, 20 September .... H 6.1

R v South West Surrey Magistrates' Court, ex p James [2000] All ER (D) 564, [2000] Crim LR 690 .... B 20.18

R (on the application of Eastenders Barking Ltd) v South Western Magistrates' Court (March 22 2011, unreported), QBD .... M 2.7

R (on the application of Rhodes-Presley) v South Worcestershire Magistrates' Court [2008] EWHC 2700 (Admin), [2008] All ER (D) 92 (Nov) .... B 7.2

R (on the application of Flegg) v Southampton and New Forest Justices [2006] EWHC 396 (Admin), 170 JP 373, (2006) 170 JPN 615, [2006] All ER (D) 271 (Feb) .... C 8.20

R (on the application of H) v Southampton Youth Court [2004] EWHC 2912 (Admin), (2004) 169 JP 37, [2005] Crim LR 395, [2004] All ER (D) 38 (Dec) .... E 3.18

R (on the application of Bartram) v Southend Magistrates' Court [2004] All ER (D) 326 (Oct), DC .... B 36.1

R (on the application of Mathialagan) v Southwark London Borough Council [2004] EWCA Civ 1689, [2005] RA 43, (2004) Times, 21 December, [2004] All ER (D) 179 (Dec) .... B 7.4; H 3.3

R v Spence [1999] RTR 353, 163 JP 754, [1999] Crim LR 975, CA .... C 20.8

R v Stapylton (Ben) [2012] EWCA Crim 728, [2012] All ER (D) 84 (Apr) .... B 18.5

R v Stewart [1987] 2 All ER 383, [1987] 1 WLR 559, 85 Cr App Rep 66, 9 Cr App Rep (S) 135, [1987] Crim LR 520, 131 Sol Jo 538, [1987] LS Gaz R 1333, CA .... A 54.5

R v Stockport Justices, ex p Conlon [1997] 2 All ER 204, 161 JP 81 .... B 33.86

R v Stoke-on-Trent Justices, ex p Knight. See R v Newcastle under Lyme Justices, ex p Massey

R v Stokes [1983] RTR 59, [1982] Crim LR 695, CA .... A 65.4

R v Stratford Justices, ex p Imbert [1999] 2 Cr App Rep 276, 163 JP 693, DC .... I 6.9

R (on the application of Singh) v Stratford Magistrates' Court [2007] EWHC 1582 (Admin), (2007) Times, 13 August , [2007] All ER (D) 30 (Jul) .... B 36.2

R (on the application of Newham London Borough Council) v Stratford Magistrates' Court [2008] EWHC 125 (Admin), [2008] RA 108, 173 JP 30, [2008] All ER (D) 17 (Jan) .... B 7.5

R v Stratford Youth Court, ex p S [1998] 1 WLR 1758, 162 JP 552, [1999] Crim LR 146, [1998] NLJR 870, [1998] All ER (D) 224 .... J 1.51

R (on the application of Clive Rees Associates Solicitors) v Swansea Magistrates' Court and rees Davies and Partners [2011] EWHC 3155 (Admin), 176 JP 39, [2011] All ER (D) 29 (Dec) .... I 7.5B

R v Swindell [1992] 1 WLR 827, 95 Cr App Rep 246, [1992] Crim LR 584, 30 LS Gaz R 32, [1992] 21 LS Gaz R 27, 136 Sol Jo LB 104, CA .... A 76.3

R v T [2008] EWCA Crim 815, [2008] 3 WLR 923, [2008] 2 Cr App Rep 235, 172 JP 335, (2008) Times, 5 May, [2008] All ER (D) 215 (Apr); affd sub nom R v JTB [2009] UKHL 20, [2009] 3 All ER 1, [2009] 2 WLR 1088, [2009] 2 Cr App Rep 189, 173 JP 289, [2009] Crim LR 581, [2009] NLJR 672, 153 Sol Jo (no 18) 27, [2009] All ER (D) 211 (Apr) .... E 3.2

R v Tait [1990] 1 QB 290, [1989] 3 All ER 682, [1989] 3 WLR 891, 90 Cr App Rep 44, [1989] Crim LR 834, CA .... A 59.4

R v Tangerine Confectionery Ltd [2011] EWCA Crim 2015, 176 JP 349 .... A 80.19

R v Teasdale [2003] Crim LR 657, CA .... B 37.68

R v Teeside Crown Court, ex p Gazette Media Co Ltd [2005] EWCA Crim 1983, (2005) Times, 8 August, [2005] All ER (D) 367 (Jul) .... I 1B.7

R v Terry [1984] AC 374, [1984] 1 All ER 65, [1984] 2 WLR 23, [1984] RTR 129, 78 Cr App Rep 101, 128 Sol Jo 34, [1984] LS Gaz R 510, HL .... A 64.4

R (on the application of R) v Thames Youth Court [2002] EWHC 1670 (Admin), 166 JP 613, [2002] Crim LR 977 .... I 6.19

R v Tilley [2009] EWCA Crim 1426, 173 JP 393, (2009) Times, 5 August, [2009] All ER (D) 200 (Jul) .... A 54.5
R v Tobierre [1986] 1 All ER 346, [1986] 1 WLR 125, 82 Cr App Rep 212, [1986] Crim LR 243, 130 Sol Jo 35, [1986] LS Gaz R 116, CA .... A 78.8
R (on the application of Morsby) v Tower Bridge Magistrates' Court [2007] EWHC 2766 (Admin), 172 JP 155, 172 JPN 372, [2007] All ER (D) 464 (Oct) .... I 6.19
R v Trott [2011] EWCA Crim 2395, 175 JP 458 .... A 41.13
R v Tsap [2008] EWCA Crim 2580, 173 JP 4, [2008] All ER (D) 194 (Oct) .... A 11.14
R v Ukoh [2004] EWCA Crim 3270, [2005] Crim LR 314, (2004) Times, 28 December, [2005] All ER (D) 58 (Jan) .... B 23.2
R v Unah [2011] EWCA Crim 1837, 175 JP 391, [2011] 30 LS Gaz R 24, 175 CL&J 503, (2011) Times, 02 August, [2011] All ER (D) 97 (Jul) A32.2A
R v Uxbridge Justices, ex p Metropolitan Police Comr [1981] 1 All ER 940, [1981] 1 WLR 112, 144 JP 432, 124 Sol Jo 828; affd [1981] QB 829, [1981] 3 All ER 129, [1981] 3 WLR 410, 146 JP 42, 125 Sol Jo 445, CA .... A 87.20
R (on the application of Thornhill) v Uxbridge Magistrates' Court [2008] EWHC 508 (Admin), 172 JP 297, 172 JPN 580, [2008] All ER (D) 08 (Mar) .... I 6.23
R v Uxbridge Magistrates' Court, ex p Adimi [2001] QB 667, [1999] 4 All ER 520, [2000] 3 WLR 434, [1999] Imm AR 560, [1999] INLR 490 .... A 81.5
R v Uxbridge Youth Court, ex p Howard (1998) 162 JP 327 . B 50.23
R v Vasili [2011] EWCA Crim 615, [2011] 2 Cr App Rep 56, 175 JP 185, [2011] All ER (D) 246 (Feb) A11.5
R v Vaughan [2008] All ER (D) 315 (Jun), CA .... B 2.20
R v Venna [1976] QB 421, [1975] 3 All ER 788, [1975] 3 WLR 737, 61 Cr App Rep 310, 140 JP 31, 119 Sol Jo 679, CA ... A 8.7, A 15.4
R v Veolia ES (UK) Ltd [2011] EWCA Crim 2015, 176 JP 349 .... A 80.19
R v Vinall [2011] EWCA Crim 2652, [2012] 1 Cr App Rep 400, 175 JP 517, [2012] Crim LR 386, [2011] All ER (D) 107 (Nov) .... A 57.32
R v Vittles [2004] EWCA Crim 1089, [2005] 1 Cr App Rep (S) 31, [2004] All ER (D) 334 (May) .... B 8.3
R v W [2006] EWCA Crim 686, [2006] 3 All ER 562, 170 JPN 716, [2006] All ER (D) 410 (Mar) .... B 8.5
R v Wallace [2007] EWCA Crim 1760, 171 JP 543, [2007] All ER (D) 219 (Jul) .... I 6.14

R (on the application of Khan) v Waltham Forest Magistrates' Court [2007] EWHC 1801 (Admin), [2007] All ER (D) 29 (Jul) .... I 5.4, I 6.5

R (on the application of S) v Waltham Forest Youth Court [2004] EWHC 715 (Admin), [2004] 2 Cr App Rep 335, 168 JP 293, [2004] All ER (D) 590 (Mar) .... A 52.10

R v Wang [2003] EWCA Crim 3228, (2003) 168 JP 224, [2003] All ER (D) 299 (Dec) .... A 11.12

R (on the application of Kelly) v Warley Magistrates Court [2007] EWHC 1836 (Admin), [2008] 1 WLR 2001, [2008] 1 Cr App Rep 195, 171 JP 585, [2008] Crim LR 643, [2007] NLJR 1155, [2007] All ER (D) 506 (Jul) .... I 6.2

R v Warley Magistrates' Court, ex p DPP [1999] 1 All ER 251, [1999] 1 WLR 216, [1998] 2 Cr App Rep 307, [1999] 1 Cr App Rep (S) 156, 162 JP 559, [1998] Crim LR 684, [1998] 24 LS Gaz R 33, [1998] NLJR 835, 142 Sol Jo LB 165 .... B 16.1

R v Watton (1978) 68 Cr App Rep 293, [1979] Crim LR 246, CA .... J 1.93

R v Webbe [2001] EWCA Crim 1217, [2002] 1 Cr App Rep (S) 22 .... A 40.11

R v Webster [2003] EWCA Crim 3597, [2004] 2 Cr App Rep (S) 126, [2004] Crim LR 238, [2003] All ER (D) 313 (Nov) ...... A 12.4

R v Webster [2006] EWCA Crim 415, (2006) Times, 15 March, [2006] All ER (D) 41 (Mar) .... C 16.6

R (on the application of Knight) v West Dorset Magistrates' Court [2002] EWHC 2152 (Admin), 166 JP 705 .... E 3.25

R (on the application of Vickers) v West London Magistrates' Court [2003] EWHC 1809 (Admin), (2003) 167 JP 473, [2003] All ER (D) 211 (Jul) .... J 1.92

R (on the application of TP) v West London Youth Court [2005] EWHC 2583 (Admin), [2006] 1 All ER 477, [2006] 1 WLR 1219, [2006] 1 Cr App Rep 402, 170 JP 82, 170 JPN 333, [2005] All ER (D) 260 (Nov) .... E 3.25

R v Whatley [2004] EWCA Crim 2755, [2005] 1 Cr App Rep (S) 640, [2004] All ER (D) 320 (Nov) .... A 54.5

R v White [2001] EWCA Crim 216 [2001] 1 WLR 1352, [2001] Crim LR 576 .... A 21.10

R v White (2002) Times, 9 December .... J 1.91

R v Wickins (1958) 42 Cr App Rep 236, 122 JP 518, CCA ..... C 5.2

R v Widdows [2011] EWCA Crim 1500, [2011] 2 FLR 869, [2011] Fam Law 937, 175 JP 345, [2011] 27 LS Gaz R 22, 175 CL&J 404, [2011] All ER (D) 136 (Jun) A41.7

R (on the application of McDonough) v Wigan Magistrates' Court [2004] EWHC 3272 (Admin), [2005] All ER (D) 304 (Feb) .. B 33.70

R v Wiggins [2001] RTR 37, CA .... C 5.38

R v Williams [2010] EWCA Crim 2552, [2011] 3 All ER 969, [2011] 1 WLR 588, 174 JP 606, [2011] Crim LR 471, 174 CL&J 751, [2010] All ER (D) 19 (Nov); affd sub nom R v Maxwell [2010] UKSC 48, [2011] 1 WLR 1837, [2011] 31 LS Gaz R 17, (2011) Times, 29 July, [2011] All ER (D) 178 (Jul) .... C 9.5

R v Wills (Alan Paul) [2011] EWCA Crim 1938, [2012] 1 Cr App Rep 16, [2012] Crim LR 565 .... I 6.13A

R v Wilson [1997] QB 47, [1996] 3 WLR 125, [1996] 2 Cr App Rep 241, [1996] Crim LR 573, 140 Sol Jo LB 93, CA .... A 15.16

R v Windsor [2011] EWCA Crim 143, [2011] 2 Cr App Rep 71, 175 CL&J 110, (2011) Times, 03 March, [2011] All ER (D) 91 (Feb) .... M 2.7

R (on the application of Daniel Thwaites plc) v Wirral Borough Magistrates' Court [2008] EWHC 838 (Admin), 172 JP 301, [2008] NLJR 707, [2008] All ER (D) 61 (May) .... F 1.15

R v Wise (Darren) [2012] EWCA Crim 995, 176 JP 337, 176 CL&J 322, [2012] All ER (D) 130 (May) .... B 41.18

R v Wise (Ryan) [2012] EWCA Crim 995, 176 JP 337, 176 CL&J 322, [2012] All ER (D) 130 (May) .... B 41.18

R v Wolverhampton Stipendiary Magistrate, ex p Mould (1992) Times, 16 November .... H 7.2

R v Woods [2005] EWCA Crim 2065, [2006] 1 Cr App Rep (S) 477, [2005] Crim LR 982 .... A 1.4, A 45.8

R v Wright [2011] EWCA Crim 1180, [2011] 2 Cr App Rep 168 .... A26.4

R v X (1989) 91 Cr App Rep 36, [1990] Crim LR 515, CA ... A 52.9

R v Yehou [1997] 2 Cr App Rep (S) 48, CA .... B 18.6

R v Yorkshire Sheeting and Insulation Ltd [2003] EWCA Crim 458, [2003] 2 Cr App Rep (S) 548, [2003] All ER (D) 369 (Feb) .... A 80.22

R (on the application of DPP) v Zhao [2003] EWHC 1724 (Admin), 167 JP 521 .... A 72.5

Radford v Kent County Council (1998) 162 JP 697 .... I 6.22

Rafiq v DPP (1997) 161 JP 412, DC .... A 72.3

Redhead Freight Ltd v Shulman [1989] RTR 1, [1988] Crim LR 696 .... C 9.5

Redknapp v Comr of the City of London Police Department [2008] EWHC 1177 (Admin), 172 JP 388, [2008] NLJR 861, 172 JPN 548, (2008) Times, 16 June, [2008] All ER (D) 319 (May) .... M 2.20A

Redmond-Bate v DPP (1999) 163 JP 789, [1999] Crim LR 998 .... A 47.13

Regina v Benjamin Adam Brown [2011] EWCA Crim 1223 .. A53.17

Richards v National Probation Service [2007] EWHC 3108 (Admin), 172 JP 100, 172 JPN 293, 172 JPN 357, [2007] All ER (D) 454 (Nov) .... A 17.2

Robinson v Abdergavenny Magistrates' Court [2007] EWHC 2005 (Admin) .... I 6.7

Robinson v DPP [2003] EWHC 2718 (Admin), (2003) 168 JP 522, [2004] Crim LR 670, [2003] All ER (D) 05 (Nov) .... C 22.25

Roper v Taylor's Central Garages (Exeter) Ltd. See Taylor's Central Garages (Exeter) Ltd v Roper

Rose v DPP [2010] EWHC 462 (Admin), [2010] RTR 269, [2010] All ER (D) 110 (Mar) .... C 22.23

Ross v Moss [1965] 2 QB 396, [1965] 3 All ER 145, [1965] 3 WLR 416, 63 LGR 321, 129 JP 537, 109 Sol Jo 475 .... A 62.3

Rudd v Secretary of State for Trade and Industry [1987] 2 All ER 553, [1987] 1 WLR 786, 85 Cr App Rep 358, 151 JP 610, 131 Sol Jo 805, [1987] LS Gaz R 2192, HL .... A 61.3

Ruiz Torija v Spain (1994) 19 EHRR 542, ECtHR .... I 1A.3

Rushmoor Borough Council v Richards (1996) 160 LG Rev 460 .... F 1.10

Rweikiza v DPP [2008] EWHC 386 (Admin), [2008] All ER (D) 259 (Jan) .... C 23.3

Rymer v DPP [2010] EWHC 1848 (Admin), 174 CL&J 526, [2010] All ER (D) 219 (Jul) .... I 6.26

S

S (a minor) (parental responsibility), Re [1995] 3 FCR 225, [1995] 2 FLR 648, [1995] Fam Law 596, CA .... D 3.7

S (care proceedings: split hearing), Re [1996] 3 FCR 578, [1996] 2 FLR 773, [1997] Fam Law 11 .... D 4.4

S (minors) (care order: implementation of care plan), Re [2002] UKHL 10, [2002] 2 AC 291, [2002] 2 WLR 720, [2002] LGR 251, [2002] 1 FCR 577, [2002] 1 FLR 815, sub nom S (children: care plan) [2002] 2 All ER 192 .... D 6.24, D 6.35

S (a child) (SGO), Re (2007) Times, 9 February .... D 18.34

S (a child) (adoption order or special guardianship order), Re [2007] EWCA Civ 90, [2007] 1 FCR 340, [2007] 1 FLR 855, [2007] All ER (D) 175 (Feb) .... D 18.38

S (a child) (placement order: revocation), Re [2008] EWCA Civ 1333, [2009] 1 FLR 503, [2009] Fam Law 100, [2008] All ER (D) 48 (Oct) .... D 18.6, D 18.7

S, Re [2008] EWCA Civ 1078, [2009] 2 FLR 397, [2008] Fam Law 1187 .... D 9.18

S v DPP (8 February 2008, unreported) .... A 10.3A

S (an infant) v Manchester City Recorder [1971] AC 481, [1969] 3 All ER 1230, [1970] 2 WLR 21, 134 JP 3, 113 Sol Jo 872, HL .... I 6.26

S v Oxfordshire County Council [1993] 2 FCR 676, [1993] 1 FLR 452, [1993] Fam Law 74 .... D 1.18

S v Poole Borough Council [2002] EWHC 244 (Admin) [2002] All ER (D) 143 (Feb) .... B 8.4

S-H (a child) (placement order), Re [2008] EWCA Civ 493, [2008] Fam Law 716, [2008] All ER (D) 176 (May), sub nom NS-H v Kingston upon Hull City Council [2008] 2 FLR 918 .... D 18.5

Sagnata Investments Ltd v Norwich Corpn [1971] 2 QB 614, [1971] 2 All ER 1441, [1971] 3 WLR 133, 69 LGR 471, 115 Sol Jo 406, CA .... F 1.15

Santa Cruz Ruiz v United Kingdom [1998] EHRLR 208 .... D 7.25

Secretary of State for the Environment, Transport and the Regions v Holt [2000] RTR 309 .... C 47.7

Sekfali v DPP [2006] EWHC 894 (Admin), [2006] All ER (D) 381 (Feb) .... A 47.9

Selby v Chief Constable of Avon and Somerset [1988] RTR 216 .... C 31.8

Shaw v DPP [2007] EWHC 207 (Admin), 171 JP 254, 171 JPN 460, [2007] All ER (D) 197 (Jan) .... I 6.23

Sheldrake v DPP [2003] EWHC 273 (Admin), [2004] QB 487, [2003] 2 All ER 497, [2003] 2 WLR 1629, [2003] 2 Cr App Rep 206, 167 JP 333, [2004] RTR 13, [2003] 13 LS Gaz R 30; revsd [2004] UKHL 43, [2004] 3 WLR 976 .... C 21.4A, C 22,64

Sills v DPP [2006] EWHC 3383 (Admin), 171 JP 201, 171 JPN 514, [2006] All ER (D) 165 (Oct) .... A 11.5

Singh v DPP [1999] RTR 424, 164 JP 82, [1999] Crim LR 914 .... C 19.6

Skinner v DPP [2004] EWHC 2914 (Admin), [2005] RTR 202, [2004] All ER (D) 441 (Nov) .... C 22.23

Smith v DPP and Morris [2000] RTR 36, 164 JP 96, [1999] 32 LS Gaz R 34, [1999] 34 LS Gaz R 34 .... C 25.11

Sobczak v DPP [2012] EWHC 1319 (Admin), 176 JP 575, 176 CL&J 371, [2012] All ER (D) 29 (May) .... A 9.8

Southard v DPP [2006] EWHC 3449 (Admin), [2006] All ER (D) 101 (Nov) .... A 20.3A

Steel v United Kingdom (1998) 28 EHRR 603, [1998] Crim LR 893, 5 BHRC 339, ECtHR .... B 10.21

Stepney Borough Council v Joffe [1949] 1 KB 599, [1949] 1 All ER 256, 47 LGR 189, 113 JP 124, [1949] LJR 561, 93 Sol Jo 119, 65 TLR 176, DC .... F 1.15

Stinton v Stinton [1995] RTR 167, [1995] 01 LS Gaz R 37, sub nom Stinton v Motor Insurers Bureau 159 JP 656, [1999] Lloyd's Rep IR 305, CA .... C 9.4

Street v DPP [2004] EWHC 86 (Admin), (2004) Times, 23 January, [2004] All ER (D) 70 (Jan) .... A 71.3

Suter v Suter and Jones [1987] Fam 111, [1987] 2 All ER 336, [1987] 3 WLR 9, [1987] FCR 52, [1987] 2 FLR 232, [1987] Fam Law 239, 151 JP 593, 131 Sol Jo 471, [1987] LS Gaz R 1142, CA .... D 7.5

Syed v DPP [2010] EWHC 81 (Admin), [2010] 1 Cr App Rep 480, 174 JP 97, [2010] 04 LS Gaz R 14, (2010) Times, 26 January, [2010] All ER (D) 48 (Jan) .... A 9.8

T

T (a child) (residential parenting assessment), Re [2011] EWCA Civ 812, [2011] 3 FCR 343, [2012] 2 FLR 308, [2011] Fam Law 1191, [2011] All ER (D) 133 (Jul) .... D 9.18

T (a minor), Re. See KDT (a minor)

T v DPP [2003] EWHC 266 (Admin), [2003] Crim LR 622 .... A 8.9

T v DPP [2004] EWHC 183 (Admin), (2004) 168 JP 313, 148 Sol Jo LB 149, [2004] All ER (D) 278 (Jan) .... A 8.9, A 15.7

T v W (contact: reasons for refusing leave) [1997] 1 FCR 118, [1996] 2 FLR 473, [1996] Fam Law 666 .... D 1.18

Talbot v DPP [2000] 1 WLR 1102, 164 JP 169, [2000] Crim LR 326, [2000] 05 LS Gaz R 33, sub nom Talbot v Oxford City Magistrates' Court [2000] 2 Cr App Rep 60 .... A 79.3

Taylor v City of Westminster Magistrates' Court [2009] EWHC 1498 (Admin), 173 JP 405 .... I 7.4

Taylor v DPP [2006] EWHC 1202 (Admin), 170 JP 485, 170 JPN 856, (2006) Times, 14 June, [2006] All ER (D) 271 (Apr) ..... A 20.8

Taylor's Central Garages (Exeter) Ltd v Roper [1951] WN 383, 115 JP 445, sub nom Roper v Taylor's Central Garages (Exeter) Ltd [1951] 2 TLR 284 .... C 9.6

Thomas v News Group Newspapers Ltd [2001] EWCA Civ 1233, [2001] 34 LS Gaz R 43, (2001) Times, 25 July, 145 Sol Jo LB 207, [2002] EMLR 78, [2001] All ER (D) 246 (Jul) A41.7

Thomson (Procurator Fiscal) v Jackson [2010] HCJAC 96, [2011] RTR 210, 2010 SCCR 915, HC of Justiciary (Sc) .... C 8.21

Thornton v Crown Prosecution Service [2010] EWHC 346 (Admin), 174 JP 121 .... I 6.33

Tora Tolinos v Spain (No 23816/94) (17 May 1995, unreported), ECtHR .... C 8.22

Trans Berckx BVBA v North Avon Magistrates' Court [2011] EWHC 2605 (Admin) .... B 34.9

Travel-Gas (Midlands) Ltd v Reynolds [1989] RTR 75 .... C 38.16

Traves v DPP. See R (on the application of Traves) v DPP

Trinity Mirror plc (A and B (Minors, acting by the Official Solicitor to the Supreme Court) Intervening), Re [2008] EWCA Crim 50, [2008] 2 All ER 1159, [2008] 3 WLR 51, [2008] 2 Cr App Rep 1, (2008) Times, 13 February, [2008] All ER (D) 12 (Feb), sub nom R (on the application of Trinity Mirror plc) v Croydon Crown Court [2008] Crim LR 554 .... A 52.12

U

U (a child) (serious injury: standard of proof), Re [2004] EWCA Civ 567, [2005] Fam 134, [2004] 3 WLR 753, [2004] 2 FCR 257, [2004] 2 FLR 263, [2004] Fam Law 565, [2004] NLJR 824, (2004) Times, 27 May, [2004] All ER (D) 197 (May); affd [2005] EWCA Civ 52, [2005] 3 All ER 550, [2005] 1 WLR 2398, [2005] 1 FCR 583, [2005] NLJR 325, (2005) Times, 31 March, 149 Sol Jo LB 266, [2005] All ER (D) 385 (Feb) .... D 6.7

V

V (a child) (care proceedings: human rights claims), Re [2004] EWCA Civ 54, [2004] 1 All ER 997, [2004] 1 WLR 1433, [2004] 1 FCR 338, [2004] 1 FLR 944, [2004] Fam Law 328, [2004] 11 LS Gaz R 33, [2004] All ER (D) 52 (Feb) .... D 6.1
V v V (children) (intractable contact dispute) [2004] EWHC 1215 (Fam), [2004] 2 FLR 851, (2004) Times, 28 May, [2004] All ER (D) 304 (May) .... D 4.4
Vehicle and Operator Services Agency v F & S Gibbs Transport Services Ltd [2006] EWHC 1109 (Admin), (2006) 170 JP 586, [2006] All ER (D) 84 (May) .... C 38.18 A
Vehicle Inspectorate v Nuttall (t/a Redline Coaches) [1999] 3 All ER 833, [1999] 1 WLR 629, [1999] RTR 264, [1999] IRLR 656, [1999] Crim LR 674, [1999] 16 LS Gaz R 36, 143 Sol Jo LB 111, HL .... C 9.6
Verderers of the New Forest v Young [2004] EWHC 2954 (Admin), [2004] All ER (D) 14 (Dec) .... H 3.4
Vigon v DPP (1997) 162 JP 115, [1998] Crim LR 289 .... A 20.9

W

W (a child) (sexual abuse), Re [2002] All ER (D) 34 (Jan) ..... D 5.10

W (children) (care order: sexual abuse) sub nom W (children) (concurrent criminal and care proceedings), Re [2009] EWCA Civ 644, [2009] 2 Cr App Rep 384, [2009] 3 FCR 1, [2009] Fam Law 795, [2009] All ER (D) 25 (Jul) .... D 4.4

W (children) (abuse: oral evidence), Re [2010] UKSC 12, [2010] 2 All ER 418, [2010] 1 WLR 701, [2010] PTSR 775, [2010] 1 FCR 615, [2010] 1 FLR 1485, [2010] Fam Law 449, [2010] 11 LS Gaz R 15, [2010] NLJR 389, 174 CL&J 206, (2010) Times, 8 March, [2010] All ER (D) 29 (Mar) .... D 2.6, D 2.7

W v DPP. See R (on the application of W) v DPP

W v Hertfordshire County Council. See Hertfordshire County Council v W

Walkling v DPP (2004) Independent, 26 January .... B 8.13

Ward (Anthony) v Royal Society for the Prevention of Cruelty to Animals [2010] EWHC 347 (Admin) .... A 5.4

Weise v UK Border Agency (Christopher Hendrik) (29 June 2012, unreported), CA .... M 3.2

West Midlands Probation Board v Sutton Coldfield Magistrates' Court [2008] EWHC 15 (Admin), [2008] 3 All ER 1193, 172 JP 169, [2008] NLJR 102, [2008] All ER (D) 03 (Jan), sub nom West Midlands Probation Board v Sadler [2008] 1 WLR 918 .... A 17.2

West Yorkshire Probation Board v Boulter [2005] EWHC 2342 (Admin), [2006] 1 WLR 232, 169 JP 601, [2005] 42 LS Gaz R 24, (2005) Times, 11 October, [2005] All ER (D) 54 (Oct) .... A 17.2

West Yorkshire Probation Board v Cruickshanks [2010] EWHC 615 (Admin), 174 JP 305, [2010] All ER (D) 239 (Mar) ...... B 37.46

West Yorkshire Trading Standards Service v Lex Vehicle Leasing Ltd [1996] RTR 70 .... C 9.4

Westminster City Council v Haw [2002] All ER (D) 59 (Oct) . C 36.4

Whiley v DPP [1995] Crim LR 39 .... A 61.3

Whittaker v Campbell [1984] QB 318, [1983] 3 All ER 582, [1983] 3 WLR 676, [1984] RTR 220, 77 Cr App Rep 267, [1983] Crim LR 812, 127 Sol Jo 714 .... A 65.8

Wildman v DPP [2001] EWHC Admin 14 (2001) 165 JP 453 .... J 1.52

Williams v DPP [1992] Crim LR 503 .... A 28.6

Williams v DPP [2009] EWHC 2354 (Admin), [2009] All ER (D) 292 (Jul) .... I 6.23

Williams v Richards (1997) Times, 29 July .... C 51.10

Wood v DPP [2008] EWHC 1056 (Admin), (2008) Times, 23 May, [2008] All ER (D) 162 (May) .... A 9.8

Wragg v DPP [2005] EWHC 1389 (Admin), [2005] All ER (D) 131 (Jun) .... A 9.5, A 9.8

X

X (emergency protection orders), Re [2006] EWHC 510 (Fam),
[2006] Fam Law 627, (2006) Times, 21 April, 150 Sol Jo LB
435 .... D 9.18
X Council v B (emergency protection orders) [2004] EWHC 2015
(Fam) .... D 9.18

Y

Yagci and Sargin v Turkey (1995) 20 EHRR 505, ECtHR ...... I 1A.4

Z

Zafar v DPP [2004] EWHC 2468 (Admin), [2005] RTR 220, 169
JP 208, (2005) Times, 7 January, 148 Sol Jo LB 1315,
[2004] All ER (D) 06 (Nov) .... C 23.3
Zofar v DPP (2004) Times, 1 November .... C 22.10
Zykin v Crown Prosecution Service [2009] EWHC 1469 (Admin),
173 JP 361 .... B 7.1

Criminal offences dealt with in magistrates' courts

Index to criminal offences and table of maximum penalties

Set out below are a number of maximum penalties for some common offences. If an offence is dealt with more fully in this book the relevant paragraph is stated.

† or + Penalty on summary conviction of an offence triable either way.

* Indicates that the police may issue a fixed penalty ticket

** Revised penalties in brackets denote changes in relation to offences committed on or after a date to be appointed by virtue of the CJA 2003

For index and penalties for road traffic offences, see **C[1]**

Absconding level 5 and 3 months **A[10]**

Abstracting/using electricity level 5 and/or 6 months (**12 months) **A[1]** †

Abusive words or behaviour level 5 and 6 months (**51 weeks) **A[21]**

Actual bodily harm level 5 and 6 months (**12 months) † **A[8]**

Affray level 5 and 6 months† (**12 months) **A[2]** †

Aggravated vehicle-taking level 5 and 6 months (**12 months) **A[66]**

Air gun in public place (FA 1968, s 22(5)) level 3 forfeiture **A[71]**

Airports (Aviation Security Act 1982)
false statements relating to baggage, cargo, etc (s 21A) level 5
false statements in connection with identity documents (s 21B) level 5
unauthorised presence in restricted zone (s 21C) level 5
unauthorised presence on board aircraft (s 21D) level 5
intentionally obstructing an authorised person (s 21E(1)(a)) level 5
impersonating an authorised person (s 21E(1)(b)) level 5

Alcohol sale offences level 3 **A[3]**

Alcohol/tobacco, fraudulently evade duty (See Customs duty) **A[4]**

Ammunition (FA 1968, s 1) (*See* Firearms) level 5 and 6 months, forfeiture **A[36]**

Animal cruelty £20,000 and/or 6 months (ss 4 and 8) level 5 and 6 months (**51 weeks)

(s 9) A[5]

Animals straying on highway level 3

Anti-social behaviour order – breach level 5 and 6 months (**12 months)† A[6], B[8] and B[8.15]

Arson (see Criminal damage)

Article with blade or point in public place (CJA 1988, s 139) level 5 and 6 months (**12 months) † A[11]

Assault (*See* Actual bodily harm, Common assault, Indecent assault, Grievous bodily harm, Wounding)

Assault on police constable or person assisting police constable level 5 and 6 months (**51 weeks) A[9]

Assault with intent to resist arrest level 5 and 6 months (**12 months) † A[7]

Avoiding customs duty (*See* Customs duty) A[4]

Bail, failure to surrender level 5 and/or 3 months A[10]

Bankrupt (undischarged, obtaining credit) level 5 and 6 months (**12 months)†

Begging level 3

Bladed article/offensive weapon, possession of (CJA 1988, ss 139, 139A and 139AA) level 5 and 6 months (**12 months) † A[11]

Breach of the peace (*See* Insulting words, and *see* B[10] for Binding over) A[21]

Breach of a non-molestation order (Family Law Act 1996, s 42A) level 5 and 6 months (**12 months) † A[46]

Bribery Bribery Act 2010
Bribing another person (s 1) level 5 and/or 6 months (**12 months) † A[89]
Being bribed (s 2) level 5 and/or 6 months (**12 months) † A[89]
Bribery of foreign public officials (s 6) level 5 and/or 6 months (**12 months) † A[89]
Failure of commercial organisations to prevent bribery (s.7) indictable only A[89]

Breach of a protective order (Protection from Harassment Act 1997, s 5) level 5 and/or 6 months (**12 months) † A[46]

Brothel level 3 and 3 months; level 4 and 6 months (**51 weeks) (second or subsequent offence in relation to a brothel) For **keeping a brothel used for prostitution** see A[44]

Builder's skip

depositing on highway level 3
not complying with a condition level 3
unlit on roadway level 3

Burglary in a dwelling (domestic burglary) level 5 and 6 months
(**12 months)† **A[12]**

Burglary in a building other than a dwelling (non-domestic burglary) level 5 and/or 6 months (**12 months) † **A[13]**

Car dumping (*See* Litter) **A[83]**

Child prostitution and pornography (includes possession of extreme photographic images) level 5 and 6 months
(**12 months) † **A[14]**

Children (cruelty to) level 5 and 6 months (**12 months)† **A[19]**

Chimes level 5 **A[34]**

Common assault level 5 and 6 months (**51 weeks) **A[15]**

Communications network offences Communications Act 2003,
s 127 (1) and (2) level 5 and/or 6 months (**51 weeks) **A[16]**

Community order, breach of Criminal Justice Act, 2003,
schedule 8. For powers of the court see **A[17]**

Computers (Computer Misuse Act 1990)
unauthorised access to computer material (s 1) level 5 and 6 months (**51 weeks)
unauthorised access with intent to commit or facilitate further offences (s 2) level 5
    and 6 months (**51 weeks)
unauthorised modification of computer material (s 3) level 5 and 6 months
    (**12 months)†

Contempt of court level 4 and 1 month **I[3]**

Controlled drugs Penalty varies with classification of drug **A[22]**

Copying false instrument level 5 and 6 months (**12 months)†
A[40]

Court security officer
assault level 5 and 6 months (**51 weeks) **A[9]**
obstruction level 3 **A[47]**

Criminal damage Penalties vary with value of property
A[18]–A[18B]

Crossbow (draw weight 1.4kg or more) (Crossbows Act 1987)
sell or lease to person under 17 level 5 and 6 months (**51 weeks), forfeiture
buying or hiring by person under 17 level 3, forfeiture
possession of by person under 17 level 3, forfeiture

Cruelty to animals £20,000 fine and/or 6 months (ss 4 and 8)
level 5 and 6 months (**51 weeks) (s 9) **A[5]**

Cruelty to a child level 5 and 6 months (**12 months)† **A[19]**

Customs duty (avoiding) 3 times value of goods or £5,000 and 6 months (**12months)† **A[4]**

Damaging property Penalty varies with value of damage **A[18]–A[18B]**

Dangerous dog A[72]

Dangerous drugs (*See* Controlled drugs) **A[22]**

Dangerous machinery level 5†

Dishonestly handling level 5 and 6 months (**12 months)† **A[49]**

Disorderly behaviour (Public Order Act 1986, s 5) level 3 **A[20]**

Displaying indecent matter level 5

Disposal of property in police possession A[66]

Dogs
Dangerous Dogs Act 1991
    breeding or parting with, etc, fighting dogs (s 1(2)) level 5 and 6 months (**51 weeks)
    fighting dog in public place without muzzle and lead (s 1(2)) level 5 and 6 months (**51 weeks)
    dog dangerously out of control in public place level 5 and 6 months (**12 months)+ (if aggravated offence)
control order (Dogs Act 1871) **A[72]**
dog worrying livestock level 3 **A[73]**

Domestic Violence (see breach of a non-molestation order)

Drugs (controlled) Penalty varies with classification of drug **A[22]–A[27B]**

Drunk in a highway, public place or licensed premises level 2 **A[28]**

Drunk and disorderly level 3 **A[28]**

Drunk at, or on the way to, a football match level 2 **A[76]**

Earnings of prostitution (living on) level 5 and 6 months (**12 months)†

Electricity, abstract/use without authority level 5 and/or 6 months (**12 months) **A[1]** †

Enclosed premises (found on) level 3 or 3 months (**level 3 only) **A[79]**

Excessive noise (nuisance order) level 5 **A[74]**

Exclusion order (licensed premises), breach of level 4 and 1 month (**51 weeks) **B[32]**

Exploitation of Prostitution – causing or inciting prostitution for gain; controlling prostitution for gain (Sexual Offences Act 2003, ss 52, 53) level 5 and 6 months (**12 months) † A[29]

Exposure (Sexual Offences Act 2003, s 66) level 5 and/or 6 months (**12 months) † A[30]

Failure to maintain oneself or a dependant
level 3 or (and, depending on the facts) 3 months (**51 weeks) (National Assistance Act 1948, s 51)
level 4 and 3 months (**level 4 only) (Social Security Administration Act 1992, s 105)

False accounting (Theft Act 1968, s 17) level 5 and 6 months (**12 months)† A[31]

False identity documents (Identity Documents Act 2010, s 6(1)) level 5 and 6 months (**12 months)† A[32]

False instrument, using level 5 and 6 months (**12 months)† A[40]

False statement to obtain social security level 5 and 3 months (**51 weeks) (Social Security Administration Act 1992, s 112) A[54]

False representation to obtain benefit level 5 and 6 months (**12 months)† (Social Security Administration Act 1992, s 111A) A[54]

Firearm (forfeiture for each of the following) (Firearms Act 1968)
air weapon in public place level 5 and 6 months (**51 weeks) (s 19) A[71]
air weapon (preventing minor from having with him) level 3 (s 24ZA) A[71A]
firearm (other than air weapon) in public place level 5 and 6 months (**12 months)† (s 19) A[33]
purchasing, possession, etc, without certificate level 5 and 6 months (**12 months)† (s 1) A[76]
trespassing in a building level 5 and 6 months (**51 weeks) A[77]
trespassing on land level 4 and 3 months (**51 weeks) A[77]

Food (selling food not of quality demanded) (Food Safety Act 1990, s 14) £20,000 and 6 months (**12 months)†

Football related offences (may attract a football banning order)
Possession of alcohol whilst entering or trying to enter ground level 3 A[34]
Being drunk in, or whilst trying to enter, ground level 2 A[35]
throwing missile, indecent or racist chanting; going into prohibited areas level 3 A[34]
unauthorised sale or attempted sale of tickets level 5 A[34]

Forgery level 5 and 6 months (**12 months)† A[78]

Found on enclosed premises level 3 or 3 months (**level 3 only) **A[79]**

Fraud level 5 and/or 6 months (**12 months)† **A[36]–A[39]**
fraud by false representation (s 1 (2) (a)) **A[36]**
fraud by failing to disclose information (s 1 (2) (b)) **A[36]**
fraud by abuse of position (s 1 (2) (c)) **A[36]**
obtaining services dishonestly (s 11) **A[37]**
possession of articles for fraud (s 6) **A[38]**
making, adapting, supplying or offering to supply articles for fraud (s 7) **A[39]**

Fraudulently receiving programmes (see Television licence below)

Game (trespassing on land in day time in search of game) level 3; level 5 if 5 or more trespassers (Game Act 1831, s 30) **A[86]**

Glue sniffing, supplying level 5 and 6 months (**51 weeks)

Going equipped for theft level 5 and 6 months (**12 months)† **A[58]**

Grievous bodily harm level 5 and 6 months (**12 months)† **A[70]**

Gross indecency level 5 and 6 months (**12 months)†

Handling stolen goods level 5 and 6 months (**12 months)† **A[40]**

Harassing residential occupier (Protection from Eviction Act 1977, s 1) level 5 and 6 months (**12 months)†

Harassment (Protection from Harassment Act 1997, s 2) level 5 and 6 months (**51 weeks) **A[41]**

Harassment (Protection from Harassment Act 1997, s 4) level 5 and 6 months (**12 months)† **A[41]**

Harassment, alarm or distress/disorderly behaviour (Public Order Act 1986, s 5) level 3* **A[20]**

Health and Safety at Work Act 1974
failure to discharge a duty imposed by ss 2–6 fine not exceeding £20,000 and/or 6 months (**12 months) **A[80]**
contravention of s 7 fine not exceeding £20,000 and 6 months (**12 months)†
contravention of s 8 fine not exceeding £20,000 and 6 months (**12 months)†
contravention of s 9 fine not exceeding £20,000 †
an offence under s 33(1)(c) fine not exceeding £20,000 and 6 months (**12 months)†
an offence under s 33(1)(d) level 5 fine
an offence under s 33(1)(e), (f) or (g) fine not exceeding £20,000 and 6 months (**12 months)†
an offence under s 33(1)(h) level 5 and/or 6 months (**51 weeks)
an offence under s 33(1)(i) level 5 †
an offence under s 33(1)(j) fine not exceeding £20,000 and 6 months (**12 months)†

an offence under s 33(1)(k), (l) or (m) fine not exceeding £20,000 and 6 months (**12 months)†

an offence under s 33(1)(n) level 5 fine

an offence under s 33(1)(o) fine not exceeding £20,000 and 6 months (**12 months)†

an offence under the existing statutory provisions for which no other penalty is specified fine not exceeding £20,000 and 6 months (**12 months)† **A[80]**

Health Act 2006 (See smoking)

Highway
builder's skip (depositing or leaving unlit) level 3
straying animals on level 3
wilful obstruction level 3 **A[85]**

Housebreaking implements (*See* Going equipped to steal) **A[58]**

Immigration offences (Immigration Act 1971, ss 24 – 26) **A[81]**

Income tax evasion (Finance Act 2000, s 144) level 5 and 6 months (**12 months)† **A[42]**

Indecent photographs of children level 5 and 6 months (**12 months)† **A[43]**

Indecent display level 5

Insulting magistrate, etc level 4 and 1 month **I[3]**

Insulting words or behaviour level 5 and 6 months (**51 weeks) **A[21]**

Interference with vehicle level 4 and 3 months (**51 weeks) **A[63]**

Intoxicating liquor
possessing at, or on the way to, a designated sporting event level 3 and 3 months (**51 weeks) **A[76]**
selling outside permitted hours level 3
selling to persons under 18 level 3 and forfeiture of licence (on second or subsequent conviction within 5 years)
selling without a licence level 4 and 6 months (**51 weeks); forfeiture of liquor and containers. For a subsequent offence defendant can be disqualified from holding a licence
persistently sell alcohol to persons aged less than 18 years, fine not exceeding £10,000, the holder of a premises licence may have the licence suspended by the court up to three months

Intoxicating substance, supplying level 5 and 6 months (**51 weeks)

Keeping a brothel used for prostitution (Sexual Offences Act 2003, s 55) level 5 and/or 6 months (**12 months)† **A[44]**

Kerb crawling level 3 **A[82]**

Kill, threatening to (Offences Against the Person Act 1861, s 16) level 5 and/or 6 months (**12 months)† **A[59]**

Landlord and tenant (unlawful eviction or harassment) level 5 and 6 months (**12 months)†

Litter (including car dumping)
(i) Environmental Protection Act 1990 A[83.18]
(ii) Refuse Disposal (Amenity) Act 1978 level 4 and 3 months (**51 weeks) A[83]

Living on earnings of prostitution level 5 and 6 months (**12 months)†

Loudspeakers level 5 A[74]

Making off without payment level 5 and 6 months (**12 months)† A[45]

Malicious communications level 5 and 6 months (**51 weeks)

Measuring equipment (false or unjust) level 5 (and 6 months (**51 weeks) if fraud), and forfeiture (Weights and Measures Act 1985, s 17)

Messages, offensive or threatening level 5 and 6 months (**51 weeks) (Malicious Communications Act 1988, s(1))

Misbehaviour in court level 4 and 1 month I[3]

Misuse of drugs (*See* Controlled drugs) A[22]–A[27B]

Mobile phones level 3 or level 4 for HGVs and PSVs*

National insurance, failing to pay contributions level 3 plus arrears of contributions for two years

Noise (excessive) A[74]

Noise or nuisance on NHS premises A[74]

Nuisance A[84]

Obscenely exposing person level 3 or 3 months (Vagrancy Act 1824, s 4); level 3 or 14 days (**not imprisonable for offences from a date to be appointed) (Town Police Clauses Act 1847, s 28)

Obstructing highway level 3 A[85]

Obstructing or resisting a police officer (or a person assisting a police officer) level 3 and 1 month A[47]

Offensive weapon and threatening with offensive weapon level 5 and 6 months (**12 months), forfeiture† A[11]

Payment, making off without level 5 and 6 months (**12 months)† A[45]

Pedlar
trading without certificate (Pedlars Act 1871, s 4) level 1

Poaching (For hunting wild mammals with dogs and hare coursing see the Hunting Act 2004, ss 1–5)
day time offence level 3; level 5 if 5 or more trespassers (Game Act 1831, s 30) **A[86]**
night time offences level 3; level 4 and 6 months where violence is used or offered
(Night Poaching Act 1828, ss 1 and 2) or 3 or more being armed (s 9) **A[86.9]**
pursuing game without a licence level 2 (Game Licence Act 1860, s 4) **A[86.23]**

Point, article with, in public place (CJA 1988, s 139) level 5 or 6 months (**12 months)+ **A[11]**

Police (Property) Act 1897 A[87]

Possessing certain false documents level 5 and 6 months (**12 months)† (Forgery etc Act 1981, s 5)

Property (damaging or destroying) Penalty varies with value **A[18]** to **A[18B]**

Property (obtaining property by deception) level 5 and 6 months (**12 months)† **A[22]**

Property in possession of police A[87]

Prostitutes (see also exploitation of prostitution)
living on earnings of level 5 and 6 months (**12 months)†
soliciting by prostitutes level 2/level 3 or Support and Engagement Order **A[82.2]**

Public telephone (see **Telephone**) (Telecommunications Act 1984 – Communications Act 2003
fraudulent use of (s 42) level 5 and 6 months (**12 months)†
indecent or false telephone calls (s 43) level 5 and 6 months (**51 weeks)

Racially or religiously aggravated offences
wounding level 5 and 6 months (**12 months) † **A[48]**
actual bodily harm level 5 and 6 months (**12 months) † **A[8.2]**
common assault level 5 and 6 months (**51 weeks) **A[8.2]**
criminal damage level 5 and 6 months (**12 months) † **A[18]**
threatening behaviour/intentional harassment alarm or distress level 5 and 6 months
(**12 months)+ **A[21]**
disorderly behaviour level 3 **A[20]**
harassment level 5 and/or 6 months (**12 months) † **A[41]**

Railway fare evasion
avoid fare level 3 or 3 months (**51 weeks) **A[48]**
giving false name or address level 3 or 3 months (**51 weeks) **A[48.2]**

Resisting a constable or a person assisting a constable level 3 and 1 month (**51 weeks) **A[47]**

Scales (unjust) level 5 (and 6 months (**51 weeks) if fraud), and forfeiture (Weights and Measures Act 1985, s 17)

School attendance, parent not ensuring (Education Act 1996, s 444) level 3 Aggravated offence level 4 and 3 months (**51 weeks) **A[49] and D[17]**

Selling food not of quality demanded (Food Safety Act 1990, s 14) £20,000 and 6 months (**12 months)†

Sexual activity with child level 5 and 6 months (**12 months)† A[52]

Sexual activity in a public lavatory level 5 and 6 months (**12 months)† A[51]

Sexual assault level 5 and 6 months (**12 months)† A[53]

Sex Offenders register – fail to comply with notification requirements level 5 and 6 months (**12 months)† A[50]

Shotgun
purchasing or possessing, etc, without certificate level 5 and 6 months (**12 months)
     †, forfeiture A[88]
loaded shotgun in a public place level 5 and 6 months (**12 months)+, forfeiture
     A[33]

Skip
depositing on highway level 3
not complying with condition level 3
unlit level 3

Smuggling 3 times value of goods or £5,000 and 6 months (**12 months)† A[19]

Social security
Dishonest statement/representation for obtaining benefit etc level 5 and/or six
     months
(**12 months) † (Social Security Administration Act 1992, s 111A) A[54]
false statement/representation to obtain level 5 and 3 months (**51 weeks) (Social
     Security Administration Act 1992, s 112) A[54]
persistently refusing or neglecting to maintain oneself or a dependant level 4 and
     3 months (**no longer imprisonable for offences from a date to be appointed)
     (Social Security Administration Act 1992, s 105)

Soliciting by prostitutes level 2/level 3 or Support and Engagement Order A[82.2]

Soliciting women for prostitution level 3 A[82]

Solvent, supplying for intoxication level 5 and 6 months (**51 weeks)

Smoking (Health Act 2006)

Smoking in a smoke free place (£200 – a fixed penalty of £50 reduced to £30 if paid before the end of 15 days)

Failing to display the required no-smoking signs (£1000 – a fixed penalty of £200 reduced to £150 if paid before the end of 15 days) – this offence is committed by anyone who manages or occupies smoke-free premises or a vehicle

Failing to prevent smoking in a smoke-free place (£2,500 – no fixed penalty) – this offence is committed by anyone who manages or controls smoke-free premises or a vehicle

Sporting event (may attract a football banning order)
football banning order **B[32]**
intoxicating liquor, possessing at/on the way to level 3 and 3 months (**51 weeks) **A[35]**
drunk at/on the way to level 2 **A[35]**

Squatting in a residential building level 5 and 6 months (51 weeks)**

Statutory nuisance (noise) A[61]

Stealing level 5 and 6 months (**12 months)† **A[57]**

Taking motor vehicle or conveyance level 5 and 6 months (**51 weeks), disqualification **A[65]**

Tattooing a minor level 3

Tax credit fraud level 5 and 6 months (**12 months)† (Tax Credits Act 2005, s 35) **A[55]**

Taxi-touting/soliciting for hire level 4 (Criminal Justice and Public Order Act 1994, s 167) **A[56]**

Telephone (Telecommunications Act 1984 – Communications Act 2003)

NB: Ss 42, 42A and 43 below were replaced by ss 125–127 of the Communications Act 2003 effective from 25/7/03 by virtue of SI 2003/1900 as amended. **A[16]**
fraudulent use of public telephone (s 42) level 5 and 6 months (**12 months)†
indecent or false calls (s 43) level 5 and 6 months (**12 months)*

Television licence payment evasion (Communications Act 2003, s 363) level 3 **A[61]**

[Fraudulently receiving programmes] (Copyright, Designs and Patents Act 1988, s 297) level 5 **F[3]**

Terrorism offences (Terrorism Act 2000, ss 15–18) level 5 or 6 months†
(Breach of notification provisions under the Counter-Terrorism Act 2008) level 5 or 6 months† See also **B[52]**

Theft (covers breach of trust; in a dwelling; from the person and from a shop) level 5 and 6 months† (**12 months) **A[57]**

Threatening to damage or destroy property level 5 and 6 months (**12 months)† **A[18A]**

Threatening letters level 4

Threats to kill (Offences Against the Person Act 1861, s 16) level 5 and/or 6 months (**12 months)† A[59]

Threatening words or behaviour (Public Order Act 1986, s 4) level 5 and 6 months (**51 weeks) A[21]

Ticket Touting (unauthorised sale or disposal of tickets for designated football matches (s 166 CJPOA 1994 as amended) level 5 A[34]

Trade mark, unauthorised use of etc (Trade Marks Act 1994, s 92) level 5 and/or 6 months (**12 months)† A[60]

Trespassing on land during day time in search of game, etc level 3/level 5 (if 5 or more trespassers) (Game Act 1831, s 30) A[65]

Trespassing with firearm in a building level 5 and 6 months (**12 months)+ (if not an air weapon) forfeiture A[38]

Trespassing with firearm on land level 4 and 3 months (**51 weeks), forfeiture A[38]

Unauthorised taking of motor vehicle level 5 and 6 months (**51 weeks), disqualification A[77]

Unfair or prohibited commercial practices level 5† A[75]

Using false (or copy of false) instrument level 5 and 6 months (**12 months)+ (Forgery etc Act 1981) A[40]

VAT evasion (Value Added Tax Act 1994, s 72) level 5 and/or 6 months (**12 months)† A[62]

Vehicle interference level 4 and 3 months (**51 weeks) A[63]

Vehicle taking, without consent level 5 and 6 months (**51 weeks), disqualification A[65]

Vehicle-taking (aggravated) level 5 and 6 months (**12 months) A[66]

Violent disorder level 5 and/or 6 months (**12 months)† A[67]

Voyeurism (Sexual Offences Act 2003, s 67) level 5 and/or 6 months (**12 months)† A[68]

Weighing equipment (unjust) level 5 (and 6 months (**51 weeks) if fraud), and forfeiture

Wilful obstruction of highway level 3 A[63]

Wilful obstruction of police constable (or person assisting police constable) level 3 and 1 month (**51 weeks) A[47]

Witness intimidation level 5 and/or 6 months (**12 months)† A[69]

Wounding level 5 and 6 months (**12 months)† A[70]

A[1]

Electricity – Abstracting/Use without authority

Charge

A[1.1]

Dishonestly uses without due authority, or dishonestly causes to be wasted or diverted, any electricity

Theft Act 1968, s 13

Maximum penalty – Fine level 5 and 6 months (**12 months). Triable either way.

Crown Court – 5 years' imprisonment and unlimited fine.

Mode of Trial

A[1.2]

Consider the **SGC Guideline** at [1.4] below.

Legal notes and definitions

A[1.3]

Dishonestly. See the notes at [57.5] onwards.

It is sufficient for the prosecution to establish electricity was used without the authority of the relevant provider (company) and with no intention to pay (*R v McCreadie and Tume* (1993) 157 JP 541).

Sentencing
SC Guideline – Electricity, abstract/use without authority

A[1.4]

OFFENCE SERIOUSNESS (CULPABILITY AND HARM)		
A. IDENTIFY THE APPROPRIATE STARTING POINT		
Starting points based on first time offender pleading not guilty		
Example of nature of activity	Starting point	Range
Where the offence results in substantial commercial gain, a custodial sentence may be appropriate		

Offence involving evidence of planning and indication that the offending was intended to be continuing, such as using a device to interfere with the electricity meter or re-wiring or to by-pass the meter.	Medium level community order	Band A fine to high level community order

OFFENCE SERIOUSNESS (CULPABILITY AND HARM)
B. CONSIDER THE EFFECT OF AGGRAVATING AND MITIGATING FACTORS (OTHER THAN THOSE WITHIN EXAMPLES ABOVE)
Common aggravating and mitigating factors are identified at [5.2A]. The following may be particularly relevant but **these lists are not exhaustive**
Factor indicating greater degree of harm
1. Risk of danger caused to property and/or life
FORM A PRELIMINARY VIEW OF THE APPROPRIATE SENTENCE, THEN CONSIDER OFFENDER MITIGATION
Common factors are identified at [5.2A] – see also note (c) below
CONSIDER A REDUCTION FOR A GUILTY PLEA
CONSIDER ANCILLARY ORDERS, INCLUDING COMPENSATION
Refer to Part B for available ancillary orders and in particular [18] for guidance on compensation. This may be ordered in respect of any injury loss or damage resulting from the offence. Maximum is £5,000 per offence. It may be ordered in addition to another sentence, or as a substantive penalty by itself. If a monetary penalty is appropriate and the defendant's means are limited, preference must be given to ordering compensation instead of a fine.
DECIDE SENTENCE
GIVE REASONS

Electricity, abstract/use without authority – factors to be taken into consideration

Key factors

(a) The starting points and sentencing ranges in this guideline are based on the assumption that the offender was motivated by greed or a desire to live beyond his or her means. To avoid double counting, such a motivation should not be treated as a factor that increases culpability.

(b) When assessing the harm caused by this offence, the starting point should be the loss suffered by the victim. In general, the greater the loss, the more serious the offence. However, the monetary value of the loss may not reflect the full extent of the harm caused by the offence. The court should also take into account the impact of the offence on the victim, any harm to persons other than the direct victim, and any harm in the form of public alarm or erosion of public confidence.

(c)   The following matters of offender mitigation may be relevant to this offence:

    (i)   *Offender motivated by desperation or need.* The fact that an offence has been committed in desperation or need arising from particular hardship may count as offender mitigation in exceptional circumstances.

    (ii)   *Voluntary restitution.* Whether and the degree to which payment for stolen electricity constitutes a matter of offender mitigation will depend on an assessment of the circumstances and, in particular, the voluntariness and timeliness of the payment.

    (iii)   Impact on sentence of offender's dependency. Many offenders convicted of acquisitive crimes are motivated by an addiction, often to drugs, alcohol or gambling. This does not mitigate the seriousness of the offence, but an offender's dependency may properly influence the type of sentence imposed. In particular, it may sometimes be appropriate to impose a drug rehabilitation requirement or an alcohol treatment requirement as part of a community order or a suspended sentence order in an attempt to break the cycle of addiction and offending, even if an immediate custodial sentence would otherwise be warranted (see [2.17]).

        The Court of Appeal gave guidance on the approach to making drug treatment and testing orders, which also applies to imposing a drug rehabilitation requirement in *Attorney General's Reference No 64 of 2003 (R v Boujettif and Harrison) v Sanchez* [2003] EWCA Crim 3514 and *R v Woods and Collins* [2005] EWCA Crim 2065 summarised in the Sentencing Guidelines Council Guideline Judgments Case Compendium (Section (A) Generic Sentencing Principles) available at: http://sentencingcouncil.judiciary.gov.uk.

A[2]

Affray

Charge

A[2.1]

Using or threatening unlawful violence towards another such that the conduct would cause a person of reasonable firmness present at the scene to fear for his personal safety

Public Order Act 1986, s 3

Maximum penalty – Fine level 5 and 6 months (**12 months). Triable either way. Specified violent offence under Sch 15, Part 1, CJA 2003

Crown Court – 3 years' imprisonment and unlimited fine.

Mode of trial

A[2.2]

Consider the **SGC Guideline** at **A[2.15]** below.

Legal notes and definitions

A[2.3]

The charge. Only one offence is created.

A[2.4]

Using or threatening. Where two or more persons use or threaten the violence, it is the conduct of them taken together that must be considered for the purpose of the offence.

A[2.5]

Threats. Cannot be made by way of words alone, there must be at least a physical gesture towards someone.

A[2.6]

Person of reasonable firmness need not actually be or be likely to be present at the scene, it is the hypothetical reasonable bystander who has to be put in fear for his personal safety, not just the victim himself (*R v Sanchez* (1996) 160 JP 321, [1996] Crim LR 572, CA). In *R v Plavecz* (2002) it is made clear that an assault does not turn into an affray because it is in a public place. There must be evidence that anyone watching would have been put in fear themselves.

The purpose of the legislation was to address public order. The authorities made it plain that the facts in particular circumstances required careful study before the legal principle was applied. It was difficult to see how, when viewed contextually, the evidence in the instant case, supported the appellant's conviction for affray. The incident had consisted of brief exchanges which were essentially private in nature. Further, there was no realistic possibility of a notional third party entering the premises and fearing for his own safety: *R (on the application of Leeson) v DPP* [2010] EWHC 994 (Admin), 174 JP 367, [2010] 17 LS Gaz R 16.

A[2.7]–[2.8]

Violence. Violence does not include violence justified in law (self-defence or prevention of crime). The violence must be directed towards another, ie not property – such as kicking a door. However, the violence is not restricted to violence causing or intended to cause injury and includes violent conduct such as throwing a missile of a kind capable of causing injury even though it misses or falls short.

A[2.9]

Intent. The accused must intend to use or threaten violence or be aware that his conduct may be violent or threaten violence.

A[2.10]–[2.14]

Intoxication. See under the offence of violent disorder at A[67]. Affray can be committed in a public or private place.

Sentencing
SC Guideline – Affray

A[2.15]

IDENTIFY DANGEROUS OFFENDERS		
This is a specified offence for the purposes of the public protection provisions in the Criminal Justice Act 2003. Refer to B[16.5] and consult legal adviser for guidance		
OFFENCE SERIOUSNESS (CULPABILITY AND HARM) A. IDENTIFY THE APPROPRIATE STARTING POINT		
Starting points based on first time offender pleading not guilty		
Examples of nature of activity	Starting point	Range
Brief offence involving low-level violence, no substantial fear created	Low level community order	Band C fine to medium level community order
Degree of fighting or violence that causes substantial fear	High level community order	Medium level community order to 12 weeks custody
Fight involving a weapon/throwing objects, or conduct causing risk of injury	18 weeks custody	12 weeks custody to Crown Court

OFFENCE SERIOUSNESS (CULPABILITY AND HARM)
B. CONSIDER THE EFFECT OF AGGRAVATING AND MITIGATING FACTORS (OTHER THAN THOSE WITHIN EXAMPLES ABOVE)
Common aggravating and mitigating factors are identified at **B[5.2A]**. The following may be particularly relevant but these lists are not exhaustive:

Factors indicating higher culpability	Factors indicating lower culpability
1. Group action	1. Did not start the trouble
2. Threats	2. Provocation
3. Lengthy incident	3. Stopped as soon as police arrived
Factors indicating greater degree of harm	
1. Vulnerable person(s) present	
2. Injuries caused	
3. Damage to property	

FORM A PRELIMINARY VIEW OF THE APPROPRIATE SENTENCE, THEN CONSIDER OFFENDER MITIGATION
Common factors are identified at **B[5.2A]**.
CONSIDER A REDUCTION FOR A GUILTY PLEA
CONSIDER ANCILLARY ORDERS, INCLUDING COMPENSATION AND FOOTBALL BANNING ORDER (where appropriate)
Refer to Part B for guidance on ancillary orders and in particular B[18] for guidance on compensation.
DECIDE SENTENCE **GIVE REASONS**

A[2.16]

Domestic violence. For domestic violence offences see SC Definitive Guideline: "Overarching Principles: Domestic Violence".

A[3]

Alcohol sale offences

Charge

A[3.1]
Sale of alcohol to a person who is drunk

Licensing Act 2003, s 141

NB: For the sale of alcohol to a drunk person under s 141 LA 2003, a fixed penalty of £80 is available (not off-licences)

A[3.2]
Sale of alcohol to children

Licensing Act 2003, s 146

NB: For the sale of alcohol to a person under 18 a fixed penalty of £80 is available for staff under s 146 Licensing Act 2003. Licensees should be the subject of a summons

A[3.3]
Allowing the sale of alcohol to children

Licensing Act 2003, s 147

Maximum penalty – level 3 fine for a s 141 offence; level 5 fine for ss 146 and 147 offences

Section 23 of the Violent Crime Reduction Act 2006 created a new offence of persistently selling alcohol to children, which came into force on April 6, 2007. This is committed if, on three or more different occasions within a period of three consecutive months, alcohol is unlawfully sold on the same premises to a person under 18. The offence is summary only and the maximum penalty is a £10,000 fine. **Consult your legal adviser for guidance on the approach to sentencing and the court's powers in relation to liquor licences.**

Legal notes and definitions

A[3.4]
The provisions apply to any person who works at the premises in a capacity, whether paid or unpaid, which gives him authority to sell the alcohol concerned (see s,141 (2) for further definitions).

The provisions apply equally to the sale or supply of alcohol in club premises.

Sentencing
SC Guideline – Alcohol sale offences

A[3.5]

OFFENCE SERIOUSNESS (CULPABILITY AND HARM)		
A. IDENTIFY THE APPROPRIATE STARTING POINT		
Starting points based on first time offender pleading not guilty		
Examples of nature of activity	**Starting point**	*Range*
Sale to a child (ie a person under 18)/to a drunk person	Band B fine	Band A fine to band C fine

Note: refer to guidance at **B[33.24]** for approach to fines for offences committed for commercial purposes.

OFFENCE SERIOUSNESS (CULPABILITY AND HARM)	
B. CONSIDER THE EFFECT OF AGGRAVATING AND MITIGATING FACTORS (OTHER THAN THOSE WITHIN THE EXAMPLES ABOVE)	
Common aggravating and mitigating factors are identified at **B[5.2A]**. The following may be particularly relevant but **these lists are not exhaustive:**	
Factors indicating higher culpability	*Factors indicating greater degree of harm*
1. No attempt made to establish age	1. Younger child/children
2. Spirits/high level of drink	2. Drunk person causing distress to others
3. Drunk person highly intoxicated	3. Drunk person aggressive
4. Large quantity of alcohol supplied	
5. Sale intended for consumption by group of children/drunk people	
6. Offender in senior or management position	
FORM A PRELIMINARY VIEW OF THE APPROPRIATE SENTENCE, THEN CONSIDER OFFENDER MITIGATION	
Common factors are identified at B[5.2A]	
CONSIDER A REDUCTION FOR A GUILTY PLEA	
CONSIDER ANCILLARY ORDERS, INCLUDING FORFEITURE OR SUSPENSION OF PERSONAL LIQUOR LICENCE	
Refer to Part B for available ancillary orders	
DECIDE SENTENCE	
GIVE REASONS	

Sentencing Note: See A[3.3] above.

A[4]

Alcohol/tobacco, fraudulently evade duty

Charge

A[4.1]

Knowingly and with intent to defraud Her Majesty of the duty payable was concerned in carrying, removing, depositing, harbouring, keeping or concealing or dealing with goods, namely, which were chargeable with a duty which had not been paid

OR

Knowingly and with intent to defraud Her Majesty of the duty payable acquired possession of goods namely, which were chargeable with a duty which had not been paid

OR

Knowingly was concerned in a fraudulent evasion (or attempt at evasion) of any duty chargeable on certain goods, namely

Customs and Excise Management Act 1979, s 170

Maximum penalty – Three times the value of the goods or £5,000 fine whichever is the greater and 6 months (**12 months). Triable either way.

Crown Court – 7 years' imprisonment and unlimited fine.

A[4.2]

Drugs – Different penalties will apply in both the magistrates' court and the Crown Court if drugs are involved and in the Crown Court where there is the import or export of counterfeit money. The legal adviser should be consulted. For drugs see A[27B].

Mode of trial

A[4.3]

See general notes at I[4] and **SGC Guideline** at A[4.16] below.

Legal notes and definitions

A[4.4]

Knowing. If it is proved that dutiable goods were in the defendant's possession there is a presumption that he knew they were in his possession. Recklessness is not sufficient (*R v Panayi (No 2)* [1989] 1 WLR 187, 88 Cr App Rep 267, CA).

A[4.5]

Intent to defraud. The intention of defrauding the Crown of duty can be inferred from the circumstances of the case. It has been held that telling a lie to a customs officer can be evidence of an intention to defraud.

A[4.6]

The prosecution. Must be authorised by HM Revenue and Customs. Neither the police nor a private citizen can instigate proceedings on their own authority.

A[4.7]

Death of informant. If the informant (or person authorised by HM Revenue and Customs) dies, is dismissed or is absent then the Revenue and Customs can nominate another person to proceed with the case.

A[4.8]

Presumptions against the defendant. The Act is so worded that it gives to the prosecution a number of advantages in presuming certain points to be in the prosecution's favour.

For example, if a defendant claims that the goods were lawfully imported or lawfully unloaded from a ship or aircraft the burden of proving these points rests on the defendant. However, the burden of proof is not to establish his defence beyond all reasonable doubt but to satisfy the magistrates that on the balance of probabilities his defence is true.

A[4.9]–[4.15]

Mistake. If the customs officer makes a mistake and undercharges the duty, no offence is committed by a person who pays the duty realising the mistake, provided that he has not given false information or induced the error.

Sentencing
SC Guideline – Alcohol/tobacco, fraudulently evade duty

A[4.16]

The guidelines and accompanying notes are drawn from the Court of Appeal's decision in *R v Czyzewski* [2003] EWCA Crim 2139, [2004] 3 All ER 135, [2004] 1 Cr App R (S.) 49. Further consideration is being given to the appropriate approach to sentencing for this offence in the context of the Council and Panel's work on fraud offences; this may result in a revised guideline being issued in a future update.

Key factors

- In terms of seriousness, the principal factors are the level of the duty evaded; the complexity and sophistication of the organisation involved; the function of the offender within the organisation; and the amount of personal profit to the particular offender.
- Evidence of professional smuggling will include:
  - (1) A complex operation with many people involved
  - (2) Financial accounting or budgets
  - (3) Obtaining goods from several different sources
  - (4) Integration of freight movements with commercial organisations
  - (5) Sophisticated concealment methods such as forged documents or specially adapted vehicles
  - (6) Varying of methods and routes
  - (7) Links with illicit overseas organisations
  - (8) When the amount of goods smuggled is in the order of half a million cigarettes (which approximates to evasion of £75,000 worth of duty): this is not a precise indication but the value of the goods could be a potential indicator of professional smuggling.
- Any customs or excise duty owed is likely to be recovered by the authorities under separate procedures and will not require an order from the sentencing court.

OFFENCE SERIOUSNESS (CULPABILITY AND HARM)		
A. IDENTIFY THE APPROPRIATE STARTING POINT		
Starting points based on first time offender pleading not guilty		
Examples of nature of activity	**Starting point**	**Range**
Duty evaded is less than £1,000	Band B fine	Band A fine to band C fine Note: a conditional discharge may be appropriate where there is particularly strong mitigation and provided there has been no earlier warning
Duty evaded is more than £1,000 but less than £10,000	Medium level community order	Band C fine to 18 weeks custody Note: the custody threshold is likely to be passed if one or more of the aggravating features listed below is present
Duty evaded is between £10,000 and £50,000	Crown Court	12 weeks custody to Crown Court

		Note: committal to Crown court is likely to be appropriate if one or more of the aggravating factors listed below is present
Duty evaded exceeds £50,000	Crown Court	Crown Court

OFFENCE SERIOUSNESS (CULPABILITY AND HARM)

B. CONSIDER THE EFFECT OF AGGRAVATING AND MITIGATING FACTORS (OTHER THAN THOSE WITHIN THE EXAMPLES ABOVE)

Common aggravating and mitigating factors are identified at **B[2A]**. The following may be particularly relevant but **these lists are not exhaustive:**

Factors indicating higher culpability	Factors indicating lower culpability
1. Offender played an organisational role	1. Pressure from others to commit offence
2. Offender made repeated importations, particularly in the face of a warning from authorities	2. Minor involvement
3. Offender was a professional smuggler (see opposite)	3. Small personal profit
4. Legitimate business used a front	
5. Offender abused position of privilege as a customs or police officer, or as an employee, for example, of a security firm, ferry company or port authority	
6. Offender threatened violence to those seeking to enforce the law	
Factors indicating greater degree of harm	
1. Offender dealt in goods with an additional health risk because of possible contamination	
2. Offender used children or vulnerable adults	
3. Offender disposed of goods to under-age purchasers	

FORM A PRELIMINARY VIEW OF THE APPROPRIATE SENTENCE, THEN CONSIDER OFFENDER MITIGATION

Common factors are identified at B[5.2A]

CONSIDER A REDUCTION FOR A GUILTY PLEA

CONSIDER ANCILLARY ORDERS, INCLUDING FORFEITURE OR SUSPENSION OF PERSONAL LIQUOR LICENCE

Consult your legal adviser on guidance for available ANCILLARY ORDERS

CONSIDER DEPRIVATION OF PROPERTY (including vehicle) AND DISQUALIFICATION FROM DRIVING

NOTIFY LICENSING AUTHORITY WHERE LICENSED PREMISES HAVE BEEN USED FOR SALE OF SMUGGLED GOODS
DECIDE SENTENCE
GIVE REASONS

A[4.17]

Value of goods. The value of the goods, for the purpose of determining the penalty, shall be the price they might reasonably be expected to have fetched on the open market, after duty has been paid, at or about the time of the commission of the offence. See *R v Dosanjh* [1998] 3 All ER 618, [1999] 1 Cr App Rep 371, CA for aggravating features and the use of imprisonment and *R v Howlett* [1999] All ER (D) 777, CA which suggest that cases involving a loss of duty under £10,000 may be dealt with by sentences of under six months' imprisonment.

A[4.18]

Financial reporting order. A conviction for an offence under s 170 of the Customs and Excise Management Act 1979 (including attempting, conspiring, inciting, aiding, abetting, counselling or procuring the commission of the offence) is one that is mentioned in s 76(3) of the Serious Organised Crime and Police Act 2005. The court when sentencing or otherwise dealing with an offender convicted on or after 4 May 4 2007 may also make a financial reporting order.

A[4.19]

Appeal. Note that HM Revenue and Customs may appeal **any** decision of the court including sentence (*Customs and Excise Comrs v Brunt* (1998) 163 JP 161).

A[5]

Animal cruelty

Charges

A[5.1]

1. A person commits an offence if –

(a) an act of his, or a failure of his to act, causes an animal to suffer;
(b) he knew, or ought reasonably to have known, that the act, or failure to act, would have that effect or be likely to do so,
(c) the animal is a protected animal, and
(d) the suffering is unnecessary.

Animal Welfare Act 2006, s 4(1).

2. A person commits an offence if –

(a) he is responsible for an animal,
(b) an act, or failure to act, of another person causes the animal to suffer,
(c) he permitted that to happen or failed to take such steps (whether by supervising the other person or otherwise) as were reasonable in all the circumstances to prevent that happening, and
(d) the suffering is unnecessary.

Animal Welfare Act 2006, s 4(2).

3. Fighting etc

A person commits an offence if he –

(a) causes an animal fight to take place, or attempts to do so;
(b) knowingly receives money for an animal fight;
(c) knowingly publicises an animal fight; . . .

Animal Welfare Act 2006, s 8(1).

NB: Offences under (d)–(i) omitted and subsections (2) and (3). Different types of offences are caught by this section including being present at an animal fight. For ease of space not all offences under section 8 have been included in this section.

4. A person commits an offence if –

he does not take such steps as are reasonable in all the circumstances to ensure that the needs of an animal for which he is responsible are met to the extent required by good practice.

Animal Welfare Act 2006, s 9

Maximum penalty

(1)   6 months' imprisonment (**51 weeks) or a fine not exceeding £20,000 or both – triable only summarily.

(2)   6 months' imprisonment (**51 weeks) or a fine not exceeding £20,000 or both – triable only summarily.

(3)   6 months' imprisonment (**51 weeks) or a fine not exceeding £20,000 or both – triable only summarily.

(4)   6 months' imprisonment (**51 weeks) or a level 5 fine or both – triable only summarily.

Legal notes and definitions

A[5.2]

Each of the types of cruelty alleged above are separate offences. The legislation appears designed to catch not only owners or persons in charge of an animal but in specified circumstances any other person "responsible" for an animal (see below). If a defendant causes suffering etc to a number of different animals on the same occasion there does not appear to be any objection to a single charge being preferred eg under s 4 (1). The mutilation of animals is a separate offence covered by s 5 while the docking of animal tails is provided for by s 6 of the AWA 2006.

Animal. Is defined in s 1 and means a vertebrate other than man.

Protected animal. The legislation covers mostly domesticated animals as defined in s 2.

Responsibility for animals. In the AWA 2006:

(1)   References to a person responsible for an animal are to a person responsible for an animal whether on a permanent or temporary basis.

(2)   References to being responsible for an animal include being in charge of it.

(3)   A person who "owns" an animal should always be regarded as being a person who is responsible for it.

(4)   A person should be "treated" as responsible for any animal for which a person under the age of 16 years of whom he has actual care and control is responsible.

Whether suffering unnecessary. In the AWA 2006, the considerations to which it is relevant to have regard when determining for the purposes of this section whether suffering is unnecessary include:

(1)   Whether the suffering could reasonably have been avoided or reduced.

(2)   Whether the conduct which caused the suffering was in compliance with any relevant enactment or any relevant provisions of a licence or code of practice issued under any enactment.

(3)   Whether the conduct which caused the suffering was proportionate to the purpose of the conduct concerned.

(4) Whether the conduct concerned was in all the circumstances that of a reasonably competent and humane person.

(5) Nothing in (1)–(4) above applies to the destruction of an animal in an appropriate and humane manner.

Time limits for prosecution.

(a) Before the end of 3 years beginning with the date of the commencement of the offence, or

(b) before the end of the period of six months beginning with the date on which evidence which the prosecutor thinks is sufficient to justify the proceedings comes to his knowledge.

A certificate issued under s 31(2) of the AWA 2006 which conformed to the criteria specified in s 31(2) could only be challenged on one of two bases alone: (i) that it constituted a fraud; (ii) that the certificate was plainly wrong. Where it was submitted that a certificate was plainly wrong a challenge should be mounted in relation to the jurisdiction of the court and not as an abuse of the process: *Atkinson v DPP* [2004] EWHC 1457 (Admin), [2004] 3 All ER 971, [2005] 1 WLR 96; see *Lamont-Perkins v RSPCA* immediately below.

Animal Welfare Act 2006, s 31.

Prosecutor. The phrase 'the prosecutor' in s 31 of the AWA 2006 is not limited to a person or body who prosecutes pursuant to a power conferred by some statutory provision but applies to anyone who initiates a prosecution under the Act. Accordingly, s 127 of the MCA 1980 had no application to a prosecution brought under the Animal Welfare Act 2006 where a certificate had been issued under s 31(2): *Lamont-Perkins v Royal Society for the Prevention of Cruelty to Animals* [2012] EWHC 1002 (Admin), (2012) 176 JP 369.

Sentencing
SC Guideline – Animal cruelty

A[5.3]

OFFENCE SERIOUSNESS (CULPABILITY AND HARM) A. IDENTIFY THE APPROPRIATE STARTING POINT Starting points based on first time offender pleading not guilty		
Examples of nature of activity	**Starting point**	**Range**
One impulsive act causing little or no injury; short term neglect	Low level community order	Band C fine to medium level community order
Several incidents of deliberate ill-treatment/frightening animal(s); medium term neglect	High level community order	Medium level community order to 12 weeks custody

Attempt to kill/torture; animal baiting/conducting or permitting cock-fighting etc; prolonged neglect	18 weeks custody	12–26 weeks custody
OFFENCE SERIOUSNESS (CULPABILITY AND HARM)		

B. CONSIDER THE EFFECT OF AGGRAVATING AND MITIGATING FACTORS (OTHER THAN THOSE WITHIN THE EXAMPLES ABOVE)

Common aggravating and mitigating factors are identified at **B[5.2]**. The following may be particularly relevant but these lists are not exhaustive:

Factors indicating higher culpability	*Factors indicating lower culpability*
1. Offender in position of special responsibility	1. Offender induced by others
2. Adult involves children in offending	2. Ignorance of appropriate care
3. Animal(s) kept for livelihood	3. Offender with limited capacity
4. Use of weapon	
5. Offender ignored advice/warnings	
6. Offence committed for commercial gain	
Factors indicating greater degree of harm	
1. Serious injury or death	
2. Several animals affected	

FORM A PRELIMINARY VIEW OF THE APPROPRIATE SENTENCE, THEN CONSIDER OFFENDER MITIGATION

Common factors are identified at **B[5.2A]**

CONSIDER A REDUCTION FOR A GUILTY PLEA

CONSIDER ANCILLARY ORDERS, INCLUDING COMPENSATION

See **Part B** for guidance on available ancillary orders and consult your legal adviser

CONSIDER DISQUALIFICATION FROM OWNERSHIP OF ANIMAL

DECIDE SENTENCE

GIVE REASONS

A[5.4]

Deprivation of ownership. If the person convicted of an offence under eg ss 4 or 9 above, is the owner of an animal in relation to which the offence was committed, the court may, instead of or in addition, make an order depriving him of ownership of the animal and for its disposal (Animal Welfare Act 2006, s 33).

Destruction of animal. After conviction the court, if satisfied on the evidence of a veterinary surgeon that it is in the interests of the animal, it may order the animal to be destroyed. The defendant or another person (such as the owner) can be ordered to pay the costs involved. There is a right of appeal to the Crown court except where the court considers that it is in the interests of the animal not to delay the destruction order (Animal Welfare Act 2006, s 37).

Disqualification. The court may disqualify the defendant:

(a)   from owning animals;
(b)   from keeping animals;
(c)   from participating in the keeping of animals; and,
(d)   from being party to an arrangement under which he is entitled to control or influence the way in which animals are kept (Animal Welfare Act 2006, s 34).

Disqualification under s 34 also *disqualifies* a person from transporting animals and for arranging for the transport of animals.

The disqualification may be for such period as the court deems fit. If the disqualification order is breached the maximum penalty is a level 5 fine or 51 weeks. The offence is triable summarily only.

Under the repealed Protection of Animals Act 1954, s 1(1) it was held that the legislation only gives the court a choice as to (a) the duration of any disqualification it imposes and, (b) what kinds of animals the disqualification is to relate to (*R (on the application of the RSPCA) v Chester Crown Court* (2006) 170 JP 725). Pursuant to s 143 (2) CJA 2003, the court is entitled to have regard to the previous convictions of the offender (as an aggravating factor) for causing unnecessary suffering to an animal. Ten years' disqualification from keeping equine animals upheld on appeal where a farmer had two previous convictions for similar offences: *Anthony Ward v Royal Society for the Prevention of Cruelty to Animals* [2010]) EWHC 347 (Admin).

After the disqualification order has been in force for 12 months the defendant can apply for its removal unless the court specified a different minimum period when imposing the order or a previous application has been refused less than 12 months ago (Animal Welfare Act 2006, s 43).

A[6]

Anti-social behaviour order, breach of

A[6.1]

See B[8] and B[8.15].

A[7]

Assault with intent to resist arrest

Charge

A[7.1]

Whosoever shall assault any person with intent to resist or prevent the lawful apprehension or detainer of himself or any other person for any offence, shall be guilty of [an offence]

Offences Against the Person Act 1861, s 38

Maximum penalty – Fine level 5 and/or 6 months (**12 months). Triable either way. Violent specified offence under Sch 15, Part 1, CJA 2003.

Crown Court – 2 years' imprisonment and unlimited fine.

Mode of trial

A[7.2]

Consider the SC guideline at A[7.4] below.

Legal notes and definitions

A[7.3]

The prosecution must establish:

(1)   That the arrest was lawful.
(2)   An intention by the defendant to resist arrest.
(3)   Knowledge that the person assaulted, who might or might not be a police officer, was a person who was seeking to arrest him.

An honest belief by the defendant that the arrest was unlawful is irrelevant (*R v Lee* (2001) 165 JP 344, CA).

Where the person carrying out the arrest was a police officer, it is not necessary for the prosecution to establish that the defendant knew he/she was a police officer (*R v Brightling* [1991] Crim LR 364).

Sentencing
SC Guideline – Assault with intent to resist arrest

A[7.4]

This guideline and guideline and accompanying notes are taken from the Sentencing Council's definitive guideline *Assault and other offences against the person*, published February 2008 and came into force for persons sentenced on or after 3 March 2008

Assault with intent to resist arrest

Offences against the Person Act 1861, section 38

This is a specified offence for the purposes of section 224 of the Criminal Justice Act 2003

Triable either way

Maximum when tried summarily: level 5 and/or 26 weeks' custody

Maximum when tried on indictment: 2 years' custody

Offence range: Fine – 51 weeks' custody

This guideline applies to all offenders aged 18 and older, who are sentenced on or after 13 June 2011. The definitions [at page 145] of 'starting point' and 'first time offender' do not apply for this guideline. Starting point and category ranges apply to all offenders in all cases, irrespective of plea or previous convictions.

Step One
Determining the offence category

The court should determine the offence category using the table below.

Category 1	Greater harm **and** higher culpability
Category 2	Greater harm **and** lower culpability; **or** lesser harm **and** higher culpability
Category 3	Lesser harm **and** lower culpability

The court should determine the offender's culpability and the harm caused, or intended, by reference **only** to the factors identified in the table below (as demonstrated by the presence of one or more). These factors comprise the principal factual elements of the offence and should determine the category.

Factors indicating greater harm

Sustained or repeated assault on the same victim

Factors indicating lesser harm

Injury which is less serious in the context of the offence

Factors indicating higher culpability

Statutory aggravating factors:

Offence racially or religiously aggravated

Offence motivated by, or demonstrating, hostility to the victim based on his or her sexual orientation (or presumed sexual orientation)

Offence motivated by, or demonstrating, hostility to the victim based on the victim's disability (or presumed disability)

Other aggravating factors:

A significant degree of premeditation

Use of weapon or weapon equivalent (for example, shod foot, head-butting, use of acid, use of animal)

Intention to commit more serious harm than actually resulted from the offence

Deliberately causes more harm than is necessary for commission of offence

Leading role in group or gang

Offence motivated by, or demonstrating, hostility based on the victim's age, sex, gender identity (or presumed gender identity)

Factors indicating lower culpability

Subordinate role in group or gang Lack of premeditation

Mental disorder or learning disability, where linked to commission of the offence

Step Two
Starting point and category range

Having determined the category, the court should use the corresponding starting points to reach a sentence within the category range below. The starting point applies to all offenders irrespective of plea or previous convictions. A case of particular gravity, reflected by multiple features of culpability in step one, could merit upward adjustment from the starting point before further adjustment for aggravating or mitigating features, set out below.

Offence Category	Starting Point *(Applicable to all offenders)*	Category Range *(Applicable to all offenders)*
Category 1	26 weeks – custody	12 weeks – custody – Crown Court (51 weeks – custody)
Category 2	Medium level community order	Low level community order – High level community order
Category 3	Band B fine	Band A fine – Band C fine

The table below contains a **non-exhaustive** list of additional factual elements providing the context of the offence and factors relating to the offender. Identify whether any combination of these, or other relevant factors, should result in an upward or downward adjustment from the starting point. In some cases, having considered these factors, it may be appropriate to move outside the identified category range.

When sentencing **category 1** offences, the court should consider whether the sentence can be suspended.

Factors increasing seriousness

Statutory aggravating factors:

Previous convictions, having regard to a) the nature of the offence to which the conviction relates and its relevance to the current offence; and b) the time that has elapsed since the conviction

Offence committed whilst on bail

Other aggravating factors include:

Location of the offence

Timing of the offence

Ongoing effect upon the victim

Gratuitous degradation of victim

Failure to comply with current court orders

Offence committed whilst on licence

An attempt to conceal or dispose of evidence

Failure to respond to warnings or concerns expressed by others about the offender's behaviour

Commission of offence whilst under the influence of alcohol or drugs

Established evidence of community impact

Any steps taken to prevent the victim reporting an incident, obtaining assistance and/or from assisting or supporting the prosecution

Offences taken into consideration (TICs)

Factors reducing seriousness or reflecting personal mitigation

No previous convictions **or** no relevant/recent convictions

Single blow

Remorse

Good character and/or exemplary conduct

Determination and/or demonstration of steps taken to address addiction or offending behaviour

Serious medical conditions requiring urgent, intensive or long-term treatment

Isolated incident

Age and/or lack of maturity where it affects the responsibility of the defendant

Mental disorder or learning disability, where not linked to the commission of the offence

Sole or primary carer for dependent relatives

Step Three
Consider any other factors which indicate a reduction, such as assistance to the prosecution

The court should take into account any rule of law by virtue of which an offender may receive a discounted sentence in consequence of assistance given (or offered) to the prosecutor or investigator.

Step Four
Reduction for guilty pleas

The court should take account of any potential reduction for a guilty plea in accordance with section 144 of the Criminal Justice Act 2003 and the *Guilty Plea* guideline.

Step Five
Dangerousness

Assault with intent to resist arrest is a specified offence within the meaning of Chapter 5 of the Criminal Justice Act 2003 and at this stage the court should consider whether having regard to the criteria contained in that Chapter it would be appropriate to award an extended sentence.

Step Six
Totality principle

If sentencing an offender for more than one offence or where the offender is already serving a sentence, consider whether the total sentence is just and proportionate to the offending behaviour.

Step Seven
Compensation and ancillary orders

In all cases, the court should consider whether to make compensation and/or other ancillary orders.

Step Eight
Reasons

Section 174 of the Criminal Justice Act 2003 imposes a duty to give reasons for, and explain the effect of, the sentence.

Step Nine
Consideration for remand time

Sentencers should take into consideration any remand time served in relation to the final sentence. The court should consider whether to give credit for time spent on remand in custody or on bail in accordance with sections 240 and 240A of the Criminal Justice Act 2003.

A[7.5]

Licensed premises. If the offence takes place on licensed premises an exclusion order may be made. See B[32].

A[8]

Assault occasioning actual bodily harm and racially/religiously aggravated assault occasioning ABH

Charge

A[8.1]
Assault occasioning actual bodily harm

Offences Against The Person Act 1861, s 47

Maximum penalty – Fine level 5 and 6 months (**12 months). Triable either way. Violent specified offence under Sch 15, Part 1, CJA 2003.

Crown Court – 5 years' imprisonment and unlimited fine.

A[8.2]
Racially or religiously aggravated assault occasioning actual bodily harm

Crime and Disorder Act 1998, s 29

Maximum penalty – Fine level 5 and 6 months (**12 months). Triable either way. Specified violent offence under Sch 15, Part 1, CJA 2003

Crown Court – 7 years' imprisonment and unlimited fine.

Mode of trial

A[8.3]–[8.4]
Consider **SC guideline** at A[8.31] below. For cases of domestic violence. See SC Definitive Guideline: "Overarching Principles: Domestic Violence".

Owing to the nature of charges of assault it is particularly important that magistrates hear an outline of the facts before making their decision.

Legal notes and definitions

A[8.5]–[8.6]
Assault. See under 'Common assault' at A[15].

A[8.7]
Intent. The defendant must intend to cause his victim to apprehend

immediate and unlawful violence, or be reckless whether such apprehension be caused (*R v Venna* [1976] QB 421, [1975] 3 All ER 788, CA). The offence of assault occasioning actual bodily harm is made out upon proof of an assault together with proof of the fact that actual bodily harm was occasioned by the assault. The prosecution are not obliged to prove that the defendant intended to cause some actual bodily harm or was reckless as to whether such harm would be caused (*R v Savage* [1992] 1 AC 699, [1991] 4 All ER 698, *R v Parmenter* [1991] 4 All ER 698, HL).

In principle it was open to justices to convict on the basis of recklessness even where the prosecution simply alleged a deliberate assault: *D v DPP* [2005] EWHC 967 (Admin) considered. However, the justices had failed to identify what was the unlawful act of K leading to the assault. Recklessness had only been a possible conclusion if the justices had found that K had thrown a punch, albeit without intending it to land, or was flailing his arms about in an agitated and aggressive manner. The conviction could not stand in the light of the findings of fact made by the justices: *Katsonis v Crown Prosecution Service* [2011] EWHC 1860 (Admin), 175 JP 396.

A[8.8]

In *DPP v K (a minor)* [1990] 1 All ER 331, [1990] 1 WLR 1067, a schoolboy who put acid in a hot air dryer recklessly but in a mindless panic rather than with any intention to cause harm was nonetheless guilty of assault. In *DPP v Santra-Bermudez* [2003] EWHC 2908, [2003] All ER (D) 168 (Nov) the offence was made out when a police officer pricked her finger on a needle while carrying out a lawful search of a man who had told her that he had no needles in his pocket.

A[8.9]

Actual bodily harm. This is less serious than grievous bodily harm. There need not be permanent injury. Any hurt or injury calculated to interfere with health or comfort can be actual bodily harm, so can an assault causing unconsciousness or an hysterical or nervous condition (*R v Miller* [1954] 2 QB 282, [1954] 2 All ER 529), ie some psychiatric damage and not just distress or panic (*R v Chan-Fook* [1994] 2 All ER 552, [1994] 1 WLR 689, CA). Significant psychological symptoms caused by a series of telephone calls, followed by silence can constitute an assault causing actual bodily harm (*R v Ireland* [1998] AC 147, [1997] 4 All ER 225, HL). Where a victim suffered great pain immediately and for some time thereafter suffered tenderness and soreness, that was sufficient for the court to infer that there was actual bodily harm notwithstanding that no physically discernible injury had been occasioned. This would include the victim's unconsciousness without the appearance of physical injury (*T v DPP* [2004] EWHC 183 (Admin), [2004] All ER (D) 278 (Jan)). Where there is evidence that a blow was struck, the justices are entitled if they see fit to infer that some bodily harm, however slight, has resulted.

Cutting off a substantial part of the victim's hair was capable in law of amounting to an assault which occasioned actual bodily harm (*DPP v Smith (MR)* [2006] EWHC 94 (Admin), [2006] 2 All ER 16).

A[8.10]–[8.15]

Racial, religious, disability or sexual orientation aggravation. This means that at the time of committing the offence, or immediately before or after doing so, the offender demonstrates towards the victim of the offence either hostility based on the victim's membership (or presumed membership) of a racial or religious group or their disability or presumed sexual orientation; or, the offence is motivated (wholly or partly) by hostility towards members of a racial or religious group based on their membership of that group, or persons of a particular sexual orientation or disability. See *R v H* [2010] EWCA Crim 1931, 174 CL&J 573, 154 Sol Jo (no 31) 28 which reviews the authorities.

A[8.16]

When considering whether an offence was racially motivated for the purposes of the CDA 1998, s 28 (1)(a) in the light of words uttered immediately prior to the offence, the following matters were irrelevant: (i) victim's perception of the words used; (ii) any additional reason unrelated to race, for uttering the words (CDA 1998, s 28(3)(b)); and (iii) the fact that in the defendant's frame of mind at the time he uttered the words, he would have abused anyone by reference to an obvious physical characteristic (*DPP v Woods* [2002] EWHC 85 (Admin), [2002] All ER (D) 154 (Jan)). However, see **A[20.6]** for more recent case law.

It is immaterial whether or not the offender's hostility is based, to any extent on any other factor not mentioned above. See **A[15.33]** for sentencing.

A[8.17]

Provocation is not a defence but can be taken into consideration when deciding sentence.

A[8.18]–[8.19]

Reasonable force for purposes of self-defence [or defence of property]* etc. A person may use reasonable force to defend himself, his property or another. Where self-defence is put forward to justify the use of violence, the onus is on the prosecution to disprove the defence beyond reasonable doubt. A person must not use force in attacking or retaliating, or revenging himself. It is permissible to use force not merely to counter an actual attack but to ward off an attack honestly believed to be imminent. The reasonableness or otherwise of the belief is only relevant in ascertaining whether he actually held the belief or not (*Beckford v R* [1988] AC 130, [1987] 3 All ER 425, PC).

Proof that the accused tried to retreat or call off the fight might be a cast-iron method of rebutting the suggestion that he was an attacker or retaliator or trying to revenge himself. It is to be stressed, however, that this is not the only method of doing so, and it depends on the circumstances of the particular case (*R v Bird* [1985] 2 All ER 513, [1985] 1 WLR 816, CA). The common law defence of self defence and the defence under s 3 of the

Criminal Law Act 1967, extended to the use of violence against an innocent third party: *R v Hichens* [2011] EWCA Crim 1626, [2011] 2 Cr App Rep 370, [2011] Crim LR 873.

*To be added when s 148 of the Legal Aid, Sentencing and Punishment of Offenders Act 2012 is brought into force.

A[8.20]

A man who is attacked can defend himself but can only do what is objectively reasonable in the circumstances as the defendant believes them to be. In relation to self defence, prevention of crime or effecting or assisting in the lawful arrest of another, s 76 of the Criminal Justice and Immigration Act 2008 codified the common law. It provides as follows:

"(3)   The question whether the degree of force used by D was reasonable in the circumstances is to be decided by reference to the circumstances as D believed them to be, and subsections (4) to (8) also apply in connection with deciding that question.

(4)   If D claims to have held a particular belief as regards the existence of any circumstances

   (a)   the reasonableness or otherwise of that belief is relevant to the question whether D genuinely held it; but

   (b)   if it is determined that D did genuinely hold it, D is entitled to rely on it for the purposes of subsection (3), whether or not -

      (i)   it was mistaken, or

      (ii)   (if it was mistaken) the mistake was a reasonable one to have made.

(5)   But subsection (4) (b) does not enable D to rely on any mistaken belief attributable to intoxication that was voluntarily induced.

(6)   The degree of force used by D is not to regarded as having been reasonable in the circumstances as D believed them to be if it was disproportionate in those circumstances.

*(6A)In deciding the question mentioned in subsection (3), a possibility that D could have retreated is to be considered (so far as relevant) as a factor to be taken into account, rather than as giving rise to a duty to retreat.

(7)   In deciding the question mentioned in subsection (3) the following considerations are to be taken into account (so far as relevant in the circumstances of the case) -

   (a)   that a person acting for a legitimate purpose may not be able to weigh to a nicety the exact measure of any necessary action; and

   (b)   that evidence of a person having only done what the

person honestly and instinctively thought was necessary for a legitimate purpose constitutes strong evidence that only reasonable action was taken by that person for that purpose.

(8)   Subsection[s (6A) and]* (7) [are]* not to be read as preventing other matters from being taken into account where they are relevant in deciding the question mentioned in subsection (3)".

*To be added or so amended when s 148 of the Legal Aid, Sentencing and Punishment of Offenders Act 2012 is brought into force.

In *Dewar v DPP* [2010] All ER (D) 83 (Jan), DC the CA confirmed that the test for self-defence is twofold ie honest belief in self defence and the force used was reasonable. The CA opined the statutory changes above had made no practical difference to the common law test.

A[8.21]
Misadventure. See A[15.8].

A[8.22]
Consent and reasonable chastisement. See A[15.10]–A[15.17].

A[8.23]
Lawful sport. See A[15.18].

A[8.24]
Trespasser on of property. See A[15.22].

A[8.25]–[8.30]
Execution of legal process. See A[8.24].

Reduction of charge/alternative verdict. The court cannot reduce this charge to common assault or consider an alternative verdict but, if a separate charge of common assault is preferred, a conviction for that may be possible. The legal adviser should be consulted. See A[15.31].

Sentencing
SC Guideline – Assault occasioning actual bodily harm and Racially/religiously aggravated ABH

Assault occasioning actual bodily harm

Offences against the Person Act 1861 (section 47)

Racially/religiously aggravated ABH

Crime and Disorder Act 1998 (section 29)

A[8.31]–[8.32]

These are specified offences for the purposes of section 224 of the Criminal Justice Act 2003

Triable either way

Section 47

Maximum when tried summarily: Level 5 fine and/or 26 weeks' custody

Maximum when tried on indictment: 5 years' custody

Section 29

Maximum when tried summarily: Level 5 fine and/or 26 weeks' custody

Maximum when tried on indictment: 7 years' custody

Offence range: Fine – 3 years' custody

This guideline applies to all offenders aged 18 and older, who are sentenced on or after 13 June 2011. The definitions [at page 145] of 'starting point' and 'first time offender' do not apply for this guideline. Starting point and category ranges apply to all offenders in all cases, irrespective of plea or previous convictions.

Step One
Determining the offence category

The court should determine the offence category using the table below.

Category 1	Greater harm **and** higher culpability
Category 2	Greater harm **and** lower culpability; **or** lesser harm **and** higher culpability
Category 3	Lesser harm **and** lower culpability

The court should determine the offender's culpability and the harm caused, or intended, by reference **only** to the factors identified in the table below (as demonstrated by the presence of one or more). These factors comprise the principal factual elements of the offence and should determine the category.

> **Factors indicating greater harm**
> Injury (which includes disease transmission and/or psychological harm) which is serious in the context of the offence (must normally be present)

Victim is particularly vulnerable because of personal circumstances

Sustained or repeated assault on the same victim

Factors indicating lesser harm

Injury which is less serious in the context of the offence

Factors indicating higher culpability

Statutory aggravating factors:

Offence motivated by, or demonstrating, hostility to the victim based on his or her sexual orientation (or presumed sexual orientation)

Offence motivated by, or demonstrating, hostility to the victim based on the victim's disability (or presumed disability)

Other aggravating factors:

A significant degree of premeditation

Use of weapon or weapon equivalent (for example, shod foot, head-butting, use of acid, use of animal)

Intention to commit more serious harm than actually resulted from the offence

Deliberately causes more harm than is necessary for commission of offence

Deliberate targeting of vulnerable victim

Leading role in group or gang

Offence motivated by, or demonstrating, hostility based on the victim's age, sex, gender identity (or presumed gender identity)

Factors indicating lower culpability

Subordinate role in group or gang

A greater degree of provocation than normally expected

Lack of premeditation

Mental disorder or learning disability, where linked to commission of the offence

Excessive self defence

Step Two
Starting point and category range

Having determined the category, the court should use the corresponding starting points to reach a sentence within the category range below. The starting point applies to all offenders irrespective of plea or previous convictions. A case of particular gravity, reflected by multiple features of culpability in step one, could merit upward adjustment from the starting point before further adjustment for aggravating or mitigating features, set out below.

Offence Category	Starting Point *(Applicable to all offenders)*	Category Range *(Applicable to all offenders)*
Category 1	Crown Court	Crown Court
Category 2	26 weeks' custody	Low level community order – Crown Court (51 weeks' custody)
Category 3	Medium level community order	Band A fine – High level community order

The table below contains a **non-exhaustive** list of additional factual elements providing the context of the offence and factors relating to the offender. Identify whether any combination of these, or other relevant factors, should result in an upward or downward adjustment from the starting point. In some cases, having considered these factors, it may be appropriate to move outside the identified category range.

When sentencing **category 2** offences, the court should also consider the custody threshold as follows:

- has the custody threshold been passed?
- if so, is it unavoidable that a custodial sentence be imposed?
- if so, can that sentence be suspended?

When sentencing **category 3** offences, the court should also consider the community order threshold as follows:

- has the community order threshold been passed?

Factors increasing seriousness

Statutory aggravating factors:

Previous convictions, having regard to a) the nature of the offence to which the conviction relates and its relevance to the current offence; and b) the time that has elapsed since the conviction

Offence committed whilst on bail

Other aggravating factors include:

Location of the offence

Timing of the offence

Ongoing effect upon the victim

Offence committed against those working in the public sector or providing a service to the public

Presence of others including relatives, especially children or partner of the victim

Gratuitous degradation of victim

In domestic violence cases, victim forced to leave their home

Failure to comply with current court orders

Offence committed whilst on licence

An attempt to conceal or dispose of evidence

Failure to respond to warnings or concerns expressed by others about the offender's behaviour

Commission of offence whilst under the influence of alcohol or drugs

Abuse of power and/or position of trust

Exploiting contact arrangements with a child to commit an offence

Established evidence of community impact

Any steps taken to prevent the victim reporting an incident, obtaining assistance and/or from assisting or supporting the prosecution

Offences taken into consideration (TICs)

Factors reducing seriousness or reflecting personal mitigation

No previous convictions **or** no relevant/recent convictions

Single blow

Remorse

Good character and/or exemplary conduct

Determination and/or demonstration of steps taken to address addiction or offending behaviour

Serious medical conditions requiring urgent, intensive or long-term treatment

Isolated incident

Age and/or lack of maturity where it affects the responsibility of the offender

Lapse of time since the offence where this is not the fault of the offender

Mental disorder or learning disability, where **not** linked to the commission of the offence

Sole or primary carer for dependent relatives

Section 29 offences only: The court should determine the appropriate sentence for the offence without taking account of the element of aggravation and then make an addition to the sentence, considering the level of aggravation involved. It may be appropriate to move outside the identified category range, taking into account the increased statutory maximum.

Step Three
Consider any other factors which indicate a reduction, such as assistance to the prosecution

The court should take into account any rule of law by virtue of which an offender may receive a discounted sentence in consequence of assistance given (or offered) to the prosecutor or investigator.

Step Four
Reduction for guilty pleas

The court should take account of any potential reduction for a guilty plea in accordance with section 144 of the Criminal Justice Act 2003 and the *Guilty Plea* guideline.

Step Five
Dangerousness

Assault occasioning actual bodily harm and racially/religiously aggravated ABH are specified offences within the meaning of Chapter 5 of the Criminal Justice Act 2003 and at this stage the court should consider whether having regard to the criteria contained in that Chapter it would be appropriate to award an extended sentence.

Step Six
Totality principle

If sentencing an offender for more than one offence, or where the offender is already serving a sentence, consider whether the total sentence is just and proportionate to the offending behaviour.

Step Seven
Compensation and ancillary orders

In all cases, the court should consider whether to make compensation and/or other ancillary orders.

Step Eight
Reasons

Section 174 of the Criminal Justice Act 2003 imposes a duty to give reasons for, and explain the effect of, the sentence.

Step Nine
Consideration for remand time

Sentencers should take into consideration any remand time served in relation to the final sentence. The court should consider whether to give credit for time spent on remand in custody or on bail in accordance with sections 240 and 240A of the Criminal Justice Act 2003.

A[8.33]

Licensed premises. An assault committed on licensed premises will enable the court to make an exclusion order. See B[32].

A[8.34]

Husband and wife and domestic violence. For cases of domestic violence. See SC Definitive Guideline: "Overarching Principles: Domestic Violence".

A[9]

Assaulting a police constable (or a person assisting the police) Assaulting a court security officer

Charge

A[9.1]
Assaulting a constable in the execution of his duty

or

Assaulting a person assisting a constable in the execution of his duty

Police Act 1996, s 89

and

Assaulting a court security officer in the execution of his duty

Criminal Justice Act 1991, s 78 [from 1 April 2005 contrary to Courts Act 2003, s 57]

Maximum penalty – Fine level 5 and 6 months (**51 weeks). Triable only summarily.

Legal notes and definitions

A[9.2]
Assault. See under Common assault at A[8].

A[9.3]
Constable. Includes a special constable and any member of the police irrespective of actual rank. Offences against designated and accredited persons acting in the execution of their duty ie community support officer, investigating officer, detention officer or escort officer are catered for under the Police Reform Act 2002, s 46. Assaults carry a maximum penalty of a level 5 fine and/or six months imprisonment (**12 months).

A[9.4]
Court security officer. A person appointed by the Lord Chancellor or provided under a contract and designated by the Lord Chancellor as a court security officer (s 51 Courts Act 2003).

A[9.5]
In the execution of his duty. The constable must be carrying out his duty at

the time of the assault. If he goes beyond his duty, for example by catching hold of a person whom he is not arresting, then this offence is not committed by a person resisting him with reasonable force. The line between duty and what lies beyond is not easily discernible. This needs reference to many decided cases in the higher courts – see, for example, *Donnelly v Jackman* [1970] 1 All ER 987, [1970] 1 WLR 562 and *Osman v DPP* (1999) 163 JP 725. Police acting on a reasonable expectation of a breach of the peace are acting within their duty (*Wragg v DPP* [2005] EWHC 1389 (Admin), [2005] All ER (D) 131 (Jun)).

In *R (on the application of Reda) v DPP* [2011] EWHC 1550 (Admin), 175 JP 329, the appellant was walking with other youths past an empty police van when he raised his voice and uttered the words "fuck the police". At the material time there were no members of the public present other than the youths and two police officers who were emerging from a nearby block of flats. The first officer heard the specific words used and decided to arrest the appellant for causing harassment, alarm or distress contrary to s 5 of the Public Order Act 1986. Following his arrest the appellant kicked the police officer on the leg.

The Queen's Bench Division concluded that there were reasonable grounds to suspect that an offence had been or was about to be committed. The offending words were said in a public place and, whilst it could not be established that the police officer had himself seen other people present at the material time, nevertheless he could reasonably proceed on the footing that there were or may have been. Furthermore, the arresting officer's colleague was in hearing distance of what was said and the other youths were present. He could not necessarily have taken it that the other boys would not themselves have been insulted or alarmed by what this appellant was shouting or saying. Accordingly, the officer was acting lawfully in the execution of his duty.

A[9.6]

A court security officer shall not be regarded as acting in the execution of his duty unless he is readily identifiable by a badge or uniform (powers of court security officers are found in the Courts Act 2003, s 51(3)).

A[9.7]

The burden of proof that the constable was acting in the execution of his duty rests on the prosecution but the prosecution does not have to prove that the defendant knew that the constable was a constable, nor that the defendant knew that the constable was acting in the execution of his duty. The offence may be established even if the court accepts that the defendant (who must take his victim as he finds him) did not know that his victim was a police officer. Where the accused is unaware that his victim is a police officer and believes there are circumstances which would justify the use of reasonable force, eg self-defence, he should have a defence (*Blackburn v Bowering* [1994] 3 All ER 380, [1994] 1 WLR 1324, CA. See also *Ali v DPP* [2009] EWHC 3353 (Admin), 174 JP 149. See A[8.8] for defences).

A[9.8]

If a police officer touches a person to draw his attention that contact must be acceptable by ordinary standards and for no longer than necessary to remain within the execution of the officer's duty (*Mepstead v DPP* (1995) 160 JP 475, [1996] Crim LR 111). When a police officer, who was not exercising his common law power, restrained a person, but had no intended or purported to arrest a person at that time, he committed an assault, even if the arrest had been justified. To be lawful arrest: (1) There must be reasonable grounds to suspect that a person had committed an arrestable offence (2) That person had to be informed that he was under arrest, either at the time of the arrest or within a reasonable time thereafter (*Wood v DPP* [2008] EWHC 1056 (Admin)).

Plain clothes officers carrying out a drugs search are not acting in the execution of their duty if they fail to comply with the requirements of s 2(3), PACE 1984 (*Bonner v DPP* [2004] EWHC 2415 (Admin), [2004] All ER (D) 74 (Oct); *R v Bristol* [2007] EWCA Crim 3214, (2007) 172 JP 161).

A police officer exercising a power of entry to premises, pursuant to s 17 of the Police and Criminal Evidence Act 1984, 'in order to save life or limb or serious damage to property', was acting lawfully where he sought to search the occupant based on a reasonable belief that she was in possession of a knife (*Baker v Crown Prosecution Service* [2009] EWHC 299 (Admin), 173 JP 215).

In current times, distinguishing between violence in the home and in the street was long gone. Cases that attempted to do so could not be relied on and were out of date, *Foulkes v Chief Constable of Merseyside* [1998] 3 All ER 705, [1999] 1 FCR 98, CA and *McConnell v Chief Constable of Greater Manchester Police* [1990] 1 All ER 423, [1990] 1 WLR 364, CA are no longer good law. The correct approach was to draw a contrast between the ability of those on the street to go their own way, and in a domestic setting where that might not be possible, *Wragg v DPP* [2005] EWHC 1389 (Admin), [2005] All ER (D) 131 (Jun) applied: *Leon Demetriou v DPP*(2012) 156 Sol Jo (no 18) 31.

Although a pat-down search was authorised by the Criminal Law Act 1967, s 3, a police officer was required by s 2 of the Police and Criminal Evidence Act 1984 to take reasonable steps to bring certain matters to the attention of the person being searched. They included his name and police station, the object of the search and his grounds for proposing to make it. It meant that the officer's search of a defendant on this occasion was unlawful. However, there was a sufficient gap in time between the search of the defendant and an assault by the defendant on H to make the events separate and distinct. What the officer was doing was no more than to prevent harm to a woman in accordance with his common law duty and to prevent her from further contributing to violence. It followed that the justices had been entitled to find that the officer had been acting lawfully in the execution of his duty: *Sobczak v DPP* [2012] EWHC 1319 (Admin), 176 JP 575, 176 CL&J 371.

A[9.9]

Reduction of charge/alternative verdict. The court cannot reduce this charge to common assault, but if a separate charge for common assault is preferred, a conviction for that offence may be possible. It was clear that Parliament intended that the right of entry by force without warrant should be confined to cases where there is an apprehension that something serious was likely to occur or had occurred within premises (*Syed v DPP* [2010] EWHC 81 (Admin), [2010] 1 Cr App Rep 480, 174 JP 97).

Sentencing
SC Guideline – Assault on a police constable in the execution of his duty

A[9.10]
Assault on a police constable in execution of his duty

Police Act 1996 (section 89)

Triable only summarily

Maximum: Level 5 and/or 26 weeks' custody

Offence range: Fine – 26 weeks' custody

This guideline applies to all offenders aged 18 years and older, who are sentenced on or after 13 June 2011. The definitions [at page 145] of 'starting point' and 'first time offender' do not apply for this guideline. Starting point and category ranges apply to all offenders in all cases, irrespective of plea or previous convictions.

Step One
Determining the offence category

The court should determine the offence category using the table below.

Category 1	Greater harm **and** higher culpability
Category 2	Greater harm **and** lower culpability; **or** lesser harm **and** higher culpability
Category 3	Lesser harm **and** lower culpability

The court should determine the offender's culpability and the harm caused, or intended, by reference **only** to the factors below (as demonstrated by the presence of one or more). These factors comprise the principal factual elements of the offence and should determine the category.

Factors indicating greater harm
Sustained or repeated assault on the same victim
Factors indicating lesser harm
Injury which is less serious in the context of the offence

Factors indicating higher culpability

Statutory aggravating factors:

Offence racially or religiously aggravated

Offence motivated by, or demonstrating, hostility to the victim based on his or her sexual orientation (or presumed sexual orientation)

Offence motivated by, or demonstrating, hostility to the victim based on the victim's disability (or presumed disability)

Other aggravating factors:

A significant degree of premeditation

Use of weapon or weapon equivalent (for example, shod foot, headbutting, use of acid, use of animal)

Intention to commit more serious harm than actually resulted from the offence

Deliberately causes more harm than is necessary for commission of offence

Leading role in group or gang

Offence motivated by, or demonstrating, hostility based on the victim's age, sex, gender identity (or presumed gender identity)

Factors indicating lower culpability

Subordinate role in group or gang Lack of premeditation

Mental disorder or learning disability, where linked to commission of the offence

Step Two
Starting point and category range

Having determined the category, the court should use the corresponding starting points to reach a sentence within the category range below. The starting point applies to all offenders irrespective of plea or previous convictions. A case of particular gravity, reflected by multiple features of culpability in step one, could merit upward adjustment from the starting point before further adjustment for aggravating or mitigating features, set out below.

Offence Category	Starting Point *(Applicable to all offenders)*	Category Range *(Applicable to all offenders)*
Category 1	12 weeks' custody	Low level community order – 26 weeks' custody
Category 2	Medium level community order	Low level community order – High level community order
Category 3	Band B fine	Band A fine – Band C fine

The table below contains a **non-exhaustive** list of additional factual elements providing the context of the offence and factors relating to the offender. Identify whether any combination of these, or other relevant factors, should result in an upward or downward adjustment from the starting point. In some cases, having considered these factors, it may be appropriate to move outside the identified category range.

When sentencing **category 1** offences, the court should also consider the custody threshold as follows:

- has the custody threshold been passed?
- if so, is it unavoidable that a custodial sentence be imposed?
- if so, can that sentence be suspended?

Factors increasing seriousness

Statutory aggravating factors:

Previous convictions, having regard to a) the nature of the offence to which the conviction relates and its relevance to the current offence; and b) the time that has elapsed since the conviction

Offence committed whilst on bail

Other aggravating factors include:

Location of the offence

Timing of the offence

Ongoing effect upon the victim

Gratuitous degradation of victim

Failure to comply with current court orders

Offence committed whilst on licence

An attempt to conceal or dispose of evidence

Failure to respond to warnings or concerns expressed by others about the offender's behaviour

Commission of offence whilst under the influence of alcohol or drugs

Established evidence of community impact

Any steps taken to prevent the victim reporting an incident, obtaining assistance and/or from assisting or supporting the prosecution

Offences taken into consideration (TICs)

Factors reducing seriousness or reflecting personal mitigation

No previous convictions **or** no relevant/recent convictions

Single blow

Remorse

Good character and/or exemplary conduct

Determination and/or demonstration of steps taken to address addiction or offending behaviour

Serious medical conditions requiring urgent, intensive or long-term treatment

---

Isolated incident

Age and/or lack of maturity where it affects the responsibility of the offender

Lapse of time since the offence where this is not the fault of the offender

Mental disorder or learning disability, where **not** linked to the commission of the offence

Sole or primary carer for dependent relatives

Step Three
Consider any other factors which indicate a reduction, such as assistance to the prosecution

The court should take into account any rule of law by virtue of which an offender may receive a discounted sentence in consequence of assistance given (or offered) to the prosecutor or investigator.

Step Four
Reduction for guilty pleas

The court should take account of any potential reduction for a guilty plea in accordance with section 144 of the Criminal Justice Act 2003 and the *Guilty Plea* guideline.

Step Five
Totality principle

If sentencing an offender for more than one offence, or where the offender is already serving a sentence, consider whether the total sentence is just and proportionate to the offending behaviour.

Step Six
Compensation and ancillary orders

In all cases, courts should consider whether to make compensation and/or other ancillary orders.

Step Seven
Reasons

Section 174 of the Criminal Justice Act 2003 imposes a duty to give reasons for, and explain the effect of, the sentence.

Step Eight
Consideration for remand time

Sentencers should take into consideration any remand time served in relation to the final sentence. The court should consider whether to give credit for time spent on remand in custody or on bail in accordance with ss 240 and 240A of the Criminal Justice Act 2003.

A[9.11]

Licensed premises. If the offence takes place on licensed premises an exclusion order may be made. See **B[32]**.

A[10]

Bail, failure to surrender

Charge

A[10.1]

Having been released on bail in criminal proceedings fails without reasonable cause to surrender to custody

Bail Act 1976, s 6 (1)

or

Having been released on bail in criminal proceedings, and having reasonable cause therefore, has failed to surrender to custody, fails to surrender to custody at the appointed place as soon as after the appointed time as is reasonably practicable

Bail Act 1976, s 6 (2).

Maximum penalty – level 5 and/or 3 months' imprisonment (if not committed for sentence).

Crown Court – 12 months' imprisonment or an unlimited fine

Legal notes and definitions

A[10.2]

'Fails without reasonable cause'. The fact that a defendant mistakenly formed the opinion he was required to surrender on a later date does not amount to a 'reasonable cause': *Laidlaw v Atkinson* (1986) The Times, 2 August.

'Surrender to custody' in a magistrates' court, means to personally surrender to a person in authority such as a court usher (but not a security guard): see *DPP v Richards* [1988] QB 701, [1988] 3 All ER 406, DC. Note the position in the Crown Court is different: *R v Evans (Scott Lennon)* [2011] EWCA Crim 2842, [2012] 1 WLR 1192, [2012] 2 Cr App Rep 279.

Burden of proof on accused. An accused who raises this defence is required to establish it on a balance of probabilities: *R v Carr-Briant* (1943) 107 JP 167.

Procedure. This is regulated by the *Practice Direction (Criminal: Consolidated)* (2002) at paras I 13.4 to I 13.6 as revised in 2004.

Prosecution. See the detailed notes at J[1.82] onwards.

Committal to the Crown Court. In certain circumstances, a magistrates' court may commit to the Crown Court for sentence. See s 6 (6) of the Bail Act 1976 and consult your legal adviser for guidance.

Sentencing
Bail, failure to surrender

A[10.3]

This guideline and accompanying notes are taken from the SGC's definitive guideline *Fail to Surrender to Bail*, published 29 November 2007.

Key factors

(a)   Whilst the approach to sentencing should generally be the same whether the offender failed to surrender to a court or to a police station <u>and</u> whether the offence is contrary to ss 6 (1) or 6 (2), the court must examine the relevant circumstances.

(b)   The following factors may be relevant when assessing the harm caused by the offence:

- Where an offender fails to appear for a first court hearing but attends shortly afterwards, the only harm caused is likely to be the financial cost to the system. Where a case could not have proceeded even if the offender had surrendered to bail, this should be taken into account.

- Where an offender appears for trial on the wrong day but enters a late guilty plea enabling the case to be disposed of to some degree at least, the harm caused by the delay may be offset by the benefits stemming from the change of plea.

- The most serious harm is likely to result where an offender fails to appear for trial, especially if this results in witnesses being sent away. Where it has been possible to conclude proceedings in the absence of the offender, this may be relevant to the assessment of harm caused.

- The level of harm is likely to be assessed as high where an offender fails to appear for sentence and is also seen to be flouting the authority of the court, such as where the avoidance of sentence results in the consequential avoidance of ancillary orders such as disqualification from driving, the payment of compensation or registration as a sex offender. This may increase the level of harm whenever the offender continues to be a risk to public safety.

- Whilst the seriousness of the original offence does not of itself aggravate or mitigate the seriousness of the offence of failure to surrender, the circumstances surrounding the original offence may be relevant in assessing the harm arising from the Bail Act offence.

- The circumstances in which bail to return to a police station is granted are less formal than the grant of court bail and the history of the individual case should be examined. There may be less culpability where bail has been enlarged on a number of occasions and less harm if <u>court</u> proceedings are not significantly delayed.

(c) Where the failure to surrender to custody was "deliberate":
- at or near the bottom of the sentencing range will be cases where the offender gave no thought at all to the consequences, or other mitigating factors are present, and the degree of delay or interference with the progress of the case was not significant in all the circumstances;
- At or near the top of the range will be cases where aggravating factors 1, 2 or 4 are present if there is also a significant delay and/or interference with the progress of the case.

(d) A previous conviction that is likely to be "relevant" for the purposes of this offence is one which demonstrates failure to comply with an order of the court.

(e) Acquittal of the original offence does not automatically mitigate the Bail Act offence.

(f) The fact that an offender has a disorganised or chaotic lifestyle should not normally be treated as offence mitigation, but may be regarded as offender mitigation depending on the particular facts.

(g) A misunderstanding which does not amount to a defence may be a mitigating factor whereas a mistake on the part of the offender is his own responsibility.

(h) Where an offender has literacy or language difficulties, these may be mitigation (where they do not amount to a defence) where potential problems were not identified and/or appropriate steps were not taken to mitigate the risk in the circumstances as known at the time bail was granted.

(i) An offender's position as the sole or primary carer of dependant relatives may be offender mitigation when it is the reason why the offender failed to surrender to custody.

(j) The sentence for this offence should usually be in addition to any sentence for the original offence. Where custodial sentences are being imposed for a Bail Act offence and the original offence at the same time, the normal approach should be for the sentences to be consecutive. The length of any custodial sentence imposed must be commensurate with the seriousness do the offence(s).

(k) If an offence is serious enough to justify the imposition of a community order, a curfew requirement with an electronic monitoring requirement may be appropriate.

In certain circumstances, a magistrates' court may commit to the Crown Court for sentence. **Consult your legal adviser for guidance.**

OFFENCE SERIOUSNESS (CULPABILITY AND HARM)
A. IDENTIFY THE APPROPRIATE STARTING POINT
Starting points based on first time offender pleading not guilty

Examples of nature of activity	Starting point	Range
Surrenders late on day but case proceeds as planned	Band A fine	Band A fine to band B fine
Negligent or non-deliberate failure to attend causing delay and/or interference with the administration of justice	Band C fine	Band B fine to medium level community order
Deliberate failure to attend causing delay and/or interference with the administration of justice	14 days custody	Low level community order to 10 weeks custody
The type and degree of harm actually caused will affect where in the range the case falls (see note (c) above)		

OFFENCE SERIOUSNESS (CULPABILITY AND HARM)
B. CONSIDER THE EFFECT OF AGGRAVATING AND MITIGATING FACTORS (OTHER THAN THOSE WITHIN THE EXAMPLES ABOVE)
Common aggravating and mitigating factors are identified at B[5.2A]. The following may be particularly relevant but **these lists are not exhaustive**

Factors indicating higher culpability	*Factors indicating lower culpability*
1. Serious attempts to evade justice	Where not amounting to a defence:
2. Determined attempt seriously to undermine the course of justice	1. Misunderstanding
3. Previous relevant convictions and/or breach of court orders or police bail	2. Failure to comprehend bail significance or requirements
Factor indicating greater degree of harm	3. Caring responsibilities – see note (i) above
4. Lengthy absence	*Factor indicating lesser degree of harm*
	4. Prompt voluntary surrender

FORM A PRELIMINARY VIEW OF THE APPROPRIATE SENTENCE, THEN CONSIDER OFFENDER MITIGATION
Common factors are identified at B[5.2A]

CONSIDER A REDUCTION FOR A GUILTY PLEA

DECIDE SENTENCE
GIVE REASONS

In appropriate cases, a magistrates' court may impose one day's detention: MCA 1980, s 135.

A[11]
Bladed article/offensive weapon, possession of

Charge

A[11.1]

Having an article which has a blade (or is sharply pointed) namely a
[. . . . .] in a public place or on school premises [or]

*[Has an article with a blade or point or offensive weapon on school
premises, unlawfully and intentionally threatens another person with the
weapon, and does so in such a way that there is an immediate risk of serious
physical harm to that other person]

Criminal Justice Act 1988, s 139 and s 139A [and 139AA]*

Having, without lawful authority or reasonable excuse, an offensive
weapon in any public place [or]

*[Has, without lawful authority or reasonable excuse, an offensive weapon
with him in a public place, unlawfully and intentionally threatens another
person with the weapon, and does so in such a way that there is an
immediate risk of serious physical harm to that other person.]

Prevention of Crime Act 1953, s 1 [and 1A]*

*To be added by the Legal Aid, Sentencing and Punishment of Offenders
Act, 142. An alternative verdict under s 139 or s 139A or s 1 is available
to the justices.

Maximum penalty – Fine level 5 and 6 months (**12 months). Triable
either way.

Crown Court – 4 years' imprisonment (for offences committed on or after
12/2/2007) and unlimited fine

A[11.2]
Mode of trial. Consider the SGC Guidelines at A[11.15] below.

Legal notes and definitions

A[11.3]
General. The possession of offensive weapons is also controlled by several
other statutes. The Crossbows Act 1987 regulates the sale or hire of
crossbows to persons under 17 years, and the purchase or possession of

crossbows by such persons. The Firearms Act 1968 controls the possession and use of airguns, shotguns and firearms and the possession of articles with blades or sharp points is governed by the Criminal Justice Act 1988 (see A[5]).

'Samurai swords' are on the list of prohibited articles. Accordingly, with a number of small exemptions the manufacture, sale, hire and importation of samurai swords is an offence. A later amendment order covered swords with a curved blade of 50 centimetres or more: Criminal Justice Act (Offensive Weapons) (Amendment) Order 2008, SI 2008/973.

A[11.4]

Controls are also imposed on the manufacturers of and dealers in or persons who lend or give 'flick-knives' by the Restriction of Offensive Weapons Act 1959 and the Criminal Justice Act 1988 extends such controls to offensive weapons specified by the Home Office such as weapons used in martial arts, stun guns and so-called stealth knives. Selling a knife to a person under the age of 18 is an offence by virtue of amendments brought into force in January 1997. The maximum penalty for contravention of such regulations is a fine on level 5 and 6 months' (**51 weeks) imprisonment.

A[11.5]

Offensive weapon. A police constable may arrest without warrant anyone carrying or suspected of carrying an offensive weapon in a public place. In order to convict the prosecution must first prove that the defendant was in possession of an offensive weapon. An offensive weapon means any article either:

(a)   made or adapted for use for causing injury to the person; or
(b)   intended by the person having it with him for such use by him or by some other person (s 1(4) Prevention of Crime Act 1953).

Articles in category (a), such as knuckle dusters and flick-knives and disguised knives, are always offensive weapons. An article in category (b), such as for example a milk bottle, only becomes an offensive weapon when the person carrying it has the intention of using it to cause injury to the person. The prosecution must prove this intention.

An object which bears all the characteristics of a flick-knife does not cease to be or lose its characteristic as a flick-knife because it has the secondary character of being a lighter. It is just as much an offensive weapon and potentially dangerous as if the lighter function were not there: *R v Vasili* [2011] EWCA Crim 615, [2011] 2 Cr App Rep 56, 175 JP 185.

In relation to category (a), in *Sills v DPP* [2006] EWHC 3383 (Admin), [2006] All ER (D) 165 (Oct), justices had been entitled to conclude that half of a pool cue, which had been unscrewed from its counterpart, and which the defendant maintained he had taken with him to scare off any attacker, was an article adapted for use for causing injury to the person within the meaning of s 1(4) above.

A[11.6]

Have with him. The prosecution must prove that the defendant knowingly was "carrying" the offensive weapon with him. 'Carrying' would not include the situation where the accused seized a clasp knife, which he had not been carrying, for instant use on his victim.

A[11.7]

Knowledge of possession. The accused must have acquired the weapon knowingly (eg it was not slipped into his pocket unawares) (*R v Cugullere* [1961] 2 All ER 343, [1961] 1 WLR 858, 45, CCA). He still has it if he subsequently forgets it is there (*R v McCalla* (1988) 87 Cr App Rep 372, 152 JP 481, CA; *Bayliss v DPP* [2003] All ER (D) 71 (Feb)) until he or another does something to rid him of it. A person who has forgotten that he has an offensive weapon is unlikely to have a 'reasonable excuse' (see below) for having it with him, but it might be otherwise where the original possession was lawful, eg picking up a policeman's truncheon intending to take it to the police station and then forgetting to do so (*R v McCalla* (1988) 87 Cr App Rep 372, 152 JP 481, CA).

A[11.8]

In a public place. This includes any highway and any other premises or place to which at the material time the public have or are permitted to have access, whether on payment or otherwise. (*R v Roberts* [2003] EWCA Crim 2753, [2003] All ER (D) 325 (Oct)). In *Harriot v DPP* [2005] EWHC 965 (Admin), (2005) 170 JP 494, the Divisional Court held that a "public place" is not a term of legal art and that the statutory definition under the Prevention of Crime Act 1953 was illustrative not exhaustive. Accordingly, the open area between a bail hostel building and a road, was, on the face of it, private premises.

A[11.9]

Bladed article – the prosecution merely has to prove that the accused had an article to which this offence applies and it is then up to the accused to justify its possession. The prosecution has a lesser burden of proof, than in the offence described at A[64]. The defendant does not discharge this burden merely by providing an explanation uncontradicted by prosecution evidence if the justices disbelieve his explanation (*Godwin v DPP* (1992) 96 Cr App Rep 244, 157 JP 197). However the prosecution must prove the defendant had knowledge of his possession of the blade (*R v Daubney* (2000) 164 JP 519, CA).

It is suggested that having regard to the legitimate aims of the legislation the legal burden of proof which rests with the accused is ECHR compliant.

Exceptions. This offence does not apply to a folding pocket knife except if the cutting edge of its blade exceeds 3 inches. Folding knife does not include a knife where the blade is secured in the open position by a locking device (*Harris v DPP* [1993] 1 All ER 562, [1993] 1 WLR 82).

A[11.10]

School premises includes any land used for the purposes of a school but excludes a dwelling occupied by a person employed at the school.

From **31 May 2007** (England only) by virtue of the Violent Crime Reduction Act 2006, school staff with reasonable grounds for suspecting that a pupil may have possession of a blade or offensive weapon, may search the pupil or his possessions for such articles. The persons authorised to search are a Head teacher or someone authorised by the Head teacher. Similar authority is a available to carry out searches of students in higher education.

A[11.11]

Defences to bladed article. It is a defence for the accused to prove that he had good reason or lawful authority for having the article with him in a public place. The defendant does not have to prove this beyond all reasonable doubt, only that it is more probable than not. (*L v DPP* [2001] EWHC 882 (Admin), [2002] 2 All ER 854). This burden is held not to be incompatible with the presumption of innocence in Article 6(2) of the ECHR (*R v Matthews* [2003] EWCA Crim 813, [2004] QB 690).

See also A[11.13] below.

A[11.12]

Good reason or lawful authority includes cases where the accused had the article with him:

(a)   for use at work;
(b)   for religious reasons (eg a Sikh) but not where the reason was connected with a martial art ancillary to a religious practice (*R v Wang* [2003] EWCA Crim 3228, [2003] All ER (D) 299 (Dec)); or
(c)   as part of any national costume (eg a Scotsman's dirk).The defendant cannot rely on forgetfulness as constituting a good reason for having a weapon with him even where at an earlier period he was in lawful possession of the article (*DPP v Gregson* (1992) 96 Cr App Rep 240, 157 JP 201); or, in the case of the school offence:
(d)   for educational purposes.

A[11.13]

Without lawful authority or reasonable excuse. If the prosecution has established that an offensive weapon was carried in a public place then the onus shifts to the defendant to prove that lawful authority or reasonable excuse existed. The degree of proof is not to establish this beyond all reasonable doubt but that on the balance of probabilities it is true. The common excuse put forward is that the article was carried for use in self-defence. As the authority or excuse relates to the reason for carrying the offensive weapon, not to a use for which it is subsequently employed, one has to look at the situation when the defendant was carrying it. Accordingly, fear of being attacked, arising from the experience of friends and general violence in the neighbourhood, has been held not to be a reasonable excuse for carrying a metal ball and chain for self-protection. Self-protection from an actual or imminent attack might provide a 'reasonable excuse'. There would be no excuse or authority for a bouncer at a dance carrying an offensive weapon.

It might be a reasonable excuse that a person carrying a weapon was at risk of immediate attack and so carried the weapon for his own defence, but the 1953 Act never intended to sanction the continued carrying of an offensive weapon. A person under that kind of threat had to seek protection via other means such as contacting the police. Each case had to be determined on its own facts and no assistance was to be derived from comparing the facts of other cases. It remained for a jury to determine how soon and how likely the anticipated attack had to be to constitute reasonable excuse for carrying an offensive weapon. Further, there was no authority to support the proposition that reasonable excuse should be determined subjectively. Nor was there any basis for importing the self-defence test. Accordingly, when a defendant claimed he had reasonable excuse it was for him to prove both belief and the reasonableness of the belief on a balance of probabilities. Otherwise any defendant could claim that he had been at risk of immediate attack: see *N v DPP* [2011] EWHC 1807 (Admin), 175 JP 337. The defendant's state of mind might be relevant to the question as to whether she had a 'good reason' for possession of a bladed article: *R v Clancy* [2012] EWCA Crim 8, [2012] 1 WLR 2536, [2012] 2 Cr App Rep 71. This last decision went too far on the facts. The defendant was no longer at risk of an immediate attack and the excuse put forward lacked merit or foundation.

ECHR: In the light of *R v Matthews* [2003] EWCA Crim 813, [2004] QB 690, it is submitted that the imposition of a reverse legal burden on the accused is proportionate in accordance with art 6(2) of the ECHR.

A[11.14]

A claim by the accused that he did not know that the article in question was an offensive weapon cannot amount to a defence of reasonable excuse (*R v Densu* [1998] 1 Cr App Rep 400, [1998] Crim LR 345, CA). However, forgetfulness that one has unintended possession of an offensive weapon, may be relevant as part of a wider set of circumstances relied on as providing reasonable excuse: *R v Glidewell* (1999) 163 JP 557, CA; *R v Tsap* [2008] EWCA Crim 2580, 173 JP 4; *Chahal v DPP* [2010] EWHC 439 (Admin), [2010] 2 Cr App Rep 33.

The burden on the defendant to show a reasonable excuse was a heavy one where the weapon (a butterfly knife) was offensive per se, but the court still has a wide discretion on the facts (*DPP v Patterson* [2004] All ER (D) 239 (Oct), DC; but see *R v Tsap* immediately above.

Sentencing
SC Guideline – Bladed article/offensive weapon,
possession of

A[11.15]

These guidelines and accompanying notes are drawn from the Court of Appeal's decision in *R v Celaire and Poulton* [2003] 1 Cr App R (S) 610.*

*No SC guidelines have been issued as yet for the aggravated form of offences added under s 142 of LASPOA 2012 (see **A[11.1]**). For offenders aged 16 years the court must assume an immediate custodial sentence is appropriate, six months for an adult, four months for a youth aged 16 or over, unless it is unjust to do so having regard to all the circumstances of the offence and the offender.

Key factors

(a)   Concurrent sentences may be appropriate if the weapons offence is ancillary to a more serious offence: consecutive sentences may be appropriate if the offences are distinct and independent. See **B[37.22] and consult your legal adviser for guidance.**

(b)   When assessing offence seriousness, consider the offender's intention, the circumstances of the offence and the nature of the weapon involved.

(c)   Some weapons are inherently more dangerous than others but the nature of the weapon is not the primary determinant of offence seriousness. A relatively less dangerous weapon, such as a billiard cue or knuckle-duster, may be used to create fear and such an offence may be at least as serious as one in which a more obviously dangerous weapon, such as a knife or an acid spray, is being carried for self-defence or no actual attempt has been made by the offender to use it.

(d)   Nevertheless, the fact that the offender was carrying a weapon which is offensive per se may shed light on his or her intentions.

Significant attention was paid to the guideline during 2008 (which is not limited to the possession of knives) and of the Court of Appeal decision in *R v Povey and other applications* [2008] EWCA Crim 1261. The purpose of this note is to set out the effect of the revised guideline following *Povey*.

* Updated guidance – sentencing for possession of a weapon – knife crime

(1)   The guideline has been strengthened from the previous Court of Appeal decision *R v Celaire and Poulton* and is likely to result in many more offences (committed by adult offenders) crossing the custody threshold.

(2)   In *Povey*, attention was drawn to the recent escalation in offences of this kind and the importance, for the time being, of courts focussing on the purposes of sentencing of reduction of crime (including its reduction by deterrence) and the protection of the public.

(3)   In *Povey*, the Court of Appeal recommended that the Magistrates' Courts Sentencing Guidelines guideline should normally be applied at the most severe end of the appropriate range to reflect current prevalence concerns. This will be likely to lead to more cases being sentenced in the Crown Court.

(4)   When the current concerns have been overcome, courts will be notified that the approach should return to the guideline as published.

(5)   The guideline provides three categories of seriousness:

(i)   **Level 1** is for the situation where a person has a weapon or bladed article, is not in a "dangerous circumstance" and the weapon or bladed article is not used to threaten or to cause fear; in those circumstances:

     –   applying *Povey*, where the offensive weapon is a knife the starting point would be close to 12 weeks custody for a first time adult offender who has pleaded not guilty;

     –   in relation to an offensive weapon other than a knife, the starting point for a first time adult offender who has pleaded not guilty is a high level community order.

(ii)   **Level 2** is for the situation where a weapon is in the possession of the offender in "dangerous circumstances" but is not used to threaten or to cause fear; in those circumstances:

     –   applying *Povey*, where the offensive weapon is a knife the starting point for a first time adult offender who has pleaded not guilty is committal to the Crown Court and, therefore, a custodial sentence in excess of 6 months;

     –   in relation to an offensive weapon other than a knife, the starting point for a first time adult offender who has pleaded not guilty is a custodial sentence of 6 weeks.

(iii)   **Level 3** is for the situation where a weapon is used in dangerous circumstances to threaten or cause fear; in those circumstances, both the starting point and range for a first time adult offender who has pleaded not guilty are for sentencing in the Crown Court and, therefore, in excess of 6 months custody.

"Dangerous circumstances" has not been judicially defined but was used in the previous Court of Appeal judgment in *R v Celaire and Poulton*. In relation to a knife, a circumstance is likely to be dangerous if there is a real possibility it could be used.

OFFENCE SERIOUSNESS (CULPABILITY AND HARM)		
A. IDENTIFY THE APPROPRIATE STARTING POINT		
Starting points based on first time offender pleading not guilty		
Examples of nature of activity	**Starting point**	**Range**
Weapon not used to threaten or cause fear	High level community order	Band C fine to 12 weeks custody* * See observations from *R v Povey* above
Weapon not used to threaten or cause fear but offence committed in dangerous circumstances	6 weeks custody	High level community order to Crown Court* *See observations from *R v Povey* above

Weapon used to threaten or cause fear and offence committed in dangerous circumstances	Crown Court	Crown Court
		*See observations from *R v Povey* above

OFFENCE SERIOUSNESS (CULPABILITY AND HARM)

B. CONSIDER THE EFFECT OF AGGRAVATING AND MITIGATING FACTORS (OTHER THAN THOSE WITHIN THE EXAMPLES ABOVE)

Common aggravating and mitigating factors are identified at **B[5.2A]**. The following may be particularly relevant but these lists are not exhaustive:

Factors indicating higher culpability	*Factors indicating lower culpability*
1. Particularly dangerous weapon	1. Weapon carried only on temporary basis
2. Specifically planned use of weapon to commit violence, threaten violence or intimidate	2. Original possession legitimate eg in course of trade or business
3. Offence motivated by hostility towards minority, individual or group	
4. Offender under influence of drink or drugs	
5. Offender operating in group or gang	
Factors indicating greater degree of harm	
1. Offence committed at school, hospital or other place where vulnerable persons may be present	
2. Offence committed on premises where people carrying out public services	
3. Offence committed on licensed premises	
4. Offence committed on public transport	
5. Offence committed at large public gathering, especially where there may be risk of disorder	

FORM A PRELIMINARY VIEW OF THE APPROPRIATE SENTENCE, THEN CONSIDER OFFENDER MITIGATION

Common factors are identified at **B[5.2A]**

CONSIDER A REDUCTION FOR A GUILTY PLEA

CONSIDER ANCILLARY ORDERS, INCLUDING COMPENSATION

Consult your legal adviser on guidance for available ANCILLARY ORDERS

CONSIDER DEPRIVATION OF PROPERTY (including weapon)

DECIDE SENTENCE

GIVE REASONS

A[12]

Domestic burglary

Charge

A[12.1]

Entering a dwelling-house (or part of a dwelling-house) as a trespasser with intent to steal therein (or with intent to do unlawful damage)

or

Having entered a dwelling-house (or part of a dwelling-house) as a trespasser stole (or attempted to steal)

Theft Act 1968, s 9(1)(a) and s 9(1)(b) respectively

Maximum penalty – Fine level 5 and 6 months (**12 months). Triable either way. Specified violent offence under Sch 15, Part 1, CJA 2003 if the offence is committed with intent to (i) inflict GBH on a person; or (ii) do unlawful damage to a dwelling or anything in it.

Crown Court – 14 years' imprisonment or life following a third separate conviction (for burglaries involving a dwelling) and unlimited fine.

Mode of trial or allocation

A[12.2]

Aggravated burglary is the commission of a burglary whilst armed with a firearm or other weapon of offence at the time of entry and is triable only at the Crown Court. Crime and Disorder Act 1998, s 51 applies.

A[12.3]

Burglary comprising the commission of, or an intention to commit, an offence of rape or grievous bodily harm may only be heard at the Crown Court. Crime and Disorder Act 1998, s 51 applies.

A[12.4]

Consult the legal adviser. Where the charge is burglary of a dwelling and the accused has two separate convictions for dwelling house burglaries, the charge may only be heard at the Crown Court (PCC(S) A 2000, s 111). See *R v Webster* [2003] EWCA Crim 3597, [2003] All ER (D) 313 (Nov) for an example of a third offence becoming indictable only. Crime and Disorder Act 1998, s 51 applies.

NB: In *R v Miller* [2010] EWCA Crim 809, [2011] 1 Cr App Rep (S) 7, [2010] Crim LR 648, it was stated that where a burglary has not been charged as burglary of a dwelling, it could not be treated as such for sentencing purposes pursuant to PCC(S)A 2000, s 111.

A[12.5]

Otherwise a magistrates' court can try the case unless it is alleged that the defendant used, or threatened, violence to someone in the dwelling-house in which case the Crime and Disorder Act 1998, s 51 applies (*R v McGrath* [2003] EWCA Crim 2062, 167 JP 554, [2004] Crim LR 142, [2003] All ER (D) 397 (Jun)).

A[12.6]

Where the offence is triable either way consider the **SC Guidelines** at A[12.19] below.

Legal notes and definitions

A[12.7]–[12.9]

Entering. Whether the defendant can properly be described as entering or having entered the building is a question of fact for the magistrates. They will have to decide whether the accused had made an effective entry into the building (*R v Brown* [1985] Crim LR 212, CA). An effective entry can be made by the burglar putting his hand through a broken shop window and stealing therefrom. It can be sufficient for only a part of the burglar's body to enter the premises.

A[12.10]–[12.14]

Building. The offence is committed by one who is lawfully in part of a building but trespasses into another part.

A[12.15]

An inhabited vehicle (eg a caravan) or vessel is within the section notwithstanding that the occupant is absent at the time of the offence.

A[12.16]

Stealing is dishonestly appropriating another person's property with the intention of permanently depriving the other person of it. See A[79].

A[12.17]

Trespass. Accidental trespass would not be an offence. The defendant must know, or be reckless as to whether, he is trespassing (*R v Collins* [1973] QB 100, [1972] 2 All ER 1105, CA). If there is doubt whether the defendant was trespassing, consult the legal adviser.

A[12.18]–[12.19]

Third conviction. Where magistrates have before them a defendant who appears to be facing a third time domestic burglary, the case must be committed for trial at Crown Court (see A[12.4]). In all cases of burglary dwelling the court should announce in open court for the record that the defendant has been convicted of a qualifying offence.

Sentencing
SC Guideline – Domestic burglary

Domestic burglary (came into force on 16 January 2012)

A[12.20]

This is a serious specified offence for the purposes of s 224 of the Criminal Justice Act 2003 if it was committed with intent to: (a) inflict grievous bodily harm on a person, or (b) do unlawful damage to a building or anything in it.

Triable either way

Maximum when tried summarily: Level 5 fine and/or 26 weeks' custody.

Maximum when tried on indictment: 14 years' custody.

Offence range: Community order – 6 years' custody.

Where sentencing an offender for a qualifying third domestic burglary, the Court must apply s 111 of the Powers of the Criminal Courts (Sentencing) Act 2000 and impose a custodial term of at least three years, unless it is satisfied that there are particular circumstances which relate to any of the offences or to the offender which would make it unjust to do so.

This guideline applies to all offenders aged 18 and older, who are sentenced on or after 16 January 2012. The definitions [at page 145] of 'starting point' and 'first time offender' do not apply for this guideline. Starting point and category ranges apply to all offenders in all cases, irrespective of plea or previous convictions.

Step One
Determining the offence category

The court should determine the offence category using the table below.

Category 1	Greater harm **and** higher culpability
Category 2	Greater harm **and** lower culpability; **or** lesser harm **and** higher culpability
Category 3	Lesser harm **and** lower culpability

The court should determine the offender's culpability and the harm caused, or intended, by reference **only** to the factors below which comprise the principal factual elements of the offence. Where an offence does not fall squarely into a category, individual factors may require a degree of weighting before making an overall assessment and determining the appropriate category range.

Factors indicating greater harm

Theft of/damage to property causing a significant degree of loss to the victim (whether economic, sentimental or personal value)

Soiling, ransacking or vandalism of property

Occupier at home (or returns home) while offender present

Trauma to the victim, beyond the normal inevitable consequence of intrusion and theft

Violence used or threatened against victim

Context of general public disorder

Factors indicating lesser harm

Nothing stolen or only property of very low value to the victim (whether economic, sentimental or personal)

Limited damage or disturbance to property

Factors indicating higher culpability

Victim or premises deliberately targeted (for example, due to vulnerability or hostility based on disability, race, sexual orientation)

A significant degree of planning or premeditation

Knife or other weapon carried (where not charged separately)

Equipped for burglary (for example, implements carried and/or use of vehicle)

Member of a group or gang

Factors indicating lower culpability

Offence committed on impulse, with limited intrusion into property

Offender exploited by others

Mental disorder or disability, where linked to the commission of the offence

Step Two
Starting point and category range

Having determined the category, the court should use the corresponding starting points to reach a sentence within the category range below. The starting point applies to all offenders irrespective of plea or previous convictions.

Where the defendant is dependant on or a propensity to misuse drugs and there is sufficient prospect of success, a community order with a drug rehabilitation requirement under s 229 of the Criminal Justice Act 2003 may be a proper alternative to a short or moderate custodial sentence.

A case of particular gravity, reflected by multiple features of culpability in step one, could merit adjustment from the starting point before further adjustment for aggravating or mitigating features, set out below.

Offence Category	Starting Point *(Applicable to all offenders)*	Category Range *(Applicable to all offenders)*
Category 1	Crown Court	Crown Court
Category 2	1 year's custody	High level community order Crown Court (2 years' custody)
Category 3	High level community order	Low level community order – 26 weeks' custody

The table below contains a **non-exhaustive** list of additional factual elements providing the context of the offence and factors relating to the offender. Identify whether any combination of these, or other relevant factors, should result in an upward or downward adjustment from the starting point. In some cases, having considered these factors, it may be appropriate to move outside of the identified category range.

When sentencing **category 3** offences, the court should consider the custody threshold as follows:

- Has the custody threshold been passed?
- If so is it unavoidable that a custodial sentence be imposed?
- If so, can the sentence be suspended?

Factors increasing seriousness

Statutory aggravating factors:

Previous convictions, having regard to a) the nature of the offence to which the conviction relates and its relevance to the current offence; and b) the time that has elapsed since the conviction*

Offence committed whilst on bail

Other aggravating factors include:

Child at home (or returns home) when offence committed

Offence committed at night

Gratuitous degradation of victim

Any steps taken to prevent the victim reporting an incident, obtaining assistance and/or from assisting or supporting the prosecution

Victims compelled to leave their home (in particular victims of domestic violence) Established evidence of community impact

Established evidence of community impact

Commission of offence whilst under the influence of alcohol or drugs

Failure to comply with current court orders

Offence committed whilst on licence

Offences taken into consideration (TICs)

Factors reducing seriousness or reflecting personal mitigation

Offender has made voluntary reparation to the victim

Subordinate role in a group or gang

No previous convictions or no relevant recent convictions

Remorse

Good character and/or exemplary conduct

Determination and/or demonstration of steps taken to address addiction or offending behaviour

Isolated incident

Serious medical conditions requiring urgent, intensive or long-term treatment

Age and/or lack of maturity where it affects the responsibility of the defendant

Lapse of time since the offence where this is not the fault of the offender

Mental disorder or learning disability, where not linked to the commission of the offence

Sole or primary carer for dependent relatives

* Where sentencing an offender for a qualifying third domestic burglary, the Court must apply section 111 of the Powers of the Criminal Courts (Sentencing) Act 2000 and impose a custodial term of at least three years, unless it is satisfied that there are particular circumstances which relate to any of the offences or to the offender which would make it unjust to do so.

Step Three
Consider any other factors which indicate a reduction, such as assistance to the prosecution

The court should take into account any rule of law by virtue of which an offender may receive a discounted sentence in consequence of assistance given (or offered) to the prosecutor or investigator.

Step Four
Reduction for guilty pleas

The court should take account of any potential reduction for a guilty plea in accordance with section 144 of the Criminal Justice Act 2003 and the *Guilty Plea* guideline.

Where a minimum mandatory sentence is imposed under section 111 Powers of Criminal Courts (Sentencing) Act, the discount for an early guilty plea must not exceed 20 per cent.

Step Five
Dangerousness

A burglary offence under section 9 of the Theft Act 1968 is a serious specified offence within the meaning of chapter 5 of the Criminal Justice Act 2003 if it was committed with the intent to (a) inflict grievous bodily harm on a person, or (b) do unlawful damage to a building or anything in it. The court should consider whether having regard to the criteria contained in that chapter it would be appropriate to award imprisonment for public protection or an extended sentence. Where offenders meet the dangerousness criteria, the notional determinate sentence should be used as the basis for the setting of a minimum term.

Step Six
Totality principle

If sentencing an offender for more than one offence or where the offender is already serving a sentence, consider whether the total sentence is just and proportionate to the offending behaviour.

Step Seven
Compensation and ancillary orders

In all cases, the court should consider whether to make compensation and/or other ancillary orders.

Step Eight
Reasons

Section 174 of the Criminal Justice Act 2003 imposes a duty to give reasons for, and explain the effect of, the sentence.

Step Nine
Consideration for remand time

Sentencers should take into consideration any remand time served in relation to the final sentence. The court should consider whether to give credit for time spent on remand in custody or on bail in accordance with sections 240 and 240A of the Criminal Justice Act 2003.

A[13]

Non-domestic burglary

Charge

A[13.1]

Entering a building (or part of a building) as a trespasser with intent to steal therein (or with intent to do unlawful damage)

or

Having entered a building (or part of a building) as a trespasser stole (or attempted to steal)

Theft Act 1968, s 9(1)(a) and s 9(1)(b) respectively

Maximum penalty – Fine level 5 and 6 months (**12 months). Triable either way. Specified violent offence under Sch 15, Part 1, CJA 2003 if the offence is committed with intent to (i) inflict GBH on a person; or (ii) do unlawful damage to a building or anything in it.

Crown Court – 10 years and unlimited fine.

Mode of trial

A[13.2]

Aggravated burglary is the commission of a burglary whilst armed with a firearm or other weapon of offence at the time of entry and is triable only at the Crown Court. Crime and Disorder Act 1998, s 51 applies.

A[13.3]

Burglary comprising the commission of, or an intention to commit, an offence of rape or grievous bodily harm may only be heard at the Crown Court. Crime and Disorder Act 1998, s 51 applies.

A[13.4]

If the building is a non-dwelling a magistrates' court can try the case unless it is alleged that the defendant used, or threatened, violence to someone in the non-dwelling in which case the Crime and Disorder Act 1998, s 51 applies (*R v McGrath* [2003] EWCA Crim 2062, 167 JP 554, [2004] Crim LR 142, [2003] All ER (D) 397 (Jun)).

A[13.5]

Where the offence is triable either way consider the **SGC Guideline** at A[13.18] below and the general notes at I[4].

Legal notes and definitions

A[13.6]

Entering. Whether the defendant can properly be described as entering or having entered the building is a question of fact for the magistrates. They will have to decide whether the accused had made an effective entry into the building (*R v Brown* [1985] Crim LR 212, CA). An effective entry can be made by the burglar putting his hand through a broken shop window and stealing therefrom. It can be sufficient for only a part of the burglar's body to enter the premises.

A[13.7]–[13.15]

Building. The offence is committed by one who is lawfully in part of a building but trespasses into another part. An inhabited vehicle (eg a caravan) or vessel is within the section notwithstanding that the occupant is absent at the time of the offence.

A[13.16]

Stealing is dishonestly appropriating another person's property with the intention of permanently depriving the other person of it. See A[79].

A[13.17]–[13.18]

Trespass. Accidental trespass would not be an offence. The defendant must know, or be reckless as to whether, he is trespassing (*R v Collins* [1973] QB 100, [1972] 2 All ER 1105, CA). If there is doubt whether the defendant was trespassing, consult the legal adviser.

Sentencing
SC Guideline – Non-domestic burglary

Non-domestic burglary (came into force on 16 January 2012)

A[13.19]

This is a serious specified offence for the purposes of section 224 Criminal Justice Act 2003 if it was committed with intent to: (a) inflict grievous bodily harm on a person, or (b) do unlawful damage to a building or anything in it.

Triable either way

Maximum when tried summarily: Level 5 fine and/or 26 weeks' custody.

Maximum when tried on indictment: 10 years' custody.

Offence range: Fine – 5 years' custody.

This guideline applies to all offenders aged 18 and older, who are sentenced on or after 16 January 2012. The definitions [at page 145] of 'starting point' and 'first time offender' do not apply for this guideline. Starting point and category ranges apply to all offenders in all cases, irrespective of plea or previous convictions.

Step One
Determining the offence category

The court should determine the offence category using the table below.

Category 1	Greater harm **and** higher culpability
Category 2	Greater harm **and** lower culpability; **or** lesser harm **and** higher culpability
Category 3	Lesser harm **and** lower culpability

The court should determine the offender's culpability and the harm caused, or intended, by reference **only** to the factors below which comprise the principal factual elements of the offence. Where an offence does not fall squarely into a category, individual factors may require a degree of weighting before making an overall assessment and determining the appropriate category range.

Factors indicating greater harm

Theft of/damage to property causing a significant degree of loss to the victim (whether economic, sentimental or personal value)

Soiling, ransacking or vandalism of property

Victim on the premises (or returns) while offender present

Trauma to the victim, beyond the normal inevitable consequence of intrusion and theft

Violence used or threatened against victim

Context of general public disorder

Factors indicating lesser harm

Nothing stolen or only property of very low value to the victim (whether economic, sentimental or personal)

Limited damage or disturbance to property

Factors indicating higher culpability

Premises or victim deliberately targeted (to include pharmacy or doctor's surgery and targeting due to vulnerability of victim or hostility based on disability, race, sexual orientation and so forth)

A significant degree of planning or premeditation

Knife or other weapon carried (where not charged separately)

Equipped for burglary (for example, implements carried and/or use of vehicle)

Member of a group or gang

Factors indicating lower culpability

Offence committed on impulse, with limited intrusion into property

Offender exploited by others

Mental disorder or disability, where linked to the commission of the offence

Step Two
Starting point and category range

Having determined the category, the court should use the corresponding starting points to reach a sentence within the category range below. The starting point applies to all offenders irrespective of plea or previous convictions.

Where the defendant is dependant on or a propensity to misuse drugs and there is sufficient prospect of success, a community order with a drug rehabilitation requirement under s 229 of the Criminal Justice Act 2003 may be a proper alternative to a short or moderate custodial sentence.

A case of particular gravity, reflected by multiple features of culpability in step one, could merit adjustment from the starting point before further adjustment for aggravating or mitigating features, set out below.

Offence Category	Starting Point *(Applicable to all offenders)*	Category Range *(Applicable to all offenders)*
Category 1	Crown Court	Crown Court
Category 2	18 weeks' custody	Low level community order – 51 weeks' custody)
Category 3	Medium level community order	Band B fine – low level – 18 weeks' custody

The table below contains a **non-exhaustive** list of additional factual elements providing the context of the offence and factors relating to the offender. Identify whether any combination of these, or other relevant factors, should result in an upward or downward adjustment from the starting point. In some cases, having considered these factors, it may be appropriate to move outside of the identified category range.

When sentencing **category 2 or 3** offences, the court should consider the custody threshold as follows:

- Has the custody threshold been passed?
- If so is it unavoidable that a custodial sentence be imposed?
- If so, can the sentence be suspended?

Factors increasing seriousness

Statutory aggravating factors:

Previous convictions, having regard to a) the nature of the offence to which the conviction relates and its relevance to the current offence; and b) the time that has elapsed since the conviction

---

Offence committed whilst on bail

Other aggravating factors include:

Offence committed at night, particularly where staff present or likely to be present

Abuse of a position of trust

Gratuitous degradation of victim

Any steps taken to prevent the victim reporting an incident, obtaining assistance and/or from assisting or supporting the prosecution

Established evidence of community impact

Commission of offence whilst under the influence of alcohol or drugs

Failure to comply with current court orders

Offence committed whilst on licence

Offences taken into consideration (TICs)

Factors reducing seriousness or reflecting personal mitigation

Offender has made voluntary reparation to the victim

Subordinate role in a group or gang

No previous convictions or no relevant recent convictions

Remorse

Good character and/or exemplary conduct

Determination and/or demonstration of steps taken to address addiction or offending behaviour

Isolated incident

Serious medical conditions requiring urgent, intensive or long-term treatment

Age and/or lack of maturity where it affects the responsibility of the defendant

Lapse of time since the offence where this is not the fault of the offender

Mental disorder or learning disability, where not linked to the commission of the offence

Sole or primary carer for dependent relatives

Step Three
Consider any other factors which indicate a reduction, such as assistance to the prosecution

The court should take into account any rule of law by virtue of which an offender may receive a discounted sentence in consequence of assistance given (or offered) to the prosecutor or investigator.

Step Four
Reduction for guilty pleas

The court should take account of any potential reduction for a guilty plea in accordance with section 144 of the Criminal Justice Act 2003 and the *Guilty Plea* guideline.

Step Five
Dangerousness

A burglary offence under section 9 of the Theft Act 1968 is a serious specified offence within the meaning of chapter 5 of the Criminal Justice Act 2003 if it was committed with the intent to (a) inflict grievous bodily harm on a person, or (b) do unlawful damage to a building or anything in it. The court should consider whether having regard to the criteria contained in that chapter it would be appropriate to award imprisonment for public protection or an extended sentence. Where offenders meet the dangerousness criteria, the notional determinate sentence should be used as the basis for the setting of a minimum term.

Step Six
Totality principle

If sentencing an offender for more than one offence or where the offender is already serving a sentence, consider whether the total sentence is just and proportionate to the offending behaviour.

Step Seven
Compensation and ancillary orders

In all cases, the court should consider whether to make compensation and/or other ancillary orders.

Step Eight
Reasons

Section 174 of the Criminal Justice Act 2003 imposes a duty to give reasons for, and explain the effect of, the sentence.

Step Nine
Consideration for remand time

Sentencers should take into consideration any remand time served in relation to the final sentence. The court should consider whether to give credit for time spent on remand in custody or on bail in accordance with sections 240 and 240A of the Criminal Justice Act 2003.

A[14]

Child prostitution and pornography

Charge

A[14.1]

Intentionally causes or incites another person (B) to become a prostitute or to be involved in pornography in any part of the world, and either –

(i)   B is under 18, and a does not reasonably believe that B is 18 or over, or

(ii)   B is under 13.

Sexual Offences Act 2003, s 48

Intentionally controls any of the activities of another person (B) relating to B's prostitution or involvement in pornography in any part of the world, and either -

(i)   B is under 18, and A does not reasonably believe that B is over 18, or

(ii)   B is under 13.

Sexual Offences Act 2003, s 49.

Intentionally arranges or facilitates the prostitution or involvement in pornography in any part of the world of another person (B), and either –

(i)   B is under 18, and A does not reasonably believe that B is over 18 or over, or

(ii)   B is under 13.

Sexual Offences Act, 2003, s 50.

Maximum penalty – Fine level 5 and 6 months (**12 months). Triable either way. Specified sexual offence under Sch 15, Part 2, CJA 2003

Crown Court – 14 years' imprisonment and unlimited fine.

A[14.1A]

NB: From 26/1/09, section 63 of the Criminal Justice and Immigration Act 2008 created a new offence of possession of extreme pornographic images.

An image is 'pornographic' if it is of such a nature that it must reasonably be assumed to have been produced solely or principally for the purpose of sexual arousal.

An 'extreme image is one which portrays, in an explicit and realistic way, any of the following –

- an act which threatens a person's life
- an act which results, or is likely to result, in serious injury to a person's anus, breasts or genitals
- an act which involves interference with a human corpse, or
- a person performing an act of intercourse or oral sex with an animal (whether dead or alive),
- and a reasonable person looking at the image would think that any such person or animal was real; <u>and</u>
- the image is grossly offensive, disgusting or otherwise of an obscene character.

An 'image' means a moving or still image (produced by any means); or, data (stored by any means) which is capable of conversion into an image.

Classified films are exempted under s 64. See ss 65 and 66 for defences.

Maximum penalty – Fine level 5 and 6 months (**12 months). Triable either way. At the moment this is not a specified sexual offence under Sch 15, Part 2 of the CJA 2003.

Crown Court – 3 years' imprisonment and unlimited fine.

NB: (1) Proceedings for an offence may not be instituted in England and Wales except by or with the consent of the Director of Public Prosecutions.

(2) There is currently no SC guideline.

Mode of trial

A[14.2]
Consider the **SC Guideline** at A[14.5] below.

Legal notes and definitions

A[14.3]
Pornography. For the purposes of ss 48 to 50, a person is involved in pornography if an indecent image of that person is recorded; and similar expressions, and 'pornography', are to be interpreted accordingly (Sexual Offences Act 2003, s 51(1)).

A[14.4]
Prostitute. Means a person (A) who, on at least one occasion and whether or not compelled to do so, offers or provides sexual services to another person in return for **payment** or a promise of payment to A or to a third person; and "prostitution" is to be interpreted accordingly (Sexual Offences Act 2003, s 51(2)).

A[14.5]
Payment. As in A[14.4] "payment" means any financial advantage, includ-

ing the discharge of an obligation to pay or the provision of goods or services (including sexual services) gratuitously or at a discount (Sexual Offences Act 2003, s 51(3)).

Sentencing
SC Guideline – Child prostitution and pornography

A[14.6]

This guideline is taken from the Sentencing Council's definitive guideline *Sexual Offences Act 2003*, published 30 April 2007.

*The court must inform the defendant that the Independent Safeguarding Authority (known as the Independent Barring Board) will automatically ban him/her from working with children and/or vulnerable adults. As the court has no role in the decision if the defendant needs any further advice he/she should consult a solicitor.

Key factors

(a) Few cases will be suitable to be dealt with in a magistrates' court for the following reasons:

– The courts should consider making an order confiscating any profits stemming from the offender's criminal life-style or forfeiting any possessions (eg cameras, computers, property) used in connection with the commission of the offence. Only the Crown Court can make a confiscation order

– The starting point for the child prostitution and pornography offences will always be a custodial sentence

– In cases where a number of children are involved, consecutive sentences may be appropriate, leading to cumulative sentences significantly higher than the starting points for individual offences. Following admissions in interview and a guilty plea at the earliest opportunity by an offender with a relevant previous conviction, the appropriate sentence for one offence of possession of extreme pornographic images was one of four months' imprisonment: *R v Burns* [2012] EWCA Crim 192, [2012] 2 Cr App Rep (S) 384.

(b) In accordance with section 80 and schedule 3 of the SOA 2003, automatic notification requirements apply upon conviction to an offender aged 18 or over.

IDENTIFY DANGEROUS OFFENDERS
These are serious offences for the purposes of the public protection provisions in the Criminal Justice Act 2003. Refer to **B[16.5]** and consult legal adviser for guidance
OFFENCE SERIOUSNESS (CULPABILITY AND HARM)
A. IDENTIFY THE APPROPRIATE STARTING POINT
Starting points based on first time offender pleading not guilty

These offences should normally be dealt with in the Crown Court. However, there may be rare occasions of non-penetrative activity involving a victim aged 16 or 17 where the offender's involvement is minimal and not perpetrated for gain in which a custodial sentence within the jurisdiction of a magistrates' court may be appropriate.

Consult your legal adviser for further guidance.

OFFENCE SERIOUSNESS (CULPABILITY AND HARM)

B. CONSIDER THE EFFECT OF AGGRAVATING AND MITIGATING FACTORS

Common aggravating and mitigating factors are identified at **B[5.2A]**. The following may be particularly relevant but **these lists are not exhaustive**

Factors indicating higher culpability	Factors indicating lower culpability
1. Background of threats or intimidation	1. Offender also being controlled in prostitution or pornography and subject to threats and intimidation
2. Large-scale commercial operation	
3. Use of drugs, alcohol or other substance to secure the victim's compliance	
4. Forcing a victim to violate another person	
5. Abduction or detention	
6. Threats to prevent the victim reporting the activity	
7. Threats to disclose victim's activity to friends/relatives	
8. Images distributed to other children or persons known to the victim	
9. Financial or other gain	
Factors indicating greater degree of harm	
1. Induced dependency of drugs	
2. Victim has been manipulated into physical and emotional dependence on the offender	
3. Storing, making available or distributing images in such a way that they can be inadvertently accessed by others	

FORM A PRELIMINARY VIEW OF THE APPROPRIATE SENTENCE, THEN CONSIDER OFFENDER MITIGATION
Common factors are identified at B[5.2A]

CONSIDER A REDUCTION FOR A GUILTY PLEA

CONSIDER ANCILLARY ORDERS, INCLUDING COMPENSATION and NOTIFICATION ORDERS
Refer to B[18] for guidance on compensation
Consult your legal adviser on guidance for availability of ANCILLARY ORDERS

DECIDE SENTENCE
GIVE REASONS

A[14.7]

Notification requirements. See A[52.15].

A[15]

Common assault and racially/religiously aggravated assault

Charge

A[15.1]

Did assault [. . . . .] [by beating]

Contrary to the Criminal Justice Act 1988, s 39.

Maximum penalty – Fine level 5 and 6 months (**51 weeks). Triable only by magistrates.

(By virtue of s 10 of the Domestic Violence, Crime and Victims Act 2004, from July 1, 2007 common assault is to become an arrestable offence.)

A[15.2]

Racially/religiously aggravated assault

Contrary to the Crime and Disorder Act 1998, s 29.

Maximum penalty – Fine level 5 and 6 months (**12 months). Triable either way. Specified violent offence under Sch 15, Part 1, CJA 2003.

Crown Court – 2 years' imprisonment and unlimited fine.

Legal notes and definitions

A[15.3]

The basic offence is triable only by magistrates but may be alleged as an alternative charge at a trial at the Crown Court if the prosecution chooses with a maximum penalty of £5,000 and 6 months (51 weeks). Racially or religiously aggravated assault is triable either way. The two offences may be tried together in the alternative (*R (CPS) v Blaydon Youth Court* [2004] EWHC 2296 (Admin), 168 JP 638).

A[15.4]

Intent. The defendant must intend to cause his victim to apprehend immediate and unlawful violence, or be reckless whether such apprehension be caused (*R v Venna* [1976] QB 421, [1975] 3 All ER 788, CA). 'Reckless' means that the accused foresaw the risk and went on to take it (*R v Cunningham* [1957] 2 QB 396, [1957] 2 All ER 412, CA).

In principle it was open to justices to convict on the basis of recklessness even where the prosecution simply alleged a deliberate assault: *D v DPP*

[2005] EWHC 967 (Admin) considered. However, the justices had failed to identify what was the unlawful act of K leading to the assault. Recklessness had only been a possible conclusion if the justices had found that K had thrown a punch albeit, without intending it to land, or was flailing his arms about in an agitated and aggressive manner. The conviction could not stand in the light of the findings of fact made by the justices: *Katsonis v Crown Prosecution Service* [2011] EWHC 1860 (Admin), 175 JP 396.

A[15.5]

Assault. Does not require any contact between the two parties, a threatening gesture is enough. Words, however insulting, are probably not an assault but any attempt to commit a battery, even if the blow does not connect, can be an assault. It is not necessary that the other party should receive an actual injury, but there must have been a hostile intent. In modern usage the term assault will now include a battery, ie the actual application of force as opposed to its threatened use, and this is how it is used in most statutes. But if a charge alleges 'did assault and batter' then 'assault' will be taken to mean assault in its pure form and the charge will be as bad as being duplicitous. If anything other than 'did assault' is to be alleged it should be 'did assault by beating' (*DPP v Taylor and Little* (1991)). A reckless act which causes injury will suffice, for example a man who having fallen to the ground when struggling with the police lashed out wildly with his legs, striking the officer and fracturing a bone in his hand, was held to have been properly convicted. Just placing a hand on someone's shoulder to call his attention to something is not an assault. Throwing something at a person, even if it misses, may be an assault.

A[15.6]

If a man strikes at another but at such a distance that it would be quite impossible for it to connect then it is not an assault (although it might be an attempt). If the other person is actually touched then it is a battery which includes an assault. Equally a punch to a mother causing her to drop her baby is an assault on the baby (*Haystead v Chief Constable of Derbyshire* [2000] 3 All ER 890, [2000] 2 Cr App Rep 339).

A[15.7]

Racially or religiously aggravated. This means that at the time of committing the offence, or immediately before or after doing so, the offender demonstrates towards the victim of the assault, hostility based on the victim's membership (or presumed membership) of a racial/religious group, or the offence is motivated (wholly or partly) by hostility towards members of a racial/ religious group based on their membership of that group. It is immaterial whether or not the offender's hostility is also based on other factor not mentioned above. The prosecution can proceed on one or both limbs and will not need to specify which (*G v DPP; T v DPP* [2004] EWHC 183 (Admin), [2004] All ER (D) 278 (Jan)) (*DPP v Woods* [2002] EWHC 85 (Admin), [2002] All ER (D) 154 (Jan)) The victim's perception of the words used is irrelevant, as is the defendant's frame of mind at the time he uttered the words. This offence may also be aggravated by a motivation towards the victim's disability or sexual orientation but not as a separate offence.

A[15.8]

Misadventure. If a horse out of control strikes a person that is not an assault. In an old decision a soldier drilling in the ranks fired his gun as a man was passing unexpectedly and this was held not to be an assault.

A[15.9]

Accidental jostling. In a crowd there is not an assault as there is an implied consent to the physical contacts of ordinary life.

A[15.10]

Hostile intent. See *Collins v Wilcock* [1984] 1 WLR 1172.

A[15.11]–[15.15]

Consent. Consent of the victim is a defence but there are limits to this. The test is whether it is in the public interest to allow the activity complained of. In 1981 the Lord Chief Justice decided consent was irrelevant where two youths settled an argument in a public street by agreeing to have a fight. It was not in the public interest for people to cause each other actual bodily harm for no good reason. A similar principle has been applied by the House of Lords to assault which took place in the course of sado-masochistic activities (*R v Brown* [1992] QB 491, [1992] 2 All ER 552, CA; affd [1994] 1 AC 212, [1993] 2 All ER 75, HL). But see *ADT v United Kingdom* [2000] 2 FLR 697, [2000] Fam Law 797, ECtHR for protection from prosecution for such genuinely 'private' activities.

It is not a defence to assault that the complainant is a teacher at a special needs school and, by taking that job, consents to the risk of being assaulted. Knowledge of the risk does not imply consent to assault: *H v Crown Prosecution Service* [2010] EWHC 1374 (Admin), 174 CL&J 271.

A[15.16]

Reasonable chastisement is a defence available to a parent accused of assaulting their child; however the chastisement must be reasonable and moderate. This is assessed by:

(i)   the nature and context of the defendant's behaviour
(ii)   the duration
(iii)   physical/ mental consequences to the child (injury will make it unlawful)
(iv)   age and characteristics of the child

Note that no battery of a child can be justified on the grounds that it constitutes reasonable punishment; Children Act 2004, s 58.

However consensual activity between husband and wife in the privacy of the matrimonial home was held not to be a proper matter for criminal investigation in *R v Wilson* [1997] QB 47, [1996] 3 WLR 125, CA. Lawful sport would be unimpeachable as being in the public interest and the exercise of a legal right.

A[15.17]

Defendants who maintained that they had been engaged in rough and undisciplined horseplay, had not intended any harm, and had thought that the victims were consenting to what had occurred, were entitled to have their defence considered by the court (*R v Muir* (1986) 83 Cr App Rep 375, CA).

A[15.18]

Lawful sport. Players in games which involve some risk of injury in play must be taken to accept that risk. So a player who injures another in a fair tackle would not be guilty of an offence. Even where the accused infringes the 'rules of the game' he might still not be acting unreasonably although it might be otherwise if he was guilty of serious and dangerous foul play which showed a reckless disregard for the victim's safety and fell far below the standards which might reasonably be expected in anyone pursuing the game. Where one player offers violence to another otherwise that in actual pursuit of the game this would be an assault (*R v Barnes* [2004] EWCA Crim 3246, [2005] 2 All ER 113).

A[15.19]

Self-defence. See A[8.18]–A[8.20].

Self-defence – onus of proof. Once the defendant raises the issue of self-defence the onus is on the prosecution to disprove the defence beyond reasonable doubt.

A[15.20]

Execution of legal process. An officer of justice acting on a court order can, if he is resisted, use whatever force is necessary to carry out the order of the court.

A[15.21]–[15.30]

Justification or triviality. In a case of common assault where the information was preferred by or on behalf of the party aggrieved, if the court finds that an assault has been committed but that either it was justified or that it was so trifling as not to merit any punishment, they may dismiss the charge and issue a certificate of dismissal (see OPA 1861, s 44).

A[15.31]

Certificate of dismissal. If, after hearing such a case, the magistrates decide to dismiss the case the defendant can apply for a certificate of dismissal which will protect him from being subsequently prosecuted or sued for damages for the same assault. It is also worth noting that a defendant who has pleaded not guilty to an offence of an assault of actual bodily harm and the prosecution offer no evidence resulting in a dismissal cannot be then tried for common assault on the same facts (*R v G (Autrefois Acquit)* [2001] EWCA Crim 1215, [2001] 1 WLR 1727).

A[15.32]

Provocation. This is not a defence but may be put forward to mitigate the penalty.

Sentencing
SC Guideline – Common assault and racially/religiously
aggravated common assault

A[15.33]
Common Assault

Criminal Justice Act 1988 (section 39)

Racially/religiously aggravated common assault

Crime and Disorder Act 1998 (section 29)

Racially/religiously aggravated assault is a specified offence for the purposes of section 224 of the Criminal Justice Act 2003

Section 39

Triable only summarily

Maximum: Level 5 and/or 26 weeks' custody

Section 29

Triable either way

Maximum when tried summarily: Level 5 fine and/or 26 weeks' custody

Maximum when tried on indictment: 2 years' custody

Offence range: Discharge – 26 weeks' custody

This guideline applies to all offenders aged 18 and older, who are sentenced on or after 13 June 2011. The definitions [at page 145] of 'starting point' and 'first time offender' do not apply for this guideline. Starting point and category ranges apply to all offenders in all cases, irrespective of plea or previous convictions.

Step One
Determining the offence category

The court should determine the offence category using the table below.

Category 1	Greater harm **and** higher culpability
Category 2	Greater harm **and** lower culpability; **or** lesser harm **and** higher culpability
Category 3	Lesser harm **and** lower culpability

The court should determine the offender's culpability and the harm caused, or intended, by reference **only** to the factors below (as demonstrated by the presence of one or more). These factors comprise the principal factual elements of the offence and should determine the category.

Factors indicating greater harm

Injury (which includes disease transmission and/or psychological harm) which is serious in the context of the offence (must normally be present)

Victim is particularly vulnerable because of personal circumstances

Sustained or repeated assault on the same victim

Factors indicating lesser harm

Injury which is less serious in the context of the offence

Factors indicating higher culpability

Statutory aggravating factors:

Offence motivated by, or demonstrating, hostility to the victim based on his or her sexual orientation (or presumed sexual orientation)

Offence motivated by, or demonstrating, hostility to the victim based on the victim's disability (or presumed disability)

Other aggravating factors:

A significant degree of premeditation

Threatened or actual use of weapon or weapon equivalent (for example, shod foot, headbutting, use of acid, use of animal)

Intention to commit more serious harm than actually resulted from the offence

Deliberately causes more harm than is necessary for commission of offence

Deliberate targeting of vulnerable victim

Leading role in group or gang

Offence motivated by, or demonstrating, hostility based on the victim's age, sex, gender identity (or presumed gender identity)

Factors indicating lower culpability

Subordinate role in group or gang

A greater degree of provocation than normally expected

Lack of premeditation

Mental disorder or learning disability, where linked to commission of the offence

Excessive self defence

Step Two
Starting point and category range

Having determined the category, the court should use the corresponding starting points to reach a sentence within the category range below. The starting point applies to all offenders irrespective of plea or previous convictions. A case of particular gravity, reflected by multiple features of culpability in step one, could merit upward adjustment from the starting point before further adjustment for aggravating or mitigating features, set out below.

Offence Category	Starting Point *(Applicable to all offenders)*	Category Range *(Applicable to all offenders)*
Category 1	High level community order	Low level community order – 26 weeks' custody
Category 2	Medium level community order	Band A fine – High level community order
Category 3	Band A fine	Discharge – Band C fine

The table below contains a **non-exhaustive** list of additional factual elements providing the context of the offence and factors relating to the offender. Identify whether any combination of these, or other relevant factors, should result in an upward or downward adjustment from the starting point. In some cases, having considered these factors, it may be appropriate to move outside the identified category range.

When sentencing **category 1** offences, the court should also consider the custody threshold as follows:

- has the custody threshold been passed?
- if so, is it unavoidable that a custodial sentence be imposed?
- if so, can that sentence be suspended?

When sentencing **category 2** offences, the court should also consider the community order threshold as follows:

- has the community order threshold been passed?

Factors increasing seriousness

Statutory aggravating factors:

Previous convictions, having regard to a) the nature of the offence to which the conviction relates and its relevance to the current offence; and b) the time that has elapsed since the conviction

Offence committed whilst on bail

Other aggravating factors include:

Location of the offence

Timing of the offence

Ongoing effect upon the victim

Offence committed against those working in the public sector or providing a service to the public

Presence of others including relatives, especially children or partner of the victim

---

Gratuitous degradation of victim

In domestic violence cases, victim forced to leave their home

Failure to comply with current court orders

Offence committed whilst on licence

An attempt to conceal or dispose of evidence

Failure to respond to warnings or concerns expressed by others about the offender's behaviour

Commission of offence whilst under the influence of alcohol or drugs

Abuse of power and/or position of trust

Exploiting contact arrangements with a child to commit an offence

Established evidence of community impact

Any steps taken to prevent the victim reporting an incident, obtaining assistance and/or from assisting or supporting the prosecution

Offences taken into consideration (TICs)

Factors reducing seriousness or reflecting personal mitigation

No previous convictions **or** no relevant/recent convictions

Single blow

Remorse

Good character and/or exemplary conduct

Determination and/or demonstration of steps taken to address addiction or offending behaviour

Serious medical conditions requiring urgent, intensive or long-term treatment

Isolated incident

Age and/or lack of maturity where it affects the responsibility of the offender

Lapse of time since the offence where this is not the fault of the offender

Mental disorder or learning disability, where **not** linked to the commission of the offence

Sole or primary carer for dependent relatives

Section 29 offences only: The court should determine the appropriate sentence for the offence without taking account of the element of aggravation and then make an addition to the sentence, considering the level of aggravation involved. It may be appropriate to move outside the identified category range, taking into account the increased statutory maximum.

Step Three
Consider any other factors which indicate a reduction, such as
assistance to the prosecution

The court should take into account any rule of law by virtue of which an offender may receive a discounted sentence in consequence of assistance given (or offered) to the prosecutor or investigator.

Step Four
Reduction for guilty pleas

The court should take account of any potential reduction for a guilty plea in accordance with section 144 of the Criminal Justice Act 2003 and the *Guilty Plea* guideline.

Step Five
Dangerousness

Inflicting grievous bodily harm/unlawful wounding and racially/religiously aggravated GBH/unlawful wounding are specified offences within the meaning of Chapter 5 of the Criminal Justice Act 2003 and at this stage the court should consider whether having regard to the criteria contained in that Chapter it would be appropriate to award an extended sentence

Step Six
Totality principle

If sentencing an offender for more than one offence, or where the offender is already serving a sentence, consider whether the total sentence is just and proportionate to the offending behaviour.

Step Seven
Compensation and ancillary orders

In all cases, the court should consider whether to make compensation and/or other ancillary orders.

Step Eight
Reasons

Section 174 of the Criminal Justice Act 2003 imposes a duty to give reasons for, and explain the effect of, the sentence.

Step Nine
Consideration for remand time

Sentencers should take into consideration any remand time served in relation to the final sentence. The court should consider whether to give credit for time spent on remand in custody or on bail in accordance with sections 240 and 240A of the Criminal Justice Act 2003.

A[16]

Communications network offences

Charge

A[16.1]

A person is guilty of an offence if he—

(a)   sends by means of a public electronic communications network a message or other matter that is grossly offensive or of an indecent, obscene or menacing character; or

(b)   causes any such matter to be so sent

Communications Act 2003, s 127(1)

A person is guilty of an offence if he—

(a)   sends by means of a public electronic communications network, a message that he knows to be false,

(b)   causes such a message to be sent; or

(c)   persistently makes use of a public electronic communications network

Communications Act 2003, s 127(2)

Maximum penalty – level 5 fine and/or six months (**51 weeks). Triable summarily only.

Legal notes and definitions

A[16.2]

Actus reus. Under s 127, the act is the sending of a message of a prescribed character by the defined means ie by a public electronic communications network. Once the message has been sent the offence is complete. Thus, it makes no difference if the message is never received, for example, a recorded message is erased before anyone listens to it (*DPP v Collins* [2006] 4 All ER 602, [2006] UKHL 40).

A[16.3]

The criminality of a defendant's conduct is not dependent on whether a message is received by A, who for any reason is deeply offended, unlike B, who is not (*DPP v Collins* [2006] 4 All ER 602, [2006] UKHL 40).

A[16.4]

It is a question of fact whether a message is eg grossly offensive; that in making this determination the court must apply the standards on an open and just multi-racial society; and, that the words must be judged taking account of their context and all relevant circumstances. Usages and sensitivities may change over time. The test is whether a message is couched in terms liable to cause eg gross offence to those to whom it relates (*DPP v Collins* [2006] 4 All ER 602, [2006] UKHL 40).

A[16.5]

Intention. The defendant must intend his words to be eg grossly offensive to those to whom they relate, or be aware that they may be taken as such (*DPP v Collins* [2006] 4 All ER 602, [2006] UKHL 40).

A[16.6]

ECHR compatibility. S 127 (1) (a) does of course interfere with a person's right to freedom of expression. But it is a restriction clearly prescribed by statute. It is directed to a legitimate objective, preventing the use of a public electronic communications network for attacking the reputations and rights of others. It goes no further than is necessary in a democratic society to achieve that end. Effect must be given to article 17 of the Convention, as in *Norwood v United Kingdom* (2004) EHRR SE 111; *DPP v Collins* [2006] 4 All ER 602, [2006] UKHL 40.

Sentencing
SC Guideline – Communications network offences

A[16.7]

OFFENCE SERIOUSNESS (CULPABILITY AND HARM) A. IDENTIFY THE APPROPRIATE STARTING POINT Starting points based on first time offender pleading not guilty		
Sending grossly offensive, indecent, obscene or menacing messages (s 127(1))		
Examples of nature of activity	**Starting point**	**Range**
Single offensive, indecent, obscene or menacing call of short duration, having no significant impact on receiver	Band B fine	Band A fine to band C fine
Single call where extreme language used and substantial distress or fear caused to receiver; OR One of a series of similar calls as described in box above	Medium level community order	Low level community order to 12 weeks custody
Single call where extreme language used and substantial distress or fear caused to receiver; OR One of a series of similar calls as described in box above	6 weeks custody	High level community order to 12 weeks custody

Sending false message/persistent use of communications network for purpose of causing annoyance, inconvenience or needless anxiety (s 127(2))		
Examples of nature of activity	Starting point	Range
Persistent silent calls over short period to private individual, causing inconvenience or annoyance	Band B fine	Band A fine to band C fine
Single hoax call to public or private organisation resulting in moderate disruption or anxiety	Medium level community order	Low level community order to high level community order
Single hoax call resulting in major disruption or substantial public fear or distress; OR One of a series of similar calls as described in box above	12 weeks custody	High level community order to 18 weeks custody
OFFENCE SERIOUSNESS (CULPABILITY AND HARM) B. CONSIDER THE EFFECT OF AGGRAVATING AND MITIGATING FACTORS (OTHER THAN THOSE WITHIN EXAMPLES ABOVE) Common aggravating and mitigating factors are identified at B[5.2A]		
FORM A PRELIMINARY VIEW OF THE APPROPRIATE SENTENCE, THEN CONSIDER OFFENDER MITIGATION Common aggravating are identified at B[5.2A]		
CONSIDER A REDUCTION FOR A GUILTY PLEA		
CONSIDER ANCILLARY ORDERS, INCLUDING COMPENSATION Refer to B[18] for guidance on compensation Consult your legal adviser on guidance for availability of ANCILLARY ORDERS		
DECIDE SENTENCE GIVE REASONS		

A[17]

Community order, breach of

Charge

A[17.1]

That the offender has failed without reasonable excuse to comply with any of the requirements of a community order made on x date by x court. Contrary to Criminal Justice Act 2003, Sch 8.

Legal notes and definitions

A[17.2]

See [B17.17].

Burden and standard of proof. The burden is on the prosecutor; the standard of proof is beyond a reasonable doubt (*West Yorkshire Probation Board v Boulter* [2005 [EWHC 2342 (Admin), (2005) 169 JP 601).

Reasonable excuse. A community order takes effect when it is imposed and it remains in full force and effect until and unless it is quashed on appeal or revoked or amended by order of the court. Although the concept of "reasonable excuse" is broad there is no statutory provision which automatically suspends the operation of a community order pending an appeal against it (or the conviction on which it is based). It is not therefore a reasonable excuse for a defendant to fail to carry out the community order despite the lodging of a notice of appeal (*West Midlands Probation Board v Sutton Coldfield Magistrates' Courts* [2005] EWHC 15 (Admin)).

Failed. An offender who "fails to keep in touch" with his responsible officer in accordance with such instructions as he may from time to time be given by that officer, in the absence of documentary or supporting evidence to explain the failure, provided within a specified period of time eg 7 days, breaches the terms of the community order (*Richards v National Probation Service* [2007] EWHC 3108 (Admin)).

Sentencing
SC Guideline – Community order, breach of

A[17.3]

These notes are taken from the Sentencing Council's definitive guideline *New Sentences: CJA 2003* published 16 December 2004.

Options in breach proceedings:

When dealing with breaches of community orders for offences committed after 4 April 2005, the court must either:

- amend the terms of the original order so as to impose more onerous requirements. The court may extend the duration of particular requirements within the order, but it cannot extend the overall length of the original order (NB: s 38 of the Criminal Justice and Immigration Act 2008 reduces from 40 hours to 20 hours the minimum period of unpaid work that can be imposed on breach, provided that the order did not previously contain an unpaid work requirement); or
- fine*, by ordering the offender to pay a fine of an amount not exceeding £2,500; or
- revoke the original order and proceed to sentence for the original offence. Where an offender has wilfully and persistently failed to comply with an order made in respect of an offence that is not punishable by imprisonment, the court can impose of to six months custody (CJA, Sch 8, para 9(1)(c)).

*Available once s 67 of LASPOA 2012 is brought into force.

NB: revocation and re-sentence: in the case of an offence triable either way this does not include committal to the Crown Court for sentence pursuant to s 3 PCC (S) Act 2000 (*R v Jordan* [1998] Crim LR 353).

Approach to breach proceedings:

- having decided that a community order is commensurate with the seriousness of the offence, the primary objective when sentencing for breach of requirements is to ensure that those requirements are completed;
- a court sentencing for breach must take account of the extent to which the offender has complied with the requirements of the original order, the reasons for the breach, and the point at which the breach has occurred;
- if increasing the onerousness of requirements, sentencers should take account of the offender's ability to comply and should avoid precipitating further breach by overloading the offender with too many or conflicting requirements;
- there may be cases where the court will need to consider re-sentencing to a differently constructed community order in order to secure compliance with the purposes of the original sentence, perhaps where there has already been partial compliance or where events since the sentence was imposed have shown that a different course of action is likely to be effective;
- where available, custody should be the last resort, reserved for those cases of deliberate and repeated breach where all reasonable efforts to ensure that the offender complies have failed.

Where the original order was made by the Crown court, breach proceedings must be commenced in that court, unless the order provided that any failure to comply with its requirements may be dealt with a magistrates' court. **Consult your legal adviser for further guidance when dealing with breach of a community order made in the Crown Court.**

A[18]

Damage to property

Criminal damage (including by fire (arson)) and racially/ religiously aggravated criminal damage

Charge

A[18.1]

Without lawful excuse destroyed (or damaged) property namely [. . . . .] belonging to [. . . . .] intending to destroy (or damage) it or being reckless as to whether such property would be destroyed or damaged

Criminal Damage Act 1971, s 1

NB: Where the damage is under £500 and not normally over £300 a fixed penalty of £80 is available

A[18.2]

Maximum penalty and venue for trial – Where the damage or destruction is caused by fire (arson) the offence is triable either way without regard to the value of the damage caused and the maximum penalty is a fine on level 5 and 6 months' (**12 months') imprisonment. If it is alleged in the charge that the accused intended to endanger life, or was reckless as to whether life would be endangered, the offence is triable only on indictment and is punishable in the Crown Court with life imprisonment. Where the offence involves racial aggravation it will always be an either way offence (see below).

Offences of arson (s 1(3)) or where life is endangered (s 1(2)) are specified violent offences under Sch 15, Part 1, CJA 2003. See **B[16.5]** for guidance.

A[18.3]

The plea before venue procedure only applies to criminal damage allegations in excess of £5,000 (*R v Kelly* [2001] RTR 45, CA). If the value is ascertained as £5,000 or under the court must proceed to summary trial and the sentence will be restricted to a maximum of a level 4 fine and/or 3 months' imprisonment – or 6 months for two offences (*R v Gwynn* [2002] EWCA Crim 2951, [2003] All ER (D) 318 (Dec)).

A[18.4]

Where the defendant does not indicate a guilty plea and it is unclear to the court whether the value of the damage is more than £5,000 or not the court must decide whether the value is more or less than that sum (it is not necessary to decide what the value is, simply whether it is above £5,000).

If the court decides that the value of the damage exceeds £5,000 (and it may hear representations from the prosecution and defence to assist in arriving at a decision) then the offence is triable either way as in the preceding paragraph. Likewise if the court reaches a decision that the value of the damage does not exceed £5,000 the offence is triable summarily, as above. In those cases where the court is unable to decide whether the value is more or less than £5,000 the accused must be told that if he wishes he may consent to be tried summarily, and if he does he will be so tried and will be liable to a maximum penalty on level 4 and 3 months (** 51 weeks) (level 5 and 6 months (**12 months) in a case of aggravated vehicle taking). If the accused then consents, the trial will proceed summarily.

A[18.5]

If he does not consent, the court proceeds as for an ordinary either way offence, with the plea before venue and mode of trial procedure as is appropriate.

A[18.6]

Assessing the value of the damage. Unless the damage was caused by fire, or racial aggravation was involved, where property has been destroyed the mode of trial depends upon its value. This means what it would probably have cost to buy in the open market at the material time. See (*R (on application of DPP) v Prestatyn Magistrates' Courts* [2002] All ER (D) 421 (May)) for further guidance

A[18.7]

If the allegation is one of damage (excluding damage caused by fire) the mode of trial depends upon the value of the damage. If, immediately after the damage was caused, the property was capable of repair (eg a car windscreen) then the value of the damage is the lesser of: (a) what would probably have been the market price for the repair of the damage immediately after the damage was caused (this would, for example, not include the cost of repairing further deterioration since the offence); or (b) what the property would probably have cost to buy in the open market at the material time, whichever is the less. Thus, if it would cost more to repair the property than its probable market value, then the value of the damage for the purposes of deciding the venue of trial would be the probable market price. If, immediately after the damage was caused, the property was beyond repair (eg a shattered crystal decanter) then the value for trial purposes is its probable cost in the open market at the time of the offence.

A[18.8]

The use of the word 'probable' in the Act indicates that the court must make up its mind in the light of the available information.

A[18.9]

Multiple offences. Where an accused is charged with a series of offences of damage or destruction the offences are only triable either way if their aggregate value is in excess of £5,000.

A[18.10]–[18.15]

Mode of trial considerations. See SC Guidelines at A[18.32] below.

Charge

A[18.16]

Racially/religiously aggravated criminal damage

Crime and Disorder Act 1998, s 30

Maximum penalty – level 5 and 6 months' (**12 months) imprisonment. Triable either way. **Crown Court** – 14 years' imprisonment and unlimited fine.

A[18.17]

Racially/religiously aggravated. This means that at the time of committing the offence, of immediately before or after doing so, the offender demonstrates towards the victim's property hostility based on the victim's membership (or presumed membership) of a racial or religious group (see *Parry v DPP* [2004] EWHC 3112 (Admin), [2004] All ER (D) 335 (Dec) for guidance on immediacy); or the offence is motivated (wholly or partly) by hostility towards members of a racial or religious group based on their membership of that group. In *DPP v M* [2004] EWHC 1453 (Admin), [2004] All ER (D) 358 (May) the term 'bloody foreigners' was held to be a group defined by nationality and was hostile. In *R v Rogers* [2007] UKHL 8, it was decided that the term "foreigners" could constitute a racial group within the meaning of s 28(4) of the Crime and Disorder Act 1998. Whether the evidence in any particular case, taken as a whole, proved that the offender's conduct demonstrated hostility to such a group, or was motivated by such hostility, was a question of fact for the court.

A[18.18]

The victim's perceptions of the words used is irrelevant here, as is the fact that the defendant would have used those words to anyone with the victim's characteristics (*DPP v Woods* [2002] EWHC 85 (Admin), [2002] All ER (D) 154 (Jan)).

It is immaterial whether the offender's hostility is also based to any extent on any other factor not mentioned above.

Legal notes and definitions

A[18.19]

Without lawful excuse. It is a defence if the defendant proves he had a lawful excuse for destroying or damaging the property. He only has to establish that this defence is probably true, he does not have to establish it beyond reasonable doubt. Section 5(2) provides that, inter alia, the following can be lawful excuses:

(a)   that at the time he destroyed or damaged the property he believed that a person or persons entitled to consent to the destruction or damage had given consent; or that person or persons would have consented if he or they had known of the destruction or damage and the circumstances; or

(b)   that at the time he destroyed or damaged the property he believed that property belonging to himself or another was in immediate need of protection and that the adopted or proposed means of protection were reasonable in all the circumstances.

Provided that the defendant honestly held such a belief, it is immaterial whether the belief was justified or not (even if the defendant was drunk) (*Jaggard v Dickinson* [1981] QB 527, [1980] 3 All ER 716, [1981] 2 WLR 118, 72 Cr App Rep 33, [1980] Crim LR 717, 124 Sol Jo 847). See *R v Mitchell* [2003] EWCA Crim 2188, [2004] RTR 224, [2004] Crim LR 139, [2003] All ER (D) 99 (Aug) on possible defences to removing a wheel clamp.

Individuals facing charges for criminal damage and aggravated trespass arising out of their actions in protesting against the war in Iraq could not argue that they were using **reasonable force** to prevent the commission of a crime under s 3 of the Criminal Law Act 1967, nor that the activities of the activities of the Crown at military bases were unlawful (*R v Jones* [2006] UKHL 16).

The destruction of badger traps were not justified under s 5(2)(b) because the defendants did not cause the damage in order to protect property belonging to themselves or another person (*Currie v DPP* [2006] EWHC AER (D) 429 (Nov)).

A[18.20]

Destroy or damage. Where a defendant was initially unaware that he had done an act that in fact set in train events which, by the time he became aware of them, would make it obvious to anyone who troubled to give his mind to them that they presented a risk that property belonging to another would be damaged, he would be guilty if he did not try to prevent or reduce the damage because he gave no thought to the possibility of such a risk or having done so he decided not to prevent or reduce the risk. An example would be the man who, unawares, drops a lighted cigarette down a chair and later, on discovering the chair is smouldering, leaves the room not caring whether the chair catches light or not.

A[18.21]

Property is defined at length in s 10(1). It means property of a tangible nature and includes money. It also includes wild creatures which have been tamed or are ordinarily kept in captivity. It does not include mushrooms, fungus, flowers, fruit or foliage of a plant, shrub or tree which are growing wild on any land.

A[18.22]

Damage. Defendants who had painted graffiti on a pavement with a water-soluble whitewash in the expectation that the graffiti would be washed away by rainwater, were guilty especially since expense and inconvenience had been caused to the local authority which removed the marks before it rained. 'Damage' may be used in the sense of mischief to property. The 'temporary functional derangement' of a police officer's cap by the defendant's stamping on it constituted damage although it could be pushed back into shape. Accordingly the erasure of a computer program on a plastic circuit card was damage and although it could be restored, this necessitated time, labour and expense (*Cox v Riley* (1986) 83 Cr App Rep 54, [1986] Crim LR 460).

A[18.23]

Belonging to another person (s 10(2)). In addition to an ordinary owner this includes a person who had the custody or control of the property, or a proprietary right or interest in the property (except for an equitable interest arising only from an agreement to transfer or grant an interest), or who had a charge on the property.

A[18.24]

As far as trust property is concerned, it can be treated for the purposes of this offence as belonging to any person having the right to enforce the trust (s 10(3)).

A[18.25]–[18.30]

Intending. The court must decide whether the defendant intended the damage by considering all the evidence and drawing from it such inferences as appear proper in the circumstances.

A[18.31]

Reckless. A person is reckless with respect to:

(a)   a circumstance when he is aware of a risk, that it exists or will exist;
(b)   a result, when he is aware of a risk that it will occur; and
(c)   it is, in the circumstances known to him, unreasonable to take the risk (*R v G* [2003] UKHL 50, [2004] 1 AC 1034, [2003] 4 All ER 765, HL).

For a more recent example of the application of the test of recklessness see *Booth v Crown Prosecution Service* [2006] EWHC 192 (Admin), (2006) 170 JP 305, QBD.

Sentencing
SC Guideline – Arson (criminal damage by fire)

A[18.32]

Where offence committed in a domestic context, refer to SC Definitive Guideline: "Overarching Principles: Domestic Violence".

IDENTIFY DANGEROUS OFFENDERS

This is a serious offence for the purposes of the public protection provisions in the Criminal Justice Act 2003. Refer to **B[16.5]** and consult legal adviser for guidance		

OFFENCE SERIOUSNESS (CULPABILITY AND HARM)

A. IDENTIFY THE APPROPRIATE STARTING POINT

Starting points based on first time offender pleading not guilty

Examples of nature of activity	Starting point	Range
Minor damage by fire	High level community order	Medium level community order to 12 weeks custody
Moderate damage by fire	12 weeks custody	6 to 26 weeks custody
Significant damage by fire	Crown Court	Crown Court

OFFENCE SERIOUSNESS (CULPABILITY AND HARM)

B. CONSIDER THE EFFECT OF AGGRAVATING AND MITIGATING FACTORS (OTHER THAN THOSE WITHIN EXAMPLES ABOVE)

Common aggravating and mitigating factors are identified at **B[5.2A]**. The following may be particularly relevant but **these lists are not exhaustive**

Factors indicating higher culpability	*Factors indicating lower culpability*
1. Revenge attack	1. Damage caused recklessly
Factors indicating greater degree of harm	
1. Damage to emergency equipment	
2. Damage to public amenity	
3. Significant public or private fear caused eg in domestic context	

FORM A PRELIMINARY VIEW OF THE APPROPRIATE SENTENCE, THEN CONSIDER OFFENDER MITIGATION

Common factors are identified at **B[5.2A]**

CONSIDER A REDUCTION FOR A GUILTY PLEA

CONSIDER ANCILLARY ORDERS, INCLUDING COMPENSATION

Refer to **B[18]** for guidance on compensation.

DECIDE SENTENCE

GIVE REASONS

SC Guideline – Criminal damage – other than by fire)
SC Guideline – Racially or religiously aggravated criminal damage

Racially or religiously aggravated damage: Refer to **B[5.2B]** for further guidance

Where offence committed in a domestic context, refer to SC Definitive Guideline: "Overarching Principles: Domestic Violence".

OFFENCE SERIOUSNESS (CULPABILITY AND HARM)		
A. IDENTIFY THE APPROPRIATE STARTING POINT		
Starting points based on first time offender pleading not guilty		
Examples of nature of activity	**Starting point**	**Range**
Minor damage eg breaking small window; small amount of graffiti	Band B fine	Conditional discharge to band C fine
Moderate damage eg breaking large plate-glass or shop window; widespread graffiti	Low level community order	Band C fine to medium level community order
Significant damage up to £5,000 eg damage caused as part of a spree	High level community order	Medium level community order to 12 weeks custody
Damage between £5,000 and £10,000	12 weeks custody	6 to 26 weeks custody
Damage over £10,000	Crown Court	Crown Court

OFFENCE SERIOUSNESS (CULPABILITY AND HARM)
B. CONSIDER THE EFFECT OF AGGRAVATING AND MITIGATING FACTORS (OTHER THAN THOSE WITHIN EXAMPLES ABOVE)
Common aggravating and mitigating factors are identified at **B[5.2A]**. The following may be particularly relevant but **these lists are not exhaustive**

Factors indicating higher culpability	*Factors indicating lower culpability*
1. Revenge attack	1. Damage caused recklessly
2. Targeting vulnerable victim	2. Provocation
Factors indicating greater degree of harm	
1. Damage to emergency equipment	
2. Damage to public amenity	
3. Significant public or private fear caused eg in domestic context	

FORM A PRELIMINARY VIEW OF THE APPROPRIATE SENTENCE
IF OFFENDER CHARGED AND CONVICTED OF THE RACIALLY OR RELIGIOUSLY AGGRAVATED OFFENCE, INCREASE THE SENTENCE TO REFLECT THE ELEMENT
Common factors are identified at **B[5.2B]**
CONSIDER OFFENDER MITIGATION
Common factors are identified at **B[5.2A]**
CONSIDER A REDUCTION FOR A GUILTY PLEA
CONSIDER ANCILLARY ORDERS, INCLUDING COMPENSATION
Refer to **B[18]** for guidance on compensation.
DECIDE SENTENCE
GIVE REASONS

A[18A]

Threatening to destroy or damage property

(Criminal Damage Act 1971, s 2(a))

Charge

A[18A.1]

Without lawful excuse made to [. . . . .] a threat to destroy (or damage) property belonging to that other person (or belonging to a third person), intending that the other person would fear it would be carried out

Maximum penalty – Fine level 5 and 6 months (**12 months). Triable either way.

The legal notes and definitions relating to the previous offence at **A[18]** also apply here, except for the reference to compensation and mode of trial. The threats can be spoken or in writing.

Crown Court – 10 years' imprisonment and unlimited fine.

A[18B]

Possessing anything with intent to destroy or damage property

(Criminal Damage Act 1971, s 3(a))

Charge

A[18B.1]

Had in his custody (or under his control) a [] intending without lawful excuse to use it to destroy (or damage) property belonging to another person

Maximum penalty – Fine level 5 and 6 months (**12 months). Triable either way.

The legal notes and definitions relating to offence no 1 at **A[18]** also apply here except for mode of trial.

Crown Court – 10 years' imprisonment and unlimited fine.

A[19]

Cruelty to a child

Charge

A[19.1]

Having responsibility for a child or young person under the age of 16 and wilfully assaulting, ill-treating, neglecting, abandoning, or exposing him in a manner likely to cause him unnecessary suffering or injury to health

Children and Young Persons Act 1933, s 1, as amended

Maximum penalty – Fine level 5 and 6 months (**12 months). Triable either way. Specified violent offence under Sch 15, Part 1, CJA 2003.

Crown Court – 10 years' imprisonment and unlimited fine.

Mode of trial

A[19.2]

Consider the **SC guideline** at **A[19.32]** below.

A[19.3]

All or any of the types of cruelty listed in the charge above can be included in a single information but on conviction one penalty must cover the lot.

A[19.4]

The offence of cruelty can only be committed by a person over the age of 16.

A[19.5]

Exemptions. The Act expressly stipulates that a parent or teacher or other person having lawful control of a child or young person is not guilty of this offence if the child is punished by them moderately and reasonably.

A[19.6]

A child. Means someone under 14 years of age.

A[19.7]

A young person. Means for this offence someone aged 14 or 15 years.

A[19.8]

Wilfully. Means deliberately (as opposed to accidentally or by mistake or inadvertence) or because the defendant knew there was a risk or he was unaware of the risk because he did not care that the treatment of the child was likely to cause him unnecessary suffering etc. The legal adviser should be consulted on this concept and it appears that in a case of assault whether the force used was moderate and reasonable is to be decided by the magistrates. The prosecution only has to prove that the defendant intended to use *force*.

A[19.9]–[19.15]

Assaulting. See under the charge of 'Common assault', at A[15].

A[19.16]

Ill-treating. Actual assault or battery need not be proved. Bullying or frightening or any course of conduct calculated to cause unnecessary suffering or injury to health will suffice.

A[19.17]

Neglecting. Means omitting to take such steps as a reasonable parent would take and can include failing to apply for state benefits. Failure to obtain medical care can amount to neglect. It is a question of fact which the magistrates have to determine in each case.

A[19.18]

Abandoning. Means leaving the child to his fate. In one case a child was carefully packed in a hamper and sent by train to the father's address and although the child came to no harm it was held that the child had been abandoned.

A[19.19]

In another case a child had been left on his doorstep and the father knew he was there and permitted the child to remain there during an October night for six hours. It was held that he had abandoned the child.

A[19.20]

Leaving children at a youth court has been held not to be an offence under this section.

A[19.21]

Exposing. It is not necessary to prove that the defendant intended to cause suffering or injury to health. The requisite is that the defendant exposed the child or young person in a manner which was likely to cause unnecessary suffering or injury to health.

A[19.22]

In a manner likely to cause him unnecessary suffering or injury to health. This part of the offence must be proved in addition to wilfully assaulting, ill-treating, neglecting, abandoning or exposing as set out in the charge.

A[19.23]

Presumption of guilt. A parent or person legally liable to maintain a child or young person will be presumed to have neglected the child or young person in a manner likely to cause injury to health if he has failed to provide adequate food, clothing, medical aid or lodging. If the parent has been unable to provide any of these things he will still be presumed to have neglected him if he fails to apply for them under state benefits. (However the prosecution must still establish that this neglect was 'wilful'.)

A[19.24]

Dealing with the children. As the defendant is almost always over the age of 18, this offence is usually tried in the adult court.

A[19.25]–[19.30]

Either before the charge is heard in the adult court or concurrently it is often the practice that the ill-treated child or young person is brought before the family proceedings court as in need of care and the family proceedings court can make a care order placing the child or young person in the care of a local authority.

A[19.31]

The court may direct that nothing may be published or broadcast which would identify any child concerned; the legal adviser should be consulted.

Sentencing
SC Guideline – Cruelty to children

A[19.32]

This guideline and accompanying notes are taken from the Sentencing Council's definitive guideline *Overarching Principles: Assaults on children and Cruelty to a child* published February 2008 and coming into force for persons sentenced on or after 3 March 2008

For cases of domestic violence. See SC Definitive Guideline: 'Overarching Principles: Domestic Violence'.

*The court <u>must</u> inform the defendant that the Independent Safeguarding Authority (<u>known</u> as the Independent Barring Board) will automatically ban him/her from working with children and/or vulnerable adults. As the court has no role in the decision if the defendant needs any further advice he/she should consult a solicitor.

Key factors

(a)   The same starting point and sentencing range is proposed for offences which might fall into the four categories (assault; ill-treatment or neglect; abandonment; and, failure to protect). These are designed to take into account the fact that the victim is particularly vulnerable, assuming an abuse of trust or power and the likelihood of psychological harm, and designed to reflect the seriousness with which society as a whole regards these offences.

(b) As noted above, the starting points have been calculated to reflect the likelihood of psychological harm and this cannot be treated as an aggravating factor. Where there is an especially serious physical or psychological effect on the victim, even if unintended, this should increase the sentence.

(c) The normal sentencing starting point for an offence of child cruelty should be a custodial sentence. The length of that sentence will be influenced by the circumstances in which the offence took place.

(d) However, in considering whether a custodial sentence is the most appropriate disposal, the court should take into account any available information concerning the future care of the child.

(e) Where the offender is the sole or primary carer of the victim or other dependants, this potentially should be taken into account for sentencing purposes, regardless of whether the offender is male or female. In such cases, an immediate custodial sentence may not be appropriate.

(f) The most relevant areas of personal mitigation are likely to be:
- Mental illness/depression
- Inability to cope with the pressures of parenthood
- Lack of support
- Sleep deprivation
- Offender dominated by an abusive or stronger partner
- Extreme behavioural difficulties in a child, often coupled with lack of support
- Inability to secure assistance or support services in spite of every effort having been made by the offender

Some of the factors identified above, in particular sleep deprivation, lack of support and an inability to cope, could be regarded as an inherent part of caring for children, especially when a child is very young and could be put forward as mitigation by most carers charged with an offence of child cruelty. It follows that, before being accepted as mitigation, there must be evidence that these factors were present to a high degree and had an identifiable and significant impact on the offender's behaviour.

IDENTIFY DANGEROUS OFFENDERS		
This is a serious offence for the purposes of the public protection provisions in the Criminal Justice Act 2003. Refer to B[16.5] and consult legal adviser for guidance		
OFFENCE SERIOUSNESS (CULPABILITY AND HARM) A. IDENTIFY THE APPROPRIATE STARTING POINT Starting points based on first time offender pleading not guilty		
Examples of nature of activity	Starting point	Range
(i) Short term neglect or ill-treatment.	12 weeks custody	Low level community order to 26 weeks custody

(ii) Single incident of short-term abandonment.		
(iii) Failure to protect a child from any of the above.		
(i) Assault(s) resulting in injuries consistent with ABH.	Crown Court	26 weeks to Crown Court
(ii) More than one incident of neglect or ill-treatment (but not amounting to long-term behaviour.		
(iii) Single incident of long-term abandonment OR regular incidents of short-term abandonment (the longer the period of long-term abandonment or the greater the number of incidents of short-term abandonment, the more serious the offence).		
(iv) Failure to protect a child from any of the above.		
(i) Series of assaults (the more serious the individual assaults an the longer the period over which they are perpetrated, the more serious the offence.	Crown	Crown Court
(ii) Protracted neglect or ill-treatment (the longer the period of ill-treatment or neglect and the longer the period over which it takes place, the more serious the offence).		
(iii) Failure to protect a child from any of the above.		
(i) Serious cruelty over a period of time.	Crown Court	Crown Court
(ii) Serious long-term neglect.		
(iii) Failure to protect a child from any of the above.		

OFFENCE SERIOUSNESS (CULPABILITY AND HARM)	
B. CONSIDER THE EFFECT OF AGGRAVATING AND MITIGATING FACTORS (OTHER THAN THOSE WITHIN THE EXAMPLES ABOVE) Common aggravating and mitigating factors are identified at **B[5.2A]**. The following may be particularly relevant but these lists are not exhaustive	
Factors indicating higher culpability	*Factor indicating lower culpability*
1. Targeting one particular child from family.	1. Seeking medical help or bringing the situation to the notice of the authorities.
2. Sadistic behaviour.	
3. Threats to prevent the victim from reporting the offence.	
4. Deliberate concealment of the victim from the authorities.	
5. Failure to seek medical help.	
FORM A PRELIMINARY VIEW OF THE APPROPRIATE SENTENCE, THEN CONSIDER OFFENDER MITIGATION Common factors are identified at **B[5.2A]**	
CONSIDER A REDUCTION FOR A GUILTY PLEA	
CONSIDER ANCILLARY ORDERS, INCLUDING COMPENSATION Consult your legal adviser on guidance for available ANCILLARY ORDERS Refer to **B[18]** for guidance on compensation.	
DECIDE SENTENCE **GIVE REASONS**	

A[19.33]

Available sentences. See Table A at **B[4.1]**.

If two or more children are concerned in the same occasion then all of them can be included in one charge and if this is done then only one penalty can be imposed for the one collective charge and not a penalty for each child (s 14). If the prosecution has brought a separate charge for each child, then a separate penalty can be ordered for each charge.

A[19.34]

As mentioned above, if in the case of an individual child one information is laid alleging assault, ill-treatment, neglect, etc, only one penalty may be imposed.

A[20]

Disorderly behaviour (harassment, alarm or distress) Racially/religiously aggravated disorderly behaviour (harassment, alarm or distress)

Charges

A[20.1]

Using threatening, abusive or insulting words or behaviour or disorderly behaviour (or displaying any writing, sign or other visible representation which is threatening, abusive or insulting) within the hearing or sight of a person likely to be caused harassment, alarm or distress thereby

Public Order Act 1986, s 5

Maximum penalty – Fine level 3. Triable only by magistrates.

NB: A fixed penalty of £80 is available for a s 5 offence of disorderly behaviour

A[20.2]

Racially or religiously aggravated threats, abuse or insulting or disorderly behaviour

Crime and Disorder Act 1998, s 31

Maximum penalty – Fine level 4. Triable only by magistrates.

Legal notes and definitions

A[20.3]

This offence is designed to deal with such cases as groups of youths persistently shouting abuse and obscenities, rowdy behaviour in the street late at night, hooligans causing disturbances in the common parts of flats, banging on doors, knocking over dustbins and throwing items downstairs.

A[20.3A]

Harassment; alarm; distress. Distress by its very nature involved an element of emotional disturbance or upset. The same could not be said of harassment. A person could be seriously harassed without any emotional disturbance or upset (*Southard v DPP* [2006] All ER (D) 101 (Nov), distinguishing on the facts *R v DPP* [2006] All ER (D) 250 (May)).

Taking a photograph of the complainant; transferring the photograph onto a computer followed by a posting of the same on the internet with the words "C'mon I'd love to eat you! We're the Covance Cannibals" held to amount to *intentional harassment* etc where the complainant was shown a hard copy some five months later (*S v DPP* judgment delivered February 8, 2008).

A[20.4]

The charge. Only one offence is created. However, the racially/religiously aggravated offence can be heard at the same time as alternative offences (*R (CPS) v Blaydon Youth Court* (2004)).

A[20.5]

Threatening; abusive; insulting; ECHR. See A[21] and A[21.5].

The principles governing the relationship between s 5 and article 10 could be summarised as follows. The starting point was the importance of the right to freedom of expression, but it was recognised that legitimate protest could be offensive, at least to some. The justification for interference had to be convincingly established and the restrictions in art 10(2) were to be construed narrowly. The justification for invoking the criminal law was the threat to public order and was for the Crown to establish. If the line between legitimate freedom of expression and a threat to public order was crossed, freedom of speech would not be impaired by 'ruling out' threatening, abusive or insulting speech: *Abdul v DPP* [2011] EWHC 247 (Admin), 175 JP 190, [2011] Crim LR 553.

A[20.6]

Racially/religiously aggravated. This means that at the time of committing the offence, or immediately before or after doing so, the offender demonstrates towards the victim of the offence, hostility based on the victim's membership (or presumed membership) of a racial or religious group, or the offence is motivated (wholly or partly) by hostility towards members of a racial or religious group based on their membership of that group.

Use of the words 'bloody foreigners' and 'go back to your own country' was capable of amounting to racially aggravated abuse (*R v Rogers* [2007] UKHL 8). The court should focus on whether the alleged remark had been made, whether it was a remark which demonstrated racial hostility, and whether s 28(1)(a) or (b) was engaged. On the facts found it was impossible to say whether the offence was motivated in part by racial hostility or by something quite different, namely the defendant's removal from hospital premises: see *R (on the application of the Director of Public Prosecutions) v Dykes* [2008] EWHC 2775 (Admin), (2009) 173 JP 88.

In *Kendall v South East Essex Magistrates' Court* [2008] All ER (D) 356 (Jun) it was open to justices to conclude that the defendant had been aware that posters which he had put on an advertising pillar, and which displayed the words "illegal, immigrant, murdered, scum" had conveyed the message that black people who committed crimes like murder were "scum".

Having regard to the language of s 28(1)(b) of the CDA 1998, if there is no evidence of racial or religious motivation there could be no conviction. See (*DPP v Howard* [2008] All ER (D) 88 (Feb)). Where a charge is brought under s 28(1)(a), the test is objective and the prosecution do not have to prove motive, simply the relevant behaviour: *Jones v DPP* [2010] EWHC 523 (Admin), [2010] 3 All ER 1057, 174 JP 278.

A[20.7]

It is immaterial whether or not the offender's hostility is also based, to any extent, on any other factor not mentioned above, nor is the victim's perception nor the defendant's usual usage of the words uttered relevant (*DPP v Woods* [2002] EWHC 85 (Admin), [2002] All ER (D) 154 (Jan)).

A[20.8]

Another person. The defendant's behaviour must be within the hearing or sight of a person likely to be caused harassment etc. The prosecution must identify the person who was likely to have been alarmed etc though he need not be called as a witness. In *Chambers and Edwards v DPP* [1995] Crim LR 896 demonstrators made it difficult for a surveyor to carry out his work. Although the surveyor was in no fear for his safety, his annoyance and inconvenience were sufficient to meet the requirements of the section. For further developments see *R (on the application of Reda) v DPP* [2011] EWHC 1550 (Admin) at A[9.5]. In *Harvey v DPP* [2011] EWHC 3992 (Admin), 176 JP 265, [2012] Crim LR 553, commonplace swear words used by the appellant were capable of causing police officers to experience harassment, alarm or distress. Much would depend on the facts, but where a witness was silent on the point, it would be wrong to draw inferences. Accordingly, there was no evidence whereby the justices could have concluded that either police officer had been caused or was likely to have been caused harassment, alarm or distress. As for a group of young people who gathered during the exchanges, the words uttered were commonplace swear words in contrast to the far more offensive terms used in the case of *Taylor v DPP* [2006] EWHC 1202 (Admin), 170 JP 485, 170 JPN 856. It was wrong to infer, in the absence of evidence of evidence from any of them, that one or more persons would have experienced harassment, alarm or distress. As for neighbours and people in the adjoining flats, there was no evidence that anybody other than the group of young people was within earshot. If there had been evidence, for example, of apparently frightened neighbours leaning out of windows or of similar passers-by within earshot, that might have formed the basis of a finding that such persons were caused alarm or distress.

A[20.9]

Vigon v DPP (1997) 162 JP 115, [1998] Crim LR 289 – A concealed camera in a changing cubicle is capable of being disorderly and insulting behaviour.

A[20.10]

Intent. The accused must intend his words or behaviour etc to be, or be aware that his words etc may be threatening, abusive or insulting, or intend his behaviour to be or is aware that it may be disorderly.

A[20.11]–[20.15]

Visible Representation. *R v Norwood* [2002] Crim LR 888 set out the four elements that need to be proved in such a case.

A[20.16]

Intoxication. See under the offence of violent disorder, at A[67]. Disorderly conduct may be committed in a public or private place. For offences committed in dwelling-houses see under the offence of threatening behaviour below, at A[21].

A[20.17]

Defences. Where the accused proves

(a)   that he had no reason to believe that there was any person within hearing or sight who was likely to be caused harassment, alarm or distress, or
(b)   that he was inside a dwelling and had no reason to believe that the words or behaviour used, or the writing, sign or other visible representation displayed, would be heard or seen by a person outside that or any other dwelling, or
(c)   that his conduct was reasonable,

he must be acquitted. He does not have to establish his defence beyond a reasonable doubt, but only on the balance of probabilities.

A[20.18]

Power of arrest. Police powers of arrest under what was s 5 of the Public Order Act 1986 are now governed by s 24 of the Police and Criminal Evidence Act 1984 as substituted by Part 3, s 110 of the Serious Organised Crime and Police Act 2005.

For the police to justify an arrest a constable has to show two things: first, under the Police and Criminal Evidence Act 1984, s 24(2), that he had reasonable grounds for suspecting that an offence had been committed and that H was guilty of it; second, that he had reasonable grounds for believing that it was necessary to arrest H to allow the prompt and effective investigation of the offence, as per s 24(4) and s 24(5)(e): see *Hayes v Chief Constable of Merseyside* [2011] EWCA Civ 911, [2012] 1 WLR 517, [2011] 2 Cr App Rep 434.

Sentencing

A[20.19]

Domestic violence. See SC Definitive Guideline: "Overarching Principles: Domestic Violence".

Available sentences. See Table C at B[4.3].

These offences are is not imprisonable and therefore sentences such as detention in a young offender institution are *not* available.

SC Guideline – (1) Disorderly behaviour (harassment, alarm or distress)
(2) Racially or religiously aggravated disorderly behaviour

OFFENCE SERIOUSNESS (CULPABILITY AND HARM)		
A. IDENTIFY THE APPROPRIATE STARTING POINT		
Starting points based on first time offender pleading not guilty		
Examples of nature of activity	**Starting point**	**Range**
Shouting, causing disturbance for some minutes	Band A fine	Conditional discharge to band B fine
Substantial disturbance caused	Band B fine	Band A fine to band C fine

OFFENCE SERIOUSNESS (CULPABILITY AND HARM)
B. CONSIDER THE EFFECT OF AGGRAVATING AND MITIGATING FACTORS (OTHER THAN THOSE WITHIN THE EXAMPLES ABOVE)
Common aggravating and mitigating factors are identified at **B[5.2A]**. The following may be particularly relevant but **these lists are not exhaustive**

Factors indicating higher culpability	*Factors indicating lower culpability*
1. Group action	1. Stopping as soon as police arrvied
2. Lengthy incident	2. Brief/minor incident
	3. Provocation
Factors indicating greater degree of harm	
1. Vulnerable person(s) present	
2. Offence committed at school, hospital or other place where vulnerable persons may be present	
3. Victim providing public service	

FORM A PRELIMINARY VIEW OF THE APPROPRIATE SENTENCE
IF OFFENDER CHARGED AND CONVICTED OF THE RACIALLY OR RELIGIOUSLY AGGRAVATED OFFENCE, INCREASE THE SENTENCE TO REFLECT THIS ELEMENT
Refer to B[5.2B] for guidance
CONSIDER OFFENDER MITIGATION
Common factors are identified at **B[5.2A]**
CONSIDER A REDUCTION FOR A GUILTY PLEA
CONSIDER ANCILLARY ORDERS, INCLUDING COMPENSATION AND FOOTBALL BANNING ORDER (where appropriate)
Consult your legal adviser on guidance for available ANCILLARY ORDERS
DECIDE SENTENCE
GIVE REASONS

A[20.20]

Bind over. See the amended Consolidated Criminal Practice Direction and associated notes at [B10] onwards.

A[21]

(1) Threatening behaviour
(2) Racially or religiously aggravated threatening behaviour
(3) Disorderly behaviour with intent to cause harassment, alarm or distress
(4) Racially or religiously aggravated disorderly behaviour with intent to cause harassment, alarm or distress

Charge 1

A[21.1]

Using towards another threatening, abusive or insulting words or behaviour (or distributing or displaying to another person any writing, sign or other visible representation being threatening, abusive or insulting) intending to cause that other person to believe that immediate unlawful violence would be used against him or another by any person, or to provoke the immediate use of unlawful violence by that person or another or whereby that other person was likely to believe that such violence would be used or it was likely that such violence would be provoked

Public Order Act 1986, s 4(1)

Maximum penalty – Fine level 5 and 6 months (**51 weeks). Triable only by magistrates.

Charge 2

A[21.2]

A person is guilty of an offence if with intent to cause a person harassment, alarm and distress, he

(a)   uses threatening, abusive or insulting words or behaviour, or
(b)   displays any writing, sign or visible representation which is threatening, abusive or insulting,

thereby causing that or another person harassment, alarm or distress

Public Order Act 1986, s 4A

Maximum penalty – Fine level 4 and 6 months (**51 weeks). Triable only by magistrates.

Charge 3

A[21.3]

Using towards another threatening, abusive or insulting words or behaviour etc which was racially or religiously aggravated.

Crime and Disorder Act 1998, s 31

Maximum penalty – see Charge 4 below.

Charge 4

A[21.4]

Intentional harassment alarm or distress etc which is racially or religiously aggravated.

Crime and Disorder Act 1998, s 31

Maximum penalty – Fine level 5 and 6 months' imprisonment (**12 months). Triable either way. Specified violent offence under Sch 15, Part 1, CJA 2003.

Crown Court – 2 years' imprisonment and unlimited fine.

Legal notes and definitions

A[21.5]

Threatening; abusive; insulting. (The following comments are based on repealed legislation but still seem applicable.) The High Court has described these as being 'all very strong words'. If the evidence shows that the words or behaviour used fell short of being abusive, insulting or threatening but merely annoying then the case should be dismissed. The words 'f . . . off' shouted at a police officer who was trying to prevent a breach of the peace have been held to be 'insulting'. Shouting encouragement to a gang throwing stones at another gang is sufficient for a conviction under this section. See *Hammond v DPP* [2004] EWHC 69 (Admin), [2004] All ER (D) 50 (Jan) and *Percy v DPP* [2001] EWHC 1125 (Admin), 166 JP 93, [2002] Crim LR 835, [2001] All ER (D) 387 (Dec). Insulting words or an insulting sign should cause harassment, alarm or distress to another not just strong disagreement.

A[21.5A]

ECHR. In *Dehal v DPP* [2005] EWHC 2154 (Admin), [2005] All ER (D) 152 (Sep), the defendant had entered a Sikh Temple and affixed a notice to a notice board which, inter alia, described the president of the Temple as a hypocrite. The Administrative Court held that in order to justify the interference with a right to freedom of expression as set out in art 10 of the ECHR, the prosecution had to demonstrate that the prosecution was being brought in pursuance of a legitimate aim and that the prosecution was the minimum necessary response to that aim. Accordingly, the prosecution of the defendant had not been a proportionate response to his conduct.

A[21.6]

Violence does not include violence justified by law (eg self-defence or prevention of crime). The violence apprehended must be immediate which does not mean 'instantaneous' but connotes proximity in time and causation (*R v Horseferry Road Metropolitan Stipendiary Magistrate, ex p Siadatan* [1991] 1 QB 260, [1991] 1 All ER 324). Where the defendant threatened to shoot the complainant coupled with a shooting gesture with his hand, the combination of the hand gesture together with his loud and threatening language satisfied the test of 'immediacy' (*Liverpool v DPP* [2008] EWHC 2540 (Admin), [2008] All ER (D) 50 (Oct)). For what is included under the offence of violent disorder see **A[67]**.

A[21.7]

Intent. The accused must *intend* his words or behaviour etc to be, or be aware that his words etc may be, threatening, abusive or insulting and intend the apprehension of unlawful violence etc. In order to ensure that an arrest is lawful the defendant must be warned first about his conduct. This warning is not however part of the offence and so a case can still be determined where the arrest was not lawful (*DPP v Chippendale* [2004] EWHC 464 (Admin), [2004] All ER (D) 308 (Jan)).

Where an appellant had struggled whilst restrained by nightclub doormen, a magistrates' court was entitled to convict him under s 4(1) of the Public Order Act 1986 on the basis that he had intended to cause the doormen to believe that he would use unlawful violence against them if they released him: *Knight v DPP* [2012] EWHC 605 (Admin), 176 JP 177.

By contrast, a court erred in concluding that the appellant had intended to cause his victim to believe that unlawful violence would be used against him, where the appellant had approached the victim in such a way that the victim had not realised that he was about to be attacked: *Hughes v DPP* [2012] EWHC 606 (Admin), [2012] All ER (D) 180 (Jan). The appellant should have been charged with assault by beating.

A[21.8]

Intoxication. See under the offence of violent disorder at **A[67]**.

A[21.9]

Threatening etc behaviour may be committed in a public or private place. If the threatening etc words or behaviour are used inside a dwelling-house, the offence can only be committed if the other person is not inside that or another dwelling-house, but parts of a dwelling not occupied as a person's house or living accommodation do not count as a dwelling for this purpose, eg the shop underneath the owner's flat; a laundry used by the residents of a block of flats: *Ian Norman Levine v DPP* [2010] May 6, 2010, QBD. A tent, caravan, vehicle, vessel or other temporary or movable structure may be a dwelling for this purpose where it is occupied as a person's house or as other living accommodation. A police cell could not be classified as a dwelling or living accommodation for the purposes of s 4A (2) of the Public Order Act 1986 (*R v Francis* [2007] EWCA Crim 3323).

A[21.10]–[21.15]

Racial/religious aggravation. See A[20.6]. Words such as 'jungle bunny', 'black bastard' and 'wog' will be a racial aggravation regardless of the fact that the defendant may have some other reason to abuse the victim (*DPP v McFarlane* [2002] EWHC 485 (Admin), [2002] All ER (D) 78 (Mar)). Use of the words "bloody foreigners" and "go back to your own country" was capable of being racially aggravated abuse (*R v Rogers* [2007] UKHL 8).

May often be sent to Crown Court for sentence and will usually result in a custodial sentence (*R v Miller* [1999] 2 Cr App Rep (S) 392, [1999] Crim LR 590, CA and *R v White* [2001] EWCA Crim 216 [2001] 1 WLR 1352, [2001] Crim LR 576).

Police officers are also entitled to the protection of the courts. See *Re Emma Lisa Jacobs* (2001) where a sentence of 3 months' imprisonment was upheld.

Sentencing
SC Guideline – (1) Threatening behaviour (2) Racially or religiously aggravated threatening behaviour

A[21.16]

(**Section 4A** disorderly behaviour and the racially/religiously aggravated SC guideline is at **A[21.17]** below)

Domestic violence. See SC Definitive Guideline: "Overarching Principles: Domestic Violence"

OFFENCE SERIOUSNESS (CULPABILITY AND HARM)		
A. IDENTIFY THE APPROPRIATE STARTING POINT		
Starting points based on first time offender pleading not guilty		
Examples of nature of activity	Starting point	Range
Fear or threat of low level immediate unlawful violence such as push, shove or spit	Low level community penalty	Band B fine to medium level community order
Fear or threat or medium level immediate unlawful violence such as punch	High level community order	Low level community order to 12 weeks custody

Fear or threat of high level immediate unlawful violence such as use of weapon; missile thrown; gang involvement	12 weeks custody	6 to 26 weeks custody

OFFENCE SERIOUSNESS (CULPABILITY AND HARM)

B. CONSIDER THE EFFECT OF AGGRAVATING AND MITIGATING FACTORS (OTHER THAN THOSE WITHIN EXAMPLES ABOVE)

Common aggravating and mitigating factors are identified at B[5.2A]. The following may be particularly relevant but **these lists are not exhaustive**

Factors indicating higher culpability	*Factors indicating lower culpability*
1. Planning	1. Impulsive action
2. Offender deliberately isolates victim	2. Short duration
3. Group action	3. Provocation
4. Threat directed at victim because of job	
5. History of antagonism towards victim	
Factors indicating greater degree of harm	
1. Offence committed at school, hospital or other place where vulnerable victims may be present	
2. Offence committed on enclosed premises such as public transport	
3. Vulnerable victim(s)	
4. Victim needs medical help/counselling	

FORM A PRELIMINARY VIEW OF THE APPROPRIATE SENTENCE

IF OFFENDER CHARGED AND CONVICTED OF THE RACIALLY OR RELIGIOUSLY AGGRAVATED OFFENCE, INCREASE THE SENTENCE TO REFLECT THE ELEMENT

Common factors are identified at B[5.2B]

CONSIDER OFFENDER MITIGATION

Common factors are identified at B[5.2A]

CONSIDER A REDUCTION FOR A GUILTY PLEA

CONSIDER ANCILLARY ORDERS, INCLUDING COMPENSATION AND FOOTBALL BANNING ORDER (where appropriate)

Refer to B[18] for guidance on compensation.

DECIDE SENTENCE

GIVE REASONS

SC Guideline – (3) Disorderly behaviour with intent etc (4) Racially or religiously aggravated threatening behaviour with intent etc

A[21.17]

(**Section 4** threatening behaviour and the racially/religiously aggravated SC guideline is at **A[21.16]** above)

Domestic violence. See SC Definitive Guideline: "Overarching Principles: Domestic Violence"

OFFENCE SERIOUSNESS (CULPABILITY AND HARM)		
A. IDENTIFY THE APPROPRIATE STARTING POINT		
Starting points based on first time offender pleading not guilty		
Examples of nature of activity	**Starting point**	**Range**
Threats, abuse or insults made more than once but on same occasion against the same person eg while following down the street	Band C fine	Band B fine to low level community order
Group action or deliberately planned action against targeted victim	Medium level community order	Low level community order to 12 weeks custody
Weapon brandished or used or threats against vulnerable victim – course of conduct over longer period	12 weeks custody	High level community order to 26 weeks custody
OFFENCE SERIOUSNESS (CULPABILITY AND HARM)		
B. CONSIDER THE EFFECT OF AGGRAVATING AND MITIGATING FACTORS (OTHER THAN THOSE WITHIN EXAMPLES ABOVE)		
Common aggravating and mitigating factors are identified at **B[5.2A]**. The following may be particularly relevant but **these lists are not exhaustive**		
Factors indicating higher culpability	*Factors indicating lower culpability*	
1. High degree of planning	1. Very short period	
2. Offender deliberately isolates victim	2. Provocation	
Factors indicating greater degree of harm		
1. Offence committed in vicinity of victim's home		
2. Large number of people in vicinity		
3. Actual or potential escalation into violence		
4. Particularly serious impact on victim		
FORM A PRELIMINARY VIEW OF THE APPROPRIATE SENTENCE		

IF OFFENDER CHARGED AND CONVICTED OF THE RACIALLY OR RE-LIGIOUSLY AGGRAVATED OFFENCE, INCREASE THE SENTENCE TO REFLECT THE ELEMENT
Common factors are identified at B[5.2B]
CONSIDER OFFENDER MITIGATION
Common factors are identified at B[5.2A]
CONSIDER A REDUCTION FOR A GUILTY PLEA
CONSIDER ANCILLARY ORDERS, INCLUDING COMPENSATION AND FOOTBALL BANNING ORDER (where appropriate)
Refer to B[18] for guidance on compensation.
DECIDE SENTENCE
GIVE REASONS

A[21.18]

Bind over. See the amended Consolidated Criminal Practice Direction and associated notes at B[10] onwards.

A[22]

Drugs

A[22.1]

The misuse of drugs is made unlawful by the Misuse of Drugs Act 1971, which introduced the term 'controlled drugs' (ie drugs, the use of which is controlled by the Act). The second schedule of the Act allocates controlled drugs to Classes A, B or C and maximum penalties vary according to the class to which a controlled drug belongs.

A[22.2]

The second schedule can be varied by an order in council. Magistrates will be able to ascertain full details from their legal adviser; the following table sets out the class of some of the commoner controlled drugs.

A[22.3]

The sections mentioned below are sections of the Act.

A[22.4]

Class A

Cocaine, heroin, LSD, morphine, opium, ecstasy (MDMA), *methylamphetamine (crystal meth) remifentanil and dihydroetrophine.

*Reclassified for offences on or after 18/1/07.

A[22.5]

Class B

Amphetamines, codeine, dexedrine, methadrine, some derivatives of morphine, preludin and for offences committed on or after 26 January 2009 cannabis and cannabis resin has been reclassified as a Class B drug.

A[22.6]

Class C

Lucofen, mandrax and villescon, Gammahydroxy-butyrate (GHB) and zolpidem.

The text below concerns two drug offences which seem likely to be among the most frequently committed offences created by the Act. These are the offences created by the Misuse of Drugs Act 1971, ss 5(2) and 5(3).

A[23]

Drugs – class A – failure to attend initial/remain for initial assessment
(Drugs Act 2005)

Charge

A[23.1]

A person who, by virtue of s 9 (2) of the Drugs Act 2005, without good cause –

(a)   fails to attend an initial drugs assessment at the specified time and place, or

(b)   attends the assessment at the specified time and place but fails to remain for its duration

shall be guilty of an offence.

Drugs Act 2005, s 12

Maximum penalty. A person guilty of an offence under s 12 is liable on summary conviction to a punishment not exceeding 3 months (**51 weeks) or to a level 4 fine or both.

Legal notes and definitions

A[23.2]

If a person fails to attend an initial assessment at the specified time and place, any requirement imposed on him by virtue of s 10(2) ie a "follow-up assessment" ceases to have effect.

Sentencing
SC Guideline – Drugs – class A – fail to attend/remain for initial assessment

A[23.3]

OFFENCE SERIOUSNESS (CULPABILITY AND HARM) A. IDENTIFY THE APPROPRIATE STARTING POINT Starting points based on first time offender pleading not guilty		
Examples of nature of activity	Starting point	Range
Failure to attend at the appointed place and time	Medium level community order	Band C fine to high level community order
OFFENCE SERIOUSNESS (CULPABILITY AND HARM)		

B. CONSIDER THE EFFECT OF AGGRAVATING AND MITIGATING FAC-TORS (OTHER THAN THOSE WITHIN EXAMPLES ABOVE)

Common aggravating and mitigating factors are identified at **B[5.2A]**. The following may be particularly relevant but these lists are not exhaustive

Factor indicating higher culpability	Factors indicating lower culpability
1. Threats or abuse to assessor or other staff	1. Offender turns up but at wrong place and time or fails to remain for duration of appointment
	2. Subsequent voluntary contact to rearrange appointment

FORM A PRELIMINARY VIEW OF THE APPROPRIATE SENTENCE, THEN CONSIDER OFFENDER MITIGATION

Common factors are identified at **B[5.2A]**

CONSIDER A REDUCTION FOR A GUILTY PLEA

CONSIDER ANCILLARY ORDERS

Refer to Part B for guidance on available ancillary orders

DECIDE SENTENCE

GIVE REASONS

A[24]

Drugs – class A – fail/refuse to provide a sample

Charge

A[24.1]

A person who by virtue of this section, fails without good cause to give any sample which may be taken from him shall be guilty of an offence.

Police and Criminal Evidence Act 1984, s 63B

Maximum penalty. A person guilty of an offence under s 63B is liable on summary conviction to a punishment not exceeding 3 months (**51 weeks) or to a level 4 fine or both.

Sentencing
SGC Guideline – Drugs – class A – fail/refuse to provide a sample

A[24.2]

OFFENCE SERIOUSNESS (CULPABILITY AND HARM)		
A. IDENTIFY THE APPROPRIATE STARTING POINT		
Starting points based on first time offender pleading not guilty		
Examples of nature of activity	Starting point	Range
Refusal where reasonable suspicion that misuse of class A drug caused or contribute to offence	Medium level community order	Band C fine to high level community order
OFFENCE SERIOUSNESS (CULPABILITY AND HARM)		
B. CONSIDER THE EFFECT OF AGGRAVATING AND MITIGATING FACTORS (OTHER THAN THOSE WITHIN EXAMPLES ABOVE)		
Common aggravating and mitigating factors are identified at B[5.2A]. The following may be particularly relevant but **these lists are not exhaustive**		
Factor indicating higher culpability	*Factors indicating lower culpability*	
1. Threats or abuse to staff	1. Subsequent voluntary with drug workers	
	2. Subsequent compliance with testing on charge	
FORM A PRELIMINARY VIEW OF THE APPROPRIATE SENTENCE, THEN CONSIDER OFFENDER MITIGATION		
Common factors are identified at B[5.2A]		
CONSIDER A REDUCTION FOR A GUILTY PLEA		

| CONSIDER ANCILLARY ORDERS |
| Refer to Part B for guidance on available ancillary orders |
| DECIDE SENTENCE |
| GIVE REASONS |

A[25]

Possession of a controlled drug
(Misuse of Drugs Act 1971, s 5(2))

Charge

A[25.1]

Having a quantity of a controlled drug, namely [. . . . .], in his possession

Maximum penalty

Class A	level 5 and 6 months (**12 months)
Class B	£2,500 and 3 months (**12months)
Class C	£1,000 and 3 months (**12 months)

Court can order forfeiture but see 'Forfeiture' below.

Crown Court -

Class A	7 years and fine
Class B	5 years and fine
Class C	2 years and fine

Triable either way in respect of any class of drug although see A[25.3] below.

Mode of trial

A[25.2]

See the SC guidelines below.

A[25.3]

Possession of Class A drugs – see **SC Guideline** at A[25.16] below.

It should be noted that the Powers of Criminal Courts (Sentencing) Act 2000, s 110 makes provision for the imposition of a minimum seven-year custodial sentence on 18-year-olds and above who have been convicted of a third Class A drug trafficking offence.

A[25.4]

Possession of class B or C drugs – see SC Guideline at A[25.16] below.

Legal notes and definitions

A[25.5]

Quantity. The charge should state the quantity involved. If it is a diminutive quantity consult the legal adviser. Scrapings from a pocket can be enough. A few droplets in a tube only discernible microscopically are not enough; the court must be satisfied that there is sufficient there to amount to something. If the quantity is very small it may be relevant to the question of the accused's knowledge that it was in his possession.

A[25.6]

Expert examination. The court should be satisfied that an expert has confirmed that the substance is the controlled drug alleged. In a contested case this would have to be proved by the prosecution or admitted by the defendant.

A[25.7]

Possession. In many cases this may be established by proving that the defendant had the drug in his custody. Possession can also be established by showing that the drug was in someone else's custody, but subject to the defendant's control (Misuse of Drugs Act 1971, s 37(3)). A drug which has changed its nature by digestion would not be a drug for the purposes of prosecution but evidence of digestion might go towards proving possession prior to consumption.

A[25.8]

Defences. Each of the following defences is expressly provided by the Act, but a defendant is also entitled to rely on other common law defences (see A[25.8A] below).

(a)   Authorised by regulation (s 7). After consulting the Advisory Council on the Misuse of Drugs, the Home Secretary is empowered to introduce regulations exempting certain persons (eg doctors, dentists, veterinary surgeons, pharmacists) and controlled drugs (in certain circumstances) from the scope of this offence.

or

(b)   Knowing or suspecting it was a controlled drug, the defendant took possession of it to prevent another person from committing or continuing to commit an offence with it; and further that as soon as possible after taking possession of it he took all reasonable steps to destroy it or to deliver it to a person lawfully entitled to take it (s 5(4)(a)).

or

(c)   Knowing or suspecting it was a controlled drug, the defendant took possession of it to deliver it to a person lawfully entitled to it and as soon as possible he took all reasonable steps to deliver it to that person (s 5(4)(b)).

or

(d)   The defendant neither knew nor suspected, nor had reason to suspect, the existence of any fact (except whether the article was a controlled drug, see (e) below) which the prosecution must prove if the defendant is to be convicted (s 28(2)); eg he did not know he possessed anything (this is where quantity might be relevant). Possession is not dependent on the accused's *recollection* that he has it. Where a man had knowingly placed some cannabis in his wallet and had later forgotten it was there, he was still in possession of it. Of course it would be otherwise if a third party had slipped it in his pocket unawares so that he never knew it was there (*R v Martindale* [1986] 3 All ER 25, [1986] 1 WLR 1042, CA). [Where the defendant knew he possessed something but denies he knew it was a controlled drug the next defence ((e) below) is appropriate.]

or

(e)   In cases where the prosecution must prove that the substance or product was the controlled drug alleged in the charge and has done so, the defendant shall not be acquitted by reason only of proving that he neither knew or suspected that the substance was the particular drug alleged but shall be acquitted if he proves either:
    (i)   that he neither believed nor suspected nor had reason to suspect that the substance or product was *any kind* of controlled drug, ie not just that it was not the controlled drug referred to in the charge; or
    (ii)   that he believed it to be a controlled drug and that he also believed the circumstances were such that he would not be committing any offence (s 28(3)).

A[25.8A]

Common law defence of necessity. In *R v Quayle and other appeals; Attorney General's Reference (No 2 of 2004)* [2005] EWCA Crim 1415, [2006] 1 All ER 988, the Court of Appeal held that the common law defence of necessity was not available for individuals who contended that they genuinely and reasonably believed that the cultivation, production, importation and possession of cannabis had been necessary to avoid them suffering serious pain or injury by reason of their medical condition.

A[25.9]

Burden of proof upon the defendant. A defendant relying upon one of the above defences does not have to establish it beyond reasonable doubt. He need only establish it was more probable than not (see **ECHR (A[25.10])** below)

A[25.10]

ECHR. In the light of *R v Lambert* [2001] UKHL 37, [2002] 2 AC 545, it appears that the imposition of a legal burden of proof on the accused may be disproportionate to a fair trial as required by art 6(2) ECHR. Accordingly, the MDA 1971 should be read as imposing an evidential burden on the accused ie the accused only bears the burden of raising the defence. Once raised it is for the prosecution to negative the defence beyond a reasonable doubt.

A[25.11]–[25.15]

Cannabis. Means the whole or any part of the plant except cannabis resin or the separated mature stalk, fibre produced from the mature stalk or the seed.

Sentencing

SC Sentencing Guideline

Possession of a controlled drug
Misuse of Drugs Act 1971 (section 5(2))

A[25.16]

This guideline applies to all offenders aged 18 years and older, who are sentenced on or after 27 February 2012. The definitions [at page 145] of 'starting point' and 'first time offender' do not apply for this guideline. Starting point and category ranges apply to all offenders in all cases, irrespective of plea or previous convictions. **Triable either way**

Class A

Maximum: 7 years' custody

Offence range: Fine – 51 weeks' custody

Class B

Maximum: 5 years' custody

Offence range: Discharge – 26 weeks' custody

Class C

Maximum: 2 years' custody

Offence range: Discharge – Community order

Step One
Determining the offence category

The court should identify the offence category based on the class of drug involved.

Category 1	Class A drug
Category 2	Class B drug
Category 3	Class C drug

Step Two
Starting point and category range

The court should use the table below to identify the corresponding starting point. The starting point applies to all offenders irrespective of plea or previous convictions. The court should then consider further adjustment within the category range for aggravating or mitigating features, set out on the opposite page.

Where the defendant is dependent on or has a propensity to misuse drugs and there is sufficient prospect of success, a community order with a drug rehabilitation requirement under section 209 of the Criminal Justice Act 2003 can be a proper alternative to a short or moderate length custodial sentence.

Offence category	Starting point (applicable to all offenders)	Category range (applicable to all offenders)
Category 1 (class A)	Band C fine	Band A fine – 51 weeks' custody
Category 2 (class B)	Band B fine	Discharge – 26 weeks' custody
Category 3 (class C)	Band A fine	Discharge – medium level community order

The table below contains a **non-exhaustive** list of additional factual elements providing the context of the offence and factors relating to the offender. Identify whether any combination of these, or other relevant factors, should result in an upward or downward adjustment from the starting point. **In particular, possession of drugs in prison is likely to result in an upward adjustment.** In some cases, having considered these factors, it may be appropriate to move outside the identified category range.

Where appropriate, consider the custody threshold as follows:

* has the custody threshold been passed?
* if so, is it unavoidable that a custodial sentence be imposed?
* if so, can that sentence be suspended?

Where appropriate, the court should also consider the community threshold as follows:

* has the community threshold been passed?

Factors increasing seriousness

Statutory aggravating factors:

Previous convictions, having regard to a) nature of the offence to which conviction relates and relevance to current offence; and b) time elapsed since conviction

Offence committed on bail

Other aggravating factors include:

Possession of drug in prison

Presence of others, especially children and/or non-users

Possession of drug in a school or licensed premises

Failure to comply with current court orders

Offence committed on licence

Attempts to conceal or dispose of evidence, where not charged separately

Charged as importation of a very small amount

Established evidence of community impact

Factors reducing seriousness or reflecting personal mitigation

No previous convictions **or** no relevant or recent convictions

Remorse

Good character and/or exemplary conduct

Offender is using cannabis to help with a diagnosed medical condition

Determination and/or demonstration of steps having been taken to address addiction or offending behaviour

Serious medical conditions requiring urgent, intensive or long-term treatment

Isolated incident

Age and/or lack of maturity where it affects the responsibility of the offender

Mental disorder or learning disability

Sole or primary carer for dependent relatives

Step Three
Consider any factors which indicate a reduction, such as assistance to the prosecution

The court should take into account sections 73 and 74 of the Serious Organised Crime and Police Act 2005 (assistance by defendants: reduction or review of sentence) and any other rule of law by virtue of which an offender may receive a discounted sentence in consequence of assistance given (or offered) to the prosecutor or investigator.

Step Four
Reduction for guilty pleas

The court should take account of any potential reduction for a guilty plea in accordance with section 144 of the Criminal Justice Act 2003 and the *Guilty Plea* guideline.

Step Five
Totality principle

If sentencing an offender for more than one offence, or where the offender is already serving a sentence, consider whether the total sentence is just and proportionate to the offending behaviour.

Step Six
Ancillary orders

In all cases, the court should consider whether to make ancillary orders.

Step Seven
Reasons

Section 174 of the Criminal Justice Act 2003 imposes a duty to give reasons for, and explain the effect of, the sentence.

Step Eight
Consideration for remand time

Sentencers should take into consideration any remand time served in relation to the final sentence at this final step. The court should consider whether to give credit for time spent on remand in custody or on bail in accordance with sections 240 and 240A of the Criminal Justice Act 2003.

A[25.17]

Available sentences (Class A, B and C drugs). See Table A at B[4.1].

A[25.18]

Forfeiture (s 27). The court can order the controlled drugs, or anything proved to relate to the offence, to be forfeited and either destroyed or otherwise dealt with as the court may order. However, if a person claims to be owner of the drug or item to be forfeited, or to be otherwise interested in it, he must first be given an opportunity to show cause why a forfeiture order should not be made.

A[26]

Supplying or offering to supply a controlled drug
Possessing a controlled drug with intent to supply it to another

(Misuse of Drugs Act 1971, ss 4(3) and 5(3))

Charge

A[26.1]

1. (a) To supply or offer to supply a controlled drug to another; or (b) to be concerned in the supplying of a controlled drug to another; or (c) to be concerned in the making to another of an offer to supply a controlled drug.

2. Having in his possession a quantity of [. . . . . .] a controlled drug of Class [. . . . . .] with intent to supply it to another person

Maximum penalty -

Class A	£5,000 and 6 months (**12 months)
Class B	£5,000 and 6 months (**12 months)
Class C	£2,500 and 3 months (*12 months)

Court can order forfeiture, but see 'Forfeiture' above.

Crown Court -

Class A	Life imprisonment and fine
Class B	14 years and fine
Class C	14 years and fine

Triable either way in respect of any class of drug but see **A[25.3]**

Mode of trial

A[26.2]

See SC Guideline at A[26.5] below.

Legal notes and definitions

A[26.3]

The notes in respect of the previous offence at **A[25]** also apply here except that the defences numbered (b) and (c) in **A[25.8]** are not applicable.

A[26.4]

Intent to supply to another person. In deciding whether or not the defendant had this intention, the court must consider all the evidence drawing such inferences from it as appear proper in the circumstances. An involuntary keeper of drugs can be guilty of supply (*R v Panton* [2001] 19 LS Gaz R 36, CA).

In *R v Wright* [2011] EWCA Crim 1180, [2011] 2 Cr App Rep 168, there was no suggestion that W had intended to supply the immature cannabis plants which he had produced and was in possession of at the material time. The core offence was the production of cannabis under s 4 and the seriousness of that offence depended, inter alia, on whether the cannabis was being grown for W's own use or for supply to others. That question could be resolved within the sentencing process for the offence of production, if necessary by a Newton hearing. It had been unnecessary therefore to add a count of possession with intent to supply in order to determine the purpose for which the cannabis was being produced.

A[26.4A]

Aggravation of offence of supply of controlled drug. A new s 4A was added to the Misuse of Drugs Act 1971 by the Drugs Act 2005, s 1. This section applies if –

(a)   a court is considering the seriousness of an offence under s 4(3) of the 1971 Act, and

(b)   at the time the offence was committed the offender had attained the age of 18 years.

If **either** of the following conditions is met the court must treat the fact that the condition is met as an aggravating factor ie a factor that increases the seriousness of the offence and when giving its reasons in open court must state that the offence is so aggravated. The conditions are:

(a)   the offence was committed on or in the vicinity of school premises at the relevant time;

(b)   in connection with the commission of the offence the offender used a courier who, at the time the offence was committed, was under the age of 18 years.

A[26.4B]

Defences and ECHR. See A[25.9] onwards and (*R v Lambert* [2001] 1 All ER 1014, [2001] 2 WLR 211, CA; affd sub nom R v Lambert [2001] UKHL 37, [2002] 2 AC 545, [2001] 3 All ER 577) and Misuse of Drugs Act 1971, s 28.

Sentencing

SC Sentencing Guideline

Supplying or offering to supply a controlled drug
Misuse of Drugs Act 1971 (section 4(3))

Possession of a controlled drug with intent to supply it to another
Misuse of Drugs Act 1971 (section 5(3))

A[26.5]

Triable either way unless the defendant could receive the minimum sentence of seven years for a third drug trafficking offence under section 110 Powers of Criminal Courts (Sentencing) Act 2000 in which case the offence is triable only on indictment.

Class A

Maximum: Life imprisonment

Offence range: Community order – 16 years' custody

A class A offence is a drug trafficking offence for the purpose of imposing a minimum sentence under section 110 Powers of Criminal Courts (Sentencing) Act 2000

Class B

Maximum: 14 years' custody and/or unlimited fine

Offence range: Fine – 10 years' custody

Class C

Maximum: 14 years' custody and/or unlimited fine

Offence range: Fine – 8 years' custody

Step One
Determining the offence category

The court should determine the offender's culpability (role) and the harm caused (quantity/type of offender) with reference to the tables below.

In assessing culpability, the sentencer should weigh up all the factors of the case to determine role. Where there are characteristics present which fall under different role categories, the court should balance these characteristics to reach a fair assessment of the offender's culpability.

In assessing harm, quantity is determined by the weight of the product. Purity is not taken into account at step 1 but is dealt with at step 2. Where the offence is **street dealing** or **supply of drugs in prison by a prison employee**, the quantity of the product is less indicative of the harm caused and therefore the **starting point is not based on quantity**.

Where the operation is on the most serious and commercial scale, involving a quantity of drugs significantly higher than category 1, sentences of 20 years and above may be appropriate, depending on the role of the offender.

[See page 233.]

Culpability demonstrated by offender's role

One or more of these characteristics may demonstrate the offender's role. These lists are not exhaustive.

LEADING role:

• directing or organising buying and selling on a commercial scale;
• substantial links to, and influence on, others in a chain;
• close links to original source;
• expectation of substantial financial gain;
• uses business as cover;
• abuses a position of trust or responsibility, for example prison employee, medical professional.

SIGNIFICANT role:

• operational or management function within a chain;
• involves others in the operation whether by pressure, influence, intimidation or reward;
• motivated by financial or other advantage, whether or not operating alone;
• some awareness and understanding of scale of operation;
• supply, other than by a person in a position of responsibility, to a prisoner for gain without coercion.

LESSER role:

• performs a limited function under direction;
• engaged by pressure, coercion, intimidation;
• involvement through naivety/exploitation;
• no influence on those above in a chain;
• very little, if any, awareness or understanding of the scale of operation;
• if own operation, absence of any financial gain, for example joint purchase for no profit, or sharing minimal quantity between peers on non-commercial basis.

Category of harm

Indicative quantity of drug concerned (upon which the starting point is based):

Category 1

- heroin, cocaine – 5kg;
- ecstasy – 10,000 tablets;
- LSD – 250,000 squares;
- amphetamine – 20kg;
- cannabis – 200kg;
- ketamine – 5kg.

Category 2

- heroin, cocaine – 1kg;
- ecstasy – 2,000 tablets;
- LSD – 25,000 squares;
- amphetamine – 4kg;
- cannabis – 40kg;
- ketamine – 1kg.

Category 3

Where the offence is selling directly to users* ('street dealing'), the starting point is not based on a quantity,

OR

where the offence is supply of drugs in prison by a prison employee, the starting point is not based on a quantity – see shaded box on page 232,

OR

- heroin, cocaine – 150g;
- ecstasy – 300 tablets;
- LSD – 2,500 squares;
- amphetamine – 750g;
- cannabis – 6kg;
- ketamine – 150g.

Category 4

- heroin, cocaine – 5g;
- ecstasy – 20 tablets;
- LSD – 170 squares;
- amphetamine – 20g;
- cannabis – 100g;
- ketamine – 5g;

OR

where the offence is selling directly to users* ('street dealing') the starting point is not based on quantity – go to category 3.

*Including test purchase officers

Step Two
Starting point and category range

Having determined the category, the court should use the corresponding starting point to reach a sentence within the category range below. The starting point applies to all offenders irrespective of plea or previous convictions. The court should then consider further adjustment within the category range for aggravating or mitigating features, set out on page 236. In cases where the offender is regarded as being at the very top of the 'leading' role it may be justifiable for the court to depart from the guideline.

Where the defendant is dependent on or has a propensity to misuse drugs and there is sufficient prospect of success, a community order with a drug rehabilitation requirement under section 209 of the Criminal Justice Act 2003 can be a proper alternative to a short or moderate length custodial sentence.

For **class A** cases, section 110 of the Powers of Criminal Courts (Sentencing) Act 2000 provides that a court should impose a minimum sentence of at least seven years' imprisonment for a third class A trafficking offence except where the court is of the opinion that there are particular circumstances which (a) relate to any of the offences or to the offender; and (b) would make it unjust to do so in all the circumstances.

CLASS A	Leading role	Significant role	Lesser role
Category 1	Starting point	Starting point	Starting point
	14 years' custody	10 years' custody	7 years' custody
	Category range	Category range	Category range
	12 – 16 years' custody	9 – 12 years' custody	6 – 9 years' custody
Category 2	Starting point	Starting point	Starting point
	11 years' custody	8 years' custody	5 years' custody
	Category range	Category range	Category range
	9 – 13 years' custody	6 years 6 months' – 10 years' custody	3 years 6 months' – 7 years' custody
Category 3	Starting point	Starting point	Starting point
	8 years 6 months' custody	4 years 6 months' custody	3 years' custody
	Category range	Category range	Category range
	6 years 6 months' – 10 years' custody	3 years 6 months' – 7 years' custody	2 – 4 years 6 months' custody

CLASS A	Leading role	Significant role	Lesser role
Category 4	Starting point	Starting point	Starting point
	5 years 6 months' custody	3 years 6 months' custody	18 months' custody
	Category range	Category range	Category range
	4 years 6 months' – 7 years 6 months' custody	2 – 5 years' custody	High level community order – 3 years' custody

CLASS B	Leading role	Significant role	Lesser role
Category 1	Starting point	Starting point	Starting point
	8 years' custody	5 years 6 months' custody	3 years' custody
	Category range	Category range	Category range
	7 – 10 years' custody	5 – 7 years' custody	2 years 6 months' – 5 years' custody
Category 2	Starting point	Starting point	Starting point
	6 years' custody	4 years' custody	1 year's custody
	Category range	Category range	Category range
	4 years 6 months' – 8 years' custody	2 years 6 months' – 5 years' custody	26 weeks' – 3 years' custody
Category 3	Starting point	Starting point	Starting point
	4 years' custody	1 year's custody	High level community order
	Category range	Category range	Category range
	2 years 6 months' – 5 years' custody	26 weeks' – 3 years' custody	Low level community order – 26 weeks' custody
Category 4	Starting point	Starting point	Starting point
	18 months' custody	High level community order	Low level community order
	Category range	Category range	Category range
	26 weeks' – 3 years' custody	Medium level community order – 26 weeks' custody	Band B fine – medium level community order

CLASS C	Leading role	Significant role	Lesser role
Category 1	**Starting point**	**Starting point**	**Starting point**
	5 years' custody	3 years' custody	18 months' custody
	Category range	**Category range**	**Category range**
	4 – 8 years' custody	2 – 5 years' custody	1 – 3 years' custody
Category 2	**Starting point**	**Starting point**	**Starting point**
	3 years 6 months' custody	18 months' custody	26 weeks' custody
	Category range	**Category range**	**Category range**
	2 – 5 years' custody	1 – 3 years' custody	12 weeks' – 18 months' custody
Category 3	**Starting point**	**Starting point**	**Starting point**
	18 months' custody	26 weeks' custody	High level community order
	Category range	**Category range**	**Category range**
	1 – 3 years' custody	12 weeks' – 18 months' custody	Low level community order – 12 weeks' custody
Category 4	**Starting point**	**Starting point**	**Starting point**
	26 weeks' custody	High level community order	Low level community order
	Category range	**Category range**	**Category range**
	High level community order – 18 months' custody	Low level community order – 12 weeks' custody	Band A fine – medium level community order

The table below contains a **non-exhaustive** list of additional factual elements providing the context of the offence and factors relating to the offender. Identify whether any combination of these, or other relevant factors, should result in an upward or downward adjustment from the starting point. In some cases, having considered these factors, it may be appropriate to move outside the identified category range.

For appropriate **class B** and **C** ranges, consider the custody threshold as follows:

- has the custody threshold been passed?
- if so, is it unavoidable that a custodial sentence be imposed?
- if so, can that sentence be suspended?

For appropriate class B and C ranges, the court should also consider the community threshold as follows:

• has the community threshold been passed?

Factors increasing seriousness

Statutory aggravating factors:

Previous convictions, having regard to a) nature of the offence to which conviction relates and relevance to current offence; and b) time elapsed since conviction (see shaded box at page 234 if third drug trafficking conviction)

Offender used or permitted a person under 18 to deliver a controlled drug to a third person

Offender 18 or over supplies or offers to supply a drug on, or in the vicinity of, school premises either when school in use as such or at a time between one hour before and one hour after they are to be used

Offence committed on bail

Other aggravating factors include:

Targeting of any premises intended to locate vulnerable individuals or supply to such individuals and/or supply to those under 18

Exposure of others to more than usual danger, for example drugs cut with harmful substances

Attempts to conceal or dispose of evidence, where not charged separately

Presence of others, especially children and/or non-users

Presence of weapon, where not charged separately

Charged as importation of a very small amount

High purity

Failure to comply with current court orders

Offence committed on licence

Established evidence of community impact

Factors reducing seriousness or reflecting personal mitigation

Involvement due to pressure, intimidation or coercion falling short of duress, except where already taken into account at step 1

Supply only of drug to which offender addicted

Mistaken belief of the offender regarding the type of drug, taking into account the reasonableness of such belief in all the circumstances

Isolated incident

Low purity

No previous convictions **or** no relevant or recent convictions

Offender's vulnerability was exploited

Remorse

Good character and/or exemplary conduct

Determination and/or demonstration of steps having been taken to address addiction or offending behaviour

Serious medical conditions requiring urgent, intensive or long-term treatment

Age and/or lack of maturity where it affects the responsibility of the offender

Mental disorder or learning disability

Sole or primary carer for dependent relatives

Step Three
Consider any factors which indicate a reduction, such as assistance to the prosecution

The court should take into account sections 73 and 74 of the Serious Organised Crime and Police Act 2005 (assistance by defendants: reduction or review of sentence) and any other rule of law by virtue of which an offender may receive a discounted sentence in consequence of assistance given (or offered) to the prosecutor or investigator.

Step Four
Reduction for guilty pleas

The court should take account of any potential reduction for a guilty plea in accordance with section 144 of the Criminal Justice Act 2003 and the *Guilty Plea* guideline.

For class A offences, where a minimum mandatory sentence is imposed under section 110 Powers of Criminal Courts (Sentencing) Act, the discount for an early guilty plea must not exceed 20 per cent.

Step Five
Totality principle

If sentencing an offender for more than one offence, or where the offender is already serving a sentence, consider whether the total sentence is just and proportionate to the offending behaviour.

Step Six
Confiscation and ancillary orders

In all cases, the court is required to consider confiscation where the Crown invokes the process or where the court considers it appropriate. It should also consider whether to make ancillary orders.

Step Seven
Reasons

Section 174 of the Criminal Justice Act 2003 imposes a duty to give reasons for, and explain the effect of, the sentence.

Step Eight
Consideration for remand time

Sentencers should take into consideration any remand time served in relation to the final sentence at this final step. The court should consider whether to give credit for time spent on remand in custody or on bail in accordance with sections 240 and 240A of the Criminal Justice Act 2003.

A[26.6]–[26.9]

Available sentences (Class A, B and C drugs). See Table A at B[4.1].

A[26.10]–[26.11]

Custodial sentence. See B[2].

A[26.12]–[26.15]

"Crack Houses" – Closure orders – S 2 Anti-Social Behaviour Act 2003

Closure orders. For more detailed guidance see JCS Good Practice Guide (Closure Notices and Orders dated November 2006 ref: 54.0022.q).

For the closure of premises associated with persistent disorder or nuisance see **Part 1A of the Anti-Social Behaviour Act 2003** at A[84.37] onwards.

(For closure orders for premises used for activities related to certain **sexual offences** see ss 22 and 22 and schedule 2 of the Policing and Crime Act 2009 which added a new Part 2A to the Sexual Offences Act 2003. These provisions came into force on **1 April 2010.**)

Within 48 hours of the serving of a closure notice an application must be made to a magistrates' court. If satisfied that:

(a)   the premises have been used for the production or supply of a class 'A' drug;
(b)   that use is associated with disorder or serious public nuisance; and
(c)   the order is necessary to prevent reoccurrence,

the court can order closure of the premises for a period no longer than 3 months.

An application can be to extend the closure order for up to a further three months pursuant to s 5(4) of the 2003 Act; but a closure order may not exceed a total of six months: s 5(5). The court should simply ask whether it had been proved that an extension was necessary and proportionate to prevent the occurrence of further disorder or nuisance; and if so how long the extension should be (R *(on the application of Smith)v Snaresbrook Crown Court* [2008] EWHC 1282 (Admin)).

Closure order applications are civil proceedings. Although closure order applications should be dealt with as a matter of urgency in R *(on the application of Turner v Highbury Corner Magistrates' Court and Commissioner of the Metropolis (Interested Party)* [2005] EWHC 2568 (Admin), [2006] 1 WLR 220, it was decided that the general power of a magistrates' court to grant an adjournment co-existed with the limited and specific power granted under s 2(6) of the Anti-Social Behaviour Act 2003. Accordingly, an adjournment of more than 14 days could be granted where the court was satisfied that there was a need for such an adjournment consonant with the interests of justice (*Metropolitan Police Comr v Hooper* [2005] EWHC 340 (Admin) explained).

The standard of proof applicable to making an order under s 2(3)(a) and (b) of the 2003 Act was the civil standard of proof, namely on a balance of probabilities (*Chief Constable of Merseyside v Harrison* [2006] EWHC 1106 (Admin), [2006] 3 WLR 171).

For general guidance on disclosure of evidence in s 2 applications and observations on the admissibility of and weight to be accorded to hearsay evidence see R *(on the application of Cleary) v Highbury Corner Magistrates' Court and the Comr of Police of the Metropolis and the Secretary of State for the Home Department* [2006] EWHC 1869 (Admin), (2006) Times, 12 September; and more recently R *(on the application of Errington) v Metropolitan Police Authority* (2007) 171 JP 89.

When applying for a closure order it was not necessary for the police and local authority to demonstrate they had first considered and/or tried other less draconian methods first, so as to comply with the ECHR, article 8. Further, it was not possible to adjust the terms of a closure order to exclude visitors from the premises but to allow an occupier to remain there: *Leary v Chief Constable of the West Midlands Police* [2012] EWHC 639 (Admin), 176 CL&J 143.

On a true construction of the Act, the requirement of s 2(3)(b) of disorder or serious nuisance had to derive from the drug use required by s 2(3)(a). The purpose of the legislation was to grant powers to deal with 'crack houses' and it followed that the disturbance(s) required by s 2(3)(b) had to be linked to the drug use referred to in s 2(3)(a). The Act was intended to deal with a present and continuing situation. An order might be obtained if there was a short hiatus in the disorder, although not if the disorder had permanently ceased. Historical evidence was therefore admissible if relevant to a continuing situation (*Chief Constable of Cumbria Constabulary v Wright* [2006] EWHC 3574 (Admin)). In *Dumble v Metropolitan Police Commissioner* [2009] All ER (D) 66 (Feb) for the purposes of s 2(3)(b) the justices were entitled to consider the ongoing nature of disorder and violence at the appellant's premises including the 'few' incidents which had taken place immediately prior to the making of the application. On the facts, the legitimate aim of preventing crime and disorder was a trump card overriding the appellant's Art 8 ECHR rights.

An offence in contravention of the order is punishable summarily by 6 months' (**51 weeks) imprisonment or a level 5 fine (ss 2 and 4 of the Anti-Social Behaviour Act 2003).

For the closure of 'noisy premises' see s 40 of the 2003 Act at A[84.7] onwards.

A[26.16]

Appeal. Section 6 of the Anti-Social Behaviour Act 2003 states that an appeal against a decision or order must be brought before the end of the period of 21 days beginning with the day on which the order or decision is made. Section 6(1) has been interpreted to mean that an appellant has 21 days from the date of the order or decision to issue the notice of appeal. Further, there was no power to extend the time for appeal under s 6(2): *Hampshire Police Authority v Smith* [2009] EWHC 174 (Admin), 173 JP 207.

A[26.17]

Costs. A magistrates' court has jurisdiction to make an award of costs between the parties under s 64 of the Magistrates' Courts Act 1980: *R (on the application of Taylor) v Comr of the Metropolitan Police* [2009] EWHC 264 (Admin), 173 JP 121.

A[26.18]

Community sentence. See B[3].

A[26.19]

Forfeiture. See A[25.18].

A[26.20]

Drug trafficking. For the power of the Crown Court to make a confiscation order in respect of the proceeds of drug trafficking offences, see B[19].

A[27]

Drugs – Cultivation of Cannabis Plant
Drugs – Production of a controlled drug

(Misuse of Drugs Act 1971, s 6(2))
(Misuse of Drugs Act 1971, s 4(2)(a) or (b))

Charge

A[27.1]
On X date at . . . . the accused unlawfully cultivated cannabis

On X date at . . . . unlawfully produced a controlled drug (namely . . . .); or was concerned in the production of a controlled drug (namely . . . .)

Maximum penalty –

Fine level 5 and/or 6 months (**12 months) imprisonment. Triable either way.

Crown Court

–   Class A: Life imprisonment and unlimited fine
–   Class B: 14 years' imprisonment and unlimited fine
–   Class C: 14 years' imprisonment and unlimited fine

A[27.2]
This offence is subject to s 7 (authorisation of activities otherwise unlawful) and s 28 (proof of lack of knowledge etc to be a defence in proceedings for certain offences.

Mode of trial

A[27.3]
See SC Guideline at A[27.4] below.

Sentencing

SC Sentencing Guideline

Production of a controlled drug
Misuse of Drugs Act 1971 (section 4(2)(a) or (b))

A[27.4]

Triable either way unless the defendant could receive the minimum sentence of seven years for a third drug trafficking offence under section 110 Powers of Criminal Courts (Sentencing) Act 2000 in which case the offence is triable only on indictment.

Class A

Maximum: Life imprisonment

Offence range: Community order – 16 years' custody

A class A offence is a drug trafficking offence for the purpose of imposing a minimum sentence under section 110 Powers of Criminal Courts (Sentencing) Act 2000

Class B

Maximum: 14 years' custody

Offence range: Discharge – 10 years' custody

Class C

Maximum: 14 years' custody

Offence range: Discharge – 8 years' custody

Cultivation of cannabis plant
Misuse of Drugs Act 1971 (section 6(2))

Maximum: 14 years' custody

Offence range: Discharge – 10 years' custody

Step One
Determining the offence category

The court should determine the offender's culpability (role) and the harm caused (output or potential output) with reference to the tables below.

In assessing culpability, the sentencer should weigh up all of the factors of the case to determine role. Where there are characteristics present which fall under different role categories, the court should balance these characteristics to reach a fair assessment of the offender's culpability.

In assessing harm, output or potential output is determined by the weight of the product or number of plants/scale of operation. For production offences, purity is not taken into account at step 1 but is dealt with at step 2.

Where the operation is on the most serious and commercial scale, involving a quantity of drugs significantly higher than category 1, sentences of 20 years and above may be appropriate, depending on the role of the offender.

Culpability demonstrated by offender's role

One or more of these characteristics may demonstrate the offender's role. These lists are not exhaustive.

LEADING role:
- directing or organising production on a commercial scale;
- substantial links to, and influence on, others in a chain;
- expectation of substantial financial gain;
- uses business as cover;
- abuses a position of trust or responsibility.

SIGNIFICANT role:
- operational or management function within a chain;
- involves others in the operation whether by pressure, influence, intimidation or reward;
- motivated by financial or other advantage, whether or not operating alone;
- some awareness and understanding of scale of operation.

LESSER role:
- performs a limited function under direction;
- engaged by pressure, coercion, intimidation;
- involvement through naivety/exploitation;
- no influence on those above in a chain;
- very little, if any, awareness or understanding of the scale of operation;
- if own operation, solely for own use (considering reasonableness of account in all the circumstances).

Category of harm

Indicative output or potential output (upon which the starting point is based):

Category 1
- heroin, cocaine – 5kg;
- ecstasy – 10,000 tablets;
- LSD – 250,000 tablets;

- amphetamine – 20kg;
- cannabis – operation capable of producing industrial quantities for commercial use;
- ketamine – 5kg.

Category 2
- heroin, cocaine – 1kg;
- ecstasy – 2,000 tablets;
- LSD – 25,000 squares;
- amphetamine – 4kg;
- cannabis – operation capable of producing significant quantities for commercial use;
- ketamine – 1kg.

Category 3
- heroin, cocaine – 150g;
- ecstasy – 300 tablets;
- LSD – 2,500 squares;
- amphetamine – 750g;
- cannabis – 28 plants;[*]
- ketamine – 150g.

Category 4
- heroin, cocaine – 5g;
- ecstasy – 20 tablets;
- LSD – 170 squares;
- amphetamine – 20g;
- cannabis – 9 plants (domestic operation);[*]
- ketamine – 5g.

---

[*]   With assumed yield of 40g per plant

Step Two
Starting point and category range

Having determined the category, the court should use the corresponding starting point to reach a sentence within the category range below. The starting point applies to all offenders irrespective of plea or previous convictions. The court should then consider further adjustment within the category range for aggravating or mitigating features, set out on page 243. In cases where the offender is regarded as being at the very top of the 'leading' role it may be justifiable for the court to depart from the guideline.

Where the defendant is dependent on or has a propensity to misuse drugs and there is sufficient prospect of success, a community order with a drug rehabilitation requirement under section 209 of the Criminal Justice Act 2003 can be a proper alternative to a short or moderate length custodial sentence.

For **class A** cases, section 110 of the Powers of Criminal Courts (Sentencing) Act 2000 provides that a court should impose a minimum sentence of at least seven years' imprisonment for a third class A trafficking offence except where the court is of the opinion that there are particular circumstances which (a) relate to any of the offences or to the offender; and (b) would make it unjust to do so in all the circumstances.

CLASS A	Leading role	Significant role	Lesser role
	Starting point	Starting point	Starting point
	14 years' custody	10 years' custody	7 years' custody
	Category range	Category range	Category range
	12 – 16 years' custody	9 – 12 years' custody	6 – 9 years' custody
Category 2	Starting point	Starting point	Starting point
	11 years' custody	8 years' custody	5 years' custody
	Category range	Category range	Category range
	9 – 13 years' custody	6 years 6 months' – 10 years' custody	3 years 6 months' – 7 years' custody
Category 3	Starting point	Starting point	Starting point
	8 years 6 months' custody	5 years' custody	3 years 6 months' custody
	Category range	Category range	Category range
	6 years 6 months' – 10 years' custody	3 years 6 months' – 7 years' custody	2 – 5 years' custody
Category 4	Starting point	Starting point	Starting point
	5 years 6 months' custody	3 years 6 months' custody	18 months' custody
	Category range	Category range	Category range
	4 years 6 months' – 7 years 6 months' custody	2 – 5 years' custody	High level community order – 3 years' custody
CLASS B	Leading role	Significant role	Lesser role
Category 1	Starting point	Starting point	Starting point
	8 years' custody	5 years 6 months' custody	3 years' custody

CLASS B	Leading role	Significant role	Lesser role
	Category range	Category range	Category range
	7 – 10 years' custody	5 – 7 years' custody	2 years 6 months' – 5 years' custody
Category 2	Starting point	Starting point	Starting point
	6 years' custody	4 years' custody	1 year's custody
	Category range	Category range	Category range
	4 years 6 months' – 8 years' custody	2 years 6 months' – 5 years' custody	26 weeks' – 3 years' custody
Category 3	Starting point	Starting point	Starting point
	4 years' custody	1 year's custody	High level community order
	Category range	Category range	Category range
	2 years 6 months' – 5 years' custody	26 weeks' – 3 years' custody	Low level community order – 26 weeks' custody
Category 4	Starting point	Starting point	Starting point
	1 year's custody	High level community order	Band C fine
	Category range	Category range	Category range
	High level community order – 3 years' custody	Medium level community order – 26 weeks' custody	Discharge – medium level community order
CLASS C	Leading role	Significant role	Lesser role
Category 1	Starting point	Starting point	Starting point
	5 years' custody	3 years' custody	18 months' custody
	Category range	Category range	Category range
	4 – 8 years' custody	2 – 5 years' custody	1 – 3 years' custody
Category 2	Starting point	Starting point	Starting point
	3 years 6 months' custody	18 months' custody	26 weeks' custody
	Category range	Category range	Category range

CLASS C	Leading role	Significant role	Lesser role
	2 – 5 years' custody	1 – 3 years' custody	High level community order – 18 months' custody
Category 3	**Starting point**	**Starting point**	**Starting point**
	18 months' custody	26 weeks' custody	High level community order
	Category range	**Category range**	**Category range**
	1 – 3 years' custody	High level community order – 18 months' custody	Low level community order – 12 weeks' custody
Category 4	**Starting point**	**Starting point**	**Starting point**
	26 weeks' custody	High level community order	Band C fine
	Category range	**Category range**	**Category range**
	High level community order – 18 months' custody	Low level community order – 12 weeks' custody	Discharge – medium level community order

The table below contains a **non-exhaustive** list of additional factual elements providing the context of the offence and factors relating to the offender. Identify whether any combination of these, or other relevant factors, should result in an upward or downward adjustment from the starting point. In some cases, having considered these factors, it may be appropriate to move outside the identified category range.

Where appropriate, consider the custody threshold as follows:

- has the custody threshold been passed?
- if so, is it unavoidable that a custodial sentence be imposed?
- if so, can that sentence be suspended?

Where appropriate, the court should also consider the community threshold as follows:

- has the community threshold been passed?

Factors increasing seriousness

Statutory aggravating factors:

Previous convictions, having regard to a) nature of the offence to which conviction relates and relevance to current offence; and b) time elapsed since conviction (see shaded box at page 241 if third drug trafficking conviction)

Offence committed on bail

Other aggravating factors include:

Nature of any likely supply

Level of any profit element

Use of premises accompanied by unlawful access to electricity/other utility supply of others

Ongoing/large scale operation as evidenced by presence and nature of specialist equipment

Exposure of others to more than usual danger, for example drugs cut with harmful substances

Attempts to conceal or dispose of evidence, where not charged separately

Presence of others, especially children and/or non-users

Presence of weapon, where not charged separately

High purity or high potential yield

Failure to comply with current court orders

Offence committed on licence

Established evidence of community impact

Factors reducing seriousness or reflecting personal mitigation

Involvement due to pressure, intimidation or coercion falling short of duress, except where already taken into account at step 1

Isolated incident

Low purity

No previous convictions **or** no relevant or recent convictions

Offender's vulnerability was exploited

Remorse

Good character and/or exemplary conduct

Determination and/or demonstration of steps having been taken to address addiction or offending behaviour

Serious medical conditions requiring urgent, intensive or long-term treatment

Age and/or lack of maturity where it affects the responsibility of the offender

Mental disorder or learning disability

Sole or primary carer for dependent relatives

Step Three
Consider any factors which indicate a reduction, such as assistance to the prosecution

The court should take into account sections 73 and 74 of the Serious Organised Crime and Police Act 2005 (assistance by defendants: reduction or review of sentence) and any other rule of law by virtue of which an offender may receive a discounted sentence in consequence of assistance given (or offered) to the prosecutor or investigator.

Step Four
Reduction for guilty pleas

The court should take account of any potential reduction for a guilty plea in accordance with section 144 of the Criminal Justice Act 2003 and the *Guilty Plea* guideline.

For class A offences, where a minimum mandatory sentence is imposed under section 110 Powers of Criminal Courts (Sentencing) Act, the discount for an early guilty plea must not exceed 20 per cent.

Step Five
Totality principle

If sentencing an offender for more than one offence, or where the offender is already serving a sentence, consider whether the total sentence is just and proportionate to the offending behaviour.

Step Six
Confiscation and ancillary orders

In all cases, the court is required to consider confiscation where the Crown invokes the process or where the court considers it appropriate. It should also consider whether to make ancillary orders.

Step Seven
Reasons

Section 174 of the Criminal Justice Act 2003 imposes a duty to give reasons for, and explain the effect of, the sentence.

Step Eight
Consideration for remand time

Sentencers should take into consideration any remand time served in relation to the final sentence at this final step. The court should consider whether to give credit for time spent on remand in custody or on bail in accordance with sections 240 and 240A of the Criminal Justice Act 2003.

A[27A]

Drugs – Permitting premises to be used

(Misuse of Drugs Act 1971, s 8)

Charge

A[27A.1]

Being the occupier or concerned in the management of premises at
. . . . on X date knowingly permits or suffers the following
activity:

(a)   producing or attempting to produce a controlled drug in contravention of section 4(1);

(b)   supplying or attempting to supply a controlled drug to another in contravention of section 4(1), or offering to supply a controlled drug in contravention of section 4(1);

(c)   preparing opium for smoking;

(d)   smoking cannabis, cannabis resin or prepared opium.

Maximum penalty – Fine level 5 and/or 6 months (**12 months). Triable either way.

Crown Court

–   Class A: 14 years' imprisonment and unlimited fine
–   Class B: 14 years' imprisonment and unlimited fine
–   Class C: 14 years' imprisonment and unlimited fine

A[27A.2]

To establish the offence of permitting the prosecution must prove: (i) knowledge, actual or by closing ones eyes to the obvious, that dealing in controlled drugs is taking place; and (ii) unwillingness to prevent it, which can be inferred from failure to take steps readily available to prevent it. A defendant's belief that he has taken reasonable steps is irrelevant; it is not for the defendant to judge his own conduct: *R v Brock* (1991) 165 JP 331, CA.

Mode of trial

A[27A.3]

See SC Guideline at A[27A.4] below.

Sentencing

SC Sentencing Guideline

Permitting premises to be used
Misuse of Drugs Act 1971 (section 8)

A[27A.4]

Triable either way unless the defendant could receive the minimum sentence of seven years for a third drug trafficking offence under section 110 Powers of Criminal Courts (Sentencing) Act 2000 in which case the offence is triable only on indictment.

Class A

Maximum: 14 years' custody

Offence range: Community order – 4 years' custody

A class A offence is a drug trafficking offence for the purpose of imposing a minimum sentence under section 110 Powers of Criminal Courts (Sentencing) Act 2000

Class B

Maximum: 14 years' custody

Offence range: Fine – 18 months' custody

Class C

Maximum: 14 years' custody

Offence range: Discharge – 26 weeks' custody

Step One
Determining the offence category

The court should determine the offender's culpability and the harm caused (extent of the activity and/or the quantity of drugs) with reference to the table below.

In assessing harm, quantity is determined by the weight of the product. Purity is not taken into account at step 1 but is dealt with at step 2.

Category 1	Higher culpability **and** greater harm
Category 2	Lower culpability **and** greater harm; **or** higher culpability **and** lesser harm
Category 3	Lower culpability **and** lesser harm

Factors indicating culpability (non-exhaustive)

Higher culpability:

Permits premises to be used primarily for drug activity, for example crack house

Permits use in expectation of substantial financial gain

Uses legitimate business premises to aid and/or conceal illegal activity, for example public house or club

Lower culpability:

Permits use for limited or no financial gain

No active role in any supply taking place

Involvement through naivety

Factors indicating harm (non-exhaustive)

Greater harm:

Regular drug-related activity

Higher quantity of drugs, for example:
- heroin, cocaine – more than 5g;
- cannabis – more than 50g.

Lesser harm:

Infrequent drug-related activity

Lower quantity of drugs, for example:
- heroin, cocaine – up to 5g;
- cannabis – up to 50g.

Step Two
Starting point and category range

Having determined the category, the court should use the table below to identify the corresponding starting point to reach a sentence within the category range. The starting point applies to all offenders irrespective of plea or previous convictions. The court should then consider further adjustment within the category range for aggravating or mitigating features, set out over the page.

Where the defendant is dependent on or has a propensity to misuse drugs and there is sufficient prospect of success, a community order with a drug rehabilitation requirement under section 209 of the Criminal Justice Act 2003 can be a proper alternative to a short or moderate length custodial sentence.

For **class A** cases, section 110 of the Powers of Criminal Courts (Sentencing) Act 2000 provides that a court should impose a minimum sentence of at least seven years' imprisonment for a third class A trafficking offence except where the court is of the opinion that there are particular circumstances which (a) relate to any of the offences or to the offender; and (b) would make it unjust to do so in all the circumstances.

Class A

Offence category	Starting point (applicable to all offenders)	Category range (applicable to all offenders)
Category 1	2 years 6 months' custody	18 months' – 4 years' custody
Category 2	36 weeks' custody	High level community order – 18 months' custody
Category 3	Medium level community order	Low level community order – high level community order

Class B

Offence category	Starting point (applicable to all offenders)	Category range (applicable to all offenders)
Category 1	1 year's custody	26 weeks' – 18 months' custody
Category 2	High level community order	Low level community order – 26 weeks' custody
Category 3	Band C fine	Band A fine – low level community order

Class C

Offence category	Starting point (applicable to all offenders)	Category range (applicable to all offenders)
Category 1	12 weeks' custody	High level community order – 26 weeks' custody*
Category 2	Low level community order	Band C fine – high level community order
Category 3	Band A fine	Discharge – band C fine

*When tried summarily, the maximum penalty is 12 weeks' custody.

The table below contains a **non-exhaustive** list of additional factual elements providing the context of the offence and factors relating to the offender. Identify whether any combination of these, or other relevant factors, should result in an upward or downward adjustment from the starting point. In some cases, having considered these factors, it may be appropriate to move outside the identified category range.

Where appropriate, consider the custody threshold as follows:

- has the custody threshold been passed?
- if so, is it unavoidable that a custodial sentence be imposed?
- if so, can that sentence be suspended?

Where appropriate, the court should also consider the community threshold as follows:

• has the community threshold been passed?

Factors increasing seriousness

Statutory aggravating factors:

Previous convictions, having regard to a) nature of the offence to which conviction relates and relevance to current offence; and b) time elapsed since conviction (see shaded box at page 247 if third drug trafficking conviction)

Offence committed on bail

Other aggravating factors include:

Length of time over which premises used for drug activity

Volume of drug activity permitted

Premises adapted to facilitate drug activity

Location of premises, for example proximity to school

Attempts to conceal or dispose of evidence, where not charged separately

Presence of others, especially children and/or non-users

High purity

Presence of weapons, where not charged separately

Failure to comply with current court orders

Offence committed on licence

Established evidence of community impact

Factors reducing seriousness or reflecting personal mitigation

Involvement due to pressure, intimidation or coercion falling short of duress

Isolated incident

Low purity

No previous convictions **or** no relevant or recent convictions

Offender's vulnerability was exploited

Remorse

Good character and/or exemplary conduct

Determination and/or demonstration of steps having been taken to address addiction or offending behaviour

Serious medical conditions requiring urgent, intensive or long-term treatment

Age and/or lack of maturity where it affects the responsibility of the offender

Mental disorder or learning disability

Sole or primary carer for dependent relatives

Step Three
Consider any factors which indicate a reduction, such as assistance to the prosecution

The court should take into account sections 73 and 74 of the Serious Organised Crime and Police Act 2005 (assistance by defendants: reduction or review of sentence) and any other rule of law by virtue of which an offender may receive a discounted sentence in consequence of assistance given (or offered) to the prosecutor or investigator.

Step Four
Reduction for guilty pleas

The court should take account of any potential reduction for a guilty plea in accordance with section 144 of the Criminal Justice Act 2003 and the *Guilty Plea* guideline.

For class A offences, where a minimum mandatory sentence is imposed under section 110 Powers of Criminal Courts (Sentencing) Act, the discount for an early guilty plea must not exceed 20 per cent.

Step Five
Totality principle

If sentencing an offender for more than one offence or where the offender is already serving a sentence, consider whether the total sentence is just and proportionate to the offending behaviour.

Step Six
Confiscation and ancillary orders

In all cases, the court is required to consider confiscation where the Crown invokes the process or where the court considers it appropriate. It should also consider whether to make ancillary orders.

Step Seven
Reasons

Section 174 of the Criminal Justice Act 2003 imposes a duty to give reasons for, and explain the effect of, the sentence.

Step Eight
Consideration for remand time

Sentencers should take into consideration any remand time served in relation to the final sentence at this final step. The court should consider whether to give credit for time spent on remand in custody or on bail in accordance with sections 240 and 240A of the Criminal Justice Act 2003.

A[27B]

Fraudulent evasion of a prohibition by bringing into or taking out of the UK a controlled drug

(Misuse of Drugs Act 1971, section 3)
(Customs and Excise Management Act 1979, section 170)

Charge

A[27B.1]

A on the . . . . day of . . . . was knowingly concealed in concealing goods, that is to say a quantity of a controlled drug, namely . . . with intent to evade the prohibition on importation of the said goods then in force pursuant to section 3 of the Misuse of Drugs Act 1971

Maximum penalty – Three times the value of the goods or £5,000 fine whichever is the greater and 6 months (**12 months). Triable either way.

Crown Court – 7 years' imprisonment and unlimited fine.

A[27B.2]

To establish the offence of permitting the prosecution must prove: (i) knowledge, actual or by closing one's eyes to the obvious, that dealing in controlled drugs is taking place; and (ii) unwillingness to prevent it, which can be inferred from failure to take steps readily available to prevent it. A defendant's belief that he has taken reasonable steps is irrelevant; it is not for the defendant to judge his own conduct: *R v Brock* (1991) 165 JP 331, CA.

Mode of trial

A[27B.3]

See SC Guideline at **A[27B.4]** below.

Sentencing

SC Sentencing Guideline

Fraudulent evasion of a prohibition by bringing into or taking out of the UK a controlled drug
Misuse of Drugs Act 1971 (section 3)
Customs and Excise Management Act 1979 (section 170(2))

A[27B.4]

Triable either way unless the defendant could receive the minimum sentence of seven years for a third drug trafficking offence under section 110 Powers of Criminal Courts (Sentencing) Act 2000 in which case the offence is triable only on indictment.

Class A

Maximum: Life imprisonment

Offence range: 3 years 6 months' – 16 years' custody

A class A offence is a drug trafficking offence for the purpose of imposing a minimum sentence under section 110 Powers of Criminal Courts (Sentencing) Act 2000

Class B

Maximum: 14 years' custody and/or unlimited fine

Offence range: 12 weeks' – 10 years' custody

Class C

Maximum: 14 years' custody and/or unlimited fine

Offence range: Community order – 8 years' custody

Step One
Determining the offence category

The court should determine the offender's culpability (role) and the harm caused (quantity) with reference to the tables below.

In assessing culpability, the sentencer should weigh up all the factors of the case to determine role. Where there are characteristics present which fall under different role categories, the court should balance these characteristics to reach a fair assessment of the offender's culpability.

In assessing harm, quantity is determined by the weight of the product. Purity is not taken into account at step 1 but is dealt with at step 2.

Where the operation is on the most serious and commercial scale, involving a quantity of drugs significantly higher than category 1, sentences of 20 years and above may be appropriate, depending on the role of the offender.

Culpability demonstrated by offender's role

One or more of these characteristics may demonstrate the offender's role. These lists are not exhaustive.

LEADING role:

- directing or organising buying and selling on a commercial scale;
- substantial links to, and influence on, others in a chain;
- close links to original source;
- expectation of substantial financial gain;
- uses business as cover;
- abuses a position of trust or responsibility.

SIGNIFICANT role:

- operational or management function within a chain;
- involves others in the operation whether by pressure, influence, intimidation or reward;
- motivated by financial or other advantage, whether or not operating alone;
- some awareness and understanding of scale of operation.

LESSER role:

- performs a limited function under direction;
- engaged by pressure, coercion, intimidation;
- involvement through naivety/exploitation;
- no influence on those above in a chain;
- very little, if any, awareness or understanding of the scale of operation;
- if own operation, solely for own use (considering reasonableness of account in all the circumstances).

Category of harm

Indicative quantity of drug concerned (upon which the starting point is based):

Category 1

- heroin, cocaine – 5kg;
- ecstasy – 10,000 tablets;
- LSD – 250,000 squares;
- amphetamine – 20kg;
- cannabis – 200kg;
- ketamine – 5kg.

Category 2

- heroin, cocaine – 1kg;
- ecstasy – 2,000 tablets;
- LSD – 25,000 squares;
- amphetamine – 4kg;
- cannabis – 40kg;
- ketamine – 1kg.

Category 3

- heroin, cocaine – 150g;
- ecstasy – 300 tablets;
- LSD – 2,500 squares;
- amphetamine – 750g;
- cannabis – 6kg;
- ketamine – 150g.

Category 4

- heroin, cocaine – 5g;
- ecstasy – 20 tablets;
- LSD – 170 squares;
- amphetamine – 20g;
- cannabis – 100g;
- ketamine – 5g.

Step Two
Starting point and category range

Having determined the category, the court should use the corresponding starting point to reach a sentence within the category range below. The starting point applies to all offenders irrespective of plea or previous convictions. The court should then consider further adjustment within the category range for aggravating or mitigating features, set out over the page. In cases where the offender is regarded as being at the very top of the 'leading' role it may be justifiable for the court to depart from the guideline.

Where the defendant is dependent on or has a propensity to misuse drugs and there is sufficient prospect of success, a community order with a drug rehabilitation requirement under section 209 of the Criminal Justice Act 2003 can be a proper alternative to a short or moderate length custodial sentence.

For **class A** cases, section 110 of the Powers of Criminal Courts (Sentencing) Act 2000 provides that a court should impose a minimum sentence of at least seven years' imprisonment for a third class A trafficking offence except where the court is of the opinion that there are particular circumstances which (a) relate to any of the offences or to the offender; and (b) would make it unjust to do so in all the circumstances.

CLASS A	Leading role	Significant role	Lesser role
Category 1	Starting point	Starting point	Starting point
	14 years' custody	10 years' custody	8 years' custody
	Category range	Category range	Category range
	12 – 16 years' custody	9 – 12 years' custody	6 – 9 years' custody
Category 2	Starting point	Starting point	Starting point
	11 years' custody	8 years' custody	6 years' custody
	Category range	Category range	Category range
	9 – 13 years' custody	6 years 6 months' – 10 years' custody	5 – 7 years' custody
Category 3	Starting point	Starting point	Starting point
	8 years 6 months' custody	6 years 6 months' – 10 years' custody	4 years 6 months' custody
	Category range	Category range	Category range
	6 years' custody	5 – 7 years' custody	3 years 6 months' – 5 years' custody
Category 4	Where the quantity falls below the indicative amount set out for category 4 on the previous page, first identify the role for the importation offence, then refer to the starting point and ranges for possession or supply offences, depending on intent.		
	Where the quantity is significantly larger than the indicative amounts for category 4 but below category 3 amounts, refer to the category 3 ranges above.		
CLASS B	Leading role	Significant role	Lesser role
Category 1	Starting point	Starting point	Starting point
	8 years' custody	5 years 6 months' custody	4 years' custody
	Category range	Category range	Category range
	7 – 10 years' custody	5 – 7 years' custody	2 years 6 months' – 5 years' custody
Category 2	Starting point	Starting point	Starting point
	6 years' custody	4 years' custody	2 years' custody
	Category range	Category range	Category range
	4 years 6 months' – 8 years' custody	2 years 6 months' – 5 years' custody	18 months' – 3 years' custody

CLASS B Category 3	Leading role Starting point	Significant role Starting point	Lesser role Starting point
	4 years' custody	2 years' custody	1 year's custody
	Category range	Category range	Category range
	2 years 6 months' – 5 years' custody	18 months' – 3 years' custody	12 weeks' – 18 months' custody

Category 4	Where the quantity falls below the indicative amount set out for category 4 on the previous page, first identify the role for the importation offence, then refer to the starting point and ranges for possession or supply offences, depending on intent.
	Where the quantity is significantly larger than the indicative amounts for category 4 but below category 3 amounts, refer to the category 3 ranges above.

CLASS C Category 1	Leading role Starting point	Significant role Starting point	Lesser role Starting point
	5 years' custody	3 years' custody	18 months' custody
	Category range	Category range	Category range
	4 – 8 years' custody	2 – 5 years' custody	1 – 3 years' custody
Category 2	Starting point	Starting point	Starting point
	3 years 6 months' custody	18 months' custody	26 weeks' custody
	Category range	Category range	Category range
	2 – 5 years' custody	1 – 3 years' custody	12 weeks' – 18 months' custody
Category 3	Starting point	Starting point	Starting point
	18 months' custody	26 weeks' custody	High level community order
	Category range	Category range	Category range
	1 – 3 years' custody	12 weeks' – 18 months' custody	Medium level community order – 12 weeks' custody

CLASS C	Leading role	Significant role	Lesser role
Category 4	Where the quantity falls below the indicative amount set out for category 4 on the previous page, first identify the role for the importation offence, then refer to the starting point and ranges for possession or supply offences, depending on intent.		
	Where the quantity is significantly larger than the indicative amounts for category 4 but below category 3 amounts, refer to the category 3 ranges above.		

The table below contains a **non-exhaustive** list of additional factual elements providing the context of the offence and factors relating to the offender. Identify whether any combination of these, or other relevant factors, should result in an upward or downward adjustment from the starting point. In some cases, having considered these factors, it may be appropriate to move outside the identified category range.

For appropriate **class C** ranges, consider the custody threshold as follows:

- has the custody threshold been passed?
- if so, is it unavoidable that a custodial sentence be imposed?
- if so, can that sentence be suspended?

Factors increasing seriousness

Statutory aggravating factors:

Previous convictions, having regard to a) nature of the offence to which conviction relates and relevance to current offence; and b) time elapsed since conviction (see box at page 227 if third drug trafficking conviction)

Offender used or permitted a person under 18 to deliver a controlled drug to a third person

Offence committed on bail

Other aggravating factors include:

Sophisticated nature of concealment and/or attempts to avoid detection

Attempts to conceal or dispose of evidence, where not charged separately

Exposure of others to more than usual danger, for example drugs cut with harmful substances

Presence of weapon, where not charged separately

High purity

Failure to comply with current court orders

Offence committed on licence

Factors reducing seriousness or reflecting personal mitigation

Lack of sophistication as to nature of concealment

Involvement due to pressure, intimidation or coercion falling short of duress, except where already taken into account at step 1

Mistaken belief of the offender regarding the type of drug, taking into account the reasonableness of such belief in all the circumstances

Isolated incident

Low purity

No previous convictions or no relevant or recent convictions

Offender's vulnerability was exploited

Remorse

Good character and/or exemplary conduct

Determination and/or demonstration of steps having been taken to address addiction or offending behaviour

Serious medical conditions requiring urgent, intensive or long-term treatment

Age and/or lack of maturity where it affects the responsibility of the offender

Mental disorder or learning disability

Sole or primary carer for dependent relatives

Step Three
Consider any factors which indicate a reduction, such as assistance to the prosecution

The court should take into account sections 73 and 74 of the Serious Organised Crime and Police Act 2005 (assistance by defendants: reduction or review of sentence) and any other rule of law by virtue of which an offender may receive a discounted sentence in consequence of assistance given (or offered) to the prosecutor or investigator.

Step Four
Reduction for guilty pleas

The court should take account of any potential reduction for a guilty plea in accordance with section 144 of the Criminal Justice Act 2003 and the *Guilty Plea* guideline.

For class A offences, where a minimum mandatory sentence is imposed under section 110 Powers of Criminal Courts (Sentencing) Act, the discount for an early guilty plea must not exceed 20 per cent.

Step Five
Totality principle

If sentencing an offender for more than one offence, or where the offender is already serving a sentence, consider whether the total sentence is just and proportionate to the offending behaviour.

Step Six
Confiscation and ancillary orders

In all cases, the court is required to consider confiscation where the Crown invokes the process or where the court considers it appropriate. It should also consider whether to make ancillary orders.

Step Seven
Reasons

Section 174 of the Criminal Justice Act 2003 imposes a duty to give reasons for, and explain the effect of, the sentence.

Step Eight
Consideration for remand time

Sentencers should take into consideration any remand time served in relation to the final sentence at this final step. The court should consider whether to give credit for time spent on remand in custody or on bail in accordance with sections 240 and 240A of the Criminal Justice Act 2003.

A[28]

Drunkenness

Charges

A[28.1]

1 Being found drunk in any highway, public place, or on licensed premises

Licensing Act 1872, s 12

Maximum penalty – Fine level 2.

A[28.2]

2 In a public place namely [. . . . .] was guilty while drunk of disorderly behaviour

Criminal Justice Act 1967, s 91

Maximum penalty – Fine level 3.

NB: A fixed penalty of £80 is available

Legal notes and definitions

A[28.3]

Found. Means 'ascertained to be', not 'discovered'.

Lawfulness of arrest.

Police were called to a disturbance in a private garden at 4am. A police officer led the defendant by the arm out of the garden onto a public path. The defendant continued to disturb the peace and was arrested. Placing the events in context and taking a common sense approach, the officer, in acting as he had done, had acted in conformity with the general accepted standards of conduct. A conviction for drunk and disorderly was upheld (*McMillan v Crown Prosecution Service* [2008] EWHC 1457 (Admin), [2008] All ER (D) 142 (May)).

A[28.4]

Drunk. Typical evidence of drunkenness is strong smell of drink, falling over, swaying, stumbling, showing evidence of a lack of co-ordination, slurred thick speech, rapid pulse, redness in the face, glazed expression, drowsiness or semi-coma and no evidence of any other cause for these symptoms. A person exhibiting these symptoms as a result of 'glue sniffing' is not drunk for the purposes of this offence or the offence of being drunk and disorderly.

The offence is constituted by the state of drunkenness. The inability of the defendant to take care of himself may permit a constable to arrest the defendant. On a charge of being drunk and disorderly it is the disorderly behaviour that normally provides the trigger for an arrest without warrant (*H v DPP* [2005] EWHC 2459 (Admin), 170 JP 4).

A[28.5]

Disorderly. The term 'drunk and disorderly' should be given its natural and ordinary meaning. It was a question of fact and degree whether or not the accused had exhibited 'disorderly behaviour' (*Carroll v DPP* [2009] All ER (D) 35 (Mar), 173 JP 285).

A[28.6]

Public place. Includes buildings and any place to which the public has access whether on payment or otherwise, as well as buses or taxis. The entrance hall of a block of flats where admission was controlled by an intercom and a security lock was not a public place (*Williams v DPP* [1992] Crim LR 503).

A[28.7]

Licensed premises. This not only includes normally licensed premises for the sale of liquor but also premises given an occasional licence and includes any part of licensed premises hired out to a private party. This definition must now be read in the light of the **Licensing Act 2003**.

Sentencing

A[28.8]

NB: There is no published guideline for being drunk in a highway. Consider whether a fine or discharge is appropriate?

SC Guideline – Drunk and disorderly in a public place

A[28.9]

OFFENCE SERIOUSNESS (CULPABILITY AND HARM) A. IDENTIFY THE APPROPRIATE STARTING POINT Starting points based on first time offender pleading not guilty		
Examples of nature of activity	Starting point	Range
Shouting, causing disturbance for some minutes	Band A fine	Conditional discharge to band B fine
Substantial disturbance caused	Band B fine	Band A fine to band C fine
OFFENCE SERIOUSNESS (CULPABILITY AND HARM) B. CONSIDER THE EFFECT OF AGGRAVATING AND MITIGATING FACTORS (OTHER THAN THOSE WITHIN EXAMPLES ABOVE)		
Common aggravating and mitigating factors are identified at B[5.2A]. The following may be particularly relevant but **these lists are not exhaustive**		

Factors indicating higher culpability	Factors indicating lower culpability
1. Offensive words or conduct involved	1. Minor and non-threatening
2. Lengthy incident involved	2. Stopped as soon as police arrived
3. Group action	
Factors indicating greater degree of harm	
1. Offence committed at school, hospital or other place where vulnerable persons may be present	
2. Offence committed on public transport	
3. Victim providing public service	

FORM A PRELIMINARY VIEW OF THE APPROPRIATE SENTENCE, THEN CONSIDER OFFENDER MITIGATION
Common factors are identified at B[5.2A]
CONSIDER A REDUCTION FOR A GUILTY PLEA
CONSIDER ANCILLARY ORDERS, INCLUDING COMPENSATION AND FOOTBALL BANNING ORDER (where appropriate)
Refer to **Part B** for guidance on available ancillary orders
DECIDE SENTENCE   **GIVE REASONS**

A[29]

Exploitation of prostitution

Charges

A[29.1]

1. Intentionally causes or incites another person to become a prostitute in any part of the world, and does so for or in the expectation of gain for himself or a third person.

Sexual Offences Act 2003, s 52.

Maximum penalty – level 5 and/or 6 months' (**12 months) imprisonment. Triable either way.

Specified sexual offence under Sch 15, Part 2, CJA 2003.

Crown Court – 7 years' imprisonment or an unlimited fine.

NB: A new s 51A of the 2003 Act has been added by the Policing and Crime Act 2009. From **1 April 2010** this makes it an offence for a person in a street or public place to solicit another (B) for the purposes of obtaining B's sexual services as a prostitute. References to a person is a street or public place include a person in a vehicle in a street or public place. The offence is a summary only offence carrying a maximum level 3 fine.

A[29.2]

2. Intentionally controls any of the activities of another person relating to that person's prostitution in any part of the world, and does so for or in the expectation of gain for himself or a third person.

Sexual Offences Act 2003, s 53.

Maximum penalty – level 5 and/or 6 months' (**12 months) imprisonment. Triable either way.

Specified sexual offence under Sch 15, Part 2, CJA 2003.

Crown Court – 7 years' imprisonment or an unlimited fine.

NB: A new s 53A of the 2003 Act has been added by the Policing and Crime Act 2009. From **1 April 2010** this makes it an offence to pay for the services of a prostitute subjected to force etc. The offence is a summary only offence carrying a maximum level 3 fine.

Mode of trial

A[29.3]

See SC Guideline at A[29.4] below.

Note

Where an offender has profited from his or her involvement in the prostitution of others, the court should consider making a confiscation order approximately equivalent to the profits enjoyed. Such an order may be made only in the Crown Court.

Sentencing
SC Guideline – Exploitation of prostitution

A[29.4]

This guideline is taken from the SC's definitive guideline *Sexual Offences Act 2003*, published 30 April 2007.

*The court **must** inform the defendant that the Independent Safeguarding Authority (known as the Independent Barring Board) will automatically ban him/her from working with children and/or vulnerable adults. As the court has no role in the decision if the defendant needs any further advice he/she should consult a solicitor.

IDENTIFY DANGEROUS OFFENDERS
These are specified offences for the purposes of the public protection provisions in the Criminal Justice Act 2003. Refer to B[16.5] and consult legal adviser for guidance

OFFENCE SERIOUSNESS (CULPABILITY AND HARM)
A. IDENTIFY THE APPROPRIATE STARTING POINT
Starting points based on first time offender pleading not guilty

Examples of nature of activity	Starting point	Range
No evidence victim was physically coerced or corrupted, and the involvement of the offender was minimal	Medium level community order	Band C fine to high level community order
No coercion or corruption but the offender is closely involved in the victim's prostitution	Crown Court	26 weeks custody to Crown Court
Evidence of physical and/or mental coercion	Crown Court	Crown Court

OFFENCE SERIOUSNESS (CULPABILITY AND HARM)
B. CONSIDER THE EFFECT OF AGGRAVATING AND MITIGATING FACTORS (OTHER THAN THOSE WITHIN EXAMPLES ABOVE)
Common aggravating and mitigating factors are identified at B[5.2A]. The following may be particularly relevant but **these lists are not exhaustive**

Factors indicating higher culpability	Factor indicating lower culpability
1. Background of threats, intimidation or coercion	1. Offender also being controlled in prostitution and subject to threats or intimidation

2. Large-scale commercial operation	
3. Substantial gain (in the region of £5,000 and up)	
4. Use of drugs, alcohol or other substance to secure the victim's compliance	
5. Abduction or detention	
6. Threats to prevent the victim reporting the activity	
7. Threats to disclose the victim's activity to friends/relatives	
Factor indicating greater degree of harm	
1. Induced dependency on drugs	
FORM A PRELIMINARY VIEW OF THE APPROPRIATE SENTENCE, THEN CONSIDER OFFENDER MITIGATION Common factors are identified at B[5.2A]	
CONSIDER A REDUCTION FOR A GUILTY PLEA	
CONSIDER ANCILLARY ORDERS, INCLUDING COMPENSATION Refer to B[18] for guidance on compensation and **Part B** for guidance on available ancillary orders	
DECIDE SENTENCE **GIVE REASONS**	

Note

Where an offender has profited from his or her involvement in the prostitution of others, the court should consider making a confiscation order approximately equivalent to the profits enjoyed. Such an order may be made only in the Crown Court.

A[29.5]

Closure orders: see [B53].

A[30]
Exposure

Charge

A[30.1]

Intentionally exposes his genitals, and he intends that someone will see them and be caused alarm or distress.

Sexual Offences Act 2003, s 66.

Maximum penalty – level 5 and/or 6 months' (**12 months) imprisonment. Triable either way.

Specified sexual offence under Sch 15, Part 2, CJA 2003.

Crown Court – 2 years' imprisonment and unlimited fine.

Mode of trial

A[30.2]

See SGC Guideline and Notes at **A[30.3]** below.

Sentencing
SC Guideline – Exposure

A[30.3]

This guideline is taken from the SC's definitive guideline *Sexual Offences Act 2003*, published 30 April 2007.

*The court <u>must</u> inform the defendant that the Independent Safeguarding Authority (known as the Independent Barring Board) will automatically ban him/her from working with children and/or vulnerable adults. As the court has no role in the decision if the defendant needs any further advice he/she should consult a solicitor.

Key factors

(a) This offence is committed where an offender intentionally exposes his or her genitals and intends that someone will see them and be caused alarm or distress. It is gender neutral, covering exposure of male or female genitalia to a male or female witness.

(b) The SC guideline provides that when dealing with a repeat offender, the starting point should be 12 weeks custody with a range of 4 to 26 weeks custody. The presence of aggravating factors may suggest that a sentence above the range is appropriate and that the case should be committed to the Crown Court [for trial or sentence as appropriate].

(c) In accordance with s 80 and schedule 3 of the Sexual Offences Act 2003, automatic notification requirements apply upon conviction to an offender aged 18 or over where:

(1) the victim was under 18; or

(2) a term of imprisonment or a community order of at least 12 months is imposed.

For notification requirements generally see **A[52.15]**.

(d) This guideline may be relevant by way of analogy to conduct charged as the common law offence of outraging public decency; the offence is triable either way and has a maximum penalty of a level 5 fine and/or 6 months' (**12 months) imprisonment when tried summarily.

IDENTIFY DANGEROUS OFFENDERS
This is a specified offence for the purposes of the public protection provisions in the Criminal Justice Act 2003. Refer to **B[16.5]** and consult legal adviser for guidance

OFFENCE SERIOUSNESS (CULPABILITY AND HARM)

A. IDENTIFY THE APPROPRIATE STARTING POINT

Starting points based on first time offender pleading not guilty

Examples of nature of activity	Starting point	Range
Basic offence as defined in the Act, assuming no aggravating or mitigating features	Low level community order	Band B fine to medium level community order
Offence with an aggravating feature	Medium level community order	Low level community order to high level community order
Two or more aggravating features	12 weeks custody	6 weeks custody to Crown Court

OFFENCE SERIOUSNESS (CULPABILITY AND HARM)

B. CONSIDER THE EFFECT OF AGGRAVATING AND MITIGATING FACTORS (OTHER THAN THOSE WITHIN EXAMPLES ABOVE)

Common aggravating and mitigating factors are identified at **B[5.2A]**. The following may be particularly relevant but **these lists are not exhaustive**

Factors indicating higher culpability	
1. Threats to prevent the victim reporting an offence	
2. Intimidating behaviour/threats of violence	
Factor indicating greater degree of harm	
1. Victim is a child	

FORM A PRELIMINARY VIEW OF THE APPROPRIATE SENTENCE, THEN CONSIDER OFFENDER MITIGATION

Common factors are identified at **B[5.2A]**

CONSIDER A REDUCTION FOR A GUILTY PLEA
CONSIDER ANCILLARY ORDERS, INCLUDING COMPENSATION
Refer to **B[18]** for guidance on compensation and **Part B** for guidance on available ancillary orders
DECIDE SENTENCE
GIVE REASONS

A[31]

False accounting

Charge

A[31.1]

Dishonestly and with a view to gain for himself or another or with intent to cause loss to another -

(a)   destroys, defaces, conceals or falsifies any account or any record or document made or required for any accounting purpose; or

(b)   in furnishing information for any purpose produces or makes use of any account, or any such record or document as aforesaid, which to his knowledge is or may be misleading, false or deceptive in any material particular.

Theft Act 1968, s 17

Maximum penalty – Fine level 5 and/or 6 months' (**12 months) imprisonment.

Crown Court – 7 years' imprisonment and unlimited fine.

Mode of trial

A[31.2]

See general notes at I[4] and SC Guidelines below.

Sentencing
SC Guideline – False Accounting (see Fraud – banking and insurance fraud etc and Fraud – confidence below)

A[31.3]

Triable either way

Maximum when tried summarily: Level 5 fine and/or 6 months

Maximum when tried on indictment: 7 years

Refer to guidelines: *Fraud – banking and insurance fraud and obtaining credit through fraud, benefit fraud and revenue fraud* at **A[31.4]** and *Fraud – confidence* at **A[31.6]** below.

Accounting purpose. Absent direct evidence of the accounting practices of the lender, a jury or bench of magistrates is entitled to conclude that an application for a mortgage or a loan made to a commercial institution is a document required for an accounting purpose. It made no difference that the details provided in the application served a dual purpose: *R v O* [2010] EWCA Crim 2233, [2011] 2 All ER 656, 174 JP 529.

Fraud – banking and insurance fraud, and obtaining credit through fraud, benefit fraud, and revenue fraud – factors to take into consideration

A[31.4]

This guideline and accompanying notes are taken from the Sentencing Council's definitive guideline *Sentencing for Fraud – Statutory offences*, published 26 October 2009.

The starting points and ranges for fraud against HM Revenue and Customs, for benefit fraud and for banking and insurance and obtaining credit through fraud are the same since the seriousness of all offences of organisational fraud derives from the extent of the fraudulent activity (culpability) and the financial loss caused or likely to be caused (harm).

Key factors common to these types of fraud

(a)   As the determinants of seriousness include the "value of property or consequential loss involved", the table provides both a fixed amount (on which the starting point is based) and a band (on which the sentencing range is based). Where the value is larger or smaller than the amount on which the starting point is based, this should lead to upward or downward movement from the starting point as appropriate. Where the amount the offender intended to obtain cannot be established, the appropriate measure will be the amount that was likely to be achieved in all the circumstances. Where the offender was entitled to part or all of the amount obtained, the starting point should be based on the amount to which they were not entitled.

(b)   A further determinant of seriousness is whether the fraud was a single fraudulent transaction or a multiple fraud. Where one false declaration or a failure to disclose a change in circumstances results in multiple payments, this should be regarded as multiple fraud.

(c)   In general terms, the greater the loss, the more serious will be the offence. However, the financial value of the loss may not reflect the full extent of the harm caused. The court should also take into account; the impact of the offence on the victim (particularly where the loss may be significantly greater than the monetary value); harm to persons other than the direct victim (including the aggravation and stress of unscrambling the consequences of an offence); erosion of public confidence; and the difference between the loss intended and that which results (which may involve adjusting the assessment of seriousness to reflect the degree of loss caused).

(d) When the offending involves a number of people acting co-operatively, this will aggravate an offence as it indicates planning or professional activity, and may also increase the degree of loss caused or intended. The role of each offender is important in determining the appropriate level of seriousness and movement above or below the starting point within the applicable level.

(e) Use of another person's identity is an aggravating factor; the extent to which it aggravates an offence will be based on the degree of planning and the impact that the offence has had on the living victim or relatives of the deceased – whether the identity belongs to a living or deceased person is neutral for this purpose. Matters of offender mitigation which may be particularly relevant to these types of fraud include:

(1) *Voluntary cessation of offending* – a claim, supported by objective evidence, that an offender stopped offending before being apprehended should be treated as mitigation, particularly where accompanied by a genuine expression of remorse. The lapse of time since commission of the last offence is relevant to whether the claim is genuine, and reasons for the cessation will assist the court in determining whether it amounts to mitigation and if so, to what degree.

(2) *Complete and unprompted disclosure of the extent of the fraud* – an admission that a greater sum has been obtained than that known to the authorities ensures that an offender is sentenced for the complete extent of the fraud. This is ready co-operation with the authorities and should be treated as mitigation. Provision of information about others involved in the fraud should also be treated as mitigation. Generally, the earlier the disclosure is given and the higher the degree of assistance, the greater the allowance for mitigation.

(3) *Voluntary restitution* – the timing of the voluntary restitution will indicate the degree to which it reflects genuine remorse. Generally, the earlier the property or money is returned the greater the degree of mitigation the offender should receive. If circumstances beyond the control of the offender prevent return of defrauded items, the degree of mitigation will depend on the point in time at which, and the determination with which the offender tried to return the items.

(4) *Financial pressure* – financial pressure neither increases nor diminishes an offender's culpability. However, where such pressure is **exceptional** and not of the offender's own making, it may in very rare circumstances constitute mitigation.

(f)   A court should be aware that a confiscation order is an important sanction. Such an order may only be made in the Crown Court. The court must commit the offender to the Crown Court where this is requested by the prosecution with a view to an order being considered.

(g)   Ancillary orders should be considered in all cases, principally compensation, deprivation and disqualification from driving, as well as other powers particular to the type of offending behaviour.

Additional notes:

Banking and insurance fraud and obtaining credit through fraud:

(i)   A payment card or bank account fraud is unlikely to be committed in circumstances where the offender's intention was not fraudulent from the outset.

(ii)   Use of another person's identity is a feature of nearly all payment card and bank account frauds since in most cases the offender claims to be the account holder or a person authorised to deal with the account. Courts should therefore increase the starting point to reflect the presence of this aggravating factor.

Benefit fraud:

(i)   This guideline is based on an understanding that the prosecutor will generally seek summary trial for appropriate benefit fraud cases involving sums up to £35,000.

(ii)   The fact that defrauded sums may have been recovered is not relevant to the choice of the type of sentence to be imposed.

(iii)   The court should have regard to personal and family circumstances of offenders which will vary greatly and may be particularly significant to sentencing this type of fraud.

Revenue fraud:

(i)   The proposals for the sentencing of revenue fraud take as a starting point an offender who acts intentionally. Where the offender has acted recklessly (relevant only to offences under the Value Added Tax Act 1994), courts should adjust the assessment of seriousness to take account of this lower level of culpability.

(ii)   Payments to HMRC may be evaded in order to increase the profitability of a legitimate business or the level of an individual's legitimate remuneration; payments may be fraudulently obtained from HMRC without any underlying legitimate activity at all as in a Carousel Fraud. Although the type of harm is the same since both result in a loss to HMRC, where payment is sought from HMRC in such circumstances, culpability is likely to be higher. Accordingly, such offences are likely to be regarded as more serious.

Fraud – banking and insurance fraud, and obtaining credit through fraud, benefit fraud, and revenue fraud

Fraud Act 2006, s 1

Theft Act 1968, s 17

Social Security Administration Act 1992, ss 111A(1), 111A(1A), 111A(1B), 111A(1D) and 111(1E)

Tax Credits Act 2002, s 35

Value Added Tax Act 1994, ss 72(1), (3) and (8)

Finance Act 2000, s 144

Customs and Excise Management Act 1979, ss 170(1)(a)(i) and (ii), 170(1)(b),170(2)(a), 170B, 50(1)(a) and 50(2)

A[31.5]
All offences: Triable either way.

Maximum when tried summarily: Level 5 fine and/or 6 months.

Maximum when tried on indictment: Fraud, 10 years; other offences, 7 years.

Offences under s 112, Social Security Administration Act 1992 are not covered by this guideline.

This guideline does not apply to offences under s 50 or s 170, Customs and Excise Management Act 1979 which involve prohibited weapons and have a maximum penalty of 10 years.

OFFENCE SERIOUSNESS (CULPABILITY AND HARM)		
A. IDENTIFY THE APPROPRIATE STARTING POINT		
Starting points based on first time offender pleading not guilty		
Examples of nature of activity	**Starting point**	**Range**
Single fraudulent transaction, not fraudulent from the outset	Value £2,500* – Band B fine	Value less than £5,000 – Band A fine to low level community order
	Value £12,500* – Medium level community order	Value £5,000 to less than £20,000 – Band B fine to 6 weeks custody
	Value £60,000* – 12 weeks custody	Value £20,000 to less than £100,000 – Medium level community order to Crown Court

Single fraudulent transaction, fraudulent from the outset	Value £2,500* – Low level community order	Value less than £5,000 – Band A fine to medium level community order
	Value £12,500* – High level community order	Value £5,000 to less than £20,000 – Band C fine to 18 weeks custody
	Value £60,000* – 26 weeks custody	Value £20,000 to less than £100,000 – 6 weeks custody to Crown Court
Not fraudulent from the outset, and either	Value £2,500* – Medium level community order	Value less than £5,000 – Band B fine to high level community order
• fraud carried out over a significant period of time or	Value £12,500* – 6 weeks custody	Value £5,000 to less than £20,000 – Medium level community order to 26 weeks custody
• multiple frauds	Value £60,000* – Crown Court	Value £20,000 to less than £100,000 – 12 weeks custody to Crown Court
Where value exceeds £100,000	Crown Court	Crown Court
Fraudulent from the outset, and either	Value £2,500* – High level community order	Value less than £5,000 – Low level community order to 6 weeks custody
• fraud carried out over a significant period of time or	Value £12,500* – 12 weeks custody	Value £5,000 to less than £20,000 – High level community order to Crown Court
• multiple frauds	Value £60,000* – Crown Court	Value £20,000 to less than £100,000 – 18 weeks custody to Crown Court
Where value £100,000 or more or fraud was professionally planned	Crown Court	Crown Court

*Where the actual amount is greater or smaller than the value on which the starting point is based, that is likely to be one of the factors that will move the sentence within the range (see (a) at A[31.4])

OFFENCE SERIOUSNESS (CULPABILITY AND HARM)

B. CONSIDER THE EFFECT OF AGGRAVATING AND MITIGATING FACTORS (OTHER THAN THOSE WITHIN EXAMPLES ABOVE)

Common aggravating and mitigating factors are identified at B[5.2A]. The following may be particularly relevant but these lists are not exhaustive

Factors indicating higher culpability	*Factor indicating lower culpability*
1. Number involved in the offence and role of the offender	1. Peripheral involvement
2. Making repeated importations, particularly in the face of warnings from the authorities	2. Misleading or incomplete advice

3. Dealing in goods with an additional health risk	
Factors indicating greater degree of harm 1. Use of another person's identity 2. Disposing of goods to under-aged purchasers	
FORM A PRELIMINARY VIEW OF THE APPROPRIATE SENTENCE, THEN CONSIDER OFFENDER MITIGATION Common factors are identified at B[5.2A]	
CONSIDER A REDUCTION FOR A GUILTY PLEA	
CONSIDE ANCILLARY ORDERS Refer to **Part B** for guidance on available ancillary orders.	
DECIDE SENTENCE **GIVE REASONS**	

Fraud – confidence – factors to take into consideration

A[31.6]

This guideline and accompanying notes are taken from the Sentencing Council's definitive guideline *Sentencing for Fraud – Statutory offences*, published 26 October 2009

Key factors

(a)   This type of offending involves a victim transferring money and/or property as a result of being deceived or misled by the offender. An example of a simple confidence fraud is a person claiming to be collecting money for charity when, in fact, he or she intends to keep the money. Other examples of common confidence frauds are *Advance fee frauds* (such as lottery/prize draw scams and foreign money-making frauds) and *Fraudulent sales of goods and services* (where goods or services are never received/performed or are worth less than represented.

(b)   As the determinants of seriousness include the 'value of property or consequential loss involved', the table provides both a fixed amount (on which the starting point is based) and a band (on which the sentencing range is based). Where the value is larger or smaller than the amount on which the starting point is based, this should lead to upward or downward movement as appropriate. Where the amount the offender intended to obtain cannot be established, the appropriate measure will be the amount that was likely to be achieved in all the circumstances.

(c)   A further determinant of seriousness is whether the fraud was a single fraudulent transaction or a multiple fraud. Most confidence frauds will by their nature involve many actual or potential victims and multiple transactions and should be regarded as multiple fraud.

(d)   Targeting a vulnerable victim is also a determinant of seriousness. A victim might be vulnerable as a result of old age, youth or disability. In addition, some victims of advance fee frauds may have personalities which make them 'vulnerable in a way and to a degree not typical of the general population' because they fall for scams many times and may be targeted using 'sucker lists' of people who have previously fallen victim to scams. Care should be taken to ensure that where targeting a vulnerable victim is used to determine the appropriate level of seriousness and starting point, that it is not used again as an aggravating factor to move within the sentencing range.

(e)   In general terms, the greater the loss, the more serious will be the offence. However, the financial value of the loss may not reflect the full extent of the harm caused. The court should also take into account; the impact of the offence on the victim (particularly where the loss may be significantly greater than the monetary value); harm to persons other than the direct victim (including the aggravation and stress of unscrambling the consequences of an offence); erosion of public confidence; and the difference between the loss intended and that which results (which may involve adjusting the assessment of seriousness to reflect the degree of loss caused).

(f)   When the offending involves a number of people acting co-operatively, this will aggravate an offence as it indicates planning or professional activity, and may also increase the degree of loss caused or intended. The role of each offender is important in determining the appropriate level of seriousness and movement above or below the starting point within the applicable level.

(g)   Use of another person's identity is an aggravating factor; the extent to which it aggravates an offence will be based on the degree of planning and the impact that the offence has had on the living victim or relatives of the deceased – whether the identity belongs to a living or deceased person is neutral for this purpose.

(h)   Matters of offender mitigation which may be particularly relevant to this type of fraud include:

       (1)   *Voluntary cessation of offending* – a claim, supported by objective evidence, that an offender stopped offending before being apprehended should be treated as mitigation, particularly where accompanied by a genuine expression of remorse. The lapse of time since commission of the last offence is relevant to whether the claim is genuine, and reasons for the cessation will assist the court in determining whether it amounts to mitigation and if so, to what degree.

(2) *Complete and unprompted disclosure of the extent of the fraud* – an admission that a greater sum has been obtained than that known to the authorities ensures that an offender is sentenced for the complete extent of the fraud. This amounts to ready co-operation with the authorities and should be treated as mitigation. Provision of information about others involved in the fraud should also be treated as mitigation. Generally, the earlier the disclosure is given and the higher the degree of assistance, the greater the allowance for mitigation.

(3) *Voluntary restitution* – the timing of the voluntary restitution will indicate the degree to which it reflects genuine remorse. Generally, the earlier the property or money is returned the greater the degree of mitigation the offender should receive. If circumstances beyond the control of the offender prevent return of defrauded items, the degree of mitigation will depend on the point in time at which, and the determination with which the offender tried to return the items.

(4) *Financial pressure* – financial pressure neither increases nor diminishes an offender's culpability. However, where such pressure is exceptional and not of the offender's own making, it may in very rare circumstances constitute mitigation.

(i) A court should be aware that a confiscation order is an important sanction. Such an order may only be made in the Crown Court. The court must commit the offender to the Crown Court where this is requested by the prosecution with a view to an order being considered.

(j) Ancillary orders should be considered in all cases, principally compensation and deprivation.

Fraud – confidence (Fraud Act 2006, s 1; Theft Act 1968, s 17)

A[31.7]

All offences: Triable either way.

Maximum when tried summarily: Level 5 fine and/or 6 months.

Maximum when tried on indictment: Fraud, 10 years; other offences, 7 years.

OFFENCE SERIOUSNESS (CULPABILITY AND HARM)		
A. IDENTIFY THE APPROPRIATE STARTING POINT		
Starting points based on first time offender pleading not guilty		
Examples of nature of activity	Starting point	Range

Single fraudulent transaction, confidence fraud not targeting a vulnerable victim, and involving no or limited planning	Value £10,000* – Medium level community order	Value less than £20,000 – Band B fine to 6 weeks custody
	Value £60,000* – 12 weeks custody	Value £20,000 to less than £100,000– Medium level community order to Crown Court
Single fraudulent transaction Involving targeting of a vulnerable victim	Value £10,000* – 6 weeks custody	Value less than £20,000 – Medium level community order to 26 weeks custody
	Value £60,000* – 26 weeks custody	Value £20,000 to less than £100,000 – High level community order to Crown Court
Lower scale advance fee fraud or other confidence fraud characterised by a degree of planning and/or multiple transactions	Value £10,000* – Crown Court	Value less than £20,000 – 26 weeks custody to Crown Court
	Value £60,000* – Crown Court	Value £20,000 to less than £100,000 – Crown Court
Large scale advance fee fraud or other confidence fraud involving the deliberate targeting of a large number of vulnerable victims	Value £10,000* – Crown Court	Value less than £20,000 – Crown Court
	Value £60,000* – Crown Court	Value £20,000 to less than £100,000 – Crown Court

*Where the actual amount is greater or smaller than the value on which the starting point is based, that is likely to be one of the factors that will move the sentence within the range (see (b) at A[37.1])

OFFENCE SERIOUSNESS (CULPABILITY AND HARM)

B. CONSIDER THE EFFECT OF AGGRAVATING AND MITIGATING FACTORS (OTHER THAN THOSE WITHIN EXAMPLES ABOVE)

Common aggravating and mitigating factors are identified at B[5.2A]. The following may be particularly relevant but **these lists are not exhaustive**

Factors indicating higher culpability	*Factor indicating lower culpability*
1. Number involved in the offence and role of the offender	1. Peripheral involvement
2. Offending carried out over a significant period of time	2. Behaviour not fraudulent from the outset
	3. Misleading or incomplete advice
Factors indicating greater degree of harm	
1. Use of another person's identity	
2. Offence has lasting effect on the victim	

FORM A PRELIMINARY VIEW OF THE APPROPRIATE SENTENCE, THEN CONSIDER OFFENDER MITIGATION Common factors are identified at B[5.2A]
CONSIDER A REDUCTION FOR A GUILTY PLEA
CONSIDE ANCILLARY ORDERS Refer to **Part B** for guidance on available ancillary orders.
DECIDE SENTENCE **GIVE REASONS**

A[32]

False identity documents

Charge

A[32.1]

Have in his possession or under his control, without reasonable excuse—

(a) an identify document that is false,
(b) an identity document that was improperly obtained,
(c) an identity document that relates to someone else,
(d) any apparatus, article or material which, to his knowledge, is or has been specially designed or adapted for he making of false identify documents or to be used in the making of such documents, or
(e) any article or material which, to his knowledge, is or has been specially designed or adapted to be used in the making of such documents.

Identity Documents Act 2010, s 6(1)*

Maximum penalty – Fine level 5 and/or 6 months' (**12 months) imprisonment.

Crown Court – 2 years' imprisonment and unlimited fine.

*NB: From 21 January 2011 this legislation repealed the Identity Cards Act 2006.

Mode of trial

A[32.2]

See the SC Guideline below.

Defences

A[32.2A]

There is defence for refugees from other countries under s.31 of the Immigration and Asylum Act 1999. Section 31 applies to prosecutions under both ss 4 and 6 of the 2010 Act. However, there are limitations to that defence. Section 31 of the said Act provides:

. . . (2) If, in coming from the country where his life or freedom was threatened, the refugee stopped in another country outside the United Kingdom, subsection (1) applies only if he shows that he could not reasonably have been expected to be given protection under the Refugee Convention in that other country.

Unlike other defences raised under s 31(1), the defendant bears only an evidential as opposed to a legal burden. Provided that the defendant can adduce sufficient evidence in support of his claim to refugee status to raise the issue, the prosecution bears the burden to the usual standard that he is in fact not a refugee.

In *R v MV* [2010] EWCA Crim 2400, [2011] 1 Cr App Rep 432, the appellant had come into the UK on a flight from Italy. Given his inability to say whether his flight had stopped during his journey from Somalia and to account for where he had spent one and a half days, a jury could have inferred that he had in all probability remained in Italy. Even if no legal advice had been given regarding the availability of a defence under s 31 of the Immigration and Asylum Act 1999, there was no reasonable prospect of that defence succeeding.

The absence of words in what was subsection (5) of s 25 of the Identity Cards Act 2006, such as are found in subsection (1) of s 25, indicates that a defendant who does not know or believe that a document is false cannot of itself, per se, amount to a reasonable excuse (even for an offence under what is now s 6(1)). However, lack of knowledge or belief might be relevant to a defence of reasonable excuse. The defence is found in various statutory contexts and it is par excellence a matter for the jury whether or not a reasonable excuse has been established. A judge ought to withdraw that issue from the jury only if no reasonable jury could conclude on the facts alleged that the explanation was capable of constituting a reasonable excuse. Nothing in s 25 suggested that honest belief in the genuineness of the document is a factor which the jury is obliged to ignore. Accordingly, the defendant was entitled to rely upon her genuine belief that the document was valid while contending that she had a reasonable excuse for having the false passport in her possession: see *R v Unah* [2011] EWCA Crim 1837, 175 JP 391, [2011] 30 LS Gaz R 24.

Sentencing
SC Guideline – False identity documents

A[32.3]

Note: possession of a false identity document with an improper intention of using it is an indictable only offence (Identity Documents Act 2010, s 4(1)). The maximum penalty is 10 years' imprisonment and an unlimited fine.

OFFENCE SERIOUSNESS (CULPABILITY AND HARM)		
A. IDENTIFY THE APPROPRIATE STARTING POINT		
Starting points based on first time offender pleading not guilty		
Examples of nature of activity	Starting point	Range
Single document possessed	Medium community order	Band C fine to high level community order
Small number of documents, no evidence of dealing	12 weeks custody	6 weeks custody to Crown Court

Considerable number of documents possessed, evidence of involvement in larger operation	Crown Court	Crown Court

OFFENCE SERIOUSNESS (CULPABILITY AND HARM)

B. CONSIDER THE EFFECT OF AGGRAVATING AND MITIGATING FACTORS (OTHER THAN THOSE WITHIN EXAMPLES ABOVE)

Common aggravating and mitigating factors are identified at B[5.2A]. The following may be particularly relevant but these lists are not exhaustive

Factors indicating higher culpability	*Factor indicating lower culpability*
1. Clear knowledge that documents false	1. Genuine mistake or ignorance
2. Number of documents possessed (where not in offence descriptions above)	
Factors indicating greater degree of harm	
1. Group activity	
2. Potential impact of use (where not in offence descriptions above)	

FORM A PRELIMINARY VIEW OF THE APPROPRIATE SENTENCE, THEN CONSIDER OFFENDER MITIGATION

Common factors are identified at B[5.2A]

CONSIDER A REDUCTION FOR A GUILTY PLEA

DECIDE SENTENCE

GIVE REASONS

A[33]

Firearm, carrying in a public place

Charge

A[33.1]

Without lawful authority or reasonable excuse having in a public place (a loaded shotgun), (a firearm loaded or not and ammunition suitable for use in the said firearm) (an air weapon loaded or not) or (an imitation firearm)

Firearms Act 1968, s 19

Maximum penalty -

Firearm: Fine level 5 and 6 months (**12 months) and forfeiture. Triable either way.

Air weapon: Fine level 5 and/or 6 months (**51 weeks) and forfeiture. Triable only by magistrates.

Crown Court – 7 years' imprisonment and unlimited fine (12 months for imitation firearm).

Mode of trial

A[33.2]

See the SC Guideline below.

Legal notes and definitions

A[33.3]

Public place. Means any highway, premises or place to which the public at the material time has access whether on payment or otherwise. This did not include a causeway linking an island to the mainland with notices declaring it was a private road (*Planton v DPP* [2001] EWHC 450 (Admin), (2001) 166 JP 324).

A[33.4]

Without lawful authority or reasonable excuse. The Firearms Act 1968 expressly places on the defendant the burden of proving that he had lawful authority or reasonable excuse. He only has to prove that on the balance of probabilities he had lawful authority or reasonable excuse. He does not have to prove this beyond all reasonable doubt.

(a)   A certificate for a firearm was not in itself lawful authority under the Firearms Act 1968, s 19, for the holder of the certificate to have the firearm and ammunition for it in a public place.

(b)   The mistaken belief by the holder of an invalid firearm certificate that it was valid and that it was lawful authority under the Firearms Act 1968, s 19 was not capable of being a reasonable excuse and therefore a defence under that section

(*R v Jones* [1995] QB 235, [1995] 3 All ER 139, CA).

A[33.5]

ECHR. Having regard to the legitimate aims of the legislation, it is suggested that the shifting of the legal burden of proof to the accused is necessary and proportionate in ECHR terms.

A[33.6]

Shotgun. Although the firearm need not be loaded a shotgun must be loaded to establish this offence. A shotgun is a smooth bore gun whose barrel is 24 inches or longer with a bore not exceeding two inches and which is not a revolver nor has an illegal magazine, not being an air gun.

A[33.7]

Air weapon. An air weapon may be loaded or not to establish this offence. An air weapon is an air gun, air rifle or an air pistol of a type which has not been declared by the Home Office to be specially dangerous (see **A[76.7]**).

A[33.8]

Firearm. Means any lethal barrelled weapon of any description from which any shot, bullet or other missile can be discharged but for this offence excludes shotguns and air weapons as described above. A lethal weapon includes one capable of inflicting injury although not designed to do so, eg a signal pistol. An imitation firearm which is so constructed or adapted as to be readily converted into a firearm is to be treated as a firearm even though it has not been so converted (*Castle v DPP* (1998) Times, 3 April).

A[33.9]

A starting pistol which could be adapted to fire bullets if the barrel was drilled was held to be a firearm (*R v Freeman* [1970] 2 All ER 413, [1970] 1 WLR 788, CA).

A[33.10]

An offence is committed whether the firearm is loaded or not but the defendant must have with him ammunition suitable for use in that firearm.

Sentencing
SC Guideline – Firearm, carrying in a public place

A[33.11]

OFFENCE SERIOUSNESS (CULPABILITY AND HARM)		
A. IDENTIFY THE APPROPRIATE STARTING POINT		
Starting points based on first time offender pleading not guilty		
Examples of nature of activity	**Starting point**	**Range**
Carrying an unloaded air weapon	Low level community order	Band B fine to medium level community order
Carrying loaded air weapon/imitation firearm/unloaded shotgun without ammunition	High level community order	Medium level community order to 26 weeks custody (air weapon) Medium level community order to Crown Court (imitation firearm, unloaded shotgun)
Carrying loaded shotgun/carrying shotgun or any other firearm together with ammunition with it	Crown Court	Crown Court

OFFENCE SERIOUSNESS (CULPABILITY AND HARM)	
B. CONSIDER THE EFFECT OF AGGRAVATING AND MITIGATING FACTORS (OTHER THAN THOSE WITHIN EXAMPLES ABOVE)	
Common aggravating and mitigating factors are identified at **B[5.2A]**. The following may be particularly relevant but **these lists are not exhaustive**	
Factors indicating higher culpability	*Factors indicating lower culpability*
1. Brandishing the firearm	1. Firearm not in sight
2. Carrying firearm in a busy place	2. No intention to use forearm
3. Planned illegal use	3. Firearm to be used for lawful purpose (not amounting to a defence)
Factors indicating greater degree of harm	
1. Person or people put in fear	
2. Offender participating in violent incident	

FORM A PRELIMINARY VIEW OF THE APPROPRIATE SENTENCE, THEN CONSIDER OFFENDER MITIGATION
Common factors are identified at B[5.2A]
CONSIDER A REDUCTION FOR A GUILTY PLEA
CONSIDER ANCILLARY ORDERS, INCLUDING COMPENSATION, FORFEITURE OR SUSPENSION OF PERSONAL LIQUOR LICENCE AND FOOTBALL BANNING ORDER (where appropriate)

Refer to **B[18]** for guidance on compensation and **Part B** for guidance on available ancillary orders
DECIDE SENTENCE **GIVE REASONS**

A[33.12]

Available sentences. See Table A at **B[4.1]** (firearms) and Table B at **B[4.2]** (air weapons).

A[33.13]

Forfeiture. The court can order the firearm (imitation, or shotgun or air weapon) to be forfeited to the police or to be disposed of as the court thinks fit. The court can also cancel any firearm or shotgun certificate held by the defendant.

A[34]

Football related offences

(For other related drunkenness offences see
A[35] below)

Charges

A[34.1]

1 Being a person at a regulated football match and throwing anything at or towards (the playing area, or any area adjacent to the playing area to which spectators are not generally admitted) (any area in which spectators or other persons are or may be present) without lawful authority or lawful excuse

Football (Offences) Act 1991, s 2

A[34.2]

2 Taking part at a regulated football match in chanting of an indecent or racialist nature

Football (Offences) Act 1991, s 3

A[34.3]

3 At a regulated football match going onto the playing area, or any area adjacent to the playing area to which spectators are not generally admitted, without lawful authority or lawful excuse

Football (Offences) Act 1991, s 4

Maximum penalty (for each offence) – Fine level 3.

A[34.4]

4 Being an unauthorised person, did sell, or offer or expose for sale, a ticket for a designated football match in any public place or place to which the public has access or, in the course of a trade or business, in any other place.

Criminal Justice and Public Order Act 1994, s 166.

Maximum penalty – Fine level 5.

Legal notes and definitions

A[34.5]

The creation of these offences follows the recommendations of the Taylor report into the Hillsborough Disaster. They can be committed only in respect of matches in England and Wales.

A[34.6]

Regulated football match. Means any association football match, designated, or of a description designated where one of the participating clubs is a member (full or associate) of the Football League or Premier League; it also includes international matches, and those which involve a team representing a club in a country outside England and Wales, and matches in a competition organised by UEFA.

A[34.7]

In addition, the match must take place on a ground occupied by a Football (or Premier) League Club or which is designated under the Safety of Sports Grounds Act 1975.

A[34.8]

Being or taking part at. The offence may be committed in a period beginning two hours before the start of the match or, if earlier, two hours before the time it is advertised to start and ending one hour after the end of the match. Where a match is postponed or cancelled, the period includes the two hours before and one hour after the advertised starting time.

A[34.9]

Without lawful authority or lawful excuse. The defendant must establish this but he only has to establish that his defence is probably true, he does not have to establish it beyond reasonable doubt.

A[34.10]

Charge 1: Throwing an object. The prosecution only has to prove that the object was thrown, not that a particular person was aimed at or caused alarm or distress thereby.

A[34.11]–[34.14]

Charge 2: Indecent or racialist chanting. 'Chanting' means the repeated uttering of any words or sounds alone or with one or more others. 'Racialist nature' means consisting of or including matter which is threatening, abusive or insulting to a person by reason of his colour, race, nationality (including citizenship) or ethnic or national origins, whether alone or in concert with one or more others. In *DPP v Stoke on Trent Magistrates' Court* [2003] EWHC 1593 (Admin), [2003] 3 All ER 1086, for example, 'Paki' was racially offensive.

Sentencing
SC Guideline – Football ground offences

A[34.15]

OFFENCE SERIOUSNESS (CULPABILITY AND HARM)
A. IDENTIFY THE APPROPRIATE STARTING POINT

Starting points based on first time offender pleading not guilty		
Examples of nature of activity	**Starting point**	**Range**
Being drunk in, or whilst trying to enter, ground (see A[35]).	Band A fine	Conditional discharge to band B fine
Going onto playing or other prohibited area	Band B fine	Band A fine to band C fine
Unauthorised sale or attempted sale of tickets Throwing missile Indecent or racist chanting	Band C fine	Band B fine to medium level community order
Possession of alcohol whilst entering or trying to enter ground (see A[35]).	Band C fine	Band B fine to high level community order

OFFENCE SERIOUSNESS (CULPABILITY AND HARM)
B. CONSIDER THE EFFECT OF AGGRAVATING AND MITIGATING FACTORS (OTHER THAN THOSE WITHIN THE EXAMPLES ABOVE)
Common aggravating and mitigating factors are identified at B[5.2A]. The following may be particularly relevant but **these lists are not exhaustive**

Factors indicating higher culpability 1. Commercial ticket operation; potential high cash value; counterfeit tickets 2. Inciting others to misbehave 3. Possession of large quantity of alcohol 4. Offensive language or behaviour (where not an element of the offence)	
Factor indicating greater degree of harm 1. Missile likely to cause serious injury eg coin, glass, bottle or stone	

FORM A PRELIMINARY VIEW OF THE APPROPRIATE SENTENCE, THEN CONSIDER OFFENDER MITIGATION
Common factors are identified at B[5.2A]
CONSIDER A REDUCTION FOR A GUILTY PLEA
CONSIDER ANCILLARY ORDERS, INCLUDING COMPENSATION AND FOOTBALL BANNING ORDER
Refer to **Part B** and consult your legal adviser on guidance for available ancillary orders
DECIDE SENTENCE **GIVE REASONS**

A[34.16]

Available sentences. See Table C at B[4.3].

A[34.17]

In addition to any sentence it may impose, the court will normally make a
football banning order (at B[41]). These orders prevent the defendant from
attending football matches in England and Wales or outside England and
Wales under s 10 of the Act, if the court is satisfied, on conviction of a
relevant offence, that there are reasonable grounds for believing that such
an order will help prevent disorder at football matches (*R (on the
application of Brown) v Inner London Crown Court* [2003] EWHC 3194
(Admin), [2003] All ER (D) 256 (Dec)). If the court is not so satisfied, it
must state that fact in open court and give its reasons. Those reasons will
be recorded in the court register.

A[35]

Football-related offences: Sporting events (control of alcohol etc)

Charges

A[35.1]

1(a) Being the operator (or hirer) (or his servant or agent) knowingly causing or permitting intoxicating liquor to be carried on a public service vehicle which was being used for the principal purpose of carrying passengers for the whole or part of a journey to or from a designated sporting event

OR

(b) Possessing intoxicating liquor whilst on such a vehicle

OR

(c) Being drunk on such a vehicle

Sporting Events (Control of Alcohol etc) Act 1985, 1(2), 1(3) and 1(4)

A[35.2]

2 (a) Possessing intoxicating liquor (or an article specified by the Act namely [. . . . .]) at a time during the period of a designated sporting event when in an area of a designated sports ground from which the event might have been directly viewed (or while entering or trying to enter such an event)

OR

(b) Being drunk in a designated sports ground at a time during the period of a designated sporting event (or, being drunk while entering or trying to enter such an event)

Sporting Events (Control of Alcohol etc) Act 1985, 2(1) and 2(2)

Maximum penalties –

Offences under   s 1(2) – Fine level 4

ss 1(3) and 2(1) – Fine level 3 and 3 months (**51 weeks)

ss 1(4) and 2(2) – Fine level 2.

Legal notes and definitions

A[35.3]

These offences were created in an attempt to deal with rowdy behaviour at football matches primarily where teams belonging to the Football (or Premier) League are involved (including their reserve and youth teams) but generally not at games exclusively concerning 'non-league' or amateur clubs. In addition, the Act provides for a total ban on the sale of alcohol at such matches although there is the opportunity for the club to apply to the relevant local authority for an order modifying this prohibition (see Section F).

A[35.4]

Public service vehicle means a motor vehicle adapted to carry more than eight passengers for hire or reward. (For this and the definition of 'operator' see the Public Passenger Vehicles Act 1981, s 181.) This offence also applies to a person who knowingly causes or permits intoxicating liquor to be carried in these circumstances on a railway passenger vehicle which he has hired. The Sporting Events (Control of Alcohol etc) Act 1985, s 1A makes provision for offences similar to those under s 1(a), (b) and (c) for drivers and keepers of a minibus, ie not a public service vehicle, but one which is adapted to carry more than eight passengers, and is being used for the principal purpose of carrying two or more passengers for the whole or part of a journey to or from a designated sporting event.

A[35.5]

Designated sporting event means any association football match where one of the participating clubs is a member (full or associate) of the Football (or Premier) League. It also includes all international association football matches and matches in competition for the European Champion Clubs Cup, European Cup Winner's Cup or UEFA Cup (whether or not either of the teams concerned is a member of the Football (or Premier) League eg where a final is played in England between two foreign teams). Also included are events in Scotland designated under the equivalent Scottish legislation (all Scottish League Clubs are designated as well as rugby internationals at Murrayfield). A match is also designated if it takes place outside Great Britain where either the team represents the Football Association or is a Football (or Premier) League Club or where a Football Association Club (not necessarily being a 'league' club) participates in one of the three European competitions. Accordingly, persons on a journey to Scotland or to Europe for a designated event are subject to the provisions of the Sporting Events (Control of Alcohol etc) Act 1985 whilst they are in England.

A[35.6]

Period of the event. The prohibitions apply to a period beginning two hours before the start of the event or, if earlier, two hours before the time it is advertised to start and ends one hour after the end of the event. Where a match is postponed or cancelled, the period includes the two hours before and one hour after the advertised start of the event. A shorter restricted period starting 15 minutes before and ending 15 minutes after the event applies to private boxes overlooking the ground.

A[35.7]

Exceptions. Apart from those clubs or matches not covered by the designation, eg games exclusively concerning 'non-league' clubs, the Sporting Events (Control of Alcohol etc) Act 1985 does not apply to matches where all competitors take part without reward *and* all spectators are admitted free of charge.

A[35.8]

Prohibited articles. As well as intoxicating liquor this includes any article capable of causing injury to a person struck by it being a bottle, can or other portable container (including such a container when crushed or broken) which is for holding *any* drink and which when empty is of a kind normally discarded or returned to the supplier, or part of such a container eg a beer glass. Thus a vacuum flask containing tea would be exempt. Also exempted are containers for holding medicinal products.

A[35.9]

Prohibited articles also include under s 2A any article or substance whose main purpose is the emission of a flare for purposes of illuminating or signalling (as opposed to igniting or heating) or the emission of smoke or visible gas, eg distress flares, fog signals, pellets for fumigating, but not matches, lighters, or heaters; fireworks are also prohibited. It is a defence if the accused proves that he was in possession of an article under s 2A with lawful authority.

A[35.10]–[35.15]

Designated sports ground. These are the home grounds of all Football Association clubs (ie not necessarily just those clubs in the Football (or Premier) League) including any ground used occasionally or temporarily by such a club, Wembley Stadium and any ground used for any international association match. However, it should be noted that all the restrictions apply only to a designated sporting event and so where, for example, a boxing match is held on a Football League ground the provisions of the Act do not apply.

Sentencing

A[35.16]

SC Guideline – Football ground offences – see **A[34.15]** above.

A[35.17]

For the power to make banning orders on persons convicted of certain offences in relation to football matches see **B[41]**.

A[36]

Fraud
(a) Fraud by false representation (s 1(2)(a))
(b) Fraud by failing to disclose information (s 1(2)(b))
(c) Fraud by abuse of position (s 1(2)(c))

Charges

A[36.1]

(1)

(a)   Dishonestly makes a false representation, and intends, by making the representation –
     (i)   to make a gain for himself or another, or
     (ii)   to cause loss to another or to expose another to a risk of loss.

Fraud Act 2006, s 1(2)(a)

A[36.2]

(1)

(b)   Dishonestly fails to disclosed to another person information which he is under a legal duty to disclose, and intends, by failing to disclose that information -
     (i)   to make a gain for himself or another, or
     (ii)   to cause loss to another or to expose another to a risk of loss.

Fraud Act 2006, s 1(2)(b)

A[36.3]

(1)

(c)   Occupies a position in which he is expected to safeguard, or not to act against, the financial interests of another person, dishonestly abuses that position, and intends, by means of the abuse of that position -
     (i)   to make a gain for himself or another, or
     (ii)   to cause loss to another or to expose another to a risk of loss.

Fraud Act 2006, s 1(2)(c)

A[36.4]
Maximum penalty – Fine level 5 and 12 months* Triable either way.

(*NB: Until repealed by the CJA 2003, the general limit on a magistrates' court to impose imprisonment is currently limited to six months for one offence: s 78 PCC (S) Act 2000.)

Crown Court – 10 years and unlimited fine.

Mode of Trial

A[36.5]

Consider first the notes at I[4]. In general, offences of fraud should be tried summarily except for the presence of one or more of the following factors (not an exhaustive list):

(a) breach of trust by a person in a person of substantial authority or in whom a high degree of trust has been placed;
(b) there has been sophisticated hiding or disguising of the offence;
(c) the offence has been committed by an organised gang;
(d) the victim was particularly vulnerable;
(e) there is unrecovered property of high value.

Legal notes and definitions

A[36.6]

Fraud by false representation: s 1(2)(a). This offence is further defined in s 2 of the Act. The effect is to create a very broad offence which consists of lying for economic purposes. This is a "conduct crime". There is no requirement that a gain or anything else should have been obtained, or that a loss should have been caused, or that any risk of loss should have been created.

A magistrates' court was correct to find a case to answer against the appellant who was alleged to have committed fraud by false representation. There was overwhelming evidence that the appellant had had another person impersonate him for the purposes of sitting a theory driving test: *Idrees v DPP* [2011] All ER (D) 156 (Feb), QBD.

A[36.7]

Dishonesty. There is no statutory definition. It is suggested that the test of dishonesty for is: (a) whether the accused's actions were dishonest according to the ordinary standards of reasonable and honest people and, if so, (b) whether the accused himself had realised that his actions were, according to those standards, dishonest (*R v Ghosh* [1982] QB 1053, [1982] 2 All ER 689, CA).

Representation. A representation is "false" if it is untrue or misleading and the person making it knows that it is, or might be, untrue or misleading. The term "representation" is widely defined as any representation as to fact or law, including a representation as to the state of the mind of –

(a) the person making the representation, or

(b)   any other person.

A representation may be express or implied and is wide enough to include deceiving a mechanical device such as a machine (s 2(5)).

Gain and loss. See s 5 of the Act. The terms are defined in the same terms as s 24 of the Theft Act 1968 and are to be construed as extending only to gain or loss in money or other property, but as extending to any such gain or loss whether temporary or permanent; and –

(i)   "gain" includes a gain by keeping what one has, as well as gain by getting what one has not; and
(ii)   "loss" includes a loss by not getting what one might get, as well as loss by parting with what one has.

A[36.8]

Fraud by failing to disclose information: s 1(2)(b). This offence is further defined in s 3 of the Act. The section is narrower than s 1(2)(a) above, but there is some overlap between the two types of offence.

Dishonesty. There is no statutory definition. See A[36.7] above.

Gain and loss. Defined in A[36.7] above.

Legal duty. There is no statutory definition. It was proposed by the Law Commission (Fraud 2002, No 276) that the offence should extend to duties arising under statute eg obligations of accuracy in company prospectuses; insurance transactions; from general contractual terms; from the custom of a particular market; or, from the existence of a fiduciary relationship between the parties.

It has been suggested that, as a matter of principle, it should not be criminal to withhold information under the civil law. It is no defence to claim a lack of knowledge as to the duty to disclose; nevertheless, the accused may claim a lack of **dishonesty**.

A[36.9]

Fraud by abuse of position: s 1(2)(c). This offence is further defined in s 4 of the Act. It is the most controversial of the three forms of fraud and was criticised in Parliament as a "catch all provision that will be a nightmare of judicial interpretation". The section is intended to criminalise the secret profiteer such as the wine waiter selling his own bottles passing them off as a belonging to the restaurant (a form of cheat): see *R v Doukas* [1978] 1 All ER 1071. There is no legal requirement for the conduct to be "secret" and the government also emphasised that the potential for s 4 to combat legacy fraud with an expectation that charities will benefit to the tune of £2–3 million per annum.

Abuse. There is no statutory definition.

Dishonesty. There is no statutory definition. See A[36.7] above.

Relevant financial position. The government refused to restrict the provision to circumstances where the defendant owes a "fiduciary duty". That is a sufficient but not a necessary condition. The Law Commission Report (Fraud 2002 No 276) treated as sufficient relationships of: (a) trustee and beneficiary (b) director and company (c) professional person and client (d) agent and principal or employee and employer (e) partnerships. However, the Law Commission also suggested that the relationship may arise "within a family" or in the context of "voluntary work", or in any context where the parties are not at "arm's length". The Home Office has also suggested that s.4 bites where the accused is given access to a person's premises, equipment records or customers.

The breadth of the offence gives rise to the potential for all sorts of civil law disputes within the family or employment to become issues of criminal law. As elsewhere the element of **dishonesty** may prove crucial.

Sentencing
Fraud – possessing, making or supplying articles for use in fraud – factors to take into consideration

A[36.10]

Fraud – possessing, making or supplying articles for use in fraud – factors to take into consideration

This guideline and accompanying notes are taken from the Sentencing Council's definitive guideline Sentencing for Fraud – Statutory offences, published 26 October 2009

Key factors

(a)   There are many ways in which offenders may commit this group of offences. 'Articles' will include any electronic programs or data stored electronically, false fronts for cash machines, computer programs for generating credit card numbers, lists of credit card or bank account details, 'sucker lists' and draft letters or emails for use in advance fee frauds.

(b)   Offenders who possess, make or supply articles for use in fraud intend their actions to lead to a fraud, and therefore have the highest level of culpability. The three offences in this group all involve an element of planning (whether by the offender or by another person) which indicates a higher level of culpability; this has been incorporated into the proposed starting points.

(c)   In relation to harm, the value of the fraud (either that intended by the offender where that can be ascertained, or that which was likely to be achieved) is not a determinant of seriousness for these offences but is a factor that should be taken into account in determining the appropriate sentence within the sentencing range.

(d) Whilst in many cases no financial harm will have been caused, in some cases, particularly where the 'article' is a list of credit card or bank account details, the victim(s) may have been inconvenienced despite not suffering any financial loss. In all cases, the harm must be judged in light of the offender's culpability.

(e) When the offending involves a number of people acting co-operatively, this will aggravate an offence as it indicates planning or professional activity, and may also increase the degree of loss caused or intended. The role of each offender is important in determining the appropriate level of seriousness and movement above or below the starting point within the applicable level.

(f) Matters of offender mitigation which may be particularly relevant to this type of fraud include:

(1) *Voluntary cessation of offending* – a claim, supported by objective evidence, that an offender stopped offending before being apprehended should be treated as mitigation, particularly where accompanied by a genuine expression of remorse. The lapse of time since commission of the last offence is relevant to whether the claim is genuine, and reasons for the cessation will assist the court in determining whether it amounts to mitigation and if so, to what degree.

(2) *Complete and unprompted disclosure of the extent of the fraud* – an admission that a greater sum has been obtained than that known to the authorities ensures that an offender is sentenced for the complete extent of the fraud. This amounts to ready co-operation with the authorities and should be treated as mitigation. Provision of information about others involved in the fraud should also be treated as mitigation. Generally, the earlier the disclosure is given and the higher the degree of assistance, the greater the allowance for mitigation.

(3) *Voluntary restitution* – the timing of the voluntary restitution will indicate the degree to which it reflects genuine remorse. Generally, the earlier the property or money is returned the greater the degree of mitigation the offender should receive. If circumstances beyond the control of the offender prevent return of defrauded items, the degree of mitigation will depend on the point in time at which, and the determination with which the offender tried to return the items.

(4) *Financial pressure* – financial pressure neither increases nor diminishes an offender's culpability. However, where such pressure is **exceptional** and not of the offender's own making, it may in very rare circumstances constitute mitigation.

(g) A court should be aware that a confiscation order is an important sanction. Such an order may only be made in the Crown Court. The court must commit the offender to the Crown Court where this is requested by the prosecution with a view to an order being considered.

(h) Ancillary orders should be considered in all cases, principally compensation and deprivation.

Fraud – possessing, making or supplying articles for use in fraud (Fraud Act 2006, ss 6, 7 and 1)

A[36.11]

Possession of articles: Triable either way

Maximum when tried summarily: Level 5 fine and/or 6 months

Maximum when tried on indictment: 5 years

Making or supplying articles, and Fraud (s 1): Triable either way

Maximum when tried summarily: Level 5 fine and/or 6 months

Maximum when tried on indictment: 10 years

OFFENCE SERIOUSNESS (CULPABILITY AND HARM)		
A. IDENTIFY THE APPROPRIATE STARTING POINT		
Starting points based on first time offender pleading not guilty		
Examples of nature of activity	Starting point	Range
Possessing articles intended for use in a less extensive and less skilfully planned fraud	Medium level community order	Low level community order to 26 weeks custody
Possessing articles for use in an extensive and skilfully planned fraud	Crown Court	6 weeks custody to Crown Court
Making or adapting, supplying or offering to supply articles intended for use in a less extensive and less skilfully planned fraud	26 weeks custody	High level community order to Crown Court
Making or adapting, supplying or offering to supply articles intended for use in an extensive and skilfully planned fraud	Crown Court	Crown Court
OFFENCE SERIOUSNESS (CULPABILITY AND HARM)		

B. CONSIDER THE EFFECT OF AGGRAVATING AND MITIGATING FACTORS (OTHER THAN THOSE WITHIN EXAMPLES ABOVE)

Common aggravating and mitigating factors are identified at B[5.2A]. The following may be particularly relevant but **these lists are not exhaustive**

Factors indicating higher culpability	*Factors indicating lower culpability*
1. Number involved in the offence and role of the offender	1. Peripheral involvement
2. Offending carried out over a significant period of time	
Factors indicating greater degree of harm	
1. Use of another person's identity	
2. Offence has lasting effect on the victim	

FORM A PRELIMINARY VIEW OF THE APPROPRIATE SENTENCE, THEN CONSIDER OFFENDER MITIGATION

Common factors are identified at B[5.2A]

CONSIDER A REDUCTION FOR A GUILTY PLEA

CONSIDER ANCILLARY ORDERS

Refer to **Part B** for guidance on available ancillary orders

DECIDE SENTENCE

GIVE REASONS

A[37]

Fraud: obtaining services dishonestly

Charge

A[37.1]

(1) Obtains services for himself or another –

(a)   by a dishonest act, and
(b)   in breach of subsection (2)

(2)

(a)   the services are made available on the basis that payment has been, is being or will be made for or in respect of them,
(b)   obtains them without any payment having been made for or in respect of them or without payment having been made in full, and
(c)   when he obtains them, he knows –
    (i)   that they are being made available on the basis as described in paragraph (a), or
    (ii)   that they might be

but intends that payment will not be made, or will not be made in full.

Fraud Act 2006, s 11.

Maximum penalty – Fine level 5 and/or 12 months. Triable either way

(NB: Until repealed by the CJA 2003, the general limit on a magistrates' court is to impose imprisonment up to a maximum of six months for one offence: s 78 PCC (S) Act 2000.)

Crown Court – five years and an unlimited fine.

Mode of trial

A[37.2]

Consider first the notes at I[4]. In general, offences of obtaining services dishonestly should be tried summarily except for the presence of one or more of the following factors (not an exhaustive list):

(a)   breach of trust by a person in position of substantial authority or in whom a high degree of trust has been placed;
(b)   there has been a sophisticated hiding or disguising of the offence;
(c)   the offence has been committed by an organised gang;
(d)   the victim was particularly vulnerable;
(e)   there is unrecovered property of high value.

Legal notes and definitions

A[37.3]

Services. As with the 1978 Act it applies only to services for which payment is required. There must be an act and an obtaining of the service.

Intention. The new offence is wider than the old offence in that it can cover obtaining services through a wholly automated process; however, it is narrower than the old offence because the defendant must intend to avoid payment which presents problems if D knows that the bank will pay.

Act. The new offence extends well beyond the machine 'deception' offences, to encompass eg cases where the defendant climbs a wall to watch a football match without paying the entrance fee (even though not deceiving the provider of the service directly); this is because the defendant is obtaining a service which is provided on the basis that people will pay for it.

As under the Theft Acts 1968 and 1978, an application for a bank account or credit card will only be caught if the service is to be paid for (see *R v Sofroniou* [2003] EWCA Crim 3681).

Dishonesty. There is no statutory definition. See **A[36.7]** above.

Sentencing
Fraud – Obtaining Services Dishonestly (Fraud Act 2006, s 11)

A[37.4]

Triable either way:

Maximum when tried summarily: Level 5 fine and/or 6 months

Maximum when tried on indictment: 5 years

The offence of **obtaining services dishonestly** may be committed in circumstances that otherwise could be charged as an offence contrary to s 1 of the Fraud Act 2006 or may be more akin to *making off without payment*, contrary to s 3 of the Theft Act 1978.

For this reason, it has not been included specifically within any of the guidelines for fraud, and one of the following approaches should be used:

- where it involves conduct which can be characterised as a fraud offence (such as obtaining credit through fraud or payment card fraud), the court should apply the guideline for the relevant type of fraud (see **A[31]** and **A[36]**); or

- where the conduct could be characterised as *making off without payment* (where an offender, knowing that payment on the spot for any goods supplied or service done is required or expected, dishonestly makes off without having paid and with intent to avoid payment), the guideline for that offence should be used: A[21.16].

A[38]

Possession of articles for fraud

Charge

A[38.1]

The defendant [person] had in his possession or under this control any article for use in the course of or in connection with any fraud

Fraud Act 2006, s 6.

Maximum penalty – Fine level 5 and/or 12 months. Triable either way.

(**NB:** until repealed by the CJA 2003, the general limit on a magistrates' courts sentencing powers is six months imprisonment for a single offence: s 78 PCC(S)A 2000).

Crown Court – 5 years' imprisonment and unlimited fine.

An "on-line" introduction to the legislation can be found on **Crimeline** (see issue 203, www.crimeline.info/issue203/htm).

Mode of trial

A[38.2]

Consider first the general notes at I[4]. In general, offences of possessing articles for fraud should be tried summarily except for the presence of one or more of the following factors (not an exhaustive list):

(a)   offence committed by a person in a position of substantial authority or in whom a high degree of trust has been placed;
(b)   sophisticated offence or disguising of the offence;
(c)   the offence has been committed by an organised gang;
(d)   targeting of a vulnerable victim;
(e)   property acquired of high value (or would have been).

Legal notes and definitions

A[38.3]

This is another very wide offence. It was created in order to meet concerns that the s 25 of the Theft Act 1968 offence of going equipped, was outdated in relation to its application to modern fraud cases eg given that many frauds are now perpetrated from home computers. Unlike s 25, there is no requirement to prove that the relevant articles were carried or used outside the defendant's "place of abode".

Article. Includes "any program or data held in electronic form" – Fraud Act 2006, s 8. The offence is designed to combat the growing menace of computer programs used to generate credit card numbers and blank utility bills.

Intention. It is not necessary to prove intended use in a particular fraud. The Crown must prove that the defendant had a general intention that the article be used by someone for a fraudulent purpose (as with the interpretation of intent in going equipped (see *R v Ellames* [1974] 3 AER 130).

Possession or control. It is submitted that the said terms will be construed analogous to offences under eg the Misuse of Drugs Act 1971 (see **A[25.7]**).

Sentencing
Fraud – Possession of articles for fraud (Fraud Act 2006, s 6)

A[38.4]

Triable either way:

Maximum when tried summarily: Level 5 fine and/or 6 months.

Maximum when tried on indictment: 5 years.

See the relevant guideline at **A[36.11]** onwards.

A[39]

Making, adapting, supplying or offering to supply articles for fraud

Charge

A[39.1]

The defendant [person] makes, adapts, supplies or offers to supply any article –

(a) knowing that it is designed or adapted for use in the course of or in connection with fraud, or

(b) intending it to be used to commit, or assist in the commission of, fraud

Fraud Act 2006, s 7.

Maximum penalty – Fine level 5 and/or 12 months. Triable either way.

(**NB:** Until repealed by the CJA 2003, the general limit on a magistrates' court to impose imprisonment is six months for a single offence (s 78 PCC(S)A 2000)).

Crown Court – 10 years' imprisonment and an unlimited fine.

Mode of trial

A[39.2]

Consider first the general notes at I[4]. In general, offences of making/adapting articles etc for fraud should be tried summarily except for the presence of one or more of the following factors (not an exhaustive list):

(a) offence committed by a person in a position of substantial authority or in whom a high degree of trust has been placed;

(b) sophisticated offence or disguising of the offence;

(c) the offence has been committed by an organised gang;

(d) targeting of a vulnerable victim;

(e) property acquired or high value (or would have been).

Legal notes and definition

A[39.3]

This offence is aimed at, amongst others, the manufacturers of the 'black boxes' (which caused electricity meters to under-record consumption) in the well-known case of *R v Hollinshead* [1985] AC 975. The defendants in that case were convicted of conspiracy to defraud at common law (still preserved under the Fraud Act 2006). It would no longer be necessary to rely on the common law in such a case.

Parliament has created numerous specific offences to tackle similar behaviour see eg Communications Act 2003, s 126; Mobile Telephones (Reprogramming) Act 2002, s 2; but this is a valuable general offence wide enough to catch eg software manufacturers producing programmes designed for criminal purposes.

It is not clear what the difference is, if any, between 'in the course of' (s 7(1)(a)) and 'in the commission of' (s 7(1)(b)).

A[39.4]

Article. Includes any "program or data held in electronic form" – Fraud Act 2006, s 8.

Makes. It is submitted that the term would be accorded its ordinary dictionary meaning.

Adapts. It is submitted that the term would be accorded its ordinary dictionary meaning.

Supplies. It is submitted that the term will be given its ordinary everyday meaning similar to eg under the Misuse of Drugs Act 1971. The offence does not appear to require proof of payment or reward. 'Supply' connotes more than a mere transfer of physical control of some chattel or object from one person to another. There is an additional concept namely that of enabling the recipient to apply the thing transferred for his own nefarious desires or purposes (see *R v Maginnis* [1987] AC 303, HL).

Offers to supply. It is inappropriate to introduce civil notions of offer and acceptance. The offence lies in the making of the offer to supply any article, It is submitted, therefore, that an offer to supply can be made by words or conduct.

Knowledge. Means actual knowledge. Mere suspicion would not appear to be sufficient for the purposes of s 7.

Intention. The accused must intend the article to be used to commit, or assist in the commission of the fraud.

Sentencing
Fraud – Making, adapting, supplying or offering to supply articles for fraud (Fraud Act 2006, s 7)

A[39.5]

Triable either way:

Maximum when tried summarily: Level 5 fine and/or 6 months.

Maximum when tried on indictment: 10 years.

See the relevant guideline at **A[36.11]** onwards.

A[40]

Handling stolen goods

Charge

A[40.1]

Handled stolen goods, namely [. . . . .], knowing or believing them to have been stolen

Theft Act 1968, s 22

Maximum penalty – Fine level 5 and 6 months (**12 months). Triable either way.

Crown Court – 14 years' imprisonment and unlimited fine.

Mode of trial

A[40.2]

Consider the SC Guidelines below.

Legal notes and definitions

A[40.3]

The prosecution must prove that the goods were:

(a)   stolen; or
(b)   obtained by deception; or
(c)   obtained by blackmail.

Also that the defendant knew or believed the goods had been obtained by one of those methods (see below).

A[40.4]

Handling. Any of the following actions can constitute handling:

(a)   dishonestly receiving the goods; or
(b)   dishonestly undertaking in the retention, removal, disposal or realisation of the goods by or for the benefit of another; or
(c)   dishonestly assisting in the retention, removal, disposal or realisation of the goods by or for the benefit of another; or
(d)   arranging to do (a) or (b) or (c).

Thus a defendant who has not himself personally handled goods can be convicted for this offence.

A[40.5]

As far as (c) is concerned failure to reveal stolen goods during a police search does not amount to 'dishonestly assisting in the retention of stolen goods'. 'Assisting' means helping or encouraging, amongst other things. It would be otherwise where deliberate lies were told to the police.

A[40.6]

If the only evidence against the defendant is that of the thief, it may be unsafe to convict and the legal adviser should be consulted.

A[40.7]

Goods. Includes money and every kind of property except land. The term also includes things severed from land by stealing.

A[40.8]

Knowledge or belief. Mere suspicion which does not amount to knowledge or belief is not sufficient to justify conviction. The state of the defendant's mind must be judged subjectively, ie what did *this* defendant know, or believe, not what did he suspect.

A[40.9]

The term 'belief' connotes its ordinary meaning of holding something to be true.

A[40.10]

In *R v Hall* (1985) 81 Cr App R. 260, the Lord Chief Justice presided in a court which gave some examples of what might amount to knowledge and what might amount to belief. A man might be said to *know* that goods were stolen when he was told by someone with first-hand knowledge, such as the thief, that such was the case. *Belief* was something short of knowledge. It might be said to be the state of mind of a person who said to himself: 'I cannot say I know for certain that those goods are stolen, but there can be no other reasonable conclusion in the light of all the circumstances of all I have heard and seen.' It was enough for belief even if the person said to himself: 'Despite all that I have seen and heard, I refuse to believe what my brain tells me is obvious.'

A[40.11]

What was insufficient was a mere suspicion: 'I suspect that these goods may be stolen but on the other hand they may not be stolen.' That state of mind does not fall within the words 'knowing or believing'. [Contrast the intention under s 22 with an offence under say, s 329 of the Proceeds of Crime Act 2002 (acquisition, use and possession of criminal property). In *Hogan v DPP* [2007] EWHC 978 (Admin), [2007] All ER (D) 253 (Feb) once a defendant raise the issue that consideration had been paid in respect of criminal property in his possession it was for the prosecution to prove to the criminal standard that the consideration paid was not adequate.]

Sentencing
SC Guideline – Handling stolen goods

A[40.12]

These guidelines are drawn from the Court of Appeal's decision in *R v Webbe* [2001] EWCA Crim 1217, [2002] 1 Cr App Rep (S) 22.

OFFENCE SERIOUSNESS (CULPABILITY AND HARM)		
A. IDENTIFY THE APPROPRIATE STARTING POINT		
Starting points based on first time offender pleading not guilty		
Examples of nature of activity	Starting point	Range
Property worth less than £1,000 acquired for offender's own use	Band B fine	Band B fine to low level community order
Property worth less than £1,000 acquired for resale; or Property worth more than £1,000 acquired for offender's own use; or Presence of at least one aggravating factor listed below – regardless of value	Medium level community order	Low level community order to 12 weeks custody Note: the custody threshold is likely to be passed if the offender has a record of dishonesty offences
Sophisticated offending; or Presence of at least two aggravating factors listed below	12 weeks custody	6 weeks custody to Crown Court
Offence committed in context of a business; or Offender acts as organiser/distributor of proceeds of crime; or Offender makes himself available to other criminals as willing to handle the proceeds of thefts or burglaries; or Offending highly organised, professional; or Particularly serious original offence, such as armed robbery	Crown Court	Crown Court
OFFENCE SERIOUSNESS (CULPABILITY AND HARM)		
B. CONSIDER THE EFFECT OF AGGRAVATING AND MITIGATING FACTORS (OTHER THAN THOSE WITHIN THE EXAMPLES ABOVE)		

Common aggravating and mitigating factors are identified at B[5.2A]. The following may be particularly relevant but **these lists are not exhaustive**	
Factors indicating higher culpability	*Factors indicating lower culpability*
1. Closeness of offender to primary offence. Closeness may be geographical, arising from presence at or near the primary offence when it was committed, or temporal, where the handler instigated or encouraged the primary offence beforehand, or, soon after, provided a safe haven or route for disposal.	1. Little or no benefit to offender.
2. High level of profit made or expected by offender.	2. Voluntary restitution to victim.
Factors indicating greater degree of harm	*Factors indicating lower degree of harm*
1. Seriousness of the primary offence, including domestic burglary.	1. Low value of goods.
2. High value of goods to victim, including sentimental value.	
3. Threats of violence or abuse of power by offender over others, such as adult commissioning criminal activity by children, or a drug dealer pressurising addicts to steal in order to pay for their habit.	

FORM A PRELIMINARY VIEW OF THE APPROPRIATE SENTENCE, THEN CONSIDER OFFENDER MITIGATION
Common factors are identified at B[5.2A]
CONSIDER A REDUCTION FOR A GUILTY PLEA
CONSIDER ANCILLARY ORDERS, INCLUDING RESTITUTION AND COMPENSATION
Refer to **Part B** and consult your legal adviser on guidance for available ancillary orders
CONSIDER DEPRIVATION OF PROPERTY
DECIDE SENTENCE
GIVE REASONS

A[41]

Harassment

Harassment – putting people in fear of violence
Racially or religiously aggravated harassment –
putting people in fear of violence
Harassment – without violence
Racially or religiously aggravated harassment –
non violent

Charges

A[41.1]

1 Did pursue a course of conduct on two or more occasions, causing another to fear that violence would be used against him, which he knew or ought to have known would cause that other person to fear violence would be used against him

Protection from Harassment Act 1997, s 4

Maximum penalty – Fine level 5 and 6 months (**12 months). Triable either way. Specified violent offence under Sch 15, Part 1, CJA 2003.

Crown Court – 5 years' imprisonment and unlimited fine.

A[41.2]

2 Racially/religiously aggravated course of conduct on two or more occasions causing fear of violence etc

Crime and Disorder Act 1998, s 32

Maximum penalty – Fine level 5 and 6 months (**12 months). Triable either way. Sch 15, Part 1, CJA 2003 does not identify this offence as a "specified violent offence". This would appear to be a drafting error given the classification of the basic offence under s 4 PHA 1997 above. The SGC Guideline (below) recognises this offence as a specified violent offence.

Crown Court – 7 years' imprisonment and unlimited fine.

A[41.3]

3 Did pursue a course of conduct amounting to harassment of another which he knew or ought to have known amounted to harassment

Protection from Harassment Act 1997, s 2

Maximum penalty – Fine level 5 and 6 months (**51 weeks) summary only.

A[41.4]

4 Racially/religiously aggravated conduct amounting to harassment of another etc

Crime and Disorder Act 1998, s 32

Maximum penalty – Fine level 5 and 6 months (**12 months). Triable either way.

Crown Court – 2 years' imprisonment and unlimited fine.

A[41.5]

Harassment of a person in his home. In response to animal rights protests and the like the Serious Organised Crime and Police Act 2005 amended the Protection from Harassment Act 1997 to make it an offence to harass two or more persons with the intention of persuading them not to do something they are required or entitled to do, or to do something they are not required to do. A course of conduct may involve conduct on just one occasion for each victim if there is more than one.

Section 126 of the Act adds s 42A to the Criminal Justice and Police Act 2001 and creates an offence of harassment of a person in his home. Punishable with fine level 4 and 6 months (**the maximum term of imprisonment may be subject to alteration under s 280(2) CJA 2003). Triable only by magistrates.

Mode of trial

A[41.6]

Consider the SC Guidelines below.

Note that the Crown Court can bring in an alternative verdict under the Protection from Harassment Act 1997, s 2 but magistrates cannot.

Legal notes and definitions

A[41.7]

Elements of the offence under s 4. A prosecution under the Protection from Harassment Act 1997, s 4 required proof of harassment. The prosecution had to prove, in addition to the statutory requirements, the requirements identified in *Thomas v News Group Newspapers Ltd* [2001] EWCA Civ 1233, [2002] EMLR 4, namely that the conduct was targeted at an individual, was calculated to alarm or cause him distress, and was oppressive and unreasonable: *R v Mohamed Enamul Haque* [2011] EWCA Crim 1871, [2012] 1 Cr App Rep 48, [2011] Crim LR 962.

Course of conduct denotes actions taking place on at least two occasions. In the case of a s 4 offence the victim must have been put in fear that violence would have been used against him on at least two of those occasions (*Caurti v DPP* [2002] EWHC 867 (Admin), [2002] Crim LR 131). The fewer the incidents and the wider apart they are spread, the less likely it is that a finding of harassment can reasonably be made (*Lau v DPP* [2000] 1 FLR 799, [2000] Fam Law 610). In *Pratt v DPP* [2001] EWHC 483 (Admin), (2001) 165 JP 800 incidents three months apart were said to be borderline, while in *Kelly v DPP* [2002] All ER (D) 177 (Jun) nine telephone calls all within five minutes amounted to a course of conduct even though the victim listened to them as recorded messages at the same time. A threat to harm a person's dog may be inferred to be a threat directed at them (*R v DPP* [2001] EWHC 17 (Admin), (2001) 165 JP 349).

Events between May 2005 and November 2005 constituted a "course of conduct" and could not be regarded as one continuous episode of intimidation (*Buckley v CPS* [2008] All ER (D) 06 (Jan)). At least one of the incidents relied on by the prosecution must have occurred within the 6 month limitation period for summary proceedings (*DPP v Baker* (2004) 169 JP 140, [2004] All ER (D) 28 (Nov), DC).

Conduct which may begin with what is or may be a legitimate inquiry (in this case by telephone) may become harassment within the meaning of section 1, by reason of the manner of its being pursued and its persistence: see *DPP v Hardy* [2008] EWHC 2874 (Admin), 173 JP 10. A series of six incidents, over the course of nine months during a volatile relationship with aggression on both sides, could not on the facts be described as a course of conduct and giving rise to an offence under s 4(1): *R v Curtis* [2010] EWCA Crim 123, [2010] 3 All ER 849, [2010] 1 Cr App Rep 457. See also *R v Widdows* [2011] EWCA Crim 1500, [2011] 2 FLR 869, [2011] Fam Law 937.

Two or more complainants. See A[41.5] above. **Two or more complainants** may be named in one charge under s 2 and such a charge is not necessarily bad for duplicity: see *DPP v Dunn* (2008) 165 JP 130. For a s 4 offence, the interpretation is slightly narrower in that the course of conduct complained of must cause at least one of the complainants to fear, on at least two occasions, that violence will be used against him, as opposed to another: see *Caurti v DPP* [2002] EWHC 867 (Admin), [2002] Crim LR 131.

A[41.8]

Knows or ought to have known. In the case of the defendant this means that he will be presumed to have that knowledge if a reasonable person in possession of the same information would think the course of conduct would amount to harassment or cause the other person to fear violence would be used against him.

A[41.9]

Racial aggravation. See A[8.10] and A[15.7].

May be heard together with a harassment charge as an alternative (*R (CPS) v Blaydon Youth Court* [2004] EWHC 2296 (Admin), [2004] All ER (D) 45 (Oct)).

A[41.10]

Defences. The Protection from Harassment Act 1997, s 1 gives three possible defences if the defendant can show:

(a)   his course of conduct was pursued for the purposes of preventing or detecting crime;

(b)   that it was pursued under an enactment or rule of law;

(c)   that in the particular circumstances the course of conduct was reasonable and in the case of a s 4 offence that it was reasonable for the protection of himself or another or his or another's property.

The Protection from Harassment Act 1997, s 1(3)(a) was confined to a course of conduct the purpose of which was preventing or detecting crime. Where a respondent could not show that his course of conduct had been pursued for the purpose identified by s 1(3)(a), the course of conduct did not fall outside the prohibition in s 1(1) and accordingly it was unlawful: *Hayes v Willoughby* [2011] EWCA Civ 1541, [2012] 1 WLR 1510, (2012) Times, 13 January.

A[41.11]

ECHR. Under the ECHR if would appear that it is sufficient for the defendant to raise one or other of the above defences. Once raised, it is for the prosecution to negative that defence(s) beyond a reasonable doubt.

Sentencing
SC Guideline – 1 Harassment – putting people in fear of violence
SC Guideline – 2 Racially or religiously aggravated harassment – putting people in fear of violence

A[41.11A]

(For offences 3 and 4 see A[41.12] below).

Where offence committed in a domestic context, see SC Definitive Guideline: "Overarching Principles: Domestic Violence"

IDENTIFY DANGEROUS OFFENDERS		
This is a specified offence for the purposes of the public protection provisions in the Criminal Justice Act 2003. Refer to B[16.5] and consult legal adviser for guidance		
OFFENCE SERIOUSNESS (CULPABILITY AND HARM) A. IDENTIFY THE APPROPRIATE STARTING POINT		
Starting points based on first time offender pleading not guilty		
Examples of nature of activity	Starting point	Range
A pattern of two or more incidents of unwanted contact	6 weeks custody	High level community order to 18 weeks custody

| Deliberate threats, persistent action over a longer period; or Intention to cause fear of violence | 18 weeks custody | 12 weeks custody to Crown Court |
| Sexual threats, vulnerable person targeted | Crown Court | Crown Court |

OFFENCE SERIOUSNESS (CULPABILITY AND HARM)

B. CONSIDER THE EFFECT OF AGGRAVATING AND MITIGATING FACTORS (OTHER THAN THOSE WITHIN EXAMPLES ABOVE)

Common aggravating and mitigating factors are identified at B[5.2A]. The following may be particularly relevant but these lists are not exhaustive

Factors indicating higher culpability	*Factors indicating lower culpability*
1. Planning	1. Limited understanding of effect on victim
2. Offender ignores obvious distress	2. Initial provocation
3. Visits in person to victim's home or workplace	
4. Offender involves others	
5. Using contact arrangements with a child to instigate offence	
Factors indicating greater degree of harm	
1. Victim needs medical help/counselling	
2. Physical violence used	
3. Victim aware that offender has history of using violence	
4. Grossly violent or offensive material sent	
5. Children frightened	
6. Evidence that victim changed lifestyle to avoid contact	

FORM A PRELIMINARY VIEW OF THE APPROPRIATE SENTENCE

IF OFFENDER CHARGED AND CONVICTED OF THE RACIALLY OR RELIGIOUSLY AGGRAVATED OFFENCE, INCREASE THE SENTENCE TO REFLECT THIS ELEMENT

Refer to B[5.2B] for guidance

CONSIDER OFFENDER MITIGATION

Common factors are identified at B[5.2A]

CONSIDER A REDUCTION FOR A GUILTY PLEA

CONSIDER MAKING A RESTRAINING ORDER

CONSIDER ANCILLARY ORDERS, INCLUDING COMPENSATION

Refer to B[18] for guidance on compensation.

DECIDE SENTENCE
GIVE REASONS

SC Guideline – 3 Harassment – without violence
SC Guideline – 4 Racially or religiously aggravated
harassment – without violence

A[41.12]

(For offences 1 and 2 see **A[41.11]** above).

Where offence committed in a domestic context, see SC Definitive Guideline: "Overarching Principles: Domestic Violence"

OFFENCE SERIOUSNESS (CULPABILITY AND HARM) A. IDENTIFY THE APPROPRIATE STARTING POINT		
Starting points based on first time offender pleading not guilty		
Examples of nature of activity	**Starting point**	**Range**
Small number of incidents	Medium level community order	Band C fine to high level community order
Constant contact at night, trying to come into workplace or home, involving others	6 weeks custody	Medium level community order to 12 weeks custody
Threatening violence, taking personal photographs, sending offensive material	18 weeks custody	12 to 26 weeks custody

OFFENCE SERIOUSNESS (CULPABILITY AND HARM)	
B. CONSIDER THE EFFECT OF AGGRAVATING AND MITIGATING FACTORS (OTHER THAN THOSE WITHIN EXAMPLES ABOVE)	
Common aggravating and mitigating factors are identified at **B[5.2A]**. The following may be particularly relevant but **these lists are not exhaustive**	
Factors indicating higher culpability	*Factors indicating lower culpability*
1. Planning	1. Limited understanding of effect on victim
2. Offender ignores obvious distress	2. Initial provocation
3. Offender involves others	
4. Using contact arrangements with a child to instigate offence	
Factors indicating greater degree of harm	
1. Victim needs medical help/counselling	
2. Action over a long period of time	
3. Children frightened	
4. Use or distribution of photographs	
FORM A PRELIMINARY VIEW OF THE APPROPRIATE SENTENCE	

IF OFFENDER CHARGED AND CONVICTED OF THE RACIALLY OR RE-LIGIOUSLY AGGRAVATED OFFENCE, INCREASE THE SENTENCE TO REFLECT THIS ELEMENT Refer to B[5.2B] for guidance
CONSIDER OFFENDER MITIGATION Common factors are identified at B[5.2A]
CONSIDER A REDUCTION FOR A GUILTY PLEA
CONSIDER MAKING A RESTRAINING ORDER
CONSIDER ANCILLARY ORDERS, INCLUDING COMPENSATION Refer to B[18] for guidance on compensation.
DECIDE SENTENCE **GIVE REASONS**

A[41.13]

Restraining orders. On conviction pursuant to s 5(1) of the Protection from Harassment Act 1997 as amended, from **30 September 2009**, restraining orders can be issued for any offence rather than just offences covered by ss 2 or 4 of the 1997 Act. The order can be made for a determinate or indeterminate period of time.

On acquittal by virtue of s 5A of the Protection from Harassment Act 1997 (as inserted by s 12 of the Domestic Violence, Crime and Victims Act 2004). Again restraining orders can be issued for any offence on acquittal, not just for offences covered by the PHA 1997. The order can be made for a determinate or indeterminate period of time. This legislation came into force on **30 September 2009**. The legislation states that the court 'may', if it considers it necessary to do so to protect a person from harassment by the defendant . . . make an order. Despite a declaration that that legislation complies with the European Convention of Human Rights difficulties arise eg what is the evidential basis and standard for making an order?

In *R v Major* [2010] EWCA Crim 3016, [2011] 1 Cr App Rep 322, [2011] 2 Cr App Rep (S) 139, it was held that s 5A(1) of the Act was inserted to deal with those cases where there is clear evidence that the victim needs protection but there is insufficient evidence to convict of the particular charges before the court. The victim need not have been blameless and the court's added powers avoided the need for alternative proceedings to protect the victim, added costs and delay. The fact that a criminal court was unsure that the alleged conduct amounted to harassment did not mean that there was no risk of future harassment. Even though the required criminal standard of proof might not have been met, a retraining order was a civil order and the civil standard of proof applied. (2) A restraining order made on acquittal is not a sentence. However, the requirements of s 174(1) of the Criminal Justice Act 2003 and the Consolidated Criminal Practice Direction at III.31.4 should be applied (see now Part 50 of the CPR 2012). Accordingly, a court imposing a restraining order should state in open court, its reasons for doing so. In the instant case, while there may have been good reason for making the order, it was not apparent from the Judge's remarks as to whether or not the order was justified. *R v Major* was followed just two weeks later in *R (on the application of Gonzales) v Folkestone Magistrates' Court* [2010] EWHC 3428 (Admin), 175 JP 453.

It is respectfully submitted that *R v Major* was wrongly decided and takes no account of binding precedent ie *R (McCann) v Crown Court at Manchester* [2002] UKHL 39. *McCann* decided that even where the proceedings are civil in nature (as in ASBOs or a fortiori restraining orders), where a subsequent breach of the order would carry serious consequences for the defendant should he breach the order ie imprisonment, the criminal standard of proof applied.

In the case of a prison sentence a copy of the order should be sent to the prison. Any order should be specific and name parties protected by it (*R v Mann* (2000) 144 Sol Jo LB 150, CA).

Section 5 and Sch 1 of the Interpretation Act 1978 provide that when the word appears in a statute, unless a contrary intention appears "person" includes a body of persons corporate or unincorporated. If there is evidence to indicate that there is a real fear of actual harassment or violence in the future, a restraining order can therefore be imposed in appropriate circumstances either to protect a limited company or its employees. However, in this particular case, the practical sense of the imposition of the order had to be balanced against the failure of the Crown, which had not originally intended applying for restraining orders, to adduce any evidence that there was actual harassment or anything close to it or any perceived danger from anything said or done by any particular defendant to put anybody in fear of violence (*R v Buxton* [2010] EWCA Crim 2923, [2011] 1 WLR 857, [2011] Bus LR 448).

In *R v Debnath* (2 December 2005, unreported), the Court of Appeal stated that when considering whether or not to make a restraining order the following principles applied: (i) the purpose of a restraining order was to prohibit particular conduct with a view to protecting the complainant from further offences; (ii) the order had to be clear and in precise terms so that there could be no doubt as to what the defendant was prohibited from doing; (iii) the order had to be practical in its terms; (iv) when considering the terms, or the extent of an order, the court had to have regard to the issue of proportionality; and (v) the power to vary or discharge an order was an important safeguard and the Court of Appeal would be unlikely to interfere with the order where an application could be made to the court that made the order for its variation or discharge.

Under s 12 above gives any person mentioned in a restraining order the right to make representations in court if an application is made to vary or discharge an order.

In *R (on the application of Smith) v Crown Prosecution Service* [2010] EWHC 3593 (Admin), it was stated that a district Judge and prosecutor were wrong in canvassing the making of a restraining order in the event no evidence being offered. There would not be an evidential basis for making a preventative order. The prosecution ought not to have acquiesced to the idea of making a restraining order in these circumstances.

In *R v K* [2011] EWCA Crim 1843, 175 JP 378, a restraining order was quashed because at the hearing no consideration appeared to have been given to the provisions of either s 5A of the 1997 Act or the Criminal Procedure Rules 2010. The serious nature of a restraining order was underpinned by the provisions of Part 50 of the Criminal Procedure Rules 2010 which identified the steps which had to be taken in order to ensure that any person to whom any such order was directed was given a proper opportunity to understand what was being proposed and why and to make representations at a hearing. In the instant case, no procedural steps were taken either before or after the Crown offered no evidence, and the limited evidence before the court could not provide a sound evidential basis upon which to make the restraining order. See also *R v Trott* [2011] EWCA Crim 2395, 175 JP 458.

A[42]

Income tax evasion

Charge

A[42.1]

Being knowingly concerned in the fraudulent evasion of income tax by him or another person.

Finance Act 2000, s 144

Maximum penalty – Fine level 5 and 6 months' (**12 months) imprisonment †

Crown Court – 7 years' imprisonment and unlimited fine.

Mode of trial

A[42.2]

See general notes at I[4] and SC Guideline below.

Sentencing

A[42.3]

Awaiting SC Guideline.

A[43]

Indecent photographs of children

Charges

A[43.1]

Did take or make an indecent photograph of a child or

Distribute or show such photographs or

Possess such photographs with a view to distribution or

Publish an advertisement conveying that the advertiser distributes or shows such photographs.

Protection of Children Act 1978, s 1

Possession of indecent photograph of child

Criminal Justice Act 1988, s 160

Possession of a prohibited image of a child

Coroners and Justice Act 2009, s 62**

Maximum penalty – Fine level 5 and/or 6 months' (**12 months) imprisonment. Triable either way. Specified sexual offence under Sch 15, Part 2, CJA 2003.

Crown Court – 10 years' imprisonment (3 years if committed before 11/01/2001) and unlimited fine. **(3 years' imprisonment and unlimited fine for an offence under s 62 above.)

Mode of Trial

A[43.2]

Consider the SC guideline at A[43.8] below. Possession of indecent photographs of children may be tried in the magistrates' court but the court must have regard to an ascending level of seriousness as set out at A[43.8] below.

Legal Notes and definitions

A[43.3]

Indecent photographs or pseudo-photographs. The section makes it an offence to make an indecent photograph, pseudo photograph, copy, negative or data stored on a computer disc. A person who downloads indecent images of children from an internet site and prints or saves them is also making an indecent photograph (*R v Smith, R v Jayson* [2002] EWCA Crim 683, [2003] 1 Cr App Rep 212, CA).

In relation to a count for possession of indecent photographs of a child, the prosecution had to prove that the defendant was capable of retrieving, or in a position to retrieve, the image or images: *R v Leonard* [2012] EWCA Crim 277, [2012] 2 Cr App Rep 138, 176 CL&J 466.

From 8 July 2008, the meaning of "photograph" in s 7(4) of the Protection of Children Act 1978 was extended by the Criminal Justice and Immigration Act 2008 to include:

"(4A) (a)a tracing or other image, whether made by electronic or other means (of whatever nature) –

    (i)   which is not itself a photograph or pseudo-photograph, but

    (ii)   which is derived from the whole or part of a photograph or pseudo-photograph (or a combination of either or both); and

  (b)   data stored on a computer disc or by other electronic means which is capable of conversion into an image within paragraph (a);

    and subsection (8) applies in relation to such an image as it applies in relation to a pseudo-photograph".

A[43.4]

Indecent photographs or pseudo-photographs: marriage etc. From April 6, 2010, ss 62–69 of the Coroners and Justice Act 2009 came into force. Section 69 amends s 1A of the Protection of Children Act 1978 and s 160A of the Criminal Justice Act 1988 to insert a reference to 'pseudo-photograph'.

A[43.5]

Evidence. It is for the court to decide on the evidence as a whole whether a child in a photograph was under age at the material time (*R v Land* [1999] QB 65, [1998] 1 All ER 403, CA).

Child includes 16 and 17 year olds: Sexual Offences Act 2003, s 45.

A[43.6]

Distribution. A person distributes an indecent photograph if he parts with possession of it, or exposes or offers it to another person.

Section 1(1)(b) ("to distribute or show") created an offence of strict liability, in which it was not necessary for the prosecution to prove the defendant's knowledge that a CD which he had given to another person, had contained indecent images at the time of his parting with possession. That section was subject only to the statutory defences, in which knowledge was in issue (*R v P* [2006] All ER (D) 238 (Oct).

A[43.7]

Knowledge. Deletion of files may be directly relevant to the accused's lack of knowledge of possession of the material particularly where specialist software would be needed to recover the deleted files (*R v Rowe* [2008] EWCA Crim 2712, 172 JP 585).

A[43.8]

Defences. It is a defence for a person to prove that he had a legitimate reason for possessing, distributing or showing the showing the photographs.

It is also a defence that he had not himself seen the photographs and did not know or have cause to suspect them to be indecent.

In respect of 16 and 17 year olds specific defences are provided that the defendant can show:

(a)   the child was 16 or over or they were married or in an enduring family relationship;
(b)   there was consent or a reasonable belief the child consented;
(c)   the photograph is not of the child and another person other than the defendant.

There is also a defence for those involved in law enforcement activities.

Sentencing
SC Guideline – Indecent photographs of children

A[43.9]

This guideline is taken from the SC's definitive guideline *Sexual Offences Act 2003* published 30 April 2007.

*The court **must** inform the defendant that the Independent Safeguarding Authority (known as the Independent Barring Board) will automatically ban him/her from working with children and/or vulnerable adults. As the court has no role in the decision if the defendant needs any further advice he/she should consult a solicitor.

Key factors

(a)   The levels of seriousness (level 1 being the least serious) for sentencing for offences involving pornographic images are:
Level 1: Images depicting erotic posing with no sexual activity.
Level 2: Non-penetrative sexual activity between children, or solo masturbation by a child.

Level 3: Non penetrative sexual activity between adults and children.

Level 4: Penetrative activity between children and adults.

Level 5: Sadism or bestiality.

(b) Pseudo-photographs generally should be treated less seriously than real photographs.

(c) Starting points should be higher where the subject of the indecent photograph(s) is a child under 13.

(d) In accordance with s 80 of and Sch 3 to the Sexual Offences Act 2003, automatic notification requirements apply upon conviction to an offender aged 18 or over or where the offence involved photographs of children under 16.

OFFENCE SERIOUSNESS (CULPABILITY AND HARM) A. IDENTIFY THE APPROPRIATE STARTING POINT Starting points based on first time offender pleading not guilty		
Examples of nature of activity	**Starting point**	**Range**
Possession of a large amount of level 1 material and/or no more than a small amount of level 2, and the material is for personal use and has not been distributed or shown to others	Medium level community order	Band C fine to high level community order
Offender in possession of a large amount of material at level 2 or a small amount at level 3	12 weeks custody	4 – 26 weeks custody
Offender has shown or distributed material at level 1 on a limited scale		
Offender has exchanged images at level 1 or 2 with other collectors, but with no element of financial gain		
Possession of a large quantity of level 3 material for personal use	26 weeks custody	4 weeks custody to Crown Court
Possession of a small number of images at level 4 or 5		
Large number of level 2 images shown or distributed		
Small number of level 3 images shown or distributed		

Possession of a large quantity of level 4 or 5 material for personal use only	Crown Court	26 weeks custody to Crown Court
Offender traded material at levels 1–3 Level 4 or 5 images shown or distributed Offender involved in the production of material of any level	Crown Court	Crown Court

OFFENCE SERIOUSNESS (CULPABILITY AND HARM)
B. CONSIDER THE EFFECT OF AGGRAVATING AND MITIGATING FACTORS (OTHER THAN THOSE WITHIN EXAMPLES ABOVE)
Common aggravating and mitigating factors are identified at B[5.2A]. The following may be particularly relevant but these lists are not exhaustive

Factors indicating higher culpability	*Factors indicating lower culpability*
1. Collection is systematically stored or organised, indicating a sophisticated approach to trading or a high level of personal interest	1. A few images held solely for personal use
2. Use of drugs, alcohol or other substance to facilitate the offence of making or taking	2. Images viewed by not stored
3. Background of intimidation or coercion	3. A few images held solely for personal use and it is established that the subject is aged 16 or 17 and that he or she was consenting
4. Threats to prevent victim reporting the activity	
5. Threats to disclose victim's activity to friends/relatives	
6. Financial or other gain	
Factors indicating greater degree of harm	
1. Images shown or distributed to others, especially children	
2. Images stored, made available or distributed in such a way that they can be inadvertently accessed by others	

FORM A PRELIMINARY VIEW OF THE APPROPRIATE SENTENCE, THEN CONSIDER OFFENDER MITIGATION
Common factors are identified at B[5.2A]
CONSIDER A REDUCTION FOR A GUILTY PLEA
CONSIDER ANCILLARY ORDERS, INCLUDING COMPENSATION AND DEPRIVATION OF PROPERTY USED TO COMMIT THE OFFENCE
Refer to B[18] for guidance on compensation and **Part B** for available ancillary orders

| DECIDE SENTENCE |
| GIVE REASONS |

A[43.10]

Available sentences. See Table A at B[4.1].

A[43.11]

Forfeiture.

Section 5 of the 1978 Act has been amended by s 39 of the Police and Justice Act 2006 to specifically provide for the forfeiture of indecent photographs and pseudo-photographs.

A[43.12]

Notification requirements. See A[52.15]. Requirements apply even on the making of a conditional discharge (*R v Longworth* [2004] EWCA Crim 2145, [2005] 1 Cr App Rep (S) 419, (2004) Times, 17 August).

A[44]

Keeping a brothel used for prostitution

Charge

A[44.1]

Did keep, or to manage, or act or assist in the management of, a brothel to which people resort for practices involving prostitution (whether or not also for other practices)

Sexual Offences Act 1956, s 33A

Maximum penalty – Fine level 5 and/or 6 months (**12 months). Triable either way. Specified sexual offence under Sch 15, Part 2, CJA 2003

Crown Court – 7 years' imprisonment and unlimited fine.

Mode of trial

A[44.2]

Consider the **SC Guideline** at A[44.4] below. Note, where an offender has profited from his or her involvement in the prostitution of others, the courts should always consider making a confiscation order approximately equivalent to the profits enjoyed. Such an order can only be made in the Crown Court.

Legal notes and definitions

A[44.3]

Prostitution. Has the same meaning as give by s 51(2) of the Sexual Offences Act 2003.

Sentencing
SC Guideline – Keeping a brothel used for prostitution

A[44.4]

This guideline is taken from the SC's definitive guideline *Sexual Offences Act 2003* published 30 April 2007.

OFFENCE SERIOUSNESS (CULPABILITY AND HARM)		
A. IDENTIFY THE APPROPRIATE STARTING POINT		
Starting points based on first time offender pleading not guilty		
Examples of nature of activity	Starting point	Range

Involvement of the offender was minimal	Medium level community order	Band C fine to high level community order
Offender is the keeper of the brothel and is personally involved in its management	Crown Court	26 weeks custody to Crown Court
Offender is the keeper of the brothel and has made substantial profits in the region of £5,000 and upwards	Crown Court	Crown Court

OFFENCE SERIOUSNESS (CULPABILITY AND HARM)
B. CONSIDER THE EFFECT OF AGGRAVATING AND MITIGATING FACTORS (OTHER THAN THOSE WITHIN EXAMPLES ABOVE)
Common aggravating and mitigating factors are identified at **B[5.2A]**. The following may be particularly relevant but **these lists are not exhaustive:**

Factors indicating higher culpability	*Factors indicating lower culpability*
1. Background of threats, intimidation or coercion	1. Using employment as a route out of prostitution and not actively involved in exploitation
2. Large-scale commercial operation	2. Coercion by third party
3. Personal involvement in the prostitution of others	
4. Abduction or detention	
5. Financial or other gain	

FORM A PRELIMINARY VIEW OF THE APPROPRIATE SENTENCE, THEN CONSIDER OFFENDER MITIGATION
Common factors are identified at **B[5.2A]**
CONSIDER A REDUCTION FOR A GUILTY PLEA
CONSIDER ANCILLARY ORDERS, INCLUDING COMPENSATION
Refer to **Part B** for available ancillary orders and **B[18]** for guidance on compensation
DECIDE SENTENCE
GIVE REASONS

Note. Where an offender has profited from his or her involvement in the prostitution of others, the courts should always consider making a confiscation order approximately equivalent to the profits enjoyed. Such an order can only be made in the Crown Court.

A[45]

Making off without payment

Charge

A[45.1]

Knowing that payment on the spot for certain goods supplied [or service done] was required or expected dishonestly made off without having paid as required or expected and with intent to avoid payment of the amount due

Theft Act 1978, s 3

A[45.2]

Maximum penalty – Fine level 5 and 6 months (**12 months). Triable either way.

Crown Court – 2 years and unlimited fine.

Mode of trial

A[45.3]

Consider the **SC Guideline** at A[45.8] below.

Legal notes and definitions

A[45.4]

The basis of this offence is dishonesty. Dishonesty can be inferred from the surrounding circumstances. It is an offence whether the advantage is obtained for the defendant or for someone else.

A[45.5]

Dishonesty. The test of dishonesty is (a) whether the accused's actions were dishonest according to the ordinary standards of reasonable and honest people and, if so, (b) whether the accused himself had realised that his actions were, according to those standards, dishonest (*R v Ghosh* [1982] QB 1053, [1982] 2 All ER 689, CA).

A[45.6]

Payment on the spot includes payment at the time of collecting goods on which work has been done, or in respect of which a service has been provided, eg collecting one's car from a garage after repair.

A[45.7]

With intent to avoid payment of the amount due. This means with intent *never* to pay the sum due. An intent merely to defer or delay payment is not enough for a 'making off' offence (*R v Allen* [1985] 1 All ER 148, [1985] 1 WLR 50, CA; affd [1985] AC 1029, [1985] 2 All ER 641, HL).

Sentencing
SC Guideline – Making off without payment

Key factors

A[45.8]

The key factors are set out below:

(a)   The starting points and sentencing ranges in this guideline are based on the assumption that the offender was motivated by greed or a desire to live beyond his or her means. To avoid double counting, such a motivation should not be treated as a factor that increases culpability.

(b)   When assessing the harm caused by this offence, the starting point should be the loss suffered by the victim. In general, the greater the loss, the more serious the offence. However, the monetary value of the loss may not reflect the full extent of the harm caused by the offence. The court should also take into account the impact of the offence on the victim, any harm to persons other than the direct victim, and any harm in the form of public alarm or erosion of public confidence.

(c)   The following matters of offender mitigation may be relevant in this offence:

  (i)   *Offender motivated by desperation or need.* The fact that an offence has been committed in desperation or need arising from particular hardship may count as offender mitigation in exceptional circumstances.

  (ii)   *Voluntary return of stolen property.* Whether and the degree to which the return of stolen property constitutes a matter of offender mitigation will depend on the assessment of the circumstances, and, in particular, the voluntariness and time-liness of the return.

  (iii) *Impact on sentence of offender's dependency.* Many offenders convicted of acquisitive crimes are motivated by an addiction, often to drugs, alcohol or gambling. This does not mitigate the seriousness of the offence, but an offender's dependency may properly influence the type of sentence imposed. In particular, it may sometimes be appropriate to impose a drug rehabilitation requirement or an alcohol treatment requirement as part of a community order or a suspended sentence order in an attempt to break the cycle of addiction and offending, even if an immediate custodial sentence would otherwise be warranted (See B[2.17]. The Court of Appeal gave guidance on the approach to making drug treatment and testing orders, which also applies to imposing a drug rehabilitation requirement in *Attorney General's Reference No 64 of 2003 (R v Boujettif and*

Harrison) v Sanchez [2003] EWCA Crim 3514 and *R v Woods and Collins* [2005] EWCA Crim 2065 summarised in the Sentencing Council's Guideline Judgments Case Compendium (Section (A) Generic Sentencing Principles) available at: sentencingcouncil.judiciary.gov.uk.

OFFENCE SERIOUSNESS (CULPABILITY AND HARM)		
A. IDENTIFY THE APPROPRIATE STARTING POINT		
Starting points based on first time offender pleading not guilty		
Examples of nature of activity	**Starting point**	**Range**
Single offence committed by an offender acting alone and with evidence of little or no planning, goods or services worth less than £200	Band C fine	Band A fine to high level community order
Offence displaying one or more of the following: – offender acting in unison with others – evidence of planning – offence part of a 'spree' – intimidation of victim – goods or services worth £200 or more	Medium level community order	Low level community order to 12 weeks custody
OFFENCE SERIOUSNESS (CULPABILITY AND HARM)		
B. CONSIDER THE EFFECT OF AGGRAVATING AND MITIGATING FACTORS (OTHER THAN THOSE WITHIN EXAMPLES ABOVE)		
Common aggravating and mitigating factors are identified at B[5.2A]		
FORM A PRELIMINARY VIEW OF THE APPROPRIATE SENTENCE, THEN CONSIDER OFFENDER MITIGATION		
Common factors are identified at B[5.2A]. See also "Key factors" above.		
CONSIDER A REDUCTION FOR A GUILTY PLEA		
CONSIDER ANCILLARY ORDERS, INCLUDING COMPENSATION		
Refer to B[18] for guidance on compensation and **Part B** for available ancillary orders		
DECIDE SENTENCE		
GIVE REASONS		

A[46]

Protective order, breach of

Charges

A[46.1]

1 Without reasonable excuse the defendant breached the terms of his restraining order in that he [specify] thereby making him guilty of an offence.

Protection from Harassment Act 1997, s 5(5).

2. Without reasonable excuse the defendant breached the terms of his non-molestation order in that he [specify] thereby making him guilty of an offence.

Family Law Act 1996, s 42A(1).

Maximum penalty – (in either case) Fine level 5 and 6 months (**12 months). Triable either way. Specified violent offence under Sch 15, Part 1, CJA 2003.

Crown Court – 5 years' imprisonment and unlimited fine.

Mode of trial

A[46.2]

Consider the **SC Guideline** at **A[46.4]** below.

Legal notes and definitions

A[46.3]

Non-molestation – duplicity. In *McCaskill v DPP* [2005] EWHC 3208 (Admin), 170 JP 301, the defendant was charged with sending letters between January and November 2004 in contravention of a restraining order imposed by the Crown Court. It was held that the breach was not duplicitous and therefore complied with the legal requirements of s 5(5) and (6) PHA 1997.

Non-molestation – general. See the notes at D[8.19] onwards.

Harassment – terms of order. An order under s.5 must identify by name those who are protected by it (*R v Mann* [2000] The Times, April 11, CA).

Sentencing
Sentencing Council – Protective order, breach of

A[46.4]

This guidelines and accompanying notes are taken from the SC's definitive guideline *Breach of a Protective Order*, published 7 December 2006.

Where the conduct is particularly serious, it would normally be charged as a separate offence. These starting points are based on the premise that the activity has either been prosecuted separately as an offence or is not of a character sufficient to justify prosecution of it as an offence in its own right.

For cases of domestic violence. See SC Definitive Guideline: "Overarching Principles: Domestic Violence".

Aims of sentencing

(a)   The main aim of sentencing for breach of a protective order (which would have been imposed to protect a victim from future harm) should be to achieve future compliance with that order.

(b)   The court will need to assess the level of risk posed by the offender. Willingness to undergo treatment or accept help may influence sentence.

Key factors

(a)   The nature of the conduct that caused the breach of the order. In particular, whether the conduct was direct or indirect, although it is important to recognise that indirect contact is capable of causing significant harm or anxiety.

(b)   There may be **exceptional cases** where the nature of the **breach** is **particularly serious** but has not been dealt with by a separate offence being charged. In those cases the **risk** posed by the offender and the **nature of the breach** will be particularly significant in determining the response.

(c)   The nature of the original conduct or offence is relevant in so far as it allows a judgement to be made on the level of harm caused to the victim by the breach, and the extent to which that harm was intended.

(d)   The sentence following a breach is for the breach alone and must avoid punishing the offender again for the offence or conduct as a result of which the order was made.

(e)   It is likely that all breaches of protective orders will pass the threshold for a community sentence. Custody is the starting point where violence is used. Non-violent conduct may also cross the custody threshold where a high degree of harm or anxiety has been caused.

(f)   Where an order was made in civil proceedings, its purpose may have been to cause the subject of the order to modify behaviour rather than to imply that the conduct was especially serious. If so, it is likely to be disproportionate to impose a custodial sentence if the breach of the order did not involve threats or violence.

(g)   In some cases where a breach might result in a short custodial sentence but the court is satisfied that the offender genuinely intends to reform his or her behaviour and there is a real prospect of rehabilitation, the court may consider it appropriate to impose a sentence that will allow this. This may mean imposing a suspended sentence order or a community order (where appropriate with a requirement to attend an accredited domestic violence programme).

OFFENCE SERIOUSNESS (CULPABILITY AND HARM)

A. IDENTIFY THE APPROPRIATE STARTING POINT

Starting points based on first time offender pleading not guilty

Examples of nature of activity	Starting point	Range
Single breach involving no/minimal direct contact	Low level community order	Band C fine to medium level community order
More than one breach involving no/minimal contact or some direct contact	Medium level community order	Low level community order to high level community order
Single breach involving some violence and/or significant physical or psychological harm to the victim	18 weeks custody	13 weeks to 26 weeks custody
More than one breach involving some violence and/or significant physical or psychological harm to the victim	Crown Court	26 weeks custody to Crown Court
Breach (whether one or more) involving significant physical violence or psychological harm to the victim	Crown Court	Crown Court

OFFENCE SERIOUSNESS (CULPABILITY AND HARM)

B. CONSIDER THE EFFECT OF AGGRAVATING AND MITIGATING FACTORS (OTHER THAN THOSE WITHIN EXAMPLES ABOVE)

Common aggravating and mitigating factors are identified at **B[5.2A]**. The following may be particularly relevant but **these lists are not exhaustive**

Factors indicating higher culpability	*Factors indicating lower culpability*
1. Proven history of violence or threats by the offender	1. Breach occurred after a long period of compliance
2. Using contact arrangements with a child to instigate offence	2. Victim initiated contact
3. Offence is a further breach, following earlier breach proceedings	
4. Offender has history of disobedience to court orders	
5. Breach committed immediately or shortly after order made	

Factors indicating greater degree of harm	
1. Victim is particularly vulnerable	
2. Impact on children	
3. Victim is forced to leave home	
FORM A PRELIMINARY VIEW OF THE APPROPRIATE SENTENCE, THEN CONSIDER OFFENDER MITIGATION Common factors are identified at B[5.2A]	
CONSIDER A REDUCTION FOR A GUILTY PLEA	
CONSIDER ANCILLARY ORDERS	
Refer to B[18] for guidance on compensation and **Part B** for available ancillary orders	
DECIDE SENTENCE **GIVE REASONS**	

Variation

A[46.5]

Variation of restraining order. Where a restraining order has been made for a specified period of time, on a true construction of s 5(4), a court had power to vary a restraining order by extending the expiry date of the order (*DPP v Kevin Hall* [2005] EWHC 2612 (Admin), [2006] 3 All ER 170). The refusal by a magistrates' court to vary or discharge a restraining order on an application under s 5(4) was not subject to a right of appeal to the Crown Court as such an order was not a sentence (or "order") for the purposes of s 108 MCA 1980 (*R (on the application of Lee) v Leeds Crown Court* [2006] All ER (D) 18 (Oct). The same argument was canvassed in *R v Bradfield* [2006] All ER (D) 394 (Nov) in relation to s 9 of the Criminal Appeal Act 1968 but the Court of Appeal did not find it necessary to decide the point. The case of *Lee*, therefore, remains good law).

A[47]

Obstructing or resisting a constable in the execution of his duty
Obstructing a court security officer in the execution of his duty

Charges

A[47.1]
1 Resisting a constable in the execution of his duty

A[47.2]
2 Resisting a person assisting a constable in the execution of his duty

A[47.3]
3 Wilfully obstructing a constable in the execution of his duty

A[47.4]
4 Wilfully obstructing a person assisting a constable in the execution of his duty

Police Act 1996, s 89(2)

Maximum penalty – Fine level 3 and one month (**51 weeks).

A[47.5]
5 Wilfully obstructing a court security officer in the execution of his duty

Courts Act 2003, s 57

Maximum penalty – Fine level 3.

Legal notes and definitions

A[47.6]
The offences of resisting and wilfully obstructing will usually involve some other activity than an assault on the police or a court security officer (which would constitute a different charge). A person exercising their right to silence does not commit the offence of obstructing a police officer.

A[47.7]
Resisting. Means striving against, opposing or trying to impede. For the intention which the defendant must have to commit the offence see A[9] (police assault).

A[47.8]

Wilfully means that there must be an intention to bring about a state of affairs whereby, judged objectively, the constable is obstructed in the sense of making it more difficult for him to carry out his duty. The accused need not be hostile to the police; motives are irrelevant. Two examples may make this clear:

(a)   The defendant sees the constable trying to arrest a robber. With the intention of helping the officer, the defendant intervenes but he is so clumsy that the villain escapes. He is not guilty of obstruction because the state of affairs that he *intended* to bring about was that the officer would be helped to effect the arrest.

(b)   The defendant sees the constable about to arrest what he considers to be the wrong man. He intervenes to stop the arrest. The arrest was in fact lawful. He is guilty because, objectively, the officer has been obstructed in his duty and this was the intention of the accused. It is irrelevant that his motives for doing so were good (otherwise the police would be in peril of all sorts of interruptions whilst exercising their duty).

Unlike a charge of assaulting a police officer, it may be that the defendant must know that the person he is obstructing is a police officer. A defendant who honestly believes the complainant is *not* a police officer, is not guilty of the offence.

A[47.9]

Obstructing. Deliberately causing a physical obstruction is an offence and so is shouting a warning to a person committing an offence or about to commit an offence. It is not a wilful obstruction if a person refuses to answer questions which he is not legally obliged to answer. However, where the police were lawfully investigating a criminal offence (shoplifting), had identified themselves to three suspects, and notified them they wished to question them in relation to an offence of shoplifting, the offenders' actions in running away could amount to an obstruction within the terms of the Act (*Sekfali v DPP* [2006] EWHC 894 (Admin).

A[47.10]

Constable. A constable includes a special constable and member of the police force of any rank however high. Offences against designated and accredited persons acting in the execution of their duty ie community support officer, investigating officer, detention officer and escort officer are catered for by the Police Reform Act 2002, s 46. Wilful obstruction carries on conviction imprisonment of one month (**51 weeks) or a level 3 fine.

A[47.11]

In the execution of his duty. If as a finding of fact/law the constable was not acting in the course of his duty then the charge must be dismissed. Once it had been established that the initial arrest of the accused was unlawful, and provided he did not unreasonable force in resisting the arrest, the accused could not be guilty of resisting other police officers who were bona fide assisting the first officer in the unlawful arrest (*Cumberbatch v Crown Prosecution Service* [2009] EWHC 3353 (Admin), 174 JP 149). See A[9.5].

A[47.12]

This type of defence sometimes raises difficult questions of law as to whether, for example, a constable had a right to be on private premises when not in possession of a search warrant, or whether a constable had a right to detain a person without there being in force a warrant for arrest. See *James and Chorley v DPP* (1997) 161 JP 89, [1997] Crim LR 831 where a defendant had ceased driving thus ending a constable's right to arrest for driving whilst disqualified. His friend did not obstruct the constable by preventing an arrest as the arrest was not lawful.

A[47.13]

The burden of proof that the constable was acting in the execution of his duty rests on the prosecution (*Redmond-Bate v DPP* (1999) 163 JP 789, [1999] Crim LR 998).

A[47.14]

Police officer and court security officer. See A[9.4] for definitions.

Sentencing
SC Guideline – Obstruct/resist a constable in the execution of duty

A[47.15]

OFFENCE SERIOUSNESS (CULPABILITY AND HARM)		
A. IDENTIFY THE APPROPRIATE STARTING POINT		
Starting points based on first time offender pleading not guilty		
Examples of nature of activity	Starting point	Range
Failure to move when required to do so	Band A fine	Conditional discharge to band B fine
Attempt to prevent arrest or other lawful police action; or giving false details	Band B fine	Band A fine to band C fine
Several people attempting to prevent arrest or other lawful police action	Low level community order	Band C fine to medium level community order
OFFENCE SERIOUSNESS (CULPABILITY AND HARM)		
B. CONSIDER THE EFFECT OF AGGRAVATING AND MITIGATING FACTORS (OTHER THAN THOSE WITHIN EXAMPLES ABOVE)		
Common aggravating and mitigating factors are identified at B[5.2A]. The following may be particularly relevant but **these lists are not exhaustive**		
Factors indicating higher culpability	*Factors indicating lower culpability*	

1. Premeditated action	1. Genuine mistake or misjudgement
2. Aggressive words/threats	2. Brief incident
3. Aggressive group action	
FORM A PRELIMINARY VIEW OF THE APPROPRIATE SENTENCE, THEN CONSIDER OFFENDER MITIGATION	
Common factors are identified at B[5.2A]	
CONSIDER A REDUCTION FOR A GUILTY PLEA	
CONSIDER ANCILLARY ORDERS	
Refer to B[18] for guidance on compensation and **Part B** for available ancillary orders	
DECIDE SENTENCE	
GIVE REASONS	

A[48]

Railway fare evasion

Charge 1

A[48.1]

Failure to give name and address following a failure to produce a valid ticket

Regulation of Railways Act 1889, s 5 (1)

Maximum penalty – Fine level 2 (Railway Company or London Transport)

Charge 2

A[48.2]

Travelling on a railway without having previously paid the fare with the intention of avoiding payment

OR

Having paid a fare knowingly and wilfully travelling beyond the distance paid for without previously paying for an additional distance with the intention of avoiding additional fare

OR

Giving a false name and address following a failure to pay

Regulation of the Railways Act 1889, s 5(3)(a), (b), and (c) respectively

Maximum penalty – Fine level 3 or 3 months (**51 weeks) (Railway Company or London Transport).

Byelaws. All railway operators and Railtrack have adopted the Framework Railway Byelaws. Penalty for a breach of a byelaw is a level 3 fine.

Legal notes and definitions

A[48.3]

A fare must be paid to the railway authority or one of its employees.

The request for a traveller's name and address must be made by an officer of the railway operator.

A[48.4]

The prosecution must satisfy the magistrates that the defendant intended to avoid paying the fare or additional fare (if he paid for part of the journey). If the magistrates believe that the defendant genuinely forgot to pay his fare then the case must be dismissed. It is sufficient for a conviction if the defendant's intention was to avoid paying until payment was demanded; there is no need to prove an intention permanently to avoid payment.

A[48.5]

The prosecution has only to establish the intention to avoid paying the fare, not the intention to defraud.

A[48.6]

It has been held that the offence of 'without having previously paid the fare with the intention of avoiding the fare' has been committed if the defendant uses the return half of a ticket issued to another person. It is not necessary to show that the offender knew that the ticket was non-transferable.

A[48.7]

Travelling. This includes the time between leaving the railway carriage and proceeding to the exit barrier. Thus an offence is committed if a passenger decides to avoid the fare at that stage of the journey.

A[48.8]

Wilfully. This means deliberately.

Sentencing
SC Guideline – Railway fare evasion

A[48.9]

OFFENCE SERIOUSNESS (CULPABILITY AND HARM)		
A. IDENTIFY THE APPROPRIATE STARTING POINT		
Starting points based on first time offender pleading not guilty		
Examples of nature of activity	Starting point	Range
Failing to produce ticket or failure to pay fare on request	Band A fine	Conditional discharge to band B fine
Travelling on railway without having paid the fare or knowingly and wilfully travelling beyond the distance paid for, with intent to avoid payment	Band B fine	Band A fine to band C fine
OFFENCE SERIOUSNESS (CULPABILITY AND HARM)		
B. CONSIDER THE EFFECT OF AGGRAVATING AND MITIGATING FACTORS (OTHER THAN THOSE WITHIN EXAMPLES ABOVE)		
Common aggravating and mitigating factors are identified at B[5.2A]. The following may be particularly relevant but **these lists are not exhaustive**		

Factor indicating higher culpability 1. Offensive or intimidating language or behaviour towards railway staff	
Factor indicating greater degree of harm 1. High level of loss caused or intended to be caused	
FORM A PRELIMINARY VIEW OF THE APPROPRIATE SENTENCE, THEN CONSIDER OFFENDER MITIGATION Common factors are identified at B[5.2A]	
CONSIDER A REDUCTION FOR A GUILTY PLEA	
CONSIDER ANCILLARY ORDERS INCLUDING COMPENSATION Refer to B[18] for guidance on compensation and Part B for available ancillary orders	
DECIDE SENTENCE **GIVE REASONS**	

A[48.10]

See Table B at B[4.2] for available sentences.

A[49]

School non-attendance

Charge 1

A[49.1]

Being the parent of a child [identify] of compulsory school age and who is a registered pupil at a school [specify], [identify child] failed to attend regularly at the school.

Education Act 1996, s 444(1).

Maximum penalty – Level 3 fine (see also D[17]).

Charge 2

A[49.2]

Being the parent of a child [identify] of compulsory school age and who is a registered pupil at a school namely [specify], knowing that the child [identify] is failing to attend regularly at that school, fails without justification to cause the child to do so.

Education Act 1996, s 444 (1A).

Maximum penalty – Level 4 fine and/or 3 months (see also D[17]).

Legal notes and definitions

A[49.3]

"Compulsory school age" and "school" is defined by Education Act 1996, s 8.

"Registered pupil" in relation to a school, means a person registered as a pupil at the school in the register kept under the Education Act 1996, s 434.

"Parent" is defined by Education Act 1996, s 576.

Absence when the register is closed may be treated as non-school attendance so as to affect "regular attendance" (*Hinchley v Rankin* (1961) 125 JP 293). As to evidence of attendance see Education Act 1996, s 566.

Subject to the defences set out in s 444(1), the offence is one of strict liability; which does not contravene article 6(2) of the ECHR (*Barnfather v Islington Education Authority* [2003] 1 WLR 2318). Where the parent asserted that the child was receiving a suitable education outside of school, the burden lay on the parent to prove that defence albeit on a balance of probabilities: *Oxford County Council v L* (unreported) 3/3/10, DC.

In *Islington London Borough Council v TD* [2011] EWHC 990 (Admin), it was held that the Education Act created two distinct offences and two distinct defences for non-school attendance. It was a defence that the child was prevented from attending regularly by reason of sickness, or any unavoidable cause. "Unavoidable cause" had to be in relation to the child and had to be something in the nature of an emergency. On the facts there was no question of something in the nature of an emergency that stopped the child from going to school and the fact that P was unable to persuade the child to go to school was not a defence. The magistrates had applied the wrong test. The fact that P had done all she reasonably could do to ensure the child's attendance went to mitigation only.

Sentencing
SC Guideline – School non-attendance

A[49.4]

OFFENCE SERIOUSNESS (CULPABILITY AND HARM) A. IDENTIFY THE APPROPRIATE STARTING POINT Starting points based on first time offender pleading not guilty		
Examples of nature of activity	**Starting point**	**Range**
Short period following previous good attendance (s 444(1))	Band A fine	Conditional discharge to band A fine
Erratic attendance for a long period (s 444(1))	Band B fine	Band B fine to low level community order
Colluding in and condoning non-attendance or deliberately instigating non-attendance (s 444(1A))	Medium level community order	Low level community order to high level community order

OFFENCE SERIOUSNESS (CULPABILITY AND HARM) B. CONSIDER THE EFFECT OF AGGRAVATING AND MITIGATING FACTORS (OTHER THAN THOSE WITHIN EXAMPLES ABOVE) Common aggravating and mitigating factors are identified at B[5.2A]. The following may be particularly relevant but **these lists are not exhaustive**	
Factors indicating higher culpability	*Factors indicating lower culpability*
1. Parental collusion (s 444(1) only)	1. Parent unaware of child's whereabouts
2. Lack of parental effort to ensure attendance (s 444(1) only)	2. Parent tried to ensure attendance
3. Threats to teachers and/or officials	3. Parent concerned by child's allegations of bullying/unable to get school to address bullying
4. Refusal to co-operate with school and/or officials	

Factors indicating greater degree of harm 1. More than one child 2. Harmful effect on other children in family	
FORM A PRELIMINARY VIEW OF THE APPROPRIATE SENTENCE, THEN CONSIDER OFFENDER MITIGATION Common factors are identified at B[5.2A]	
CONSIDER A REDUCTION FOR A GUILTY PLEA	
CONSIDER ANCILLARY ORDERS, INCLUDING PARENTING ORDER Refer to B[18] for guidance on compensation and Part B for available ancillary orders	
DECIDE SENTENCE **GIVE REASONS**	

A[50]

Sex offenders register – fail to comply with notification requirements

Charge

A[50.1]

A person commits an offence if he –

(a) fails, without reasonable excuse, to comply with section 83 (1), 84 (1), 84 (4) (b), 85 (1), 87 (4) or 89 (2) (b) or any requirement imposed by regulations made under section 86 (1); or

(b) notifies to the police, in purported compliance with section 83 (1), 84 (1) or 95 (1) or any requirement imposed by regulations made under section 86 (1), any information which he knows to be false.

Sexual Offences Act 2003, s 91 (1).

Maximum penalty – Fine level 5 and 6 months (**12 months). Triable either way.

Crown Court – 5 years' imprisonment and unlimited fine

Mode of trial

A[50.2]

See SC Guideline at A[50.4] below.

Legal notes and definitions

A[50.3]

As to the obligation to register see A[52.15] and A[53.16].

Sentencing
SC Guideline – Sex offenders register – fail to comply with notification requirements

A[50.4]

OFFENCE SERIOUSNESS (CULPABILITY AND HARM) A. IDENTIFY THE APPROPRIATE STARTING POINT Starting points based on first time offender pleading not guilty		
Examples of nature of activity	Starting point	Range

Negligent or inadvertent failure to comply with requirements	Medium level community order	Band C fine to high level community order
Deliberate failure to comply with requirements OR Supply of information known to be false	6 weeks custody	High level community order to 26 weeks custody
Conduct as described in box above AND Long period of non-compliance OR Attempts to avoid detection	18 weeks custody	6 weeks custody to Crown Court

OFFENCE SERIOUSNESS (CULPABILITY AND HARM)
B. CONSIDER THE EFFECT OF AGGRAVATING AND MITIGATING FACTORS (OTHER THAN THOSE WITHIN EXAMPLES ABOVE)
Common aggravating and mitigating factors are identified at **B[5.2A]**. The following may be particularly relevant but **these lists are not exhaustive**

Factor indicating higher culpability	*Factor indicating lower culpability*
1. Long period of non-compliance (where not in the examples above)	1. Genuine misunderstanding
Factors indicating greater degree of harm	
1. Alarm or distress caused to victim	
2. Particularly serious original offence	

FORM A PRELIMINARY VIEW OF THE APPROPRIATE SENTENCE, THEN CONSIDER OFFENDER MITIGATION
Common factors are identified at **B[5.2A]**
CONSIDER A REDUCTION FOR A GUILTY PLEA
CONSIDER ANCILLARY ORDERS, INCLUDING PARENTING ORDER
Refer to **Part B** for guidance on available ancillary orders
DECIDE SENTENCE **GIVE REASONS**

Note. An offender convicted of this offence will always have at least one relevant previous conviction for the offence that resulted in the notification requirements being imposed. The starting points and ranges take this into account; any other previous convictions should be considered in the usual way. See **A[52.15]** and **A[53.16]**.

A[51]

Sexual activity in a public lavatory

Charge

A[51.1]

The accused was in a lavatory to which the public or a section of the public has or were permitted to have access, whether on payment or otherwise; that he intentionally engaged in an activity and, the activity was sexual.

Sexual Offences Act 2003, s 71.

Maximum penalty – Fine level 5 and 6 months (**51 weeks).

Legal Notes and definitions

A[51.2]

For the purposes of s 71, an activity is sexual if a reasonable person would, in all the circumstances but regardless of any person's purpose, consider it to be sexual.

Sentencing
SC Guideline – Sexual activity in a lavatory

A[51.3]

This guideline and accompanying notes are taken from the SC's definitive guideline *Sexual Offences Act 2003* published 30 April 2007.

Key factors

(a)   This offence is committed where an offender intentionally engages in sexual activity in a public lavatory. It was introduced to give adults and children the freedom to use public lavatories for the purpose for which they are designed, without the fear of being an unwilling witness to overtly sexual behaviour of a kind that most people would not expect to be conducted in public. It is primarily a public order offence rather than a sexual offence.

(b)   When dealing with a repeat offender, the starting point should be a low level community order with a range of Band C fine to medium level community order. The presence of aggravating features may suggest that a sentence above the range is appropriate.

(c)   This guideline may be relevant by way of analogy to conduct charged as the common law offence of outraging public decency; the offence is triable either way and has a maximum penalty of a level 5 and/or 6 months' imprisonment when tried summarily.

OFFENCE SERIOUSNESS (CULPABILITY AND HARM)

A. IDENTIFY THE APPROPRIATE STARTING POINT

Starting points based on first time offender pleading not guilty

Examples of nature of activity	Starting point	Range
Basic offence as defined in the Act, assuming no aggravating or mitigating factors	Band C fine	Band C fine
Offence with aggravating factors	Low level community order	Band C fine to medium level community order

OFFENCE SERIOUSNESS (CULPABILITY AND HARM)

B. CONSIDER THE EFFECT OF AGGRAVATING AND MITIGATING FACTORS (OTHER THAN THOSE WITHIN EXAMPLES ABOVE)

Common aggravating and mitigating factors are identified at **B[5.2A]**. The following may be particularly relevant but **these lists are not exhaustive**

Factors indicating higher culpability	
1. Intimidating behaviour/threats of violence to member(s) of the public	
2. Blatant behaviour	

FORM A PRELIMINARY VIEW OF THE APPROPRIATE SENTENCE, THEN CONSIDER OFFENDER MITIGATION

Common factors are identified at **B[5.2A]**

CONSIDER A REDUCTION FOR A GUILTY PLEA

CONSIDER ANCILLARY ORDERS, INCLUDING COMPENSATION

Refer to **B[18]** for guidance on compensation and **Part B** for available ancillary orders

DECIDE SENTENCE

GIVE REASONS

A[52]

Sexual activity with a child

Charge

A[52.1]

(1) Intentionally touching a child under 13 in a sexual manner

Sexual Offences Act 2003, s 7

Maximum penalty – Fine level 5 and 6 months (**12 months). Triable either way. Specified sexual offence under Sch 15, Part 2, CJA 2003.

Crown Court – 14 years' imprisonment and unlimited fine.

(2) Being over 18 years did intentionally engage in sexual touching with a child under 16

Sexual Offences Act 2003, s 9

Maximum penalty – As (1) above unless penetration is involved when triable on indictment only – life imprisonment.

Mode of trial

A[52.2]

See general notes at I[4] and the SC's definitive guideline at A[52.14] below.

Legal notes and definitions

A[52.3]

Sexual activity. An activity is sexual if a reasonable person would conclude:

(a) whatever the circumstances or purpose, it is because of its nature sexual; or

(b) because of its nature it may be sexual and because of the circumstances and or purpose it is sexual (s 78).

A[52.4]

Consent is agreement by choice. A child under 13 does not have legal capacity to consent nor is consent material in the case of a child under 16 other than to absolve the defendant of a more serious offence

A[52.5]

Age. It is a defence that the defendant did not reasonably know or was mistaken about the age of the child (*B v DPP* [2000] 2 AC 428, [2000]

1 All ER 833, HL) in the case of a s 9 offence and the burden of proving the absence of reasonable belief rests on the prosecution. In the case of a s 7 offence this defence is not available.

A[52.6]

Evidence of children. The evidence of children (ie those persons under 14 years) must be given unsworn (Youth Justice & Criminal Evidence Act 1999, s 55). Such evidence need not be corroborated only because it is unsworn (*R v Hampshire* [1996] QB 1, [1995] 2 All ER 1019, CA).

A[52.7]

A court may not refuse to admit the evidence of a child complainant by reason of age only. The court should assess whether the child is capable of giving intelligible testimony either by watching a video of the child or by questioning the complainant themselves (*DPP v M* [1998] QB 913, [1997] 2 All ER 749). See *R v Barker* [2010] EWCA Crim 4, [2011] Crim LR 233, (2010) Times, 5 February. The law was put on a statutory footing by s 53 of the Youth Justice and Criminal Evidence Act 1999. Where the issue is raised, it is for the party calling a witness to establish competence to the civil standard. There are no presumptions or preconceptions regarding competence. Provided the witness could understand the questions put to her by the prosecution and defence and could give comprehensible answers, he/she was competent.

A[52.8]

Proceedings involving child witnesses. In cases of assault, cruelty or neglect and sexual offences, the legal presumption is that a video recording of a child witness' evidence will be admitted albeit the leave of the court is required. A 'child witness' is one who is, under 17 years at the time of the hearing. A defendant may not cross-examine a child witness in person; this must be done by his solicitor or counsel – see A[52.10] below.

A[52.9]

Adult magistrates' courts may consider such a video even though the child is not called to give evidence. In trials before magistrates a screen may be used so that the witness may not feel intimidated by the presence of the accused (*R v X* (1989) 91 Cr App Rep 36, [1990] Crim LR 515, CA).

A[52.10]

Special measures. For a more detailed commentary see section I[6.13A].

A witness under 18 years is eligible for assistance by a special measures direction if the quality of his evidence (ie completeness, coherence or accuracy) is likely to be diminished by reason of fear or distress (Youth Justice and Criminal Evidence Act 1999, ss 16–19). In magistrates' courts, special measures are screens, TV links and video-recorded evidence. For child witnesses in cases involving sexual offences, violence (including threats) and cruelty who are defined as witnesses in need of special protection, the provision of special measures is near to mandatory (*R v*

Camberwell Green Youth Court [2005] UKHL 4, [2005] 1 All ER 999, [2005] All ER (D) 259 (Jan)). This is intended to provide protection for children in cases involving assaults, muggings and domestic violence and to bring the adult magistrates' court into line with the provision in the Youth Court. The provisions apply to defence and prosecution witnesses but not to the defendant (*R (on application of S) v Waltham Forest Youth Court* [2004] EWHC 715 (Admin), [2004] All ER (D) 590 (Mar)).

Special measures may be applied for in proceedings for an anti-social behaviour order.

A[52.11]

Privacy: clearing the court. The magistrates can order the court to be cleared (except for those directly concerned with the case and the press) whilst the child or young person is testifying (Children and Young Persons Act 1933, s 37 as amended).

A[52.12]

Anonymity of victim. The general prohibition on the revealing of the identity of the victim of a sexual offence applies (see **A[53.11]**). In the case of persons under 18 the existing power under s.39 of the Children and Young Persons Act 1933 (as amended) is preserved. The court may direct that any press, radio or television report of the case must not reveal the name, address, school or identity of any child or young person concerned in the proceedings including the defendant. However, such an order must be clear as to precisely what is prohibited (*Briffet v DPP* [2001] EWHC 841 (Admin), (2001) 166 JP 66, sub nom *Briffett and Bradshaw v Crown Prosecution Service* [2002] EMLR 203) and should be in writing (*Re BBC Litigation Department* [2002] All ER (D) 69 (Apr), CA).

Great care should be taken by magistrates' courts when making an order under s 39. Before making such an order the court should generally ask members of the press whether they had any submissions so the court fully understood the issues, given the great importance of making these orders. Orders are not to be made as a matter of routine, and require a careful balance of matters relating to the public interest, after submissions have been made (*C v CPS* [2008] EWHC 854 (Admin), 172 JP 273).

Any embarrassment that might flow to the children was an unfortunate consequence of a parent being convicted of a crime. Unless there were exceptional circumstances the balance between articles 8 and 10 of the ECHR fell firmly in favour of removing the s 39 prohibition (*C v CPS* [2008] EWHC 854 (Admin), 172 JP 273; *Re Trinity Mirror Plc* [2008] EWCA Crim 50, [2008] 2 All ER 1159).

A decision to vary reporting restrictions in relation to a young offender pursuant to the Children and Young Persons Act 1933, s 39 was quashed as the proper test had not been applied and inadequate reasons had been given to justify the variation. In deciding whether to impose reporting restrictions under s 39, a court had to balance the welfare of the child, the public interest and the requirements of the ECHR, art 10, and to restrict publication if the factors were evenly balanced: *R (on the application of Y) v Aylesbury Crown Court, Crown Prosecution Service and Newsquest Media Group Ltd* [2012] EWHC 1140 (Admin), [2012] All ER (D) 89 (May).

A[52.13]

Corroboration. The evidence of a complainant in sexual cases is no longer required.

Sentencing
SC Guideline – Sexual assault and Sexual assault of a child under 13

A[52.14]

These guidelines are taken from the SC's definitive guideline *Sexual Offences Act 2003* published 30 April 2007.

**The court must inform the defendant that the Independent Safeguarding Authority (known as the Independent Barring Board) will automatically ban him/her from working with children and/or vulnerable adults. As the court has no role in the decision if the defendant needs any further advice he/she should consult a solicitor.

For offences under s 9 see **SC definitive guideline** in Part 3A, pp 42–54 and Part 7, p 135 located at http://sentencingcouncil.judiciary.gov.uk/guidelines/guidelines-to-download.htm.

IDENTIFY DANGEROUS OFFENDERS		
These are serious offences for the purposes of the public protection provisions in the Criminal Justice Act 2003. Refer to B[16.5] and consult legal adviser for guidance		
OFFENCE SERIOUSNESS (CULPABILITY AND HARM)		
A. IDENTIFY THE APPROPRIATE STARTING POINT		
Starting points based on first time offender pleading not guilty		
Examples of nature of activity	Starting point	Range
Contact between part of offender's body (other than the genitalia) with part of the victim's body (other than the genitalia)	26 weeks custody if the victim is under 13 Medium level community order if the victim is aged 13 or over	4 weeks custody to Crown Court Band C fine to 6 weeks custody
Contact between naked genitalia and another part of the victim's body	Crown Court if the victim is under 13	Crown Court

Contact with naked genitalia of victim by offender using part of his or her body other than the genitalia, or an object	Crown Court if the victim is under 13	Crown Court
Contact between either the clothed genitalia of offender and naked genitalia of victim or naked genitalia of offender and clothed genitalia of victim	Crown Court if the victim is aged 13 or over	26 weeks custody to Crown Court
Contact between naked genitalia of offender and naked genitalia, face or mouth of the victim	Crown Court	Crown Court

OFFENCE SERIOUSNESS (CULPABILITY AND HARM)

B. CONSIDER THE EFFECT OF AGGRAVATING AND MITIGATING FACTORS (OTHER THAN THOSE WITHIN EXAMPLES ABOVE)

Common aggravating and mitigating factors are identified at B[5.2A].The following may be particularly relevant but **these lists are not exhaustive:**

Factors indicating higher culpability	*Factors indicating lower culpability*
1. Background of intimidation or coercion	1. Youth and immaturity of the offender
2. Use of drugs, alcohol or other substance to facilitate the offence	2. Minimal or fleeting contact
3. Threats to prevent the victim reporting the incident	*Where the victim is aged 16 or over*
4. Abduction or detention	3. Victim engaged in consensual activity with the offender on the same occasion and immediately before the offence
5. Offender aware that he or she is suffering from a sexually transmitted infection	*Where the victim is under 16*
6. Prolonged activity or contact	4. Sexual activity between two children (one of whom is the offender) was mutually agreed and experimental
Factors indicating greater degree of harm	
1. Offender ejaculated or caused victim to ejaculate	
2. Physical harm caused	

FORM A PRELIMINARY VIEW OF THE APPROPRIATE SENTENCE, THEN CONSIDER OFFENDER MITIGATION

Common factors are identified at B[5.2A]

CONSIDER A REDUCTION FOR A GUILTY PLEA

CONSIDER ANCILLARY ORDERS, INCLUDING COMPENSATION

Refer to **B[18]** for guidance on compensation and **Part B** for available ancillary orders
DECIDE SENTENCE
GIVE REASONS

Note. (See **A[52.15]** immediately below)

(a)   In accordance with s 80 of and Sch 3 to the Sexual Offences Act 2003, automatic notification requirements apply upon conviction to an offender aged 18 or over where:
(1)   the victim was under 18; or
(2)   a term of imprisonment or a community sentence of at least 12 months is imposed.

NB: A community order with a requirement to carry out 120 hours unpaid work was not a community sentence of at least 12 months for the purposes of Sch 3 and therefore the offender was not subject to the notification requirements of the legislation (*R v Odam* [2008] EWCA Crim 1087).

A[52.15]

Sexual Offences Act 2003 (Part 2). Under a new r 42.3 of the CPR 2012, on conviction the court must explain the notification requirements to the defendant.

(a)   **notify the police** within the next three days (or if in custody or otherwise detained, within three days of release) of his name, any other names he uses, his date of birth and his home address;

(b)   **notify the police** of any change of name or home address within 14 days of any change;

(c)   **notify the police** of any address where he resides or stays for 14 days or longer. This means either 14 days at a time, or a total of 14 days in any 12-month period;

(d)   **notify the police** of an intention to leave the UK for a period of 24 hours or longer, at least 24 hours prior to departure of the particulars of the journey;*

(e)   **notify the police** of his national insurance number.

*See the Sexual Offences Act 2003 (Notification Requirements) (England and Wales) Regulations 2012, SI 2012/1876). These Regulations amend the Sexual Offences Act 2003 (Travel Notification Requirements) Regulations 2004, SI 2004/1220 ('the 2004 Regulations') and introduce new notification requirements under the Sexual Offences Act 2003 ('the 2003 Act').

Part 2 of the 2003 Act imposes notification requirements on offenders convicted of certain sex offences. These offenders are called 'relevant offenders'. The 2003 Act requires relevant offenders to notify certain personal information to the police, both at the outset and periodically thereafter (and to notify certain changes of circumstances). These Regulations amend the 2004 Regulations and impose new notification requirements on relevant offenders.

In *R v Longworth*, January 26, 2006, the House of Lords held that for persons convicted before May 1, 2004, the notification requirements under the Sex Offenders Act 1997 do not arise if an order of **absolute** or **conditional discharge** is made. In some cases this means that a notification requirement will arise on conviction but where sentencing is adjourned, will cease on the imposition of an absolute or conditional discharge. Persons conditionally discharged after May 1, 2004 are subject to the notification requirements of the 2003 legislation.

The Sexual Offences Act 2003 (Amendment of Schedules 3 and 5) Order 2007 (SI 2007/296) amended the primary legislation. Section 80 of the 2003 Act now provides that if a person is convicted, found not guilty by reason of insanity or cautioned for an offence listed in Sch 3 to the Act, or found to be under a disability and to have done the act charged against him in respect of such an offence, then that person is subject to the notification requirements of Part 2 of the Act.

For observations on the appropriate level of sentence for failing to comply with the notification requirements see *R v Bickerton* [2007] EWCA Crim 2884, [2007] All ER (D) 230 (Nov).

A[52.16]

Sexual offences prevention order may be applied for separately under Part II of the Sexual Offences Act 2003 The application is a civil matter (*B v Chief Constable of Avon and Somerset Constabulary* [2001] 1 All ER 562, [2001] 1 WLR 340) or made on conviction. See A[53.17]. The police may also apply independently for a **Risk of Sexual Harm Order**.

A[53]

Sexual assault

Charge

A[53.1]
Sexual assault

Sexual Offences Act 2003, s 3

OR

A[53.2]
Causing a person to engage in sexual activity without consent

Sexual Offences Act 2003, s 4

Maximum penalty – Fine level 5 and 6 months (**12 months). Triable either way. Specified sexual offence under Sch 15, Part 2, CJA 2003.

Crown Court – 10 years' imprisonment and unlimited fine.

Mode of trial

A[53.3]
Consider first the general notes at I[4] and the SC definitive guidance set out at A[53.15] below.

Legal notes and definitions

A[53.4]
Sexual assault. The accused must intentionally touch the victim. The touching and the circumstances accompanying it, must be capable of being considered by reasonable persons as sexual taken together with the intentions of the accused (see **defences** below). Voluntary intoxication cannot be relied upon as negating the necessary intent eg due to his intoxication, the accused contends that he could not remember anything about what had occurred (*R v Heard* [2007] EWCA Crim 125).

A[53.5]
An accused's explanation for the assault, whether or not it reveals a sexual motive, is admissible to support or negative that the touching was sexual and was so intended by the accused (*R v Court* [1989] AC 28, [1988] 2 All ER 221, HL; grabbing a girl's tracksuit bottoms coupled with the request 'Do you fancy a shag?' (*R v H* [2005] EWCA Crim 732, [2005] 2 All ER 859).

A[53.6]

Defences. Consent of the alleged victim is a defence except if obtained by force or fraud. A reasonable belief that the person consents is a defence, as would be non-intentional touching. The defence that voluntary intoxication had rendered a defendant unable to form the intent to touch is not open to him (*R v Heard* [2007] EWCA Crim 125).

The following two categories of persons cannot give consent, or in the case of a mental disorder consent may be impeded.

A[53.7]

Persons under 16. A person under the age of 16 years is incapable in law of consent in these circumstances and therefore it is no defence that a person under 16 consented. It is for the prosecution to prove that the defendant did not honestly believe that the girl was aged 16 or over. The defendant's belief must be honest and genuine but the more unreasonable the belief, the less likely it was to be accepted as genuine (*R v K* [2001] 1 Cr App Rep 493, [2001] Crim LR 134, CA; revsd sub nom R v K [2001] UKHL 41 [2002] 1 AC 462, [2001] 3 All ER 897). Offences involving children will normally be charged under ss 9–15 of the Sexual Offences Act 2003 and where the child is under 13 the defendant is not entitled to raise any issues about mistaken belief in age.

A[53.8]

Mental disorder. If the person subject to sexual activity has a mental disorder he or she is deemed not to have freely given consent; the defendant can only be convicted if he knew or had reason to suspect that the person has a mental disorder and because of that was likely to be unable to refuse.

A[53.9]

Sexual activity with children. If a child under the age of 13 is involved in sexual activity a number of offences arise under ss 5–15 of the Sexual Offences Act 2003. See A[52].

In *R v Grout* [2011] EWCA Crim 299, [2011] 1 Cr App Rep 472, 175 JP 209, the appellant was charged with causing or inciting a child to engage in sexual activity. The Court of Appeal decided that s 8 of the 2003 Act created two, if not four, separate offences. This meant that a count charging a defendant must be drawn with particular care. In the present case the count was defective and gave rise to difficulties for both Judge and jury. In essence there were two prosecution allegations. The first was whether the victim's act of showing her bra strap amounted to "sexual activity" and whether the appellant had "intentionally caused" H to engage in such activity. The second was whether the taking off of clothing could amount to "sexual activity" by H and whether the appellant had "intentionally incited" H to engage in that sexual activity.

A[53.10]

Evidence of children. See under this heading on at **A[52.6]**.

A[53.11]

Anonymity of victim. Where an allegation has been made or a person is accused of this offence neither the name or address nor any moving or still picture of the victim shall be published or broadcast during his lifetime if it is likely to lead members of the public to identify him as the victim of the offence (Sexual Offences (Amendment) Act 1992). Before the trial a magistrate may direct that the prohibition does not apply where he is satisfied the direction is necessary to induce witnesses to come forward, or the applicant's defence is otherwise likely to be substantially prejudiced. The restriction may also be lifted during the trial to such an extent as is necessary in the public interest.

A[53.12]

The existing power under s 39 of the Children and Young Persons Act 1933, in respect of persons under 18, to direct that any press, radio or television report of the case must not reveal his name, address, school or identity is preserved. See **A[52.12]**.

A[53.13]

The magistrates can order the court to be cleared (except for those directly concerned with the case and the press) whilst the child or young person is testifying (Children and Young Persons Act 1933, s 37).

A[53.14]

Corroboration. The Criminal Justice and Public Order Act 1994 removed any requirement for corroboration in sexual offences.

Sentencing
SC Guideline – Sexual assault and Sexual assault of a child under 13

A[53.15]

These guidelines are taken from the SC's definitive guideline *Sexual Offences Act 2003* published 30 April 2007.

*The court **must** inform the defendant that the Independent Safeguarding Authority (known as the Independent Barring Board) will automatically ban him/her from working with children and/or vulnerable adults. As the court has no role in the decision if the defendant needs any further advice he/she should consult a solicitor.

For offences under s 4 see SC definitive guideline in Part 2C, pp 38–41 located at http://sentencingcouncil.judiciary.gov.uk/guidelines/guidelines-to-download.htm.

IDENTIFY DANGEROUS OFFENDERS

These are serious offences for the purposes of the public protection provisions in the Criminal Justice Act 2003. Refer to **B[16.5]** and consult legal adviser for guidance

---

OFFENCE SERIOUSNESS (CULPABILITY AND HARM)

A. IDENTIFY THE APPROPRIATE STARTING POINT

Starting points based on first time offender pleading not guilty

Examples of nature of activity	Starting point	Range
Contact between part of offender's body (other than the genitalia) with part of the victim's body (other than the genitalia)	26 weeks custody if the victim is under 13	4 weeks custody to Crown Court
	Medium level community order if the victim is aged 13 or over	Band C fine to 6 weeks custody
Contact between naked genitalia and another part of the victim's body	Crown Court if the victim is under 13	Crown Court
Contact with naked genitalia of victim by offender using part of his or her body other than the genitalia, or an object	Crown Court if the victim is under 13	Crown Court
Contact between either the clothed genitalia of offender and naked genitalia of victim or naked genitalia of offender and clothed genitalia of victim	Crown Court if the victim is aged 13 or over	26 weeks custody to Crown Court
Contact between naked genitalia of offender and naked genitalia, face or mouth of the victim	Crown Court	Crown Court

OFFENCE SERIOUSNESS (CULPABILITY AND HARM)

B. CONSIDER THE EFFECT OF AGGRAVATING AND MITIGATING FACTORS (OTHER THAN THOSE WITHIN EXAMPLES ABOVE)

Common aggravating and mitigating factors are identified at B[5.2A]. The following may be particularly relevant but **these lists are not exhaustive**

Factors indicating higher culpability	Factors indicating lower culpability
1. Background of intimidation or coercion	1. Youth and immaturity of the offender
2. Use of drugs, alcohol or other substance to facilitate the offence	2. Minimal or fleeting contact
3. Threats to prevent the victim reporting the incident	*Where the victim is aged 16 or over*
4. Abduction or detention	3. Victim engaged in consensual activity with the offender on the same occasion and immediately before the offence
	Where the victim is under 16
5. Offender aware that he or she is suffering from a sexually transmitted infection	

6. Prolonged activity or contact	4. Sexual activity between two children (one of whom is the offender) was mutually agreed and experimental
Factors indicating greater degree of harm 1. Offender ejaculated or caused victim to ejaculate 2. Physical harm caused	
FORM A PRELIMINARY VIEW OF THE APPROPRIATE SENTENCE, THEN CONSIDER OFFENDER MITIGATION Common factors are identified at **B[5.2A]**	
CONSIDER A REDUCTION FOR A GUILTY PLEA	
CONSIDER ANCILLARY ORDERS, INCLUDING COMPENSATION Refer to **B[18]** for guidance on compensation and **Part B** for available ancillary orders	
DECIDE SENTENCE **GIVE REASONS**	

Note. (See **A[53.16]** immediately below)

(a)   In accordance with section 80 and schedule 3 of the Sexual Offences Act 2003, automatic notification requirements apply upon conviction to an offender aged 18 or over where:
   (1)   the victim was under 18; or
   (2)   a term of imprisonment or a community sentence of at least 12 months is imposed.

NB: A community order with a requirement to carry out 120 hours unpaid work was not a community sentence of at least 12 months for the purposes of Sch 3 and therefore the offender was not subject to the notification requirements of the legislation (*R v Odam* [2008] EWCA Crim 1087).

A[53.16]

Sexual Offences Act 2003 (Sch 3) Under a new r 42.3 of the CPR 2012, on conviction the court must explain the notification requirements to the defendant.

Depending upon the nature of the conviction, on conviction, including a conditional discharge, the court must require the defendant to:

(a)   **notify the police** within the next three days (or if in custody or otherwise detained, within three days of release) of his name, any other names he uses, his date of birth and his home address;

(b)   **notify the police** of any change of name or home address within 14 days of any change;

(c)   **notify the police** of any address where he resides or stays for 14 days or longer. This means either 14 days at a time, or a total of 14 days in any 12-month period;

(d)   **notify the police** of an intention to leave the UK for a period of 24 hours or longer, at least 24 hours prior to departure of the particulars of the journey;

(e)   **notify the police** of his national insurance number.

In the case of a conviction under s 3 or s 13 (sexual assault or sexual assault of a child under 13) notification is mandatory for any custodial sentence of at least 12 months or where the victim is under 18. Otherwise any custodial sentence or community sentence of 12 months or a mental health detention will trigger notification in the case of an adult offender.

Juvenile offenders. Where the offender is under 18 years these provisions will apply to a person identified as having parental responsibility.

Order for absolute or conditional discharge. See A [52.15] and *R v Longworth*, January 26, 2006, HL.

See A[52.15] for amendments to the Sexual Offences Act 2003 by reason of the Sexual Offences Act 2003 (Amendment of Schedules 3 and 5) Order 2007 (SI 2007/296).

A[53.17]

Sexual Offences prevention order may be applied for separately under Part II of the Sexual Offences Act 2003. The application is a civil matter (*B v Chief Constable of Avon and Somerset Constabulary* [2001] 1 All ER 562, [2001] 1 WLR 340). In civil proceedings, the judgment whether it is necessary to make an order is the criminal standard, proof beyond a reasonable doubt: *Cleveland Police v Haggas* [2009] EWHC 3231 (Admin), [2010] 3 All ER 506. Alternatively where on conviction the court is satisfied it is necessary to protect the public from serious sexual harm from the defendant an order may be made prohibiting the defendant from prescribed activities for a period not less than 5 years. Similar to anti-social behaviour orders, given the fact that breach of an order is punishable by a sentence of up to five years, there was a need for the terms of the order to be clear and precise (*R v H* [2006] EWCA Crim 1470, [2006] All ER (D) 87 (Jun); *R v Emery* [2007] EWCA Crim 2469). Similarly in *R v R* [2007] EWCA Crim 1603 it was held that a sexual offences prevention order should be (a) clear and readily intelligible in its terms; (b) specific as to time and place; (c) and, no wider than necessary to restrain the particular harm which it was feared the defendant might cause.

The Sexual Offences Act 2003 (amendment of Schedules 3 and 5) Order 2007 (SI 2007/296) added eight offences to those offences which may lead to a person being made subject to a sexual offences prevention order.

It was not a pre-condition to the making of a sexual offences prevention order that the court should be satisfied that the defendant would also qualify for an extended sentence, life imprisonment or imprisonment for public protection (*R v Richards* [2006] All ER (D) 338 (Oct)).

In *R v Brown* [2011] EWCA Crim 1223, the final provision of the Sexual Offences Prevention Order made against B read as follows: 'Save where to do so is inadvertent or unavoidable, not to possess any images of a child under the age of 16 years unless the prior permission of that child's parents or guardian has been obtained'. It was decided that the said restriction would, for example, serve to criminalise the continued possession of a daily newspaper which happened to have an inoffensive photograph of a child in it unless it was disposed of straight away upon realisation that such a photograph was in the newspaper. It was not adequate to rely upon the good sense of prosecutors in cases of this type so that very widely drafted prohibitions could be incorporated into such orders. The Court of Appeal regarded that prohibition as being far too widely drafted and proposed to delete it.

Where there was a discrepancy between the terms of a sexual offences prevention order announced by the court and the order issued by the court administration, the appellant was subject to the order announced in court: *R v P* (2012) May 10, CA.

The police may also apply independently for a **risk of sexual harm order**. In *Metropolitan Police Comr v Ebanks* [2012] All ER (D) 45 (Jul), DC, it was decided that the standard of proof on an application for a risk of sexual harm order under the Sexual Offences Act 2003, s 123(4) was the criminal standard of proof. It appears the penny seems to have dropped with the higher courts. Unlike eg restraining orders under ss 4–5 PHA 1997, (see *R v Major* [2010] EWCA Crim 3016, [2011] 1 Cr App Rep 322, [2011] 2 Cr App Rep (S) 139) the standard of proof clearly is the criminal standard. The sooner the CA revisits its decision in *Major* et al, the better.

A[54]

Social security benefit, false statement/representation to obtain

Charges

A[54.1]

1. The accused, for the purpose of obtaining any benefit or other payment under the relevant social security legislation whether or himself or some other person, or for any other purpose connected with that legislation –

(a)   makes a statement or representation which he knows to be false; or
(b)   produces or furnishes, or knowingly causes or knowingly allows to be produced or furnished, any document or information which he knows to be false in a material particular.

Social Security Administration Act 1992, s 112(1).

2. The accused dishonestly –

(a)   makes a statement or representation or;
(b)   produces or furnishes, or causes or allows to be produced or furnished, any document or information which is false in a material particular;

With a view to obtaining any benefit or other payment or advantage under the relevant social security legislation (whether for himself or for some other person).

Social Security Administration Act 1992, s 111A.

Maximum penalty – Fine level 5 and 6 months (**12 months). Triable either way.

Crown Court – 10 years' imprisonment and unlimited fine.

Mode of trial

A[54.2]

For **charge 2** consider the SC definitive guidance set out at **A[54.5]** below.

More serious charges may well be charged under the Fraud Act 2006.

Legal notes and definitions

A[54.3]

Charge 2 requires proof of dishonesty unlike charge 1. For the definition of dishonesty see **A[60.5]**.

The provisions of ss 111A or 112 do not apply in any case where the benefit or other payment or advantage is or relates to, or the failure to notify relates to, tax credit (see Tax Credits Act 2002, s 35 and A[55]).

The provisions of ss 111A or 112 can apply equally to a failure to notify a change in circumstances affecting entitlement to benefit (see ss 111A(1A)–(1G) and 112(1A)–(1F).

A[54.4]

Under s 112 the offence is committed where there is a false representation made which the person making the claim knows to be false; the proof of intent to defraud is not necessary (*Clear v Smith* [1981] 1 WLR 399, HL). The offence under s 112 does not require proof of dishonesty. However, "constructive knowledge" ie that the defendant neglected to make such inquiries as a reasonable and prudent person would make (as distinct from deliberately closing one's eyes to an obvious means of knowledge) is insufficient to found liability (*Flintshire County Council v Reynolds* [2006] EWHC 195 (Admin), 170 JP 73).

In *Pearson v Greenwich Borough Council.* [2008] All ER [D] 256 (Jan), the accused owned two properties. A council tax form required the accused to provide details of the name and address of the property for which he sought to receive a council tax reduction. The subsequent allegation was that he had made representations that he only owned one property for the purposes of obtaining benefit. The charge failed because the accused's omission did not necessarily mean he had made representations to the effect that he only owned one house.

By virtue of s 116(2) of the 1992 Act, a prosecution could be started at any time from 3 months or 12 months, whichever period last expired. The time limits for an offence under s 112 had been satisfied where it had been brought within 12 months even thought there had been some evidence available for a prosecution within three months, as the offence was a continuing offence and the investigations were ongoing: *Bennett v Secretary of State for Work and Pensions* [2012] EWHC 371 (Admin), 176 JP 181.

A[54.5]

Causes or Allows. The word 'causes' suggests that the defendant did something that 'caused' the recipient of the benefit not to report a change of circumstances (alternatively, the defendant could be guilty of aiding and abetting an offence under s 111A(1A)). The word 'allows' normally means there has to be some act that the defendant could have taken which could have resulted in the recipient of benefit discharging his/her liability to report. The one exception might be where the defendant is aware of circumstances that he knew affected the recipient's entitlement to benefit (*R v Tilley* [2009] EWCA Crim 1426, 173 JP 393).

Sentencing
SC Guideline – Social security benefit, false statement/
representation to obtain

A[54.6]

This guideline reflects the are Court of Appeal's decisions in *R v Stewart* [1987] 2 All ER 383 and *R v Graham and Whatley* [2004] EWCA Crim 2755. Further consideration is being given to the appropriate approach to sentencing for this offence in the context of the Council and Panel's work on fraud offences; this may result on a revised guideline being issued in a future update.

OFFENCE SERIOUSNESS (CULPABILITY AND HARM)		
A. IDENTIFY THE APPROPRIATE STARTING POINT		
Starting points based on first time offender pleading not guilty		
Examples of nature of activity	**Starting point**	**Range**
Claim fraudulent from the start, up to £5,000 obtained (s 111A or s 112)	Medium level community order	Band B fine to high level community order
Claim fraudulent from the start, more than £5,000 but less than £20,000 obtained (s 111A or s 112)	12 weeks custody	Medium level community order to Crown Court
Claim fraudulent from the start, large-scale, professional offending	Crown Court	Crown Court
OFFENCE SERIOUSNESS (CULPABILITY AND HARM)		
B. CONSIDER THE EFFECT OF AGGRAVATING AND MITIGATING FACTORS (OTHER THAN THOSE WITHIN EXAMPLES ABOVE)		
Common aggravating and mitigating factors are identified at **B[5.2A]**. The following may be particularly relevant but **these lists are not exhaustive**		
Factors indicating higher culpability	*Factors indicating lower culpability*	
1. Offending carried out over a long period	1. Pressurised by others	
2. Offender acting in unison with one or more persons	2. Claim initially legitimate	
3. Planning	*Factor indicating lower culpability*	
4. Offender motivated by greed or desire to live beyond his/her means	1. Voluntary repayment of amounts overpaid	
5. False identities or other personal details used		
6. False or forged documents used		
7. Official documents altered or falsified		

FORM A PRELIMINARY VIEW OF THE APPROPRIATE SENTENCE, THEN CONSIDER OFFENDER MITIGATION
Common factors are identified at B[5.2A]
CONSIDER A REDUCTION FOR A GUILTY PLEA
CONSIDER ANCILLARY ORDERS, INCLUDING COMPENSATION (see Note below)
Refer to B[18] for guidance on compensation and **Part B** for available ancillary orders
DECIDE SENTENCE
GIVE REASONS

Note. A maximum of £5,000 compensation may be imposed for each offence of which the offender has been convicted. The above guidelines have been drafted on the assumption that, in most cases, the Department for Work and Pensions will take separate steps to recover the overpayment.

A[55]

Tax credit fraud

Charge

A[55.1]

The accused was knowingly concerned in any fraudulent activity undertaken with a view to obtaining payments of a tax credit by him or any other person.

Tax Credits Act 2002, s 35.

Maximum penalty – Fine level 5 and 6 months (**12 months). Triable either way.

Crown Court – 7 years' imprisonment and unlimited fine.

Mode of trial

A[55.2]

Consider first the general notes at I[4] and the SC definitive guidance set out at A[55.4] below.

More serious charges may well be charged under the Fraud Act 2006.

Legal notes and definitions

A[55.3]

Administrative penalties may be levied under ss 31–34 in respect of incorrect statements, failure to comply with requirements and failure by employer to make correct payments.

In order to prove 'fraudulent activity' for the purposes of s 35, an offender had to behave in a manner calculated to achieve false benefits payments. A passive receipt of funds and a deliberate failure to notify the benefits agency of an overpayment, while dishonest, fell short of fraudulent activity: *R v Nolan; R v Howard* [2012] EWCA Crim 671, [2012] All ER (D) 43 (Apr).

Sentencing

A[55.4]

Awaiting SC Guideline.

A[56]

Taxi-touting/soliciting for hire

Charge

A[56.1]

The accused, in a public place, solicited persons to hire vehicles to carry them as vehicles.

Criminal Justice and Public Order Act 1994, s 167.

Maximum penalty – Fine level 4

Legal notes and definitions

A[56.2]

No offence is committed where soliciting persons to hire licensed taxis is permitted by a scheme under the Transport Act 1985, s 10.

It is a defence for the accused to show (on a balance of probabilities) that he was soliciting for passengers to be carried at separate fares by public service vehicles for public service vehicles on behalf of the holder of a PSV operator's licence for those vehicles whose authority he had at the time of the alleged offence.

"Public place" includes any highway and any other premises or place to which at the material time the public have or are permitted to have access (whether on payment or otherwise); "Public service vehicle" and "PSV operator's licence" have the same meaning as in Part II of the Public Passengers Act 1981 (Criminal Justice and Public Order Act 1994, s 167(5))

Sentencing
SC Guideline – Taxi-touting

A[56.3]

Note: refer to B[33.24] for approach to fines for offences committed for commercial purposes.

OFFENCE SERIOUSNESS (CULPABILITY AND HARM)		
A. IDENTIFY THE APPROPRIATE STARTING POINT		
Starting points based on first time offender pleading not guilty		
Examples of nature of activity	Starting point	Range
Licensed taxi-driver touting for trade (ie making approach rather than waiting for a person to initiate hiring)	Band A fine (see Note above)	Conditional discharge to band A fine and consider disqualification from driving 1–3 months

PHV licence held but touting for trade rather than being booked through an operator; an accomplice to touting	Band B fine (see Note above)	Band A fine to Band C fine and consider disqualification from driving 3–6 months
No PHV licence held	Band C fine (see Note above)	Band B fine to medium level community order and disqualification from driving 6–12 months

OFFENCE SERIOUSNESS (CULPABILITY AND HARM)

B. CONSIDER THE EFFECT OF AGGRAVATING AND MITIGATING FACTORS (OTHER THAN THOSE WITHIN EXAMPLES ABOVE)

Common aggravating and mitigating factors are identified at **B[5.2A]**. The following may be particularly relevant but **these lists are not exhaustive**

Factors indicating higher culpability	*Factor indicating lower culpability*
1. Commercial business/large-scale operation	1. Providing a service when no licensed taxi available
2. No insurance/invalid insurance	
3. No driving licence and no MOT	
4. Vehicle not roadworthy	
Factors indicating greater degree of harm	
1. Deliberately diverting trade from taxi rank	
2. PHV licence had been refused/offender ineligible for licence	

FORM A PRELIMINARY VIEW OF THE APPROPRIATE SENTENCE, THEN CONSIDER OFFENDER MITIGATION

Common factors are identified at **B[5.2A]**

CONSIDER A REDUCTION FOR A GUILTY PLEA

CONSIDER ANCILLARY ORDERS

Refer to **B[18]** for guidance on compensation and **Part B** for available ancillary orders

CONSIDER DISQUALIFICATION FROM DRIVING AND DEPRIVATION OF PROPERTY

DECIDE SENTENCE

GIVE REASONS

A[57]

Theft

(Covers (1) Theft – breach of trust (2) Theft – person (3) Theft – shop (4) Theft – dwelling

Charge

A[57.1]
Stealing

Theft Act 1968, s 1(1)

Maximum penalty – Fine level 5 and/or 6 months (**12 months). Triable either way.

Crown Court – 7 years' imprisonment and unlimited fine.

Motor vehicles. See A[77].

Theft, going equipped for. See A[58].

NB: A fixed penalty of £80 is available for theft from a shop but only where the goods are under £200, and not normally where the goods are over £100

Mode of trial

A[57.2]
Consider first the general notes at I[4] and the SC Guidelines at A[57.37] onwards below.

Legal notes and definitions

A[57.3]
Theft or stealing means dishonestly appropriating property belonging to another person with the intention of permanently depriving the other person of it. It does not matter whether the purpose of the theft was gain or not. Nor does it matter if the theft was for the benefit of the defendant or another person.

A[57.4]
The prosecution does not have to prove that the property was appropriated without the owner's consent. However, if the defendant believed he had the owner's consent that could be relevant in deciding whether the defendant acted dishonestly.

1 *Dishonestly*

A[57.5]

The appropriation can be dishonest even though the defendant was willing to pay for the property.

A[57.6]

The general test of dishonesty is: first, whether the accused's actions were dishonest according to the ordinary standards of reasonable and honest people and second, if so, whether the accused himself had realised that his actions were, according to those standards, dishonest. Thus a genuine belief by the accused that he was morally justified in acting as he did is no defence if he knew that ordinary people would consider such conduct to be dishonest (*R v Ghosh* [1982] QB 1053, [1982] 2 All ER 689, CA).

A[57.7]

The Theft Act 1968 provides that appropriation in the following circumstances is not 'dishonest':

(a)   if the defendant believed he had the legal right to deprive the other of the property, either for himself or a third party; or

(b)   if the defendant believed the other person would have consented had the other person known of the appropriation and the circumstances of the appropriation; or

(c)   if the defendant believed the person to whom the property belonged could not be discovered by taking reasonable steps (but this defence is not available if the property came to the defendant as a trustee or a personal representative).

2 *Appropriates*

A[57.8]

Any assumption of the rights of an owner amounts to appropriation. If the defendant came by the property (innocently or otherwise) without stealing it and later assumed a right to it by keeping it or dealing with it as an owner, he has appropriated it. An appropriation may occur even though the owner has consented to the property being taken (*R v Hinks* [2001] 2 AC 241, [2000] 4 All ER 833, HL).

A[57.9]

The following are examples of dishonest appropriation:

(a)   a parent whose child has brought home someone else's property and who retains the property; or

(b)   a person who has found property (but see (1)(c) above); or

(c)   a person who has acquired property through another person's mistake and has taken advantage of the error; or

(d)   a person who switches price labels in a supermarket in order to obtain the goods at a price lower than the original marked price.

A[57.10]–[57.15]

Repentance. It is important in some cases to appreciate the moment when the offence is complete. Sometimes, for example, the shoplifter decides either to put the goods back or to pay for them. Once the offence is completed such action is evidence of repentance only and may affect the sentence, but it does not establish innocence.

A[57.16]

Acquiring in good faith. If the defendant in good faith gave value for the property and later found that the vendor (or other person from whom he acquired the property) had no right to the goods, then the defendant is not guilty of theft in the event of his keeping or disposing of the property.

3 Property

A[57.17]

Includes money, stocks and shares, bills of exchange, insurance policies and all kinds of goods and property.

Nothing in the 1968 Act suggested that what would otherwise constitute or be regarded as 'property' for the purposes of the Act ceased to be so because its possession or control was, for whatever reason, unlawful or illegal or prohibited. The criminal law was concerned with keeping the Queen's peace, not vindicating individual property rights: *R v Smith* [2011] EWCA Crim 66, [2011] 1 Cr App Rep 379, [2011] Crim LR 719.

A[57.18]

Land. Land or anything forming part of land cannot be stolen except in the following circumstances:

(a)   dishonest appropriation by trustees, personal representatives, liquidators of companies, persons holding a power of attorney and certain similar persons; or

(b)   dishonest appropriation of something forming part of land by a person not in possession of the land (eg removing soil); or

(c)   dishonest appropriation by tenants of fixtures let to be used with land.

A[57.19]

Attempting the impossible. A person may be guilty of an attempt to steal even though the facts are such that the commission of the offence of theft is impossible, for example by placing one's hand into an empty pocket.

A[57.20]

Things growing wild. If mushrooms, flowers, fruit or foliage from a plant which is growing wild are picked, that only amounts to theft if it is done for reward, or for sale or any other commercial purpose.

A[57.21]

Wild creatures. Appropriating a wild creature can only amount to theft if it has been reduced into the possession of someone else who has not lost or abandoned such possession of the creature; or if someone else is in the course of reducing it into his possession.

4 Belonging to another

A[57.22]

The property must be treated as belonging to anyone having possession or control of it or having any proprietary right or interest in it. Petrol ceases to belong to another when it is put in a vehicle's petrol tank at a self-service filling station (this accounts for the offence under s.3 of the Theft Act 1978 – see A[45]). When goods in a supermarket are for convenience or hygiene bagged, weighed and priced by an assistant they remain the property of the supermarket until paid for, and may therefore be the subject of the theft.

A[57.23]

Trust property. Must be treated as belonging to anyone having a right to enforce the trust. An intention to defeat the trust shall be treated as an intention to deprive the person entitled to enforce the trust of the property.

A[57.24]

Being entrusted with property. If a defendant (eg the treasurer of a holiday fund or Christmas club) has received property and is under an obligation to retain it or deal with it in a particular way, the property shall be treated as belonging to the beneficiary and not to the defendant.

A[57.25]–[57.30]

Getting property by mistake. If the defendant obtained property by a mistake on the part of another person, and is under a legal (as opposed to a moral or social) obligation to restore it, then the property must be treated as belonging to the other person.

A[57.31]

If the court considers the defendant formed an intention not to restore the property, he must be deemed to have intended to deprive the other person of the property.

5 With the intention of permanently depriving

A[57.32]

The court must be satisfied that the defendant had this intention; or alternatively that he intended treating the property as his own to dispose of regardless of the owner's rights. The court must decide the defendant's intention by considering all the evidence and drawing from it such inferences as appear proper in the circumstances.

An offer, not to return a person's car to him in exactly the same condition that it had been when it was removed from his possession and control, but to sell his property back to him, and to make its return subject to a condition or conditions inconsistent with his right to possession of his own property fell within the definition of s 6(1): See *R v Raphael* [2008] EWCA Crim 1014.

In *R v Vinall* [2011] EWCA Crim 6252, [2012] 1 Cr App Rep 400, 175 JP 517 on a charge of robbery the judge should have invited the jury to consider whether the subsequent abandonment of D's bicycle was evidence from which it could be inferred that when the appellants appropriated the bicycle they intended to treat the bicycle as their own to dispose of regardless of D's rights. If such a direction had been given, an explicit direction would also have been required explaining that an intention formed only upon abandonment of the bicycle at the bus shelter was inconsistent with and fatal to the robbery count. In the absence of a proper direction the verdicts were unsafe. The jury was discharged from reaching a verdict on count 2. This was not a case in which the court should substitute a conviction for theft or taking a pedal cycle as those alternatives were not left to the jury.

A[57.33]

Borrowing or lending. Can be used to establish that the defendant had the intention of permanently depriving the owner if, and only if, the borrowing or lending were for a period and the circumstances of the case make it equivalent to an outright taking or disposal. Ordinary borrowing or lending would not have this effect.

A[57.34]

Reduction of the charge (motor vehicles). If the property is a motor vehicle a magistrates' court cannot reduce the charge of theft to one of 'taking a conveyance', see A[65].

A[57.35]

Proof of stealing one article enough. If the charge alleges the theft of several articles, the court can convict of theft if it decides that only one of the articles was stolen. The announcement of decision and court register should make the decision clear.

A[57.36]

Partnership property. A partner can be convicted of stealing property which he and another or other partners own.

Sentencing
(1) SC Guideline: Theft – breach of trust

A[57.37]

Maximum when tried summarily: Level 5 and/or 6 months.

Maximum when tried on indictment: 7 years.

OFFENCE SERIOUSNESS (CULPABILITY AND HARM)		
A. IDENTIFY THE APPROPRIATE STARTING POINT		
Starting points based on first time offender pleading not guilty		
Examples of nature of activity	**Starting point**	**Range**
Theft of less than £2,000	Medium level community order	Band B fine to 26 weeks custody
Theft of £2,000 or more but less than £20,000 OR Theft or less than £2,000 in breach of a high degree of trust	18 weeks custody	High level community order to Crown Court
Theft of £20,000 or more OR Theft of les than £20,000 in breach of a high degree of trust	Crown Court	Crown Court
OFFENCE SERIOUSNESS (CULPABILITY AND HARM)		
B. CONSIDER THE EFFECT OF AGGRAVATING AND MITIGATING FACTORS (OTHER THAN THOSE WITHIN EXAMPLES ABOVE)		
Common aggravating and mitigating factors are identified at B[5.2A]. The following may be particularly relevant but **these lists are not exhaustive**		
Factors indicating higher culpability 1. Long course of offending 2. Suspicion deliberately thrown on others 3. Offender motivated by intention to cause harm or out of revenge		
FORM A PRELIMINARY VIEW OF THE APPROPRIATE SENTENCE, THEN CONSIDER OFFENDER MITIGATION		
Common factors are identified at B[5.2A]		
CONSIDER A REDUCTION FOR A GUILTY PLEA		
CONSIDER ANCILLARY ORDERS		
Refer to B[18] for guidance on compensation and **Part B** for available ancillary orders.		
DECIDE SENTENCE		
GIVE REASONS		

(2) SC Guideline: Theft – dwelling

A[57.37A]

Triable either way.

Maximum when tried summarily: Level 5 and/or 6 months.

Maximum when tried on indictment: 7 years.

OFFENCE SERIOUSNESS (CULPABILITY AND HARM)		
A. IDENTIFY THE APPROPRIATE STARTING POINT		
Starting points based on first time offender pleading not guilty		
Examples of nature of activity	**Starting point**	**Range**
Where the effect on the victim is particularly severe, or the stolen property is of high value (defined as more than £2,000 (including sentimental value to the victim) although this will depend on an assessment of all the circumstances of the particular case), or substantial consequential loss results thereby, a sentence higher than the range into which the offence would fall may be appropriate.		
Theft in a dwelling not involving a vulnerable victim.	Medium level community order	Band B fine to 18 weeks custody
Theft from a vulnerable victim (A 'vulnerable victim' is a person targeted by the offender because it is likely that he or she is unlikely or unable to resist the theft. The exploitation of a vulnerable victim indicates a high level of culpability and will influence the category of seriousness into which the offence falls).	18 weeks custody	High level community order to Crown Court
Theft from a vulnerable victim (as defined above) involving intimidation or the use or threat of force (falling short of robbery) or the use of deception.	Crown Court	Crown Court
OFFENCE SERIOUSNESS (CULPABILITY AND HARM)		
B. CONSIDER THE EFFECT OF AGGRAVATING AND MITIGATING FACTORS (OTHER THAN THOSE WITHIN EXAMPLES ABOVE)		
Common aggravating and mitigating factors are identified at B[5.2A]. The following may be particularly relevant but **these lists are not exhaustive**		
Factors indicating higher culpability 1. Offender motivated by intention to cause harm or out of revenge		
Factors indicating greater degree of harm 1. Intimidation or face to face confrontation with victim [except where this raises the offence into a higher sentencing range].		

2. Use of force, or threat of force, against victim (not amounting to robbery) [except where this raises the offence into a higher sentencing range]. 3. Use of deception [except where this raises the offence into a higher sentencing range]. 4. Offender takes steps to prevent the victim from reporting the crime or seeking help.	

FORM A PRELIMINARY VIEW OF THE APPROPRIATE SENTENCE, THEN CONSIDER OFFENDER MITIGATION
Offender Mitigation
(i) Return of stolen property – *Will depend on an assessment of the circumstances and, in particular, the voluntariness and timeliness of the return*
(ii) Impact of sentence on offender's dependency – *Where an offence is motivated by an addiction (often to drugs, alcohol or gambling) this does not mitigate the seriousness of the offence, but a dependency may influence the type of sentence imposed. In particular, it may sometimes be appropriate to impose a drug rehabilitation requirement, an alcohol treatment requirement (for dependent drinkers) or an activity or supervision requirement including alcohol specific information, advice and support (for harmful and hazardous drinkers) as part of a community order or suspended sentence order in an attempt to break the cycle of addiction and offending, even if an immediate custodial sentence would otherwise be warranted.*
(iii) *The fact that an offence has been committed in desperation or need arising from particular hardship may count as offender mitigation in exceptional circumstances.*
CONSIDER A REDUCTION FOR A GUILTY PLEA
CONSIDER ANCILLARY ORDERS
Refer to B[18] for guidance on compensation and **Part B** for available ancillary orders.
DECIDE SENTENCE
GIVE REASONS

(3) SC Guideline: Theft – person

A[57.37B]

Triable either way.

Maximum when tried summarily: Level 5 and/or 6 months.

Maximum when tried on indictment: 7 years.

OFFENCE SERIOUSNESS (CULPABILITY AND HARM)		
A. IDENTIFY THE APPROPRIATE STARTING POINT		
Starting points based on first time offender pleading not guilty		
Examples of nature of activity	Starting point	Range

Where the effect on the victim is particularly severe, or the stolen property is of high value (defined as more than £2,000 (including sentimental value to the victim) although this will depend on an assessment of all the circumstances of the particular case), or substantial consequential loss results thereby, a sentence higher than the range into which the offence would fall may be appropriate.

Theft in a dwelling not involving a vulnerable victim.	Medium level community order	Band B fine to 18 weeks custody
Theft from a vulnerable victim (A 'vulnerable victim' is a person targeted by the offender because it is likely that he or she is unlikely or unable to resist the theft. The exploitation of a vulnerable victim indicates a high level of culpability and will influence the category of seriousness into which the offence falls).	18 weeks custody	High level community order to Crown Court
Theft involving the use or threat of force (falling short of robbery) against a vulnerable victim as described above.	Crown Court	Crown Court

OFFENCE SERIOUSNESS (CULPABILITY AND HARM)

B. CONSIDER THE EFFECT OF AGGRAVATING AND MITIGATING FACTORS (OTHER THAN THOSE WITHIN EXAMPLES ABOVE)

Common aggravating and mitigating factors are identified at B[5.2A]. The following may be particularly relevant but **these lists are not exhaustive**

Factors indicating higher culpability 1. Offender motivated by intention to cause harm or out of revenge	
Factors indicating greater degree of harm 1. Intimidation or face to face confrontation with victim [except where this raises the offence into a higher sentencing range]. 2. Use of force, or threat of force, against victim (not amounting to robbery) [except where this raises the offence into a higher sentencing range]. 3. High level of inconvenience caused to victim, eg replacing house keys, credit cards etc.	

FORM A PRELIMINARY VIEW OF THE APPROPRIATE SENTENCE, THEN CONSIDER OFFENDER MITIGATION

Offender Mitigation

(i) Return of stolen property – *Will depend on an assessment of the circumstances and, in particular, the voluntariness and timeliness of the return.*

(ii) Impact of sentence on offender's dependency – *Where an offence is motivated by an addiction (often to drugs, alcohol or gambling) this does not mitigate the seriousness of the offence, but a dependency may influence the type of sentence imposed. In particular, it may sometimes be appropriate to impose a drug rehabilitation requirement, an alcohol treatment requirement (for dependent drinkers) or an activity or supervision requirement including alcohol specific information, advice and support (for harmful and hazardous drinkers) as part of a community order or suspended sentence order in an attempt to break the cycle of addiction and offending, even if an immediate custodial sentence would otherwise be warranted.*

(iii) *The fact that an offence has been committed in desperation or need arising from particular hardship may count as offender mitigation in exceptional circumstances.*

CONSIDER A REDUCTION FOR A GUILTY PLEA
CONSIDER ANCILLARY ORDERS
Refer to B[18] for guidance on compensation and **Part B** for available ancillary orders.
DECIDE SENTENCE
GIVE REASONS

(4) SC Guideline: Theft – shop

A[57.37C]

Triable either way.

Maximum when tried summarily: Level 5 and/or 6 months.

Maximum when tried on indictment: 7 years.

OFFENCE SERIOUSNESS (CULPABILITY AND HARM)		
A. IDENTIFY THE APPROPRIATE STARTING POINT		
Starting points based on first time offender pleading not guilty		
Examples of nature of activity	Starting point	Range
Little or no planning or sophistication and goods stolen of low value.	Band B fine	Conditional discharge to low level community order
Low level intimidation or threats or some planning eg a session of stealing on the same day or going equipped or some related damage.	Low level community order	Band B fine to medium level community order
Significant intimidation or threats or use of force resulting in slight injury or very high level of planning or significant related damage.	6 weeks custody	High level community order to Crown Court

Organised gang/group and intimidation or the use or threat of force (short of robbery).	Crown Court	Crown Court

OFFENCE SERIOUSNESS (CULPABILITY AND HARM)

B. CONSIDER THE EFFECT OF AGGRAVATING AND MITIGATING FACTORS (OTHER THAN THOSE WITHIN EXAMPLES ABOVE)

Common aggravating and mitigating factors are identified at **B[5.2A]**. The following may be particularly relevant but **these lists are not exhaustive**

Factors indicating higher culpability	
1. Child accompanying offender is involved or aware of theft.	
2. Offender is subject to a banning order that includes the store targeted.	
3. Offender motivated by intention to cause harm or out of revenge.	
4. Professional offending.	
Factors indicating greater degree of harm	
1. Victim particularly vulnerable (eg small independent shop).	
2. Offender targeted high value goods.	

FORM A PRELIMINARY VIEW OF THE APPROPRIATE SENTENCE, THEN CONSIDER OFFENDER MITIGATION

Offender Mitigation

(i) Return of stolen property – *Will depend on an assessment of the circumstances and, in particular, the voluntariness and timeliness of the return.*

(ii) Impact of sentence on offender's dependency – *Where an offence is motivated by an addiction (often to drugs, alcohol or gambling) this does not mitigate the seriousness of the offence, but a dependency may influence the type of sentence imposed. In particular, it may sometimes be appropriate to impose a drug rehabilitation requirement, an alcohol treatment requirement (for dependent drinkers) or an activity or supervision requirement including alcohol specific information, advice and support (for harmful and hazardous drinkers) as part of a community order or suspended sentence order in an attempt to break the cycle of addiction and offending, even if an immediate custodial sentence would otherwise be warranted.*

(iii) *The fact that an offence has been committed in desperation or need arising from particular hardship may count as offender mitigation in exceptional circumstances.*

CONSIDER A REDUCTION FOR A GUILTY PLEA

CONSIDER ANCILLARY ORDERS

Refer to **B[18]** for guidance on compensation and **Part B** for available ancillary orders.

DECIDE SENTENCE

GIVE REASONS

A[57.38]

Structure of the sentencing decision. See B[3.6].

A[57.39]

Compensation. This may be ordered up to £5,000 either as part of a wider sentence or by itself as a substantive penalty. The court may deprive the defendant of any property in his possession when arrested if it was used, or intended for use, in the commission of a crime.

A[57.40]

Motor vehicles. If the property was a motor vehicle (defined as a mechanically propelled vehicle intended or adapted for use on a road) the court may disqualify but there is no endorsement or penalty points.

A[58]

Theft, going equipped for

Charge

A[58.1]

Having, when not at his place of abode, an article, namely a [
. . . .], for use in the course of burglary, theft or cheat

Theft Act 1968, s 25

Maximum penalty – Fine level 5 and 6 months (**12 months). Triable either way.

Crown Court – 3 years' imprisonment and unlimited fine.

Motor vehicles. If the defendant intended to steal or take a motor vehicle the offence is not endorsable nor are penalty points applicable but disqualification may be ordered.

Mode of trial

A[58.2]

See the SC Guideline at **A[58.8]** below.

Legal notes and definitions

A[58.3]

Theft includes taking a conveyance without the owner's consent.

A[58.4]

Cheat means an offence of obtaining by deception.

A[58.5]

If the article was made or adapted for use in committing a burglary, theft or obtaining property by deception, the court can treat that as evidence that the defendant had the article with him for such use.

A[58.6]

The offence can be committed by day or night. The offence cannot take place at the defendant's place of abode. It must be proved that he had the articles with him for the purpose of using them in connection with burglary, theft or obtaining property by deception though it is not necessary for the prosecution to prove that the defendant intended to use them himself. An intention to use the item if the opportunity arose would be sufficient to convict the accused, but it would not be sufficient where he had not actually decided whether to use the item if the opportunity presented itself.

A[58.7]

More than one article may be specified in the charge without offending the rule against duplicity.

Sentencing
SC Guideline – Theft, going equipped for

A[58.8]

OFFENCE SERIOUSNESS (CULPABILITY AND HARM)		
A. IDENTIFY THE APPROPRIATE STARTING POINT		
Starting points based on first time offender pleading not guilty		
Examples of nature of activity	Starting point	Range
Possession of items for theft from shop or of vehicle	Medium level community order	Low level community order to high level community order
Possession of items for burglary, robbery	High level community order	Medium level community order to Crown Court
OFFENCE SERIOUSNESS (CULPABILITY AND HARM)		
B. CONSIDER THE EFFECT OF AGGRAVATING AND MITIGATING FACTORS (OTHER THAN THOSE WITHIN EXAMPLES ABOVE)		
Common aggravating and mitigating factors are identified at B[5.2A]. The following may be particularly relevant but **these lists are not exhaustive**		
Factors indicating higher culpability 1. Circumstances suggest offender equipped for particularly serious offence 2. Items to conceal identify		
FORM A PRELIMINARY VIEW OF THE APPROPRIATE SENTENCE, THEN CONSIDER OFFENDER MITIGATION		
Common factors are identified at B[5.2A]		
CONSIDER A REDUCTION FOR A GUILTY PLEA		
CONSIDER ANCILLARY ORDERS		
Refer to B[18] for guidance on compensation and **Part B** for available ancillary orders		
CONSIDER DISQUALIFICATION FROM DRIVING AND DEPRIVATION OF PROPERTY		
DECIDE SENTENCE		
GIVE REASONS		

A[59]

Threats to kill

Charge

A[59.1]

Without lawful excuse makes to another a threat intending that that other would fear it would be carried out, to kill that other or a third person

Offences Against the Person Act 1861, s 16

Maximum penalty – Fine level 5 and 6 months (**12 months). Triable either way. Specified violent offence under Sch 15, Part 1, CJA 2003.

Crown Court – 10 years' imprisonment and unlimited fine.

Motor vehicles. If the defendant intended to steal or take a motor vehicle the offence is not endorsable nor are penalty points applicable but disqualification may be ordered.

Mode of trial

A[59.2]

See the SC Guideline at A[59.5] below.

Legal notes and definitions

A[59.3]

Lawful excuse. Making a threat where it is for the prevention of crime or self-defence can amount to a defence if it is reasonable in the circumstances to make such a threat. Once the issue is raised by the defence the onus is on the prosecution to prove that there was no lawful excuse, beyond a reasonable doubt (*R v Cousins* [1982] 2 All ER 115, CA).

A[59.4]

Person. A foetus in utero is not a person distinct from its mother; therefore a threat to cause the mother to have a miscarriage is not an offence under s 16. However, a threat to kill a child after its birth when it is still in foetus does amount to an offence under s 16 (*R v Tait* [1989] 3 All ER 682, CA).

Sentencing
SC Guideline – Threats to kill

A[59.5]

Where committed in a domestic context, see SC Definitive Guideline: "Overarching Principles: Domestic Violence".

IDENTIFY DANGEROUS OFFENDERS

This is a serious offence for the purposes of the public protection provisions in the Criminal Justice Act 2003. Refer to **B[16.5]** and consult legal adviser for guidance

OFFENCE SERIOUSNESS (CULPABILITY AND HARM)

A. IDENTIFY THE APPROPRIATE STARTING POINT

Starting points based on first time offender pleading not guilty

Examples of nature of activity	Starting point	Range
One threat uttered in the heat of the moment, no more than fleeting impact on victim	Medium level community order	Low level community order to high level community order
Single calculated threat or victim fears that threat will be carried out	12 weeks custody	6 to 26 weeks custody
Repeated threats or visible weapon	Crown Court	Crown Court

OFFENCE SERIOUSNESS (CULPABILITY AND HARM)

B. CONSIDER THE EFFECT OF AGGRAVATING AND MITIGATING FACTORS (OTHER THAN THOSE WITHIN EXAMPLES ABOVE)

Common aggravating and mitigating factors are identified at **B[5.2A]**. The following may be particularly relevant but **these lists are not exhaustive**

Factors indicating higher culpability	*Factor indicating lower culpability*
1. Planning	1. Provocation
2. Offender deliberately isolates victim	
3. Group action	
4. Threat directed at victim because of job	
5. History of antagonism towards victim	
Factors indicating greater degree of harm	
1. Vulnerable victim	
2. Victim needs medical help/counselling	

FORM A PRELIMINARY VIEW OF THE APPROPRIATE SENTENCE, THEN CONSIDER OFFENDER MITIGATION

Common factors are identified at **B[5.2A]**

CONSIDER A REDUCTION FOR A GUILTY PLEA

CONSIDER ANCILLARY ORDERS, INCLUDING COMPENSATION AND FOOTBALL BANNING ORDER (where appropriate)

Refer to **B[18]** for guidance on compensation and **Part B** for available ancillary orders

DECIDE SENTENCE

GIVE REASONS

A[60]

Trade mark, unauthorised use of etc

Charge

A[60.1]

(1) With a view to gain for himself or another, or with intent to cause loss to another, and without the consent of the proprietor -

(a)   applies to goods or their packaging a sign identical to, or likely to be mistaken for, a registered trade mark, or

(b)   sells or lets for hire, offers or exposes for sale or hire or distributes goods which bear, or the packaging of which bears, such a sign, or

(c)   has in his possession, custody or control in the course of a business any such goods with a view to the doing of anything, by himself or another, which would be an offence under paragraph (b).

Trade Marks Act 1994, s 92(1)

(2) With a view to gain for himself or another, or with intent to cause loss to another, and without the consent of the proprietor -

(a)   applies a sign identical to, or likely to be mistaken for, a registered trade mark to material intended to be used –
    (i)   for labelling or packaging goods,
    (ii)   as a business paper in relation to goods, or
    (iii)   as advertising goods, or

(b)   uses in the course of a business material bearing such a sign for labelling or packaging goods, as a business paper in relation to goods, or for advertising goods, or

(c)   has in his possession, custody or control in the course of a business any such material with a view to the doing of anything, by himself or another, which would be an offence under paragraph (b).

Trade Marks Act, 1994, s 92(2)

(3) With a view to gain for himself or another, or with intent to cause loss to another, and without the consent of the proprietor -

(a)   makes an article specifically designed for or adapted for making copies of a sign identical to, or likely to be mistaken for, a registered trade mark, or

(b)   has such an article in his possession, custody or control in the course of a business,

Knowing or having reason to believe that it has been, or is to be, used to produce goods, or material for labelling or packaging goods, as a business paper in relation to goods, or for advertising goods.

Trade Marks Act 1994, s 92(3)

Maximum penalty – Fine level 5 and 6 months' (**12 months) imprisonment+.

Crown Court – 10 years' imprisonment and unlimited fine.

Mode of trial

A[60.2]

See the SC Guideline at A[60.5] below.

Legal notes and definitions

A[60.3]

Defences. A criminal offence under s 92 cannot be committed unless there is a civil infringement of a trade mark (see ss 10–12); the civil defences will not apply in every case. Once a defence has been raised it is for the prosecution to disprove it (*R v Johnstone* [2003] 3 All ER 884; *R v Isaac* [2004] EWCA Crim 1082, 168 JP 417).

Section 92(4) provides that a person does not commit an offence unless –

(a)   the goods are goods in respect of which the trade mark is registered, or

(b)   the trade mark has a reputation in the UK and the use of the sign takes or would take unfair advantage of, or is or would be detrimental to, the distinctive character or repute of the trade mark.

The validity of the registration of a trade mark cannot be tried in criminal proceedings. If there is a challenge to the validity, the court must adjourn to allow that challenge to be determined against the trademark owner; albeit, not where the challenge is made late or is frivolous (*R v Johnstone* [2003] 3 All ER 884).

Section 92(5) provides that it a defence to show that the accused believed on reasonable grounds that the use of the sign in the manner in which it was used, or was to be used, was not an infringement of the registered trade mark.

The burden of proof rests with the accused to establish the defence on a balance of probabilities (*R v Johnstone* [2003] 3 All ER 884).

A[60.4]

Companies. For offences committed by partnerships and bodies corporate see s 101.

Sentencing
SC Guideline – Trade mark, unauthorised use of

A[60.5]

*This may be an offence for which it is appropriate to combine a fine with a community order. Consult your legal adviser for further guidance.

OFFENCE SERIOUSNESS (CULPABILITY AND HARM)

A. IDENTIFY THE APPROPRIATE STARTING POINT

Starting points based on first time offender pleading not guilty

Examples of nature of activity	Starting point	Range
Small number of counterfeit items	Band C fine	Band B fine to low level community order
Larger number of counterfeit items but no involvement in wider operation	Medium level community order, plus fine*	Low level community order to 12 weeks custody, plus fine*
High number of counterfeit items or involvement in wider operation eg. Manufacture or distribution	12 weeks custody	6 weeks to Crown Court
Central role in large-scale operation	Crown Court	Crown Court

OFFENCE SERIOUSNESS (CULPABILITY AND HARM)

B. CONSIDER THE EFFECT OF AGGRAVATING AND MITIGATING FACTORS (OTHER THAN THOSE WITHIN EXAMPLES ABOVE)

Common aggravating and mitigating factors are identified at B[5.2A]. The following may be particularly relevant but **these lists are not exhaustive**

Factors indicating higher culpability	*Factor indicating lower culpability*
1. High degree of professionalism	1. Mistake or ignorance about provenance of goods
2. High level of profit	
Factor indicating greater degree of harm	
1. Purchasers at risk of harm eg from counterfeit drugs	

FORM A PRELIMINARY VIEW OF THE APPROPRIATE SENTENCE, THEN CONSIDER OFFENDER MITIGATION

Common factors are identified at B[5.2A]

CONSIDER A REDUCTION FOR A GUILTY PLEA

CONSIDER ANCILLARY ORDERS

Refer to **B[18]** for guidance on compensation and **Part B** for available ancillary orders

Consider ordering forfeiture and destruction of the goods

DECIDE SENTENCE

GIVE REASONS

A[61]

TV licence payment evasion

Charge

A[61.1]

Installation or use of a television receiver without a licence.

Communications Act 2003, s 363(2)

Has a television receiver in his possession or under his control who –

(a)   intends to install or use it in contravention of subsection (1), or
(b)   knows, or has reasonable grounds for believing, that another person intends to install or use it in contravention of that subsection.

Communications Act 2003, s 363(3)

NB: The Wireless Telegraphy Act 1949, was repealed by the Wireless Telegraphy Act 2006. See ss 8 and 35 for further provision concerning the use of television and wireless apparatus.

Maximum penalty – Fine level 3.

Legal notes and definitions

A[61.2]

The charge should allege either that the apparatus was used or was installed.

A[61.3]

Using should be given its natural and ordinary meaning. This might create problems for enforcing authorities. They would if necessary have to persuade the court to draw the inference that the apparatus in question had been used by the defendant during the relevant period. If, for example, a television set in working order was found in the sitting-room of a house occupied by the defendant, it would not be difficult for a court to draw the necessary inference in the absence of some credible explanation by the defendant to the effect that it was not being used (*Rudd v Secretary of State for Trade and Industry* [1987] 2 All ER 553, [1987] 1 WLR 786, HL) and (*Whiley v DPP* [1995] Crim LR 39) in respect of a radio scanner.

A[61.4]

A user does not have to be an owner or hirer. Therefore where a set belonged to a husband but the wife switched it on, she was convicted of using it (*Monks v Pilgrim* [1979] Crim LR 595).

A[61.5]

Licence. Applies to the person named on the licence, his family and domestic staff living with him on the premises. The prosecution does not have to prove that the defendant did not have a valid licence (see s 101 MCA 1980).

A[61.6]

Applies to the premises named on the licence. Also covers members of family living away as full-time students at educational establishments using a portable television set (black and white or colour as described in the licence) in any other place provided:

(a)   they normally reside at the licence holder's address; and
(b)   the equipment is powered by internal batteries; and
(c)   is not permanently installed.

There are concessions for touring caravans.

A[61.7]

Duration. Normally one year. If the licence is paid for by a subsequently dishonoured cheque, it continues in force until it is properly revoked. It may be short-dated if it is not renewed immediately on the expiry of the previous licence.

A[61.8]

A licence is required where a television set is used to receive BBC, ITV, satellite or cable television programmes, whether or not it is used for other purposes such as a home computer.

A[61.9]–[61.14]

Concessions and exemptions are made under regulations for particular categories of persons. The number of sets that may be used on the same or different premises is also regulated by secondary legislation.

Sentencing
SC Guideline – TV licence payment evasion

A[61.15]

OFFENCE SERIOUSNESS (CULPABILITY AND HARM)		
A. IDENTIFY THE APPROPRIATE STARTING POINT		
Starting points based on first time offender pleading not guilty		
Examples of nature of activity	Starting point	Range
Up to 6 months unlicensed use	Band A fine	Band A fine
Over 6 months unlicensed use	Band B fine	Band A fine to band B fine
OFFENCE SERIOUSNESS (CULPABILITY AND HARM)		

B. CONSIDER THE EFFECT OF AGGRAVATING AND MITIGATING FACTORS (OTHER THAN THOSE WITHIN EXAMPLES ABOVE)

Common aggravating and mitigating factors are identified at B[5.2A]. The following may be particularly relevant but **these lists are not exhaustive**

Factors indicating lower culpability

1. Accidental oversight or belief licence held

2. Confusion of responsibility

3. Licence immediately obtained

FORM A PRELIMINARY VIEW OF THE APPROPRIATE SENTENCE, THEN CONSIDER OFFENDER MITIGATION

Common factors are identified at B[5.2A]

CONSIDER A REDUCTION FOR A GUILTY PLEA

CONSIDER ANCILLARY ORDERS

Refer to **Part B** for guidance on available ancillary orders

DECIDE SENTENCE

GIVE REASONS

A[62]

VAT evasion

Charge

Being knowingly concerned in, or in the taking of steps with a view to, the fraudulent evasion of VAT by him or any other person.

Value Added Tax Act, s 72(1)

Maximum penalty – Fine level 5 and/or 6 months' (**12 months) imprisonment.

Crown Court – 7 years' imprisonment and unlimited fine.

Mode of trial

A[62.1]

See general notes at I[4] and SC Guideline at A[62.4] below.

Legal notes and definitions

A[62.2]

Evasion of VAT. Includes a reference to the obtaining of –

(a)   the payment of a VAT credit; or
(b)   a refund under ss 35, 36 or 40 of this Act or s 22 of the 1983 Act; or
(c)   a refund under any regulations made by virtue of s 13 (5); or
(d)   a repayment under s 39;

and any reference in those subsections to the amount of VAT shall be construed –

(i)   in relation to VAT itself or a Vat credit, as a reference to the aggregate of the amount (if any) falsely claimed by way of credit for input tax and the amount (if any) by which output tax was falsely understated, and
(ii)   in relation to a refund or repayment falling within paragraph (b), (c) or (d) above, as a reference to the amount falsely claimed by way of refund or repayment.

A[62.3]

Knowingly. Can include "deliberately looking the other way" (*Ross v Moss* [1965] 2 QB 396, (1965) 129 JP 537).

Evasion. Means a deliberate non-payment when payment is due. There is no need therefore for the Crown to prove an intention permanently to deprive (*R v Dealy* [1995] 1 WLR 658).

Sentencing
VAT evasion

A[62.4]

Awaiting SC Guideline.

A[62.5]

Where an offender is sentenced to imprisonment and a fine, with an alternative period of imprisonment in default of payment of the fine, the aggregate of the terms of imprisonment must not exceed 15 months (see Customs and Excise Management Act 1979, s 179).

A[63]

Vehicle interference

Charge

A[63.1]

Interfered with a motor vehicle or anything carried in or on the same with the intention that an offence of theft of the said motor vehicle or part of it or of anything carried in or on the said motor vehicle or an offence of taking and driving it away without consent should be committed

Criminal Attempts Act 1981, s 9(1)

Maximum penalty – Fine level 4 and/or 3 months (**51 weeks).

Legal notes and definitions

A[63.2]

This offence applies to trailers. A trailer means a vehicle drawn by a motor vehicle.

A[63.3]

Interfere. It will be for the court to decide whether a particular activity amounts to interference; simply keeping a vehicle under observation in the hope that an opportunity will arise to commit an offence would not be interference. In many cases the alleged activity would support a charge of attempting to steal which, unlike this offence is triable either way but this offence may be easier to prove because of the provision regarding 'intent'.

A[63.4]

Intent. There must be evidence of an intention to commit theft of the vehicle, trailer, any parts of them or anything carried in or on them, or to commit the offence of unauthorised taking of the vehicle or trailer. The prosecution does not have to prove precisely which of these offences the accused intended. In some cases, for example, the prosecution would be unable to prove whether the intention was to take the vehicle, steal it, or steal goods from inside it.

A[63.5]

Motor vehicle. Means a mechanically propelled vehicle intended or adapted for use on the road.

Sentencing
SC Guideline – Vehicle interference

A[63.6]

<table>
<tr><td colspan="3">OFFENCE SERIOUSNESS (CULPABILITY AND HARM)
A. IDENTIFY THE APPROPRIATE STARTING POINT
Starting points based on first time offender pleading not guilty</td></tr>
<tr><td>Examples of nature of activity</td><td>Starting point</td><td>Range</td></tr>
<tr><td>Trying door handles; no entry gained to vehicle; no damage caused</td><td>Band C fine</td><td>Band A fine to low level community order</td></tr>
<tr><td>Entering vehicle, little or no damage caused</td><td>Medium level community order</td><td>Low level community order to high level community order</td></tr>
<tr><td>Entering vehicle with damage caused</td><td>High level community order</td><td>Medium level community order to 12 weeks custody</td></tr>
<tr><td colspan="3">OFFENCE SERIOUSNESS (CULPABILITY AND HARM)
B. CONSIDER THE EFFECT OF AGGRAVATING AND MITIGATING FACTORS (OTHER THAN THOSE WITHIN EXAMPLES ABOVE)
Common aggravating and mitigating factors are identified at B[5.2A]. The following may be particularly relevant but **these lists are not exhaustive**</td></tr>
<tr><td colspan="2">*Factor indicating higher culpability*
1. Targeting vehicle in dark/isolated location</td><td></td></tr>
<tr><td colspan="2">*Factors indicating greater degree of harm*
1. Emergency services vehicle
2. Disabled driver's vehicle
3. Part of series</td><td></td></tr>
<tr><td colspan="3">FORM A PRELIMINARY VIEW OF THE APPROPRIATE SENTENCE, THEN CONSIDER OFFENDER MITIGATION
Common factors are identified at B[5.2A]</td></tr>
<tr><td colspan="3">CONSIDER A REDUCTION FOR A GUILTY PLEA
CONSIDER ANCILLARY ORDERS, INCLUDING COMPENSATION
Refer to B[18] for guidance on compensation and **Part B** for available ancillary orders
CONSIDER DISQUALIFICATION FROM DRIVING</td></tr>
<tr><td colspan="3">DECIDE SENTENCE
GIVE REASONS</td></tr>
</table>

A[63.7]

See Table B at B[4.2] for available sentences.

A[64]

Vehicle licence/registration fraud

Charge

A[64.1]

Fraudulently using a vehicle excise licence

Vehicle Exercise and Registration Act 1994, s 44

Maximum penalty – Fine level 5 (for fines see **B[33]**).

Crown Court – Unlimited fine and 2 years' imprisonment. Triable either way.

Mode of trial

A[64.2]

See the SC Guideline at **A[64.4]** below.

Note: Custody only available in Crown Court.

Legal notes and definitions

A[64.3]

Other offences. The offence can also be committed by forging or fraudulently altering, lending or allowing to be used by another a licence or registration document under the Act. It is also an offence fraudulently to use etc a number plate. Exhibiting an altered vehicle excise licence on a car parked on private land does not amount to fraudulent use within the meaning of the Act (*R v Johnson* [1995] RTR 15, 158 JP 788, CA).

A[64.4]

Fraudulently. Does not merely cover economic loss by the evasion of excise duty but also includes the case where the defendant intends by deceit to cause a public official such as a police officer to act, or refrain from acting, in a way in which he otherwise would not have done. See *R v Terry* [1984] AC 374, [1984] 1 All ER 65, HL and *R v Macrae* (1993) 159 JP 359, [1994] Crim LR 363, CA on forgery of a licence.

Sentencing
SC Guideline – Vehicle licence/registration fraud

A[64.5]

OFFENCE SERIOUSNESS (CULPABILITY AND HARM)		
A. IDENTIFY THE APPROPRIATE STARTING POINT		
Starting points based on first time offender pleading not guilty		
Examples of nature of activity	**Starting point**	**Range**
Use of unaltered licence from another vehicle	Band B fine	Band B fine
Forged licence bought for own use, or forged/altered for own use	Band C fine	Band C fine
Use of number plates from another vehicle; or licence/number plates forged or altered for sale to another	High level community order	Medium level community order to Crown Court Note: custody only available in Crown Court

OFFENCE SERIOUSNESS (CULPABILITY AND HARM)
B. CONSIDER THE EFFECT OF AGGRAVATING AND MITIGATING FACTORS (OTHER THAN THOSE WITHIN EXAMPLES ABOVE)
Common aggravating and mitigating factors are identified at B[5.2A]. The following may be particularly relevant but **these lists are not exhaustive**

Factors indicating higher culpability	*Factors indicating lower culpability*
1. LGV/PSV/LGV/taxi etc	1. Licence/registration mark from another vehicle owned by defendant
2. Long-term fraudulent use	2. Short-term use
Factors indicating greater degree of harm	
1. High financial gain	
2. Innocent victim deceived	
3. Legitimate owner inconvenienced	

FORM A PRELIMINARY VIEW OF THE APPROPRIATE SENTENCE, THEN CONSIDER OFFENDER MITIGATION
Common factors are identified at B[5.2A]

CONSIDER A REDUCTION FOR A GUILTY PLEA
CONSIDER ANCILLARY ORDERS
Refer to B[18] for guidance on compensation and **Part B** for available ancillary orders

CONSIDER DISQUALIFICATION FROM DRIVING AND DEPRIVATION OF PROPERTY (including vehicle)

DECIDE SENTENCE
GIVE REASONS

A[65]
Vehicle taking, without consent

Charge

A[65.1]
Without the consent of the owner or other lawful authority taking a conveyance, namely a [. . . . .] for his own use (or for another person's use)

Theft Act 1968, s 12(1)

Note – It is also an offence to drive a conveyance, or allow oneself to be carried in or on it, if one knows the conveyance has been taken without such authority; the penalty for such offences is the same as for the offence of unauthorised taking.

Maximum penalty – Fine level 5 and 6 months (**51 weeks). Triable only by magistrates.

Motor vehicles. The defendant may be disqualified but no endorsement or penalty points are applicable.

Legal notes and definitions

A[65.2]
Pedal cycles. The Theft Act 1968, s 12(5) applies a special provision if the conveyance is a pedal cycle. The maximum penalty is a fine up to level 3.

A[65.3]
If the circumstances amounted to theft and theft is alleged, the notes at A[57.3] will apply.

A[65.4]
Taking. An offence is committed if the conveyance is taken. 'Driving away' does not have to be proved but there must be evidence of some movement and that the vehicle was used as a conveyance. Accordingly, the moving of a motor car round the corner as a practical joke to lead the owner to believe it had been stolen was not an offence as it was not established that anyone rode inside it (*R v Stokes* [1983] RTR 59, [1982] Crim LR 695, CA). But where a defendant allowed a vehicle to roll down a hill by climbing in it and releasing the handbrake, he was guilty of the offence (*R v Bow* [1977] RTR 6, 64 Cr App Rep 54, CA). It would be otherwise if he did not get inside the vehicle. It is not a defence that the conveyance was stolen, as opposed to being taken. Nor is it a defence that the vehicle had been previously taken (*DPP v Spriggs* [1994] RTR 1, 157 JP 1143, [1993] Crim LR 622).

A[65.5]
Conveyance. Means a conveyance constructed or adapted for carrying one

or more persons by land, water or air. It does not include a conveyance which can only be controlled by a person not carried in or on it.

A[65.6]

Motor vehicle. A motor vehicle is a mechanically propelled vehicle intended or adapted for use on a road.

A[65.7]

Owner. Includes a person in possession of the conveyance under a hiring or hire-purchase agreement.

A[65.8]

Owner's consent. Where the owner is induced by fraud to part with possession of his vehicle, no offence under this section has been committed (*Whittaker v Campbell* [1984] QB 318, [1983] 3 All ER 582). The owner has in fact consented even though in the civil law he may have a remedy against the fraudster.

A[65.9]

No offence was committed where consent was obtained by a false pretence as to the destination and purpose of the journey (*R v Peart* [1970] 2 QB 672, [1970] 2 All ER 823, CA). Nor where consent of an owner to allow a vehicle to be hired was obtained by the fraudulent misrepresentation of the hirer as to his identity and the holding of a full driving licence.

A[65.10]

Reduction of charge from theft of conveyance. If a defendant is tried in a magistrates' court for stealing a conveyance, the court cannot reduce the charge to this offence of taking the conveyance.

A[65.11]–[65.15]

Time Limits. Like many summary road traffic offences, proceedings may be commenced within six months of the day the prosecution had knowledge of the offence subject to an overall time limit of three years from the commission of the offence.

A[65.16]

Successful defence. If the court is satisfied the defendant acted in the belief that he had lawful authority, or that the owner would have consented if the owner knew the circumstances, then he must be acquitted. The defendant only has to raise the defence. The absence of lawful authority or the owner's consent is an essential ingredient of the offence and it remains the prosecutor's duty to prove the allegation beyond a reasonable doubt.

A[65.17]

Aggravated vehicle-taking. See A[66].

Sentencing
SC Guideline – Vehicle taking, without consent

A[65.18]

OFFENCE SERIOUSNESS (CULPABILITY AND HARM)		
A. IDENTIFY THE APPROPRIATE STARTING POINT		
Starting points based on first time offender pleading not guilty		
Examples of nature of activity	**Starting point**	**Range**
Relative's vehicle; exceeding authorised use of eg. employer's vehicle; retention of hire car beyond return date	Low level community order	Band B fine to medium level community order
As above with damage caused to lock/ignition; or stranger's vehicle involved but no damage caused	Medium level community order	Low level community order to high level community order
Taking vehicle from private premises; causing damage to eg. lock/ignition of stranger's vehicle	High level community order	Medium level community order to 26 weeks custody

OFFENCE SERIOUSNESS (CULPABILITY AND HARM)	
B. CONSIDER THE EFFECT OF AGGRAVATING AND MITIGATING FACTORS (OTHER THAN THOSE WITHIN EXAMPLES ABOVE)	
Common aggravating and mitigating factors are identified at B[5.2A]. The following may be particularly relevant but **these lists are not exhaustive**	
Factors indicating greater degree of harm	*Factor indicating lower culpability*
1. Vehicle later burnt	1. Misunderstanding with owner
2. Vehicle belonging to elderly/disabled person	*Factor indicating lesser degree of harm*
3. Emergency services vehicle	1. Offender voluntarily returned vehicle to owner
4. Medium to large goods vehicle	
5. Passengers carried	

FORM A PRELIMINARY VIEW OF THE APPROPRIATE SENTENCE, THEN CONSIDER OFFENDER MITIGATION
Common factors are identified at B[5.2A]

CONSIDER A REDUCTION FOR A GUILTY PLEA
CONSIDER ANCILLARY ORDERS, INCLUDING COMPENSATION
Refer to B[18] for guidance on compensation and **Part B** for available ancillary orders
CONSIDER DISQUALIFICATION FROM DRIVING

DECIDE SENTENCE
GIVE REASONS

A[65.19]

Available sentences. See Table B at B[4.2].

A[65.20]

Disqualification may be ordered in the case of a motor vehicle (no points available).

A[66]

(1) Vehicle-taking (aggravated) – damage caused to property other than the vehicle in accident or damage caused to the vehicle (ss 12A(2)(c) and (d)) (2) Vehicle-taking (aggravated) – dangerous driving or accident causing injury (ss 12A(2)(a) and (b))

Charges

A[66.1]

Taking a mechanically propelled vehicle without the owner's consent or other lawful authority (or driving, or allowing oneself to be carried in or on it, knowing it to have been taken without the owner's consent etc) and at any time after it had been unlawfully taken and before it was recovered:

(a)   that the vehicle was driven dangerously on a road or other public place;

(b)   that, owing to the driving of the vehicle, an accident occurred by which injury was caused to any person;

(c)   that, owing to the driving of the vehicle an accident occurred by which damage was caused to any property, other than the vehicle;

(d)   that damage was caused to the vehicle.

Theft Act 1968, s 12A(1)

Maximum penalty – Fine level 5 and 6 months' (**12 months) imprisonment+. Specified violent offence under Sch 15, Part 1, CJA 2003 if the offence involves an accident causing the death of any person.

Mandatory disqualification for one year and endorsement. Penalty points 3–11.

Crown Court – 2 years' imprisonment (14 years where death has been caused) and unlimited fine.

Mode of trial

A[66.2]

See the SC Guideline at **A[66.16]** and **A[66.17]** below.

Where no allegation is made other than damage to property or the vehicle concerned, the offence is triable only before magistrates where the total value of the damage concerned does not exceed £5,000 (*R v Kelly* [2001] RTR 45, CA). The value of the damage to property other than the vehicle involved in the offence is what it would probably have cost to buy the property in the open market at the time of the offence. The value of the damage to the vehicle taken is assessed in a similar manner to that where property has been damaged. Otherwise the offence is triable either way.

A[66.3]–[66.4]

For the procedure where it is not clear whether the damage is above or below £5,000, see **A[18.4]**.

Legal notes and definitions

A[66.5]

Mechanically propelled vehicle ie a vehicle intended or adapted for use on a road. This includes, inter alia, a Mantis City electric scooter (*DPP v King* [2008] EWHC 447 (Admin), 172 JP 401).

A[66.6]

Vehicle recovered ie when it is restored to its owner or to other lawful possession or custody.

A[66.7]

Owner includes a person in possession under a hiring or hire-purchase agreement.

A[66.8]

Dangerous driving ie driven in a way which falls far below what would be expected of a competent and careful driver and it would be obvious to a competent and careful driver that driving the vehicle in that way would be dangerous.

A[66.9]

Road or public place. See **C[22.5]**, **C[22.6]**.

A[66.10]

Defence. The defendant is not guilty of this offence if he proves that the driving accident or damage occurred before he committed the basic offence or that he was neither in, nor on, nor in the immediate vicinity of the vehicle when that driving etc occurred. The defendant does not have to establish one of these defences beyond reasonable doubt. He need only establish that it was probably true. (It is suggested that the burden and standard of proof legitimately lies with the accused because the facts giving rise to the defence are peculiarly within the knowledge of that person. Accordingly, the legal burden of proof appears compatible with the European Convention on Human Rights (ECHR).)

A[66.11]–[66.15]

Reduction of charge/alternative verdict. The court may find the defendant guilty of the basic offence if it decides to dismiss the aggravated version. (*H v Liverpool City Youth Court* [2001] Crim LR 897)

Sentencing
SC Guideline – Vehicle taking (aggravated) – Damage caused to property etc – ss 12A(2)(c) and (d)

A[66.16]

Must endorse and disqualify for at least 12 months

Must disqualify for at least two years if offender has had two or more disqualifications for periods of 56 days or more in preceding 3 years – consult your legal adviser for further guidance

If there is a delay in sentencing after conviction, consider interim disqualification

OFFENCE SERIOUSNESS (CULPABILITY AND HARM)		
A. IDENTIFY THE APPROPRIATE STARTING POINT		
Starting points based on first time offender pleading not guilty		
Examples of nature of activity	**Starting point**	**Range**
Relative's vehicle; exceeding authorised use of eg. employer's vehicle; retention of hire car beyond return date; minor damage to taken vehicle	Medium level community order	Low level community order to high level community order
Greater damage to taken vehicle and/or moderate damage to another vehicle and/or property	High level community order	Medium level community order to 12 weeks custody
Vehicle taken as part of burglary or from private premises; severe damage	18 weeks custody	12 to 26 weeks custody (Crown Court if damage over £5,000)
OFFENCE SERIOUSNESS (CULPABILITY AND HARM)		
B. CONSIDER THE EFFECT OF AGGRAVATING AND MITIGATING FACTORS (OTHER THAN THOSE WITHIN EXAMPLES ABOVE)		
Common aggravating and mitigating factors are identified at B[5.2A]. The following may be particularly relevant but **these lists are not exhaustive**		
Factors indicating greater degree of harm	*Factors indicating lower culpability*	
1. Vehicle deliberately damaged/destroyed	1. Misunderstanding with owner	
2. Offender under influence of alcohol/drugs	2. Damage resulting from actions of another (where this does not provide a defence)	
Factors indicating greater degree of harm		

1. Passengers carried 2. Vehicle belonging to elderly or disabled person 3. Emergency services vehicle 4. Medium to large goods vehicle 5. Damage caused in moving traffic accident	
FORM A PRELIMINARY VIEW OF THE APPROPRIATE SENTENCE, THEN CONSIDER OFFENDER MITIGATION Common factors are identified at B[5.2A]	
CONSIDER A REDUCTION FOR A GUILTY PLEA	
CONSIDER ANCILLARY ORDERS, INCLUDING COMPENSATION	
Refer to **B[18]** for guidance on compensation and **Part B** for available ancillary orders	
DECIDE SENTENCE **GIVE REASONS**	

SC Guideline – Vehicle taking (aggravated) – Dangerous driving or accident causing injury – ss 12A(2)(a) and (b)

A[66.17]

Must endorse and disqualify for at least 12 months

Must disqualify for at least two years if offender has had two or more disqualifications for periods of 56 days or more in preceding 3 years – consult your legal adviser for further guidance

If there is a delay in sentencing after conviction, consider interim disqualification

OFFENCE SERIOUSNESS (CULPABILITY AND HARM) A. IDENTIFY THE APPROPRIATE STARTING POINT Starting points based on first time offender pleading not guilty		
Examples of nature of activity	**Starting point**	**Range**
Taken vehicle involved in single incident of bad driving where little or no damage or risk of personal injury	High level community order	Medium level community order to 12 weeks custody
Taken vehicle involved in incident(s) involving excessive speed or showing off, especially on busy roads or in built-up area	18 weeks custody	12 to 26 weeks custody

Taken vehicle involved in prolonged bad driving involving deliberate disregard for safety of others	Crown Court	Crown Court

OFFENCE SERIOUSNESS (CULPABILITY AND HARM)
B. CONSIDER THE EFFECT OF AGGRAVATING AND MITIGATING FACTORS (OTHER THAN THOSE WITHIN EXAMPLES ABOVE)
Common aggravating and mitigating factors are identified at B[5.2A]. The following may be particularly relevant but **these lists are not exhaustive**

Factors indicating greater degree of harm	
1. Disregarding warnings of others	
2. Evidence of alcohol or drugs	
3. Carrying out other tasks while driving	
4. Carrying passengers or heavy load	
5. Tiredness	
6. Trying to avoid arrest	
7. Aggressive driving, such as driving much too close to vehicle in front, inappropriate attempts to overtake, or cutting in after overtaking	
Factors indicating greater degree of harm	
1. Injury to others	
2. Damage to other vehicles or property	

FORM A PRELIMINARY VIEW OF THE APPROPRIATE SENTENCE, THEN CONSIDER OFFENDER MITIGATION
Common factors are identified at B[5.2A]

CONSIDER A REDUCTION FOR A GUILTY PLEA

CONSIDER ORDERING DISQUALIFICATION UNTIL APPROPRIATE DRIVING TEST PASSED
CONSIDER ANCILLARY ORDERS, INCLUDING COMPENSATION
Refer to B[18] for guidance on compensation and **Part B** for available ancillary orders

DECIDE SENTENCE
GIVE REASONS

A[67]

Violent disorder

Charge

A[67.1]

Being one of three or more persons present together and using or threatening unlawful violence so that the conduct taken together is such as would cause a person of reasonable firmness present at the scene to fear for his personal safety

Public Order Act 1986, s 2(1)

Maximum penalty – Fine level 5 and 6 months (**12 months). Triable either way. Specified violent offence under Sch 15, Part 1, CJA 2003.

Crown Court – 5 years' imprisonment and unlimited fine.

Mode of trial

A[67.2]

Cases of violent disorder should generally be considered for trial on indictment. See SC Guideline at **A[67.10]** below.

Legal notes and definitions

A[67.3]

The charge. Only one offence is created.

A[67.4]

Three or more persons. The defendants need not be using or threatening violence simultaneously. The term 'present together' meant no more than being present in the same place at the same time; the prosecution are not required to prove a common purpose among those using or threatening violence: *R v NW* [2010] EWCA Crim 404, [2010] 2 Cr App Rep 54, [2010] Crim LR 723.

A[67.5]

Violence does not include violence justified by law (eg self-defence or prevention of crime) but apart from that includes violent conduct towards property or persons and is not restricted to conduct causing or intended to cause injury or damage but includes any other violent conduct (for example, throwing at or towards a person a missile of a kind capable of causing injury which does not hit or falls short).

A[67.6]

Person of reasonable firmness need not actually be or be likely to be, present at the scene. See **A[2.6]**.

A[67.7]

Intent. A person may be guilty only if he intends to use or threaten violence, or is aware that his conduct may be violent or threaten violence.

A[67.8]

Intoxication. A person whose awareness is impaired by intoxication shall be taken to be aware of that of which he would be aware if not intoxicated, unless he shows that his intoxication was not self-induced, or that it was caused solely by the taking of a substance in the course of medical treatment. 'Intoxication' may be caused by drink, drugs or other means.

A[67.9]

Violent disorder may be committed in a public or private place.

Sentencing
SC Guideline – Violent disorder

A[67.10]

IDENTIFY DANGEROUS OFFENDERS
This is a specified offence for the purposes of the public protection provisions in the Criminal Justice Act 2003. Refer to B[16.5] and consult legal adviser for guidance
OFFENCE SERIOUSNESS (CULPABILITY AND HARM)   A. IDENTIFY THE APPROPRIATE STARTING POINT   Starting points based on first time offender pleading not guilty
These offences should normally be dealt with in the Crown Court. However, there may be rare cases involving missile violence or threats of violence leading to no or minor injury, with few people involved and no weapon or missiles, in which a custodial sentence within the jurisdiction of a magistrates' court may be appropriate.

A[67.11]

Available sentences. See Table A at B[4.1].

A[68]

Voyeurism

Charge

A[68.1]

For the purpose of obtaining sexual gratification, observed another person doing a private act, and he knows that the other person does not consent to being observed for sexual gratification.

Sexual Offences Act 2003, s 67(1)

Maximum penalty – Fine level 5 and 6 months (**51 weeks). Triable either way. Specified sexual offence under Sch 15, Part 2, CJA 2003.

Crown Court – 2 years' imprisonment and unlimited fine.

Mode of trial

A[68.2]

See the SC Guideline at A[68.5] below.

Legal notes and definitions

A[68.3]

Method of offence. The offence of sexual gratification can be committed in a number of different ways. It can involve the operation of equipment (s 67 (2)), the recording of another person doing a private act (s 67 (3)) or the installation of equipment, construction or adaptation of a structure or part of a structure with the intention of enabling himself or another (s 67 (4)).

A[68.4]

Definitions. See the notes at the end of the SC guideline at A[68.5] below.

"Private Act" and "structure" are defined by s 68.

There must be a private act in order for offences of voyeurism to be committed. Section 68 is then concerned to bring within the meaning of the private act those parts of the body for which people conventionally expect or normally expect privacy. The clear intention of Parliament therefore was to mean the female "breast" or breasts" and not the male breast (see the notes to A[68.5] below)

"Observes" and "image" are further defined by s 79.

For "consent" see s 74.

Sentencing
SC Guideline – Voyeurism

A[68.5]

This guideline is taken from the Sentencing Council's definitive guideline *Sexual Offences Act 2003* published 30 April 2007

Key factors

(a)   This offence is committed where, for the purpose of obtaining sexual gratification, an offender observes a person doing a private act and knows that the other person does not consent to being observed. It may be committed in a number of ways such as by direct observation on the part of the offender, by recording someone doing a private act with the intention that the recording image will be viewed by the offender or another person, or by installing equipment or constructing or adapting a structure with the intention of enabling the offender or another person to observe a private act. For the purpose of this offence "private act" means an act carried out in a place which, in the circumstances, would reasonably be expected to provide privacy and, the person's genitals, buttocks or breasts are exposed or covered only in underwear; or the person is using a lavatory; or the person is doing a sexual act that is of a kind not ordinarily done in public (the offence does not extend solely to "ogling male breasts": *R v Bassett* [2008] EWCA Crim 1174).

(b)   For a recent sentencing case where the offence was held to fall within the lower range or scale of sentences see: *R v Hodgson* [2008] EWCA Crim 1180. In this case there had been recording or dissemination of images of a sexual nature, albeit the offence had been a continuing one and involved a breach of trust. A community order with various requirements including a community sex offender programme was substituted on appeal.

(c)   In accordance with s 80 of and Sch 3 to the Sexual Offences Act 2003, automatic notification requirements apply upon conviction to an offender aged 18 or over where:

     (1)   a victim was under 18; or

     (2)   a term of imprisonment or a community sentence of at least 12 months is imposed.

     For notification requirements generally see **A[52.15]**.

NB: A community order with a requirement to carry out 120 hours unpaid work was not a community sentence of at least 12 months for the purposes of Sch 3 and therefore the offender was not subject to the notification requirements of the legislation (*R v Odam* [2008] EWCA Crim 1087).

IDENTIFY DANGEROUS OFFENDERS

This is a serious offence for the purposes of the public protection provisions in the Criminal Justice Act 2003. Refer to **B[16.5]** and consult legal adviser for guidance

OFFENCE SERIOUSNESS (CULPABILITY AND HARM)

A. IDENTIFY THE APPROPRIATE STARTING POINT

Starting points based on first time offender pleading not guilty

Examples of nature of activity	Starting point	Range
Basic offence as defined in the Act, assuming no aggravating or mitigating factors eg the offender spies through a hole he or she has made in a changing room wall	Low level community order	Band B fine to high level community order
Offence with aggravating factors such as recording sexual activity and showing it to others	26 weeks custody	4 weeks custody to Crown Court
Offence with serious aggravating factors such as recording sexual activity and placing it on a website or circulating it for commercial gain	Crown Court	26 weeks to Crown Court

OFFENCE SERIOUSNESS (CULPABILITY AND HARM)

B. CONSIDER THE EFFECT OF AGGRAVATING AND MITIGATING FACTORS (OTHER THAN THOSE WITHIN EXAMPLES ABOVE)

Common aggravating and mitigating factors are identified at **B[5.2A]**. The following may be particularly relevant but **these lists are not exhaustive**

Factors indicating higher culpability 1. Threats to prevent the victim reporting an offence 2. Recording activity and circulating pictures/videos 3. Circulating pictures or videos for commercial gain – particularly if victim is vulnerable eg a child or a person with a mental or physical disorder	
Factor indicating greater degree of harm 1. Distress to victim eg where the pictures/videos are circulated to people known to the victim	

FORM A PRELIMINARY VIEW OF THE APPROPRIATE SENTENCE, THEN CONSIDER OFFENDER MITIGATION

Common factors are identified at **B[5.2A]**

CONSIDER A REDUCTION FOR A GUILTY PLEA

CONSIDER ANCILLARY ORDERS, INCLUDING COMPENSATION

Refer to **B[18]** for guidance on compensation and **Part B** for available ancillary orders

DECIDE SENTENCE

GIVE REASONS

A[69]

Witness intimidation

Charge 1

A[69.1]

Did intimidate [. . . . .] knowing or believing [. . . . .] is assisting an investigation/is a witness or potential witness in proceedings with the intention that the investigation/course of justice would be interfered/perverted/obstructed

Criminal Justice and Public Order Act 1994, s 51(1)

See Charge 2 for penalty.

Charge 2

A[69.2]

Did threaten [. . . . .] with harm intending to harm him knowing or believing that [. . . . .] has assisted in an investigation or has given evidence in proceedings for an offence because he believes/ knows that assistance or evidence was given

Criminal Justice and Public Order Act 1994, s 51(2)

Maximum penalty – Fine level 5 and 6 months (**12 months). Triable either way.

Crown Court – maximum 5 years' imprisonment.

Note that similar offences carrying the same maximum penalty may now be charged under the Criminal Justice and Police Act 2001, ss 39 and 40. These offences are specifically aimed at incidents not covered by CJPOA 1994, s 51 and cover both civil and criminal proceedings.

Mode of trial

A[69.3]

See the SC Guideline at **A[69.11]** below.

Legal notes and definitions

A[69.4]

A person does an act to another person with the intention of intimidating/harming not only when it is done directly but also when it is done to a third party with the same intention. The threat may be at a distance, eg over the telephone (*DPP v Mills* [1997] QB 300, [1996] 3 WLR 1093). An act might amount to intimidation under the section even though the victim is sufficiently steadfast not to be intimidated (*R v Petrascu* [2004] EWCA Crim 2417, [2004] 4 All ER 1066).

It was not enough to describe the defendant's behaviour as objectively intimidating, but rather, there had to have been an act that had intimidated and had been intended to intimidate the victim (*R v Mahmood* [2007] EWCA Crim 13).

A[69.5]

Harm may be financial/physical to a person or property.

A[69.6]

Intention. The intention or motive required for the two charges need not be the only or predominant motive or intention with which the act is done or threatened. A threat to harm a witness relayed via a third party constitutes an offence under this section. If a threat to harm a witness takes place within one year after the trial the prosecution do not have to prove a connection between the threat and the trial: *A-G's Reference (No 1 of 1999)*. If the prosecution can prove the act/threat and the defendant's knowledge/belief in the circumstances then the resultant motive/intention shall be presumed unless the contrary is proven.

A[69.7]

Knowingly and ECHR. Section 51(7) of the CJPOA 1994 provides that if the defendant knowingly commits an act of intimidation it will be presumed that the defendant intended to interfere with the course of justice unless otherwise proven. The fact that the legislation imposes a reverse burden of proof on the defence is both justiciable and proportionate in ECHR terms having regard to the stated aims of the legislation and *Attorney General's Reference (No 1 of 2004)* [2004] EWCA Crim 1025, [2004] 1 WLR 2111.

A[69.8]

Witness includes jurors or potential jurors in the Crown Court.

A[69.9]

Investigation into an offence means an investigation by police or such other person charged with the duty of investigating offences or charging offenders.

A[69.10]

Offence includes an alleged or suspected offence.

Sentencing
SC Guideline – Witness intimidation

A[69.11]

Where offence committed in a domestic context, see SC Definitive Guideline: "Overarching Principles: Domestic Violence".

OFFENCE SERIOUSNESS (CULPABILITY AND HARM)

A. IDENTIFY THE APPROPRIATE STARTING POINT

Starting points based on first time offender pleading not guilty

Examples of nature of activity	Starting point	Range
Sudden outburst in chance encounter	6 weeks custody	Medium level community order to 18 weeks custody
Conduct amounting to a threat; staring at, approaching or following witnesses; talking about the case; trying to alter or stop evidence	18 weeks custody	12 weeks custody to Crown Court
Threats of violence to witnesses and/or their families; deliberately seeking out witnesses	Crown Court	Crown Court

OFFENCE SERIOUSNESS (CULPABILITY AND HARM)

B. CONSIDER THE EFFECT OF AGGRAVATING AND MITIGATING FACTORS (OTHER THAN THOSE WITHIN EXAMPLES ABOVE)

Common aggravating and mitigating factors are identified at **B[5.2A]**. The following may be particularly relevant but these lists are not exhaustive

Factors indicating higher culpability 1. Breach of bail conditions 2. Offender involves others	
Factors indicating greater degree of harm 1. Detrimental impact on administration of justice 2. Contact made at or in vicinity of victim's home	

FORM A PRELIMINARY VIEW OF THE APPROPRIATE SENTENCE, THEN CONSIDER OFFENDER MITIGATION

Common factors are identified at **B[5.2A]**

CONSIDER A REDUCTION FOR A GUILTY PLEA

CONSIDER ANCILLARY ORDERS, INCLUDING COMPENSATION

Refer to **B[18]** for guidance on compensation and **Part B** for available ancillary orders

DECIDE SENTENCE

GIVE REASONS

A[70]

Wounding/causing grievous bodily harm, and racially/religiously aggravated grievous bodily harm and malicious wounding

(Offences Against the Person Act 1861, s 20; Crime and Disorder Act 1998, s 29)

Charges

A[70.1]

Unlawfully and maliciously inflicting grievous bodily harm

A[70.2]

Unlawfully and maliciously wounding

Offences against the Person Act 1861, s 20

Maximum penalty – Fine level 5 and 6 months (**12 months). Triable either way. Specified violent offence under Sch 15, Part 1, CJA 2003.

Crown Court – 5 years and unlimited fine.

Racially/religiously aggravated offences.

Maximum penalty – Fine level 5 and 6 months (**12 months). Triable either way. Specified violent offence under Sch 15, Part 1, CJA 2003.

Crown Court – 7 years and unlimited fine.

Mode of trial

A[70.3]

For cases of domestic violence. See SC Definitive Guideline: "Overarching Principles: Domestic Violence".

A[70.4]

See the SC Guideline at A[70.20] below

Legal notes and definitions

A[70.5]

Intent. 'Maliciously' means intentionally or recklessly (*R v Mowatt* [1968]

1 QB 421, [1967] 3 All ER 47, CA) and 'recklessly' means that the accused foresaw the particular risk and yet went on to take it (*R v Cunningham* [1957] 2 QB 396, [1957] 2 All ER 412, CCA). In offences under the Offences Against The Person Act 1861, s 20 what must be intended or foreseen is that some physical harm might occur, not necessarily amounting to grievous bodily harm or wounding. An intention to frighten is not enough. (*DPP v A* [2000] All ER (D) 1247). In *Re Dica* (5 May 2004, unreported), CA it was held that where a person, knowing he suffers from a serious sexual disease, infects another through consensual sex (but not deliberately intending to pass on the disease) he will be guilty of the offence, so long as the victim did not consent to the risk of infection. An honest belief in an informed consent will amount to a defence (*R v Konzani* [2005] EWCA Crim 706, [2005] All ER (D) 292 (Mar)).

In principle it was open to justices to convict on the basis of recklessness even where the prosecution simply alleged a deliberate assault: *D v DPP* [2005] EWHC 967 (Admin) considered. However, the justices had failed to identify what was the unlawful act of K leading to the assault. Recklessness had only been a possible conclusion if the justices had found that K had thrown a punch albeit, without intending it to land, or was flailing his arms about in an agitated and aggressive manner. The conviction could not stand in the light of the findings of fact made by the justices: *Katsonis v Crown Prosecution Service* [2011] EWHC 1860 (Admin), 175 JP 396.

A[70.6]

Grievous bodily harm. Means really serious bodily harm. The injuries caused do not have to be permanent or dangerous, but they have to be more severe than actual bodily harm. (See A[8].)

A[70.7]

Provocation is no defence, but can be taken into account when sentencing.

A[70.8]

Racial/religious aggravation (See A[8.7].)

A[70.9]

Misadventure (See A[8.8].)

A[70.10]

Consent (See A[8.10]–A[8.17].)

A[70.11]–[70.15]

Self-defence etc (See A[8.18]–A[8.20].)

A[70.16]

Lawful sport (See A[15.18].)

A[70.17]

Trespasser on property (See A[15.22].)

A[70.18]

Execution of legal process (See A[8.24].)

A[70.19]

Reduction of charge/alternative verdict. The court cannot reduce this charge to a less serious one (eg actual bodily harm or common assault); but if a separate charge for a lesser offence has been preferred there could be a conviction for that. Consult a legal adviser and A[15.31] on the effect of a dismissal for common assault.

Sentencing
SC Guideline – Wounding/causing grievous bodily harm and Racially/religiously aggravated GBH/Unlawful wounding

Grievous bodily harm

Inflicting grievous bodily harm/Unlawful wounding

Offences against the Person Act 1861 (section 20)

Racially/religiously aggravated GBH/Unlawful wounding

Crime and Disorder Act 1998 (section 29)

A[70.20]

These are specified offences for the purposes of section 224 of the Criminal Justice Act 2003

Triable either way

Section 20

Maximum when tried summarily: Level 5 fine and/or 26 weeks' custody

Maximum when tried on indictment: 5 years' custody

Section 29

Maximum when tried summarily: Level 5 fine and/or 26 weeks' custody

Maximum when tried on indictment: 7 years' custody

Offence range: Community order – 4 years' custody

This guideline applies to all offenders aged 18 and older, who are sentenced on or after 13 June 2011. The definitions [at page 145] of 'starting point' and 'first time offender' do not apply for this guideline. Starting point and category ranges apply to all offenders in all cases, irrespective of plea or previous convictions.

Step One
Determining the offence category

The court should determine the offence category using the table below.

Category 1	Greater harm **and** higher culpability
Category 2	Greater harm **and** lower culpability; **or** lesser harm **and** higher culpability
Category 3	Lesser harm **and** lower culpability

The court should determine the offender's culpability and the harm caused, or intended, by reference **only** to the factors below (as demonstrated by the presence of one or more). These factors comprise the principal factual elements of the offence and should determine the category.

Factors indicating greater harm

Injury (which includes disease transmission and/or psychological harm) which is serious in the context of the offence (must normally be present)

Victim is particularly vulnerable because of personal circumstances

Sustained or repeated assault on the same victim

Factors indicating lesser harm

Injury which is less serious in the context of the offence

Factors indicating higher culpability

Statutory aggravating factors:

Offence motivated by, or demonstrating, hostility to the victim based on his or her sexual orientation (or presumed sexual orientation)

Offence motivated by, or demonstrating, hostility to the victim based on the victim's disability (or presumed disability)

Other aggravating factors:

A significant degree of premeditation

Use of weapon or weapon equivalent (for example, shod foot, headbutting, use of acid, use of animal)

Intention to commit more serious harm than actually resulted from the offence

Deliberately causes more harm than is necessary for commission of offence

Deliberate targeting of vulnerable victim

Leading role in group or gang

Offence motivated by, or demonstrating, hostility based on the victim's age, sex, gender identity (or presumed gender identity)

Factors indicating lower culpability

Subordinate role in a group or gang

A greater degree of provocation than normally expected

Lack of premeditation

Mental disorder or learning disability, where linked to commission of the offence

Excessive self defence

Step Two
Starting point and category range

Having determined the category, the court should use the corresponding starting points to reach a sentence within the category range below. The starting point applies to all offenders irrespective of plea or previous convictions. A case of particular gravity, reflected by multiple features of culpability in step one, could merit upward adjustment from the starting point before further adjustment for aggravating or mitigating features, set out below.

Offence Category	Starting Point *(Applicable to all offenders)*	Category Range *(Applicable to all offenders)*
Category 1	Crown Court	Crown Court
Category 2	Crown Court	Crown Court
Category 3	High level community order	Low level community order – Crown Court (51 weeks' custody)

The table below contains a **non-exhaustive** list of additional factual elements providing the context of the offence and factors relating to the offender. Identify whether any combination of these, or other relevant factors, should result in an upward or downward adjustment from the starting point. In some cases, having considered these factors, it may be appropriate to move outside the identified category range.

When sentencing **category 3** offences, the court should also consider the custody threshold as follows:

- has the custody threshold been passed?
- if so, is it unavoidable that a custodial sentence be imposed?
- if so, can that sentence be suspended?

Factors increasing seriousness

Statutory aggravating factors:

Previous convictions, having regard to a) the nature of the offence to which the conviction relates and its relevance to the current offence; and b) the time that has elapsed since the conviction

---

Offence committed whilst on bail

Other aggravating factors include:

Location of the offence

Timing of the offence

Ongoing effect upon the victim

Offence committed against those working in the public sector or providing a service to the public

Presence of others including relatives, especially children or partner of the victim

Gratuitous degradation of victim

In domestic violence cases, victim forced to leave their home

Failure to comply with current court orders

Offence committed whilst on licence

An attempt to conceal or dispose of evidence

Failure to respond to warnings or concerns expressed by others about the offender's behaviour

Commission of offence whilst under the influence of alcohol or drugs

Abuse of power and/or position of trust

Exploiting contact arrangements with a child to commit an offence

Established evidence of community impact

Any steps taken to prevent the victim reporting an incident, obtaining assistance and/or from assisting or supporting the prosecution

Offences taken into consideration (TICs)

Factors reducing seriousness or reflecting personal mitigation

No previous convictions **or** no relevant/recent convictions

Single blow

Remorse

Good character and/or exemplary conduct

Determination and/or demonstration of steps taken to address addiction or offending behaviour

Serious medical conditions requiring urgent, intensive or long-term treatment

Isolated incident

Age and/or lack of maturity where it affects the responsibility of the offender

Lapse of time since the offence where this is not the fault of the offender

Mental disorder or learning disability, where **not** linked to the commission of the offence

Sole or primary carer for dependent relatives

Section 29 offences only: The court should determine the appropriate sentence for the offence without taking account of the element of aggravation and then make an addition to the sentence, considering the level of aggravation involved. It may be appropriate to move outside the identified category range, taking into account the increased statutory maximum.

Step Three
Consider any other factors which indicate a reduction, such as assistance to the prosecution

The court should take into account any rule of law by virtue of which an offender may receive a discounted sentence in consequence of assistance given (or offered) to the prosecutor or investigator.

Step Four
Reduction for guilty pleas

The court should take account of any potential reduction for a guilty plea in accordance with section 144 of the Criminal Justice Act 2003 and the *Guilty Plea* guideline.

Step Five
Dangerousness

Inflicting grievous bodily harm/unlawful wounding and racially/religiously aggravated GBH/unlawful wounding are specified offences within the meaning of Chapter 5 of the Criminal Justice Act 2003 and at this stage the court should consider whether having regard to the criteria contained in that Chapter it would be appropriate to award an extended sentence.

Step Six
Totality principle

If sentencing an offender for more than one offence, or where the offender is already serving a sentence, consider whether the total sentence is just and proportionate to the offending behaviour.

Step Seven
Compensation and ancillary orders

In all cases, the court should consider whether to make compensation and/or other ancillary orders.

Step Eight
Reasons

Section 174 of the Criminal Justice Act 2003 imposes a duty to give reasons for, and explain the effect of, the sentence.

Step Nine
Consideration for remand time

Sentencers should take into consideration any remand time served in relation to the final sentence. The court should consider whether to give credit for time spent on remand in custody or on bail in accordance with sections 240 and 240A of the Criminal Justice Act 2003.

A[71]
Air guns

Charge

A[71.1]

Being a person under 18 having with him an air weapon or ammunition

Firearms Act 1968, s 22(4)

Maximum penalty – Fine level 3 or any other adjudication to which a young person is liable, bearing in mind the offence is not punishable with imprisonment.

Forfeiture of the air weapon or ammunition can be ordered.

Legal notes and definitions

A[71.2]

Possession, a close physical link and immediate control over the firearm but not necessarily that he had been carrying it. It is not an offence where he is under the supervision of someone of or over 21 years.

A[71.3]

Air weapon means an air rifle, air gun or air pistol of a type which has not been declared to be specially dangerous in rules made by the Home Office. See *Street v DPP* [2004] EWHC 86 (Admin), (2004) Times, 23 January, [2004] All ER (D) 70 (Jan) where a low powered ball bearing gun was included in the definition.

A[71.4]

Public place includes any highway or premises or place to which at the material time the public had access whether for payment or otherwise.

A[71.5]

It is not an offence for a person of 14 or over to have with him an air weapon on private premises with the consent of the occupier.

A[71.6]

He does not commit an offence if he is engaged in target practice as a member of a club approved by the Home Office or if the weapon and ammunition are being used at a shooting gallery where only air weapons or miniature rifles of 0.23 calibre or less are used (Firearms Act 1968, s 23(2)).

Sentencing

A[71.7]

No SC guideline. For available sentences see Table C at **B[4.3]**.

A[71.8]

Fines. See B[33].

A[71A]

Air guns

Charge

A[71A.1]

(1) It is an offence for a person in possession of an air weapon to fail to take reasonable precautions to prevent any person under the age of eighteen from having the weapon with him.

(2) Subsection (1) does not apply where by virtue of section 23 of this Act the person under the age of eighteen is not prohibited from having the weapon with him.

Firearms Act 1968, s 24ZA

Maximum penalty – Fine level 3 or any other adjudication to which a young person is liable, bearing in mind the offence is not punishable with imprisonment.

Forfeiture of the air weapon or ammunition can be ordered.

Legal notes and definitions

A[71A.2]

In proceedings for an offence under subsection (1) it is a defence to show that the person charged with the offence—

(a)   believed the other person to be aged eighteen or over; and
(b)   had reasonable ground for that belief.

A person shall be taken to have shown the matters specified in subsection (3) if—

(a)   sufficient evidence of those matters is adduced to raise an issue with respect to them; and
(b)   the contrary is not proved beyond a reasonable doubt.

Sentencing

A[71A.3]

No SC guideline. For available sentences see Table C at **B[4.3]**.

A[72]

Dangerous dogs

Offences under the Dangerous Dogs Act 1991

A[72.1]

Being the owner (person for the time being in charge) of a dog which on [. . . . .] was dangerously out of control in a public place namely [. . . . .] (and which injured a person)

Dangerous Dogs Act 1991, s 3(1)

Maximum penalty – Fine level 5 and 6 months' (**51 weeks) imprisonment. Triable only by magistrates.

Where it is alleged and proved that the dog injured a person (an 'aggravated offence') the offence is triable either way with a maximum penalty of level 5 fine and 6 months' (**12 months) imprisonment on summary conviction. The maximum penalty at the Crown Court is 2 years' imprisonment and an unlimited fine.

Legal notes and definitions

A[72.2]

Owner. Includes, where the dog is owned by a person who is less than 16 years old, the head of the household of which that person is a member. See *R v Huddart* [1999] Crim LR 568, CA, where the dog has been placed in the control of someone other than the owner.

A[72.3]

Dangerously out of control. Is defined to include any occasion on which there are grounds for reasonable apprehension that the dog will injure any person, whether or not it actually does so (exception is made, inter alia, for police dogs). The Act imposes strict liability on the owner (*R v Bezzina* [1994] 3 All ER 964, [1994] 1 WLR 1057, CA; *Rafiq v DPP* (1997) 161 JP 412). The Act imposes strict liability on a person who is either the owner or in charge of the dogs. The whole point of the Act is to penalise those who allow dogs to get dangerously out of control: *R v Pritipal Singh* [2011] EWCA Crim 1756.

The behaviour of the dog in that it bit a person and the fact that it was not controlled by its handler when on a lead was ample evidence of the dog being dangerously out of control in a public place (*R v Gedminintaite and Collier* [2008] EWCA Crim 814).

A[72.4]

The offence (under s 3(3)) of allowing the dog to enter a place, not being a public place, where it injures someone, can be committed by omission, ie where the dog escapes from an enclosed area (*Greener v DPP* (1996) Times, 15 February). Whether a person remained in physical control of a dog was a question of fact and degree. There was no reason in principle why a short and temporary transfer of actual physical control to another prevented the first person from remaining in charge of the dog: *L v Crown Prosecution Service* [2010] EWHC 341 (Admin), 174 JP 209.

A[72.5]

Public place. Any street, road or other place (whether or not enclosed) to which the public have or are permitted to have access whether for payment or otherwise and includes the common parts of a building containing two or more separate dwellings. This will often be a question of fact based on the usage of the street (*R (on the application of the DPP) v Zhao* [2003] EWHC 1724 (Admin), 167 JP 521).

External parts of building were generally excluded for the purposes of liability under the Dangerous Dogs Act 1991, ss 3(1) and 10(2): *R v C* [2007] EWCA Crim 1757. The Court of Appeal indicated that the 1991 Act was a penal statute and as such had to be construed strictly. *R v C* was followed in *R v Bogdal* [2008] EWCA Crim 1, 172 JP 178.

A[72.6]

It is an offence under s 3(3) to allow a dog to enter a place which is not a public place where it is not permitted to be and while there it injures a person or there are grounds for reasonable apprehension that it will do so.

A[72.7]

If this type of dog is in a car which is parked in a public place then the dog itself is in a public place (*Bates v DPP* (1993) 157 JP 1004). An inference can be drawn from the fact that a place is publicly owned (*Cummings v DPP* (1999) 143 Sol Jo LB 112, Times, 26 March).

Sentencing

SC Sentencing Guideline

A[72.8]

This guideline applies to all offenders aged 18 years and older, who are sentenced on or after 20 August 2012. The definitions [at page 145] of 'starting point' and 'first time offender' do not apply for this guideline.

Owner or person in charge of a dog dangerously out of control in a public place, injuring any person
Dangerous Dogs Act 1991 (section 3(1))

Owner or person in charge allowing a dog to be in a private place where the dog is not permitted to be, injuring any person
Dangerous Dogs Act 1991 (section 3(3)(a))

Triable either way

Maximum: 2 years' custody

Offence range: Discharge – 18 months' custody

Step One
Determining the offence category

The court should determine the offence category using the table below.

Category 1	Greater harm **and** higher culpability
Category 2	Greater harm **and** lower culpability; **or** lesser harm **and** higher culpability
Category 3	Lesser harm **and** lower culpability

The court should determine culpability and harm caused or intended, by reference **only** to the factors below, which comprise the principal factual elements of the offence. Where an offence does not fall squarely into a category, individual factors may require a degree of weighting before making an overall assessment and determining the appropriate offence category.

Factors indicating greater harm

Serious injury (which includes disease transmission and/or psychological harm)

Sustained or repeated attack

Victim is a child or otherwise vulnerable because of personal circumstances

Factor indicating lesser harm

Minor injury

Factors indicating higher culpability

Statutory aggravating factors:

Offence racially or religiously aggravated

Offence motivated by, or demonstrating, hostility to the victim based on his or her sexual orientation (or presumed sexual orientation)

Offence motivated by, or demonstrating, hostility to the victim based on the victim's disability (or presumed disability)

Other aggravating factors:

Failure to respond to warnings or concerns expressed by others about the dog's behaviour

Goading, or allowing goading, of dog

Dog used as weapon or to intimidate victim

Offence motivated by, or demonstrating, hostility based on the victim's age, sex, gender identity (or presumed gender identity)

Factors indicating lower culpability

Attempts made to regain control of dog and/or intervene

Provocation of dog without fault of the offender

Evidence of safety or control measures having been taken

Mental disorder or learning disability, where linked to the commission of the offence

Step Two
Starting point and category range

Having determined the category, the court should use the corresponding starting points to reach a sentence within the category range below. The starting point applies to all offenders irrespective of plea or previous convictions. A case of particular gravity, reflected by multiple features of culpability or harm in step 1, could merit upward adjustment from the starting point before further adjustment for aggravating or mitigating features, set out on the next page.

Offence Category	Starting Point *(Applicable to all offenders)*	Category Range *(Applicable to all offenders)*
Category 1	26 weeks' custody	Medium level community order – Crown Court (18 months' custody)
Category 2	Medium level community order	Band B fine – 26 weeks' custody
Category 3	Band B fine	Discharge – Band C fine

The table below contains a **non-exhaustive** list of additional factual elements providing the context of the offence and factors relating to the offender. Identify whether any combination of these, or other relevant factors, should result in an upward or downward adjustment from the starting point. In some cases, having considered these factors, it may be appropriate to move outside the identified category range.

When sentencing **category 1 or 2** offences, the court should also consider the custody threshold as follows:

- has the custody threshold been passed?
- if so, is it unavoidable that a custodial sentence be imposed?
- if so, can that sentence be suspended?

When sentencing **category 2** offences, the court should also consider the community order threshold as follows:

- has the community order threshold been passed?

Factors increasing seriousness

Statutory aggravating factors:

Previous convictions, having regard to a) the nature of the offence to which the conviction relates and its relevance to the current offence; and b) the time that has elapsed since the conviction

Offence committed whilst on bail

Other aggravating factors include:

Injury to another animal(s)

Location of the offence

Ongoing effect upon the victim and/or others

Failure to take adequate precautions to prevent dog escaping

Allowing person insufficiently experienced or trained, to be in charge of dog

Ill treatment or failure to ensure welfare needs of dog, where not charged separately

Dog known to be prohibited

Lack or loss of control of dog due to influence of alcohol or drugs

Offence committed against those working in the public sector or providing a service to the public

Established evidence of community impact

Failure to comply with current court orders

Offence committed whilst on licence

Factors reducing seriousness or reflecting personal mitigation

No previous convictions **or** no relevant/recent convictions

Isolated incident

No previous complaints against, or incidents involving, the dog

Remorse

Good character and/or exemplary conduct

Evidence of responsible ownership

Determination and/or demonstration of steps taken to address addiction or offending behaviour

Serious medical conditions requiring urgent, intensive or long-term treatment

Age and/or lack of maturity where it affects the responsibility of the offender

Mental disorder or learning disability, where not linked to the commission of the offence

Sole or primary carer for dependent relatives

Step Three
Consider any factors which indicate a reduction, such as assistance to the prosecution

The court should take into account sections 73 and 74 of the Serious Organised Crime and Police Act 2005 (assistance by defendants: reduction or review of sentence) and any other rule of law by virtue of which an offender may receive a discounted sentence in consequence of assistance given (or offered) to the prosecutor or investigator.

Step Four
Reduction for guilty pleas

The court should take account of any potential reduction for a guilty plea in accordance with section 144 of the Criminal Justice Act 2003 and the *Guilty Plea* guideline.

Step Five
Compensation and ancillary orders

In all cases, the court should consider whether to make a compensation order and/or other ancillary orders.

Compensation order

The court should consider compensation orders in all cases where personal injury, loss or damage has resulted from the offence.[1] The court must give reasons if it decides not to award compensation in such cases.

Other ancillary orders available include:

Disqualification from having custody of a dog

The court **may** disqualify the offender from having custody of a dog.[2] The test the court should consider is whether the offender is a fit and proper person to have custody of a dog.

Destruction order/contingent destruction order

In any case where the offender is not the owner of the dog, the owner must be given an opportunity to be present and make representations to the court.

The court **shall** make a destruction order unless the court is satisfied that the dog would not constitute a danger to public safety.[3]

In reaching a decision, the court should consider the relevant circumstances which include:

- the incident – what degree of harm was caused by the dog's behaviour?

- past behaviour of the dog – is this an isolated incident or have there been previous warnings or incidents? and

- owner's character – is the owner a fit and proper person to own this particular dog?

If the court is satisfied that the dog would not constitute a danger to public safety, it **shall** make a contingent destruction order imposing certain available conditions.[4] A contingent destruction order should specify the measures to be taken by the owner for keeping the dog under proper control, which include:

- muzzling;

- keeping on a lead;

- neutering in appropriate cases; and

- excluding it from a specified place.[5]

Where the court makes a destruction order, it **may** order the offender to pay what it determines to be the reasonable expenses of destroying the dog and of keeping it pending its destruction.[6]

Step Six
Totality principle

If sentencing an offender for more than one offence, or where the offender is already serving a sentence, consider whether the total sentence is just and proportionate to the offending behaviour.

Step Seven
Reasons

Section 174 of the Criminal Justice Act 2003 imposes a duty to give reasons for, and explain the effect of, the sentence.

Step Eight
Consideration for remand time

Sentencers should take into consideration any remand time served in relation to the final sentence at this final step. The court should consider whether to give credit for time spent on remand in custody or on bail in accordance with sections 240 and 240A of the Criminal Justice Act 2003.

---

[1]   Powers of Criminal Courts (Sentencing) Act 2000, s 130.

[2]   Dangerous Dogs Act 1991, s 4(1)(b).

[3]   Dangerous Dogs Act 1991, s 4(1)(a).

[4]   Dangerous Dogs Act 1991, s 4A(4).

[5]   Dangerous Dogs Act 1991, s 4A(5).

[6]   Dangerous Dogs Act 1991, s 4(4)(b).

A[72.8A]

For structure of the sentencing decision see also **B[3.6]**.

Owner or person in charge of a dog dangerously out of control in a public place
Dangerous Dogs Act 1991 (section 3(1))

Owner or person in charge allowing a dog to be in a private place where the dog is not permitted to be, which makes a person fear injury
Dangerous Dogs Act 1991 (section 3(3)(b))

Triable summarily only

Maximum: 26 weeks' custody

Offence range: Discharge – 26 weeks' custody

Step One
Determining the offence category

The court should determine the offence category using the table below.

Category 1	Greater harm **and** higher culpability
Category 2	Greater harm **and** lower culpability; **or** lesser harm **and** higher culpability
Category 3	Lesser harm **and** lower culpability

The court should determine culpability and harm caused or intended, by reference **only** to the factors below, which comprise the principal factual elements of the offence. Where an offence does not fall squarely into a category, individual factors may require a degree of weighting before making an overall assessment and determining the appropriate offence category.

Factors indicating greater harm

Presence of children or others who are vulnerable because of personal circumstances

Injury to another animal(s)

Factors indicating lesser harm

Low risk to the public

Factors indicating higher culpability

Statutory aggravating factors:

Offence racially or religiously aggravated

Offence motivated by, or demonstrating, hostility to the victim based on his or her sexual orientation (or presumed sexual orientation)

Offence motivated by, or demonstrating, hostility to the victim based on the victim's disability (or presumed disability)

Other aggravating factors:

Failure to respond to warnings or concerns expressed by others about the dog's behaviour

Goading, or allowing goading, of dog

Dog used as weapon or to intimidate victim

Offence motivated by, or demonstrating, hostility based on the victim's age, sex, gender identity (or presumed gender identity)

Factors indicating lower culpability

Attempts made to regain control of dog and/or intervene

Provocation of dog without fault of the offender

Evidence of safety or control measures having been taken

Mental disorder or learning disability, where linked to the commission of the offence

Step Two
Starting point and category range

Having determined the category, the court should use the corresponding starting points to reach a sentence within the category range below. The starting point applies to all offenders irrespective of plea or previous convictions. A case of particular gravity, reflected by multiple features of culpability or harm in step 1, could merit upward adjustment from the starting point before further adjustment for aggravating or mitigating features, set out on the next page.

Offence Category	Starting Point *(Applicable to all offenders)*	Category Range *(Applicable to all offenders)*
Category 1	Medium level community order	Band C fine – 26 weeks' custody
Category 2	Band B fine	Band A fine – Low level community order
Category 3	Band A fine	Discharge – Band B fine

The table below contains a **non-exhaustive** list of additional factual elements providing the context of the offence and factors relating to the offender. Identify whether any combination of these, or other relevant factors, should result in an upward or downward adjustment from the starting point. In some cases, having considered these factors, it may be appropriate to move outside the identified category range.

When sentencing **category 1** offences, the court should also consider the custody threshold as follows:

- has the custody threshold been passed?
- if so, is it unavoidable that a custodial sentence be imposed?
- if so, can that sentence be suspended?

When sentencing **category 1 or 2** offences, the court should also consider the community order threshold as follows:

- has the community order threshold been passed?

Factors increasing seriousness

Statutory aggravating factors:

Previous convictions, having regard to a) the nature of the offence to which the conviction relates and its relevance to the current offence; and b) the time that has elapsed since the conviction

Offence committed whilst on bail

Other aggravating factors include:

Location of the offence

Ongoing effect upon the victim and/or others

Failure to take adequate precautions to prevent dog escaping

Allowing person insufficiently experienced or trained, to be in charge of dog

Ill treatment or failure to ensure welfare needs of dog, where not charged separately

Dog known to be prohibited

Lack or loss of control of dog due to the influence of alcohol or drugs

Offence committed against those working in the public sector or providing a service to the public

Established evidence of community impact

Failure to comply with current court orders

Offence committed whilst on licence

Factors reducing seriousness or reflecting personal mitigation

No previous convictions **or** no relevant/recent convictions

Isolated incident

No previous complaints against, or incidents involving, the dog

Remorse

Good character and/or exemplary conduct

Evidence of responsible ownership

Determination and/or demonstration of steps taken to address addiction or offending behaviour

Serious medical conditions requiring urgent, intensive or long-term treatment

Age and/or lack of maturity where it affects the responsibility of the offender

Mental disorder or learning disability, where not linked to the commission of the offence

Sole or primary carer for dependent relatives

Step Three
Consider any factors which indicate a reduction, such as assistance to the prosecution

The court should take into account sections 73 and 74 of the Serious Organised Crime and Police Act 2005 (assistance by defendants: reduction or review of sentence) and any other rule of law by virtue of which an offender may receive a discounted sentence in consequence of assistance given (or offered) to the prosecutor or investigator.

Step Four
Reduction for guilty pleas

The court should take account of any potential reduction for a guilty plea in accordance with section 144 of the Criminal Justice Act 2003 and the *Guilty Plea* guideline.

Step Five
Compensation and ancillary orders

In all cases, the court should consider whether to make a compensation order and/or other ancillary orders.

Compensation order

The court should consider compensation orders in all cases where personal injury, loss or damage has resulted from the offence.[7] The court must give reasons if it decides not to award compensation in such cases.

Other ancillary orders available include:

Disqualification from having custody of a dog

The court **may** disqualify the offender from having custody of a dog.[8] The test the court should consider is whether the offender is a fit and proper person to have custody of a dog.

Destruction order/contingent destruction order

In any case where the offender is not the owner of the dog, the owner must be given an opportunity to be present and make representations to the court.

The court **may** make a destruction order.[9] Alternatively, it **may** make a contingent destruction order imposing certain available conditions.[10] A contingent destruction order should specify the measures to be taken by the owner for keeping the dog under proper control, which include:

- muzzling;
- keeping on a lead;
- neutering in appropriate cases; and
- excluding it from a specified place.[11]

In reaching a decision, the court should consider the relevant circumstances which include:

- the incident – what degree of harm was caused by the dog's behaviour?
- past behaviour of the dog – is this an isolated incident or have there been previous warnings or incidents? and
- owner's character – is the owner a fit and proper person to own this particular dog?

Where the court makes a destruction order, it **may** order the offender to pay what it determines to be the reasonable expenses of destroying the dog and of keeping it pending its destruction.[12]

---

[7]   Section 130 Powers of Criminal Courts (Sentencing) Act 2000.

[8]   Section 4(1)(b) of the Dangerous Dogs Act 1991.

[9]   Section 4(1)(a) of the Dangerous Dogs Act 1991.

[10]   Section 4A(4) of the Dangerous Dogs Act 1991.

[11]   Section 4A(5) of the Dangerous Dogs Act 1991.

[12]   Section 4(4)(b) of the Dangerous Dogs Act 1991.

Step Six
Totality principle

If sentencing an offender for more than one offence, or where the offender is already serving a sentence, consider whether the total sentence is just and proportionate to the offending behaviour.

Step Seven
Reasons

Section 174 of the Criminal Justice Act 2003 imposes a duty to give reasons for, and explain the effect of, the sentence.

Step Eight
Consideration for remand time

Sentencers should take into consideration any remand time served in relation to the final sentence at this final step. The court should consider whether to give credit for time spent on remand in custody or on bail in accordance with sections 240 and 240A of the Criminal Justice Act 2003.

Possession of a prohibited dog
Dangerous Dogs Act 1991 (section 1(3))

Breeding, selling, exchanging or advertising a prohibited dog
Dangerous Dogs Act 1991 (section 1(2))

Triable only summarily

Maximum: 26 weeks' custody

Offence range: Discharge – 26 weeks' custody

Step One
Determining the offence category

The court should determine the offence category using the table below.

Category 1	Greater harm **and** higher culpability
Category 2	Greater harm **or** higher culpability
Category 3	**Neither** greater harm **nor** higher culpability

The court should determine culpability and harm caused or intended, by reference **only** to the factors below, which comprise the principal factual elements of the offence. Where an offence does not fall squarely into a category, individual factors may require a degree of weighting before making an overall assessment and determining the appropriate offence category.

Factors indicating greater harm

Injury to person

Injury to another animal(s)

Factors indicating higher culpability

Possessing a dog known to be prohibited

Breeding from a dog known to be prohibited

Selling, exchanging or advertising a dog known to be prohibited

Offence committed for gain

Dog used to threaten or intimidate

Permitting fighting

Training and/or possession of paraphernalia for dog fighting

Step Two
Starting point and category range

Having determined the category, the court should use the corresponding starting points to reach a sentence within the category range below. The starting point applies to all offenders irrespective of plea or previous convictions. A case of particular gravity, reflected by multiple features of culpability or harm in step 1, could merit upward adjustment from the starting point before further adjustment for aggravating or mitigating features, set out on the next page.

Offence Category	Starting Point *(Applicable to all offenders)*	Category Range *(Applicable to all offenders)*
Category 1	Medium level community order	Band C fine – 26 weeks' custody
Category 2	Band C fine	Band A fine – Medium level community order
Category 3	Band A fine	Discharge – Band B fine

* Imprisonment is not available if the provisions of s 1(7) Dangerous Dogs Act 1991 apply

The table below contains a **non-exhaustive** list of additional factual elements providing the context of the offence and factors relating to the offender. Identify whether any combination of these, or other relevant factors, should result in an upward or downward adjustment from the starting point. In some cases, having considered these factors, it may be appropriate to move outside the identified category range.

When sentencing **category 1** offences, the court should also consider the custody threshold as follows:

- has the custody threshold been passed?

- if so, is it unavoidable that a custodial sentence be imposed?

- if so, can that sentence be suspended?

When sentencing **category 1 or 2** offences, the court should also consider the community order threshold as follows:

- has the community order threshold been passed?

Factors increasing seriousness

Statutory aggravating factors:

Previous convictions, having regard to a) the nature of the offence to which the conviction relates and its relevance to the current offence; and b) the time that has elapsed since the conviction

Offence committed whilst on bail

Other aggravating factors include:

Presence of children or others who are vulnerable because of personal circumstances

Ill treatment or failure to ensure welfare needs of dog, where not charged separately

Established evidence of community impact

Failure to comply with current court orders

Offence committed whilst on licence

Factors reducing seriousness or reflecting personal mitigation

No previous convictions **or** no relevant/recent convictions

Unaware that dog was prohibited type despite reasonable efforts to identify type

Evidence of safety or control measures having been taken by owner

Prosecution results from owner notification

Remorse

Good character and/or exemplary conduct

Evidence of responsible ownership

Determination and/or demonstration of steps taken to address addiction or offending behaviour

Serious medical conditions requiring urgent, intensive or long-term treatment

Age and/or lack of maturity where it affects the responsibility of the offender

Lapse of time since the offence where this is not the fault of the offender

Mental disorder or learning disability

Sole or primary carer for dependent relatives

Step Three
Consider any factors which indicate a reduction, such as assistance to the prosecution

The court should take into account sections 73 and 74 of the Serious Organised Crime and Police Act 2005 (assistance by defendants: reduction or review of sentence) and any other rule of law by virtue of which an offender may receive a discounted sentence in consequence of assistance given (or offered) to the prosecutor or investigator.

Step Four
Reduction for guilty pleas

The court should take account of any potential reduction for a guilty plea in accordance with section 144 of the Criminal Justice Act 2003 and the *Guilty Plea* guideline.

Step Five
Ancillary orders

In all cases, the court should consider whether to make any ancillary orders.

Ancillary orders available include:

Disqualification from having custody of a dog

The court **may** disqualify the offender from having custody of a dog.[13] The test the court should consider is whether the offender is a fit and proper person to have custody of a dog.

Destruction order/contingent destruction order

The court **shall** make a destruction order unless the court is satisfied that the dog would not constitute a danger to public safety.[14]

In reaching a decision, the court should consider the relevant circumstances which include:

- danger to the public – what is the potential risk of harm posed by the dog?

- behaviour of the dog – have there been any warnings or incidents involving the dog? and

- owner's character – is the owner a fit and proper person to own this particular dog?

If the court does not make a destruction order, the court **shall** make a contingent destruction order providing that unless the dog is exempted from the prohibition within two months it shall be destroyed.[15] Statutory procedures and conditions automatically apply to exempted dogs and no other conditions can be imposed.[16] Where the offender is the owner of the dog, it would not normally be appropriate to make a contingent destruction order in conjunction with a disqualification order.

Furthermore, the court **must not** transfer ownership of the dog to another. [17]

Where the court makes a destruction order, it **may** order the offender to pay what it determines to be the reasonable expenses of destroying the dog and of keeping it pending its destruction.[18]

---

[13]   Section 4(1)(b) of the Dangerous Dogs Act 1991.

[14]   Section4(1)(a) of the Dangerous Dogs Act 1991.

[15]   Section4A(1) of the Dangerous Dogs Act 1991.

[16]   The Dangerous Dogs Compensation and Exemption Schemes Order 1991 SI 1991/1744 (as amended by The Dangerous Dogs Compensation and Exemption Schemes (Amendment) Order 1991, SI 1991/2297).

[17]   Section 1(2)(b) of the Dangerous Dogs Act 1991.

[18]   Section 4(4)(b) of the Dangerous Dogs Act 1991.

Step Six
Totality principle

If sentencing an offender for more than one offence, or where the offender is already serving a sentence, consider whether the total sentence is just and proportionate to the offending behaviour.

Step Seven
Reasons

Section 174 of the Criminal Justice Act 2003 imposes a duty to give reasons for, and explain the effect of, the sentence.

Step Eight
Consideration for remand time

Sentencers should take into consideration any remand time served in relation to the final sentence at this final step. The court should consider whether to give credit for time spent on remand in custody or on bail in accordance with sections 240 and 240A of the Criminal Justice Act 2003.

A[72.9]

Available sentences. See Table B at **B[4.2]**; for aggravated offences see Table A at **B[4.1]**. In *R v Cox* (2004) Times, 20 February, CA a sentence of 3 months was upheld for an aggravated offence where a pack of dogs attacked a child resulting in hospitalisation.

A[72.10]–[72.14]

Order for destruction. Before making a destruction order the court must consider ss 4(1A)(a), 4A(4) and 4A(5) – see **A[72.15]** below. Where a person is convicted of an offence under s 3(1) or s 3(3) the court may order the destruction of the dog and must do so in the case of an aggravated offence, unless the court is satisfied the dog does not constitute a danger to public safety. A court should not make an order for destruction without giving the dog's owner an opportunity to be heard (*R v Ealing Magistrates' Court, ex p Fanneran* (1995) 160 JP 409, 8 Admin LR 351). Any person having custody of the dog may be required to deliver it up to a person appointed by the court to undertake its destruction which will be suspended pending the determination of any appeal. Note that disobedience of a court order to deliver up for destruction is a criminal offence. The maximum penalty under these provisions is a level 5 fine.

A[72.15]

Order for contingent destruction. Section 4(1A) of the Dangerous Dogs Act 1991 allows for a contingent destruction order even if a mandatory or discretionary order is appropriate. For example, the court may order that the dog will be destroyed unless the owner keeps it under proper control, and that it was to be muzzled and on a lead at all times in any public place. The legal principles were outlined in *R v Flack* [2008] EWCA Crim 204, [2008] 2 Cr App Rep (S) 395; *R v Grant David Robert Davies* [2010] EWCA Crim 1923, 174 CL&J 574.

The Crown Court had no power to impose conditions when it made contingent destruction orders under the Dangerous Dogs Act 1991, s 4A in relation to two pit bull terriers, the possession of which was prohibited under s 1 of the Act: *R (on the application of Sandhu) v Isleworth Crown Court* [2012] EWHC 1658 (Admin), 176 JP 537, 176 CL&J 339.

A[72.16]

Additional powers. A person convicted under s 3(1) or (3) may be ordered to keep the dog under proper control or failing that the dog shall be destroyed. The court may also specify measures for keeping the dog under proper control such as muzzling, keeping on a lead or excluding the dog from entering specific places. The court may also order a male dog to be neutered.

A[72.17]

Disqualification. Whether or not there is an order for destruction of the dog the court may disqualify the person convicted (ie not necessarily the owner) for having custody of a dog for a period specified in the order. A person disqualified for having custody of a dog may apply to the court after one year to terminate the disqualification having regard to his character, conduct and any other circumstances (*R v Holland* [2002] EWCA Crim 1585, [2002] All ER (D) 113 (Jun), CA). Where an application is refused, no further application can be considered for a further year. Costs may be awarded.

Note there is no power to make a disqualification order under s 4(1)(b) that would allow for a single dog to be kept, nor is there power to attach other conditions (*R v Haynes* [2004] EWCA Crim 390, (2004) Times, 27 February, [2004] All ER (D) 235 (Mar), CA).

A[72.18]

Having custody of a dog in contravention of a disqualification is an offence, maximum penalty a fine on level 5.

A[72.19]

Right to appeal to the Crown Court. A person convicted of an offence has an automatic right to appeal to the Crown Court against his conviction, sentence or any order made. In addition, where an order has been made for the destruction of a dog owned by a person other than the offender, then, unless the order was one which the court was required to make the owner may appeal to the Crown Court against the destruction order.

Other offences

A[72.20]

The Dangerous Dogs Act 1991 creates a number of offences in connection with 'fighting dogs' which are defined as pit bull terriers, Japanese Tosas and other dogs specified by the Secretary of State. It is unlawful to breed, sell, exchange, advertise for sale or to make a gift of such a dog. Accordingly, these dogs will decline in numbers with the effluxion of time. Those persons who already possess such dogs must obtain a certificate of exemption and comply with the stringent conditions attached thereto. It is an offence for an owner to have such a dog which is not registered, or to abandon it. The most common charge is for the owner or person for the time being in charge of such a dog to allow it to stray or to be in a public place without being muzzled and kept on a lead: maximum penalty 6 months' imprisonment (**51 weeks) and a level 5 fine – triable only by magistrates. It should be noted that a dog 'of the type known as a pit bull terrier' is not to be taken as being synonymous with the definition breed (*R v Crown Court at Knightsbridge, ex p Dunne* [1993] 4 All ER 491, [1994] 1 WLR 296). The provisions relating to destruction and disqualification apply as for 'aggravated offences' under s 3 of the 1991 Act. Except that where no destruction order is made in the case of a designated dog, the court must order that unless a certificate of exemption is obtained for the dog within two months of the date of the order the dog shall be destroyed. If a certificate is not obtained the court has a discretion to extend the two-month period.

Control or destruction order

(Dogs Act 1871, as amended)

A[72.21]

As an alternative to prosecution under the Dangerous Dogs Act 1991 the pre-existing civil remedy under the Dogs Act 1871 is still available and is not confined to public places nor where the dog has injured a person, but is determined by where the dog resides (*R (on the application of Shufflebottom) v Chief Constable of Greater Manchester Police* [2003] EWHC 246 (Admin), 167 JP 153). The introduction of a national jurisdiction under the Courts Act 2003 means that the case could be heard at any venue within England and Wales. In practice, jurisdiction will usually be exercised by reference to residence or where the cause of action arose.

Legal notes and definitions

A[72.22]

Application for dangerous dog to be kept under control or destroyed.

Application may be made to a magistrates' court for an order that the dog be destroyed or kept under proper control by the owner. The magistrates may in their discretion make a destruction order without the option of a control order. A dog is not allowed his 'one bite' although in most cases a control order is sufficient for the first transgression. Costs can be awarded by the court to the successful party.

A[72.23]

The proceedings must be in the form of a **complaint** and not as an **information** for an offence.

A[72.24]

The court must be satisfied (a) that the dog *is* dangerous and (b) that it *is* not kept under proper control. The dog need not be dangerous to mankind. It is sufficient if it is proved that the dog injured cattle or chased sheep. It need not be proved that the owner knew his dog was dangerous. Moreover the dog need not be dangerous by temperament if he is shown to have been dangerous on one occasion. Evidence of the temperament of the animal, however, is admissible if it shows the likelihood of its being dangerous on a particular occasion. The correct approach is for the justices to ask themselves whether on the facts the behaviour of the dog showed that it had a dangerous disposition (*Briscoe v Shattock* [1999] 1 WLR 432, 163 JP 201, [1999] Crim LR 396).

A[72.25]–[72.30]

Change of ownership. If the owner of the dog establishes in court that he is no longer the owner of the dog but has made a bona fide transfer of the dog to some other person no order can be made against him for the dog's destruction or its proper control; but the order can be made against the new owner provided that a complaint is made against the new owner within six months from the date of the cause of the complaint.

A[72.31]

Procedure at the hearing. If the **complaint** is accompanied by an **information** alleging some additional offence (such as worrying livestock) then the **information** should be dealt with first and the **complaint** afterwards. The legal adviser should be consulted in such cases.

A[72.32]

Control order. The court may specify the measures to be taken for keeping the dog under proper control, whether by muzzling, keeping on a lead, excluding it from specified places, or otherwise. Where the dog is male, the court may order it to be neutered if thereby it would be less dangerous.

A[72.33]

Destruction order. Any person having custody of the dog may be required to deliver it up to a person appointed by the court to undertake its destruction which will be suspended pending the determination of any appeal.

A[72.34]

Disqualification. A court which makes a destruction order may disqualify the owner for having custody of a dog for a period specified in the order. Disqualification may also be imposed on conviction of an offence of failure to comply with a court order (either to keep the dog under proper control or deliver it up for destruction), maximum penalty a fine on level 3.

A[72.35]

A person disqualified for having custody of a dog may apply to the court after one year to terminate the disqualification having regard to his character, conduct and any other circumstances. Where an application is refused, no further application can be considered for a further year. Costs may be awarded.

A[72.36]

Disobedience of a court order for control or to deliver up for destruction is a criminal offence, maximum penalty a fine on level 3.

A[72.37]

Having custody of a dog in contravention of a disqualification is an offence, maximum penalty a fine on level 5.

A[72.38]

Right of appeal to the Crown Court. If an order is made for control or destruction, the owner can appeal to the Crown Court. Appeal against conviction and sentence for the criminal offences lie to the Crown Court in the normal way.

A[73]

Dog worrying livestock

Charge

A[73.1]

Being the owner of (or being in charge of) a dog worrying livestock namely [. . . . .] on agricultural land situated at [. . . . .]

Dogs (Protection of Livestock) Act 1953, s 1, as amended

Maximum penalty – Fine level 3.

Legal notes and definitions

A[73.2]

A dog's owner or the person in charge of a dog commits an offence if the dog worries livestock on agricultural land. A prosecution for livestock worrying can only be brought by or with the consent of the chief officer of the police, or by the occupier of the agricultural land or the owner of the livestock.

A[73.3]

Worrying livestock means:

(a)   attacking livestock; or
(b)   chasing livestock in such a way as may reasonably be expected to cause injury or suffering to the livestock, or abortion or loss or diminution in their produce; or
(c)   being at large in a field where there are sheep except a dog owned by or in the charge of the occupier or the owner of the sheep or a person authorised by them or a police dog, guide-dog, trained sheep dog, working gun dog or pack of hounds.

Livestock is extensively defined by s 3 of the Act and means cattle, sheep, goats, swine, horses or poultry.

A[73.4]

Possible lines of defence

(a)   That the livestock were trespassing and the dog in question was owned by or in the charge of the occupier of the land on which the livestock were trespassing or the dog was in the charge of a person authorised by the occupier of the land. This defence is not available if the dog was deliberately set on the livestock.
(b)   The owner of the dog is not liable if at the time of the attack on the livestock the dog was in the custody of a person whom the owner considered to be a fit and proper person to have charge of the dog.

(c)   That the worrying took place on land that was not agricultural land. A street or a private garden is not therefore agricultural land and some moors and heaths are excluded from the definitions of agricultural land.

(d)   That the Ministry of Agriculture, Fisheries and Food has directed that this offence shall not apply to the land in question.

A[73.5]

No SC guideline. For structure of the sentencing decision see B[3.6].

A[73.6]

Fines. See B[33.16].

A[73.7]

Compensation. This may be ordered up to a maximum of £5,000 on each charge, eg for the loss of livestock, either as part of a wider sentence or by itself as a substantive penalty. If the offender's means are limited and a monetary penalty is appropriate, preference must be given to ordering compensation instead of a fine.

A[74]

Excessive noise
(Prosecution)

A[74.1]

Problems caused by noise amounting to a nuisance, eg caused by noisy neighbours, are dealt with by proceedings for a nuisance order, see A[84].

Causing a noise or disturbance on National Health Service premises is now an offence contrary to s 119 of the Criminal Justice and Immigration Act 2008. By s 120 a constable or 'authorised person' may remove persons causing a noise or disturbance from NHS premises.

Maximum penalty – Fine level 3.

Night time charge

A[74.2]

Operating a loudspeaker in a street between 9 p.m. and 8 a.m.

Control of Pollution Act 1974, s 62

Maximum penalty – Fine level 5 (and a further fine not exceeding £50 for each day on which the offence continues after the conviction). The notes which follow only apply to proceedings brought under the Control of Pollution Act 1974, s 62 and magistrates should confirm with their legal adviser that the proceedings are in fact being brought under that Act.

Legal notes and definitions

A[74.3]

In certain circumstances loudspeakers are exempt from prosecutions as follows:

(a)　　those used by the police, fire, ambulance, water authority or local authority;

(b)　　those used for communicating with a vessel to direct it or any other vessel;

(c)   those forming part of the public telephone system;

(d)   those fitted to vehicles solely for the entertainment of persons in the vehicle or for communicating with persons in the vehicle or for giving warning to other vehicles if the loudspeaker forms part of the vehicle's horns or warning system but all such loudspeakers fitted to vehicles must not operate so loudly that they give reasonable cause for annoyance to persons in the vicinity or the exemption is forfeited;

(e)   transport undertakings may use loudspeakers off the highways to make announcements to passengers, prospective passengers and staff;

(f)   a travelling showman may use a loudspeaker on his fairground;

(g)   loudspeakers may be used in an emergency.

Except for the above exemptions there is a complete ban on the use of loudspeakers in a street between 9 pm and 8 am.

A[74.4]

Loudspeaker. Includes a megaphone and any other device for amplifying sound.

A[74.5]

Street. Means any highway, road, footway, square or court which is for the time being open to the public.

Day time charge

A[74.6]

Operating a loudspeaker in a street between 8 a.m. and 9 p.m. for the purpose of advertising an entertainment, a trade or a business

Control of Pollution Act 1974, s 62

Maximum penalty – Fine level 5 (and a further fine not exceeding £50 for each day on which the offence continues after the conviction).

Legal notes and definitions

A[74.7]

See under this heading at A[74.3].

A[74.8]

Defences. It is permissible to use a loudspeaker in a street between the hours of 8 a.m. and 9 p.m. except as outlined above for advertising. However, there is an exception to this ban on advertising in the following circumstances. Where the loudspeaker is:

(a)   fixed to a vehicle conveying a perishable commodity for human consumption; and

(b)   is used solely to inform the public (otherwise than by words) that the commodity is on sale from the vehicle; and

(c)   is so operated as not to give reasonable cause for annoyance to persons in the vicinity,

it may be operated between the hours of noon and 7 p.m. on the same day. This is the provision, for example, under which ice cream vans are allowed to use chimes to advertise their wares.

Sentencing

A[74.9]

No SC Guideline.

Noise amounting to a statutory nuisance. If a noise is persistent and seriously affects persons in an area then the local authority may serve a noise abatement notice or the person affected can lay a complaint alleging that the noise or vibration amounts to a statutory nuisance. See **A[84]**.

A[75]

Offences relating to unfair or prohibited commercial practices

Offences

A[75.1]

(From 26/5/08 s 1 of the Trade Description Act 1968 offences were repealed and replaced by a series of new offences contrary to the Consumer Protection from Unfair Trading Regulations 2008.)

Offence 1: Commercial practice contrary to professional diligence

(1) A trader is guilty of an offence if –

(a)   he knowingly or recklessly engages in a commercial practice which contravenes the requirements of professional diligence under regulation 3 (3) (a); and

(b)   the practice materially distorts or is likely to materially distort the commercial behaviour of the average consumer with regard to the product under regulation 3 (3) (b).

Regulation 8 of the Consumer Protection from Unfair Trading Regulations 2008

Offence 2: Commercial practice which is misleading

A trader is guilty of an offence if he engages in a commercial practice which is a misleading action under regulation 5 otherwise than by reason of the commercial practice satisfying the condition in regulation 5 (3) (b).

Regulation 9 of the Consumer Protection from Unfair Trading Regulations 2008

Offence 3: Commercial practice – misleading omission

A trader is guilty of an offence if he engages in a commercial practice which is a misleading omission under regulation 6.

Regulation 10 of the Consumer Protection from Unfair Trading Regulations 2008

Offence 4: Commercial practice – aggressive practice

A trader is guilty of an offence if he engages in commercial practice which is aggressive under regulation 17.

Regulation 11 of the Consumer Protection from Unfair Trading Regulations 2008

Offence 5: Banned commercial practices – contravenes schedule 1 (except paragraphs 11 and 28)

A trader is guilty of an offence if he engages in a commercial practice set out in any of the paragraphs 1 to 10, 12 to 27 and 29 to 31 of Schedule 1.

Regulation 12 of the Consumer Protection from Unfair Trading Regulations 2008

Maximum penalty in each case – Fine statutory maximum (currently £5,000 per offence). Triable either way.

Crown Court – 2 years' imprisonment and unlimited fine.

Mode of trial

A[75.2]
See general notes at I[4].

Legal notes and definitions

A[75.3]
General. This is a detailed piece of legislation. A detailed three-part commentary to the 2008 regulations can be found at (2008) 172 JPN 516, 536 and 560 respectively.

Time limits for prosecution. These are provided for by regulation 14 and are similar to the repealed Trade Descriptions Act 1968.

Offences committed by bodies of persons. See regulation 15

A[75.4]
Mens rea – regulation 8. Creates the only one of the five offence provisions which includes an element of mens rea. Regulation 8(2) defines the term "recklessly". It is submitted that it will suffice if the prosecution can show that the defendant trader did not have regard to the truth or falsity of his statement even though it cannot be shown that he was deliberately closing his eyes to the truth, or that he had any kind of dishonest mind.

A[75.5]
Defences. Offence due to the act or default of another person – regulation 16 (applies to prosecutions under regulations 9–12).

Due diligence offence – regulation 17 (applies to prosecutions under regulations 9–12)

Innocent publication of advertisement – regulation 18 (applies to prosecutions under regulations 9–12)

A[75.6]

Definitions. Commercial practice: "Any act, omission, course of conduct, representation or commercial communication (including advertising and marketing), by a trader, which is directly connected with the promotion, sale or supply of a product to or from consumers, whether occurring before, during or after a commercial transaction (if any) in relation to a product".

Consumer: "Any individual who in relation to a commercial practice is acting for purposes which are outside his business".

Product: "Any goods or service and includes immovable property, rights and obligations".

Transactional decision: "Any decision taken by a consumer, whether it is to act or to refrain from acting, concerning (a) whether, how and on what terms to purchase, make payment in whole or in part for, retain or dispose of a product; or (b) whether, how and on what terms to exercise a contractual right in relation to a product".

Trader: "Any person who in relation to a commercial practice is acting for purposes relating to his business (including acting in the name of or on behalf of a trader)".

Sentencing

A[75.7]

No SC guideline.

Unlike most either way offences, and by analogy most trade description offences did not carry imprisonment on summary conviction. Therefore, community penalties were not available because the offence or offences were not "serious enough" to warrant such a disposal and because they are now expressly excluded under the Criminal Justice and Immigration Act 2008. See *R v Docklands Estates Ltd* (2000) 164 JP 505, [2000] 3 EGLR 17, [2000] 45 EG 175, CA, for fines levels and *R v Richards* [2004] EWCA Crim 192, [2004] All ER (D) 15 (Mar) for elements likely to take the case over the custody threshold in the Crown Court. In *R v Bore* [2004] EWCA Crim 1452, [2005] All ER (D) 12 (Feb) a conditional discharge was imposed on appeal for selling 27 falsely autographed photographs and costs of £1,000 quashed as wholly excessive.

In *R v Penfold* [2007] All ER (D) 179 (Jun) for applying a false trade description to a pony the Court of Appeal said that a fine of £200 and £500 costs was appropriate where the defendant pleaded guilty on the first day of trial.

A[75.8]

Compensation. This may be ordered up to £5,000 either as part of a wider sentence or by itself as a substantive penalty. If the offender's means are limited and a monetary penalty is appropriate, preference must be given to ordering compensation instead of a fine.

A[75.9]

Crown Court. Prison is appropriate only where there has been a deliberate dishonesty. Prison has been upheld in cases involving dishonest dealers eg traders who deliberately "clock" motor vehicles.

A[75.10]

Fines. See B[33].

A[76]

Firearm (purchasing etc without certificate)

Charge

A[76.1]

Purchasing or acquiring or possessing a firearm (or ammunition) without certificate

Firearms Act 1968, s 1

For shotguns see **A[71]**.

Maximum penalty – Fine level 5 and 6 months (****12 months**) and forfeiture. Triable either way.

Crown Court – 5 years' imprisonment and unlimited fine.

Mode of trial

A[76.2]

See general notes at I[4].

Legal notes and definitions

A[76.3]

Purchasing, acquiring and wrongly possessing. These are three separate offences and the charge should only include one of these allegations. Possession can include where a person has a firearm in his custody for another for the purpose of cleaning it, and is not restricted to physical possession but includes proprietary control (*R v Pawlicki and Swindells* [1992] 3 All ER 902, [1992] 1 WLR 827, CA). More than one person can control a firearm at the same time (*R v Hall-Chung* [2002] EWCA Crim 3088, [2003] All ER (D) 113 (Feb)).

A[76.4]

Excessive ammunition. It is also an offence to have in one's possession more ammunition than the quantity authorised by a firearms certificate.

A[76.5]

Certificate. This is granted by the police. It may specify conditions. Failure to observe such conditions is an offence. The certificate may bear a photograph of the holder and, unless revoked or cancelled, remains in force for the period specified which may be up to three years.

A[76.6]

Firearm. This means any lethal barrelled weapon of any kind from which any shot, bullet or missile can be discharged. A lethal weapon includes one capable of inflicting injury although not designed to do so, eg a signal pistol. An imitation firearm which is so constructed or adapted as to be readily converted into a firearm is to be treated as a firearm even though it has not been so converted. Two fingers inside the defendant's pocket cannot constitute possession of an imitation firearm under s 17(2) of the Act (*R v Bentham* [2005] UKHL 18, [2005] 2 All ER 65, HL)).

A[76.7]

A smooth bore shotgun with a barrel of 24 inches or more with a bore not exceeding two inches and which is not a revolver nor has an illegal magazine is not a firearm as far as this offence is concerned; nor normally are air guns, air rifles or air pistols unless the Home Secretary declares them to be of a specially dangerous type. This now includes high powered air weapons (Brococks) and all disguised weapons including those designed for use only when submerged in water (HOC 1/2004). However, an air weapon may be found to be a 'lethal' barrelled weapon capable of killing vermin etc, for the purposes of s 21(2) Firearms Act 1968 (possession of a firearm within five years of release from prison). The Court of Appeal has ruled that a starting pistol which could be adapted to fire bullets if the barrel was drilled was a firearm. In this case the barrel was partly drilled (*R v Freeman* [1970] 2 All ER 413, [1970] 1 WLR 788, CA).

A[76.8]

Ammunition. Means ammunition for any firearm as defined above. It also means grenades, bombs and other similar missiles. It also includes ammunition containing or adapted to contain any noxious liquid, gas or other noxious thing.

A[76.9]

Exemptions. If a defence is raised that a weapon or ammunition is not covered by the Act the legal adviser should be consulted.

A[76.10]–[76.15]

Certain persons and organisations are exempted from having to hold firearms certificates such as the following:

(a)   A registered dealer and his staff, an auctioneer, carrier or warehouseman in the course of his business, a licensed slaughterer in respect of his slaughtering instruments, ships and aircraft (Firearms Act 1968, ss 8–10 and 13).

(b)   A person may carry a firearm or ammunition for another person who does hold a firearms certificate if he is acting under that other person's instructions and if that other person is to use the firearm or ammunition for sporting purposes only. Sporting purposes does not include the shooting of rats (Firearms Act 1968, s 11(1)). **NB:** If the person carrying the firearm etc is under 18 years, the other person must be 18 years or over.

(c)   Members of rifle clubs, miniature rifle clubs and cadet corps in possession of Home Office approval do not require certificates for club or corps activities such as drilling or target practice (Firearms Act 1968, s 11(3) and Firearms (Amendment) Act 1988, s 15).

(d)   A certificate is not necessary for weapons at a miniature rifle range if the miniature rifles do not exceed 0.23 calibre or if the weapons are air guns, air rifles or air pistols which have not been declared as dangerous by the Home Office (Firearms Act 1968, s 11(4)).

(e)   Persons participating in a theatrical performance or rehearsal or in producing a film may have a firearm without a certificate (Firearms Act 1968, s 12).

(f)   Starters aged 18 years or over at athletic meetings may have a firearm without a certificate (different rules for persons aged under 18 years apply for blank-firing weapons): Firearms Act 1968, s 11(2).

(g)   A person who has obtained a permit from the police may have a firearm and ammunition, as authorised by that permit without holding a firearms certificate. The permit will usually be for short periods such as one month to allow, for example, the next of kin of the holder of a firearms certificate time to sell the weapons and ammunition after the holder has died (Firearms Act 1968, s 7).

(h)   A person may borrow a shotgun or, if under 18 years, a rifle from the occupier of private premises (which includes land) and use it on those premises in the occupier's presence (Firearms Act 1968, s 11(5) and Firearms (Amendment) Act 1988, s 16).

(i)   A person visiting Great Britain may have in his possession a firearm or shotgun without a certificate where he has been granted a visitor's permit. Such permits are granted by the police and may continue in force for up to 12 months (Firearms (Amendment) Act 1988, s 17).

(j)   A person temporarily in Great Britain purchasing weapons for export (Firearms (Amendment) Act 1988, s 18).

(k)   Museums granted a licence by the Secretary of State (Schedule to the Firearms (Amendment) Act 1988, para.1).

A[76.16]

Degree of proof. A defendant wishing to establish one of the above exemptions does not have to satisfy the court beyond reasonable doubt; he need only satisfy the court that on the balance of probabilities his defence is true. Having regard to the legitimate aims of the above legislation, the shifting of the legal burden to the accused is necessary and proportionate in ECHR terms.

A[76.17]

Antique firearms. The legislation does not apply to an antique firearm sold, transferred, purchased, acquired or possessed as a curiosity or ornament (Firearms Act 1968, s 58(2)). See *Bennett v Brown* (1980) 71 Cr App Rep 109.

Sentencing

A[76.18]

No SC guideline.

Structure of the sentencing decision. See B[3.6].

Should the case be committed for sentence? (*R v Gent* [2002] EWCA Crim 943 [2002] All ER (D) 46 (Apr)) 2 years' imprisonment for possession of a sawn-off shotgun.

A[76.19]

Available sentences. See Table A at B[4.1].

R v Charles [2004] EWCA Crim 1977, [2005] 1 Cr App Rep (S) 253 – 5 years when coupled with a siege and threats to the police.

A[76.20]

Custodial sentence. See B[2]. See *R v Clarke* [1997] 1 Cr App Rep (S) 323, CA on the use of imprisonment.

A[76.21]

Community sentence. See B[3].

A[76.22]

Fines. See B[33].

A[76.23]

Forfeiture. The court can order the firearm and ammunition to be forfeited to the police or disposed of as it thinks fit.

A[76.24]

The court can cancel any firearm or shotgun certificate held by the defendant.

A[77]

Firearm (trespassing in a building and on land)

Charges

A[77.1]

1 Whilst having a firearm or imitation firearm with him, entering or being in any building or part of a building, as a trespasser and without reasonable excuse

Firearms Act 1968, s 20(1)

Maximum penalty -

Firearm: Fine level 5 and 6 months (**12 months) and forfeiture. Triable either way.

Air weapon or imitation firearm: Fine level 5 and 6 months (**51 weeks) and forfeiture. Triable only by magistrates.

Crown Court – 7 years' imprisonment and unlimited fine.

A[77.2]

2 Whilst having a firearm or imitation firearm with him entering or being on any land as a trespasser and without reasonable excuse

Firearms Act 1968, s 20(2)

Maximum penalty – Fine level 4 and 3 months (**51 weeks) and forfeiture.

Mode of trial

A[77.3]

See general notes at I[4].

Legal notes and definitions

A[77.4]

Trespasser. The court must be satisfied that the defendant was a trespasser which means that the defendant was personally within the domain of another person without his consent.

A[77.5]

Land. The Act provides that 'land' includes 'land covered by water'.

A[77.6]

With him. The prosecution must establish more than mere possession, namely, a close physical link and immediate control over the firearm, but not necessarily that he had been carrying it (*R v Kelt* [1977] 3 All ER 1099, [1977] 1 WLR 1365, CA). In the context of an offence under s 18 of the Act a defendant was said not to have a firearm with him when it was 2 or 3 miles away (*R v Bradish* [2004] EWCA Crim 1340, 148 Sol Jo LB 474, [2004] All ER (D) 40 (Apr), CA).

A[77.7]

Reasonable excuse. The onus of establishing reasonable excuse for his presence, when a trespasser, in a building and in possession of a firearm rests on the defendant. He does not have to prove reasonable excuse beyond all reasonable doubt. He has only to prove that on the balance of probabilities he had reasonable excuse. For ECHR, see A[33.5] above.

A[77.8]

Firearm. Means any lethal barrelled weapon of any description from which any shot, bullet or other missile can be discharged. A lethal weapon includes one capable of inflicting injury although not designed to do so, eg a signal pistol. An imitation firearm which is so constructed or adapted as to be readily converted into a firearm is to be treated as a firearm even though it has not been so converted. The Court of Appeal has ruled that a starting pistol which could be adapted to fire bullets if the barrel was drilled was a firearm. In this case the barrel was partly drilled.

A[77.9]

Shotguns and air weapons count as firearms for the purpose of this offence. An air weapon is an air rifle, air gun or air pistol of a type which has not been declared by the Home Office to be specially dangerous.

Sentencing

A[77.10]–[77.15]

No SC guideline but see A[33].

Structure of the sentencing decision. See B[3.6].

A[77.16]

Available sentences. See Table A at B[4.1] (firearms) and Table B at B[4.2] (air weapons and trespass on land).

A[77.17]

Forfeiture. The court can order the weapon and ammunition to be forfeited to the police or disposed of as the court thinks fit.

A[77.18]

The court can also cancel any firearm or shotgun certificate held by the defendant.

Forgery

Charge

A[78.1]
1 Unlawfully making a false instrument with the intention that he (or another) should use it to induce somebody to accept it as genuine, and, by reason of so accepting it to do, or not to do, some act to that person's or some other person's prejudice

Forgery and Counterfeiting Act 1981, s 1

A[78.2]
2 Unlawfully using a false instrument, which is and which he knows or believes to be false, with the intention of inducing somebody to accept it as genuine, as above

Forgery and Counterfeiting Act 1981, s 3

A[78.3]
3 Unlawfully using a copy of a false instrument, which is and which he knows or believes to be false, as above

Forgery and Counterfeiting Act 1981, s 4

Maximum penalty – Fine level 5 and 6 months (**12 months). Triable either way.

Crown Court – 10 years' imprisonment and unlimited fine.

Mode of trial

A[78.4]
Consider first the general guidelines at I[4]. In general, forgery offences should be tried summarily except for the presence of one or more of the following factors:

(a)   breach of trust by a person in a position of substantial authority or in whom a high degree of trust has been placed;
(b)   there has been a sophisticated hiding or disguising of the offence;
(c)   the offence has been committed by an organised gang;
(d)   the victim was particularly vulnerable;
(e)   there is unrecovered property of high value.

Legal notes and definitions

A[78.5]
Instrument. Means any document whether of a formal or informal charac-

ter, any stamp issued or sold by the Post Office, any Inland Revenue stamp and any disk, tape, soundtrack or other device on or in which information is recorded, or is stored by mechanical, electronic or other means.

A[78.6]

False. This is extensively defined in the Forgery and Counterfeiting Act 1981. The essence of falsity in this connection is that the document should tell a lie about itself.

A[78.7]

Make. A person makes a false instrument if he alters it so as to make it false in any respect, whether or not it is false in some other respect apart from that alteration. There is no further element of dishonesty required.

A[78.8]

Intention. In *R v Tobierre* [1986] 1 All ER 346, [1986] 1 WLR 125, CA for an offence under s 3, it was held that the prosecution must prove both that the accused intended to induce somebody to accept the forgery as genuine *and* intended that by so doing he should act, or not act, to that person's or some other person's prejudice.

A[78.9]

Prejudice. An act or omission intended to be induced is to be regarded as being to a person's prejudice only if it is one which *will* result (and not merely which has the *potential* to result (*R v Garcia* (1987) 87 Cr App Rep 175, [1988] Crim LR 115, CA):

(a)   in his temporary or permanent loss of property;
(b)   in his being deprived of the opportunity to earn remuneration, or greater remuneration;
(c)   in his being deprived of an opportunity to gain a financial advantage otherwise than by way of remuneration; or would result in someone being given an opportunity;
(d)   to earn remuneration, or greater remuneration from him; or
(e)   to gain a financial advantage from him otherwise than by way of remuneration; or
(f)   would be the result of his having accepted a false instrument as genuine, or a copy of a false instrument as a copy of a genuine one, in connection with the performance of a duty.

In deciding whether to deal summarily with an offence of forgery the court will have regard, amongst other things, to the harm intended to be caused, or which potentially would be caused by the offence and will compare the very different levels of maximum penalty available at the Crown Court.

Sentencing

A[78.10]

No SC guideline.

A[78.11]–[78.15]

Structure of the sentencing decision. See B[3.6].

A[78.16]

Available sentences. See Table A at B[4.1].

A[78.17]

Compensation. This may be ordered up to £5,000 either as part of a wider sentence or by itself as a substantive penalty. If the offender's means are limited and a monetary penalty is appropriate, preference must be given to ordering compensation instead of a fine.

A[79]

Found on enclosed premises

Charge

A[79.1]

Being found in or upon any dwelling-house, warehouse, outhouse, or in any enclosed yard, garden or area for an unlawful purpose

Vagrancy Act 1824, s 4

Maximum penalty – For a first offence fine level 3 or 3 months. For a subsequent offence the accused may sometimes be committed to the Crown Court as an incorrigible rogue for sentence.

**For an offence committed from a date to be appointed, the power to impose imprisonment will be repealed by the CJA 2003, Sch 25. In addition the power to commit the offender as an incorrigible rogue to the Crown Court will be repealed by the CJA 2003, Sch 37, Part 9.

Legal notes and definitions

A[79.2]

Found. For an offence to be made out an individual had to be found, which meant that he had to be **seen** or **discovered**, with an unlawful purpose in mind at the time he was so found: *L v CPS* [2007] EWHC1843 (Admin).

A[79.3]

Enclosed. The yard may still rate as being enclosed even if there is access through spaces in surrounding buildings, an archway, open gate, etc but does not include a room within a building (*Talbot v DPP* [2000] 1 WLR 1102, 164 JP 169, sub nom Talbot v Oxford City Magistrates' Court [2000] 2 Cr App Rep 60).

A[79.4]

Yard. Would not include a very large area, such as a shipyard or railway sidings, the essential feature of a yard is that it should be a relatively small area ancillary to a building.

Area. There was no evidence that a university campus amounted to an 'enclosed area' within the terms of the section in *Akhurst v Enfield Magistrates' Court* [2009] EWHC 806 (Admin), 173 JP 499.

A[79.5]

Unlawful purpose. Means that the defendant was there for the purpose of committing a criminal offence. In deciding whether the defendant had such a purpose, the court must consider all the evidence drawing such inferences from it as appear proper in the circumstances. "Unlawful purpose" meant that an individual was about to commit a criminal offence. Hiding from the police in order to escape detection for a criminal offence which had already occurred could not constitute an unlawful purpose: *L v CPS* [2007] EWHC 1843 (Admin).

Sentencing

A[79.6]

No SC guideline. For structure of the sentencing decision. See **B[3.6]**.

A[79.7]

Available sentences. See Table B at **B[4.2]**.

A[79.8]

Committal for sentence. For a subsequent offence, as long as the previous offence was **not** dealt with by absolute or conditional discharge the court may commit the defendant to the Crown Court for sentence on bail or in custody as an incorrigible rogue. The Crown Court can impose imprisonment for up to one year. **For offences committed on or after a date to be appointed the power to imprison or commit for sentence has been repealed.

A[79.9]

Even if there is no previous conviction for a similar offence but there is evidence of previous convictions under the Vagrancy Act 1824, then this procedure may still be available to the magistrates. **See **A[79.1]** above.

A[80]

Health and safety at work

Charges

A[80.1]

Did fail to comply with an improvement or prohibition notice (specified)

Health and Safety at Work Act 1974, s 33(2A)

A[80.2]

Did fail to comply with an order of the court to remedy (specified)

Health and Safety at Work Act 1974, s 33(2A)

Maximum penalty – Fine £20,000 and 6 months (**12 months). Triable either way.

Crown Court – 2 years' imprisonment and unlimited fine.

A[80.3]

Did fail to comply with a duty specified in the Health and Safety at Work Act 1974, ss 2–6 (for example), under s 3(1) did fail to conduct an undertaking in such a way as to ensure, so far as is reasonably practicable, that persons not in your employment, who may be affected thereby, were not exposed to risks to their health and safety.

Health and Safety at Work Act 1974, s 33(1A)

Maximum penalty – Fine £20,000 and 6 months (**12 months). Triable either way.

Crown Court – Unlimited fine.

A[80.4]

Other breaches of the Act or Regulations

See the new Sch 3A to the Health and Safety at Work Act 1974 as added by Sch 1 to the Health and Safety (Offences) Act 2008.

Mode of trial

A[80.5]

See general notes at I[4].

A[80.6]

Offences having an impact on the public at large and breaches of licensing requirements (for example in relation to asbestos, explosives or nuclear plant) may indicate trial on indictment.

Legal notes and definitions

A[80.7]

The Health and Safety at Work Act 1974 imposes general duties on employers towards their employees, self-employed persons, persons connected with premises other than employees and articles and substances for use at work in ss 2–6. Most prosecutions are now brought under these sections.

A[80.8]

Specific offences are detailed in the Health and Safety at Work Act 1974, s 33.

A[80.9]

Offences by bodies corporate. Where an offence committed by a body corporate is proved to have been committed with the consent or connivance of or attributable to neglect by a director, manager, secretary or other officer of the company, he as well as the company shall be guilty of that offence and may be proceeded against.

A[80.10]–[80.15]

Prosecution by inspectors. An inspector if authorised by the enforcement authority may prosecute before a magistrates' court.

A[80.16]

Power to order remedial action. Where it appears to the court that the defendant can remedy matters they may in addition to or instead of a punishment order him within a given time to remedy the matters complained of (s 42).

A[80.17]

Work means work as an employee, or self-employed person. Regulations may extend the meaning of work to include at work.

A[80.18]

Article for use at work, means any plant designed for use or operation by persons at work and any article designed for use as a component in any such plant.

Defences

A[80.19]

Typical prosecutions involve breaches of duty to safeguard health and safety so far as is reasonably practicable as well as specific requirements under regulations. It is therefore a common defence that an employer has safe systems of work and has done all that was reasonably practicable to avoid a breach of duty.

(1)   Although s 2 is concerned with ensuring safety and s 3 with ensuring an absence of risk to safety, the language of the statute signified that these two concepts are one and the same thing. It was also implicit from the leading decision in *R v Chargot Ltd (t/a Contract Services)* [2007] EWCA Crim 3032, [2008] 2 All ER 1077, [2008] ICR 517; affd [2008] UKHL 73, [2009] 2 All ER 645, [2009] 1 WLR 1. In each section the obligation is qualified by the words 'so far as is reasonably practicable'. An offence under s 2 is committed if there is a relevant risk to the safety of an employee and the defendant has not taken such steps as are reasonably practicable to avoid it; whilst an offence under s 3 is committed if there is a relevant risk to the safety of a non-employee who may be affected by the conduct of the undertaking and the defendant has not taken such steps as are reasonably practicable to avoid that. In the case of each section, s 40 places on the defendant a reverse onus of proof (on the balance of probabilities) on the issue of reasonable practicability.

(2)   The offence in s 2 or s 3 lies in the failure to ensure safety so far as reasonably practicable, ie in exposure to risk of injury, not in the doing of actual injury. Causation of the injury, therefore, is not an ingredient of either offence: *R v Chargot; R v EGS Ltd* [2009] EWCA Crim 1942 followed.

(3)   The risks with which both sections are concerned are those relating to the activities of the defendant. Although it will sometimes be necessary to address the source of a risk, the introduction of a separate test of 'derivation' is more likely to confuse than to illuminate. The jury should be asked to concentrate on two central issues:

(i)   exposure to risk and

(ii)   (assuming the issue is raised) whether it was reasonably practicable to avoid it.

(4)   Foreseeability of risk (strictly foreseeability of danger) is relevant to the question whether a risk to safety exists. That accords with the ordinary meaning of risk, as is demonstrated by the concept of a risk assessment, which is itself an exercise in foresight. Whether a material risk exists or not is a jury question and the foreseeability (or lack of it) of some danger or injury is a part of the enquiry: *Baker v Quantum Clothing Group Ltd* [2011] UKSC 17, [2011] 4 All ER 223, [2011] 1 WLR 1003 followed. Nonetheless, the Crown is not required to prove that the accident which occurred was foreseeable. The sections impose, in effect, a duty on employers to think deliberately about things which are not obvious. In most cases, absent the sort of time factor which obtained in *Baker v Quantum*, it is likely that consideration of foreseeability will add little to the question whether there was a risk. In most cases, the principal relevance of foreseeability will be whether the employer took all

reasonably practicable precautions to avoid that material risk: *R v Tangerine Confectionary Ltd; R v Veolia ES (UK) Ltd* [2011] EWCA Crim 2015, 176 JP 349.

ECHR. This is a legal rather than an evidential burden on the defendant and the reverse burden of proof is compatible with the presumption of innocence under the ECHR (*R v Davies* [2002] EWCA Crim 2949, [2002] All ER (D) 275 (Dec) , sub nom *Davies v Health and Safety Executive* [2003] IRLR 170, 147 Sol Jo LB 29;*R v Chargot Ltd (t/a Contract Services)* [2007] EWCA Crim 3032, [2008] 2 All ER 1077, [2008] ICR 517; affd [2008] UKHL 73, [2009] 2 All ER 645, [2009] 1 WLR 1).

Sentencing

A[80.20]

No SC guideline.

Aggravating and mitigating factors. Factors which may aggravate an offence are:

- a deliberate or reckless breach of the law rather than carelessness;
- action or lack of action prompted by financial motives-profit or cost saving;
- disregarding warnings from a regulatory authority or the workforce;
- an awareness of the specific risks likely to arise from action taken;
- lack of co-operation with a regulatory authority;
- serious extent of damage resulting from offence (but lack of actual damage does not render the offence merely technical; it is still serious if there is risk);
- previous offences of a similar nature;
- death or serious injury or ill health of humans has been a consequence of the offence;
- animal health or flora affected.

Factors in mitigation may include:

- the offender's minor role with little personal responsibility;
- genuine lack of awareness or understanding of specific regulations;
- an isolated lapse.

There may be some offender mitigation:

- prompt reporting;
- ready co-operation with regulatory authority;
- good previous record;
- timely guilty plea.

Costs

A[80.21]

The prosecution will normally claim the costs of investigation and presentation. These may be substantial and can incorporate time and activity expended on containing and making the area safe.

Fines

A[80.22]

It is difficult to assess the appropriate level of fine in Health and Safety prosecutions. In *R v Clifton Steel Ltd* [2007] EWCA Crim 1537, [2007] All ER (D) 108 (Jun) it was said that having regard to the authorities, care had to be taken to ensure that the level of fine was sufficiently punitive so as to encourage improved performance, but was not counterproductive in that it placed the defendant [company] under further financial constraints.

Very high fines are often imposed on companies and individuals for serious breaches of health and safety legislation: *R v Keltbray Ltd* [2000] All ER (D) 705, [2001] 1 Cr App Rep (S) 132, CA. Fines on companies need to be large enough to bring the message to managers and shareholders alike. Where the court is of the opinion that the offence or the combination of the offence and other offences associated with it was so serious that greater punishment should be inflicted for it than the court has power to impose, the defendant, whether an individual or a company, may be committed to the Crown Court for sentence: **see however B[16]** and the changes to the powers of magistrates' courts to commit for sentence as a result of the CJA 2003.

A deliberate breach with a view to profit will be viewed seriously as will a failure to heed warnings or comply with notices. The penalty should 'reflect' public disquiet at the unnecessary loss of life (*R v F Howe & Son (Engineers) Ltd* [1999] 2 All ER 249, [1999] 2 Cr App Rep (S) 37, CA). Such cases are suitable for sentence at the Crown Court (*R v Yorkshire Sheeting and Insulation Ltd* [2003] EWCA Crim 458, [2003] 2 Cr App Rep (S) 548, [2003] All ER (D) 369 (Feb); *R v P & O Ferries (Irish Sea) Ltd* [2004] EWCA Crim 3236, [2005] 2 Cr App Rep (S) 113, [2004] All ER (D) 380 (Nov)).

A[80.23]

Those whose work brings with it a familiarity with machinery notoriously become indifferent to safety precautions and will sometimes take the most appalling risks. It may be appropriate to take into account any contribution a worker may have made to his own misfortune in accident cases, but employers must be expected to know the nature of their workers and take and maintain measures to protect workers not only from dangerous machines but from themselves.

A[81]

Immigration offences

Charges

A[81.1]

1 Illegal entry and similar offences by a person who is not a British citizen

Immigration Act 1971, s 24

Maximum penalty – Triable summary only. Fine level 5 or 6 months' (**51 weeks) imprisonment

A[81.2]

2 Assisting unlawful entry to a member state, assisting an asylum seeker to enter the UK and entry to the UK in breach of an exclusion or deportation order.

Immigration Act 1971, s 25, 25A, 25B

Maximum penalty – Fine level 5 and 6 months (**12 months). Triable either way.

Crown Court – Unlimited fine and/or 14 years' imprisonment.

A[81.3]

3 Possession of false passports, work permits, registration cards etc and other offences in connection with the administration of the Act.

Immigration Act 1971, s 26, 26A

Maximum penalty – Triable summary only. Level 5 and 6 months (**51 weeks).

NB: The Nationality, Immigration and Asylum Act 2002 created a large number of related offences under the Act with effect from 10 February 2003. If charged under s 26A they are punishable with a maximum of ten years' imprisonment and a fine unless they only involve possession without reasonable excuse when the maximum penalty is two years' imprisonment and a fine. Both offences are triable either way carrying on summary conviction a fine level 5 and 6 months (**12 months) imprisonment.

Mode of trial

A[81.4]

See general notes at I[4] and sentencing below for further guidance, although many cases will be most appropriately dealt with at Crown Court (*R v Uluc* [2001] EWCA Crim 2991 [2001] All ER (D) 273 (Dec)).

Legal notes and definitions

A[81.5]

No asylum seeker can be convicted for using false documents without consideration of whether he is protected by Article 31 of the United Nations Convention Relating to the Status of Refugees, this provides for a defence to any individual who has come to the United Kingdom directly from a country where his life or freedom was threatened **and;**

(1)   presented himself to the authorities in the United Kingdom without delay;
(2)   showed good cause for his illegal entry or presence; and
(3)   made a claim for asylum as soon, as was reasonably practicable after his arrival in the United Kingdom (*R v Uxbridge Magistrates' Court, ex p Adimi* [2001] QB 667, [1999] 4 All ER 520).

A person commits an offence of knowingly remaining beyond the time limit of a limited leave to stay on the day when he first knows that the time limit of his leave has expired. He continues to commit the offence (Immigration Act 1971, s 24(1)(b)(i)) throughout any period he is in the United Kingdom thereafter.

A[81.6]

Extended time limits for prosecution. The normal time limit for laying an information for a summary offence is 6 months. However in cases charged under s 28(1)(a) (knowingly entering the United Kingdom in breach of a deportation order), s 28(1)(c)(having lawfully entered the United Kingdom remains without leave beyond the time allowed), s 26(1)(c) (making a false representation to an immigration officer) or 26(1)(d) (altering any relevant certificate, work permit or passport) an information relating to the offence may in England and Wales be tried by a magistrates' court if it is laid within six months after the commission of the offence, or if it is laid within three years after the commission of the offence and not more than two months after the date certified by a police officer above the rank of chief superintendent to be the date on which evidence sufficient to justify proceedings came to the notice of the police.

A[81.7]

Search warrants. In the case of offences of illegal entry (s 24(1)(a)), obtaining leave to enter or remain by deception (s 24(1)(aa)) and remaining beyond a time-limited leave or failing to observe conditions of leave (s 24(1)(b)) may all be the subject of an arrest without warrant by a constable or immigration officer with reasonable grounds to suspect an offence has been committed. A justice of the peace may grant a warrant of entry of search to premises if satisfied by written information on oath that a person suspected of one of the above offences is to be found on those premises.

Immigration and Asylum Act 1999, s 7

A[81.8]

An immigration officer is a person appointed by the Secretary of State or may be employed as a revenue and customs officer.

Facilitating entry is not an offence if it is done otherwise than for gain or by a bona fide organisation whose purpose is assisting asylum claimants.

Illegal entrant is not confined to persons who have actually entered the country but includes those seeking to enter (*R v Eyck* [2000] 3 All ER 569, [2000] 1 WLR 1389, CA).

Sentencing

A[81.9]

No SC guideline. For structure of the sentencing decision. See B[3.6].

A[81.10]–[81.15]

Available sentences. See Table A at B[4.1] (either way offences) and Table B at B[4.2] (summary offences).

A[81.16]

Immigration offences are generally considered seriously by the courts and may lead to custodial sentences, often after committal for sentence. See for example *R v Anthoni Angel* [1998] 1 Cr App Rep (S) 347, CA. A man of good character acting out of humanitarian motives sentenced to 15 months' imprisonment for facilitating the illegal entry of another (*R v Daljit Singh* [1999] 1 Cr App Rep (S) 490, [1999] Crim LR 236, CA). Knowingly using a false passport merited a deterrent sentence of between 6 and 9 months' imprisonment despite a guilty plea and previous good character. See *R v Kolawole* [2004] EWCA Crim 3047, [2005] 2 Cr App Rep (S) 71, [2004] All ER (D) 439 (Nov).

A[81.17]

Bail See J[1].

It may be the case that some asylum seekers face charges before the criminal courts. In these circumstances, the courts have no powers under immigration and asylum legislation to bail or detain them. Where the criminal proceedings have to be adjourned for any reason, magistrates are advised that defendants who are also asylum seekers should have their applications for bail under the Bail Act 1976 considered by the courts in the same way as any other defendant. Where the case proceeds to sentence, the courts have no additional powers to exercise in relation to the offender's immigration status, save for making a recommendation for deportation under the Immigration Act 1971, s 3(6), where this is appropriate. Before considering or making a recommendation for deportation consult the legal adviser.

A[82]

Kerb crawling and soliciting women for prostitution

Charges

A[82.1]

Being a man, soliciting a woman (or different women) for the purpose of prostitution

(a)   from a motor vehicle while it is in a street or public place or
(b)   in a street or public place while in the immediate vicinity of a motor vehicle that the accused has just got out of or off

persistently (or in such a manner or in such circumstances as to be likely to cause annoyance to the woman (or any of the women) solicited, or nuisance to other persons in the neighbourhood)

Sexual Offences Act 1985, s 1(1)

A[82.2]

Being a man in a street or public place persistently soliciting a woman (or different women) for the purpose of prostitution

Sexual Offences Act 1985, s 2(1)

Maximum penalty – (for either offence) Fine level 3. Triable only by magistrates.

NB: For offences prosecuted under s 1 of the Street Offences Act 1959 (loitering or soliciting for the purpose of prostitution), instead of the level 2 (first offence) or level 3 penalty, the Policing and Crime Act 2009 (Commencement No 4) Order introduces a new penalty for those persons convicted of the s 1 offence. The court is empowered to make a rehabilitation order known as an 'Engagement and Support Order' (an order requiring attendance at meetings with a supervisor to address the causes of the offending behaviour. Magistrates should consult with their legal adviser before imposing the same. The supervising body or person should be consulted first, not least to ensure that a scheme in the local justice area where the offender resides is in place.

Legal notes and definitions

A[82.3]

The words in brackets in the Sexual Offences Act 1985, s 1 enable proceedings to be taken where the soliciting was likely to cause annoyance etc to the woman or nuisance to other persons in the neighbourhood, eg to local residents who are annoyed at their district becoming a 'red light' area.

A[82.4]

Soliciting a woman for the purpose of prostitution means soliciting her for the purpose of obtaining her services as a prostitute. The accused must have given some indication, by act or word, to the woman that he required her services as a prostitute (*Darroch v DPP* (1990) 90 Cr App Rep 378, 154 JP 844).

A single act by a male on foot of soliciting a woman for prostitution within a recognised area could not amount in law to the common law offence of public nuisance: *DPP v Fearon* [2010] EWHC 340 (Admin)), [2010] 2 Cr App Rep 169, 174 JP 145.

A[82.5]

Woman includes girl. These offences can only be committed by a man and for this act 'man' includes 'boy'.

A[82.6]

Street includes any bridge, road, lane, footway, subway, square, court, alley or passage, whether a thoroughfare or not, which is for the time being open to the public; and the doorways and entrances of premises abutting on a street and any ground adjoining and open to a street are to be treated as forming part of the street.

A[82.7]

Persistently means a degree of repetition, of either more than one invitation to one person or a series of invitations to different people.

A[82.8]

Likely to cause annoyance. No persons need be present witnessing the incident for the offence to be made out; it is sufficient if there is a likelihood of nuisance to other persons in the neighbourhood. Justices may use their local knowledge that an area is a frequent haunt of prostitutes with a constant procession of cars there (*Paul v DPP* (1989) 90 Cr App Rep 173, [1989] Crim LR 660, sub nom Paul v Luton Justices, ex p Crown Prosecution Service 153 JP 512).

Sentencing

A[82.9]

No SC Guideline.

Child prostitutes should be treated as victims rather than offenders and will rarely be put before the court.

A[82.10]

Since neither of these offences is punishable with imprisonment, a fine will be the usual penalty. The court might consider the amount of distress caused to the victim. When a prosecution is brought on the basis of annoyance to a neighbourhood, an element of deterrent sentencing may be necessary.

A[82.11]

Fines. See B[33].

A[82.12]–[82.15]

Anti-Social Behaviour Orders. ASBOs have been made for this offence as an ancillary order. See **B[8.8]**.

A[82.16]

Binding-over orders

Complaints for bind over are sometimes included by the prosecution or brought as an alternative remedy to the above charges. Magistrates may use their common law powers to bind over the offender where a future breach of the peace is anticipated (see **B[10]**).

A[83]

Litter

(including dumping articles and car dumping)

A[83.1]

Under the general term of **litter** there are three different offences: car dumping, dumping objects other than vehicles, and depositing general litter.

Charge 1

A[83.2]

Without lawful authority abandoning on land in the open air or on land forming part of a highway a motor vehicle

Refuse Disposal (Amenity) Act 1978, s 2(1)(a)

Maximum penalty – Fine level 4 and 3 months' (**51 weeks) imprisonment. May be dealt with by a fixed penalty notice.

A removal charge can also be imposed if the local authority applies.

Legal notes and definitions

A[83.3]

It is also an offence to abandon on such land a part of a motor vehicle if the vehicle was brought to that land and there dismantled and some part of the vehicle abandoned there.

A[83.4]

Motor vehicle. This is defined in the Act as a mechanically propelled vehicle intended or adapted for use on roads whether or not it is in a fit state for such use. It includes a trailer, a chassis or body with or without wheels appearing to have formed part of a motor vehicle or trailer and anything attached to a motor vehicle or trailer.

A[83.5]

Burden of proof. If the vehicle (or part of a vehicle) was left on the land in such circumstances or for such a period that it may be reasonably assumed that the defendant had abandoned it then he shall be deemed to have abandoned the vehicle (or part of a vehicle) unless he can prove the contrary. The degree of proof required of the defendant is not such as is necessary to establish this point beyond all reasonable doubt but only such as establishes that on the balance of probabilities it is true. Give the stated aims of the legislation and the fact that the reason for leaving [abandoning] the vehicle may peculiarly be within the knowledge of the accused, it is suggested that the shifting of the legal burden of proof to the accused is both necessary and proportionate and therefore ECHR compliant.

A[83.6]
Land. The land must be land in the open air or land which forms part of the highway.

Sentencing

A[83.7]
No SC guideline.

Prison will rarely be appropriate but a fine will in most cases need to be such as to reflect the seriousness of the offence.

A[83.8]
On application by police or local authority, a removal charge can also be imposed.

A[83.9]
Disqualification from driving. See C[5.45].

Charge 2

A[83.10]
Without lawful authority abandoning on land in the open air (or on land forming part of the highway) property namely [. . . . .] which he brought to the land for the purpose of abandoning it there

Refuse Disposal (Amenity) Act 1978, s 2(1)(b)

Maximum penalty – Fine level 4 and 3 months' (**51 weeks) imprisonment.

Legal notes and definitions

A[83.11]–[83.14]
Although this offence does not apply to motor vehicles it does apply to a part of a motor vehicle which was dismantled elsewhere and then brought

and abandoned. If the motor vehicle was dismantled on the land then the charge should have been the previous one on at A[60.3].

A[83.15]

Land. Means land in the open air or land forming part of a highway.

Sentencing

A[83.16]

No SC guideline.

The position is the same as for the previous charge at A[60.7] except that ordering a removal charge is limited to removing motor vehicles.

A[83.17]

Disqualification from driving. See C[5.45].

Charge 3

A[83.18]

Throwing down (or dropping or depositing) [in a public open place] [in a place to which this section applies] and there leaving certain articles namely [. . . . .] in such circumstances as to tend to lead to defacement by litter

Environmental Protection Act 1990, s 87

Maximum penalty – Fine level 4.

Legal notes and definitions

A[83.19]

The charge should allege one or other of the following:

A[83.20]

Throwing down; dropping; depositing. If two or more of these words are included in the charge then it may be defective.

A[83.21]

Public open place. Means a place in the open air to which the public are entitled or permitted to have access without payment. Any covered place open to the air on at least one side and available for public use is to be treated as a public open place. An enclosed telephone kiosk is not an open space (*Felix v DPP* [1998] Crim LR 657).

A[83.22]

Place to which the section applies. Includes publicly maintained highways and motorways, local authority open spaces, certain Crown lands and land belonging to certain designated statutory undertakers and educational establishments. Also included is land designated by a local authority as a 'litter control area', eg a shopping mall.

A[83.23]

Time limit. Proceedings must be commenced within six months of the litter being thrown down or dropped or deposited. If litter is left for a considerable period then the time limit of six months still commences from the time the litter was deposited.

A[83.24]

Leaving. No offence is committed if the litter is not left; thus prompt clearing up can be a defence.

A[83.25]–[83.30]

Consent of the owner. If the owner, occupier or person having control of the place consented to the depositing of the litter then no offence is committed.

Sentencing

A[83.31]

No SC guideline.

Aggravating factors to which the court may have regard may include the defacement by litter, but also the nature of the litter and any resulting risk of injury to persons or animals or of damage to property.

A[83.32]

Whatever the circumstances the fine will usually need to be such as to reflect the prevalence of the offence in an area.

A[83.33]

Fines. See B[33].

A[83.34]

Disqualification from driving. See C[5.45].

A[84]

Nuisance

A[84.1]

In addition to the remedies which the law affords in respect of nuisances in civil proceedings before the county court and the High Court, local authorities and private persons may bring proceedings for the abatement or restriction of a statutory nuisance before the magistrates' court. Further see A6 and A[74].

Statutory nuisance

(Environmental Protection Act 1990, s 79)

A[84.2]

The following matters constitute statutory nuisances where they are such as to be prejudicial to health or a nuisance:

(a)   the state of any premises;
(b)   the emission of smoke from premises;
(c)   the emission of fumes or gases from private dwellings;
(d)   any dust, steam, smell or other effluvia arising on industrial, trade or business premises;
(e)   any accumulation or deposit;
(f)   the manner or keeping in such a place of any animal;
(g)   noise emitted from premises;

and also

(h)   any other matter declared by any enactment to be a statutory nuisance.

Note however that a steep staircase cannot in itself constitute a statutory nuisance (*R v Bristol City Council, ex p Everett* [1999] 2 All ER 193, [1999] 1 WLR 1170, CA).

The issue of an abatement notice by a local authority under s 79(10) of the 1990 Act does not require the prior consent of the Secretary of State: *R (on the application of Ethos Recycling Ltd) v Barking and Dagenham Magistrates' Court and London Borough of Barking and Dagenham* [2009] EWHC 2885 (Admin), [2010] PTSR 787, 174 JP 25.

A[84.3]

Prejudicial to health. Means injurious, or likely to cause injury to health.

A[84.4]

Noise. Includes vibration.

A[84.5]

Exceptions are made to the definitions of a statutory nuisance given above. These include activities of the armed forces, smoke emissions covered by the Clean Air Acts (excluding bonfires), dark smoke from trade or industrial premises, smoke and steam from steam locomotives and noise from aircraft.

A[84.6]

Premises. Includes land and any vessel (except one powered by steam reciprocating engines).

Proceedings by the local authority

(Environmental Protection Act 1990, s 82)

A[84.7]

The local authority must from time to time cause its area to be inspected to detect the existence of any statutory nuisance and, where a complaint has been made, take such steps as are reasonably practicable to investigate the complaint (s 79).

They may also require premises subject to a premises licence on a temporary event notice to close for up to 24 hours if they believe noise from the premises is causing a public nuisance. Contravention is punishable by 3 months' (**51 weeks) imprisonment and/or a £20,000 fine (Anti Social Behaviour Act 2003, s 40).

A[84.8]

Abatement notice. Where the local authority are satisfied that a statutory nuisance exists or is likely to occur or reoccur, the local authority must serve a notice requiring abatement or prohibiting or restricting its occurrence and if the means of abatement are required by the local authority the description of any steps necessary for this purpose and any times within which the required action is to be taken (*R v Falmouth and Truro Port Health Authority, ex p South West Water Services* [2001] QB 445, [2000] 3 All ER 306, [2000] All ER (D) 429, CA). he consent of the Secretary of State or the Environment Agency is not required prior to the issue of an abatement notice by a local authority: *R (on the application of Ethos Recycling Ltd v Barking and Dagenham Magistrates' Court* [2009] EWHC 2885 (Admin).

In *R (on the application of Mohuddin Khan) v Isleworth Crown Court and the London Borough of Hillingdon* [2011] EWHC 3164 (Admin), 176 JP 6, there was no dispute as to the facts of the nuisance itself, nor was there any dispute that the claimant was not at the premises. It was also accepted that the dog (the cause of the nuisance) did not belong to him. The Crown Court considered that the claimant should have made sensible arrangements to collect his post while he was absent from the relevant premises. It concluded that he was therefore responsible for the nuisance and dismissed an appeal from the magistrates' court. It as held that the claimant was not 'the person responsible' for the nuisance. He was not the person 'to whose act, default or sufferance the nuisance was attributable'. That person was manifestly another person whose dog it was, and who was plainly in control of the dog at all material times. The abatement notice should in the ordinary way have been served on him and he should have been prosecuted for its breach. Despite the claimant's failure to make a better arrangement to collect his post from the said premises, that failure could not properly deprive him of an opportunity to raise a cast iron point had he appealed to the magistrates' court.

A[84.9]

Appeal. The person served with the notice may appeal within 21 days to the magistrates' court. These are civil proceedings by way of complaint and the court is unable to impose a criminal penalty (*Hounslow London Borough Council v Thames Water Utilities Ltd* [2004] All ER (D) 94 (Feb)).

A[84.10]–[84.15]

Offence. Contravention of or failure to comply with the terms of a notice without reasonable excuse is an offence triable only by magistrates. The maximum penalty is a fine of £5,000 and £500 per day for each day the offence continues after conviction. For an offence on industrial, trade or business premises the fine is £20,000.

A[84.16]

Defence. It is a defence for the defendant to prove that the best practicable means were used to prevent, or to counteract the effects of, the nuisance. This defence is not available:

(a)   in paras (a), (d), (e), (f) and (g) at **A[61.2]** except where the nuisance arose on trade, industrial or business premises;

(b)   in para (b) except where the smoke is emitted from a chimney.

Certain other defences are available where it is alleged that the activity is in conformity with consents or notices under control of pollution legislation.

A[84.17]

If the defendant raises the defence of reasonable excuse under s 80(4) and (6) then it is for the prosecution to satisfy the court beyond reasonable doubt that the excuse was not reasonable (*Polychronakis v Richards and Jerrom Ltd* [1998] JPL 588, [1998] Env LR 347).

A[84.18]

Appeal. A person convicted of an offence may appeal against conviction and sentence to the Crown Court in the usual way.

Complaint by person aggrieved by a statutory nuisance

(Environmental Protection Act 1990, s 82)

A[84.19]

A private individual may complain to the local authority about an alleged statutory nuisance and it will be the duty of the authority to take such steps as are reasonably practicable to investigate the complaint and if they consider it appropriate to serve an abatement notice as described above (Environmental Protection Act 1990, s 79).

A[84.20]

However, a person may also lay a complaint before the magistrates on the ground that he is aggrieved by the existence of a statutory nuisance. Proceedings are normally brought against the person responsible for the nuisance; where he cannot be found it will be the owner or occupier of the premises.

A[84.21]

Notice of intention to bring proceedings and the matters complained of should be served not less than 3 days before, in respect of noise, and 21 days before, in respect of any other allegation.

A[84.22]

Magistrates' order. If the court is satisfied that the alleged nuisance exists or that, although abated, it is likely to reoccur, the court must make either one or both of the following orders:

(a) to abate the nuisance, within a time specified in the order, and to execute any works necessary for that purpose;
(b) prohibiting a recurrence of the nuisance, and requiring the defendant, within a time specified in the order, to execute any works necessary to prevent the recurrence.

The court may also impose a fine not exceeding £5,000 (level 5).

A[84.23]

Where the nuisance renders premises unfit for human habitation, the order may prohibit their use for this purpose until the court is satisfied they are fit for such use.

A[84.24]

Offence. See A[74.9] for private premises.

A[84.25]–[84.30]

Defence. See A[84.16]–A[84.17]. The 'best practicable means' defence is not available for a nuisance which is such as to render the premises unfit for human habitation.

A[84.31]

Costs. Where the alleged nuisance is proved to have existed at the making of the complaint then, whether or not at the date of the hearing it still exists or is likely to recur, the court shall order the defendant to pay the complainant's proper costs. Such costs should include costs incurred in establishing that a statutory nuisance existed (*Hollis v Dudley Metropolitan Borough Council* [1998] 1 All ER 759, [1999] 1 WLR 642).

Such proceedings are not civil in nature. Any award of costs therefore cannot be made under 64 of the Magistrates' Courts Act 1980: see s 50 of the Magistrates' Courts Act 1980 and s 82(2) of the Environmental Protection Act 1990. The combined effect of those two provisions was that s 82 must be read as if the word 'information' is substituted for 'complaint' in subsection (1). The power to award costs in favour of a successful defendant, other than by a wasted costs order when an information is dismissed, is to be found only in s 16(1) of the Prosecution of Offences Act 1985: *R (on the application of DeSouza) v Croydon Magistrates' Court* [2012] EWHC 1362 (Admin), 176 JP 624.

A[84.32]

Local authority. Where a person has been convicted of failing to comply with an order the court, after allowing the local authority an opportunity to be heard, may direct the authority to do anything which the person convicted was required to do by the order. Similarly, where the defendant cannot be found the court may direct the local authority to do that which it would have ordered him to do.

Noise Act 1996

A[84.33]

See the amendments as a result of s.84 and schedule, 1 to the Clean Neighbourhoods and Environment Act 2005 which applies to licensed premises with a penalty (after service of the relevant notice under para 4A of a fine not exceeding **level 5.

If a warning notice has been served under this Act, in respect of noise emitted from premises, any person who is responsible for such a breach is liable to a fine not exceeding **level 3**.

A[84.34]

Defence. It is open to the defendant to show he has reasonable excuse.

A[84.35]

Forfeiture. Magistrates may direct the forfeiture of any equipment related to a noise conviction.

A[84.36]

Before doing so the court must have regard:

(a)   to the value of the equipment; and
(b)   to the likely financial and other effects on the offender of the making of the order.

"Closure of premises associated with persistent disorder or nuisance" – Part 1A of the Anti-Social Behaviour Act 2003

A[84.37]

In some communities there are particular premises that are a constant focus for severe anti-social behaviour, making the lives of those living nearby a misery. Premises closure orders are designed to offer immediate respite via the temporary closure of premises for up to three months where the person occupying those premises is responsible for:

- Significant and persistent disorder or
- Persistent serious nuisance to a community.

These procedures should only be used as a last resort and not as an eviction tool or fast-track procedure to eviction. An order can be made by a relevant police force and/or local authorities. Once a premises closure order has been made, the police or the local authority must apply to a magistrates' court for authority to continue the order for up to three months.

The application must be heard by the magistrates' court not later than 48 hours after the notice was served in pursuance of s 11A(7)(a) of the 2003 Act. The magistrates' court may adjourn for a period of not more than 14 days to enable the owner, occupier, or any other person with an interest in the premises to show cause why a Part 1A closure order should not be made.

In adjourning the case the magistrates' court may direct that the closure order shall continue. Analogous to closure orders associated with 'crack houses' under s 2 of the 2003 Act, it is submitted that magistrates have a general discretion to adjourn closure order proceedings beyond the 14 days period in accordance with the Magistrates' Courts Act 1980.

The definition of 'premises' is a neutral term and applies to privately-owned properties (including owner-occupied or privately rented properties. The following premises are covered under the legislation: Flats and apartments, common areas adjacent to houses or flats, garages and sheds, factories, pubs and clubs, public buildings, community centres, halls and even car parks.

The police and local authorities assessing the need to issue a closure order must have reasonable grounds for believing that:

- at any time in the preceding three months a person had engaged in anti-social behaviour on the premises; and

- that the use of the premises is associated with significant and persistent disorder or persistent serious nuisance to members of the public.

The closure order gives a power to close a property completely or partially for a maximum of up to three months and to prevent access by any person, even those with rights of abode or ownership. Orders may be discharged when problems associated with the premises have been addressed. No property should remain empty longer than is necessary. There are provisions to extend or discharge the order on application.

It will be up to the courts to define 'significant and persistent disorder' or 'persistent and serious nuisance'.

There is a right of appeal against the making of an order or decision to the Crown Court.

Breach of a closure order is an offence carrying six months' imprisonment and/or a fine of £5,000 on summary conviction.

For guidance on the procedures associated with the closure process magistrates should consult their legal adviser.

For the closure of 'noisy premises' see s 40 of the 2003 Act at A[84.7] onwards.

A[85]

Obstructing the highway

Charge

A[85.1]

Without lawful authority or excuse wilfully obstructing the free passage along a highway

Highways Act 1980, s 137

Maximum penalty – Fine level 3.

Legal notes and definitions

A[85.2]

This offence can be committed in a number of different ways apart from leaving a motor vehicle. It should not be confused with the offence of causing an unnecessary obstruction on a road with a motor vehicle or with a breach of parking regulations. See C[36].

A[85.3]

The correct approach for magistrates dealing with an offence of obstruction is as follows:

(a)   Was there an obstruction? Unless within the *de minimis* rule, any stopping on the highway is prima facie an obstruction.
(b)   Was it wilful, ie deliberate?
(c)   Have the prosecution proved that the obstruction was without lawful authority or excuse? Lawful authority includes permits and licences granted under statutory provision; lawful excuse embraces activities otherwise lawful in themselves which may or may not be reasonable in all the circumstances, including the length of time the obstruction continues, the place where it occurs, the purpose for which it is done and whether it does in fact cause an actual obstruction as opposed to a potential obstruction (*Hirst and Agu v Chief Constable of West Yorkshire* (1986) 85 Cr App Rep 143, 151 JP 304).

A[85.4]

Highway. A highway means the whole or part of a highway. Only a part of a highway needs to be obstructed to commit this offence and the highway, available to the general public, may be a wide road or a narrow passageway, only suitable for pedestrians. Bridges and tunnels used by the public are also highways.

Sentencing

A[85.5]

No SC guideline. This offence carries a fine only. See B[33.12].

A[86]

Poaching

1 Day time offence

A[86.1]

Trespassing by entering or being in the day time upon any land in search or pursuit of game, or woodcocks, snipes or conies

Game Act 1831, s 30, as amended

Maximum penalty – Fine level 3. Triable only by magistrates.

Note – Where it is alleged that there were five or more persons together trespassing in pursuit of game the maximum penalty is a fine set at level 5 for each defendant.

For hunting wild mammals with dogs and hare coursing see ss 1–5 of the Hunting Act 2004.

Legal notes and definitions

A[86.2]

A prosecution must be commenced within three calendar months after the commission of the offence (Game Act 1831, s 41). The charge creates only one offence, that of trespass, and the summons may refer to pursuit of more than one species.

A[86.3]

Claim of right. The magistrates' jurisdiction is ousted if the accused contends that he had a right to act as he did. However, this claim must be bona fide and made on reasonable grounds. The magistrates may decide on the reasonableness and sufficiency of the evidence to support it.

A[86.4]

Trespassing is a complicated concept. However, for this offence the accused must himself have been personally entering on the land and 'constructive' trespass, eg sending a dog into the land, would not be sufficient.

A[86.5]

Day time commences at the beginning of the last hour before sunrise and concludes at the expiration of the first hour after sunset (s 34).

A[86.6]

Game means hares, pheasants, partridges, grouse, heath or moor game, and black game (s 2).

A[86.7]

Game licence. A conviction of this offence renders a licence to kill game void (Game Licences Act 1860, s 11).

A[86.8]

Hunting. This offence does not apply to hunting or coursing in fresh pursuit of deer, hare, or fox (Game Act 1831, s 35). **NB:** By virtue of the Hunting Act 2004, Sch 3, the words, "to any person hunting or coursing upon any land with hounds or greyhounds, and being in pursuit of any deer, hare or fox already started upon any other land, nor" have been repealed.

A[86.8A]

Disqualification from driving. See C[5.45].

2 Night time offences

A[86.9]

(a) Unlawfully taking or destroying any game or rabbits by night in any land, open or enclosed or by night unlawfully entering or being on any land, whether open or enclosed, with any gun, net, engine, or other instrument for the purpose of taking or destroying game

Night Poaching Act 1828, s 1, as amended

Maximum penalty – Fine level 3 (offence under s 2 where violence is offered to gamekeepers etc with the weapons described in charge (b) the maximum is a fine on level 4 and 6 months (**51 weeks)). Triable only by magistrates.

A[86.10]–[86.15]

(b) Three or more persons together by night unlawfully entering or being on any land, whether open or enclosed, for the purpose of taking or destroying game or rabbits, any of such persons being armed with gun, cross bow, firearms, bludgeon or any other offensive weapon

Night Poaching Act 1828, s 9, as amended

Maximum penalty – Fine level 4 and 6 months (**51 weeks). Triable only by magistrates.

Legal notes and definitions

A[86.16]

Claim of right. See above at A[86.3].

A[86.17]

Game includes hares, pheasants, partridges, grouse, heath or moor game, black game and bustards (Night Poaching Act 1828, s 13).

A[86.18]

Land includes public roads, highways, or paths, or the sides thereof or at the opening, outlets, or gates, from any such land into any such road, highway or path.

A[86.19]

Charge. Section 1 creates two offences and any information must allege only one offence.

A[86.20]

Unlawfully entering or being. (See above.) This offence does not relate to the taking or destroying of rabbits.

A[86.21]

Night time commences at the expiration of the first hour after sunset and concludes at the beginning of the last hour before sunrise.

A[86.22]

Three or more together. It is not necessary for all the persons actually to enter provided they are associated together on a common purpose, some entering while others remain near enough to assist.

A[86.22A]

Disqualification from driving. See C[5.45].

3 Pursuing game without a licence

A[86.23]

Taking, killing, pursuing, or using any dog, gun, net or other engine for the purpose of taking, killing, or pursuing any game, or any woodcock, snipe or any coney, or deer, without a proper licence

Game Licences Act 1860, s 4, as amended

Maximum penalty – Fine level 2. Triable only by magistrates.

Legal notes and definitions

A[86.24]

Game licences are granted by local authorities.

A[86.25]–[86.30]

Exceptions. Include taking woodcocks and snipe with nets or springs; taking or destroying conies by proprietors or tenants of lands; pursuing and killing of hares by coursing with greyhounds or hunting with beagles or other hounds; a person assisting a licence holder in his company or presence; a person authorised under the Hares Act 1848 to kill hares without a game certificate.

Sentencing

A[86.31]

No SC guideline.

Where the police have arrested a person for an offence under the Night Poaching Act 1828 or Game Act 1831 they may search him and may seize and detain any game or rabbits, or any gun or cartridges or other ammunition, or any nets, traps, snares or other devices of a kind used for the killing or taking of game or rabbits, which are found in his possession.

A[86.32]

If convicted the court may order any of these items to be forfeited (whether or not the offence of which he was convicted concerned that game, rabbit etc) (Game Laws Amendment Act 1960, s 4).

A[86.32A]

Disqualification from driving. See C[5.45].

A[87]

Police (Property) Act 1897

A[87.1]

Application for an order for the delivery of property in possession of the police in connection with their investigation of a suspected offence under s 1 of the Act.

Legal notes and definitions

A[87.2]

While this proceeding is a civil case of a kind that is more usually dealt with at a county court, nevertheless it can be dealt with at a magistrates' court. Clearly it will be cheaper and more expeditious if a magistrates' court deals with the matter fairly soon after the hearing of a criminal charge, thus saving a hearing in the county court or High Court. Sufficient notice of the date of hearing should be given to each claimant of the property to enable him to prepare for the hearing before the magistrates.

A[87.3]

When applicable. This procedure applies when the police have in their possession property which has come into their hands during investigation into a suspected offence. It is not necessary that the person has been charged with any offence.

The powers of the executive to seize and retain goods were carefully circumscribed both at common law and by statute. As a matter of principle the police must not keep an article, or prevent its removal, for any longer than is reasonably necessary to complete their investigations or preserve it for evidence. If a copy will suffice, it should be made and the original returned. As soon as the case is over, or it is decided not to go on with it, the article should be returned. The terms of s 22(2)–(4) of PACE were directed to the retention of the article for use as evidence at trial or for investigation in connection with an offence. There was nothing in s 22 which suggested that the power of retention can be for any purpose other than a purpose for which it was originally seized: *Chief Constable of Merseyside Police v Owens* [2012] EWHC 1515 (Admin, 176 CL&J 353).

A[87.4]

Often there is no such difficulty as stolen property can be restored direct to the rightful owner. In other cases where the defendant has been convicted for several offences eg theft, at the end of the case the police may be in possession of a large sum of money taken from the defendant. The various losers may each claim part or all of this money as being stolen from them or arising from the sale by the thief of the stolen property.

A[87.5]

The police, any claimant or even the defendant can lay a complaint or make an application asking the magistrates to decide the ownership of property and/or to whom the property should be delivered.

A[87.6]

At the hearing the police or a claimant has the right to call witnesses, cross-examine the other party's witnesses and to address the magistrates. The hearing can be expedited by the filing of written evidence which can include hearsay evidence.

A[87.7]

Powers of the magistrates. Having heard all the parties the magistrates may make an order for delivery of the property to the person who appears to the court to be the owner or if he cannot be ascertained they may make such order as they think fit (see A[87.17]). The court could only decline to return the property to its owner where it was satisfied that the use of its process would in fact indirectly assist in or encourage a crime: *Chief Constable of Merseyside Police v Owens* [2012] EWHC 1515 (Admin, 176 CL&J 353).

A[87.8]

This gives the magistrates wide powers of discretion. If, for instance, the magistrates are not impressed by any of the claims then they can order the money or the monies the police obtain from selling the stolen property (eg a stolen motor vehicle) to be paid to the Police Property Act Fund which is administered by the Police Authority. The money is invested and the income is used (a) to defray the expenses in handling and storing such property; (b) for compensating the persons who deliver such property to the police; (c) for charitable purposes.

A[87.9]

If there are several claimants, magistrates might find in favour of one claimant and order his claim to be paid and find against the other claimants and then order the balance of the money to be delivered to the fund.

A[87.10]–[87.16]

Deliver. It is to be noted that the word used in disposing of the property is 'delivered'. This means that an unsuccessful claimant can sue in the county court the authority or person to whom the magistrates order delivery, but must do so within six months from the date of the hearing, or his/her right ceases.

A[87.17]

Case unsuitable for magistrates' courts. The High Court has ruled that magistrates should hesitate to deal with a claim of a similar kind if the value of the property is substantial or if difficult matters of law are likely to arise. For example, a motor car which was stolen whilst subject to a hire-purchase agreement led to there being several claimants. See *Gough v Chief Constable of West Midlands* [2004] EWCA Civ 206, [2004] All ER (D) 45 (Mar) for the interaction with civil proceedings.

A[87.18]

If the magistrates decide that if either of the above points arise the best course is to adjourn the hearing *sine die* and to invite the claimant or claimants to commence proceedings in the county court or the High Court. Alternatively, the magistrates can decline to exercise their jurisdiction. A magistrates' court is not obliged to make an order.

A[87.19]

Criminal Damage Act 1971. The above provisions also apply if the police have possession of property following the execution of a search warrant granted under the Criminal Damage Act 1971, s 6.

A[87.20]

Costs. Proceedings should be commenced by way of complaint because in magistrates' courts there is no power to award costs where proceedings have been commenced by way of "application" (see for example, *R v Salisbury and Tisbury and Mere Combined Juvenile Court, ex p Ball* (1985) 149 JP 346. Where proceedings have begun by way of a complaint it is inappropriate to order costs against the police where they do not object to the order sought (*R v Uxbridge Justices, ex p Metropolitan Police Comr* [1981] 1 All ER 940, [1981] 1 WLR 112; affd [1981] QB 829, [1981] 3 All ER 129, CA).

A[88]

Shotgun (purchasing etc without shotgun certificate)

Charge

A[88.1]

Possessing, or purchasing or acquiring a shotgun without holding a shotgun certificate

Firearms Act 1968, s 2(1)

Maximum penalty – Fine level 5 and 6 months (**12 months). Triable either way.

Crown Court – 5 years' imprisonment and unlimited fine.

Mode of trial

A[88.2]

See general notes at I[4].

Legal notes and definitions

A[88.3]

Purchasing, possessing, acquiring. These are three separate offences and the charge should only allege one of these.

A[88.4]

Shotgun. Means a smooth bore gun with a barrel of 24 inches or longer with a bore not exceeding two inches and which is not a revolver nor has an illegal magazine, which is not an air gun.

A[88.5]

Certificate. This is granted by the police and it may contain conditions. Failure to observe the conditions is an offence which is also triable either way punishable on summary conviction by a fine of level 5 and/or 6 months' (**12 months) imprisonment; the offence carries five years on indictment and an unlimited fine (Firearms Act 1968, s 2(2)). The police can revoke the certificate if they are satisfied that it entails danger to public safety or peace.

A[88.6]

Exemptions. These include visitors to Great Britain who are holders of a visitor's shotgun permit; persons using shotguns on occasions and at places approved by the police; a person who borrows a shotgun and uses it on the lender's private premises, in the presence of the lender; persons holding a Northern Ireland firearm certificate which authorises holders to possess shotguns. See also A[76.9].

A[88.7]

ECHR. The degree of proof required from the defendant is to establish that on the balance of probabilities he was exempt. He does not have to establish this beyond reasonable doubt. Having regard to the legitimate aims of the legislation it is suggested that the imposition of a legal burden on the accused is necessary and proportionate so as to accord with art 6(2) of the ECHR.

Sentencing

A[88.8]

No SC guideline. For structure of the sentencing decision see B[3.6].

A[88.9]

Available sentences. See Table A at B[4.1].

A[88.10]

Forfeiture. The court can order the shotgun to be forfeited to the police or disposed of as it thinks fit.

A[88.11]

The court can also cancel any firearm or shotgun certificate held by the defendant.

A[89]

General bribery offences

Charges

A[89.1]

The following charges are available:

1. Bribing another person, or purchasing
Bribery Act 2010, s 1
Maximum penalty – Fine level 5 and 6 months (**12 months). Triable either way.
Crown Court – 10 years' imprisonment and unlimited fine.*

2. Offences relating to being bribed
Bribery Act 2010, s 2
Maximum penalty – Fine level 5 and 6 months (**12 months). Triable either way.
Crown Court – 10 years' imprisonment and unlimited fine.*

3. Bribery of foreign officials
Bribery Act 2010, s 6
Maximum penalty – Fine level 5 and 6 months (**12 months). Triable either way.
Crown Court – 10 years' imprisonment and unlimited fine.*

4. Failure of commercial organisation to prevent bribery
Bribery Act 2010, s 7
Maximum penalty – Indictable only
Crown Court – Unlimited fine.

*The maximum penalties above relate to individuals only.

No proceedings for an offence under this Act may be instituted in England and Wales except by or with the consent of—

(a)   the Director of Public Prosecutions,
(b)   the Director of the Serious Fraud Office, or
(c)   the Director of Revenue and Customs Prosecutions

A[89.2]

1. Offences of bribing another person

(1)   A person ("P") is guilty of an offence if either of the following cases applies.
(2)   Case 1 is where—
       (a)   P offers, promises or gives a financial or other advantage to another person, and
       (b)   P intends the advantage

(i)   to induce a person to perform improperly a relevant function or activity, or

(ii)   to reward a person for the improper performance of such a function or activity.

(3)   Case 2 is where—

(a)   P offers, promises or gives a financial or other advantage to another person, and

(b)   P knows or believes that the acceptance of the advantage would itself constitute the improper performance of a relevant function or activity.

(4)   In case 1 it does not matter whether the person to whom the advantage is offered, promised or given is the same person as the person who is to perform, or has performed, the function or activity concerned.

(5)   In cases 1 and 2 it does not matter whether the advantage is offered, promised or given by P directly or through a third party.

2. Offences relating to being bribed

(1)   A person ("R") is guilty of an offence if any of the following cases applies.

(2)   Case 3 is where R requests, agrees to receive or accepts a financial or other advantage intending that, in consequence, a relevant function or activity should be performed improperly (whether by R or another person).

(3)   Case 4 is where—

(a)   R requests, agrees to receive or accepts a financial or other advantage, and

(b)   the request, agreement or acceptance itself constitutes the improper performance by R of a relevant function or activity.

(4)   Case 5 is where R requests, agrees to receive or accepts a financial or other advantage as a reward for the improper performance (whether by R or another person) of a relevant function or activity.

(5)   Case 6 is where, in anticipation of or in consequence of R requesting, agreeing to receive or accepting a financial or other advantage, a relevant function or activity is performed improperly—

(a)   by R, or

(b)   by another person at R's request or with R's assent or acquiescence.

(6)   In cases 3 to 6 it does not matter—

(a)   whether R requests, agrees to receive or accepts (or is to request, agree to receive or accept) the advantage directly or through a third party,

(b)   whether the advantage is (or is to be) for the benefit of R or another person.

(7)   In cases 4 to 6 it does not matter whether R knows or believes that the performance of the function or activity is improper.

(8)   In case 6, where a person other than R is performing the function or activity, it also does not matter whether that person knows or believes that the performance of the function or activity is improper.

3. Bribery of foreign public officials

(1)   A person ("P") who bribes a foreign public official ("F") is guilty of an offence if P's intention is to influence F in F's capacity as a foreign public official.

(2)   P must also intend to obtain or retain—
     (a)   business, or
     (b)   an advantage in the conduct of business.

(3)   P bribes F if, and only if—
     (a)   directly or through a third party, P offers, promises or gives any financial or other advantage—
         (i)   to F, or
         (ii)   to another person at F's request or with F's assent or acquiescence, and
     (b)   F is neither permitted nor required by the written law applicable to F to be influenced in F's capacity as a foreign public official by the offer, promise or gift.

(4)   References in this section to influencing F in F's capacity as a foreign public official mean influencing F in the performance of F's functions as such an official, which includes—
     (a)   any omission to exercise those functions, and
     (b)   any use of F's position as such an official, even if not within F's authority.

(5)   "Foreign public official" means an individual who—
     (a)   holds a legislative, administrative or judicial position of any kind, whether appointed or elected, of a country or territory outside the United Kingdom (or any subdivision of such a country or territory)
     (b)   exercises a public function—
         (i)   for or on behalf of a country or territory outside the United Kingdom (or any subdivision of such a country or territory), or
         (ii)   for any public agency or public enterprise of that country or territory (or subdivision), or
     (c)   is an official or agent of a public international organisation.

(6)   "Public international organisation" means an organisation whose members are any of the following—
     (a)   countries or territories,
     (b)   governments of countries or territories
     (c)   other public international organisations,
     (d)   a mixture of any of the above.

(7)   For the purposes of subsection (3)(b), the written law applicable to F is—
     (a)   where the performance of the functions of F which P intends to influence would be subject to the law of any part of the United Kingdom, the law of that part of the United Kingdom,
     (b)   where paragraph (a) does not apply and F is an official or agent of a public international organisation, the applicable written rules of that organisation,
     (c)   where paragraphs (a) and (b) do not apply, the law of the country or territory in relation to which F is a foreign public official so far as that law is contained in—

    (i)   any written constitution, or provision made by or under legislation, applicable to the country or territory concerned, or

    (ii)   any judicial decision which is so applicable and is evidenced in published written sources.

(8)   For the purposes of this section, a trade or profession is a business.

Mode of trial

A[89.3]

See general notes at I[4].

Legal notes and definitions

A[89.4]

The Bribery Act 2010 received Royal Assent on 8 April 2010 and came into force on 1 July 2011. Amendments by virtue of the Bribery Act 2010 (Consequential Amendments) Order 2011 reflect the abolition of the following offences:

(1)   The common law offences of bribery and embracery.
(2)   The Public Bodies Corrupt Practices Act 1889.
(3)   The Prevention of Corruption Act 1906.
(4)   The Prevention of Corruption Act 1916.

Section 1: Offences of bribing another person

A[89.5]

Makes it an offence for a person ('P') to offer, promise or give a financial or other advantage to another person in one of two cases:

* Case 1 applies where P intends the advantage to bring about the improper performance by another person of a relevant function or activity or to reward such improper performance.
* Case 2 applies where P knows or believes that the acceptance of the advantage offered, promised or given in itself constitutes the improper performance of a relevant function or activity.

'Improper performance' is defined at ss 3, 4 and 5 of the Bribery Act 2010. In summary, this means performance which amounts to a breach of an expectation that a person will act in good faith, impartially, or in accordance with a position of trust. The offence applies to bribery relating to any function of a public nature, connected with a business, performed in the course of a person's employment or performed on behalf of a company or another body of persons. Therefore, bribery in both the public and private sectors is covered.

For the purposes of deciding whether a function or activity has been performed improperly the test of what is expected is a test of what a reasonable person in the UK would expect in relation to the performance of that function or activity. Where the performance of the function or activity is not subject to UK law (for example, it takes place in a country outside UK jurisdiction) then any local custom or practice must be disregarded – unless permitted or required by the written law applicable to that particular country. Written law means any written constitution, provision made by or under legislation applicable to the country concerned or any judicial decision evidenced in published written sources.

By way of illustration, in order to proceed with a case under Bribery Act 2010, s 1 based on an allegation that hospitality was intended as a bribe, the prosecution would need to show that the hospitality was intended to induce conduct that amounts to a breach of an expectation that a person will act in good faith, impartially, or in accordance with a position of trust. This would be judged by what a reasonable person in the UK thought. So, for example, an invitation to foreign clients to attend a Six Nations match at Twickenham as part of a public relations exercise designed to cement good relations or enhance knowledge in the organisation's field is extremely unlikely to engage s 1 as there is unlikely to be evidence of an intention to induce improper performance of a relevant function.

Section 2: Offences relating to being bribed

A[89.6]

This section defines the offence of bribery as it applies to the recipient or potential recipient of the bribe, who is called R. It distinguishes four cases, namely Case 3 to Case 6.

In Cases 3, 4 and 5 there is a requirement that R "requests, agrees to receive or accepts" an advantage, whether or not R actually receives it. This requirement must then be linked with the "improper performance" of a relevant function or activity. As with section 1, the nature of this function or activity is addressed in section 3, and "improper performance" is defined in section 4. The link between the request, agreement to receive or acceptance of an advantage and improper performance may take three forms:

- R may intend improper performance to follow as a consequence of the request, agreement to receive or acceptance of the advantage (Case 3, in subsection (2));
- requesting, agreeing to receive or accepting the advantage may itself amount to improper performance of the relevant function or activity (Case 4, in subsection (3));
- alternatively, the advantage may be a reward for performing the function or activity improperly (Case 5, in subsection (4)).

In Cases 3 and 5, it does not matter whether the improper performance is by R or by another person. In Case 4, it must be R's requesting, agreeing to receive or acceptance of the advantage which amounts to improper performance, subject to subsection (6).

In Case 6 (subsection (5)) what is required is improper performance by R (or another person, where R requests it, assents to or acquiesces in it). This performance must be in anticipation or in consequence of a request, agreement to receive or acceptance of an advantage. Subsection (6) is concerned with the role of R in requesting, agreeing to receive or accepting advantages, or in benefiting from them, in Cases 3 to 6. First, this subsection makes it clear that in Cases 3 to 6 it does not matter whether it is R, or someone else through whom R acts, who requests, agrees to receive or accepts the advantage (subsection (6)(a)). Secondly, subsection (6) indicates that the advantage can be for the benefit of R, or of another person (subsection (6)(b)).

Subsection (7) makes it clear that in Cases 4 to 6, it is immaterial whether R knows or believes that the performance of the function is improper. Additionally, by subsection (8), in Case 6 where the function or activity is performed by another person, it is immaterial whether that person knew or believed that the performance of the function is improper.

Section 6: Bribery of a foreign public official

A[89.7]

Creates a stand alone offence of bribery of a foreign public official. The offence is committed where a person offers, promises or gives a financial or other advantage to a foreign public official with the intention of influencing the official in the performance of his or her official functions. The person offering, promising or giving the advantage must also intend to obtain or retain business or an advantage in the conduct of business by doing so. However, the offence is not committed where the official is permitted or required by the applicable written law to be influenced by the advantage.

A 'foreign public official' includes officials, whether elected or appointed, who hold a legislative, administrative or judicial position of any kind of a country or territory outside the UK. It also includes any person who performs public functions in any branch of the national, local or municipal government of such a country or territory or who exercises a public function for any public agency or public enterprise of such a country or territory, such as professionals working for public health agencies and officers exercising public functions in state-owned enterprises. Foreign public officials can also be an official or agent of a public international organisation, such as the UN or the World Bank.

Sections 1 and 6 may capture the same conduct but will do so in different ways. The policy that founds the offence at section 6 is the need to prohibit the influencing of decision making in the context of publicly funded business opportunities by the inducement of personal enrichment of foreign public officials or to others at the official's request, assent or acquiescence. Such activity is very likely to involve conduct which amounts to 'improper performance' of a relevant function or activity to which section 1 applies, but, unlike section 1, section 6 does not require proof of it or an intention to induce it. This is because the exact nature of the functions of persons regarded as foreign public officials is often very difficult to ascertain with any accuracy, and the securing of evidence will often be reliant on the co-operation of the state any such officials serve. To require the prosecution to rely entirely on section 1 would amount to a very significant deficiency in the ability of the legislation to address this particular mischief. That said, it is not the Government's intention to criminalise behaviour where no such mischief occurs, but merely to formulate the offence to take account of the evidential difficulties referred to above. In view of its wide scope, and its role in the new form of corporate liability at section 7, the Government offers the following further explanation of issues arising from the formulation of section 6.

Local law. For the purposes of section 6 prosecutors will be required to show not only that an 'advantage' was offered, promised or given to the official or to another person at the official's request, assent or acquiescence, but that the advantage was one that the official was not permitted or required to be influenced by as determined by the written law applicable to the foreign official.

In seeking tenders for publicly funded contracts Governments often permit or require those tendering for the contract to offer, in addition to the principal tender, some kind of additional investment in the local economy or benefit to the local community. Such arrangements could in certain circumstances amount to a financial or other 'advantage' to a public official or to another person at the official's request, assent or acquiescence. Where, however, relevant 'written law' permits or requires the official to be influenced by such arrangements they will fall outside the scope of the offence. So, for example, where local planning law permits community investment or requires a foreign public official to minimise the cost of public procurement administration through cost sharing with contractors, a prospective contractor's offer of free training is very unlikely to engage section 6. In circumstances where the additional investment would amount to an advantage to a foreign public official and the local law is silent as to whether the official is permitted or required to be influenced by it, prosecutors will consider the public interest in prosecuting. This will provide an appropriate backstop in circumstances where the evidence suggests that the offer of additional investment is a legitimate part of a tender exercise.

Hospitality, promotional, and other business expenditure. Bona fide hospitality and promotional, or other business expenditure which seeks to improve the image of a commercial organisation, better to present products and services, or establish cordial relations, is recognised as an established and important part of doing business and it is not the intention of the Act to criminalise such behaviour. The Government does not intend for the Act to prohibit reasonable and proportionate hospitality and promotional or other similar business expenditure intended for these purposes. It is, however, clear that hospitality and promotional or other similar business expenditure can be employed as bribes.

In order to amount to a bribe under section 6 there must be an intention for a financial or other advantage to influence the official in his or her official role and thereby secure business or a business advantage. In this regard, it may be in some circumstances that hospitality or promotional expenditure in the form of travel and accommodation costs does not even amount to 'a financial or other advantage' to the relevant official because it is a cost that would otherwise be borne by the relevant foreign Government rather than the official him or herself.

Where the prosecution is able to establish a financial or other advantage has been offered, promised or given, it must then show that there is a sufficient connection between the advantage and the intention to influence and secure business or a business advantage. Where the prosecution cannot prove this to the requisite standard then no offence under section 6 will be committed. There may be direct evidence to support the existence of this connection and such evidence may indeed relate to relatively modest expenditure. In many cases, however, the question as to whether such a connection can be established will depend on the totality of the evidence which takes into account all of the surrounding circumstances. It would include matters such as the type and level of advantage offered, the manner and form in which the advantage is provided, and the level of influence the particular foreign public official has over awarding the business. In this circumstantial context, the more lavish the hospitality or the higher the expenditure in relation to travel, accommodation or other similar business expenditure provided to a foreign public official, then, generally, the greater the inference that it is intended to influence the official to grant business or a business advantage in return.

The standards or norms applying in a particular sector may also be relevant here. However, simply providing hospitality or promotional, or other similar business expenditure which is commensurate with such norms is not, of itself, evidence that no bribe was paid if there is other evidence to the contrary; particularly if the norms in question are extravagant. Levels of expenditure will not, therefore, be the only consideration in determining whether a section 6 offence has been committed. But in the absence of any further evidence demonstrating the required connection, it is unlikely, for example, that incidental provision of a routine business courtesy will raise the inference that it was intended to have a direct impact on decision making, particularly where such hospitality is commensurate with the reasonable and proportionate norms for the particular industry; e.g. the provision of airport to hotel transfer services to facilitate an on-site visit, or dining and tickets to an event.

Section 3: Function or activity to which bribe relates

A[89.8]

This section defines the fields within which bribery can take place, in other words the types of function or activity that can be improperly performed for the purposes of sections 1 and 2. The term "relevant function or activity" is used for this purpose.

The purpose of the section is to ensure that the law of bribery applies equally to public and to selected private functions without discriminating between the two. Accordingly the functions or activities in question include all functions of a public nature and all activities connected with a business, trade or profession. The phrase "functions of a public nature" is the same phrase as is used in the definition of "public authority" in section 6(3)(b) of the Human Rights Act 1998 but it is not limited in the way it is in that Act. In addition, the functions or activities include all activities performed either in the course of employment or on behalf of any body of persons: these two categories straddle the public/private divide.

Not every defective performance of one of these functions for reward or in the hope of advantage engages the law of bribery. Subsections (3) to (5) make clear that there must be an expectation that the functions be carried out in good faith (condition A), or impartially (condition B), or the person performing it must be in a position of trust (condition C).

Subsection (6) provides that the functions or activities in question may be carried out either in the UK or abroad, and need have no connection with the UK. This preserves the effect of section 108(1) and (2) of the Anti-terrorism, Crime and Security Act 2001 (which is repealed by the Act).

Section 4: Improper performance to which bribe relates

A[89.9]

Section 4 defines "improper performance" as performance which breaches a relevant expectation, as mentioned in condition A or B (subsections (3) and (4) of section 3 respectively) or any expectation as to the manner in which, or reasons for which, a function or activity satisfying condition C (subsection (5) of section 3) will be performed. Subsection (1)(b) states that an omission can in some circumstances amount to improper "performance".

Subsection (3) addresses the case where R is no longer engaged in a given function or activity but still carries out acts related to his or her former function or activity. These acts are treated as done in performance of the function or activity in question.

Section 5: Expectation test

A[89.10]

Section 5 provides that when deciding what is expected of a person performing a function or activity for the purposes of sections 3 and 4, the test is what a reasonable person in the UK would expect of a person performing the relevant function or activity. Subsection (2) makes it clear that in deciding what a reasonable person in the UK would expect in relation to functions or activities the performance of which is not subject to UK laws, local practice and custom must not be taken into account unless such practice or custom is permitted or required by written law. Subsection (3) defines what is meant by "written law" for the purposes of this section.

Sentencing

A[89.11]

No Sentencing Council guideline.

Sentencing

Index to sentencing

(**Indicates changes introduced by virtue of the CJA 2003 from a date to be appointed)

Absolute discharge B[31]

Activity requirement B[17.3]

Action plan order B[7A]

Alcohol Treatment requirement B[17.14]

Anti-social behaviour order including breach B[8] and B[8.15]

Assessment of fines B[33A]

Attendance centre order (aged 10 to 21) B[9]

Binding over B[10]

Closure order (specified prostitution offences) B[53]

Community orders B[17]
Breach of a requirement B[17.16] and A[17]

Committal to Crown Court for sentence B[11]–B[16]

Community sentence B[3]

Compensation order B[18]

Conditional discharge B[31]

Confiscation order B[19]

Costs B[20]

Curfew requirement B[17.6]

Custodial sentence B[2]

Deferred sentence B[21]–B[22]

Deportation B[23]

Deprivation of property B[34]

Detention and training order B[25]

Detention
in courthouse B[24]
in young offender institution B[26]–B[30]

Disqualification and endorsement C[5]

Domestic violence protection notice B[54]

Domestic violence protection order B[55]

Drug rehabilitation requirement B[17.11]

Exclusion orders
Drinking banning orders B[32A]
Licensed premises B[32]

Exclusion requirement B[18]

Fines B[33]

(Assessment of fines) B[33A]

Fines unpaid B[33.37]
enforcement procedure B[33.37]
means inquiry B[33.62]
18 to 21 age group B[33.85]
10 to 17 age group B[33.93]

Football banning orders B[41]–B[46]

Foreign Travel Prohibition requirement B[17.7]

Foreign Travel Restriction order B[52]

Forfeiture B[34]

Forfeiture or suspension of liquor licence B[47]

Guardianship order B[35]

Hospital order B[36]

Imprisonment B[37]
suspended sentence B[37.40]

Legal aid contribution order B[7]

Mental Health Treatment requirement B[17.9]

Mental Health Treatment at place other than that specified in the order B[17.10]

Multiplicity of charges B[6]

Parenting order B[37A]

Power to review decisions B[7]

Process of sentencing B[5]

Programme requirement B[17.4]

Prohibited activity requirement B[17.5]

Referral order B[48]–B[49]

Referral order B[48]–B[49]

Remission to another court B[1]

Reparation order B[38]

Residence requirement B[17.8]

Restitution order B[39]

Restraining order A[41.13]

Review of decisions B[7]

Sentencing tables B[4]

Structure B[5.2]

aggravating and mitigating features **B[5.2A]**
aggravated related to race, religion, disability or sexual orientation **B[5.2B]**

Supervision requirement B[17.15]

Surcharge (see fines, costs and compensation at B[18], B[20] and B[33].

Suspended sentence (See Imprisonment) B[37.40]

Transfer of criminal proceedings B[1A]

Unpaid work requirement B[17.2]

Violent Offender Order B[51]

Youth Rehabilitation Order B[50]
YRO requirements (Sch 1, Pt 1 CJ & IA 2008) B[50.4] onwards)
The details are to be found in Schedule 1 of the Act and the relevant paragraph to the
   Schedule is indicated below in each of the available requirements:
(1)   Intensive supervision and surveillance requirement
(2)   Activity requirement (paras 6–8)
(3)   Supervision requirement (para 9)
(4)   Unpaid work requirement for those aged 16–17 years when convicted
        (para 10)
(5)   Programme requirement (para 11)
(6)   Attendance centre requirement (para 12)
(7)   Prohibited activity requirement (para 13)
(8)   Curfew requirement (para 14)
(9)   Exclusion requirement (para 15)
(10)   Residence requirement (para 16)
(11)   Local authority residence requirement (paras 17 and 19)
(12)   Fostering requirement (paras 4, 18–19)
(13)   Mental health treatment requirement (paras 20–21)
(14)   Drug treatment/drug testing requirement (paras 22–23)
(15)   Intoxicating substance treatment requirement (para 24)
(16)   Education requirement (para 25)
(17)   Electronic monitoring requirement (para 26)
Breach of a YRO requirement B[50.23]
Commission of further offence B[50.24]

Application to revoke **B[50.25]**
Amendment **B[50.26]**

B[1]

Remission to another court

B[1.1]

If the following conditions are met a magistrates' court may remit an offender to another magistrates' court (Powers of Criminal Courts (Sentencing) Act 2000, s 10). The conditions are:

(a)   The court proposing to remit has convicted the offender of an offence which is punishable by either imprisonment or disqualification.

(b)   The offender has attained 18 years of age.

(c)   The court to which the convicting court proposes to remit has convicted the offender of another such offence but has not sentenced him nor committed him to the crown court to be dealt with.

(d)   The receiving court consents to the remission.

B[1.2]

The offender may be remitted on bail or in custody. He is not required to consent to the remission nor has he any right of appeal against it.

B[1.3]

Juveniles. A magistrates' court which has found a juvenile offender (under 18) guilty of an offence must remit the juvenile to a youth court unless satisfied that it is undesirable to do so (Powers of Criminal Courts (Sentencing) Act 2000, s 8) and must exercise that power unless it is of the opinion that the case is one which can properly be dealt with by means of:

(a)   an absolute or conditional discharge;

(b)   a fine.

B[1.4]

The court to which he is remitted will normally be the youth court for the area in which he resides. If the court finding the juvenile guilty is itself a youth court it may remit to another youth court or deal with him as it thinks fit.

Remittal to an adult court.

B[1.5]

If a juvenile attains the age of 18 before trial in the youth court or after conviction but before sentence the youth court may remit for trial or sentence to the adult court in the same petty sessions area. The remittal may be on bail or in custody.

Although s 29(2) of the MCA 1980 gave an express power for the magistrates' court to remit a juvenile to the youth court for trial where an adult co-accused pleaded guilty, there was no similar power to do so in the Crown Court. The Crown Court Judge could not use s 66 of the Courts Act 2003 to sit as a district judge (magistrates' courts) to revisit the mode of trial as s 25 of the MCA 1980 did not apply: *R (on the application of W (A Minor) v Leeds Crown Court and CPS* [2011] EWHC 2326 (Admin), [2012] 1 Cr App Rep 162, 175 JP 467.

B[1A]

Transfer of criminal proceedings

B[1A.1]

Where a person appears or is brought before a magistrates' court –

(a)   to be tried by the court for an offence, or
(b)   for the court to inquire into the offence as examining justices,

the court may transfer the matter to another magistrates' court (MCA 1980, s 27A as inserted by Courts Act 2003, s 46).

The court may transfer the matter before or after beginning the trial or inquiry. If the magistrates' court transfers before hearing all of the evidence and the parties the court to whom the case has been transferred must, in effect, hear the evidence and the parties again. The power to transfer must be exercised in accordance with any directions given under Courts Act 2003, s 30(3).

B[1A.2]

It would appear that the consent of the magistrates' court to which the proceedings are to be transferred is not a legal requirement. Good practice suggests that the court to whom the case has been transferred should be contacted prior to transfer. (See JCS document: 'Guidance on the use of s 27A MCA 1980'; ref 54.004, Intel October 2008.)

B[1A.3]

The reference to "examining justices" will become otiose on or after a date to be appointed by virtue of the CJA 2003 (allocation proceedings).

B[2]

Custodial sentences

B[2.1]

There are three main forms of custodial sentence: imprisonment, detention in a young offender institution and detention and training orders. By virtue of the CJA 2003, sentences of custody plus and intermittent custody will be available nationally from a date to be appointed. Assuming the provisions of the CJA 2003 are implemented, the new sentencing disposals will only apply to offences committed on or after the operative date.

B[2.2]

Imprisonment (at **B[37]**) is confined to defendants over the age of 21 years (****18 years). The minimum period is 5 days (****14 days) and the maximum is that fixed by statute. There is one other form of imprisonment – the suspended sentence.

B[2.3]

Detention in a young offender institution (at **B[25]**) is the equivalent of imprisonment for those under 21. The minimum age is 18 years for both males and females. (****From a date to be appointed sentences of detention in a YOI will be replaced by imprisonment for offences committed on or after the operative date.)

B[2.4]

The general minimum for 18–21 year old offenders is 21 days. In the case of detention in a young offender institution imposed for breach of a supervision order made on release from such an institution a term not exceeding 30 days may be imposed. (****B[2.2]** will apply to offences committed on or after the appointed date.)

B[2.5]

The maximum term is generally the maximum term that an adult could receive for the offence. The maximum is 12 months for two indictable offences. (****From an appointed date, the maximum sentence prescribed for summary offences will be 51 weeks. For indictable offences the maximum sentence will be 12 months imprisonment for a single offence and 65 weeks maximum for two or more indictable offences.)

B[2.6]

Detention and training orders. Available for 12 to 17 year old offenders inclusive. The court may order a period of 4, 6, 8, 10, 12, 18 or 24 months, half of which will be detention in a training centre and half of which will be supervised in the community. The offence must carry a sentence of four months or more were an adult to be charged with a similar offence. Accordingly, a detention and training order is not available in the case of a youth convicted of an offence of criminal damage where the damage alleged is below £5,000 (*Pye v Leeds Youth Court* [2006] EWHC 2527 (Admin), [2006] All ER (D) 16 (Oct)).

B[2.7]

Presence of the accused. Imprisonment (or its equivalent) cannot be imposed in the absence of the accused.

B[2.8]

Legal representation. A person shall not be sentenced to a custodial sentence of any form (whether suspended or not) unless he is legally represented. There are two exceptions:

(i)   where he has either been granted the right to representation funded by the Legal Services Commission and had it withdrawn because of his conduct or has been informed of his right to apply for representation and he failed to apply for it;

(ii)   (as from 2 October 2006) his means have been assessed as such that he is required to make a contribution to his legal costs and he declines or fails to make the appropriate contributions in accordance with regulations made under the Criminal Defence Service Act 2006.

B[2.9]

Restrictions on imposing custodial sentences. A court may not pass a custodial sentence in any form on an offender of any age unless it is satisfied that:

(a)   the offence, or the combination of the offence and one or more offences associated with it, was so serious that neither a fine alone nor a community sentence can be justified for the offence; or

(b)   the offender fails to express a required willingness to comply with a requirement in a community order; or

(c)   the offender fails to comply with an order for pre-sentence drug testing (CJA 2003, s 161(2));

(d)   in the case of an offender aged under 18, the court must obtain a pre-sentence report. The pre-sentence report must be in writing and cannot be given orally.

B[2.10]–[2.15]

In forming such an opinion a court must take into account all such information about the circumstances of the offence (including any associated offences and any aggravating or mitigating factors) as is available to it, which will almost invariably include information in a pre-sentence report (see below). A court may also take into account any information about the offender which is before it. The court may take into account previous convictions and previous failures to respond to sentences when assessing the seriousness of current offending.

B[2.16]

Exceptionally ((b) above) the court may impose a custodial sentence where the defendant refuses to give his consent to a requirement in a community order proposed by the court which requires his consent.

B[2.17]

Apart from the exceptional case, the court must state in open court that it is of the opinion that either one or other of the criteria (a), (b) or (c) apply and why it is of that opinion. In any case, the court must explain to the offender in ordinary language why it is imposing a custodial sentence on him.

Even where the custody threshold is reached the court should take into account:

- the clear intention of the threshold test is to reserve custody as a punishment for the most serious offences;
- passing the custody threshold does not mean that a custodial sentence should be deemed inevitable; custody can still be avoided in light of personal mitigation or where there is a suitable intervention in the community which provides sufficient restriction (by way of punishment) while addressing the rehabilitation of the offender to prevent future crime. However, where the offence would otherwise appear to warrant a term of imprisonment within the Crown Court's jurisdiction, it is for the Crown Court to make that judgement;
- the approach to the imposition of a custodial sentence should be as follows:
  - (a) Has the custody threshold been passed?
  - (b) If so, is it unavoidable that a custodial sentence be imposed?
  - (c) If so, can that sentence be suspended? (Sentencers should be clear that they would have imposed a custodial sentence if the power to suspend had not been available.)
  - (d) If not, impose a sentence which takes immediate effect for the shortest possible term commensurate with the seriousness of the offence (CJA 2003, s 153(2)).

Length of custodial sentences

B[2.18]

A custodial sentence passed by a court shall be for such term (not exceeding the permitted maximum) as in the opinion of the court is commensurate with the seriousness of the offence, or a combination of the offence and other offences associated with it.

B[2.19]

In determining sentence the court must have regard to the guidelines set by the Sentencing Guidelines Council and, if it departs from those guidelines, the court must state its opinion and reasons in open court and give an explanation to the offender in ordinary language.

B[2.20]

In forming an opinion on the appropriate length of sentence the court must take into account all such information about the circumstances of the offence (including any associated offences and any aggravating or mitigating factors) as is available to it (such as a pre-sentence report). In passing a sentence of imprisonment, subject to the exceptions contained in CJA 2003, s 240(4), the court must direct that the number of days for which the offender was remanded in custody in connection with an offence or a related offence shall count as time served by the offender as part of the sentence imposed (CJA 2003, s 240(3)).

It is wrong to indicate, on the imposition of a suspended sentence, that time served on remand would not count as time served as part of the sentence: see CJA 2003, s 240(7) and *Carruthers v Hampshire Probation Service* [2010] 1961 (Admin), 174 CL&J 510, (2010) Times, 26 August.

Police detention did not fall within the 'credit for time served' provisions of the Criminal Justice Act 2003, s 240: *R v Tariq Al-Daour; R v Wassem Mughal* [2011] EWCA Crim 2392.

*LASPOA 2012, s 108 when brought into force, does away with s 240 and replaces it with a new s 240ZA(3). The principal effect of the new section is to remove from the sentencing court any responsibility for dealing with time in custody on remand. Days will not count if on the day concerned the offender was detained in connection with any other matter, although if he was simultaneously remanded in connection with other offences, those days will count. The section applies to determinate sentences under PCCSA 2000, s 91 and sentences of detention in a young offender institution. The effect of s 240ZA appears to be that time served on remand before the imposition of a community order or before a suspended sentence order, where either order is revoked and the offender re-sentenced to custody, will be deducted automatically from the sentence.

Section 21 of the Criminal Justice and Immigration Act 2008 inserted a new s 240A into the Criminal Justice Act 2003 whereby, subject to s 240A(4), the court is obliged to direct that any time served by the offender while on bail subject to a qualifying curfew condition and an electronic monitoring condition shall count as time served by the offender as part of the sentence imposed (CJA 2003, s 240A(3)), unless it is just in all the circumstances not to give such a direction. The offender must have been subject to a curfew of at least nine hours long on any given day. Only half the period on bail counts eg a person on bail for six days would be entitled to have three days counted as time served. There is provision to round up in the case of odd number days. It is advisable that magistrates **consult with their legal adviser** on the effect of this provision.*

*An amended version of s 240A will come into effect when s 109 of LASPOA 2012 is implemented. The new formula appears to be similar, in effect, to the old formula.

The fact that a defendant had entered a late guilty plea did not on its own justify the withholding of a direction under s 240 (*R v Vaughan* [2008] All ER (D) 315 (Jun)).

For concurrent or consecutive sentences imposed on the same occasion or on subsequent occasions the drafting of the legislation is far from clear (see *R v Barber* [2006] EWCA Crim 162, [2006] 2 Cr App Rep (S) 539). Justices should consult their legal adviser.

In passing a detention and training order on a juvenile offender the [youth] court must also take into account any time spent on secure remand when fixing the length of sentence, and time spent on remand must be calculated and announced at time of sentence in cases of imprisonment.

Pre-sentence report

B[2.21]

This means a report in writing which is made by a probation officer (or social worker) with a view to assisting the court in determining the most suitable method of dealing with an offender and contains such information as to such matters as may be prescribed by the Secretary of State.

B[2.22]

Before forming an opinion on the necessity for, and appropriate length of, a custodial sentence the court should obtain a pre-sentence report. Although a custodial sentence is not invalidated by the court's failure to obtain such a report, magistrates will no doubt continue to wish to meet the statutory requirement in all cases where an offender is in jeopardy of losing his liberty despite the 'let out' clause 'unless the court is of the opinion that it is unnecessary to obtain a pre-sentence report' (see **B[2.9]** above).

Mentally disordered offenders

B[2.23]

Where the offender is, or appears to be, mentally disordered, the court must, unless in the circumstances of the case it appears unnecessary to do so, obtain a medical report made orally or in writing by a doctor approved under the Mental Health Act 1983 as having special experience in the diagnosis or treatment of mental disorder.

B[2.24]

Where a court is considering a custodial sentence in such circumstances it must consider:

(a)   any information before it which relates to his mental condition (whether given in a medical report, a pre-sentence report or otherwise); and

(b)   the likely effect of such a sentence on that condition and on any treatment which may be available for it.

B[3]

Community sentences

B[3.1]

The Criminal Justice Act 2003 introduced the concept of a 'community order', ie a sentence which consists of or includes one or more requirements: see B[17.35]. This generic community order only applies to defendants over 18 years.

B[3.2]

A court may not impose a community sentence unless:

(a)   the offence is punishable with imprisonment (s 150A CJA 2003);

(b)   it is of the opinion that the offence was serious enough to warrant such a sentence taking into account all such information about the circumstances of the offence (including any associated offences or any aggravating or mitigating factors) as is available to it;

(c)   the particular order or orders comprising or forming part of the sentence are such as in the opinion of the court is, or taken together are, the most suitable for the offender taking into account any information about the offender which is before it (such as a pre-sentence report, see below);

(d)   the restrictions on liberty imposed by the order or orders are such as in the opinion of the court are commensurate with the seriousness of the offence, or the combination of the offence and other offences associated with it, taking into account information about the circumstances etc as in (a) above.

Note that there will still be cases where the community threshold has been passed but a fine or discharge is still an appropriate penalty (see s 148(5) CJA 2003).

B[3.3]–[3.4]

When considering seriousness of the current offence or offences previous convictions and previous failures to respond to court orders may be taken into account.

Pre-sentence report

B[3.5]

Before forming an opinion as to the suitability for an offender of one or

more of the above orders, the court should obtain and consider a
pre-sentence report unless it is of the opinion that it is unnecessary to obtain
one.

B[3.6]

An adult community order must specify an end* date of not more than 3
years after commencement when all requirements must be completed.
Individual requirements, aside from supervision, may be specified to be
completed in a shorter period than that of the overall order.

*When s 66 of LASPOA 2012 is brought into force.

The sentencing decision

B[3.7]

SENTENCING FORM FOR PSR

A: PRE-SENTENCE ASSESSMENT STAGE

DATE: [ ] 1a) **DEFENDANT:** [ ]

b) **D.O.B:** [ ] c) **ADDRESS:** [ ]

2. **CUSTODY:** [ ] **BAIL:** [ ]

3. **CHARGES:** [ ]

4. **GUIDELINE SENTENCE:** Fine/discharge [ ] Community [ ] Custody [ ] Commit for Sentence [ ]

5. **OFFENCE FACTORS INFLUENCING ASSESSMENT**

a) Aggravating factors: [ ]

b) Mitigating factors: [ ]

c) Culpability   intentional [ ]   reckless [ ]

knew likely outcome [ ]   negligent [ ]

d) Harm caused/risked: [ ]

6. **OFFENDER FACTORS INFLUENCING ASSESSMENT**

[ ]

7. **SERIOUSNESS** (sentencing range justified by offence and offending factors)   **L   M   H**

Fine/discharge (no **PSR**) [ ]   Community (serious enough) [ ] [ ] [ ]

Custody (so serious) [ ]   Commit to Crown Court (too serious) [ ]

8. **MAIN (1) AND SECONDARY (2) PURPOSE(S) OF SENTENCE**

Punishment [ ]   Rehabilitation [ ]   Reduction in crime/deterrence [ ]

Protection of public [ ]   Reparation [ ]

9. **REPORT TYPE:**   Fast [ ]   Standard [ ]   Due: [ ]

B: SENTENCING STAGES

10. FACTORS ARISING FROM REPORT
Including, if appropriate, a) why you have reached a different conclusion from the indications of seriousness and purpose already given, or b) why you are departing from the proposals in the report.

11. SENTENCE TO BE IMPOSED (referring to reasons)

12. CREDIT FOR GUILTY PLEA
Record a) the extent of credit given and reasons for it, or b) what the sentence would have been if a timely guilty plea had been entered. (NB: Do not double count credit)

13. ANCILLARY ORDERS
Details of compensation (or reasons for not awarding it), plus other ancillary orders.

14. REASONS FOR DEPARTING FROM SENTENCING COUNCIL GUIDELINES

15. EXPLAIN SENTENCE USING APPROPRIATE PRONOUNCEMENTS

B[4]

Sentencing tables

B[4.1]

See the following pages for the sentencing tables.

B[4.1]

Table A

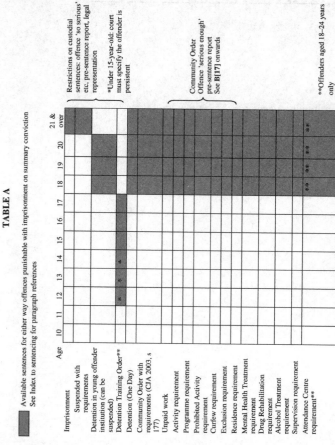

TABLE A

Available sentences for either way offences punishable with imprisonment on summary conviction
See Index to sentencing for paragraph references

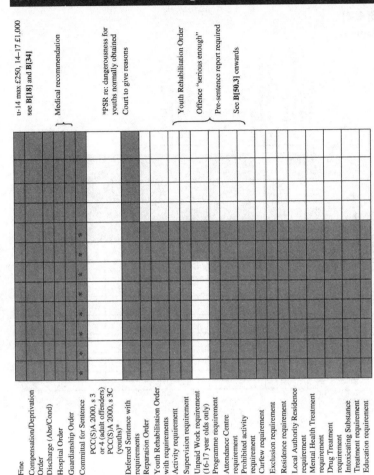

u-14 max £250, 14–17 £1,000 see **B[18]** and **B[34]**

Medical recommendation

*PSR re: dangerousness for youths normally obtained
Court to give reasons

Youth Rehabilitation Order
Offence "serious enough"
Pre-sentence report required
See **B[50.3]** onwards

Fine
Compensation/Deprivation Order
Discharge (Abs/Cond)
Hospital Order
Guardianship Order
Committal for Sentence PCC(S)A 2000, s 3 or 4 (adult offenders) PCC(S)A 2000, s 3C (youths)*
Deferred Sentence with requirements
Reparation Order
Youth Rehabilitation Order with requirements
Activity requirement
Supervision requirement
Unpaid Work requirement (16-17 year olds only)
Programme requirement
Attendance Centre requirement
Prohibited activity requirement
Curfew requirement
Exclusion requirement
Residence requirement
Local Authority Residence requirement
Mental Health Treatment requirement
Drug Treatment requirement
Intoxicating Substance Treatment requirement
Education requirement

B[4.2]

Table B

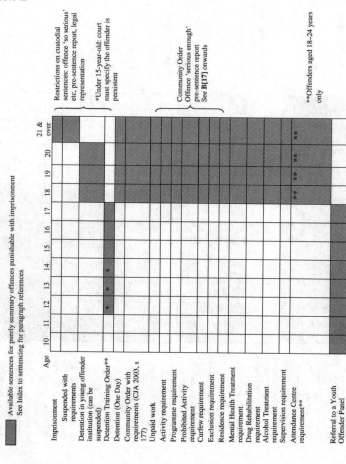

TABLE B

Available sentences for purely summary offences punishable with imprisonment
See Index to sentencing for paragraph references

Age	10	11	12	13	14	15	16	17	18	19	20	21 & over
Imprisonment												
Suspended with requirements												
Detention in young offender institution (can be suspended)												
Detention Training Order**		*	*	*	*							
Detention (One Day)												
Community Order with requirements (CJA 2003, s 177)												
Unpaid work												
Activity requirement												
Programme requirement												
Prohibited Activity requirement												
Curfew requirement												
Exclusion requirement												
Residence requirement												
Mental Health Treatment requirement												
Drug Rehabilitation requirement												
Alcohol Treatment requirement												
Supervision requirement												
Attendance Centre requirement**									**	**	**	**
Referral to a Youth Offender Panel												

Restrictions on custodial sentences: offence 'so serious' etc, pre-sentence report, legal representation

*Under 15-year-old: court must specify the offender is persistent

Community Order
Offence 'serious enough'
pre-sentence report
See **B[17]** onwards

**Offenders aged 18–24 years only

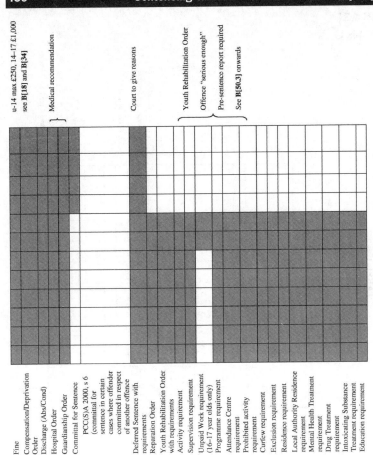

B[4.3]

Table C

TABLE C

Available sentences for purely summary offences not carrying imprisonment
See Index to sentencing for paragraph references

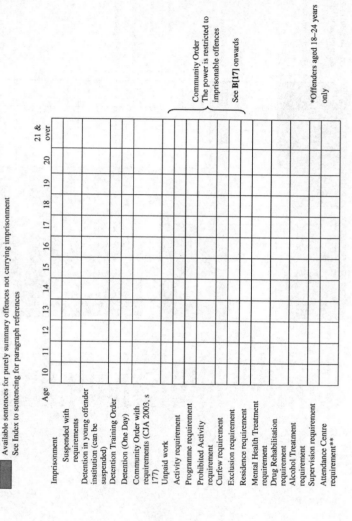

Age	10	11	12	13	14	15	16	17	18	19	20	21 & over
Imprisonment												
Suspended with requirements												
Detention in young offender institution (can be suspended)												
Detention Training Order												
Detention (One Day)												
Community Order with requirements (CJA 2003, s 177)												
Unpaid work												
Activity requirement												
Programme requirement												
Prohibited Activity requirement												
Curfew requirement												
Exclusion requirement												
Residence requirement												
Mental Health Treatment requirement												
Drug Rehabilitation requirement												
Alcohol Treatment requirement												
Supervision requirement												
Attendance Centre requirement**												

Community Order
The power is restricted to imprisonable offences

See B[17] onwards

*Offenders aged 18–24 years only

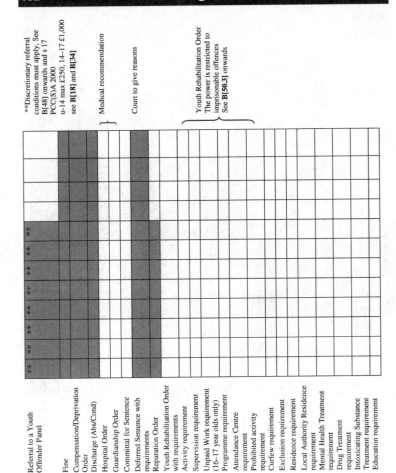

B[4.4]

Table D

TABLE D

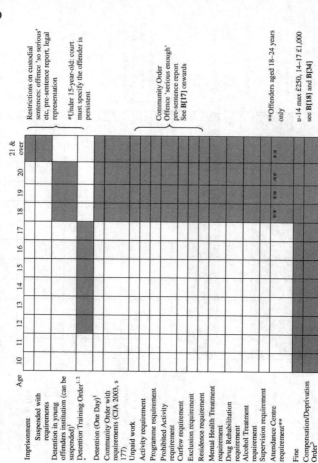

Available sentences according to age of offender
See Index to sentencing for paragraph references

	Age	10	11	12	13	14	15	16	17	18	19	20	21 & over	
Imprisonment														Restrictions on custodial sentences: offence 'so serious' etc, pre-sentence report, legal representation
Suspended with requirements														
Detention in young offenders institution (can be suspended)[1,2]														*Under 15-year-old: court must specify the offender is persistent
Detention Training Order[1,2]														
Detention (One Day)[1]														
Community Order with requirements (CJA 2003, s 177)														Community Order Offence 'serious enough' pre-sentence report See **B[17]** onwards
Unpaid work														
Activity requirement														
Programme requirement														
Prohibited Activity requirement														
Curfew requirement														
Exclusion requirement														
Residence requirement														
Mental Health Treatment requirement														
Drug Rehabilitation requirement														
Alcohol Treatment requirement														
Supervision requirement														
Attendance Centre requirement**										**	**	**	**	**Offenders aged 18–24 years only
Fine														u-14 max £250, 14-17 £1,000
Compensation/Deprivation Order[3]														see **B[18]** and **B[34]**

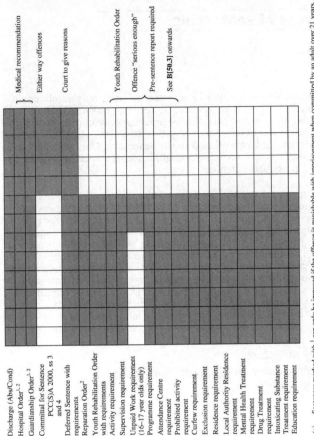

Discharge (Abs/Cond)
Hospital Order[1,2]
Guardianship Order[1,2]
Committal for Sentence PCC(S)A 2000, ss 3 and 4
Deferred Sentence with requirements
Reparation Order[2]
Youth Rehabilitation Order with requirements
Activity requirement
Supervision requirement
Unpaid Work requirement (16–17 year olds only)
Programme requirement
Attendance Centre requirement
Prohibited activity requirement
Curfew requirement
Exclusion requirement
Residence requirement
Local Authority Residence requirement
Mental Health Treatment requirement
Drug Treatment requirement
Intoxicating Substance Treatment requirement
Education requirement

Medical recommendation
Either way offences
Court to give reasons
Youth Rehabilitation Order
Offence "serious enough"
Pre-sentence report required
See B[50.3] onwards

(a)   Sentences marked with [1] can only be imposed if the offence is punishable with imprisonment when committed by an adult over 21 years.

(b)   As far as offenders under 18 are concerned, a magistrates' court (as opposed to a youth court) cannot impose any of the penalties marked with a [2]. The magistrates' court must remit such juveniles on bail or in care to a youth court which will usually be the youth court for the area in which he lives.

(c)   [3] Under PCC(S)A 2000, s 143: see B[34]

**   Available up to the age of 25 in cases of default in payment of money where the court would have the power to commit to prison

B[5]

The process of sentencing

Introduction

B[5.1]

Sentencing is not and never will be an exact science; only rarely could a group of sentencers agree that a particular sentence was exactly right and, even if they did, they would probably be agreeing only that it was right to show a particular level of leniency. The prerogative of saying what is 'right' in terms of sentencing levels belongs to the Sentencing Council who aim to promote consistency in sentencing and guidance in respect of offences or offenders in a particular category.

However, a degree of vagueness might be thought to be inevitable when there are so many variables to be considered before a sentencing decision is reached. Not only should this fact not discourage a proper study of the subject of sentencing, but it should positively encourage it and the area of study most profitable to the lay magistrate is that of the process of sentencing, the route to be followed in order to reach a sentence which, if it cannot be said to be exactly right, at least is unlikely to be disturbed on appeal if the offender's circumstances remain the same. The framework for a structured sentencing decision is given at B[3.7]. This is amplified and explained in paragraphs 1–8 which follow. Determination of guilt and the factual basis for the sentencing decision is dealt with in Section I court procedure.

Sentencing structure
Magistrates' Courts Sentencing Guidance – Definitive Guideline

B[5.2]

Section 172 of the Criminal Justice Act 2003 places a statutory obligation on courts to follow Sentencing Council sentencing guidelines. In general, a court's reasons for departing from sentencing guidelines would be specific to the offence and offenders under consideration. A court which had departed from the guidelines essentially because it considered that they needed reconsideration had erred: *R v Heathcote-Smith (Benjamin) and Melton (Christopher Timothy)* [2011] EWCA Crim 2846, [2012] 2 Cr App Rep (S) 133, [2012] Crim LR 304.

1. Offence seriousness (culpability and harm)
A Identify the appropriate starting point
Consider which of the examples of offence activity corresponds most closely to the circumstances of the case to identify the appropriate **starting point**
Starting points are based on a **first time offender pleading guilty**
Refer to the following where the starting point is, or the **range** includes, a:

(i) fine – **B[33]**

(ii) community order – **B[17]**

(iii) custodial sentence – **B[2]**

Refer to B[5.7] below for the meaning of the terms "starting point", "range" and "first time offender"

B Consider the effect of aggravating and mitigating factors

Move up or down from the starting point to reflect aggravating or mitigating factors that affect the seriousness of the offence to reach a provisional sentence

Common aggravating and mitigating factors are set out below at **B[2A]** below; relevant factors are also identified in the individual offence guidelines to be found in **Section A** of this book. **These lists are not exhaustive.**

Do not double-count any aggravating or mitigating factors in the description of the activity used to reach the starting point/

The **range** is the bracket into which the provisional sentence will normally fall but the court is not precluded from going outside the range where the facts justify it.

Previous convictions which aggravate the seriousness of the current offence may take the provisional sentence beyond the range, especially if there are significant other aggravating factors present.

2. Form a preliminary view of the appropriate sentence, then consider offender mitigation

Matters of offender mitigation may include remorse and admissions to police in interview

3. Consider a reduction for a guilty plea

Apply the sliding scale reduction for a guilty plea to punitive elements of the sentence – see B[5.46] below.

Application of the reduction may take the sentence below the range in some cases

4. Consider ancillary orders including compensation

Refer to B[18] for compensation and section B generally for available ancillary orders.

Consider compensation in every case where the offending has resulted in personal injury, loss or damage – give reasons if order not made. See B[18].

5. Decide sentence

Give reasons

Review the total sentence to ensure that it is proportionate to the offending behaviour and properly balanced.

Give reasons for the sentence passed, including any ancillary orders.

State if the sentence has been reduced to reflect a guilty plea; indicate what the sentence would otherwise have been.

NB: By law, criminal courts are obliged **to follow** SC guidance. Explain ie give reasons, if the sentence is of a different kind or outside the range indicated in the guidelines.

List of aggravating and mitigating factors

B[5.2A]

(Taken from the SGC Guideline "Overarching Principles: Seriousness")

Aggravating factors

Factors indicating higher culpability:

- Offence committed while on bail for other offences
- Failure to respond to previous sentences
- Offence was racially or religiously aggravated
- Offence motivated by, or demonstrated hostility to the victim based on his or her sexual orientation (or presumed sexual orientation)
- Offence motivated by, or demonstrating, hostility based on the victim's disability (or presumed disability)
- Previous conviction(s), particularly where a pattern of repeat offending is disclosed
- Planning of an offence
- An intention to commit more serious harm than actually resulted from the offence
- Offenders operating in groups or gangs
- "Professional" offending
- Commission of the offence for financial gain (where this is not inherent in the offence itself)
- High level of profit from the offence
- An attempt to conceal or dispose of evidence
- Failure to respond to warnings or concerns expressed by others about the offender's behaviour
- Offence committed while on licence
- Offence motivated by hostility towards a minority group, or a member or members of it
- Deliberate targeting of vulnerable victim(s)
- Commission of an offence while under the influence of alcohol or drugs
- Use of a weapon to frighten or injure victim
- Deliberate and gratuitous violence or damage to property, over and beyond what is needed to carry out the offence
- Abuse of power
- Abuse of position of trust

Factors indicating a more than usually serious degree of harm:

- Multiple victims
- An especially serious physical or psychological effect on the victim, even if unintended
- A sustained assault or repeated assaults on the same victim
- Victim is particularly vulnerable
- Location of the offence (for example, in an isolated place)
- Offence is committed against those working in the public sector or providing a service to the public

- Presence of others eg relatives, especially children or partner of the victim
- Additional degradation of the victim (eg taking photographs of a victim as part of a sexual offence)
- In property offences, high value (including sentimental value) of property to the victim, or substantial consequential loss (eg where the theft of equipment causes serious disruption to the victim's life or business)

Mitigating factors

Factors indicating lower culpability:

- A greater degree of provocation than normally expected
- Mental illness or disability
- Youth or age, where it affects the responsibility of the individual defendant
- The fact that the offender played only a minor role in the offence

Offender mitigation

- Genuine remorse
- Admissions to police in interview
- Ready co-operation with authorities

Aggravation related to race, religion, disability or sexual orientation

B[5.2B]

Racial or religious aggravation – statutory provisions

(1) Sections 29 to 32 of the Crime and Disorder Act 1998 create specific racially or religiously aggravated offences which have higher maximum penalties than the non-aggravated versions of those offences. The individual offence guidelines (see **Part A**) indicate whether there is a specifically aggravated form of the offence.

(2) An offence is racially or religiously aggravated for the purposes of ss 29–32 of the Act if the offender demonstrates hostility towards the victim based on his or her membership (or presumed membership) of a racial group, or if the offence is racially or religiously motivated: s 28 CDA 1998.

(3) For all other offences, s 145 of the CJA 2003 provides that the court must regard racial or religious aggravation as an aggravating factor.

(4) The court should not treat an offence as racially or religiously aggravated for the purposes of s 145 where a racially or religiously aggravated form of the offence was charged but resulted in an acquittal: *R v McGillivray* [2005] EWCA Crim 604. The court should not normally treat an offence as racially or religiously aggravated if a racially or religiously form of the offence was available but was not charged: *R v O'Callaghan* [2005] EWCA Crim 317. **Consult your legal adviser for further guidance in these situations.**

Aggravation related to disability, sexual orientation or transgender identity* – statutory provisions

*References to transgender or transgender identity to be added by s 65 of the Legal Aid, Sentencing and Punishment of Offenders Act 2012 from a date to be appointed.

(5)   Under s 146 of the CJA 2003, the court must treat as an aggravating factor the fact that:

-   an offender demonstrated hostility towards the victim based on his or her sexual orientation or disability (or presumed sexual orientation, transgender identity or disability); or
-   the offence was motivated by hostility towards persons who are of a particular sexual orientation, transgender or who have a particular disability.

Approach to sentencing

(6)   A court should not conclude that offending involved aggravation relating to race, religion, disability, sexual orientation or transgender without first putting the offender on notice and allowing him or her to challenge allegation.

(7)   When sentencing any offence where such aggravation is found to be present, the following approach should be followed. This applies both to the specific racially or religiously aggravated offences under the CDA 1998 and to offences which are regarded as aggravated under s 145 or 146 of the CJA 2003 (*R v Kelly and Donnelly* [2001] EWCA Crim 1751):

-   sentencers should first determine the appropriate sentence, leaving aside the element of aggravation relating to race, religion etc but taking into account al other aggravating and mitigating features;
-   the sentence should then be increased to take account of the aggravation related to race, religion, disability or sexual orientation'
-   the increase may mean that a more onerous penalty of the same type is appropriate, or that the threshold for a more severe type of sentence is passed;
-   the sentencer must state in open court that the offence was aggravated by reason of race, religion, disability or sexual orientation;
-   the sentencer should state what the sentence would have been without that element of aggravation.

(8)   The extent to which the sentence is increased will depend on the seriousness of the aggravation. The following factors could be taken as indicating a high level of aggravation:

Offender's intention

-   The element of aggravation based on race, religion etc was planned
-   The offence was part of a pattern of offending by the offender
-   The offender was a member of, or was associated with, a group promoting hostility based on race, religion, disability or sexual orientation

- The incident was deliberately set up to be offensive or humiliating to the victim or to the group of which the victim is a member

Impact on the victim or others

- The offence was committed in the victim's home
- The victim was providing a service to the public
- The timing or location of the offence was calculated to maximise the harm or distress it caused
- The expressions of hostility were repeated or prolonged
- The offence caused fear and distress throughout a local community or more widely
- The offence caused particular distress to the victim and/or the victim's family

(9) At the lower end of the scale, the aggravation may be regarded as less serious if:

- It was limited in scope or duration
- The offence was not motivated by hostility on the basis of race, religion, disability or sexual orientation, and the element of hostility or abuse was minor or incidental.

(10) In these guidelines, the specific racially or religiously aggravated offences under the CDA 1998 are addressed on the same page as the "basic offence"; the starting points and ranges indicated on the guidelines (see Part A) relate to the "basic" (ie non-aggravated) offence. The increase for the element of racial or religious aggravation may result in a sentence above the range; this will not constitute a departure from the guideline for which reasons must be given.

1 The offence

B[5.3]

An important principle of sentencing is that a sentence should not be more severe than is warranted by the seriousness of the offence and other offences associated with it. When considering the seriousness of the current offence or offences, previous convictions and failures to respond to previous sentences may be taken into account where relevant. Custodial sentences are reserved primarily for offenders who have committed an offence 'so serious' that only a custodial sentence can be justified for it, and community sentences are only available where the offence is 'serious enough' to warrant such a sentence.

The Purposes of Sentencing

B[5.4]

In respect of adults, the Criminal Justice Act 2003 sets out the objectives of sentencing as punishment, the reduction of crime (including deterrence), reforms and rehabilitation, protection of the public and reparation.

B[5.5]

A custodial sentence may also be imposed where the offender has refused to consent to a drug testing order or certain conditions requiring consent (see B[2.9]).

B[5.6]

Otherwise any sentence imposed will generally be commensurate with the seriousness of the offence, although the court, having considered all the mitigation, may take this into account in mitigating an offender's sentence.

Determining seriousness

B[5.7]

Meaning of 'range', 'starting point' and 'first time offender'. As in previous editions, and consistent with other SGC guidelines, these guidelines are for a first time offender convicted after a trial. The guidelines provide a starting point based on an assessment of the seriousness of the offence and a range within which the sentence will normally fall in most cases.

B[5.8]

The facts. The court must be satisfied that the facts of the offence or offences for which sentence is to be passed have been proved or agreed.

In determining the seriousness of an offence the court must take into account all information about the circumstances of the offence, any aggravating or mitigating factors as are available to it, and information in a pre-sentence report. The court must consider the offender's culpability and any harm or potential harm caused by the offence.

B[5.9]

Associated offence. In considering whether an offence is 'serious enough' to warrant a community sentence, or 'so serious' that only a custodial sentence can be justified, the court may consider the combination of the offence and other offences associated with it. An 'associated offence' is in essence another offence for which the offender is to be sentenced at that time or is to be taken into consideration. Whether it is appropriate for offences to be TIC'd see *R v Lavery* [2008] EWCA Crim 2499, [2009] 3 All ER 295.

B[5.10]–[5.15]

Guidance on the seriousness of offences and aggravating and mitigating features is to be found at B[5.2] and B[5.2A] above.

B[5.16]

Parliament also gives broad guidance to the courts by prescribing the maximum penalties available. For example, many minor offences are punishable only by a fine on level 1 (max £200) and level 5 (max £5,000). Other, more serious, offences are also punishable with imprisonment of up to 6 (**12) months.

2 Mitigation

B[5.17]

There are two particular objectives of mitigation: to draw to the attention of the court any factors relevant to mitigating the seriousness of the offence, and to highlight mitigation personal to the offender.

B[5.18]

The first consideration for the court in determining sentence is the seriousness of the offence. The seriousness of the offence will generally determine whether the court must impose a custodial sentence or if the offence warrants the making of a community sentence, a fine or discharge.

B[5.19]

In addressing the seriousness of the offence, the circumstances of the offence should be examined to see whether they disclose any mitigating circumstances. Guidance on what may amount to a mitigating (or aggravating) feature of an offence is given by the Sentencing Guidelines Council (see www.sentencing-guidelines.gov.uk) and B[5.2] and B[5.2A] above.

B[5.20]

The seriousness of the offence including culpability and harm considerations will broadly determine which range of sentencing options is open to the court: custody, community, financial or a discharge. Where the court is concerned with a violent or sexual offence and is considering a custodial sentence to protect the public, the personal circumstances and history will become relevant. However, personal mitigation is usually more relevant at the second stage when the general level of seriousness has been determined, where mitigation will affect the final choice of sentence and the impact it will have on the offender. While no sentence may be more severe than is justified by the defendant's offence, personal mitigation may serve to reduce the punishment or suggest that a more individualised approach may be appropriate. In forming an opinion, whether a particular community order or orders comprising a community sentence is or are the most suitable for the offender, the court may take into account any information about the offender which is before it. Mitigating factors which have commonly been considered by the courts are referred to under 'Consideration of sentences' at B[5.36]–B[5.48].

3 Availability of sentences

B[5.21]

Available sentences are determined by the maximum penalties prescribed by Parliament and by the court's assessment of the gravity of the offence.

As mentioned above the maximum penalty for an offence is fixed by statute as being a fine, or a fine and custody. Some sentences and orders of the court are available only where an offence is punishable in the case of an adult with imprisonment (the defendant himself does not need to be liable to imprisonment). A comparison of Tables A and C at B[4.1] and B[4.3] will make this apparent. Furthermore some sentences are only available to offenders of a certain age – see B[1.5].

B[5.22]

By a systematic process of noting whether an offence is punishable with imprisonment and the age of the offender, the sentencing options available to the court can be narrowed progressively.

B[5.23]

Criminal Justice Act 2003. This further categorises sentences and orders into four broad divisions: discharges (instead of sentencing), financial, community and custodial. In addition there are orders providing for the medical treatment of mentally disturbed offenders.

B[5.24]

Discharges (absolute/conditional). These are available to all offenders and for all offences where the court is satisfied that having regard to the circumstances of the offence and the offender it is inexpedient to inflict punishment. See B[31].

B[5.25]–[5.31]

Financial penalties. These include fines (B[33]), compensation (B[18]) and deprivation of property (B[34]) and are available to all offenders and for all offences.

B[5.32]

Community orders (adults). The court may only impose a community sentence which consists of one or more requirements where the offence carries imprisonment and the court considers the offence, or a combination of the offence and other 'associated offences' to be 'serious enough' to warrant such a sentence. The fact that an offence is 'serious enough' does not mean that the court must pass a community sentence, only that it may do so (see B[17.35] onwards).

B[5.33]

Custodial sentences (see B[2]). The custodial sentences available to the magistrates are imprisonment and for offenders under 21, detention in a young offender institution (**to be replaced by a sentence of imprisonment from a date to be appointed by virtue of the CJA 2003) and detention and training orders for offenders aged 12 to 17 inclusive. They are only available where statute defines an offence as being punishable with imprisonment and for adult offenders only **where the offence carries a custodial sentence of 28 weeks or more. (**It is anticipated custody plus and intermittent custody will be available nationally from a date to be appointed but consult the legal adviser.)

B[5.34]

A custodial sentence may generally only be imposed where the offence or a combination of the offence and 'associated offences' is 'so serious' that neither a community penalty nor a fine cannot be justified for it. The court will usually find it helpful to consider the nature and extent of the defendant's criminal culpability and the nature and extent of any injury or damage caused to the victim (*R v Howells* [1999] 1 All ER 50, [1999] 1 WLR 307, CA). However, although this criterion may be satisfied the court may nevertheless, in the case of a mentally ill defendant, make a hospital or guardianship order.

B[5.35]

Exceptionally a custodial sentence may be imposed where the offender has refused to consent to a drug testing order and certain conditions in a community order requiring consent ie a willingness to comply with the requirements.

4 Consideration of sentences

B[5.36]

When the court has ascertained the range of sentences appropriate for the seriousness of the offence, it must then proceed to select the particular sentence appropriate for the case. In this task it will be assisted by its appreciation of the seriousness of the offence but also by mitigation personal to the offender, any pre-sentence report and the court's objective in sentencing.

B[5.37]

Mitigation. Nothing shall prevent a court from mitigating an offender's sentence by taking into account any such matters as, in the opinion of the court, are relevant in mitigation of sentence. Mitigating factors which have commonly been considered by courts include the following.

B[5.38]

1 Youth of the offender. This may operate as mitigation and will usually indicate a lower level of sentence (eg a smaller fine or shorter period of custody) than would be appropriate otherwise. The mitigating effect of youth, however, may be cancelled out by other factors, such as a record of previous convictions which is serious having regard to the offender's age, or which shows a proclivity for crime beyond what one would expect for his age.

B[5.39]

2 Older offenders who have not previously offended would receive credit for a previously blameless life especially when receiving a more serious penalty such as a community sentence or custody.

B[5.40]–[5.45]

3 Effect of previous convictions. Previous convictions must be taken into account and may make an offence more serious although this will depend upon the nature of the offence and the time elapsed since conviction. Within the range of sentences appropriate to the seriousness of the offence good character is almost always strong mitigation and the worse an offend-

er's previous record is, the less 'discount' he can expect for good character. Occasionally, the record of previous convictions may show a significant gap since the last conviction and might be taken as evidence of a genuine effort to keep out of trouble. The record may also show that the present offence is out of character, for example, when a man with a long record of petty theft appears on a charge of indecent assault.

B[5.46]

4 Plea of guilty. Revised definitive guidance (Reduction in Sentence for a Guilty Plea) was handed down by the Sentencing Guidelines Council in 2007 and applies to all cases sentenced on or after 23 July 2007 (see www.s entencing-guidelines.gov.uk).

A plea of guilty will nearly always attract a sentencing discount of between 10% and 33% depending upon the stage of proceedings and the circumstances that the indication of plea was given. Remorse or contrition will mitigate the sentence particularly when there is real evidence of it. A ready admission of guilt, a willingness to assist the police, and voluntary efforts to make compensation can all be interpreted as evidence of contrition. Particularly in cases involving sexual offences a plea of guilty will spare witnesses, especially young persons, from the ordeal of giving evidence, even though the law now provides more sympathetic means for the reception of such evidence. Where the court does reduce or does not reduce the sentence because of the circumstances and stage at which the guilty plea is entered it must state in open court the reasons for its decision.

Where the prosecution case is overwhelming, it may not be appropriate to give the full reduction that would otherwise be given. Whilst there is a presumption in favour of the full reduction being given where a plea has been indicated at the first reasonable opportunity, the fact that the prosecution case is overwhelming without relying on admissions from the defendant may be a reason justifying a lower reduction should be given. The recommended reduction of 20% is likely to be appropriate. Reasons must be given.

The question whether or not a defendant has pleaded guilty at the first available opportunity was an issue which depended on the [youth] court's assessment at the time of sentencing as to whether or not it would have been proper for the defendant to have entered a guilty plea before he had viewed a CCTC recording of the incident (*R (on the application of H) v Bromley Youth Court* [2006] All ER (D) 266 (Oct)).

Annex 1 to the revised SGC definitive guidance states that the critical time for determining the reduction for a guilty plea is the **first reasonable opportunity** for the defendant to have indicated a willingness to plead guilty. This opportunity will vary with a wide range of factors and the court will need to make a judgment on the particular facts of the case before it. The first reasonable opportunity may be the first time that a defendant appears before the court and has the opportunity to plead guilty; but the court may consider that it would have been reasonable to have expected an indication of willingness even earlier, perhaps whilst under interview.

B[5.47]

5 Loss of employment etc. An offender must generally be taken to have foreseen the normal consequences of conviction and so factors such as distress to his family, loss of job, pension, good character, etc will usually have little mitigating value. Where consequences follow which could not reasonably have been foreseen, for example, where the offence was unconnected with the offender's employment but he nevertheless finds himself dismissed, or where the offence was committed on the spur of the moment under provocation with no opportunity to consider the consequences, some allowance may be made if those consequences turn out to be disastrous. The person who is especially vulnerable must be expected to take special care. So, for example, the person whose employment depends upon his having a driving licence must be expected to take particular care not to commit endorsable offences. People such as doctors, nurses and solicitors, from whom a high ethical standard is expected, must expect the consequences of conviction for an offence which amounts to a breach of those standards and cannot claim professional disciplinary action in mitigation.

B[5.48]

Unrepresented defendant. The court has a duty itself to seek out mitigating factors before finally arriving at a sentence. It should be especially careful not to assume that there are none in the case of the inarticulate unrepresented defendant.

5 The totality of sentencing

B[5.49]

The Sentencing Council laid down a definitive guideline ('Totality') which applies to all offenders, whose cases are dealt with on or after **11 June 2012**. The reader is also recommended to consult the section dealing with 'Offences Taken Into Consideration'. The principle of totality comprises two elements:

(1) All courts, when sentencing for more than a single offence, should pass a total sentence which reflects all the offending behaviour before it and is just and proportionate. This is so whether the sentences are structured as concurrent or consecutive. Therefore, concurrent sentences will ordinarily be longer than a single sentence for a single offence.

(2) It is usually impossible to arrive at a just and proportionate sentence for a multiple offending simply by adding together notional single sentences. It is necessary to address the offending behaviour, together with the factors personal to the offender as a whole.

Concurrent/consecutive sentences. There is no inflexible rule governing whether sentences should be structured as concurrent or consecutive components. The overriding principle is that the overall sentence must be just and proportionate. Space precludes some examples which are set out in the SC Guideline. The reader is invited to consult the SC website where necessary.

6 Choice of sentence

B[5.50]

The deliberations of the court will have brought into focus more than one form of sentence. For example, it may be that the offence is 'serious enough' to warrant a community sentence. The pre-sentence report may have considered a range of community orders. The probation officer will have considered the seriousness of the offence and have proposed a sentence which is commensurate with the seriousness of the offence and takes into account the circumstances of the offender. The court will need to be clear that the sentence adequately reflects the seriousness of the offence while (in the case of a community penalty) also being the most suitable for the offender. It does not mean that if an offence is serious enough to warrant a community sentence that is the only sentence which may be imposed. If there is mitigation which allows the court to impose a fine then the fine must reflect the seriousness of the offence and the financial circumstances of the offender.

B[5.51]

The advice of the legal adviser will be essential to ensure that all the statutory criteria which must be satisfied before sentence can be passed and the correct ancillary orders made.

B[5.52]

The good chairman will have noted during the hearing such matters as applications for costs, or forfeiture of drugs. Liability for endorsement and disqualification will also have occupied attention and after the substantive sentence has been agreed by (at least) a majority of the justices, the chairman will deal with each of these matters in turn. Save in the simplest cases, the chairman will make a written note of the total decision so that no error or omission is made.

7 Statement accompanying the sentence

B[5.53]

The Criminal Justice Act 2003, s 174 (as amended by s 64 of the Legal Aid, Sentencing and Punishment of Offenders Act 2012, from a date to be appointed) requires a court to give reasons for and explain the effect of its sentence

The requirement of Article 6 of the European Convention on Human Rights means that reasons should be given. Indeed the effect, not to say the benefit, of a sound sentencing decision can sometimes be lost because the defendant does not understand the reasoning behind it, or because the public do not.

B[5.54]

When a particular sentence falls within the Sentencing Guidelines Council guidance for the kind of offence and offender – when it is the sort of sentence the defendant probably expected to receive – there will seldom be justification for garnishing the reasons. However, when the court imposes a sentence which might be unexpected the reasons for this departure from normal sentencing habits might be fuller. Likewise, when different types of sentence are imposed on co-accused whose circumstances may appear to be similar. The needs of the public as well as those of the defendant and any victim of his offence should be borne in mind. A structured approach to the sentencing decision, consultation with the clerk and a careful note will assist the chairman when giving reasons

Victim Personal Statement

B[5.55]–[5.60]

Victim personal statements give victims a formal opportunity to say how a crime has affected them. Where the victim has chosen to make such a statement, a court should consider and take it into account prior to passing sentence.

The Consolidated Practice Direction (as amended from March 2007) [2002] 3 All ER 90 emphasises that:

- evidence of the effects of an offence on the victim must be in the form of a witness statement under s 9 of the Criminal Justice Act 1967 or an expert's report;
- the statement must be served on the defence prior to sentence;
- except where inferences can properly be drawn from the nature of or circumstances surrounding the offence, the court must not make any assumptions unsupported by evidence about the effects of the offence on the victim;
- the court must pass what it judges to be the appropriate sentence having regard to the circumstances of the offence and the offender, taking into account, so far as the court considers it appropriate, the consequences to the victim;
- the opinions of the victim or the victim's close relatives as to what the sentence should be are not relevant.

For cases involving sexual offences see also B[18] regarding the relevance of the victim's views to any compensation order that may be imposed.

B[5.61]

It is worth noting the pre ECHR law which requires reasons to be given. Before announcing the court's reasons the chairman should consult the legal adviser:

(a) When sentencing an offender to imprisonment [**for offences committed before a date to be appointed under the CJA 2003 – detention in a young offender institution] (except where he has refused to consent to a community sentence);

(b) when not requiring the subject of a suspended sentence to serve that sentence after committing a further offence;

(c)   when declining to endorse or disqualify for special reasons;

(d)   when not disqualifying for the minimum period where 12 penalty
        points have accumulated;

(e)   when deferring sentence an indication should be given to the
        offender as to what is expected of him during the period of
        deferment, ie the reason for the deferment;

(f)   in the youth court it is desirable that the court should indicate in
        advance what sentence or disposal it has in mind to order;

(g)   when refusing bail or in certain circumstances granting bail for
        murder, manslaughter or rape;

(h)   when deciding not to award compensation when otherwise empow-
        ered to do so;

(i)   when refusing to grant an appeal it is good practice for the court to
        give its reasons;

(j)   where an offence is treated more seriously because the court finds
        that it was statutorily aggravated that fact should be stated in open
        court.

B[5.62]

It is generally inadvisable to deliver a lecture or homily or offer any other
words of worldly wisdom to a defendant who is being sentenced. Research
has shown that most prisoners cannot remember even a short time after
sentence much of what the judge said and even whether he said anything at
all.

8 Pronouncement of sentence

B[5.63]

The chairman should announce the sentence(s) in a way which leaves no
one in court in any doubt as to the court's decision. In the following pages
each possible sentence is considered and a form of words is provided as a
guide to the way in which the sentence may be announced. It is not
suggested that the chairman should read the sentence from this book but
that a glance at the wording suggested here will assist in ensuring that all
the necessary legal points have been covered. Where an offender is to be
sentenced for more than one offence it is advised that each sentence is
related to each offence by description. It is bad practice to sentence in such
terms as, 'For the first offence you will be fined £50. For the second offence
you will be fined £100 and your licence endorsed. For the third offence etc.'
Bear in mind that the offender has no idea of the order in which offences
appear on the list and therefore has no way of relating the penalties to the
offences if they are announced in this fashion. The better practice is
exemplified as follows: 'For the burglary and theft at Jackson's, the
butchers, you will go to prison for 20 days; for using the credit card to
obtain a camera from Browns, you will go to prison for 15 days which will
be in addition to the first sentence, which means you will go to prison for
a total of 35 days.' Whenever there are several sentences to be announced,
the chairman should totalise the effect of them, that is, the total amount of
a monetary penalty, the total period of imprisonment or of disqualification

should be stated. Words such as concurrent or consecutive need not be used if other words are used which make it clear what the total effect of the sentence is, as in the example above.

B[5.64]

When offences have been taken into consideration in arriving at a sentence that fact should be stated as a preamble to the sentence.

B[5.65]

Where relevant the chairman should announce by how much the sentence has been reduced by virtue of the defendant's guilty plea.

B[6]

Multiplicity of charges

B[6.1]

Sometimes a defendant faces more than one charge stemming from the same circumstances and while this is generally unobjectionable there are occasions when the court feels that the prosecution is having two bites at the cherry. Some courts impose the appropriate penalty on one charge and mark the other 'No separate penalty'. Another practice is to decide the appropriate penalty and divide it between the two offences but this may result in penalties which appear inadequately low.

Power to review decisions – criminal and civil proceedings

(MCA 1980, s 142)

B[7.1]

For civil proceedings, see B[7.5] below.

It occasionally happens that information reaches a court after a case is disposed of which, if it had been known earlier, might have affected the court's decision. Sometimes, for example, it is simply the realisation by a justices' clerk that one of his legal advisers failed to advise the justices that they had no power to make a particular decision. Or it may be that for some compelling reason, where the defendant was convicted after a not guilty plea, the verdict should be reconsidered (eg after a conviction for driving without insurance, a valid insurance certificate is discovered).

The legislation, ie s 142, draws a distinction between those cases where the court is being asked to review or rescind an order because a 'slip' or 'error' has been made (s workNOTlife25142(1)) as distinct from where the court is being asked to rescind the conviction of the offender (s 142(2)).

As far as s 142(2) is concerned the test as to whether a court should reopen a case is whether it would be in the interests of justice to do so (*R v Ealing Magistrates' Court, ex p Sahota* (1997) 161 JP 73, [1997] 45 LS Gaz R 29; followed in *R (on the application of Blick) v Doncaster Magistrates' Court* [2008] EWHC 2698 (Admin), 172 JP 651). As far as s 142(1) is concerned (review of a sentence or order), the power should be exercised to correct a 'slip' or 'error'; the section is not designed to permit either party to ask the court to simply review its previous order (*Zykin v Crown Prosecution Service* [2009] EWHC 1469 (Admin), 173 JP 361).

Generally the power should be exercised as soon as practicable once the error has been discovered. 28 days has been regarded as a good rule of thumb for rectifying a conviction, sentence or order of the magistrates' court. In *R (on the application of the CPS) v City of London Magistrates' Court* [2007] All ER (D) 302 (Jul), the prosecution delayed their application to rectify a committal order for many months. The High Court indicated that this may have afforded grounds for justices to decline to invoke the power under s 142.

B[7.2]

The court has power to vary or rescind a sentence or order and may substitute some other sentence or order (*R v Sheffield City Justices, ex p*

Foster (1999) Times, 2 November. If, however, the decision has already been subject to an appeal to a higher court, the power to reopen no longer applies. Likewise, a magistrates' court had no power to quash a conviction and order a rehearing under s 142(2) where the justices had agreed to state a case for the opinion of the High Court: see *R (on the application of Rhodes-Presley) v Worcestershire Magistrates' Court* [2008] EWHC 2700 (Admin), [2008] All ER (D) 92 (Nov).

It was inappropriate for magistrates to exercise their powers under s 142 to increase a sentence originally imposed some 20 months earlier. There had to be finality of proceedings and a power of rectification had to be exercised speedily after the date of the original sentence: see *R (on the application of Trigger) v Northampton Magistrates' Court (Northamptonshire Probation Trust and Northamptonshire Crown Prosecution Service, Interested Parties)* [2011] EWHC 149, (2011) 175 JP 101.

Section 142(2) was not a vehicle by which a court should rescind a sentence and remit to a fresh bench because the defendant asserts he received incompetent legal advice and/or that his plea was equivocal: see *R (on the application of Williamson) v City of Westminster Magistrates' Court* [2012] EWHC 1444 (Admin), [2012] 2 Cr App Rep 299.

B[7.3]

The provisions may operate against a defendant, for example where the court has omitted to impose penalty points or an endorsable road traffic offence. Note, however, the power does not extend to overturning an acquittal (*R v Gravesend Justices, ex p Dexter* [1977] Crim LR 298). The power is directed towards sentences or other orders; it had no bearing on convictions which had been entered by way of procedural irregularity (*R (on the application of D) v Sheffield Youth Court* [2008] EWHC 601 (Admin), [2008] All ER (D) 70 (Mar)).

B[7.4]

When the court alters a sentence or order under this procedure, and substitutes another, that other sentence or order will take effect from the date of the first sentence or order, unless the court otherwise directs.

Note the power under the Magistrates Courts Act 1980, s 142 does not extend to civil proceedings (*R (on the application of Mathialagam) v Southwark London Borough Council* [2004] EWCA Civ 1689, [2004] All ER (D) 179 (Dec)). Nor does s 142 have any bearing on criminal convictions which had been entered by way of procedural irregularity (*R (on the application of D) v Sheffield Youth Court* [2008] EWHC 601 (Admin), [2008] All ER (D) 70 (Mar).

B[7.5]

Civil Proceedings. The general power to re-open civil proceedings was considered in *R (on the application of Newham London Borough Council) v Stratford Magistrates' Court* [2008] EWHC 125 (Admin), [2008] RA

108. This was noted in R *(on the application of Jones) v HM Justices of the Peace* [2008] EWHC 2740 (Admin), [2008] All ER (D) 331 (Oct). Case law declares that there is a limited common law power to re-open and review civil proceedings. The principles are as follows:

(1)   The power is an exceptional one and should be exercised cautiously.

(2)   Before exercising the power there must be, first, a genuine and arguable dispute as to the defendant's liability to the order in question; second, that the order must be made as a result of a substantial procedural error, defect or mishap; and thirdly, the application to set aside is made promptly after a defendant learns that an order has been made or has notice that an order had been made.

The Jones case was concerned with council tax proceedings. There is a statutory power to review, on the application of the relevant local authority, pursuant to reg 36A of the Council Tax (Administrative and Enforcement) Regulations 1992.

B[7A]

Action plan orders

(PCC(S) Act 2000, ss 69–72)

Reports

B[7A.1]

Sections 69–72 of the 2000 Act have been repealed by the Criminal Justice and Immigration Act 2008. Action plan orders were replaced by the Youth Rehabilitation Order. See [B50] onwards.

B[8]

Anti-social behaviour orders (ASBOs)

(Crime and Disorder Act 1998, ss 1–4)

Limitations

B[8.1]

Civil Applications – Can only be applied for by either:

(i)   the relevant local authority;
(ii)   the police;
(iii) the British Transport Police; or
(iv)   a recognised housing association or action trust.

B[8.2]

Age limits – May be made for a person aged 10 years or over.

B[8.3]

Maximum/minimum period – An order must be for a minimum period of 2 years, but it is inappropriate to make an order for an indefinite period (*R v Vittles* [2004] EWCA Crim 1089, [2004] All ER (D) 334 (May)).

B[8.4]

The application – The application is to a magistrates' court by way of complaint. If the respondent is under 18 years of age the justices constituting the court should normally be qualified to sit in the youth court. There are dispensations for interim orders or if it is not practicable to constitute a bench contributing to a delay in hearing the case (*Practice Direction (Magistrates' Courts: Anti-Social Behaviour Orders: Composition of Benches)* 24 February 2006, BLD 2702060704). A separate application must be made in respect of each named individual. The defendant will receive a summons with a copy of the written application. Due to the severe sanction for breach a criminal standard of proof is required (*R v Manchester Crown Court, ex p McCann* [2001] 1 WLR 358, sub nom R v Crown Court at Manchester, ex p McCann 165 JP 225, [2001] 02 LS Gaz R 40, 144 Sol Jo LB 287; affd sub nom R (on the application of McCann) v Crown Court at Manchester [2001] EWCA Civ 281 [2001] 4 All ER 264, [2001] 1 WLR 1084, 165 JP 545). Even though the proceedings are civil in nature, the court may rely upon facts which previously formed the basis of criminal prosecutions (*S v Poole Borough Council* [2002] EWHC 244 (Admin), [2002] All ER (D) 143 (Feb)); *R (on the application of the Chief Constable of Mercia Constabulary) v Boorman* [2005] EWHC Admin 2559).

B[8.4A]

Reliance upon hearsay evidence – Where the applicant proposes to adduce hearsay evidence in support of the application, notice must be given under the Civil Evidence Act 1995 and the Magistrates' Courts (Hearsay Evidence in Civil Proceedings) Rules 1999. See *M v DPP* [2007] EWHC 1032 (Admin) and *R v James Lima* [2010] EWCA Crim 284, as illustrations where the applicant failed to comply with the said rules.

B[8.5]

The order and its terms – may be made against a person who it has been proved has acted in an anti-social manner (that is in a manner that caused or was likely to cause harassment, alarm or distress, to one or more persons not in the same household as himself) and an order is necessary to prevent further anti-social acts. It may prohibit further anti-social acts described in the order, necessary to protect relevant persons. The terms of the ASBO must be clear and commensurate with the risk they seek to guard against (*R v McGrath* [2005] EWCA Crim 353, [2005] All ER (D) 81 (May)). A curfew may be a legitimate condition so long as it was preventive and protective (*R (on the application of Lonergan) v Lewes Crown Court and Secretary of State for the Home Department (interested party)* [2005] EWHC 457 (Admin), [2005] All ER (D) 382 (Mar)).

The reference to behaviour 'likely to cause' harassment, alarm or distress in s 1(1) of the 1998 Act permitted police witnesses to give evidence that there were potential victims present who were caused harassment, alarm or distress. However, s 1(1)(a) of the Act was not made out where it could not be shown that a potential victim was present (*R (on the application of Gosport Borough Council) v Fareham Magistrates' Court* (2007) 171 JP 102).

Guidance – For a more detailed commentary the reader should consult: *Anti-Social Behaviour Orders: a guide for the judiciary* (3rd edn, JSB).

Judicial guidance – In *R v Boness, R v Bebbington* [2005] EWCA Crim 2395, [2006] 1 Cr App Rep (S) 690, the Court of Appeal ruled as follows:

(1)   An ASBO had to be precise and capable of being understood by the offender. It followed that the court should ask itself, before making an order, whether the terms of the order were clear so that the defendant would know precisely what it was that he was prohibited from doing (it would be wrong to make an ASBO against an offender who by reason of mental health would not have the capacity to understand or comply with the terms of the order: *R (on the application of Cooke) v Director of Public Prosecutions* [2008] EWHC 2703 (Admin), 172 JP 596).

(2)   There must be evidence of anti-social behaviour (see *R (on the application of Mills) v Birmingham Magistrates' Court* [2005] EWHC 2732 (Admin), (2005) 170 JP 237). Evidence of later behaviour showing a propensity to behave in an anti-social manner was capable of being relevant, to the question of whether the defendant acted in an anti-social manner at the times and at places alleged in a section complaint. Post-complaint behaviour was also relevant to whether an order was necessary to protect persons from

further anti-social acts: see *Birmingham City Council v Dixon* [2009] EWHC 761(Admin), 173 JP 233. Following a finding that the defendant had acted in an anti-social manner (whether or not the act constituted a criminal offence), the test for making an order that prohibited the offender from doing something was one of necessity (see *R v W; R v F* [2006] EWCA Crim 686). [In that context, the prohibition on associating with a named individual, who was not the subject of an ASBO with a reciprocal prohibition on association, was held to be lawful in *Hills v Chief Constable of Essex Police* [2006] EWHC 2633 (Admin)].

(3)   Each separate order prohibiting a person from doing a specified thing had to be necessary to protect persons from further anti-social acts by him. Accordingly, any order had to be tailor-made for the individual defendant, not designed on a word processor for use in every case.

(4)   The purpose of an order was preventative, not to punish. The use of an ASBO to punish a defendant was unlawful.

(5)   Where the ASBO was being sought as ancillary to a criminal sentence or disposal, the court should not allow itself to be diverted by a defendant's representative at the sentencing stage in the hope that the court might make such an order as an alternative to prison or other sanction. It might be better for the court to decide the substantive sentence and then move on to consider whether an ASBO should be made or not after sentence has been pronounced, albeit at the same hearing [subject to the power of the court to adjourn consideration of an ASBO to a later date (Crime and Disorder Act 1998, s 1C as amended)].

(6)   The court should not impose an order which prohibited a defendant from committing a specified criminal offence, if the sentence which could be passed following conviction for the offence should be a sufficient deterrent. It followed that an ASBO should not be used merely to increase the sentence of imprisonment which a defendant was liable to receive. Whilst different considerations might apply where the maximum sentence was a fine, the court had still to go through all the steps to ensure that the order was necessary. [In that context, a prohibition on carrying knives or bladed articles in a public place was held to be lawful in *Hills v Chief Constable of Essex* supra, as the order was intended to cover behaviour not caught by s 139 Criminal Justice Act 1988, namely the carrying of knives or bladed articles with a blade of less than three inches in a public place.]

(7)   The corollary to (6) above was that a court should be reluctant to impose an order which prohibited a defendant from committing a specified criminal offence. The aim of an ASBO was to prevent anti-social behaviour, by enabling action to be taken before the anti-social behaviour it was designed to prevent was to take place.

(8)   The terms of the order had to be proportionate in the sense that they had to be commensurate with the risk to be guarded against. That was particularly important where an order might interfere with a defendant's right under the European Convention of Human Rights.

B[8.6]

Statutory defence – to an application is available namely that the behaviour complained of was reasonable in the particular circumstances.

B[8.7]

Interim Orders – For guidance on ex parte applications *see R (on the application of Manchester City Council) v Manchester Magistrates' Court* (2005) Times, 8 March, [2005] All ER (D) 103 (Feb). Interim orders may be made pending the determination of an order if the court considers it just. An application may be made without notice if the justices are satisfied that it is necessary. The court itself may direct that notice be served on the defendant and refuse to make an order without notice (*R (Kenny) v Leeds Magistrates* [2003] EWHC 2963 (Admin), [2004] 1 All ER 1333, [2003] All ER (D) 104 (Dec); affd sub nom R (on the application of M) v Secretary of State for Constitutional Affairs and Lord Chancellor [2004] EWCA Civ 312, [2004] All ER (D) 345 (Mar)). See also *R (on the application of M) v Secretary of State for Constitutional Affairs and Lord Chancellor* [2004] EWCA Civ 312, [2004] All ER (D) 345 (Mar), CA.

There is no presumption that an order against publicity will be made on an interim order against a juvenile but age is an important consideration (*R (on the application of K) v Knowsley Metropolitan Borough Council* [2004] EWHC 1933 (Admin), 168 JP 461, sub nom Keating v Knowsley Metropolitan Borough Council [2004] All ER (D) 383 (Jul)).

B[8.8]

Criminal Proceedings – An ASBO may also be made as an ancillary order following a conviction for a criminal offence committed after 2 December 2002 if:

(a)   the offender has acted at any time since 1 April 1999 in an anti-social manner (causing or likely to cause harassment, alarm or distress to a person not in the same household) and

(b)   the order is necessary to protect persons in England and Wales from further anti-social behaviour.

Rules of procedure are to be found in r 50 of the Criminal Procedure Rules 2012.

For example, the prosecution must serve notice of its intention on the court, the defendant and any person who is likely to be adversely affected by the order as soon as practicable (without waiting for a verdict; r 50.3(2). NB: The rules at 50.2 and 50.4 have been amended, to make it clear that the defendant must be allowed the opportunity to consider the evidence on which the court is going to rely when it makes one of the orders listed in rule 50.4.

Guidance was given in *R v Parkin* [2004] EWCA Crim 287, [2004] All ER (D) 32 (Feb) on the principles to be followed. This must be read in the light of *R v Boness, R v Bebbington* and others at B[8.5] above.

The order must be necessary, precise, recorded, explained to the defendant and reduced to writing. The order may be at the invitation of the prosecution or in the court's discretion. The court may hear evidence not admissible in criminal proceedings (CDA 1998, s 1C). The court may adjourn proceedings in respect of an ASBO after conviction even after sentencing the defendant. If it does so, it may make an interim order and may issue a warrant if the defendant does not reappear.

It is not inappropriate to make an ASBO in motoring offences if their regularity and type constitutes anti-social behaviour. It is not appropriate to make an order just to increase the penalty for breach of it (*R v Hall* [2004] EWCA Crim 2671, [2004] All ER (D) 377 (Nov)).

B was part of a gang who had engaged in anti-social behaviour whilst wearing hooded tops to conceal their identities. A prohibition on B wearing hooded tops in the London Borough of Greenwich, whether up or down, was held to be clear, necessary and proportionate (*R (on the application of B) v Greenwich Magistrates' Court* [2008] EWHC 2882 (Admin), 173 JP 52).

B[8.8A]

Reliance upon hearsay evidence – see B[8.4A].

B[8.9]

The Order – May be for any term not less than 2 years and may require the defendant to refrain from any specified activities. In the case of a juvenile under 16 the court must make a parenting order unless it is able to justify its reasons for not doing so. It must also consider whether the individual support conditions are satisfied. If fulfilled the court must make an individual support order. If the court is not satisfied that the conditions are fulfilled it must state its reasons and cause those to be recorded in the court register: Crime and Disorder Act 1998, s 1A as amended by CJA 2003, s 322.

B[8.10]

Restrictions – The order may not be made following an order of absolute discharge or no separate penalty.

B[8.11]

An order may be suspended while the defendant remains in custody.

B[8.12]

Variation or discharge – of a civil order may only be done within the first two years with the consent of both parties. There is no provision for discharge of a criminal order before the two year period without the consent of the DPP or the offender. Notice to vary or discharge must be served by either party on the other.

In *Leeds City Council v G* [2007] EWHC 1612 (Admin), (2007) Times, 11 September, the Administrative Court held that a magistrates' court did have jurisdiction under s 1(8) of the Crime and Disorder Act 1998 to *vary* a *civil order* by extending the duration of the original order beyond the minimum period ie two years. The Administrative Court did have some misgivings because there is no appeal from any variation. The protection for the defendant is that if the variation seeks more stringent conditions than the original order (including the length of the order), sufficient material would have to be put before the court which, by reference to the normal burden and standard of proof, justifies the extension in order to achieve the statutory objective. Further, the applicant will need to persuade the magistrates that it is appropriate to vary an order rather than make an application for a new anti-social behaviour order. See *James v Birmingham City Council* below.

The misgivings of the Administrative Court regarding a right of appeal were confirmed in *R (on the application of Langley) v Preston Crown Court* [2008] EWHC 2623 (Admin), [2009] 3 All ER 1026 where it was held that there was no right of appeal to the Crown Court against the **variation** of a 'stand-alone' order pursuant to s 1(8) of the 1998 Act. It is submitted that the decision is wrong. Section 4 confers a right of appeal because by analogy the term 'variation' has been interpreted or defined as if it were a fresh order of the court. For the moment, the above decisions are binding and must be followed.

Variation of an ASBO under s 1(8) does not require proof of a fresh act of anti-social behaviour. The court was entitled, in the exercise of its discretion, to consider a variation even if the applicant had the option of applying for a fresh ASBO. A complaint to vary must simply be made within six months from an event or circumstance which it is alleged renders the original order inappropriate for one reason or another. On a purposive construction of s 1(8) the question is whether it is necessary to vary the order to protect the public: *James v Birmingham City Council* [2010] EWHC 282 (Admin), 174 JP 250.

B[8.13]

Breach of an order – will result in the commission of a criminal offence triable either way. The order commences when announced in court and not when reduced in writing (*Walkling v DPP* (2004) Independent, 26 January). Repeated and deliberate breaches will indicate committal to Crown Court for sentence (*R v Braxton* [2004] EWCA Crim 1374, [2005] 1 Cr App Rep (S) 167).

Breach of an order – commission of a criminal offence – s 8(2) CDA 1998 – Although there is nothing inherently wrong by passing a consecutive sentence for breach of an anti-social behaviour order, if the new offence is derived from the same course of conduct, broadly speaking concurrent sentences should be imposed (*R v Lawson* [2006] EWCA Crim 2674, [2006] All ER (D) 61 (Mar)).

Breach – collateral attack on validity of the order or its terms: In *W v DPP* [2005] EWCA Civ 1333, it was decided that an ASBO was to be treated as a valid order unless and until it was varied or declared invalid. The Court of Appeal said it was open to a magistrates' court considering an allegation of a breach of an order to determine whether the original order was ultra vires and therefore not a valid order. In *DPP v T* [2006] EWHC 728 (Admin), [2006] 3 All ER 471; sub nom *CPS v T* (2006) 170 JP 470, the Divisional Court reached a slightly different conclusion. The Divisional Court made reference to the normal rule that an order of the court was to be obeyed unless and until it was set aside. The Court noted that the person against whom an ASBO was made had had a full opportunity to challenge that order on appeal or to apply to vary it. The policy consideration that a magistrates' court had jurisdiction to determine issues of the validity of a byelaw or an administrative decision was wholly absent when the issue was the validity of an order of the court. It was open to a magistrates' court to consider whether the provision lacked sufficient clarity to warrant a finding that the defendant's conduct did not amount to a breach of the order; or that the lack of clarity provided him with a reasonable excuse; or whether, assuming a breach was established, it was appropriate in the circumstances not to impose any penalty for the breach.

Breach – reasonable excuse – Section 1(10) of the CDA 1998 makes it a criminal offence to breach an ASBO in the following terms: 'If without reasonable excuse a person does anything which he is prohibited from doing by an anti-social behaviour order, he is guilty of an offence'. The Act only imposes an evidential burden of the defendant, the legal burden rests with the prosecution to prove that the defendant acted without reasonable excuse (*R v Charles* [2009] EWCA Crim 1570, [2010] 4 All ER 553, [2010] 1 Cr App Rep 38).

Breach – reasonable excuse – In the context of an ASBO, ignorance, forgetfulness or misunderstanding, whether arising from an error as to the terms of the order or lack of knowledge of where the defendant was at the material time, might be capable of constituting a defence of reasonable excuse (*R v Nicholson* [2006] EWCA Crim 1518, 170 JP 573)).

Breach – reasonable excuse – s 1(10) did not require the Crown to prove a specific mental element on the part of a defendant at the time he committed an act which constituted a breach of an ASBO. However, if the defence of reasonable excuse was raised, the state of mind of the accused would usually be relevant and could, if the circumstances warranted, be taken into account in determining whether the Crown had proved there was no reasonable excuse. The burden of so proving lay with the Crown: *R v Charles* [2009] EWCA Crim 1570, [2010] 4 All ER 553, [2010] 1 Cr App Rep 38. In this case the Judge was entitled to conclude that there was no reasonable excuse as the risk was obvious and JB had actually foreseen it. The alarm and distress had not been an accident but was caused by JB's reckless conduct in breaching the ASBO: *JB v DPP* [2012] EWHC 72 (Admin), [2012] 1 WLR 2357, [2012] 2 Cr App Rep 9.

SGC Guideline – Anti-social behaviour order, breach of

B[8.14]

Triable either way

Maximum when tried summarily: Level 5 and/or 6 months

Maximum when tried on indictment: 5 years or an unlimited fine

Note: A conditional discharge is not available as a sentence for this offence

<table>
<tr><td colspan="3">OFFENCE SERIOUSNESS (CULPABILITY AND HARM)
A. IDENTIFY THE APPROPRIATE STARTING POINT
Starting points based on first time offender pleading not guilty</td></tr>
<tr><th>Examples of nature of activity</th><th>Starting point</th><th>Range</th></tr>
<tr><td>Breach where no harassment, alarm or distress was caused or intended</td><td>Low level community order</td><td>Band B fine to medium level community order</td></tr>
<tr><td>Breach involving a lesser degree of actual or intended harassment, alarm or distress than in the box below, or where such harm would have been likely had the offender not been apprehended</td><td>6 weeks custody</td><td>Medium level community order to 26 weeks custody</td></tr>
<tr><td>Breach involving serious actual or intended harassment, alarm or distress</td><td>26 weeks custody</td><td>Custody threshold to Crown Court</td></tr>
</table>

<table>
<tr><td colspan="2">OFFENCE SERIOUSNESS (CULPABILITY AND HARM)
B. CONSIDER THE EFFECT OF AGGRAVATING AND MITIGATING FACTORS (OTHER THAN THOSE WITHIN EXAMPLES ABOVE)
Common aggravating and mitigating factors are identified at B[5.2A]. The following may be particularly relevant but these lists are not exhaustive</td></tr>
<tr><td>Factors indicating higher culpability</td><td>Factors indicating lower culpability</td></tr>
<tr><td>1. Offender has a history of disobedience to court orders</td><td>1. Breach occurred after a long period of compliance</td></tr>
<tr><td>2. Breach was committed immediately or shortly after the order was made</td><td>2. The prohibition(s) breached was not fully understood especially where an interim order was made without notice</td></tr>
<tr><td>3. Breach was committed subsequent to earlier breach proceedings arising from the same order</td><td></td></tr>
<tr><td>4. Targeting of a person the order was made to protect or a witness in the original proceedings</td><td></td></tr>
<tr><td>Factor indicating greater degree of harm
1. Involvement of vulnerable/young persons</td><td></td></tr>
<tr><td colspan="2" align="center">FORM A PRELIMINARY VIEW OF THE APPROPRIATE SENTENCE, THEN CONSIDER OFFENDER MITIGATION</td></tr>
</table>

Common factors are identified at B[5.2A]
CONSIDER A REDUCTION FOR A GUILTY PLEA
CONSIDER ANCILLARY ORDERS, INCLUDING FORFEITURE AND DESTRUCTION OF DRUG
Refer to B[18] for guidance on compensation and Part B for available ancillary orders
DECIDE SENTENCE
GIVE REASONS

B[8.14A]

Previous convictions. For the purposes of this guideline a 'first time offender' is one who does not have a previous conviction for breach of an ASBO.

Key factors

B[8.15]

(a) An ASBO may be breached in a very wide range of circumstances and may involve one or more terms not being complied with. The examples given below are intended to illustrate how the scale of the conduct that led to the breach, taken as a whole, might come within the three levels of seriousness:

No harm caused or intended – in the absence of intimidation or the causing of fear or violence, breaches involving being very drunk or begging at this level, as may prohibited use of public transport or entry into a prohibited area, where there is no evidence that harassment, alarm or distress was caused or intended.

Lesser degree of harm caused or intended – examples may include lesser degree of threats or intimidation, the use of seriously abusive language, or causing more than minor damage to property.

Serious harm caused or intended – breach at this level of seriousness will involve the use of violence, significant threats or intimidation or the targeting of individuals or groups of people in a manner that leads to a fear of violence.

(b) The suggested starting points are based on the assumption that the offender has the level of culpability.

(c) In the most serious cases, involving repeat offending and a breach causing serious harassment together with the presence of several aggravating factors, such as the use of violence, a sentence beyond the highest range will be justified.

(d) When imposing a community order, the court must ensure that the requirements imposed are proportionate to the seriousness of the breach, compatible with each other, and also with the prohibitions of the ASBO if the latter is to remain in force. Even where the threshold for a custodial sentence is crossed, a custodial sentence is not inevitable.

(e) An offender may be sentenced for more than one offence of breach, which occurred on different days. While consecutive sentences may be imposed in such cases, the overall sentence should reflect the totality principle.

B[8.15A]

Sentencing of Young Offenders. The normal approach is that the penalty is scaled down to reflect both reduced culpability (for example, due to a lesser ability to foresee the consequences of actions) and the more onerous effects of punishments on their education and personal development. For the same reasons, the sentencing framework differs significantly depending on the age of the young offender. Space does not permit a full discussion of the SAP advice. See **paragraphs 52–69** of the advice.

B[8.16]

The court may not impose a conditional discharge following a breach.

B[8.17]

Reporting restrictions – see E[2.4].

B[9]

Attendance centre orders (adults only)

(Powers of Criminal Courts (Sentencing) Act 2000, s 60; Criminal Justice Act 2003, s 177)

B[9.1]

Jurisdiction – Offence must be punishable with imprisonment (even though the individual offender may not be).

B[9.2]

Age limits – 18 to under 25 years (25 years old also when used as a fine default power).

B[9.3]

Maximum period – 12 hours unless the court thinks that would be inadequate in which event the maximum periods are:

Offender aged 18 to under 25: 36 hours

Note – A further order may be made during the currency of a previous one, in which case the period of the later order may be determined as above without regard to the unexpired part of the previous order.

B[9.4]

Minimum period – 12 hours.

B[9.5]

Availability. Court must have been notified of the availability of a centre for persons of the offender's age and sex.

B[9.6]

Regard must be paid to the accessibility of the centre to the offender.

B[9.7]

Juveniles. A magistrates' court may not make this order against a juvenile but must remit him to a youth court.

B[9.8]

Community sentences. Note the restrictions on imposing a community sentence, see B[3].

Ancillary orders

B[9.9]

Anti-social behaviour orders B[8]

Binding over orders

Compensation at B[18]

Costs at B[20]

Deprivation of property and forfeiture at B[34]

Disqualification from driving at C[5]

Endorsement of driving licence at C[5]

Legal aid contribution order at I[7]

Restitution orders B[39]

How to announce

B[9.10]–[9.15]

We shall order you to attend the attendance centre at [   ] for a total of [   ] hours starting on [   ]. You will be given a copy of the order which will show the date and time of your first attendance. After that you will attend as directed by the officer in charge. You will make up the period of [   ] hours by attending on Saturday afternoons (or as the case may be) for two (or three, as the case may be) hours at a time. If you arrive late the officer in charge may not count that day's attendance. If you fail to attend without a very good excuse, or if you fail to carry out the officer's instructions properly, he will bring you back here and we shall deal with you. Do you understand?

General considerations

B[9.16]

The aims of the attendance centre have been described by the Home Office as follows:

(a)   to vindicate the law by imposing loss of leisure, a punishment that is generally understood by offenders;

(b)   to bring the offender for a period under the influence of representatives of the authority of the state; and

(c)   to teach the offender constructive use of leisure and to guide him, on leaving, towards organisations or activities where he may use what he has learned. Centres usually require attendance for three-hour periods on alternate Saturday afternoons. Only one period of attendance may be required in any one day. The court must take into account the availability of suitable transport and the journey time from home to the centre. A distance of 15 miles or a 90–minutes journey would be the limit.

B[9.17]

The court must announce for how many hours the defendant must attend. The court should also tell the defendant the date, time and place of the first attendance.

B[10]
Binding over

B[10.1]

There have been significant developments to the making of binding over orders following amendments to the *Consolidated Criminal Practice Direction* which for the sake of completeness is set out below at **B[10.21]**. The following notes therefore must be read in the light of that Practice Direction.

B[10.2]

Maximum period – None, but the Practice Direction suggests generally not longer than 12 months.

B[10.3]

Minimum period – None, but consistent with community orders generally not less than six months.

Ancillary orders

B[10.4]

Costs at B[20]. It would appear that there is no power to award costs where a defendant is bound over under the court's inherent powers where the substantive charge is withdrawn or dismissed.

How to announce

B[10.5]

We are going to order you to enter a recognisance – that is a binding promise – that you will refrain from the following conduct or activity for the next [*period*]. [Court to specify the specific conduct or activity from which the individual must refrain.]

The amount of that recognisance will be [*amount*] and that means that if you repeat the kind of conduct or activity we have heard about today, during the next [*period*] **we will order** you to pay that amount. Do you understand? Do you agree to making that promise and to guaranteeing to pay the [*amount*] if you break that promise?

Age limits – None. However, a refusal to enter a recognisance (see below) will result in imprisonment and as those under 21 [**18] may not be imprisoned the court would be powerless to enforce an order to enter into a recognisance.

General considerations

B[10.6]

One or more sureties may also be required if the court thinks fit. This order is commonly and conveniently referred to as a binding over order but this tends to disguise its real form. The court orders the defendant to enter a recognisance in terms chosen by the court as to the duration and amount. The defendant or his legal representative must be given an opportunity to address the court in order not to breach Article 6 rights (*Hooper v UK* (2004) Times, 19 November, [2004] All ER (D) 254 (Nov), ECtHR). If the defendant so agrees, he is said to be bound over to keep the peace. If he refuses to enter the recognisance the only course left to the court is to send him to prison from which he will be released after a term fixed by the court of up to six months (**51 weeks) or when he enters the recognisance, whichever is the sooner. Great care should therefore be exercised before making such an order especially if there is any possibility of refusal to comply with it. An order to be of good behaviour should be avoided as it is imprecise and may breach the ECHR (*Hashman and Harrup v United Kingdom* (1999) 30 EHRR 241, [2000] Crim LR 185, 8 BHRC 104, ECtHR).

NB: The defendant's consent is not required if the binding over order is made as an ancillary penalty to a criminal sentence (*R v Crown Court at Lincoln, ex p Jude* [1997] 3 All ER 737). This case must be read against the Consolidated Practice Direction set out below.

B[10.7]

Before a court has any power to order a person to enter a recognisance to keep the peace, it must have grounds for believing that there is a possibility of a future breach of the peace.

B[10.8]

Sometimes the court is asked to make this order by an applicant who has taken out a summons for that purpose. In addition to this, the court may on its own initiative consider the need to make the order when dealing with an offender. Moreover, a witness or complainant may also be ordered to enter a recognisance. Whenever the court takes the initiative it should explain to the person concerned what it has in mind to do and offer an opportunity to address the court before it is decided whether to make the order or not.

B[10.9]–[10.15]

The procedure for binding over a complainant or witness must be followed punctiliously, and if this is in contemplation, the advice of the legal adviser should be followed.

B[10.16]

There is no power generally to impose any conditions, and an order must be specific as to the conduct or activity which the individual must refrain from repeating. Also it appears that there may be a condition not to possess, carry or use firearms or as part of a community order (Firearms Act 1968, s 21(3)).

B[10.17]

Breach of the order will be dealt with by forfeiting the recognisance, or any part of it. The defendant may be given time to pay and in default, after a means inquiry, he may be committed to prison, as if he owed a fine.

Binding over a parent

B[10.18]

Either a magistrates' court or a youth court may require the parent of a young person (or an 18-year-old who was 17 when the proceedings commenced) who has been found guilty of an offence to enter a recognisance to take proper care of him and to exercise proper control over him. The court must exercise these powers where the juvenile has not attained 16 years if it is satisfied, having regard to the circumstances of the case, that it would be desirable in the interests of preventing the juvenile from committing further offences. If the court does not exercise the powers it must say so and give its reasons in open court. The court's duty to bind over the parent is replaced by a power where the juvenile has attained 16 years. In such a case the maximum amount of the recognisance is £1,000 and the maximum period is three years or until a young person attains 18, whichever is the shorter.

B[10.19]

The parent must consent to the order. An unreasonable refusal is punishable by a fine of up to £1,000. A parent may appeal to the Crown Court against the bind over.

Consolidated Criminal Practice Direction

B[10.20]

Amendment No 15 to the Consolidated Criminal Practice Direction (Binding Over Orders and Conditional Discharges) ([2007] AER (D) 520 (Mar)) made a number of changes to the original Practice Direction handed down by the Lord Chief Justice on 8 July 2002 (as subsequently amended). In schedule 1, Part III, a new paragraph 31 has been inserted. The amendments to the Practice Direction take effect from **2 April 2007.**

(III.31) Binding Over Orders and Conditional Discharges.

B[10.21]

(III.31.1) This direction takes into account the judgments of the European Court of Human Rights in *Steel v UK* (1998) 28 EHRR 603, [1998] Crim LR 893 and in *Hashman and Harrup v UK* (2000) 30 EHRR 241, [2000] Crim LR 185. Its purpose is to give practice guidance, in the light of those two judgments, on the practice of imposing binding over orders. The direction applies to orders made under the court's common law powers, under the Justices of the Peace Act 1361, under s 1(7) of the Justices of the Peace Act 1968 and under s 115 of the Magistrates' Courts Act 1980. This direction also gives guidance concerning the court's power to bind over parents or guardians under s 150 of the PCC (S.) Act 2000 and the Crown Court's power to bind over to come up for judgment. The court's power to impose a conditional discharge under s 12 of the PCC (S.) Act 2000 is also covered by this direction.

Binding over to keep the peace

(III.31.2) Before imposing a binding over order, the court must be satisfied that a breach of the peace involving violence or an imminent threat of violence has occurred or that there is a real risk of violence in the future. Such violence may be perpetrated by the individual who will be subject to the order or by a third party as a natural consequence of the individual's conduct.

(III.31.3) In the light of the judgment in *Hashman and Harrup*, courts should no longer bind an individual over "to be of good behaviour". Rather than binding an individual over "to keep the peace" in general terms, the court should identify the specific conduct or activity from which the individual must refrain.

Written order

(III.31.4) When making an order binding an individual over to refrain from specified types of conduct or activities, the details of that conduct or those specified activities should be specified by the court in a written order served on all relevant parties. The court should state its reasons for the making of the order, its length and the amount of the recognisance. The length of the order should be proportionate to the harm sought to be avoided and should not generally exceed 12 months.

Evidence

(III.31.5) Sections 51 to 57 of the Magistrates' Courts Act 1980 set out the jurisdiction of the magistrates' court to hear an application made on complaint and the procedure to be followed. This includes a requirement under s 53 to hear evidence and the parties before making an order. This practice should be applied to all cases in the magistrates' court and the Crown Court where the court is considering imposing a binding over order.

The court should give the individual who would be subject to the order and the prosecutor the opportunity to make representations, both as to the making of the order and as to its terms. The court should hear any admissible evidence the parties wish to call and which has not already been heard in the proceedings. Particularly careful consideration may be required where the individual who would be subject to the order is a witness in the proceedings.

(III.31.6) Where there is an admission which is sufficient to found the making of a binding over order and/or the individual consents to the making of the order, the court should nevertheless hear sufficient representations and, if appropriate, evidence, to satisfy itself that an order is appropriate in all the circumstances and to be clear about the terms of the order.

(III.31.7) Where there is an allegation of breach of a binding over order and this is contested, the court should hear representations and evidence, including oral evidence, from the parties before making a finding.

Burden of proof

(III.31.8) The court should be satisfied beyond reasonable doubt of the matters complained of before a binding over order may be imposed. Where the procedure has commenced on complaint, the burden of proof rests on the complainant. In all other circumstances, the burden of proof rests on the prosecution.

(III.31.9) Where there is an allegation of breach of a binding over order, the court should be satisfied beyond reasonable doubt that a breach has occurred before making an order for forfeiture of a recognisance. The burden of proof shall rest on the prosecution.

Recognisance

(III.31.10) The court must be satisfied on the merits of the case that an order for a binding over order is appropriate and should announce the decision before considering the amount of the recognisance. The individual who is made subject to the binding over order should be told he has a right of appeal from the decision.

(III.31.11) When fixing the amount of the recognisance, courts should have regard to the individual's financial resources and should hear representations from the individual or his legal representatives regarding finances.

Refusal to enter into a recognisance

(III.31.12) If there is any possibility that an individual will refuse to enter [into] a recognisance, the court should consider whether there are any appropriate alternatives to a binding over order (for example, continuing with a prosecution). Where there are no appropriate alternatives and the individual continues to refuse to enter into the recognisance, the magistrates' court may use its powers under s 115(3) of the Magistrates' Courts Act 1980, and the Crown Court may use its common law power, to commit the individual to custody.

(III.31.13) Before the court exercises a power to commit the individual to custody, the individual should be given the opportunity to see a duty solicitor or another legal representative and be represented in proceedings if the individual so wishes. Public funding should generally be granted to cover representation.

(III.31.14) In the event that the individual does not take the opportunity to seek legal advice, the court shall give the individual a final opportunity to comply with the request and shall explain the consequences of a failure to do so.

Antecedents

(III.31.15) Courts are reminded of the provisions of s 7(5) of the Rehabilitation of Offenders Act 1974 which excludes from a person's antecedents any order of the court "with respect to any person otherwise than on a conviction".

Binding over to come up for judgment

(III.31.16) If the Crown Court is considering binding over an individual to come up for judgment, the court should specify any conditions with which the individual is to comply in the meantime and not specify that the individual is to be of good behaviour.

Binding over of parent or guardian

(III.31.17) Where a court is considering binding over a parent or guardian under s 150 of the Powers of Criminal Courts (Sentencing) Act 2000 to enter into a recognisance to take proper care of and exercise proper control over a child or young person, the court should specify the actions which the parent or guardian is to take.

Security for good behaviour

(III.31.18) where a court is imposing a conditional discharge under section 12 of the Powers of Criminal Courts (Sentencing) Act 2000, it has the power, under section 12 (6) to make an order that a person who consents to do so give security for the good behaviour of the offender. When making such an order, the court should specify the type of conduct from which the offender is to refrain.

B[11]–B[16]

Committal to Crown Court for sentence

(Powers of the Criminal Courts (Sentencing) Act 2000, ss 3 and 4**)

(Note – There are a few circumstances in which a person may be committed to the Crown Court which are mentioned at the end of this section. The following notes are intended to refer to committal for sentence after conviction for an either way or related offence.)

Limitations

B[16.1]

A magistrates' court when dealing with an either way offence (excluding criminal damage where the value makes the offence triable only by magistrates) may commit on bail or in custody an offender aged at least 18 to be sentenced by the judge with all the powers available to the Crown Court (*R v Warley Magistrates' Court, ex p DPP* [1999] 1 All ER 251, [1999] 1 WLR 216). However where a previous bench had indicated that the defendant has a legitimate expectation that he will be dealt with in the magistrates' court, the option to commit is no longer open (*R v Norwich Magistrates' Court, ex p Elliott* 2000] 1 Cr App Rep (S) 152; *R (on the application of Harrington) v Bromley Magistrates' Court* [2007] EWHC 2896 (Admin), [2007] All ER (D) 199 (Nov). For this reason the 'all options open' form of words when requesting a pre-sentence report does not preserve the option of committal (*R v Feltham Justices, ex p Rees* [2001] 2 Cr App Rep (S) 1, [2001] Crim LR 47) but will be adequate where committal takes place immediately after conviction on disclosure of the defendant's record (*R v McHoul* [2002] EWCA Crim 1918, [2003] 1 Cr App Rep (S) 382). Where a court departs form a non-custodial recommendation in a pre-sentence report in favour of a committal, they should state their reasons in open court (*R v Law* [2002] All ER (D) 40 (Jan), CA).

Case law such as *R (on the application of Harrington) v Bromley Magistrates' Court* [2007] All ER (D) 199 (Nov), does not sit well with *Nicholas v Chester Magistrates' Court* [2009] EWHC 1504 (Admin), where it could be argued that a magistrates' court when adjourning should not be 'deemed' to have ruled out committal for sentence where that decision was 'Wednesbury' unreasonable (see **I[6.32]**).

B[16.2]

The court must be of the opinion that the offence (or combination of the offence and one or more offences associated with it) was so serious that greater punishment should be inflicted for the offence than the court has power to impose or **the Crown Court should, in the court's opinion, have the power to deal with the offender in any way it could deal with him if he had been convicted on indictment** i.e. at the Crown Court. See s 4 for the power to commit related either way offences for sentence following a committal for trial. **NB:** The words highlighted above were substituted by the Criminal Justice and Immigration Act 2008, s 53 from May 8, 2008.

B[16.3]

Alternatively, the court may use the same powers in the case of an offender who has committed an offence of violence or a sexual offence, where the court considers it is necessary that a sentence longer than it has power to impose is necessary to protect the public from serious harm by him.

Ancillary orders

B[16.4]

Disqualification from driving pending sentence is available.

Dangerous offenders

B[16.5]

The Criminal Justice Act 2003, ss 224-236 make provision for the sentencing of dangerous offenders. To qualify the offender must be convicted of a specified violent or sexual offence in Sch 15 of the Act.*

*Imprisonment or detention for public protection for serious offenders; extended sentences for certain violent or sexual offences (persons under 18 years and those aged 18 years or over respectively ie ss 225(3)–(4); 226(3)–(4); 227; and 228 will be abolished by virtue of LASPO 2012, s 123 when brought into force. A new regime entitled 'extended sentences for certain violent of sexual offences' (persons over 18 and under 18) will be introduced by virtue of s 124 of LASPOA 2012 when brought into force.

Magistrates do not have power to impose the necessary extended or life sentences and must send dangerous offenders to Crown Court under the provisions of the Powers of the Criminal Courts (Sentencing) Act 2000, s 3A for sentence and s 51A for trial in the case of young offenders.

A significant change has been the requirement that (except where the offender has a previous conviction for one or more of the offences listed in Sch 15A to the 2003 Act) a sentence under these provisions may be imposed only if the equivalent determinate sentence would have been at least 4 years. Accordingly, it is very unlikely that a magistrates' court will need to consider these provisions specifically since an offence likely to result in a sentence of 4 years or more will be committed for trial or sentence under other provisions.

For general guidance see *R v Lang* [2005] EWCA Crim 2864, [2006] 2 All ER 410 as explained in *R v Johnson* [2006] EWCA Crim 2486, [2007] 1 All ER 1237.

*Given the complexity of these provisions it is advisable for magistrates to consult with their legal adviser.

General considerations

B[16.6]

The power to commit for sentence is often used where a custodial sentence is likely to be imposed which would exceed the maximum available to the magistrates' court. The maximum period of custody which a magistrates' court may impose for an offence triable either way is six months**. If an offender is convicted of more than one such offence, the maximum custodial sentence is 12 months. Magistrates may acquaint themselves with the sentences imposed in their local Crown Court either by sitting there, or through the liaison judge.

B[16.7]

Generally where a defendant appears on bail before the magistrates he may be committed to the Crown Court for sentence on bail. The provisions of the Bail Act 1976 do not apply.

B[16.8]

An offender committed for sentence under the procedure described here may be dealt with by the Crown Court in any manner as if he had been convicted on indictment at the Crown Court, so long as the committal is clearly under PCC(S)A 2000, s 3(2) (*R v Sallis* [2003] EWCA Crim 233, [2003] All ER (D) 275 (Jan)).

B[16.9]

The legal adviser should always be consulted if a committal to the Crown Court is contemplated.

B[16.10]–[16.19]

An offender committed for sentence under the procedure described here may also be committed to be dealt with in respect of another offence of which he has been convicted by the committing court and which that court could have dealt with (Powers of the Criminal Courts (Sentencing) Act 2000, s 6). The Powers of the Criminal Courts (Sentencing) Act 2000, s 4 is used to commit offences where a guilty plea has been indicated but those offences are related to matters which are to be dealt with at Crown Court for trial.

Committals for sentence under other provisions**

B[16.20]

Other circumstances in which an offender may be committed to the Crown Court to be dealt with:

(a)   Where the offender has failed to surrender to bail (Bail Act 1976, s 6);

(b)   where the offender is in breach of an order or sentence of the Crown Court, eg community rehabilitation, suspended sentence (Criminal Justice Act 1991, Sch 6 and Powers of Criminal Courts (Sentencing) Act 2000)**;

(c)   where a prisoner subject to early release commits an imprisonable offence during the original period of a custodial sentence and is liable to be returned to prison to serve more than six months (Powers of the Criminal Courts (Sentencing) Act 2000, s 116)**;

(d)   where the offender has been convicted of an offence under the Vagrancy Act 1824 which renders him liable to be sentenced as an incorrigible rogue (Vagrancy Act 1824, s 5)**.

** Please consult the legal adviser as to the availability of this power. When revised early release provisions of LASPOA 2012, ss 108–118 are brought into force, the result will be to produce a single system of early release. In other words, the power to order an offender to return to custody under PCCSA 2000, s 116 will disappear.

B[17]
Community Orders (adults only)

B[17.1]

The power to impose a community sentence is restricted to imprisonable offences.

Sections 147–150 of the Criminal Justice Act 2003 define community orders and the restrictions that apply to them. Any requirements imposed must be the most suitable for the offender and must be commensurate and proportionate with the seriousness of the offending. The court may take account of time spent on remand before sentence.

The court must set the end date* for completion of all requirements (not later that three years from sentence), but may set different dates for different requirements. If a supervision requirement is included it must be for the full length of the order. The court must impose an electronic monitoring requirement with a curfew or exclusion requirement and may do so for various requirements.

*Contingent on s 66 of the Legal Aid, Sentencing and Punishment of Offenders Act 2012 being brought into force.

B[17.2]

SGC guidelines provide that the seriousness of the offence should be the initial factor in determining which requirements to include in a community order. It establishes three sentencing ranges within the community order band based on offence seriousness (low, medium and high), and identifies non-exhaustive examples of requirements that might be appropriate in each.

LOW	MEDIUM	HIGH
Offences only just cross community order threshold, where a discharge or fine is inappropriate	Offences that obviously fall within the community order band	Offences only just fall below the custody threshold or the custody threshold is crossed but a community order is more appropriate in the circumstances
In general, only one requirement will be appropriate and the length may be curtailed if additional requirements are necessary		More intensive sentences which combine two or more requirements may be appropriate
Suitable requirements might include:	Suitable requirements might include:	Suitable requirements might include:

40–80 hours unpaid work	80–150 hours unpaid work	150–300 hours unpaid work
Curfew requirement eg up to 12 hours per day for a few weeks (see electronic monitoring below)	Curfew requirement eg up to 12 hours per day for 2–3 months (see electronic monitoring below)	Activity requirement up to the maximum of 60 days
Exclusion requirement, without electronic monitoring for a few months (see electronic monitoring below)	Exclusion requirement lasting in the region of 6 months (see electronic monitoring below)	Curfew requirement up to 12 hours per day for 4–6 months (see electronic monitoring below)
Prohibited activity requirement	Prohibited activity requirement	Exclusion order lasting in the region of 12 months (see electronic monitoring below)

Attendance centre requirement (where available)

Note: Electronic monitoring. The court must usually impose an electronic monitoring requirement where it makes a community order consisting of a curfew or exclusion requirement, and may do so in all other cases (CJA 2003, s 173(3), (4)). Electronic monitoring should be used with the primary purpose of promoting and monitoring compliance with other requirements, in circumstances where the punishment of the offender and/or the need to safeguard the public and prevent re-offending are the most important concerns.

Permissible requirements

(1) *Unpaid work requirement*

B[17.3]

This is a requirement that the offender must perform unpaid work in accordance for the number of hours specified in the order such work at such times as he may be instructed by the responsible officer. Unless revoked, a community order imposing an unpaid work requirement remains in force until the offender has worked under it for the number of hours specified in it. The work required to be performed under an unpaid work requirement of a community order or a suspended sentence order must be performed during a period of twelve months.

The number of hours which a person may be required to work under an unpaid work requirement must be specified in the relevant order and must be in the aggregate–

(a)   not less than 40, and

(b)   not more than 300.

The court may not impose an unpaid work requirement in respect of an offender unless after hearing (if the court thinks necessary) an appropriate officer, the court is satisfied that the offender is a suitable person to perform work under such a requirement.

Where the court makes orders in respect of two or more offences of which the offender has been convicted on the same occasion and includes unpaid work requirements in each of them, the court may direct that the hours of work specified in any of those requirements is to be concurrent or consecutive. However the total number of hours must not exceed the maximum of 300 hours.

(2) Activity requirement

B[17.4]

An activity requirement means a requirement that the offender must do either or both of the following-

(a)   present himself to a person or persons specified in the relevant order at a place or places so specified on such number of days as may be so specified and comply with instructions given by, or under the authority of, the person in charge of that place.
(b)   participate in activities specified in the order on such number of days as may be so specified.

The specified activities may consist of or include reparation, for example contact between the offender and victims affected by their offences.

A court may not include an activity requirement in a relevant order unless it has consulted either an officer of a local probation board or a member of a youth offending team, and it is satisfied that it is feasible to secure compliance with the requirement.

A court may not include an activity requirement in a relevant order if compliance with that requirement would involve the co-operation of a person other than the offender and the offender's responsible officer, unless that other person consents to its inclusion.

The aggregate of the number of days specified must not exceed 60.

A place specified in a requirement for the offender's attendance must be either,

(a)   a community rehabilitation centre, or
(b)   a place that has been approved by the local probation board for the area in which the premises are situated as providing facilities suitable for persons subject to activity requirements.

A requirement to participate in activities operates to require the offender,

(a)   to participate in activities on the number of days specified in the order in accordance with instructions given by his responsible officer, and

(b)   while participating, to comply with instructions given by, or under the authority of, the person in charge of the activities.

(3) Programme requirement

B[17.5]

This requirement involves the offender in participation in an accredited programme [*in accordance with this section on the number of days specified in the order] specified in the order at a place approved by the local probation board and on such number of days as may be so specified.

*Words inserted by LASPOA 2012, s 70 when in force and the remainder of the paragraph is deleted. .

The activities in programme, will be accredited by an accreditation body designated for that purpose by the Secretary of State.

**The court may not include a programme requirement in a relevant order unless-

(a)   the accredited programme which the court proposes to specify in the order has been recommended to the court as being suitable for the offender by an officer of a local probation board or by a member of a youth offending team, and

(b)   the court is satisfied that the programme is available at the place proposed to be specified.

**A court may not include a programme requirement in a relevant order if compliance with that requirement would involve the co-operation of a person other than the offender and the offender's responsible officer, unless that other person consents to its inclusion.

**Both paragraphs will be deleted when LASPO 2012, s 70 is brought into force.

A requirement to attend *[a programme requirement] an accredited programme operates to require the offender,

(a)   in accordance with instructions given by the responsible officer, to participate in the accredited programme *['that is from time to time specified by the responsible officer at the place that is so specified'] at the place specified in the order on the number of days specified in the order, and

(b)   while at that place, to comply with instructions given by, or under the authority of, the person in charge of the programme.

*Words inserted by LASPOA 2012, s 70 when in force.

4 *Prohibited activity requirement*

B[17.6]

This means a requirement that the offender must refrain from participating in activities specified in the order-

(a)   on a day or days so specified, or
(b)   during a period so specified.

A court may not include a prohibited activity requirement in a relevant order unless it has consulted, either an officer of a local probation board or a member of a youth offending team.

The statute provides that the requirements that may be included in a relevant order include a requirement that the offender does not possess, use or carry a firearm within the meaning of the Firearms Act 1968.

(5) *Curfew requirement*

B[17.7]

A curfew requirement is a requirement that the offender must remain, for periods specified in the relevant order, at a place so specified. It may specify different places or different periods for different days, but may not specify periods which amount to less than two hours or more than twelve hours *[sixteen] in any one day.

The order may not exceed a period of six *[twelve] months beginning with the day on which it is made. For youths and curfew orders see B[50.12].

*Changes made by LASPOA 2012, s 71 when brought into force.

Before making a relevant order imposing a curfew requirement, the court must obtain and consider information about the place proposed to be specified in the order (including information as to the attitude of persons likely to be affected by the enforced presence there of the offender). An electronic monitoring requirement must be made unless it requires the co-operation of a third party which is not forthcoming.

(6) *Exclusion requirement*

B[17.8]

An exclusion requirement, is a provision prohibiting the offender from entering a place named in the order for a specified period of not more than two years.

An exclusion requirement,

(a)   may provide for the prohibition to operate only during the periods specified in the order, and

(b)   may specify different places or areas for different periods or days.

Subject to limited exceptions, the court must impose an electronic monitoring requirement where

it makes a community order with an exclusion requirement.

(7) Residence requirement

B[17.9]

This is a requirement that, during a period specified in the relevant order, the offender must reside at a place specified in the order.

If the order makes provision, a residence requirement does not prohibit the offender from residing, with the prior approval of the responsible officer, at a place other than that specified in the order.

Before making a community order containing a residence requirement, the court must consider the home surroundings of the offender.

A court may not specify a hostel or other institution as the place where an offender must reside, except on the recommendation of an officer of a local probation board.

*(7A) Foreign Travel Prohibition requirement In this Part "foreign travel prohibition requirement", in relation to a relevant order, means a requirement prohibiting the offender from travelling, on a day or days specified in the order, or for a period so specified— (a) to any country or territory outside the British Islands specified or described in the order, (b) to any country or territory outside the British Islands other than a country or territory specified or described in the order, or (c) to any country or territory outside the British Islands. (2) A day specified under subsection (1) may not fall outside the period of 12 months beginning with the day on which the relevant order is made. (3) A period specified under that subsection may not exceed 12 months beginning with the day on which the relevant order is made." (6) In section 305(1) of that Act (interpretation of Part 12), at the appropriate place insert— ""foreign travel prohibition requirement", in relation to a community order or suspended sentence order, has the meaning given by section 206A;". An electronic monitoring requirement must be made unless e.g. it requires the co-operation of a third party which is not forthcoming. *Available when LASPO 2012, s 72 is broughlt into force.

*7A Foreign Travel Prohibition requirement**

*Available when LASPOA 2012, s 72 is brought into force. Section 72(5) inserts s 206A into the CJA 2003:

'206A Foreign Travel Prohibition requirement

(1) In this Part "foreign travel prohibition requirement", in relation to a relevant order, means a requirement prohibiting the offender from travelling, on a day or days specified in the order, or for a period so specified—

(a)   to any country or territory outside the British Islands specified or described in the order,

(b)   to any country or territory outside the British Islands other than a country or territory specified or described in the order, or

(c)   to any country or territory outside the British Islands.

(2) A day specified under subsection (1) may not fall outside the period of 12 months beginning with the day on which the relevant order is made.

(3) A period specified under that subsection may not exceed 12 months beginning with the day on which the relevant order is made.'

Sub-section (6) amends the interpretation section as follows:

'(6) In section 305(1) of that Act (interpretation of Part 12), at the appropriate place insert— ""foreign travel prohibition requirement", in relation to a community order or suspended sentence order, has the meaning given by section 206A;"'

An electronic monitoring requirement must be made unless eg it requires the co-operation of a third party which is not forthcoming.

(8) Mental health treatment requirement

B[17.10]

This requires the offender to submit, during periods specified in the order, to treatment by or under the direction of a registered medical practitioner or a chartered psychologist (or both, for different periods) with a view to the improvement of the offender's mental condition.

The treatment required must be one of the following kinds of treatment as may be specified in the relevant order:

(a)   treatment as a resident patient in an independent hospital or care home within the meaning of the Care Standards Act 2000 or a hospital within the meaning of the Mental Health Act 1983, but not in hospital premises where high security psychiatric services within the meaning of that Act are provided;

(b)   treatment as a non-resident patient at such institution or place as may be specified in the order;

(c)   treatment by or under the direction of such registered medical practitioner or chartered psychologist (or both) as may be so specified;

The nature of the treatment may not be specified in the order except as mentioned in (a), (b) or (c) above.

A court may not by virtue of this section include a mental health treatment requirement in an order unless-

(a)   the court is satisfied, *on the evidence of a registered medical practitioner approved for the purposes of s 12 of the Mental Health Act 1983, that the mental condition of the offender—

     (i)   is such as requires and may be susceptible to treatment, but

     (ii)   is not such as to warrant the making of a hospital order or guardianship order within the meaning of [**the Mental Health Act 1983] that Act;

(b)   the court is also satisfied that arrangements have been or can be made for the treatment intended to be specified in the order (including arrangements for the reception of the offender where he is to be required to submit to treatment as a resident patient); and

(c)   the offender has expressed his willingness to comply with such a requirement.

While the offender is under treatment as a resident patient in pursuance of a mental health requirement, his responsible officer shall carry out the supervision of the offender to such extent only as may be necessary for the purpose of the revocation or amendment of the order.

***Note that sub-ss (2) and (3) of s 54 of the Mental Health Act 1983 have effect with respect to proof for the purposes of sub-s (3)(a) of an offender's mental condition as they have effect with respect to proof of an offender's mental condition for the purposes of s 37(2)(a) of that Act.

*The words in bold to be deleted by LASPOA 2012, s 73 when in force.

**The words in parentheses to be substituted by LASPOA 2012, s 72 when in force.

*** This section will be deleted by LASPOA 2012, s 73 when in force.

(9) Mental health treatment at place other than that specified in order

B[17.11]

Where the medical practitioner or chartered psychologist, treating the offender in pursuance of a mental health treatment requirement, is of the opinion that part of the treatment can be better or more conveniently given in or at an institution or place which—

(a)   is not specified in the relevant order, and

(b)   is one in or at which the treatment of the offender will be given by or under the direction of a registered medical practitioner or chartered psychologist,

he may, with the consent of the offender, make arrangements for him to be treated accordingly.

These arrangements as are mentioned may provide for the offender to receive part of his treatment as a resident patient in an institution or place notwithstanding that the institution or place is not one which could have been specified for that purpose in the relevant order.

Where any such arrangements are made for the treatment of an offender the medical practitioner or chartered psychologist by whom the arrangements are made shall give notice in writing to the offender's responsible officer giving details of the place and the treatment provided.

(10) *Drug rehabilitation requirement*

B[17.12]

A drug rehabilitation requirement means a requirement that during a period specified in the order the offender must submit to treatment by or under the direction of a specified person having the necessary qualifications or experience with a view to the reduction or elimination of the offender's dependency on or propensity to misuse drugs.

During that period he must provide samples for the purpose of ascertaining whether he has any drug in his body.

A court may not impose a drug rehabilitation requirement unless–

(a)   it is satisfied–
         (i)   that the offender is dependent on, or has a propensity to misuse, drugs, and
         (ii)   that his dependency or propensity is such as requires and may be susceptible to treatment,
(b)   it is also satisfied that arrangements have been or can be made for the treatment intended to be specified in the order (including arrangements for the reception of the offender where he is to be required to submit to treatment as a resident),
(c)   the requirement has been recommended to the court as being suitable for the offender either by an officer of a local probation board or by a member of a youth offending team, and
(d)   the offender expresses his willingness to comply with the requirement.

The treatment and testing period must be ***not less than six months or** more than three years and must be treatment as a resident in such institution or place as may be specified in the order, or treatment as a non-resident place, as may be so specified.

*Words in bold deleted by LASPO 2012, s 74 when in force.

The nature of the treatment may not be specified in the order except as mentioned in paragraph (a) or (b) above.

A community order imposing a drug rehabilitation requirement must provide that the results of tests carried out on any samples provided by the offender in pursuance of the requirement to a person other than the responsible officer are to be communicated to the responsible officer.

(10A) *Drug rehabilitation requirement: provision for review by court*

B[17.13]

A community order imposing a drug rehabilitation requirement may (and must if the treatment and testing period is more than 12 months),

(a)   provide for the requirement to be reviewed periodically at intervals of not less than one month,

(b)   provide for each review of the requirement to be made, at a hearing held for the purpose by the court responsible for the order (a "review hearing"),

(c)   require the offender to attend each review hearing,

(d)   provide for the responsible officer to make to the court responsible for the order, before each review, a report in writing on the offender's progress under the requirement, and

(e)   provide for each such report to include the test results communicated to the responsible officer and the views of the treatment provider as to the treatment and testing of the offender.

References to the court responsible for a community order or suspended sentence order imposing a drug rehabilitation requirement are:

(a)   where a court is specified in the order, to that court;

(b)   in any other case, to the court by which the order is made.

Where the area specified in a community order is not the area for which the court acts, the court may, if it thinks fit, include in the order provision specifying a magistrates' court which acts for the area specified in the order.

(10B) Periodic review of drug rehabilitation requirement

B[17.14]

At a review hearing the court may, after considering the responsible officer's report, amend the community order, so far as it relates to the drug rehabilitation requirement but only if the offender expresses his willingness to comply with the requirement as amended *and,]

*Added by LASPOA 2012, s 74 when in force.

The court may not amend any provision of the order so as to reduce the period for which the drug rehabilitation requirement has effect below the minimum period of 6 months.**

**This paragraph is deleted when LASPOA 2012, s 74 when in force.

Nor may the court amend any requirement or provision of the order while an appeal against the order is pending, except with the consent of the offender.

If the offender fails to express his willingness to comply with the drug rehabilitation requirement as proposed to be amended by the court, the court may, revoke the community order and deal with him, for the offence in respect of which the order was made. If the court decides to re-sentence it must take into account the extent to which the offender has complied with the requirements of the order, and may impose a custodial sentence (where the order was made in respect of an offence punishable with such a sentence) notwithstanding anything in section CJA 2003 s 152(2). In the case of a juvenile who has attained the age of 18 the court's powers are to do either or both of the following,

(a)   to impose a fine not exceeding £5,000 for the offence in respect of which the order was made;

(b)   to deal with the offender for that offence in any way in which the court could deal with him if it had just convicted him of an offence punishable with imprisonment for a term not exceeding twelve months.

If at a review hearing the court, after considering the responsible officer's report, is of the opinion that the offender's progress under the requirement is satisfactory, the court may so amend the order as to provide for each subsequent review to be made by the court without a hearing.

If at a review without a hearing the court, after considering the responsible officer's report, is of the opinion that the offender's progress under the requirement is no longer satisfactory, the court may require the offender to attend a hearing of the court at a specified time and place.

At that hearing the court, after considering that report, may:-

(a)   exercise the powers conferred by this section as if the hearing were a review hearing, and

(b)   so amend the order as to provide for each subsequent review to be made at a review hearing.

(11) *Alcohol treatment requirement*

B[17.15]

This is a requirement that the offender submits during a specified period (of not less than 6 months) to treatment by or under the direction of a specified person having the necessary qualifications or experience with a view to the reduction or elimination of the offender's dependency on alcohol.

*Words in bold deleted by LASPOA 2012, s 75 when in force.

The court may not impose an alcohol treatment requirement in respect of an offender unless it is satisfied that he is dependent on alcohol, and his dependency is such as requires and may be susceptible to treatment. Arrangements must be made for the treatment intended to be specified in the order (including arrangements for the reception of the offender where he is to be required to submit to treatment as a resident).

A court may not impose an alcohol treatment requirement unless the offender expresses his willingness to comply with its requirements.

The treatment required by an alcohol treatment requirement for any particular period must be,

(a)   treatment as a resident in such institution or place as may be specified in the order,

(b)   treatment as a non-resident in or at such institution or place, and at such intervals, as may be so specified, or

(c)   treatment by or under the direction of such person having the necessary qualification or experience as may be so specified;

but the nature of the treatment shall not be specified in the order except as mentioned in paragraph (a), (b) or (c) above.

(12) Supervision requirement (excludes juvenile offenders)

B[17.16]

A supervision requirement is a requirement that, during the relevant period, the offender must attend appointments with the responsible officer or another person determined by the responsible officer, at such time and place as may be determined by the officer.

The purpose for which a supervision requirement may be imposed is that of promoting the offender's rehabilitation.

For these purposes the relevant period means the period for which the community order remains in force.

B[17.17]

Breach of a requirement

See also A[17]. Under national standards an offender will be given one warning and then returned to court following a subsequent breach. It is open to probation to allege in the information both the original warning before the breach proceedings and the subsequent breach after the warning: *West Yorkshire Probation Board v Robinson and Tinker* [2009] EWHC 2468 (Admin). The court's powers are contained in Sch 8 Criminal Justice Act 2003. On breach of a requirement the court may impose more onerous requirements with the aim being completion of the order, impose a fine of up to £2,500* or deal with the original offence as if he had just been convicted. In the latter case the court must make the original order. Crown Court orders may contain a direction that breaches are dealt with in the magistrates' court or reserved to itself.

*A fine may be imposed under s 67 of the Legal Aid, Sentencing and Punishment of Offenders Act 2012 once brought into force. At the time of writing a date has yet to be fixed.

B[17.18]

Revocation

The offender or responsible officer may apply to revoke the order and the court if satisfied it is in the interests of justice may revoke and or deal with the original offence, giving credit for any part of the order already completed. For the procedure see Part 44 of the Criminal Procedure Rules 2012.

It would be wrong in principle to resentence the offender where the revocation was on the grounds of ill health (*R v Bishop* [2004] EWCA Crim 2956, [2004] All ER (D) 116 (Dec)).

B[18]

Compensation order
(Powers of Criminal Courts (Sentencing) Act 2000, ss 130–138)

B[18.1]

Compensation order. Either as a sentence in its own right or in addition to another sentence, the court may order the defendant to pay compensation to a person who has suffered as a consequence of the defendant's crime.

A court must consider making a compensation order in any case where this section empowers it do so: s 130(2A) of the PCCSA 2000.*

*Inserted by s 63 of the Legal Aid, Sentencing and Punishment of Offenders Act 2012 from a date to be appointed.

Compensation orders are intended to be used in simple, straightforward cases where no great amount is at stake. A compensation order can only be made when sentence is being passed and, therefore, cannot be made when committing for sentence or deferring sentence. The court shall give its reasons, on passing sentence, if it does not make a compensation order where it is empowered to do so. Examples of such reasons will be the defendant's lack of means, or that the loss is difficult to quantify (see below).

Surcharge. By virtue of the Criminal Justice Act 2003, s 161A(1) and secondary legislation, for offences committed on or after **1 April 2007** where a court requires the offender to pay a fine and/or costs, or by requiring an offender to pay a fine and compensation and/or costs, it must order the offender to pay a surcharge of £15. The court has no discretion except in those cases where the means of the offender are such that he has no additional income to pay a surcharge over and beyond a fine and/or compensation order. In other words, the court gives priority to the compensation order.

Note: the term "fine" does not include any road fund or excise offence committed under the Vehicle Excise and Registration Act 1994 (C[47]) because the legislation provides for payment of an "excise penalty".

B[18.2]

For what may compensation be ordered? For any personal injury, loss or damage (or to make payments for funeral expenses or bereavement in respect of a death resulting from any such offence, other than a death due to an accident arising out of the presence of a motor vehicle on a road – (ie the only such situation likely to arise in a magistrates' court, death arising from careless driving, not being covered)) resulting from the offence or any offences taken into consideration. Personal injury need not be physical injury, compensation may be ordered for terror or distress caused by the offence *(Bond v Chief Constable of Kent* [1983] 1 All ER 456, [1983] 1 WLR 40).

B[18.3]

In the case of an offence under the Theft Act 1968, if the property is recovered but is damaged, a compensation order may be made against the defendant no matter how the damage was caused provided it was caused while the property was out of the owner's possession.

Exceptions

B[18.4]

Exceptions include:

(a)   Loss caused to the dependants of a victim who has died (except funeral expenses etc in the circumstances referred to above).

(b)   Injury, loss or damage due to an accident arising out of the presence of a motor vehicle on a road except compensation may be awarded:

    (i)   for damage caused to a motor vehicle stolen or taken without the owner's consent but not damage caused by the vehicle, eg to another car on the road; and

    (ii)   in cases where the defendant's use of the vehicle was uninsured and no compensation is payable under the Motor Insurers' Bureau scheme (see **C[33.18]–C[33.22]**).

The amounts ordered under (i) and (ii) may include payment to cover loss of a 'no claims' bonus.

B[18.5]

Proof of loss. As a result of amendments made to the law in 1982 it was considered that the approach to establishing the amount of the loss was not so strict as it was formerly. However, in 1985 the judges of the Divisional Court reaffirmed that (unless the amount was admitted by the accused at the outset) it was the duty of the prosecution to establish the loss and its amount, and make it clear to the defendant by means of evidence. If, after this, there was any real dispute as to the loss suffered by the victim, a compensation order should not be made and the victim should be left to resort to civil remedies to obtain compensation *(R v Horsham Justices, ex p Richards* [1985] 2 All ER 1114, [1985] 1 WLR 986)); followed in *R v Stapylton (Ben)* [2012] EWCA Crim 728, [2012] All ER (D) 84 (Apr). However where the exact loss cannot be ascertained but finding the minimum loss was a simple task that latter sum may be ordered (*R v Brazil* [2004] EWCA Crim 1975, [2004] All ER (D) 348 (Jun)).

Fixing the amount

B[18.6]

The following need to be taken into account when fixing the amount:

(a) The amount of the loss should be established after proof or agreement.

(b) Where the loss is not determined the court cannot fix an arbitrary amount at a figure below that which is in dispute. Either the lowest amount admitted should be adopted or no order made at all.

(c) Compensation for personal injury may be ascertained having regard to guidelines issued by the Criminal Injuries Compensation Board (see B[18.19]).

(d) The maximum compensation that may be awarded is £5,000 for each offence against each defendant. For the maximum where offences are to be taken into consideration the legal adviser should be consulted.

(e) Having ascertained what the loss is, and what the maximum amount is that can be ordered, the court must have regard to the defendant's ability to pay. He may be allowed to pay by instalments but generally such instalments should not extend beyond two years (*R v Olliver and Olliver* (1989) 11 Cr App Rep (S) 10, 153 JP 369, [1989] Crim LR 387, CA), a case in the Crown Court where a large sum was to be paid) although in the magistrates' courts simple straightforward orders will probably be paid within a shorter period. Judicial guidance suggests that magistrates' court orders should be paid within a short period of time, preferably 13 weeks and 52 weeks should be regarded as the maximum period for repayment. Where the defendant is of limited means and would be unable to pay both compensation and a fine, preference must be given to the award of compensation. Neither *R v Olliver and Olliver* (1989) 11 Cr App Rep (S) 10, 153 JP 369, CA and *R v Yehou* [1997] 2 Cr App Rep (S) 48, were authority for the proposition that there was an outer limit for the period of repayment of a compensation order. Under s 130(4) of the Powers of Criminal Courts (Sentencing) Act 2000, a court making a compensation order must ask whether it is appropriate. That requires an enquiry into whether the compensation order will be oppressive or an undue burden given the offender's means; whether realistically the offender can be expected to repay in the terms proposed and whether the compensation order accords with the nature of the offence and the nature of the offender. In neither case was the order an undue burden. Under s 133 of the PCCSA 2000, if there was a change in financial circumstances of either of the appellants, they could apply for a variation or discharge of the order: *R v Ganyo* [2011] EWCA Crim 2491, [2012] 1 Cr App Rep (S) 650, 176 JP 396. With respect,

Ganyo is wrong. The CA overlooked the Sentencing Council guidelines which recommend maximum periods for repayment in comity with *Olliver* and *Yehou* above,

(f)   If the defendant cannot afford to pay for the whole amount of the loss, then this lower amount, which he can afford, must be ordered.

(g)   The circumstances in which a court may subsequently vary a compensation order are limited. Accordingly, an unrealistically high order for compensation may result in the defendant being committed to prison for default; this is wrong in principle (see B[18.17]–B[18.18] 'appeal and review').

B[18.7]

Making an order. When deliberating whether to make an order, the court should bear in mind that the wealthy offender should never be allowed to buy his way out of prison by offering compensation. Also, the court should be wary of an accused mitigating for a suspended sentence on the basis of extravagant promises to pay compensation.

B[18.8]

On the other hand, when a custodial sentence is imposed, compensation should be ordered only if the offender has the means to pay immediately or out of existing resources. He should not have to face the payment of compensation upon his discharge from a custodial sentence unless it is clear that he will then have the means to pay, eg he has savings or by being able to return to gainful employment immediately.

B[18.9]

The court should announce the amount of compensation for each offence and against each defendant. Where there are competing claims for compensation, the court may make an order for one compensatee in preference to another, eg a private individual in preference to a financial institution (*R v Amey* [1983] 1 All ER 865, [1983] 1 WLR 345, CA).

B[18.10]–[18.15]

In all cases where a compensation order is contemplated, the legal adviser should be consulted.

B[18.16]

Compensation and deprivation orders. Where a court makes a deprivation order (see B[34]) in a case where a person has suffered personal injury, loss or damage, but a compensation order for the full loss cannot be made because of the offender's inadequate means, it may direct that the proceeds arising from the disposal of the forfeited goods be paid to the victim to make good the deficiency. The amount to be paid is a sum not exceeding the amount of compensation that the court would have ordered were it not for the offender's lack of means. See also B[19] for confiscation orders.

Appeal and review

B[18.17]

The entitlement of the victim is suspended for 21 days to allow the defendant time to appeal if he wishes, or until after the appeal is heard. But the enforcement of the order against the offender is not suspended; the obligation to pay arises immediately. Accordingly, where an appeal is successful, the court will have to repay to the appellant any monies that he has already paid.

B[18.18]

At any time before the order has been fully complied with, the court may discharge or reduce the order:

(a)   if a civil court determines an amount of damage or loss less than that stated in the order; or

(b)   if the property or part of it is subsequently recovered; or

(c)   where the defendant's means are insufficient to satisfy in full the compensation order and a confiscation order made in the same proceedings; or

(d)   where the defendant has suffered a substantial reduction in his means which was unexpected at the time the compensation order was made, and his means seem unlikely to increase for a considerable period.

The permission of the Crown Court is required where it made the original order, if the magistrates' court contemplates the action at (c) or (d).

Guidelines for compensation for personal injury

B[18.19]

Guidelines were to be found originally in Home Office circular 53/1993 for the assistance of magistrates. They were prepared by the Criminal Injuries Compensation Board (now renamed the Criminal Injuries Compensation Authority) and reflect the level of damages which would be awarded in the civil courts for the injuries described. The Criminal Injuries Compensation Authority has no power to compensate for injuries attracting compensation under £1,000 and therefore guidelines for some of the more minor injuries commonly encountered in the magistrates' court are reproduced at B[18.21]–B[18.23].

B[18.20]

In each example the victim is assumed to be in the age bracket 20–35 years but the age of the victim may materially affect the assessment, cf for example, the psychological effect of an assault on an elderly victim as opposed to a youth. Scarring is particularly problematical and reference should be made to the full circular for this and other injuries not referred to in the list below. Before making an award magistrates must also take into account the defendant's ability to pay any order made.

Type of injury

B[18.21]

Less serious injury including:		*Suggested award*
Graze	depending on size	up to £50
Bruise	depending on size	up to £75
Black eye		£100
Cut (without permanent scarring)	depending on size and whether stitched	£75–£500
Sprain	depending on loss of mobility	£100–£1,000
Loss of a tooth (not a front tooth)	depending on position of tooth and age of victim	£250–£500
Minor injury	causing reasonable absence from work of about 3 weeks	£550–£850

B[18.22]

More serious injury		
Loss of a front tooth		£1,000
Nasal	undisplaced fracture of the nasal bone (see note)	£750
Nasal	displaced fracture of the bone requiring manipulation under general anaesthetic (see note)	£1,000
Nasal	not causing fracture but displaced septum requiring a sub-mucous resection (see note)	£1,750

B[18.23]

NB: Assuming that after the appropriate treatment there is no visible deformity of the nose and no breathing problem. If either of these factors is present, an increased award is appropriate and the amount of the increase will depend on the severity of the remaining problems. It is not uncommon for a fractured nasal bone to be manipulated and for the patient thereafter to have breathing problems which after some months require a sub-mucous resection – in this situation the suggested award would be £2,000 assuming full recovery after a second operation.

B[19]

Confiscation orders

B[19.1]

Part VI of the CJA 1988 is repealed by the Proceeds of Crime Act 2002. See M[3.2].

The prosecutor may ask the magistrates' court to commit the offender to the Crown Court so that a confiscation order may be made. The court must comply with such a request and may also commit any other offence for which he stands to be sentenced (PCA 2002, s 10).

For enforcement of confiscation orders see B[33] onwards and M[3.2]. For case law see *R (on the application of Johnson) v Birmingham Magistrates' Court and CPS* [2012] EWHC 596 (Admin), 176 JP 298.

B[20]

Costs

B[20.1]

The award of costs is the exercise of a judicial discretion and any decision must always be made after taking each case on its merits, hearing each party and taking proper account of the law. As a general rule, the successful party in any proceedings can expect to be reimbursed for the costs he has incurred in conducting the proceedings. In civil proceedings, a successful party can receive his costs from the other party. Under the Litigants in Person (Costs and Expenses, Magistrates' Courts) Order 2001 an individual who has been successful in civil proceedings may also benefit from an order for costs to cover work done by him in connection with the case and any resultant expenses or losses. In criminal proceedings, according to the circumstances of the particular case, it may be possible for costs to be awarded either against the unsuccessful party or from central funds, which are monies provided by Parliament to defray the costs of criminal proceedings.

Criminal proceedings

(Prosecution of Offences Act 1985, ss 16–19)

B[20.1A]

Surcharge. By virtue of the Criminal Justice Act 2003, s 161A(1) and secondary legislation, for offences committed on or after **1 April 2007** where a court orders the offender to pay a fine and/or costs, or by requiring the offender to pay a fine and compensation and/or costs it must order the offender to pay a surcharge of £15. Where the court imposes a compensation order and the means of the offender are such that he is not able to pay additional penalties such as a fine, costs or surcharge order, it may reduce the level of the fine, costs or surcharge or to make no order for the payment of a fine, costs or surcharge. In other words, the court gives priority to compensation order.

Note: the term "fine" does not include any road fund or excise offence committed under the Vehicle Excise and Registration Act 1994 (C[47]) because the legislation provides for payment of an "excise penalty".

Where the court proposes to impose a fine and costs but the means of the offender are such that he cannot realistically pay all three orders it is permissible to reduce the level of the fine or costs to reflect the surcharge order.

B[20.2]

See Part 76 of the CPR 2012. In a criminal case, the court's duty is firstly to consider the appropriate sentence. If that is a fine, the offender's means so far as they are known to the court must be taken into account. It is wrong in principle to reduce a fine in order to accommodate an order for costs. Costs should never be awarded as a disguised penalty and the offender's means should be taken into account as above (*R v Nottingham Magistrates' Court, ex p Fohmann* (1986) 84 Cr App Rep 316, 151 JP 49). The costs awarded should be proportionate to the level of any fine (*Nedic v South Staffordshire Council* [2005] EWHC 1481 (Admin), [2005] All ER (D) 182 (Jun)).

B[20.2A]

The following sections must be read in the light of *Practice Direction (Costs in Criminal Proceedings)* CLW/10/32/26, unreported, July 30, 2010.

Prosecution costs

B[20.3]

Central funds. See Part 76 of the CPR 2012. Almost all criminal prosecutions are conducted by the Crown Prosecution Service or a public authority such as the Trading Standards Department of a local authority. The funding for these prosecutions is provided by national or local revenues, and so there is no power to award the costs of the prosecution to these authorities out of central funds, even where the prosecution is successful. This avoids the wasteful practice of transferring moneys from one public fund to another.

B[20.4]

Private prosecutors. See Part 76 of the CPR 2012. The court may, in a case where an indictable offence is concerned, order the costs of the prosecutor to be paid out of central funds whether the prosecution is successful or not. An indictable offence includes an offence triable either way and also offences of criminal damage where the damage is under £5,000 and is therefore triable only summarily. This provision does not apply to public authorities such as the CPS and local authorities (POA 1985, s 17(2)).

B[20.5]

There is no power to order costs from central funds to a prosecutor for purely summary offences. The costs to be awarded would normally be such amounts as the court considers reasonably sufficient to compensate the prosecutor for any expenses properly incurred by him and can include the costs of compensating a witness for the expense, trouble or loss of time properly incurred in his attendance at court. The amount payable to witnesses in respect of travelling expenses and loss of earnings is fixed by regulations and witnesses' expenses are dealt with in the clerk's office. A witness may be reimbursed even if he did not actually give evidence, if he was properly called to do so. Witnesses may be called, for example, in anticipation of a trial only to find that there is a last minute guilty plea. The cost of investigating offences is not included.

B[20.6]

Making an order for the costs of a private prosecutor. The court may fix the amount to be paid to the prosecutor out of central funds at the hearing where the prosecutor is in agreement, or in any other case the amount of the costs can be assessed afterwards by the central taking officer.

B[20.7]

Reducing the amount of the prosecutor's order. Where the court is prepared to order the prosecutor's costs out of central funds but is of the opinion that there are circumstances that make it inappropriate to order the full amount of costs, eg where the defendant is convicted of some offences and acquitted of others, the court can assess what in its opinion would be just and reasonable, and specify that amount.

B[20.8]

Ordering the accused to pay the prosecution costs. See Part 76 of the CPR 2012. Where a person has been convicted of an either way or purely summary offence, the court can order the accused to pay to the prosecutor (the Crown Prosecution Service, a public authority or a private prosecutor) such costs as it considers just and reasonable. The amount of the costs is specified by the court at the hearing and cannot be left to be assessed later. In general the principle applied to fines imposition (**B[33.16]**) should be applied and should be in keeping with the level of the fine (*R v Northallerton Magistrates' Court, ex p Dove* [2000] 1 Cr App Rep (S) 136, 163 JP 657, [1999] Crim LR 760). In *R (on the application of Middleton) v Cambridge Magistrates' Court* [2012] EWHC 2122 (Admin), 176 JP 569, it was held that there was no requirement for there to be an arithmetical relationship between a fine and the costs sought. In fact, there might well be situations where the fine and costs imposed differed. However, that did not mean that a prosecution could not be brought because it was too expensive as the requirements of justice had to be kept in mind. That being said, the costs imposed should not be grossly disproportionate to the maximum penalty for the offence committed. The instant court could not ignore the fact that the maximum sentence for the offences M had committed was at the lowest level. Notwithstanding the delays because of M's failure to plead guilty at the earliest opportunity, and the inherent complexities, the costs awarded to the prosecution (£6,871) were grossly disproportionate to the fine imposed and could not be sustained as just and reasonable.

An order for costs can include sums expended as part of the investigation but only where the prosecutor has incurred liability for those costs to a third party e.g. an accountancy report, and where the report formed part of the case presented at court. In such a case the court need only be satisfied that it is just and reasonable for the defendant to pay those costs: *Balshaw v Crown Prosecution Service* [2009] EWCA Crim 470, [2009] 2 Cr App Rep 95.

B[20.9]

Monetary penalty not exceeding £5. Where, on conviction of an offence, the court orders payment of any sum as a fine, penalty, forfeiture or compensation not exceeding £5, the court shall not order the accused to pay the prosecution costs unless in the particular circumstances of the case it considers it right to do so.

B[20.10]–[20.15]

Juveniles. Where a person under 17 years of age is convicted of an offence before a magistrates' (or youth) court and he is ordered to pay the costs, the amount that is ordered shall not exceed the amount of any fine that is properly imposed on him. This restriction does not apply if a parent is made responsible for paying the fine etc (see **B[33.95]**).

Defence costs

B[20.16]

Where an accused is acquitted, or where the information is not proceeded with, ie withdrawn or discontinued, or where the defendant is discharged in committal proceedings, the court may order the defendant's costs to be paid out of central funds. This applies whether the charge is triable purely summarily or is an indictable offence. Apart from exceptional circumstances, a prosecutor cannot be ordered to pay an acquitted defendant's costs. The amount of the order will be such amount as the court considers reasonably sufficient to compensate him for any costs incurred in the proceedings and includes the expense of compensating any witness for the expense, trouble or loss of time properly incurred or incidental to his attendance, in a similar manner to that for prosecution witnesses. *R (on the application of Hale) v North Sefton Justices* [2002] EWHC 257 (Admin), [2002] All ER (D) 10 (Jan) gives guidance on the appropriate taxation of such costs (although see the revised regulations immediately below). A defendant cannot claim any loss of earnings or income foregone by himself personally. He can claim defence witness expenses even where convicted. See **[B20.2A]**.

The Costs in Criminal Cases (General) (Amendment) Regulations 2012 (SI 2012/1804) corrects an error in reg 20 of the Costs in Criminal Cases (General) Regulations 1986 and amends Part III of the 1986 Regulations, which sets out procedures for making such payments, so as to require the court, in most cases where it is still permitted to make an award in respect of legal costs, to either assess the amount to be paid in respect of such costs at rates set by the Lord Chancellor, or to fix the amount having regard to such rates.

B[20.17]

A publicly aided defendant can only claim those costs which cannot be covered by the representation order, eg his travelling expenses to court.

In *Re Patel and a defendant's costs order* [2012] EWCA Crim 1508, [2012] All ER (D) 115 (Jul), it was decided that whilst the court had jurisdiction to re-open its decision to make a defendant's costs order, as the court had been unaware that the defendant and his solicitors had agreed to remove a cap on fees, which increased the fees retrospectively, it was appropriate to let the assessment by the determining officer take its course.

B[20.18]

Reducing the amount of the defendant's order. A court should not deny a defendant his costs order where it would undermine the presumption of innocence in the Human Rights Convention (*R v South West Surrey Magistrates, ex p James* [2000] Crim LR 690, [2000] All ER (D) 564). An order will normally be made unless there are positive reasons for not making such an order, eg where the defendant's own conduct has brought suspicion on himself and has misled the prosecution into thinking that the case against him is stronger than it is. In these circumstances the court may make no order or a reduced order for costs. It would appear that where a defendant is convicted of an offence of 'due care' when charged with reckless driving he is not entitled to costs, as the information is not dismissed. However where he always intended to plead guilty to the lesser charge a partial order for costs may be appropriate (see *Practice Direction (Costs: Criminal Proceedings)* (2010) at **[B20.2A]**).

When refusing to make an order or refusing an order for costs the court must give its reason: see *Dowler v Merseyrail* [2009] EWHC 558 (Admin), 173 JP 332. See also *R (on the application of Elliott Spiteri) v Basildon Crown Court* [2009] EWHC 665 (Admin), 173 JP 327.

Costs unnecessarily or improperly incurred (see amendments to r 3.5 CPR 2012)

B[20.19]

Where the court is satisfied that one party to criminal proceedings has incurred costs as a result of an unnecessary or improper act or omission, it may order the party responsible to pay the additional costs thereby incurred whatever the final result of the case. This includes the whole of the defence costs where a private prosecutor instituted proceedings knowing an identical prosecution brought by CPS on the same ground had been dismissed without challenge (*Oddy v Bug Bugs Ltd* [2003] All ER (D) 156 (Nov)). This enables the court to mark its displeasure at the unreasonable behaviour of a party, eg where one party has put the other to unnecessary expense by requiring an adjournment when they should have been ready to proceed. Before making such an order both parties should be invited to make representations to the court and the court should determine the sum to be paid.

In *R (on the application of the DPP) v Bury Magistrates' Court* [2007] All ER (D) 208 (Dec) if was held that a court was entitled to make a costs order against the prosecution where it had failed to comply with a court order that it should serve its witness evidence on the defence by a specified date. As the prosecution had given no explanation for its failure there had been a breach of the Criminal Procedural Rules 2012.

A wasted costs order in favour of a defendant in receipt of a representation order under the Access to Justice Act 1999, and whose legal representatives fall to be remunerated under the graduated fee schemes for advocates and litigators in Schs 1 and 2 to the Criminal Defence Service (Funding) Order 2007 (SI 2007/1174), must be strictly limited to the amount falling to be paid to the legal representatives under those schemes. It is not permissible to include an amount by way of compensation for work reasonably done in the case which will otherwise not fall to be remunerated (as in the case of work done by way of preparation for a hearing at which the prosecution offered no evidence, where the decision to offer no evidence should have been made earlier and where the fees payable to the defence under the graduated fee scheme would be the same as if the decision had been made when it should have been, ie at an earlier hearing): *R v Fitzgerald* [2012] 3 Costs LR 437, Central Criminal Court (HH Judge Gordon).

B[20.20]

Costs against legal representatives. See Part 76 of the CPR 2012. The magistrates may disallow or order a legal representative to meet the whole or any part of any costs incurred by a party as a result of any improper, unreasonable or negligent act or omission of the representative or, where the conduct occurred after the incurring of the costs, the court considers it is unreasonable for the party to pay. Such orders are not common and the court must follow a detailed procedure before ordering costs against a legal representative. If such an order is contemplated, the legal adviser must be consulted.

B[20.20A]

Costs against third parties. Section 19B of the Prosecution of Offences Act 1985 (inserted by s 98 of the Courts Act 2003) empowers a criminal court to make costs orders against a third party where it has been guilty of serious misconduct. If such an order is contemplated, the legal adviser must be consulted. See Part 76 of the CPR 2012.

Miscellaneous provisions

B[20.21]

Medical reports. In criminal proceedings, where the court has required a medical practitioner to make a report to the court orally or in writing, for the purpose inter alia of determining the most suitable method of dealing with the offender, his costs may be ordered to be paid from central funds.

B[20.22]

Interpreters. In any criminal proceedings provision is made for the payment of interpreters from central funds.

B[20.23]

Proceedings for breach or revocation of community orders including youth community orders etc. In appropriate circumstances a magistrates' court may now make an award of costs against the offender in breach proceedings where the breach is admitted or found proved.

Civil proceedings

(Magistrates' Courts Act 1980, s 64)

B[20.24]

On hearing a complaint (eg concerning a dangerous dog), the court may order the defendant to pay to the successful complainant such costs as it thinks just and reasonable and, where the complaint is dismissed, the complainant may similarly be ordered to pay the defendant's costs (see the case law and principles discussed in detail in section F[1.16]). However, where the complaint is for the revocation, revival, variation or enforcement of an order for the paying of maintenance, a court can order either party to pay the others costs whatever order is made. In proceedings under the Children Act 1989 the court may at any time during the proceedings order that a party pay the whole or any part of the costs of any other party.

B[20.25]–[20.30]

In civil cases, it is not usual to order one party to pay or contribute towards the other's costs if both are publicly funded, but there is no reason why an order for costs should not be paid against a party who is not publicly funded where the successful party is so aided, so that the legal aid fund will receive the benefit of the order.

B[20.31]

Applications. There is no power to award costs where proceedings are begun by way of an application (eg an application under the Police (Property) Act 1897) except in family proceedings (see above and *R v Salisbury and Tisbury and Mere Juvenile Court, ex p Ball* (1985) 149 JP 346).

B[21]–B[22]

Deferment of sentence

(Powers of Criminal Courts (Sentencing) Act 2000, ss 1A–1F)

Limitations

B[21.1]

The offender must consent, and undertake to comply with any requirements the court considers appropriate to impose during the period of deferment.

B[21.2]

Deferment may be used only once in respect of any one offence.

B[21.3]

The court must be satisfied that it is in the interests of justice to defer sentence, having regard to the nature of the offence and the character and circumstances of the offender.

B[21.4]

There are no limitations as to age or the nature of the offence. The court may have regard to the defendant's conduct after conviction (including if appropriate any reparation made by him) and any change in his circumstances. The court may impose requirements as to the offender's conduct during the deferment and appoint an appropriate supervisor with their consent.

Ancillary orders

B[21.5]

None, because this is not a final disposal of the case, except that a restitution order may be made.

How to announce

B[21.6]

We feel that it is not in the interests of justice that we impose a sentence on you today and we are considering deferring our decision for [*state period, and give the reason*] during that period you will comply with the following requirements [*state what is expected from the offender during the period of deferment*]. Do you understand? We cannot defer sentence without your consent. Do you consent? [*If answered affirmatively*] Then you must attend court here on [*date*] when we shall consider what sentence to impose after hearing how you have progressed in the meantime.

B[21.7]

Note – The essential ingredients of this announcement are the request for consent and the date when the case will be heard again. Consent must be obtained before the order is formally made and, as with any consent, has no value unless the offender understands exactly to what he is consenting. Accordingly the words above may be varied according to the circumstances and in the light of the general considerations below.

General considerations

B[21.8]

This power of the court might be less confusing if it were referred to as deferment of sentencing. There is no question, contrary to what is sometimes believed, that the court decides upon a sentence but postpones announcing it in case it changes its mind.

B[21.9]

Only exceptionally may a custodial sentence be imposed after deferment; it is advised that where an offender is liable to be ordered to serve a suspended sentence it will rarely be appropriate to defer sentencing him for the offence which he has committed during the operational period.

B[21.10]–[21.15]

Deferment is appropriate when some event may occur in the near future which, according to whether it occurred or not, would influence the court when imposing a sentence. It may be, for example, that the offender has an uncertain chance of employment upon which voluntary compensation depends. There should always be some reason for deferment which can be stated so that the offender knows what is expected of him and may, as he thinks fit, take steps to improve his situation from a sentencing point of view. Great care should be exercised, however, not to use this power as a threat or coercion or to give an offender an opportunity to buy his way out of prison by making compensation (especially if he may do so by resorting to further offences).

B[21.16]

The concern of a victim of the offence should be borne in mind when considering deferment; one effect of deferment, for example, may be to postpone the day when compensation is ordered.

B[21.17]

The maximum period for which sentencing may be deferred is six months. The defendant cannot be remanded. A summons or warrant may be issued if he fails to appear on the date for sentencing specified by the court.

Sentence after the period of deferral. The deferred sentence did not represent part of the sentence which was imposed at the end of the period of deferment. Section 204(3) of the Criminal Justice Act 2003 provided that the period with regard to curfew requirements runs from the date of the making of the community order. The six-month curfew condition of the deferred sentence was a factor which needed to be taken into account at the point of sentence when determining the community requirements of the order and the length of any requirement: *R v Saeed Ali* [2011] EWCA Crim 2747, 176 JP 1.

B[21.18]

Magistrates should never fall into the trap of deferring sentencing because they are unable to make up their minds as to the appropriate sentence. The court will obviously wish to be informed at the end of the period of deferment whether the offender has done what it was hoped he would do, or whether the event has taken place which was the reason for the deferment. In many cases it will be convenient to ask the supervising officer to report, but in some cases only the offender or a third party will be able to satisfy the court. It is advised that the court when deferring sentence makes clear arrangements at that time as to how such information is to be provided.

B[21.19]

The court might consider that a conditional discharge for six months but imposed immediately would achieve the court's objectives. It is not necessary, but may be desirable, that the same magistrates should impose the sentence as those who deferred sentence. Provided the requirement and reasons for deferment are explicitly stated, the legal adviser will note them and bring them to the attention of the sentencing court.

B[21.20]

The offender can be returned to court if the supervisor has reported to the court that the offender has failed to comply with one or more requirements in respect of which an offender gave an undertaking (s 1B(2)(c)). The can issue a summons or warrant for the offender to appear before it (s 1B(3)).

B[21.21]

If the offender commits an offence during the period of deferment, the court convicting him of that offence may deal with the deferred case even though the period of deferment has not expired. Section 1C sets out the powers of the Crown Court and magistrates' courts in these cases. If the original sentence was deferred by a Crown Court, it must be a Crown Court that passes sentence for both offences. The power to commit to the Crown Court for sentence under s 3 PCC(S)A 2000 is retained by s 1D(2)(b) PCC(S)A 2000**.

B[23]

Deportation

[23.1]

' . . . a person who is not a British citizen shall be . . . liable to deportation from the United Kingdom if, after he has attained the age of seventeen, he is convicted of an offence for which he is punishable with imprisonment and on his conviction is recommended for deportation by a court'

Immigration Act 1971, s 3(6)

NB: Section 32 of the UK Borders Act 2007 provides that the Secretary of State must make a deportation order in respect of foreign national prisoners who meet one of the two conditions set out in s 32 of the Act and are not then covered by the exceptions covered in s 33. This does not affect the power of the court to make a recommendation for deportation as outlined below.

NB: In cases to which the 2007 Act applies, it is no longer necessary or appropriate for a court to make a recommendation for deportation: *R v Kluxen* [2010] EWCA Crim 1081, [2010] Crim LR 657, 174 CL&J 380.

B[23.2]

Recommendation. A magistrates' court cannot order deportation, but it can make a recommendation to the Home Secretary for the deportation of the convicted person. In sentencing the offender the court does not have to take into account what might happen in the offender's own country if he is returned (*R v Ukoh* [2004] EWCA Crim 3270, [2005] All ER (D) 58 (Jan)).

B[23.3]

Not a British citizen. The following categories of citizens cannot be deported:

(a) British citizens;
(b) Commonwealth citizens having a right of abode in the United Kingdom;
(c) Commonwealth citizens not included in (b) and citizens of the Republic of Ireland provided in either case they were such citizens at the time of the coming into force of the Immigration Act 1971 and were ordinarily resident in the United Kingdom and at the time of conviction had been ordinarily resident in the United Kingdom and Islands for the last five years.

B[23.4]

The following may be deported:

(a)   Commonwealth citizens not included in (b) or (c) above;
(b)   aliens;
(c)   aliens being citizens of countries which are members of the European Community.

B[23.5]
Age of seventeen. A person shall be deemed to have obtained the age of 17 at the time of his conviction, if on consideration of any available evidence he appears to have done so to the court.

B[23.6]
Convicted. Means found to have committed the offence.

B[23.7]
Punishable with imprisonment. This means punishable with imprisonment in the case of a person over 21 years even though the defendant himself may not be liable to imprisonment.

Criteria for making a recommendation

General considerations

B[23.8]
The court. In deciding whether to make a recommendation for deportation the court may consider:

(a)   Would the offender's continued presence in the United Kingdom be detrimental? In considering this the court might take account of:
      (i)   the seriousness of the crime, eg a simple offence of shoplifting would not merit such a recommendation;
      (ii)   the length of the defendant's criminal record.

The court should not consider:

(b)   A recommendation for deportation does not engage the Convention rights of a defendant. Accordingly, it is no longer necessary for a sentencing court considering the making of a recommendation for deportation to take account of the possible impact of the recommendation on the defendant's family and dependents (*R v Nelson Carmona* [2006] 2 Cr App R (S) 662).
(c)   The consequences to the offender of his being returned to his own country, eg persecution. This is generally a matter for the Home Secretary (*R v Jelk* [2002] EWCA Crim 184 [2002] All ER (D) 200 (Jan)).

(d)   The fact that the offender is in receipt of social security.

See generally *R v Bouchereau* 30/77 [1978] QB 732, [1981] 2 All ER 924n, ECJ.

B[23.9]–[23.15]

Home Secretary's considerations. In considering a recommendation the Home Secretary takes into account:

(a)   the nature of the offence;
(b)   the length of time the offender has spent in this country;
(c)   the offender's criminal record;
(d)   the strength of his connections with this country, his personal history and domestic circumstances (eg if the offender's wife or children are citizens of this country and resident here, it might be a great hardship to them to order deportation of the offender);
(e)   any compassionate feature that may be present;
(f)   any representation made by the offender.

B[23.16]

The Home Secretary will not normally deport an offender sentenced to borstal training (now abolished and replaced by youth custody), or detention, or a first offender unless the offence was very grave or other offences were taken into consideration.

Citizens of EC countries

B[23.17]

Before recommending the deportation of a national of a country in the EC the court must have regard to Community laws. Article 48 of the Treaty makes the following relevant provisions:

'1   Freedom of movement for workers shall be secured within the Community by the end of the transitional period at the latest.

2   Such freedom of movement shall entail the abolition of any discrimination based on nationality between workers of the member states as regards employment, remuneration and other conditions of work and employment.

3   It shall entail the right, subject to limitations justified on grounds of public policy, public security or public health:
    (a)   to accept offers of employment actually made;
    (b)   to move freely within the territories of member states for this purpose;
    (c)   to stay in the member state for the purpose of employment in accordance with the provisions governing the employment of nationals of that said state laid down by law, regulation or administrative action;

(d)   to remain in the territory of a member state after having been employed in that state subject to conditions which shall be embodied in implementing regulations which shall be drawn up by the Commission.

4   The provisions of this Article shall not apply to employment in the public service.'

B[23.18]

With regard to the references in paragraph 3 above to public policy or security, a directive has been issued (No. 64/221) which states:

'(1)   Measures taken on grounds of public policy or public security shall be based exclusively on the conduct of the individual concerned.

(2)   Previous criminal convictions shall not themselves constitute grounds for the taking of such measures.'

B[23.19]

The European Court of Justice has ruled:

(a)   that any action affecting the rights of persons covered by article 48 to enter and reside freely in a member state under the same conditions as nationals of that state constituted a 'measure' for the purposes of the directive quoted above;

(b)   that a recommendation for deportation by a court of a member state according to its national law was such an action (ie the 'action' referred to in (a) above);

(c)   that the directive must be interpreted to mean that previous convictions are relevant only in so far as the circumstances which gave rise to them are evidence of personal conduct constituting a present threat to the requirements of public policy;

(d)   that the justification for restricting free movement provided in article 48 (above) presupposed the existence of a genuine and sufficiently serious threat affecting one of the fundamental interests of society additional to the disturbance of order which any infringement of the law involved.

See guidance handed down in *R v Secretary of State for the Home Department, ex p Santillo* [1981] 2 All ER 897.

B[23.20]

It should be noted that not all EC nationals come within the ambit of the directive. In practice it covers those who come to the United Kingdom to take or seek work, to set up in business or in a self-employed capacity or to receive services for money, eg medical, educational or business.

Procedure

B[23.21]

There should be a full inquiry into the case before a recommendation is made. A person who is likely to be the subject of an order must be given seven clear days' notice of what may happen to him. The defendant should have legal representation. Solicitors should be asked to address the court specifically on the possibility of a recommendation for deportation being made. In the case of an **EU National** the court must give reasons for making a recommendation as to deportation (*R v Secretary of State for the Home Department, ex p Dannenburg* [1984] 2 All ER 481, (1984) 148 JP 321).

B[23.22]

What should not be done is to add a sentence as if by an afterthought at the end of observations about any sentence of imprisonment.

EC national within the scope of article 48

B[23.23]

The recommendation can only be based on the grounds of public policy, public security or public health. The offender must be informed of the grounds on which the recommendation is based. A short statement in writing should be given to the offender and also attached to the written recommendation (see **B[23.21]** above). It should include some indication of the extent to which the current and previous criminal convictions of the defendant have been taken into account and the light which such conviction or convictions threw on the likely nature of the defendant's personal conduct in the future. Of particular importance will be the court's assessment of the gravity of the conduct and the likelihood of reoffending.

EC national to which article 48 does not apply

B[23.24]

It is desirable that the same procedure be followed.

Aliens (see generally *R v Nazari* [1988] QB 631, [1988] 2 WLR 1005, sub nom R v Kuxhaus [1988] 2 All ER 705, 56 P & CR 229, CA).

B[23.25]–[23.30]

Similarly reasons, not necessarily in writing, should be given.

B[23.31]

The effect of a recommendation. Where the court makes a recommendation and the defendant is not sentenced to imprisonment or is not liable to be detained in any other way he will be detained under the Immigration Act 1971 until he is deported. The court may, however, order his release subject to such restrictions as to residence and/ or to reporting to the police as it may direct.

B[24]

Detention for one day at the court or at a police station
(Magistrates' Courts Act 1980, s 135)

B[24.1]

Magistrates may order the detention of a defendant aged 18 years or more in the precincts of the court house or at a police station for any period until 8 pm on the day of the hearing; but the offence must be punishable with imprisonment or alternatively the detention must be an alternative to payment of a fine. The magistrates should announce at what time the defendant can be released, taking into account that the defendant should be given the opportunity of returning home that day.

B[25]

Detention and training orders
(Powers of the Criminal Courts (Sentencing) Act 2000, s 100)

B[25.1]

Detention and training orders (DTO) are the sole custodial sentence available to the courts which may be imposed on a young person aged under 18. Age is generally determined at the time of conviction rather than at sentence. The order is available in the youth court only and not the adult court. The DTO is a rehabilitative order and not simply a young offender's prison.

B[25.2]

Where a DTO is a likely sentence the Youth Offending Team (YOT) will make contact with the Youth Justice Board before the court hearing to establish if accommodation is available.

B[25.3]

All the restrictions outlined at B[37] and contained in s 152 CJA 2003 apply to the detention and training order because it is defined as a custodial sentence.

B[25.4]

Before making an order the court must be satisfied that the following additional circumstances pertain:

(a)   the offender is not less than 12 years of age when the offence for which he is to be dealt with is found proved;

(b)   where the offender is under the age of 15 years at the time of conviction the courts must be of the opinion that he is a persistent young offender. Note this is 15 years old at the time of conviction (*R v Thomas* (2004) although *R v LM* [2002] EWCA Crim 3047, [2002] All ER (D) 35 (Dec) suggests that a non-persistent offender who is under the age of 15 when a non-grave offence is committed cannot receive a DTO even when 15 at date of conviction.

This is not the same definition as a persistent offender for the purposes of monitoring speed of case throughput (*R v Charlton* (2000) 164 JP 685,

CA). Where there has been a series of offences on separate occasions the offender may be persistent (*R v Smith* (2000) 164 JP 681, [2000] Crim LR 613, CA). However, such offending should be of a similar character (*R v JD* (2000) 165 JP 1, CA).

B[25.5]

Where the court passes a detention and training order it must state in open court that it is of the opinion that the above conditions are satisfied.

B[25.6]

Length of the order. The term of a detention and training order (DTO) may only be made up of terms of 4, 6, 8, 10, 12, 18 or 24 months. However the court may not exceed the maximum term the Crown Court could impose for the offence on an offender aged 21. This means that the youth court must be careful when dealing with a case of summary criminal damage (maximum three months' imprisonment) making the DTO unavailable (see *Pye v Leeds Youth Court* [2006] All ER (D) 16 (Oct)) and cases involving other summary offences where the maximum sentence for an adult offender will generally be less than six months [**28 weeks]. Another exception to this is an offence under the Bail Act where the maximum penalty is currently three months. [**It is not clear whether the combined effect of the changes envisaged by the CJA 2003, ss 181 and 195 together with s 34 of the Police and Justice Act 2006 will make a detention and training order available for youths (see J[1.91]).

B[25.7]

In assessing the length of sentence the court must give credit for a timely guilty plea. The level of credit will generally depend on the time the plea of guilty is entered. **Sentencing Guideline Council** guidance suggests up to a third for a timely guilty plea, reducing to roughly 10% for a plea entered on the date set for trial. In rare circumstances credit for plea can be withheld altogether. Magistrates should consult their legal adviser before determining to withhold any credit for a plea of guilty (see *R v Barber* [2006] EWCA Crim 162, [2006] 2 Cr App Rep (S) 539).

The court must also take into account in deciding the overall the length of the DTO any time spent on remand in custody (*R v B* [2000] Crim LR 870). See also *R (on the application of A) v The Governor of Huntercombe Young Offenders' Institute and the Secretary of State for the Home Department* [2006] EWHC 2544 (Admin).

B[25.8]

Consecutive orders may be made provided that the overall term does not exceed 24 months. Note that an aggregate term of more than the statutory maximum** may be imposed on the same occasion for summary only offences (*C v DPP* [2001] EWHC 453 (Admin), [2002] 1 Cr App Rep (S)

189, [2001] Crim LR 671). For indictable and either way offences each offence must be one of the specified terms above, although when aggregated it may come to an unspecified term of, for example, 6+ 8+ 10 = 24 months.

B[25.9]

Half the order will be served in a secure establishment and half will be the subject of supervision under a member of the Young Offender Team.

B[25.10]

Breach of supervision. Supervision takes place throughout the order, but if a supervision order is breached the offender may be detained for a period not exceeding the shorter of three months or *[the period beginning with the date of the offender's failure and ending with the last day of the term of the detention and training order. For the purposes of the legislation above a failure that is found to have occurred over two or more days is to be taken to have occurred on the first of those days;] the remainder of the term of the DTO; or may be fined up to the maximum of level 3. Offenders brought before the court for further offending during the period of supervision may be dealt with for the new offence as well as the remainder of the existing order.

*Words substituted by LASPO 2012, s 80 when in force.

B[25.11]

See *R v Ganley* [2000] All ER (D) 594, [2001] 1 Cr App Rep (S) 60, CA for general guidance on the use of the order.

B[26]–B[30]

Detention in a young offender institution

(Powers of the Criminal Courts (Sentencing) Act 2000, s 96)

B[26.0]

**Section 96 will be repealed by the Criminal Justice and Courts Services Act 2000, Sch 7 from a date to be appointed. Section 96 will, in effect, be replaced by the provisions to be found in Chapter 3 (ss 181–195 inclusive) of the CJA 2003. This will make available prison sentences, intermittent custody and suspended sentences for offenders aged 18 years or more at the date of conviction (not sentence). It is likely the new regime will only apply to offences committed on or after the operative date ie from a date to be appointed. See B[37] onwards.

There are currently transitory provisions making suspended sentence available for offenders aged 18–20 years inclusive. However, see *R v Campbell* [2006] EWCA Crim 726, [2006] All ER (D) 137 (Mar).

General

B[26.1]

Imprisonment is not available for offenders under the age of 21 years. The main custodial provision for these offenders is detention in a young offender institution. This is subject to the criteria restricting the use of custodial sentences imposed by the Powers of the Criminal Courts (Sentencing) Act 2000.*

*Custody plus and intermittent custody orders provided for by the CJA 2003, ss 181–188 and Schs 10 and 11 will be repealed at a future date by LASPO 2012, s 89.

B[26.2]

As with all custodial sentences the court must explain:

(a)   how long the defendant will spend in custody;

(b)   how long after release he will be liable to recall; and
(c)   how long after release he will be subject to supervision.

Limitations

B[26.3]

Imprisonable offence. The offence of which the offender is found guilty must be punishable with imprisonment in the case of a person aged 21 or over.

B[26.4]

Age of offender. The minimum age for male and female offenders is 18 years. In either case the offender must be under 21 years.

B[26.5]

Criteria for imposing a custodial sentence. The court must be of the opinion:

(a)   that the offence, or the combination of the offence and any other offences associated with it, was so serious that only such a sentence can be justified for the offence;
(b)   where the offence is a violent or sexual offence, that only such a sentence would be adequate to protect the public from serious harm from the offender.

B[26.6]

Other circumstances in which custody may be imposed. Nothing in paragraphs (a) and (b) above prevents the court imposing a custodial sentence on an offender who refuses to consent to a community sentence proposed by the court which requires his willingness to comply with a proposed requirement. A court may also impose custody for a wilful and persistent breach of a community order.

B[26.7]

So serious. See B[37.6]. The court must take account of all the information about the circumstances of the offence including any aggravating or mitigating factors as are available to it.

B[26.8]

Associated offence. An offence of which the offender has been convicted in the same proceedings or for which he is sentenced at the same time, or an offence taken into consideration.

B[26.9]

Violent offence. An offence which leads, or is intended or likely to lead, to a person's death or to physical injury to a person, and includes an offence which is required to be charged as arson.

B[26.10]–[26.15]

Sexual offence under the Sexual Offences Act 2003. It does not include offences relating to prostitution. Nor does it include offences in public lavatories.

B[26.16]

Protection from serious harm. This refers to protecting members of the public from death or serious personal injury, whether physical or psychological, occasioned by further such offences committed by the offender.

B[26.17]

Pre-sentence report. Except where the court considers it unnecessary to do so, the court must obtain and consider a pre-sentence report before forming an opinion on:

(a)   whether the offence etc was so serious;
(b)   (violent or sexual offence) only custody would be adequate to protect the public etc;
(c)   the length of term commensurate with the offence;
(d)   (violent or sexual offence) the length of term necessary to protect the public etc.

B[26.18]

In all cases where a court is contemplating sentencing a defendant to custody for the first time a report should be obtained: *R v Gillette* (1999) Times, 3 December, CA.

B[26.19]

Failure to obtain pre-sentence report. Does not invalidate the sentence but the appeal court must obtain and consider such a report if the court below was not justified in forming an opinion that a report was unnecessary.

B[26.20]

Mentally disordered offender. Where an offender is or appears to be mentally disordered, ie suffering from a mental disorder within the meaning of the Mental Health Act 1983, the court must additionally obtain and consider a medical report before passing a custodial sentence unless the court considers it unnecessary to do so. The court must take any such information into account and consider the likely effect of any custodial sentence on his condition and any treatment for it. Failure to obtain a medical report does not invalidate any sentence but one must be obtained and considered by an appeal court.

B[26.21]

Legal representation. The offender must first be given the opportunity to be legally represented unless he has failed to take up the offer of legal representation or has been refused legal representation based on financial grounds. Note that the requirement is not that he should be represented, but that he should have an opportunity to be.

B[26.22]

Offenders under 18 years. A magistrates' court (as opposed to a youth court) cannot commit defendants aged under 18 years to custody. Such juveniles must be remitted on bail or in local authority accommodation to a youth court which will usually be the youth court for the area in which they reside.

Passing sentence

B[26.23]–[26.24]

Maximum length of sentence. Twelve months or the maximum term of imprisonment available for the offence, whichever is the lesser term, six months if suspended.

B[26.25]–[26.30]

Minimum length of sentence. 21 days over 18 years of age, 14 days if suspended except for detention imposed where an offender has breached a supervision order made on his release. See B[26.39].

B[26.31]

Consecutive terms. Detention in a young offender institution may be ordered to be consecutive to an existing period of detention or, if more than one period of detention is imposed on the same occasion, one period of detention may be ordered to be consecutive to another so, however, that the offender will not be liable to a period of more than 12 months in total. If a longer period is ordered the excess period will be treated as remitted.

B[26.32]

Length of custodial sentence. Shall be for a term which is commensurate with the seriousness of the offence or the combination of the offence and other offences associated with it or, in the case of a violent or sexual offence, for such longer term as is necessary to protect the public from serious harm from the offender. The court may suspend the sentence for an operational period of 2 years maximum, see B[37.60].

B[26.33]

Committal to Crown Court. The longest term of detention available to a magistrates' court in respect of an offender for a single indictable or either way offence is six months. However, in certain circumstances a magistrates' court may commit offenders aged 18 years to the Crown Court for sentence under s 3 Powers of Criminal Courts (Sentencing) Act 2000** (see B[16]).

Reasons for decisions

B[26.34]

It is the duty of the court to state in open court:

(a)   that it is of the opinion that either or both of paragraphs (a) and (b) at B[26.35] apply:

(b)   that it is of the opinion that in the case of a violent or sexual offence it is necessary to pass a longer term than is commensurate with the seriousness of the offence to protect the public from serious harm from the offender;

(c)   why it is of that opinion;

and in all cases to explain to the offender in open court and in ordinary language why it is passing a custodial sentence on him or such longer term.

How to announce

B[26.35]

We have decided to pass a sentence of detention in a young offender institution on the defendant and we are of the opinion that:

(a)   the offence (or the combination of the offence and other associated offence(s) namely []) was so serious that only such a sentence can be justified for the offence; and/or

(b)   this is a violent/sexual offence and only such a sentence would be adequate to protect the public from serious harm from him

because [*then explain why either or both of the paragraphs apply*]. (Violent/sexual offence): We are also passing a sentence of detention for a term longer than is commensurate with the seriousness of the offence as this is necessary to protect the public from serious harm from him because [*give reasons*].

Accordingly [*addressing the defendant*] you will be sent to a young offender institution for [*state period*]. On release you will be subject to supervision for [*state how long*] and you will be subject to recall to detention for the next [*state time*] and this is because [*explain in ordinary language why he is receiving a custodial sentence and, where applicable, why he is receiving a term longer than is commensurate with the seriousness of the offence*].

Note – If there is more than one offence it should be clearly stated what the total period of detention is to be.

Ancillary orders

B[26.36]

Compensation at B[18]

Costs at B[20]

Disqualification at C[5]

Endorsement at C[5]

Deprivation of property and forfeiture at B[34]

Restitution order at B[39]

Early release

B[26.37]

An offender subject to a term of detention in a young offender institution for 12 months or less will be automatically released after he has served one half of the term. In determining the period that has been served, time spent on remand in custody or secure accommodation is to be taken into account. However, additional days may be imposed under the prison rules where the offender has been guilty of disciplinary offences.

B[26.38]

Supervision following release. An offender who is released and is under 22 years will be under the supervision of a probation officer or social worker for a period of three months or until he attains the age of 22 years, whichever is the shorter period.

B[26.39]–[26.45]

Failure to comply with requirements as to supervision is punishable by custody of up to 30 days or a fine of up to £1,000.

B[26.46]

Further offences. Where an offender commits an imprisonable offence before he would (but for his release) have served his sentence in full, the court which deals with him for the later offence may return him to custody for the whole or part of the period which begins with the making of the order of return and is equal in length to the period between the date of commission of the new offence and the date of expiry of the original term.

B[31]

Discharge (absolute or conditional)

(Powers of Criminal Courts (Sentencing) Act 2000, s 12)

Limitations

B[31.1]

Absolute	– None.
Conditional	– minimum period, none,
	– maximum period, three years.

B[31.2]

Special consideration. Before making either of these orders the court must be of opinion, having regard to the circumstances including the nature of the offence and the character of the offender, that it is inexpedient to inflict punishment.

Unless there are exceptional circumstances a magistrates' court (which includes a youth court), may not make an order for conditional discharge in respect of an offence committed within two years of a final warning (CDA 1998, s 66(4)).

B[31.3]

Before making an order for conditional discharge the court must explain to the offender in ordinary language that if he commits another offence during the period of discharge he will be liable to be sentenced for the offence for which the conditional discharge is given. This is the court's duty and only in the most exceptional circumstances may it be delegated to another person, eg the accused's lawyer.

Ancillary orders

B[31.4]–[31.6]

Compensation at B[18]

Costs at B[20]

Disqualification at C[5]

Endorsement at C[5]

Deprivation of property and forfeiture at B[34]

Restitution at B[39]

Legal note

B[31.7]

A defendant who is convicted of an offence while subject to a Crown Court conditional discharge may be committed to the Crown Court to be sentenced for the offence for which the conditional discharge was originally ordered, under the Powers of Criminal Courts (Sentencing) Act 2000, s 13(5). He may also be committed to be dealt with for the new offence, under Powers of Criminal Courts (Sentencing) Act 2000, s 6 (*R v Penfold* (1995) 16 Cr App Rep (S) 1016, [1995] Crim LR 666, CA).

General considerations

B[31.8]

It is most important to note that only after the court has decided that it is inexpedient to inflict punishment because of all the circumstances may it make an order for discharge. But magistrates are specifically empowered to make a deprivation order or order for costs and compensation where appropriate: Power of Criminal Courts (Sentencing) Act 2000, s 12(7) as amended. Disqualification and endorsement may be ordered where appropriate.

B[31.9]

This is not a conviction for the purposes of the Sex Offenders Act 1997.

B[31.10]–[31.15]

No conditions or requirements may be added to either of these orders.

B[31.16]

Period of conditional discharge. This must always commence on the pronouncement of sentence. There is no provision to make this period consecutive to any other period.

Exclusion orders

Licensed Premises (Exclusion of Certain Persons)
Act 1980

B[32.1]

(This order will be repealed and replaced by drinking banning orders (on conviction) when ss 6–8 of the Violent Crime Reduction Act 2006 is brought into force)

When a person is convicted of an offence (of whatever nature) which was committed on licensed premises and the court which convicts him is satisfied that when he committed the offence he resorted to violence, or offered or threatened violence, the court may make an exclusion order prohibiting him from entering those licensed premises or any other licensed premises which the court may specify in the order. Such an order is made in addition to any sentence imposed, including a discharge.

"**Licensed premises**" for this purpose means those in respect of which a premises licence under the Licensing Act 2003 has been granted by the relevant local authority authorising the supply of alcohol (within the meaning of s 14 of that Act) for consumption on the premises.

The court must state the period during which the defendant is to be excluded; the minimum period is three months and the maximum is two years. Any person who is subject to such an order and is in the specified premises otherwise than with the express consent of the licensee or one of his staff is guilty of an offence punishable with a fine on level 4 and one months' imprisonment (**from a date to be appointed, 51 weeks).

Thus, a person convicted of breach of an exclusion order who is also the subject of a suspended sentence (which might be imposed for the offence which gave rise to the exclusion order) will be in jeopardy of having to serve that additional sentence. Courts would probably want to make this point to the defendant both in fairness to him and also perhaps the better to enforce the order. At the time of convicting a person for breach of an exclusion order the court may also determine whether to revoke the order or vary it by deleting the name of any specified premises.

B[32.2]

The licensee or his staff may expel from his premises any person whom he reasonably suspects of having entered in breach of an exclusion order and a constable shall at the request of the licensee or his staff, help to expel any person whom the constable reasonably suspects of being present in breach of such an order.

B[32A]

Drinking Banning Orders

B[32A.1]

A substantial part of Chapter I, Part 1 of the Violent Crime Reduction Act 2006 (drinking banning orders) was brought into force on 31 August 2009.

An application may be made by a chief officer of police (including the British Transport Police) or a local authority (after consultation with each other). Application is by way of complaint to a magistrates' court (s 3) or a county court (s 4). The proceedings are therefore classified as civil proceedings: s 3.

The subject of the order must be at least 16 years of age and since 31 August 2009 engaged in criminal or disorderly behaviour while under the influence of alcohol. If the complaint is proved the court must consider whether an order is necessary to protect others from behaviour of the same kind while under the influence of alcohol.

Rules of court have been made governing the forms and procedure which must be adhered to in relation to orders under sections 3 and 9 of the 2006 respectively: see the Magistrates' Courts (Drinking Banning Orders) Rules 2009, SI 2009/2937 and the Criminal Procedure Rules 2011, r 50.2 onwards.

Orders made on conviction. From 1 November 2010 a Drinking Banning Order may be made on conviction where an offender aged 16 years of over is convicted of an offence and at the time he committed the offence he was under the influence of alcohol. The following conditions must be satisfied:

(1)   The defendant has engaged in criminal or disorderly conduct while under the influence of alcohol; and

(2)   An order is necessary to protect other persons from further conduct of that kind by the defendant while under the influence of alcohol.

NB: An order may only be made on conviction in relation to specified local justice areas by way of secondary legislation: see SI 2010/469 and SI 2010/2541.

Order and its terms

B[32A.2]

An order may contain such prohibitions as are necessary to protect the public from criminal or disorderly behaviour from the subject of the order while under the influence of alcohol. The prohibitions may include entering premises with a premises licence or club premises licence authorising the sale of alcohol. The individual may not be prohibited from entering a place where he lives, works, attends for education, training or medical treatment or is legally obliged to attend: s 1.

The duration of the order may be between two months and two years although different prohibitions may have effect for different periods: s 2.

The order may provide for the order or any prohibition or provision to cease to have effect at an earlier date if the subject completes a specified approved course and he consents to its inclusion. If it does so the order must specify the date on which the order or prohibition will case to have effect. This will be at least half-way through the original period specified by the court. The court must be satisfied that a place on a specified approved course if available.

The court must explain the terms of the order and if it does not include or offer attendance at an approved course the court must state its reasons in open court: s 2.

Variation or discharge

B[32A.3]

Either party may apply by complaint for variation or discharge. The order may not be extended to last longer than two years and may not be discharged before the specified period is half-way through the original term unless the police/local authority consents: see s 5.

Interim order

B[32A.4]

An interim order may be made if the court considers it just to do so. An application may be made without notice or be heard in the absence of the subject with the leave of the justices' clerk if he considers that such a procedure is **necessary**. An interim order may last for up to four weeks although there is provision to extend such an order: s 9. It is suggested that a copy of an order made should be served on the offender preferably by personal service by the police/local authority to ensure that the subject is aware of the terms of the order and the sanctions for non-compliance (see breach proceedings below).

Breach proceedings

B[32A.5]

Breach of an order without reasonable excuse is punishable on summary conviction with a fine of up to £2,500 (£1,000 in respect of a youth aged 16–17 years). A conditional discharge on breach is not available.

If breach proceedings are brought in the youth court, the list of persons entitled to be present has been expanded to include 'one person authorised by a relevant authority'. Reporting restrictions under s 49 CYPA 1933 do not apply but the court may make an order under s 33 CYPA 1933 (or s 45 YJCEA 1999 when in force) and if the court imposes a reporting restriction or declines to make an order it should give its reasons: see s 11.

Appeal

B[32A.6]

An appeal against a full order from the magistrates' court lies to the Crown Court: s 10. No appeal lies against the making of an interim order. There does not appear to be a right of appeal to the Crown Court against the variation or discharge of a full order.

B[33]

Fines

For 'Assessment of Fines: Sentencing Process' see B[33A] below
Limitations

B[33.1]
Offences. The court may fine for any criminal offence.

Surcharge. See B[33.4] below.

B[33.2]
Maximum fine. The power of magistrates' courts (unlike that of the Crown Court) to impose a fine is entirely controlled by statute. Therefore the maximum fine for the offence may not be exceeded.

B[33.3]
The maximum fine for the vast majority of offences which are only triable by magistrates is expressed as being on one of five levels, each level representing a monetary limit. (The maximum for most offences triable either way is expressed as the 'statutory maximum' or 'prescribed sum'.)

Level 1: maximum fine is £200

Level 2: maximum fine is £500

Level 3: maximum fine is £1,000

Level 4: maximum fine is £2,500

Level 5: maximum fine is £5,000

(Either way offences: prescribed sum is £5,000.)

B[33.4]
This is known as the standard scale of fines and it has been devised as an attempt to rationalise the maximum amounts of fines and to provide a simple means of increasing them in inflationary times.

Victims surcharge. By virtue of the Criminal Justice Act 2003, s 161A(1) and secondary legislation, for offences committed on or after 1 April 2007 where a court requires an offender to pay a fine and/or costs, or by requiring the offender to pay a fine and compensation and/or costs, it must order the offender to pay a victims surcharge of £15. Where the means of the offender are such that he has insufficient income to pay a fine, costs and/or a surcharge in addition to *compensation,* the court may give precedence to the compensation order by making no order for the payment of the surcharge. In other words, the court gives priority to the compensation order.

Where the court proposes a fine and/or costs, but the offender has limited means, it is permissible to give priority to the surcharge by reducing the level of the fine and/or costs, but not the surcharge.

A surcharge is not payable where the court is imposing a fine or back duty in relation to a vehicle excise prosecution. This is because the vehicle excise legislation provides for payment of an "excise penalty".

*As of **1 October 2012** the following provisions apply in the magistrates' court (SI 2012/1696):

Offender aged 18 or over when offence committed	Offender aged under 18 when offence committed	Incorporated and unincorporated companies etc
(a) Conditional discharge at a flat rate of £15 (b) Fine at 10% of the fine value, rounded up or down to the nearest pound, with a minimum amount of £20 and a maximum amount of £120 (c) Community order at a flat rate of £60 (d) Suspended sentence of imprisonment or detention in a young offenders' institution at– (i) £80 for a sentence of 6 months and below; and (ii) £100 for a sentence of over six months but not more than 12 months	(a) Conditional discharge at a flat rate of £10 (b) Fine at a flat rate of £15 (c) Youth rehabilitation order at a flat rate of £15 (d) Referral order at a flat rate of £15	(a) Conditional discharge at a flat rate of £15 (b) Fine at 10% of the fine value, rounded up or down to the nearest pound with a minimum amount of £20 and a maximum amount of £120

Mixed disposal. Where the defendant is dealt with in different ways (so for example a fine in relation to one offence and custody in relation to another) only one surcharge (whichever is the higher) will be paid.

Transitional provisions:

(1)   An offender is dealt with by a court for more than one offence, and at least one of the offences was committed either side of the 1 October 2012 implementation date. In such cases, the surcharge will be payable if the person is fined, at a rate of £15 as specified by the 2007 Order.

(2)   A court deals with an adult offender for more than one offence, and at least one of those offences was committed when under 18, the surcharge will be payable at the rate for under 18s.

Juveniles

B[33.5]

Offender under 14 (a child). Maximum fine is the amount in the statute creating the offence or £250, whichever is less.

B[33.6]

Offender 14 to under 18 (young person). Maximum fine is the amount in the statute creating the offence or £1,000, whichever is less.

Parental responsibility for payment

B[33.7]

In the case of a person under 16 the court must order the parent or guardian to pay unless either he cannot be found or the court is satisfied that it would be unreasonable to order the parent to pay having regard to the circumstances of the case. Provided the parent has been given the opportunity to attend court, an order for payment may be made against him in his absence. If he is present, he must be given the opportunity of making representations about whether he should be ordered to pay.

B[33.8]

Before exercising its power to make an order that a parent should pay a financial order in respect of an offence committed by a child the court must be satisfied that it is reasonable to do so. Before making an order a parent or guardian should be given the opportunity of being heard (PCC(S)A 2000, s 137(4)).

B[33.9]

Where the offender is aged 16 or 17, and it would not be unreasonable to do so, the court has a power to make the parent responsible for the financial order.

B[33.10]–[33.15]

Where a local authority has parental responsibility (see D[3.1]–D[3.7]) for a child in their care or accommodated by them, the local authority is responsible for payment, unless it has done everything reasonably and properly expected of it to protect the public from the young offender (*D v DPP* (1995)).

Determining the amount of any fine

B[33.16]

Introduction. The amount of a fine must reflect the **seriousness** of the offence (CJA 2003, s 164(2)). The court must also take into account the **financial circumstances** of the offender; this applies whether it has the effect of increasing or reducing the fine (CJA 2003, s 164(1) and (4)). The **aim** is for the fine to have an equal impact on offenders with different financial circumstances; it should be a hardship but should not force the offender below a reasonable "subsistence" level.

Fine Bands. For the purposes of the SGC offence guidelines, a fine is normally based on one of three bands, that is Bands A, B or C (see on for Bands D and E). The selection of the relevant band, and the position of the individual offence within that band, is determined by the **seriousness** of the offence.

Starting points based on first time offender pleading not guilty

	Starting point	Range
Fine Band A	50% of relevant weekly income	25%–75% of relevant weekly income
Fine Band B	100% of relevant weekly income	75%–125% of relevant weekly income
Fine Band C	150% of relevant weekly income	125%–175% of relevant weekly income

Fine band starting point and ranges. Each fine band has a starting point and a range. Some guidelines are expressed as a single fine band (eg see careless driving at C[25]). Other guidelines the range may encompass more than one fine band (eg see drunk and disorderly at A[28]).

Multiple offences. The starting point and ranges indicated in the individual offence guidelines assume that the offender is being sentenced for a single offence. Where an offender is being sentenced for multiple offences, the overall sentence must be just and appropriate having regard to the totality of the offending; the court should not simply aggregate the sentences considered suitable for the individual offences. The court's assessment of the totality of the offending may result in an overall sentence above the range indicated by the individual offences, including, where permitted, a sentence of a different type (see CJA 2003, ss 148(1) and 152(2)).

Where an offender is to be fined for two or more offences that arise out of the **same incident**, it will often be appropriate to impose on the most serious offence a fine which reflects the totality of the offending where this can be achieved within the maximum for that offence. "no separate penalty" should be imposed for other offences.

Ancillary orders – order of priority. Where **compensation** is being ordered, that will need to be attributed to the relevant offence as will any necessary **ancillary** orders.

Where the offender does not have sufficient means to pay the total financial penalty, the order of priority is compensation, surcharge, fine and then costs.

Offences not included in the SGC guidelines. Where an offence is not included in this or any other SGC guideline, it may assist in determining sentence to consider the starting points and ranges indicated for offences that are of a similar level of seriousness.

B[33.17]

Definition of relevant weekly income. The **seriousness** of an offence determines the choice of fine band and the position of the offence within the range for that band. The offender's **financial circumstances** are taken into account by expressing that position as a proportion of the offender's **relevant weekly income.**

Where an offender is in receipt of income from employment or is self-employed **and** that income is more than £100 per week after deduction of tax and national insurance (or equivalent where the offender is self-employed), the actual income is the **relevant weekly income.**

Where the offender's only source of income is state benefit (including where there is relatively low additional income as permitted by the benefit regulations) or the offender is in receipt of income from employment or is self-employed but the amount of income after deduction of tax and national insurance is £100 or less, the **relevant weekly income is deemed to be £100.** Additional information about this approach is set out below. In calculating relevant weekly income, no account should be taken of tax credits, housing benefit, child benefit or similar.

B[33.18]

Determining relevant weekly income – means Information and no reliable information. Under s 95 of the Courts Act 2003 (which amends s 20A of the Criminal Justice Act 1991) it is an offence for a defendant to fail to provide means information to the court when charged. The best way for the court to receive that information is on the standard *Means Form* which should be issued to all defendants so that if they are found guilty the court can impose a fine appropriate to the offender's means and ability to pay.

Where an offender has failed to provide information, or the court is not satisfied that it has been given sufficient reliable information, it is entitled to make such determination as it thinks fit regarding the financial circumstances of the offender (CJA 2003, s 164(5)). Any such determination should be clearly stated on the court records for use in any subsequent variation or enforcement proceedings. A record should also be made of the applicable fine band and the court's assessment of the position of the offence within that band based on the seriousness of the offence.

Where there is **no information** on which a determination can be made, the court should proceed on the basis of an **assumed relevant weekly income of £400.** This is derived from national median pre-tax earnings; a gross figure is used as, in the absence of financial information from the offender, it is not possible to calculate appropriate deductions.

Where there is some information that tends to suggest a significantly lower or higher income than the recommended £350 default sum, the court should make a determination based on that information. A court is empowered to remit a fine in whole or in part if the offender subsequently provides information as to means (CJA 2003, s 165(2)). The assessment of offence seriousness and, therefore, the appropriate fine band and the position of the offence within that band is **not** affected by the provision of this information.

B[33.18A]

Approach to offenders on low income (including state benefit). An offender whose primary source of income is state benefit will generally receive a base level of benefit (eg job seekers' allowance, a relevant disability benefit or income support) and may also be eligible for the supplementary benefits depending on his or her individual circumstances (such as child tax credits, housing benefit, council tax benefit and similar. If **relevant weekly income** were defined as the amount of benefit received, this would usually result in higher fines being imposed on offenders with a higher level of need; in most circumstances that would not properly balance the seriousness of the offence with the financial circumstances of the offender. While it might be possible to exclude from the calculation any allowance above the basic entitlement of a single person, that could be complicated and time consuming. Similar issues can arise where the offender is in receipt of a low earned income since this may trigger eligibility for means related benefits such as working tax credits and housing benefit depending on the particular circumstances. It will not always be possible with any confidence whether such a person's financial circumstances are significantly different from those of a person whose primary source of income is state benefit.

For those reasons, a simpler and fairer approach to cases involving offenders in receipt of low income (whether primarily earned or as a result of benefit) is to identify an amount that is **deemed** to represent the offender's relevant weekly income. While a precise calculation is neither possible nor desirable, it is considered that an amount that is approximately half-way between the base rate for job seekers' allowance and the net weekly income of an adult earning the minimum wage for 30 hours per week represents a starting point that is both realistic and appropriately; that is **currently £100**. The calculation is based on a 30 hour working week in recognition of the fact that many of those on a minimum wage do not work a full 37 hour week and that lower minimum wage rates apply to younger people. It is expected that this figure will remain in use until 31 March 2011. Future revisions of the guideline will update the amount in accordance with current benefit and minimum wage levels.

B[33.19]

Assessment of financial circumstances. While the initial consideration for the assessment of a fine is the offender's relevant weekly income, the court is required to take account of the offender's **financial circumstances** more broadly. An offender's financial circumstances may have the effect of increasing or reducing the amount of the fine; however they are **not** relevant to the assessment of offence seriousness. They should be considered separately from the selection of the appropriate fine band and the court's assessment of the position of the offence band within the range for that band.

B[33.20]

Out of the ordinary expenses. In deciding the proportions of relevant weekly income that are the starting point and ranges for each fine band, account has been taken of reasonable living expenses. Accordingly, no further allowances should normally be made for these. In addition, no allowance should normally be made where the offender has dependants. Outgoings will be relevant to the amount of the fine only where the expenditure is **out of the ordinary** and **substantially** reduces the ability to pay a financial penalty so that the requirement to pay a fine based on the standard approach would lead to undue hardship.

Example: Court determines offence seriousness is a Band A fine. Defendant's relevant weekly income is £600 per week. Defendant pleads guilty at the first availability opportunity. The court determines to take into account out of the ordinary expenditure of £50 per week.

Fine = 50% of £600–£300 less a one-third discount for plea = £200 less £50 for out of the ordinary expenses = a total fine of £150.

Unusually low outgoings

Where the offender's living expenses are substantially lower than would normally be expected, it may be appropriate to adjust the amount of the fine to reflect this. This may apply, for example, where an offender does not make any financial contribution towards his or her own living costs.

B[33.21]
Savings

Where an offender has savings these will not normally be relevant to the assessment of the amount of a fine although they may influence the decision on time to pay. However, where an offender has substantial savings, the court may consider it appropriate to adjust the amount of the fine to reflect this.

B[33.22]
Household has more than one source of income. Where the household of which the offender is a part has more than one source of income, the fine should normally be based on the income of the offender alone. However, where the offender's part of the income is very small (or the offender is wholly dependent on the income of another), the court may have regard to the extent of the householder's income and assets which will be available to meet any fine imposed on the offender (*R v Engen* [2004] EWCA Crim 1536).

B[33.23]
Potential earning capacity. Where there is reason to believe that an offender's potential earning capacity is greater than his or her current income, the court may wish to adjust the amount of the fine to reflect this (*R v Little* (unreported) 14 April 1976, CA). This may apply, for example, where an unemployed offender states an expectation to gain paid employ-

ment within a short time. The basis for the calculation of fine should be recorded in order to ensure that there is a clear record for use in variation or enforcement proceedings.

High income offenders. Where the offender is in receipt of a very high income, affine based on a proportion of relevant weekly income may be disproportionately high when compared with the seriousness of the offence. In such cases, the court should adjust the fine to an appropriate level; as a general indication, in most cases the fine for a first time offender pleading not guilty **should not exceed** 75% of the maximum fine.

B[33.24]

Offence committed for "commercial" purposes. Some offences are committed with the intention of gaining a significant commercial benefit. These often occur, where, in order to carry out an activity lawfully, a person has to comply with certain processes which may be expensive. They include, for example, "taxi-touting" (where unauthorised persons seek to operate as taxi drivers) and "fly-tipping" (where the cost of lawful disposal is considerable). In some of these cases, a fine based on the standard approach set out above may not reflect the level of financial gain achieved or sought through the offending. Accordingly:

(a) where the offender has generated income or avoided expenditure to a level that can be calculated or estimated, the court may wish to consider that amount when determining the financial penalty;

(b) where it is not possible to calculate or estimate that amount, the court may wish to draw on information from the law enforcing authorities about the general costs of operating within the law.

B[33.25]

Reduction for a guilty plea. Where a guilty plea has been entered, the amount of the fine should be reduced by an appropriate proportion. See B[5.46].

Announcing the fine and time to pay

B[33.26]

Time to pay. When a fine is announced, unless payment can be made forthwith, in the case of an adult offender the court should normally make a collection order. The same applies in the youth court where a parent or guardian has been made responsible for the payment of the fine. In those cases where the juvenile is made responsible it is recommended that fixing time for payment should be deferred by the youth court and responsibility delegated to the fines officer.

B[33.27]

An immediate committal to prison in default of payment can only be ordered in the four types of cases mentioned below. In other cases the court must announce (and cause to be entered in the register) the time allowed for payment. This may be a fixed period, eg 14 days, or it may be an order that the defendant pays by instalments.

B[33.28]

The court, when imposing a fine, should establish if the defendant is an existing defaulter. If he/she is in default of an existing order the court is normally obliged to make either a deductions of earnings order (if working) or a deductions from benefits order (if claiming benefits). If the offender is not in default of an existing order the court may make these orders with the defendant's consent. In either case the court should make a reserve payment order in case the order fails ie payment in full within 10 working days. In the case of a **compensation order** see B[33.29] below.

B[33.29]

Costs and compensation. Costs against a defendant in criminal cases and compensation are normally enforceable in the same way as a fine. However, on imposition it is now **mandatory** that an attachment/deduction order should be considered where the offender is liable to pay compensation as part of the financial imposition. If the attachment/deduction order is subsequently made it should be applied to the whole sum adjudged to be paid.

B[33.30]

Limited companies. In law a company is a person. Therefore a fine imposed against a company can only be enforceable against the company and not against any of its officials. For non-payment of a fine a distress warrant can be issued against the company and its property seized and sold to meet the fine and any costs involved in conducting the sale.

B[33.31]

Payment of the fine can sometimes be enforced in the High Court or county court. Consult the legal adviser. In certain circumstances the appropriate officer (the collecting officer, in this case the Area Director) may apply to the High Court to have a company wound up under the Insolvency Act 1986.

B[33.32]

Partnership firm. The conviction will have been against the partners personally and fines can be enforced against them personally in the usual way.

B[33.33]

Searching. The court may order the defendant to be searched and any money found used to pay the fine, compensation and costs. If there is a balance this must be returned to the defendant.

B[33.34]

Such money must not be taken if the court is satisfied that the money does not belong to the defendant or if the loss of money would be more injurious to his family than his detention.

B[33.35]

Fine supervision order. Instead of the court fixing the time to pay or ordering fixed instalments, it may decide that the defendant is so incompetent or feckless that he will not put aside the money to meet the fine. In such circumstances the court can make a supervision order placing the defendant under the care of some person (often a probation officer) whose duty is not to collect the fine or decide the rate of payments, but to persuade the offender to pay so as to keep out of prison. When making such an order the rate of payment should be fixed by the court.

B[33.36]

Imposing a fine and suspended imprisonment. If an offence is punishable both by a fine and imprisonment, a fine and a suspended prison sentence can be imposed.

B[33.37]

Fine and immediate imprisonment. This combination is appropriate where the defendant has made a substantial profit from the offence. Generally, however, a fine should be imposed with an immediate custodial sentence only when the defendant has resources from which to pay the fine despite his imprisonment. The situation should be avoided which saddles a discharged prisoner with a fine. Generally offenders who profit from crimes are subject to the Proceeds of Crime Act 2002 confiscation provisions.

Procedure for enforcing fines

B[33.38]

Enforcement of a fine. This should begin the moment it is imposed with a fines collection order. The chairman of the court should never invite an application for time to pay. The court should always inquire how much can be paid immediately (if the defendant cannot pay in full) and should consider requiring even a small sum to be paid forthwith. It is usually better to fix any reserve payment order by reference to the offender's pay day rather than seven days from the date of his conviction. On a first default the fines officer must make an attachment of earnings order or apply for an attachment of benefit unless it is impracticable or inappropriate. Thereafter once a fines collection order has been made the fines officer has a wide range of powers but the court still has a role to play in many cases (see Courts Act 2003, Sch 5).

On default the fines officer can impose the following steps:

- Clamping of the offender's car
- Registration of the fine with the Register of Fines and Judgments
- Distress warrant
- Attachment of Earnings
- Deductions from Benefit
- Transfer the case to the civil courts for enforcement where it is cost effective to do so

If the fines officer clamps a car and wants to sell the vehicle he will have to first seek the permission of the court. The fines officer will have to have the case listed and go before the court to seek permission.

There is a new power for the fines officer to transfer cases for enforcement without referring them back to the court. This can be used where the court receives new information on the whereabouts of the offender and it is necessary to transfer for enforcement purposes.

If the fines officer considers that the above disposals are insufficient to recover payment he will refer the matter back to court, for example, to increase the fine or to impose imprisonment in default.

Immediate enforcement

B[33.39]

When a fine is imposed the court can use the following methods to enforce immediate payment, if there is a good reason not to make a collection order.

B[33.40]

1 Search. The court can order the defendant to be searched for money to meet the fine. See above.

B[33.41]–[33.45]

2 Immediate committal to prison. In the circumstances listed below the court may order imprisonment forthwith for a period determined in accordance with the following scale:

An amount not exceeding £200	7 days
An amount exceeding £200 but not exceeding £500	14 days
An amount exceeding £500 but not exceeding £1,000	28 days
An amount exceeding £1,000 but not exceeding £2,500	45 days
An amount exceeding £2,500 but not exceeding £5,000	3 months
An amount exceeding £5,000 but not exceeding £10,000	6 months
An amount exceeding £10,000	12 months

B[33.46]

It must be borne in mind that these are the maximum periods applicable, the court is not obliged to impose the maximum period in default. In other words, the number of days in default should be proportionate to the sum outstanding eg if the sum imposed was £520 and nothing has been paid, pro rata 15 days (rather than 28 days) should be ordered to be served in default of payment.

B[33.47]

If part payments have been made then the period of imprisonment is calculated by taking the period of imprisonment considered appropriate for the whole sum and reducing that period by the proportion which the part payment bears to the original sum due. For example, if a defendant is fined £600 and over a period pays £400, the maximum period of imprisonment for that balance is one-third of 28 days in band 4. Where a defendant is fined at one time for several offences, each fine must be calculated separately and the periods of imprisonment may be made consecutive. However, it is not appropriate to fix consecutive terms of imprisonment in respect of fines imposed for several offences arising out of the same incident. In every case where several fines are outstanding the court must look realistically at the total situation.

NB: Where several fines are ordered to run consecutive to each other the total number of days in default should not exceed the statutory maximum. For example, if four separate fines of £240 are ordered to run consecutive to each other the total number of days in default should not exceed the statutory maximum outlined in B[33.40] above ie 28 days.

B[33.48]

The above table applies to monetary penalties (ie fines, costs and compensation) and not to civil orders eg arrears of maintenance for which the maximum period is six weeks. Nor does it apply to the community charge for which the maximum period is three months. (It may be convenient to mention here that periods of imprisonment for more than one amount of unpaid community charge may not be made consecutive.)

B[33.49]

An immediate committal to prison can only be ordered in the following cases:

(a)   if the offence is punishable with imprisonment and the defendant appears to the court to have sufficient means to pay immediately; or

(b)   if it appears to the court that the defendant is unlikely to remain at an address in the United Kingdom long enough for the fine to be enforced by other methods; or

(c)   if the defendant is already serving a prison or detention sentence; or

(d)   if the defendant is being sent to prison or detention on the same or another charge.

B[33.50]

The court should announce its reasons (that is, (a), (b), (c) or (d) above) for making an immediate committal to prison and these reasons should be entered in the court register and on the committal warrant. Failure to comply may result in a challenge to the decision by judicial review (*R v Oldham Justices, ex p Cawley* [1997] QB 1, [1996] 1 All ER 464). If the defendant has second thoughts about paying and tenders payment to the court staff, the police or the prison officials he is entitled to be released. If only part of the fine is paid then he is entitled to a proportionate remission of the prison sentence. This applies even if he offers part payment after he has served a part of the prison sentence. A committal order, forthwith or suspended, will be inappropriate for a single mother with very little income, trying her best to balance her financial obligations (*R (on the application of Stokes) v Gwent Magistrates' Court* [2001] EWHC 569 (Admin), [2001] All ER (D) 125 (Jul)). A defaulter's human rights may be breached if he is not offered legal representation (*Best v UK* (2005) Times, 10 March).

B[33.51]

The period of imprisonment for non-payment can be concurrent with or consecutive to another sentence already being served; or if more than one fine is being enforced, the periods of imprisonment for non-payment can be consecutive to each other subject to the overall restrictions on the aggregate length of sentences. Consult the legal adviser.

B[33.52]

3 **Suspended committal order.** The court can order a committal to prison under the scale at B[33.40] to be suspended for a definite period of time during which the defendant has to find the money for the fine or it may suspend the prison sentence whilst he pays instalments at a rate decided by the court (usually weekly, fortnightly or monthly). Such a suspended committal order can only be ordered if the case falls into one of the categories listed at B[33.49] as (a), (b), (c), or (d). If more than one fine is being enforced in this way, the periods of imprisonment for non-payment can be concurrent with or consecutive to each other subject to the overall restrictions on the aggregate length of sentence (at B[33.40]). The defendant may apply subsequently to the court to vary the terms of the postponement. Where the defendant subsequently defaults in payment of the order, the court must give him notice that the warrant of commitment falls to be issued. Magistrates should adjourn hearing a warrant for committal case if they know that the defendant has not been served with proceedings (*R v Doncaster Justices, ex p Hannan* (1998) 163 JP 182, [1998] 32 LS Gaz R 30). He then has an opportunity to make representations orally or in writing as to why the warrant should not issue. Consult the legal adviser.

B[33.53]

4 **Detention for one day or overnight at a police station.** The court can order the defendant to be detained for the remainder of the day within the precincts of the court or police station but must be released at a time which will allow him to get home the same day or at the latest by 8 p.m. The release time should be announced by the court. Similarly, overnight detention authorises the police to arrest the defendant and keep him until 8 a.m. on the morning following his arrest or if he is arrested between midnight and 8 o'clock in the morning, until 8 o'clock in the morning of the day on which he is arrested. The effect of this is to wipe out the fine.

B[33.54]

5 **Distress warrant.** The magistrates can issue a distress warrant which orders the seizure of the defendant's property to meet the unpaid fine. Such an order may be suspended on terms that the defaulter pays as ordered by the court.

B[33.55]–[33.60]

6 **Supervision order.** This means placing the defendant under supervision, usually of the probation officer, see B[33.34].

B[33.61]

7 **Fixing a means inquiry.** When imposing a fine etc the court may fix a date

on which the offender must appear in court for a means inquiry if at that time any part of the monetary penalty remains unpaid.

Enforcement as a result of a referral by the fines officer

B[33.62]

If the defendant fails to pay the fine or other enforcement has failed, the fines officer will arrange for the issuing of a summons or warrant to bring the defendant back before the court who will conduct a means inquiry to investigate the defendant's ability to pay the fine and may demand that the defendant produce documentary evidence of his financial resources, eg pay slips, account books, post office savings book, bank statements etc. The defendant must produce a statement of means either before the inquiry or during the inquiry by a specified date and failure to produce such a statement is punishable with a fine up to level 3 if directed by the court and level 2 if directed by the fines officer.

Additionally the court may discharge a fines collection order and revert to its standard powers following an appeal against a decision of the fines officer to vary terms or take action by the use of alternative sanctions (including wheel clamping).

B[33.63]

Power to remit whole or part of the fine. Magistrates are empowered to remit the whole or part of a fine having regard to any change of circumstances since the defendant's conviction. Arrears of national insurance cannot be remitted. The court may also remit or reduce the fine where the court fixed the fine in the absence of adequate information about the offender's means either because he was convicted in absence or failed to comply with an order to furnish a statement of means and the result was that the original fine was set too high.

B[33.64]

For compensation see B[18].

B[33.65]

If the fine was imposed by a higher court, magistrates can only remit the whole or part of the fine if the higher court consents.

B[33.66]

At a means inquiry magistrates can enforce payment by the following methods:

B[33.67]

1 Attachment orders. If the magistrates are satisfied that the defendant is being paid earnings they may make an attachment order directing that the employer make deductions from the defendant's wages and remit them to the court. If the magistrates have this course in mind they should first consult the legal adviser and/or direct that the defendant completes a means form as the court must obtain certain details about the defendant and his employment.

B[33.68]

2 **Distress warrants.** See above.

B[33.69]

3 **Search.** See B[33.32].

B[33.70]–[33.75]

4 **Immediate committal to prison.** The magistrates can order an immediate committal to prison for a specified period according to the scale set out at B[33.40]. For calculation of the term in default see B[33.47]. Immediate committal to prison can only be ordered if:

(a) the offence for which he has been fined is also punishable with imprisonment and the defendant appears to the court to have the means to pay immediately; or

(b) the court is satisfied that the default is due to the offender's wilful refusal or culpable neglect and the court has considered or tried all other methods of enforcement and it appears to the court that they are inappropriate or unsuccessful.

Culpable neglect cannot be found where a defaulter has no capital or income to pay a fine. Nor should the assumption be made that someone else will pay the fine (*R (on the application of McDonough) v Wigan Magistrates' Court* [2004] EWHC 3272 (Admin), [2005] All ER (D) 304 (Feb)).

A high threshold has to be crossed before making a finding of *wilful refusal* (*R (on the application of Louis) v Ealing Magistrates' Court* [2009] EWHC 521 (Admin), 173 JP 248, [2009] All ER (D) 215 (Feb)).

B[33.76]

The test in s 82(4) of the MCA 1980 was that the court had to have regard to other methods of enforcement; it was not obliged to have tried them all: *R (Johnson) v Birmingham Magistrates' Court and CPS* [2012] EWHC 596 (ADMIN).

The other methods referred to are distress warrants, application to the High Court or county court for enforcement, supervision, attachment of earnings and, if under 21, attendance centre.

B[33.77]

5 **Detention for one day or overnight at a police station.** See B[33.53].

B[33.78]

6 **Suspended committal to prison.** The court can order a suspended

committal to prison for a period in accordance with the scale on at B[33.40]. This imprisonment can then be suspended for a definite period of time during which the defendant must pay the fine or alternatively the court may direct that the defendant shall pay at so much per week or month. Such a suspended committal can only be ordered if the offence for which the defendant was fined is punishable with imprisonment and the defendant appears to have sufficient means to pay; or the court is satisfied that the default is due to the offender's wilful refusal or culpable neglect and the court has considered all the other methods of enforcement and it appears that they are inappropriate or unsuccessful. See above.

B[33.79]

7 **Supervision order.** See B[33.34].

B[33.80]

8 **Deduction from benefit.** After a means inquiry has been made the court may request the Department of Works and Pensions to make payments towards a fine or compensation direct from the offender's benefit, subject to any right of review or appeal he may have.

B[33.81]

9 **Transfer to High Court or county court.** If the defendant is a holder of shares or has certain kinds of assets, enforcement can sometimes be transferred to the High Court or county court. Consult the legal adviser.

B[33.82]

Defendant already in prison. If a defendant, who has not paid part or the whole of a fine, is serving a sentence of imprisonment or is confined in a detention centre a committal warrant can be issued without any means inquiry taking place. The clerk will give notice to the debtor who may appear or make written representations.

B[33.83]

Fines Payment work. If, on a means inquiry, it is clear that the offender has very few, and is unlikely to acquire sufficient means, to pay a fine in the foreseeable future, the payment terms may be in the form of fines payment work, at he rate of £6 per hour. The court will make the order but the offender must see the fines officer to make arrangements for the fines payment work to take place. The scheme has been piloted in five areas namely Cambridgeshire, Cheshire, Cumbria, Devon and Cornwall and South Yorkshire. The pilot scheme will continue until March 2007 and then evaluated. The Home Office has produced guidance on fines payment work.

Fines imposed by Central Criminal Court and Crown Court

B[33.84]

These fines are payable to and enforceable by magistrates' courts.

B[33.85]

The whole fine or part of it can be remitted only with the consent of the higher court.

B[33.85A]

When calculating the period of default sentence under s 15 of the Criminal Justice (International Co-Operation) Act 1990, interest was to be included: *R (on the application of the CPS) v. City of London Magistrates' Court* [2007] All ER (D) 302 (Jul).

Defendants aged 18 to 21

B[33.86]–[33.90]

The above provisions can also be employed in respect of defendants in this age group except that an order of detention in default of payment should only be ordered if a supervision order has already been tried or the court is satisfied that a supervision order is either undesirable or impracticable. These considerations must be noted on any commitment warrant (*R v Oldham Justices, ex p Cawley* [1997] QB 1, [1996] 1 All ER 464 and *R v Stockport Justices, ex p Conlon* [1997] 2 All ER 204, 161 JP 81).

B[33.91]

If the court has available to it an attendance centre for defaulters to the age of 25, the court can send the defendant for up to 36 hours in all in default of payment.

B[33.92]

The clerk should be consulted as to the exact number of hours that the defendant should attend at the attendance centre.

Defendants aged 10 to 17

B[33.93]

Maximum fine. Children under 14, £250; young persons, 14 or over, £1,000, or, in either case the lesser sum applicable in the case of an adult (Powers of the Criminal Courts (Sentencing) Act 2000, s 135).

B[33.94]

Costs. The costs ordered must not exceed the amount of the fines unless a parent or guardian is ordered to pay.

B[33.95]

Parental liability to pay. The child's parent or guardian must be ordered to pay the fine and costs unless he cannot be found or the court considers it would be unreasonable to order him to pay. In the case of a young person the court has a power to order the parent to pay. If the parent or guardian does not pay, enforcement takes place in the adult court as described at B[33.7]–B[33.10].

Enforcement

B[33.96]

The power to make a fines supervision order or an attachment of earnings order is available in the case of juveniles. In addition, where the court is satisfied that the juvenile has had the money to pay but has refused or neglected to pay it may make an order requiring:

(a)   the parent to enter a recognisance to ensure that the defaulter pays the fine or balance; or

(b)   the court may transfer the debt to the parent in which case further enforcement, if necessary, would be taken as if the fine has been imposed on that parent.

B[33.97]

The parent must, according to the statute, consent before an order may be made for him to enter into a recognisance. The parent's consent is not required for the responsibility for the fine to be transferred to him provided the court is satisfied in all the circumstances that it is reasonable to make the order.

B[33.98]

If an attendance centre is available for persons of the debtor's class or description, he may be ordered to attend, up to the age of 25 years.

B[33.99]

The powers mentioned under this heading must be exercised after a means inquiry. An order transferring the debt to the parent may be made in his absence provided he has been given adequate notice of the proceedings; if he is present, he must be given the opportunity of speaking to the court before such an order is made.

B[33A]

Assessment of Fines: Sentencing Process

Sentencing guidelines

B[33A.1]

Assessment of fines

1. DECIDE THAT A FINE IS APPROPRIATE
2. OFFENCE SERIOUSNESS **A. IDENTIFY THE APPROPRIATE STARTING POINT** In the offence guidelines, the starting point is identified as band A, B or C Each fine band provides a **starting point** and a **range** related to the **seriousness** of the offence expressed as a proportion of the offender's **relevant weekly income** – see B[33.16].
2. OFFENCE SERIOUSNESS **B. CONSIDER THE EFFECT OF AGGRAVATING AND MITIGATING FACTORS** **Move up or down from the starting point** to reflect aggravating or mitigating factors that affect the **seriousness** of the offence – this will usually be within the indicated range for the fine band but the court is not precluded from going outside the range where the facts justify it.
3. CONSIDER OFFENDER MITIGATION The court may consider it appropriate to make a further adjustment to the starting point in the light of any matters of offender mitigation.
4. FORM A VIEW OF THE POSITION OF THE OFFENCE WITHIN THE RANGE FOR THE FINE BAND THEN TAKE INTO ACCOUNT THE OFFENDER'S FINANCIAL CIRCUMSTANCES Require the offender to provide a statement of **financial circumstances**. Obtain further information through questioning if necessary. Failure to provide the information when required is an offence. The provision of financial information does not affect the seriousness of the offence or, therefore, the position of the offence within the range for the applicable fine band. The initial consideration for the assessment of the fine is the offender's **relevant weekly income** – see B[33.17]. However, the court must take account of the offender's financial circumstances more broadly. These may have the effect of increasing or reducing the amount of the fine – see B[33.18]–B[33.23]. Where the court has insufficient information to make a proper determination of the offender's financial circumstances, it may make such determination as it thinks fit – see B[33.18].
5. CONSIDER A REDUCTION FOR A GUILTY PLEA Reduce the fine by the appropriate proportion – see B[5.46].
6. CONSIDER ANCILLARY ORDERS, INCLUDING COMPENSATION

Must consider compensation in every case where the offending has resulted in personal injury, loss or damage – give reasons if order not made – see B[18].

7. CONSIDER A REDUCTION FOR A GUILTY PLEA

GIVE REASONS

The resulting fine must reflect the seriousness of the offence and must take into account the offender's financial circumstances

Consider the proposed total financial penalty, including compensation, victims surcharge and costs. Where there are insufficient resources to pay the total amount, the order of priority is compensation, surcharge, fine, costs.

Must give reasons for the sentence passed, including any ancillary orders.

Must state if the sentence has been reduced to reflect ca guilty plea; indicate what the sentence would otherwise have been.

Must make a collection order unless this would be impracticable or inappropriate – see B[33.38] onwards above.

B[34]

Deprivation of property and forfeiture

(Powers of Criminal Courts (Sentencing) Act 2000, s 143)

B[34.1]

Any court which has convicted a person of an offence and

(a)   is satisfied
    (a)   that any property
    (b)   which has been lawfully seized from him or was in his possession or under his control at the time when he was apprehended for the offence or when a summons in respect of it was issued
    (c)   has been used for the purposes of committing, or facilitating the commission of any offence or was intended to be used for that purpose

or

(b)   the offence (or an offence taken into consideration) consists of unlawful possession of property in the circumstances of (ii) above

may make an order to deprive him of that property.

B[34.2]

Property. Does not include land. For applications under the Proceeds of Crime Act 2002 see **M[3.2]**.

B[34.3]

Possession. Usually means physical possession but can include a legal right to possession. If there is any dispute the legal adviser should be consulted.

B[34.4]

Facilitating. This includes the taking of any steps after the offence has been committed to dispose of property which is the subject of the crime or to avoid apprehension or detection. The property need not have been used personally by the defendant provided he intended it be used for criminal purposes, even by another.

B[34.5]

The effect of an order. The accused is deprived of his rights in the property which passes into the possession of the police. Accordingly, the true owner retained the full rights including a right to possession. The owner had a right to bring civil proceedings for conversion. The orders under PCCSA 2000, s 143 made by the magistrates' court provided no defence to the police to that right, unless possibly there was a public policy defence (*Chief Constable of Merseyside Police v Owens* [2012] EWHC 1515 (Admin), 176 CL&J 353 considered): *O'Leary International Ltd v Chief Constable of North Wales and CPS* [2012] EWHC 1516 (Admin), 176 JP 514, 176 CL&J 370.

The provisions of the Police Property Act 1897 (at **A[66]**) apply and a person may claim the property provided that he satisfies the court that either:

(a) he had not consented to the offender having possession; or
(b) he did not know, and had no reason to suspect, that the property was likely to be used for the purpose of committing an offence.

B[34.6]

If no successful claim is made the property will be sold and the proceeds disposed of in the same way as described at **A[66]**.

B[34.7]

Sentencing. The court may make an order under this section in respect of the property whether or not it also deals with the offender in respect of the offence in any other way, and may combine the making of the order with an absolute or conditional discharge.

B[34.8]

Under previous legislation it was stated that an order depriving a defendant of property should not be made for the purpose of realising assets to pay fines or compensation (*R v Kingston-upon-Hull Stipendiary Magistrates, ex p Hartung* [1981] RTR 262, 72 Cr App Rep 26).

B[34.9]

In considering whether to make a deprivation order the court shall have regard:

(a) to the value of the property; and
(b) to the likely financial and other effects on the offender of the making of the order (together with any other order the court is contemplating) (see *Trans Berckx BVBA v North Avon Magistrates' Court* [2011] EWHC 2605 (Admin), DC);
(c) any representations of the parties (*R v Ball* [2002] EWCA Crim 2777, [2003] 2 Cr App Rep (S) 92).

B[34.10]–[34.15]

But where the offence has resulted in a person suffering personal injury, loss or damage and the court has not been able to make a compensation order because of the defendant's lack of means, the proceeds of sale resulting from a deprivation order may be used for compensation.

B[34.16]

This order only takes effect after a period of six months in order to allow a person to make a claim under the Police Property Act 1897.

B[34.17]

Motor vehicles. Where a person has committed an offence under the Road Traffic Act 1988 which is imprisonable, eg driving with excess alcohol or whilst disqualified, the Road Traffic Act 1991 provides that the vehicle concerned is to be regarded as used for the purpose of committing the offence. Accordingly, the offender runs the risk of the court, after considering all relevant factors, depriving him of his vehicle. The significant use of a motor vehicle (manoeuvring to strike and injure a victim) justified the forfeiture of a motor car in *R v Norman* [2007] EWCA Crim 624.

B[34.18]

Disqualification for any offence: See C[5.45].

B[34.19]

Other provisions for forfeiture. Formerly the provisions described here were confined to offences punishable with at least 2 years' imprisonment, but now they are available without regard to maximum penalty and so will overlap with some existing forfeiture powers, eg forfeiture of controlled drugs and firearms and the Customs and Excise Management Act 1979. See for example *Customs and Excise Comrs v Newbury* [2003] EWHC 702 (Admin), [2003] 2 All ER 964.

B[35]

Guardianship order
(Mental Health Act 1983, s 37)

Limitations

B[35.1]
Offence must be punishable in the case of an adult with imprisonment, even though the offender may be immune from imprisonment.

B[35.2]
Two medical reports must be received indicating that the offender is suffering from one of four specified illnesses.

B[35.3]
The minimum age for a guardianship order is ten.

B[35.4]
Court must be of opinion (which it will usually form from the contents of the medical reports and a consideration of the circumstances of the offence) that a guardianship order is the most suitable method of dealing with the offender.

B[35.5]
Court must also be satisfied that arrangements have been made for a guardian to take care of the patient.

Ancillary orders

B[35.6]
Compensation at **B[18]**

Costs at **B[20]**

Disqualification at **C[5]**

Endorsement at **C[5]**

Deprivation of property and forfeiture at **B[34]**

Restitution at **B[39]**

B[35.7]
Period of order. This is an indeterminate order but the patient's condition is reviewed periodically by the medical authorities.

General considerations

B[35.8]

Medical evidence. The evidence can be two written reports by the doctors who made the examination, but the defendant has the right to insist that the doctors be present in court so that he can cross-examine them, and if the written reports only are before the court, then the defendant must be asked if he is agreeable to the court acting on those written reports.

B[35.9]

Copies of the doctors' reports must be given to the defendant's advocate. If the defendant is not represented the substance of the reports should be explained to the defendant.

B[35.10]–[35.15]

The defendant has the right to call his own medical evidence to rebut all or any part of the two reports.

B[35.16]

The court can require the personal appearance of the doctors.

B[35.17]

Effect of guardianship order. Once the guardianship order has been made the defendant is in effect handed over as a mental patient to the mental health authorities and the court has no more powers over the defendant and cannot stipulate what happens later. Thus, there can be no restriction order, and the court cannot stipulate the length of the guardianship order. The guardian will be a social worker or person approved by the local authority.

B[35.18]

Normally it will lapse after six months, but the mental specialists can recommend an extension when it will be extended for a further six months. After that the order can be extended for one-year periods or until the mental health authorities consider it safe to grant the defendant a discharge.

B[35.19]

As the defendant has now become a patient and not a prisoner his discharge from guardianship can be made on the advice of the mental specialist in charge of his case.

B[35.20]

The defendant need not wait for the mental specialist to act, but can apply for his discharge at any time during the first six months of the guardianship order or on any occasion when the order is renewed.

B[35.21]

The defendant's nearest relative can make application once a year to the

Mental Health Review Tribunal for his release.

B[36]

Hospital order

(Mental Health Act 1983, s 37)

Criteria

B[36.1]

These are as follows:

(a) defendant must have been convicted of an imprisonable offence, or (in certain circumstances) is proved to have committed an act which would amount to such an offence in the case of a normal person; see *R (on the application of Bartram) v Southend Magistrates' Court* [2004] All ER (D) 326 (Oct), DC for some of the procedural difficulties on fitness to plead

(b) court must be satisfied on written or oral evidence of two registered doctors that the defendant suffers from:
   (i) mental illness;
   (ii) psychopathic disorder;
   (iii) severe mental impairment; or
   (iv) mental impairment;

(c) the mental disorder is of a nature or degree that makes it appropriate for him to be detained in a hospital;

(d) (psychopathic disorder or mental impairment) such treatment is likely to alleviate or prevent a deterioration of his condition;

(e) the court is of the opinion having regard to all the circumstances including the nature of the offence and the character and antecedents of the offender and other available methods of dealing with him, that a hospital order is the most suitable means of dealing with him;

(f) justices have no jurisdiction to make a hospital order in respect of a defendant charged with an offence triable only on indictment (*R v Chippenham Magistrates' Court, ex p Thompson* (1995) 160 JP 207).

General considerations

B[36.2]

Legal representation should be offered to the defendant, or he should be recommended to consult a solicitor if the court is considering a hospital order.

In limited circumstances it is open to a defendant tried in a magistrates' court to plead **insanity**. There are limits on the availability of this defence. For a review of the authorities and procedures see *R (on the application of Singh) v Stratford Magistrates' Court* [2006] EWHC 1582 (Admin). The judgment also discusses the nature and limitations of the availability of an order under s 37 MHA 1983. It is advisable to consult the legal adviser.

B[36.3]

Medical reports. The court must obtain reports from two doctors, one of whom must be an approved mental specialist, certifying that the defendant is suffering from some form of mental disorder which warrants detention in hospital for mental treatment. The court can, with the consent of the defendant, act on the two written mental reports. The defendant has the right to insist that the doctors attend court so that they can be cross-examined, and he is also entitled to bring his own medical evidence to rebut the reports. The court can also require that the doctors attend in person.

B[36.4]

If written reports are used copies must be given to the defendant's advocate. If the defendant is not represented then the court should explain to the defendant the substance of the reports.

B[36.5]

Before announcing that a hospital order is being made the court should ensure that a vacancy in a mental hospital has definitely been arranged; if it has not, consult the clerk. An adjournment may be necessary. Alternatively a hospital order may be possible with the defendant's date of admission deferred for up to 28 days.

B[36.6]

Effect of a hospital order. The court does not fix the period that the defendant has to stay in hospital. The date of his release will be decided by the hospital authorities.

B[36.7]

Normally the hospital order lapses after six months but it can be renewed for a further six months on the recommendation of the mental specialist in charge of the case, and thereafter the order can be renewed for one-yearly periods. The procedure is that the responsible mental specialist examines the patient and sends a report to the mental health authorities, which can be the hospital managers, who may then act on the recommendation to retain or discharge the patient. Thus the patient can be discharged at any time without reference back to the sentencing court.

B[36.8]

The defendant, once a mental patient, can apply for his discharge at any time after the first six months of the order or whenever it is proposed to extend the order. For these reasons the order is in the discretion of the court and custody may still be dictated by public policy considerations (*R v Nafel* (2004)).

B[36.9]

The defendant's nearest relative can apply for his discharge once a year to the Mental Health Review Tribunal.

B[36.10]–[36.15]

Including a restriction clause in a hospital order (Mental Health Act 1983, s 41). If the defendant is 14 or more and was convicted (as opposed to having 'done the act'), and the magistrates consider a court restriction should be imposed on his release, he can be committed to the Crown Court for sentence pursuant to PCC(S)A 2000, s 3. [**It would appear that this power will no longer be available on or after a date to be appointed unless the committal for sentence is made immediately after the entering of a plea or the offence is a specified offence and the defendant is committed for sentence on the basis that he is a dangerous offender: see **B[16]**]).

B[36.16]

The Crown Court can make a hospital order, and include in it a restriction upon the date of release either for a specified period of time or indefinitely.

B[36.17]

The magistrates can commit the defendant to prison pending his appearance at the Crown Court or, if satisfied that a vacancy is available at a mental hospital, can order him to be detained there pending his appearance at the Crown Court.

B[36.18]

If the Crown Court includes a restriction clause the defendant cannot be discharged by the mental specialist or allowed out of the specified hospital without the consent of the Home Secretary.

B[36.19]

The Home Secretary may at any time refer the case to a Mental Health Review Tribunal for their advice, but does not have to accept the advice if he considers that discharge of the patient is not in the public interest.

B[36.20]

If the Home Secretary does decide that the patient should be discharged from the mental hospital, he has powers to impose conditions for the discharge such as the place of residence, a scheme of supervision and the liability to recall if a lapse occurs.

B[36.21]

Remand for report on accused's mental condition (s 35). Where a doctor satisfies the court that there is reason to suspect that the accused suffers from one or other of several mental disorders and

(a)   the accused has been convicted of an offence punishable on summary conviction with imprisonment or 'did the act' or has consented to this course of action; and
(b)   it is otherwise impracticable to obtain medical reports; and
(c)   arrangements have been made for his reception into a hospital;

the court may remand the accused in a hospital for up to 28 days. There may be further such remands for a total period of up to 12 weeks.

Interim hospital order (s 38)

B[36.22]

Where:

(a)   an accused has been convicted of an offence punishable with imprisonment; and

(b)   the court is satisfied on the evidence (written or oral) of two doctors that he is suffering from one of several mental disorders and it may be appropriate to make a hospital order; and

(c)   arrangements have been made for his reception into a hospital;

the court may make an interim hospital order for up to 12 weeks initially before finally passing sentence. An interim hospital order may be further renewed for up to 28 days at a time subject to a total period of six months before sentence is imposed.

B[37]

Imprisonment
(Powers of Criminal Courts (Sentencing) Act 2000, s 78**)

Limitations

B[37.1]

(a) **Imprisonable offence.**

B[37.2]

(b) **Presence of offender.** Imprisonment may only be imposed in the presence of the defendant.

B[37.3]

(c) **Age limit.** Defendant must be 21 or over**. For offenders under 21 the appropriate custodial sentence would be detention in a young offender institution**.

B[37.4]

Criteria for imposing a custodial sentence. The court must be of the opinion

(a)   that the offence, or the combination of the offence and other offences associated with it was so serious that neither a fine nor a community sentence can be justified; or

B[37.5]

Other circumstances in which custody may be imposed. Nothing in paragraph (a) above prevents the court imposing a custodial sentence on an offender who refuses to consent to a community sentence proposed by the court which requires his consent. A court may also impose custody for a wilful and persistent breach of a community order.

B[37.6]

So serious. Courts should always bear in mind that criminal sentences were in almost every case intended to protect the public whether by punishing the offender or reforming him, or deterring him and others, or all of those things. The sentence imposed should be no longer than is commensurate with the seriousness of the offence (Criminal Justice Act 2003, s 153). The court must take account of all the information about the circumstances of the offence including any aggravating or mitigating factors as is available to it.

In *R v Mills* [2002] EWCA Crim 26 [2002] 2 Cr App Rep (S) 51, the Lord Chief Justice said that imprisonment was often unnecessary for non-violent crimes of dishonesty committed by mothers caring for young families. In *R v Kefford* [2002] EWCA Crim 519, [2002] Crim LR 432 this principle is extended to those persons with no previous convictions convicted of economic crimes.

B[37.7]–[37.15]

Associated offence. An offence of which the offender has been convicted in the same proceedings or for which he is sentenced at the same time, or an offence taken into consideration.

B[37.16]

Pre-sentence report. A magistrates' court, unless it considers it unnecessary to do so, must obtain and consider a pre-sentence report before forming an opinion on:

(a)   whether the offence etc was so serious;
(b)   the length of term commensurate with the offence.

In all cases where a court is contemplating sentencing a defendant to prison for the first time, other than a very short period, it should be the inevitable practice that a pre-sentence report is obtained (*R v Gillette* (1999) Times, 3 December, CA).

B[37.17]

Failure to obtain pre-sentence report. Does not invalidate the sentence but the appeal court must obtain and consider such a report if the court below was not justified in forming the opinion that a report was not necessary (Criminal Justice Act 2003, s 156).

B[37.18]

Mentally disordered offender. Where an offender is or appears to be mentally disordered, ie suffering from a mental disorder within the meaning of the Mental Health Act 1983, the court must additionally obtain and consider a medical report before passing a custodial sentence unless the court considers it unnecessary to do so. The court must take any such information into account and consider the likely effect of any custodial sentence on his condition and any treatment for it. Failure to obtain a medical report does not invalidate any sentence but one must be obtained and considered by an appeal court (Criminal Justice Act 2003, s 157).

B[37.19]

Legal representation. The offender, who has not previously been imprisoned, must first be given the opportunity to be legally represented unless he has been refused legal aid for financial reasons. Note the requirement is not that he should be represented but that he should have the opportunity to be.

Reasons for decisions

B[37.20]

It is the duty of the court to state in open court that it is of the opinion that either or both of paragraph B[37.4] and B[37.2] above apply and why it is of that opinion and in all cases (including where a custodial sentence has been imposed following the offender's refusal to comply with a proposed requirement in a community sentence) explain to the offender in open court and in ordinary language why it is passing a custodial sentence on him or, if applicable, why imprisonment is for a longer term than would normally be commensurate with the seriousness of the offence.

B[37.21]

Suspended sentences. All these limitations apply equally to suspended sentences.

General considerations

B[37.22]

Consecutive sentences. If the defendant is sentenced to immediate or suspended imprisonment on each of two or more offences the terms will run concurrently unless the court orders they are to run consecutively. Consecutively means that one term of imprisonment follows another.

B[37.23]

When a magistrates' court sentences an offender for two or more offences it may order that one sentence runs consecutively to the other. In addition (when sentencing for one or more offences) the court may order that a term of imprisonment shall be consecutive to a term already being served by the defendant. In such a case the term imposed should be stated to be consecutive to the total period to which the defendant is subject.

B[37.24]

The total period of two or more consecutive sentences imposed on the same occasion by a magistrates' court must not exceed 6 months, unless either two or more of the offences are triable either way, when the total period may not exceed 12 months. If the defendant is convicted of two offences, the former being an offence triable either way and the latter which is purely summary, the maximum total remains as 6 months. If the court orders a suspended prison sentence to take effect, it can order that sentence to take effect consecutively to a period of imprisonment for the later offence, even though the total period will exceed the above limits. When a previously suspended sentence is ordered to be served it should normally be made consecutive to a sentence imposed for the later offence. Minimum sentence is 14 days if the sentence is suspended.

B[37.25]–[37.30]

Where several offences arise out of one incident consecutive sentences should not be imposed but the incident should be looked at as a whole and one appropriate period fixed. The same principle would apply to a series of offences committed against the same person over a relatively short period, eg an employee who falsifies a weekly claim for expenses.

B[37.31]

Consecutive sentences are appropriate where, although there is a single incident, there is more than one offence but they do not arise as a matter of course from the principle offence. For example, the burglar who attacks a householder who discovers him, or an assault on a police officer effecting an arrest for another offence. Offences committed on bail should normally attract a consecutive sentence where imprisonment is appropriate as offending on bail is an aggravating factor.

B[37.32]

When consecutive sentences are imposed the court should pay particular regard to the total period and reduce it if it is excessive; this is especially the rule to follow with young offenders and those receiving a first custodial sentence. One method of adjusting the total period in such cases is to consider concurrent rather than consecutive sentences.

B[37.33]

Multiple offences. When sentencing a defendant for several offences it is best to refer to the nature of each offence and the sentence and to state the total time to be served. To say 'For the first offence you will go to prison for two months, for the second two months consecutive, for the third two months concurrent . . . ' can be quite meaningless. Some chairmen prefer to begin with what is perhaps the most important aspect of the sentence first: 'You will go to prison for a total of 6 months. That is made up of two months for stealing the watch, a further two months for stealing the camera . . . etc.'

B[37.34]

When consecutive sentences are being considered the total period should be reviewed and reduced if it is excessive.

B[37.35]

Period of imprisonment. Great care must be exercised in determining the period of imprisonment, especially if it is to be suspended. The length of a custodial sentence must not exceed a term justified by the seriousness of the offence(s) and where there is appropriate mitigation, may be shorter.

B[37.36]

Magistrates' courts tend to consider sentences in units of months and the commonest terms are 3, 6 (and where appropriate) 9 and 12 months. It should be remembered that there is a complete discretion within the range available for a particular offence. It may be that for some offenders receiving a custodial sentence for the first time, a sentence of 7 or 14 days would be a salutary lesson, but with no other sentencing objective.

B[37.37]

Magistrates should reserve the maximum period available for an offence for those cases which are the worst type of case they would deal with.

B[37.38]

Offences of attempt will not usually attract the same period as would the completed offence.

B[37.39]

Time spent in custody on remand will be deducted from the sentence by the court, announced in open court and recorded on the warrant and in the register.

B[37.40]–[37.45]

Suspended sentences (Criminal Justice Act 2003, s 189).

If the court imposes a term of imprisonment between 14 days (21 days for offenders aged 18–20 years) and six months it may suspend the sentence for between 6 months and two years (the "operational period"). Where the court imposes two or more sentences to be served consecutively, the power to suspend the sentence is not available in relation to any of them unless the aggregate term of them does not exceed six months (CJA 2003, s 189 (2) as amended by art 2(2)(b) of the CJA 2003 (Sentencing) (Transitory Provisions) Order 2005).

The above provisions must be read in the light of the Magistrates' Courts Act 1980, s 133 as amended, which permits consecutive custodial terms totalling 12 months in relation to two or more offences triable either way. In this case a sentence of custody means a sentence of imprisonment or detention in a young offender institution.

B[37.46]

When the court suspends a sentence, it must [*may] impose one or more requirements for the offender to undertake in the community. The requirements are identical to those available for community orders.

If the offender **fails** to comply with a community requirement or commits a further offence, the court must either activate the suspended sentence in full or in part unless it is unjust to do so; or amend the order so as to:

(a)   extend the period during which the offender is subject to community requirements;
(b)   make the community requirements more onerous;
(c)   may order the offender to pay a fine not exceeding £2,500*; or
(d)   extend the operational period (CJA 2003, Sch 12, para 8).

*Available once s 69 of LASPOA 2012 is brought into force.

If the suspended sentence was imposed by the **Crown Court**, magistrates should consult their legal adviser. The courses open to the justices may vary according to whether the breach is by reason of re-offending or by breaching the terms of the community requirements).

NB: In *West Yorkshire Probation Service v Cruickshanks* [2010] EWHC 615 (Admin), 174 JP 305 it was held that the Probation Service could not enforce an unpaid work requirement under a suspended sentence order following expiration of the operational period of the order. This means that the Probation Service should be alive to laying breaches during the currency of the order. Levenson LJ, who gave the judgment of the court was also of the view that there was no power to extend the operational period once it had expired.

B[37.47]–[37.49]

There are many similarities between suspended sentences and community orders; requirements can be imposed on the offender and the court can respond to breach by sending him or her to custody. The crucial difference is that a suspended sentence is a custodial sentence; it may be imposed **only** where the court is satisfied that the custodial threshold has been passed and that it is not appropriate to impose a community order, fine or other non-custodial disposal.

A further difference is the approach to any breach; while sentencing for breach of a community order, the primary objective is to ensure that the requirements of the order are complied with. When responding to breach of a suspended sentence, the **statutory presumption** is that the custodial sentence will be activated.

In *R v Levesconte* [2011] EWCA Crim 2754, [2012] 2 Cr App Rep (S) 80, 176 JP 204 it was held that the sentencer was not entitled to treat the fact that the offence was committed during the operational period of the suspended sentence as a factor justifying the increase of the second sentence, not at least in circumstances where the suspended sentence was activated in full. To take that factor into account again was to increase the sentence referable to that fact beyond the maximum for which the defendant had been at risk. The court recognised that the same argument may not apply where the suspended sentence is not fully implemented. The decision in *Levesconte* misconstrues s 143(2) of the CJA 2003. A strict application of its principles can lead to the same overall length of sentence being imposed for either the activation of a suspended sentence in full or in part.

B[37.50]

Detailed guidance regarding suspended sentence and the appropriate response to breaches is set out in the Sentencing Guidelines Council guideline *New Sentences: Criminal Justice Act 2003*. The guideline emphasises that:

- a custodial sentence that is suspended should be for the same term that would have applied if the sentence was to be served immediately;
- the time for which a sentence is suspended should reflect the length of the sentence; up to 12 months might normally be appropriate for a suspended sentence of up to 6 months;
- the imposition of a custodial sentence is both punishment and a deterrent; to ensure that the overall terms of the sentence are commensurate with offence seriousness, requirements imposed as part of the sentence should generally be less onerous than if a custodial order had been imposed;

- a court wishing to impose onerous or intensive requirements should reconsider whether a community sentence might be more appropriate (refer to section **B[17]**);

- where an offender has breached a suspended sentence, there is a presumption that the suspended custodial term will be activated in full or in part. Relevant considerations will include the extent to which (if any) the offender complied with the requirements, and the circumstances of the breach;

- when the court imposes a suspended sentence, it may also order that the sentence be reviewed periodically at a review hearing (CJA 2003, s 191).

In *R v Finn* [2012] EWCA Crim 881, the 29 year old appellant had 36 convictions for 86 different offences. In February 2010 he was sentenced to 9 months' imprisonment, suspended for two years, for one offence of affray and one offence of possession of a bladed article. He was sentenced to an 18-month supervision order with an unpaid work requirement of 140 hours.

In January 2012, he was sentenced to six months' imprisonment for one offence of shop theft committed in November 2011. In addition, on that occasion the Recorder activated the full nine month suspended sentence, making a total sentence of 15 months. He appealed against the activation of all nine months of the suspended sentence. The Court of Appeal held:

'In the circumstances of this particular case, we do not believe that the judge erred in principle in concluding that it was not unjust to impose the suspended sentence in full. We recognise that some judges might have given the appellant modest credit for the unpaid work he had carried out, but that is not the test. A suspended sentence order must be complied with in full; non-compliance risks activation of the suspended sentence in full. In those circumstances, a defendant such as the appellant in the present case, who does not comply with the terms of the suspended sentence order, only has himself to blame if non-compliance leads to activation of the suspended sentence in full.'

B[37.51]

Suspended sentence and fine. For many offences it is possible to impose a fine as well as a suspended term of imprisonment. Courts must consider a fine but care should be taken in deciding such matters. If the defendant pays the monetary part of the penalty and then after a further offence is ordered to serve the prison sentence he may feel that he has been sentenced twice for his offence. On the other hand, if he is given a suspended sentence and avoids conviction during the operational period he may feel he has got away with it. Some would argue that the court ordering the suspended sentence to take effect would reduce the period because the monetary penalty had been paid, but this is neither a logical nor legally attractive argument. A careful explanation from the chairman emphasising the dual obligations of a single sentence is recommended. If the defendant defaults on the monetary part of his penalty he will be liable to imprisonment in accordance with the scale at B[33.40], not to the sentence which has been suspended.

Ancillary orders

B[37.52]
Compensation at B[18]

Costs at B[20]

Disqualification at C[5]

Endorsement at C[5]

Deprivation of property and forfeiture at B[34]

Restitution order at B[39]

Early release**

B[37.53]
A person subject to a term of imprisonment for less than 12 months will automatically be released after he has served one half of the term. In determining the period that has been served, time spent on remand in custody is to be taken into account. A person serving a term of 12 months and under 4 years is released on licence after serving one half of the original term and is unconditionally released after three-quarters of the sentence.

B[37.54]
Further offences under the Powers of the Criminal Courts (Sentencing) Act 2000, s 116. Where the offender commits an imprisonable offence before he would (but for his release) have served his sentence in full, the court which deals with him for the later offence may return him to custody for the whole or part of the period which begins with the making of the order of return, and is equal in length to the period between the date of commission of the new offence and the date of expiry of the original term. As a matter of good practice, the court should have precise information about the unexpired term of the offender's sentence before ordering a return to custody (*R v Divers* [1999] 2 Cr App Rep (S) 421, [1999] Crim LR 843, CA).

B[37.55]
When sentencing for the new offence, the court can take into account the fact that it was committed in breach of a home detention curfew as an aggravating factor. In *R v Teasdale* [2003] Crim LR 657, CA it is made clear that if a defendant commits an offence while on licence form prison and it is dealt with under s 116 of the PCC(S)A, the court should take into account any period of custody served following an administrative recall and deduct

it from the maximum available under s 116. If the defendant is a short term prisoner, a double period could be deducted as the defendant would be entitled to release half way through the term.

Section 116 of the Powers of the Criminal courts (Sentencing) Act 2000 continues to apply to sentences of less than 12 months or more than 12 months if committed before 4 April 2005. It does not apply to sentences of 12 months or more committed on or after 4 April 2005 leaving the court to sentence on the new offence alone. See SI 2005/950 art 2(1), Sch 1, para 42(1) and the Criminal Justice and Immigration Act 2008, Sch 26, paras 40 and 45.

B[37A]

Parenting order

(Crime and Disorder Act 1998, s 8 **as amended by CJA 2003, Sch 34)

Limitations

B[37A.1]

A parenting order is an order made against the parent or guardian of a child or young person:

- where the juvenile has been convicted of an offence, or
- where a court makes a child safety order, or
- where a court makes an anti-social behaviour order in respect of the juvenile, or
- where a court makes a sex offender order in respect of the juvenile, or
- where a conviction is recorded for failure to ensure regular school attendance or comply with a school attendance order, or
- where either a local authority or registered social landlord applies (from 29/6/07 – new sections 26A and 26B as added by the Police and Justice Act 2006).

In the case where the court intends to make a referral order and a parenting order it must first obtain a report as to why such an order is necessary. Parenting orders may also be made on complaints in respect of parents whose children have been excluded from school or have been referred to a Youth Offending Team because of anti social behaviour (Anti-Social Behaviour Act 2003, ss 20 and 26).

Applications are governed by rules of court, that is, the Magistrates' Courts (Parenting Orders) Rules 2004. Generally applications are brought by way of complaint. The said rules were amended from 1/9/07 by the Magistrates' Courts (Parenting Orders) (Amendment) Rules 2007 (SI 2007/2222).

Reasons

B[37A.2]

A court must make a parenting order in respect of a child or young person under the age of 16 who is convicted of an offence, or state in open court that a parenting order would not be desirable in the interests of preventing the commission of any further offence by the child or young person, and the reasons why. See also r 50.2 of the Criminal Procedure Rules 2010.

Consent

B[37A.3]

Consent of the parent/guardian is not required although many courts recognise the importance of a willing participation.

How to announce

B[37A.4]

We are satisfied that you need help and support in stopping [*child's name*] offending/anti-social behaviour. We are therefore making an order that you attend counselling and guidance sessions for [*a period not exceeding three months*]. The parenting order itself will last for [*a period not exceeding 12 months*] and during that time you must ensure that [*child's name*] [*insert requirements as appropriate*]. If you fail to comply with the order without reasonable excuse you may be guilty of an offence and fined up to £1,000.

General considerations

B[37A.5]

The order must require the parent or guardian to comply for a period not exceeding 12 months, with requirements that the court considers desirable in the interests of preventing the commission of further offences. The order must include a requirement to attend for a period, not exceeding three months, counselling or guidance sessions, unless the parent has previously been the subject of a parenting order. An order may include attendance at a residential course.

B[37A.6]

In the case of a juvenile under 16 years the court must make an order unless it can state reasons as to why it would not be desirable in the interests of preventing further offending by the juvenile.

Requirements

B[37A.7]

Additional requirements may be imposed to ensure or encourage the parent in preventing undesirable behaviour or offending such as:

(a)   making sure the juvenile does not have contact with co-defendants,
(b)   ensuring the juvenile is indoors between certain hours,
(c)   ensuring the juvenile is accompanied to school,
(d)   preventing the juvenile from visiting certain clubs or shopping centres.

Breach, variation and appeals

B[37A.8]

Breach is punishable by a fine not exceeding level 3

Variation and discharge are by way of complaint and governed by the Magistrates' Courts (Parenting Orders) Rules 2004

Appeals are governed by CDA 1998, s 10.

B[38]

Reparation order

(Powers of Criminal Courts (Sentencing) Act 2000, s 73)

Limitations

B[38.1]

May only be made in the Youth Court. The offence involved need not be serious enough to merit a community penalty.

B[38.2]

A reparation order may not be made if the court proposes to pass a custodial sentence or to make a youth rehabilitation order or a referral order.

Maximum periods

B[38.3]

A reparation order may not require the offender to work for more than 24 hours in all, or to make reparation to any person without the consent of that person.

B[38.4]

The reparation must be made within three months of the making of the order.

Reports

B[38.5]

The order does not require a full pre-sentence report (PSR) but before making a reparation order the court must obtain and consider a report indicating:

(a)   the type of work that is suitable for the offender; and
(b)   the attitude of the victim or victims to the requirements proposed to be included in the order.

General consideration

B[38.6]–[38.7]

A reparation order should be considered in less serious cases where the court wishes to

- take into account the feelings and wishes of the victims of crime; and

- prevent the young offender from committing further offences by confronting him with the consequences of his criminal behaviour, and allowing him to make some amends.

B[38.8]

Reparation can be in the form of direct or indirect reparation. The court will require a report setting out the reparation activities appropriate, such as writing a letter of apology or meeting the victim in person to apologise, repairing criminal damage for which the young person has been responsible, cleaning graffiti, and working on an environmental or other community project.

B[38.9]–[38.15]

Reparation carried out under a reparation order should be reparation in kind rather than financial reparation. Courts are already able to make a compensation order if they believe that financial reparation is appropriate.

Reasons

B[38.16]

The court must give reasons if it does not make an order where it has power to do so.

Breach of the order

B[38.17]

The responsible officer will instigate breach proceedings.

B[38.18]

The powers available to the court are:

(a) fine up to level 3 or,
(b) revoke and re-sentence for the original offence; or
(c) in the case of an order made by the Crown Court the magistrates can commit the offender on bail or in custody until he can be brought up or appear before the Crown Court.

B[39]–B[40]

Restitution order

(Powers of Criminal Courts (Sentencing) Act 2000, s 148)

B[39.1]

Where goods have been stolen and a person is convicted of any offence with reference to the theft (whether or not the stealing is the gist of his offence) or such an offence is taken into consideration the court may make a restitution order.

B[39.2]

Stolen includes obtaining by deception or blackmail.

B[39.3]

Restitution. The court:

(a)   may simply order the defendant to restore the goods to the person entitled to them whether or not any application is made for restitution; or

(b)   (where an application has been made) order the delivery over of any goods directly or indirectly representing the proceeds of the stolen goods; or

(c)   where money was taken from the possession of the accused on his apprehension, order its payment to the aggrieved,

but the beneficiary of the restitution must not receive more than the value of the original goods, a matter particularly to note when a combination of orders under (b) and (c) is made.

B[39.4]

Innocent purchasers. Sometimes the thief has sold the goods to an innocent purchaser. The goods will be restored to the owner but the court may also order the defendant to pay out of any monies in his possession when apprehended a sum to the innocent third party up to the amount he paid for the goods.

B[39.5]

Making a restitution order. Can be made on conviction of the offender whether or not sentencing is otherwise deferred.

B[39.6]

Evidence. In the opinion of the court the relevant facts must sufficiently appear from the evidence at the trial, or available documents (ie witness statements, depositions or other documents which were made for use and would have been admissible as evidence in the proceedings) together with any other admissions made.

B[41]–B[46]

Football banning orders

(Football Spectators Act 1989, ss 14 and 22 and Football (Disorder) Act 2000)

Criminal orders

B[41.1]

Where a person has been convicted of a relevant offence the court shall make a restriction order which requires him to report at a police station at the time that a designated football match is being played outside the United Kingdom, ie the order prohibits football hooligans from attending certain football matches played abroad.

B[41.2]

A Regulated football match is an association football match (whether in the United Kingdom or elsewhere) which is a prescribed match or a match of a prescribed description.

An association football match (outside the United Kingdom) described below is also a regulated football match for the purposes of Part II of the 1989 Act.

B[41.3]

Failure to comply with a banning order is a criminal offence triable only by magistrates with a maximum penalty on level 5 and six months' [**51 weeks] imprisonment.

B[41.4]

Relevant offence means:

(1) An offence in the Football Spectators Act 1989, Sch 1 which includes:

(a)   an offence under the Sporting Events (Control of Alcohol etc) Act 1985, s 2;

(b)   offences under the Public Order Act 1986, s 5 and Part III (racial hatred or sexual orientation);

(c)   an offence involving the threat or use of violence to a person or property: this includes an offence under Public Order Act 1986, s 4(1)(a) (*R v O' Keefe* (2004))

(d)   offences under the Football (Offences) Act 1991.

See Football Spectators Act 1989, Sch 1 (as amended) for an exhaustive list.

B[41.5]

Offences (b)–(d) must be committed during a period relevant to a designated football match at any premises while the accused was at, or was entering or leaving or trying to enter or leave, the premises. Therefore a defendant convicted of a public order offence on a train travelling away from a match he had been refused entry to was on a factual basis not related to a football match (*R v Smith* [2002] EWCA Crim 683, [2003] 1 Cr App Rep 212).

There is, however, no need to prove in a criminal case the civil requirements that the defendants caused or contributed to violence or disorder: s 14B (*R (on the application of Brown) v Inner London Crown Court* [2003] EWHC 3194 (Admin), [2003] All ER (D) 256 (Dec)).

B[41.6]

Relevant period. A period beginning 24 hours before the start of the match or, if earlier, 24 hours before the time it is advertised to start or the time at which spectators are first admitted to the premises, and ends 24 hours after the end of the match. Where a match is postponed or cancelled, the period includes the 24 hours before and 24 hours after the advertised start of the event. Regulated football match' for the purposes of these offences and those described below (a)–(d) is described above.

B[41.7]

(2) The following offences committed on a journey to or from a designated football match where the court makes a declaration that the offence related to football matches:

(a)   offences under (b) and (c) above;
(b)   drunkenness;
(c)   an offence under the Sporting Events (Control of Alcohol etc) Act 1985, s 1;
(d)   driving whilst unfit or over the prescribed limit of alcohol: Road Traffic Act 1988, ss 4 and 5

"Related to a football match" is to be given its ordinary meaning (*DPP v Beaumont* [2008] EWHC 523 (Admin); *R v Arbery and Mobley* [2008] EWCA Crim 702).

In *R v Pakes; R v Cartwright* [2010] EWCA Crim 2803, [2011] 2 Cr App Rep (S) 54, 175 JP 33, it was decided that the spark which caused the violence was related to football, that is a match between two Championship sides. From what occurred it was clear that there was hostility between two sets of rival supporters. It mattered not that one of the appellants did not go to an area of the West Midlands looking for trouble; the fact that he became caught up in the hostility which erupted between two rival sets of fans was sufficient.

Where violence arose out of a racial incident between two sets of football supporters outside a London pub and not in relation to the match or matches, the offences could not be said to be "football-related" and banning orders under s 14A were quashed on appeal (*R v Arbery and Mobley* supra; *R v Craig Mabee* [2007] EWCA Crim 3230).

B[41.8]

The prosecution must normally give five days' notice of its intention to seek a declaration that the offence related to football matches.

B[41.9]

(3) Offences under paras (a) and (c) committed on journeys to designated matches played outside the United Kingdom.

B[41.10]–[41.15]

(4) 'Corresponding offences' committed in countries designated from time to time by the Secretary of State.

B[41.16]

Therefore an order can be made in respect of a relevant offence whether committed in the United Kingdom or abroad, and the restriction order will apply to designated matches both domestically and internationally.

B[41.17]

Offences committed abroad. Where the relevant offence was committed abroad the court may, on information being laid, issue a summons or warrant to bring the offender before the court to consider whether to make a restriction order.

B[41.18]

Criterion. The court must make a football banning order in relation to the offender if satisfied that there are reasonable grounds to believe that it would help to prevent violence or disorder at or in connection with regulated football matches. If it does not make an order the court must state in open court its reasons for not being satisfied an order was required: see r 50.2 of the Criminal Procedure Rules 2011.

It is important that courts who are considering the rather complex provisions of the Football Spectators Act 1989 should have in mind the nature of the regime for which it provides. It should also address its mind to the differences between the consequences of a football banning order on the one hand and a prohibited activities requirement attached either to a suspended sentence or a community order on the other. They are not to be treated as equivalents.

There is some difference between the two kinds of order as to sanction. Disobedience to a football banning order is itself an offence, whereas disobedience to a prohibited activity requirement is not. But there is ample sanction for disobedience to a prohibited activity requirement because if it is attached to a suspended sentence the suspended sentence can be activated for breach, and if it is attached to a community order then on breach the court can re-sentence for the original offence and that may well involve loss of liberty. The principal difference between the two forms of order lies in the regime which exists. There is quite a sophisticated regime for the co-ordination of intelligence relating to those who are subject to football banning orders. Where such an order is in contemplation, courts who are addressing the test of whether making an order would help to prevent violence or disorder ought to have in mind the extent of the regime as well of course as its potentially draconian effect: *R v Boggild* [2011] EWCA Crim 1928, 175 CL&J 502, (2011) Times, 5 September.

In order for the court to make a 'declaration of relevance' an offence of affray had to be committed in the circumstances stipulated by Schedule 1. Further, there had to be reasonable grounds to believe that the making of a banning order would help to prevent violence or disorder at or in connection with any regulated football matches. In the present case, the court did not so determine and the evidence showed only that the affray arose out of the fact that the defendants were drunk, rather than that it had any connection to football: *R v Doyle; R v Wise; R v Wise* [2012] EWCA Crim 995, 176 JP 337, 176 CL&J 322.

B[41.19]

Procedure. Since 6 April 2007, amendments to the primary legislation have been made to allow a court to remand an offender where proceedings are adjourned under s 14A Football Spectators Act 1989.

May only be made in addition to a sentence (which includes a community rehabilitation order and an order for conditional or absolute discharge) imposed in respect of the offence of which the accused was convicted. The court must:

(a)   certify that the offence is a relevant offence where appropriate;
(b)   specify the police station in England and Wales at which the person must report initially;
(c)   explain to the person the effect of the order in ordinary language;
(d)   give a copy of the order to the defendant, and send copies to the Football Banning Orders Authority and the Chief Executive of the Football Association, the specified police station and, if appropriate, the relevant prison governor. The relevant authority is currently based at: UK Football Policing Unit, Football Banning Orders Authority, PO Box 51997, London, SW9 6TN. The Chief Executive of the Football Association is currently based at: Football Association, 25 Soho Square, London, W1D 4FA.

B[41.20]

The court must also impose conditions in the order including the surrender of the defendant's passport not more than five days before the date of each designated football match in respect of which the defendant is required to report unless there are exceptional circumstances for not doing so.

B[41.21]

Duration. Where the person receives an immediate prison sentence but not other forms of detention the mandatory period is a maximum of 10 years and a minimum of 6 years. In any other football case the maximum is 5 years and the minimum three years. In a non-football-related offence, the period is between two and three years.

B[41.22]

Effect. The person is under a duty to report initially to the police station specified in the order within five days of the making of the order and thereafter to report to a police station specified when notified by the Banning Orders Authority. Note a banning order is not a punishment for the purposes of ECHR Art 7 (*Gough v Chief Constable of Derbyshire* [2001] EWHC 554 (Admin), [2002] QB 459; affd sub nom *Gough v Chief Constable of Derbyshire Constabulary* [2002] EWCA Civ 351, [2002] 2 All ER 985).

B[41.22A]

Effect – enhanced obligations. Persons subject to a banning order made since 6 April 2007, are now subject to enhanced obligations to notify the enforcement authority, within 7 days, of certain changes. These changes include:

(a)   change of any name;
(b)   use of a name not previously disclosed;
(c)   change of address;
(d)   acquisition or change of a temporary address;
(e)   commencing an appeal or an application to terminate the order.

B[41.23]

Exemption may be granted from reporting in respect of a particular match either an application to the Banning Orders Authority or in cases of urgency to the police. Exemption might be granted, for example, to cover a stay in hospital or the funeral of a close relative.

B[41.24]

Application to terminate. The person subject to the order may apply to the court to terminate the order after two-thirds of the period determined has expired.

B[41.25]–[41.30]

The court will have regard to the person's character, his conduct since the order was made, the nature of the offence which led to it and any other circumstances of the case.

B[41.31]

Further application may not be made within six months of a refusal.

B[41.32]

Appeal is to the Crown Court against the making of a banning order or a refusal to award compensation (see below). Prosecutors can now appeal to the Crown Court against the refusal of a magistrates' court to make a banning order on conviction of a *"relevant offence"* (s 14A(5A) Football Spectators Act 1989). These relevant offences are listed in schedule 1 to the Football Spectators Act 1989.

B[41.33]

Civil applications. In addition to its imposition as a result of a football-related conviction, a banning order may be imposed by a magistrates' court in accordance with a civil procedure, following a complaint by the police. The requirement that applications by complaint could only be made by the Chief Constable of the area where the individual resides was removed by the Violent Crime Reduction Act 2006. Applications can be made by any Chief Constable including the Chief Constable of the British Transport Police and the Director of Public Prosecutions.

The Violent Crime Reduction Act 2006 removed the statutory time limit of 27 August 2007 for making an application on complaint for a football banning order on complaint under s 14B Football Spectators Act 1989. Also, the power of summary detention by a police constable (as distinct from arrest) under s 21A of the 1989 Act has been removed.

The court must be satisfied that the person who is the subject of the complaint has at any time caused or contributed to any violence or disorder in the United Kingdom or elsewhere, and that there are reasonable grounds to believe that making a banning order would help to prevent violence or disorder at or in connection with any regulated football matches. This is a civil order and not a sentence (*Gough v Chief Constable of Derbyshire* [2001] EWHC 554 (Admin), [2002] QB 459; affd sub nom *Gough v Chief Constable of Derbyshire Constabulary* [2002] EWCA Civ 351, [2002] 2 All ER 985).

B[41.34]

If, during a control period when international bans are activated, a police officer has reasonable grounds for suspecting that a person before him or her has caused or contributed to any violence or disorder in the United Kingdom or elsewhere, and for believing that imposing a banning order on that person would help to prevent violence or disorder at or in connection with any regulated football matches, the officer may, with the authorisation of an inspector of police, give the person a notice in writing requiring him or her to appear before a magistrates' court within 24 hours and in the meantime not to leave England and Wales. The magistrates' court will then treat the notice as an application for a banning order under the new civil procedure. Section 14B of the 1989 Act was further amended by the Violent Crime Reduction Act 2006 so that magistrates' Courts are now empowered to remand a respondent when adjourning proceedings on complaint.

B[41.35]

Appeal. The respondent may appeal to the Crown Court against the making by a magistrates' court of a banning order on complaint (s 14D Football Spectators Act 1989).

B[41.36]

Compensation Where a notice has been issued by a police officer under these powers and a court subsequently refuses to impose a banning order, the court may order compensation up to £5000 to be paid to that person out of central funds if it is satisfied that the notice should not have been given in the first place, that the person has suffered loss as a result of the notice, and that it is appropriate to order the payment of compensation in respect of that loss. There is no statutory definition of the word refuse and so presumably if the police seek to withdraw the proceedings the right to compensation is lost although the right to apply for legal costs remains.

B[41.37]

Length of order The minimum civil order has been altered by the Violent Crime Reduction Act 2006. The minimum order will last for three years and the maximum five years.

B[47]

Forfeiture or suspension of personal liquor licence
(Licensing Act 2003, s 129)

B[47.1]

Where an offender who holds a personal licence to supply alcohol is charged with a "relevant offence", he or she is required to produce the licence to the court, or inform the court of its existence, no later than his or her first court appearance.

"Relevant offences" are listed in Sch 4 of the Licensing Act 2003 and are set out below.

Where the offender is convicted the court may order forfeiture of the licence or suspend it for up to 6 months pursuant to s 129 (2) LA 2003. When deciding whether to order forfeiture or suspension, the court may take account of the offender's previous convictions for "relevant offences" (s 129 (3)).

Whether or not forfeiture or suspension is ordered, the court is required to notify the licensing authority of the offender's conviction and the sentence imposed.

B[47.2]

"Relevant offence"

These include:

- An offence under the Licensing Act 2003
- An offence under the Firearms Act 1968
- Theft – s 1 Theft Act 1968
- Burglary – s 9 Theft Act 1968
- Abstracting electricity – s 13 Theft Act 1968
- Handling stolen goods – s 22 Theft Act 1968
- Going equipped for theft etc – s 25 Theft Act 1968
- Production of a controlled drug – s 4(2) Misuse of Drugs Act 1971
- Supply of a controlled drug – s 4(3) Misuse of Drugs Act 1971
- Possession with intent to supply – s 5(3) Misuse of Drugs Act 1971
- Evasion of duty – s 170 Customs and Excise Management Act 1979 (except s 170(1)(a))
- Driving/attempting to drive while unfit through drink or drugs – s 4 RTA 1988
- In charge of a motor vehicle when unfit through drink or drugs – s 4 RTA 1988

- Driving/attempting to drive with excess alcohol – s 5 RTA 1988
- In charge of a vehicle with excess alcohol – s 5 RTA 1988
- Unauthorised use of a trade mark where the goods in question are or include alcohol – ss 92(1) and 92(2) Trade Marks Act 1994
- Sexual assault – s 3 SOA 2003
- Exploitation of prostitution – ss 52 and 53 SOA 2003
- Exposure – s 66 SOA 2003
- Voyeurism – s 67 SOA 2003
- A violent offence, being any offence which leads, or is intended to lead, to death or to physical injury

B[48]–B[49]

Referral order
(Powers of Criminal Courts (Sentencing) Act 2000, s 16)

Limitations

B[48.1]
Although an order can be made by an adult magistrates' court it is recommended that offenders aged 10–17 years should normally be remitted from a magistrates' court to the youth court to be dealt with, including the imposition of a referral order.

B[48.2]
Age limits – Person in respect of whom the order is made must be under 18.

B[48.3]
Maximum period – 12 months.

B[48.4]
Minimum period – 3 months.

B[48.5]
Consent – Consent of offender not required.

Ancillary orders

B[48.6]
Compensation at B[18]

Costs at B[20]

Disqualification at C[5]

Endorsement at C[5]

Deprivation of property and forfeiture at B[34]

Parenting order B[37A]

Restitution at B[39]

General considerations

B[48.7]
Where a youth aged 10–17 years is before a court for an offence where

neither the offence nor a connected offence is one for which the sentence is fixed by law eg murder; the court is not proposing to impose a custodial sentence or make a hospital order (within the meaning of the Mental Health Act 1983); and, the court is not proposing to discharge the youth absolutely *[or conditionally], if referral is available, the court must, if the compulsory referral conditions are satisfied, or may, if the discretionary referral conditions are satisfied, sentence the youth for the offence by ordering him to be referred to a youth offender panel.

*Words to be added by LASPOA 2012, s 79 when in force.

Referral is available within England and Wales following notification from the Secretary of State. The relevant youth offender panel will be located in the area in which the youth resides or will reside.

Connected offence. An offence is connected with another if the youth falls to be dealt with at the same time as he is dealt with for the other offence whether or not he is convicted of the offences at the same time by or before the same court.

Compulsory referral conditions. The offence is punishable with imprisonment and the youth pleaded guilty to the offence and any connected offence; and, the youth has never been convicted by or before a court in the UK of any offence other than the offence and any connected offence.

*Discretionary referral conditions.** The compulsory referral conditions do not apply; the offender pleaded guilty to at least one offence for which he is being dealt with; AND one of the three conditions outlined below apply:

(a)   the youth has never been convicted by or before a court in the UK of any offence other than the offence and any connected offence; or
(b)   has one previous conviction but did not then receive a referral order; or
(c)   the youth has been dealt with on one or more occasions by a court in the UK but has previously only once received a referral order; an appropriate officer recommends the youth as suitable for referral; and the court is satisfied there are exceptional circumstances which justify the making of a second referral order.

*To be amended by LASPOA 2012, s 709 when in force.

Previous conviction. This will include an absolute or conditional discharge or a binding over order.

Appropriate officer. A member of a youth offending team; an officer of a local probation board; or an officer of a provider of probation services.

Attendance of parent or guardian. On making a referral order, the court may order a parent or guardian (which includes a representative of a local authority where the youth is being looked after by that authority), to attend meetings of the youth offender panel.

Prohibited orders

B[48.8]

When a court makes a referral order it may not at the same time deal with the youth by:

* imposing a community sentence;
* imposing a fine;
* imposing a reparation order; or
* deferring sentence.

Variation and discharge

B[48.9]

Courts have a discretion to discharge referral orders early on application for good behaviour.

Likewise, courts have the option of extending the term of the referral order for up to three months, on application and, at the recommendation of the youth offender panel, eg, in cases of breach. Note the extension cannot exceed the overall maximum of 12 months.

Where an offender has been brought before the court for breach of a referral order the court may either: extend the period for the order as outlined immediately above; or, may revoke the referral order and deal with the offender for the original offence(s) in any manner, other than making a referral order, he could have been dealt with by the court which made the order.

When dealing with the youth, the court must have regard to:

(i)   the circumstances of his referral back to the court; and
(ii)   the extent of his compliance, if any, with the terms of his referral contract.

Appeal. On a breach, where the court revokes the referral order and deals with the youth for the original offence(s), he may appeal to the Crown Court against the sentence.

B[48.10]

Breach. The young offender may be referred back to the court for a revocation of the order if he fails to attend the panel, fails to agree a contract or fails to comply with the terms of the contract.

On receiving a report of a breach the court must summons or issue a warrant for the appearance of the juvenile.

On his appearance they must consider if the panel was right to refer the breach back. If they decide it was not then the order continues.

If a breach is proved the court has power to extend the period for compliance with the order or to revoke it and deal with the original offence in any way it could have done other than the making of a referral order. Any fresh sentence (other than an absolute discharge) has the effect of revoking the referral order.

There is also power to extend the period of the referral order for offences committed before and during the currency of the order. This may be done once only and must not extend the order beyond the 12 month maximum.

B[50]

The Youth Rehabilitation Order

Statutory considerations

B[50.1]

This order may only be imposed by the youth court or a Crown Court (see s 8 PCC (S) A 2000).

Before imposing a youth rehabilitation order (YRO) a youth court must have regard to:

- the seriousness of the offence;
- any order made must be proportionate to offence seriousness;
- the aim of preventing further offences;
- the welfare of the juvenile offender

Before imposing a YRO a youth court must have regard to the purposes of sentencing, that is:

- the punishment of offenders
- the reform and rehabilitation of offenders
- the protection of the public
- the making of reparation to persons affected by the offender's criminality

General considerations

B[50.2]

The offence or the combination of the offence and associated offences is serious enough to warrant a YRO. To be 'serious enough', as with adult offenders, the offence or offences must be punishable with imprisonment.

There is one exception to be found in CJA 2003 where an offender aged 16 or over is convicted of an offence not punishable with imprisonment, has three or more previous convictions dealt with by a fine since he attained 16 and it is in the interests of justice to impose a community penalty: s 151 CJA 2003. This provision, as amended by the CJ & IA 2008 has not yet been brought into force.

The court should obtain a pre-sentence report unless the court is of the opinion that it is unnecessary to obtain one (CJA 2003, s 156(4)), and in the case of a juvenile offender the court shall not form that opinion unless there is a previous pre-sentence report and the court has regard to the information in that report or, if there is more than one report, the most recent report (CJA 2003, s 156 (5)).

Any requirements to be imposed must be *compatible* with each other. The youth court must ensure, as far as is practicable, that any requirements imposed in the order avoid conflicting with the offender's religious beliefs or his ability to attend work, school or other educational establishment.

The length of the order may not last longer than three years by which time all requirements (see **B[50.4]** below) must have been complied with.

The order takes effect on the day after the order is made except where an offender is serving a detention and training order (DTO) sentence or is subject to supervision following release from a DTO when the court may order that the youth rehabilitation order takes effect from the expiry of the DTO or the supervision requirement.

A YRO may not be imposed when another YRO or a reparation order is already in force unless it proposes to revoke those earlier orders.

Generally is good practice to make <u>requirements</u> in orders to run concurrent to each other; fostering requirements (see **B[50.16]** below) may not be directed to run consecutively. Where the court makes a consecutive requirement, the number of hours, days or months specified may not exceed the specified statutory maximum and bearing in mind that a YRO may not last longer than three years.

The YRO and requirement(s) will identify a specified officer known as the 'responsible officer'. That is usually a member of a youth offending team, but it could be a social worker, a probation officer and in unusual cases an education welfare officer.

Specific requirements (Sch 1, Pt 1 CJ & IA 2008)

B[50.3]

A youth court may only impose a YRO with an *intensive supervision and surveillance requirement* and/or a *fostering requirement* if:

(a)   the offence or offences are punishable with imprisonment;

(b)   the offence or the combination of the offences associate with it are so serious that, but for these provisions, a custodial sentence would be appropriate, or if the offender is under 12 at the time of conviction, would have been appropriate if he had been aged 12 or more); and

(c)   if the offender was aged 12–15 years, he is a persistent offender.

A youth court may not include a *local authority residence requirement* or a *fostering requirement* in a YRO unless the offender is legally represented or funding by the Legal Services Commission has been withdrawn because of the offender's conduct; or, having been informed of his right to apply for such representation, has refused or failed to apply.

An *electronic monitoring requirement* may be added at the court's discretion but <u>must</u> be added where the court makes either a curfew or an exclusion requirement as part of a YRO.

YRO requirements (Sch 1, Pt 1 CJ & IA 2008)

B[50.4]

The details are to be found in Schedule 1 of the Act and the relevant paragraph to the Schedule is indicated below in each of the available requirements:

(1)   Intensive supervision and surveillance requirement
(2)   Activity requirement (paras 6–8)
(3)   Supervision requirement (para 9)
(4)   Unpaid work requirement for those aged 16–17 years when convicted (para 10)
(5)   Programme requirement (para 11)
(6)   Attendance centre requirement (para 12)
(7)   Prohibited activity requirement (para 13)
(8)   Curfew requirement (para 14)
(9)   Exclusion requirement (para 15)
(10)   Residence requirement (para 16)
(11)   Local authority residence requirement (paras 17 and 19)
(12)   Fostering requirement (paras 4, 18–19)
(13)   Mental health treatment requirement (paras 20–21)
(14)   Drug treatment/drug testing requirement (paras 22–23)
(15)   Intoxicating substance treatment requirement (para 24)
(16)   Education requirement (para 25)
(17)   Electronic monitoring requirement (para 26)

(1) Intensive supervision and surveillance requirement

B[50.5]

The order may be used for juveniles where the following criteria apply:

(a)   the offence or offences are punishable with imprisonment;
(b)   the offence or the combination of the offences associate with it are so serious that, but for these provisions, a custodial sentence would be appropriate, or if the offender is under 12 at the time of conviction, would have been appropriate if he had been aged 12 or more); and
(c)   if the offender was aged 12–15 years, he is a persistent offender.

The restrictions outlined above do not apply if the offender has failed to comply with an order for pre-sentence drug testing pursuant to s 161(2) of the CJA 2003.

The court may include one or more of the other requirements (with the exception of fostering) set out below subject to the caveat that the requirements must be proportionate to the seriousness of the offence or offences.

The court may in addition make an extended activity requirement of up to 180 days. If it does so it <u>must</u> also impose a supervision requirement with electronic monitoring.

Copies of the order must be served on the offender ant other person involved with the order: CJ & IA 2008, Sch 2, para 24.

(2) Activity requirement

B[50.6]

The offender must do any or all of the following:

(a)   participate, on such days as may be specified, in activities at the place or places specified by presenting himself at the place specified or to a specified person in accordance with instructions given by the responsible officer and comply with such instructions given by, or under the authority of, the person in charge of that activity;

(b)   participate in activity, or activities, specified in the order on such number of days so specified;

(c)   participate in one or more residential exercises for a continuous period or periods compromising such number of days as specified;

(d)   engage in activities in accordance with instructions of the responsible officer on such number of days as may be specified.

As far as requirement (c) above is concerned, the <u>consent</u> of a parent or guardian of the offender must be obtained.

Specified activities may include *reparation*, direct or indirect, or as directed by the responsible officer.

Before making an order the court should consult either an officer of the local probation board or a member of a youth offending team. The court must be satisfied that the activities to be specified can be made under arrangements that exist in the local justice area in which the offender resides and that it is feasible to secure compliance with those requirements. Where compliance with an activity involves the co-operation of a person other than the offender and/or the responsible officer, that person's consent must be obtained.

The aggregate number of days upon which a juvenile may be required to comply with directions must not exceed 90 unless the 'custody' criteria are satisfied (see B[50.3]) when the total number of days permitted is 180: CJ & IA 2008, s 1(4)(a)–(c).

(3) Supervision requirement

B[50.7]

When a youth court makes a supervision requirement the effect is to place the juvenile under the supervision of the responsible officer or another person determined by him for the relevant period. The "relevant period" for these purposes means the period for which the order remains in force i.e. for up to three years. The purpose of the requirement is to promote the offender's rehabilitation.

(4) Unpaid work requirement (16 and 17 year old offenders only)

B[50.8]

This is a requirement that the offender must perform unpaid work in accordance for the number of hours specified in the order, at such times as he may be instructed by the responsible officer. Unless revoked, an unpaid work requirement remains in force until the offender has completed the number of hours specified.

The number of hours which a person may be required to work under an unpaid work requirement must be specified in the relevant order and must be in the aggregate:

(a)   not less than 40, and
(b)   not more than 240.

The court may not impose an unpaid work requirement in respect of an offender unless after hearing (if the court thinks necessary) from an appropriate officer, the court is satisfied that the offender is a suitable person to perform work under such a requirement.

Where the court makes orders in respect of two or more offences of which the offender has been convicted on the same occasion and includes unpaid work requirements in each of them, the court may direct that the hours of work specified in any of those requirements is to be concurrent or consecutive. However the total number of hours must not exceed the maximum of 240 hours.

(5) Programme requirement

B[50.9]

This requirement involves the offender's participation in a systematic set of activities specified in the order, on such number of days as may be specified. The court may not include a programme requirement unless:

(a)   the proposed programme has been recommended to the court as being suitable for the offender by an officer of a local probation board or a youth offending team or a provider of probation services; and
(b)   the programme is available at the specified place.

Where compliance with an activity involves the co-operation of a person other than the offender and/or the responsible officer, that person's consent must be obtained.

The programme requirement means the offender must:

(a)   in accordance with instructions given by the responsible officer, participate in the programme at the place specified in the order on the number of days specified in the order; and
(b)   while at that place, comply with instructions given by, or under the authority of, the person in charge of the programme.

(6) Attendance centre requirement

B[50.10]

This is a requirement to attend at an attendance centre for any period on any occasion at the beginning of the period and, during that period, to engage in occupations, or receive instruction, under the supervision of and in accordance with instructions given by, or under the authority of the officer in charge of the centre.

The aggregate number of hours will depend on the age of the offender:

(a)   offender aged 16 or over at the time of conviction: not less than 12 and not more than 36 hours.
(b)   offender aged 14 or over but under 16 at the time of conviction: not less than 12 and not more than 24 hours
(c)   offender aged under 14 at the time of conviction: not more than 12 hours.

The court must have been notified of the availability of a centre for persons of the offender's age and sex. Regard must be paid to the accessibility of the centre to the offender.

(7) Prohibited activity requirement

B[50.11]

This requires the offender to refrain from participating in activities specified in the order on a day or days so specified <u>or</u> during a period so specified.

The court must first consult either a provider of probation services such as an officer of a local probation board or a member of a youth offending team. One requirement which may be included in an order is that the offender is not to possess, use or carry a firearm within the meaning of the Firearms Act 1968. It is recommended that the court should consult first with its legal adviser before including such a requirement.

(8) Curfew requirement

B[50.12]

A curfew requirement is a requirement that the offender must remain, for periods specified in the relevant order, at a place so specified. It may specify different places or different periods for different days, but may not specify periods which amount to less than two hours or more than *[sixteen hours] twelve hours in any one day.

The order may not exceed a period of *[12 months] <u>six months</u> beginning with the day on which it first takes effect. The court must also make an electronic monitoring requirement unless the court considers it inappropriate to do so in the particular circumstances of the case or the court is prevented from doing so eg it is not practicable to secure the co-operation of a person other than the offender: see CJ &IA 2008, Sch 1, para 26.

*Different maxima apply when LASPOA 2012, s 81 is brought into force.

Before making a relevant order imposing a curfew requirement, the court must obtain and consider information about the place proposed to be specified in the order (including information as to the attitude of persons likely to be affected by the enforced presence there of the offender).

(9) Exclusion requirement

B[50.13]

An exclusion requirement is a provision prohibiting the offender from entering a place named in the order for a specified period of not more than three months.

An exclusion requirement:

(a)   may provide for the prohibition to operate only during the periods specified in the order; and

(b)   may specify different places or areas for different periods or days.

The court must also make an electronic monitoring requirement unless the court considers it inappropriate to do so in the particular circumstances of the case or the court is prevented from doing so eg it is not practicable to secure the co-operation of a person other than the offender: see CJ & IA 2008, Sch 1, para 26.

(10) Residence requirement

B[50.14]

This requirement is only applicable to offenders aged 16 or over at the time of conviction.

Residence means that, during a period specified in the relevant order, the offender must reside with an individual or at a place specified in the order. If the court proposes to specify residence with a named individual, that person's consent must first be obtained.

If the order makes specific provision, a residence requirement does not prohibit the offender from residing, with the prior approval of the responsible officer, at a place other than that specified in the order.

Before making a YRO containing a residence requirement, the court must consider the home surroundings of the offender.

A court may not specify a hostel or other institution as the place where an offender must reside, except on the recommendation of an officer of a local probation board, or a provider of probation services, a local authority social worker or a member of a youth offending team.

(11) Local authority residence requirement

B[50.15]

Local authority residence means that, during a period specified in the relevant order, the offender must reside in accommodation provided by or on behalf of a local authority specified in the order.

The court must be satisfied that the behaviour which constituted the offence was due to a significant extent to the circumstances in which the offender was living, and that the imposition of such a requirement will assist in his rehabilitation.

The court must first consult with the local authority and a parent or guardian of the offender (unless it is not practicable to do so) and the local authority that is to receive the offender (if different). The order may stipulate that the offender is not to reside with a person specified in the order.

The order must specify the local authority in whose area the offender resides or is to reside.

Any period specified in the order as a period for which the offender must reside in accommodation provided by or on behalf of a local authority must not exceed six months, and it must not include any period after the offender attains 18 years of age.

A youth court may not include a *local authority residence requirement* in a YRO unless the offender is legally represented or funding by the Legal Services Commission has been withdrawn because of the offender's conduct; or, having been informed of his right to apply for such representation, has refused or failed to apply.

A local authority has power to place an offender with a local authority foster patent where a local authority residence requirement is imposed: CJ & IA 2008, Sch 2, Pt 2, para 18.

(12) Fostering requirement

B[50.16]

During a period specified in the relevant order, the offender must reside with a local authority foster parent.

The specified period of fostering must end no later 12 months beginning with the date on which the requirement takes effect but must not include any period after the offender has attained 18 years of age. An 18-month period may be substituted following breach proceedings: CJ & IA 2008, Sch 2, paras 8 and 16.

The requirement must specify the local authority that is to place the offender with a local authority foster parent under s 23(2)(a) of the Children Act 1989. The authority so specified must be the local authority in whose area the offender resides or is to reside.

If at any time during that period the responsible officer notifies the offender that no suitable local authority foster parent is available, and that he proposes or has applied for the revocation or amendment of the YRO, the fostering requirement is, until the determination of that application, to be taken as requiring the offender to reside in accommodation provided by or on behalf of the a local authority.

Such a requirement cannot be made unless the court has been notified by the Secretary of State that arrangements for placing the offender with a local authority foster parent are available in the relevant local authority area.

(13) Mental health treatment requirement

B[50.17]

This requires the offender to submit, during periods specified in the order, to treatment by or under the direction of a registered medical practitioner or a chartered psychologist (or both, for different periods) with a view to the improvement of the offender's mental condition.

The treatment required must be one of the following kinds of treatment as may be specified in the relevant order:

(a)   treatment as a resident patient in an independent hospital or care home within the meaning of the Care Standards Act 2000 or a hospital within the meaning of the Mental Health Act 1983, but not in hospital premises where high security psychiatric services within the meaning of that Act are provided;

(b)   treatment as a non-resident patient at such institution or place as may be specified in the order;

(c)   treatment by or under the direction of such registered medical practitioner or chartered psychologist (or both) as may be so specified;

The nature of the treatment may not be specified in the order except as mentioned in (a), (b) or (c) above.

A court may not by virtue of this section include a mental health treatment requirement in an order unless-

(a)   the court is satisfied, *[on the evidence of a registered medical practitioner approved for the purposes of s 12 of the Mental Health Act 1983], that the mental condition of the offender-
  (i)   is such as requires and may be susceptible to treatment, but
  (ii)   is not such as to warrant the making of a hospital order or guardianship order within the meaning **[the Mental Health Act 1983] of that Act;

(b)   the court is also satisfied that arrangements have been or can be made for the treatment intended to be specified in the order (including arrangements for the reception of the offender where he is to be required to submit to treatment as a resident patient); and

(c)   the offender has expressed his willingness to comply with such a requirement.

While the offender is under treatment as a resident patient in pursuance of a mental health requirement, his responsible officer shall carry out the supervision of the offender to such extent only as may be necessary for the purpose of the revocation or amendment of the order.

*[Note that sub-ss (2) and (3) of s 54 of the Mental Health Act 1983 have effect with respect to proof for the purposes of sub-s (3)(a) of an

offender's mental condition as they have effect with respect to proof of an offender's mental condition for the purposes of s 37(2)(a) of that Act.]

*All words in brackets to be deleted by LASPOA 2012, s 82 when in force.

**'Of that Act' replaced by the words in brackets when LASPOA 2012, s 82 is brought into force.

Mental health treatment at place other than that specified in order

B[50.18]

Where the medical practitioner or chartered psychologist, treating the offender in pursuance of a mental health treatment requirement, is of the opinion that part of the treatment can be better or more conveniently given in or at an institution or place which-

(a)   is not specified in the relevant order, and
(b)   is one in or at which the treatment of the offender will be given by or under the direction of a registered medical practitioner or chartered psychologist,

he may, with the consent of the offender, make arrangements for him to be treated accordingly.

These arrangements as are mentioned may provide for the offender to receive part of his treatment as a resident patient in an institution or place notwithstanding that the institution or place is not one which could have been specified for that purpose in the relevant order.

Where any such arrangements are made for the treatment of an offender the medical practitioner or chartered psychologist by whom the arrangements are made shall give notice in writing to the offender's responsible officer giving details of the place and the treatment provided.

(14) Drug treatment/drug testing requirement

B[50.19]

A drug rehabilitation requirement means a requirement that during a period specified in the order the offender must submit to treatment by or under the direction of a specified person having the necessary qualifications or experience with a view to the reduction or elimination of the offender's dependency on or propensity to misuse drugs.

During that period he must provide samples for the purpose of ascertaining whether he has any drug in his body (a drug testing requirement).

A drug testing requirement may not be made unless the court has been notified that arrangements for implementing drug-testing are in force in the local justice area where the offender resides. The offender must also express his willingness to comply with the order.

Where a requirement is imposed the court must specify for each month the minimum number of occasions on which samples are to be provided. The court may also specify at which, and the circumstances in which, the responsible officer or treatment provider may require samples and descriptions of the samples that may be required.

A court may not impose a drug rehabilitation requirement unless-

(a) it is satisfied—
   (i) that the offender is dependent on, or has a propensity to misuse, drugs, and
   (ii) that his dependency or propensity is such as requires and may be susceptible to treatment;
(b) it is also satisfied that arrangements have been or can be made for the treatment intended to be specified in the order (including arrangements for the reception of the offender where he is to be required to submit to treatment as a resident);
(c) the requirement has been recommended to the court as being suitable for the offender either by an officer of a local probation board (or provider of probation services) or by a member of a youth offending team; and
(d) the offender expresses his willingness to comply with the requirement.

The treatment and testing period is the period specified in the YRO and will be treatment either as a resident in such institution or place as may be specified in the order, or treatment as a non-resident place, as may be so specified.

A YRO imposing a drug rehabilitation requirement must provide that the results of tests carried out on any samples provided by the offender in pursuance of the requirement to a person other than the responsible officer are to be communicated to the responsible officer.

(15) Intoxicating substance treatment requirement

B[50.20]

This is a requirement that the offender submits during a specified period or periods to treatment by or under the direction of a specified person having the necessary qualifications or experience with a view to the reduction or elimination of the offender's dependency on or propensity to misuse intoxicating substances.

Intoxicating substances are defined as alcohol or other substance or product (other than a drug) which is, of the fumes of which are, capable of being inhaled or otherwise used for the purpose of causing intoxication.

The court may not impose an alcohol treatment requirement in respect of an offender unless it is satisfied that he is dependent on or has a tendency to misuse intoxicating substances, and his dependency is such as requires and may be susceptible to treatment. Arrangements must be made for the treatment intended to be specified in the order (including arrangements for the reception of the offender where he is to be required to submit to treatment as a resident).

The court must be satisfied that arrangements have been or can be made for the treatment intended and the requirement must have been recommended to the court as suitable for the offender by a member of the youth offending team, an officer of the local probation service or a provider of probation services.

A court may not impose an alcohol treatment requirement unless the offender expresses his willingness to comply with its requirements.

The treatment required by an intoxicating substance treatment requirement for any particular period must be,

(a)   treatment as a resident in such institution or place as may be specified in the order; or

(b)   treatment as a non-resident in or at such institution or place, and at such intervals, as may be so specified;

but the nature of the treatment shall not be specified in the order except as mentioned in paragraph (a) or (b) above.

(16) Education requirement

B[50.21]

The offender must comply during a period or periods specified in the order with approved education arrangements. These may be arrangements made for the offender's education n by his parent or guardian and approved by the local education authority specified in the order. The authority should be the local education authority for the area in which the offender resides.

The court must consult with the local education authority and be satisfied that arrangements exist for the offender to receive sufficient full-time education suitable for his age, ability, aptitude and special education needs (if any).

The court must be satisfied that the requirement is necessary for securing the good conduct of the offender or for preventing the commission of further offences. Any period specified in the YRO cannot include a period once the offender has ceased to be of compulsory school age.

(17) Electronic monitoring requirement

B[50.22]

This requirement must normally be added to a curfew or exclusion requirement and may be added to other requirements.

Before making the order arrangements for electronic monitoring must be available in the local justice area proposed to be specified in the order and the order must make provision for making a person responsible for the monitoring of the offender.

The period for monitoring the offender's compliance with other requirements will be specified in the order or determined by the responsible officer
in accordance with the relevant requirement. Accordingly, where the
responsible officer is to determine when an electronic monitoring is to take
effect, he must notify the offender, the monitoring person and any other
person whose co-operation is required to ensure that monitoring takes
place. The consent of any such person is required and the requirement may
not be included in the order without that consent.

Breach of a requirement or order (Sch 2, CJIA 2008)

B[50.23]

If at any time while a relevant order is in force in respect of an offender it
appears on information to a justice of the peace acting for the local justice
area concerned that the offender has failed to comply with any of the
requirements, the justice may:

(a)   issue a summons requiring the offender to appear at the place and
        time specified in it; or
(b)   if the information is in writing and on oath, issue a warrant for his
        arrest.

If the offender is aged 18 or over breach proceedings will normally
commence in an adult magistrates' court. Offenders aged under 18 will
appear before a youth court (see *R v Uxbridge Youth Court, ex p Howard*
(1998) 162 JP 327).

If it is proved that the offender has failed without reasonable excuse to
comply with any of the requirements, the court may deal with the offender
in respect of the failure in one of the following ways (the legislation
prescribes **must** deal with him in one of the following ways if the relevant
order is in force):

(a)   a fine not exceeding £250 if aged under 14 or £1,000 *[£2,500] in
        any other case;
        *Added by LASPOA 2012, s 84 when in force.
(b)   by amending the YRO requirements so as to add to or substitute any
        requirement imposed by the order. However, this may not include an
        extended activity requirement or fostering requirement if the origi-
        nal order did not already contain such a requirement. Where the
        original requirement included a fostering and this is substituted by a
        new fostering requirement the order may run for 18 months (as
        opposed to the original 12) beginning with the date on which the
        original requirement first took effect;
(c)   where the relevant order was made by a youth court or adult
        magistrates' court, by revoking the order and dealing with him for
        he offence in respect of which the order was made, in any way in
        which he could have been dealt with for the offence as if that
        order had not been made.

Any requirement imposed under (b) above must be capable of being
complied with before the date specified under CJIA 2008, Sch 1, para 32(2)

and not more than three years after the order first took effect. Where the original order did not contain an unpaid work requirement and the court imposes such a requirement, the minimum number of hours that may be imposed is reduced from 40 to 20 hours.

When dealing with the original offence(s) under (c) above, the court shall take into account the extent to which the offender has complied with the requirements of the relevant order. A person so sentenced may appeal to the Crown Court against that sentence.

In the case of an offender who has wilfully and persistently failed to comply with the requirement(s) of a YRO, and the court is dealing with him under (c) above, the court may impose an intensive supervision and surveillance requirement without regard to the fact that the court is not dealing with the offender for an offence that is punishable with imprisonment nor need it form the opinion that the offence is so serious that it would (but for the statutory restrictions) merit a custodial sentence. Where the court does revoke and re-sentence on breach for any offence not punishable with imprisonment, the court is deemed to have power to deal with the offender for the offence by imposing a detention and training order for a term not exceeding four months: CJIA 2008, Sch 2, paras 12–14.

Commission of further offence

B[50.24]

An offender who is convicted and sentenced of a further offence while subject to a YRO, a youth court may revoke that order and re-sentence the offender for the original offence. That power extends to a YRO made in the Crown Court where the Crown Court has directed that breaches may be dealt with in a youth court. If the court revokes the order and re-sentences, it must take into account the extent to which the offender has complied with the order.

The court must not revoke and re-sentence unless it is in the interests of justice to do so, having regard to the circumstances that have arisen since the YRO was made.

Where a youth court is authorised to deal with a Crown Court order, it may nonetheless commit the offender back to the Crown Court in custody or on bail. **Section 6 of the Powers of Criminal Courts Act 2000 will require amendment to enable a youth court to be able to commit for sentence any summary offence committed during the currency of a YRO requirement.

Application to revoke

B[50.25]

Where a relevant order made by a youth court or adult magistrates' court is in force and, and on the application of the responsible officer, it appears to the court that, having regard to circumstances that have arisen since the order was made, it would be in the interests of justice for the order to be revoked, or for the offence to be dealt with in some other way for the original offence, the court may:

(a) revoke the order; or
(b) revoke the order, and deal with the offender for the offence in respect of which the order was made, in any way in which he could have been dealt with for the original offence.

An application to revoke may be based on the offender making good progress or responding satisfactorily to a supervision requirement as the case may be.

If the offender is over 18 the application will be heard in the adult magistrates' court; if under 18, in a youth court.

If an application to revoke is refused (dismissed), no further application may be brought within three months except with the consent of the appropriate court: CJIA 2008, Sch 2, Part 3, para 11(7).

In dealing with an offender for the original offence, the court shall take into account the extent to which the offender has complied with the requirements of a YRO. A person so dealt with may appeal to the Crown Court against that sentence.

Unless the application is made by the offender, the court shall summons the offender to appear before the court, and if he does not appear, may issue a warrant for his arrest.

No application to revoke an order may be made while an appeal against the relevant order is pending.

Amendment

B[50.26]

Where an offender has or proposes to change residence from one local justice area to another, at any time while the order is in force, a youth or an adult magistrates' court for the local justice area named in the order, may transfer the relevant order.

On the application of an eligible person, the same court may amend an order by cancelling or inserting any of the requirements in the order (either in addition to or in substitution for any of its requirements) that the court could include if it were then making the order (although see treatment requirements below).

As with breach or revocation applications, the procedural requirements for the issue of summonses or warrant are required to be followed unless the application is to cancel a requirement of an order, reducing the period of an order, reducing the period of any one requirement, or transferring the order to a new local justice area. Natural justice dictates that notice of the amendment should be given to the offender.

In either case where the original order contains a specific area requirement (for example, a curfew requirement), or a programme requirement, the court must not make an amendment that would prevent the offender from complying with that requirement. In such circumstances, the court must substitute a similar requirement within the new area.

Where the court amends by including a new requirement, the new requirement must be capable of being complied with before the end of the order. In the case of a fostering requirement that substitutes a new fostering requirement it may run for a period of 18 months beginning with the date on which the original requirement first had effect.

An order containing an unpaid work requirement may, on the application of the offender or the responsible officer, be amended by extending the period of 12 months during which the order must be complied with. Such an order should only be extended if it is in the interests of justice to do so having regard to circumstances that have arisen since the order was made.

Treatment requirements. The court may not impose a treatment requirement such as mental health treatment, drug treatment or drug testing *by way of amendment* unless the offender has expressed his willingness to comply with the requirement.

B[51]

Violent Offender Order

B[51.1]

Part VII of the Criminal Justice & Immigration Act 2008, ie ss 98–117, created the Violent Offender Order (VOO). The legislation came into force on 3 August 2009.

A VOO may be made against an offender aged 18 years or more on the application of a chief officer of police. The application is made by way of complaint to a magistrates' court. The proceedings rank as civil proceedings.

The application may be made against an offender convicted of manslaughter, soliciting, conspiracy or attempted murder, corresponding offences under legislation relating to the armed forces, causing GBH or wounding with intent (s 18 OPA 1861) or offences contrary to s 20 OPA 1861 (inflicting or causing GBH).

A VOO when made contains prohibitions, restrictions and conditions intended to protect the public from serious violent harm. The order must be for a minimum duration of two years and a maximum of five years unless renewed or discharged: s 98(1)(b).

Qualifying Offender (s 99)

B[51.2]

A person is a qualifying offender if he is aged 18 years or more, has been convicted of a qualifying offence (see above) and received either a custodial sentence of 12 months or more, a hospital order, a supervision order (within the meaning of the Criminal Procedure (Insanity) Act 1964) or found not guilty by way of insanity.

A person is also a qualifying offender if convicted of an equivalent offence or offences and has been dealt with in an equivalent fashion according to the law of any country outside England and Wales: s 99(4).

Application (ss 100–101)

B[51.3]

Application is made by complaint via a chief officer of police. The application should specify that the chief officer believes since the date of conviction or finding of insanity etc that the offender has acted in such a way as to give reasonable cause to believe that it is necessary for a VOO to be made in respect of him.

The court may make the order if satisfied that the conditions are met, but in determining whether an order is **necessary** the court must have regard to whether the offender would, at any time while such an order is in force, be subject under any other enactment to any measures that would operate to protect the public from the risk of serious violent harm caused by him.

A VOO cannot come into force while an offender is serving a custodial sentence, is on licence, subject to a hospital or supervision order (see above); nevertheless the order may be sought and made at any time.

Prohibitions, conditions restrictions (s 102) and notification requirements (ss 107–112)

B[51.4]

The order may contain specific terms which prevent an offender from going to specified premises or places at any time or specified times, attending any specified event, or having contact with any specified individual.

A person subject to a VOO or interim order is under a duty to notify the police of his name, address, national insurance number and any plans to travel abroad. An offender must comply with the notification requirement within 3 days of the order coming into force. There is also a periodic duty to notify the police of a change of circumstances, make periodic reports and notify any plans to travel outside the UK.

Variation, discharge and renewal (s 103)

B[51.5]

A full order may be varied, discharged or renewed on application by way of complaint to a magistrates' court. An order may not be discharged within the first two years unless both the offender and police consent.

Interim orders (s 104)

B[51.6]

An interim order may be made where the court is not in a position to make a final determination but the person concerned is a qualifying offender and the court considers that it would be likely to be make a full order and that it is desirable to act to provide the public with immediate protection. As with full orders the VOO will not come into effect while the offender is serving a custodial sentence etc. An interim order ceases to have effect at the end of the specified period subject to any application to vary or discharge the order. There is no provision to extend an interim order. A fresh application would have to be made.

Notice provisions and appeals (ss 105–106)

B[51.7]

An application for a full or interim order, discharge, variation or renewal may not be heard unless the court is satisfied that the person concerned has been given reasonable notice of the application. An appeal lies to the Crown Court against the making of an order, interim order, renewal or variation, or a refusal to make or the discharge of an order.

Breach of a VOO (s 113)

B[51.8]

Section 113 makes it an offence to fail without reasonable excuse to comply with the terms of the order **or** with the notification requirements, **or** notifying false information. The offences are triable either way and punishable summarily to a £5,000 fine, 6 months custody or both (**12 months). On indictment the offence carries an unlimited fine and/or five years' imprisonment. Unlike ASBOs there is nothing to prevent a court from imposing a conditional discharge for a breach of the order.

Jurisdiction for breach proceedings to be commenced lies with the court in the area where the offender resides or is found: s 113(8).

B[52]
Foreign Travel Restriction Order

B[52.1]

Schedule 5 of the Counter-Terrorism Act 2008 authorises a chief officer of police to apply by way of <u>complaint</u> to a magistrates' court for a foreign travel restriction order. An order can only be sought against a person who is already subject to a notification requirement (see ss 41–45 and Sch 4 of the 2008 Act). The legislation came into force on 1 October 2009.

An order places restrictions on where the person concerned may travel outside the UK. The court may make an order where it is satisfied that the person's behaviour since being dealt with for the original offence makes it necessary for an order to be made to prevent him from taking part in terrorism activity outside the UK (Sch 5, para 2(3)).

A foreign travel restriction order must have effect for a fixed term not exceeding 6 months (Sch 5, para 7(1)). Although proceedings are instituted by way of complaint and therefore the procedures are essentially civil in nature, the imposition of criminal sanctions means that the criminal standard of proof applies to the application: see case law under B[8.4].

There are provisions relating to variation, renewal or discharge: Sch 5, para 8. There is no provision to make an interim order. Failure without reasonable excuse to comply with an order is an offence triable either way carrying an unlimited fine and/or five years' imprisonment on conviction on indictment: Sch 5, para 15(2). On summary conviction the offence carries six months' imprisonment and/or a fine not exceeding £5,000. The magistrates' court may not impose a conditional discharge: Sch 5, para 15(4)(a).

B[53]

Closure Order (specified prostitution offences)

B[53.1]

Part 2A of the Sexual Offences Act 2003 was inserted by the Policing and Crime Act 2009.

The provisions outlined below came into force on 1 April 2010. Section 136B of the SOA 2003 permits a police officer, not below the rank of superintendent, to authorise a closure order in relation to premises which are being used for certain activities; those activities are associated with "specified prostitution or pornography offences" as defined by the Act. The police must have consulted the local authority first.

If a closure order has been issued, a constable must apply under SOA 2003, s 136D to a magistrates' court for a closure order.

A closure order is an order that the premises (or part of the premises) in respect of which the order is made are closed to all persons for such period not exceeding 3 months as is specified in the order.

The application must be heard by the magistrates' court not later than 48 hours after the notice was served by the police in pursuance of SOA 2003, s 136C(3)(a).

The magistrates' court may adjourn the hearing for a closure order for a period of not more than 14 days to enable any of the following to show why a closure order should not be made: (a) an occupier of the premises; (b) a person who has control of or responsibility for the premises; (c) any other person who has an interest in the proceedings (see SOA 2003, s136B(7)(b)).

If the application is adjourned the magistrates' court may order that the closure order continues in effect until the end of the period of the adjournment.

Closure order applications are civil proceedings. Although closure order applications should be dealt with as a matter of urgency, it is submitted that, analogous to crack house orders (see A[26.12]), a magistrates' court has a general power to grant a further adjournment under the MCA 1980, s 54: see R (on the application of Turner v Highbury Corner Magistrates' Court and Commissioner of the Metropolitan Police Comr (Interested Party) [2005] EWHC 2568.

B[53.2]

A magistrates' court may make a closure order if satisfied three criteria have been made out:

(1)   That the premises have been used, during the period 3 months ending on the day the closure order was issued by the police, for specified prostitution offences (except if only one person obtained all of the sexual services in question, whether or not on a single occasion) or for specified pornography offences.

(2)   That the closure order is necessary to prevent the premises being used for one or other of the above activities.

(3)   Reasonable steps have been taken to consult the relevant local authority and to establish the identity of any person (see SOA 2003, s 136B(7)(b) above); and, there has been compliance by the police with SOA 2003, s 136C(3)(d) ie a copy of the notice was given to the persons mentioned in s 136B(7)(b) of the SOA 2003.

B[53.3]

Enforcement and offences. Enforcement is to be found in SOA 2003, s 136F. A person who obstructs a constable or an authorised person acting under s 136C(3) or (4) or s 136F(2) or (4) of the SOA 2003 commits an offence. The offence is summary only carrying a maximum penalty of 6 months' imprisonment (51 weeks if the CJA 2003 is brought into force) and/or a maximum fine of £5,000 (level 5).

B[53.4]

Extension, variation and discharge. This is catered for by SOA 2003, ss 136H–J. On application a closure order may be extended for a further period of 3 months but a closure order cannot exceed 6 months in total. This would not prevent the police from making a fresh application for a closure order. There is provision for any of the person mentioned in SOA 2003, s 136B(7)(b) to apply for the order to be discharged.

B[53.5]

Appeal. Any of the above mentioned may appeal to the Crown Court. The appeal must be lodged before the end of 21 days beginning with the day on which the order or decision was made: SOA 2003, s 136K.

B[53.6]

There are miscellaneous provisions covering costs or compensation associated with the making of such orders eg see SOA 2003, s 136M. Magistrates would be well advised to consult their legal adviser.

B[54]

Domestic violence protection notice

Power to issue

B[54.1]

Power to issue a domestic violence protection notice is provided by ss 24–26 of the Crime and Security Act 2010. Appointment (for a period of 12 months for the purposes of certain regional pilots): 30 June 2011: see SI 2011/1440, arts 2, 3.

The pilot currently only applies to the police areas of Greater Manchester, West Mercia and Wiltshire.

A member of a police force not below the rank of superintendent ("the authorising officer") may issue a domestic violence protection notice ("a DVPN").

A DVPN may be issued to a person ("P") aged 18 years or over if the authorising officer has reasonable grounds for believing that—

(a)   P has been violent towards, or has threatened violence towards, an associated person,

(b)   the issue of the DVPN is necessary to protect that person from violence or a threat of violence by P.

Before issuing a DVPN, the authorising officer must, in particular, consider—

(a)   the welfare of any person under the age of 18 whose interests the officer considers relevant to the issuing of the DVPN (whether or not that person is an associated person),

(b)   the opinion of the person for whose protection the DVPN would be issued as to the issuing of the DVPN,

(c)   any representations made by P as to the issuing of the DVPN, and

(d)   in the case of provision included by virtue of subsection (8), the opinion of any other associated person who lives in the premises to which the provision would relate.

The authorising officer must take reasonable steps to discover the opinions mentioned in (a)–(d) above. But the authorising officer may issue a DVPN in circumstances where the person for whose protection it is issued does not consent to the issuing of the DVPN.

A DVPN must contain provision to prohibit P from molesting the person for whose protection it is issued. Provision in the DVPN may be expressed so as to refer to molestation in general, to particular acts of molestation, or to both.

If P lives in premises which are also lived in by a person for whose protection the DVPN is issued, the DVPN may also contain provision—

(a)   to prohibit P from evicting or excluding from the premises the person for whose protection the DVPN is issued

(b)   to prohibit P from entering the premises,

(c)   to require P to leave the premises, or

(d)   to prohibit P from coming within such distance of the premises as may be specified in the DVPN

An "associated person" means a person who is associated with P within the meaning of s 62 of the Family Law Act 1996. There are further provisions dealing with the armed forces and armed forces personnel (see s 24(10)–(11)).

Contents and service of a domestic violence protection notice

B[54.2]

A DVPN must state—

(a)   the grounds on which it has been issued,

(b)   that a constable may arrest P without warrant if the constable has reasonable grounds for believing that P is in breach of the DVPN,

(c)   that an application for a domestic violence protection order under section 27 will be heard within 48 hours of the time of service of the DVPN and a notice of the hearing will be given to P (see **B[55]** below).

(d)   that the DVPN continues in effect until that application has been determined, and

(e)   the provision that a magistrates' court may include in a domestic violence protection order.

A DVPN must be in writing and must be served on P personally by a constable. On serving P with a DVPN, the constable must ask P for an address for the purposes of being given the notice of the hearing of the application for the domestic violence protection order.

Breach and enforcement of a DVPN

B[54.3]

A person arrested for a breach of a DVPN must be held in custody and brought before the magistrates' court which will hear the application for the DVPO under s 27 (see below)—

(a)   before the end of the period of 24 hours beginning with the time of the arrest, or

(b)   if earlier, at the hearing of that application.

If the person is brought before the court and the hearing is adjourned the court may remand the person.

In calculating when the period of 24 hours mentioned above ends, Christmas Day, Good Friday, any Sunday and any day which is a bank holiday in England and Wales under the Banking and Financial Dealings Act 1971 are to be disregarded.

No penalty is prescribed for breach of an order under the 2010 legislation. Breach of a magistrates' court order (other than for payment of money) is provided for by s 63 of the Magistrates' Courts Act 1980. Where breach of an order is established (to the criminal standard it is submitted) the maximum penalty is:

(a)   a fine not exceeding £50 for every day during which P is in default or a sum not exceeding £5,000;

(b)   committal to custody until he has remedied his default or for a period not exceeding 2 months.

B[55]

Domestic violence protection order

Application for a domestic violence protection order

B[55.1]

Power to apply for a domestic violence protection order is provided by ss 27–30 of the Crime and Security Act 2010. Appointment (for a period of 12 months for the purposes of certain regional pilots): 30 June 2011: see SI 2011/1440, arts 2, 3.

The pilot currently only applies to the police areas of Greater Manchester, West Mercia and Wiltshire.

If a DVPN has been issued, a constable must apply for a domestic violence protection order ("a DVPO"). The application must be made by complaint to a magistrates' court.

The application must be heard by the magistrates' court not later than 48 hours after the DVPN was served pursuant to s 25(2).

In calculating when the period of 48 hours ends, Christmas Day, Good Friday, any Sunday and any day which is a bank holiday in England and Wales under the Banking and Financial Dealings Act 1971 are to be disregarded.

A notice of the hearing of the application must be given to the person ("P"). The notice is deemed given if it has been left at the address given by P under section 25(3).

But if the notice has not been given because no address was given by P under section 25(3), the court may hear the application for the DVPO if the court is satisfied that the constable applying for the DVPO has made reasonable efforts to give P the notice.

The magistrates' court may adjourn the hearing of the application. If the court adjourns the hearing, the DVPN continues in effect until the application has been determined.

On the hearing of an application for a DVPO, section 97 of the Magistrates' Courts Act 1980 (summons to witness and warrant for his arrest) does not apply in relation to a person for whose protection the DVPO would be made, except where the person has given oral or written evidence at the hearing.

The Magistrates' Courts (DVPO Proceedings) Rules 2011 SI No 2011/1434 have been made. These rules make provision for applications under the 2010 Act.

Rule 4 disapplies section 2(1) of the Civil Evidence Act 1995 (c 38) (the 1995 Act), which requires parties proposing to adduce hearsay evidence in civil proceedings to give notice of the proposal.

Rule 5 amends rule 2 of the Magistrates' Courts (Hearsay Evidence in Civil Proceedings) Rules 1999 (SI 1999/681) (the 1999 Rules) to exclude the 1999 rules in respect of applications for DVPOs. The 1999 Rules make further provision concerning hearsay evidence, including the contents of hearsay notices (rule 3), the procedure to call witnesses for cross-examination on hearsay evidence (rule 4), credibility and the use of previous inconsistent statements (rule 5) and the service of documents (rule 6).

The provisions under the 1995 Act and 1999 Rules have been respectively disapplied or excluded because they are either incompatible with the procedures prescribed for applying for DVPOs under the 2010 Act or else cease to have effect in consequence of the disapplication or exclusion of other of these provisions.

Section 27 of the 2010 Act provides that an application for a DVPO must be made by complaint to the magistrates' court. Rule 6 prescribes the procedure to be followed in such circumstances.

Conditions for and contents of a DVPO

B[55.2]

The court may make a DVPO if two conditions are met.

The first condition is that the court is satisfied on the balance of probabilities that P has been violent towards, or has threatened violence towards, an associated person.

The second condition is that the court thinks that making the DVPO is necessary to protect that person from violence or a threat of violence by P.

Before making a DVPO, the court must, in particular, consider—

(a) the welfare of any person under the age of 18 whose interests the court considers relevant to the making of the DVPO (whether or not that person is an associated person), and

(b) any opinion of which the court is made aware—

    (i) of the person for whose protection the DVPO would be made, and

    (ii) in the case of provision included by virtue of subsection (8), of any other associated person who lives in the premises to which the provision would relate.

But the court may make a DVPO in circumstances where the person for whose protection it is made does not consent to the making of the DVPO.

A DVPO must contain provision to prohibit P from molesting the person for whose protection it is made. Provision required to be included may be expressed so as to refer to molestation in general, to particular acts of molestation, or to both.

If P lives in premises which are also lived in by a person for whose protection the DVPO is made, the DVPO may also contain provision—

(a)   to prohibit P from evicting or excluding from the premises the person for whose protection the DVPO is made

(b)   to prohibit P from entering the premises,

(c)   to require P to leave the premises, or

(d)   to prohibit P from coming within such distance of the premises as may be specified in the DVPO.

A DVPO must state that a constable may arrest P without warrant if the constable has reasonable grounds for believing that P is in breach of the DVPO.

A DVPO may be in force for—

(a)   no fewer than 14 days beginning with the day on which it is made,

(b)   no more than 28 days beginning with that day.

A DVPO must state the period for which it is to be in force.

Breach and Enforcement of a DVPO

B[55.3]

A person arrested by virtue of section 28(9) for a breach of a DVPO must be held in custody and brought before a magistrates' court within the period of 24 hours beginning with the time of the arrest.

If the matter is not disposed of when the person is brought before the court, the court may remand the person.

In calculating when the period of 24 hours mentioned in subsection (1) ends, Christmas Day, Good Friday, any Sunday and any day which is a bank holiday in England and Wales under the Banking and Financial Dealings Act 1971 are to be disregarded.

There are further provisions about remand to be found in s 30 of the 2010 Act.

No penalty is prescribed for breach of an order under the 2010 legislation. Breach of a magistrates' court order (other than for payment of money) is provided for by s 63 of the Magistrates' Courts Act 1980. Where breach of an order is established (to the criminal standard it is submitted) the maximum penalty is:

(a)   a fine not exceeding £50 for every day during which P is in default or a sum not exceeding £5,000; or

(b)   committal to custody until he has remedied his default or for a period not exceeding 2 months.

Road traffic offences

C[1]

Index and penalties for road traffic offences

Maximum fines and the standard scale

C[1.1]

MCA 1980, s 32(9); Interpretation Act 1978, s 32, Sch 1	The statutory maximum fine on summary conviction of an offence triable either way, being the prescribed sum under the Magistrates' Court Act 1980,	£5,000
CJA 1982, s 37(2)	The standard scale giving maximum fines on an adult on conviction for a summary offence:	

level 1		£200
level 2		£500
level 3		£1,000
level 4		£2,500
level 5		£5,000

C[1.2]
The following table contains an alphabetical list of the road traffic offences dealt with in this book, together with some others included to provide the maximum penalty. Readers will wish to note the penalties recommended in the Magistrates' Association National Sentencing Guidelines.

C[1.3]
Speed/distance chart. See C[2]

C[1.4]
Stopping distances. See C[3]

C[1.5]
Endorsement codes. See C[6]

C[1.6]

Offences and endorsement code	Standard scale	Licence and penalty points	para
Abandoning a motor vehicle	level 4+3 months [**51 weeks]		
Accident, failing to give particulars AC 20	level 5+6 months [**51 weeks]	E 5–10	C[32]
Report AC 20	level 5+6 months [**51 weeks]	E 5–10	C[32]
stop after AC 10	level 5+6 months [**51 weeks]	E 5–10	C[31]
Bicycle			
defective brakes riding	level 3		
Careless	level 3		
Dangerous	level 4		
Inconsiderate	level 3		
two persons on	level 1		
when unfit through drink	level 3		
Brakes, defective			
on private vehicle CU 10 §	level 4	E*3	C[9]
on goods vehicle CU 10 §	level 5	E*3	C[9]
on bicycle	level 3		
Breath test, refusing DR 70	level 3	E 3–11	C[24]
Car door, opening to cause			
injury or danger §	level 3		C[37]
Car dumping	level 4 + 3 months [**51 weeks]	104	A[60]
Careless driving CD 10	level 5	E 3–9	C[25]
Common land, driving on §	level 3		
Dangerous condition			
using private vehicle in CU 20 §	level 4	E*3 (D) – see C[10]	C[10]
using goods vehicle in CU 20 §	level 5	E*3 (D) – see C[10]	C[10]
Dangerous load			
on private vehicle CU 50 §	level 4	E*3	
on goods vehicle CU 50 §	level 5	E*3	
Dangerous position, leaving			
motor vehicle in MS 10 §	level 3	E 3	
Date of birth, failing to give	level 3		
Defective tyre			
private vehicle CU 30 §	level 4	E*3	C[53]

Offences and endorsement code	Standard scale	Licence and penalty points	para
goods vehicle CU 30 §	level 5	E*3	C[53]
Driver, failing to give particulars of date of birth	level 3		
Driving			
Careless CD 10	level 5	E 3–9	C[25]
causing death by careless or inconsiderate driving †(from **18/8/08**)	level 5 + 12 months	E 3–11	C[16A]
dangerous†DD 40	level 5 + 6 months [**12 months]	D 3–11	C[16]
causing death by driving: unlicensed, disqualified or uninsured† (from **18/8/08**)	level 5 + 12 months	D 3–11	C[16B]
causing serious injury by dangerous driving (from a date to be added when s 143 of LASPOA 2012 is brought into force)	level 5 + 12 months	D 3–11	C[16C]
disqualified BA 10	level 5 + 12 months [**51 weeks]	E 6	C[19]
drink, under influence of DR 20	level 5 + 6 months [**51 weeks]	D 3–11	C[20]
excess alcohol DR 10	level 5 + 6 months [**51 weeks]	D 3–11	C[22]
excessive periods on footpath, common land, etc	level 4		
(RT Act) §	level 3		
Without			
due care and attention CD 10	level 4 5 for offences on or after 24/9/07	E 3–9	C[25]
insurance IN 10 §	level 5	E 6–8	C[33]
Keeping vehicle which does not meet insurance requirements (RTA, s 144A)	level 3		
licence (excise)	£1,000 or 5 times duty		C[47]
reasonable consideration CD 20	level 5 for offences on or after 24/9/07	E 3–9	C[46]
test certificate			
(private)	level 3		C[51]
(goods)	level 4		C[51]
Drunk in charge DR 50	level 4 + 3 months [**51 weeks]	E 10	C[21]

Offences and endorsement code	Standard scale	Licence and penalty points	para
Excess alcohol			
driving DR 10	level 5 + 6 months [**51 weeks]	D 3–11	C[20]
in charge DR 40	level 5 + 3 months [**51 weeks]	E 10	C[21]
Excise licence			
failing to display §	level 1		
making false statement to obtain	level 5		
using/keeping vehicle without	level 3 or 5 times duty		C[47]
Eyesight, driving with defective MS 70	level 3	E 3	
Failing to comply with traffic sign §	level 3	+ 3	C[52]
(constable or traffic warden on traffic duty) TS 40 §	level 3	E 3	
Give			
name and address to	level 5	E 5–10	C[31]
police AC 20	+ 6 months [**51 weeks]		
particulars after accident AC 20	level 5 + 6 months [**51 weeks]	E 5–10	C[31]
specimen of			
breath DR 70	level 3	E 4	C[24]
blood/urine/breath			
driving or attempting DR 30	level 5 + 6 months [**51 weeks]	D 3–11	C[24]
in charge DR 60	level 4 + 3 months [**51 weeks]	E 10	C[24]
statement by owner	level 3		
Produce			
driving licence	level 3		C[17]
insurance certificate	level 3		C[17]
test certificate	level 3		C[17]
wear seat belt (front §)	level 2		C[48]
(rear §)	level 2 (child)		
report accident AC 20	level 5 + 6 months [**51 weeks]	E 5–10	C[31]
sign driving licence	level 3		

Offences and endorsement code	Standard scale	Licence and penalty points	para
stop (a mechanically propelled vehicle when required to do so: s 163 RTA 1988)	level 5		
after accident AC 10	level 5 + 6 months [**51 weeks]	E 5–10	C[31]
at school crossing TS 60	level 3	E 3	
False declaration to obtain excise licence †	level 5		
False statement to obtain			
driving licence	level 4		
Insurance	level 4		
Footpath, driving on			
(Highways Act 1835, s 72)	level 2		
Forging, etc			
driving licence, excise licence †	level 5		
insurance certificate	level 5		
test certificate †	level 5		
Front seat, carrying child in §	level 3		C[48]
Getting on to vehicle to **be carried**	level 1		
Heavy goods vehicle			
driving without LGV licence	level 3		
overloading §	level 5		C[38]
parking on verge, etc §	level 3		
using without plating certificate	level 3		
using without test certificate	level 4		
Holding on to vehicle to be towed or carried	level 1		
Hours, driving for excessive number	level 4		
Insecure load			
private vehicle CU 50 §	level 4	E*3	
goods vehicle CU 50 §	level 5	E*3	
Insurance			
using without, causing or permitting IN 10 §	level 5	E 6–8	C[33]
failing to produce certificate	level 3		C[17]
false statement to obtain	level 4		
Jay walking	level 3		
Licence			

Offences and endorsement code	Standard scale	Licence and penalty points	para
driving otherwise than in accordance with LC 10 §	level 3	E 3–6	C[18]
excise, keeping/using vehicle without	level 3 or 5 times duty		C[47]
failing to produce for endorsement	level 3		
failing to produce to constable	level 3		C[17]
LGV, driving otherwise than in accordance with	10 units		C[19]
obtaining while disqualified	level 3		
Lights, driving or parking			
without §	level 4 (goods vehicle etc)		C[34]
	level 3 (other)		
(Breach of requirements as to control of vehicle, Mobile Telephone etc)	level 4 if committed in respect of a good vehicle or a vehicle adapted to carry more than 8 persons, otherwise level 3	E 3 (for offence committed on or after 27/2/07 prosecuted under s 41D RTA 1988)	
[Currently] Mobile Telephone§			
Motor cyclists not wearing helmet §	level 2		C[35]
Neglecting policeman's directions			
driver TS 40 §	level 3	E 3	
Pedestrian	level 3		
Obstruction, causing			
unnecessary §	level 4 (goods vehicle etc)		C[36]
	level 3 (other)		
Opening door to cause danger or injury §	level 4 (goods vehicle)		C[37]
	level 3 (other)		
One way street, driving in wrong direction §	level 3	E 3	C[52]
Overloading §	level 5		C[38]
Owner failing to identify driver	level 3	E 6	
Parking			
heavy vehicle on footpath,	level 3		

Offences and endorsement code	Standard scale	Licence and penalty points	para
on offside at night §	level 4 (goods vehicle etc)		
on yellow lines §	level 3		
breach of regulations for			
on street parking places §	level 2		
(abuse of parking for the disabled) §	level 3		
off street parking places	level 2		
(abuse of parking for the disabled)	level 3		
failure to pay initial or excess charge	level 2 + amount un-paid		
interfering with meter with in-tent to defraud	level 3		
Pedal cycle, *see* Bicycle			
Pedestrian			
failing to comply with direction of constable on traffic duty	level 3		
Pedestrian crossing			
not giving precedence PC 20 §	level 3	E 3	C[39]
overtaking within limits PC 20 §	level 3	E 3	C[39.10]
Stopping within limits PC 30 §	level 3	E 3	C[40]
Provisional licence holder			
Reasonable consideration			
driving without CD 20	level 5	E 3–9	C[46]
Record of hours, failing to keep	level 4		
Refusing blood/urine/breath specimen			
in charge DR 60	level 4 + 3 months [**51 weeks]	E 10	C[23]
driving DR 30	level 5 + 6 months [**51 weeks]	D 3–11	C[23]
Riding bicycle, *see* Bicycle			
Road fund licence			
keeping/using without	level 3 or 5 times duty		C[47]
fail to display §	level 1		
false statement to obtain †	level 5		
Seat belt, failure to wear (front §)	level 2		C[48]

Offences and endorsement code	Standard scale	Licence and penalty points	para
(rear §)	level 2 (child in rear seat)		
School crossing, fail to stop at TS 60	level 3	E 3	
Silencer, defective §	level 4 (goods vehicle etc) level 3 (other)		
Speeding SP 30 §	level 3	E 3–6(FP3) [2–6 under the Road Safety Act 2006]	C[49]
motorway SP 50 §	level 4	E 3–6(FP3) [2–6 under the Road Safety Act 2006]	C[49]
Speed assessment equipment detection devices	level 4 if committed on a special road, otherwise level 3	E 3–6 (FP3) from a date to be appointed under the Road Safety Act 2006	C[38A]
Stealing (or attempt) vehicle † NE 99	level 5 + 6 months [**12 months]	D (discretionary)	A[57], A[65]
Steering, defective private vehicle CU 40 §	level 4	E*3	C[50]
goods vehicle CU 40 §	level 5	E*3	
Taking motor vehicle without consent NE 99	level 5	D (discretionary)	A[57], A[65]
(Theft Act 1968, s 12) Aggravated Vehicle Taking UT 50	6 months [**51 weeks] Level 5	D	A[3]
(Theft Act 1968, s 12A)	6 months [**12 months]		
Tampering with motor vehicle	level 3 + 3 months [**51 weeks]		A[63]
Test certificate § using etc vehicle without	level 3		C[51]

Offences and endorsement code	Standard scale	Licence and penalty points	para
using goods vehicle without	level 4		C[51]
failing to produce	level 3		C[17]
Traffic sign, non compliance			
with §	level 3	E 3	C[52]
Tyre, defective			
private vehicle CU 30 §	level 4	E*3	C[53]
goods vehicle CU 30 §	level 5	E*3	C[53]
Waiting on yellow lines §	level 3		

D   means that the offence attracts an obligatory disqualification.

E   means that the offence attracts an obligatory endorsement; in all such cases disqualification is discretionary.

*   The defendant in cases thus marked is not liable to an endorsement if he satisfies the court that he did not know of the defect and had no reasonable cause to suspect that it was present.

+   Endorsable only if the sign is a traffic light (TS 10), double white lines (TS 20), Stop (TS 30), no entry sign or failure to comply with a green arrow traffic sign, abnormal load failing to observe procedure at railway crossing (TS 50), or vehicle contravening height restriction (TS 50).

†   Triable either way.

§   The prosecution may offer a fixed penalty instead of prosecuting in the normal way. See [8].

**   Denotes changes to the sentencing powers of magistrates under the Criminal Justice Act 2003 earmarked to be brought into force from a date to be appointed.

C[2]

Speed and distance chart

C[2.1]

An approximate guide to the distance covered by a vehicle moving at a constant speed is that half the number of miles per hour is roughly the number of yards per second, eg 30 mph = 15 yds per second. The following table is more accurate than that and the distances are expressed in feet. But it must be borne in mind that the distance given will be covered only by a vehicle travelling at the speed given for the whole of the distance, ie at a constant speed. The table cannot therefore be used in the case of a vehicle slowing down or accelerating.

Miles per hour	*Feet per second*
20	29
30	44
40	59
50	73
60	88
70	103
80	117
90	132
100	146

C[3]

Braking distances

(Taken, with permission, from the Highway Code)

C[3.1]

The following braking table appears in the Highway Code. It must be taken as a guide only since no information is given with it as to whether a vehicle with disc or servo assisted brakes, or any particular tyres could improve upon these figures. It is submitted that the court can take judicial notice of the table and may form part of the cross-examination of a witness including the defendant. Moreover, the table, like any other part of the Highway Code, is embraced by the Road Traffic Act 1988, s 38(7) which states:

'A failure on the part of a person to observe a provision of the Highway Code shall not of itself render that person liable to criminal proceedings of any kind, but any such failure may in any proceedings (whether civil or criminal and including proceedings under the Traffic Acts . . .) be relied upon by any party to the proceedings as tending to establish or negative any liability which is in question in those proceedings.'

C[4]

Shortest stopping distances – in feet

[4.1]

'On a dry road, a good car with good brakes and tyres and an alert driver will stop in the distances shown. Remember these are shortest stopping distances. Stopping distances increase greatly with wet and slippery roads, poor brakes and tyres and tired drivers.'

Mph	Thinking distance		Braking distance		Overall stopping distance	
	m	ft	m	ft	m	ft
20	6	20	6	20	12	40
30	9	30	14	45	23	75
40	12	40	24	80	36	120
50	15	50	38	125	53	175
60	18	60	55	180	73	240
70	21	70	75	245	96	315

C[5]

Endorsement and disqualification

C[5.1]

The Traffic legislation imposes on the courts an obligation to endorse the licence of any person convicted of certain offences. In the case of a convicted person who does not hold a driving licence this acts as an order to endorse any licence which he may obtain during the period when the endorsement is effective. An endorsement means that particulars of the offence and sentence will be recorded in code (as to which see C[6]) on the defendant's licence, unless it is a foreign licence. In the case of a foreign licence, the order for endorsement should be made (subject to there being special reasons for not making it, see below) and the clerk will notify the DVLA. The court must order endorsement unless it decides after hearing sworn evidence (which may be no more than the evidence given during the trial of the offence) that there are special reasons for not doing so.

C[5.2]

Special reasons. This has become a term of art; it has a significance which is determined by law rather than by the ordinary meaning of the words. In order to avoid endorsement or compulsory disqualification the defendant must give to the court at least one specific reason why he should not be penalised by endorsement (or disqualification in cases where that is mandatory) and that reason must meet all of the following criteria:

(a)   it must be a mitigating or extenuating circumstance;
(b)   it must not amount to a legal defence to the charge;
(c)   it must be directly connected with the circumstances in which the offence was committed, and not relate solely to the circumstances of the offender;
(d)   it should be a factor which the court ought properly to take into consideration when deciding the sentence (*R v Wickins* (1958) 42 Cr App Rep 236, 122 JP 518, CCA).

C[5.3]

Case law has provided very many examples of circumstances under (c) above which may, and other circumstances which may not, be accepted as special reasons and some circumstances (eg the distance driven by the defendant) may be accepted or rejected according to the offence with which he is charged. For this reason examples are not set out here since they may confuse rather than clarify the position. Magistrates are recommended always to consult the legal adviser before reaching any final decision on this question.

C[5.4]

Disqualification. Disqualification is mandatory for certain offences. In every case where the court can order an endorsement it has the discretion also to disqualify. Thus it can be seen how important it may be for a defendant to persuade the court that there are special reasons for not endorsing, because if he is successful and the court does not order endorsement, it may not disqualify. In cases where disqualification is mandatory, eg dangerous driving and drinking and driving offences, the defendant may submit special reasons for not disqualifying while conceding the endorsement.

C[5.5]

For offences of theft of vehicles, going equipped to steal vehicles and taking vehicles without consent, the court may disqualify even though there is no power to impose penalty points. Disqualification may also be imposed for offences of assault involving a motor vehicle and, indeed, where following a motoring incident one driver follows another and assaults him the power to disqualify will arise (*R v Rajesh Patel* (1994) 16 Cr App Rep (S) 756, [1995] Crim LR 440, CA). A discretionary disqualification may not be imposed where the defendant is also liable to be disqualified under the penalty points provisions (see below).

There is a discretionary power to disqualify for any offence under PCC(S) Act 2000, s 146. See C[5.45].

C[5.6]

Length of disqualification. A minimum period of disqualification must, in the absence of special reasons, be imposed in the following cases:

driving with excess alcohol/whilst unfit	One year; three years where second offence within 10 years; *two years where there has been two or more bans of 56 days or more 3 years immediately preceding the commission of the latest offence (s 34(4) RTOA 1988).
refusing to supply a specimen	One year; three years where second offence within 10 years; *two years where there has been two or more bans of 56 days or more, 3 years immediately preceding the commission of the latest offence (s 34(4) RTOA 1988).
dangerous driving	*one year *two years where there has been two or more bans of 56 days or more, 3 years immediately preceding the commission of the latest offence (s 34(4) RTOA 1988)
(from a date to be appointed) causing death by careless or inconsiderate driving	One year; three years

(from a date to be appointed) causing death by driving: unlicensed, disqualified or uninsured drivers	One year; three years
(from a date to be appointed) using vehicle in a dangerous condition	6 months if second conviction within three years of a conviction for any such offence

Dangerous driving also carries a mandatory disqualification until a test is passed.

C[5.7]

There is a tendency for magistrates to think of disqualification in units of say, 6, 12, 18 and 24 months. Research has shown that the longer the period of disqualification the more it is likely to be disobeyed. Moreover, the driver who is disqualified, say for two years, will probably decide within a few weeks that he will ignore the ban. There is, therefore, a strong case for short-term disqualifications especially, for example, for bad cases of careless driving and young men charged with driving licence offences (see below for disqualification under the penalty points system).

C[5.8]

Disqualification starts on the day on which the order is made and that day counts as one full day of the disqualification.

C[5.9]

Disqualification for life. Such a disqualification will be rare. Only where there are exceptional circumstances should a disqualification for life be imposed (*R v Rivano* (1993) 14 Cr App Rep (S) 578, 158 JP 288, CA), for example, where there is psychiatric evidence that the driver would indefinitely be a danger to the public if allowed to drive (*R v King* [1993] RTR 245, 13 Cr App Rep (S) 668, CA) or evidence of many previous convictions which indicated the same possibility (*R v Buckley* (1994) 15 Cr App Rep (S) 695, [1994] Crim LR 387, CA).

The penalty points system

C[5.10]–[5.15]

Persons convicted of certain offences must be disqualified from driving, eg for driving with excess alcohol. A court has a discretion to disqualify any person who has been convicted of an endorsable offence and will do so where the particular offence with which it is dealing is serious. The person who persistently commits minor endorsable offences may therefore escape these mandatory or discretionary disqualifications but will be caught by the disqualification imposed under the penalty points system. This provides in essence that where a person accumulates 12 or more penalty points over a three-year period, he must generally be disqualified for a minimum period.

C[5.16]

Penalty points. Every endorsable offence attracts a number of penalty points varying from 2 to 11. Some offences (including careless driving, uninsured use of a vehicle and failing to stop or report after an accident) give the court a discretion to attach a number of penalty points within a range, so indicating the court's view of the relative gravity of the offence. The choice of the number of penalty points in these cases will on occasion determine whether a disqualification must be imposed. For example, Brian A Driver has already accumulated 8 penalty points and is convicted of careless driving for which anything from 3 to 9 penalty points may be awarded. If the court imposes 3 points, Driver escapes disqualification because he does not reach a total of 12; but if the court imposes more than 3 then he must be disqualified, subject to his proving mitigating circumstances amounting to exceptional hardship.

C[5.17]

When a driver is convicted of a single endorsable offence his licence will be endorsed with the number of penalty points appropriate to that offence, or with a number within the appropriate range. However, where he is convicted of a number of offences committed on the same occasion (which is not the same as saying on the same day) the number of points to be endorsed will usually be the number for the offence attracting the highest number. For example, if in addition to his careless driving conviction (3–9 penalty points) Brian A Driver is also convicted of driving whilst disqualified (6 penalty points) and driving in a play street (2 penalty points) then his endorsement will show at least 6 penalty points, that being the highest figure. If the court decides to endorse 8 penalty points for the careless driving (that being a number within the range for that offence) then the endorsement would show 8 penalty points. It is these 8 penalty points which count towards disqualification, not the total number for the three offences.

C[5.18]

Two things will be evident from this in the normal situation:

(a)   although every endorsable offence has a penalty points value, the endorsement relating to that offence may show a higher number; and

(b)   when a conviction relates to a number of offences committed on the same occasion the number of penalty points which count towards disqualification is the number relating to the offence with the highest number of penalty points.

C[5.19]

However, the court may if it thinks fit decide to accumulate the points for offences committed on the same occasion. If it does so it must state its reasons in open court and enter them in the register.

Note that the court should not order penalty points to be endorsed if it orders the offender to be disqualified in respect of any offence of which he has been convicted on that occasion (*Martin v DPP* [2000] RTR 188, [2000] 2 Cr App Rep (S) 18, 164 JP 405, [2000] Crim LR 320).

Penalty points to be taken into account

C[5.20]

There is a general misconception as to the law and practice following the decision in *Jones v Chief Constable of West Mercia Police Authority* (2000) 165 JP 6. A totting ban is usually for not less than 6, 12 or 24 months which is substantially longer than the majority of discretionary bans. Accordingly, the starting point is to calculate the number of points to be taken into account and to determine whether the offender tots. As the court in *Jones* indicated the usual practice is to impose a totting ban without reference to the seriousness or triviality of the offence (as provided for by s 35 of the Offenders Act). Only in an exceptional case will the court first consider if it wishes to impose a discretionary disqualification bearing in mind the seriousness of the offence and previous offences. If a discretionary disqualification is imposed any existing points remain on the licence. If discretionary disqualification is not appropriate the court imposes points and goes on to consider the totting-up procedure.

The effect of the decision in *Jones* above was nullified by the introduction of the Magistrates' Courts Sentencing Guidelines – see page 185, para 12 which clearly states that if the court is considering discretionary disqualification but D would be liable to totting up if further points were imposed the court should go down the totting up route not the discretionary ban route. This plugged the *Jones* 'gap' whereby some courts were being persuaded to impose short discretionary bans in the absence of exceptional hardship thus circumventing the totting up.

Subject to there being grounds for mitigation, disqualification is incurred when the number of penalty points to be taken into account reaches or exceeds 12. The following penalty points are to be taken into account at the time of conviction:

(a) those endorsed at the time of that conviction. Where a person is made the subject of a mandatory or discretionary disqualification no penalty points for the offence for which he was disqualified will be taken into account, for the purpose of imposing an additional disqualification under the penalty points provisions;

(b) those endorsed previously in respect of any offence committed within three years of the present offence, except where a disqualification under the penalty points provisions has been ordered, in which case the court is only concerned with the penalty points incurred since that disqualification.

C[5.21]

Therefore, only a disqualification under the penalty points provisions will have the effect of 'wiping clean' any points previously incurred.

Period of disqualification

C[5.22]

Once a defendant becomes liable for disqualification under this scheme he may be disqualified for any period at the court's discretion, but this discretion is limited by the fixing of minimum periods. These minimum periods are as follows:

(a)   six months if no previous disqualification is to be taken into account;
(b)   one year if one previous disqualification is to be taken into account; and
(c)   two years if there is more than one such disqualification.

C[5.23]

For a prior disqualification to be taken into account it must have been imposed within three years of the latest offence which has brought the offender's total of penalty points up to 12. Such disqualification may have been imposed:

(a)   for an offence for which it was obligatory (eg driving with excess alcohol); or
(b)   for an offence for which it was optional (eg a bad case of careless driving); or
(c)   for 12 or more penalty points;

and must have been for a period of 56 days or more and was not imposed for stealing a motor vehicle, taking without consent or going equipped for theft.

Mitigating grounds

C[5.24]

When a defendant becomes liable to disqualification under this procedure he may claim that there are grounds for mitigating the normal consequences of conviction and if the court finds such grounds it may reduce the minimum period to which the offender is liable or it may decide not to disqualify. In either event it must state its reasons which will be recorded. The court's discretion, however, is limited. It may not take into account:

(a)   any circumstances which are alleged to make the offence (or any of them) not a serious offence;
(b)   the fact that disqualification would cause hardship (but it may take account of exceptional hardship);
(c)   any circumstances which have been taken into account during the previous three years so as to avoid or reduce disqualification.

The case of *Miller v DPP* [2004] EWHC 595 (Admin), [2004] 17 LS Gaz R 30, [2004] All ER (D) 477 (Mar) suggests that where there has been excessive delay (over 2 years) in sentencing the defendant this is a proper ground for reducing the length of a disqualification under RTOA 1988, s 35(1).

C[5.25]–[5.30]

So, for example, Mr Zimmer is liable to disqualification but successfully avoids it by pleading that being disabled a disqualification would cause exceptional hardship because his specially adapted vehicle is his only means of getting to work. If he is convicted and attracts a totting disqualification again within three years he is unable to put forward that ground for avoiding disqualification but once three years have passed, that ground is resurrected and may be used again.

C[5.31]

Under the penalty points scheme only one disqualification is imposed irrespective of the number of offences. In the event of an appeal against any one or more of the offences, the disqualification will be treated as having been imposed on each offence and in any event the Crown Court has the power to alter sentences imposed by the magistrates' court for several offences even if there is only an appeal against the sentence on one offence.

C[5.32]

Summary. Upon conviction of certain offences the court must order endorsement unless either there are special reasons (although the Road Traffic Offenders Act 1988 uses the plural it has always been treated as the singular) for not doing so, or in the case of some offences under the Road Vehicles (Construction and Use) Regulations 1986, the defendant did not know of and had no reason to suspect the condition of the vehicle. These offences are noted in the table at C[1.6].

C[5.33]

No disqualification may be ordered unless it is for an endorsable offence (except for offences of theft, going equipped to steal vehicles and taking vehicles without consent). Some few offences carry a compulsory order for disqualification and this must be imposed by the court unless there are special reasons for not doing so.

C[5.34]

The term 'special reasons' has a very narrow meaning, in particular, hardship to the defendant is excluded from consideration.

C[5.35]

A period of disqualification takes effect immediately. This includes disqualification for 12 or more penalty points. Only one period of disqualification is ordered under the penalty points scheme irrespective of the number of offences. The three year period during which penalty points are to be counted runs between dates of offence, not conviction. The three year period during which, the circumstances once used as mitigating grounds for not disqualifying under the penalty points system may not be used again, is measured between dates of their original use and the present conviction.

C[5.36]

Where appeal against sentence is lodged, the court may suspend the effect of disqualification until the appeal is *heard*. This should not be done automatically but only after careful consideration.

Disqualification until passes a test

C[5.37]

The court *must* disqualify an offender until he passes an extended driving test where:

(a) he is convicted of an offence of dangerous driving; or
(b) in the Crown Court, the offences of manslaughter, causing death by dangerous driving or causing death by careless driving whilst under the influence of drink or drugs; or
(c) the court orders him to be disqualified until a test of competence is passed, having convicted him of an offence involving obligatory disqualification under s 34 or he is disqualified under s 35 of the RTOA 1988.

C[5.38]

The court has a *discretion* to disqualify until an ordinary test of competence is passed where the offender has been convicted of any offence involving obligatory endorsement. The defendant is entitled to drive but must display L plates and be supervised. In cases where the court is exercising its discretion it must have regard to the safety of road users and an order is inappropriate as a punishment, but is suitable for the following cases:

(a) for people who are growing aged or infirm, or show some incompetence in the offence which needs looking into. In addition a licence may be revoked by the Secretary of State on medical grounds and a provisional licence issued for the sole purpose of a road reassessment;
(b) where the defendant is disqualified for a long period for the offence and there is doubt about his ability to drive at the expiry of the disqualification period;
(c) where the manner of the defendant's driving suggests a threat to the safety of other road users (*R v Miller* (1993) 15 Cr App Rep (S) 505, [1994] Crim LR 231, CA). See the Road Traffic Offenders Act 1988, s 36;
(d) it is not usually appropriate in the cases of passengers in vehicles taken without the owner's consent (*R v Wiggins* [2001] RTR 37, CA).

The onus is on the defendant charged with driving whilst disqualified when not having completed a retest to show he held a provisional licence and was complying with the conditions of that licence (*DPP v Barker* (2004) 168 JP 617, [2004] All ER (D) 246 (Oct), DC).

Interim disqualification

C[5.39]

A magistrates' court may impose an interim disqualification on a person where:

(a)   it commits him to the Crown Court for sentence or remits his case to another magistrates' court; or

(b)   it defers or adjourns his case before passing sentence (including a transfer to another magistrates' court post conviction). An interim order of disqualification may continue until the defendant is finally dealt with subject to a limit of six months and any subsequent order of disqualification will be reduced by the period of the interim order.

Disqualification by the Crown Court

C[5.40]–[5.44]

Where the Crown Court either convicts or sentences a person who was convicted by a magistrates' court of an offence punishable with at least two years' imprisonment it may disqualify the defendant for an unlimited period if it is satisfied that a motor vehicle was used (whether by him or by an accomplice) to commit or to facilitate the commission of the offence.

C[5.45]

Disqualification for any offence. This is a power to disqualify a person from driving instead of or as an addition to dealing with him in any other way and it applies to any criminal offence (PCC(S)A 2000, s 146). Certain non endorsable offences recommend themselves for such a penalty including kerb crawling, unlawful tipping and driving off road unlawfully. See *R v Doick* [2004] EWCA Crim 139, [2004] 2 Cr App Rep (S) 203 for guidance when coupled with custody. The power should not be used arbitrarily but could be used where a vehicle was driven to an affray (*R v Clift* [2004] EWCA Crim 3139, [2005] RTR 147, [2004] All ER (D) 400 (Nov)) or when used in connection with the fraudulent evasion of duty on cigarettes (*R v Skitt* [2004] EWCA Crim 3141, [2004] All ER (D) 401 (Nov)).

The effect of endorsement on new drivers

C[5.46]

Drivers within the first two years of first passing a driving test are in a probationary period. If, during that period, such a driver accumulates 6 or more penalty points on his licence the DVLA will automatically revoke his driving licence when it is sent to them or they are notified by the court.

C[5.47]

This is not a disqualification but the new driver will only be entitled to hold a provisional licence until he passes a retest, which will restore his previous entitlements. Revocation will occur whether the penalty points are added following a conviction by a court or following a fixed penalty.

C[5.48]

Points accumulated before the test was taken will count, unless they were committed more than three years before the current offence (*R (on the application of Adebowale) v Secretary of State for Transport* [2004] EWHC 1741 (Admin), [2004] All ER (D) 335 (Jun)). Points accumulated after the test is passed will count if the *offence* is within two years of the date on which the test was passed. In *R v Damien Joseph Edmunds* [2000] 2 Cr App Rep (S) 62, CA the Court of Appeal reduced the points imposed from 6 to 5 to avoid the defendant from losing his full licence on the grounds that he lived in a rural area without public transport. It is submitted that the Court's basis for so doing was not what Parliament intended when introducing changes to the law on endorsement for new drivers.

C[5.49]

If in any proceedings for an offence committed in respect of a motor vehicle it appears to the court that the accused may be suffering from any relevant disability or prospective disability (within the meaning of Part III of the Road Traffic Act 1988), the court **must** notify the Secretary of State.

There must be sufficient material before the court, even if only by way of something said in mitigation, suggesting that the defendant is suffering from a relevant disability or a prospective disability, before the court can properly refer the matter to the Secretary of State. A good example is alcoholism or epilepsy (see *R v Chichester JJ, ex p Crouch* (1981) 146 JP 26). Note that the court has no discretion in the matter. It is advisable to consult the legal adviser.

C[6]

Driving licence codes

C[6.1]

Offences and the sentences imposed therefor are recorded on driving licences in code. The codes are reproduced below by permission of the Department of the Environment.

Endorsement code

C[6.2]

Causing or permitting

Offences as coded below, but with zero changed to 4, eg IN 10 becomes IN 14.

Inciting

Offences as coded below, but with zero changed to 6, eg DD 30 becomes DD 36.

Periods of time

Periods of time are signified as follows: D = days; M = months; Y = years.

Code	Accident offences
AC 10	Failing to stop after an accident.
AC 20	Failing to give particulars or to report an accident within 24 hours.
AC 30	Undefined accident offence.
	Disqualified driver
BA 10	Driving whilst disqualified by order of court.
BA 20	Driving whilst disqualified by reason of age (obsolete).
BA 30	Attempting to drive whilst disqualified by order of court.
	Careless driving
CD 10	Driving without due care and attention.

Code	**Accident offences**
CD 20	Driving without reasonable consideration for other road users.
CD 30	Driving without due care and attention or without reasonable consideration for other road users (primarily for use by Scottish courts).
CD 40	Causing death by careless driving when unfit through drink.
CD 50	Causing death by careless driving when unfit through drugs.
CD 60	Causing death by careless driving with alcohol level above the limit.
CD 70	Causing death by careless driving, then failing to supply specimen for analysis.
CD 71	Causing death by careless driving, then failing to supply a specimen for drug analysis.
CD 80	Causing death by careless or inconsiderate driving.
CD 90	Causing death by driving: unlicensed, disqualified or uninsured drivers.

	Construction and use offences
CU 10	Using a vehicle with defective brakes.
CU 20	Causing or likely to cause danger by reason of use of unsuitable vehicle or using a vehicle with parts or accessories (excluding brakes, steering or tyres) in a dangerous condition.
CU 30	Using a vehicle with defective tyres.
CU 40	Using a vehicle with defective steering.
CU 50	Causing or likely to cause danger by reason of load or passengers.
CU 60	Undefined failure to comply with Road Vehicles (Construction and Use) Regulations 1986.
CU 80	Breach of requirements as to control of vehicle, mobile telephones etc

	Reckless driving
DD 30	Reckless driving (obsolete).
DD 40	Dangerous driving.
DD 60	Manslaughter or culpable homicide while driving a vehicle.
DD 70	Causing death by reckless driving (obsolete).
DD 80	Causing death by dangerous driving.

	Drink or drugs
DR 10	Driving or attempting to drive with alcohol concentration above limit.
DR 20	Driving or attempting to drive while unfit through drink.
DR 30	Driving or attempting to drive then refusing to supply a specimen for laboratory testing.
DR 40	In charge of a vehicle with alcohol concentration above limit.
DR 50	In charge of a vehicle when unfit through drink.
DR 60	In charge of a vehicle then refusing to supply a specimen for laboratory testing.

Code	Accident offences
DR 61	In charge of a vehicle then refusing to supply a specimen for drug analysis.
DR 70	Failing to provide specimen for breath test (roadside).
DR 80	Driving or attempting to drive when unfit through drugs.
DR 90	In charge of a vehicle when unfit through drugs.

Insurance offences

IN 10	Using a vehicle uninsured against third party risks.

Licence offences

LC 10	Driving without a licence (obsolete).
LC 20	Driving otherwise than in accordance with a licence.
LC 30	Driving after making a false declaration about fitness when applying for a licence.
LC 40	Driving a vehicle having failed to notify a disability.
LC 50	Driving after a licence has been revoked or refused on medical grounds.

Miscellaneous offences

MS 10	Leaving a vehicle in a dangerous position.
MS 20	Unlawful pillion riding.
MS 30	Playstreet offences.
MS 40	Driving with uncorrected defective eyesight or refusing to submit to a test. (Obsolete code, see now MS 70 and MS 80.)
MS 50	Motor racing on the highway.
MS 60	Offences not covered by other codes.
MS 70	Driving with uncorrected defective eyesight.
MS 80	Refusing to submit to eyesight test.
MS 90	Failure to give information as to identity of driver in certain cases.

Motorway offences

MW 10	Contravention of Special Road Regulations (excluding speed limits). Road Traffic Regulation Act 1984

Non-endorsable offences

NE 98	Disqualification under Powers of Criminal Courts (Sentencing) Act 2000, s 146
NE 99	Disqualification under Criminal Justice Act 1972, s 24 and Powers of Criminal Courts (Sentencing) Act 2000, s 147 (and for offences of unauthorised taking see A[77]).

Pedestrian crossings

PC 10	Undefined contravention of Zebra, Pelican and Puffin Pedestrian Crossing Regulations and General Directions 1997 (primarily for use by Scottish courts).
PC 20	Contravention of Zebra, Pelican and Puffin Pedestrian Crossing Regulations and General Directions 1997 with moving vehicle.

Code	Accident offences
PC 30	Contravention of Zebra, Pelican and Puffin Pedestrian Crossing Regulations and General Directions 1997 with stationary vehicle.

Provisional licence offences (obsolete, see now LC 20)

PL 10	Driving without 'L' plates.
PL 20	Not accompanied by a qualified person.
PL 30	Carrying a person not qualified.
PL 40	Drawing an unauthorised trailer.
PL 50	Undefined failure to comply with conditions of a provisional licence.

Speed limits

SP 10	Exceeding goods vehicle speed limit.
SP 20	Exceeding speed limit for type of vehicle (excluding goods or passenger vehicles).
SP 30	Exceeding statutory speed limit on a public road.
SP 40	Exceeding passenger vehicle speed limit.
SP 50	Exceeding speed limit on a motorway.
SP 60	Undefined speed limit offence.

Traffic directions and signs

TS 10	Failing to comply with traffic light signals.
TS 20	Failing to comply with double white lines.
TS 30	Failing to comply with a 'stop' sign.
TS 40	Failing to comply with directions of a constable or traffic warden.
TS 50	Failing to comply with a traffic sign (excluding 'stop' signs, traffic lights or double white lines).
TS 60	Failing to comply with a school crossing patrol sign.
TS 70	Undefined failure to comply with a traffic direction or sign.

Theft or unauthorised taking (obsolete (except UT 50), see now NE 99)

UT 10	Taking and driving away a vehicle without consent or an attempt thereat (primarily for use by Scottish courts).
UT 20	Stealing or attempting to steal a vehicle.
UT 30	Going equipped for stealing or taking a vehicle.
UT 40	Taking or attempting to take a vehicle without consent; driving or attempting to drive a vehicle knowing it to have been taken without consent, allowing oneself to be carried in or on a vehicle knowing it to have been taken without consent.
UT 50	Aggravated taking of a vehicle.

Special codes

TT 99	Disqualification for accumulating 12 or more penalty points.
NSP	(No separate penalty.) Where court does not impose penalty points for minor offences committed at the same time as a more serious one.

C[7]
Sentence code

C[7.1]

The sentence is represented by four characters, eg G 02 Y (community rehabilitation order two years). The first letter indicates the nature of the sentence, the middle two numbers (0 always precedes what would otherwise be a single figure) and the final letter indicate the period of the sentence, if any, as hours (H), days (D), months (M), or years (Y). Apart from the special code TT 99 which indicates a disqualification under the penalty points procedure there is no code to represent disqualification because this appears in a special column on the licence. In the case of an absolute discharge there is no period so the code J 000 is used.

C[7.2]

The first letter of the code indicates the sentence as follows:

A	imprisonment
B	detention in a place approved by the Secretary of State
C	suspended sentence of imprisonment
E	conditional discharge
F	bound over
G	community rehabilitation
H	supervision order (youth court)
I	no separate penalty
J	absolute discharge
K	attendance centre
M	community punishment order
P	young offender institution
S	compensation
T	hospital or guardianship order
W	care order

C[8]
Fixed penalties

C[8.1]

For some time it has been possible to avoid the expense of court proceedings for some criminal and motoring offences by the expedient of the prosecution offering the defendant a 'fixed penalty ticket'. If he accepts the offer he pays the required sum and the matter is settled, otherwise he is summoned to court and the matter proceeds in the usual way.

C[8.2]

In the interests of relieving the burden on the courts of having to deal with many minor motoring cases, the fixed penalty system (formerly almost exclusively confined to motoring offences) has been greatly extended to cover a wide range of offences. These are noted in the index at C[1.6] and include a number of offences which carry an endorsement.

C[8.3]

A summary of the procedure is as follows:

Offering the fixed penalty

C[8.4]

When a constable observes that a 'fixed penalty' offence has been committed, he must decide whether it is endorsable or not.

C[8.5]

Non-endorsable offences. He may give the fixed penalty ticket to the driver or affix it to the vehicle if the driver is not present. In the case of criminal offences the offender must be present and at least 18 years old.

C[8.6]

Endorsable offences. The driver must be present and the officer will require him to produce his driving licence for examination. If the driver is not liable to disqualification because he will not have accumulated 12 or more penalty points, the officer may offer him the option of a fixed penalty and invite him to surrender his licence in exchange for a receipt which he may use as evidence that he is a licence holder. It is then for the driver to decide whether to accept the offer of a fixed penalty.

C[8.7]

If the driver does not have his driving licence with him, the procedure is modified in that he may be required to produce his driving licence within seven days at a chosen police station where it will be inspected and, if appropriate, a fixed penalty offered.

C[8.8]

Note. There are no fixed penalties for endorsable offences when the driver is not present (but see 'Conditional offer of fixed penalty', below), nor where he is present but declines the offer. Also the police have a discretion whether to offer a fixed penalty so that, for example, a constable might decline to offer it for an isolated offence which is serious in nature.

From a date to be appointed s 3 of the **Road Safety Act 2006,** will amend s 53 of the Road Traffic Offenders Act 1988, to cater for the introduction of graduated fixed penalties. Similarly s 4 of the **Road Safety Act 2006** will likewise introduce a graduated fixed penalty points scheme.

Paying the fixed penalty

C[8.9]

The defendant has to pay the fixed penalty within 21 days (or such longer period as is allowed by the ticket) to the court responsible for fixed penalties.

Offences	Fixed penalty
A fixed penalty offence under s 143 of the RTA 1988 (no insurance)	£200
A fixed penalty offence under s 172 of the RTA 1988 (failure to supply name and address of driver)	£120
Any other fixed penalty offence involving obligatory endorsement	£60
A fixed penalty parking offence committed in Greater London on a red route)	£60
Other fixed penalty parking offence committed in Greater London	£40
A fixed penalty offence under s 47 of the RTA 1988 (no test certificate)	£60
A fixed penalty offence under s 33, 42 and 43 of the Vehicle Excise and Registration Act 1994 (failure to display a VEL; no registration mark or obscured registration mark)	£60
Any other fixed penalty offence	£30

C[8.10]–[8.15]

For the purpose of the higher parking penalties, London is regarded as the

Metropolitan Police District. The licence that was surrendered to the police is sent to the fixed penalty clerk who places the endorsement on it and returns it to the defendant when the penalty has been paid.

Instituting proceedings

C[8.16]

In any case where a fixed penalty has been offered the defendant can at any time before the time for payment has expired, request a hearing before the magistrates and plead guilty or not guilty as he thinks fit.

Where the fixed penalty is not paid

C[8.17]

In the case of an endorsable offence, the defendant's licence will already be in the possession of the police who will have forwarded it to the clerk responsible for fixed penalties. If the penalty is unpaid at the end of the required period, the police will register the penalty at the court for the area in which the defendant lives and the clerk who already holds the licence will endorse it and return it to the defendant. Unfortunately for him the penalty is registered as a fine 50% above the fixed penalty. Similar provisions apply to non-endorsable offences where the ticket is given to the driver.

C[8.18]

Where the offence is non-endorsable and the ticket was affixed to the vehicle, the police send a notice to the person they believe to be the owner requesting him either to pay the penalty or to inform them who is the actual owner. If he fails to co-operate by not replying at all, he will have the enhanced penalty registered against him. He is similarly liable if he replies and admits he was the owner unless either (a) he pays the penalty, or (b) persuades the actual driver to pay it for him, or (c) he returns a form signed by the person who was actually driving and who requests a court hearing.

Enforcement of payment

C[8.19]

Once a penalty has been registered, it is regarded as a fine. Non-payment of the registered penalty will result in enforcement proceedings being taken in the manner described at B[33.96].

Penalty points

C[8.20]

If the accused has committed several endorsable offences on the *same occasion*, and one is dealt with under the fixed penalty procedure and his licence is to be endorsed, the penalty points for those offences dealt with at a court hearing are to be treated as being reduced by those points to be endorsed under the fixed penalty procedure.

Conditional offer of fixed penalty

C[8.21]

The Road Traffic Act 1988, s 172 provides for the police to issue a notice to the keeper of the vehicle requiring information as to the identity of the driver. If the keeper fails to give the information he will be guilty of an endorsable offence deemed to have taken place in the place to where the reply ought to have been sent (*Kennet District Council v Young* [1999] RTR 235, 163 JP 622). Any reply must be in writing and signed (*DPP v Broomfield* [2002] EWHC 1962 (Admin), [2003] RTR 108). A telephone call will not be sufficient compliance with the section but a letter accompanying the form and disclosing the required information will be (*Jones v DPP* [2004] EWHC 236 (Admin), [2004] All ER (D) 319 (Jan)) but not if it is left unsigned (*Francis v DPP* [2004] EWHC 591 (Admin), [2004] All ER (D) 443 (Mar)). In *R (on the application of Flegg) v Southampton and New Forest Justices* [2006] EWHC 396 (Admin), 170 JP 373 the defendant returned a section 172 request with a covering note stating that he could not say who the driver was. The conviction was upheld on the basis that the information given was both misleading and inaccurate. The defendant as the owner or keeper of the vehicle has a duty to name potential drivers not just actual drivers.

Where the driver is identified, a conditional offer of a fixed penalty is sent to him and if he wishes to accept the offer he will send his driving licence and payment to the fixed penalty office within 28 days of the issue of the offer. The fixed penalty will be accepted unless the details of the licence disclose that the offender is liable to be disqualified under the penalty points provisions. In this case the police will be notified and a summons issued in the normal way.

In *DPP v Holden* [2006] All ER (D) 363 (Feb), the notice sent to the defendant stated that the response to the police had to be returned within 28 days but failed to specify the period during which a speeding offence could be commenced (see s 75(7)(c) RTOA 1988). In the absence of bad faith this was not a matter which directly affected the fairness of the trial; further, the delay in instituting proceedings was not so exceptional as to warrant a stay of proceedings on the ground of delay.

In *Thomson (Procurator Fiscal) v Jackson* [2010] HCJAC 96, [2011] RTR 210, the High Court of Justiciary dissented from the opinion in *Wilkinson's Road Traffic Offences* (24th edn, 2009), to the effect that there could be more than one valid requirement addressed to the same person, and in relation to the same incident under RTA 1988, s 172. There is nothing in the legislation to suggest that there can only be one requirement. The relevance of the argument goes to questions of statutory time limits and/or issues of abuse of process based on delay. The above decision is of *persuasive* authority only and it is open to question whether it would be followed in England and Wales.

Note, where a defendant is convicted of an offence under s 172, the penalty has been increased to allow for an endorsement with 6 penalty points for offences committed on or after 24 September 2007 (Road Safety Act 2006 (Commencement No 2) Order 2007 (SI 2007/2472 (C 91)).

C[8.22]

This procedure would appear not to breach the rule against self-incrimination contained in Art 6 of the ECHR: see *Tora Tolinos v Spain* (No 23816/94) (17 May 1995, unreported), ECtHR, *Brown v Stott* [2001] 2 All ER 97, [2001] 2 WLR 817, PC and *Hayes v DPP* [2004] EWHC 277 (Admin), [2004] All ER (D) 55 (Feb). In *O'Halloran v United Kingdom* [2007] All ER (D) 7 (Jul), [2007] ECHR 15809/02 it was decided:

'The right to remain silent and the right not to incriminate oneself were not absolute rights and the right to require an actual or potential suspect to provide information which contributed or might contribute to his conviction by direct compulsion would not cumulatively result in a violation of article 6 of the Convention. While the right to a fair trial was an unqualified right, what constituted a fair trial could not be the subject of a single unvarying rule, but had to depend on the circumstances of the particular case. In order to determine whether the essence of the applicant's right to remain silent and privilege against self-incrimination had been infringed, it was necessary to focus on the nature and degree of compulsion used to obtain the evidence, the existence of any relevant safeguards in the procedure, and the use to which any material so obtained was put.'

Looking at s 172(2)(a) the ECHR noted that it was not an offence of strict liability; certain defences were still available. The essence of the applicant's right to remain silent and the privilege against self-incrimination had not been destroyed. Hence, it decided there was no violation of Art 6.

The prosecution should annex to s 9 statements proving service, a notice of intended prosecution and the requirement to provide details. If the defence fail to raise the issue, that the requirement was not lawfully made, before the end of the prosecution case the court should permit the prosecution to re open their case to prove the point (*Mohindra v DPP* [2004] EWHC 490 (Admin), [2004] All ER (D) 269 (Mar)).

C[9]

Brakes defective

Charge

C[9.1]

Using, causing or permitting to be used on a road a motor vehicle or trailer with defective brakes

Road Vehicles (Construction and Use) Regulations 1986, reg 18; Road Traffic Act 1988, s 41A(b)

Maximum penalty – For goods vehicles fine level 5. Other motor vehicles or trailers fine level 4 (for fines see para B[33]). For endorsement and disqualification-see below, and under 'Sentencing'.

'Goods vehicles' for this purpose includes vehicles adapted to carry more than eight passengers; as to whether this includes the driver, consult the clerk.

If the defendant can satisfy the court that he did not know and had no reasonable cause to suspect the deficiency of the brakes then disqualification and endorsement cannot be ordered. The defendant does not have to establish this point beyond reasonable doubt but merely that it is true on the balance of probabilities.

Penalty points – 3.

Fixed penalty – £60.

Legal notes and definitions

C[9.2]

Goods vehicle. Means a motor vehicle or trailer constructed or adapted for the carrying or hauling of goods or burden.

C[9.3]

The law requires that every part of every braking system and of the means of operating the braking system must be maintained in good and efficient working order and must be properly adjusted. The offence is an absolute one and the vehicle must have proper brakes at all times. If the charge is using the prosecution need not prove that the defendant knew of the defect. If the vehicle had no brakes at all then he will be charged under a different regulation.

C[9.4]

Using. This does not mean only driving along a road; mere presence on a road, even in a useless condition, may constitute using (*Pumbien v Vines* [1996] RTR 37, [1996] Crim LR 124). The term means 'to have the use of the vehicle on the road'. The test to be applied is whether or not such steps had been taken as would make it impossible for anyone to use the car. 'Use' involves an element of control, management or operation as a vehicle. Therefore, an accused who was in the driving seat of a 'vehicle' where the steering was locked, there was no ignition key, the brakes were seized on and the engine could not be started was not 'using' it when it was being towed along the road. It was an inanimate hunk of metal. It would be different if there was a possibility of control, ie its steering could be operated and its brakes were working, even if its engine were not working. In doubtful cases the legal adviser should be consulted. A person, limited company or corporate body which owns a vehicle that is being driven in the course of the owner's business is using the vehicle (*West Yorkshire Trading Standards Service v Lex Vehicle Leasing Ltd* [1996] RTR 70). Knowledge of the facts which constitute the offence is not necessary. For a recent judgment where the High Court were unable to agree on whether knowledge on the part of the employer company was required (s 5 RTRA 1984) see *Cambridgeshire County Council v Associated Lead Mills Ltd* [2005] EWHC 1627 (Admin), [2006] RTR 82.

A passenger in a car knowing the driver to be uninsured and allowing himself to be carried in it in pursuance of a joint enterprise is a person using the vehicle for insurance purposes (*Stinton v Stinton* [1995] RTR 167, [1995] 01 LS Gaz R 37, sub nom Stinton v Motor Insurers Bureau 159 JP 656, [1999] Lloyd's Rep IR 305, CA).

C[9.5]

Causing. This implies some express or positive mandate from the person causing the vehicle to be used or some authority from him and knowledge of the *fact* which constitutes the offence (but there need be no *intention* to commit an offence). Acquiescence could amount to permission (see below) but falls short of a positive mandate (*Redhead Freight Ltd v Shulman* [1989] RTR 1, [1988] Crim LR 696).

The meaning of 'cause' in causing death by dangerous driving (Road Traffic Act 1988, s 1) meant a cause that was more than negligible or *de minimis*: *R v Hennigan* [1971] 3 All ER 133, [1971] RTR 305, (1971) 55 Cr App R 262, CA. Given that Parliament is normally presumed to legislate in the knowledge of, and having regard to, relevant judicial decisions, Parliament could not have intended any different meaning for s 3ZB (causing death while unlicensed or uninsured etc). The judge, therefore, had been correct to direct the jury that in order to convict what was necessary was a cause that was more than minute or negligible: *R v Williams* [2010] EWCA Crim 2552, [2011] 3 All ER 969, [2011] 1 WLR 588.

C[9.6]

Permitting. This includes express permission and also circumstances in which permission may be inferred. If the defendant is a limited company or corporate body it must be proved that some person for whose criminal act the company is responsible permitted the offence. A defendant charged with permitting must be shown to have known that the vehicle was being used or it must be shown that he shut his eyes to something that made it obvious to him that the vehicle was being used on a road (*Roper v Taylor's Central Garages Ltd* [1951] 2 TLR 284). In other road traffic offences permitting in the case of an employer may mean failing to take reasonable steps to prevent a contravention of the transport regulations (*Vehicle Inspectorate v Nuttall (t/a Redline Coaches)* [1999] 3 All ER 833, [1999] 1 WLR 629, HL).

C[9.7]

Motor vehicle. Means a mechanically propelled vehicle intended or adapted for use on roads. 'Intended' does not mean intended by the user of the vehicle either at the moment of the alleged offence or for the future nor the intention of the manufacturer or the wholesaler or the retailer. The test is whether a reasonable person looking at the vehicle would say that one of its users would be a road user. If a reasonable man applying the test would say 'Yes, this vehicle might well be used on a road' then the vehicle was intended or adapted for such use. For example a Go-Ped requires both a driving licence and insurance (*DPP v Saddington* [2001] RTR 227, sub nom Chief Constable of North Yorkshire Police v Saddington (2001) 165 JP 122, [2001] Crim LR 41). If that were the case then it is nothing to the point if the individual defendant says that he normally used the vehicle for scrambling and was only pushing it home on this occasion because there was no other means of taking it home, or something of that sort (*Chief Constable of Avon and Somerset v Fleming* [1987] 1 All ER 318, [1987] RTR 378, 84 Cr App Rep 345).

C[9.8]

For 'mechanically propelled' see the note at C[47.9].

C[9.9]

A trailer. Means any vehicle being drawn by a motor vehicle.

C[9.10]–[9.15]

A road. Means any highway (including footpaths and bridleways) and any other road to which the public has access and includes bridges but not a car park the purpose of which is to enable cars to stand and wait rather than move along it to a destination (*Cutter v Eagle Star Insurance Co Ltd* [1998] 4 All ER 417, [1998] 1 WLR 1647, HL).

Sentencing
SC Guideline – Brakes defective

C[9.16]

Starting point – Band B fine (driver); Band B fine (owner-driver but consider an uplift of 25% of at least 25% on the driver's fine); Band C fine (owner-company)

C[9.16A]

If the defendant proves that he did not know, and had no reasonable cause to suspect, that the brakes were deficient, endorsement and disqualification cannot be ordered. The defendant only has to prove that it is more probable than not that this was the case. Otherwise he can be disqualified and the licence **must** be endorsed unless there are 'special reasons'; see C[5.2].

C[9.17]

It may sometimes be appropriate to grant a conditional or absolute discharge but if this course is adopted then a disqualification can still be imposed. Endorsement must still be ordered unless 'special reasons' exist.

C[9.18]

If it appears to the court that the accused suffers from some disease or physical disability likely to cause his driving to be a source of danger to the public then the court shall notify the licensing authority (see C[5.49]).

C[9.19]

When the vehicle concerned is a goods vehicle the fine will reflect the potential danger to the public and to the driver of the vehicle, and the gross weight and nature of the load may well be relevant.

C[9.20]

For fines see B[33].

C[10]–C[15]

Dangerous condition/bodywork

Charge

C[10.1]

Using, causing or permitting to be used a motor vehicle or trailer on a road when

[the condition of the motor vehicle or trailer, or of its accessories or equipment]

[the purpose for which it is used]

[the number of passengers carried by it, or the manner in which they are carried]

[the weight, position or distribution of its load, or the manner in which it is secured]

is such that the use of the motor vehicle or trailer involves a danger of injury to another person

Road Traffic Act 1988, s 40A

Maximum penalty-For goods vehicle or vehicle adapted to carry more than eight passengers fine level 5. For other vehicles or trailers fine level 4 (for fines see B[33]).

Licence must be endorsed unless special reasons exist. *May be disqualified for any period and/or until he passes a driving test. Endorsement and disqualification cannot be ordered if defendant can satisfy the court that he did not know of, and he had no reasonable cause to suspect, the dangerous condition. The defendant does not have to prove this beyond reasonable doubt. He need only prove that on the balance of probabilities it is true.

Must disqualify for at least 6 months where the offence under s 40A has been committed within three years of a previous conviction of the offender under the same section; otherwise, disqualification is discretionary: Road Safety Act 2006 (Commencement No 2) Order 2007 (SI 2007/2472 (C 91)).

Penalty points – 3.

Fixed penalty – £60.

Legal notes and definitions

C[10.2]

Goods vehicle. Means a motor vehicle or trailer constructed or adapted for the carriage of goods or burden. The clerk should be consulted if there is a question whether a vehicle is a goods vehicle.

C[10.3]
Using, causing, permitting. See the notes under these headings for the offence of defective brakes at C[9.4]–C[9.6].

C[10.4]
Road. Means any highway (including footpaths and bridleways) and any other road to which the public has access and includes bridges.

Motor vehicle. See C[9.7].

C[10.5]
The offence is an absolute one. It is no defence that the defect was latent, and only became apparent during the journey. The section requires that the vehicle (or trailer) and all its parts and accessories are both in good repair and efficient working order.

C[10.6]
The wording of the summons or charge should specify the exact part or accessory which is said to be dangerous. The court can allow the prosecution to amend the wording to remedy such an omission and to offer the defence an adjournment if it needs further time to prepare its case.

Sentencing
SC Guideline – Dangerous condition/bodywork

C[10.7]
Starting point – Band B fine (driver); Band B fine (owner-driver but consider an uplift of 25% of at least 25% on the driver's fine); Band C fine (owner-company)

C[10.7A]
If the defendant can establish that he did not know and he had no reason to suspect the dangerous condition, in this case endorsement and disqualification cannot be ordered. The defendant does not have to prove this beyond reasonable doubt. He need only prove that on the balance of probabilities it is true.

C[10.8]
If it appears to the court that the accused suffers from some disease or physical disability likely to cause his driving to be a source of danger to the public then the court shall notify the licensing authority (see C[5.49]).

C[10.9]
For fines see B[33].

C[16]

Dangerous driving

Charge

C[16.1]

Driving a mechanically propelled vehicle dangerously on a road or other public place

Road Traffic Act 1988, s 2 (as substituted by the Road Traffic Act 1991)

Maximum penalty – Fine level 5 and 6 months [**12 months] (for fines see B[33]). Triable either way. Must disqualify for at least one year unless special reasons. The disqualification may be for any period exceeding a year. If disqualified he *must* also be ordered to pass an extended driving test. Must endorse licence unless special reasons exist.

Crown Court – 2 years' imprisonment and unlimited fine.

Penalty points – 3–11.

Mode of trial

C[16.2]

Consider the SC guideline at C[16.7] below.

Legal notes and definitions

C[16.3]

Driving. See the note under the offence of no driving licence at C[18.8].

C[16.4]

Mechanically propelled vehicle. See C[47.9].

C[16.5]

Dangerously. Means that the defendant's driving falls far below what would be expected of a competent and careful driver *and* it would be obvious to a competent and careful driver that driving in that way would be dangerous.

A person is also to be regarded as driving dangerously if it would be obvious to a competent and careful driver that driving the vehicle in its current state would be dangerous. The unintentional pressing of the wrong pedal is not a defence to dangerous driving (*A-G's Reference (No 4 of 2000)* (2001)).

C[16.6]

Aid and Abet. In *R v Webster* [2006] EWCA Crim 415, (2005) Times,

15 March, the defendant allowed a friend to drive his vehicle while drunk. It was held that whilst the condition of the driver could be relevant to the manner in which the vehicle was driven on the facts this had not been established by the Crown. In this case there was no evidence that the defendant had been given the opportunity to intervene once he became aware the defendant was driving in a dangerous manner.

C[16.7]

Dangerous refers to danger either of injury to any person or of serious damage to property.

C[16.8]

In determining what would be expected of, or obvious to, a competent and careful driver in a particular case, regard shall be had not only to the circumstances of which he could be expected to be aware but also to any circumstances shown to have been within the knowledge of the accused. The effect of s 2A(3) of the 1988 Act was not to offend against the rule that the test for dangerous driving was objective; it simply refined the objective test by reference to existing circumstances. By enacting s 2A(3) Parliament directed the court to have regard to any circumstances shown to have been within the knowledge of the accused. Subjective considerations, such as what the driver thought about the situation were irrelevant, but in so far as circumstances relevant to the issue of dangerousness was capable of being established as being within the knowledge of the accused, the fact finder had to have regard to it.

In *Milton v DPP* [2007] EWHC 532 (Admin), [2007] All ER (D) 285 (Mar), it was decided the fact that the defendant was an advanced police driver was a circumstance to which regard had to be had pursuant to s 2A(3). *Milton v DPP* has recently been overruled by *R v Bannister* [2009] EWCA Crim 1571, (2009) Times, 24 August. In the latter case the Court of Appeal reconsidered the position of a police officer who claimed specialist driving skills should be taken into account when judging the standard of driving. The Court of Appeal held: ' . . . the special skill (or indeed lack of skill) of a driver is an irrelevant circumstance when considering whether the driving is dangerous'.

C[16.9]

In determining the state of the vehicle regard may be had to anything attached to or carried on or in it and to the manner in which it is attached or carried.

C[16.10]–[16.14]

Road. See C[10.4] and C[22.5].

C[16.15]

Public place. See C[20.7]–C[20.8].

C[16.16]

Warning of proceedings. If the defence claim that notice should have been given within 14 days of intention to prosecute, consult the legal adviser.

Sentencing
SC Guideline – Dangerous Driving

C[16.17]

Must endorse and disqualify for at least 12 months

Must disqualify for **at least** 2 years if offender has had two or more disqualifications for periods of 56 days or more in preceding 3 years – consult your legal adviser for further guidance

If there is a delay in sentencing after conviction, consider interim disqualification

OFFENCE SERIOUSNESS (CULPABILITY AND HARM)		
A. IDENTIFY THE APPROPRIATE STARTING POINT		
Starting points based on first time offender pleading not guilty		
Examples of nature of activity	**Starting point**	**Range**
Single incident where little or no damage or risk of personal injury	Medium level community penalty	Low level community order to high level community order Disqualify 12 – 15 months
Incident(s) involving excessive speed or showing off, especially on busy roads or in built-up area; OR Single incident where little or no damage or risk of personal injury but offender was disqualified driver	12 weeks custody	High level community order to 26 weeks custody Disqualify 15 – 24 months
Prolonged bad driving involving deliberate disregard for safety of others; OR Incident(s) involving excessive speed or showing off, especially on busy roads or in built-up area, by disqualified driver; OR Driving as described in box above while being pursued by the police	Crown Court	Crown Court* *Consider interim disqualification
OFFENCE SERIOUSNESS (CULPABILITY AND HARM)		
B. CONSIDER THE EFFECT OF AGGRAVATING AND MITIGATING FACTORS (OTHER THAN THOSE WITHIN EXAMPLES ABOVE)		
Common aggravating and mitigating factors are identified at B[5.2A]. The following may be particularly relevant but **these lists are not exhaustive**		

Factors indicating higher culpability	Factors indicating lower culpability
1. Disregarding warnings of others	1. Genuine emergency
2. Evidence of alcohol or drugs	2. Speed not excessive
3. Carrying out other tasks while driving	3. Offence due to inexperience rather than irresponsibility of driver
4. Carrying passengers or heavy load	
5. Tiredness	
6. Aggressive driving, such as driving much too close to vehicle in front, racing, inappropriate attempts to overtake, or cutting in after overtaking	
7.Driving when knowingly suffering from a medical condition which significantly impairs the offender's driving skills	
8. Driving a poorly maintained or dangerously loaded vehicle, especially where motivated by commercial concerns	
Factors indicating greater degree of harm	
1. Injury to others	
2. Damage to other vehicles or property	
FORM A PRELIMINARY VIEW OF THE APPROPRIATE SENTENCE, THEN CONSIDER OFFENDER MITIGATION	
Common factors are identified at B[5.2A]	
CONSIDER A REDUCTION FOR A GUILTY PLEA	
CONSIDER ANCILLARY ORDERS, INCLUDING COMPENSATION AND DEPRIVATION OF PROPERTY	
Refer to B[18] for guidance on compensation and Part B for available ancillary orders	
DECIDE SENTENCE	
GIVE REASONS	

C[16.18]

See Table A at B[4.1] for available sentences.

C[16.19]

If the prosecution have not brought an alternative charge of careless driving and the court finds the defendant not guilty of dangerous driving but the allegations amount to an offence of careless driving or inconsiderate driving, he may be convicted of one of these offences. For the procedure see *R v Gloucester Magistrates' Court, ex p Chung* (1989) 153 JP 75.

C[16.20]

If convicted of dangerous driving the defendant's licence must be endorsed and he must be disqualified from holding a licence for at least one year (two years if the defendant has had two or more disqualifications of 56 days or more imposed three years immediately preceding the commission of the latest offence). If special reasons are found (at C[5.2]) he may avoid endorsement or a disqualification. If he is not disqualified the court must determine the number of penalty points to be recorded on any endorsement.

C[16.21]–[16.30]

Forfeiture of vehicle. See B[34].

C[16A]
Causing death by careless, or inconsiderate driving

Charge

C[16A.1]
Being the driver of a mechanically propelled motor vehicle on a road or other public place did cause the death of another person by driving the said vehicle without due care and attention, or without reasonable consideration for other persons using the road or place.

Road Traffic Act 1988, s 2B (as inserted by the Road Safety Act 2006 from 18 August 2008 by virtue of the Road Safety Act (Commencement No 4) Order 2008, SI 2008/1918)

Maximum penalty – Fine level 5 and 12 months (for fines see B[33]). Triable either way. Must disqualify for at least 12 months unless special reasons. The disqualification may be for any period exceeding one year. If disqualified he *must* also be ordered to pass an extended driving test. Must endorse licence unless special reasons exist.

Crown Court – 5 years' imprisonment and unlimited fine.

Penalty points – 3–11.

Mode of trial

C[16A.2]
Consider the SC Guideline at **C[16A.10]** below. In general, offences of causing death by careless or inconsiderate driving should be tried summarily except for the presence of one or more of the aggravating factors (a)–(e), outlined under 'Sentencing' at **C[16.18]**.

Legal notes and definitions

C[16A.3]
Driving. See the note under the offence of no driving licence at C[18.8].

Mechanically propelled vehicle. See C[47.9].

C[16A.4]
Road. See C[22.5].

C[16A.5]
Public Place. See [C20.7]-C[20.8]. The car park of a dealership has been found to be a public place (*May v DPP* [2005] EWHC 1280 (Admin), [2005] All ER (D) 182 (Apr)).

C[16A.6]

Cause. See the definition at C[9.5].

Due care and attention. See the detailed notes at C[25]-C[30].

Reasonable consideration. See the detailed notes at C[46] onwards.

C[16A.7]

Where magistrates see fit, they may allow separate informations for an offence under s 2B and s 3 to be heard together. In this event, if the defendant is convicted of one offence, the second information may be adjourned *sine die* or the justices may make *"no adjudication"*. Should the driver successfully appeal against conviction, he can later be tried on the second information.

C[16A.8]

Alternatively, where there is a single information alleging causing death by careless driving or causing death by inconsiderate driving and the magistrates do not find this proved, they may convict of careless or inconsiderate driving in the alternative (s 24 RTOA 1988 as amended by s 20 of the Road Safety Act 2006).

C[16A.9]

Warning of proceedings. If the defence claim that notice should have been given within 14 days of intention to prosecute, consult the legal adviser.

Sentencing
SC Guideline – Causing death by careless or inconsiderate driving

C[16A.10]

This guideline applies only to offenders aged 18 or over. The advice and full guideline are available onhttp://sentencingcouncil.judiciary.gov.uk.

Road Traffic Act 1988 (s 2B)

Maximum penalty. 5 years' imprisonment; minimum disqualification of 12 months, discretionary re-test

This guideline and accompanying notes are taken from the SGC's definitive guideline *Causing Death by Driving*, published 15 July 2008 and coming into force on 18 August 2008.

Key factors

(a)   It is unavoidable that some cases will be on the borderline between *dangerous* and *careless* driving, or may involve a number of factors that significantly increase the seriousness of the offence. As a result, the guideline for this offence identifies three levels of seriousness, the range for the highest of which overlaps with ranges for the lower levels of seriousness for *causing death by dangerous driving*.

(b)   The three levels of seriousness are defined by the degree of carelessness involved in the standard of driving:

- the most serious level for this offence is where the offender's driving fell not that far short of dangerous;
- the least serious group of offences relates to those cases where the level of culpability is low – for example in a case involving an offender who misjudges the speed of another vehicle, or turns without seeing an oncoming vehicle because of restricted visibility;
- other cases will fall into the intermediate level.

(c)   Where the level of carelessness is low and there are no aggravating factors, even the fact that death was caused is not sufficient to justify a prison sentence.

(d)   A fine is unlikely to be an appropriate sentence for this offence; where a non-custodial sentence is considered appropriate, this should be a community order. The nature of the requirements will be determined by the **purpose** (CJA 2003, s 142(1)) identified by the court as of primary importance. Requirements most likely to be relevant include unpaid work requirement, programme requirement and curfew requirement.

(e)   Offender mitigation particularly relevant to this offence includes conduct after the offence such as where the offender gave direct, positive, assistance at the scene of a collision to victim(s). It may also include remorse – whilst it can be expected that anyone who has caused a death by driving would be remorseful, this cannot undermine its importance for sentencing purposes. It is for the court to determine whether an expression of remorse is genuine.

(f)   Where an offender has a good driving record, this is not a factor that automatically should be treated as mitigation, especially now that the presence of previous convictions is a statutory aggravating factor. However, any evidence to show that an offender has previously been an exemplary driver, for example, having driven an ambulance, police vehicle, bus, taxi or similar vehicle conscientiously and without incident for many years, is a fact that the courts may well wish to take into account by way of offender mitigation. This is likely to have even greater effect where the offender is driving on public duty (for example, on ambulance, fire services or police duties) and was responding to an emergency.

(g)   Disqualification of the offender from driving and endorsement of the offender's driving licence are mandatory, and the offence carries between 3 and 11 points when the court finds special reasons for not imposing disqualification. There is a discretionary power to order an extended driving test/re-test where a person is convicted of an offence: s 36(4) of the Road Traffic Offenders Act 1988.

NB: In *R v Campbell* [2009] EWCA Crim 2459 a case which could be described as a single incident of misjudgement (as opposed to momentary inattention) fell into category 2 of the guidelines as opposed to category 1.

OFFENCE SERIOUSNESS (CULPABILITY AND HARM)		
A. IDENTIFY THE APPROPRIATE STARTING POINT Starting points based on first time offender pleading not guilty		
Nature of offence	**Starting point**	**Sentencing range**
Careless or inconsiderate driving arising from momentary inattention with no aggravating factors	Medium level community order	Low level community order to high level community order
Other cases of careless or inconsiderate driving	Crown Court	High level community order to Crown Court
Careless or inconsiderate driving falling not far short of dangerous driving	Crown Court	Crown Court

OFFENCE SERIOUSNESS (CULPABILITY AND HARM)	
B. CONSIDER THE EFFECT OF AGGRAVATING AND MITIGATING FACTORS (OTHER THAN THOSE WITHIN EXAMPLES ABOVE) Common aggravating and mitigating factors are identified at B[5.2A]. The following may be particularly relevant but **these lists are not exhaustive**	
Factors indicating higher culpability	*Factors indicating lower culpability*
1. Other offences committed at the same time, such as driving other than in accordance with the terms of a valid licence; driving while disqualified; driving without insurance; taking a motor vehicle without consent; driving a stolen vehicle	1. Offender seriously injured in collision
2. Previous convictions for motoring offences, particularly offences that involve bad driving	2. The victim was a close friend or relative
3. Irresponsible behaviour, such as failing to stop or falsely claiming that one of the victims was responsible for the collision	3. The actions of the victim or a third party contributed to the commission of the offence
	4. The offender's lack of driving experience contributed significantly to the likelihood of a collision occurring and/or death resulting
	5. The driving was in response to a proven and genuine emergency falling short of a defence

Factors indicating greater degree of harm	
1. More than one person was killed as a result of the offence	
2. Serious injury to one or more persons in addition to death(s)	
FORM A PRELIMINARY VIEW OF THE APPROPRIATE SENTENCE, THEN CONSIDER OFFENDER MITIGATION Common factors are identified at B[5.2A]	
CONSIDER A REDUCTION FOR A GUILTY PLEA	
CONSIDER ANCILLARY ORDERS, INCLUDING COMPENSATION AND DEPRIVATION OF PROPERTY Refer to B[18] for guidance on compensation and **Part B** for available ancillary orders	
DECIDE SENTENCE **GIVE REASONS**	

C[16A.11]

Forfeiture of vehicle. See B[34].

C[16B]

Causing death by driving: unlicensed, disqualified or uninsured drivers

C[16B.1]

Did cause the death of another person by driving a motor vehicle on a road, and at the time when he was driving, the circumstances are such that he was committing an offence under – s 87(1) of the Road Traffic Act 1988 (driving otherwise than in accordance with a licence), s 103(1)(b) of the Road Traffic Act 1988 (driving while disqualified), or s 143 of the said Act (driving while uninsured or unsecured against third party risks).

Road Traffic Act 1988, s 3ZB (as inserted by the Road Safety Act 2006 from 18 August 2008 by virtue of the Road Safety Act (Commencement No 4) Order 2008, SI 2008/1918).

Maximum penalty – Fine level 5 and 12 months (6 months in Scotland). For fines see B[33]. Triable either way. Must disqualify for at least one year unless special reasons. The disqualification may be for any period exceeding one year. If disqualified he *may* be ordered to pass an extended driving test. Must endorse licence unless special reasons exist.

Crown Court – 2 years' imprisonment and unlimited fine.

Penalty points – 3–11.

Mode of trial

C[16B.2]

Consider first the guidance notes at I[4]. In general, offences of causing death by unlicensed, disqualified or uninsured drivers should be tried summarily except for the presence of one or more of the aggravating factors (a)–(e), outlined under 'Sentencing' at C[16.8].

C[16B.3]

Driving. See the note under the offence of no driving licence at C[18.8].

C[16B.4]

Motor vehicle. See the definition at A[60.4].

C[16B.5]

Driving otherwise than in accordance with the conditions of a driving licence. See the notes at C[18] onwards.

Driving while disqualified. See the notes at C[19] onwards.

Driving while uninsured. See the notes at C[33] onwards.

C[16B.5A]

Cause. See the notes at C[9.5].

Sentencing
SC Guideline – Causing death by driving: unlicensed,
disqualified or uninsured drivers

C[16B.6]

This guideline applies only to offenders aged 18 or over. The advice and full guideline are available on http://sentencingcouncil.judiciary.gov.uk.

Road Traffic Act 1988 (s 3ZB)

Maximum penalty. 2 years' imprisonment; minimum disqualification of 12 months, discretionary re-test

This guideline and accompanying notes are taken from the SGC's definitive guideline *Causing Death by Driving*, published 15 July 2008 and coming into force on 18 August 2008.

Key factors

(a) Culpability arises from the offender driving a vehicle on a road or other public place when, by law, not allowed to do so; the offence does not involve any fault in the standard of driving.

(b) Since driving while disqualified is more culpable that driving while unlicensed or uninsured, a higher starting point is proposed when the offender.

(c) Being uninsured, unlicensed or disqualified are the only determinants of the seriousness for this offence, as there are no factors relating to th standard of driving. The list of aggravating factors identified is slightly different as the emphasis is on the decision to drive by an offender who is not permitted by the law to do so.

(d) A fine is unlikely to be an appropriate sentence for this offence; where a non-custodial sentence is considered appropriate, this should be a community order.

(e) Where the decision to drive was brought about by a genuine and proven emergency, that may mitigate offence seriousness and so it is included as an additional mitigating factor.

(f)   Offender mitigation particularly relevant to this offence includes conduct after the offence such as where the offender gave direct, positive, assistance at the scene of a collision to victim(s). It may also include remorse – whilst it can be expected that anyone who has caused a death by driving would be remorseful, this cannot undermine its importance for sentencing purposes. It is for the court to determine whether an expression of remorse is genuine.

(g)   Where an offender has a good driving record, this is not a factor that automatically should be treated as mitigation, especially now that the presence of previous convictions is a statutory aggravating factor. However, any evidence to show that an offender has previously been an exemplary driver, for example, having driven an ambulance, police vehicle, bus, taxi or similar vehicle conscientiously and without incident for many years, is a fact that the courts may well wish to take into account by way of offender mitigation. This is likely to have even greater effect where the offender is driving on public duty (for example, on ambulance, fire services or police duties) and was responding to an emergency.

(h)   Disqualification of the offender from driving and endorsement of the offender's driving licence are mandatory, and the offence carries between 3 and 11 points when the court finds special reasons for not imposing disqualification. There is a discretionary power to order an extended driving test/re-test where a person is convicted of an offence: s 36 (4) Road Traffic Offenders Act 1988.

OFFENCE SERIOUSNESS (CULPABILITY AND HARM)		
A. IDENTIFY THE APPROPRIATE STARTING POINT		
Starting points based on first time offender pleading not guilty		
Nature of offence	Starting point	Sentencing range
The offender was disqualified from driving OR	12 months custody	36 weeks – 2 years custody
The offender was unlicensed or uninsured plus 2 or more aggravating factors from the list below		
The offender was unlicensed or uninsured plus at least 1 aggravating factor from the list below	26 weeks custody	High level community order to 36 weeks custody
The offender was unlicensed or uninsured – no aggravating factors	Medium level community order	Low level community order to High level community order
Additional aggravating factors	Additional mitigating factors	

Previous convictions for motoring offences, whether involving bad driving or involving an offence of the same kind that forms part of the present conviction (i.e. unlicensed, disqualified or uninsured driving)	The decision to drive was brought about by a proven and genuine emergency falling short of a defence
More than one person was killed as a result of the offence	The offender genuinely believed that he or she was insured or licensed to drive
Serious injury to one or more persons in addition to the death(s)	The offender was seriously injured as a result of the collision
Irresponsible behaviour such as failing to stop or falsely claiming that someone else was driving	The victim was a close friend or relative

C[16B.7]

Forfeiture. See B[34].

C[16C]

Causing serious injury by dangerous driving

Charge

Being the driver of a mechanically propelled vehicle on a road or other public place, did cause serious injury to another person by driving the said vehicle dangerously

Road Traffic Act 1988, s 1A*

Maximum penalty – Fine level 5 and 12 months (for fines see B[33]). Triable either way. Must disqualify for at least 12 months unless special reasons. The disqualification may be for any period exceeding one year. If disqualified he must also be ordered to pass an extended driving test. Must endorse licence unless special reasons exist.

Crown Court – 5 years' imprisonment and unlimited fine.

Penalty points – 3–11.

*This section will be added to the RTA 1988 by the Legal Aid, Sentencing and Punishment of Offenders Act 2012. At the time of writing this provision has yet to be brought into force.

Mode of trial

C[16C.2]

No SC guidance at the time of writing.

Legal notes and definitions

C[16C.3]

See C[16] for the definition of dangerous driving.

An alternative verdict of either dangerous driving or careless driving is available to the magistrates' court.

Sentencing
SC Guideline – causing serious injury by dangerous driving: unlicensed

C[16C.4]

No SC guideline has been published at the time of writing.

C[17]

Failing to produce driving licence, insurance certificate or test certificate

Charge

C[17.1]

1 Being the driver of a motor vehicle on a road,

OR

C[17.2]

2 Being a person whom a police constable reasonably believed to have driven a motor vehicle when an accident occurred owing to its presence on a road, or other public place.

OR

C[17.3]

3 Being a person whom a police constable reasonably believed had committed an offence in relation to the use on a road or other public place of a motor vehicle, failed on being so required by a police constable to produce (his driving licence) (the relevant certificate of insurance) (the relevant test certificate) for examination.

Road Traffic Act 1988, s 164 (driving licence); s 165 (insurance and test certificates)

Maximum penalty– Fine level 3 (for fines see **B[33]**). No power to disqualify or endorse.

Legal notes and definitions

C[17.4]

Right to demand production. Before the police officer is entitled to require the defendant to produce his driving licence or certificate of insurance the defendant must:

(a)   be driving a motor vehicle on a road or other public place; or

(b)   have been reasonably believed by the police to be the driver of a motor vehicle which was on a road or other public place and involved in an accident; or

(c)   have been reasonably believed by the police to have committed a motor vehicle offence on a road or other public place;

in addition, where a requirement is made to produce a test certificate, the vehicle must require a test certificate.

C[17.5]

Purpose of production. In the case of a driving licence, to enable the constable to ascertain inter alia the holder's name and address; in the case of test and insurance certificates the person must give his name and address and those of the owner where required. Additionally, if a driver fails to produce his insurance/licence when required and the constable has reasonable grounds to believe that he doesn't have a licence/insurance, or he fails to stop for long enough for enquiries to be made, and the constable believes that he has no licence or insurance, the constable may seize and remove the vehicle, and may enter premises by force to do so (but not a private dwelling). The constable must first warn the driver unless it is impracticable to do so.

C[17.6]

Driver. See the notes under the heading 'driving' for the offence of driving without a licence C[18.8].

C[17.7]

Person supervising a learner driver. In the circumstances (a)–(c) outlined above the supervisor may be required to produce his driving licence.

C[17.8]

Motor vehicle. See C[9.7].

C[17.9]

Road. Means any highway (including footpaths and bridleways) and any other road to which the public has access and includes bridges.

Other public place. Will exclude private property but will normally include such places as car parks.

C[17.10]–[17.15]

Constable. Includes a police constable of any rank. Traffic wardens also have power to require production of a driving licence and the giving of a name and address in certain, very limited, circumstances. Certain vehicle examiners may also require production of documents.

C[17.16]

Insurance certificate. The law requires that the insurance certificate be produced and not the policy or a premium receipt, unless the vehicle is covered by a certificate of security instead of a conventional insurance policy. Instead of an insurance policy the compulsory insurance of a motor vehicle can be covered by depositing £500,000 with the Accountant-General of the Supreme Court and a duplicate copy of this certificate will suffice instead of an insurance certificate. It will also be acceptable to produce a certificate in the prescribed form signed by the vehicle's owner (or by an agent on his behalf) stating that he has £500,000 on deposit with the Accountant-General of the Supreme Court.

C[17.17]

If the vehicle is subject to a hire-purchase agreement either party to that agreement can be the 'owner'.

C[17.18]

If the motor vehicle is owned by a local authority or a police authority then that authority may issue a 'Certificate of Ownership' in a prescribed form which makes an insurance certificate unnecessary.

Defences

C[17.19]

There are several defences that the defendant can use:

(a)   If the defendant is unable to produce his documents at the time, he can elect to produce them at some police station of his own choosing within seven days. Although it is not compulsory, the constable will issue the defendant with a special form (HORT1) requiring him to produce the documents. A driving licence has to be produced in *person*; insurance and test certificates merely have to be *produced.*

(b)   If the documents were not produced within the seven days it is a defence if they were produced (in person for a driving licence) at the specified police station as soon as was reasonably practicable.

Or

(c)   It is also a defence if it was not reasonably practicable for the documents to be produced in the required manner before the day on which the proceedings for non-production were commenced by the laying of an information. A defendant may instead produce a *current* receipt for a licence surrendered for a fixed penalty.

C[17.20]

The burden of proof to establish any of these defences rests with the defendant, however he does not have to prove his point beyond reasonable doubt but only on the balance of probabilities.

Sentencing
SC Guideline – failing to produce documents

C[17.21]

Starting point – Band A fine (special considerations: fine per offence, not per document).

C[17.22]

For fines see B[33].

C[18]

Driving licence offences

Charges

C[18.1]

Driving on a road a motor vehicle otherwise than in accordance with a licence to drive a vehicle of that class

Road Traffic Act 1988, s 87

Maximum penalty-Fine level 3. May disqualify for any period and must endorse, unless special reasons exist (except where the driving of the accused was in accordance with any licence that could have been granted to him).

Penalty points – 3–6 (fixed penalty 3).

Fixed penalty-£60.

Legal notes and definitions

C[18.2]

On an appropriate application the Secretary of State may grant a provisional licence with a view to the applicant passing a test of competence to drive. A provisional licence is subject to conditions and restrictions such as to class of vehicle which may be driven, or, in the case of motor cycles, the power of the engine. Breach of any of these conditions or restrictions is an offence (Road Traffic Act 1988, s 87 and the Motor Vehicles (Driving Licences) Regulations 1987).

C[18.3]

For driving a motor car a provisional licence holder must comply with the following conditions:

(a)   *Learner plates.* He must clearly display front and rear in a conspicuous position a red letter 'L' of regulation size (102mm x 89mm x 38mm) on a white background (178mm × 178mm; the corners may be rounded off).
(b)   *Supervision.* He must be supervised by a qualified driver. This offence applies to three-wheeled cars.

C[18.4]

From July 1999 all driving licence applications are in the form of the new photocard type licence.

C[18.5]

Supervised. Means that the supervisor must have been in a suitable part of the vehicle for supervising. For example, if the supervisor was in a rear seat from which it was difficult to supervise, the court may decide the defendant was not supervised. If a supervised driver is convicted of an offence, eg driving without due care, the supervisor can be convicted of aiding and abetting.

C[18.6]

Qualified driver. Means that the supervisor must have held a full licence to drive the same type of vehicle for at least three years and be at least 21 years of age (exemption is provided for the military).

C[18.7]

Motor cyclists who are learners must not drive or ride a motorcycle to which a sidecar is not attached and carry a passenger. A motor cycle which has a bare chassis or framework attached to its side does not have a side car.

C[18.8]

Driving. A person steering a car whilst another person pushes the vehicle is driving. A person who walks alongside his car, pushing it and steering it with one hand is not driving it. A motor cyclist sitting on his machine and propelling it along with his feet is driving but he is not driving it if he walks beside it pushing it [but he may be "riding" the vehicle] (*Gunnell v DPP* [1993] Crim LR 619). A person sitting in the driver's seat of a car, stationary but with the engine running, was found to be driving. (*Planton v DPP* [2001] EWHC 450 (Admin), (2001) 166 JP 324). In *DPP v Alderton* [2003] EWHC 2917 (Admin), [2003] All ER (D) 360 (Nov) the defendant was driving even though the car was stationary on the verge as the wheels were spinning and he was exercising control over the vehicle by use of the handbrake. In *R (on the application of Traves) v DPP* [2005] EWHC 1482 (Admin), 169 JP 421, applying the brakes to a vehicle being towed was held to be "driving".

C[18.9]

A person pushed a motor cycle along a road, its lights were on and he had used the brakes. At some point he had turned the ignition on for long enough to warm up the exhaust pipe. When apprehended he was astride the machine and was wearing a crash helmet. It was held to be within the magistrates' discretion to find that he was driving (*McKoen v Ellis* [1987] RTR 26, 151 JP 60, [1987] Crim LR 54). A person is driving who steers and brakes a vehicle being towed by a rope or chain. The position with regard to a vehicle drawn by a rigid tow bar has not been authoritatively decided but a case decided in 1985 implies that a person in the driving seat of the towed vehicle in such a case is not driving. The nature of the force used to put or keep a vehicle in motion is irrelevant in determining whether a person is driving. The essence of driving is the use of the driver's controls in order to direct the movement, however that movement is produced (*Traves v DPP* [2005] EWHC 1482 (Admin), 169 JP 421, sub nom Traves v DPP [2005] All ER (D) 381 (Jun)). An important test in deciding whether a person is driving is whether he was in a substantial sense controlling the movement and direction of the vehicle. If he is, then the question has to be answered whether his actions fall within the ordinary meaning of the word 'driving'. It is also helpful to consider whether the defendant himself deliberately set the vehicle in motion and also the length of time that he was handling the controls. A person who knelt on the driving seat of a vehicle, released the handbrake and thereafter attempted to reapply the handbrake to stop the movement of the vehicle was held to be driving the vehicle. However a momentary seizing of the steering wheel causing the vehicle to swerve cannot properly be said to be driving (*DPP v Hastings* [1993] RTR 205, 158 JP 118). In *Cawthorn v DPP* [2000] RTR 45, sub nom Cawthorn v Newcastle upon Tyne Crown Court (1994) 164 JP 527 a man who had left his vehicle briefly to post a letter, leaving the hazard warning lights on, was held to be the driver responsible for reporting an accident when the vehicle rolled down a hill and into a wall.

C[18.10]–[18.15]

Motor vehicle. See C[9.7].

C[18.16]

A road. Is any highway (including footpaths and bridleways) and any other road to which the public has access and includes bridges. However it will not normally include a car park (*Clarke v Kato* [1998] 4 All ER 417, [1998] 1 WLR 1647, sub nom Clarke v General Accident Fire and Life Assurance Corpn plc [1999] RTR 153, 163 JP 502, HL).

C[18.17]

Burden of proof. Proof that the driver held the appropriate driving licence rests with the defendant. The prosecution does not have to prove that the defendant did not hold a licence. As with all document offences there is not statutory requirement that the prosecution issue the defendant with a production notice; it is sufficient that they show he drove the vehicle on a road (*DPP v Hay* [2005] EWHC 1395 (Admin), [2005] All ER (D) 90 (Jun)).

C[18.18]

The driver does not have to prove this beyond reasonable doubt. He need only prove that on the balance of probabilities he did hold a licence.

C[18.19]

Employers. No employer shall let an employee drive unless the employee holds the appropriate driving licence, and it is his responsibility to make the necessary check that the employee has such a licence. Thus the employer is liable for permitting unless he can prove that his employee was licensed. Being misled by the employee is probably not a defence though the court might consider it a mitigating circumstance.

C[18.20]

A partner is neither the employee nor employer of another partner in the same firm.

Sentencing
SC Guideline – No driving licence

C[18.21]

Starting point – Band A fine (Special considerations: Aggravating factor if no licence ever held).

C[18.22]

If it appears to the court that the accused suffers from some disease or physical disability likely to cause his driving to be a source of danger to the public, then the court shall notify the licensing authority. Even if the accused has never obtained a licence, the court may consider it appropriate to bring the disease or disability to the attention of the licensing authority in case the accused should apply for a licence at some future date (see C[5.49]).

C[18.23]

A defendant will generally not have a licence because he has not passed a test. Therefore, the case is serious and may attract a high fine and compulsory endorsement.

C[18.24]

For fines see B[33].

Large goods vehicles

C[18.24A]

It is an offence to drive a large goods vehicle (or to employ a person to do so) unless the driver holds a large goods vehicle driving licence authorising him to drive large goods vehicles of that class. The LGV licence is an additional entitlement to the ordinary licence.

C[18.25]–[18.30]

Penalty. Same as for an ordinary licence. For definition of large goods vehicle consult the legal adviser.

C[18.31]

Under the provisions of the Road Traffic (Driver Licensing and Information Systems) Act 1989 existing Heavy Goods Vehicle Licences will be phased out. Instead a driver who passes an appropriate test of competency and who satisfies the Secretary of State that he is a fit person may be granted a 'large goods vehicle licence' which is in effect an ordinary driving licence which authorises the holder to drive vehicles of the classes formerly covered by a Heavy Goods Vehicle Licence. The penalty for driving without a licence is the same as for an ordinary licence.

C[18.32]

The new style licences were issued from 1 October 1990 for licences commencing on or after 1 January 1991 and as existing HGV licences become due for renewal.

C[19]

Driving whilst disqualified

Charge

C[19.1]

Driving a motor vehicle on a road when disqualified for holding or obtaining a driving licence

Road Traffic Act 1988, s 103

Maximum penalty-Fine level 5 and 6 months' imprisonment [**51 weeks] (for fines see B[33]). May disqualify for any period and/or until a driving test has been passed. Must endorse unless special reasons. Triable only by magistrates.

Penalty points – 6.

Legal notes and definitions

C[19.2]

Time limit. Subject to overall maximum of three years, proceedings may be brought within six months from when, in the prosecutor's opinion, he had sufficient evidence to warrant proceedings. A certificate signed by or on behalf of the prosecutor, as to when that date was, is conclusive evidence on that point.

C[19.3]

Driving. See the notes under the offence of driving without a licence at C[18.8]–C[18.9]. Once it is established that a person was driving, he may continue to be the driver of a vehicle although his conduct has changed and he no longer fulfils the test mentioned on that page.

C[19.4]

Motor vehicle. See C[9.7].

C[19.5]

Road. Means any highway (including footpaths and bridleways) and any other road to which the public has access and includes bridges.

C[19.6]

Disqualified. The prosecution must prove the defendant was driving and that the record of disqualification relates to that defendant, although there are a number of ways in which this can be done (*R v Derwentside Magistrates' Court, ex p Swift* [1997] RTR 89, 160 JP 468). It is the prosecution's task to prove all the elements of the offence and it is therefore not for the court to consult its own records to show that the defendant was in fact a disqualified driver (*Kingsnorth v DPP* [2003] All ER (D) 235 (Mar)). In *R (on the application of Howe) v South Durham Justices* [2004] EWHC 362 (Admin), 168 JP 424, [2004] All ER (D) 226 (Feb) a court permitted the defendant's solicitor to be a witness summoned for the purposes of identifying the disqualified person. A defendant disqualified in his absence and subsequently arrested for driving whilst disqualified may make a statutory declaration to the effect that he did not know of the proceedings. However this will make the earlier proceedings void but not void ab initio leaving the disqualification as valid at the time he was driving (*Singh v DPP* [1999] RTR 424, 164 JP 82, [1999] Crim LR 914).

In *Pattison v DPP* [2005] EWHC 2938 (Admin), [2006] 2 All ER 317, it was held that evidence of identity could be proved by admission (formal or otherwise), fingerprints, a witness who was present in court, or a match between the personal details of the accused and a certificate of conviction. Even where the personal details were not uncommon eg the name, address and date of birth of the accused, that might be sufficient to found a prima facie case. See also *Mills v DPP* [2008] EWHC 3304 (Admin), [2009] RTR 143.

C[19.7]

Knowledge. It is not necessary to prove that the defendant knew he was disqualified, nor that he knew he was on a road. When disqualified until a test is passed the onus is on the defendant to show that he held a provisional licence and was complying with the conditions of that licence at the time he was driving (*DPP v Baker* (2004) 168 JP 140, [2004] All ER (D) 28 (Nov), DC).

Sentencing
SC Guideline – Driving while Disqualified

C[19.8]

Must endorse and may disqualify. If no disqualification, impose 6 points.

OFFENCE SERIOUSNESS (CULPABILITY AND HARM) A. IDENTIFY THE APPROPRIATE STARTING POINT Starting points based on first time offender pleading not guilty		
Examples of nature of activity	Starting point	Range
Full period expired but retest not taken	Low level community penalty	Band C fine to medium level community order 6 points or lengthen disqualify for 3–6 months
Lengthy period of ban already served	High level community order	Medium level community order to 12 weeks custody

		Lengthen disqualification for 6–12 months beyond expiry of current ban
Recently imposed ban	12 weeks custody	High level community order to 26 weeks custody
		Lengthen disqualification for 12–18 months beyond expiry of current ban

OFFENCE SERIOUSNESS (CULPABILITY AND HARM)

B. CONSIDER THE EFFECT OF AGGRAVATING AND MITIGATING FACTORS (OTHER THAN THOSE WITHIN EXAMPLES ABOVE)

Common aggravating and mitigating factors are identified at B[5.2A]. The following may be particularly relevant but **these lists are not exhaustive**

Factors indicating higher culpability	*Factors indicating lower culpability*
1. Never passed test	1. Defendant not present when disqualification imposed and genuine reason why unaware of ban
2. Planned long-term evasion	2. Genuine emergency established
3. Vehicle obtained during ban	
4. Driving for remuneration	
Factors indicating greater degree of harm	
1. Distance driven	
2. Evidence of associated bad driving	
3. Offender caused accident	

FORM A PRELIMINARY VIEW OF THE APPROPRIATE SENTENCE, THEN CONSIDER OFFENDER MITIGATION
Common factors are identified at B[5.2A]

CONSIDER A REDUCTION FOR A GUILTY PLEA

CONSIDER ANCILLARY ORDERS, INCLUDING DEPRIVATION OF PROPERTY
Refer to B[18] for guidance on compensation and **Part B** for available ancillary orders

DECIDE SENTENCE
GIVE REASONS

Note: An offender convicted of this offence will always have at least one relevant previous conviction for the offence that resulted in disqualification. The starting points and ranges take this into account. Any other previous convictions should be considered in the usual way – consult the legal adviser for guidance.

C[19.9]

See Table B at B[4.2] for available sentences.

C[19.10]

If it appears to the magistrates that the accused suffers from a disease or physical disability likely to cause his driving to be a source of danger to the public, they must notify the licensing authority in case the accused applies for a licence at some future date (see C[5.49]).

C[19.11]–[19.17]

The offence does not apply to offenders who are driving under age. They are guilty of driving otherwise than in accordance with a licence, see C[18].

C[20]
'Unfit through drink or drugs' (drive/attempt drive)

Charge

C[20.1]
Driving or attempting to drive a mechanically propelled vehicle on a road (or public place) when unfit through drink or drugs

Road Traffic Act 1988, s 4(1), as amended

Maximum penalty-Fine level 5 and 6 months' imprisonment [**51 weeks] (for fines see B[33]). Must disqualify for at least one year unless special reasons. The disqualification may be for any period exceeding a year. He may also be ordered to pass a driving test. Must endorse licence unless special reasons exist.

Previous convictions-Where there is a previous conviction during the ten years preceding the current offence, the compulsory disqualification must be for at least three years unless special reasons exist.

A previous conviction for driving (or attempting to drive) a motor vehicle with alcohol over the prescribed limit or a previous conviction for refusing a blood etc specimen in such circumstances counts as a previous conviction for this offence.

Penalty points – 3–11.

Legal notes and definitions

C[20.2]
The charge may allege either driving or attempting to drive. It must not allege both.

C[20.3]
The court must be satisfied that the defendant drove (or attempted to drive) a mechanically propelled vehicle on a road or public place when his ability to drive properly was impaired by drink or drugs. The offence is one of strict liability and therefore the defence of insanity is not available (*DPP v H* [1997] 1 WLR 1406, [1998] RTR 200, sub nom DPP v Harper (1997) 161 JP 697).

C[20.4]
Driving. See the notes under this heading for the offence of driving without a licence at C[18.9].

C[20.5]

Mechanically propelled vehicle. See C[47.9].

C[20.6]

Road. Means any highway (including footpaths and bridleways) and any other road to which the public has access and includes bridges.

C[20.7]

Public place. Need not be a road. A field or enclosure at the rear of licensed premises for parking cars has been held to be a public place. In *Lewis v DPP* [2004] EWHC 3081 (Admin), [2005] All ER (D) 66 (Jan), it was decided that magistrates were entitled to infer that a public house car park was a public place and that the prosecution did not need to adduce evidence of public utilisation. See also *May v DPP* [2005] EWHC 1280 (Admin), [2005] All ER (D) 182 (Apr).

C[20.8]

Whether the scene of the charge is a road or public place is a question of fact for the court to decide (such as a car park in (*R v Spence* [1999] RTR 353, 163 JP 754, [1999] Crim LR 975, CA; or the parking area of a privately owned tyre and exhaust centre: *Filmer v DPP* [2006] EWHC 3450 (Admin), [2006] All ER (D) 08 (Nov)). See *Hallett v DPP* [2011] EWHC 488 (Admin) in which the key question was whether there was before the justices evidence of public use of an unmade service road. Any road might be regarded as open to which the public had access if the public was there without overcoming physical obstruction or in defiance of a prohibition. Whether a place was public would generally be a question of fact and degree. Help might also be derived from asking whether access was only for a special class of members of the public, including guests of residents, postmen and milkmen. A sign or barrier lent weight to restriction of the area to a special class and thus to it being private, but the absence of a sign or barrier was not determinative.

C[20.9]

Unfit. A person is taken to be unfit to drive if his ability to drive properly is for the time being impaired. It need not be proved that the defendant was *incapable* of driving.

C[20.10]

The court may take note of such evidence as, for example, where there is evidence of drink or drugs:

(a)   driving erratically;
(b)   colliding with a stationary object for no apparent reason;
(c)   the defendant's condition-slurred speech, staggering, mental confusion. Also account may be taken of evidence of an analyst's certificate where the accused has given a sample of blood/breath/urine.

C[20.11]–[20.15]

Even where the defendant has taken a drink subsequent to the incident the certificate may be evidence of the amount of alcohol consumed at the time of the incident unless the accused proves on the balance of probabilities that had he not consumed the subsequent drink his ability to drive would not have been impaired.

C[20.16]

A witness who is not an expert can give his impressions as to whether an accused had taken drink but he may not give evidence whether the accused was fit to drive.

C[20.17]

Drink or drugs. Drink means an alcoholic drink. Drugs can refer to medicine, ie something given to cure, alleviate or assist an ailing body, or it can be something which, when consumed, affected the control of the body. Accordingly, 'glue sniffing' would come within the ambit of this offence.

C[20.18]

Alternative verdict. If the allegation is 'driving' the court may convict on the basis of attempting to drive. Where the defendant is found not guilty of an offence under s 4(1) but the allegations amount to or include an offence under the Road Traffic Act 1988, s 4(2) (being in charge when unfit to drive through drink or drugs) the court may convict him of that offence (Road Traffic Offenders Act 1988, s 24 as substituted by the Road Traffic Act 1991, s 24).

Sentencing
SC Guideline – Unfit through drink or drugs (drive/attempt to drive)

C[20.19]

Must endorse and disqualify for at least 12 months.

Must disqualify for **at least** 2 years if offender has had two or more disqualifications for periods of 56 days or more in preceding 3 years – consult your legal adviser for further guidance.

Must disqualify for **at least** 3 years if offender has been convicted of a relevant drink/drive offence in preceding 10 years – consult your legal adviser for further guidance.

If there is a delay in sentencing after conviction, consider interim disqualification.

Note: the first column below provides guidance regarding the length of disqualification that may be appropriate in case to which the 3 year minimum applies. The period to be imposed in any individual case will depend on an assessment of all the relevant circumstances, including the length of time since the earlier ban was imposed and the gravity of the current offence.

OFFENCE SERIOUSNESS (CULPABILITY AND HARM)

A. IDENTIFY THE APPROPRIATE STARTING POINT

Starting points based on first time offender pleading not guilty

Examples of nature of activity	Starting point	Range	Disqualification	Disqualification. 2nd offence in 10 years
Evidence of moderate level of impairment and no aggravating factors	Band C fine	Band C fine	12–16 months	36–40 months
Evidence of moderate level of impairment and presence of one or more aggravating factors listed below	Band C fine	Band C fine	17–22 months	36–46 months
Evidence of high level of impairment and no aggravating factors	Medium level community order	Low level community order to high level community order	23–28 months	36–52 months
Evidence of high level of impairment and presence of one or more aggravating factors listed below	12 weeks custody	High level community order to 26 weeks custody	29–36 months	36–60 months

OFFENCE SERIOUSNESS (CULPABILITY AND HARM)

B. CONSIDER THE EFFECT OF AGGRAVATING AND MITIGATING FACTORS (OTHER THAN THOSE WITHIN EXAMPLES ABOVE)

Common aggravating and mitigating factors are identified at B[5.2A]. The following may be particularly relevant but **these lists are not exhaustive**

Factors indicating higher culpability	*Factors indicating lower culpability*
1. LGV, HGV, PSV etc	1. Genuine emergency established*
2. Poor road or weather conditions	2. Spiked drinks*
3. Carrying passengers	3. Very short distance driven*
4. Driving for hire or reward	* Even where not amounting to special reasons
5. Evidence of unacceptable standard of driving	
Factors indicating greater degree of harm	
1. Involved in accident	
2. Location eg near school	
3. High level of traffic or pedestrians in vicinity	

FORM A PRELIMINARY VIEW OF THE APPROPRIATE SENTENCE, THEN CONSIDER OFFENDER MITIGATION
Common factors are identified at B[5.2A]
CONSIDER A REDUCTION FOR A GUILTY PLEA
CONSIDER OFFERING DRINK/DRIVE REHABILITATION COURSE
CONSIDER ANCILLARY ORDERS
Refer to B[18] for guidance on compensation and **Part B** for available ancillary orders
DECIDE SENTENCE
GIVE REASONS

C[20.20]

See Table B at B[4.2] for available sentences and the notes to the offence of 'Alcohol over the prescribed limit' at C[22.2] and C[22.56] for rehabilitation courses and their effect upon disqualifications.

C[21]
'Unfit through drink or drugs (in charge)'

Charge

C[21.1]

Being in charge of a mechanically propelled vehicle on a road (or public place) when unfit through drink or drugs

Road Traffic Act 1988, s 4(2), as amended

Maximum penalty – Fine level 4 and 3 months' imprisonment [**51 weeks] (for fines see B[33]). May disqualify for any period and/or until a driving test has been passed. Must endorse unless there are special reasons.

Penalty points – 10.

Legal notes and definitions

C[21.2]

See the notes for the offence of 'drunken driving' at C[20.2].

C[21.3]

In charge. This is a potentially wide concept. There must be proof of some connection, which can be less than attempting to drive, between the defendant and a motor vehicle on a road or public place. The owner or a person who had recently driven the vehicle would be 'in charge' unless he put the vehicle in someone else's charge or unless there was no realistic possibility of his resuming actual control, eg where he was at home in bed or a great distance from the car (*DPP v Watkins* [1989] QB 821, [1989] 1 All ER 1126 where there is further guidance in respect of defendants who are not the owner or have not recently driven the vehicle). A qualified driver supervising a provisional licence holder is 'in charge'.

C[21.4]

A person is deemed not to be in charge if he can demonstrate from the evidence that at the material time the circumstances were such that there was no likelihood of his driving the vehicle so long as he remained unfit to drive through drink or drugs but in determining whether there was such a likelihood the court may disregard any injury to him and any damage to the vehicle. A supervisor of a learner driver is in charge and may need to take over at any time (*DPP v Janman* [2004] EWHC 101 (Admin), [2004] Crim LR 478, [2004] All ER (D) 171 (Jan)).

C[21.4A]

ECHR. The House of Lords held that this was a reasonable and legitimate burden on the defendant (*Sheldrake v DPP* [2003] EWHC 273 (Admin), [2004] QB 487; revsd [2004] UKHL 43, [2004] 3 WLR 976).

Sentencing
SC Guideline – Unfit through drink or drugs (in charge)
C[21.5]

Must endorse and may disqualify. If no disqualification, impose 10 points.

OFFENCE SERIOUSNESS (CULPABILITY AND HARM) A. IDENTIFY THE APPROPRIATE STARTING POINT Starting points based on first time offender pleading not guilty		
Examples of nature of activity	**Starting point**	**Range**
Evidence of moderate level of impairment and no aggravating factors	Band B fine	Band B fine 10 points
Evidence of moderate level of impairment and presence of one or more aggravating factors listed below	Band B fine	Band B fine 10 points or consider disqualification
Evidence of high level of impairment and no aggravating factors	Band C fine	Band C fine to medium level community order 10 points or consider disqualification
Evidence of high level of impairment and presence of one or more aggravating factors listed below	High level community order	Medium level community order to 12 weeks custody Consider disqualification OR 10 points
OFFENCE SERIOUSNESS (CULPABILITY AND HARM) B. CONSIDER THE EFFECT OF AGGRAVATING AND MITIGATING FACTORS (OTHER THAN THOSE WITHIN EXAMPLES ABOVE) Common aggravating and mitigating factors are identified at B[5.2A]. The following may be particularly relevant but **these lists are not exhaustive**		
Factors indicating higher culpability 1. LGV, HGV, PSV etc 2. High likelihood of driving 3. Driving for hire or reward		*Factor indicating lower culpability* 1. Low likelihood of driving
FORM A PRELIMINARY VIEW OF THE APPROPRIATE SENTENCE, THEN CONSIDER OFFENDER MITIGATION Common factors are identified at B[5.2A]		

CONSIDER A REDUCTION FOR A GUILTY PLEA
CONSIDER ANCILLARY ORDERS
Refer to **B[18]** for guidance on compensation and **Part B** for available ancillary orders
DECIDE SENTENCE
GIVE REASONS

C[21.6]

See Table B at **B[4.2]** for available sentences and the notes to the offence of 'Alcohol over the prescribed limit' at **C[22.2]**.

C[22]
Excess alcohol (drive/attempt to drive or in charge)

Charge 1

C[22.1]
Driving (or attempting to drive) a motor vehicle on a road (or public place) with alcohol above the prescribed limit

Road Traffic Act 1988, s 5(1)(a)

Maximum penalty-Fine level 5 and 6 months' imprisonment [**51 weeks] (for fines see B[33]). Must disqualify for at least one year unless special reasons. The disqualification may be for any period exceeding a year. The defendant may also be ordered to take a test again. Must endorse licence unless special reasons.

It is not a special reason that the defendant's driving was not impaired.

Previous convictions-Where there is a previous conviction during the ten years preceding the current offence, the compulsory disqualification must be for at least three years unless special reasons.

A previous conviction for driving (or attempting to drive) a motor vehicle when unfit through drink or a previous conviction for refusing a blood or urine specimen in such circumstances counts as a previous conviction for this offence.

Penalty points – 3–11.

Legal notes and definitions

C[22.2]
The charge may allege either driving or attempting to drive. It is important to note that it must not allege both. The prosecution need not prove that the defendant's ability to drive was impaired.

C[22.3]
Driving. See the notes under the offence of no driving licence at C[18.2].

C[22.4]
Motor vehicle. See C[9.7].

C[22.5]
Road. Means any highway (including footpaths and bridleways) and any

other road to which the public has access and includes bridges. The information may read 'road or other public place', but if it does not the specific allegation must be proved (*Plunkett v DPP* [2004] EWHC 1937 (Admin), [2004] All ER (D) 82 (Jul)).

C[22.6]

Public place. Need not be a road. A field or enclosure at the rear of licensed premises for parking cars has been held to be a public place (see C[20.7]).

C[22.7]

Whether the scene of the charge is a road or public place is a question of fact for the court to decide. It is basically a question of whether at the relevant time the public enjoyed access to the place where the offence was committed.

C[22.8]

Prescribed limit. If a blood specimen was provided by the defendant the prescribed limit is 80 mg of alcohol in 100 ml of blood; if a urine specimen, 107 mg of alcohol in 100 ml of urine; if breath, 35 µg of alcohol in 100 ml of breath. Comparison of these levels is achieved by multiplying a breath/alcohol level by 2.3 and rounding up to convert to blood alcohol. The following conversion table relates blood, urine and breath levels.

C[22.9]

Blood	Urine	Breath	Blood	Urine	Breath
80	107	35	110	147	48
83	110	36	113	150	49
85	113	37	115	153	50
87	116	38	117	156	51
90	119	39	120	159	52
92	122	40	122	162	53
94	125	41	124	165	54
97	129	42	126	168	55
99	132	43	129	171	56
101	135	44	131	174	57
103	138	45	133	177	58
106	141	46	136	181	59
108	144	47	138	184	60
140	187	61	163	217	71
143	190	62	166	220	72
145	193	63	168	223	73
147	196	64	170	226	74
147	199	65	172	230	75
152	154	205	175	233	76

Blood	Urine	Breath	Blood	Urine	Breath
154	205	67	178	236	77
156	208	68	180	239	78
159	211	69	182	242	79
161	214	70	184	245	80

C[22.10]–[22.15]

Breath tests. A constable in uniform may require a person to submit to a breath test if the constable reasonably suspects him to have alcohol in his body or to have committed a traffic offence while the vehicle was in motion. The test may also be required in these circumstances after a person has ceased to be a driver. If the test indicates the presence of alcohol the driver need not, but may be, arrested and taken to a police station where he will be required to offer a specimen of blood, urine or breath at the choice of the police. The roadside breath test may be taken by blowing into a bag or into a machine, but these devices are a preliminary test and the sample of breath used in these tests is not the one which is analysed to determine its alcohol content.

Once a negative breath test has been given, the police lose the power of arrest under the Road Traffic Act 1988, s 6, but may in appropriate circumstances arrest under s 4 of the Act (*DPP v Robertson* [2002] 15 LS Gaz R 33).

Breath is not confined to deep lung air but includes all that is exhaled (*Zafar v DPP* (2004) Times, 1 November).

C[22.16]

If the police require a breath sample for analysis it will be analysed in a machine approved by the Secretary of State such as a Lion Intoxilyzer 6000 UK. It works by, analysing the level of alcohol in the breath by the absorption of infra red radiation and giving a printed record of the result of two samples of breath given within a short time. The lower reading is the one which will be used to determine whether a prosecution will follow. Each machine works with a simulator, a device enabling the machine to check itself for accuracy. If for any reason the police decide not to use the machine they may ask for a sample of blood or urine.

The modification of a device, which did not affect its operation, did not take it out of the approved category (*Breckon v DPP* [2007] EWHC 2013 (Admin)); whether a modification to an intoxyliser machine took it out of a type approved under the Breath Analysis Devices Approval Order 2005 required a common sense consideration of whether the function of the modified device still had the character, essence and identity of the device with type approval: *R (on the application of Coxon v Manchester City Magistrates' Court* [2010] EWHC 712 (Admin), 174 CL&J 221.

C[22.17]

The form of print-out from the machine will give the subject's name and the time and date of the test. They will show the results of each of two samples given by the subject and the results of each of two checks which the machine carries out to prove its accuracy. These calibration checks must show a reading within a range of 32–38 µg; figures outside this range on either check will render the test void.

C[22.18]

The print-out will be signed by the operator and by the subject and a machine-produced copy will be handed to the driver, the other copy being retained by the police. It is unlikely that a prosecution will follow if the lowest reading is less than 40, but if it is 50 or less the driver is entitled to ask for an analysis of a sample of blood or urine. In the absence of any suggestion that the machine was not used properly and providing the calibration checks show readings within the parameters mentioned above, the print-out from the machine is evidence of the level of alcohol in the breath without further proof provided that a print-out was handed to the accused at the time it was produced, or served on him more than seven days before the hearing, either personally or by registered or recorded post.

C[22.19]

Evidence by certificate. A certificate signed by an authorised analyst stating the proportion of alcohol in the specimen is admissible without the analyst being called as a witness: the same applies to a certificate signed by a doctor who took a blood specimen from the defendant.

C[22.20]

The defendant is entitled to insist on the attendance at court of the analyst or doctor. As the police were bound to provide the defendant with specimens of blood or urine taken at the same time, it is possible that sometimes a defendant may call his own analyst to give evidence as to the proportion of alcohol.

C[22.21]

If difficulty arises about the provision of a specimen to a defendant, or about the admissibility of a certificate, the legal adviser should be consulted. The police are entitled to divide the specimen into three parts and not two.

C[22.22]

The High Court has quashed a conviction because a pathologist declared the blood specimen handed to the defendant to be inadequate for examination.

C[22.23]

The defendant is entitled to be acquitted if he can raise a reasonable doubt about the accuracy of the machine. However the prosecution do not have to prove a specific alcohol content, but that the alcohol content exceeded the prescribed limit so that where an accused called expert evidence to show that the variation in readings on the breath machine was unacceptable but where it was conceded that the readings must have been 5 microgrammes above the limit, he was convicted. In some circumstances it may not be necessary for the defendant to call expert evidence in order to rebut the presumption that the machine is reliable (*DPP v Spurrier* [2000] RTR 60, sub nom R v Crown Prosecution Service, ex p Spurrier 164 JP 369), but such evidence should relate to a particular fault relevant to the issues in the case (*DPP v Teixeira* (2002) 166 JP 1). For further case law on the statutory presumption and reliability of breath testing equipment see *DPP v Memery* (2003) 167 JP 238; *Skinner v DPP* [2004] EWHC 2914 (Admin); *Rose v DPP* [2010] EWHC 462 (Admin).

C[22.24]

Special reasons. It is not a defence to the charge that unknown to him the defendant's drink had been laced. If this is put forward as a reason for not disqualifying the question must be answered whether the extra drink by itself is what took the level of alcohol in the blood over the limit and the defendant, if there is any doubt, should be invited to call expert evidence. Note that even if special reasons are proved this only gives the justices a discretion not to disqualify. They may still do so depending on the circumstances of the case (*R v Crown Court at St Albans, ex p O'Donovan* [2000] 1 Cr App Rep (S) 344).

A motorist drove 350 metres to his home address fearing the loss of valuable work tools in his van. Held, not special reasons: *DPP v Oram* [2005] EWHC 964 (Admin), [2005] All ER (D) 57 (May).

C[22.25]–[22.29]

Driving in an emergency may amount to a special reason not to disqualify, but only where a sober, reasonable and responsible friend of the defendant present at the time, but unable to drive, would have advised the defendant to drive (*DPP v Bristow* [1998] RTR 100, 161 JP 35). Shortness of distance driven may be a special reason but not where the defendant's intention was to drive a longer distance than he in fact managed (*DPP v Humphries* [2000] RTR 52, sub nom Crown Prosecution Service v Humphries [2000] 2 Cr App Rep (S) 1, 164 JP 502). No specific reasons could be argued by a defendant who assumed without enquiry that a drink he consumed contained no alcohol (*Lloyd Robinson v DPP* [2003] EWHC 2718 (Admin), (2004) 168 JP 522, [2004] Crim LR 670, [2003] All ER (D) 05 (Nov)); nor where the defendant drove to the scene of an accident involving his son, having failed to wake his wife who could have legally driven (*Khan v DPP* [2004] EWHC 2505 (Admin), sub nom Khan v DPP [2004] All ER (D) 134 (Oct)).

In *Ng v DPP* [2007] EWHC 36 (Admin), the defendant contended that his breath reading had been affected by eructation (belching) during the procedure. It was decided that the evidence on which the defendant had sought to rely went directly to the commission of the offence. If accepted it could provide an explanation as to why the level of alcohol exceeded the prescribed limit. It was capable therefore of amounting a special reason.

Driving a short distance to avoid car park charges was held not to be a special reason because, on the facts, there was danger of the defendant coming into contact with other road users (*DPP v Cove* [2008] EWHC 441 (Admin), [2008] All ER (D) 199 (Feb).

C[22.30]

Drinking after driving. If the accused claims that the alcohol level was increased because he had taken drink after ceasing to drive then he must prove on the balance of probabilities that the post-driving drink took him over the limit and that he was not over the limit while he was driving. This is because the law requires the court to assume that the alcohol level at the time of the driving was not less than that at the time of the test (*Griffiths v DPP* [2002] EWHC 792 (Admin), 166 JP 629, [2002] All ER (D) 132 (Apr)). If an accused wishes to raise this defence he will almost certainly have to call medical or scientific evidence.

C[22.31]

Alternative verdict. If the allegation is 'driving' the court may convict him on the basis of attempting to drive. Where the defendant is found not guilty of an offence under the Road Traffic Act 1988, s 5(1)(a) but the allegations amount to or include an offence under s 5(1)(b) (being in charge of a vehicle with excess alcohol in breath, blood or urine) the court may convict him of that offence (RTOA 1988, s 24).

Sentencing
SC Guideline – Excess Alcohol (drive/attempt to drive)

C[22.32]

Must endorse and disqualify for at least 12 months.

Must disqualify for **at least** 2 years if offender has had two or more disqualifications for periods of 56 days or more in preceding 3 years – consult your legal adviser for further guidance.

Must disqualify for **at least** 3 years if offender has been convicted of a relevant drink/drive offence in preceding 10 years – consult your legal adviser for further guidance.

If there is a delay in sentencing after conviction, consider interim disqualification.

Note: the first column below provides guidance regarding the length of disqualification that may be appropriate in case to which the 3 year minimum applies. The period to be imposed in any individual case will depend on an assessment of all the relevant circumstances, including the length of time since the earlier ban was imposed and the gravity of the current offence.

OFFENCE SERIOUSNESS (CULPABILITY AND HARM)				
A. IDENTIFY THE APPROPRIATE STARTING POINT				
Starting points based on first time offender pleading not guilty				
Level of alcohol Breath (mg) Blood (ml) Urine (ml)	Starting point	Range	Disqualification	Disqualification. 2nd offence in 10 years
36–59 mg (breath) or 81–137 ml (blood) or 108– 183 ml (urine)	Band C fine	Band C fine	12–16 months	36–40 months
60–89 mg (breath) or 138–206 ml (blood) or 184–274 ml (urine)	Band C fine	Band C fine	17–22 months	36–46 months
90–119 mg (breath) or 207–275 ml (blood) or 275–388 ml (urine)	Medium level community order	Low level community order to high level community order	23–28 months	36–52 months
120–150 mg (breath) and above or 276–345 ml (blood) and above or 367–459 (urine) and above	12 weeks custody	High level community order to 26 weeks custody	29–36 months	36–60 months

OFFENCE SERIOUSNESS (CULPABILITY AND HARM)	
B. CONSIDER THE EFFECT OF AGGRAVATING AND MITIGATING FACTORS (OTHER THAN THOSE WITHIN EXAMPLES ABOVE)	
Common aggravating and mitigating factors are identified at B[5.2A]. The following may be particularly relevant but **these lists are not exhaustive**	
Factors indicating higher culpability	*Factors indicating lower culpability*
1. LGV, HGV, PSV etc	1. Genuine emergency established*

2. Poor road or weather conditions	2. Spiked drinks*
3. Carrying passengers	3. Very short distance driven*
4. Driving for hire or reward	* Even where not amounting to special reasons
5. Evidence of unacceptable standard of driving	
Factors indicating greater degree of harm	
1. Involved in accident	
2. Location eg near school	
3. High level of traffic or pedestrians in vicinity	
FORM A PRELIMINARY VIEW OF THE APPROPRIATE SENTENCE, THEN CONSIDER OFFENDER MITIGATION Common factors are identified at B[5.2A]	
CONSIDER A REDUCTION FOR A GUILTY PLEA	
CONSIDER OFFERING DRINK/DRIVE REHABILITATION COURSE	
CONSIDER ANCILLARY ORDERS, INCLUDING FORFEITURE OR SUSPENSION OF PERSONAL LIQUOR LICENCE Refer to B[18] for guidance on compensation and **Part B** for available ancillary orders	
DECIDE SENTENCE **GIVE REASONS**	

C[22.33]

Structure of the sentencing decision. See B[3.7].

C[22.34]

Available sentences. See Table B at B[4.2].

C[22.35]–[22.40]

Custodial sentence. See B[2].

C[22.41]

Community sentence. See B[3].

C[22.42]

Fine. See B[33].

C[22.43]

Forfeiture of vehicle. See B[34].

C[22.44]

Disqualification. See C[5].

C[22.45]

High risk offenders. Drivers who are convicted of the following offences are regarded as high risk offenders (for endorsement codes see C[6]):

(a)   one disqualification for drinking and driving with alcohol two and a half or more times the legal limit (DR 10 and DR 50);

(b)   two disqualifications for drinking and driving within 10 years (DR 10, DR 20, DR 40 and DR 50);

(c)   one disqualification for refusal to provide a specimen for analysis (DR 30 and DR 60).

C[22.46]

The DVLA will write to a high risk offender and explain that the disqualification is considered to be an indication of a drink problem. Shortly before the expiry of the disqualification, a further letter will be sent explaining what must be done to apply for the return of the licence. The applicant will have to submit to a medical examination and pay an administration fee and medical fees to the examining doctor.

C[22.47]

If it appears to the court that the accused suffers from a disease or physical disability likely to cause his driving to be a source of danger to the public, it must notify the licensing authority (see C[5.49]).

C[22.48]

The fact that the amount of alcohol is only slightly over the statutory limit is **not** a special reason for avoiding imposing disqualification and endorsement.

C[22.49]

The 12 months' mandatory disqualification is to be regarded as a minimum and not as a tariff and should be increased in appropriate cases. The national sentencing guidelines suggest an increased disqualification for cases between 56mg and 70mg.

C[22.50]–[22.55]

If the defendant submits as a special reason for not disqualifying him that he was obliged to drive by some sudden crisis or emergency he must show that he acted responsibly and that the crisis or emergency was not one which arose through his own irresponsibility or lack of reasonable foresight. The driving must have been only to the extent occasioned by the emergency.

C[22.56]

Reduced disqualification for attendance on course (Road Traffic Offenders Act 1988, s 34A). The court may reduce the period of disqualification where a person completes an approved course by a date specified in the order.

C[22.57]

This power applies where there is a conviction for driving (or being in charge) under the influence of drink or drugs; driving etc with excess alcohol (C[22]and C[20]); or failing to provide a specimen (C[23]).

C[22.58]

The court must have made an order for disqualification for not less than 12 months.

C[22.59]

The reduction specified must be not less than three months and not more than one quarter of the original period (ie 9 months' disqualification must remain where the original unreduced period was 12 months). The reduction should be announced in open court.

C[22.60]

Criteria. The court should decide whether or not to offer the offender an opportunity to participate. It must then check that:

(a)   a place on the course is available;
(b)   the offender is aged 17 years or more;
(c)   the court has explained the effect of the order in ordinary language, the amount of fees payable and that they must be paid before beginning the course;
(d)   the offender consents.

The course must be completed at least two months before the end of the reduced period of disqualification. The scheme is voluntary after referral. There is no additional penalty if the offender fails to attend the course but the full period of disqualification applies.

C[22.61]

On completion, the organiser of the course will give the offender a certificate for presentation to the court.

Charge 2

C[22.62]

Being in charge of a motor vehicle on a road (or public place) having consumed alcohol over the prescribed limit

Road Traffic Act 1988, s 5(1)(b)

Maximum penalty-Fine on level 4 and 3 months' imprisonment [**51 weeks] (for fines see B[33]). May disqualify for any period and/or until a driving test has been passed. Must endorse unless there are special reasons.

Penalty points – 10.

Legal notes and definitions

C[22.63]
In charge. See notes at C[21.3].

C[22.64]
ECHR. The defendant is entitled to be acquitted if he can establish from the evidence that there was no likelihood of his driving whilst he probably had an excessive proportion of alcohol in his blood. He only has to prove this on the balance of probabilities and the House of Lords held that the burden on the defendant was both reasonable and legitimate (*Sheldrake v DPP* [2003] EWHC 273 (Admin), [2004] QB 487; revsd [2004] UKHL 43, [2004] 3 WLR 976). Note that a passenger supervising a learner driver who has been drinking may be in charge for the purposes of this section (*DPP v Janman* [2004] EWHC 101 (Admin), [2004] All ER (D) 171 (Jan)).

See also the legal and sentencing notes for the previous offence, at C[21.2].

Sentencing
SC Guideline – Excess Alcohol (in charge)

C[22.65]
Must endorse and may disqualify. If no disqualification, impose 10 points.

OFFENCE SERIOUSNESS (CULPABILITY AND HARM)		
A. IDENTIFY THE APPROPRIATE STARTING POINT		
Starting points based on first time offender pleading not guilty		
Level of alcohol Breath (mg) Blood (ml) Urine (ml)	Starting point	Range
36–59 mg (breath) or 81–137 ml (blood) or 108–183 ml (urine)	Band B fine	Band B fine 10 points
60–89 mg (breath) or 138–206 ml (blood) or 184–274 ml (urine)	Band B fine	Band B fine 10 points OR consider disqualification
90–119 mg (breath) or 207–275 ml (blood) or 275–388 ml (urine)	Band C fine	Band C fine to medium level community order Consider disqualification up to 6 months OR 10 points
120–150 mg (breath) and above or 276–345 ml (blood)and above or	Medium level community order	Low level community order to 6 weeks custody Disqualify 6–12 months

367–459 (urine) and above		

OFFENCE SERIOUSNESS (CULPABILITY AND HARM)
B. CONSIDER THE EFFECT OF AGGRAVATING AND MITIGATING FACTORS (OTHER THAN THOSE WITHIN EXAMPLES ABOVE)
Common aggravating and mitigating factors are identified at B[5.2A]. The following may be particularly relevant but **these lists are not exhaustive**

Factors indicating higher culpability	*Factor indicating lower culpability*
1. LGV, HGV, PSV etc	1. Low likelihood of driving
2. Ability to drive seriously impaired	
3. High likelihood of driving	
4. Driving for hire or reward	

FORM A PRELIMINARY VIEW OF THE APPROPRIATE SENTENCE, THEN CONSIDER OFFENDER MITIGATION
Common factors are identified at B[5.2A]

CONSIDER A REDUCTION FOR A GUILTY PLEA

CONSIDER ANCILLARY ORDERS, INCLUDING FORFEITURE OR SUSPENSION OF PERSONAL LIQUOR LICENCE
Refer to B[18] for guidance on compensation and **Part B** for available ancillary orders

DECIDE SENTENCE
GIVE REASONS

C[22.66]–[22.71]

See Table B at B[4.2] for available sentences and the notes for the previous offence.

C[23]

Fail to provide specimen for analysis (drive/attempt to drive)

Charge

C[23.1]

Failing, without reasonable excuse, to provide a specimen of blood, urine or breath for analysis

Road Traffic Act 1988, s 7 (6) and s 7A

Maximum penalty-This varies according to whether it is alleged the defendant was driving or in charge. Accordingly the summons should make clear which of the alternative offences at C[21] and C[22], is alleged.

(a)   If the defendant drove or attempted to drive a motor vehicle on a road or public place fine on level 5 and 6 months' imprisonment. Must disqualify for at least one year (the guideline penalty is **two years**) unless special reasons. The disqualification may be for any period exceeding a year. The defendant may also be ordered to take a test again. Must endorse licence unless special reasons.

For a subsequent offence committed within ten years of a previous conviction must disqualify for at least three years and must endorse unless special reasons. The minimum ban is two years if the defendant has been disqualified for more than 56 days on at least two occasions, three years immediately preceding the commission of the current offence (s 34(4) RTOA 1988).

A previous conviction for driving (or attempting to drive) a motor vehicle when unfit through drink (see C[20]) or a previous conviction for driving (or attempting to drive) with alcohol over prescribed limit (see C[21]) count as a previous conviction for this offence.

Penalty points – 3–11.

(b)   If the defendant was in charge of a motor vehicle on a road or a public place fine level 4 and 3 months' imprisonment (**51 weeks). May disqualify for any period and/or until a driving test has been passed. Must endorse unless there are special reasons.

Penalty points – 10.

Legal notes and definitions

C[23.2]

A constable, in the course of an investigation into whether a person has committed an offence under the Road Traffic Act 1988, s 3A (causing death by careless driving where under the influence of drink or drugs) the Road Traffic Act 1988, s 4 or s 5, may require him to provide two specimens of breath or a specimen of blood or urine for analysis.

C[23.3]

Fails to provide. If the case concerns a refusal to provide a blood specimen, an offence is committed if the defendant would only allow blood to be taken from an inappropriate part of the body (toe, penis, etc). In one case a woman refused to provide a blood or urine specimen and claimed embarrassment, there being no doctor or policewoman present. The High Court ruled this amounted to refusal. An agreement to provide a specimen which is conditional will generally be treated as a refusal. In the case of a sample of breath being required for analysis it must be provided in such a way as to make that analysis possible, that is, the required quantity at the required pressure. If a driver has a phobia/medical condition he must inform the police officer so that the police officer can require an alternative specimen (*Martiner v DPP* [2004] EWHC 2484 (Admin), [2004] All ER (D) 122 (Oct)).

In *DPP v Karamouzis* [2006] All ER (D) 109 (Oct), the defendant provided a positive roadside breath test. She was arrested and taken to a police station where she was required to provide specimens of breath for analysis. She argued that she had already been required to provide an evidential breath test under s 7 and accordingly there was no power to arrest and convey her to a police station. It was held that the roadside test was a preliminary test under s 6 and that the defendant had failed to provide specimens as required under s 7.

There must be sufficient breath to enable a test to be carried out although deep lung breath is not a legal requirement. Where an officer had requested a specimen from a Lion Intoxilyser device and requested the defendant blow into the machine and the defendant had removed the mouthpiece on eight occasions, where the device registered there was an insufficient specimen an offence under s 7(6) was made out (*DPP v Darwin* [2007] EWHC 337 (Admin). See also *DPP v Heywood* [1997] RTR 1; *Zafar v DPP* [2004] All ER (D) 6 (Nov)).

In *Rweikiza v DPP* [2008] EWHC 396 (Admin), [2008] All ER (D) 259 (Jan) the defendant's conviction was upheld because he had been properly instructed on how to use the intoxilyser and had deliberately failed to comply with those instructions and had deliberately frustrated the objectives of the test. In those circumstances the court had been correct to find that the specimen was not sufficient to enable the test or analysis to be carried out or the objective to be satisfactorily achieved.

C[23.4]

Reasonable excuse. The Court of Appeal has said: 'In our judgment no excuse can be adjudged a reasonable one unless the person from whom the specimen is required is physically or mentally unable to provide it, or the provision of the specimen would entail a substantial risk to health.' The fact that a driver has not consumed alcohol at all, or that he has consumed alcohol since being involved in an accident, does not amount to a reasonable excuse for not providing a specimen. Nor can he demand to see a law book before complying (*DPP v Noe* [2000] RTR 351, [2000] 20 LS Gaz R 43), or refuse to take a test until legal advice has been received (*Kirkup v DPP* [2003] EWHC 2354 (Admin), [2003] All ER (D) 53 (Oct)).

Once the defendant had raised the issue a reasonable excuse, eg by expert medical evidence, it is for the prosecution to prove the absence of a reasonable excuse beyond a reasonable doubt (*McKeon v DPP* [2007] EWHC 3216 (Admin), [2007] All ER (D) 314 (Dec)).

Defendant must have been warned of consequences of refusing a specimen

C[23.5]

The Act expressly directs a policeman requesting a specimen to warn the defendant that a failure to provide such a specimen may make the defendant liable to prosecution. If this warning has not been given, the magistrates can dismiss the charge. If the driver is incapable of understanding the warning (for example, because he does not understand English sufficiently) he may not be convicted if he refuses to provide a sample. Separate procedures apply under s 7A where the defendant is unable to give consent due to a medical condition following an accident. In such circumstances the police surgeon may take a sample of blood. The defendant must be told that the sample has been taken when he is conscious and his permission for a lab test has been obtained. Failure to give consent is an offence with the same penalties as failure to supply a sample.

C[23.6]

There are three possible ways of providing a specimen: breath, blood or urine. The current law places the choice entirely in the hands of the police who will use the breath-analysis machine, only offering the defendant blood or urine if the machine is broken or unavailable, or where there are medical reasons for not requiring a sample of breath. Where the police require a specimen of blood for analysis they are not required to offer the motorist a preference but must ask whether there are any reasons why a specimen cannot or should not be taken by a medical practitioner (*DPP v Warren* [1993] AC 319, [1992] 4 All ER 865, HL). The officer must act reasonably in his choice and not ignore for example a defendant's assertions that he could not give blood due to religious reasons (*Joseph v DPP* [2003] EWHC 3078 (Admin), [2003] All ER (D) 326 (Nov)).

There was nothing in the legislation to state that where a driver failed to provide a specimen of breath and the custody sergeant sought a blood test it was not possible to abandon the blood testing procedure and prosecute the driver under s 7 (6) (*Longstaff v DPP* [2008 EWHC 303 (Admin), [2008] All ER (D) 276 (Jan)); see also *McNeil v DPP* [2008] EWHC 1254 (Admin), [2008] All ER (D) 375 (Apr).

C[23.6A]

Legal Advice. A police officer does not have to delay the procedures to permit the suspect to consult a solicitor. As a matter of principle, however, once a police officer had decided to give a person the opportunity to consult a solicitor in respect of the requirement to provide two specimens of breath, it would be incumbent on the officer to allow that person the benefit of a full cycle on an approved device despite an earlier refusal (*Plackett v DPP* [2008] EWHC 1335 (Admin), [2008] All ER (D) 194 (May)).

Sentencing

C[23.7]

Where either the defendant was driving or attempting to drive or where he was in charge see Table B at B[4.2] and see the notes to the offence of 'Alcohol over the prescribed limit' at C[22].

SC Guideline – Failure to Provide Evidential Specimen (drive/attempt to drive)

See C[23.9] for SC Guideline (in charge)

C[23.8]

Must endorse and disqualify for at least 12 months.

Must disqualify for **at least** 2 years if offender has had two or more disqualifications for periods of 56 days or more in preceding 3 years – consult your legal adviser for further guidance.

Must disqualify for **at least** 3 years if offender has been convicted of a relevant drink/drive offence in preceding 10 years – consult your legal adviser for further guidance.

If there is a delay in sentencing after conviction, consider interim disqualification.

Note: the first column below provides guidance regarding the length of disqualification that may be appropriate in case to which the 3 year minimum applies. The period to be imposed in any individual case will depend on an assessment of all the relevant circumstances, including the length of time since the earlier ban was imposed and the gravity of the current offence.

OFFENCE SERIOUSNESS (CULPABILITY AND HARM)				
A. IDENTIFY THE APPROPRIATE STARTING POINT				
Starting points based on first time offender pleading not guilty				
Examples of nature of activity	Starting point	Range	Disqualification	Disqualification. 2nd offence in 10 years
Defendant refused test when had honestly held but unreasonable excuse	Band C fine	Band C fine	12–16 months	36–40 months

| Deliberate refusal or deliberate failure | Low level community order | Band C fine to high level community order | 17–28 months | 36–52 months |
| Deliberate refusal or deliberate failure where evidence of serious impairment | 12 weeks custody | High level community order to 26 weeks custody | 29–36 months | 36–60 months |

OFFENCE SERIOUSNESS (CULPABILITY AND HARM)
B. CONSIDER THE EFFECT OF AGGRAVATING AND MITIGATING FACTORS (OTHER THAN THOSE WITHIN EXAMPLES ABOVE)
Common aggravating and mitigating factors are identified at B[5.2A]. The following may be particularly relevant but **these lists are not exhaustive**

Factors indicating higher culpability	*Factors indicating lower culpability*
1. Evidence of unacceptable nature of driving	1. Genuine but unsuccessful attempt to provide specimen
2. LGV, HGV, PSV etc	
3. Obvious state of intoxication	
4. Driving for hire or reward	
Factor indicating greater degree of harm	
1. Involved in accident	

FORM A PRELIMINARY VIEW OF THE APPROPRIATE SENTENCE, THEN CONSIDER OFFENDER MITIGATION
Common factors are identified at B[5.2A]
CONSIDER A REDUCTION FOR A GUILTY PLEA
CONSIDER OFFERING DRINK/DRIVE REHABILITATION COURSE; CONSIDER ANCILLARY ORDERS
Refer to B[18] for guidance on compensation and **Part B** for available ancillary orders
DECIDE SENTENCE
GIVE REASONS

SC Guideline – Failure to Provide Evidential Specimen (in charge) See C[23.8] for SC Guideline (drive/attempt to drive)

C[23.9]

Must endorse and may disqualify. If no disqualification, impose 10 points.

OFFENCE SERIOUSNESS (CULPABILITY AND HARM)
A. IDENTIFY THE APPROPRIATE STARTING POINT
Starting points based on first time offender pleading not guilty

Examples of nature of activity	**Starting point**	**Range**
Defendant refused test when had honestly held but unreasonable excuse	Band B fine	Band B fine

Deliberate refusal or de-liberate failure	Band C fine	10 points
		Band C fine to medium level community order
Deliberate refusal or de-liberate failure where evidence of serious impairment	Medium level community order	Consider disqualification OR 10 points
		Low level community order to 6 weeks custody
		Disqualify 6–12 months

OFFENCE SERIOUSNESS (CULPABILITY AND HARM)

B. CONSIDER THE EFFECT OF AGGRAVATING AND MITIGATING FACTORS (OTHER THAN THOSE WITHIN EXAMPLES ABOVE)

Common aggravating and mitigating factors are identified at B[5.2A]. The following may be particularly relevant but **these lists are not exhaustive**

Factors indicating higher culpability	*Factors indicating lower culpability*
1. Obvious state of intoxication	1. Genuine but unsuccessful attempt to provide specimen
2. LGV, HGV, PSV etc	2. Low likelihood of driving
3. High likelihood of driving	
4. Driving for hire or reward	

FORM A PRELIMINARY VIEW OF THE APPROPRIATE SENTENCE, THEN CONSIDER OFFENDER MITIGATION

Common factors are identified at B[5.2A]

CONSIDER A REDUCTION FOR A GUILTY PLEA

CONSIDER ANCILLARY ORDERS

Refer to B[18] for guidance on compensation and **Part B** for available ancillary orders

DECIDE SENTENCE

GIVE REASONS

C[24]

Failure to co-operate with roadside breath test

Charge

C[24.1]

Failing, without reasonable excuse, to provide a specimen of breath for a breath test when required to do so by a policeman in uniform

Road Traffic Act 1988, s 6(4)

Maximum penalty-Fine of level 3. Must endorse unless special reasons. Disqualification is discretionary.

Penalty points – 4.

Legal notes and definitions

C[24.2]

The policeman must have been in uniform at the time he requested the defendant to take a breath test and used a Home Office approved breathalyser.

C[24.3]

A defendant can only be required to take this test by a constable in uniform who has reasonable cause for suspecting:

(a)   the defendant *is* driving or attempting to drive a motor vehicle on a road or other public place and has alcohol in his body or has committed a traffic offence whilst the vehicle was in motion; or

(b)   he *has been* driving or attempting to drive on a road or other public place with alcohol in his body and he still has alcohol in his body; or

(c)   he *has been* driving or attempting to drive a motor vehicle on a road or other public place and has committed a traffic offence whilst the vehicle was in motion.

For these purposes 'driving' includes being 'in charge'.

C[24.4]

In addition, where there has been an accident, a constable (whether in uniform or not) may require any person who he has reasonable cause to believe was driving or attempting to drive or in charge of the vehicle at the time of the accident to provide a breath test.

C[24.5]

The instructions on the breath test device need not be strictly observed. If the constable had no reason to suspect that the motorist had drunk alcohol in the previous 20 minutes he can be required to take the test immediately.

See also C[23.3].

C[24.6]

Motorist in hospital. If a motorist is in a hospital as a patient, he can still be required to take a breath test, provided that the doctor in immediate charge of him is notified and does not object.

C[24.7]

Reasonable excuse. If the defendant satisfies the magistrates that he had a reasonable excuse for failing to take a breath test he is entitled to be acquitted. Such a defendant will probably be rare. One example may be that the defendant was hurrying to get a doctor to deal with an emergency. The degree of proof required of the defendant is to prove that this point is probably true. He does not have to establish it beyond reasonable doubt.

C[24.8]

The legal adviser should be consulted if the defence raise this point.

Sentencing
SC Guideline – Failing to co-operate with roadside
breath test

C[24.9]

Starting point – Band B fine.

Since 'reasonable excuse' is a defence (see above) a conviction implies that the defendant had no excuse and therefore this is not a trivial offence and carries an endorsement.

C[25]–C[30]

Careless driving (drive without due care and attention)

Charge

C[25.1]

Driving a mechanically propelled vehicle on a road or other public place without due care and attention

Road Traffic Act 1988, s 3, as amended

Maximum penalty-Fine level 5 for offences committed on or after 24/9/07. For fines see B[33]). May disqualify for any period and/or until a driving test has been passed. Must endorse unless special reasons.

Penalty points – 3–9.

Legal notes and definitions

C[25.2]

Mechanically propelled vehicle. See C[47.9].

C[25.3]

Road. See C[22.5].

C[25.4]

Public place. See C[20.7]–C[20.8]. The car park of a dealership has been found to be a public place (*May v DPP* [2005] EWHC 1280 (Admin), [2005] All ER (D) 182 (Apr)).

C[25.5]

Due care and attention. The standard of driving expected by the law is that of the degree of care and attention to be exercised by a reasonable and prudent driver in the circumstances. The standard of careful driving expected in law from a motorist is the same for all, even the holder of a provisional licence.

Definition: For offences committed or after 24 September 2007 the **Road Safety Act 2006** inserts after s 3 of the Road Traffic Act 1988, a new s 3ZA which provides a statutory meaning of careless, or inconsiderate, driving as follows:

"(1)   This section has effect for the purposes of sections 2B and 3 above and section 3A below.

(2)   A person is to be regarded as driving without due care and attention if (and only if) the way he drives falls below what would be expected of a competent and careful driver.

(3)   In determining for the purposes of subsection (2) above what would be expected of a competent and careful driver in a particular case, regard shall be had not only to the circumstances of which he could be expected to be aware but also to any circumstances shown to have been within the knowledge of the accused.

(4)   A person is to be regarded as driving without reasonable consideration for other persons only if those persons are inconvenienced by his driving".

C[25.6]

A skid may or may not be due to lack of care, but being overcome by sleep is not a defence.

C[25.7]

Where a motorist is confronted by an emergency during the course of driving, he should be judged by the test of whether it was reasonable for him to have acted as he did and not according to the standard of perfection yielded by hindsight.

C[25.8]

If the driving complained of was due to a mechanical defect in the vehicle, that is a defence unless the defendant knew of the defect, or he could have discovered it by exercising prudence; but the burden of proof remains on the prosecution to establish beyond reasonable doubt a lack of due care and attention.

C[25.9]

Observance or non-observance of the Highway Code can be used to establish or disprove guilt. General impressions formed by a witness as to the speed of a vehicle may be admitted (*Blake v DPP* [2002] EWHC 2014 (Admin), [2002] All ER (D) 125 (Sep)).

C[25.10]

Warning of proceedings. If the defence claim that notice should have been given within 14 days of intention to prosecute, consult the clerk.

Evidence will not be excluded because of the failure of a police officer to issue a caution before asking a driver if he was driving a particular vehicle involved in an accident (*Kemsley v DPP* [2005] 169 JP 148).

C[25.11]–[25.15]

Death. As a matter of practice justices should not proceed with a summary trial until the inquest has been held (*Smith v DPP* [2000] RTR 36, 164 JP 96).

C[25.16]

Careless or inconsiderate driving (Road Traffic Act 1988, s 3) and

dangerous driving (s 2). Where the magistrates see fit, they may allow information for an offence under s 3 and s 2 to be heard together. In this event, if the defendant is convicted of one offence, the second information may be adjourned *sine die* or the justices may make *"no adjudication"*. Should the driver successfully appeal against conviction, he can later be tried on the second information.

C[25.17]
Alternatively, where there is a single information alleging dangerous driving and the magistrates do not find this proved, they may convict of careless driving in the alternative (s 24 RTOA 1988).

C[25.18]
Emergency vehicles. The same standard of care and attention is required of the drivers of fire engines, ambulances, coastguard and police vehicles as of any other driver. That standard is that the driver takes 'due' care and pays 'due' attention.

C[25.19]
Driving. See the note under the offence of no driving licence at C[18.2].

Sentencing
SC Guideline – Careless driving (drive without due care and attention)

C[25.20]
Must endorse and may disqualify. If no disqualification, impose 3–9 points.

OFFENCE SERIOUSNESS (CULPABILITY AND HARM) A. IDENTIFY THE APPROPRIATE STARTING POINT Starting points based on first time offender pleading not guilty		
Examples of nature of activity	**Starting point**	**Range**
Momentary lapse of concentration or misjudgement at low speed	Band A fine	Band A fine 3–4 points
Loss of control due to speed, mishandling or insufficient attention to road conditions, or carelessly turning right across on-coming traffic	Band B fine	Band B fine 5–6 points
Overtaking manoeuvre at speed resulting in collision of vehicles, or driving bordering on the dangerous	Band C fine	Band C fine

		Consider disqualification OR 7–9 points

OFFENCE SERIOUSNESS (CULPABILITY AND HARM)

B. CONSIDER THE EFFECT OF AGGRAVATING AND MITIGATING FACTORS (OTHER THAN THOSE WITHIN EXAMPLES ABOVE)

Common aggravating and mitigating factors are identified at B[5.2A]. The following may be particularly relevant but **these lists are not exhaustive**

Factors indicating higher culpability	*Factors indicating lower culpability*
1. Excessive speed	1. Minor risk
2. Carrying out other tasks while driving	2. Inexperience of driver
3. Carrying passengers or heavy load	3. Sudden change in road or weather conditions
4. Tiredness	
Factors indicating greater degree of harm	
1. Injury to others	
2. Damage to other vehicles or property	
3. High level of traffic or pedestrians in vicinity	
4. Location eg near school when children are likely to be present	

FORM A PRELIMINARY VIEW OF THE APPROPRIATE SENTENCE, THEN CONSIDER OFFENDER MITIGATION

Common factors are identified at B[5.2A]

CONSIDER A REDUCTION FOR A GUILTY PLEA

CONSIDER ORDERING DISQUALIFICATION UNTIL APPROPRIATE DRIVING TEST PASSED

CONSIDER ANCILLARY ORDERS, INCLUDING COMPENSATION

Refer to B[18] for guidance on compensation and Part B for available ancillary orders

DECIDE SENTENCE

GIVE REASONS

C[25.21]

If it appears to the court that the offender suffers from a disease or physical disability likely to cause his driving to be a source of danger to the public, then the court shall notify the licensing authority who may take steps to withdraw the driving licence (see C[5.49]).

C[31]

Failing to stop and give details after accident

Charge

C[31.1]

As a driver of a mechanically propelled vehicle, owing to the presence of which on a road or other public place, an accident occurred whereby injury was caused to another person (or damage caused to another vehicle or to roadside property or injury to an animal)

[failed to stop]

[upon being reasonably required to give his name and address, the name and address of the owner of the vehicle and the number of the vehicle, failing to do so]

Road Traffic Act 1988, s 170 (4), as amended

Maximum penalty-Fine level 5 and 6 months' imprisonment [**51 weeks]. May disqualify for any period and/or until a driving test has been passed. Must endorse unless there are special reasons.

Penalty points – 5–10.

Legal notes and definitions

C[31.2]

Charge. The one charge may include both factual situations without offending the rule against duplicity (*DPP v Bennett* [1993] RTR 175, 157 JP 493).

C[31.3]

Relationship between the offences of failing to stop and give details and failing to report an accident. Where an accident has occurred in the circumstances described above, there is an obligation on the driver to stop at the scene of the accident. If he does not do so immediately and as soon as he could safely and conveniently, he commits the offence described here (*Hallinan v DPP* [1998] Crim LR 754). Having stopped at the scene of the accident, he has a duty to give his name and address, the name and address of the owner of the vehicle and the identification marks of the vehicle to any person having reasonable grounds for such a request. If he fails to do so, he has also committed the offence described here. Unless he has actually given his particulars to such other person, he must report the accident at a police station or to a police constable *as soon as reasonably practicable*, and in any case within 24 hours of the accident, otherwise he commits the offence at **C[32.18]**.

C[31.4]

Mechanically propelled vehicle. See C[47.9].

C[31.5]

A road or other public place. See C[22.5].

C[31.6]

An animal. Means any horse, cattle, ass, mule, sheep, pig, goat or dog.

C[31.7]

Roadside property. Means any property constructed on, fixed to, growing in or otherwise forming part of the land on which the road in question is situated, or land adjacent thereto.

C[31.8]

The law requires the driver to give the appropriate particulars upon being reasonably required to do so. It is acceptable to give a business address or a lawyer's office where one can be contacted *(DPP v McCarthy* [1999] RTR 323, 163 JP 585). It is not sufficient to report the incident to the police within 24 hours. Where the defendant was the driver of the vehicle involved in the accident, there is a rebuttable presumption that the defendant knew that he had been involved in the accident. If the defendant can satisfy the court that he was unaware of any accident he must be acquitted *(Selby v Chief Constable of Avon and Somerset* [1988] RTR 216).

C[31.9]

The degree of proof required of the defendant is to satisfy the court that this was probably true; he does not have to prove this beyond reasonable doubt.

C[31.10]–[31.15]

Driver. The notes under the heading 'driving' for the offence of driving without a licence at C[18.2] may be of assistance. A person may continue to be the driver of a motor vehicle if having fulfilled the requirements mentioned on that page he ceases to do so by reason of a change of activity.

C[31.16]

Accidents involving personal injury (to a person other than the driver). The driver must at the time produce his certificate of insurance to a constable or other person having reasonable cause to require it. If he does not do so, he must report the accident as described above and produce his insurance certificate. Otherwise he commits an offence under the Road Traffic Act 1988, s 170(7)-maximum penalty a fine of up to level 3. There is a defence if the certificate is produced within seven days of the accident at a police station specified by him at the time when the accident was reported. This provision does not apply to the driver of an invalid carriage.

Sentencing
SC Guideline – Failing to stop/report accident

C[31.17]

OFFENCE SERIOUSNESS (CULPABILITY AND HARM)		
A. IDENTIFY THE APPROPRIATE STARTING POINT		
Starting points based on first time offender pleading not guilty		
Examples of nature of activity	**Starting point**	**Range**
Minor damage/injury or stopped at scene but failed to exchange particulars or report	Band B fine	Band B fine 5–6 points
Moderate damage/injury or failed to stop and failed to report	Band C fine	Band C fine 7–8 points Consider disqualification
Serious damage/injury and/or evidence of bad driving	High level community order	Band C fine to 26 weeks custody Disqualify 6–12 months OR 9–10 points
OFFENCE SERIOUSNESS (CULPABILITY AND HARM)		
B. CONSIDER THE EFFECT OF AGGRAVATING AND MITIGATING FACTORS (OTHER THAN THOSE WITHIN EXAMPLES ABOVE)		
Common aggravating and mitigating factors are identified at B[5.2A]. The following may be particularly relevant but **these lists are not exhaustive**		
Factors indicating higher culpability	*Factors indicating lower culpability*	
1. Evidence of drink or drugs/ evasion of test	1. Believed identity known	
2. Knowledge/suspicion that personal injury caused (where not an element of the offence)	2. Genuine fear of retribution	
3. Leaving injured party at scene	3. Subsequently reported	
4. Giving false details		
FORM A PRELIMINARY VIEW OF THE APPROPRIATE SENTENCE, THEN CONSIDER OFFENDER MITIGATION		
Common factors are identified at B[5.2A]		
CONSIDER A REDUCTION FOR A GUILTY PLEA		
CONSIDER ANCILLARY ORDERS, INCLUDING COMPENSATION		
Refer to B[18] for guidance on compensation and **Part B** for available ancillary orders		

DECIDE SENTENCE
GIVE REASONS

C[31.18]

If it appears to the court that the accused suffers from a disease or physical disability likely to cause his driving to be a source of danger to the public, then the court shall notify the licensing authority who may take steps to withdraw the driving licence (see C[5.49]).

C[31.19]

For fines see B[33].

C[32]

Failing to report after accident

Charge

C[32.1]

As a driver of a mechanically propelled vehicle, owing to the presence of which on a road or other public place an accident occurred whereby injury was caused to another person (or damage caused to another vehicle or to roadside property or to an animal), not giving his name and address to any person having reasonable grounds for requiring this information, failing to report to the police as soon as reasonably practicable and in any case within 24 hours

Road Traffic Act 1988, s 170(4), as amended

Maximum penalty-Fine level 5 and 6 months' imprisonment [**51 weeks]. May disqualify for any period and/or until a driving test has been passed. Must endorse unless there are special reasons.

Penalty points – 5–10.

Legal notes and definitions

C[32.2]

Relationship between the offences of failing to stop and give details and failing to report an accident. See C[31].

C[32.3]

Mechanically propelled vehicle. See C[47.9].

C[32.4]

A road or other public place. See C[22.5].

C[32.5]

An animal. Means any horse, cattle, ass, mule, sheep, pig, goat or dog.

C[32.6]

Report. Means approaching the police oneself as soon as reasonably practicable, even if no one else was present at the scene of the accident and therefore there was nobody present to ask for the driver's particulars.

C[32.7]

If the defendant were approached by a police officer within 24 hours of the accident, that would not constitute reporting the accident.

C[32.8]

If the defendant can satisfy the court that he was unaware that an accident had occurred, he must be acquitted of this charge.

C[32.9]

The degree of proof is to satisfy the court that this was probably true. The defendant need not prove this beyond reasonable doubt.

C[32.10]–[32.15]

If the defendant gave his name and address to the other party he need not report the accident to the police.

C[32.16]

Roadside property. Means any property constructed on, fixed to, growing in or otherwise forming part of the land on which the road in question is situated or land adjacent thereto.

C[32.17]

Driver. See note under the offence of no driving licence at C[18.8]. A person does not necessarily cease to be a driver if having met the requirements mentioned on that page, he ceased to do so by reason of a change of activity.

C[32.18]

Reasonably practicable. A driver is not saved from conviction because he reported the accident within 24 hours if he could reasonably have reported it sooner. If, for example, he continued his journey after the accident and drove past a police station he would need a very strong reason for not reporting at that station. It appears that he is not obliged to go in search of a public telephone in order to telephone the police. It is for the court to decide what is 'reasonably practicable' in the particular circumstances of each case and the test is not 'Is it reasonable for the defendant to have reported the accident earlier?' but 'Did he report it as soon as practicable?'

In *DPP v Hay* [2005] EWHC 1395 (Admin), (2005) Times, 13 July, it was decided that, after discharging himself from hospital, a driver was still under an obligation to report an accident despite the fact that the police had seen the motorist at the hospital and despite the fact that the police did not issue the driver with an HORT 1 notice to produce the relevant documents such as insurance within 7 days.

Sentencing

C[32.19]

See **SC guideline** and sentencing notes to previous offence at C[31.17].

C[33]

No insurance (using, causing, or permitting)

Charge

C[33.1]

Using (or causing or permitting to be used) a motor vehicle on a road or other public place when there is not in force a policy of insurance or security against third party risks

Road Traffic Act 1988, s 143

Maximum penalty-Fine level 5. May disqualify for any period and/or until defendant has passed a driving test. Must endorse unless special reasons.

Penalty points – 6–8.

Fixed penalty – £200/6 points

Legal notes and definitions

C[33.2]

Motor vehicle. See C[9.7].

Other public place. Not private property but can include such places as car parks.

C[33.3]

A road. Means any highway (including footpaths and bridleways) and any other road to which the public has access and includes bridges.

C[33.4]

Security in respect of third party risks. The requirement to have insurance or a security does not apply to a vehicle owned by a person who has deposited with the Accountant General of the Supreme Court the sum of £500,000, at a time when the vehicle is being driven under the owner's control. Nor does it apply to vehicles owned by bodies such as local authorities or the police. Certain other undertakings may have instead of insurance a security given by an insurer that the undertaking will meet any liability it may incur.

C[33.5]

Time limit. Subject to an overall maximum of three years, proceedings may be brought within 6 months from when, in the prosecutor's opinion, he had sufficient evidence to warrant proceedings. A certificate signed by or on behalf of the prosecutor as to when that date was constitutes conclusive evidence on that point.

C[33.6]

Burden of proof. If the prosecution prove that the defendant used a motor vehicle on a road or other public place, the burden of proof shifts to the defendant to establish that he was insured. The defendant does not have to prove beyond reasonable doubt; he need only prove that he was probably insured.

C[33.7]

Insurance certificate. This is in law the main item of proof of insurance and until it has been delivered to the insured he is held not to be insured. Mere proof that he has paid the premium or holds an actual policy is not sufficient.

C[33.8]

Using on a road or other public place. This expression does not in law only mean driving the vehicle along the road; its mere presence on a road, jacked up and without a battery, may constitute using on a road (*Pumbien v Vines* [1996] RTR 37, [1996] Crim LR 124). A vehicle which is being towed is being used. In any given case where doubt exists consult the legal adviser. See also at C[9] (Brakes).

C[33.9]

A person, limited company or body corporate which owns a vehicle that is being driven in the course of the owner's business is using the vehicle.

C[33.10]–[33.15]

Causing involves an express or positive mandate from the defendant to the driver.

C[33.16]

Permitting. Permission must be given by someone able to permit or withhold permissions but may be express or inferred. See further the note under this heading at C[9.6] in the section on Brakes.

C[33.17]

Defence open to employed drivers. An employed driver cannot be convicted if he can prove that:

(a)   the vehicle did not belong to him; and
(b)   it was not in his possession under a hiring contract or on loan to him; and
(c)   he was using it in the course of his employment; and
(d)   he did not know and had no reason to believe he was not insured. The degree of proof required from the defendant is to prove that this defence is probably true; he does not have to prove beyond reasonable doubt.

C[33.18]

The Motor Insurers' Bureau is a company funded by insurers transacting compulsory motor insurance. Under an agreement with the Secretary of State for Transport the Bureau, subject to certain limitations and exceptions, will compensate the victims of uninsured motorists. A brief outline of the scheme is given here (for the full details see the text of the agreement which is published by HMSO).

C[33.19]

To obtain compensation the victim must obtain judgment in a civil court against the uninsured driver, having given the MIB notice within seven days of starting the proceedings. If the judgment is not met within seven days the victim will be entitled to be compensated by the MIB.

C[33.20]

Compensation is payable for personal injury or for damage to property (except for the first £300 of the claim in respect of property damage and this figure will be the relevant limit of a compensation order made against an uninsured driver in the magistrates' court).

C[33.21]

There are exceptions to claims against the MIB such as claims in relation to Crown vehicles but more particularly where damage is to the claimant's own vehicle which he himself has failed to insure as required by the Road Traffic Act or where the claimant is the passenger in a vehicle which he knew had been stolen or unlawfully taken or was being used without insurance.

C[33.22]

A separate agreement covers the case of victims of untraced drivers.

Sentencing
SC Guideline – No insurance

C[33.23]

Must endorse and may disqualify. If no disqualification, impose 6–8 points – see notes below.

OFFENCE SERIOUSNESS (CULPABILITY AND HARM)		
A. IDENTIFY THE APPROPRIATE STARTING POINT		
Starting points based on first time offender pleading not guilty		
Examples of nature of activity	**Starting point**	**Range**
Using a motor vehicle on a road or other public place without insurance	Band C fine	Band C fine 6 points – 12 months disqualification – see notes below

OFFENCE SERIOUSNESS (CULPABILITY AND HARM)	
B. CONSIDER THE EFFECT OF AGGRAVATING AND MITIGATING FACTORS (OTHER THAN THOSE WITHIN EXAMPLES ABOVE)	
Common aggravating and mitigating factors are identified at B[5.2A]. The following may be particularly relevant but **these lists are not exhaustive**	
Factors indicating higher culpability	*Factors indicating lower culpability*
1. Never passed test	1. Responsibility for providing insurance rests with another
2. Giving false details	2. Genuine misunderstanding
3. Driving LGV, HGV, PSV etc	3. Recent failure to renew or failure to transfer vehicle details where insurance was in existence
4. Driving for hire or reward	4. Vehicle not being driven
5. Evidence of sustained uninsured use	
Factors indicating greater degree of harm	
1. Involved in accident	
2. Accident resulting in injury	
FORM A PRELIMINARY VIEW OF THE APPROPRIATE SENTENCE, THEN CONSIDER OFFENDER MITIGATION	
Common factors are identified at B[5.2A]	
CONSIDER A REDUCTION FOR A GUILTY PLEA	
CONSIDER ANCILLARY ORDERS	
Refer to B[18] for guidance on compensation and **Part B** for available ancillary orders	
DECIDE SENTENCE	
GIVE REASONS	

Notes. Consider range from 7 points – 2 months disqualification where vehicle was being driven and no evidence that the offender held insurance.

Consider disqualification of 6 – 12 months if evidence of sustained uninsured use and/or involvement in accident.

C[33.23A]

Endorsement must be ordered unless special reasons exist. A short distance driven can amount to a special reason. In *DPP v Heritage* [2002] EWHC 2139 (Admin), 166 JP 772 a car was pushed onto the road to be cleaned and a vehicle collided with it.

C[33.24]

If it appears to the court that the accused suffers from some disease or physical disability likely to cause his driving to be a source of danger to the public, then the court shall notify the licensing authority who may take steps to withdraw the driving licence (see C[5.49]).

C[33.25]–[33.30]

Clearly a lower level of fine may be appropriate for the vehicle sitting unused outside the owner's house, whereas deliberate driving around without insurance cover aggravates the seriousness considerably.

C[33.31]

For fines see **B[33]**.

C[34]

Lights defective

Charge

C[34.1]

1 Using or causing or permitting to be used on a road a vehicle without every front position lamp, rear position lamp, headlamp, rear registration plate lamp, side marker lamp, end-outline marker lamp, rear fog lamp, retro reflector and rear marking with which it is required to be fitted by the Regulations, and every stop lamp and direction indicator, running lamp, dim- dip device, headlamp levelling device and hazard warning signal device with which it is fitted in good working order and, in the case of a lamp, clean

C[34.2]

2 Using, causing or permitting to be used on a road any vehicle with a headlamp, front fog lamp, or rear fog lamp so as to cause undue dazzle or discomfort to other persons using the road

C[34.3]

3 Using or causing or permitting to be used on a road a vehicle which is in motion between sunset and sunrise (or between sunrise and sunset in seriously reduced visibility), (or allowing to remain at rest, or causing or permitting to be allowed to remain at rest, on a road any vehicle between sunset and sunrise) unless every front position lamp, rear position lamp, rear registration plate lamp, side marker lamp and end-outline marker lamp with which the vehicle is required by the Regulations to be fitted is kept lit and unobscured

C[34.4]

4 Using, or causing or permitting to be used on a road a vehicle which is fitted with obligatory dipped beam headlamps without such lamps being lit during the hours of darkness (or in seriously reduced visibility)

Road Vehicles Lighting Regulations 1989, reg 23(1) (charge 1); reg 27 (charge 2); reg 24(1) (charge 3); reg 25(1) (charge 4);

Road Traffic Act 1988, s 42

Maximum penalty-Fine level 4 (goods vehicles etc), level 3 (private vehicles) (for fines see B[33]). No power to disqualify or endorse.

Fixed penalty-£30.

Legal notes and definitions

C[34.5]

Using, causing or permitting. The charge should allege only one of these. For 'using', 'causing' and 'permitting' see C[9.4]–C[9.6].

C[34.6]

The obligatory minimum requirements for an ordinary motor car are two front position lights, two headlights (with a dipped beam facility), direction indicators, hazard warning lights, two rear position lamps, one rear fog lamp (vehicles first used after 1 April 1980), two stop lamps, a rear registration plate lamp and two rear reflex reflectors.

C[34.7]

These requirements vary according to the category of vehicle concerned. If the matter is in dispute the legal adviser will be able to provide a list of the requirements.

C[34.8]

Vehicle. Means a vehicle of any description and includes a machine or implement of any kind drawn or propelled along roads whether by animal or mechanical power.

C[34.9]

Road. Means any road or highway to which the public has access and includes bridges and footways.

C[34.10]–[34.15]

Front position lamp. Means a lamp used to indicate the presence and width of a vehicle when viewed from the front.

C[34.16]

Hours of darkness. Means the time between half an hour after sunset and half an hour before sunrise. An almanac can be produced to establish this period if it is in dispute.

C[34.17]

Exempted vehicles include

(a)   Pedal cycles and hand drawn vehicles are not required to be fitted with lamps between sunrise and sunset.
(b)   Vehicles temporarily imported or proceeding to port for export provided they comply with international Conventions.
(c)   Military vehicles which comply with certain requirements.
(d)   Vehicles drawn or propelled by hand which have an overall width (including load) not exceeding 800 millimetres are not required to be fitted with lamps and reflectors except when they are used on a carriageway between sunset and sunrise (unless they are close to the near side or are crossing the road).

Possible defences include

C[34.18]

Offence 1 where a defective lamp or reflector is fitted to the vehicle which is in use between sunrise and sunset if the lamp etc becomes defective during the journey or if arrangements have been made to remedy the defect with all reasonable expedition.

C[34.19]

Offence 3 where the vehicle is a car or does not exceed 1,525 kilograms and is parked on a road with a speed limit of 30 miles per hour or less in force and the vehicle is parked in a designated parking place or lay-by or is parked parallel to the kerb, close to it and facing the direction of traffic and is not less than 10 metres from a junction.

C[34.20]

Offence 4. Except where there is seriously reduced visibility, the car is on a road restricted to 30 miles per hour by virtue of a system of street lighting which is lit at the time of the alleged offence.

Sentencing
SC Guideline – Lights defective

C[34.21]

Starting point – Band A fine (driver); Band A fine (owner-driver but consider an uplift of at least 25% on the driver's fine); Band B fine (owner-company).

C[34.22]

For fines see B[33].

C[35]

Motor cyclist not wearing helmet

Charge

C[35.1]

Being a person driving (or riding on) a motor cycle on a road, did not wear protective headgear

Motor Cycles (Protective Helmets) Regulations 1980, reg 4; Road Traffic Act 1988, s 16(4)

Maximum penalty-Fine level 3 (for fines see B[33]). There is no power to endorse or disqualify.

Fixed penalty-£30.

Legal notes and definitions

C[35.2]

Where the person actually in breach of the regulations by not wearing a helmet is over 16, there can be no prosecution of another person for aiding and abetting. However, aiders and abettors of defendants under 16 can be prosecuted.

C[35.3]

Riding on. This includes a pillion rider but not a passenger in a side-car.

C[35.4]

Protective headgear is defined in the regulations as being that which complies with a certain British Standard. Headgear manufactured for use by persons on motorcycles which appears to afford the same or a greater degree of protection than laid down by the Standard is also included. But before any helmet satisfies the definition it must also be securely fastened to the head of the wearer by the straps or fastenings provided on the helmet. An unfastened helmet, therefore, would not suffice.

C[35.5]

Driving. See the notes under this heading for the offence of driving without a licence at C[18.8]–C[18.9] but bear in mind the exemption mentioned at (b) below.

C[35.6]

Exemptions. There is no requirement to wear a helmet:

(a)   if the motor cycle is a mowing machine;

(b)   if the motor cycle is being propelled by a person on foot;
(c)   if the driver is a Sikh and is wearing a turban.

Sentencing

C[35.7]
No SC Guideline.

Starting point – Band A fine suggested.

C[35.8]
For fines see **B[33]**.

C[36]

Obstruction

Charge 1

C[36.1]

Causing unnecessary obstruction of a road by a person in charge of a motor vehicle or trailer

Road Vehicles (Construction and Use) Regulations 1986, reg 103; Road Traffic Act 1988, s 42

Maximum penalty-Fine level 4 (goods vehicle etc), level 3 (otherwise) (for fines see B[33]). No power to disqualify or endorse.

Fixed penalty-£30.

Charge 2

C[36.1A]

Did without lawful authority or excuse wilfully obstruct the free passage along a highway.

Highways Act 1980, s 137

Maximum penalty-Fine level 3

Legal notes and definitions

C[36.2]

Unnecessary obstruction. There need be no notice or sign displayed as is the case where a driver is charged in parking offences. This offence can be committed on a road to which local parking regulations are applicable.

Wilful. If anyone does something by exercise of their free will which causes an obstruction the offence is usually made out (*Arrowsmith v Jenkins* [1963] 2 QB 561, [1963] 2 All ER 210).

C[36.3]

If the vehicle is parked in a lawfully designated parking place then there can be no charge of obstruction.

C[36.4]

The High Court has ruled that a motorist who left his car on a road 24 ft wide for 75 minutes did not commit this offence (*Evans v Barker* [1971]

RTR 453). An obstruction was not committed by a reasonable protest taking up 2 ft of an 11ft-wide path (*Westminster City Council v Haw* [2002] All ER (D) 59 (Oct)).

C[36.5]

A taxi-driver was held by the High Court to have committed this offence in waiting in the road to turn right, thereby holding up heavy traffic.

C[36.6]

The question is one for the justices to decide on the facts of each case. An obstruction caused by a doctor answering an emergency call may, for example, be necessary.

C[36.7]

A road. Means any highway (including footpaths and bridleways) and any other road to which the public has access and includes bridges. A road is provided as a means of transit from one place to another and not as a place to park motor vehicles.

C[36.8]

Trailer. Means any vehicle drawn by a motor vehicle.

C[36.9]

A motor vehicle. See C[9.7]. If left on a road for an unreasonable time may constitute an unnecessary obstruction.

Power to order the removal of the obstruction rests with the magistrates when recording a conviction under the Highways Act 1980, s 137. Failure to comply with the order without reasonable excuse is an offence punishable by a fine not exceeding level 5 and a daily fine thereafter.

Sentencing

C[36.10]–[36.15]

No SC Guideline.

Starting point – Band A fine suggested.

An average case will not usually attract more than a small fine; where there is a complete disregard for the convenience or safety of others (eg access of fire appliances or ambulances) a heavier fine is called for.

C[36.16]

For fines see B[33].

C[37]

Opening door

Charge

C[37.1]

Opening a door of a motor vehicle or trailer on a road so as to cause injury or danger

Road Vehicles (Construction and Use) Regulations 1986, reg 105; Road Traffic Act 1988, s 42

Maximum penalty-Fine level 4 (goods vehicle etc), level 3 (otherwise) (for fines see B[33]). No power to disqualify or endorse.

Fixed penalty-£30.

Legal notes and definitions

C[37.2]
Motor vehicle. See C[9.7].

C[37.3]
Trailer. Means any vehicle drawn by a motor vehicle.

C[37.4]
Road. Means any highway (including footpaths and bridleways) and any other road to which the public has access and includes bridges.

C[37.5]
The offence. Consists of opening or causing or permitting a door to be opened so as to cause injury or danger to any person. The offence can be committed by a passenger as well as the driver. If a child opened the door and his parent was present and knew the child was about to open the door, then the parent could be charged with permitting. If the child opened the door on the instructions of a parent then the latter could be guilty of causing the offence. Door opening, permitting or causing are all identical offences for the purpose of the penalties that may be inflicted. Only one of the offences should be alleged.

C[37.6]
The prosecution does not have to prove carelessness; nor that someone was actually struck or injured. It is enough if the act caused danger.

Sentencing

C[37.7]
No SC Guideline.

Starting point – Band A fine suggested.

The amount of the fine will vary according to the circumstances. It will rarely be appropriate to impose a fine less than the fixed penalty. When the offence is very dangerous, eg where it causes a motor cyclist to swerve to the offside of a busy main road, this will aggravate the seriousness. Where actual injury is caused a similar level of penalty should apply.

C[37.8]

If it appears to the court that a driver suffers from some disease or physical disability likely to cause his driving to be a source of danger to the public, then the court shall notify the licensing authority who may take steps to withdraw his driving licence (see C[5.49]).

C[37.9]

For fines see B[33].

C[38]

Overloading/exceeding axle weight

Charge

C[38.1]

Using, causing or permitting to be used on a road a vehicle which exceeds the maximum (gross weight) (train weight) (weight for specified axle) shown on the (plating certificate) (manufacturer's plate fitted to the vehicle)

Road Vehicles (Construction and Use) Regulations 1986, reg 80; Road Traffic Act 1988, s 41B

Maximum penalty-Fine level 5 (for fines see B[33]). Not endorsable.

Fixed penalty-£60.

Legal notes and definitions

C[38.2]

Certain vehicles specified in the Road Vehicles (Construction and Use) Regulations 1986, reg 66 must be fitted with a plate which contains information prescribed in Sch 8 or the relevant EC Directives. In particular the plate must show the maximum gross weight, train weight and weight for each axle. The weights may be specified by the manufacturer and are the limits at or below which the vehicle is considered fit for use, having regard to its design, construction and equipment and the stresses to which it is likely to be subjected in use. Further, the weights must also be specified at which the use of the vehicle will be legal in the UK having regard, inter alia, to the maximum weights set out in regs 75–79. This is a 'manufacturer's plate'.

C[38.3]

In addition, goods vehicles are now covered by the compulsory 'type approval' system whereby the Secretary of State issues a certificate that a type of vehicle conforms with the appropriate requirements and the manufacturer issues a Certificate of Conformity that the vehicle conforms with the approved type. This certificate is *treated* as a 'plating certificate' and a plate (which is in fact a piece of paper) is affixed to the vehicle, which is *deemed* to be a 'ministry plate' (for this and 'plating certificate' see below).

C[38.4]

After one year and annually thereafter goods vehicles must be submitted for a goods vehicle test and at the *first* test the vehicle will also be examined for the purpose of issuing a 'plating certificate'. The examiner will issue a certificate containing information similar to that on the plate previously affixed to the vehicle. If the vehicle passes its goods vehicle test the ministry plate will remain affixed in a conspicuous and readily accessible position on the vehicle and in the cab. Only one plating certificate is issued, but it will be amended where there has been a 'notifiable alteration' to the vehicle.

C[38.5]

Using; causing; permitting. See C[9.4]–C[9.6].

C[38.6]

Road. See C[9.10].

C[38.7]

Vehicle. The provisions concerning manufacturers' plates cover such vehicles as non-agricultural tractors of various weights which do not carry loads, buses and various trailers. This article is concerned with offences committed by goods vehicles, being the most commonly encountered in the magistrates' court.

C[38.8]

Maximum gross weight. The sum of the weights to be transmitted to the road surface by all the wheels of the motor vehicle (including any load imposed by a trailer on the vehicle).

C[38.9]

Maximum train weight. The maximum gross weight and the weight transmitted to the road surface by any trailer drawn.

C[38.10]–[38.15]

Maximum axle weight. The sum of the weights to be transmitted to the road surface by all the wheels of that axle.

C[38.16]

Multiple charges. Under the former regulations 'gross', 'train' or 'axle' weight were the subject of separate charges and not combined into one. It was not oppressive for there to be a charge in respect of each axle that was overweight and for exceeding the gross weight. The new regulations are worded slightly differently but it is still permissible to prefer several charges where appropriate (*Travel-Gas (Midlands) Ltd v Reynolds* [1989] RTR 75).

C[38.17]

Evidence. Unless proved to the contrary the weight indicated on a ministry plate is presumed to be the weight recorded on the relevant plating certificate.

C[38.18]

Defences. In the case of a goods vehicle it is a defence for the accused to prove:

(a)   that at the time when the vehicle was being used on the road it was proceeding to a weighbridge which was the nearest available one to the place where the loading of the vehicle was completed for the purpose of being weighed, or was proceeding from a weighbridge after being weighed to the nearest point at which it was reasonably practicable to reduce the weight to the relevant limit without causing an obstruction on any road; or

(b)   in a case where the limit of that weight was not exceeded by more than 5%, that limit was not exceeded at the time the loading of the vehicle was originally completed and that since that time no person has made any addition to the load (eg a load which becomes wet owing to falling rain).

C[38.18A]

"**Nearest available weighbridge**" means the nearest available weighbridge that was actually available as a matter of objective fact regardless of the knowledge of the driver (*Vehicle and Operator Services Agency v F & S Gibbs Transport Services Ltd* [2006] EWHC 1109 (Admin), 170 JP 586.

C[38.19]

The degree of proof required from the defendant is to prove that the defence is probably true; he does not have to prove beyond reasonable doubt.

Sentencing
SC Guideline – Overloading/exceeding axle weight

C[38.20]

Starting point – Mechanically propelled vehicle-Band A fine (driver); Band A fine (owner-driver but consider an uplift of at least 25% on the driver's fine); Band B fine (owner-company). The starting point presumes an excess overload etc of no more than 10%. A further uplift of 1% for every 1% more than 10% is permissible but the total fine must not be out of proportion to the offence and the means of the defendant may be relevant.

Starting point – HGV, LGV or PSV – Band B fine (driver); Band B fine (owner-driver but consider an uplift of at least 25% on the driver's fine); Band C fine (owner-company). A further uplift of 1% for every 1% more than 10% is permissible but the total fine must not be out of proportion to the offence and the means of the defendant may be relevant.

C[38.21]

For fines see B[33].

C[38A]

Breach of requirement as to speed assessment equipment detection devices

Charge

C[38A.1]

A person who –

(a) contravenes or fails to comply with a construction or use requirement as to speed assessment equipment detection devices, or
(b) uses on a road a motor vehicle or trailer which does not comply with such a requirement, or causes or permits a motor vehicle or trailer to be so used, is guilty of an offence.

Road Traffic Act 1988, s 41C as inserted (from a date to be appointed) by s 18 Road Safety Act 2006.

Maximum penalty – Fine level 4 if committed on a special road otherwise level 3. Must endorse unless special reasons.

Penalty points – 3–6 (fixed penalty 3).

Fixed penalty-£60.

Legal notes and definitions

C[38A.2]

Motor vehicle. See C[9.7] for definition.

Trailer. See C[9.9] for definition.

Road. See C[9.10]–C[9.15] for definition.

Sentencing

C[38A.3]

Awaiting SC Guidance.

C[39]

Pelican/zebra crossing contravention

Charge

C[39.1]

Failure of a driver of any vehicle to accord precedence to a pedestrian within the limits of an uncontrolled pedestrian crossing

'Zebra' Pedestrian Crossings Regulations 1971, reg 8 (or 'Pelican' Pedestrian Crossings Regulations 1987, reg 17); Road Traffic Regulation Act 1984, s 25(5)

Maximum penalty-Fine of level 3 (for fines see **B[33]**). If the offence was committed in a motor vehicle, the court may disqualify for any period and/or until a driving test has been passed. Must endorse unless special reasons exist.

Penalty points – 3.

Fixed penalty-£60 (3PP)

Legal notes and definitions

C[39.2]

Vehicle. A bicycle is a vehicle (but not in the case of offences of stopping in an area *adjacent* to a zebra crossing, see **C[40.7]–C[40.9]**).

C[39.3]

Zebra crossing. A driver should approach such a crossing in a manner that enables him to stop before reaching it, unless he can see there is no pedestrian on the crossing.

C[39.4]

The law imposes a very strict duty on the driver and the prosecution has the advantage of not having to prove any negligence or want of care. It would, however, be a sufficient defence to satisfy the magistrates that the failure to accord precedence was due to circumstances over which the defendant had no control (eg being attacked by a swarm of bees, or a sudden brake failure).

C[39.5]

The High Court in Scotland has held that where a woman was pushing her child in a pram and the pram was on the crossing but she herself had not actually stepped on to the crossing, the mother had the right of way.

C[39.6]

The limits of the crossing are marked by studs bordering the striped lines. The broken white line along the striped crossing is to indicate where vehicles should give way.

C[39.7]

The sections of pedestrian crossings on each side of a dual carriageway, central street refuge or reservation are considered to be two separate crossings.

C[39.8]

A crossing may still legally remain a crossing even if one or more of its stripes are missing, discoloured or imperfect, or if a globe or one of its lights is missing, or even if some of the studs have disappeared. The magistrates should consult the legal adviser if a submission is made on any of these matters.

C[39.9]

The regulations require pedestrians to cross 'with reasonable dispatch'.

C[39.10]–[39.15]

On each side of crossings are zigzag lines parallel to the carriageway. These indicate the 'area controlled by the crossing'. On the approach side of the crossing it is an offence for a vehicle to overtake another vehicle in that area if that vehicle is either the only other vehicle in the area or is the nearest vehicle of several to the crossing. 'Overtaking' includes allowing part of the rearmost vehicle to pass the front of the overtaken vehicle, a complete passing is not necessary. The prohibition on overtaking does not apply if the overtaken vehicle is stationary otherwise than to allow pedestrians to cross (eg if it is waiting to turn left or right) or if the crossing is for the time being controlled by a policeman or traffic warden, but it applies where a vehicle has stopped to wait for pedestrians to step on to the crossing, for example as a courtesy. It also applies when the pedestrians have passed the stationary vehicle which is overtaken.

C[39.16]

Pelican crossings. Similar provisions apply. A vehicle approaching such a crossing shall proceed with due regard to the safety of other users of the road. When a red light shows the vehicle must stop, similarly where a constant amber light shows, a vehicle must stop except where the vehicle cannot safely be stopped in line with the signal. Where there is a flashing amber light, a vehicle must accord precedence to pedestrians already on the crossing. Failure to comply with any of the regulations is an offence with a maximum penalty of a fine on level 3.

C[39.17]

Pedestrian. A person walking and pushing a bicycle is a pedestrian. He ceases to be a pedestrian if he uses the bicycle to carry him, for example, by placing one foot on a pedal and pushing himself along with the other.

C[39.18]

Precedence means allowing the pedestrian to go before the vehicle. Once the pedestrian has safely passed the vehicle's line of travel the vehicle may proceed even though the pedestrian is still on the crossing.

Sentencing
SC Guideline – Pelican/zebra crossing contravention

C[39.19]

Starting point – Band A fine.

C[39.20]

If it appears to the court that the defendant driver of a motor vehicle suffers from some disease or physical disability likely to cause his driving to be a source of danger to the public, then the court shall notify the licensing authority who may take steps to withdraw the driving licence (see **C[5.49]**).

C[39.21]

For fines see **B[33]**.

C[40]–[45]
Stopping on pedestrian crossing

Charge

C[40.1]

That a driver of a vehicle caused it or any part of it to stop within the limits of zebra crossing

'Zebra' Pedestrian Crossings Regulations 1971, reg 9; Road Traffic Regulation Act 1984, s 25(5)

Maximum penalty-Fine level 3 (for fines see B[33]). If the offence was committed in a motor vehicle, the court may disqualify for any period and/or until the defendant has passed a driving test. Must endorse unless special reasons exist.

Penalty points – 3.

Fixed penalty-£60 (3PP).

Legal notes and definitions

C[40.2]

The defendant must be acquitted if he establishes any of the following:

(a)   that circumstances beyond his control compelled him to stop;
(b)   that he had to stop to avoid an accident (see **C[40.9]**).

C[40.3]

The degree of proof required from the defendant is to prove that one of these is probably true; he does not have to prove one of them beyond reasonable doubt.

C[40.4]

The term 'vehicle' includes a pedal cycle.

C[40.5]

This charge does not apply to a push-button controlled crossing which is subject to special regulations.

C[40.6]

A crossing may still legally remain a crossing even if one or more stripes are missing, discoloured or imperfect, or if a globe or its light is missing or even if some of the studs have disappeared. Consult the legal adviser.

C[40.7]

Stopping in area adjacent to zebra crossing. It is also an offence to stop in a zebra-controlled area, ie the part of a road indicated by zig-zag lines at either side of the crossing ('Zebra' Pedestrian Crossings Regulations 1971, reg 12).

C[40.8]

For the purposes of this regulation 'vehicle' does *not* include a pedal cycle.

C[40.9]

Defences are:

(a)   that circumstances beyond his control compelled him to stop;
(b)   that he had to stop to avoid an accident;
(c)   that the stopping was for the purpose of allowing free passage to pedestrians on the crossing;
(d)   that he had to stop for fire brigade, ambulance or police purposes, because of demolitions, repairs to road, gas, water, electricity services etc;
(e)   that he stopped for the purpose of making a left or right turn;
(f)   a stage carriage or express carriage vehicle (not on a trip or excursion) in the controlled area beyond the zebra crossing for the purposes of picking up or setting down passengers.

Sentencing
SC Guideline – Pelican/zebra crossing contravention

C[40.10]–[40.15]

Starting point – Band A fine.

C[40.16]

If it appears to the court that the defendant driver of a motor vehicle suffers from some disease or physical disability likely to cause his driving to be a source of danger to the public, then the court shall notify the licensing authority who may take steps to withdraw the driving licence (see **C[5.49]**).

C[40.17]

For fines see **B[33]**.

C[46]

Reasonable consideration

Charge

C[46.1]

Driving a mechanically propelled vehicle on a road or other public place without reasonable consideration for other persons using the road or place

Road Traffic Act 1988, s 3, as amended

Maximum penalty-Fine level 4 [level 5 for offences committed on or after 24/9/07] (for fines see **B[33]**). May disqualify for any period and/or until a driving test has been passed. Must endorse unless special reasons exist.

Penalty points – 3–9.

Legal notes and definitions

C[46.2]

Reasonable consideration. At the time of the offence there must have been other people also using the road. They could be passengers in the defendant's vehicle. Another example of this offence is driving the vehicle through a muddy puddle and splashing pedestrians.

Definition: See C[25.5] for a new statutory definition which has been added to s 3ZA of the Road Traffic Act 1988 by the Road Safety Act 2006 (applies to offences committed on or after 24 September 2007)

C[46.3]

If no other person but the driver is using the road then this charge fails.

C[46.4]

Observance or non-observance of the Highway Code can be used to establish or disprove liability.

C[46.5]

The driver alleged to have committed this offence must give his name and address on request to any person having reasonable grounds for requiring it, otherwise he commits an offence under the Road Traffic Act 1988, s 168, maximum penalty fine on level 3.

C[46.6]

Mechanically propelled vehicle. See C[47.9].

C[46.7]

Road. See C[22.5].

C[46.8]

Public place. See C[20.7]–C[20.8].

C[46.9]

Warning of prosecution. If the defence claim that notice should have been given within 14 days of intention to prosecute, consult the legal adviser.

C[46.10]–[46.15]

Other persons using the road. May include passengers in the defendant's vehicle. There must be evidence that another road user was inconvenienced by the manner of driving adopted by the accused.

C[46.16]

Careless or inconsiderate driving (Road Traffic Act 1988, s 3) and dangerous driving (s 2). Where the magistrates see fit, they may allow informations for an offence under s 3 and s 2 to be heard together. In this event, if the defendant is convicted of one offence, the second information can either be adjourned *sine die* or the justices may make *"no adjudication"*. Should the driver successfully appeal against conviction for dangerous driving, he can later be tried on the second information.

C[46.17]

Alternatively, where there is a single information alleging dangerous driving and the magistrates do not find this proved, they may convict of driving without reasonable consideration in the alternative (s 24 RTOA 1988).

C[46.18]

Driving. See the note under the offence of no driving licence at C[18.8]–C[18.9].

Sentencing

C[46.19]

SC Guideline – Careless (or inconsiderate) driving – see C[25.20].

C[46.20]

In rare cases it may be appropriate to grant an absolute discharge; if this course is adopted disqualification can be imposed but this would be an unusual course to take. Endorsement must be ordered unless special reasons exist.

C[46.21]

If it appears to the court that the accused suffers from some disease or physical disability likely to cause his driving to be a source of danger to the public then the court shall notify the licensing authority who may take steps to withdraw the driving licence (see C[5.49]).

C[46.22]

It is the lack of consideration rather than the consequences of it which normally determines the punishment.

C[46.23]

For fines see B[33].

C[47]

No excise licence

Charge 1

C[47.1]

Using or keeping on a public road a mechanically propelled vehicle when no excise licence is in force and doing so when a SORN is in force

Vehicle Excise and Registration Act 1994, s 29 and s 29(3A)

C[47.2]

Maximum penalty-A fine of level 3 (s 29(3)) or level 4 (s 29(3A)) or 5 times the value of the licence, whichever is the greater. No power to disqualify or endorse.

Charge 2

Keeping an unlicensed vehicle while the registered keeper

Vehicle Excise and Registration Act 1994, s 31A

Maximum penalty –A fine of level 3 or 5 times the annual duty. Additional penalty of a least £1,000 if the vehicle remains unlicensed from the date of offence to the start of proceedings.

C[47.3]

In addition to a fine the court is compelled, in certain cases, to order the defendant to pay loss of duty. See **C[47.18]** under 'Sentencing'.

Legal notes and definitions

C[47.4]

The charge must stipulate whether the defendant is being charged with using or keeping. One charge cannot allege both.

C[47.5]

Prosecutor and time limit. Only the Secretary of State, the police acting with his approval, or a person or authority authorised by that Secretary of State can conduct the prosecution. Proceedings must start within 6 months of their receiving sufficient evidence to warrant proceedings; subject to an overall limit of three years from the offence.

C[47.6]

Using. In law means not only driving the vehicle but can also include the vehicle's mere presence on the road. The owner is not liable to be charged with using the vehicle if he allowed some other person to have the vehicle and who used it outside the scope of the authority given by the owner.

C[47.7]

Keeping. Means causing the vehicle to be on a public road for any period, however short, when the vehicle is not in use. See *Secretary of State for the Environment, Transport and the Regions v Holt* [2000] RTR 309, where the High Court ruled that proof that the defendant was the registered keeper together with the adverse inference drawn from his failure to give information as to the identity of the driver was sufficient to prove he was the keeper on the day in question.

C[47.8]

Public road. Refers to a road repairable at the public expense. This is different from the more usual definition of a road which means any highway (including footpaths and bridleways) and any other road to which the public has access and includes bridges.

C[47.9]

Mechanically propelled vehicle. Means a vehicle with some form of engine; thus even a motor assisted pedal cycle comes within the legal definition even if the rider is just pedalling the machine without the use of the engine. A car does not cease to be a mechanically propelled vehicle after removal of its engine, nor if there is some temporary defect which prevents the engine working. If the condition of the vehicle is such that there is no reasonable prospect of it ever being made mobile again, then it ceases to be a mechanically propelled vehicle.

C[47.10]–[47.15]

Employees, drivers, chauffeurs. It has been decided that it is oppressive to prosecute an employee who was not responsible for licensing the vehicle.

C[47.16]

A dishonoured cheque. If offered in payment of the licensing fee renders the licence void. The licensing authority will send a notice requiring the excise licence to be delivered up within seven days of the posting of the notice. Failure to comply is an offence punishable with a maximum fine of level 3 or 5 times the annual rate of duty applicable (Customs and Excise Management Act 1979, s 102). For liability for back duty see below.

C[47.17]

Exempted vehicles. Certain vehicles are exempt from duty and the clerk can supply a list: ambulances, fire engines, military vehicles, some agricultural vehicles; vehicles going for a *pre-arranged* test and some vehicles acquired by overseas residents, vehicles more than 25 years old, calculated from the 31 December of the year of first registration. This latter class of vehicles must still be licensed annually and display a VED disc. See Sch 2 of the

1994 Act. A vehicle kept off the public road may be subject to a Statutory Off-Road Notification (SORN). A SORN declaration is valid for 12 months. Failure to make or renew a SORN may be subject to a level 3 fine.

Sentencing
SC Guideline – No excise licence

C[47.18]

Starting point – Band A fine (1–3 months unpaid); Band B fine (4–6 months unpaid); Band C fine (7–12 months lost).

(Special considerations: in all cases add duty lost).

The fine and the arrears of duty should be announced as separate items; we do not recommend the practice of some courts of announcing a single sum and stipulating that it includes the back duty.

Liability for back duty

C[47.19]

If the defendant was the person who *kept* the vehicle at the time of the offence the court must order him to pay an amount to cover the loss of duty. Such order is in addition to a fine and the chairman of the court must announce two amounts, namely the amount of the fine and the amount of the lost duty.

C[47.20]

If the court decides not to impose a fine but to grant an absolute or conditional discharge the court must still order the payment of the lost duty as well and this must be announced. It must be stressed that this provision applies only if the defendant is the person who *kept* the vehicle at the time of the offence. Thus this provision would not apply to an employed lorry driver but would apply to a private motorist who kept and used his own vehicle. It would also apply to a company which kept and used its own vehicles.

C[47.21]

Dishonoured cheques. In relation to licences taken out on or after 27 July 1989 the court must, in addition to any penalty it may impose under the Customs and Excise Management Act 1979, s 102, order the defendant to pay an amount to cover the loss of duty incurred for the period for which he had the benefit of the licence.

C[47.22]

Calculating back duty. This period will usually commence with the date of the expiry of the expired licence, or when the defendant notified his acquisition of the vehicle to the appropriate authority. It will terminate with the date of offence. If there is doubt about the length of the 'relevant period' consult the legal adviser. Back duty is calculated for each month or part thereof. Use on one day in a month will render him liable for back duty for the whole month.

C[47.23]

Previous convictions. If the defendant has a previous conviction in respect of the same vehicle for a similar offence for which the court made an order for lost revenue then in the present proceedings the relevant period will commence with the day after the date of the previous offence.

C[47.24]

Costs can be ordered as well as a fine and back duty.

C[47.25]–[47.30]

Defence against back duty. If the defendant can prove any one of the following in respect of any part of the relevant period back duty cannot be ordered against him for that part of the relevant period:

(a)   the vehicle was not kept by him; or
(b)   he paid duty in respect of the vehicle for any month or part of a month (where relevant) whether or not on a licence. The defendant does not have to establish this beyond reasonable doubt but only that his contention is probably true.

Defences for a registered keeper (s 31B). The burden is on the defendant to show either:

(i)   he is no longer the keeper and has complied with the requirements under the Act;
(ii)   the vehicle was not kept on a public road and the requirements have been complied with;
(iii)   the vehicle was stolen and not recovered and the notification requirements complied with.

Note that it is an offence to use a vehicle in public if it is not properly registered; defence of no reasonable opportunity or reasonable grounds for believing that registration details were correct – level 3 fine (fixed penalty offence). A constable or authorised person may require production of vehicle registration certificate – level 2 fine for failure to do so.

C[47.31]

A person is liable for all the periods when he kept a vehicle without a current tax whether it was on a public road or not. It is not obligatory for a person to tax a car that is kept off the road for the whole of that period. However since 31 January 1998 keepers of vehicles which become unlicensed and are to be kept off the public road are required to provide a declaration to the DVLA. If he ventures onto the road without tax he may find himself with a liability extending back over the time when it was not taxed or to the date when he notified his acquisition of the vehicle.

Charge 3

C[47.32]
Fraudulently using a vehicle excise licence

Vehicle Exercise and Registration Act 1994, s 44.

Maximum penalty – Fine level 5 (for fines see **B[33]**). No power to disqualify or endorse.

Crown Court – Unlimited fine and 2 years' imprisonment. Triable either way.

See **A[64]** for more details and **SC guideline**.

C[48]

Seat belt offences

Charge

C[48.1]

Unlawfully did drive or ride in a motor vehicle of a class specified in the Motor Vehicles (Wearing of Seat Belts) Regulations 1993 otherwise than in accordance with the provisions of those Regulations

Road Traffic Act 1988, s 14

Maximum penalty-Fine level 2 (for fines see B[33]). No power to endorse or disqualify.

C[48.2]

Unlawfully did drive a motor vehicle with a child in the front seat not wearing a seat belt

OR

C[48.3]

Unlawfully did drive a motor vehicle with a child in the rear seat not wearing a seat belt

Motor Vehicles (Wearing of Seat Belts by Children in Front Seats) Regulations 1993

Road Traffic Act, s 15

Maximum penalty   —   (Front seat) level 2
                          —   (Rear seat) level 2 for offence (child)

No endorsement or disqualification.

Fixed penalty-£30.

Legal notes and definitions

C[48.4]

Criminal liability. Only the person actually committing the contravention can be prosecuted. There are no provisions for another person to be prosecuted for aiding and abetting etc and causing or permitting.

C[48.5]

Specified passenger's seat is the front seat alongside the driver's seat, or, if there is more than one such seat, the one furthest from the driver's seat. If there is no seat alongside the driver's seat, then the specified passenger's seat is the foremost forward facing seat furthest from the driver's seat, unless there is a fixed partition separating it from the space in front of it and alongside the driver's seat as, for example, in a London type taxi cab.

C[48.6]

Class of vehicle. Every motor car registered on or after 1 January 1965, every three-wheeled vehicle not weighing more than 225 kg manufactured on or after 1 March 1970 and first used on or after 1 September 1970 and heavy motor cars first used on or after 1 October 1988, eg goods vehicles and minibuses.

C[48.7]

Seat belt. The seat belt must comply with the requirements of the relevant regulations, about which the legal adviser will clarify.

C[48.8]

Exemptions. Every driver and every person occupying the specified passenger's seat, as defined above, must wear a seat belt when in the vehicle, even when the vehicle is stationary, except a person who is:

(a) using a vehicle constructed or adapted for the delivery or collection of goods or mail to consumers or addressees, as the case may be, whilst engaged in making local rounds of deliveries or collections;

(b) driving the vehicle while performing a manoeuvre which includes reversing;

(c) a qualified driver, and is supervising a provisional licence holder while that person is performing a manoeuvre which includes reversing;

(d) the holder of a valid certificate in a form supplied by the Secretary of State, containing the information required by it, and signed by a registered medical practitioner to the effect that it is inadvisable on medical grounds for him to wear a seat belt;

(e) a constable protecting or escorting another person;

(f) not a constable, but is protecting or escorting another person by virtue of powers the same as or similar to those of a constable for that person;

(g) in the service of a fire brigade and is donning operational clothing or equipment;

(h) the driver of:

(i) a taxi which is being used for seeking hire, or answering a call for hire, or carrying a passenger for hire; or

(ii) a private hire vehicle which is being so used to carry a passenger for hire;

(i) a person by whom a test of competence to drive is being conducted and his wearing a seat belt would endanger himself or any other person;

(j) occupying a seat for which the seat belt either:

(i) does not comply with the relevant standards; or

(ii) has an inertia reel mechanism which is locked as a result of the vehicle being, or having been, on a steep incline;

(k)   riding in a vehicle being used under a trade licence, for the purpose of investigating or remedying a mechanical fault in the vehicle.

C[48.9]

Children under 14 years. The above regulations do not apply but it is an offence under the Road Traffic Act 1988, s 15(2) punishable with a maximum fine on level 2 for a person without reasonable excuse to drive on a road with a child under 14 years in the front of a motor vehicle who is not wearing a seat belt.

C[48.10]–[48.15]

The seat belt must conform to the Motor Vehicles (Wearing of Seat Belts by Children in Front Seats) Regulations 1993 which provide for the use of special child restraining devices, or, according to age, adult seat belts for use in the front passenger seat.

C[48.16]

Exemptions similar to those at (d) and (j) apply. Generally it is now unlawful to drive a vehicle with a small child in the front unless he is wearing a suitable restraint.

C[48.17]

Rear seat belts. It is also compulsory for both adults and children in the rear seats of a vehicle fitted with seat belts to wear them. If a child (ie a person under 14 years) on the rear seat is not wearing a seat belt (with a booster cushion where necessary, or a child restraint), the driver of the vehicle will incur liability (maximum penalty a fine on level 1) [level 2 for offences committed on or after 24/9/07]. In the case of a passenger aged 14 years or more, only he will be liable (maximum penalty a fine on level 2), there are no provisions for the driver to be guilty of aiding and abetting the offence. There is no liability where all available seat belts are in use.

C[48.18]

The following table summarises the main legal requirements for wearing seat belts.

	Front seat	Rear seat	Whose responsibility
Driver	Must be worn if fitted	—	Driver
child under 3 years of age	Appropriate child restraint must be worn	Appropriate child restraint must be worn	Driver
child aged 3–11 and under 1.5 metres (about 5 feet) in height	Appropriate child restraint must be worn if available. If not an adult seat belt must be worn	Appropriate child restraint must be worn if available. If not an adult seat belt must be worn	Driver

	Front seat	Rear seat	Whose responsibility
child aged 12 or 13 or younger 1.5 metres or more in height	Adult seat belt must be worn if available	Adult seat belt must be worn if available	Driver
adult passengers	must be worn if available	must be worn if available	Passenger

Sentencing
SC Guideline – Seat belt offences

C[48.19]

Starting point – Band A fine.

C[49]

Speeding

Charge

C[49.1]

Driving a motor vehicle on a road at a speed exceeding a statutory limit

Road Traffic Regulation Act 1984, ss 81 (84 or 86) and 89

Maximum penalty-Fine level 3 (for fines see B[33]). May disqualify for any period and/or until a driving test has been passed. Must endorse unless there are special reasons.

Note-Speeding on a motorway may be charged under the Road Traffic Regulation Act 1984, s 17 in which case the maximum penalty is a fine on level 4.

Penalty points – 3–6. [from a date to be appointed 2–6 under the **Road Safety Act 2006**] (Fixed penalty – 3.)

Fixed penalty-£60

Legal notes and definitions

C[49.2]

Speeding can be considered under five main headings:

(A)   Speeding on restricted roads (Road Traffic Regulation Act 1984, s 81).
(B)   Speeding on motorways (s 17).
(C)   Breaking the speed limit imposed by the Secretary of State for the Environment or highway authorities on roads other than restricted roads (s 84).
(D)   Driving a vehicle at a speed in excess of that permitted for that class of vehicle (s 86).
(E)   Breaking a temporary or experimental speed limit imposed by the Secretary of State for the Environment on certain specified roads (s 88). These classes of speeding are dealt with in the above order on the following pages.

C[49.3]

Warning of prosecution must have been given to the defendant except in circumstances prescribed in the Road Traffic Offenders Act 1988, s 2, as amended (eg following an 'accident'). Section 2 required only that there was a sufficiently causal link between the relevant offence and the offender, so that the driver need not be warned of the risk of prosecution (*R v Myers* [2007] All ER [D] 241 (Feb)). The word 'accident' in s 2 had to be given a common sense meaning and was not restricted to untoward or unintended consequences having an adverse physical effect (*R v Currie* [2007] EWCA Crim 926).

C[49.4]

Evidence. The Road Traffic Offenders Act 1988, s 20 (as substituted by the Road Traffic Act 1991) provides that it will be sufficient for evidence of an offence of speeding or contravening a red traffic light to be obtained by approved devices, such as a Gatso camera, which also records speeds and times as appropriate. The record must be signed by the police and the defendant given seven days notice of its intended use. The accused may require the attendance of the person who signed the document not less than three days before the trial.

In *DPP v Thornley* [2006] EWHC 312 (Admin), [2006] 09 LS Gaz R 32, it was held that s 20(8) of the RTOA 1988 was permissive in its terms and therefore the prosecution were entitled to admit the record of speeding as a species of "real evidence". *DPP v Thornley* has since been applied and followed in *Griffiths v DPP* [2007] EWHC 619 (Admin).

A police officer was entitled to corroborate his opinion that a motorist had travelled at an excessive speed by reference to the speed reading given by a speed measuring device that was a prescribed device but which was not of an approved type. Section 20 of the Road Traffic Offenders Act 1988 was a self-contained code which did not apply to a prosecution brought under s 89 of the Road Traffic Regulation Act 1984: *Connell v DPP* [2011] EWHC 158 (Admin), 175 JP 151.

See 'Conditional offer of fixed penalty' at C[8.21]–C[8.22].

C[49.5]

If the evidence merely consists of one witness's opinion that the defendant was exceeding the speed limit there cannot be a conviction. If the single witness is supported by a speedometer, stop watch, radar meter or Vascar, then there can be a conviction.

C[49.6]

The evidence of two witnesses estimating the speed at the same time can result in a conviction, but if their estimates refer to speeds at different parts of the road then that will not suffice.

C[49.7]

If a vehicle was being used for the purpose of the fire brigade, the police, or the ambulance services, and the driver can establish that observing the speed limit would have hindered him in the execution of his official duties, then that could be accepted as a successful line of defence by the court. It is for the court to decide this issue as there is no inherent right for all such vehicles to exceed the speed limit, for instance an empty ambulance merely returning to its garage or a fire engine out on routine test carry no exemption from a speed limit. A police officer using a vehicle to 'hone' his skills may be guilty of speeding (see **C[16]** and *DPP v Milton* [2006] EWHC 242 (Admin), (2006) 170 JP 319).

C[49.8]

The defendant merely has to prove that this defence is probably true; he need not prove it beyond reasonable doubt.

C[49.9]

Although the driver must be identified, the fact that he was driving when stopped is prima facie evidence that he drove over the whole distance for which he was timed.

C[49.10]–[49.15]

Speed limit signs. The ordinary meaning of the words in s 85(4) of the Road Traffic Regulation Act 1984 meant that two tests had to be satisfied before the defendant could be convicted. The first was that at the time the offence was being committed there were such signs as were mentioned in s 85(1) or (2). The second was that those signs indicated the relevant speed limit. Accordingly, no offence was committed where speed signs were obscured by hedgerows (*Coombe v DPP* [2006] EWHC 3263 (Admin), [2007] RTR 383); further, in *DPP v Butler* (unreported) 4/3/10, DC, it was held that a magistrates' court was entitled to find that a terminal speed limit located within 50 metres of a street lamp did not comply with the Traffic Signs Directions and Regulations 2002, Sch 17, item 10, as it was not illuminated in darkness. Accordingly, on the facts found no offence of speeding was made out. However, see *Peake v DPP* immediately below.

In *Peake v DPP* [2010] EWHC 286 (Admin) the High Court adopted a **purposive approach** and rejected the argument that the enforcement of a speed limit was dependent upon every sign within a 40 mph area having to be compliant with the Traffic Signs Directions and Regulations 2002. On the facts found the argument was rejected because there were no deficiencies in the road along which the defendant had driven or they were de minimis (minor).

If the defendant submits that the speed sign was unlawful because of its size, composition, character or colour, etc, the legal adviser should be consulted.

On a natural reading of the relevant primary and secondary legislation and adopting a purposive approach to interpretation to the relevant provisions, if at the point of enforcement there are signs complying with the directions of the Secretary of State which in fact provide adequate guidance of the speed limit at that point, this satisfies the requirements of s 85(4) of the Road Traffic Regulation Act 1984. If the prosecution can establish the route taken by the defendant, it will only have to show that compliant signs provide adequate guidance at the point of enforcement for a motorist taking that route. If the prosecution cannot establish the route, they would have to show compliant signs on all routes the driver may have taken (*Coombes v DPP* and *Peake v DPP* considered): *Jones v DPP* [2011] EWHC 50 (Admin), 175 JP 129.

Category A – speeding on restricted roads (Road Traffic Regulation Act 1984, s 81)
Legal notes and definitions

C[49.16]

Restricted road. A road becomes a restricted road in one of two ways:

(a)   it has a system of street lamps placed not more than two hundred yards apart, in which case the speed limit is 30 miles per hour; or

(b)   it is directed by the relevant authority that it becomes a restricted road, in which case the speed limit is again 30 miles per hour.

A road restricted by (a) above need not display 'repeater' signs but a road in category (b) does have to display the repeater '30' signs.

C[49.17]

The relevant authority may direct that an (a) category road may be derestricted. 'Restricted road' is a term of art referring to a road having a 30 mile per hour limit because of the above provisions. Confusingly, restricted road is commonly, but erroneously, used to refer to any road having a speed limit less than the overall maxima of 70 miles per hour for motorways and dual carriageways and 60 miles per hour for single carriageways.

C[49.18]

The limit on a restricted road of 30 mph can be altered by the Secretary of State for the Environment and the Home Secretary acting jointly.

C[49.19]

A vehicle which is limited to a lower speed than the limit for the road must always conform to its own scheduled speed limit, for example, a lorry drawing more than one trailer is limited to 20 mph and must keep to that limit even on a restricted road where a 30 mph limit is in force.

Category B – speeding on motorways (Road Traffic Regulation Act 1984, s 17)

C[49.20]

Motorway. The legal adviser can provide a detailed definition if it should be necessary. The motorway includes the hard shoulder and access and exit roads.

C[49.21]

The general speed limit on a motorway is 70 miles per hour although there are lower speed limits on certain stretches of motorway.

C[49.22]

Contraventions of certain temporary restrictions on motorways (eg for roadworks) are offences under s 16 and also carry an endorsement.

Category C – driving a motor vehicle at a speed in excess of a limit imposed on a road, other than a restricted road, by the highway authority (Road Traffic Regulation Act 1984, s 84)
Legal notes and definitions

C[49.23]

For the purposes of this offence the appropriate highway authority for trunk roads is the Secretary of State for the Environment. For non-trunk roads the appropriate authority is either the Secretary of State for the Environment or the local authority (for instance a county council or, in London, the relevant London borough) but the local authority has to have his consent.

C[49.24]

These speed limits can be ordered to be in general use or merely during specified periods.

C[49.25]–[49.30]

This is the provision which enables a 40 or 50 (or whatever) miles per hour limit to be imposed on a specified road. If the road would otherwise be a 'restricted' (ie having a limit of 30 miles per hour) road, eg because of having lamp posts not more than 200 yards apart, it ceases to be a 'restricted' road when an order is made imposing a limit under this provision.

Category D – driving a motor vehicle at a speed exceeding the limit prescribed for that class of vehicle (Road Traffic Regulation Act 1984, s 86)
Legal notes and definitions

C[49.31]

Permitted speed limits for restricted classes of vehicles include:

	Motor-way	Dual car-riageway	Other road
Coach or motor caravan having an unladen weight exceeding 3.05 tonnes or adapted to carry more than 8 passengers			
(a) if not exceeding 12 metres in overall length	70	60	50
(b) if exceeding 12 metres in overall length	60	60	50
Car, motor caravan, car-derived van drawing one trailer, eg a caravan	60	60	50

	Motor-way	Dual car-riageway	Other road
Goods vehicle maximum laden weight not exceeding 7.5 tonnes (except car-derived van and articulated vehicles)	70	60	50
Goods vehicle maximum laden weight exceeding 7.5 tonnes	60	50	40
Articulated goods vehicles			
(a) maximum laden weight not exceeding 7.5 tonnes	60	50	50
(b) maximum laden weight exceeding 7.5 tonnes	60	50	40

Category E – where temporary or experimental speed limits have been imposed by the Ministry of Transport (Road Traffic Regulation Act 1984, s 88)
Legal notes and definitions

C[49.32]

The Secretary of State for the Environment may, for a period of up to 18 months, impose a speed limit on all roads or on certain specified roads in the interests of safety or traffic flow. The limit may be general or apply only at specified times.

C[49.33]

Unless such an order directs otherwise, it will not interfere with existing speed limits on restricted roads or roads which are already the subject of an order. It is an order under this provision which has imposed a general speed limit of 70 miles per hour on dual carriageways and 60 miles per hour on single carriageways. Originally of a temporary nature, the order has now been made indefinite.

C[49.34]

A speed limit may be imposed on a stretch of road for a temporary period to prevent danger from works on or near the highway.

C[49.35]

These provisions do not apply to motorways.

Sentencing
SC Guideline – Speeding

C[49.36]

Must endorse or may disqualify. If no disqualification, impose 3–6 points.

OFFENCE SERIOUSNESS (CULPABILITY AND HARM)

A. IDENTIFY THE APPROPRIATE STARTING POINT

Starting points based on first time offender pleading not guilty

Speed limit (mph)	Recorded speed limit	Recorded speed limit	Recorded speed limit
20 mph	21–30	31–40	41–50
30 mph	31–40	41–50	51–60
40 mph	41–55	56–65	66–75
50 mph	51–65	66–75	76–85
60 mph	61–80	81–90	91–100
70 mph	71–90	91–100	100–110
Starting point	Band A fine	Band B fine	Band B fine
Range	Band A fine	Band B fine	Band B fine
Points/disqualification	3 points	4–6 points OR Disqualify 7–28 days	Disqualify 7–56 days OR 6 points

OFFENCE SERIOUSNESS (CULPABILITY AND HARM)

B. CONSIDER THE EFFECT OF AGGRAVATING AND MITIGATING FACTORS (OTHER THAN THOSE WITHIN EXAMPLES ABOVE)

Common aggravating and mitigating factors are identified at B[5.2A]. The following may be particularly relevant but **these lists are not exhaustive**

Factors indicating higher culpability	*Factor indicating lower culpability*
1. Poor road or weather conditions	1. Genuine emergency established
2. LGV, HGV, PSV etc	
3. Towing caravan/trailer	
4. Carrying passengers or heavy load	
5. Driving for hire or reward	
6. Evidence of unacceptable standard of driving over and above speed	
Factors indicating greater degree of harm	
1. Location eg near school	
2. High level of traffic or pedestrians in vicinity	

FORM A PRELIMINARY VIEW OF THE APPROPRIATE SENTENCE, THEN CONSIDER OFFENDER MITIGATION

Common factors are identified at B[5.2A]

CONSIDER A REDUCTION FOR A GUILTY PLEA

CONSIDER ANCILLARY ORDERS

Refer to **B[18]** for guidance on compensation and **Part B** for available ancillary orders
DECIDE SENTENCE **GIVE REASONS**

C[49.37]

If it appears to the court that the accused suffers from some disease or physical disability likely to cause his driving to be a source of danger to the public, then the court shall notify the licensing authority who may take steps to withdraw the driving licence (see **C[5.49]**).

C[50]

Steering defective

Charge

C[50.1]

Using, causing or permitting to be used on a road a motor vehicle with defective steering

Road Vehicles (Construction and Use) Regulations 1986, reg 29; Road Traffic Act 1988, s 41A(b)

Maximum penalty – For a goods vehicle, fine on level 5, otherwise level 4 (for fines see **B[33]**).

Penalty points – 3.

Fixed penalty – £60 (3PP).

Legal notes and definitions

C[50.2]

All the details as to maximum penalty, legal notes, exemption from endorsement and disqualification, and definitions and sentencing set out at C[9] for defective brakes apply to this charge of defective steering.

C[50.3]

As with brakes, the law demands that the steering fitted to a motor vehicle on a road shall at all times be maintained in good and efficient working order and properly adjusted.

Sentencing
SGC Guideline – Steering defective

C[50.4]

Starting point – either mechanically propelled vehicle or HGV, LGV or PSV – Band B fine (driver); Band B fine (owner-driver but consider an uplift of at least 25% on the driver's fine); Band C fine (owner-company)

C[51]

No test certificate

Charge

C[51.1]

Using, causing or permitting a motor vehicle to be on the road first registered 3 or more years previously without having a test certificate in force

Road Traffic Act 1988, s 47(1)

Maximum penalty-Fine level 3. Vehicles adapted to carry more than eight passengers, level 4 (for fines see **B[33]**). No power to endorse or disqualify.

Fixed penalty-£60

Legal notes and definitions

C[51.2]

Passenger vehicles carrying more than eight passengers. These vehicles and some taxis and ambulances must be tested after one year.

C[51.3]

Motor vehicle. See C[9.7].

C[51.4]

Road. Means any highway (including footpaths and bridleways) and any other road to which the public has access and includes bridges.

C[51.5]

Using. This does not in law only mean driving a vehicle along a road; its mere presence on a road, even in a useless condition may constitute using (*Pumbien v Vines* [1996] RTR 37, [1996] Crim LR 124). The test is whether steps had been taken to make it impossible for a driver to drive the vehicle. Where doubt exists consult the legal adviser. A person, limited company, a corporate body which owns a vehicle that is driven in the course of the owner's business is using the vehicle. See C[9.4].

C[51.6]

Causing. This implies some express or positive mandate from the person causing the vehicle to be used; or some authority from him and knowledge of the facts which constitute the offence.

C[51.7]

Permitting. This includes express permission and also circumstances in which permission may be inferred.

C[51.8]

If the defendant is a limited company, it must be proved that some person for whose criminal act the company is responsible permitted the offence. A defendant charged with permitting must be shown to have known the vehicle was being used or that he shut his eyes to something that would have made the use obvious to him.

C[51.9]

Examples of exempted vehicles include:

Goods vehicles the design gross weight of which exceeds 3,500 kg.

Motor tractors.

Articulated vehicles, and their several parts.

Works trucks.

Pedestrian-controlled vehicles.

Invalid vehicles.

Some taxis.

Certain vehicles from abroad and Northern Ireland only here temporarily.

Vehicles en route for export.

Agricultural motor vehicles.

C[51.10]–[51.15]

Examples of exempted uses include:

(a)   that by a previous arrangement the vehicle was being used for the purpose of taking it for a test or for bringing it back from a test (*Williams v Richards* (1997) Times, 29 July);

(b)   that the examiner or a person under his personal direction was using the vehicle in the course of or in connection with a test;

(c)   that following an unsuccessful test the vehicle was being used by being towed to a place where it could be broken up; or

(d)   that by a previous arrangement the vehicle was being taken to or from a place where it was to be or had been taken to remedy defects on the ground of which a test certificate had been refused.

C[51.16]

The defendant need not prove either kind of exemption (ie exempted vehicle or exempted use) beyond reasonable doubt; he need only prove this defence is probably true.

C[51.17]

Renewal of certificate. A certificate lasts for one year. Within one month from the expiry of the certificate, the vehicle may be retested and a further certificate issued to commence on the expiry of the existing certificate.

Sentencing
SC Guideline – (1) No test certificate (2) No goods vehicle test certificate

C[51.18]

Starting point – mechanically propelled vehicle – Band A fine (driver); Band A fine (owner-driver but consider an uplift of at least 25% on the driver's fine); Band B fine (owner-company).

Starting point – goods vehicle – Band B fine (driver); Band B fine (owner-driver but consider an uplift of at least 25% on the driver's fine); Band C fine (owner-company).

C[52]

Traffic signs

Charge

C[52.1]

Failing to comply with the indication given by a traffic sign

Road Traffic Act 1988, s 36

Maximum penalty-Fine level 3 (for fines see **B[33]**). Endorsement and disqualification can only be ordered if the vehicle was a motor vehicle and the traffic sign was one of the following: **Stop, Traffic Lights** (including portable traffic lights and green filter arrows), **No Entry Sign** or **Double White Lines.** For these signs disqualification can be for any period or until the accused has passed a driving test. Must endorse for these signs unless there are special reasons.

Endorsement and disqualification also apply to drivers of 'abnormal loads' at railway level crossings who fail to phone the signalman before crossing and to drivers of vehicles which contravene relevant height restrictions.

Penalty points – 3 (only for endorsable offences).

Fixed penalty-£60 (endorsable offences); £30 (otherwise).

Legal notes and definitions

C[52.2]

It is not a defence that the sign was not seen.

C[52.3]

The defendant can only be convicted if at the time of the offence he was warned of possible prosecution, or a summons or a notice of intended prosecution was served within 14 days upon the registered owner of the vehicle. It will be presumed that this requirement was complied with unless the contrary is proved by the defendant on the balance of probabilities.

C[52.4]

The offence applies to all vehicles including pedal cycles and is not limited to mechanically propelled vehicles.

C[52.5]

Even wheeling a pedal cycle in contravention of the sign is an offence.

C[52.6]

A traffic sign. This is presumed to be of correct size, colour and type unless proved to the contrary by the defence.

C[52.7]

Automatic traffic lights are presumed to be in proper working order unless the contrary is proved by the defence.

C[52.8]

Traffic lights. It is an offence if any part of the vehicle crosses the 'stop' line when the light is red, for example, if the front part of the vehicle is already over the line and the light turns red an offence is committed if the rear part of the vehicle then crosses the line with the light still at red.

C[52.9]

Double white lines. It is an offence to overtake or park in contravention of double white lines in the middle of the road. There are certain exceptions, however, such as passing a slow moving road sweeper or a taxi stopping to allow a passenger to alight or board. Ask the legal adviser for details.

C[52.10]–[52.15]

A road. Means any highway (including footpaths and bridleways) and any other road to which the public has access and includes bridges.

C[52.16]

Signs to which the offence applies. These include:

Emergency traffic signs placed by a constable on the instructions of a chief officer of police.

[1] Stop at major road ahead.

Give way at major road ahead.

Stop one way working.

[1] No entry.

Arrow indicating direction to be followed.

Arrow indicating keep left or right.

[1] Red light including portable light signals and at automatic level crossings.

[1] Double white lines.

Keep left dual carriageway.

Turn left at dual carriageway.

[1] Drivers of 'abnormal loads' at railway level crossings.

[1] Prohibition on vehicles exceeding specified height.

[1] Green arrow traffic signals.

No 'U' turn.

Mini roundabout sign.

---

[1]   Only these offences qualify for endorsement and disqualification. See reg 10 of the Traffic Signs Regulations and General Directions 2002.

Sentencing
SC Guideline – Failing to comply with traffic sign

C[52.17]

Starting point – Band A fine (Endorsement and disqualification can only be ordered if the vehicle was a motor vehicle and the traffic sign was one of those mentioned under 'Maximum penalty').

C[52.18]

If it appears to the court that the accused suffers from some disease or physical disability likely to cause his driving to be a source of danger to the public, then the court shall notify the licensing authority who may take steps to withdraw the driving licence (see **C[5.49]**).

C[53]

Tyres defective

Charge

C[53.1]

Using, causing or permitting to be used on a road a motor vehicle or trailer with defective tyres

Road Vehicles (Construction and Use) Regulations 1986, reg 27; Road Traffic Act 1988, s 41A(b)

Maximum penalty – For a goods vehicle, fine level 5, otherwise level 4 (for fines see B[33]). May disqualify for any period and/or until a driving test has been passed. Must endorse unless special reasons exist.

For 'special reasons', see C[5.2].

Penalty points – 3.

Fixed penalty – £60 (3PP).

Legal notes and definitions

C[53.2]

All the details as to legal notes, exemption from endorsement and disqualification, definitions and sentencing set out on at C[9] for defective brakes also apply to these charges.

C[53.3]

It is an offence for a tyre on a car or light van (gross weight not exceeding 3,500 kg) and their trailers to be in any of the following conditions:

(a) tyre being unsuitable having regard to the use to which the vehicle is put;
(b) tyre being unsuitable having regard to types of tyres on other wheels;
(c) tyre not so inflated as to make it fit for use to which vehicle is being put;
(d) break in fabric of tyre;
(e) ply or cord structure exposed;
(f) the grooves of the tread pattern of the tyre do not have a depth of at least 1 millimetre throughout a continuous band comprising the central three-quarters of the breadth of the tread and round the entire outer circumference of the tyre;
(g) tyre must be free from any defect which might damage the road surface or cause danger to persons in the vehicle or on the road.

Consult the legal adviser for the complete list.

C[53.4]

The law requires all tyres of a motor vehicle or trailer on a road to be free from any defect which might in any way cause damage to the road surface or cause danger to persons in or on a vehicle or to other persons using the road.

C[53.5]

If no tyre is fitted at all the offence will be brought under a different regulation.

C[53.6]

Two or more defective tyres. If a vehicle has two or more defective tyres, a separate charge should be alleged for each.

Sentencing
SC Guideline – Tyres defective

C[53.7]

Starting point – mechanically propelled vehicle – Band A fine (driver); Band A fine (owner-driver but consider an uplift of at least 25% on the driver's fine); Band B fine (owner-company).

Starting point – goods vehicle – Band B fine (driver); Band B fine (owner-driver but consider an uplift of at least 25% on the driver's fine); Band C fine (owner-company).

C[53.8]

As for 'brakes' see C[9.16]. A vehicle with two defective tyres is much more dangerous than a vehicle with only one defective tyre. Where the means of the offender permit the penalty should usually ensure that it is cheaper to keep the vehicle in good condition than to risk a fine. A short disqualification can also be considered.

Family proceedings

Index to family proceedings

Adoption D[18]
Application to the court D[18.7]
Applications for an adoption order D[18.3]
Placement orders D[18.3]
General matters D[18.39]
Hearing D[18.24]
Special Guardianship Orders D[18.33]
Preliminary proceedings D[18.19]

Allocation and case management continuity D[1.20]
President's Guidance D[1.20]

Public law proceedings D[6]
Appeals D[6.49] and D[1.19]
Applications D[6.3]
Children's evidence D[2.6]
Directions appointments D[6.2]
Discharge and variation D[6.47]
Exclusion requirement D[6.38]
Interim orders D[6.35]
Orders of the court D[6.23]
Public Law Outline D[6.2A]–D[6.2B]

Capacity to conduct family proceedings D[19.1]–D[19.6]

Child abduction D[16]

Domestic violence D[8]
Non molestation orders D[8.1]
Occupation orders D[8.23]
Undertakings D[8.21]

Family proceedings D[1]
Appeals D[1.19]
Children's evidence D[2.6]
Evidence D[1.17]
Family proceedings court D[1.4]
Family proceedings panel D[1.5]
Privacy D[1.7]
Reasons for decision D[1.18]
Split hearings D[4.4], D[6.4B]

Financial provision D[7]
Agreed orders D[7.9]
Applications under DPMCA 1978, s 2 D[7.1]
Enforcement of an order D[7.19]
Variation of maintenance orders D[7.17]

Non-specified proceedings – making the child a party D[20.1]

Orders with respect to the upbringing of children D[4], D[5]
Family assistance orders D[5.19]
Section 8 orders D[4.3], D[5.1]–D[5.17]
Enforcement of contact orders D[5.17]
Private Law Programme D[4.1]
Welfare reports D[4.2]

Parental responsibility D[3]
Acquisition of parental responsibility by father D[3.8]
Appointment of guardian D[3.24]
Persons having parental responsibility for a child D[3.3]

Private Law Programme D[4.1]

Protection of children D[9]
Child assessment order D[9.4]
Duties of local authority D[9.2]
Emergency protection order D[9.16]
Exclusion requirement D[9.23]
Police powers D[9.1]

Recovery order D[10]

School attendance and truancy D[17]
Education supervision orders D[17.6]

Special Guardianship Orders D[18.33]

Split hearings D[4.4], D[6.4B]

Welfare of the child D[2]
Delay D[2.3]
Welfare checklist D[2.4]
Welfare principle D[2.1]

D[1]

Family proceedings

D[1.1]

Magistrates' courts have an extensive jurisdiction in family proceedings which for this purpose are defined to include proceedings under the Children Act 1989, applications for maintenance of a spouse under the Domestic Proceedings and Magistrates' Courts Act 1978, applications for consent to marry (Marriage Act 1949, s 3), adoption (Magistrates' Courts Act 1980, s 65) and domestic violence applications (Family Law Act 1996).

D[1.2]

The Children Act 1989 has created a largely concurrent jurisdiction between the three courts which deal with the welfare of children – the High Court, county court and magistrates' court – and as far as practicable the procedures in the three courts have been assimilated. All these courts also have jurisdiction in adoption proceedings and this coming together of the separate jurisdictions will lay the foundations for one unified family court.

D[1.3]

In using the term 'family proceedings' it should be noted that the term is also used in a different and more restricted sense when referring to the power of the courts to make orders in family proceedings under the Children Act, see D[4].

The family proceedings court

D[1.4]

Jurisdiction in the magistrates' court resides in the 'Family Proceedings Court'. Parties to a private dispute (ie one not involving a local authority) used to be able, subject to practical and financial limitations, to choose whether the High Court, county court or magistrates' court should hear their case. Jurisdiction to hear such cases in now governed by rules of court (see the Allocation and Transfer of Proceedings Order 2008 (SI

2008/2836). Some cases must now be commenced in a magistrates' court, while others must be commenced in the county court. The rules were supplemented by a *Practice Direction: Allocation and Transfer of Proceedings* issued by the President of the Family Division, dated 3 November 2008.

All public law proceedings (which include most matters formerly heard in wardship) will commence in the family proceedings court. In the case of public law proceedings the justices' clerk will allocate such cases to the more appropriate court, eg lengthy or complex matters to the county court where they will be heard there or transferred on to the High Court.

Family proceedings panel

D[1.5]

By rules of court made under s 49 of the Courts Act 2003 authorisation of magistrates to sit in family proceedings courts now rests with the Lord Chief Justice. Through the rules he has delegated the function to Bench Training and Development Committees (BTDC). From 13 July 2007, authorisation for winger and chairmanship selection functions is undertaken by BTDCs although it is open to a BTDC and a family panel to jointly apply to the Lord Chief Justice to form a Family Training and Development Committee that would carry out these functions (see the Justices of the Peace (Training and Development Committee) Rules 2007 (SI 2007/1609) and the Family Proceedings (Constitution of Committees and Right to Preside) Rules 2007 (SI 2007/1610 (L8)). Copies of these rules can be viewed and downloaded from www.opsi.gov.uk.

D[1.6]

Each court, except in unforeseen circumstances, will be presided over by a panel member specially trained as a chairman and must so far as is practicable comprise both a man and woman.

Privacy

D[1.7]

The courtroom. So far as is consistent with the due dispatch of business, family proceedings should be heard separately from the hearing of other business (MCA 1980, s 69).

D[1.8]

Persons present during the hearing. Only the following are allowed to be present:

(a)   officers of the court;

(b)   parties to the case before the court, their solicitors and counsel, and witnesses and other persons directly concerned with that case;

(c)   representatives of newspapers or news agencies (see *Practice Direction (Attendance of Media Representatives at Hearings in Family Proceedings)* issued by the President of the Family Division dated 20 April 2009);

(d) persons permitted by the court to be present, but permission shall not be withheld from a person who appears to the court to have adequate grounds for attendance (MCA 1980, s 69)

(e) McKenzie Friends: a litigant who is not legally represented has the right to have reasonable assistance from a layperson, sometimes called a *McKenzie Friend* (MF). This is the case even where the proceedings relate to a child and are being held in private. See the President of the Family Division's revised Guidance on McKenzie Friends handed down on 12 July 2010: *Practice Note (McKenzie Friends: Civil and Family Courts)* [2010] 1 WLR 1881. A judge was entitled to reject F's application for Y to act as a McKenzie Friend on the basis that Y was intimidating towards the respondent mother: *Re H (Children)* [2012] All ER (D) 124 (Jun), CA.

D[1.9]

More stringent requirements apply to adoption proceedings, when persons included in paragraphs (a) and (b) only may be in court.

D[1.10]–[1.15]

Restrictions on reporting. The press may not report particulars of the proceedings other than:

(a) the names, addresses and occupations of the parties and witnesses;
(b) the grounds of the application and a concise statement of the charges, defences and counter-charges in support of which evidence has been given;
(c) submissions on points of law and the court's decision on them;
(d) the decision of the court and any observations of the court on making it (Magistrates' Courts Act 1980, s 71(1)).

In *Clayton v Clayton* [2006] EWCA Civ 878, the President of the Family Division, Sir Mark Potter, explicitly stated that from henceforth it will be appropriate for every tribunal, when making what it believes to be a final order in proceedings under the Children Act 1989, to consider whether or not there is an outstanding issue which needs to be addressed by a continuing order for anonymity. See an informative article by Robert Stevens at [2007] 171 JPN 372.

For more information about media access to family court cases, or family proceedings in general, see: www.hmcourts-service.gov.uk, www.direct.gov. uk. For statutory reporting restrictions see www.dca.gov.uk/consult/courttra nsparencey1106/consultation1106.pdf.

D[1.16]

In adoption proceedings the press may also not report matters at (a) and (b) and must not identify the child in any way (MCA 1980, s 71).

Evidence

D[1.17]

In any family proceedings in a magistrates' court, hearsay evidence given in connection with the upbringing, maintenance or welfare of a child is admissible.

Reasons for decision

D[1.18]

See *Practice Direction (Appeal) (Allocation to Judiciary)* [2009] All ER (D) 128 (Apr) set out at paragraph (h) below.

The reasons for any decision of the family proceedings court must be announced and recorded at the time the decision is made and a copy of that record will be available on demand from the legal adviser to any person who is considering an appeal. The reasons must be drawn up in consultation with the legal adviser but they will be the justices' reasons (or the reasons of a majority of them) and not those of the legal adviser. It is advised that the justices retire with the legal adviser and after making their decision they formulate their reasons and ask the legal adviser to write them down before returning to court to announce the decisions. The availability of technology allows legal advisers to record the reasons on a PC rather than writing them in conventional form.

(a)   Guidance to the courts on the giving of reasons is contained in *Re B (Procedure in Family Proceedings Courts)* [1992] 2 FCR 631, [1993] Fam Law 209, CA.

(b)   Reasons may not be amplified later when an appeal is lodged (*Hillingdon London Borough Council v H* [1993] Fam 43, [1993] 1 All ER 198).

(c)   Reasons must be formulated before making an order (*Hertfordshire County Council v W* [1992] 2 FCR 885, [1992] 39 LS Gaz R 33, sub nom W v Hertfordshire County Council [1993] 1 FLR 118, [1993] Fam Law 75).

(d)   Reasons must be given for all decisions including interim orders, granting or refusing leave or on the refusal of an application to adjourn (*T v W* (contact: reasons for refusing leave) [1997] 1 FCR 118, [1996] 2 FLR 473).

(e)   If the recommendations of a guardian ad litem or welfare officer are not followed reasons for that should be given (*S v Oxfordshire County Council* [1993] 2 FCR 676, [1993] 1 FLR 452).

(f)   Magistrates must comply with rule 21(6) by stating their reasons and findings of fact but in doing so orally they are able to summarise their written reasons (*Oxfordshire County Council v S* (2005) FLR 426).

(g)   In a judgment in a specific [care] case, the law should be specifically related to the facts. In relation to the welfare principles, a shorthand form was not acceptable. The guardian had a specific role, to make recommendations, but the justices had to apply the welfare checklist in accordance with the evidence placed before them. It was appropriate for them to set out the factors in the welfare checklist which they considered to be of particular relevance on the facts of the case before them with such specificity as was required (*Re G (Children) (Care Proceedings) (Adequacy of Reasons)* [2007] All ER (D) 210 (May)).

(h)   The President of the Family Division, Sir Mark Potter has made a Practice Direction (*Practice Direction (Appeal) (Allocation to Judiciary)* [2009] All ER (D) 128 (Apr)) relating to appeals which came into force on 6 April 2009. Paragraph 3.1 provides for magistrates' courts to give written reasons for its decisions in all family proceedings listed in s 65(1) of the Magistrates' Courts Act 1980. The purpose of this Practice Direction is to make the same provision for written reasons to be given by magistrates' courts in relation to proceedings which are not listed in s 65(1) but which are family proceedings for the purposes of the Access to Justice Act 1999 (Destination of Appeals) (Family Proceedings) Order 2009 outlined at [1.18] below. Those proceedings are or may be treated as family proceedings under s 65(2) of the 1980 Act; for example, proceedings for enforcement or variation of maintenance orders and proceedings under the Child Support Act 1991 (other than proceedings under s 20 which are referred to in s 65(1)(o) of the 1980 Act).

The Family Proceedings Courts (Matrimonial Proceedings, etc) Rules 1991, rr 11 and 12 and the Family Proceedings (Children Act 1989) Rules 1991, rr 20 and 21 already require the justices' clerk in consultation with the justice or justices to record in writing the reasons for the court's decision and the justices' clerk to keep a written note of the substance of the oral evidence given at a hearing. Proceedings to which these rules apply include proceedings under the Children Act 1989 and the Domestic Proceedings and Magistrates' Courts Act 1978. The requirements for the magistrates' court to give written reasons for its decision and for the justices' clerk to keep a written note of the substance of oral evidence are not to be restricted to those proceedings but are to apply to all proceedings referred to in this paragraph and [1.19] below.

A new r 8.2A(4) inserted into the Family Proceedings (Amendment) Rules 2009 provides for written reasons and notes of evidence to be filed and served as soon as practicable after the filing of the notice of appeal in the county court and service of the notice.

Appeals

D[1.19]

The Access to Justice Act 1999 (Destination of Appeals) (Family Proceedings) Order 2009 (SI 2009/871) came into force on 6 April 2009. The Order changes the route of appeal against a decision of the magistrates' court in family and related proceedings so that the appeal lies to a county court instead of to the High Court.

In addition, as a result of an amendment to s 111 of the Magistrates' Courts Act 1980, an application to have a case stated for the opinion of the High Court may not be made in relation to family proceedings. 'Family proceedings' for these purposes are not restricted to the matters listed as such in s 65(1) of the Magistrates' Courts Act 1980 and are defined as:

(a) proceedings, which by virtue of s 65 of the 1980 Act, are or may be treated as family proceedings for the purposes of that Act; and

(b) proceedings under the Child Support Act 1991 (except for s 20 which is referred to in s 65(1)(o)).

A new s 111A has been inserted into the 1980 Act which provides that in family proceedings (as more widely defined above), a person may appeal to a county court on the ground that a decision is wrong in law or is in excess of the jurisdiction – replacing the procedure for making an application to have a case stated. Section 111A(3)(a) provides that no appeal may be brought under s 111A if there is a right of appeal to a county court against a decision otherwise than under that section.

The two-stage case stated procedure is replaced by one notice of appeal outlining the restricted grounds of appeal to a county court. As there will be no document stating the case for a county court, there is a need to ensure that a county court hearing an appeal from a magistrates' court has sufficient information about the magistrates' courts decision – including reasons (as which see paragraph (h) at **[1.18]** above.

Allocation and case management continuity

President's guidance: Allocation and continuity of case managers in the Family Proceedings Courts

July 2011 (issued by the President of the Family Division following consultation with the Senior Presiding Judge, HMCTS and with the endorsement of the Justices' Clerks Society)

Background

D[1.20]

The background is as follows:

(1) In April 2011 the President issued his Guidance Bulletin Number 3, Listing and Hearing Care Cases. That Guidance emphasised the principles of judicial continuity and efficient case management and, in the Family Proceedings Court (FPC), the importance of the role of the Justices' Clerk/Assistant Justices' Clerk as case manager. The purpose of this Guidance is to set out the expectations on FPCs in relation to the allocation and continuity of case managers and to provide some practical guidance.

(2) Practice Direction 12A 'Public Law Proceedings Guide to Case Management: April 2010 '(PLO) applies to care and supervision proceedings. It also applies, in so far as practicable to all other Public Law Proceedings.

(3) Part 4 Family Procedure Rules 2010 set out the courts' general case management powers

(4)   Paragraph 2 of the PLO sets out the main principles underlying case management and the means of the court furthering the overriding objective. These principles are set out in Part 1 of the Family Procedure Rules 2010.

(5)   A key element of these principles is the requirement under paragraph 3.1(2) of the PLO for judicial continuity. That requires that each case be allocated to one or not more than two . . . in the case of magistrates courts . . . case managers who will be responsible for every case management stage in the proceedings through to the Final Hearing.

(6)   Those stages are First Appointment, Case Management Conference, Issues Resolution Hearing together with any other hearing at which case management directions are being given.

Allocation

(7)   In the Family Proceedings Court the case manager is the Justices Clerk or the Assistant Justices Clerk. Continuity of case manager in the FPC is as essential as continuity of case management judge in the County or High Court.

(8)   In accordance with the PLO, case managers must be nominated to be responsible for the management of the case throughout its hearings in the FPC.

(9)   The requirement to allocate case managers in the FPC applies equally to cases transferred from the County Court.

(10)   The name of the case managers must be clearly noted on the front of the court file together with the target date by which the case should be completed. Where possible, the target date for completion should be determined at the First Appointment and certainly no later than the Case Management Conference. In determining the target date, the court should have regard to the timetable for the child.

(11)   The name of the case managers and the target date by which the case should be completed should appear on the face of any order or case management documents.

(12)   It is a matter for Justices' Clerks to determine how legal advisers are deployed, however, my attention has been drawn to a number of ways in which FPCs have acted to ensure the appropriate allocation of cases. These include—

        (a)   determining the number of legal advisers authorised to make case management decisions in family work so as to ensure regular exposure to public law cases, that supports the principles of and ensures robust case management

        (b)   allocation to case managers who work consistently together as a pair

        (c)   legal advisers dealing with family work on a set day each week and are allocated as case manager(s) from the First Appointment onwards

        (d)   cases are allocated to case managers on a rota basis to ensure an even spread

        (e)   cases are allocated to a legal manager as the primary case manager with a member of the legal team as case manager 2

     (f)   the legal adviser dealing with the First Appointment is the case manager and any legal adviser who deals with a subsequent hearing is the second case manager

(13) All of these systems have resulted in the early allocation and continuity of case manager and are to be commended.

(14) Justices' Clerks should determine the arrangements to be applied locally in order to achieve allocation on issue, and certainly no later than by First Appointment.

(15) This Guidance recognises that Justices' Clerks and those who line manage legal advisers will also have arrangements in place to ensure there is oversight of the allocation of cases to case managers, but more importantly, that cases are being managed in accordance with the practice directions and rules at points 2, 3 and 4 of this Guidance.

Continuity

(16) Listing arrangements should be in place to support continuity of case managers. Discussions must have taken place to ensure that one of the two case managers is available to take the case for the date fixed for the next appointment. In other words, legal advisers must fit their availability around the case, not the other way round. Continuity of representation is also important and lawyers are expected to play their part in ensuring that continuity, and that cases are heard without delay.

(17) In order to help facilitate this, once a date is fixed, court hearing diaries should be noted with the name/initials of the case managers concerned.

(18) Any case management decisions required to be taken between hearings, such as a variance of the timetable or any failure to comply with directions should be dealt with by a case manager. There must therefore be close liaison between the case managers and those members of the administration having case progression responsibilities.

(19) It is acknowledged that in some circumstances it may be appropriate for the reallocation of a case manager. It expected that this will be the exception rather than the norm. Circumstances where it might be appropriate are where—

     (a)   it is necessary to achieve ongoing continuity eg absence of a case manager

     (b)   a legal adviser other than one of the case managers has been present at an interim contested hearing

     (c)   The circumstances of a case are such that there is a need for increased attention to case management. In such cases the Justices' Clerk or the nominated legal manager, should determine whether they should be one of the designated case managers. Increased attention to case management may be appropriate where

         (i)   any case where it appears that the timetable for the child or completion is at risk

(ii)   where the local authority care plan is unclear (the court may have had difficulty in identifying a timetable for completion)

(iii)   where there is an application in writing to adjourn the IRH or final hearing

(iv)   where a final hearing is adjourned

(v)   in any case where one of the two case managers has concerns about the substantial non-compliance of any party with directions

(d)   Where a District Judge (MC) has assumed one of the case manager roles.

Case management

(20)   Case managers should ensure that cases are actively case managed and that the principles of the PLO and Family Procedure Rules are applied.

(21)   The President is aware of and commends various case management tools which have assisted case managers in FPCs. These include:

     (a)   The use of recitals in orders and directions setting out the stage that the case has reached, including reference to whether the threshold is conceded, matters agreed , and the expectations about how the case is to progress

     (b)   Electronic case histories, updated by and accessed by the case managers(s)/case progression officers

     (c)   For case management hearings, which includes the IRH, filing of bundles by local authorities as agreed locally, parties position statements (which are not evidential statements nor the Guardians analysis), case summaries and a schedule of issues

(22)   Where there has been a failure to comply with case management directions, case managers should consider full use of Part 4 of the Family Procedure Rules 2010, in particular, the ability to make orders of their own motion without requiring attendance at court giving the parties the opportunity to make representations.

(23)   In some cases, however the current practise of listing a non compliance hearing, may continue to be appropriate. Where judicial continuity is maintained through a bench of magistrates or by a District Judge (MC), the case managers' responsibilities will include close liaison with them. This will apply when the District Judge (MC) is a nominated case manager or where the District Judge (MC)/Magistrates are required to maintain judicial continuity following the hearing of evidence or determination of a point at an interim hearing.

Transfer

(24)   Where continuity of case manager cannot otherwise be achieved, consideration should be given to transferring laterally or to the County Court, depending on the issues involved in the case.

D[2]

The welfare of the child
(Children Act 1989)

The welfare principle

D[2.1]

'When a court determines any question with respect to:

(a)   the upbringing of a child; or
(b)   the administration of a child's property or the application of any income arising from it,

the child's welfare shall be the court's paramount consideration' (Children Act 1989, s 1(1)).

The Family Proceedings Rules 2010 (came into force 6 April 2011): The Rules set out a unified procedural code for the High Court, the county court and the magistrates' court.

The overriding objective is to be found in r 1.1. These rules are a new procedural code with the overriding objective of enabling the court to deal with cases justly, having regard to any welfare issues involved.

Dealing with a case justly includes, so far as is practicable—

(a)   ensuring that it is dealt with expeditiously and fairly;
(b)   dealing with the case in ways which are proportionate to the nature, importance and complexity of the issues;
(c)   ensuring that the parties are on an equal footing;
(d)   saving expense; and
(e)   allotting to it an appropriate share of the court's resources, while taking into account the need to allot resources to other cases.

The Rules must be read with a series of Practice Directions which supplement specific Parts of the Rules.

Note that r 2.1(2)(a) provides that the rules only apply to family proceedings as defined by s 65 of the Magistrates' Courts Act 1980. The view of the Family Rules Committee is that this covers the position where the court orders that proceedings shall be treated as family proceedings pursuant to s 65(2) of the Magistrates' Courts Act 1980.

D[2.2]

The test is amplified by two more provisions:

(i) Delay

D[2.3]

'The court shall have regard to the general principle that any delay in determining the question is likely to prejudice the welfare of the child' (s 1(2)).

(See the FPR 2010 above.)

September 2003 saw the launch of a national protocol and standard directions forms. The objective is to reduce delay in public law care cases and thereby produce better outcomes for children. Children should have to spend less time in temporary care arrangements. The period of instability which impacts on their personal and educational development should be reduced. The principle of making high quality decisions about their welfare must however be retained (at the time of writing a national protocol is being drawn up for private law family proceedings)

(ii) Welfare checklist

D[2.4]

Where a court is considering an *opposed* application to make, vary or discharge a 'section 8' order (see D[4.3]), or is considering making, varying or discharging a care or supervision order it must have regard in particular to a 'checklist' of factors:

(a)   the ascertainable wishes and feelings of the child concerned (considered in the light of his age and understanding);
(b)   his physical, emotional and educational needs;
(c)   the likely effect on him of any change in his circumstances;
(d)   his age, sex, background and any characteristics of his which the court considers relevant;
(e)   any harm which he has suffered or is at risk of suffering;
(f)   how capable each of his parents, and any other person in relation to whom the court considers the question to be relevant, is of meeting his needs;
(g)   the range of powers available to the court under this Act in the proceedings in question (s 1(3)).

D[2.5]

Presumption of no order. The court should only make an order if it is in the child's best interests (Children Act 1989, s 1(5)).

D[2.6]

Children's evidence. It should be noted that the wishes and feelings of the child will normally be communicated to the court through the children's guardian or the children and family reporter. In *Re W (children) (abuse: oral evidence)* [2010] UKSC 12, [2010] 2 All ER 418, [2010] 1 WLR 701 the Supreme Court declared that the essential test is whether justice can be done to all the parties without further questioning of the child. The presumption or starting point that a child is rarely called to give evidence has been removed. The court will be required to conduct a balancing exercise weighing two considerations: the advantages that that will bring to the determination of the truth and the damage this may do to the welfare of the child or any other child.

The court set out a number of factors that a family court should consider when conducting the balancing exercise: (1) An unwilling child should rarely, if ever, be obliged to give evidence. The risk to the child is an ever present factor which should be given great weight. (2) The risk and therefore the weight will vary from case to case but must always be taken into account. (3) At both stages of the test the court must also factor in any steps which can be taken to improve the quality of a child's evidence, and at the same time decrease the risk of harm to the child.

For a more recent decision where the Court of Appeal held that the Judge had struck the right balance when refusing to permit the child to be called to give evidence in care proceedings see: *Re H (a child) (abuse: oral evidence)* [2011] EWCA Civ 741.

D[2.7]

Guidelines for Judges Meeting Children who are subject to Family Proceedings

Following *Re W (Children)* [2010] UKSC 12, the Family Justice Council, with the approval of the President of the Family Division has issued guidance dated April 2010 entitled **Guidelines for Judges Meeting Children who are subject to Family Proceedings**. The guidelines, with suitable modification, apply to all family proceedings in England and Wales and are set out immediately below.

In these Guidelines –

- All references to 'child' or 'children' are intended to include a young person or young people the subject of proceedings under the Children Act 1989.
- 'Family proceedings' includes both public and private law cases.
- 'Judge' includes magistrates.
- 'Cafcass' includes CAFCASS CYMRU.

Purpose

The purpose of these Guidelines is to encourage Judges to enable children to feel more involved and connected with proceedings in which important decisions are made in their lives and to give them an opportunity to satisfy themselves that the Judge has understood their wishes and feelings and to understand the nature of the Judge's task.

Preamble

- In England and Wales in most cases a child's needs, wishes and feelings are brought to the court in written form by a Cafcass officer. Nothing in this guidance document is intended to replace or undermine that responsibility.

- It is Cafcass practice to discuss with a child in a manner appropriate to their developmental understanding whether their participation in the process includes a wish to meet the Judge. If the child does not wish to meet the Judge discussions can centre on other ways of enabling the child to feel a part of the process. If the child wishes to meet the Judge, that wish should be conveyed to the Judge where appropriate.
- The primary purpose of the meeting is to benefit the child. However, it may also benefit the Judge and other family members.

Guidelines

(1) The Judge is entitled to expect the lawyer for the child and/or the Cafcass officer:
  - (i) to advise whether the child wishes to meet the Judge;
  - (ii) if so, to explain from the child's perspective, the purpose of the meeting;
  - (iii) to advise whether it accords with the welfare interests of the child for such a meeting take place; and
  - (iv) to identify the purpose of the proposed meeting as perceived by the child's professional representative/s.

(2) The other parties shall be entitled to make representations as to any proposed meeting with the Judge before the Judge decides whether or not it shall take place.

(3) In deciding whether or not a meeting shall take place and, if so, in what circumstances, the child's chronological age is relevant but not determinative. Some children of 7 or even younger have a clear understanding of their circumstances and very clear views which they may wish to express.

(4) If the child wishes to meet the Judge but the Judge decides that a meeting would be inappropriate, the Judge should consider providing a brief explanation in writing for the child.

(5) If a Judge decides to meet a child, it is a matter for the discretion of the Judge, having considered representations from the parties:
  - (i) the purpose and proposed content of the meeting;
  - (ii) at what stage during the proceedings, or after they have concluded, the meeting should take place;
  - (iii) where the meeting will take place;
  - (iv) who will bring the child to the meeting;
  - (v) who will prepare the child for the meeting (this should usually be the Cafcass officer);
  - (vi) who shall attend during the meeting – although a Judge should never see a child alone;
  - (vii) by whom a minute of the meeting shall be taken, how that minute is to be approved by the Judge, and how it is to be communicated to the other parties.

It cannot be stressed too often that the child's meeting with the judge is not for the purpose of gathering evidence. That is the responsibility of the Cafcass officer. The purpose is to enable the child to gain some understanding of what is going on, and to be reassured that the judge has understood him/her.

(6) If the meeting takes place prior to the conclusion of the proceedings:

(i)   The Judge should explain to the child at an early stage that a Judge cannot hold secrets. What is said by the child will, other than in exceptional circumstances, be communicated to his/her parents and other parties.

(ii)   The Judge should also explain that decisions in the case are the responsibility of the Judge, who will have to weigh a number of factors, and that the outcome is never the responsibility of the child.

(iii)   The Judge should discuss with the child how his or her decisions will be communicated to the child.

(iv)   The parties or their representatives shall have the opportunity to respond to the content of the meeting, whether by way of oral evidence or submissions.

D[3]

Parental responsibility

D[3.1]

The primary responsibility for the upbringing and care of children resides with their parents. Accordingly the Children Act 1989 refers to parental 'responsibilities' rather than parental 'rights'. Under the former law the obligations of parents to their children were not articulated as clearly as they might have been. In practice most disputes between parents concern residence and contact. The law now seeks consciously to emphasise that in reality both parents have an enduring responsibility for their children which continues whether or not the child is living with them unless and until the child reaches 18 years of age or, in certain circumstances is adopted.

D[3.2]

Accordingly it is necessary to determine who has parental responsibility for a child.

Persons having parental responsibility for a child

D[3.3]

The persons having responsibility for a child can be listed as follows:

(a)   (where they were married to each other at the time of the child's birth) the mother and the father (Children Act 1989, s 2(1)) ('married etc' includes where the parents married subsequent to the birth);

(b)   (where the parents were not so married) the mother alone, unless:
   (i)   the parents make an agreement to share parental responsibility; or
   (ii)   the father makes a successful application to the court for an order granting him parental responsibility which is then shared equally with the mother (s 4);

(c)   anyone who acquires a residence order under s 8 acquires parental responsibility for as long as the order is in force;

(d)   by the father being registered as the child's father under any of the Births and Deaths legislation applicable to England, Wales, Scotland or Northern Ireland.

D[3.4]

Once parental responsibility is acquired under para (a) above it can never be lost unless the child is adopted or reaches 18 years of age. Parental responsibility acquired under para (b) may be brought to an end by an order of the court.

D[3.5]

The court may also make orders in **family proceedings** which grant parental responsibility to other persons *in addition* to the parents, in which case parental responsibility is shared.

D[3.6]

Definition. Parental responsibility means 'all the rights, duties, powers, responsibilities and authority which by law a parent has in relation to the child and his property' (s 3(1)).

D[3.7]

A desire to exercise parental responsibility is something the courts should encourage (*Re S (a minor)* [1995] 3 FCR 225, [1995] 2 FLR 648, CA); an order may be made in favour of a father if the court is satisfied of:

(a)   the degree of commitment he has shown to the child;
(b)   the degree of attachment which exists between him and the child;
(c)   the reasons for his applying for the order. (*Re G (a minor)* [1994] 2 FCR 1037, [1994] 1 FLR 504, CA)

Acquisition of parental responsibility by father (Children Act 1989, s 4)

D[3.8]

The Family Law Reform Act 1987 provides that as a general principle in legislation passed after the Act came into force and in certain other statutes in the relationship between two people no regard is to be paid to whether any of their parents or forebears have been married. The legislation refers to a child whose parents have not been married. Where a child is born to such parents the father will have parental responsibility if he is named on the birth certificate. If he is not so named, he may apply to the court under the Children Act 1989, s 4 for an order that he shall have parental responsibility for the child and if given this he will share it equally with the mother. Such an order may subsequently be discharged on a further application made by the father or mother.

If a mother agrees to the father's name being registered on the birth certificate he will obtain parental responsibility (PR) without the need for a court order. Step-parents may acquire PR by agreement or by order of the court.

D[3.9]

Proof of parentage. There is a rebuttable presumption that a child born to parents who are married is the child of both of them. Where parentage is in dispute various methods of proof are available.

D[3.10]–[3.15]

1 Evidence of the father. As these are civil proceedings, he may be compelled to give evidence on behalf of the mother. His evidence on oath may provide the corroboration for her testimony.

D[3.16]

2 Scientific tests. The Family Law Reform Act 1969, Part III and the Family Law Act 1986 empowers the court to give a direction for the use of scientific tests (on application of either party) to be made on the mother, child and defendant. The rules are complicated so that when a court has scientific tests in mind, it should first consult its legal adviser.

D[3.17]–[3.18]

No person can be compelled to submit to a scientific test, even though a direction has been given. The court has jurisdiction to order that a sample be taken from a child under 16 where it would be in his interests, even though the person with care and control of the child does not consent.

D[3.19]

Magistrates may direct scientific tests on an application for a declaration of parentage under s 55A of the Family Law Act 1986. This is a single mechanism for all applicants including the Child Maintenance Enforcement Commission (which has taken over the functions of the Child Support Agency – see **D[7.47]**). A refusal to comply with an order for blood tests may result in an adverse inference being drawn sufficient to rebut the presumption of legitimacy (*F v Child Support Agency* [1999] 2 FCR 385, [1999] 2 FLR 244). Although in *Re H and A (paternity: blood tests)* [2002] EWCA Civ 383, [2002] 2 FCR 469 it was said that the interests of justice are best served by the truth and the court should have the best scientific evidence rather than rely on inference.

D[3.20]

While blood tests cannot determine who is the actual father of a child, in about 80% of cases these tests can establish that a man cannot possibly be the father of a child and thus he can only be excluded from paternity.

It is now possible to employ DNA genetic fingerprinting which is not merely an 'exclusionary' test but can prove parentage with almost complete certainty.

D[3.21]–[3.23]

3 Evidence of a conviction or a finding of adultery in previous matrimonial proceedings. If the complainant wishes to use the Civil Evidence Act 1968, s 11 or s 12 by proving that the defendant was convicted of an offence of having unlawful sexual intercourse with the complainant at the material time or if she wishes to rely on a finding of adultery in previous matrimonial proceedings, she may do so but the legal adviser should be consulted.

Appointment of guardian (Children Act 1989, s 5)

D[3.24]

Where a child has no parent with parental responsibility for him or a parent or guardian in whose favour a residence order has been made has died while the order was in force, any person may apply to the court to be appointed as the child's guardian and thereby acquire parental responsibility.

D[4]

Orders with respect to the upbringing of children

Private law proceedings

D[4.1]

Although parents have parental responsibility for their children, it will be necessary on occasion for the court to intervene either, for example, to resolve a dispute between parents as to how their responsibility should be exercised, or where individuals such as foster parents wish to acquire parental responsibility. It may also be appropriate to provide specifically for the upbringing of children involved in other family proceedings such as adoption, domestic violence and for maintenance of a spouse and in family proceedings under the Children Act 1989 itself: applications to acquire parental responsibility by unmarried fathers (s 4); appointment of guardians (s 5); applications for financial relief (Sch 1); are all normally referred to as **private law proceedings**. In all these private law proceedings the court may make one or more of the following orders.

Public law proceedings are dealt with at **D[6]**.

(References are all to the Children Act 1989.)

Practice Direction: The Revised Private Law Programme H [2010] Fam Law 539

The Practice Direction below is made by the President of the Family Division under the powers delegated to him by the Lord Chief Justice under Sch 2, Part 1, paragraph 2(2) of the Constitutional Reform Act 2005, and is approved by Bridget Prentice, Parliamentary Under Secretary of State, by authority of the Lord Chancellor.

1 Introduction

1.1 The Private Law Programme has achieved marked success in enabling the resolution of the majority of cases by consent at the First Hearing Dispute Resolution Appointment ("FHDRA"). It has been revised to build on the successes of the initial programme and to take account of recent developments in the law and practice associated with private family law.

1.2 In particular, there have been several legislative changes affecting private family law. The Allocation and Transfer of Proceedings Order 2008 (the "Allocation Order"), requires the transfer of cases from the County Court to the Family Proceedings Court (FPC). Sections 1 to 5 and Sch 1 of the Children and Adoption Act 2006 which came into force on 8 December 2008, amends the Children Act 1989 by introducing Contact Activity Directions, Contact Activity Conditions, Contact Monitoring Requirements, Financial Compensation Orders and Enforcement Orders.

1.3 There has been growing recognition of the impact of domestic violence and abuse, drug and alcohol misuse and mental illness, on the proper consideration of the issues in private family law; this includes the acceptance that Court orders, even those made by consent, must be scrutinised to ensure that they are safe and take account of any risk factors. Coupled with this is the need to take account of the duty on Cafcass, pursuant to s 16A of the Children Act 1989, to undertake risk assessments where an officer of the Service ("Cafcass Officer") suspects that a child is at risk of harm. (References to Cafcass include CAFCASS CYMRU and references to the Cafcass Officer include the Welsh family proceedings officer in Wales).

1.4 There is awareness of the importance of involving children where appropriate in the decision making process.

1.5 The Revised Programme incorporates these developments. It also retains the essential feature of the FHDRA as the forum for the parties to be helped to reach agreement as to, and understanding of, the issues that divide them. It recognises that having reached agreement parties may need assistance in putting it into effect in a co-operative way.

1.6 The Revised Programme is designed to provide a framework for the consistent national approach to the resolution of the issues in private family law whilst enabling local practices and initiatives to be operated in addition and within the framework.

1.7 The Revised Programme is designed to assist parties to reach safe agreements where possible, to provide a forum in which to find the best way to resolve issues in each individual case and to promote outcomes that are sustainable, that are in the best interests of children and that take account of their perspectives.

2 Principles

2.1 Where an application is made to a court under Part II of the Children Act 1989, the child's welfare is the court's paramount concern. The court will apply the principle of the "Overriding Objective" to enable it to deal with a case justly, having regard to the welfare principles involved. So far as practicable the Court will —

(a)   Deal expeditiously and fairly with every case;
(b)   Deal with a case in ways which are proportionate to the nature, importance and complexity of the issues;
(c)   Ensure that the parties are on an equal footing;
(d)   Save unnecessary expense;
(e)   Allot to each case an appropriate share of the court's resources, while taking account of the need to allot resources to other cases.

2.2 The court will give effect to the overriding objective when applying this programme and when exercising its powers to manage cases. The parties are required to help the court further the overriding objective and promote the welfare of the child by the application of the welfare principle, pursuant to s 1(1) of the Children Act 1989.

This Programme provides that consideration and discussion of all issues will not take place until the FHDRA when parties are on an equal footing and can hear what is said to and by each other. This excludes the safety checks and enquiries carried out by Cafcass before the first hearing that are required for that hearing and deal only with safety issues.

At the FHDRA the Court shall consider in particular —

(a) Whether and the extent to which the parties can safely resolve some or all of the issues with the assistance of the Cafcass Officer and any available mediator.

(b) Risk identification followed by active case management including risk assessment, and compliance with the Practice Direction 14th January 2009: "Residence and Contact Orders: Domestic Violence and Harm".

(c) Further dispute resolution.

(d) The avoidance of delay through the early identification of issues and timetabling, subject to the Allocation Order.

(e) Judicial scrutiny of the appropriateness of consent order.

(f) Judicial consideration of the way to involve the child.

(g) Judicial continuity.

3 Practical Arrangements

Before the FHDRA

3.1 Applications shall be issued on the day of receipt in accordance with the appropriate Rules of Procedure. It is important that the form C100 is fully completed, especially on pages 1, 2, 3, 10 and 11 otherwise delay may be caused by requests for information.

3.2 If possible at the time of issue, and in any event by no later than 24 hours after issue, or in courts where applications are first considered on paper, by no later than 48 hours after issue, the court shall

(i) send or hand to the Applicant

(ii) send to Cafcass

the following:

(a) a copy of the Application Form C100, (together with Supplemental Information Form C1A) (if provided) (references to form C1A are to be read as form C100A following the introduction of this replacement form),

(b) the Notice of Hearing

(c) the Acknowledgment Form C7,

(d) a blank Form C1A,

(e) the Certificate of Service Form C9,

(f) information leaflets for the parties.

3.3 Save in urgent cases that require an earlier listing, the fully effective operation of this Practice Direction requires the FHDRA to take place within 4 weeks of the application. Where practicable, the first hearing must be listed to be heard in this period and in any event no later than within 6 weeks of the application. Where, at the time of introduction of this Programme, the Designated Family Judge/Justices' Clerk determines that it is not practicable to list the first hearing within 4 weeks, they should, in consultation with HMCS and Cafcass, formulate a timetable for revisiting the position and managing to list the FHDRA within 4 weeks.

3.4 Copies of each Application Form C100 and Notice of Hearing shall be sent by the court to Cafcass in accordance with 3.2 above.

3.5 The Respondent shall have at least 14 days notice of the hearing where practicable, but the court may abridge this time.

3.6 The Respondent should file a response on the Forms C7/C1A no later than 14 days before the hearing.

3.7 A copy of Forms C7/C1A shall be sent by the court to Cafcass on the day of receipt.

3.8 NOTE: This provision relates to cases that are placed in the FHDRA list for hearing other than by direct application in accordance with the procedure referred to in paragraph 3.1. Such listing may follow an application under the Family Law Act 1996, or a direction by the Court in other proceedings. In all such cases, or where the Court adjourns proceedings to a 'dispute resolution hearing' (sometimes called 'conciliation'), this will be treated as an adjournment to a FHDRA, and the documents referred to in para 3.2 must be filed and copied to parties and Cafcass for safety checks and enquiries, in the same way.

3.9 Before the FHDRA Cafcass shall identify any safety issues by the steps outlined below. Such steps shall be confined to matters of safety. Neither Cafcass nor a Cafcass Officer shall discuss with either party before the FHDRA any matter other than relates to safety. The Parties will not be invited to talk about other issues, for example relating to the substance of applications or replies or about issues concerning matters of welfare or the prospects of resolution. If such issues are raised by either party they will be advised that such matters will be deferred to the FHDRA when there is equality between the parties and full discussion can take place which will also be a time when any safety issues that have been identified also can be taken into account.

(a)   In order to inform the court of possible risks of harm to the child in accordance with its safeguarding framework Cafcass will carry out safeguarding enquiries, including checks of local authorities and police, and telephone risk identification interviews with parties.

(b)   If risks of harm are identified, Cafcass may invite parties to meet separately with the Cafcass Officer before the FHDRA to clarify any safety issue.

(c)   Cafcass shall record and outline any safety issues for the court.

(d)   The Cafcass Officer will not initiate contact with the child prior to the FHDRA. If contacted by a child, discussions relating to the issues in the case will be postponed to the day of the hearing or after when the Cafcass officer will have more knowledge of the issues.

(e)   At least 3 days before the hearing the Cafcass Officer shall report the outcome of risk identification work to the court by completing the Form at Schedule 2.

4 The First Hearing Dispute Resolution Appointment

4.1 The parties and Cafcass Officer shall attend this hearing. A mediator may attend where available.

4.2 At the hearing, which is not privileged, the court should have the following documents:

(a)   C100 application, and C1A if any
(b)   Notice of Hearing
(c)   C7 response and C1A if any
(d)   Schedule 2 safeguarding information

4.3 The detailed arrangements for the participation of mediators will be arranged locally. These will include:

(a)   Arrangements for the mediator to ask the parties in a particular case to consent to the mediator seeing the papers in the case where it seems appropriate to do so.
(b)   Arrangements for the mediator to ask the parties to waive privilege for the purpose of the first hearing where it seems to the mediator appropriate to do so in order to assist the work of the mediator and the outcome of the first hearing.
(c)   In all cases it is important that such arrangements are put in place in a way that avoids any pressure being brought to bear in this connection on the parties that is inconsistent with general good mediation practice.

4.4 At the FHDRA the Court, in collaboration with the Cafcass Officer, and with the assistance of any mediator present, will seek to assist the parties in conciliation and in resolution of all or any of the issues between them. Any remaining issues will be identified, the Cafcass Officer will advise the court of any recommended means of resolving such issues and directions will be given for the future resolution of such issues. At all times the decisions of the Court and the work of the Cafcass Officer will take account of any risk or safeguarding issues that have been identified.

4.5 The Cafcass Officer shall, where practicable, speak separately to each party at court and before the hearing.

4.6 In the County Court, the Court shall have available a telephone contact to the Family Proceedings Court listing manager, diary dates for the appropriate Family Proceedings Court, or other means by which the County Court, at the time of the hearing, will be able to list subsequent hearings in the Family Proceedings Court.

5 Conduct of the Hearing

The following matters shall be considered

5.1 Safeguarding:

(a) The court shall inform the parties of the content of any screening report or other information which has been provided by Cafcass, unless it considers that to do so would create a risk of harm to a party or the child. The court may need to consider whether and how any information contained in the checks should be disclosed to the parties if Cafcass have not disclosed it.

(b) Whether a risk assessment is required and when.

(c) Whether a fact finding hearing is needed to determine allegations whose resolution is likely to affect the decision of the court.

5.2 Dispute Resolution:

(a) There will be at every FHDRA a period in which the Cafcass Officer, with the assistance of any Mediator and in collaboration with the Court, will seek to conciliate and explore with the parties the resolution of all or some of the issues between them. The procedure to be followed in this connection at the hearing will be determined by local arrangements between the Cafcass manager, or equivalent in Wales, and the Designated Family Judge or the Justices' Clerk where appropriate.

(b) What is the result of any such meeting at Court?

(c) What other options there are for resolution eg may the case be suitable for further intervention by Cafcass; mediation by an external provider; collaborative law or use of a parenting plan?

(d) Would the parties be assisted by attendance at Parenting Information Programmes or other activities, whether by formal statutory provision under s 11 of the Children Act 1989 as amended by Children and Adoption Act 2006 or otherwise?

5.3 Consent Orders:

Where agreement is reached at any hearing or submitted in writing to the court, no order will be made without scrutiny by the court. Where safeguarding checks or risk assessment work remain outstanding, the making of a final order may be deferred for such work. In such circumstances the court shall adjourn the case for no longer than 28 days to a fixed date. A written notification of this work is to be provided by Cafcass in accordance with the timescale specified by the court. If satisfactory information is then available, the order may be made at the adjourned hearing in the agreed terms without the need for attendance by the parties. If satisfactory information is not available, the order will not be made, and the case will be adjourned for further consideration with an opportunity for the parties to make further representations.

5.4 Reports:

a)

(a) Are there welfare issues or other specific considerations which should be addressed in a report by Cafcass or the Local Authority? Before a report is ordered, the court should consider alternative ways of working with the parties such as are referred to in paragraph 5.2 above. If a report is ordered in accordance with s 7 of the Children Act 1989, it should be directed specifically towards and limited to those issues. General requests should be avoided and the Court should state in the Order the specific factual and other issues that are to be addressed in a focused report. In determining whether a request for a report should be directed to the relevant local authority or to Cafcass, the court should consider such information as Cafcass has provided about the extent and nature of the local authority's current or recent involvement with the subject of the application and the parties, and any relevant protocol between Cafcass and the Association of Directors of Children's Services.

(b)   Is there a need for an investigation under s 37 Children Act 1989?

(c)   A copy of the Order requesting the report and any relevant court documents are to be sent to Cafcass or, in the case of the Local Authority, to the Legal Adviser to the Director of the Local Authority Children's Services and, where known, to the allocated social worker by the court forthwith.

(d)   Is any expert evidence required in compliance with the Experts' Practice Direction?

5.5 Wishes and feelings of the child:

(a)   Is the child aware of the proceedings? How are the wishes and feelings of the child to be ascertained (if at all)?

(b)   How is the child to be involved in the proceedings, if at all, and whether at or after the FHDRA?

(c)   If consideration is given to the joining of the child as a party to the application, the court should consider the current Guidance from the President of the Family Division. Where the court is considering the appointment of a guardian ad litem, it should first seek to ensure that the appropriate Cafcass manager has been spoken to so as to consider any advice in connection with the prospective appointment and the timescale involved. In considering whether to make such an appointment the Court shall take account of the demands on the resources of Cafcass that such appointment would make.

(d)   Who will inform the child of the outcome of the case where appropriate?

5.6 Case Management:

(a)   What, if any, issues are agreed and what are the key issues to be determined?

(b)   Are there any interim orders which can usefully be made (e.g. indirect, supported or supervised contact) pending final hearing?

(c)   What directions are required to ensure the application is ready for final hearing — statements, reports etc?

(d)   List for final hearing, consider the need for judicial continuity (especially if there has been or is to be a fact finding hearing or a contested interim hearing).

5.7 Transfer to FPC:

The case should be transferred to the FPC, pursuant to the Allocation and Transfer of Proceedings Order 2008 unless one of the specified exceptions applies. The date should be fixed at court and entered on the order.

6 The Order

6.1 The Order shall set out in particular:

(a)   The issues about which the parties are agreed
(b)   The issues that remain to be resolved
(c)   The steps that are planned to resolve the issues
(d)   Any interim arrangements pending such resolution, including arrangements for the involvement of children.
(e)   The timetable for such steps and, where this involves further hearings, the date of such hearings.
(f)   A statement as to any facts relating to risk or safety; in so far as they are resolved the result will be stated and, in so far as not resolved, the steps to be taken to resolve them will be stated.
(g)   If it be the case, the fact of the transfer of the case to the Family Proceedings Court with the date and purpose of the next hearing
(h)   If it be the case, the fact that the case cannot be transferred to the Family Proceedings Court and the reason for the decision.
(i)   Whether in the event of an order, by consent or otherwise, or pending such an order, the parties are to be assisted by participation in mediation, Parenting Information Programmes, or other types of parenting intervention, and to detail any contact activity directions or conditions imposed by the court.

6.2 A suggested template order is available as set out in Schedule 1 below.

7 Commencement and Implementation

7.1 This Practice Direction will come into effect on April 1st 2010. So that procedural changes can be made by all agencies, the requirement for full implementation of the provisions is postponed, but in any event it should be effected by no later than October 4th 2010.

SCHEDULE 1

The suggested form of Order which courts may wish to use is PLP10 which is available from Her Majesty's Court Service.

SCHEDULE 2

Report Form on outcome of safeguarding enquiries. See version for Cafcass in England and for CAFCASS CYMRU in Wales.

Welfare reports (Children Act 1989, s 7)

D[4.2]

A court considering any question with respect to a child under this Act may ask an officer of CAFCASS (the Children and Family Court Advisory and Support Service) or local authority social worker to report to the court on matters relating to the welfare of that child (s 7(1)). See CAFCASS Practice Note (2001). Information contained in such reports will be supplied to the parties in the proceedings. The officer may not give assurances of confidentiality and the court will only withhold information contained in reports in the most exceptional circumstances where real harm would be caused to the child by disclosure (*Re G (minors)* [1994] 1 FCR 37, [1993] 2 FLR 293, CA).

Section 8 orders

D[4.3]

The court may make one or more of the following orders under the Children Act 1989, s 8. For additional powers linked to contact order applications see D[5.17] below.

D[4.4]

Contact order requiring the person with whom the child lives to allow the child to visit or stay with or otherwise have contact with the person named in the order. The court should regard contact with both parents to be a right of the child which should not be denied due to earlier difficulties suffered after the parent separation (*Re H (minors)* [1992] 1 FCR 70, [1992] 1 FLR 148, CA). An application for contact and parental responsibility are to be treated separately. A refusal to grant contact does not mean parental responsibility should also be refused (*Re C and V (minors)* [1998] 1 FCR 52, [1998] 1 FLR 392, CA). See also *Glaser v United Kingdom* [2000] 3 FCR 193, [2001] 1 FLR 153, ECtHR on the human rights issues surrounding the court's obligations to enforce contact. The court may make an order for reasonable contact and should encourage parties to reach agreement but when faced with an issue the court must make a determination (*Re P (Parental Dispute: Judicial Determination)* [2002] EWCA Civ 1627, [2002] All ER (D) 80 (Oct)). Where repeated orders for contact have failed due to the actions of one parent a transfer of residence to the other parent may be used if it is in the best interests of the children and ensures a normal relationship with both parents (*V v V (children) (intractable contact dispute)* [2004] EWHC 1215 (Fam), [2004] All ER (D) 304 (May)).

Contact: domestic violence. The philosophy of the Children Act 1989 is non-interventionist; it encourages settlement. The 'no order' principle is so imbued in those working in the family justice system, that if two parents present a court with an agreement about an issue or issues relating to children, the court's normal reaction is to welcome that agreement. For guidelines see *Re L (Contact: Domestic Violence)* [2000] 2 FLR 334. Four points were identified as being of particular significance in an application for contact:

(1) The extent of the violence.
(2) The effect upon the primary carer.
(3) The effect upon the children.
(4) The ability of the [other party] offender to recognise his behaviour and attempt to change it.

Where violence has been alleged, it is a matter for the court to decide whether, if proved, that violence would be relevant to the issue of contact. If the court decides it would be relevant, the court must decide whether the allegations are proved or not (in other words, it must hold a fact-finding hearing to determine this issue).

One recommendation that has been made by the Family Justice Council, in a report dated January 2007, is that there should be renewed emphasis on the message that ensuring safety should be paramount when considering whether contact is in the child's best interests. To that end it recommended that a Practice Direction embodying the guidelines in *Re L*, suitably updated to reflect current best practice, should be issued. That recommendation has been followed.

On 9 May 2008 the President of the Family Division issued a Practice Direction (Residence and Contact Orders: Domestic Violence and Harm (www.family-justice-council.org.uk/publications.htm). The *Practice Direct ion* was reissued in revised form on 14 January 2009 and reported at [2009] All ER (D) 122 (Jan). The revisions reflect the decision of the House of Lords in *Re B (children) (sexual abuse: standard of proof)* [2008] UKHL 35, [2008] 4 All ER 1, in which Baroness Hale confirmed at [76] that a fact -finding hearing is part of the process of trying a case and is not a separate exercise and that when the case is then adjourned for a further hearing it remains part heard. This principle applies equally in private and public law cases. Paragraphs 15 and 23 of the *Practice Direction* have been amended to reinforce this principle.

The PD applies whenever an application is made for a residence or contact order or a question arises about contact and residence between a child and family member and it is alleged or there is some reason to suppose that the child or a party has experienced domestic violence perpetrated by another party or that there is a risk of such violence.

In *Re W (children) (care order: sexual abuse) sub nom W (children) (concurrent criminal and care proceedings)* [2009] EWCA Civ 644, [2009] 2 Cr App Rep 384, Wall LJ emphasised the need for robust and critical consideration of the need to hold split hearings in cases where the decision as to the outcome appears to be inevitable whatever the precise findings as to the role or complicity of a party concerned in a case of domestic violence or other forms of abuse.

'Domestic violence' is widely defined to include threatening or intimidating behaviour and any other form of abuse which, directly or indirectly, may have caused harm to the other party or to the child or which may give rise to the risk of harm. See an informative article at (2008) 172 JPN 412.

Split hearings: President's guidance May 2010

NB: *From time to time issues will arise with which magistrates and judges at every level will have to grapple and which will cause difficulties. Against* *this background I intend from time to time to issue what I propose to call "Guidance" designed to help colleagues make difficult decisions. Self-evidently such Guidance is not designed to tell courts what to decide: the objective is to assist them in the process of going about the decision making progress. Plainly, it will be appropriate not to follow the Guidance in some circumstances: what I hope is that in a sufficiently large number of instances the Guidance will be of use and will help magistrates and judges in the decision making process.*

Introduction

1. Over recent months and years it has become apparent to me that split hearings are: (1) taking place when they need not do so; and (2) are taking up a disproportionate amount of the court's time and resources.

2. I have therefore decided to issue the following Guidance in an attempt to assist judges and magistrates who are invited to direct split hearings.

3. Like all Guidance, what follows is not binding on the judiciary at any level. It is an attempt to identify good practice. Moreover, it is designed to apply in both private and public law proceedings.

4. In this Guidance, I propose to use the following terminology:

A "split hearing" is a hearing divided into two parts, during the first of which the court makes findings of fact on issues either identified by the parties or the court, and during the second part of which the court, based on the findings which it has made, decides the case.

A "fact finding hearing" is the first limb of a split hearing.

Guidance

5. Judges and magistrates should always remember that the decision to direct a split hearing or to conduct a fact finding hearing is a judicial decision. It is not a decision for Cafcass or for the parties. It is a decision to be taken by the court. Thus the court should not direct a fact finding hearing simply because the parties agree that one is necessary or because Cafcass says that it cannot report without one. Such considerations are, of course, to be taken into account, but they are not conclusive. In any event, the focus of any report is a matter for the court.

6. Judges and magistrates should always remember that a fact finding hearing is a working tool designed to assist them to decide the case. Thus a fact finding hearing should only be ordered if the court takes the view that the case cannot properly be decided without such a hearing.

7. Even when the court comes to the conclusion that a fact finding hearing is necessary, it by no means follows that such a hearing needs to be separate from the substantive hearing. In nearly every case, the court's findings of

fact inform its conclusions. In my judgment it will be a rare case in which a separate fact finding hearing is necessary.

8. Thus, for example, the fact that domestic abuse is put forward by the residential parent of a child as a reason for denying the non-residential parent contact with the child is not automatically as reason for a split hearing with a preliminary fact finding hearing. As the *President's Practice Direction: Residence and Contact order: Domestic Violence and Harm of 14 January 2009* [2009] 2 FLR 1400 makes clear, the court must consider the nature of any allegations, and the *extent* to which those allegations, if admitted or proved " *would be relevant in deciding whether to make an order about residence or contact and, if so, in what terms*" – see para [3] (emphasis supplied). In para [11] the court is again instructed to "consider the likely impact of that issue (domestic abuse) *on the outcome of the proceedings*" (emphasis supplied) and whether or not the decision of the court is likely to be affected by findings of domestic abuse. Plainly, if the allegations are unlikely to have any impact on the court's order, there is no need for a separate fact finding hearing.

9. In addition, in cases in which the court concludes that a fact-finding hearing is necessary, the Practice Direction requires the court to give directions designed to ensure that " *the matters in issue are determined expeditiously and fairly*" (emphasis supplied).

10. None of the foregoing is designed to minimise or trivialise domestic abuse or its effects on children and upon its other victims, or to discourage victims from coming forward with abuse allegations. I repeat that the aim of the Guidance is to enable magistrates and judges fully to address their minds to the need for a separate fact finding hearing.

11. The rationale for split hearings in care proceedings was enunciated by Bracewell J in *Re S (care proceedings: split hearing)* [1996] 3 FCR 578, [1996] 2 FLR 773 when, voicing the views of the Children Act Advisory Committee, she stated that consideration could usefully be given to whether or not there were questions of fact within a case which needed to be determined at an early stage. The advantages of doing so, she said were that early resolution of such facts "would enable the substantive hearing to proceed more speedily" and would enable the court to "focus on the child's welfare with greater clarity". Cases suitable for split hearings, she commented "would be likely to be cases in which there is a clear and stark issue, such as sexual abuse or physical abuse". Once again, the object was "to prevent delay and the ill-focused use of scarce expert resources". These factors should be borne in mind by the court when deciding whether or not to order a split hearing.

12. Magistrates and judges are reminded of the decision of the Court of Appeal in *Re C (child) (contact order; fact finding hearing)* [2009] EWCA Civ 994, [2010] 1 FLR 1728, [2010] Fam Law 586. They might also care to look at paragraphs 27 to 35 of my recent judgment in the case of *W (children) (care order)* [2009] EWCA Civ 644, [2009] 2 FLR 1106, now also reported at [2009] 3 FCR 1.

13. Courts are also reminded of the provisions of the *Practice Direction: The Revised Private Law Programme* which came into effect from 1 April 2010.

D[4.5]

Prohibited steps order that no step which a person with parental responsibility might take, shall be taken without the consent of the court.

D[4.6]

Residence order settling the arrangements to be made as to with whom a child is to live. A family proceedings court should not countenance a change of residence on an **interim** basis unless there was a compelling reason for doing so (*Re K (children: interim residence order)* [2004] All ER (D) 276 (Dec); *Re H (children) (residence order)* [2007] All ER (D) 26 (May)).

D[4.7]

Specific issue order giving directions to determine a specific question in connection with any aspect of parental responsibility for a child.

D[4.8]

Availability. A s 8 order may be made:

(a)   in the course of any family proceedings:
  (i)   on the application of a person entitled to apply or who has obtained the leave of the court to apply;
  (ii) where the court considers that the order should be made even though no application has been made; and
  (iii) at any time during proceedings even though the court is not in a position finally to dispose of these proceedings.

D[4.9]–[4.15]

A court will not normally hold a detailed hearing of a case to determine an application for leave to apply but may in a disputed case hear the main parties to form a broad view of the merits of the application (the Children Act 1989, s 10(a) and *Re F and R (s 8 Order Grandparents application)* [1998] Crim LR 657).

D[5]

Persons who may apply for a s 8 order

D[5.1]

	Contact	Prohib-ited steps	Resi-dence	Specific issue
Parent/Guardian	✔	✔	✔	✔
Person with residence order	✔	✔	✔	✔
Party to marriage re child of family	✔	*	✔	*
Person with whom child has lived for 1 year	✔	*	✔	*
Persons with consent of:				
(1) persons with residence order	✔	*	✔	*
(2) (child in care) local authority	✔	*	✔	*
(3) those with PR	✔	*	✔	*
Other applicants	*	*	*	*
Local authority	-	*	-	*

Notes

* Leave of the court required.

- A residence order grants parental responsibility to the person in whose favour it is made.
- A specific issue or prohibited steps order shall not be made with a view to achieving a result which could be achieved by making a residence or contact order.
- No court may make a s 8 order other than a residence order in respect of a child in the care of a local authority.
- Local authority foster parents need consent of the authority unless they are relatives or the child has lived with them for at one year or more.

D[5.2]

The making of a residence order will give the person in whose favour the order is made parental responsibility for the child (subject to some limitations – eg there is no power to consent to adoption) whilst the order is in force (s 12). Certain persons who do not have parental responsibility may not apply for prohibited steps or specific issue orders as these would be an unwarranted interference in the exercise of the parental responsibility of others.

Only in exceptional circumstances should the court attach a condition restricting movement within the UK (*Re H (children: relocation)* (2001) Times, 29 August, CA).

D[5.3]

Children in care and applications by local authorities (Children Act 1989, ss 9 and 10). No s 8 order, except a residence order (which has the effect of discharging a care order), may be made with respect to a child in the care of a local authority. Conversely a local authority may not apply for a residence or contact order in respect of a child not in their care; those matters are more appropriately dealt with in care proceedings where 'threshold' criteria have to be fulfilled. Specific limitations are placed on applications by local authority foster parents.

D[5.4]

Welfare criterion and welfare checklist. See D[2].

D[5.5]

Welfare reports. See D[4.2].

D[5.6]

Delay and court timetable. In order to avoid delay rules of court provide for the court to draw up a timetable with a view to determining the issue without delay (s 11(1)). The importance of the court taking a proactive role at the directions hearing is emphasised (*Re G, S and M (care proceedings)* (1999)).

D[5.7]

Is a court order necessary? A court shall not make an order under the Children Act 1989 unless it considers that doing so would be better for the child than making no order at all (s 1(5)).

D[5.8]

Duration of orders. A s 8 order cannot be made in respect of a child who has attained 16 years, or extend beyond that age unless there are exceptional circumstances (s 9).

D[5.9]

Transfer of proceedings. Provision is made for a case under the Children Act 1989 to be transferred from one court to another either horizontally to another family proceedings court or vertically to the county court.

D[5.10]–[5.15]

The overall test is whether the interests of the child demand that the proceedings be transferred. The legal adviser will advise on factors likely to affect this finding, such as complexity or consolidation of proceedings. Difficult evidential issues surrounding sexual abuse are best transferred to the county court (*Re W (a child) (sexual abuse)* [2002] All ER (D) 34 (Jan)).

D[5.16]

Supplementary provisions. A s 8 order may contain directions about how it is to be carried into effect, impose conditions which must be complied with by any person named in the order and make such incidental, supplemental or consequential provision as the court thinks fit (s 11(8)).

Contact and enforcement of contact orders – Children and Adoption Act 2006

D[5.17]

On 8 December 2006 additional powers were conferred on the courts when dealing with contact orders when made under s 8. New ss 11A–P was inserted into the Children Act 1989. The emphasis of the new legislation is geared towards giving the courts and the parties more flexibility in private law contact cases. The following is an overview of those new powers.

D[5.18]

Contact activities. They include programmes, classes and counselling or guidance sessions of a kind that assist in establishing, maintaining or improving contact. They also include perpetrator programmes that seek to address violent behaviour (s 11A(5)).

The Act distinguishes between 'contact activity directions' and 'contact activity conditions'. Before making either order the court must be satisfied that an order is appropriate in the circumstances of the case.

D[5.19]

Contact activity directions (s 11A-B). A contact activity direction may only be made where there is some dispute about the provision for contact that the court is considering whether to make. In contrast to contact activity conditions which are made when a contact order is made, contact activity directions are made at an interim stage i.e. before the finalisation of the case. Section 11B also provides that a contact activity direction may not be made where an 'excepted order' is being considered eg an adoption application. The person who is to undertake the contact activity must be habitually resident in England and Wales. There are also restrictions on requiring a child to undertake a contact activity, unless that person is the parent of the child at the centre of the contact case.

D[5.20]

Contact activity conditions (s 11C). These are contact activities that are ordered at the same time at the same time a contact order is made. In other words, contact activity conditions become part of the contact order, as with conditions ordered under s 11(7)(b) of the 1989 Act. Similar to s 11B above, the restrictions on a child, excepted orders and habitual residence apply.

D[5.21]

Contact activity directions and conditions – factors and monitoring (ss 11E and 11G). The subsection specifies that certain criteria must be met, for example, that a contact activity is relatively local to the party who will be attending the activity; that it would not expose a party or attendee to a risk of domestic violence; that it does not conflict with religious beliefs, work or educational commitments. Section 11G enables the court to ask CAFCASS to monitor compliance with a court activity direction or condition and to report to the court on any failure to comply. Once the request has been made, CAFCASS are under a duty to comply with that request (s 11G(3)).

D[5.22]

Monitoring contact (s 11H). The court can ask a CAFCASS officer to monitor compliance of an individual with a contact order (other than an 'excepted order') and to report to the court 'on any such matters relating to an individual's compliance as the court may specify in the request'. Once the request has been made, CAFCASS are under a duty to comply (s 11H(7)). The request must specify a monitoring period of up to 12 months.

D[5.23]

Warning notices (s11I). Whenever a court makes a contact order it must attach to the order a warning notice. The warning notice should warn the person that a breach of the order could lead to him/her being committed to prison or fined and/or made subject to an unpaid work order and/or required to pay financial compensation to the other party. There are provisions which state that a contact order is unenforceable unless the person alleged to have breached the order received, or was otherwise informed of the terms of a warning notice when the contact order was made (ss 11K(1) and 11P(1)).

D[5.24]

Enforcement orders (s11J). An enforcement order is made (on application only) in response to a breach of a contact order and imposes upon the party in breach an unpaid work order. The aim of an enforcement order is to secure the person's compliance with the order and as such must be proportionate to the seriousness of the breach. Because of the potential for criminal sanctions proof of breach must be established beyond a reasonable doubt. Section 11J(3) states that the court may not make an enforcement order if the party alleged to have breached an order had a reasonable excuse for non-compliance. The burden of proof lies with the person claiming a reasonable excuse on a balance of probabilities.

The court may suspend an enforcement order for such a period as it thinks fit (s 11J(9)). Similar to ss 11A–C above, the restrictions on a person under 18 years of age, excepted orders and habitual residence apply.

The number of hours to be worked under an enforcement order is not less than 40 and not more than 200. Part 2 of Sch A1 to the Children Act 1989 deals with the breach, revocation and amendment of enforcement orders.

A new s 11M provides that when a court makes an enforcement order it must ask a CAFCASS officer to monitor compliance with the order and to report any such matters relating to the monitoring as the court may request. When the court makes an order it must attach a warning notice, warning on the consequences of failing to comply with the order (s 11N).

D[5.25]

Breach of an enforcement order. The case may only come back to court on the application of one of the parties. Proof of breach must be established beyond a reasonable doubt – and in the absence of a reasonable excuse (the burden lies with the person claiming a reasonable excuse on a balance of probabilities). If a breach is proved, without prejudice to the court's power to fine or to commit to custody (s 63(3) of the Magistrates' Courts Act 1980), it may either amend the terms of the original order, by imposing more onerous terms, or to make a second enforcement order, either in addition to, or in substitution for the first enforcement order. For financial compensation, see below.

D[5.26]

Financial compensation orders (s 11O). This enables a party who has suffered financial loss as a result of a breach of a contact order by another party, to apply to the court for an order that the party in breach pays him/her financial compensation. The amount payable may only be sufficient to compensate the party for his/her loss; a punitive element must not be added. The court must consider the welfare of the child and the finances of the person in breach. Any such sum is enforceable as a civil debt.

Proof of financial loss is to the civil standard ie proof on a balance of probabilities. Such an order cannot be made where the party alleged to be in breach of the contact order has a reasonable excuse. The burden of proof lies with the person claiming a reasonable excuse and to the civil standard.

D[5.27]

Investigation by the local authority (s 37). Where it appears to the court that it may be appropriate to make a care or supervision order it may direct the local authority to undertake an investigation of the child's circumstances. If the court is considering making an interim care order then the proceedings become specified and a children's guardian may be appointed: see D[6.17]–D[6.19].Where the authority decides not to apply for such an order it must report to the court generally within eight weeks giving its reasons, details of any services or assistance the authority will provide and any other action it proposes to take, and the proceedings cease to be specified proceedings. It is not appropriate to invoke public law procedures in private law proceedings (*Re CE (section 37 direction)* [1995] 1 FCR 387, [1995] 1 FLR 26.)

Family assistance orders (s 16)

D[5.28]

Whether or not the court makes a s 8 order, it may make a family assistance order requiring a CAFCASS officer or social worker to advise, assist or befriend a parent, the child or a person with whom the child is living or who has the benefit of a contact order. A family assistance order shall not be made so as to require a local authority to make an officer of the authority available unless (i) the authority agree (ii) the child concerned lives or will live within the local authority area.

Revised arrangements were introduced in respect of family assistance orders in September 2007 as follows:

(a)   Extension of the maximum period from 6 months to 12 months.
(b)   Widening the range of cases in which such orders can be made by removing the requirement that the family circumstances had to be exceptional.
(c)   Provision for the court to require CAFCASS or a local authority officer to help people named in the order to establish and maintain contact with a child.
(d)   Provision for the court to require CAFCASS or a local authority to report on the operation of a section 8 order (contact, residence, specific issue or prohibited steps) and report on whether the order should be varied or discharged.
(e)   Provision of greater protection for children by requiring CAFCASS to carry out a risk assessment and report back to the court. Section 16A of the CA 1989 places a duty on CAFCASS to make risk assessments (and report them to the court) wherever there is cause to suspect that a child is at risk of harm.

The President of the Family Division issued a Practice Direction (Family Assistance Orders: Consultation) on 3 September 2007, which requires the court to consult with CAFCASS or the local authority before making an order.

D[6]
Public law proceedings

D[6.1]

Normally Art 8 of the Human Rights Act protects family life from state interventions. However this is a qualified right and the local authority or the NSPCC are prescribed by statute as being able to bring proceedings for the welfare of children.

A local authority may provide accommodation for any child within their area if they consider that to do so would safeguard or promote his welfare and in certain cases, such as where children have been abandoned or are in need, are under a duty to do so. However, such accommodation may not be provided where any person with parental responsibility who can arrange for his accommodation objects. The only means whereby a local authority may compulsorily obtain the care of a child is as a result of an order made by a court in care proceedings.

Articles 6 and 8 are engaged in every application and once the threshold test is satisfied the court uses a welfare checklist to balance the competing art 8 rights of the parties and the child. The family proceedings court will normally deal with these issues without need for an upwards transfer (*Re V (a child)* [2004] EWCA Civ 54, [2004] All ER (D) 52 (Feb)).

Directions appointments

D[6.2]

On receipt of an application in care proceedings the legal adviser must issue the application nominating a case manager and gives standard directions on issue including the date for a first court hearing or first appointment. The purpose of a directions appointment at which the parties, their legal advisers and a children's guardian may be present is to ensure that those facts which are and are not in dispute are clearly identified, that a guardian is appointed where appropriate if this has not already been done and that a timetable is set. The parties will be under a duty to disclose to each other and the court in written form the evidence on which they intend to rely. The magistrates may then read the evidence in advance of the hearing so that the oral evidence may be directed to matters in dispute. There may be more than one directions appointment during the course of the proceedings. The President of the Family Division of the High Court has intimated that care proceedings should where practicable be concluded within three months (this intimation must now be read in the light of the Public Law Outline below). Other parties such as grandparents may apply for leave to join the application (or apply for a residence order). Their applications should be assessed with due regard to the statutory checklist: s 10(a) (*Re J (leave to serve application for Residence Order)* [2003] 1 FLR 114, [2003] Fam Law 27, CA).

Expert evidence

D[6.2A]

In family proceedings relating to children, the court's permission is required to instruct an expert. Any such application must confirm with the President's *Practice Direction: Experts in Family Proceedings Relating to Children* [2008] All ER (D) 18 (May)). In summary the application must outline:

(i)   the category of expert evidence sought;
(ii)   the name of the expert and their CV;
(iii) the expert's timetable for reporting and availability for attending court;
(iv) the relevance of the expert evidence to the issues of the case;
(v)   an explanation if the report sought is not to be on a joint instruction. The normal expectation will be that an expert will be jointly instructed, with the guardian ad litem in public law and applicant in private law, acting as the lead party. The costs of a jointly appointed expert will be borne by the parties dependent on the reasonableness of the case (*Calderdale Metropolitan Borough Council v S* [2004] EWHC 2529 (Fam), [2004] All ER (D) 346 (Nov)).

Applications for additional assessments or for expert reports: President's guidance November 2010 (extract)

Re-read the experts' Practice Direction at [2009] 2 FLR 1383. Remember always that it is your case and your decision. An 'expert' can only be instructed if you agree, and the function of the expert is 'to provide an opinion about a question that is not within the skill and experience of the court' (PD paragraph 1.3). So always ask yourself: do I need this additional report to enable me to make a fair and proper decision? What can this expert add or contribute to the case? If the answer to the first question is 'no' and to the second 'nothing', you are unlikely to order a report (in relation to an application for a second expert's report see also the observations of the President, Sir Nicholas Wall in *R v A Local Authority* [2011] EWCA Civ 1451, [2012] 1 FLR 1302, [2012] Fam Law 265).

Process is important in family law, and every hearing you conduct must be ECHR Article s 6 and 8 compliant. This does not, of course, mean that you must accede to every parent's application for a second opinion: each decision is a matter of judgment. What is important is that your conduct of the proceedings is transparent and your conclusion is fair. This will inevitably involve balancing different factors in the manner I have already described before reaching a reasoned conclusion.

Always bear in mind the effect which any order you are being asked to make has on the time-table for the child and the case overall.

Always remember that issues of fact and credibility (who is believed and who is not) are matters for you, and not for the expert.

In public law care proceedings, judges and magistrates cannot make care orders under the Act unless they are satisfied both that the threshold criteria under section 31 of the Act are satisfied and that it is in the best interests of the child for a care order to me made. If the material available to you does not enable you to fulfil your statutory obligations to the child, say so, specifying the gap that needs filling, and – if you make an order for an expert opinion – list that as a principal reason for doing so.

Note that by virtue of paragraph 4.3(8) of the Practice Direction the party seeking permission to instruct an expert must explain why the expert evidence proposed cannot be given by social services undertaking a core assessment or by the children's guardian in accordance with their respective statutory duties.

Additional guidance: *A Local Authority v DS* [2012] EWHC 1442 (Fam), [2012] All ER (D) 06 (Jun):

(i)   The words 'the cost thereof is deemed to be a necessary and proper disbursement on [a named individual's] public funding certificate' (or words to equivalent effect) should no longer be used when the court orders a report from an expert. The words do not bind the LSC or, for that matter anybody else. In addition, there must be doubt about the court's power to make such an order. It is, in my judgment, far better to follow the words of the Regulations, particularly if the court is being asked to approve rates in excess of those allowed by the Funding Order. A copy of such an order is attached at the end of this judgment.

(ii)   The test for expert evidence will shortly import the word 'necessary'. The question which the court will have to ask itself is whether or not the report of the expert is necessary for the resolution of the case. FPR rule 25.1 will shortly be amended to insert the word 'necessary' for 'reasonably required' and there will be a new Practice Direction.

(iii)   It is the court which makes the order for the instruction of an expert, and this responsibility neither can nor should be delegated to the parties. It is of the essence of good case management that the court should identify the issues on which it wants the expert to report. It would thus be helpful and important for the tribunal to be able to say – if it is the case and the hard pressed Tribunal with a long list has had the time – that it has read all the (relevant) papers.

(iv)   If the court takes the view that an expert's report is *necessary* for the resolution of the case, it should say so, and *give its reasons*. This can be done by a preamble to the order, or by a short judgment, delivered at dictation speed or inserted by the parties with the judge's approval. I have considered this point carefully, and have come to the conclusion that this does not impose an undue burden either on the court or the profession.

(v)   There is no substitute for reasons. A consent order is still an order of the court: it is a judicial decision and must be supported by reasons. Equally, a decision by the LSC is a decision. It too should be supported by reasons.

(vi)   'Reasons' in circumstances such as these need not be lengthy or elaborate. They must, however, explain to anyone reading them *why* the decision maker has reached the conclusion he or she has particularly if the expert is seeking to be paid at rates which are higher than those set out in the table in Sch 6 of the Funding Order.

(vii)   Speed is of the essence in proceedings relating to children. An application for prior authority must be made at the earliest opportunity and, once again, must be carefully drafted and supported by reasons.

(viii)   By like token, it behoves the LSC to deal with such applications promptly and, particularly if the application is being refused, or only granted to a limited extent, to give its reasons for its decision. Once again, the reasons can be concise. Of course the solicitor seeking prior authority can go ahead regardless, and instruct the expert at the rates the expert demands, but such a suggestion, in reality, is unreal. The expert's contract is with the solicitor, and if he or she does not recover the expert's costs from the LSC, it is the solicitor who is liable. Given the exiguous rates of remuneration, this is a risk no solicitor is willing to take, particularly where the client is impecunious.

(ix)   Similar considerations to those set out above apply to any challenge to the LSC's ruling.

(x)   If a case is urgent, it should be so marked and the reasons for its urgency explained.

(xi)   Courts should familiarise themselves with Part 25 of the FPR and with Practice Direction 25A which supplements it. Specifically, they should be aware of paragraph 4.3(h) or its equivalent when amended which provides that the person wishing to instruct an expert must explain to the court why the expert evidence proposed cannot be given by Social Services undertaking a core assessment or by the Children's Guardian in accordance with their respective statutory duties. The Rule and the Practice Direction are being revised to make them (it is to be hoped) more practical and "user friendly". Practitioners should look out, in due course, for the amendments.

The Public Law Outline – Guide to Case Management in Public Law Proceedings

Revised guidance came into force on 6 April 2010. The revised guidance seeks to continue the change in the culture of case management amongst judges and lawyers. (NB: As a result of the Family Justice Review the timetable is to be altered shortly leading to an overall completion target of 26 weeks.) Issues should be focused earlier on in the process, documents necessary to resolving the issues should be identified early on, all parties should be clear on the timetable and the actions being taken by others, the number of directions hearings should be reduced and the settlement rate should increase. The process has been compressed into four stages:

Stage 1 [on Day 1 and by Day 3]	Issue of Application and the First Appointment
Stage 2 [no later than Day 45]	Case Management Conference
Stage 3 [between 16 and 25 weeks]	Issues Resolution Hearing
Stage 4 [in accordance with timetable for the child and usually within 40 weeks]	Final Hearing

Thus completing the process in a 40 week time period.

NB: Applications for emergency protection orders will continue to fall outside the scope of the PLO. A Practice Direction issued by the President on 1 April 2010 states that consideration should be given to applying the PLO in all public law proceedings and therefore it will be a decision to be taken by the court about how and when it is appropriate for the PLO to an application commenced by way of an EPO (Practice Direction: Public Law Proceedings: Guide to Case Management).

The Public Law Outline – Stages

Stage 1 – Issue and the First Appointment (FA)

D[6.2B]

ISSUE	First Appointment
On DAY 1 and by DAY 3	**By DAY 6**
Objectives: To ensure compliance with pre-proceedings checklist; to obtain the information necessary for initial case management at the first appointment	Objectives: To confirm allocation; to give initial case management directions
On Day 1:	
The Local Authority (LA) files:	Parties notify LA and court of need for a contested hearing
Application Form	
Supplementary Form PLO 1	Court makes arrangements for a contested hearing
Checklist documents	
Court officer issues application	Initial case management by court including:
Court nominates case manager(s)	
Court gives standard directions on issue including:	Confirm Timetable for child(ren)
	Confirm allocation/transfer
Pre-proceedings checklist compliance	
	Identify additional parties and representation (including allocation of children's guardian)
Allocate and/or transfer	Identify "Early Final Hearing" cases
Appoint children's guardian	
Appoint solicitor for child	Scrutinise Care Plan
Case analysis for FA	Court gives standard directions on FA including:

Invite Official solicitor to act for protected persons (non-subject children and
incapacitated adults)

List FA by Day 6

Make arrangements for contested hearing
(if necessary)

By Day 3:

Allocation of children's guardian expected

LA serves the Application Form, Supplementary Form PLO1 and the Checklist
Documents on parties

Case analysis and recommendations
for Stages 2 & 3

LA case summary

Other parties' case summaries

Parties initial witness statements

For the Advocates meeting

List Case Management Conference
(CMC) or (if appropriate) an early

Final Hearing

Upon transfer

Stage 2 – Case Management Conference (CMC)

ADVOCATES' MEETING

No later than 2 days before the CMC

Objectives: To prepare the draft Case
Management Order; to identify experts
and draft questions for them

Consider all other parties' case summaries; consider all other parties' case
analysis and recommendations

Identify proposed experts and draft
questions in accordance with Practice
Direction at D[6.2] above

Draft Case Management Order

Notify court of need for a contested
hearing

File draft Case Management Order with
the case manager/case management
Judge by 11am **one working day** before
the CMC

CMC

No later than day 45

Objectives: To identify the issue(s); to
give full case management directions

Detailed case management by the
court:

– Scrutinise compliance with directions

– Confirm timetable for the child(ren)

– Identify key issue(s)

– Confirm allocation or transfer

– Consider case management directions in the:

Draft Case Management Order

– Scrutinise care plan

– Check compliance with Experts
Practice Direction

Court Issues Case Management Order

Court lists Issues Resolution Hearing,
and where necessary, a warned period
for Final Hearing

Stage 3 – Issues Resolution Hearing (IRH)

ADVOCATES' MEETING

Between 2 and 7 days before the IRH

Objective: To prepare or update the
draft Case Management Order

IRH

Between 16 and 25 weeks

Objectives: To resolve and narrow key
issues; to identify any remaining key
issues

Consider all other parties' case summaries and case analysis and recommendations

Draft Case Management Order

Notify court of need for a contested hearing/time for oral evidence to be given

File draft Case Management Order with the case manager/case management Judge by 11am one working day before the IRH

Identification by the court of the key issue(s) (if any) to be determined

Final case management by the court:
– Scrutinise compliance with directions

– Consider case management directions in the:

Draft Case Management Order ie

– Scrutinise Care Plan
– Give directions for Hearing
– Threshold agreement or facts/issues remaining to be determined
– Final evidence and Care Plan
– Case analysis and recommendations
– Witness templates
– Skeleton arguments
– Judicial reading list/reading time/judgment + drawing up reasons
– Overall time estimate
– Bundles Practice Direction compliance
– List or confirm hearing

Court issues case Management Order

Stage 4 – Final Hearing (FH)

FINAL HEARING

In accordance with the timetable for the Child(ren)

Objective: To determine the outstanding issues

All parties file and serve updated case management documents and bundle

Draft final order(s) in approved format

Judgment/reasons

Disclose documents as required after hearing

Judicial continuity and hearing care cases

President's Guidance – Bulletin number 3: Listing and hearing care cases (April 2011) Issued by the President of the Family Division following consultation with the Senior Presiding Judge and the Chief Executive of Her Majesty's Courts and Tribunals Service, and with the approval of the Lord Chief Justice.

D[6.2C]

Background On 1st October 2010 the President's Agreements with CAF-CASS and with CAFCASS CYMRU (the Children and Families Court Advisory and support services for England and for Wales) came into effect.

The Agreements were circulated with a message from the President entitled "What case management means in practice", which (inter alia) emphasised the importance of the Public Law Outline [2010] 2 FCR 477 (the PLO), a copy of which accompanied the message.

3.1 of the PLO sets out the main principles governing court case management. Judicial continuity is one of the main principles and the PLO provides guidance on how to achieve such continuity.

It is understood that most legal advisers, magistrates and judges of all levels do not sit exclusively in the family jurisdiction, and there is a need for arrangements to be made to allow care cases to be heard in accordance with these principles.

In the December issue of Family Law the President emphasised the need to give priority to cases involving children [2010] Fam Law 1251.

In subsequent correspondence with the Chief Executive of Her Majesty's Courts (and now Tribunals) Service, Peter Handcock, the President (1) made it clear that both he and the Senior Presiding Judge are committed to ensuring that all cases receive appropriate judicial attention and proceed as expeditiously as possible; (2) re-emphasised the need for care cases to be heard within the timetable for the child; and (3) proposed issuing guidance the purpose of which was:

—   to re-emphasise the need for avoiding unnecessary delay;
—   to repeat the need for judicial continuity and efficient case management; and
—   to encourage local discussions between the relevant parties, notably the case managers, case management judges and listing officers designed to underscore the PLO and ensure that final hearings of care proceedings in particular are timeously allocated.

The President is conscious of the fact that the Family Justice System has now received the interim report of the Family Justice Review headed by David Norgrove with its emphases on judicial continuity and on proactive judicial case management.

The President and the Senior Presiding Judge encourage discussions between the Family Division Liaison Judges and the Presiding Judges to clarify any support they may give to the Designated Family Judges, Resident Judges and Justices' Clerks so that the Designated Family Judges are able to work with HMCTS and secure listing arrangements to support this Guidance.

The Guidance In the FPC, the case manager is the Justices' Clerk or assistant Justices' Clerk who manages the case. Continuity of case manager in the FPC is as essential as continuity of case management judge in the county court or the High Court.

In accordance with the PLO, on issue of a care case in the Family Proceedings Court (FPC) the court must nominate case manager(s) to be responsible for the management of the case throughout its hearings in the FPC. The name of the case manager(s) must be clearly noted on the outside of the court file.

Discussions on how to achieve continuity of magistrates and DJ(MC)s in their decisions in the Family Proceedings Courts will be held separately. Guidance on this will be issued when it has been prepared.

In accordance with the PLO, as soon as a care case is transferred to the county court from the FPC it must be allocated to one or not more than two case management judges who will be responsible for every case management stage in the proceedings through to the final hearing. One of the two judges may be a district judge with a care ticket. The arrangements for allocation will be determined by the Designated Family Judge for the care centre to which the case is transferred. It may be sensible to write the name(s) of the case management judge(s) on the outside of the court file.

In accordance with the PLO, as soon as a case is transferred to the High Court from the county court it must be allocated to a Judge of the High Court as set out in the scheme for the Royal Courts of Justice.

The PLO is not written in stone. It is a working tool designed to ensure that care cases are heard swiftly and efficiently. The case managers and case management judges will require and should expect the cooperation of the other parties. Statements and reports must be filed on time. But the key person is the case manager. He or she must be available to hear the case when it requires to be heard and what he or she says must go.

The PLO envisages four stages in each case. These are (1) the First Appointment; (2) the Case Management Conference; (3) the Issues Resolution Hearing; and (4) the Final Hearing. In some instances, these stages can be telescoped: in complex cases, it may be necessary for them to be extended. What is important at all levels of court is that (a) no hearing at any stage of the case should conclude without a date for the next hearing having been fixed for the earliest possible date; and (b) that the date fixed for the next hearing is a date on which one of the two case managers or management judges can sit to hear the case.

It is not good practice for the case to have to wait until the case manager is available to hear it. Discussions must have taken place as at 8 above to ensure that one of the two case managers or case management judges is available to take the case on the date fixed for the next appointment. In other words, the legal advisers and judges must fit their availability around the case, not the other way around. Continuity of representation is also important, and the lawyers will be expected to play their part in ensuring cases are heard without delay.

Under the PLO the final hearing is not usually fixed until the Issue Resolutions Hearing (the IRH). This makes sense in the majority of cases, since it is only at the IRH that the time needed for the final hearing can be realistically assessed. It is of vital importance that the final hearing should not be delayed by waiting for the allocated judge to become available. This will mean close liaison between the allocated judge and the listing officer in accordance with the arrangements made at 8 above. It is recognised that the judge will have other important commitments (including trying civil actions) but a balance must be struck and the judge's other commitments can and must as far as possible be fitted round the need swiftly to hear care cases.

Nicholas Wall

Applications

D[6.3]

Applicant. The local authority or an 'authorised person' (at present only the NSPCC).

Ordinarily a parent will be allowed to join proceedings as a party but this is not an absolute right. Notice has to be served even on an absent parent *(Re B (a child) (Parentage: knowledge of proceedings)* [2003] EWCA Civ 1842, [2003] All ER (D) 129 (Nov), sub nom *Re AB (care proceedings: service on husband ignorant of child's existence)* [2004] 1 FLR 527, [2004] Fam Law 17). In exceptional circumstances and after consideration of Arts 6 and 8 a parent, who has formed no family life with the child, may be excluded *(Re G* [2004] EWHC 1474 (Fam), [2004] All ER (D) 163 (May)).

Notifying the extended family. In *Birmingham City Council v S* [2006] EWHC (Fam) 3065, the local authority wished to notify paternal grandparents of the existence of care and related private law proceedings to try and identify possible alternative carers within the family. The father objected on the grounds that he feared difficulties within the family, in particular that he might be evicted from the family home. The High Court decided that the right of a child to be brought up within his/her family prevailed, unless there was some good reason to the contrary.

D[6.4]

Grounds for application (s 31). The court must be satisfied (on the balance of probabilities):

(a)   that the child concerned is suffering, or is likely to suffer, significant harm; and

(b)   that the harm, or likelihood of harm, is attributable to:

    (i)   the care given to the child, or likely to be given to him if the order were not made, not being what it would be reasonable to expect a parent to give him; or

    (ii)   the child's being beyond parental control.

In some cases an order may result even though it is not clear which parent caused which injuries to their child *(Re O and N (care: preliminary hearing)* [2003] UKHL 18, [2004] 1 AC 523, sub nom *Re O & N* [2003] 1 FLR 1169, HL).

The standard of proof in finding the facts necessary to establish the threshold for making a care or supervision order under s 31(2) of the 1989 Act or the welfare considerations in s 1 of the 1989 Act is the simple balance of probabilities child (*Re B (children) (sexual abuse: standard of proof)* [2008] UKHL 35).

D[6.4A]

Domestic violence. On May 9, 2008 the President of the Family Division issued a Practice Direction (Residence and Contact Orders: Domestic Violence and Harm (www.family-justice-council.org.uk/publications.htm). The *Practice Direction* was reissued in revised form on 14 January 2009 and reported at [2009] All ER (D) 122 (Jan). The *Practice Direction* applies equally to private and public law proceedings. See D[4.4].

D[6.4B]

Split hearings. See D[4.4].

D[6.5]

The use of the terms 'is suffering or is likely to suffer' means at the date the local authority had initiated protective arrangements. If the need for these protective arrangements ceases because the child's welfare is satisfactorily provided for otherwise, it will not be possible to found *subsequent* jurisdiction on the situation at the time of initiation of those arrangements. It is only permissible to look back from the date of disposal to the date of initiation of protection where local authority arrangements had been continuously in place (*Re M* [1994] 2 AC 424, [1994] 3 All ER 298, HL).

It was undesirable that a child should have to give evidence in care proceedings, and particular justification would be required before that course of action was taken. In considering whether to make an order (including the issue of a witness summons), the court would have to balance the need for the evidence in the circumstances of the case against what it assessed to be the potential for harm to the child (*Re M (a child) (care proceedings: witness summons)* [2007] EWCA Civ 9).

D[6.6]

In order to establish that a child was likely to suffer significant harm in the future within the meaning of the Children Act 1989, s 31 so as to enable the court to make a care or supervision order, there has to be a real possibility of the risk, based on actual facts rather that mere suspicions (*Re H* [1996] AC 563, [1996] 1 All ER 1, HL). Once the threshold test has been conceded it is not necessary to hear lengthy evidence on issues of child protection (*Re B (threshold criteria in agreed facts)* [1999] 2 FCR 328, [1998] 2 FLR 968, CA).

A supervision order may be a proportionate response to the circumstances of the case (*Re O (supervision order)* [2001] EWCA Civ 16, [2001] 1 FCR 289).

D[6.7]

Harm means ill-treatment or the impairment of health or development including, for example, impairment suffered form seeing or hearing the ill-treatment of another. It is not necessary for the harm to be proved to be due to a failure of care by one or more identified individuals but that it is attributable to an absence of care to the objective standard in the statute (*Lancashire County Council v A* [2000] 2 AC 147, [2000] 2 All ER 97, HL). Serious injury is still judged on the balance of probabilities, although the more improbable the event the stronger the evidence must be that it happened before, on that evidential burden, its occurrence will be established (*Re U; Re B (serious injury; standard of proof)* [2004] EWCA Civ 567, [2004] All ER (D) 197 (May); affd [2005] EWCA Civ 52, [2005] All ER (D) 385 (Feb).

D[6.8]

Development means physical, intellectual, emotional, social or behavioural development.

D[6.9]

Health means physical or mental health.

D[6.10]–[6.15]

Ill-treatment includes sexual abuse and forms of ill-treatment which are not physical.

D[6.16]

Significant. Where the question whether harm suffered by a child is significant turns on the child's health or development, his health or development shall be compared with that which could reasonably be expected of a similar child.

D[6.17]

Appointment of a child's guardian (s 41). The court must appoint a guardian unless it is satisfied that it is not necessary to do so in order to safeguard the interests of the child.

D[6.18]

The guardian will be appointed from CAFCASS referred to at D[4.2].

D[6.19]

The duties of the guardian include instructing a solicitor on behalf of the child and also preparing a report for the assistance of the court. The guardian's paramount consideration is to have regard to the need to safeguard and promote the best interests of the child. See D[6.24].

D[6.20]

Welfare paramount and checklist. See D[2].

D[6.21]

Delay. The court must draw up a timetable to dispose of the application. In child abuse cases the concentration should be on the factual issues which may establish the threshold test and not psychiatric or psychological assessment of the parties (*Re CB and JB (care proceeding guidelines)* [1998] 2 FCR 313, [1998] 2 FLR 211).

D[6.22]

Necessity for a court order. The court should ask itself whether an order would be better for the welfare of the child than making no order.

Orders of the court

D[6.23]

Care order. The local authority designated in the care order has parental responsibility for the child. Parents will retain their parental responsibility but the local authority may determine the extent to which the parents may meet their parental responsibility for him. The authority may only do this if it is necessary to safeguard or promote the child's welfare (s 33(4)).

D[6.24]

The court must consider a care plan when making a care order (s 31A). No order can be made unless the court has considered a care plan which may be challenged before the family proceedings court (*Re I (care proceedings; human rights claims)* (2004) 1 FLR 289). In *Re M-H (Assessment: Father of Half Brother)* [2006] EWCA Civ 1864, it was held that the evidence of the child's guardian could not fill the gaps of an independent and flawed viability assessment carried out by the local authority, and therefore, an independent assessment should have been ordered.

If the statutory threshold is met however, despite reservations concerning the care plan, the court should make the care order: *Re M (A Child)* [2009] EWCA Civ 1486.

Before making a care order the court must consider the arrangements made or proposed for contact with the child by his parents and other specified persons (s 34). There is a presumption (which is rebuttable) that there will be reasonable contact. The court may make an order regulating contact on application or of its own motion and may also make an order that there be no contact. In a matter of urgency and for no more than seven days a local authority may terminate contact without a court order. There is no power given to the court to impose conditions when making a care order (*Re T (a minor)* [1994] 2 FCR 721, sub nom *Re T (a minor)* [1994] 2 FLR 423, [1994] Fam Law 558, [1994] 21 LS Gaz R 40, CA). In *Re S (children: care plan)* [2002] UKHL 10, [2002] 2 AC 291, sub nom S (children: care plan) [2002] 2 All ER 192, HL the court said that when deciding whether to make a care order, the court should have before it a care plan which was sufficiently firm and particularised for all concerned to have a clear picture of the child's foreseeable future. However the court specifically disapproved the setting of 'starred milestones' in the order for the local authority to achieve.

D[6.25]–[6.30]

Age limit. No care or supervision order may be made in respect of a child who has attained 17 years (16 if married).

D[6.31]

Duration. A care order, unless it is brought to an end earlier, will continue in force until the child reaches 18 years (s 91(12)).

D[6.32]

Supervision order. Places a child under the supervision of a probation officer or social worker for an initial period of one year. The order may be renewed for an aggregate maximum period of three years. The supervisor is to advise, assist and befriend the child and the order may require him to notify any change of address and to allow the supervisor to visit him.

D[6.33]

The order may include a requirement to comply with directions for intermediate treatment, and psychiatric and medical treatment (see B[47.21]–B[47.24]).

D[6.34]

Obligations may be imposed on a person with parental responsibility or with whom the child is living to take reasonable steps to ensure the child complies with the requirements made of him. The making of a supervision order brings to an end any earlier care or supervision order.

Interim orders (s 38)

D[6.35]

On an application for a care or supervision order or where in other family proceedings the court has directed the local authority to investigate the child's circumstances, the court may make an interim care or supervision order as a holding measure (*Re S (children: care plan)* [2002] UKHL 10, [2002] 2 AC 291, sub nom *S (children: care plan)* [2002] 2 All ER 192).

If the interim threshold criteria are met, the best interests of the child generally dictate that it is appropriate to make an order even if eg the guardian ad litem has concerns about the local authority's interim care plan: *Re M (a child)* [2009] EWCA Civ 1486.

A residential assessment under s 38(6) is not just an assessment of the parents but of the family as a whole. It would be unfair not to have that evidence before making any firm decisions on the child's future (*Re L (a child), Re H (a child)* [2007] EWCA Civ 213).

D[6.36]

The court must be satisfied that there are reasonable grounds for believing that the circumstances are as mentioned in the grounds for a care or supervision order set out at **D[6.3]**. Interim orders (which are renewable) may not extend for more than four weeks at a time except to extend for up to eight weeks from the making of the initial order. See **D[6.24]** above.

D[6.37]

In deciding the period of an interim order, the court shall consider whether any party opposed to the making of the order was in a position to argue his case against the order in full. Where there is too much change in a case to make a final order, an interim order should be made (*Re C (a child)* [2001] EWCA Civ 810, [2001] 3 FCR 381). In *Re D (a minor: contact: interim order)* [1995] 1 FCR 501, [1995] 1 FLR 495 the court is advised to be cautious about making interim contact orders where principle of contact is in dispute/substantial factors unresolved, and to look upon interim orders as part of a coherent strategy – to be planned and implemented. For emergency protection orders see **D[9.16]**.

Exclusion requirement

D[6.38]

An exclusion order may be part of an interim care order and specify that:

(a)   someone leave a dwelling-house in which he is living with the child concerned;

(b)   someone be prohibited from entering a dwelling-house in which the child lives;

(c)   someone be excluded from a defined area in which a dwelling is located (the dwelling must be where the child lives).

D[6.39]

The following criteria must be satisfied:

(1)   there are reasonable grounds for believing that the child is suffering or is likely to suffer significant harm; and

(2)   that the harm or likelihood of harm is attributable to the care given to the child, or likely to be given to him if the order were not made, not being what it would be reasonable to expect a parent to give him; and

(3)   the court decides to make an interim care order on the basis of (1) and (2) being satisfied; and

(4)   there is reasonable cause to believe that if someone is excluded from a dwelling-house in which the child concerned lives, the child will cease to suffer, significant harm; and

(5)   that someone else living in the dwelling (who need not be a parent or a relation) is both:

    (a)   able and willing to give the child the care which it would be reasonable to expect a parent to give him; and

    (b)   consents to the exclusion requirements.

D[6.40]–[6.45]

Duration. The exclusion requirement will usually be of the same length as the interim care order but will cease to have effect if the local authority removes the child from the dwelling in question for a continuous period of 24 hours.

D[6.46]

Undertaking. The court may instead of making an exclusion requirement accept an undertaking to the same effect.

Discharge and variation of care and supervision orders (s 39)

D[6.47]

A care order may be discharged or a supervision order varied or discharged on the application of:

(a)   a person with parental responsibility for the child;
(b)   the child himself;
(c)   the local authority designated in the order.

D[6.48]

On discharging a care order a supervision order may be substituted. Further application may not be made within six months except by leave of the court (s 91(15)).

Appeals (s 94)

D[6.49]

See D[1.19]. Appeals in family proceedings now lie to the county court.

D[7]

Financial provision

D[7.1]

The family proceedings court may order a person to pay maintenance for a spouse. Maintenance for a spouse may be ordered in proceedings under the Domestic Proceedings and Magistrates' Courts Act 1978, ss 2, 6 or 7. Maintenance for a child may be ordered. Such applications were rare since the introduction of the Child Support Agency. Following the enactment of the Child Maintenance and Other Payments Act 2008 and the creation of the Child Maintenance Enforcement Commission see D[7.47].

D[7.2]

Method of payment. Payment is normally to be made through the designated officer but exceptionally, at the wish of the payee, may be made direct to her. The court may instead direct that payment be made by standing order or direct debit or make an attachment of earnings order.

Financial Provision (DPMCA, s 2)

D[7.3]

No single lump sum may exceed £1,000, but an order may provide for lump sums, say for a wife and two children (£3,000) totalling more than that. A lump sum provision might be used, for example, to apportion savings or to purchase school uniforms etc. A lump sum may be ordered to be paid by instalments.

D[7.4]

When deciding what financial provision (if any) to make **for an applicant** it is the duty of the court to have regard to all the circumstances of the case, first consideration being given to the welfare while a minor of any child of the family who has not attained the age of 18 and in particular:

(a)   the income, earning capacity, property and any other financial resources which each of the parties has, or is likely to have in the foreseeable future, including in the case of earning capacity which it would in the opinion of the court be reasonable to expect a party to the marriage to take steps to acquire;

(b)   the financial needs, obligations and responsibilities which each of the
       parties has or is likely to have in the foreseeable future;
(c)   the standard of living they enjoyed before the occurrence of the
       conduct which is the ground for making the order (this may be
       different from the standard of living at the time of parting);
(d)   the parties' ages and the duration of the marriage;
(e)   any physical or mental disability of either party;
(f)   the contributions made, or which are likely in the foreseeable future
       to be made, by each party to the welfare of the family including that
       made by looking after the home or caring for the family;
(g)   anything else which the court considers to be relevant to take into
       account; this may include the conduct of each of the parties if that
       conduct is such that it would be inequitable to disregard it (see
       Miller v Miller; McFarlane v McFarlane [2006] 3 All ER 1, HL).

D[7.5]–[7.7]

'First consideration being given to the welfare . . . of any child', means
that the child's welfare is not paramount but of first importance in deciding
maintenance payments (*Suter v Suter and Jones* [1987] Fam 111, [1987]
2 All ER 336, CA).

D[7.8]

An order in respect of the wife will cease if she remarries and orders for
children will cease normally when the child attains 17, or 18 years if the
court specifies this. This may be extended if the child is being educated, or
trained, even though the child may be in gainful employment at the same
time. It may also be extended if there are special circumstances justifying it,
for example, a disabled person unable to work.

Agreed orders (DPMCA 1978)

D[7.9]

DPMCA 1978, s 6. Either party to a marriage may ask the court for an
order making financial provision simply on the ground that the other party
has agreed to make that provision. In such a case there is no limit to the
amount of any lump sum. The court before making such an order must be
satisfied:

(a)   that the respondent (or the applicant) has agreed to make the
       financial provisions detailed in the application for the order; and
(b)   that there is no reason to think that it would be contrary to the
       interests of justice to make the order; and
(c)   where there is financial provision for children, that the order would
       either provide or make a proper contribution towards the financial
       needs of the child.

D[7.10]–[7.15]

If the court is not satisfied with the adequacy of any financial provision it
may suggest some other provision and, if the parties consent, it may make
an order accordingly. If the parties do not consent the application is to be
treated as an application for an order under s 2 in the ordinary way.

D[7.16]

DPMCA 1978, s 7. Where parties to a marriage have lived apart for a continuous period of three months without either one having deserted* the other, the court may make an order for financial provision even though the grounds stated earlier do not exist and neither is there agreement about financial provisions. In applying for an order under these circumstances the applicant must specify in the application the aggregate amount of voluntary payments made by the respondent for the maintenance of the applicant and/or the children during the three months immediately preceding the application. This aggregate figure then sets the limit on the amount which the court may order. The court may make an order for periodical payments provided that the amount payable during any three-month period under the order will not exceed the aggregate sum referred to in the application. There is no power to include lump sums in this kind of order. If the court thinks that the best it can do in these circumstances would be inadequate it may treat the application as an application for an order under s 2 in the ordinary way.

[*To be repealed by the Family Law Act 1996, Sch 10 when brought into force.]

Variation of maintenance orders

D[7.17]

The court may vary the provisions of any maintenance order it has made. In respect of maintenance for a spouse, the commonest applications are to vary the financial provisions of the order where the husband's income has been reduced or increased or where the husband pleads that a child whom he is having to support is no longer a dependent eg holding down full-time employment.

D[7.18]

When dealing with an application to vary the amount of maintenance the court is generally concerned with considering a change of circumstances since the previous order was made. This is not an inflexible rule and the court has to look at the reality of the situation. The court may have to look afresh at the means of the parties and fix the amount of maintenance as they would do so when making a new order. It is not necessary to establish a change of circumstances since an order made in divorce proceedings was registered for enforcement in the magistrates' court where the payer clearly cannot afford the order and there was clearly some mistake in the fixing of the original amount*.It is a matter of good practice that courts record their reasons in variation proceedings (*Hackshaw v Hackshaw* [1999] 3 FCR 451, [1999] 2 FLR 876, [1999] Fam Law 697).

[*Such cases can, in appropriate circumstances, be remitted back to the county court to determine the variation hearing pursuant to the Maintenance Order Act 1958, s 4(4). See *Goodall v Jolly* (1983) 147 JP 513.]

Enforcement of an order

D[7.19]

If a payer falls behind in his maintenance payments the magistrates can grant a summons or a warrant to secure his appearance before the court for an inquiry into his means.

D[7.20]

If the court is satisfied that the payer has a good reason for failing to pay the instalments (such as ill health), and is satisfied that he has no resources with which to meet the arrears then it has the power to remit part or all of the arrears; but the recipient must be given an opportunity to make written or oral representations against such a remission, unless the court considers it unnecessary or impracticable to give her such an opportunity. The starting point for courts is that arrears over a year old should not be enforced unless there are special circumstances (*B v C* [1995] 2 FCR 678, [1995] 1 FLR 467). Courts can adjourn these cases to give the payer another chance to clear the arrears but if the court is not inclined to an adjournment it may make the following orders:

(a)   Direct that payment be made by standing order or direct debit.
(b)   Order the issuing of a **distress warrant** for the seizure and sale of his property.
(c)   Make an **attachment of earnings order.** Such an order requires the employer to make weekly (or other periodical) payment into court of a fixed amount from the payer's wages.

D[7.21]

An attachment of earnings order will be able to follow him to his next job. If the court decides upon an attachment of earnings order it should inform the legal adviser before announcing this decision as the legal adviser has to obtain certain information as to the precise details of the job and works number (if any).

D[7.22]

The court must announce two figures. First, the **protected earnings rate,** which is the amount reasonable for the payer to retain having regard to his resources and needs.

D[7.23]

The second figure is the **normal deduction rate** which is the amount the court thinks reasonable to cover his liability under the order.

D[7.24]

If the court is satisfied that the defendant either has wilfully refused to pay or culpably neglected to pay and an attachment of earnings order is inappropriate (because, for example, the defendant is likely to change his job to thwart an attachment of earnings order) the court can send the defendant to **prison** unless he pays the arrears immediately. The actual period of imprisonment is limited by the amount of arrears in accordance with this table (adapted from that used in criminal proceedings):

Arrears	Imprisonment
not exceeding £200	7 days
exceeding £200 but not exceeding £500	14 days
exceeding £500 but not exceeding £1,000	28 days
exceeding £1,000	6 weeks

D[7.25]–[7.30]

Imprisonment may not be ordered in the absence of the debtor. Even where the debtor is arrested following the issue of a suspended committal order he should be informed of the nature of the proceedings and offered the opportunity of legal advice from the duty solicitor. An interpreter should be available where necessary (*Santa Cruz Ruiz v United Kingdom* [1998] EHRLR 208).

D[7.31]

If the defendant goes to prison and serves part of the sentence then the amount to secure his release is reduced proportionately.

D[7.32]

If the defendant serves the full sentence or part of it the arrears are not automatically wiped out, but the sanction of imprisonment is no longer available. Other civil rights of the person entitled to the arrears remain – see D[7.33] below.

D[7.33]

A person cannot be committed to prison twice for the same period of arrears but such arrears remain due from him and could still be enforced against him by, for example, a distress warrant (see (b) above) or by an attachment of earnings order (see (c) above).

D[7.34]

Make a suspended committal to prison for the same reasons as applied in (d) above. The length of imprisonment will be determined in accordance with the table above.

D[7.35]

The sentence of imprisonment can be suspended for a fixed time to give the payer time to pay the whole amount or suspended whilst he pays a fixed sum regularly each week off the arrears (in addition to a sum as maintenance as laid down in the order).

D[7.36]

If the defendant fails to comply the designated officer sends him a notice inviting the defendant to provide within eight days written reasons why the suspended committal order should not be put into effect. If no written answer is received within eight days the committal warrant can be released. Since the inception of the Human Rights Act 1998, common practice is to issue an arrest warrant directing the defaulter to be brought before the court to show cause why the committal warrant should not be issued.

D[7.37]

If the defendant submits his reasons they are put before a single magistrate who can either direct that the matter be considered in open court or to be make directions similar to D[7.36] above.

D[7.38]

If the defendant goes to prison and serves part of the sentence the amount to secure his release is reduced proportionately.

D[7.39]

The serving of all or even part of the prison sentence does not automatically wipe out the arrears as a debt (see D[7.32]-D[7.33] above).

D[7.40]–[7.45]

A defendant serving a sentence under (d) or (e) is entitled to apply for review of his committal to prison. It is first considered by a single magistrate who may either refuse a further review or direct that the application be considered in open court.

D[7.46]

Magistrates reviewing a committal order have wide powers. They can remit all or part of the committal, put the committal into effect, or allow it to continue on the same terms as before, or further suspend the committal on new terms. Generally arrears becoming due more than a year before commencement of an enforcement action are not enforced in the absence of special circumstances (*R v Cardiff Magistrates, ex p Czech* [1999] 1 FCR 721, [1999] 1 FLR 95).

D[7.47]

**Where a maintenance assessment has been made by the Secretary of State for Work and Pensions in relation to an 'absent parent' and that a sum or sums remain outstanding and unpaid he may apply, pursuant to the Child Support Act 1991, s 33 for a liability order. On an application for a liability order the magistrates' court must proceed on the basis that the maintenance assessment in question was lawfully and properly made. The magistrates' court is precluded from questioning any aspect of that assessment. Such an investigation is a matter to be pursued through the statutory appeal structure provided for by the 1991 Act (see *Farley (FC) v Child Support Agency* [2006] UKHL 31, [2006] 2 FCR 713; *R (on the application of the Child Support Agency) v Learad* [2008] EWHC 2193 (Admin), [2009] 1 FLR 31).

Where the Secretary of State has failed to recover an amount owing under the Child Support Act an application may be made to the court for an order for disqualification from holding or obtaining a driving licence (Child Support Act 1991, s 39A).

**The Child Maintenance and Other Payments Act 2008 came into force on 5 June 2008. The Act creates a new organisation, the Child Maintenance Enforcement Commission (CMEC). The CMEC will take over the responsibility for the Child Support Agency and the current maintenance schemes during 2008. The CMEC will then process applications where parents, including those in receipt of state benefits, decide that a private arrangement or court based consent order are not appropriate. This is likely to lead to an increase in the number of consent orders for family maintenance.

An application made pursuant to s 39A, seven years after the date of a liability order, was not 'an action to recover any sum recoverable by virtue of any enactment' within the Limitation Act 1980 s 9 and was therefore not time barred: see *Child Maintenance and Enforcement Commission v Mitchell* [2010] EWCA Civ 333, [2010] 2 FCR 526, [2010] Fam Law 696. Arguably the respondent could have pleaded an abuse of the process of the court if the CEMC had been dilatory in its enforcement of the order having regard to ECHR principles.

D[8]

Domestic violence
Non molestation orders

D[8.1]

Non molestation orders provide a remedy to any associated person from molestation. Molestation includes, but is much wider than, violence and will cover any serious pestering or harassment which is of such a degree as to merit the intervention of the family proceedings court. Revelations to a newspaper do not constitute molestation (*C v C (non-molestation order: jurisdiction)* [1998] Fam 70, [1998] 2 WLR 599).

Who can apply?

D[8.2]

The following persons may apply for non-molestation orders:

(1) Associated persons. This includes husbands and wives, civil partners (within the meaning of the Civil Partnership Act 2004), divorced couples and cohabitants and former cohabitants. Other applicants may include a wide range of relatives, those who live or have lived in the same household (other than lodgers, tenants and employees) and those who have agreed to marry one another. In relation to a child the definition includes parents, natural parents and adoptive and those with paternal responsibilities. The court should take a purposive construction of associated persons (*G v F (non molestation order jurisdiction)* [2000] Fam 186, [2000] 3 WLR 1202, sub nom G v G (non- molestation order: jurisdiction) [2000] 2 FLR 533, [2000] Fam Law 703).

There is no requirement that the said persons are cohabiting. Section 4 of the Domestic Violence Crime and Victims Act 2004 extended the definition to include persons who are no longer cohabiting but 'have or have had an intimate personal relationship with each other which is or was of significant duration'.

(2) Authorised third parties.
(3) Children under 16 with leave of the High Court.
(4) The court of its own motion when dealing with an application in family proceedings.

D[8.3]

Criteria for grant. When considering whether or not to grant an application for a non molestation order the court shall have regard to all the circumstances including the need to secure the health, safety and well being of:

(a)   the applicant;

(b)   the person for whose benefit the order is made;

(c)   any relevant child. A relevant child, includes any child whose interests the court considers relevant, any child who is living with or ought reasonably be expected to live with either party and a child who is the subject of adoption or Children Act proceedings. *Chechi v Bashier* [1999] 2 FCR 241, [1999] 2 FLR 489, CA emphasises that this is a discretionary order.

D[8.4]

Duration. The order may be for a specified duration or until further order but if made in the course of other family proceedings, it will expire if these proceedings are dismissed or withdrawn.

D[8.5]

Content of the order. The order may prohibit the respondent from molesting a named associated person(s) and relevant child. The court should endeavour to be specific as to what acts are prohibited so that the order is both understandable and enforceable.

D[8.6]

Variation. A non molestation order may be varied by:

(a)   the person who applied for it;

(b)   the respondent;

(c)   the court itself where the order was made of its own motion.

D[8.7]

Ex parte applications. An application may be made in the absence of the respondent and if necessary to a single justice in exceptional circumstances. In addition to looking at all the circumstances the court must consider whether there is any risk of significant harm to the applicant or a relevant child and whether it is likely that the applicant would be deterred or prevented from pursuing the application. The court also has power to make an ex parte order where it has reason to believe that the respondent knows of the proceedings but is deliberately evading service.

D[8.8]

Service of the order. Ordinarily the order must be served on the defendant – it is good practice to personally serve the defendant particularly if an ex parte order has been made. A copy of the order when made should also be served on the police officer in charge of the local police station in the area where the defendant resides.

If an ex parte order is made then a hearing should be listed as soon as is just and convenient to allow for representations to be made.

D[8.9]

Power of arrest modified. For orders made on or after **1 July 2007**, breach of an order is now a criminal offence triable either way (see **D[8.19]** below). A power of arrest is no longer added to the order as breach of the order is an arrestable offence and the defendant can be either charged and bailed by the police to appear before a magistrates' court (exercising a criminal jurisdiction) or produced by the police from custody.

Enforcement

D[8.10]–[8.17]

For orders made **before 1 July 2007**, if a non-molestation order is breached, the order is enforced (under the power of arrest) by bringing the defendant back before the family court that made the order.

For orders made **on or after 1 July 2007**, the applicant/victim has a choice on how to proceed:

(a) He/she can contact the police. The defendant is arrested as in D[8.9] above. The Crown Prosecution Service should be notified by the police and they decide how the case is to proceed. Family courts have no extra role unless contacted for papers. There is no legal requirement for a family panel member to sit on the breach proceedings but this may represent good practice.

(b) He/she can make a committal application (to commit the defendant to custody or prison for contempt of court. The maximum powers of the family proceedings court remain unaffected ie up to two months' imprisonment.

D[8.18]

If arrested in pursuance of a committal application the defendant must be produced to the court within 24 hours (excluding Christmas day, Good Friday and Sunday). When the arrested person is brought before the court the attendance of the arresting officer is not necessary unless the arrest itself is in issue. A written statement from the arresting officer should normally be sufficient (*Practice Direction* 19 January 2000).

Sanction for breach

Civil Contempt

D[8.19]

Upon hearing a breach application the court may adjourn the case and may remand the respondent to a later date on civil bail, with or without conditions. If the breach is proved on the balance of probabilities the court may order the respondent:

(a)   to pay a sum not exceeding £50 for every day he is in breach up to £1,000, or a sum not exceeding £5,000; or

(b)   to be committed to custody for a period not exceeding two months or until he has remedied his default in such shorter period.

Offence of breaching a non-molestation order: s 42A Family Law Act 1996

This new provision was added by s 1 of the Domestic Violence, Crime and Victims Act 2004. The offence came into force on 1 July 2007. The offence is triable either way. It carries 6 months' (**12 months) imprisonment on summary conviction and up to 5 years' imprisonment on indictment.

Section 42A(1) provides: 'A person who without reasonable excuse does anything that he is prohibited from doing by a non-molestation order is guilty of an offence'.

Where the defendant raises a defence of reasonable excuse the burden rests with the Crown to negative that defence: *R v Richards* (unreported), 9/3/10, CA.

Section 42A(2): 'In the case of a non-molestation order made under s 45(1), a person can be guilty of an offence under this section only in respect of conduct engaged in at a time when he was aware of the existence of the order'.

Section 42A(3) declares that the offence is not punishable as a contempt of court when there is a conviction under s 42A. Similarly, that the defendant cannot be convicted under s 42A where the conduct has been punished as a contempt of court.

SGC sentencing guidelines have been published and are to be found at A[46.4] onwards.

D[8.20]

A civil committal to custody as a contempt may be suspended upon condition of obedience to the order. However the Court of Appeal has indicated that in the case of a serious breach it must be understood that punishment will take place immediately (*Neil v Ryan* [1999] 1 FCR 241, [1998] 2 FLR 1068, CA).

Undertakings

D[8.21]

Where the court has the ability to make a non molestation order, and there have been no threats of violence or violence used, they may accept an undertaking from the parties. An undertaking is a promise by a party to the court that they will do or refrain from doing some defined act.

D[8.22]

Sanctions. The sanctions for breach as a civil contempt are the same as those outlined above for breach of a civil order.

Occupation orders

D[8.23]

The family proceedings court shares a jurisdiction with the county court and the High Court to make declaratory and regulatory occupation orders. These orders deal with rights of occupation or exclude a person from all or part of the dwelling. A power of arrest may be attached to the order.

D[8.24]

These applications are unusual in the family proceedings court and should be the subject of detailed consultations with the legal adviser.

D[8.25]

A judge was not wrong in exercising his discretion to order an occupation order under the Family Law Act 1996, s 33(6), to exclude a father from the matrimonial home for a three-month period after finding that the children would suffer serious harm if the parents continued to live together. Although an occupation order was draconian and interfered with property rights, it was appropriate to grant it in exceptional circumstances: *Re L (Children) (Occupation order: absence of domestic violence)* [2012] EWCA Civ 721, [2012] All ER (D) 189 (Jun).

D[9]

Protection of children

(Children Act 1989)

Police powers (Children Act 1989, s 46)

D[9.1]

Where the police have reasonable cause to believe that a child would otherwise suffer significant harm, they may remove the child to suitable accommodation and keep him in police protection for up to 72 hours. They must also inform the local authority, persons having parental responsibility for the child and anyone with whom he was living before he was taken into police protection.

Duties of the local authority (Children Act 1989, s 47)

D[9.2]

Where a local authority are:

(a)   informed that a child is:
       (i)   the subject of an emergency protection order (see **D[9.16]**), or
       (ii)   in police protection, or
(b)   have reasonable cause to suspect that a child is suffering or is likely to suffer, significant harm

the authority must make such inquiries as they consider necessary to enable them to decide whether they should take any action to safeguard or promote the child's welfare.

D[9.3]

The action which the local authority may take may include applying for one of the following orders.

Child assessment order (Children Act 1989, s 43)

D[9.4]

Only a local authority or the NSPCC may apply for this order. Where the court is satisfied that:

(a)   the *applicant* has reasonable cause to suspect that the child is suffering, or is likely to suffer, significant harm;
(b)   an assessment of the state of the child's health or development or of the way in which he has been treated is required to enable the applicant to determine whether or not the child is suffering or is likely to suffer significant harm; and
(c)   it is unlikely that such an assessment will be made, or be satisfactory, in the absence of an order under this section

it may make a child assessment order.

D[9.5]–[9.6]

Welfare of child and necessity for order. See D[2] and D[4].

D[9.7]

Notice must be given where reasonably practicable to the child's parents and other persons specified in the Children Act 1989, s 43(11).

D[9.8]

The order must specify the date by which the assessment is to begin and will have effect for up to seven days from that date. It is then the duty of any person who is in a position to produce the child to do so to such person as is named in the order and to comply with court directions concerning the assessment.

D[9.9]

A child may be kept away from home only in accordance with directions in the order and only if it is necessary for the purposes of the assessment. Where the child is away from home, the order must contain such directions as the court thinks fit with regard to contact with other persons.

D[9.10]–[9.15]

Assessment and emergency protection. A court cannot make a child assessment order where there are grounds for making an emergency protection order and it considers it ought to make such an order.

Emergency protection order (Children Act 1989, s 44)

D[9.16]

An emergency protection order authorises the removal of a child to accommodation provided by the applicant for the period specified in the order.

D[9.17]

Grounds. Any person may apply for an emergency protection order. The court may make the order where it is satisfied:

(a)   (all applicants) there is reasonable cause to believe that the child is likely to suffer significant harm if he is not removed to accommodation provided by the applicant; or

(b)   (local authority applicant) inquiries are being made because of the local authority's suspicion that the child is suffering or is likely to suffer significant harm (see D[6.3]) which are being frustrated by an unreasonable refusal of access and access is required as a matter of urgency; or

(c)   (NSPCC) the applicant has reasonable cause to suspect that a child is suffering or is likely to suffer significant harm and inquiries into the child's welfare are being frustrated as in (b) above.

D[9.18]

The court may consider any evidence (including hearsay) which it considers relevant to the application.

X Council v B (emergency protection orders) [2004] EWHC 2015 (Fam) gives a review of relevant authorities in this area.

In *Re X: Emergency Protection Orders* [2006] EWHC 510 (Fam), [2006] Fam Law 627, Mr Justice McFarlane made the following observations together with some additional guidance:

(a) the 14 points made by Munby J in *X Council v B* above should be copied and made available to the justices hearing an EPO on each and every occasion such an application is made;

(b) it is the duty of the applicant for an EPO to ensure that the *X Council v B* guidance is brought to the court's attention;

(c) mere lack of information or a need for an assessment can never of themselves establish the existence of a genuine emergency to justify an EPO. The proper course in such a case is to consider application for a Child Assessment Order or issuing s 31 proceedings and seeking the court's directions under s 38(6) for assessment;

(d) evidence given to the justices should come from the best available source. In most cases this will be from the social worker with direct knowledge of the case;

(e) where there has been a case conference with respect to the child, the most recent case conference minutes should be produced to the court;

(f) where the application is made without notice, if possible the applicant should be represented by a lawyer, whose duties will include ensuring that the court understands the legal criteria required for both an EPO and an application without notice;

(g) the applicant must ensure that as full a note as possible of the hearing is prepared and given to the child's parents at the earliest possible opportunity;

(h) unless it is impossible to do so, every without notice hearing should either be tape recorded or be recorded in writing by a full note being taken by a dedicated note taker who has no other role (such as clerk [legal adviser]) to play in the hearing;

(i) when the matter is before the court at the first 'on notice' hearing, the court should ensure that the parents have received a copy of the clerk's [legal adviser's] notes of the EPO hearing together with a copy of any material submitted to the court and a copy of the justices' reasons;

(j) cases of emotional abuse will rarely, if ever, warrant an EPO, let alone an application without notice;

(k) cases of sexual abuse where the allegations are inchoate and non-specific, and where there is no evidence or immediate risk of harm to the child, will rarely warrant an EPO;

(l) cases of fabricated or induced illness, where there is no medical evidence of immediate risk of direct physical harm to the child, will rarely warrant an EPO;

(m)   justices faced with an EPO application in a case of emotional abuse, non specific allegations of sexual abuse and/or fabricated or induced illness, should actively consider refusing an EPO application on the basis that the local authority should then issue an application for an interim care order. Once an application for an ICO has been issued in such a case, it is likely that justices will consider that it should be transferred up for determination by a county court or the High Court;

(n)   the requirement that justices give detailed findings and reasons applies as much to an EPO application as it does to any other application. In a case of urgency, the decision may be announced and the order made with the detailed reasons prepared thereafter;

(o)   where an application is made without notice, there is a need for the court to determine whether or not the hearing should proceed on a without notice basis (and to give reasons for that decision) independently of any subsequent decision upon the substantive EPO application.

Applications under section 38(6) of the Act – President's guidance November 2010 (extract)

(1)   There are additional factors which should be taken into account when dealing with applications under ss 38(6) and (7).

(2)   It is, I think, worthwhile remembering that s 38 of the Act deals with interim care orders and interim supervision orders. So the court cannot make an order under s 38(6) unless such an order is or will be in place. Section 38(6) is thus an exception to the general rule that where a care order is made, the local authority is in the driving seat and can effectively dictate how parental responsibility is to be exercised under s 33.

(3)   The two leading cases are the decisions in the House of Lords in *Re C (a minor) (interim care order: residential assessment)* [1997] AC 489, [1996] 4 All ER 871, HL (*Re C*) and *Re G (a child) (interim care order: residential assessment)* [2005] UKHL 68, [2006] 1 AC 576, [2006] 1 All ER 706, [2006] 1 FLR 601 (*Re G*). They should be re-read.

(4)   Two points of law were decided by *Re C*. They are: (i) That ss 38(6) and (7) of the Act are to be broadly construed and "confer jurisdiction on the court to order or prohibit any assessment which involves the participation of the child and is directed to providing the court with the material which, in the view of the court, is required to enable it to reach a proper decision at the final hearing of the application for a full care order" (per Lord Browne-Wilkinson); and (ii) that the phrase "the medical or psychiatric examination or other assessment of the child" in s 38(6) is not to be interpreted so as to restrict assessments to the medical or psychiatric.

(5)   In addition, *Re C* makes it clear that it is impossible to assess a young child divorced from his or her environment and thus the assessment includes the relationship between the parents and the child or children concerned.

(6)   *Re G*, whilst adopting the broad approach set out in *Re C* decides that an assessment under s 38(6) does not include therapy or treatment, particularly for a parent. Inpatient treatment was thus beyond s 38(6) and the court had no power to order it under the sub-section.

(7)   Lord Scott, who conducts a helpful review of the authorities, specifically agreed with a statement by Holman J in *Re M (Residential Assessment Directions)* [1998] 2 FLR 371 at 381 which I think it useful to follow. Holman J said:

> The court's powers . . . are limited to a process that can properly be described as "assessment" rather than "treatment" although no doubt all treatment is accompanied by a continuing process of assessment. And they are limited to a process which bona fide involves the participation of the child as an integral part of what is being assessed

(8)   Section 38(6) should thus be seen as part of the essential evidence gathering process. Plainly, if the proposed assessment is in fact a therapeutic intervention for the benefit of the parents, you will refuse the application. If, on the other hand, the assessment falls within Holman J's statement in *Re M*, that will be a factor which opens the door to the exercise of your discretion.

For a more recent judgment where the Court of Appeal upheld the decision of a Judge to refuse a residential parental assessment under s 38(6) see: *TL (a child) (residential parenting assessment), Re* [2011] EWCA Civ 812. A summary of the guidance in *TL* is set out below.

When a residential assessment should be ordered	When a residential assessment should not be ordered
Two questions to be asked: Does this child's welfare warrant an assessment under s38(6)? Looking at this child's timetable is there evidence that this mother will be able to adequately care for the child within the child's timetable?	

When a residential assessment should be ordered	When a residential assessment should not be ordered
If there is a real risk of the parent losing the child forever BUT there is no right to an assessment – the question is whether the assessment will provide important information to assist the court.	If the assessment will jeopardise the final hearing.
If the assessment is not going to unduly delay the final hearing.	A residential assessment is opposed.
There is a clear and unchallenged expert recommendation for such an assessment.	Experts do not recommend such an assessment.
There is a change in dynamic eg the mother has separated from the father whereby the prospects of successful rehabilitation have materially improved	Expert evidence suggests that the parent is not capable of safely looking after the child in the community within the child's timeframe.
EH v LB Greenwich [2010] EWCA Civ 344, [2010] PTSR (CS) 23, [2010] 2 FCR 106	Previous assessments have failed.
Re L (children) (care order: residential assessment)[2007] EWCA Civ 213, [2007] 3 FCR 259, [2007] 1 FLR 1370	The parents appear reluctant to address such issues as to the volatility of their relationship or substance misuse.
Re B (a child) [2007] EWCA Civ 556, [2007 2 FLR 979, [2007] Fam Law 798	The parent has a record of failing to co-operate with assessments or attempts by professionals to help them.
M (a child) (care order), Re [2009] EWCA Civ 315, [2009] 2 FLR 950, [2009] Fam Law 570	The assessment would involve removing the child from a current secure placement .
K (a child) (care order), Re [2007] EWCA Civ 697, [2007] 2 FLR 1066, [2007] Fam Law 797	*Re S* [2008] EWCA Civ 1078, [2009] 2 FLR 397, [2008] Fam Law 1187
	Re J (a child) (care proceedings: assessment) [2009] EWCA Civ 1210, [2010] Fam Law 131, [2010] 1 FLR 1290 *Re T (a child) (residential parenting assessment)* [2011] EWCA Civ 812, [2011] 3 FCR 343, [2012] 2 FLR 308 (which reviews the most recent authorities and should be treated as the current leading case)

D[9.19]

Welfare of child and necessity for order. See D[2] and D[4].

D[9.20]

Child's Guardian. See D[3.24]

Effect of the order

D[9.21]

The order:

(a)   Directs any person in a position to do so to produce the child on request to the applicant.

(b)   Authorises removal of the child to the applicant's accommodation and his retention there.

(c)   Gives parental responsibility to the applicant which he may only exercise to the extent reasonably required to safeguard or promote the child's welfare.

(d)   May contain directions as to any medical or psychiatric examination of the child.

(e)   Presumes contact with parents and other persons specified in the Children Act 1989, s 44(13) subject to any more restrictive direction in the order.

(f)   May require a person who has information relating to the child's whereabouts to disclose that information (s 48).

(g)   May authorise the applicant to enter premises specified in the order and search for the child (s 48(3)).

D[9.22]

Where the court is satisfied that there is reasonable cause to believe that there may be another child on the premises who should be subject to an emergency protection order, it may authorise the applicant to search for that child and if the applicant is satisfied that the grounds for an order are satisfied the order has effect as if it were an emergency protection order (s 48).

Exclusion requirement

D[9.23]

As with interim care orders if the court is able and decides to make an emergency protection order but is satisfied that the reasons and grounds for making the order would be removed if someone is excluded from the dwelling in which the child lives and that someone else living there is both:

(a)   able and willing to give to the child the care which it would be reasonable to expect a parent to give him; and

(b)   consents to the exclusion requirement,

the court may make the requirement.

D[9.24]

The requirement may:

(a)   specify that someone leave the dwelling-house in which he is living with the child concerned;

(b)   specify that someone be prohibited from entering a dwelling-house in which the child lives;

(c)   exclude someone from a defined area in which a dwelling-house is located (the dwelling-house must be where the child lives).

D[9.25]–[9.30]

This allows the child to remain in its dwelling despite the making of the order.

D[9.31]

Undertaking. The court may, instead of making an exclusion requirement, accept an undertaking to the same effect.

D[9.32]

Warrant of entry. The intentional obstruction of a person exercising powers of search and removal of a child subject to an emergency protection order is a criminal offence. Where it appears to the court that a person has been or is likely to be prevented from exercising these powers by being refused entry to premises or access to the child, it may issue a warrant authorising the police to assist using reasonable force if necessary.

D[9.33]

Duration. An emergency protection order shall have effect for such period not exceeding eight days as may be specified in the order with special provision for public holidays. This period normally includes any period already in police detention. The order may be extended once for a further period of up to seven days.

D[9.34]

Discharge. The child, his parents, or anyone having parental responsibility or with whom the child was living prior to the making of the emergency protection order may apply to the court after 72 hours to have the order discharged unless they were present at the making of the order. There is no right of appeal in respect of the making of an emergency protection order.

D[10]–D[15]

Recovery order
(Children Act 1989, s 50)

D[10.1]

Where it appears to the court that there is reason to believe that a child in care or subject to an emergency protection order or in police protection has been unlawfully taken away, has run away or is missing, it may make a recovery order.

D[10.2]

Application is by a person with parental responsibility by virtue of a care order or emergency protection order; or where the child is in police protection, for the purposes of s 46 CA 1989, the designated officer.

D[10.3]

The recovery order may:

(i)   direct a person to produce the child;
(ii)   authorise the removal of the child;
(iii)   require disclosure of the child's whereabouts;
(iv)   authorise a constable to enter specified premises to search for the child, using reasonable force if necessary.

D[16]

Child abduction

D[16.1]

Child Abduction Act 1984. It is a criminal offence triable either way for a person 'connected' with a child under 16 to take or send the child out of the United Kingdom without the appropriate consent.

D[16.2]

'Connected' persons include a parent, guardian, a special guardian of the child, or a person having custody, or in whose favour a residence order is in force, or a person reasonably believed to be the father of an illegitimate child.

D[16.3]

'Appropriate consent' is that of persons who are parents, guardians, a special guardian of the child, or in whose favour a residence order is in force, or any person who has custody of the child.

D[16.4]

Provision is also made for the protection of children subject to various court proceedings such as care and adoption. It is also an offence for other persons to take a child from the lawful control of any person having lawful control of the child.

Where the appropriate consent has been given and the child is kept out of the UK beyond the defined period no offence is committed because the removal of the child must relate to a specific event rather than a continuing activity: *R (on the application of Nicolaou) v Redbridge Magistrates' Court and CPS* [2012] EWHC 1647 (Admin), [2012] 2 Cr App Rep 290, 176 JP 441.

D[16.5]

The Child Abduction Act 1984 provides certain defences for the person who has taken the child out of the jurisdiction.

A mother who subjectively believed her daughter to be at risk of sexual abuse by her father was not entitled to rely on the defence of necessity against a charge of abduction where, in order to protect her, she had removed her from the jurisdiction in breach of a consent order. The whole purpose of making removal an offence under the 1984 Act was to reinforce the objective of retaining the child within the jurisdiction so that they could be subject to the court's protection. The defence of necessity was not available within that legislative scheme: *R v CS* [2012] EWCA Crim 389, [2012] 1 Cr App Rep 429, 176 CL&J 157.

D[17]

School attendance and truancy proceedings

(Education Act 1996)

D[17.1]

A magistrate who is a member of the local authority which is also the education authority should not adjudicate in this type of case.

D[17.2]

The educational duty of every parent or guardian of a child or young person of compulsory school age is 'to cause him to receive efficient full time education suitable to his age, ability and aptitude and to any special educational needs he may have, either by regular attendance at school or otherwise'.

D[17.3]

Compulsory school age is normally from 5 to 16. The actual date when a pupil reaches school-leaving age may be after his sixteenth birthday, for example, the date the term ends. Education legislation prescribes the exact dates and if there is any doubt in a particular case as to whether a 16-year-old has passed the date or not, consult the legal adviser. In this type of proceedings the pupil must be presumed to be of compulsory school age unless his parents prove the contrary.

D[17.4]

As against a parent there are two types of proceedings, which can only be brought by a local education authority:

(1)   The local education authority can serve a school attendance order requiring the parent to register the child at the school named in the order. Before doing this the local education authority must have served on the parent a notice giving the parent at least 15 days in which to satisfy it that the child is already receiving efficient full time education suitable to his age, ability and aptitude and to any special educational needs he may have. If the education authority wishes to continue proceedings it must serve a notice stating the school it intends to specify in the order (or, if it thinks fit, several schools from which the parent can choose one). Thus, the first set of proceedings is in effect for **failure to comply with a school attendance order.**

(2) The second type of proceedings is where the child or young person is a registered pupil at a school but has failed to attend regularly. This is an absolute offence and does not contravene art 6 of the ECHR (*Barnfather v Islington Education Authority* [2003] EWHC 418 (Admin), [2003] All ER (D) 89 (Mar); however, a child shall not be deemed to have failed to attend school regularly if:

(a) he was absent with leave; or

(b) he was absent through sickness or any unavoidable cause; or

(c) he was absent on a day of religious observance kept by the religious body to which his parent belongs; or

(d) his parents prove that the school is not within walking distance and the local authority have not arranged transport. If one of these defences is raised, consult the legal adviser.

The local education authority may issue a fixed penalty notice of £50 against a parent who fails to send their child to school. Payment is a bar to proceedings but non payment after 42 days may result in a summons to court.

D[17.5]

If convicted in either set of proceedings the parent can be fined on level 3. Note that the court is also empowered to make a parenting order. If the court is satisfied that the parent knows that the child is not attending regularly and fails without reasonable cause to ensure attendance this aggravated version of the offence is punishable by a level 4 fine and/or three months' imprisonment [**51 weeks when the CJA 2003, Sch 26 is brought into force]. The court may direct the local education authority to bring proceedings before the family proceedings court for an education supervision order.

For a prosecution under s 444(1A) see *R (on the application of P) v Liverpool City Magistrates* [2006] EWHC 2732 (Admin), (2006) 170 JP 453. In this case it was held that the parent bears an evidential rather than a legal burden when seeking to establish 'legal justification'.

Local education authorities may also apply for parenting order following a second exclusion in a 12 month period under s 20 of the Anti Social Behaviour Act 2003.

Education supervision orders

D[17.6]

The local education authority may bring proceedings for an education supervision order on the ground that a child is not being educated properly (where, for example, he is not complying with a school attendance order or is not attending regularly at a school at which he is a registered pupil, see above). Unless previously discharged, an education supervision order will last for one year initially but may be extended for periods of up to three years at a time until the child reaches school leaving age. The supervisor is under a duty to advise, assist and befriend and give directions to the child and his parents to secure that the child is properly educated. A parent who persistently fails to comply with a direction may be guilty of an offence (a maximum fine, level 3).

Care proceedings may be brought and the statutory grounds may be satisfied on evidence of non-school attendance alone (*Re O (a minor)* [1992] 4 All ER 905, [1992] 1 WLR 912).

D[17A]

Child safety order
(Crime and Disorder Act 1998, s 11)

D[17A.1]

This order may be made in the family court on application by the local authority. It is aimed at protecting children under 10 years who may be involved in crime or in anti-social behaviour. The applicant must prove one or more conditions:

(a) the child has committed an act which would have constituted an offence but for his age;
(b) an order is necessary to prevent an act as mentioned in (a) above;
(c) the child has contravened a curfew notice; and
(d) the child has caused harassment alarm or distress to someone outside the child's household.

D[17A.2]

The order places the child under the supervision of a responsible officer for three months but this may be up to 12 months.

D[17A.3]

The court can impose conditions to ensure the child:

(i) receives support, protection or control;
(ii) is prevented from repeating the behaviour which resulted in the order.

If a child breaches the order the court may make a parenting order.

D[18]

Adoption proceedings

(Adoption and Children Act 2002)

D[18.1]

Under the Adoption and Children Act 2002, a child may only be placed for adoption in one of two ways, where there is consent of a parent or under a placement order of the court. During the placement with prospective adopters the local authority has a duty to manage, oversee and review the child's progress.

Consensual Placement

D[18.2]

An adoption agency may place a child for adoption if it is satisfied that each parent has consented to a placement (Adoption and Children Act 2002 s 19). CAFCASS will be involved in witnessing such consents to placement at the request of the adoption agency.

This route cannot be used where there is a pending application for a care order or a placement order has been made. In such circumstances any application made by the local authority must be under the Adoption and Children Act 2002 s 22.

Placement Orders

D[18.3]

Freeing for adoption is abolished and replaced by a system of placement orders. (This is an order authorising a local authority to place a child up for adoption with any prospective adopters chosen by the authority.) The court may not make a placement order unless the child is subject to a care order or it is satisfied the conditions (Children Act 1989 s 31) for a care order are met or the child has no parent or guardian and each parent has consented to a placement order, or the court dispenses with that consent (Adoption and Children Act 2002 ss 21 and 52). [For consideration of the transitional provisions where a child had been freed under s 18 of the Adoption Act 1976, but proceedings for adoption commenced under the 2002 Act see *Re F (adoption: notice of hearing)* [2006] All ER (D) 205 (Oct).]

Once a placement order is made only a local authority may remove the child and it continues in force until it is revoked, the child marries, attains 18 years or the adoption order is made in respect of the child.

Consequences of a placement order

D[18.4]

The consequences of a placement order are as follows:

(i)   Parental responsibility for the child is given to the adoption agency and the prospective adopters for the duration of the placement. The parents' parental responsibility is not extinguished but it is shared with the prospective adopters and the agency. It is for the agency to decide on any necessary and proportionate restrictions of the parental responsibility of a parent or of a prospective adopter.

(ii)   Any contact provision under the Children Act 1989 ceases to have effect but the court can order contact under s 26 either on application or of its own motion.

(iii)   The child may not be given a new surname or removed from the UK for more than a month unless each parent consents or the court grants leave.

(iv)   Any care order is 'suspended' whilst the placement order is in force, any supervision order or s 8 order ceases to have effect and there are prohibitions on certain orders being applied (s 29(3)–(5)).

(v)   Once a placement order is made no parent or guardian may oppose the making of any adoption order unless the court grants leave. The court cannot grant such leave unless satisfied that there has been a change of circumstances since the placement order was made.

Applications for Placement Orders

D[18.5]

In order to avoid delay, a local authority **must** apply for such an order (s 22) when:

(i)   a child is placed for adoption with them or is being provided with accommodation, no agency is authorised to place the child for adoption, the child has no parent or guardian or the conditions under s 31(2) of the 1989 Act (to make a care order) appears to be met and the local authority is satisfied that the child ought to be placed for adoption, or;

(ii)   an application has been made and not disposed of on which a care order might be made or the child is subject to a care order but there is no authority to place him/her for adoption and the local authority is satisfied that the child ought to be placed for adoption.

A local authority is prohibited from making a placement order until it has decided that adoption is the most appropriate placement for the child. In making such a decision a local authority is acting as an Adoption Agency and is therefore unable to reach this conclusion until the matter has been considered by the Adoption Panel and ratified by the local authority decision maker (*Re P-B (a child)* [2006] EWCA Civ 1016). NB: Regulations implementing the Family Justice Review recommendations on adoption panels have now been laid before Parliament. The Adoption Agencies (Panel and Consequential Amendments) Regulations 2012, SI 2012/1410 came into force on 1 September 2012. Arrangements are being made for the revised statutory adoption guidance to be made available on the Department's website. A formal announcement to local authorities of the Regulations and revised guidance was made in June 2012.

The 2012 regulations remove the requirement for a Local Authority adoption panel to give approval to a child being placed for adoption before a placement order can be made. This should speed up placing children as a result of care proceedings where the final plan is adoption

It was an insufficient foundation for a placement order that the long-term aim of the court was that the child should be adopted. The necessary foundation was that the child was presently in a condition to be adopted, and was ready to be adopted, even though in some cases the court had to countenance the possibility of substantial difficulty and therefore delay in finding a suitable adoptive placement or even of failure to find one. In making the placement order, the court had to be satisfied that the requirements of ss 1(1) and (2) and s 22 of the 2002 Act had been met (*Re S-H a child) (placement order)* [2008] EWCA Civ 493).

Permission to advertise for Adoption

D[18.5A]

A number of *principles* apply when a family court is asked to consider an application to advertise a child for adoption (see *Re K (Permission to advertise for adoption)* [2007] EWHC (Fam) 544).

The principles may be stated as follows:

(i)   Before a child may be advertised by a local authority as available for adoption, the local authority must be satisfied that the child ought to be placed for adoption.

(ii)   When advertising a child as available for adoption, the local authority is acting as an adoption agency and therefore before advertising the case, must first go before the local authority adoption panel. The panel must make a recommendation as to the child's placement for adoption.

(iii)   In determining whether to grant permission the child's welfare is the court's paramount consideration.

(iv)   The court and local authority must bear in mind that any delay in the process is likely to prejudice the child's welfare.

(v)   Delay is but one, albeit important, factor in the overall process. The court must also be aware of the duty to act fairly and be seen to do so with respect to the other parties in the overall process. Family members and the child have ECHR Art 6 rights to a fair trial which must be kept in focus.

(vi)   Under Art 8 ECHR, any such advertising must be necessary and proportionate to the needs of the child.

Judicial guidance on advertising. The following guidance was handed down in *Re K* [2007] EWHC (Fam) 544:

(a)   It is not open to a local authority to place an advertisement advertising a particular child as available for adoption until the authority has obtained the necessary recommendation from its adoption panel and has decided that the child should be placed for adoption in compliance with the Adoption Agencies Regulations 2005.

(b)   Where an application is made where the court has yet to hold a final hearing in care proceedings and has yet to endorse the local authority's care plan for adoption, the court is unlikely to give permission to advertise unless the adoption plan is unopposed or there is some [unusual or] exceptional feature of the case that justifies advertisement eg where the mother has died, or cannot be traced.

(c)   In considering such an application the court should bear in mind the local authority has existing sources for discovering potential adopters eg its own register. The child's status should also be borne in mind eg if permission is given, prior to the authority having legal authority to place the child any advertisement cannot boldly state that the child is available for adoption.

(d)   Where a care order has been made and the local authority's adoption plan has been approved by the court, but a placement order has yet to be made, it is more likely that such an application will be looked on favourably by the court, without having to look for unusual or exceptional circumstances.

(e)   In any case where the court has yet to approve the adoption plan, the court is likely to require sight of the precise words that are to be used in the advertisement to describe the child's status at that time.

(f)   Other than specialist adoption publications the court is likely to require clarity as to the identity or type of publications that are to be approached; the precise terms of the advertisement should be ascertained by the court.

(g)   As a matter of common sense the court should consider granting permission for a full advertisement (which identifies the child and carries a photograph) or refusing to give permission at all, rather than sanctioning an anonymous advertisement.

Parental Consent

D[18.6]

Two of the key components of making a placement order are:

(i)   consent of the parent or guardian, or alternatively,
(ii)   dispensing with consent.

The issue of dispensing with parental consent is now dealt with at the early stages of the placement decision.

The court will consider the s 1 principles, which apply to the dispensing of consent, and consider the welfare checklist (see D[18.19]).

Consent to the placement is of central importance because it can have the effect of removing the parent from any subsequent adoption hearing unless the court gives permission to oppose. The local authority must clearly go through three stages before a child can be placed for adoption: see *Re S (a child) (placement order: revocation)* [2008] EWCA Civ 1333, [2009] 1 FLR 503.

Specified proceedings (ACA s 122)

D[18.7]

Applications to make or revoke placement orders are specified proceedings within s 41 of the Children Act 1989. Therefore the child will be a party and the children's guardian will be appointed by the court. The guardian will appoint a solicitor to represent the child. See *Re S (a child) (placement order: revocation)* at D[18.6]) above. The three stages are: (1) The local authority must consider whether adoption is in the best interests of the child. (2) If yes, once that is granted, the authority must approve the adopter. (3) The adoption panel determines that the child is matched to the adopter. Only then will the child be considered to have been 'placed for adoption'.

Adoption orders

D[18.8]

An adoption order is an order giving parental responsibility for a child to the adopters. Any pre-existing orders for maintenance or orders under the Children Act 1989 are extinguished.

An adoption order can be made in respect of any child under the age of 18 years who is not, or has not been, married and can even be made even if the child has previously been adopted.

Applications for an Adoption Order

D[18.9]

Applicant must qualify for eligibility by virtue of age, domicile and residence.

D[18.10]

The Applicants. An application can be made either by a couple or one person. A couple may be married or living in an enduring relationship. A step parent or partner may adopt as a single applicant under the Adoption and Children Act 2002, s 51(2).

D[18.11]

Identity of the applicants. Where the applicants wish their identity to be confidential, they may apply for a serial number to be assigned to them. This number will be used instead of their names.

D[18.12]

Residence of the child with the applicants. Before an adoption order can be made the court must be satisfied that a probationary period where the child has been placed with the applicant has occurred. In the case of an agency adoption the period is 10 weeks, for a non agency parent or partner adoption the period is 6 months. Local authority foster parents may not adopt unless the child has its home with them for at least a year or the court gives its leave.

Application to the court

D[18.13]

An adoption application is made in a prescribed form.

D[18.14]

The court. An application can be made to the High Court, a county court or a magistrates' court but an application involving the *applicants* or *child* living abroad cannot be made to a magistrates' court. In respect of applications made or transferred to a county court, the case must be sent to a county court adoption centre or inter-country adoption centre as set out in the amended Children (Allocation and Proceedings) Order 1991.

Consent

D[18.15]

ACA 2002, s 52 is of general application to both placement and adoption.

'Consent' to the placement of a child for adoption or the making of an adoption order means:

> 'consent given unconditionally and with full understanding of what is involved; but a person may consent to adoption without knowing the identity of the persons in whose favour the order will be made'.

'Freely' has been omitted from the definition under ACA 2002 in recognition that many parents struggle against their own feelings in giving consent in the children's best interests.

The persons who have the right to consent are the parent 'having parental responsibility' or the guardian of the child (which includes a special guardian).

Those 'parents' who qualify are:

(1)   The birth mother.
(2)   The birth father, where he is married to the child's mother at the time of the child's birth or if he subsequently marries the mother.
(3)   An unmarried father if:
         (i)   he becomes registered as the child's father under the Birth and Deaths Registration Act 1953 or

    (ii)   he makes a parental responsibility agreement with the child's mother; or

    (iii)   he is granted a parental responsibility order by the court.

(4)   The child's adoptive parent, where the child has been the subject of a previous adoption.

Dispensing with Consent

D[18.16]

There are now only two grounds for dispensing with a parent's consent (ACA 2002, s 52(1)). These are:

Where the court is satisfied that:

(a)   the parent or guardian of a child cannot be found or is incapable of giving consent; or

(b)   the welfare of the child requires the consent to be dispensed with. (The availability of post adoption contact is a relevant factor to be taken into account when deciding whether to dispense with the parent's agreement and to make a freeing order (*Down Lisburn Health and Social Services Trust v H* [2006] UKHL 36, [2007] 1 FLR 121).

General Principles

D[18.17]

Whenever the court is making a decision in relation to placement orders, adoption orders or their revocation, contact under ACA 2002, s 26 (in relation to placements) or granting leave it must consider ACA 2002, s 1.

D[18.18]

Factors to consider therefore are:

(1)   The effect of the delay. ACA 2002, s 1(3) applies the general principle that delay is prejudicial to the child's welfare and s 109 lays down a statutory obligation on the court to draw up a timetable to minimise delay.

(2)   The whole range of powers and the 'no order' principle. ACA 2002, s 1(6) sets out two key principles which set out the context in which the welfare principle itself must operate.

    (i)   That the court or adoption agency must always consider the whole range of powers available to it in the child's case (either under ACA 2002 or under the Children Act 1989) [see the Children and Adoption Act 2006 when in force] and;

    (ii)   The court must not make any order unless it considers that making the order would be better for the child than not doing so (the 'No Order' principle).

The Welfare Checklist and Other Factors

D[18.19]

ACA 2002, s 1(2) provides that 'the paramount consideration of the court or adoption agency must be the child's welfare throughout his life'.

ACA 2002, s 1(4) states what the court or the adoption agency should consider in relation to the child's welfare: this checklist is very similar to the one used in the Children Act 1989.

The things that the court will consider include (among others)—

(a) the child's ascertainable wishes and feelings regarding the decision (considered in light of the child's age and understanding),
(b) the child's particular needs,
(c) the likely effect on the child (throughout his life) of having ceased to be a member of the original family and become an adopted person,
(d) the child's age, sex, background and any of the child's characteristics which the court or agency considers relevant,
(e) any harm (within the meaning of the CA 1989) which the child has suffered or is at risk of suffering,
(f) the relationship which the child has with relatives and with any person in relation to whom the court or agency considers the question to be relevant including—
    (i) the likelihood of any such relationship continuing and the value to the child of its doing so,
    (ii) the ability and willingness of any of the child's relatives, or of any such person, to provide the child with a secure environment in which the child can develop and otherwise to meet the children's needs,
    (iii) the wishes and feelings of any of the child's relatives or any such person regarding the child.

Procedural Requirements – Rules/Practice Directions

D[18.20]

A new single set of rules will cover all three levels of court (High Court, county court and magistrates' court).

The Family Procedure (Adoption) Rules 2005 (FPAR)

D[18.21]

These extend the application of the Civil Procedure Rules to some areas of adoption work and harmonisation with the CPR of all rules relating to family proceedings is in hand.

These rules are supplemented by a number of Practice Directions which are as follows:

— Who receives a copy of the application form for orders in the proceedings

—   The first directions hearing – adoptions with a foreign element
—   Forms
—   Reports by the adoption agency or local authority
—   Reports by registered medical practitioner ('health reports')
—   Litigation friends
—   Court documents
—   Communication of information relating to the proceedings
—   Service
—   Service out of the jurisdiction
—   Human rights
—   Joining the Crown
—   Disclosing information to an adopted adult
—   Alternative procedure for applications (Part 8)
—   Applications (Part 9)
—   Civil restraint orders
—   Interim injunctions
—   Written evidence
—   Depositions and court attendance by witnesses
—   Change of solicitor.

The courts and all parties are subject to the overriding objectives, namely,

'to enable the court to deal with cases justly, having regard to the welfare issues involved'.

D[18.22]

FPAR rule 1. This means that court staff have a responsibility to support the judiciary in ensuring that:

(1)   the parties are on an equal footing
(2)   the case is dealt with fairly and in a timely way
(3)   the case is dealt with in ways which are proportionate to the nature, importance and complexity of the issues
(4)   an appropriate share of the court's resources are allotted to the case and
(5)   expense is spared.

D[18.23]

Rule 4 of FPAR 2005 lays down the court's duty to actively manage cases in order to further the overriding objective.

D[18.24]

This will include:

—   monitoring timetables and directions which have been fixed by the judiciary
—   assisting in progress of the case by referring back to the Judge or the legal adviser as necessary
—   ensuring that family lists provide sufficient court time to cover as many aspects of the case as it can on the same occasion
—   facilitating the attendance of the applicants at any hearing or hearing their evidence by telephone or any other method of direct oral communication.

D[18.25]

Part 10 of FPAR 2005 indicates that the Civil Procedure Rules 1998 (Part 3) apply in relation to the court's case management powers.

The Role of CAFCASS in Adoption and Placement

D[18.26]

If it appears that the parent is willing to consent and it is within the jurisdiction of the court then the court will appoint a reporting officer to witness the documents.

D[18.27]

The reporting officer:

(1)   Ensures that consent is given unconditionally and with full understanding

(2)   Investigates all circumstances relevant to consent

(3)   Writes a report/makes an interim report if parent is unwilling to consent and the court will then inform the applicant.

D[18.28]

Placement/revocation of placement orders are specified proceedings and therefore a child's guardian will be appointed unless the court is satisfied it is not necessary to protect his interests.

D[18.29]

The court will have a new power to appoint a CFR (Children and Family Court Reporter) in an adoption case. On of his/her duties will be to advise the court whether the child should be joined as a party.

NB: the same officer may hold more than one role in relation to the child at the same time.

D[18.30]

The child will be a respondent and therefore a party joined in the proceedings where:

—   permission has been granted to a parent or guardian to oppose the making of the adoption order (s 47(3) or (5));

—   he or she opposes the making of an adoption order;

—   a child and a family reporter recommends that it is in the best interests of the child to be a party to the proceedings and that recommendation is accepted by the court;

—   he or she is already an adopted child;

—   any party to the proceedings or the child is opposed to –

       (1)   the arrangements for allowing any person contact with the child; or

       (2)   a person not being allowed contact with the child after the making of the adoption order;

— the application is for a Convention adoption order or a s 84 order;
— he or she has been brought into the United Kingdom in the circumstances where s 83(1) applies (restriction on bringing children in);
— the application is for an adoption order other that a Convention adoption order and the prospective adopters intend the child to live in a country or territory outside the British Islands after the making of the adoption order; or
— the prospective adopters are relatives of the child.

D[18.31]

The court also retains a general discretion, at any time, to direct that;

— a person should be made/removed as a respondent.
— a child should be made a respondent where he/she;
  (a) wishes to make an application, or;
  (b) has evidence to give or a legal submission to make that will not be made by any other party, or;
  (c) there are special circumstances.

D[18.32]

The rules introduce a presumption that any child who has been joined in adoption proceedings should be represented by a guardian unless the court is satisfied that it is not necessary to protect his interests. Also, older children who hold divergent views from his/her guardian will be able to seek the leave of the court to instruct a solicitor directly.

Special Guardianship Orders

D[18.33]

ACA 2002, s 115 has inserted new sections 14A–G into the Children Act 1989, which includes the new provision of Special Guardianship Orders (SGOs).

D[18.34]

They are intended to be another option for permanence available to the court.

They are deemed to be **Private Law Proceedings** and the principles of the Children Act 1989 will apply. Aside from where the court is considering an order of its own motion, an applicant must seek the leave of the court. Once leave is given by the court the applicant must give 3 months' notice to his/her local authority (see *Birmingham City Council v R* (2006) Times, 29 December).

In *R (a child)* [2006] EWCA Civ 1748 the following was decided:

(a) A person who requires the permission of the court to make an application for a special guardianship order cannot either make an application for such an order or give notice of his intention to do so unless and until he has obtained the court's permission to make the application.

(b)   Section 14A(8), which imposes a duty on a local authority to prepare a special guardianship report, is not triggered where a person who requires the court's permission to make an application but has not obtained it, purports to give notice of his intention to apply for a special guardianship order.

(c)   The court should not invoke s 14A(9) to compel a local authority to perform its statutory obligations at the instance of a person who needs but has not yet obtained permission unless s 14A(6)(b) applies, that is, the court considers that a special guardianship order should be made even though no such application has been made.

(d)   There is nothing in the primary or secondary legislation which permits the court to restrict the nature and scope of a report under s 14A(8).

The case of *Re S (a child) (SGO)* (2007) Times, 9 February, makes clear that a court is entitled to make a SGO in adoption proceedings of its own motion, subject to the appropriate local authority report being sought and provided (see **D[18.38]** below).

D[18.35]

The Children Act welfare checklist applies, not the ACA 2002 checklist.

Effects of Special Guardianship Orders

D[18.36]

SGOs are intended to meet the needs of children who cannot live with their birth parents but for whom an adoption order is not appropriate.

D[18.37]

The special guardian appointed by the order has parental responsibility for the child and is entitled to exercise that parental responsibility to the exclusion of any other person with parental responsibility with **two exceptions**:

(1)   It does **not** affect any of the rights, which a natural parent has in relation to a child's adoption or placement for adoption. Parents retain the right to consent, or not, to these applications.

(2)   It does **not** affect the operation of any rule of law which requires the consent of all those with parental responsibility, for example, the sterilisation or circumcision of the child.

Parents will retain their parental responsibility, but the exercise of that responsibility will be limited.

In *Re L (a child)* [2007] EWCA Civ 196, the Court of Appeal confirmed the refusal of a care Judge to refuse the grandparent's application to change the child's surname on the making of a special guardianship order. The test was what was best for the child's welfare and there was no presumption in favour of a change merely because the relevant statute identified the change of name as a factor.

D[18.38]

The making of an SGO discharges all care orders.

The Local Authority has to investigate and write a report and the court may also appoint a CAFCASS officer and request a welfare report. The need for a local authority report is mandatory although in some cases an authority need not complete an entirely new report (see the guidance in *Re S (a child) (adoption order or special guardianship order)* [2007] EWCA Civ 90).

Disclosure of Information about a person's adoption

D[18.39]

Under ACA 2002 access to information is filtered through adoption agencies so as to provide an intermediary safeguard before disclosure is made.

Sections 54 and 56 to 65 (the disclosure group of sections) deal with different types of information.

D[18.40]

Section 54 *information*, which an adoption agency is required to disclose to prospective adopters.

Section 56 *information* or *'protected'* information, which an adoption agency must keep in relation to a person's adoption:

(1)   Information about the adopted person including his birth parents and siblings, his adoptive parents and siblings and other relatives.
(2)   Any information kept by the adoption agency (a) which is necessary to enable an adopted person to obtain a certified copy of the record of his birth or (b) which is information about an entry relating to an adopted person in the Adoption Contact Register.

It includes *'identifying'* information, which means information which identifies the person or enables the person to be identified.

D[18.41]

Section 58 *information* or 'background' information (which does not fall into either category).

The System for Disclosure

D[18.42]

In brief:

—   The adoption agency is the single point of access for 'identifying information', including the information necessary to access a birth record.

— Protected information may only be disclosed by the agency pursuant to ss 57–65. The system for disclosure of protected information is subject to criminal sanctions imposed on adoption agencies who contravene the disclosure provisions.

D[18.43]

Certain background information must be disclosed to adopters and may be disclosed to certain persons for the purposes of the agency's functions.

D[18.44]

The adopted adult, has the right, at his request, under s 60:

— to receive from the agency the information disclosed to the adopters by the agency under s 54

— to receive from the adoption agency the information necessary to obtain his birth record ('the birth record information') unless the High Court orders otherwise. For the High Court to do so, there must be an application by the agency for permission not to disclose and the High Court must be satisfied that the circumstances are exceptional

— to receive from the court, which make the adoption order, a copy of:

(1) the application form for an adoption order (but not the documents attached);

(2) the adoption order and any other orders relating to the adoption proceedings;

(3) orders allowing a person contact with the child after the adoption order was made;

(4) any document or order referred to in the relevant Practice Direction. The court will remove any protected information from any such copy document or order before it is given to the adopted person.

D[19]

Family proceedings where a party may lack capacity to conduct proceedings

Legislation and Guidance

D[19.1]

The following should be referred to:

- Part 15 Family Procedure Rules 2010
- Practice Direction 15A – Protected Parties
- Mental Capacity Act 2005
- Guidance issued by the Children in Safeguarding Proceedings Committee of the Family Justice Council – Parents who lack capacity to conduct proceedings (May 2010) http://www.family-justice-council. org.uk/docs/Parents_who_Lack_Capacity_with_appendices.pdf
- The Official Solicitor's Role in Children's Cases http://www.court funds.gov.uk/docs/parentsnetworkarticle.doc
- *Re P (a child) (care and placement order proceedings: mental capacity of parent)* [2008] EWCA Civ 462, [2009] LGR 213, [2008] 3 FCR 243

Protected persons and capacity

D[19.2]

A protected person is a party who does not have capacity within the meaning of the Mental Capacity Act (MCA) 2005 to conduct proceedings. Section 1 of the MCA 2005 states the general principle that a person must be assumed to have capacity unless it is established otherwise.

Section 2(1) establishes that a person lacks capacity in relation to a matter if, at the material time, he is unable to make a decision for himself in relation to the matter because of an impairment of or disturbance in the functioning of the mind or brain, whether the impairment is permanent or temporary.

Assessment of capacity is both issue and time specific, for example, a person suffering from dementia may lack capacity to manage their own finances but have capacity to decide upon where they would like to live.

A person may lack capacity to conduct proceedings at the outset of a case due to an acute episode of mental illness but regain capacity at a later point having received treatment.

There will be cases where there is a dispute as to capacity, either because the person involved does not agree to be assessed or accept the outcome of an assessment or where experts disagree. In these situations the court is required to make a finding as to capacity. These decisions are likely to be complex and consideration should be given at the outset of the case as to whether it is appropriate to transfer to the county court.

Litigation friends

D[19.3]

Where it is established that a party is found to lack capacity, r. 15.2 of the FPR 2010 provides that the party concerned must have a litigation friend to conduct proceedings on their behalf.

Appointment of a litigation friend

The following persons can act as a litigation friend.

(a) The Official Solicitor – May only be appointed with his consent and by court order under r 15.6. Consent will only be given where: there is satisfactory evidence or a finding of the court as to a lack of capacity to conduct proceedings; there is no other suitable person to take on the role of Litigation Friend; the OS has received confirmation that there is security for the costs of legal representation (this is covered if the party is in receipt of public funding).

In spite of these restrictions it is extremely rare for any other person to act as a LF to a parent within care proceedings. Generally the OS will instruct the solicitor originally chosen by the protected person to ensure continuity.

(b) A person with legal authority as a deputy to conduct proceedings in the name of a protected person or on that person's behalf – no court order is required however the deputy must file a copy of the order, declaration or other document conferring their authority. (Rules 15.4(2) and 15.5(2))

(c) If there is no person with authority then any other person may act as litigation friend if the court is satisfied that they meet the conditions set out in r. 15.4(3) namely that they:

— can fairly and competently conduct proceedings on behalf of the protected party;

— have no interest adverse to that of the protected party; and

— undertake to pay any costs which the protected party may be ordered to pay in relation to the proceedings, subject to any right that person may have to be repaid from the assets of the protected party.

Such a person can become a litigation friend without a court order by filing a certificate of suitability to act (r 15.5.(3)); or, by way of court order under r 15.6.

The court may exercise a power to appoint a litigation friend of its own motion or on the application of the person wishing to become the LF or a party to the proceedings (r 15.6(2)).

Under r 15.7 the court may direct that a person may not act as a litigation friend, terminate a LF's appointment or substitute a new LF for an existing one. In the FPC only a court may exercise the power to appoint/terminate the appointment of/substitute a litigation friend.

Practice Direction 15A – Protected Parties imposes additional procedural requirements in respect of litigation friends

Responsibilities of a litigation friend

A litigation friend (including the OS) is under a duty to fairly and competently conduct the proceedings on behalf of the protected party. The OS will consider the protected party's views and wishes as communicated by the instructed solicitor and set them out in his final statement to the court. They will not however be determinative of the OS's approach, which will be based on an assessment of the protected person's best interests and may differ from the protected party's views. The OS will present any realistic argument and relevant evidence to the court by reference to what is reasonably arguable rather than likelihood of success.

The OS will consider whether, and if so how, a protected party should be provided with an opportunity to have their say, even where the OS has decided not to contest proceedings on their behalf, and will seek the court's agreement to this.

The case of *Re P (a child) (care and placement order proceedings: mental capacity of parent)* [2008] EWCA Civ 462, [2009] LGR 213, [2008] 3 FCR 243 provides guidance as to the role of the OS (and litigation friends generally) in relation to care proceedings and includes a supplement in which the OS sets out a summary of his practice.

Allocation

D[19.4]

For the first time, the 2010 Rules allow the FPC to invite the OS to act for a protected party. As a result there is no absolute requirement to transfer proceedings to the county court simply because a party lacks capacity.

Nevertheless there will clearly be cases where the issues are such that the matter is not suitable for retention by the FPC.

Examples of circumstances where this might apply are: if an assessment as to capacity is disputed and the court is required to make a finding in this regard; where a litigant in person may lack capacity; if the court must consider whether to dispense with consent to placement for adoption on the grounds of lack of capacity and the party opposes this course of action.

Suggested procedure in cases where capacity is an issue:

(a)   Where a legal adviser to a party reasonably entertains a doubt as to the ability of their client to give proper instructions he/she is under a professional duty to satisfy himself/herself as quickly as possible whether the client has capacity in this regard.

(b)   Where the court is notified that potential lack of capacity is an issue (and this may be as a result of information from the party's legal adviser or, often, from an applicant local authority) the court should ensure that the party's solicitor obtains an assessment as to capacity as quickly as possible from a suitably qualified expert (who may be either a treating clinician or an independent expert). The Official Solicitor has produced standard letters of instruction and a certificate as to capacity which should be used (see pages 21–42 of the Guidance issued by the Children in Safeguarding Proceedings Committee of the Family Justice Council – Parents who lack capacity to conduct proceedings).

(c)   Where the party concerned is in person the court should instruct the solicitor for another party (generally the children's solicitor) to arrange for an assessment as to capacity. In this situation the case is likely to be complex and, therefore, may require transfer to the county court.

(d)   The court will need to adjourn the proceedings in order for an assessment to take place. Because a single justice/JC/AJC is not able to appoint a litigation friend an adjourned hearing in the FPC will need to be before a court. Although the court may be limited as to the progress it can make at this stage it should consider whether it can make case management directions which are not dependent upon the outcome and which would not be prejudicial to the relevant party. A 'liberty to apply to vary/set aside' clause may be appropriate.

(e)   The court may also be asked to make interim orders (eg care, supervision or residence). Because a party may lack capacity the court must consider carefully whether it is appropriate and necessary to deal with such an application at this stage, balancing child protection needs against rights to a fair trial and respect for private and family life.

(f)   When adjourning, the court should also consider the issue of allocation, in particular whether it is inevitable that, if the assessment concludes that the party does not have capacity to conduct proceedings, the matter would need to be transferred to the county court. If that is the case then provision could be made for such a transfer to take place without the need for a further hearing in the FPC (and any directions hearing that had been listed in the FPC vacated).

(g)   The solicitor for the party concerned will explain the conclusions of any assessment to their client. If the party wishes to dispute the opinion of the expert or has declined to be assessed then, as stated above, the court will need to make a finding as to capacity. This may of itself be a reason to transfer to the county court.

(h)   Where there is no dispute that a party lacks capacity the issue of a litigation friend will arise. In the absence of an authorised deputy, initially the question of the identity of the LF is for the protected party and their solicitor to consider ie is there a friend or relative who is suitable and willing to take on the role? If so, then the solicitor will consider whether to issue a certificate as to suitability under r 15.5(3) and the court will consider whether to accept it.

(i) Only where there is no suitable 'other person' will the question of appointment of the Official Solicitor arise. The OS will need to be appointed as litigation friend subject to his agreement and be formally invited to take on that role. The court will need to include the following provisions within any order:

   (1) The Official Solicitor is invited to become Litigation Friend for XXXX and, with his agreement, shall be appointed as such.

   (2) [The court has determined that] [It is agreed that] XXXX lacks capacity to conduct proceedings.

   (3) There is no other person suitable or available to act as Litigation Friend.

   (4) Security for the costs of the Official Solicitor is available by way of ... (in care cases usually through public funding)

   (5) Permission is granted to the solicitor for [XXXX] [the children] to disclose this order and a case summary [and the following documents] to the Official Solicitor.

   An adjournment of 28 days or so will be required to enable the invitation to be considered and responded to. The solicitor for the protected party will be responsible for forwarding the order, a case summary and other relevant documentation to the OS. The court will need to grant permission for disclosure to the OS of the order and any other documentation relating to the proceedings.

(j) Rule 15.3 places strict restrictions upon the steps that parties can take prior to the appointment of a litigation friend without the court's permission. The court will therefore also need to consider whether to make directions permitting certain actions to be taken prior to the formal appointment of the OS.

(k) If an invitation to act is accepted the Official Solicitor will generally instruct the party's original solicitor to act as his agent. The case is therefore likely to continue with little interruption or delay. As set out in section 3 above the OS will consider at every stage what representations to make to the court and in particular whether it is appropriate to request that the court consider evidence direct from the protected party. If so then the OS and court will need to consider whether special measures are required to safeguard the welfare of the protected party.

(l) Where an issue other than conduct of proceedings arises which requires the consent of the protected party (eg disclosure of medical records, medical treatment for a child) it may be necessary for their capacity in that regard to be separately assessed. In the case of consent to placement for adoption this should generally not be necessary as this is considered to be an aspect of 'conduct of proceedings'.

(m) Where there is a clear indication that a protected party may have regained capacity the court should request that a further assessment as to capacity take place. If it is established that the party does now have capacity the litigation friend should apply for discharge so that the party can resume conduct of the proceedings themselves.

Guidance in cases involving the Official Solicitor

D[19.5]

The Official Solicitor and the President met in order to discuss the difficulties which the Official Solicitor had been having in accepting requests to act as guardian ad litem/litigation friend for protected parties in proceedings relating to children. The Official Solicitor's role in proceedings under the Mental Capacity Act 2005 was also discussed. At the end of the meeting the President invited Pauffley J to draft guidance for courts dealing with such cases.

That guidance is now attached. It has been seen by, and has the endorsement of, both the Official Solicitor and the President.

Nicholas Wall [President]
December 2010

Guidance in cases involving protected parties in which the Official
Solicitor is being invited to act as guardian ad litem or litigation friend

Public and private law children's cases

(1)   Many practitioners and judges will know of the Official Solicitor's recent difficulties in accepting requests to act as guardian ad litem/litigation friend for protected parties in proceedings relating to children. Although, currently, there are unallocated cases, the backlog has reduced significantly in recent months.

(2)   The Official Solicitor is subject to severe budgetary constraints – a situation which is unlikely to ameliorate in the medium term.

(3)   In all cases, the Official Solicitor will need to be satisfied of the following criteria before accepting a case, and parties may need reminding of the need to provide confirmation of these matters immediately on approaching the Official Solicitor's office: satisfactory evidence or a finding by the court that the party lacks capacity to conduct the proceedings and is therefore a protected party; confirmation that there is security for the costs of legal representation; there is no other person who is suitable and willing to act as guardian ad litem/litigation friend.

(4)   In order to assist the Official Solicitor in the decisions he makes about allocating case workers, in certain cases, judges should consider whether it may be appropriate to indicate with as much particularity as possible the relative urgency of the proceedings and the likely effect upon the child (and family) of delay. The Official Solicitor will very carefully consider giving priority to such cases.

(5)   It is and remains the judge's duty in children's cases, so far as he is able, to eradicate delay.

Court of Protection welfare cases (including medical cases)

(6) The number of welfare cases brought under the provisions of the Mental Capacity Act 2005 is rising exponentially with concomitant resource implications for the Official Solicitor.

(7) Judges should be alert to the problems the Official Solicitor may have in attending at each and every preliminary hearing. Consideration should be given, in appropriate cases, to dispensing with the requirement that he should be present at a time when he is unable to contribute meaningfully to the process. In circumstances where his position has been/will be communicated in writing it may be particularly appropriate for the judge to indicate that the Official Solicitor's attendance at the next directions' hearing is unnecessary

(8) The Court of Protection Rules make clear that the judge is under a duty to restrict expert evidence to that which is reasonably required to resolve the proceedings. The explanatory note to r 121 states that the court will consider what 'added value' expert evidence will give to the case. Unnecessary expert assessments must be avoided. It will be rare indeed for the court to sanction the instruction of more than one expert to advise in relation to the same issue.

(9) The Practice Direction – Experts (PD15A) specifies that the expert should assist by "providing objective, unbiased opinion on matters within his expertise, and should not assume the role of advocate". The form and content of the expert's report are prescribed, in detail, by paragraph 9 of the Practice Direction. It is no part of the expert's function to analyse or summarise the evidence. Focused brevity in report writing is to be preferred over discussion.

Mrs Justice Pauffley
December 2010

Practice Note – The Official Solicitor: Appointment in family proceedings

D[19.6]

The Official Solicitor: Appointment in family proceedings

Practice directions and notes – Official Solicitor – Appointment as guardian ad litem – Appointment as next friend – Terms of appointment

(1) This Practice Note supersedes the Practice Note dated 4 December 1998 issued by the Official Solicitor in relation to his appointment in family proceedings. It is issued in conjunction with a Practice Note dealing with the appointment of Officers of CAFCASS Legal Services and Special Casework in family proceedings. This Practice Note is intended to be helpful guidance, but always subject to Practice Directions, decisions of the court and other legal guidance.

(2) The Children and Family Court Advisory and Support Service (CAFCASS) has responsibilities in relation to children in family proceedings in which their welfare is or may be in question

(Criminal Justice and Court Services Act 2000, s 12). From 1 April 2001 the Official Solicitor will no longer represent children who are the subject of family proceedings (other than in very exceptional circumstances and after liaison with CAFCASS).

(3)   This Practice Note summarises the continuing role of the Official Solicitor in family proceedings. Since there are no provisions for parties under disability in the Family Proceedings Courts (Children Act 1989) Rules 1991, the Official Solicitor can only act in the High Court or in a county court, pursuant to Part IX of Family Proceedings Rules 1991. The Official Solicitor will shortly issue an updated Practice Note about his role for adults under disability who are the subject of declaratory proceedings in relation to their medical treatment or welfare.

Adults under disability

(4)   The Official Solicitor will, in the absence of any other willing and suitable person, act as next friend or guardian ad litem of an adult party under disability, a "patient". "Patient" means someone who is incapable by reason of mental disorder of managing and administering his property and affairs (Family Proceedings Rules 1991, rule 9.1). Medical evidence will usually be required before the Official Solicitor can consent to act and his staff can provide a standard form of medical certificate. Where there are practical difficulties in obtaining such medical evidence, the Official Solicitor should be consulted.

Non-subject children

(5)   Again in the absence of any other willing and suitable person, the Official Solicitor will act as next friend or guardian ad litem of a child party whose own welfare is not the subject of family proceedings (Family Proceedings Rules 1991, rr 2.57, 9.2 and 9.5). The most common examples will be:

(i)   A child who is also the parent of a child, and who is a respondent to a Children Act or Adoption Act application. If a child respondent is already represented by a CAFCASS officer in pending proceedings of which he or she is the subject, then the Official Solicitor will liaise with CAFCASS to agree the most appropriate arrangements.

(ii)   A child who wishes to make an application for a Children Act order naming another child (typically a contact order naming a sibling). The Official Solicitor will need to satisfy himself that the proposed proceedings would benefit the child applicant before proceeding.

(iii)   A child witness to some disputed factual issue in a children case and who may require intervener status. In such circumstances the need for party status and legal representation should be weighed in the light of *Re H (Care Proceedings: Intervener)* [2000] 1 FLR 775;

(iv)   A child party to a petition for a declaration of status under Part III of the Family Law Act 1986.

(v)   A child intervener in divorce or ancillary relief proceedings (r 2.57 or r 9.5).

(vi)   A child applicant for, or respondent to, an application for an order under Part IV of the Family Law Act 1996. In the case of a child applicant, the Official Solicitor will need to satisfy himself that the proposed proceedings would benefit the child before pursuing them, with leave under Family Law Act 1996, s 43 if required.

(6)   Any children who are parties to Children Act or inherent jurisdiction proceedings may rely on the provisions of Family Proceedings Rules 1991 rule 9.2A if they wish to instruct a solicitor without the intervention of a next friend or guardian ad litem. Rule 9.2A does not apply to Adoption Act 1976, Family Law Act 1996 or Matrimonial Causes Act 1973 proceedings.

Older children who are also patients

(7)   Officers of CAFCASS will not be able to represent anyone who is over the age of 18. The Official Solicitor may therefore be the more appropriate next friend or guardian ad litem of a child who is also a patient and whose disability will persist beyond his or her 18th birthday, especially in non-emergency cases where the substantive hearing is unlikely to take place before the child's 18th birthday. The Official Solicitor may also be the more appropriate next friend or guardian ad litem in medical treatment cases such as sterilisation or vegetative state cases, in which his staff have particular expertise deriving from their continuing role for adult patients.

Advising the court

(8)   The Official Solicitor may be invited to act or instruct counsel as a friend of the court (amicus) if it appears to the court that such an invitation is more appropriately addressed to him rather than (or in addition to) CAFCASS Legal Services and Special Casework.

Liaison with CAFCASS

(9)   In cases of doubt or difficulty, staff of the Official Solicitor's office will liaise with staff of CAFCASS Legal Services and Special Casework to avoid duplication and ensure the most suitable arrangements are made.

Invitations to act in new cases

(10)   Solicitors who have been consulted by a child or an adult under disability (or by someone acting on their behalf, or concerned about their interests) should write to the Official Solicitor setting out the background to the proposed case and explaining why there is no other willing and suitable person to act as next friend or guardian ad litem. Where the person concerned is an adult, medical evidence in the standard form of the Official Solicitor's medical certificate should be provided.

Invitations to act in pending proceedings

(11)   Where a case is already before the court, an order appointing the Official Solicitor should be expressed as being made subject to his consent. The Official Solicitor aims to provide a response to any invitation within 10 working days. He will be unable to consent to act for an adult until satisfied that the party is a "patient". A further directions appointment after 28 days may therefore be helpful. If he accepts appointment the Official Solicitor will need time to prepare the case on behalf of the child or patient and may wish to make submissions about any substantive hearing date. The following documents should be forwarded to the Official Solicitor without delay:

(a)   a copy of the order inviting him to act (with a note of the reasons approved by the judge if appropriate);

(b)   the court file;

(c)   if available, a bundle with summary, statement of issues and chronology (as required by President's Direction of 10 March 2000).

Contacting the Official Solicitor

(12)   It is often helpful to discuss the question of appointment with the Official Solicitor or one of his staff by telephoning 020 7911 7127. Inquiries about family proceedings should be addressed to the Team Manager, Family Litigation.

The Official Solicitor's address is: 81 Chancery Lane, London WC2A 1DD. DX 0012 London Chancery Lane Tel: 020 7911 7127 Fax: 020 7911 7105

Email enquiries@offsol.gsi.gov.uk

2 April 2001
Laurence Oates, Official Solicitor

D[20]

Making the child a party and representation for the child in non-specified proceedings

Legislation and guidance

D[20.1]

The following should be kept in mind:

— Making the child a party to the proceedings is a step that will be taken only in cases which involve an issue of significant difficulty and consequently **will occur in only a minority of cases**. Where this is an intractable dispute over residence or contact, including when all contact has ceased, or where there is irrational but implacable hostility to contact or where the child may be suffering harm associated with the contact dispute. *Source: Practice Direction 16A, Part 4, paras 7.1 and 7.2 (specifically 7.2 (c) in this case).*

— Family Proceedings Rules 2010, Part 16, r 16.2 – Before taking the decision to make the child a party, consideration should be given to whether an alternative route might be preferable, such as asking an Officer of the Service or a Welsh family proceedings officer to carry out further work or by making a referral to social services or, possibly, by obtaining expert evidence. This is where it is essential to be aware of local practices. *Source: Para 7.1 as above.*

— It must be recognised that separate representation of the child may result in a delay in the resolution of the proceedings. When deciding whether to direct that a child be made a party, the court will take into account the risk of delay or other facts adverse to the welfare of the child. The court's primary consideration will be the best interests of the child.

Para 7.4 states:

> When a child is made a party and a children's guardian is to be appointed:
>
> Consideration should first be given to appointing an officer of the Service or Welsh family proceedings officer. Before appointing an officer, the court will cause preliminary enquiries to be made of Cafcass or CAFCASS CYMRU.

— Transfer of proceedings should also be considered at this and every hearing. It might be prudent to clarify local practice with the Designated Family Judge. *Source: Paras 7.3 and 7.5 above.*

— CAFCASS and the National Assembly for Wales Practice Note June 2006: [2006] 2 FLR 143.

— Pages 2817–2820 The Family Court Practice 2010.

— Article 15 of the Allocation and Transfer of Proceedings Order 2008.

The youth court

E[1]

Juveniles

(Children and Young Persons Acts 1933, 1963 and 1969)

E[1.1]

Children (those aged under 14) and young persons (those aged 14 or under 18) are juveniles. Cases involving juveniles are heard in the youth court apart from exceptional cases in criminal proceedings where the juvenile appears before the adult magistrates' court charged with an adult defendant. The adult court may also remand a juvenile, when no youth court is sitting.

Determining the age of the defendant

E[1.2]

If the exact age of a child (under 14) or young person (14 or under 18) is not known, his age will be the age that he appears to be to the court after it has considered all the available evidence.

E[2]

The youth court

E[2.1]

Under s 50 of the Courts Act 2003, responsibility for the selection and authorisation of magistrates to sit in youth courts passed to the Lord Chief Justice. Through rules of court he has delegated that function to Bench Training and Development Committees (BTDC). From 13 September 2007, authorisation for winger and chairmanship selection is undertaken by BTDCs for the relevant local justice area (see the Justices of the Peace (Training and Development Committee) Rules 2007 (SI 2007/1609) and the Youth Courts (Constitution of Committees and Right to Preside) Rules 2007 (SI 2007/1611 (L9)). Copies of these rules can be viewed and downloaded from www.opsi.gov.uk.

E[2.2]

Each youth court should (except in unforeseen circumstances) consist of three such magistrates, at least one of whom should be male and one female and the court should be presided over by the chairman or a deputy chairman of the panel. In *R v Birmingham Justices, ex p F* (2000) 164 JP 523, [2000] Crim LR 588 it was made clear that the court should consider representations before proceeding with a single sex bench. A district judge may sit alone in the youth court.

E[2.3]

Persons present during the hearing. Only the following are allowed to be present:

- members and officers of the court;
- parties to the case before the court, their solicitors and counsel, and witnesses and other persons directly concerned with that case;
- bona fide representatives of newspapers or news agencies;
- such other persons as the court may specially authorise to be present.

E[2.4]

Restrictions on reporting. The press may not report details of the name, address or school of a juvenile who is a defendant or witness in any proceedings before the youth court or any other details including the printing of a photograph which would identify him. An exception to this is when the court is dealing with an anti-social behaviour order. In such case the court may make an order under s 39 Children and Young Persons Act 1933 and give its reasons. For the principles governing a s 39 order see A[52.12].

E[2.5]

These restrictions may be lifted:

- in order to avoid an injustice to a juvenile or in certain circumstances where a juvenile is unlawfully at large on application of the Director of Public Prosecutions; or
- the juvenile is convicted and the court, having listened to representations of the parties, believes it is in the public interest to do so.

Publication leading to the identification of an adult witness may also be prohibited under s 49 Youth Justice and Criminal Evidence Act 1999: see I[1B.7].

E[3]
Criminal proceedings

E[3.1]

It shall be the principal aim of the youth justice system to prevent offending by children and young persons. Youth courts must have regard to this aim.

Age of criminal responsibility

E[3.2]

A child under the age of ten cannot be guilty of any offence (Children and Young Persons Act 1933, s 50).

In relation to offenders aged 10–14 years, the presumption and the defence of 'doli incapax' (mischievous discretion) was abolished by s 34 of the Crime and Disorder Act 1998 (*R v T* [2008] EWCA Crim 815, [2008] 3 WLR 923; affd sub nom R v JTB [2009] UKHL 20, [2009] 3 All ER 1).

Attendance of parent

E[3.3]

Unless the court considers it unreasonable to do so, it must insist on the attendance of the parent or guardian of a child or young person under 16 years. In respect of those who are 16 and 17 years' old, the court has a discretion. 'Parent' will include a local authority where the juvenile is in their care. At all stages of the proceedings, if a parent refuses to attend a warrant can be issued against him or her.

*Remands of Children and Young Persons

*When ss 90–104 of LASPOA 2012 are brought into force there will be a number of changes in relation to the remand of offenders, particularly those affecting children and young persons. Section 23 of the CYPA 1969 will be repealed. First, the definition of a 'young person' will apply to offenders under the age of 18 (as opposed to 17 years). Secondly, remands of youths, where the provisions bite, will be to 'local authority accommodation' or in the case of secure remands to 'youth detention accommodation'. Sections E[3.4]–E[3.18] must be construed in the light of those changes when LASPOA 2012 is implemented. At the time of writing the proposed implementation date is late November or December 2012.

Remands (Children and Young Persons Act 1969, s 23)

E[3.4]

A juvenile may be remanded in the way described in Section J (Remands in Custody and Bail). Defendants who have attained 17 years are remanded in the same manner as an adult, although Youth Offending Teams must have bail support programmes in place for children and young persons remanded on bail while awaiting trial or sentencing. In areas covered by the street crime initiative (see J[1.6]) a 17–year-old may also be made subject to a condition of curfew with electronic monitoring. Where bail is refused in respect of a defendant under 17 years, he will generally be remanded into local authority accommodation. Where the juvenile is remanded into local authority accommodation the local authority may apply to the court to use secure accommodation in certain circumstances.

**For a juvenile charged with murder see J[1.32].

E[3.5]

Secure accommodation (civil application). Where a juvenile is remanded into local authority accommodation he may not be kept in accommodation provided for the purpose of restricting liberty unless the youth court (or magistrates' court) which remands him is satisfied:

(a)   that:
      (i)   the juvenile has a history of absconding and is likely to abscond from any other description of accommodation; and
      (ii)   if he absconds he is likely to suffer significant harm; or
(b)   that if he is kept in any other description of accommodation he is likely to injure himself or other persons.

E[3.6]

Where the juvenile is charged with an offence carrying 14 years' imprisonment or more or with an offence of violence or he has previously been found guilty of an offence of violence the criteria that must be established are that non-secure accommodation is inappropriate because:

(a)   the juvenile is likely to abscond from such accommodation; or
(b)   the juvenile is likely to injure himself or other people if he is kept in any such accommodation.

E[3.7]

This application is under the Children Act 1989, s 25. However, the welfare of the child is relevant, not paramount, in a remand situation (*Re M (a minor) (secure accommodation)* [1995] Fam 108, [1995] 3 All ER 407, CA).

E[3.8]

The maximum period of authorisation is the length of the remand or, in the case of committal to the Crown Court, 28 days.

E[3.9]–[3.15]

Conditions. After consultation with the local authority, the court may require a juvenile remanded to their accommodation to comply with conditions analogous to those for conditional bail (see J[1.55]). The court may also impose requirements on the authority to ensure the juvenile's compliance with those conditions and may stipulate that he be not placed with a named person.

E[3.16]

Remand with a security requirement In some situations the remand may be to secure accommodation or prison accommodation, namely:

(a)   he is charged with or has been convicted of a violent or sexual offence, or an offence punishable in the case of an adult with imprisonment for a term of 14 years or more; or

(b)   he is charged with or has been convicted of one or more imprisonable offences which, together with any other imprisonable offences of which he has been convicted in any proceedings:

    (i)   amount, or

    (ii)   would, if he were convicted of the offences with which he is charged, amount, to a recent history of repeatedly committing imprisonable offences while remanded on bail or to local authority accommodation.

and (in either case) the court is of opinion that having considered all the other options only remanding him to secure accommodation would be adequate to protect the public from serious harm from him or prevent the commission by him of imprisonable offences.

E[3.17]

15 and 16-year-old males. 15 and 16-year-old males who meet the above criteria will normally be remanded to prison accommodation unless they are defined as vulnerable by reason of immaturity or propensity for self-harm, in which case they may be remanded to previously identified secure accommodation.

This differentiation between males and females was found to be justified in *R (SR) v Nottingham Magistrates' Court* (1986) 84 Cr App Rep 316, 151 JP 49.

E[3.17A]

Age at date of sentence If a defendant's case is retained by the Youth Court when the defendant is 17 years old and sentenced when he is 18 years old the Youth Court has all of the sentencing powers available to it: s 29 of the Children and Young Persons Act 1963 and *Aldis v DPP* [2002] EWHC 403 (Admin), [2002] All ER (D) 128 (Feb).

In *R v Ghafoor* [2002] EWCA Crim 1857, [2003] 1 Cr App Rep (S) 428 it was said that the starting point for sentencing was the age of the defendant at the date of the offence. *R v Ghafoor* has since been followed in *R v Britton* [2006] EWCA Crim 2875, [2006] All ER (D) 334 (Oct).

Juveniles and committal for trial [*see below]

E[3.18]

In *R v Iles* [2012] EWCA Crim 1610, 176 JP 601, the President of the QBD said, per curiam:

' . . . there appears to have developed a practice under which the Magistrates' Courts adjourn summary only matters, knowing the offender is due to appear at a Crown Court on other matters, and invite the Crown Court to enable the summary cases to be dealt with at the same time by the expedient of arranging for a Circuit Judge to sit as a District Judge. Such a practice has advantages, but there are dangers. Therefore before this practice is followed, the Magistrates' Court must carefully consider whether this is in the interests of justice and ensure that there is power to do so. A Crown Court Judge who is invited to deal with two sets of proceedings in this way must decide whether it is appropriate in the light of submissions from both the prosecution and the defence. For this purpose it must be kept firmly in mind that when sentencing as a District Judge the sentence is imposed by the Magistrates' Court, and consideration must be given not only to advantages but also to dangers that may arise because (1) the Judge would, as regards the Magistrates' Court matters, be limited to the powers of a Magistrates' Court, powers which must be carefully checked by counsel and the court; and (2) sentences that the Judge imposes when sitting as a Magistrates' Court would have a different route of appeal from that applicable to sentences imposed by the Judge when sitting in the Crown Court. If the invitation is accepted, then consideration must again be given to these dangers at the stage of deciding what sentence should be imposed by the Judge when sitting as a Magistrates' Court.'

The following rules govern the committal for trial of a juvenile:

(a)   If the charge is homicide the juvenile must be committed for trial (Magistrates' Courts Act 1980, s 24). In this context the term 'homicide' includes a person charged with an offence of causing or allowing the death of a child or vulnerable adult contrary to s 5 of the Domestic Violence, Crime and Victims Act 2004. This new offence was brought into force on 1 July 2007.

(b)   If the offence is punishable by 14 years' imprisonment or more (or certain prescribed offences under the Sexual Offences Act 2003 eg sexual assault (s 3) – for an unusual case under s 13 of the SOA 2003 involving offenders aged 13-14 years see *R (on the application of G) v Burnley Magistrates' Court* [2007] EWHC 1033 (Admin), 171 JP 445; or certain prescribed offences under s 5 of the Firearms Act

1968) he must be committed for trial if the magistrates consider that in the event of his being found guilty he could be detained for a term of two years or more, or in the case of an offender aged 10–15 years – where there is some unusual feature of the case – a sentence approaching two years (*R (on the application of H) v Southampton Youth Court* [2004] EWHC 2912 (Admin), [2004] All ER (D) 38 (Dec)). If the magistrates are not of that opinion he must be tried summarily (Powers of Criminal Courts (Sentencing) Act 2000, s 91) (*R v Mills* [1998] 2 Cr App Rep (S) 128, [1998] Crim LR 220, CA). Cases involving offenders under 15 years of age for whom detention and training was not available will only rarely attract a period of detention under PCC(S) A 2000, s 91 (*R (on application of M) v Camberwell Green Youth Court* [2004] All ER (D) 95 (Dec), DC). In order to place themselves in the same position as the Crown Court magistrates may have regard to previous relevant convictions when making this decision (*R (Tullett) v Medway Magistrates Court* [2003] EWHC 2279 (Admin), 167 JP 541). The Sentencing Guidelines Council issued guidance in July 2006 for offences of **robbery**. The guidelines apply to offenders who have <u>not</u> been assessed as dangerous. The sentencing ranges and presumptive starting points apply to three types of robbery namely (i) street robbery or 'mugging' (ii) robberies of small businesses (iii) less sophisticated commercial robberies. The starting points are based upon a first-time offender aged 17 years who pleaded not guilty. In such cases it will be necessary to consult the legal adviser.

(c)   **Sexual Offences in the Youth Court: A Protocol issued by the Senior Presiding Judge dated March 31, 2010.** The following is a short synopsis of the Protocol:

> 'Wherever possible such cases should be listed before an authorized district Judge (Magistrates' Court), to decide whether the case falls within the grave crime provisions. If jurisdiction is retained and the allegation involves actual, or attempted, penetrative activity, the case must be tried by an authorised DJ (MC). In all other cases, the authorised DJ (MC) must consider whether the case is so serious and/or complex that it must be tried by an authorised DJ (MC), or whether the case can be heard by any DJ (MC) or any Youth Court Bench.

> If it is not practicable for an authorized DJ (MC) to determine venue, any DJ (MC) or any Youth Court Bench may consider that issue. Thereafter an authorised DJ (MC) should be sent the case papers etc to determine whether the case must be tried by an authorised DJ (MC) or is suitable for hearing before any DJ (MC) or any Youth Court Bench. However, if the case involves actual or alleged penetrative activity, the trial must be heard by an authorised DJ (MC).

> Committal proceedings and other hearings in cases in which jurisdiction has been declined may be dealt with by any DJ (MC) or any Youth Court Bench.

All cases which are remitted for sentence from the Crown Court to the Youth Court should be listed for sentence before an authorised DJ (MC).

Where a case is to be tried by an authorised DJ (MC) but no such Judge is available, the Bench Legal Adviser should contact the Chief Magistrates' Office)'.

(d) A juvenile of 16 or 17 who faces a minimum sentence under s 51A of the Firearms Act 1968 or s 29(3) of the Violent Crime Reduction Act 2006 (minimum sentences in certain cases of using someone to mind a weapon) would apply if he were convicted of the offence.

(e) If a juvenile is jointly tried with someone aged 18 or older, the juvenile must be tried summarily unless the magistrates consider it necessary in the interests of justice to commit both for trial (Magistrates' Courts Act 1980, s 24).

(f) [Having indicated a not guilty plea] the offence is a specified offence within the meaning of s 224 of the CJA 2003 and it appears to the court that if found guilty the criteria for the imposition of a sentence under s 226(3) [detention for public protection] or s 228(2) [extended sentence] would be met. For general guidance see *R v Lang* [2005] EWCA Crim 2864, [2006] 2 All ER 410; as explained in *R v Johnson and other appeals* [2006] EWCA Crim 2486.**

The legal adviser should be consulted when this point arises. Paragraph (f) can lead to a send to the Crown Court rather than committal for trial if the offender is found (solely) to be 'dangerous' at the mode of trial stage.

*[These amendments will apply once the provisions of Sch 3 to the Criminal Justice Act 2003 are brought into force. NB: Committal proceedings will be abolished.]

**This regime will be modified by LASPOA 2012, ss 123 and 124 when brought into force. See B[16.5].

Allocation and the sending of juveniles to the Crown Court for trial

E[3.18A]

There is a general presumption that a juvenile will be tried in the magistrates' [youth] court unless certain criteria apply. In those circumstances the youth must be **sent** to the Crown Court. The criteria are as follows:

(a) The charge is one of homicide (for definition see E[3.18] (a)).

(b) The juvenile faces a serious complex fraud allegation and the prosecution has served a relevant notice under the CJA 2003.

(c) The case involves a child witness and the prosecution has served a relevant notice under the CJA 2003.

(d) [Having indicated a not guilty plea] the offence is a specified offence within the meaning of s 224 of the CJA 2003 and it appears to the court that if found guilty the criteria for the imposition of a sentence

under s 226(3) [detention for life or public protection] or s 228(2) [extended sentence] would be met. For general guidance see *R v Lang* [2005] EWCA Crim 2864, [2006] 2 All ER 410.*
*This regime will be modified by LASPOA 2012, ss 123 and 124 when brought into force. See **B[16.5]**.

(e)   A juvenile aged 16 or 17 who faces a minimum sentence under s 51A (1) of the Firearms Act 1968 or s 29(3) of the Violent Crime Reduction Act 2006 (minimum sentences in certain cases of using someone to mind a weapon) would apply if he were convicted of the offence;

(f)   [Having indicated a not guilty plea] a juvenile is jointly charged with someone aged 18 or older, and the court considers it necessary in the interests of justice to send both for trial.

(g)   [Having indicated a not guilty plea] if the offence is punishable with 14 years' imprisonment or more; or the offence is a prescribed under the Sexual Offences Act 2003 ie sexual assault (s 3), a child sex offence (s 13), sexual activity with a child family member (s 25), inciting a child family member to engage in sexual activity (s 26); or is a prescribed offence under s 5 of the Firearms Act 1968 – where s 51A(1) above does not apply; a juvenile **must be sent** for trial if the magistrates consider that in the event of his being found guilty he could be detained for a term of two years or more; or in the case of an offender aged 10–15 years – where there is some unusual feature of the case – a sentence approaching two years. For an unusual case under s 13 of the SOA 2003 involving offenders aged 13–14 years see *R (on the application of G) v Burnley Magistrates' Court* [2007] EWHC 1033 (Admin).

Given the complexity of these provisions it is advisable for the magistrates to consult with their legal adviser.

**Committal for Sentence

E[3.18B]

Under the old legislation committal for sentence was not available to a youth or adult magistrates' court. Under the new sentencing regime committal for sentence is available in limited circumstances:

(a)   A juvenile **pleads guilty** to an offence punishable with 14 years' imprisonment or more; or the offence is a prescribed offence under the Sexual Offences Act 2003 ie sexual assault (s 3); a child sex offence (s 13); sexual activity with a family member (s 25); inciting a child family member to engage in sexual activity (s 26); and, the court is of the opinion that the offence or the combination of the offence and one or more offences associated with it, was such that the Crown Court should, in the court's opinion, have power to deal with the offender as if the provisions of s 91(3) of the PCC(S)A 2000 applied ('power to detain for specified period') the court **may** commit him in custody or on bail for sentence: s 3B Magistrates' Courts Act 1980. The court may also commit him to the Crown Court to be dealt with in respect of certain other offences: s 6 Magistrates' Courts Act 1980.

(b)   On the summary trial of an information a juvenile is **convicted** of a specified offence and it appears to the court that the offender is eligible for a sentence under s 226(3)* (detention for life or public protection) or s 228(2) (extended sentence)* the court **must** commit the offender in custody or on bail to the Crown Court for sentence: s 3C Magistrates' Courts Act 1980. The court may also commit him to the Crown Court to be dealt with in respect of certain other offences: s 6 Magistrates' Courts Act 1980.
*This regime will be modified by LASPOA 2012, ss 123 and 124 when brought into force. See B[16.5].

(c)   Where a juvenile is sent to the Crown Court for an offence and the offender faces a further **related charge** which carries 14 years' imprisonment or more, or is a prescribed offence under the Sexual Offences Act 2003 (see (a) above), and the offender indicates his intention in due course to plead guilty to that offence or pleads guilty to that offence, in due course the court may commit him in custody or on bail to the Crown Court to be dealt with in respect of the offence pursuant to s 4A Magistrates' Courts Act 1980.

These procedural provisions are complicated and it is recommended that magistrates consult with their legal adviser before exercising any of the above powers.

E[3.19]

It is suggested that the chairman announces the decision as to whether the juvenile shall be committed [sent] for trial or tried summarily so as to make it clear that this point has been considered. This will prevent any suggestion being made that the juvenile was committed [sent] for trial and a summary trial not considered. *R v Allen and Lambert* (1999) 163 JP 841, CA suggests that it is undesirable for the Crown Court to remit back to the youth court cases committed to it.

Procedure

E[3.20]

The court has to consider two general duties, the welfare of the child and the principal aim of the youth justice system to prevent offending by juveniles.

E[3.21]

The court must take care to ensure that he understands the proceedings and the charge should be explained in simple terms appropriate to his age and understanding. If not represented, his parents should be allowed to assist him in his defence.

E[3.22]

Oath. In the youth court, the evidence of children under 14 years must be given unsworn, otherwise the defendant and all the witnesses use a modified form of oath which commences 'I promise before Almighty God to tell the truth' etc. This oath is also used by a juvenile who gives evidence in the adult court (Children and Young Persons Act 1963, s 28).

Evidence from a witness in need of special protection (a child victim of a violent or sexual offence) will give evidence via a live video link (*R v Camberwell Green Youth Court, ex p G* [2005] UKHL 4, [2005] All ER (D) 259 (Jan)). For vulnerable accused see J[1.22B]. For witnesses other than the accused see J[1.22C].

E[3.23]

Remission to a local court. Where the court before which a juvenile appears is not the youth court for the area in which he resides it may (and if it is an adult magistrates' court, it must unless it exercises its limited powers of sentence) remit him to be dealt with by his local youth court. This would normally be done, for example, where reports are required and the case has to be adjourned in order to obtain them. The court may give directions as to whether the defendant should be bailed or kept in custody until he appears before the local court.

E[3.24]

Remission to the adult court. Where a juvenile attains the age of 18 before conviction or after conviction but before sentencing he may be remitted on bail or in custody to be dealt with in the adult court, but not for an indictable offence (*R (on the application of Denny) v Acton Youth Court* (2004) Independent, 24 May).

E[3.25]

Abuse of Process – for general principles consult I[1B.10]–I[1B.11].

Abuse of Process – youth incapable of following proceedings. Guidance was given in *DPP v P* [2007] EWHC 946 (Admin) as follows:

(1)   Although the youth court had an inherent jurisdiction to stay proceedings as an abuse of the process, the jurisdiction was limited directly to matters affecting the fairness of the trial of the particular defendant concerned, and should only be exercised in exceptional circumstances, on the ground of one or more of the capacity issues, before any evidence was heard.

(2)   The fact that a higher authority had previously held that a person was unfit to plead did not make it an abuse to try that person for subsequent criminal acts. The issue of the child's capacity to participate effectively had to be decided afresh.

(3)   A child in early adolescence might well develop significantly over a relatively short period. However, where the medical evidence suggested that the child's condition had not changed since his appearance before that higher court, the decisions of that previous court would be relevant matters to be considered, although not determinative or binding.

(4)   Medical evidence should be considered as part of the evidence in the case and not as the sole evidence in a [preliminary] application. It was the court's opinion of the child's level of understanding which had to determine whether a trial was to proceed.

(5)   Although the medical evidence might be of great importance, it had always to be set in the context of other evidence relating to the child, which might bear upon the issues of his understanding, mental capacity and ability to participate effectively in a trial. Medical evidence on its own might appear quite strong, but when other matters were considered the court might conclude that the defendant's understanding and ability to take part in the trial were greater than was suggested by the doctors and that, with proper assistance from his legal adviser and suitable adjustments to the procedure of the court, the trial could properly proceed to a conclusion.

(6)   Other factors might also be relevant to the decision that the court had to take. If a trial began, the court would wish to ensure that the child understood each stage of the process. That might involve some direct exchanges between the bench and the child (engagement). The child's responses might assist the court in deciding the child's level of understanding. Further, it might become apparent from the way in which the trial was conducted that the child's representative did not have adequate instructions on which to cross-examine witnesses.

(7)   The court had a duty to keep under continuing review the question of whether the criminal trial ought to continue. If at any stage the court concluded that the child was unable to participate effectively in the trial, it might decide to call a halt. Nevertheless, the court might consider that it was in the best interests of the child that the trial should continue. If the prosecution evidence was weak, there might be no case to answer. It might be that the defendant's representative would invite the court to acquit on the ground that the child did not know that what he had done was seriously wrong: *R (on the application of P) v West London Youth Court* [2005] EWHC 2583 (Admin), [2006] 1 All ER 447 applied.

(8)   If the court decided it should call a halt to the criminal trial on the ground that the child could not take an effective part in the proceedings, it should then consider whether to switch to a consideration of whether the child had done the acts alleged. That decision was one for the discretion of the court, but the proceedings should be stayed as an abuse of process before fact finding only if no useful purpose could be served by finding the facts. The court would wish to consider the possibility that it might be appropriate to make a hospital [or guardianship] order, but even if such an order appeared unlikely, there might be other advantages in continuing to complete the fact finding process. If the court found that the child had done the acts alleged, it might be appropriate to alert the local authority to the position with a view to the consideration of care proceedings. If the court found that the child had not done the acts alleged, the proceedings would be brought to an end by a finding of not guilty: *R (on the application of P) v Barking Youth Court* [2002] All ER (D) 93 (Apr) applied.

(9)   It would be right for a court to stay proceedings at the outset if the child was so severely impaired as to be unable to participate in the trial and where there would be no useful purpose in finding the facts.

Vulnerable accused. Where it is said that the accused is vulnerable and may not be able to participate effectively in the proceedings the court should bear in mind that it has the power to direct that the accused can give evidence via a live video link. See J[1.22B].

Abuse of Process – delay. A stay of proceedings even on the grounds of unjustifiable delay will not normally be acceptable in a Youth Court (*R (on the application of DPP) v Croydon Youth Court* (2001) 165 JP 181, 165 JPN 34) but see *R (on the application of Knight) v West Dorset Magistrates' Court* [2002] EWHC 2152 (Admin), 166 JP 705. See I[1B.10]–I[1B.11].

E[4]

Possible orders for juveniles

E[4.1]

See the Process of sentencing at B[5], and also the notes on each type of sentence in the 'Sentencing' section at B[8]–B[47].

E[4.2]

Payment of fines, costs and compensation. See B[33].

E[4.3]

If a juvenile is found guilty of an offence in a magistrates' court (as opposed to a youth court) because he has been jointly tried in the magistrates' court with a defendant aged 18 or older, the magistrates' court can only impose one of the following:

(a) absolute discharge;
(b) conditional discharge;
(c) fine;
(d) bind over.

E[4.4]

Costs, compensation, endorsement and disqualification can also be imposed. If the magistrates' court considers some other sentence appropriate the juvenile must be remitted on bail or in care to a youth court which will usually be the youth court of the area where he resides.

E[4.5]

Binding over parent(s) or guardian(s). The court is required to bind over the parent or guardian of an offender aged under 16 years who has been convicted of an offence to take proper care of him and exercise proper control over him; in the case of 16 and 17-year-olds there is a discretion to do so. Although the consent of the parent or guardian is required, an unreasonable refusal will attract a fine of up to £1,000. This note must be read against the amended Consolidated Criminal Practice Direction set out at B[10.21].

E[4.6]

Parenting orders. Where a juvenile has been convicted of an offence the court has a duty in the case of an under 16-year-old and a power in the case of a 16 or 17-year-old to make a parenting order if it considers it would be desirable in the interests of preventing further offending. If no order is made the court must state its reasons.

The order requires parents to control their child and prevent offending within a 12 month maximum period and to attend counselling or guidance sessions for up to three months. Such orders will not breach Article 8 of EHRC (*R (M) v Inner London Crown Court* [2004] 1 FCR 178, [2003] 1 FLR 994).

Orders must not conflict with the parent's religious beliefs, work or education.

Breach is punishable with a fine up to level 3.

E[4.7]

Fines. In relation to fines, it should be noted that in the case of 16 and 17-year-olds there is now a power for the court to order a parent to pay any fine. If the juvenile is ordered to pay a fine the amount of costs ordered may not exceed the amount of the fine. Also, where a local authority has parental responsibility for a juvenile who is in their care or is provided with accommodation by them, they are to be treated as the person's parent for the purpose of a parent's responsibility to pay a fine etc. Where a parent etc is responsible for payment it will be his means that are taken into account, not those of the juvenile: see also **B[33.7]–B[33.10]**.

E[4.8]

Intensive Support and Surveillance Orders (ISSPs) ISSPs are not orders in their own right but may be attached to other orders, and are available for persistent young offenders who appear in court and have been charged, warned or convicted on four or more separate occasions within the previous 12 months and who have received at least one community or custodial penalty. Young offenders can also qualify for ISSPs if they are at risk of custody because they have been charged with or convicted of an offence for which an adult could face a sentence of 14 years or more or has been guilty of repeat offending whilst on bail and are at risk of a secure remand under s 23 CYPA 1969 as substituted by Criminal Justice and Police Act 2001, s 130 (See **E[3.16]**).

Liquor licensing

Readers will wish to note that the Licensing Act 2003 is now in force. Its effect is to transfer responsibility for licensing to local authorities.

Magistrates' courts still hold an appellate function from a licensing authority and may be involved in closure orders.

For the forfeiture and suspension of a personal liquor licence (s 129 LA 2003) following conviction for a 'relevant offence' see B[48].

F[1]

Appeals under the Licensing Act 2003

Background

F[1.1]

The Licensing Act 2003 makes provision for the grant of both personal and premises licences by local authorities.

F[1.2]

A personal licence is granted under section 111 to an individual and authorises that person to supply alcohol for a period of ten years.

NB: The Licensing Act 2003 (Premises licences and club premises certificates) (Amendment) Regulations 2012 (SI 2012/955) came into force on 25 April 2012. These Regulations amend the Licensing Act 2003 (Premises licences and club premises certificates) Regulations 2005 to give effect to certain amendments made to the Licensing Act 2003 by the Police Reform and Social Responsibility Act 2011. For example, the category of 'interested party' is removed from the 2003 Act to enable any person to participate in the various processes set out in that Act, regardless of their physical proximity to the premises concerned. Moreover, the Secretary of State must by regulations require licensing authorities to advertise certain applications in a prescribed form and in a prescribed manner which is likely to bring the application to the attention of persons likely to be affected by it.

F[1.3]

A premises licence under section 11 and may be granted in respect of any premises and authorises the premises to be used for one or more licensable activities.

F[1.4]

The licensable activities are defined in section 1 as,

(a)   sale by retail of alcohol
(b)   supply of alcohol by club
(c)   provision of regulated entertainment and
(d)   provision of late-night refreshment.

F[1.5]

The local authority will determine the application or licence under section 120 and must grant where the applicant is 18 all over, possesses a described licensing qualification, has not forfeited his personal licence within the previous five-year period nor been convicted of any relevant offence. In the case of the first three criteria the local authority must reject the application where they are not met.

Appeals

F[1.6]

In respect of any of the local authority's functions outlined above or variation or imposition of conditions the applicant has a right to appeal to a magistrates' court. Schedule 5 of the Licensing Act 2003 set out in detail the decisions against which an appeal from the local authority may be made.

F[1.7]

When the appellant considers the local authorities licensing policy to be incompatible or 'ultra vires' the provisions of the statute, an appeal to the High Court by way of judicial review may be appropriate

Notices

F[1.8]

An appeal is commenced by way of written notice being given to a magistrates' court, in the case of a personal licence to the court for the area in which the local authority concerned is situated and in the case of a premises licence, the magistrates' court for the area in which premises are situated.

Period of notice

F[1.9]

Notice of appeal must be lodged within the period of 21 days beginning with the date on which the appellant is notified of the local authority's decision. It is the appellant's responsibility to serve notice on all respondents and prove to the court that such notice has been given.

The hearing

F[1.10]

Whilst any justice of a local magistrates' court may hear and determine an appeal most courts will have appointed an appeals panel in accordance with guidance issued by the Justices' Clerk's Society. In potentially complex appeals the court may hold a pre-hearing review to identify the issues, the numbers of witnesses and a time estimate for the hearing together with other preliminary matters. At such a hearing the justices may make directions regarding disclosure by the parties to each other (*Rushmoor Borough Council v Richards* (1996) 160 LG Rev 460). The proceedings are civil proceedings and therefore hearsay evidence may be admitted. To shorten proceedings justices or their legal adviser may give directions as to the conduct of the case – including the filing of evidence and any skeleton legal arguments.

F[1.11]

The court's powers (section 181). On hearing the application the court may:

(i)   dismiss the appeal; or
(ii)   uphold the appeal and make any other decision which could have
        been made by the licensing authority; or
(iii)   remit the case to the licensing authority to dispose of in accordance
        with the direction of the court, if, for example, the local authority
        has simply failed to process an application.

Procedure

F[1.12]

The appellant's case may be presented in person or by a representative
qualified under the provisions of the Courts and Legal Services Act 1990.
The appeal is by way of a rehearing on the merits of the case and is neither
a review of the local authority's decision nor an appeal on a point of law.
The court is, therefore, able to hear all the evidence that was before the
local authority committee and any relevant evidence, which has arisen
subsequent to the local authority's decision.

Order of speeches

F[1.13]

As the appeal is commenced by way of a complaint the order of proceedings
is governed by the Magistrates' Courts Rules 1981 (rule 14). This means
that the appellant will open the case and call evidence in support of the
appeal. Any respondent will be permitted to cross-examine witnesses called
by the appellant and the appellant may re-examine any of those witnesses.

F[1.14]

Subject to any questions the justices may have, at the end of the appellant's case the respondent will outline his case and call witnesses in support.
Such witnesses may be cross-examined and re-examined and the respondent
may make a closing speech leaving the appellant with the final address to
the court.

The Magistrates' Courts Rules 1981, r 34 provides that where a statutory
appeal lies to a magistrates' court against a decision of a local authority the
appeal shall be made by way of complaint, the procedure for which involves
calling evidence. Such an appeal takes the form of a fresh hearing at which
the parties are free to adduce whatever evidence they think fit, subject to the
control of the court. Section 181(2)(b) does not restrict the evidence which
may be laid before the justices but simply makes clear that the justices have
the power to make any order of the kind that the licensing authority could
have made, without saying anything about the grounds on which such an
order might be made. The justices' function is to consider the application by
reference to the statutory licensing objectives untrammelled by any of the
regulations that govern the procedure for a review under s 51. The justices
are therefore entitled to consider evidence of events occurring before the
application to the licensing authority as well as evidence of events occurring
since its decision. Whilst it is right that a person whose licence is under

threat ought to have notice of the nature of the case against him so that he has a fair chance of meeting it, this can be achieved without limiting the hearing before the magistrates to the allegations that were made before the licensing authority. The magistrates, therefore, are not limited to considering only those grounds of complaint that were raised in the notice of application or the representations before the licensing authority: *R (on the application of Khan) v Coventry Magistrates' Court* [2011] EWHC Civ 751.

The decision

F[1.15]

In *R (on the application of Raphael trading as Orleans) v Highbury Corner Magistrates Court* [2011] EWCA Civ 462, the Court of Appeal decided that at a Licensing Committee's meeting, a resolution was passed establishing and empowering sub-committees for the future discharge of licensing functions. That resolution was passed after ss 7 and 10 of the Licensing Act 2003 came into force. Accordingly, the sub-committee had jurisdiction to amend the conditions of the appellant's nightclub licence and the justices (on appeal from the local authority) had been correct to reject that ground of appeal.

The court will have regard to the licensing authority's statement of licensing policy and any guidance issued by the Secretary of State under s 182 of the Act. The court will also make its decision with the aim of promoting the licensing objectives set out in the Act namely:

(i)   the prevention of crime and disorder,
(ii)   public safety,
(iii)   the prevention of public nuisance, and
(iv)   the protection of children from harm.

The court will give reasons for its decision and if the court departs from either the statutory guidance or the licensing statement it will give reasons for doing so. Justices hearing an appeal should not consider or engage in planning matters which fell properly within the jurisdiction of the licensing authority (*R (on the application of Blackwood) v Birmingham Magistrates' Court* [2006] AER (D) 324 (Jun)). Except in the case of a closure order there is no further statutory entitlement to appeal the decision of the magistrates' court.

For more up to date guidance on the relevance of the Licensing Act's objectives when justices are hearing an appeal see (*R (on the application of Daniel Thwaites plc) v Wirral Borough Magistrates' Court* [2008] EWHC 838 (Admin), 172 JP 301).

When dealing with an appeal against a decision of a local licensing authority, the magistrates' court had to pay careful attention to the licensing committee's reasons and exercise its own judgement as to how much weight to accord to them. The fuller and clearer the reasons, the more force they were likely to carry. The appellant bore the burden of persuading the appellate court that the committee ought to have exercised its discretion differently, rather than the court being required to exercise the discretion afresh: *Stepney Borough Council v Joffe* [1949] 1 KB 599 , [1949] 1 All ER 256, DC considered; *Sagnata Investments Ltd v Norwich Corporation* [1971] 2 QB 614, [1971] 2 All ER 1441, CA applied: *R (on the application of Hope and Glory Public House) v City of Westminster Magistrates' Court (Lord Mayor and Citizens of the City of Westminster, interested party)* [2011] EWCA Civ 31, [2011] 3 All ER 579, [2011] PTSR 868.

In *R (on the application of Developing Retail Ltd) v East Hampshire Magistrates' Court* [2011] EWHC 618 (Admin), on an appeal against the grant of a provisional premises licence, in accordance with s 29 of the LA 2003, the justices had sought to impose two conditions. Analogous to bail conditions, the High Court stressed the need for conditions to be clear, precise and enforceable.

The first condition modified an original condition to ensure that an external seating area was vacated by customers at 11pm. That condition was directed at late night noise emanating from the premises. The justices added to the condition by including a balcony on the premises. It was held that the justices had been entitled to regard the condition as preventative rather than reactive like the regulatory conditions preventing noise. The condition was clear and proportionate and was tailored to the activities intended to take place at the premises.

However, the justices had imposed a second condition, namely that all noise from regulated entertainment at the premises should be inaudible one metre outside any noise sensitive premises. Although a condition was justified by reference to a decibel level to protect local residents, the condition was quashed and the matter remitted to the justices to consider an alternative condition. The original condition was so vague as to be unenforceable. There was no clarity as to the premises or location intended to be protected and the meaning of 'inaudible', in that context, was unclear.

Costs

F[1.16]

The court may make such order for costs as it thinks fit under s 181 of the Licensing Act 2003. Case law such as *Bradford Metropolitan District Council v Booth* (2002) suggests that public authorities need to be able to make honest, reasonable and sound administrative decisions in the public interest without fear of exposure to undue financial prejudice if they are successfully appealed.

In *Crawley Borough Council v Attenborough* [2006] EWHC 1278 (Admin), (2006) 170 JP 593, the justices varied conditions imposed by the Borough Council in relation to licensed premises run by the respondent. The justices ordered the local authority to pay all of the costs of the respondent. On appeal it was agreed that there was no practical distinction between the terms of s 64 of the MCA 1980 (civil proceedings) and s 181 of the Licensing Act 2003. The Divisional Court upheld the justices' decision to award costs having regard to the fact that they had considered all of the circumstances including the facts and the history of the case and bearing in mind the order was varied on appeal by the justices.

Just over one week later, in *R (on the application of Cambridge City Council) v Alex Nesting Ltd* [2006] EWHC 1374 (Admin), (2006) 170 JP 539, it was decided that although as a matter of strict law the power of the appellate court in such circumstances to award costs is not confined to cases where the local authority acted unreasonably or in bad faith, the fact that the local authority has acted reasonably and in good faith in the discharge of its public function is plainly a most important factor. In ordinary civil litigation the principle that costs follow the event does not apply in this type of case. Therefore, an award of costs should not routinely follow in favour of a successful appellant in this type of case, if anything, quite the contrary.

It is submitted that if there is a perceived conflict between the two authorities above, there was fuller argument in the latter case and therefore the approach adopted in *Alex Nesting Ltd* is to be preferred.

Note that the principles outlined in *Bradford Metropolitan District Council v Booth* above, apply equally to costs sought in forfeiture proceedings brought under s 298(2) of the Proceeds of Crime Act 2002. See [3.2].

F[2]

Closure Orders: police powers to close disorderly and noisy on-licensed premises and for persistently selling alcohol to children

(Licensing Act 2003, ss 161–171)

F[2.1]

Power. On licensed premises only

- closure for a period not exceeding 24 hours
- no entry to members of the public during closure
- purchases or supplies prohibited during closure
- contravention without reasonable excuse is liable to a fine not exceeding £20,000 or to imprisonment for a term not exceeding 3 months (**no increase is provided for by the Criminal Justice Act 2003, Sch 26), or to both.

F[2.2]

Grounds. Requires authorisation by a senior police officer who believes that:

- likely to be disorder in or near premises and that closure is necessary in the interests of public safety, or
- disorder already taking place and that closure is necessary in the interests of public safety, or
- public nuisance is being caused by noise from the premises and that closure is necessary to prevent nuisance.

F[2.3]

Duration.

- up to 24 hours (notice must be given in writing);
- may be cancelled by police at any time after the order has been made (notice must be given in writing);
- order may be extended by responsible senior police officer if he/she believes grounds continue to apply and that magistrates will not have considered the order by end of closure period;
- no such extension shall come into force unless notice is given by end of previous closure period.

F[2.4]

Consideration hearing by magistrates (ss 164–165).

- as soon as reasonably practicable (must have written notice);
- must be in 'open court';
- powers may be exercised by a magistrates' court (which can be exercised by a single justice);
- evidence given must be on oath.

F[2.5]

Powers. The court may:

- revoke the order and any extension of it if the order or extension is still in force; or
- order the relevant premises to remain, or to be, closed until the matter is dealt with by the licensing authority. In considering whether to exercise this power the magistrates will have regard to s 161 in determining whether the grounds for making the order are continuing, or are likely to continue;
- order the premises to remain or be closed until dealt with by the licensing authority under s 167 but subject to specified exceptions;
- order the premises to remain or be closed until determination by the licensing authority unless conditions specified in the order are satisfied.

F[2.6]

Appeal from the Justices. Any person aggrieved by the decision of the magistrates may appeal to the Crown Court (Licensing Act 2003, s 166).

F[2.7]

Closure notices for persistently selling alcohol to children under s 147A Licensing Act 2003.

Power. Applies to any premises:

- prohibition for a period not exceeding 48 hours of sales of alcohol;
- offers the opportunity to discharge all criminal liability.

For more detail see s 169A of the Licensing Act 2003 as added by s 24 of the Violent Crime Reduction Act 2006. This legislation came into force on 6 April 2007.

The Licensing Act 2003 (Persistent Selling of Alcohol to Children) (Prescribed Form of Closure Notice) Regulations 2012 (SI 2012/963) came into force on 25 April 2012.

These Regulations revoke the Licensing Act 2003 (Persistent Selling of Alcohol to Children) (Prescribed Form of Closure Notice) Regulations 2007 and prescribe the form of a closure notice given under s 169A of the Licensing Act 2003 ('the 2003 Act') to give effect to certain amendments made to that Act by the Police Reform and Social Responsibility Act 2011.

A closure notice represents an alternative to prosecution under s 147A of the 2003 Act for the offence of persistently selling alcohol to children. The offence may be committed by the holder of a premises licence if on two or more occasions within three consecutive months alcohol is sold unlawfully to an individual aged under 18 on the premises to which the licence relates.

Previously, the effect of a closure notice was that alcohol sales at the licensed premises to which it relates could be prohibited for a period of up to 48 hours. Following the amendment to the 2003 Act, a closure notice may prohibit alcohol sales from the premises to which it relates for a period of between 48 and 336 hours. These Regulations prescribe the form of a closure notice which contains reference to the period for which premises may be prohibited from making sales of alcohol in accordance with the amendment to the 2003 Act.

F[3]

Offence of fraudulently receiving programmes
(Copyright, Designs and Patents Act 1988, s 297)

F[3.1]

Prosecution of designated premises supervisors and premises licence holders. The Federation Against Copyright Theft is engaged in the private prosecution of designated premises supervisors and premises licence holders throughout England and Wales for offences contrary to s 297(1). This is a relevant offence for *personal licence holders* as defined by Sch 4 to the Licensing Act 2003 and magistrates have certain powers and obligations when dealing with personal licence holders, namely:

- The requirement for a personal licence holder to produce his licence on his first appearance in court (s 128(1)).
- The power to order forfeiture or suspension of the personal licence (s 129).
- The notification of a conviction for a relevant offence to the licensing authority that issued the personal licence (s 131(2)(a)).

Betting and gaming licensing

Readers will wish to note that the Gambling Act 2005 is now fully implemented. Its effect was to transfer responsibility for all aspects of betting and gaming to the Gambling Commission (operating and personal licences) or local authorities (premises licences).

Magistrates' Courts still hold an appellate function from a licensing authority but <u>not</u> from the Gambling Commission

Gambling Act 2005

G[1.1]

The Gambling Act 2005 contains a new regulatory system to govern the provision of all forms of gambling in Great Britain, other than the National lottery and spread betting. From **1 September 2007** the Act repealed the Betting, Gaming and Lotteries Act 1963, the Gaming Act 1968 and the Lotteries and Amusements Act 1976 respectively (see the Gambling Act 2005 (Commencement No 6 and Transitional) Provisions Order 2006 (2006/3272) (C119) as modified by several amending orders.

The following is a brief summary of the changes in procedure and jurisdiction.

General changes

G[1.2]

The following general changes have been made:

- Creation of a Gambling Commission.
- A two-tier jurisdiction with local authorities dealing with premises.
- The Act removes all responsibility from licensing, betting and gaming justices for granting betting and gaming permissions, which they exercised previously.
- Decisions of the licensing authority, ie the relevant local authority, may be the subject of an appeal to the local magistrates' court. Decisions of the Gambling Commission may be the subject of an appeal to the Gambling Appeals Tribunal (but not a magistrates' court).

Appeals under the Gambling Act 2005 from local authorities

Background

G[1.3]

Operating and personal licences fall under the jurisdiction of the Gambling Commission by virtue of Part 7 (s 140 onwards) of the Gambling Act 2005. Appeals lie to the Gambling Appeal Tribunal.

Premises licences fall under the licensing authority's jurisdiction ie the relevant local authority under Part 8 (s 153 onwards).

Appeals in respect of premises licences are governed by ss 206 and 207 of the Gambling Act 2005.

Appeals

G[1.4]

Section 206 stipulates who is entitled to appeal.

Section 207 states that an appeal under s 206 in relation to premises must be instituted:

(a)   in the magistrates' court for a local justice area in which the premises are wholly or mainly situated
(b)   by notice of appeal given to the designated officer; and
(c)   within the period of 21 days beginning with the day on which the appellant receives notice of the decision against which the appeal is brought (**NB:** there does not appear to be a power to extend the 21 day period);
(d)   a fee will be payable to the magistrates' court hearing the appeal.

Section 207 prescribes who the respondent is.

Section 207(3) states that on hearing the appeal the **magistrates may:**

(a)   dismiss the appeal;
(b)   substitute for the decision appealed against any decision that the licensing authority could have made;
(c)   remit the case to the local authority to decide in accordance with the direction of the court;
(d)   make an order about costs.

Section 208 permits a stay of the order pending appeal.

There is no appeal from the decision of the magistrates' court to the Crown Court. An aggrieved party may appeal on a point of law to the High Court.

NB: As these are essentially civil proceedings, the hearing, procedure, order of speeches and the discretion to award costs are to all intents and purposes the same as in licensing appeals. The reader is invited to refer to **Section F,** paragraphs **[1.10]–[1.16]** inclusive.

Council tax

H[1]
Background

H[1.1]
The administration and enforcement of the council tax is regulated by the Council Tax (Administration and Enforcement) Regulations 1992.

H[2]

Recovery and enforcement

H[2.1]

The first action the courts are involved in is the issue of a summons by a single justice or a justices' clerk against the alleged debtor following a complaint by a local authority of non-payment. Prior to this the local authority will have served a demand notice on the liable person and when payment has not been forthcoming the authority must serve a reminder notice. If payment is not made within seven days of the issue of the reminder notice the whole amount outstanding becomes due after a further seven-day period. The final step the local authority takes before making a complaint for a liability order is the issue of a final notice. Such notice will state the sum outstanding and the amount of any costs reasonably incurred in obtaining the liability order. The court will fix a date when the applications for the liability order will be heard.

H[2.2]

A summons may be served on a person by delivering it to him; leaving it in his usual or last known place of abode; sending it to him by post to that address or leaving it or sending it by post to an address given by the person as an address at which the service of the summons will be accepted (eg a solicitor's office). In the case of a company service can be effected at the company's registered office.

H[3]

The court hearing

H[3.1]

The court hearing is conducted as a complaint and the complainant council may make out their case for a liability order on the balance of probabilities, whether or not the non-payer appears in court. In order to be successful the council must satisfy the court that:

(a)   council tax has been set by resolution of the authority;
(b)   a sum due has been demanded in accordance with the regulations as set out above; and
(c)   a summons has been served.

H[3.2]

It follows that if the amount has not been demanded in accordance with the regulations or has been duly paid then this will amount to a defence. A complaint for a liability order made more than six years after the amount became due will not be valid.

H[3.3]

Reopening

It is noteworthy that the power to reopen and rehear a case under s 142 of the Magistrates' Courts Act 1980 does not apply to this type of civil proceedings (*R (on the application of Mathialagan) v Southwark London Borough Council* [2004] EWCA Civ 1689, [2004] All ER (D) 179 (Dec)).

Nor can the power be used when a case has been dismissed (*Verderers of the New Forest v Young* [2004] EWHC 2954 (Admin), [2004] All ER (D) 14 (Dec)). However, reg 36A of the Council Tax (Administration and Enforcement) Regulations 1992 permits a liability order to be rescinded on the application of the local authority; further, there does appear to be a limited power to review civil orders in exceptional circumstances: see case law under B[7.5].

H[4]

Evidential requirements

H[4.1]

Much of the evidence may be produced by way of certificate, for example, a certified copy signed by the appropriate officer showing the council's resolution setting the amount of the council tax for the given local authority area. In addition:

(a)   computer generated documents are admissible under the Civil Evidence Act 1995 so long as the document constitutes or forms part of a record compiled by the authority;

(b)   direct oral evidence of any facts stated would have been admissible; and

(c)   where the document has been produced by a computer it is accompanied by a certificate which:

       (i)   must identify the document and the computer by which it was produced;

       (ii)   give appropriate explanations to the contents of the document; and

       (iii)   be signed by a person occupying a responsible position in relation to the operation of the computer.

H[4.2]

The only legitimate defences against the making of the liability order are outlined above and such matters as pending appeals at the valuation tribunal as to the correct banding, or disputes as to the amount owed, will not amount to a reason for the court to decline to issue a liability order. The justices are obliged to prevent the claimant from putting forward irrelevant matters such as whether the defendant should have received council tax benefit (*R (on application of Williams) v Pontefract Magistrates' Court* [2002] All ER (D) 465 (May)).

H[5]
The liability order

H[5.1]

Where magistrates are satisfied that the local authority has made out its case then they have no further discretion but to issue a liability order. This order will include an order for reasonable costs. A liability order gives the local authority the power to take enforcement action such as an attachment of earnings order, distress or deductions from income support. Matters which may be raised at a valuation tribunal are not relevant in liability order proceedings.

H[6]

Committal proceedings

H[6.1]

Following the failure of liability or other enforcement methods the local authority may apply to the court for a means inquiry to be held with a view to a committal to prison in default of payment of the outstanding council tax. A warrant of commitment may only be applied for if the local authority has first attempted to levy distress and have received a report that the bailiffs were unable to find sufficient goods on which to levy the amount outstanding. In order to secure the debtor's attendance the court may issue a summons or a warrant for his arrest. At the committal hearing the court will inquire into the defaulter's means and may impose a period of three months maximum to be served in imprisonment where they are satisfied that failure to pay is due to the person's wilful refusal or culpable neglect. Justices using this power should be satisfied of the criteria on a criminal standard of proof or a high civil standard (*R v South Tyneside Justices, ex p Martin* (1995) Independent, 20 September). The defaulter must be present before the court and although local authorities are not under a statutory obligation to exhaust all other remedies before making an application for committal, it may well be advisable for them to do so. Courts will therefore be keen to see such action being tried as clearer evidence that the defendant is culpable in his neglect to pay and not just unable to pay through impecuniosity or mismanagement.

H[6.2]

When dealing with a committal application then the magistrates may:

(a)   issue a warrant for commitment;

(b)   fix a term of imprisonment and postpone the issue of the warrant until such time and on such conditions as the court thinks fit; note that where a warrant is issued after postponement and, since the term of imprisonment was fixed, part-payments have been made, these payments will reduce the imprisonment in a proportion to the full amount outstanding;

(c)   adjourn the application;

(d)   dismiss the application;

(e)   remit all or part of the sum owing. As a guideline payments should be able to be made within a three-year period (*R (on the application of Broadhurst) v Sheffield Justices* (2000) 164 JP 870). Previous case law points to the fact that, as with rates enforcement, this may only be appropriate if the debtor cannot afford to pay; remission remains an option only up to the point at which a term of imprisonment has been fixed (*Harrogate Council v Barker* (1995) 159 LG Rev 889, 159 JP 809);

(f)   theoretically the court might find wilful refusal or culpable neglect but not issue a commitment warrant as the matter does rest within its discretion: once a warrant of commitment has been issued or a term of imprisonment fixed, a charging authority may not take further steps to recover the debt under the liability order (Council Tax (Administration and Enforcement) Regulations 1992, reg 52).

H[6.3]

The Council Tax (Administration and Enforcement) Regulations 1992, regulation 47(2) makes it clear that on an application for commitment to prison being made the court shall, in the debtor's presence, inquire into his means and inquire whether the failure to pay which has led to *the application* is due to his wilful refusal or culpable neglect. In other words, the court's inquiries concern the period of time after the issue of the liability order but before the application for a commitment to prison. This in fact makes it even more important that local authorities pursue all available options to them under the authority's liability order before coming into court to ask for a commitment warrant to be issued.

There must be a separate enquiry by the magistrates into the circumstances relevant under reg 47 of the Council Tax (Administration and Enforcement) Regulations 1992, SI 1992/613, for each of the separate years of liability. Otherwise this will be fatal to the decision of the magistrates: *R v Leeds Justices, ex p Kennett* [1996] RVR 53.

In *R (on the application of Aldous) v Dartford Magistrates' Court* [2011] EWHC 1919 (Admin), it was held that the form of enquiry as to means was hopelessly inadequate and did not meet the requirements of reg 47. The claimant was invited to fill in a standard means form, but it was deficient in terms of discovering how the claimant could meet her liability for payment in excess of £7,000. There did not appear to have been anything like an adequate number of questions posed to discover what the claimant's means were. Accordingly, there was nothing which could properly be called an enquiry. Further, the period of any imprisonment imposed under reg 47(3) must vary according to the culpability of the person in question. It was less serious to fail to pay rates through culpable neglect rather than through wilful refusal. In order to fix the amount of any term of committal it was necessary to determine whether it was due to wilful refusal or culpable neglect which had led to the failure to pay. The magistrates in the present case failed to distinguish between the two statutory criteria and failed to make a finding which was a necessary precondition to fixing a term of imprisonment in default: *R v Highbury Corner Magistrates' Court, ex p Uchendu* (1994) 158 LGR 481, [1994] RA 51, (1994) 158 JP 409 considered.

H[6.4]

Although the council may only deduct 5% of debtors' benefit payments direct from income support a magistrates' court may order a payment in excess of this figure in appropriate circumstances (*R v Felixstowe etc Magistrates' Court, ex p Herridge* [1993] RA 83, 158 JP 307).

H[7]

Suspended commitments

H[7.1]

Where a commitment to prison is issued but postponed on terms it appears that the court must hold a further inquiry before the commitment warrant is issued to take the defaulter to prison. This was considered in *R v Faversham and Sittingbourne Justices, ex p Ursell* [1992] RA 99, 156 JP 765. The court considered that a further inquiry into a commitment warrant postponed on terms was necessary before that warrant could be issued. This was a further opportunity to enable the court to be satisfied that the conditions had not been met by the debtor as well as giving the debtor a further opportunity to explain his default.

H[7.2]

The role of a defaulter was considered in *R v Wolverhampton Stipendiary Magistrate, ex p Mould* (1992) Times, 16 November. This was a case under the community charge legislation. The role of the defaulter was defined as going beyond the mere giving of evidence. He could also:

(a)   challenge the evidence given by the charging authority as to indebtedness and any steps to levy distress;

(b)   challenge the information given about his means;

(c)   submit that failure to pay was not due to wilful refusal or culpable neglect; and

(d)   even if it was, that a warrant of commitment postponed on suitable conditions was to be preferred to immediate custody.

H[7.3]

Where the defaulter fails to attend, in the light of the European Convention on Human Rights, it is advisable to issue an arrest warrant rather than issue the warrant of commitment in the absence of the defaulter. Magistrates should adjourn hearing a warrant for committal case where they know the debtor has not been served with the relevant committal notice (*R v Doncaster Justices, ex p Hannan* (1999) 163 JP 182, [1998] 32 LS Gaz R 30, [1998] RVR 254, 142 Sol Jo LB 218).

H[7.4]

A number of cases have emphasised that before committing a debtor to prison the court must have considered all available alternatives to attempt recovery of the sum due (*R v Newcastle under Lyme Justices, ex p Massey* [1995] 1 All ER 120, 158 JP 1037, [1994] NLJR 1444, sub nom R v Stoke-on-Trent Justices, ex p Knight [1994] 1 WLR 1684).

Court room procedure

I[1]

The Human Rights Act

I[1.1]

The purpose of the Human Rights Act 1998 is to allow citizens of the United Kingdom to enforce their rights under the Human Rights Convention in the domestic courts.

The Act requires all courts and tribunals to give effect to Convention rights by interpreting existing legislation and laws, where possible, compatibly with the Convention.

I[1.2]

With regard to statute (primary legislation) the courts are required to interpret the legislation so as to uphold the Convention rights unless legislation is so clearly incompatible with the Convention that it is impossible to do so. If a Convention right is contravened by a provision in primary legislation which the court is unable to interpret compatibly it must give effect to the will of Parliament. However, in such circumstances an appeal may be made to the High Court for a *declaration of incompatibility* which leads to a fast track procedure in Parliament for the passing of a *remedial order* to cure the apparent incompatibility.

In the case of secondary legislation or precedent the court's duty is to give effect to Convention rights; firstly through the medium of interpretation or secondly through disapplying the relevant domestic law.

I[1.3]

Additionally, courts must take into account judgments, decisions and opinions of the European Court of Human Rights and the Commission. All public authorities have a positive obligation to act compatibly with the Convention. This includes magistrates' courts, local authorities, the Probation Service and justices' clerks.

I[1.4]

Advocates wishing to raise a Convention point in magistrates' courts should be prepared to identify the article of the Convention which it is suggested may be breached, the reason for the breach and the remedy required of the courts. Court may give directions requiring the parties to file skeleton arguments in support of any Convention arguments.

Procedural steps

I[1.5]

Step 1 Ask if a Convention right is engaged.

If no Convention right is engaged, the case must be decided on the basis of domestic law.

If the Convention is engaged move to step 2

Step 2 Identify the relevant article and its class

- Absolute Rights:
  Article 3: prohibition of torture, inhuman or degrading treatment
  Article 4(1): prohibition of slavery or servitude
  Article 7: prohibition of punishment without law
- Limited Rights:
  Article 2: right to life
  Article 4(2): prohibition of forced or compulsory labour
  Article 5: right to liberty
  Article 6: right to a fair trial
- Qualified Rights:
  Article 8: right to respect for private and family life
  Article 9: freedom of thought, conscience and religion
  Article 10: freedom of expression
  Article 11: freedom of assembly
- Parts of Article 6 such as art 6(1) confer limited rights. Other parts, such as art 6(3) confer qualified rights.

I[1.6]

The threshold is high for breach of an *absolute right* but once breached for any reason, a violation is established.

Limited rights contain definitive statements of the circumstances which *permit* a breach of the right. If the restrictions are not complied with, there has been a violation of the Article.

Qualified Rights *may* be breached if:

- the breach is prescribed by domestic law
- the law is clear and accessible
- the breach pursues a legitimate aim which is set out in the Article
- the measure is a proportional response

If these provisions do not apply there is likely to be a violation of the convention.

I[1.7]

A magistrates' court which finds a breach or potential breach of the Convention may grant such relief or remedy, or make that order within its powers and it considers just and appropriate. In essence this may mean a simple adjournment to provide more time to prepare for a trial or it may involve the exclusion of evidence which would have had an unfair effect on the trial itself.

In *R (Laporte) v Chief Constable of Gloucestershire* [2004] EWCA Civ 1639, [2005] 1 All ER 473 the High Court found that the police acted reasonably in stopping a coach party, in apprehension of a breach of the peace and did not violate their Article 10 rights. However their actions in forcibly returning the coach to London breached Article 5.

I[1.8]

Burden of Proof. Where a statutory provision imposes a burden of proof on a defendant the court must first ascertain if it is an evidential or a legal burden. An evidential burden can be discharged by some evidence which could result in a decision in the defendant's favour. A legal burden on the other hand may breach the presumption of innocence in Article 6 (*R v Johnstone* [2003] UKHL 28, [2003] All ER (D) 323 (May), HL and *A-G's Reference No 1 (2004)*).

Reasons for decision

I[1A.1]

There are many statutory requirements to give reasons in court. Examples are the imposition of imprisonment or where a court orders the removal of press restriction normally applicable in court. Such requirements are outlined in the text of this work. Article 6(1) states: ' . . . everyone is entitled to a fair and public hearing within a reasonable time by an independent and impartial tribunal established by law. Judgment shall be pronounced publicly . . . '.

I[1A.2]

The giving of reasons enables an aggrieved person to understand the decision and make an informed decision on the right to appeal. It also provides an explanation for the public at large and those observing the proceedings in court. Reasons need not be elaborate (*McKerry v Teesdale and Wear Valley Justices* (2000) 164 JP 355, [2000] Crim LR 594, CA).

I[1A.3]

However, a reasoned judgment at the end of a trial should cover the major issues in dispute, and any legal submissions, together with the findings of fact. In *Ruiz Torija v Spain* (1994) 19 EHRR 542, ECtHR the European Court stated: 'The court reiterates that Article 6(1) obliges the courts to give reasons for their judgments, but cannot be understood as requiring a detailed answer to every argument. The extent to which this duty to give reasons applies may vary according to the nature of the decision'. One area where it is clear the court will have to give reasons is where there is any suggestion that an inference from the exercise of the right to silence is to be drawn: see *Condron v United Kingdom* [2000] Crim LR 679, 8 BHRC 290, ECtHR.

I[1A.4]

One other area that would appear to be clear is that the courts must not resort to formatted or standard reasons. In *Yagci and Sargin v Turkey* (1995) 20 EHRR 505, ECtHR the European Court disapproved of the use of stereotyped reasons by a court when refusing bail.

I[1A.5]

The court, like all other tribunals and public authorities, must act compatibly with the European Convention. In general a rigorous approach to giving reasons for a decision will normally alert the court to any human rights issues. A structured approach to those issues should lead to a successful resolution of human rights problems in court.

I[1B]

Proceedings to be in open court

I[1B.1]

Magistrates conducting a summary trial must generally sit in open court (Magistrates' Courts Act 1980, s 121) and comply with the provisions of Art 6 of the ECHR that everyone is entitled to a fair and public hearing. See r 37 of the Criminal Procedure Rules 2012 (Trial and Sentence in a Magistrates' Court).

I[1B.2]

There may be **exceptions** such as governing the conduct of proceedings in a youth court (at E[2]) and a family proceedings court (at D[1]) including particular restrictions in adoption proceedings (at D[18]). Also, statute provides for a court to sit in camera when considering evidence in proceedings under the Official Secrets Act 1920. All these may be read into Art 6(1) of the Convention and are unlikely to be subject to challenge.

I[1B.3]

Power to clear court while child or young person is giving evidence in certain cases. Where, in any proceedings in relation to an offence against or any conduct contrary to decency or morality, a juvenile is called as a witness, the court may be cleared of persons other than members or officers of the court, parties to the case, their counsel or solicitors, and persons otherwise directly concerned with the case, but bona fide representatives of the press may not be excluded (Children and Young Persons Act 1933, s 37).

I[1B.4]

Apart from the statutory exceptions evidence must be given in open court except where it may be necessary to depart from this principle where the nature or circumstances of the particular proceedings are such that the application of the general rule in its entirety would frustrate or render impracticable the administration of justice (*A-G v Leveller Magazines Ltd* [1979] AC 440, [1979] 1 All ER 745, HL).

I[1B.5]

The High Court has commented on the magistrates' decision to hear mitigation in camera because embarrassing and intimate details of the defendant's personal life would have to be given by her and she had an overwhelming fear of revealing them publicly. The judges felt the magistrates' exercise of their discretion was unsustainable and out of accord with principle (*R v Malvern Justices, ex p Evans* [1988] QB 540, [1988] 1 All ER 371).

I[1B.6]

Non-disclosure of evidence given in open court. Sometimes where the court decides not to sit in camera there is a request that a witness may write down his name on a piece of paper or use a pseudonym. In criminal cases at least this should only be done where the criteria for sitting in camera are met and such a device is normally only encountered in blackmail cases. Such a power is not designed for the benefit of the comfort and feelings of defendants such as where publication of a defendant's address might cause him to be harassed by his former wife (*R v Evesham Justices, ex p McDonagh* [1988] QB 553, [1988] 1 All ER 371).

Reporting of court proceedings

I[1B.7]

Apart from the special provisions governing the youth and family proceedings courts referred to above, the press may report all legal proceedings held in public (Contempt of Court Act 1981, s 4(1)). There are certain exceptions to the general rule:

(a)   *Children and young persons:* The court may direct that no newspaper may reveal the name and address or other specified particulars calculated to lead to the identification of any juvenile concerned in the proceedings either as a witness or a defendant, nor that any picture shall be published, except as permitted by the court (CYPA 1933, s 39). The court may not order that the names of the adult defendants should not be published although a report naming the defendant and linking it to the victim may breach the s 39 order (*R v Teesside Crown Court, ex p Gazette Media Co* [2005] EWCA Crim 1983, [2005] All ER (D) 367 (Jul)). Any embarrassment that might well flow to children was an unfortunate consequence of a parent being accused or convicted of a crime. The decision to prosecute brought the matter into the public domain. A balance had to be struck between Arts 8 and 10 of the ECHR. Previous authorities identified special circumstances to justify the imposition of an order under s 39. Great care is needed therefore when making orders under s 39. Magistrates would be well advised to invite representations from the parties and where appropriate any members of the press. For recent guidance see **A[52.2]** and *C v CPS* [2008] EWHC 854 (Admin)).

(b) After an allegation of rape and other sexual offences (eg see **A[53]**) has been made the general statutory rule is that no material likely to lead to the identification by the public of the complainant may be published or broadcast (Sexual Offences (Amendment) Act 1992).

(c) *Publication of matters exempted from disclosure in court:* Where a court has allowed a name or other matter to be withheld from the public in proceedings before the court, the court may give such directions prohibiting the publication of that name or matter in connection with the proceedings as appear to the court to be necessary for the purpose for which it was so withheld (Contempt of Court Act 1981, s 11). The order must be in writing and must state with precision its exact terms, extent and purpose. There has to be a very compelling reason to withhold the addresses of serving police officers charged with criminal offences: see *R (on the application of Harper and Johncox) v Aldershot Magistrates' Court* [2010] EWHC 1319 (Admin), 174 JP 410, 174 CL&J 383.

(d) *Power to postpone publication of reports of court proceedings:* Where it appears to be necessary for avoiding a substantial risk of prejudice to the administration of justice in those proceedings or in any other proceedings pending or imminent the court may order that the publication of any report of the proceedings or any part of the proceedings be postponed for such period as the court thinks necessary for that purpose (Contempt of Court Act 1981, s 4(2)). The order should be no wider than is necessary for the prevention of prejudice to the administration of justice (*R v Horsham Justices, ex p Farquharson* [1982] QB 762, [1982] 2 All ER 269, CA) and must be in writing and must state with precision its exact terms, extent and purpose.

(e) Under s 46 of the Youth Justice and Criminal Evidence Act 1999 the court may prevent publication of any matter which may lead to the identification of an adult witness for the duration of that person's life, if it is satisfied that the quality of their evidence or their participation would be diminished by fear or distress related to public information.

(f) Note, that by virtue of the Coroners and Justice Act 2009, Chapter 2, Part 3, witness anonymity is available in criminal proceedings including summary proceedings. Recourse to the relevant provisions in the magistrates' court should prove rare. Where the issue is canvassed justices should consult their legal adviser. See Part 29, Section 5 of the CPR 2012.

I[1B.8]

Twitter and other live, text-based communications. The Lord Chief Justice in 2012 has issued guidance on the use of live, text-based communications such as mobile email, social media (including Twitter) and internet-enabled laptops in open court. This guidance replaces interim guidance issued in 2010.

The new guidance makes clear that:

- There is no longer any need for representatives of the media/legal commentators to make an application to use text-based devices to communicate from court.
- Members of the public should make a formal or informal application if they wish to use these devices.
- Use of the devices should not cause a disturbance or distraction.
- The court always retains full discretion to prohibit live, text-based communications from court, in the interests of justice. The 'paramount question' for the court in deciding whether to allow live text-based communications is whether it may interfere with the administration of justice. 'The danger . . . is likely to be at its most acute in the context of criminal trials, eg where witnesses who are out of court may be informed of what has already happened in court and so coached or briefed before they then give evidence . . . '
- Anyone using electronic text is strictly bound by the existing restrictions on reporting court proceedings under the Contempt of Court Act 1981.
- Photography in court remains strictly forbidden under the Criminal Justice Act 1925.

I[1B.9]

Photographs and sketches in court. No person shall take or attempt to take a photograph, or make or attempt to make any portrait or sketch of a justice or party or witness to proceedings, in a court room or in a court building or precincts or entering or leaving them (Criminal Justice Act 1925, s 41).

I[1B.10]

Tape recorders. It is a contempt of court to use a tape recorder (other than for the purpose of making an official transcript) in a court without the leave of the court (Contempt of Court Act 1981, s 9). Guidelines for the decision whether to grant leave were given in a Practice Direction by the Lord Chief Justice in 1982 which may be summarised thus:

- Has the applicant a reasonable need to use the tape recorder?
- Is there a risk of a recording being used to brief witnesses?
- What is the possibility of distracting proceedings or distracting or worrying witnesses?

I[1B.11]

Abuse of the process. The jurisdiction exercised by magistrates, to protect the court's process from abuse is confined to matters directly affecting the fairness of the trial of the accused, and it does not extend to the wider supervisory jurisdiction for upholding the rule of law which is vested in the High Court (*R v Horseferry Road Magistrates, ex p Bennett* [1994] AC 42, [1993] 3 WLR 90, sub nom *Bennett v Horseferry Road Magistrates' Court* [1993] 3 All ER 138, HL). It must not be used, therefore, to exercise a disciplinary function over eg executive decisions made by a prosecuting authority.

The parameters of this power are narrowly drawn. Justices may only stay proceedings where it would be unfair to try the defendant or where the defendant cannot receive a fair trial. It may be an abuse of process if either (a) the prosecution have manipulated or misused the process of the court so as to deprive the defendant of a protection provided by the law or to take unfair advantage of a technicality, or (b) the defendant has been, or will be, prejudiced in the preparation or conduct of his defence by delay on the part of the prosecution which is unjustifiable.

Magistrates would be well advised to consult with their legal adviser before adjudicating on such matters. The defence should give advance notice of such application. Where notice is not given magistrates should look favourably on an adjournment application by the prosecution. In addition, the court should give directions for the filing of skeleton arguments by the parties. A skeleton argument should focus on the issues arising in the case and the relevant principles. An excessive citation of authorities is to be deprecated.

I[1B.12]

Principles. May be summarised as follows:

(1)   The discretionary decision as to whether or not to grant a stay as an abuse is an exercise in judicial assessment dependent on judgement, rather than on any conclusion as to fact based on evidence. Accordingly, in cases of delay it is potentially misleading to apply to the exercise of that discretion the language of burden and standard of proof, which is more apt to an evidence-based, fact-finding process (*R v S* [2006] EWCA Crim 756, (2006) 170 JP 434).

(2)   The applicant must identify the ground or grounds upon which he relies eg delay, manipulation of the proceedings or destruction of evidence.

(3)   Where there is no fault attributable to, or the prosecution have acted in good faith, it will be very rare for a stay to be granted.

(4)   Is there serious prejudice to the accused? No stay should be granted in the absence of serious prejudice to the accused. When assessing possible serious prejudice, the court should consider its powers to regulate the admissibility of evidence, and that the trial process itself should ensure that all relevant factual issues arising from eg delay or the destruction of evidence, are placed before the court for its consideration.

(5)   When assessing possible serious prejudice, the court can take into account its powers in relation to sentence, assuming there is a conviction or a guilty plea.

(6)   A permanent stay should be the exception rather than the rule.

(7)   If having considered all the relevant factors, the court's assessment is that a fair trial will be possible, a stay should not be granted.

Abuse of the process – long delay – relevant principles: *R v F* [2011] EWCA Crim 726, [2011] 2 Cr App Rep 145, 175 CL&J 213.

The Court of Appeal derived from a review of authority five propositions concerning the treatment of criminal proceedings brought after a long delay. Those propositions were:

- Proceedings should be stayed only if the court was satisfied that delay precluded a fair trial.
- An application for a stay should *normally* be made at trial after all the evidence has been heard.
- In assessing [serious] prejudice to the defendant, the court had to balance evidence that had survived the delay against missing evidence and critically examine the importance of the missing evidence.
- Having identified [serious] prejudice, the court had to consider whether it could come compensate for the prejudice by special [jury] directions.
- Unjustified delay by a complainant in coming forward was relevant to whether a fair trial could be achieved, but it had to be firmly borne in mind that sexual abuse victims were often unwilling to talk about their experiences for some time and for good reason.

Disclosure – delay – abuse of the process – test to be applied: *Brants v DPP* [2011] EWHC 754 (Admin), 175 JP 246.

A positive decision not to disclose relevant material culminating in delay may amount to an abuse of the process. In the case of *Brants*, the appellant, a driver of a heavy goods vehicle, was stopped by a police constable and required to produce his digital driver card. The officer downloaded the material held on the card onto his laptop. From this he produced reports and a list of offences under the Transport Act 1968, s 96. An information was laid alleging four contraventions relating to drivers' hours and rest periods. On 16 March 2009, solicitors for the appellant requested disclosure of the digital material downloaded by the police officer. It was first directed by the magistrates' court to be handed over on 14 May 2009. The material was not disclosed until 26 July 2009. At a later date, and as a preliminary issue, it was submitted that the proceedings were an abuse of the process by reason of delay. The justices ruled against the appellant and he changed his plea to guilty. On appeal by way of case stated.

The Queen's Bench Division decided this was not a case where the prosecution had positively refused to comply with a direction of the court. The prosecution did ultimately comply. However, there was a long delay before the material was disclosed. Whilst the court strongly disapproved of the failure to disclosure, the delay in this case was attributable to the inefficiency or incompetence of the prosecution: *R R (L)* [2010] EWCA Crim 924, [2011] 1 WLR 359, [2010] 2 Cr App Rep 63 distinguished.

It is submitted that the justices in *Brants* could have inferred a deliberate decision not to disclose the relevant material, having regard to the lapse of time and the number of adjourned hearings after a direction to disclose the material was given.

I[2]
Misbehaviour in court

I[2.1]
Misbehaviour by members of the public:

(a) Where persons misbehave in court the first approach should be to attempt to calm down offenders by an appeal to reason and good manners. A court can also consider putting the case back for a 'cooling off' period and the chairman may also make mention in very general terms of the court's powers to maintain order.

(b) If this is not successful a court has power to order persons disrupting the court to leave the court room. If they refuse, and their removal is necessary to enable justice to be administered properly, the court may order a court security officer or the police to remove such persons using reasonable force if necessary.

(c) Where persons are misbehaving in court the magistrates should not exercise their power to **bind over** (Consolidated Practice Direction para 54 (2002)).

I[3]

Contempt of court

Charges

I[3.1]–[3.3]

Contempt of court

(a) **Wilfully did insult AB being a justice of the peace (or a witness before the court, or an officer of the court, or a solicitor or counsel having business before the court) during his sitting or attendance in court or when he was going to or returning from the court; or**
(b) **wilfully interrupted the proceedings of a magistrates' court; or**
(c) **wilfully misbehaved in a magistrates' court.**

Contempt of Court Act 1981, s 12.

I[3.4]

Maximum penalty. Fine of level 4 and one month. Proceedings under s 12: offender may be ordered to be taken into custody by an officer of the court or a constable and detained until the rising of the court in addition to or instead of the penalty mentioned above. A person under 18 years may not be committed for contempt. A substantial prison sentence (12 months) was upheld in *R v D (contempt of court: illegal photography)* (2004) Times, 13 May where the defendant had photographed the interior of the Crown Court (see I[1B.8]).

Legal notes

I[3.5]

Wilfully insult. The word 'insult' has to be given its ordinary English meaning. A person who had *threatened* a defendant had not 'insulted' him and was not in breach of s 12 (*R v Havant Justices, ex p Palmer* (1985) 149 JP 609, [1985] Crim LR 658).

I[3.6]

Officer of the court. This term is not defined in the Act. It will apply to the justices' clerk and his staff, presumably whether or not they are concerned in the particular proceedings in which the insult occurs. If there is any doubt, the matter could certainly be resolved by simply alleging misbehaviour in court.

I[3.7]

Procedure. See *Practice Direction (Magistrates' Courts: Contempt)* [2001] 2 Cr App Rep 272. By the nature of such proceedings, feelings may be running high and it is a grave matter to punish someone for contempt of court. Accordingly magistrates should be careful not to act in haste. The court should allow time for reflection. If necessary the case can be put back to the end of the court list. If the offender is removed to the cells, he should have the opportunity of speaking to his solicitor or receiving other legal advice (legal representation is available for contempt proceedings). The offender should always be given the opportunity to apologise to the court and it may be that a genuine apology together with the brief period spent in the cells may suffice. If it is necessary to punish the offender imprisonment should be the last resort. Where a person has been in prison, for example, because he refuses to apologise he may apply subsequently to the magistrates to purge his contempt by apologising and the magistrates may then order his release from custody.

In the case of a contested contempt the overall trial process must be in accordance with Art 6 and this may mean involving a different bench to try the issue.

I[3.8]

Where the disorder in court is so overwhelming magistrates should retire immediately and allow the police to restore order. Where the offenders are subsequently dealt with, they should be dealt with individually.

I[3.9]

Witnesses. In addition to the powers outlined above, where a witness refuses to take the oath or to answer a question, he may be committed to prison for a period of up to one month (and ordered to pay a fine on level 4). He may be released immediately he changes his mind and decides to co-operate with the court. This advice may ensure his compliance.

I[3.10]–[3.14]

Defendants. Disorderly defendants may be dealt with as outlined above. However, a court is naturally reluctant to deal with the case in the absence of a defendant. Accordingly, if the defendant has to be ejected the court should carefully consider adjourning the case for a 'cooling off' period. The more serious the case the less appropriate it will be to proceed in the defendant's absence. The defendant should be informed that he will be readmitted to the court any time he is prepared to conduct himself properly.

I[3.15]

Taking a photograph in court with a mobile phone is a contempt of court and has resulted in immediate prison sentences in the Crown Court (*R v D* (2004) Times, 13 May). See I[1B.8].

I[3.16]

Appeal. An appeal against conviction and/or sentence under s 108 Magistrates' Courts Act 1980 lies to the Crown Court pursuant to s 12(5) of the 1981 Act (*Haw and Tucker v City of Westminster Magistrates' Court* [2007] EWHC 2960 (Admin), [2008] 2 All ER 326).

I[4]

Plea before venue and mode of trial proceedings

I[4.1]

**The following will apply when the new allocation proceedings under the Criminal Justice Act 2003 are brought into force. Schedule 3 of the CJA 2003 revises the procedures to be found in ss 4–8 and 17–25 of the Magistrates' Courts Act 1980. The revised procedure for adult offenders charged with an offence triable either way will be as follows:

Allocation – adult accused – Key points

(1) Indictable only offences – no change – send to the Crown Court.
(2) Summary only – unless linked to an indictable only or either way offence – no change – take a plea.
(3) Either way offences – modified procedures. Committal proceedings are to be abolished.

For either way offences the court will apply a modified procedure **unless:**

(1) Serious or complex fraud; vulnerable child witness; or offence linked to either situation and, the prosecutor has served a notice signifying Crown Court trial.
(2) Either a third specified drug or domestic burglary offence when the offence becomes indictable only.
(3) The offence is linked to an adult co-accused charged with an indictable only offence.

In 1–3 above the court must send the offender to the Crown Court for trial pursuant to s 51 Crime and Disorder Act 1998.

Procedure for either way offence:

(1) Defendant to indicate plea.
(2) If guilty, the court should normally decide whether it has power to sentence or to commit for sentence. Note, the plea must be unambiguous. If the accused pleads guilty and then qualifies the plea eg makes a statement which, if true, would amount to a defence to the charge, the court should then enter a plea of not guilty.
(3) On a guilty plea, if there is a dispute as to the facts which is material to sentence the court should conduct a Newton hearing, unless, on either version of the facts the sentencing powers of the magistrates' court are inadequate, when the justices should commit the defendant to the Crown Court for sentence.
(4) [If the adult is jointly charged with a juvenile and the allegation is a specified offence within the meaning of s 224 of the CJA 2003, the court must ask the youth to indicate a plea. If the plea is one of not

guilty, the court must inquire as to dangerousness. If the court determines that the juvenile is liable to be sentenced under the dangerousness provisions it must send the juvenile to the Crown Court pursuant to s 51A Crime & Disorder Act 1998. The adult should then be asked to indicate a plea. If the plea is one of not guilty he also must be sent to the Crown Court and for any related offence which is triable either way pursuant to s 51A(6)].

(5)   [Disregarding 4 above] If no plea or a not guilty plea is indicated the court will hear representations as to venue. The court is entitled to take into account the offender's previous convictions. The primary test is whether the court's sentencing powers are adequate. The court will make its decision taking the prosecution case at its highest. Personal mitigation is not relevant to the decision as to venue.

(6)   If the court determines Crown Court trial, it will immediately send the offender for trial pursuant to s 51 CDA 1998.

(7)   If the court determines summary trial, the defendant will be asked to elect where he wishes to be tried. Before making his choice, the defendant may ask for, or in some cases the court might decide to give an indication of sentence if he were to elect summary trial. If the court gives an indication it will express the sentence in general terms eg custody or a community penalty.

(8)   If the defendant elects trial at the Crown Court, the court will immediately send the defendant for trial pursuant to s 51. Any indication as to sentence will not be binding on the Crown Court.

(9)   If the accused elects summary trial, he will be asked to enter a plea. If the plea is one of guilty any indication as to sentence will be binding on the court unless the magistrates determine to commit for sentence under the dangerousness provisions (see s 3A PCC(S)A 2000).

(10)   Where there is more than one adult co-accused and a co-accused elects to be tried at the Crown Court, the court must send all defendants pleading not guilty to the Crown Court for trial, even if one or more co-accused have elected, or would have elected to have their cases tried summarily. The legislation reverses the rule in *R v Brentwood Justices, ex p Nicholls* (1990) 154 JP 487, HL.

(11)   If the defendant consents to trial in the magistrates' court and enters a plea of not guilty the court will proceed to summary trial. Any indication as to sentence will not be binding on the court even if the offender later changes his plea to one of guilty.

(12)   At a later date the prosecution can ask the court to review the mode of trial decision where (i) further information has become available since the decision as to venue was made; (ii) the court is satisfied that as its sentencing powers are inadequate. The power may not be exercised where the court has determined a pre-trial issue eg the admissibility of bad character evidence or hearsay evidence.

Allocation guidance – Sentencing Council guidelines:

- General presumption = summary trial.
- Broad rule of thumb – if in doubt as to venue – send to the Crown Court.
- Presumption that adult co-accused pleading not guilty should be tried together.

I[4.1A]

Current Procedures:

Where a person is accused of an offence triable either way, the magistrates cannot conduct committal proceedings or try the offence themselves until plea before venue proceedings have taken place. The court will invite the defendant to indicate his plea, having explained to him that he may be committed to the Crown Court for sentence if the court considers its powers are insufficient. If the defendant indicates a plea of guilty he will be treated as convicted and the court will proceed to sentence, or committal to the Crown Court for sentence. If the defendant fails to intimate a plea or intimates a plea of not guilty the court will hear representations on the seriousness of the case, both from the prosecutor and the defendant. The court at this stage is only concerned with the gravity of the offence and not with the character of the defendant, and previous convictions of the accused are, therefore, irrelevant and should not be mentioned. The prosecutor should therefore give the court an outline of the prosecution case so that the gravity of the offence can be ascertained, eg in an assault case: the description of the injuries caused and whether a weapon was used. The defence may then make representations if it wishes before the magistrates make their decision.

Once mode of trial has been decided there is no inherent jurisdiction to change it. Such procedure is prescribed by MCA 1980, s 25 (*R (DPP) v Camberwell Green Youth Court* [2005] UKHL 4, 2005] All ER (D) 259 (Jan)).

Although *R (on the application of C) v Grimsby and Cleethorpes Magistrates* [2004] EWHC 2240 (Admin), [2004] All ER (D) 494 (Jul) suggests that s 25 has no application in the magistrates' court to proceedings against juveniles it is submitted that this observation is per incuriam having regard to the decision of the Divisional Court in *H v Balham Youth Court* [2003] EWHC 3267 (Admin), [2003] All ER (D) 173 (Dec).

For abuse of process arguments see I[14.8] below.

Matters to which the court is to have regard

I[4.2]

The court must have regard to the following matters:

(a)   The nature of the case;
(b)   whether the circumstances make the offence one of a serious character;
(c)   whether the punishment which a magistrates' court would have power to inflict for it would be adequate (*R v Flax Bourton Magistrates' Court, ex p Customs and Excise Comrs* (1996) 160 JP 481, [1996] Crim LR 907);

(d)   any other circumstances which appear to the court to make it more suitable for the offence to be tried in one way rather than the other (Magistrates' Courts Act 1980, s 19(3)).

I[4.3]

If the magistrates feel able to deal with the case the defendant is given a choice of which court he wishes to try the offence. Before he makes his choice he *must* be warned that if he elects summary trial and pleads guilty or is convicted after a trial he may still be committed for sentence if the court is of the opinion that the offence (or the combination of the offence and other associated offences) is so serious that the magistrates' powers of punishment are insufficient, or, in the case of a violent or sexual offence, a longer sentence is necessary for protection of the public.

I[4.4]

In accordance with s 122(2) of the Coroners and Justice Act 2009, the Sentencing Council has issued definitive guidance entitled 'Allocation'. It applies to all defendants in the magistrates' courts (including youths jointly charged with adults) whose cases are dealt with on or after 11 June 2012. It will not be applicable in the youth court where a separate statutory procedure applies.

Allocation guidelines

I[4.5]

The guidelines to be followed are:

- In general, either way offences should be tried summarily unless it is likely that the court's sentencing powers will be insufficient.
- Its powers will generally be insufficient if the outcome is likely to result in a sentence in excess of six months' imprisonment.
- The court should assess the likely sentence in the light of the facts alleged by the prosecution case, taking into account all aspects of the case including those advanced by the defence.
- The court should refer to definitive guidelines to assess the likely sentence for the offence.

Committal for sentence. There is ordinarily no statutory restriction on committing an either way case for sentence following conviction. The general power of a magistrates' court to commit to the Crown Court for sentence after a finding that a case is suitable for summary trial and/or conviction continues to be available where the court is of opinion that the offence (and any associated offences) is so serious that greater punishment should be inflicted than the court has power to impose (s 3 of the PCCSA 2000). Where the court decides that the case is suitable to be dealt with in the magistrates' court, it should remind the defendant that all sentencing options remain open, including committal to the Crown Court for the sentence at the time it informs the defendant of this decision.

I[4.6]

Criminal damage offences. However, where the court proceeds (only) to the summary trial of certain offences relating to criminal damage, upon conviction there is no power to commit to the Crown Court for sentence (ss 2 and 33 of the MCA 1980). See B[9.4].

I[4.7]

Linked cases. Where a youth and an adult are jointly charged, the youth must be tried summarily unless the court considers it to be in the interests of justice for both the youth and the adult to be committed to the Crown Court for trial. Examples of factors that should be considered when deciding whether to separate the youth and adult defendants include:

- whether separate trials can take place without causing undue convenience to witnesses or injustice to the case as a whole
- the young age of the defendant, particularly where the age gap between the adult and youth offender is substantial
- the immaturity of the youth
- the relative culpability of the youth compared with the adult and whether or not the role played by the youth was minor
- the lack of previous convictions on the part of the youth.

I[4.8]

Indictable offences only. Under the Crime and Disorder Act 1998, s 51 indictable offences (such as aggravated burglary and grievous bodily harm) only have an initial hearing in the magistrates' court to decide on bail and legal representation.

The case will then transfer straight to the Crown Court for a preliminary hearing (within eight days if the defendant is in custody). There will be no committal proceedings and any challenge to the evidence will be made to a judge at the Crown Court.

The section does not apply generally to persons under 18 years of age or corporations.

Abuse of process. Prior to sending an indictable offence to the Crown Court under the Crime and Disorder Act 1998, s 51, a magistrates' court has jurisdiction to stay criminal proceedings as an abuse of the process: *R (on the application of Craik, Chief Constable of Northumbria Police) v Newcastle Upon Tyne Magistrates' Court (Price, interested party)* [2010] EWHC 935 (Admin), 174 CL&J 334, [2010] 5 Archbold Review, 2. However, it will rarely be appropriate to do so. The rule seems analogous to committal proceedings, ie such matters should normally be left to the Crown Court Judge to determine. See *R v Belmarsh Magistrates' Court, ex p Watts* [1999] 2 Cr App Rep 188.

I[5]

Committal for trial at Crown Court

**Committal proceedings will be abolished once the new allocation procedures under the Criminal Justice Act 2003 have been introduced. See I[4.1].

I[5.1]

Magistrates have no power to try the guilt or innocence of an adult accused charged with an offence triable only at the Crown Court or with an offence triable either way where either the magistrates themselves have declined jurisdiction in mode of trial proceedings or the accused has elected to be tried at the Crown Court. See B[11]–B[16] for committal for sentence.

I[5.2]

Magistrates dealing with committal proceedings are referred to examining justices. They examine the prosecution case to decide whether there is sufficient evidence to put the defendant on trial by jury. The sole test for the justices to apply is whether the prosecution has adduced sufficient evidence to satisfy them that there is a triable issue to be put before a jury. This is normally done where the defendant is represented, by statements tendered by the prosecution being accepted by the defence lawyer. In this case the defendant is formally committed to stand trial at the Crown Court with a date for either a plea and directions hearing or a preliminary hearing. If the defence do not accept that there is a prima facie case the court will consider the prosecution evidence only.

I[5.3]

A magistrates' court will consider only documentary evidence and exhibits tendered by the prosecution, together with representations by both parties, when determining whether there is a case to answer. Evidence should be presented in accordance with s 5B–5E of the Magistrates' Courts Act 1980 and will be read out in full unless the court directs that it is summarised. No witness will be called to give evidence or be cross examined. The defence may make submissions that there is insufficient evidence to put the accused on trial by jury. If the court is of the opinion that the statements disclose evidence upon which a jury could convict of an indictable offence the defendant will be committed to stand trial at the Crown Court. If they are not of that view the defendant will be discharged.

General provisions concerning committal proceedings

I[5.4]

The hearing. The committal proceedings may take place before only one magistrate but any hearing must take place in open court unless for any part, or the whole, of the proceedings, the ends of justice would not be served by having a sitting in open court. The evidence shall be tendered in the presence of the accused unless his disorderly conduct has made it impracticable for him to remain in court or he is ill and is represented by an advocate and has consented to the evidence being tendered in his absence (Magistrates' Courts Act 1980, s 4). See *R v Liverpool City Magistrates, ex p Quantrell* [1999] 2 Cr App Rep 24, [1999] Crim LR 734.

In *R (on the application of Khan) v Waltham Forest Magistrates' Courts* [2007] EWHC 1801 (Admin), [2007] All ER (D) 29 (Jul) magistrates adjourned a committal hearing for one week where the prosecution sought an adjournment for 'administrative failures'. In upholding the decision the High Court said this: 'In the instant case, the material submitted by the justices indicated that they had not failed to give proper weight to the application before them. [However] no consideration had been given by either party or, the court, to the possibility of adjourning the hearing later on in the day'. Clearly the committal paperwork was missing but it was a straightforward case and copies of the statements would have sufficed for committal purposes: see *Re Harding (decd)* (unreported) (1998).

I[5.5]

Publicity. Only certain formal matters may be contained in any report of committal proceedings including:

(a)   the identity of the court and the names of the examining justices;
(b)   the names, addresses and occupations of the parties and witnesses and ages of the accused and witnesses; and
(c)   the offence or offences, or a summary of them, of which the accused is or are charged;
(d)   where the court commits the accused or any of the accused for trial, the charge or charges, or a summary of them, on which he is committed and the court to which he is committed;
(e)   any arrangement as to bail on committal or adjournment;
(f)   whether legal representation was granted to the accused or any of the accused.

I[5.6]

These restrictions automatically apply unless an accused chooses to have the reporting restrictions lifted. Where there are several accused, and they are not unanimous in wanting restrictions to be lifted, the magistrates must decide whether it is in the interests of justice to do so. Further, the restrictions do not apply where the accused are all discharged in the proceedings or after the conclusion of the trial in the Crown Court.

Summary offences

(Criminal Justice Act 1988, ss 40 and 41)

I[5.7]

Where an accused is committed or sent for trial for an offence triable either way, the magistrates may also commit or send him for trial for any connected summary offences provided they are either imprisonable or endorsable. At the Crown Court, if the accused is convicted of the indictable offence, he may also plead guilty to the summary offences and be dealt with, the Crown Court having the same powers as the magistrates with respect to the summary offences. If he denies the summary offences he may not be tried for them in the Crown Court, but proceedings may then continue in the magistrates' court (Criminal Justice Act 1988, s 41).

I[5.8]

Certain summary offences including common assault, damage and taking without consent may be heard at the Crown Court if they arise from the same facts or evidence as an indictable charge being committed to the crown court or they are part of a series of offences of the same or similar character as the indictable charge (Criminal Justice Act 1988, s 40).

I[6]

Summary proceedings

1 *Criminal Procedural Rules (CPR)*

I[6.1]

Increasingly the higher courts (see for example *R v L* [2007] EWCA Crim 764) are emphasising the importance of both the courts and the parties to criminal proceedings discharging their obligations under the Criminal Procedure Rules 2012, particularly those rules dealing with case management (Part 3). In *Narinder Malcolm v DPP* [2007] EWHC 363 (QB), reference was made by the High Court to the overriding objective of Part I of the CPR:

> 'Criminal trials are no longer to be treated as a game, in which any move is final and any omissions by the prosecution leads to its failure. It is the duty of the defence to make its defence and the issues it raises clear to the prosecution and to the court at an early stage. The duty is implicit in r 3.3 of the CPR, which requires the parties actively to assist the exercise by the courts of its case management powers, the exercise of which requires early identification of the real issues.' (per Stanley Brunton J at para 31)

CPR, Part 1 – Overriding objective:

I[6.2]

1.1 To ensure that criminal cases are dealt with **justly**.

1.2 The duty of participants in a criminal case:

(a)   Prepare and conduct the case in accordance with the overriding objective.
(b)   Comply with the CPR, Practice Directions and any directions given by the court.
(c)   Inform the court and parties of any significant failure to take any procedural step as required in (b) above.

Anyone involved in any way with a criminal case is a **participant** in its conduct for the purposes of this rule.

Notification of intention to call defence witnesses. Section 6C of the Criminal Procedure and Investigations Act 1996 was brought into force on 1 May 2010. The section provides that the accused must give to the court and the prosecutor a notice indicating whether he intends to call any persons (other than himself) as witnesses at his trial and, if so, the name, address and date of birth of each such proposed witness, or as many of those details as are known to the accused when the notice is given; and provide any information in the accused's possession which might be of material assistance in identifying or finding any such proposed witness. The provision of the witness' details must be given within 14 days of the service or purported service of initial disclosure (subject to an application to extend for good reason within the 14 day period).

The revised legislation reverses in effect the decision in *R (on the application of Kelly) v Warley Magistrates' Court and the Law Society* [2007] EWHC 1836 (Admin).

The requirement to provide the relevant details applies on or after the operative date, irrespective of the fact that the prosecution commenced before 1 May. A revised section 11 of the 1996 Act permits a party to comment on the failure of the accused to comply with any provision of s 6C and/or for the court to draw such inferences as appear proper from that failure. The court may not convict solely on inferences drawn under s 11, similar to ss 34–38 of the Criminal Justice and Public Order Act 1994 (inferences from silence etc).

NB: Part 3 of the CPR 2012 sets out the general duties and powers of the court, and the duties of the parties, relevant to the pre-trial preparation of a criminal case. However, the CPR contained no sanctions for a party's failure to comply with a procedural rule or with a case management direction made by the court. The court's powers to make a costs order in consequence of such a failure, to adjourn the case or, in some circumstances, to exclude evidence or to draw adverse inferences from a late introduction of an issue or evidence, are powers that are conferred by other legislation and under some other procedural rules. Having considered the *Kelly* judgment the Criminal Procedure Rules Committee introduced what is now CPR 2012, rr 3.5 and 3.10 to make the court's powers to impose sanctions for failure to comply with a procedural rule or procedural direction explicit (see I[6.3] below).

In addition, further changes were introduced by the Criminal Justice and Immigration Act (Commencement No 3 and Transitional Provisions) Order 2008 from 3 November 2008. Section 6A(1) of the Criminal Procedure and Investigations Act 1996 has been amended to provide that a defence statement:

"(ca) set out particulars of the matters of fact on which he intends to rely for the purposes of his defence".

Section 11(2)(f)(ii) (defaults in disclosure by accused) has also been amended to reflect subsection (ca) above.

CPR, Part 3.2 – The duty of the court

I[6.3]

The court must further the overriding objective by actively managing the case.

Active case management includes –

(a)   early identification of the real issues;
(b)   early identification of the needs of witnesses;
(c)   setting a timetable (see immediately below);
(d)   monitoring the progress of the case and compliance with directions;
(e)   discouraging delay;
(f)   making use of technology;
(g)   the facilitation of the attendance of witnesses when they are needed.

'In setting the timetable, the court should scrutinise the reasons why it is said a witness is necessary and the time examination and cross-examination would take. It is also important in setting a timetable to have regard to the nature of the issues and the fact that the trial is a summary trial; any estimate of more than a day in the Magistrates' Courts should be scrutinised with the utmost rigour. Parties must realise that a summary trial requires a proportionate approach. If a timetable for the trial is not set, it is difficult to have any real confidence that the estimate is accurate. At the commencement of the trial, the Magistrates' Court should check with the parties that the timetable and the estimates remain valid. If there is any variation which lengthens the estimate, the court should make every effort to see if the trial can still be accommodated that day by sitting late or otherwise. Once the trial has started, the court must actively manage the trial, keeping an eye on progress in relation to the timetable': *R (on the application of Drinkwater) v Solihull Magistrates' Court and CPS* [2012] EWHC 765 (Admin), 176 JP 401.

CPR, Part 3.3 – The duty of the parties

I[6.4]

Each party must –

(a)   actively assist the court in fulfilling its duty under Part 3.2 without or if necessary with a direction; and
(b)   apply for a direction if needed to further the overriding objective.

A person or organisation directly involved in a criminal case, either as prosecutor or defendant is a party (see the glossary to the CPR).

For the responsibility of a solicitor involved in criminal litigation under CPR, Part 3, see *R (on the application of Robinson) v Abergavenny Magistrates' Court* [2007] All ER (D) 210 (Jul).

In *R (on the application of Martin) v Harrow Crown Court* [2007] EWHC 31893 (Admin), [2007] All ER (D) 106 (Dec), it was decided that in order to avoid an adjournment in a speeding case where measurements of the distances between street lamps was required for the purpose of determining whether a road was a 'restricted road' within the meaning of s 82(1)(a) of the Road Traffic Regulation Act 1984, good practice dictated that the defendant notify the prosecution in advance that the latter would be put to proof on the matter at trial.

A **Practice Note** for guidance to **solicitors** entitled '*Criminal Procedure Rules 2005: impact on solicitors; duties to the client*' was issued by the Law Society on 16 August 2007. A revised Practice Note to solicitors entitled "Criminal plea in absence of full disclosure" was issued on 20 January 2011. A copy of this Practice Note can be accessed via http://www.lawsociet y.org.uk/advice/practice-notes/plea-in-absence-disclosure/.

Adjournment applications

I[6.5]

Examination of a number of decisions of the superior courts suggests that the judges in those courts will be prepared to uphold pre-trial decisions of magistrates including applications for adjournments (whether pre-trial or on the day of hearing), provided the magistrates, through their reasons, can demonstrate that they have properly identified and taken into account the relevant factors and exercised their discretion appropriately: see for example, *R (on the application of Khan) v Waltham Forest Magistrates' Court* [2007] EWHC 1801 (Admin), [2007] All ER (D) 29 (Jul).

The following will hopefully assist magistrates in identifying the relevant factors when faced with an adjournment application.

Adjournment applications – checklist

I[6.6]

The following checklist applies to adjournment applications:

- CPR, Part 1: Overriding duty on court to ensure criminal cases are dealt with justly
- ECHR, Article 6: The accused is entitled to a trial within a reasonable period of time
- ECHR, Article 6: The accused is entitled to a reasonable period of time in order to prepare his case

The 'overriding duty' does not mean that the court must adjourn on application, even where both parties seek an adjournment.

Broad approach to adjournment applications

I[6.7]

The following broad approach should be taken to adjournment applications:

- What is the full (or relevant) history of the case?
- Has there been any pre-trial correspondence? – What was the court's response?
- Is it just or fair to depart from that pre-trial decision (reasons needed)? (see *Robinson v Abergavenny Magistrates' Court* [2007] EWHC 2005 (Admin)).

A.   First Hearing

I[6.8]

Establish whether any issues that might affect jurisdiction eg such as dangerousness or under the Proceeds of Crime Act 2002.

Clarify whether any issues such as special measures, expert evidence or pre-trial issues such as bad character or hearsay (see I[6.13] below).

Does the defendant require the services of an interpreter?

Plea

I[6.9]

Has the defendant received **initial details** (formerly advance disclosure) of the prosecution case? The prosecutor's duty is to serve those details on the court officer and make those details available to the defendant at, or before, the beginning of the day of the first hearing – if yes, proceed to take plea.

If no, are the details on file? – How detailed is the information? (Consider standing back the case for the defence to take instructions.) A revised Practice Note to solicitors entitled "Criminal plea in absence of full disclosure" was issued on 20 January 2011. A copy of the Practice note can be accessed at http://www.lawsociety.org.uk/advice/practice-notes/plea-in-a bsence-disclosure/.

CCTV: Is the prosecution relying on CCTV to prove its case? Does the CCTV evidence form part of the details disclosed? If available stand back for defence to view. If not, proceed to plea.

Initial details: A summary of the prosecution case in documentary form. By definition does not normally include CCTV or video evidence.

NB: There is a common misconception that initial details (formerly known as advance disclosure) includes CCTV (see CPR 2011, Part 21). This was based on a generous concession made by counsel in *R v Calderdale Magistrates' Court, ex p Donahue and Cutler* [2001] Crim LR 141, that 'document' included a video. This concession was doubted in *DPP v Croydon Magistrates' Court* [2001] EWHC 552 (Admin).

NB: The prosecutor's obligation to furnish details (primary disclosure) was initially aimed at offences 'triable either way'. Given the obligations under the ECHR, the prosecutor's duty is wider and can extend to summary only cases. However, the extent and nature of the disclosure will depend on factors such as the seriousness of the charge (*R v Stratford Magistrates' Court, ex p Imbert* [1999] 2 Cr App R 276.

Defence advocates should, save in exceptional circumstances, go through the details with the defendant and advise on such matters as venue and plea without the need for an adjournment.

Having put the case back, proceed to take a plea or indication of plea and/or mode of trial.

Legal Aid

I[6.10]

Has the defendant submitted an application? When? Why any delay in submission? – If defendant in receipt of benefits or paid employment stand back in the list for a decision by the court administration.

If the defendant is self-employed, has he attached accounts to the legal aid application? If not, why not? Put back to clarify the position with the court administration.

Seek clarification as to when a decision as to legal representation can be made. If necessary to adjourn, list on the earliest practicable date.

Prosecution Evidence (initial disclosure)

I[6.11]

This duty only arises after a not guilty plea has been entered. Do not adjourn before plea. After a not guilty plea has been entered give directions on the service of the evidence eg within 14 days.

Initial disclosure: All material in the prosecutor's possession to be used to prove the case against the accused.

As to a failure to make disclosure following a direction of the court see I[1B.11] above.

B.   First or Subsequent Hearing

I[6.12]

Disclosure of unused prosecution material. The duty on the prosecutor arises only after a not guilty plea has been entered.

Unused material: Any prosecution material which might reasonably be considered capable of undermining the case for the prosecution against the accused or of assisting the case for the accused.

Has the CPS fully complied with its legal duties (see below)?

Has the defence filed a voluntary defence statement? If not, the accused cannot make an application for disclosure of unused material.

Any voluntary defence statement should normally be served within 14 days of the date upon which the prosecution has complied with its duty to provide initial disclosure.

Has the accused in his defence statement set out particulars of the matters of fact on which he intends to rely for the purposes of his defence?

Any defence application to extend the timeframe must be in writing and must be made <u>before</u> the time limit expires.

The late service of a defence statement does not formally preclude the court from considering a proper application.

Where there is late service of a defence statement, any application to adjourn for further disclosure or to adjourn the trial, must be scrutinised closely (see immediately below).

If it is just to adjourn the case, the court should immediately consider the question of wasted costs (see ss 19, 19A and 19B Prosecution of Offences Act 1985 and regulations made thereunder); or, where the defendant is publicly funded, to notify the Legal Services Commission. The court must give <u>reasons</u> for its decision.

On wasted costs, it is necessary for magistrates to consult their legal adviser.

C.   Pre-trial Issues

I[6.13]

General. Magistrates are often called upon to deal with applications either pre-trial or on the date of trial. Examples include bad character and hearsay applications.

- What are the issues?
- Is the evidence and/or testimony of live witnesses material?
- Could a section 9 (CJA 1967) statement cover the relevant ground?
- Can the parties formally agree the evidence under s 10 CJA 1967?
- Are court directions necessary eg filing of evidence or skeleton arguments?

I[6.13A]

Power to make, vary or discharge pre-trial rulings. Section 8A of the Magistrates' Courts Act 1980 authorises a magistrates' court to make binding pre-trial rulings. That ruling remains binding upon the parties and the court unless a party applies to the court to discharge or vary that ruling on the grounds that there has been a material change of circumstances since the ruling was made (MCA 1980, s 8B).

It is open to a court of its own motion to vary or discharge a previous ruling of the magistrates' court but not solely on the basis that it would have reached a different conclusion; there must be a compelling reason such as changed circumstances or fresh evidence (*R (on the application of the CPS) v Gloucester Justices* [2008] EWHC 1488 (Admin), 172 JP 406).

In *Jones v South East Surrey Local Justice Area* [2010] EWHC 916 (Admin), 174 JP 342 it was recognised at common law that a lower court had limited power to reverse and to revoke a previously made order. It could so in the interests of justice, in particular, in changed circumstances.

However, the parameters of the interests of justice test were to be measured not simply by reference to a "change of circumstances" but by reference to ss 8A and 8B of the Magistrates' Courts Act 1980 and the overriding objective of the Criminal Procedure Rules. As a result each case had to be decided in the light of it own particular circumstances. In the instant case, the justices had been right to grant the adjournment sought. There had been a "change of circumstances". For one it was clear on the day of trial, unlike the previous day, that the error for the delay lay with the police and not the Crown Prosecution Service. That may have influenced the decision that the magistrates made to refuse the adjournment.

Per Cranston J: "None of what I have said is to give encouragement to poor initial applications, which have to be supplemented later by applications to remedy the defect".

Special measures for vulnerable and intimidated witnesses

Definition: In the case of certain witnesses in criminal proceedings (other than the accused), a magistrates' court may make a "special measures direction" for the purpose of improving the quality of a witness's evidence. The statutory test or emphasis is designed to improve "the quality of a witness's evidence".

Special measures can take one of a number of forms:

- Screening the witness from the accused
- The giving of evidence by live link
- The giving of evidence in private
- Removal of wigs and gowns (arises normally only in the Crown Court)
- Video recorded evidence in chief
- Video recorded cross-examination and re-examination
- Examination of a witness through an intermediary
- Aids to communication

Other protection afforded to a witness can include:

- Protection from cross-examination by the accused in person
- Restrictions on evidence and questions about the complainant's bad character and more important (in a sexual case), sexual behaviour
- Restrictions on reporting

Inherent powers to protect a witness (as well as the accused) continue to apply:

— Provision of an interpreter (including an intermediary): see *R (on the application of AS) v Great Yarmouth Youth Court* [2011] EWHC 2059 (Admin)
— Use of screens

Eligibility for assistance: All persons aged under 18 years (as opposed to 17 years above) will automatically qualify as witnesses eligible for assistance.

Automatic eligibility for complainants in sexual cases has been extended to cover witnesses in specified gun and knife crimes which are listed in a new Sch 1A to the Youth Justice and Criminal Evidence Act 1999. A witness can still continue to inform the court that he/she does not wish to be eligible for assistance.

The Coroners and Justice Act 2009 removed the special category of child witnesses who are "in need of special protection". The effect is to place all child witnesses on the same footing, regardless of the offence to which the proceedings relate. There are further provisions allowing the child witness to opt out of giving evidence by a combination of video recorded and live link. The provisions are quite involved and magistrates should consult their legal adviser before giving further directions as to the conduct of the trial.

Evidence by live link: The court is able to give a direction allowing a witness to give evidence by live link. The court can also direct that a person specified by the court can accompany the witness when he/she is giving evidence by live link. The court must take the witness's wishes into account when it determines who is to accompany the witness.

Protected witness: Section 35 of the 1999 Act prevents the cross-examination of a "protected witness" by an accused in person. The definition of a protected witness includes a child. The definition of "child" has been amended to mean a person under the age of 18 years (as opposed to 17 years).

Quality of evidence: Special measures may only be authorised where the court considers that they would improve the quality of a witness's evidence, ie in terms of completeness, coherence and accuracy. Coherence refers to a witness's ability in giving evidence to give answers which address the questions put to the witness and can be understood both individually and collectively.

Procedure: The Criminal Procedure Rules 2012 govern the process. In broad terms the application for special measures must normally be made within a specific time frame and address the matters canvassed above; notably, the application must identify what sort of measures are sought and how those measures will improve the quality of the witness's evidence. It is good practice for the prosecution to attach a statement from the witness where it is being asserted that he/she is in fear or distress (not necessarily of the accused but of the court process).

If another party (usually the defence) object to the application they should normally object in writing within a given time frame. The notice of objection should address the points raised in the application for special measures.

Decision: It is for the court to determine and weigh the application in the light of the representations or evidence put before it. Be careful not to attach too much weight to assertions unsupported by evidence. The fact that there is some suggestion from the defence that there has been contact between the witness and defence during the court proceedings is not in itself sufficient to rebut the application. If there is a statement from a witness saying that he/she is in fear of giving evidence in front of the defendant without special measures, the court should attach some weight to this evidence when assessing whether it would be likely to improve the quality of the witness's evidence.

The Criminal Law Review (Issue No 7, 2012) recently reported two cases which may be of substantial benefit to the work of the court: *R v Edwards* [2011] EWCA Crim 3028, [2012] Crim LR 563 and *R v Wills* [2011] EWCA Crim 1938, [2012] 1 Cr App Rep 16, [2012] Crim LR 565.

If you read the judgments you will see in the Commentaries that the Judicial College accepted the invitation of the Court of Appeal in *Wills* and subsequently issued a Bench Checklist for Young Witness cases now available at: http://www.judiciary.gov.uk/publications-and-reports/guida nce/2012/jc-bench-checklist-young-wit-cases

This guidance, inter alia, instructs both advocates at 'ground rules' discussions to adapt their questions to a child's developmental stage enabling the child to give his/her best evidence. Consistent with the CPR it will also enable the court to control the conduct of the case and the manner in which the advocates conduct their cases, notably, the defence advocate's cross-examination of the witness.

Judging by the observation in the Commentary to *R v E* it seems to me there may be merit in the court directing the appointment of an intermediary who can be of real value in privately advising the prosecution or defence on how to formulate particular questions for a very young witness or one with learning difficulties

I[6.14]

CPR, Part 35 – bad character – defendant. Has the prosecutor complied with the notice requirements? – If not, is there an acceptable reason for not complying with the rules?

Has a certificate of readiness for trial already been filed by the party seeking to make the application?

Applications made very late or on the date of trial without good reason should be dealt with robustly, including a refusal of the application if its primary effect is to prejudice the fair trial of the accused.

Check that the application is not caught by s 98 of the CJA 2003 (definition of the term 'bad character'). [See *R v Chopra* [2006] EWCA Crim 2133, [2006] All ER (D) 44 (Dec); *R v Wallace* [2007] EWCA Crim 1760, 171 JP 543.]

Under which gateway or gateways is the application made (see s 101 CJA 2003)? The application should identify the gateway and its relevance.

In some cases (seek legal advice), the court is entitled to exclude the bad character evidence on the grounds that its prejudicial effect outweighs its probative value (s 101(1)(d), (g) CJA 2003).

Reasons needed.

Case law: see *R v Hanson* [2005] EWCA Crim 824, (2005) 1 WLR 3169.

I[6.15]

CPR, Part 35 – bad character – non-defendant (witness). Have the notice requirements been complied with? If not, is there an acceptable reason for not complying with the rules?

Has a certificate of readiness for trial already been filed by the party seeking to make the application?

Applications made very late or on the day of trial without good reason should be dealt with robustly, including a refusal of the application, having regard to the statutory assumption (see below) and if its primary effect is to prejudice a fair trial.

What is the relevance of the non-defendant's bad character? Assume the evidence is not admissible unless under s 100 of the CJA 2003 it is –

(a)   important explanatory evidence,
(b)   it has substantial probative value in relation to a matter which –
    (i)   is a matter in issue in the proceedings, and
    (ii)   is of substantial importance in the context of the case as a whole, or
(c)   all the parties to the proceedings agree to the evidence being admissible.
    •   Ask the parties to define 'important explanatory evidence'.
    •   Ask the parties to define 'substantial probative value'.
    •   Except where paragraph (c) above applies, evidence of the bad character of a witness may not be given without the leave of the court.
    •   Court must give reasons for its decision.

I[6.16]

CPR, Part 34 – hearsay evidence. Have the notice requirements been complied with? If not, is there an acceptable reason for not complying with the rules?

Has a certificate of readiness for trial already been filed by the party seeking to make the application?

Applications made very late or on the day of trial without good reason should be dealt with robustly, including a refusal of the application, if its primary affect is to prejudice a fair trial.

Does the application identify the nature and type of hearsay evidence to be adduced (see s 114 CJA 2003 onwards)?

How important is the hearsay evidence in the context of the case a whole?

Weigh the relevant factors and other considerations prescribed by s 114(2) CJA 2003 (see *R v Cole* [2007] EWCA Crim 1924).

Court to reach a determination and give reasons for its decision.

D.   Trial

I[6.17]
See 'Broad approach to adjournment applications' at I[6.7] above.

Was a certificate of readiness for trial filed either by both parties or a party? In the absence of a compelling reason, be prepared to refuse an application to adjourn the trial.

Be prepared to proceed in absence.

Remember r 3.8(4) (Case preparation and progression): 'In order to prepare for the trial, the court must take every reasonable step to encourage and to facilitate the attendance of witnesses when they are needed'.

Evidence eg sick notes, must state unfit to attend court.

Start promptly, unless there is a very good reason to the contrary.

If unable to start the trial, consider reading section 9 statements and the record of taped interview while waiting.

If the court deems it necessary for the s 9 statements etc to be read out, ask the parties to summarise the contents, where appropriate.

Do not delay the trial to allow for the editing of statements. This can be done later in the day.

Prioritise and call on as soon as practicable those witnesses available to give live evidence. Take their evidence out of order where that is feasible and will not affect the fairness or outcome of the trial.

Give reasons for your decision to proceed and/or your verdict.

E.   Guilty plea entered

I[6.18]
Where possible proceed to sentence.
- How serious is the offence?
- What is the guideline or starting point?
- Does the court need a psychiatric report? Would it materially affect the sentence?

- Does the court need more information? Would it materially affect the sentence?
- How long would it take to obtain a psychiatric report?
- Is a full pre-sentence report necessary? Would an oral or fast-delivery report suffice?

2 Not guilty plea

I[6.19]

See **section 1** above and in particular issues associated with pre-trial disclosure and pre-trial issues eg bad character applications.

When an accused person enters a not guilty plea, he is not necessarily proclaiming his innocence. This arises from two factors: first, it is not the function of the court to decide whether he is guilty or not, the court's function is to decide *whether the prosecutor has proved that he is guilty*. Second, there may be legal or procedural reasons why an accused should enter a not guilty plea as will be seen from the following circumstances. A plea of not guilty should be entered when:

(a) the accused disputes the facts;
(b) the accused hopes to show that some legal condition precedent to conviction has not been fulfilled, eg a notice of intended prosecution;
(c) the accused believes that the prosecutor's witnesses will be incapable of establishing the facts beyond reasonable doubt, for example because:
  (i)   there is a question of legal competence;
  (ii)   there is lack of corroboration in a case where the law requires it;
  (iii) evidence vital to the prosecution is legally inadmissible;
  (iv)   the accused believes he can discredit a prosecution witness by cross- examination;
(d) the accused agrees the facts but wishes to show that as a matter of law they do not constitute the offence charged;
(e) the accused has a statutory defence;
(f) the accused has no recollection of the circumstances alleged by the prosecutor and wishes to hear evidence before deciding whether he should plead guilty.

At the commencement of the trial, the Magistrates' Court should check with the parties that the timetable and the estimates remain valid. If there is any variation which lengthens the estimate, the court should make every effort to see if the trial can still be accommodated that day by sitting late or otherwise. Once the trial has started, the court must actively manage the trial, keeping an eye on progress in relation to the timetable: *R (on the application of Drinkwater) v Solihull Magistrates' Court and CPS* [2012] EWHC 765 (Admin), 176 JP 401.

Trial in absence. Section 11 of the Magistrates' Courts Act 1980 provides the general authority for proceeding in the absence of the accused subject, in the case of a summons, to its being served in accordance with the rules (*R* *(on the application of Durham County Council) v North Durham Justices* [2004] EWHC 1073 (Admin), [2004] All ER (D) 260 (Apr)). The Divisional Court handed down broad guidance in *R v Ealing Magistrates Court, ex p Burgess* (1999) 163 JP 82, [2000] Crim LR 855 on hearing a trial in the defendant's absence. The Court indicated that the defendant must be given a fair opportunity (but not an unlimited opportunity) to be present. A defendant may waive his right to be present or to be represented (*R v Haywood* [2001] EWCA Crim 168, [2001] All ER (D) 256 (Jan); affd [2002] UKHL 5, [2002] All ER (D) 275 (Feb)) and may by his behaviour be said to have voluntarily absented himself (*R v Jones* [2002] UKHL 5, [2003] 1 AC 1) but not where the defendant is known by the court to be in custody at the time of his trial (*R (R) v Thames Youth Court* [2002] EWHC 1670 (Admin), (2002) 166 JP 613; *R (on the application of Morsby) v Tower Bridge Magistrates' Court* [2007] EWHC 2766 (Admin)).

In *R (on the application of Davies) v Solihull Justices* [2008] EWHC 157 (Admin), the defendant while awaiting trial for an offence under s 4 of the Public Order Act 1986, was excluded from the court precincts by a member of the court security staff pursuant to s 53 of the Courts Act 2003. The Divisional Court held that the justices' view that the defendant had voluntarily absented himself was not a correct characterisation of what had occurred. This was not a case where the defendant had disrupted the court proceedings. The defendant had not wanted to be in court but had been excluded because of his disorderly behaviour by a member of court staff. That was not the same as saying that it was his choice. The justices' decision to proceed in absence was quashed. This is a generous decision. It is suggested that in such a situation the court should issue a warrant for the accused's arrest (if on bail, s 7 of the Bail Act 1976) and then to consider removing bail pending the accused's trial.

Section 11 of the MCA 1980 (above) has been supplemented by s 54 of the Criminal Justice and Immigration Act 2008. This section brings in a presumption that an accused aged 18 years or over and who fails to attend for trial, shall have that trial held in his absence unless it is deemed not to be in the interests of justice to do so. If there is an acceptable reason for the accused's non-appearance then the court shall not proceed in his absence. This provision adds little to the common law principles outlined immediately above.

I[6.20]

Whatever the reason the accused chooses to enter a not guilty plea, once he has entered the plea all the facts relevant to the proof of guilt are said to be 'in issue' which means that the prosecutor must either prove those facts beyond reasonable doubt or (in some few cases) must establish facts which then place the burden of proving his innocence on the accused. An example of this last situation occurs where the police allege the uninsured use of a motor vehicle. Once they establish that the accused used a motor vehicle on a road it becomes the responsibility of the accused to satisfy the court that his use of the vehicle was insured. The prosecutor will establish his facts by the oral testimony of witnesses who may then be cross-examined, and/or by the production of witness statements of which the accused will have had prior notice in order to object to them if he wishes, and/or by formal admissions from the accused which should be written down and signed by him. If the accused wishes to give evidence he may use all or any of these methods of doing so. The basis on which a not guilty plea is entered is important to the sentencer in some cases. It is often urged in mitigation that the accused pleaded guilty consequently saving stress and inconvenience to witnesses, court time and expense. The court must take account of the stage in the proceedings that the guilty plea was entered and the circumstances in which it was given. If as a result the court imposes a punishment which is less severe than would otherwise have been the case, it must state, in open court, that it has done so. It should not be held against an accused that he pleaded not guilty if he clearly was justified in doing so. However, in some cases where the basis of a not guilty plea proves unjustified, the accused's proper course is to change his plea. An example of this would be where he wishes to plead a technical point and has been overruled.

I[6.21]

No case to answer. There must be a sufficient case for the defendant to answer by the end of the prosecution case. If the prosecution have failed to prove an essential ingredient of the offence or the evidence adduced has been so discredited by cross- examination or is shown to be manifestly unreliable then if no reasonable tribunal could convict at that stage the case should be dismissed (*R v Galbraith* [1981] 2 All ER 1060, [1981] 1 WLR 1039 CA).

Where the court dismisses the case it must give reasons for its decision. The converse does not normally apply ie the court is not usually required to give reasons if it finds a case to answer (*Moran v DPP* [2002] EWHC 89 (Admin), (2002) 166 JP 467).

For a recent decision where it was held that the justices' decision that the case could not proceed beyond the half-way stage, in the light of weaknesses and inconsistencies in the accounts of prosecution witnesses, was perverse see *DPP v S* [2007] All ER (D) 148 (Dec).

A submission of no case to answer may not be made and/or considered prior to the close of the prosecution case (*Prosecution Appeal (No 32 of 2007; R v N Ltd* [2008] EWCA Crim 1223).

In *R (on the application of the Crown Prosecution Service) v Norwich Magistrates' Court* [2011] EWHC 82 (Admin), the High Court ruled that the justices erred by not permitting the Crown to re-open or to call additional evidence after the closure of its case. The prosecution had not appreciated there was any issue over identification until it had closed its case. The justices' refusal to exercise their discretion ran contrary to the overriding objective of the Criminal Procedure Rules 2010, was plainly contrary to the interests of justice and lacked any reasonable basis.

I[6.22]
Inferences from silence.

(a) Accused's failure to mention facts when questioned or charged (s 34 Criminal Justice and Public Order Act 1994)

(1)   Are there legal proceedings against the accused for an offence?
(2)   Did the alleged failure to mention a fact or facts occur before the accused was charged?
(3)   Did the alleged failure to mention a fact or facts occur while under caution by a constable or other investigating officer?
(4)   Was the constable's or other officer's questioning directed towards trying to discover whether or by whom the alleged offence had been committed?
(5)   Was the alleged fact or facts (not mentioned before charge) relied upon by the accused in his defence in these proceedings?
(6)   Was the accused's failure to mention the alleged fact or facts something which he/she could reasonably have been expected to mention when so questioned?
(7)   Can the accused's failure to mention the alleged fact or facts only be sensibly explained in that he had no answer at the time of his interview or none that would stand up to scrutiny?
(8)   Apart from the failure to mention that fact or facts is the prosecution's case sufficiently strong to amount to a case to answer against the accused?

Only if the court is sure as to 1–8 above may it draw an inference. The court may draw such inference as it deems appropriate. The inference itself may be one solely as to credit, credibility or an inference as to guilt. However, the court may not convict solely on the basis of the inferences it has drawn (see *R v Argent* (1996) 161 JP 190; *Condron v UK* (2001) 21 EHRR 1; *R v Beckles* [2005] 1 All ER 705).

In *R v Hackett* [2011] EWCA Crim 380, [2011] 2 Cr App Rep 35, the Court of Appeal held that it was wrong to give both a s 34 and a *Lucas* direction (lies as corroboration): *R v Rana* [2007] EWCA Crim 2261 applied. The Judge should have confined his directions to a s 34 direction whilst reminding the jury that unless they rejected H's explanation for not revealing his trip to the petrol station and its purpose at the first interview then no adverse inference could be drawn.

R v Rana did not decide that a s 34 direction should always be given in place of a *Lucas* direction. *Rana* decided that it had been appropriate for the trial judge to modify his directions under s 34 to take account of lies allegedly given by R in his account to the police. The principle flowing from the judgment applies equally to magistrates' courts; that is, a suitably modified direction under s 34 should be given in any advice to the justices, or, they should be invited to focus solely on whether the lies support the prosecution case in accordance with the principles laid down in *R v Lucas*.

(b) Accused's failure or refusal to account for objects, substances or marks (s 36 Criminal Justice and Public Order Act 1994)

(1) When the accused was arrested by a police constable did the accused have with him, or in or on his clothing, or on his footwear (delete as appropriate); or was there at the place he was arrested an object, substance or mark concerned (delete as appropriate)?

(2) Did the constable reasonably believe, for example, that the accused may have eg used the object to commit the crime for which he is being tried?

(3) Did the officer inform the accused of his reasonable belief and ask him/her to account for the presence of eg the object/substance/mark (delete as appropriate)?

(4) Did the officer warn the accused that if he did not account eg for the presence of the object, a court may later ask why?

(5) Did the accused fail or refuse to account eg for the presence of the object?

(6) Was the accused's failure or refusal to account eg for the presence of the object, one which he/she could reasonably have been expected to mention when arrested?

(7) Was the accused's failure or refusal to account eg for the presence of an object, because he/she had no innocent explanation to give or none that would stand up to scrutiny?

(8) Apart from the failure or refusal to account for eg the presence of an object, is the prosecution's case sufficiently strong to amount to a case to answer against the accused?

Only if the court is sure as to 1–8 above may it draw an inference. The court may draw such inference as it deems appropriate. The inference itself may be one solely as to credit, credibility or an inference as to guilt. However, the court may not convict solely on the basis of the inferences it has drawn.

(c) Accused's failure or refusal to account for presence at a particular place (s 37 Criminal Justice and Public Order Act 1994)

(1) When the accused was arrested by a police constable (or Revenue and Customs officer) was he found at or near the place (at or about the time the offence for which he was arrested was alleged to have been committed)?

(2) Was the 'place' any building or part of a building, any vehicle, vessel, aircraft, hovercraft or any other place whatsoever?

(3) Did the officer or an officer investigating the offence reasonably believe that the accused was participating in the crime for which he was arrested?

(4) Did the officer tell the accused of his belief and ask him to account for his presence?

(5) Did the accused fail or refuse to account for his presence?

(6) Was the accused's failure or refusal one which he could reasonably have been expected to account for?

(7) Was the accused's failure or refusal because he/she had no innocent explanation to give or none that would stand up to scrutiny?

(8) Apart from the failure or refusal to account for presence at a particular place, is the prosecution's case sufficiently strong to amount to a case to answer against the accused?

Only if the court is sure as to 1–8 above may it draw an inference. The court may draw such inference as it deems appropriate. The inference itself may be one solely as to credit, credibility or an inference as to guilt. However, the court may not convict solely on the basis of the inferences it has drawn.

(d) Accused's silence at trial (s 35 Criminal Justice and Public Order Act 1994)

If the accused is **legally represented,** at the conclusion of the evidence for the prosecution (assuming there is a case to answer), if the court is informed that the accused does not intend to give evidence, the legal adviser should, in the presence of the magistrates, inquire of the representative in these terms:

> 'Have you advised your client that the stage has now been reached at which he may give evidence and, if he chooses not to do so, or having been sworn, without good cause refuses to answer any question, the court may draw such inferences as appear proper from his failure to do so?'

If the reply is that the accused has been so advised the trial may proceed. If the answer is in the negative the court must direct the representative to advise his client and the consequences of such a failure.

If the accused is **not legally represented,** at the conclusion of the evidence for the prosecution (assuming there is a case to answer), the legal adviser should, in the presence of the magistrates, say to the accused:

> 'You have heard the evidence against you. Now is the time to make your defence. You may give evidence on oath, and be cross-examined like any other witness. If you do not give evidence, or having been sworn, without good cause refuse to answer any question, the court may draw such inferences as appear proper. That means they may hold it against you. You may also call any witness or witnesses whom you have arranged to attend court [today]. Afterwards, you may also, if you wish, address the court by arguing your case from the dock. But you cannot at that stage give evidence. Do you now intend to give evidence?'

(*Practice Direction (Criminal: Consolidated)* [2002] 3 All ER 90 (as subsequently revised).

(1)   Is there a prima facie case?
(2)   Has the defendant declined to give evidence or failed to answer any question properly put to him/her?
(3)   Has the accused given any reason for not giving evidence or answering any question properly put to him/her?
(4)   Despite the explanation given by the accused in 3 above, is the accused's failure to testify or answer any question properly put to him/her because he/she has no answer to the prosecution's case or none that would stand up to cross-examination?

Only if the court is sure as to 1–4 above may it draw an inference. The court may draw such inference as it deems appropriate. The inference itself may be one solely as to credit, credibility or an inference as to guilt. However, the court may not convict solely on the basis of the inferences it has drawn (*R v Cowan* [1996] QB 373, [1995] 4 All ER 939, (1996) 160 JP 165; *R v Condron* [1997] 1 WLR 827; *Radford v Kent County Council* (1998) 162 JP 697; *R v Gough* (2001) 165 JPN 895; *R v Becouarn* [2005] UKHL 55, [2005] 1 WLR 2589).

A magistrates' court may not draw an inference from the defendant's failure to give evidence under s 35 of the CJPOA 1994 on account of his absence. However, a magistrates' court may draw an inference under s 35 from the defendant's failure to give evidence where he is present but a co-accused is not. There may be occasions where, in the interests of being seen to be even-handed to both defendants, the court will decline to draw an inference: *R v Hamidi* [2010] EWCA Crim 66, [2010] Crim LR 578.

I[6.23]

Amendment of charge or information. Justices have a discretion to allow the amendment of a charge or information under the Magistrates' Courts Act 1980, s 123. This may even allege a different summary offence after the 6 month limitation period and even as late as the close of the prosecution case, but only where they are satisfied the allegation arises out of the same facts and it is in the interests of justice to allow the amendment (see *DPP v Everest* [2005] EWHC 1124 (Admin), [2005] All ER (D) 363 (May)).

In *DPP v Hammerton* [2009] EWHC 921 (Admin), [2009] 2 Cr App Rep 322, the Administrative Court stated that the CPS could not assume that they would be permitted to substitute or amend charges as a matter of course. The court retained a discretion to permit such a course of action but the overriding objective of the CPR 2005 (now CPR 2011), that a criminal case is dealt with justly, must be also be borne in mind. See also *Williams v DPP* [2009] EWHC 2354 (Admin), [2009] All ER (D) 292 (Jul)).

It is impermissible to amend an information by substituting a different defendant where the six-month statutory time limit has expired (*R (on the application of Sainsbury's Supermarkets Ltd) v Plymouth Magistrates' Court and R (on the application of J Sainsbury's Supermarkets Ltd) v Plymouth Magistrates' Court* [2006] EWHC 1749 (Admin), [2006] All ER (D) 137 (Jun)).

There are limitations on the power to amend an information. In *Shaw v DPP* [2007] EWHC 207 (Admin), a new charge was introduced in the defendant's absence after the expiry of the six-month time limit under s 127 MCA 1980, rendering him liable to imprisonment when he had not been before. In the circumstances it was not an appropriate course to take. Even if the justices had been justified in allowing the amendment, the term 'misled' in s 123(2) bore a very wide meaning and they should have adjourned to give the defendant a further opportunity to attend.

In *R (on the application of Thornhill) v Uxbridge Magistrates' Court* [2008] EWHC 508 (Admin), 172 JP 297, 172 JPN 580 the Divisional Court held that magistrates were wrong to allow the prosecution to amend an information alleging a failure to provide a specimen of breath to one of failure to provide a specimen of urine pursuant to s 7(6) of the Road Traffic Act 1988. The Divisional Court said that there was a distinct difference between the two offences and accordingly there was no need to consider if the amendment was 'in the interests of justice'. The procedures may be different but s 7(6) creates one offence of 'failing to provide a specimen'. This judgment does not sit well with previous judgments and by analogy *DPP v Butterworth* [1995] 1 AC 381, HL.

3 Guilty plea

I[6.24]

A guilty plea must be unequivocal; when an accused purports to admit an offence but then adds words or offers an explanation redolent of a defence the legal adviser should normally be left to clarify the plea. If the defendant is unrepresented it might be advisable for the case to be stood back for the accused to seek independent legal advice from a solicitor. If the court concludes that the plea is equivocal it has no discretion but to substitute a plea of not guilty.

A guilty plea, however, is an admission of the offence charged and not necessarily of every fact which the prosecutor may allege as a circumstance of it. A guilty plea to assault, for example, would not indicate an acceptance of the prosecution's allegations of the number of blows struck or their severity. Where there is a dispute about an important circumstance of the offence either side may call evidence notwithstanding the guilty plea. The court can also decline to sentence until the matter has been resolved by evidence. This procedure is known as a **Newton hearing**. There are one or two exceptions. The legal adviser should be consulted where the question of a Newton hearing is being canvassed. Evidence may also be called if there is a dispute relating to an ancillary matter, such as the amount of compensation or liability for back duty. The evidence should be confined solely to deciding the issue in question and, if the prosecution cannot establish its version of the facts beyond a reasonable doubt, the defence version must be accepted.

The other aspect of the question is that the court must sentence only on the basis of the case put forward by the prosecution and not on the basis of conclusions it might draw that the case is in reality more serious. For example, if a person is accused of two cases of theft from his employer the court must not infer that in fact this was a common occurrence and sentence accordingly. Sometimes the inference might be inescapable. The important thing is that it does not affect the sentence for the offence charged. There are exceptions to the above rule eg in the case of sample or specimen charges or offences admitted and taken into consideration. Magistrates should clarify the legal principles with their legal adviser.

I[6.25]

Guilty plea – complex cases or to avoid misunderstanding. The Attorney General issued new guidelines which imposed new duties on prosecutors. The guideline also applies in some magistrates' court cases. The change came into effect on 25 June 2007.

New paragraph C6:

'(1)   In all cases before the Crown Court, and in cases before the magistrates' court where the issues are complex or there is scope for misunderstanding, the prosecution must commit to writing the aggravating and mitigating factors that will form the opening of the prosecution case as well as any statutory limitations on sentencing. The prosecution will address, where relevant, the factors outlined at B4 including the matters set out in the next sub-paragraph.

(2)   The matters to be dealt with are:
- The aggravating and mitigating factors of the offence (not personal mitigation).
- Any statutory provisions relevant to the offender and the offence under consideration so that the judge [magistrates] is made aware of any statutory limitations on sentencing.
- Any relevant sentencing Guidelines and guideline cases.
- Identifying any victim personal statement or other information available to the prosecution advocate as to the impact of the offence on the victim.
- Where appropriate, any evidence of the impact of the offending on the community.
- An indication, where applicable, of an intention to apply for any ancillary orders, such as anti-social behaviour orders and confiscation orders, and so far as possible, indicating the nature of the order to be sought.'

I[6.26]

Application to change a plea of guilty to not guilty. A magistrates' court may allow a defendant to withdrawn his plea of guilty at any time up to sentence being passed (*S (an infant) v Manchester City Recorder* [1971] AC 481, HL). The onus lies on a party seeking to vacate a guilty plea to demonstrate that justice requires that this should be permitted.

Where the defendant pleads guilty by post under s 12 of the MCA 1980 and the plea is accepted by the court, at an adjourned hearing the accused would have to seek leave to change his plea, in accordance with the CPR outlined immediately below: see *Rymer v DPP* [2010] EWHC 1848 (Admin), 174 CL&J 526.

For the principles and procedures governing the exercise of the discretion see *R v South Tameside Magistrates' Court, ex p Rowland* (1984) 148 JP 202. For a more recent authority see *DPP v Revitt* [2006] EWHC 2266 (Admin), [2006] NLJR 1476, (2006) 170 JP 729.

I[6.27]

Application to withdraw a guilty plea. CPR, Part 37.9 provides:

'(2)   The defendant must apply to do so –

       (a)   as soon as practicable after becoming aware of the reasons for doing so; and

       (b)   before sentence.

(3)   Unless the court otherwise directs, the application must be in writing and the defendant must serve it on –

       (a)   the court officer; and

       (b)   the prosecutor.

(4)   The application must –

       (a)   explain why it would be unjust not to allow the defendant to withdraw the guilty plea;

       (b)   identify –

             (i)   any witness that the defendant wishes to call, and

             (ii)   any other proposed witness; and

       (c)   say whether the defendant waives legal professional privilege, giving any relevant name and date.'

4 Legal Advice

I[6.28]

The legal adviser has a duty to advise on matters of law and matters of mixed law and fact. Justices who refuse to act on his advice in a straightforward matter (eg a driver's liability to disqualification) may run the risk of being ordered to pay the costs of a consequent appeal. The justices are entitled to invite the legal adviser to retire with them if they think that a matter may arise on which they will seek his advice. In a case of any complexity it is wise to invite the legal adviser to retire at an early stage in order that he can give such advice as the occasion may require during the justices' discussions. If the legal adviser has taken a full note of the evidence he may be called upon to refresh the justices' memory from it. However, so far as it is practical to do so, the legal adviser should be asked to give his advice openly in court. This will not always be a practical way to give advice, especially in complicated matters, or where reference to books may be necessary, or where a discussion with one or more of the justices may be involved. The justices' clerk has the right to advise the justices even though he is not sitting with them in court so that, if he is available, he may always be sent for if necessary. It should be noted, however, where representations have been made to the court which the justices' clerk has not heard they should be repeated in the presence of the justices' clerk before he gives his advice to the bench. It is especially useful to bear this in mind when sitting with an inexperienced legal adviser. Equally, where the legal adviser finds it necessary to give advice in the retiring room on a point not canvassed with the advocates then the legal adviser should return to court telling them of the advice given and allowing them to address the bench if they have anything additional to contribute.

I[6.29]

For a fuller account of the role of the justices' clerk and his staff see **Section L**.

5 Consideration of guilt

I[6.30]

The question for justices to ask themselves at this stage is, 'Has the prosecutor satisfied the majority of us beyond reasonable doubt that the accused committed the offence with which he has been charged?' A reasonable doubt must not be a fanciful doubt nurtured by prejudice. The burden of proof, that is the degree to which a court should be convinced of guilt, is a matter of law and one on which the legal adviser can assist.

I[6.31]

When announcing the decision in court it is generally better to avoid using a reference to 'the case'. It is better to say, 'We find you guilty of theft' or as the case may be, rather than, 'We find the case proved'. The accused feels he has 'a case' too, and the latter expression of the decision sometimes creates the impression that 'the case' which the court has been concerned with has been the prosecution case. The former method of announcing the decision leaves nothing to doubt or prejudice and is especially to be recommended when there has been more than one charge or accused.

6 Reports etc

I[6.32]

Irrespective the plea, once the guilt of the accused has been established the court may hear further information about him relevant to sentence. The prosecutor will give information about previous convictions or the fact that there are none. He will also indicate if the accused has admitted other similar offences which he wishes the court to take into consideration when determining the sentence. These will have been written down and should be put one by one by the clerk and the accused should be asked to signify his admission of each such offence separately. This is important because offences admitted and taken into consideration ('TICs' as these offences are usually known) may be significant in the sentencing decision and because (especially if there is a long list) it is very easy for the police to include in a list of outstanding offences some which a prisoner will admit through not giving the matter proper thought. Compensation may be ordered in respect of offences taken into consideration and this is another reason for being procedurally correct when dealing with them. The maximum amount of compensation depends on the number of substantive charges eg a plea of guilty to two charges of theft and 24 TICs means that the magistrates' powers to award compensation are limited to £10,000 (£5,000 per offence).

I[6.33]

Also at this stage the prosecutor will ask for any appropriate ancillary orders such as costs or the forfeiture of a weapon or drugs, etc. The chairman should make a written note of such matters so that they are not overlooked when the final sentencing decision is made. See *Nicholas v Chester Magistrates' Court* [2009] EWHC 1504 (Admin). As a general proposition, magistrates adjourning for a full pre-sentence report cannot bind the sentencing court as to the general level of sentence, unless the same magistrates return to deal with the offender. Magistrates must also have regard to the SC Magistrates' Courts Sentencing Guidelines under s 172(1)(b) of the Criminal Justice Act 2003 when giving an indication as to the level of sentence proposed: see *Thornton v CPS* [2010] EWHC 346 (Admin), 174 JP 121.

I[6.34]

Pre-sentence report. The court may at this stage consider a pre-sentence report and if one is not available the question of an adjournment in order to obtain one should not be overlooked. Although they need not do so if they are of the opinion that it is unnecessary, it is still a statutory requirement for a magistrates' court to consider a pre-sentence report before imposing any custodial sentence or a community sentence (except a probation order with no additional requirements, although the obtaining of a pre-sentence report is nevertheless still strongly advised).

I[6.35]

The pre-sentence report is to assist the court in determining the most suitable method of dealing with an offender. The responsibility for determining the seriousness of an offence remains solely with the magistrates. However, the pre-sentence report will contain impartial advice and information and will balance the aggravating and mitigating factors in the case and report on the nature of the defendants offending: *R v Salisbury Magistrates' Court, ex p Gray* [2000] 1 Cr App Rep (S) 267, 163 JP 732. The report may give advice in support of a particular sentence although it will bear in mind the ultimate responsibility of the sentencer. The Crown prosecutor may make representations on matters contained in the pre-sentence report.

I[6.36]

Short or fast-delivery reports. These reports have the same status as a pre-sentence report but can be requested by the court on the day if they are considering a lower end order such as a community order with a single requirement.

Note that the Youth Court must have a written report before it can make a reparation or action plan order but these are not classified as pre-sentence reports.

I[6.37]

Medical report. Where the offender is, or appears to be, mentally disordered, the court must, if it is considering a custodial sentence, obtain a medical report. Such a report is made orally or in writing by a doctor approved under the Mental Health Act 1983 as having experience in the diagnosis or treatment of mental disorder.

I[6.38]

Reports from other sources may be available, for example, a reference from an offender's employer or educational establishment etc. In any case where the court thinks fit it may adjourn and call upon the maker of a report to attend for questioning upon its contents.

I[6.39]

The court must give the accused or his solicitor and the Crown Prosecutor a copy of the pre-sentence report. In the youth court the report will be given to a parent or guardian. It is very important, however, that the accused is aware of the contents of any written report submitted to the court. It is not considered entirely satisfactory simply to hand a written report to an unrepresented defendant in court. He may have difficulty in reading, especially in the stressful situation of court proceedings, so that he may not absorb the contents of the report at all, or he may not have finished reading it by the time he is invited to comment on it. Furthermore, he may not understand the meaning of everything he reads and he almost certainly will have had inadequate time to gather his thoughts and to express a useful opinion about anything contained in the report. The better practice, therefore, is that the probation officer (or youth offending officer) has discussed the contents of the pre-sentence report and especially the implications of any proposal therein, with the offender before the case is dealt with in court.

7 Guilty plea by post procedure

I[6.40]

This is a quick and effective procedure for dealing with summary cases, in the absence of the accused (specified proceedings). The procedures outlined below only apply to offences dealt with in the adult court and those offences which do not carry a term of imprisonment of more than three months.

I[6.41]

A summons is served on the defendant along with a witness statement of evidence. The defendant may plead guilty in absence on the basis of the evidence supplied and the clerk to the court reads the statement (or if directed by the court a summary) in open court before the court decides to accept the plea.

I[6.42]

The legal adviser will then read any statement in mitigation from the defendant and any statement of means is considered along with the driving licence, in endorsable cases. The court may then pass sentence or adjourn if it requires the defendant's attendance, for example if it is considering a disqualification. This may be done in the absence of a prosecutor.

I[6.43]

Failure to respond. If the summons and statements are properly served but the defendant fails to respond the proceedings become non-specified and the prosecution may use the evidence in the statements to prove the case against the defendant at the first hearing.

I[6.44]

Not guilty plea. Where the defendant indicates in writing that he wishes to plead not guilty but attends court to give evidence the statement may be used at an adjourned trial date unless the defendant has indicated he wishes any of the prosecution witnesses to attend court. Note that the police will be able to ask for costs in writing against a defendant who has either pleaded guilty or been convicted on the statements served. There is also a hybrid procedure of serving the defendant with a statement of facts, upon which he may enter a guilty plea, and witness statements which will be used if he fails to enter a plea.

8 Appeals

I[6.45]

There are three common forms of appeal from the Magistrates' Courts.

I[6.46]

Appeal against conviction and or sentence to the Crown Court. Notice for such an appeal must be lodged within 21 days of the date of sentence. This time limit may be extended with the consent of the Crown Court (s 108 MCA 1980).

I[6.47]

Appeal by way of case stated to the High Court on a point of law. The justices may be asked to state a case within 21 days of their decision. There is no power to extend this period. Once an application for a case stated is made the right to appeal to the Crown Court normally ceases (s 111 MCA 1980).

I[6.48]

Application for judicial review. This application must be lodged with the High Court as soon as practicable and in any event within 3 months of the grounds for the appeal arising (Senior Courts Act 1981, ss 29, 31; Civil Procedure Rules 1998, Part 54). If successful the High Court may make quashing, prohibiting and mandatory orders to correct or prevent an error in law or a failure to exercise jurisdiction. See for example *R (on the application of Durham County Council) v North Durham Justices* [2004] EWHC 1073 (Admin), [2004] All ER (D) 260 (Apr).

I[7]

The Criminal Defence Service*

Introduction

I[7.1]

*When Part 1 of the Legal Aid, Sentencing and Punishment of Offenders Act 2012 is brought into force Part 1 will make fundamental changes to the nature of the legal aid scheme in England and Wales. Section 38 abolishes the Legal Services Commission and replaces it with an executive agency within the Ministry of Justice, to be known as the Legal Aid Agency.

Criminal Legal Aid is dealt with in ss 13–20 of the 2012 Act. The statute is an empowering Act and it is anticipated that detailed provisions will be made as now by regulation.

The Legal Services Commission (LSC) is responsible for the provision of a Criminal Defence Service. This includes advice and assistance at a solicitor's office, police station advice and assistance, advocacy assistance in the magistrates' courts including representation by the court duty solicitor and finally magistrates' court representation.

Representation orders

I[7.1A]

See reg 3 of the Criminal Defence Service (General) (No 2) Regulations 2001 as amended. Circumstances in which a representation order is available in a magistrates' court include:

(a) any person who is to appear before a magistrates' court or a youth court in respect of an offence; this includes an application for the removal of a disqualification from driving (*R v Crown Court at Liverpool, ex p McCann* [1995] RTR 23);

(b) a person who is to appear before a magistrates' court to answer a complaint for failure to pay a sum due or obey a court order where such failure carries a risk of imprisonment or for a binding over order or breach;

(c) a person whose case has been transferred, or has been sent, committed for trial or committed for sentence to the Crown Court*;

(d) a person who proposes to appeal to the Crown Court against a decision of a magistrates' court;

(e) proceedings where following a conviction of a child or the making of an anti-social behaviour order, an interim order or sex offences prevention order or the court makes a parenting order. This includes appeals against and variations of parenting orders;

(f) proceedings under the Football Spectators Act 1989 for banning orders and references to the court;

(g) orders under Part 1 of the Anti Social Behaviour Act 2003 (closure of premises);

(h)   proceedings relating to serious crime prevention orders under the Serious Crime Act 2007 (Criminal Defence Service (General) (No 2) (Amendment) Regulations 2008, SI 2008/725);

(i)   application for a domestic violence protection order; breach of a domestic violence protection order and breach of a domestic violence protection notice (see ss 24–30 of the Crime and Security Act 2010): SI 2011/1453.**

*Where a representation order is granted to cover criminal proceedings in the magistrates' court, new regulations provide that the order extends to the Crown Court if the proceedings continue there.

**Comes into force from 30 June 2011 in the following police areas: Greater Manchester Police, Wiltshire Police and West Mercia.

I[7.2]

The Criminal Defence Service Act 2006 (CDSA) received the Royal Assent on 30 March 2006. The majority of the Act's provisions, together with secondary legislation (as subsequently amended) were brought into force on 2 October 2006. The CDSA 2006 made a number of amendments to the Access to Justice Act 1999. A major amendment is the requirement that the power to grant a right to representation may only be exercised where a person is **financially eligible**, under regulations, to be granted such a right. The Government stated during the passage of the CDSA 2006 that these powers would be exercised, in the first instance, in relation to criminal proceedings, in magistrates' courts.

Another key change was to transfer authority to grant legal aid to the Legal Services Commission with Her Majesty's Courts Service staff acting as agents on behalf of the LSC. Essentially, the grant of criminal representation (legal aid) is an administrative function. HMCS takes all the decisions relating to the interests of justice test and most of the means test assessments (see below).

All applications for a representation order in magistrates' courts must be in writing on one or more of the prescribed forms (CDS14–17) below. Oral applications can no longer be made; neither can the court grant a representation order without seeing a written application.

Financial Eligibility

I[7.2A]

The Criminal Defence Service (Financial Eligibility) Regulations 2006 set out the criteria which must be satisfied before individuals involved in criminal proceedings in a magistrates' court may receive publicly funded representation. Note that the regulations have been amended to make provision for contribution orders for the cost of publicly funded representation in criminal trials and appeals from magistrates' courts to the Crown Court: see the Criminal Defence Service (Contribution Orders) Regulations 2009, SI 2009/3328.

Individuals in receipt of certain 'passported' benefits such as income support, income-based jobseeker's allowance and guarantee credit under s 1(3)(a) of the State Pension Credit Act 2002 are **automatically eligible,** as are those under the age of 16 years or under 18 years and in full-time education or living at home with no income. If the individual has a partner, the partner's resources are to be treated as those of the individual, unless the partner has a contrary interest in the proceedings.

An individual is **financially eligible** for a representation order if his gross annual income, adjusted to take account of any partner or children, is **£12,475 or less.** An individual is **ineligible** if his gross annual income, as adjusted, is **£22,325 or more.** Where it falls between these amounts, the representation authority will calculate the individual's annual disposable income, making deductions in respect of any income tax, national insurance, council tax, housing expenses, child care costs, maintenance and cost of living expenses, from the applicant's adjusted income. The individual is financially eligible if his **annual income does not exceed £3,398.**

Where there is a material change in an individual's financial circumstances, he must notify the representation authority of the change if he has been granted a representation order, and he may make a renewed application if his previous application has been refused because he was financially ineligible.

Regulations* provide for a review of the decision to refuse representation on the basis that the applicant is financially ineligible, on the grounds that his income has been miscalculated or that he cannot afford to pay for legal assistance notwithstanding that he is financially ineligible. Regulations* provide, in some cases, for the application to be renewed to the representation authority or the Legal Services Commission.

Regulations also contain provisions about the withdrawal of representation orders. The representation authority must normally withdraw an order where an individual fails to provide evidence of means that has been requested. Where a subsequent application is made following the withdrawal of a representation order, the same representative must be selected unless the representation authority considers there are good reasons why a different representative should be selected.

*See **appeals and reviews** below.

I[7.3]

An application **must** be made in the prescribed form. The application forms are:

—   CDS14 Application for Legal Aid
—   CDS15 Financial Statement
—   CDS16 Review on Grounds of Hardship
—   CDS17 Statement of Truth.

Revised CDS forms became effective from 2 February 2007 and are available on the Internet. Courts were able to accept any old forms signed prior to the said date and up to 2 March 2007. The forms have been reduced in length and the CDS15 altered to try and separate self-employed applicants from anyone else using this form.

The forms must be fully completed within five working days of charge. It is likely the court will return incomplete forms or refuse to grant representation. The court will make a decision within two working days unless the applicant's means are complex.

The CDS14 form must be submitted with all applications for representation orders. It contains the unchanged interests of justice test (see below) and sets out the following:

–   the applicant's (and partner's where applicable) personal details
–   a partner's involvement in the case, if they are a victim, prosecution witness, or co-defendant whose evidence conflicts with the applicant's case
–   disability and equal opportunities monitoring data (completion is optional)
–   information about the applicant's case
–   contact details for the solicitor or their firm, including their LSC account number.

The following applicants need only complete form CDS14. This is because they are exempt from undergoing a means test. They are known as "passported" applicants:

•   those under 16
•   those under 18 and in full-time education
•   those aged 16 or 17 with no income and living with their parents/guardian
•   those receiving any of the following benefits: income support, income based jobseeker's allowance, guaranteed state pension credit (guaranteed credit)
•   for applicants in custody, see the section below on form CDS17 (Statement of Truth)

Where the applicant is remanded in custody he/she will be required to provide details of his/her financial circumstances. If unable to provide a wage slip, unless self employed, the CDS17 form will be accepted as evidence. If claiming a 'passported' benefit, the applicant must provide his/her National Insurance number. Applicants who are self employed and in custody cannot use form CDS17. They must produce evidence of income as set out in form CDS15.

Form CDS15 (Financial statement for legal aid in criminal proceedings) is for **all other applicants** , ie those persons not exempt or able to fall back on form CDS17. Form CDS15 contains questions on such items as:

•   income (employment, other state benefits, self employment, partnerships, directorships, private pension, maintenance and other income)
•   family size (children, grouped according to age at next birthday)

- outgoings (housing, childcare)
- freezing orders, self-assessment tax forms and tax bracket
- their partner's income (unless the partner has a conflicting interest in their case)

The application may be considered by the representation authority who may make an order provided that it is satisfied that (i) the applicant is financially eligible (see above); and, (ii) it is in the interests of justice that a representation order should be made. Representation is considered in the Access to Justice Act 1999, s 14 and Sch 3. A parent or guardian may apply on behalf of a defendant under 17 years.

The Legal Services Commission has posted full guidance, including the new forms, on its website (www.legalservices.gov.uk).

A representation order may be backdated to cover urgent work undertaken and may in certain circumstances outlined in reg 17 of the Criminal Defence Service (General) (No 2) Regulations 2001 be withdrawn.

I[7.4]

A representation order covers representation by a litigator (solicitor). Regulation 12(1) of the Criminal Defence Service (General) (No 2) Regulations 2001 provides for representation by a court advocate (advocates with higher rights of audience) in the case of an indictable offence (which includes an offence 'triable either way') or extradition hearings under the Extradition Act 2003, where the court is of the opinion that, because of the circumstances which make the proceedings unusually grave or difficult, representation by both a litigator (solicitor) and an advocate would be desirable. There is no power to extend representation to a court advocate arising out of enforcement proceedings including confiscation proceedings: *Taylor v City of Westminster Magistrates' Court Crown Court* [2009] EWHC 1498 (Admin), 173 JP 405.

It should be noted that a magistrates' court may only make an order for the services of a Queen's Counsel or of more than one advocate only in extradition proceedings under the Extradition Act 2003 and where the court is of the opinion that the assisted person could not be adequately represented except by a Queen's Counsel or by more than one advocate.

I[7.5]

Two or more co defendants must be assigned the same representative unless there is a conflict of interest.

I[7.5A]

An **early cover payment scheme** was introduced to cover solicitors' concerns that they might be asked to represent applicants without having a representation order granted. Under regulations early first cover will be available where:

(i)   the applicant or their solicitor submits application forms CDS14 and CDS15 (as appropriate) to HMCS within 5 days from instruction, as long as this is before the first hearing; and

(ii)   HMCS (or NCT, where the case has been referred) fail to reach a decision by the time the first hearing takes place; and

(iii)   the eventual decision is that the application satisfies the *interests of justice test* but does not pass the *means test*.

In these cases the solicitor can claim a fixed fee of £75 from the LSC. If the representation order is granted the solicitor does not need to claim early first cover, as the representation order itself would be dated from the date the application was first submitted and would therefore cover payment for the first hearing.

Solicitors cannot claim early first cover for applications where the hardship form (CDS16) has been submitted directly to the NCT (along with forms CDS 14 and 15) prior to HMCS carrying out a means assessment.

I[7.5B]

Transfer of representation order. The regulations make provision for the transfer of a representation order to eg another litigator. In *R v Iqbal* [2011] 2 Cr App Rep 250, (2011) Times, 21 April, CA, the following two points were highlighted. First, the regulations refer to a breakdown in the relationship between the defendant and the 'litigator', ie the person named in the order as representing the assisted person. In practice, this means the defendant's solicitor. Secondly, under the regulations, it is the duty of the litigator, not the defendant, to give details of the nature of the breakdown. The court is often prepared to allow a change of solicitor where the application is often made early in the proceedings and where the application is not designed to, or does not have the net effect of delaying the proceedings, particularly where a trial is listed. As was stated in *Iqbal*, vigorous scrutiny is needed to avoid disruption to trials and adverse effect on the public purse. The evidence in the instant case showed that there had been no breakdown, merely a spurious attempt, based on dishonest assertions, at manipulation of the system.

In *R (on the application of Clive Rees Associates) v Swansea Magistrates' Court and Rees Davies and Partners* [2011] EWHC 3155 (Admin), 176 JP 39, M had received conflicting advice from two reputable firms of solicitors, both of which were authorised by the Legal Services Commission to carry on criminal legal aid work. The fact that different advice had been given by a second firm of solicitors was capable of having a fundamental effect on M's confidence in his original representatives. The justices found that it did. Furthermore, it was a relevant consideration that the interested party were already acting for M in other criminal matters. The justices therefore were entitled to transfer the representation order under reg 16(2)(*a*)(iv) of the 2001 Regulations above.

Interests of justice

I[7.6]

The Criminal Defence Service (Interests of Justice) Regulations 2009, SI 2009/2875 provide that it will be "deemed" to be in the interests of justice for an individual who is the subject of trial on indictment in, or committal for sentence to, the Crown Court, to be granted a publicly funded right to representation.

The Justices' Clerks' Society has reissued guidance in relation to the interests of justice test. The document is entitled 'Guidance on the Consideration of Defence Representation Order Applications' (Ref: 53.0010, issue 06/06/07) and can be found on the Legal Services Commission website via http://www.legalservices.gov.uk/docs/cds_main/IofJJusticeGuidanceFina lVersion060607.pdf.

As to whether it is in the interests of justice that a representation order should be made, the factors to be taken into account include:

(a) the offence is such that if proved it is likely that the court would impose a sentence which would deprive the accused of his liberty or lead to loss of his livelihood or serious damage to his reputation; or

(b) there is a substantial question of law involved; or

(c) the accused may be unable to understand the proceedings or state his own case (because of his inadequate knowledge of English (*R (Matara) v Brent Magistrates' Court* (2005) 169 JP 576), mental illness or other mental or physical disability); or

(d) the nature of the defence is such as to involve the tracing and interviewing of witnesses or expert cross-examination of a witness for the prosecution; or

(e) where it may be in the interests of a third party, eg the victim of a sexual offence who might be distressed at being cross-examined directly by the accused, or who might be spared an appearance in court if the accused is given proper legal advice as to his plea.

I[7.7]

These criteria, which are used in the assessment of whether or not it is in the interests of justice that representation should be granted, are largely self-explanatory. A motorist who wishes to raise a plea of special reasons based on an allegation that a drink had been 'laced' would need an expert witness and would need to cross-examine witnesses to the incident. Such a driver should be granted representation (*R v Gravesend Magistrates' Court, ex p Baker* (1997) 161 JP 765). In *R v Liverpool City Magistrates Justices, ex p McGhee* (1993) 158 JP 275, [1993] Crim LR 609 it was pointed out that 'expert' in (d) above meant that the cross-examiner should be expert, it was not necessary that the witness should be an expert.

In (*R (on the application of GKR Law Solicitors) v Liverpool Magistrates' Court* [2008] EWHC 2974 (Admin), [2008] All ER (D) 315 (Nov) a mother proposed to call her 12-year old son to give evidence in support of her claim that special reasons for not endorsing her driving licence existed. The son qualified for special measures and she needed professional assistance to make the necessary arrangements. It was held that having regard to the guidance in Sch 3, paragraph 5(2)(d) of the Access to Justice Act 1999, and the lack of resources available to S, it was in the interests of justice to grant her a representation order to enable a fair and proper consideration of the questions to be determined at the hearing.

I[7.8]

Guidance was also given on (a) above in that it was pointed out that the likelihood of a community sentence was not a sentence which deprived the accused of his liberty. However, in view of the Practice Direction on the subject of failure to answer bail which could result in a custodial sentence a grant should therefore follow (*R (on the application of Evans) v Chester Magistrates Court* [2004] All ER (D) 260 (Mar)).

Appeals and review

1.   Interests of justice test appeals

I[7.9]

Where an application for a representation order is refused, the appropriate officer shall provide the applicant with written reasons for the refusal and details of the appeal process. The applicant is entitled to request an appeal following a refusal on this ground. The applicant should explain in writing why he wishes to appeal and confirm that his financial circumstances have not changed since he first applied.

If the applicant's financial circumstances have not changed, the appeal must be put before a single magistrate or a court for a decision. If the applicant's financial circumstances have not changed, the appeal must be put before a single magistrate or a court for a decision. If the applicant's circumstances have not changed, the appeal may be considered by the same officer who originally considered and refused the application: Criminal Defence Service (Representation Orders: Appeals etc) (Amendment) Regulations 2010, SI 2010/1186. If the appropriate officer refuses the renewed application on the grounds that the 'interests of justice' have not been met then the refusal notice should be re-issued to the applicant and solicitor. It is then for the applicant and solicitor to decide whether to appeal to the court.

It should be stressed that nothing in this amendment removes or dilutes the applicant's right of appeal to the court if the decision on the 'Interests of Justice' test goes against him or her. An applicant or solicitor has no statutory right to attend an appeal hearing; the local court retains a discretion as to how it conducts the appeal. Natural justice suggests that it is prudent to allow the applicant or his solicitor to attend for the purposes of making brief representations to the court or magistrate.

In relation to a refusal following an appeal to the Crown Court against conviction and/or sentence, the applicant may appeal to the appropriate officer of the Crown Court: see the Criminal Defence Service (Representation Orders: Appeals etc Regulations 2009, SI 2009/3329.

2.   Review of means

I[7.10]

If the applicant believes an administrative error has occurred the matter can be referred back to HMCS.

If the applicant omitted information in their previous application (for example, childcare costs were omitted), form CDS15 should be amended and resubmitted to the HMCS office carrying out the assessment.

3.   Hardship application to the National Court Team (NCT)

I[7.11]

The hardship review provides a safety net for applicants who have not passed the financial eligibility test, but are genuinely unable to pay for their defence costs. This may be because the costs of the case are particularly high, or because they have especially high outgoings; for example, care costs for a disabled relative. Any applicant wishing to apply for a hardship review after a refusal under the means test must submit form CDS16 and a copy of form CDS15.

There are two NCT offices, one based at Nottingham, the other based at Liverpool. The choice of which NCT office to which the hardship application should be referred is determined by the region in which the local magistrates' court is located. A list is to be found on the LSC website and by HMCS staff.

Remands in custody and bail

J[1]

Remands in custody and on bail

'Remand'

J[1.1]

When a case is adjourned to a fresh date the defendant may be remanded to ensure his attendance at the next hearing. The accused may be remanded in custody or released on bail. The prosecution will very often ask the court for a 'remand', when in fact it is seeking an adjournment. The other party to the case frequently does not object to the adjournment, but it should be remembered that the final decision rests with the court. Although the court may have been presented with a *fait accompli* where an agreement has previously been made between the parties, the magistrates should always be scrupulous to ensure that an adjournment is necessary. They should hear representations from both sides and make their decision judicially, taking all the relevant considerations into account. While it may not be possible to prevent an adjournment, the court may be able to avoid future adjournments. If magistrates do not keep a tight hold on the course of proceedings, it will not be surprising that undue delays occur in the administration of justice.

Bail and the Human Rights Act 1998

J[1.2]

Some sections of the Bail Act 1976 have been subject to challenge under the ECHR, for example the power to remove bail based solely on a police officer's belief that a defendant will breach a bail condition (Sch 1, Part 1, para 6). It is now established that while there is no need for a full inquiry following an arrest for breach of bail conditions, Art 5 does apply to any remand in custody (*R v Havering Magistrates' Court, ex p DPP* [2001] 3 All ER 997, [2000] All ER (D) 2307).

However, the Bail Act as outlined before should comply with Convention requirements if the overall concepts of fairness and proportionality are borne in mind. For example, a defendant may be remanded in custody on substantial grounds that he will commit a further offence, but that must relate to a serious offence based solely on the facts of the individual case. See *MB v Switzerland* (2001) 37 EHRR 1000, ECtHR for the application of Article 5 to the defendant's rights on arrest and production before a court.

J[1.3]

Remand on unconditional bail. The accused is released with an obligation to surrender to the custody of the court on a certain day at a specified time. If he fails to do so, there are two consequences: the court can immediately issue a warrant for his arrest and he may be prosecuted for the criminal offence of failing to answer his bail.

J[1.4]

Remand on conditional bail. The accused is on bail but with conditions attached to that bail, to ensure that he appears at court on the appointed day at the appropriate time or does not commit offences in the meantime or does not interfere with the witnesses in the case.

J[1.5]

Remand in custody. Where bail is refused, the defendant is detained in prison or in police cells until his next appearance in court.

J[1.6]

Juveniles. The remand of juveniles on bail is largely the same as that outlined below for those aged 17 and above. The exception is the condition of electronic monitoring of a curfew which can be imposed for 17-year-olds and adults. Elsewhere, in order to impose such a condition the court must be satisfied that the offender has reached the age of 12, and has been charged with:

- a violent or sexual offence or an offence carrying more that 14 years' imprisonment in the case of an adult, or
- (an) imprisonable offence(s) which, together with other such offences where there has been a conviction in any proceedings, mean that he has a recent history of repeatedly committing imprisonable offences while on remand (bail or local authority).

The court must have been informed by a YOT that imposing an electronic monitoring requirement will be suitable for this individual. The court must have been notified that electronic monitoring is available and be satisfied that the necessary provision can be made under those arrangements.

For remand of juveniles with a security requirement, see [3.16]–[3.17].

Section 52 of the Criminal Justice and Immigration Act 2008 imposes a duty on a magistrates' court (which includes a youth court) considering whether to withhold or grant bail in relation to a person under 18 accused of an offence where the value involved is relevant to the mode of trial (eg criminal damage and aggravated vehicle taking) to consider the value involved in the offence. In other words, where the value is under eg £5,000, the court should generally, for the purposes of the Bail Act 1976, treat the offence as if it were a summary imprisonable offence, not an offence triable either way.

**For a juvenile charged with murder see J[1.32] below.

When must the court remand?

J[1.7]

Where the court is acting with a view to committal for trial or sending an accused to the Crown Court for trial the accused must always be remanded on bail or in custody.

J[1.8]

If the offence is triable either way, the court must always remand where the accused was initially arrested by the police and brought to court in custody or bailed for his appearance, or he has previously been remanded in the proceedings.

J[1.9]

Where the offence is purely summary, the court always has a discretion whether to remand or simply adjourn the case.

J[1.10]–[1.15]

In the case of juveniles (under 17) the court may remand if it thinks it is necessary to do so in those cases where it must do so when the defendant is 17 or over.

Length of the remand – before conviction

J[1.16]

In custody. A remand in custody is not normally for longer than 8 clear days, ie the day when the decision to remand is made and the day when the defendant is next due to appear in court, are excluded. Therefore a remand in custody may be from the Monday of one week to the Wednesday of the next.

J[1.17]

There are three major exceptions:

(a) If the defendant is to be kept in police cells, the maximum period is 3 clear days or 24 hours in the case of a juvenile.

(b) Where the accused is already serving a custodial sentence and will not be released in the intervening period, he may be remanded for up to 28 days.

(c) The court may remand a defendant present before the court who has previously been remanded in custody for a period not exceeding when the next stage of the proceedings is reached or 28 days, whichever is the less. In exercising this power the court will have to have regard to the total length of time which the accused would spend in custody if it were to exercise the power. This would not affect the right of the defendant to apply for bail during this period.

J[1.18]

On bail. Unless the accused consents, a remand on bail cannot be for more than 8 clear days. However, defendants always do consent to longer remands and that is why, as mentioned above, it is important for the magistrates to exercise control over the granting of adjournments. It should be remembered that bail is always granted to a fixed date and so it is not possible to adjourn a case *sine die* where the accused is remanded. An exception to this rule is a committal or send to the Crown Court although a plea and directions hearing may be specified.

Length of remand – after conviction

J[1.19]

A remand after conviction (for further inquiries and pre-sentence reports) cannot be for longer than 3 weeks if in custody, or should not be for longer than 4 weeks on bail.

Committal or send to the Crown Court

J[1.20]

When a magistrates' court commit or sends proceedings to the Crown Court for trial (or commits for sentence) the court may order the accused to be kept in custody until his trial (or sentence) or it may grant him bail.

Remands in the absence of the accused

J[1.21]

An application for a remand for not more than 8 clear days may in prescribed circumstances be heard in the absence of the accused. The conditions to be complied with before this is possible are as follows:

(a)   the court is adjourning a case before conviction; and
(b)   the accused is present before the court;
(c)   he is legally represented before the court (although his solicitor need not necessarily be present in court).

J[1.22]

The accused must be asked whether he consents to future remands being determined in his absence. If he does, the court may remand him for up to three occasions in his absence. This means that the defendant must be brought before the court every four weeks. If the accused withdraws his consent or for any reason ceases to be legally represented, arrangements will be made by the justices' clerk to bring him before the court at the earliest opportunity, even though the period of his remand has not expired.

J[1.22A]

Video remands. The Crime and Disorder Act 1998, s 57 provides for the use of video conferencing between the prison and the court for defendants previously refused bail in person. No consent is required and the defendant's next physical appearance before either the magistrates' court or the Crown Court will be for trial or plea and sentence.

Section 57 has had new sections added by s 45 of the Police and Justice Act 2006. The 2006 Act has extended a video remand hearing to include eg juveniles remanded to secure accommodation by virtue of s 23 CYPA 1969; and live video links are available for the sentencing hearing of adult and youth offenders where the defendant consents. The new provisions came into force on **15 January 2007**. Further amendments have since been made by the Coroners and Justice Act 2009 from **14 December 2009**.

Justices are advised to consult their legal adviser before making an order.

J[1.22B]

Vulnerable accused – live video links. From **15 January 2007** the Youth Justice and Criminal Evidence Act 1999 was amended to permit a direction for a vulnerable accused to give evidence by a live link. A court may give a direction on the application of the accused for the accused to give evidence via live video link where –

(1) the accused is aged *under 18*; his ability to participate effectively is compromised by his level of intellectual ability or social functioning; and the live link would enable him to participate more effectively in proceedings; or

(2) the accused has *attained the age of 18*; is suffering from a mental disorder and for that reason is unable to participate effectively; and that the live link would enable more effective participation.

J[1.22C]

Live links in criminal proceedings – witnesses. From **26 April 2010** the Criminal Justice Act 2003, s 51, provides that if a magistrates' court so directs, a witness may give evidence through a live link at suitable premises other than court premises. The direction may be given in relation either to a trial or where the accused has pleaded guilty eg a "Newton hearing". A direction may be given on the application by a party to the proceedings or of the court's own motion. A direction may not be given unless the court is satisfied that it is in the interests of the efficient or effective administration of justice for the person concerned to give evidence in the proceedings through a live link. There is provision for the court to review and rescind a live video link direction: CJA 2003, s 52.

J[1.23]

If the defendant has been remanded on bail or in custody and cannot appear because of accident or illness, the court may further remand him in absence. A court can always further remand in absence an accused who is on bail. *R (on the application of Grimshaw) v Leeds Magistrates' Court* [2001] EWHC 880 (Admin), [2001] All ER (D) 350 (Oct) is authority for a remand in the absence of the accused where he has not been produced due to a mistake.

The decision whether to remand in custody or on bail

J[1.24]

Presumption of liberty. The general principle is that an accused man has a right to be released on bail where he has not been convicted of the charge or where his case has been adjourned for pre-sentence reports. This means that the accused never has to apply for bail, it is up to the prosecution to object to his right to bail (although in practice the defence are referred to as making an application for bail). Therefore, it is no reason for remanding an accused in custody that he has not applied for bail. However this right to bail does not apply to a committal to the Crown Court for sentence.

J[1.25]

Grant of opposed bail. Where the court grants bail following a prosecution objection to bail the court must state its reasons for doing so.

J[1.26]–[1.30]

Exceptions to the right to bail. An accused can only be denied his right to bail if the court finds that there is an exception to that right. These exceptions are set out in the Bail Act 1976, Sch 1 as amended by the Coroners and Justice Act 2009.* They differ according to whether or not the offence is (a) indictable imprisonable; (b) summary only imprisonable; or (c) summary only non-imprisonable. In taking these decisions the court must also have regard to any misuse of controlled drugs by the defendant so far as it is relevant.*

*Further amendments are contemplated by virtue of LASPOA 2012, s 90, when brought into force.

J[1.31]

A defendant need not be granted bail if he is charged with an either way or indictable offence and it appears to the court that he was on bail in criminal proceedings at the date of the offence.

For offences on or after 1 January 2007, which carry a sentence of life imprisonment, where the accused is aged *18 years or over and it appears that he committed the offence whilst on bail in criminal proceedings, he may not be granted bail unless the court is satisfied that there is no significant risk of his committing an offence while on bail. The court must give its reasons if it grants bail.

For offences on or after 1 January 2007, which carry a sentence of life imprisonment, where the accused is aged **18 years or over and, the defendant fails to surrender to custody after 1 January 2007, he may not be granted bail unless the court is satisfied that there is no significant risk that, if released on bail, he would fail to surrender to custody. If the accused had reasonable cause for failure to answer his bail the court shall take into account whether he surrendered as soon as practicable thereafter.

*Where the accused is aged under 18 years of age, in determining whether there are substantial grounds for believing that he would reoffend if granted bail, the court shall give particular weight to the fact that he was on bail in criminal proceedings.

**Where the accused is aged under 18 years of age, in determining whether there are substantial grounds for believing that he would fail to surrender, the court shall give particular weight to the fact that he failed to surrender at the appointed time, or if there was a reasonable excuse, as soon as practicable thereafter.

J[1.32]–[1.38]

Indictable imprisonable offences. The exceptions to the right to bail are:

(1)   Where the court has substantial grounds for believing the accused would:
    (a)   fail to answer bail; or
    (b)   commit further offences on bail; or
    (c)   interfere with witnesses or otherwise obstruct the course of justice.
    Each of the exceptions must be substantiated by a reason given by the court such as:
    (i)   the nature and seriousness of the offence or default (and the probable method of dealing with the accused for it);
    (ii)   the character, antecedents, associations and community ties of the defendant;
    (iii)   the accused's previous record when granted bail (eg committing offences on bail or absconding);
    (iv)   (except when remanding after conviction for a report) the strength of the evidence against the accused;
    (v)   if the court is satisfied that there are substantial grounds for believing that the defendant, if released on bail (whether subject to conditions or not), would commit an offence on bail, the risk that the defendant may do so by engaging in conduct that would, or would be likely to, cause physical or mental injury to any person other than the defendant;
    (vi)   any other relevant reasons.

Note that where the prosecution objects to bail but the court nevertheless grants bail it must provide reasons for granting bail. A written record must be kept.

(2)   Remand in custody for the accused's own protection (or in the case of a juvenile, welfare). Used only in exceptional circumstances and with strong reasons eg the accused is a high suicide risk.
(3)   Where the accused is already in custody as a result of a prison sentence.
(4)   Where there has been insufficient time to gather information to make the bail decision.
(5)   Where the accused has absconded or breached the conditions of his bail in the same proceedings already.
(6)   Where the case has been adjourned for reports or inquiries and it is impracticable to gain the information or prepare reports without remanding the accused in custody.
(7)   A defendant need not be granted bail, unless there is no significant risk of offending while on bail, or the defendant declines to take up an offer of a 'relevant assessment, or having agreed to one, fails to comply with such an assessment. It is a precondition that:
    (a)   the defendant be aged 18 or over;

(b)   the presence of Class A drugs has been detected in his body; and

(c)   either he has been charged under s 5(2) or s 5(3) of the Misuse of Drugs Act 1971, or the court is satisfied that his misuse of Class A drugs caused or contributed to his behaviour, or his offending was wholly or partly motivated by his intended misuse of a Class A drug.

** Note the Criminal Justice Act 2003, s 19, which imposes restrictions on the granting of bail to persons who have tested positive for a Class A drug, is in force but only in areas notified by the Secretary of State.

(8)   A person who has been charged with or convicted of an offence specified in s 25 of the Criminal Justice and Public Order Act 1994 (murder (see paragraph 9 below), rape and certain specified sexual offences) and has previously been convicted within the United Kingdom of any such specified offence as mentioned in s 25(3) shall be granted bail only if the court or police constable considering the grant of bail is satisfied that there are exceptional circumstances which justify it. Magistrates would be well advised to consult their legal adviser.

(9)   From 1 February 2010 any offender charged with murder may **only** be granted bail by a Crown Court Judge: see Coroners and Justice Act 2009 (Commencement No 3 and Transitional Provisions) Order 2010, SI 2010/145. The legislation prescribes that the Crown Court must make a decision about bail as soon as reasonably practicable and within 48 hours beginning with the day after the offender appears before a magistrates' court (see **juveniles** at paragraph (10) immediately below).

(10)   A youth court has no jurisdiction to grant bail to a juvenile charged with murder. However, in *R (on the application of A) v Lewisham Youth Court* [2011] EWHC 1193 (Admin), 175 JP 321, it was decided that CYPA 1969, s 23 contains a carefully calibrated, if confusingly complex set of provisions for determining how young defendants in criminal cases who are not granted bail should be detained. However, the Coroners and Justice Act 2009, s 115 was capable of being read in harmony with CYPA 1969, s 23. Thus, a Youth Court cannot grant bail to a child or young offender charged with murder, because that can only be granted by the Crown Court, but in determining the form of custody it must apply s 23 as it would in any other case.

J[1.39]

Summary only imprisonable offences. The exceptions to the right to bail are:

(a)   failure to surrender (if the accused has previously failed to surrender);

(b)   commission of further offences (if the instant offence was committed on bail);

(c)   fear of commission of offences likely to cause another person to suffer or fear physical or mental injury;

(d)   the accused's own protection (for his own welfare if a child);

(e)   the defendant is serving custody;

(f)   fear of failure to surrender, commission of offences, interference with witnesses or obstruction of justice (if the defendant has been arrested for breach of bail in respect of the instant offence); and

(g)   lack of sufficient information to make a bail decision.

J[1.40]

Summary only non-imprisonable offences. The exceptions to the right to bail are:

(a)   having been previously granted bail in criminal proceedings the accused has failed to surrender to his bail; and the court believes, in view of that failure, that the defendant, if released on bail (whether subject to conditions or not) he would again fail to surrender to custody;

(b)   remand in custody for the accused's own protection (or in the case of a juvenile, welfare);

(c)   where the accused is already in custody as a result of a prison sentence;

(d)   where the accused has already absconded or breached the conditions of his bail in the same proceedings and this leads the court to find that there are substantial grounds for believing the defendant would fail to surrender to custody, commit an offence on bail or interfere with witnesses or otherwise obstruct the course of justice.

General considerations

J[1.41]–[1.45]

It is not common for a court to have to deal with a remand of a non-imprisonable case and it is even less common for the court to consider a remand in custody. Therefore the following remarks are confined mainly to remands of imprisonable cases.

J[1.46]

The usual grounds for the police objecting to bail are exceptions (1) (a)–(c) above (failure to surrender, further offences or interference with the course of justice). It is worthwhile to examine these a little more closely.

J[1.47]

Failure to surrender to custody. The accused may fail to surrender because he knows he will be convicted of a serious charge and will receive a custodial sentence.

In considering this objection to the right to bail, the bench might have regard to the likely sentence that will be imposed, in which case the accused's record will be relevant. Then, the circumstances of the defendant: Is he a 'local' man? How long has he lived in the district? Does he have anywhere else to move to? Are all his friends and relations in the area? The court must also consider whether bail with a condition of finding a security or surety would suffice instead of a remand in custody.

J[1.48]

Further offences on bail. A defendant may consider that he will receive a custodial sentence and that he might as well be 'hung for a sheep as a lamb', in other words the final sentences he receives will not be materially affected whether he is sentenced for one or several offences. This is particularly the case with the 'professional' burglar or the youth with a penchant for taking the cars of other people without their consent.

J[1.49]

Interference with the course of justice. In certain situations, a defendant released on bail would interfere with the course of justice. This has three main aspects. First, he might 'tip off' a co-accused who could then abscond or destroy evidence. Second, the co-accused might collaborate to concoct a consistent but false story. Third, the defendant might intimidate the prosecution witnesses, eg in disputes involving a domestic background. The court must consider whether conditions attached to bail would be sufficient to prevent this occurring, eg of non-association with co-accused, or with the prosecution witnesses.

J[1.50]

Mistakes commonly made in finding these exceptions are that the bench fail to announce that they find substantial grounds for believing etc and that they announce reasons but no exceptions, eg the defendant is remanded in custody because of his character and antecedents and the nature and seriousness of the offence. These are reasons for finding one of the exceptions (1) (a)–(c), but they are not in themselves exceptions to the right to bail.

J[1.51]

Custody time limits. The Prosecution of Offences Act 1985, s 22 provides for restrictions on the period for which a person charged with an either way, indictable or summary offence may be remanded in custody. The maximum period of a custodial remand is 70 days between his first appearance and the start of a summary trial or committal proceedings, as appropriate. Where, in the case of an either way offence, summary trial is decided upon within 56 days the summary trial must commence within 56 days of the first appearance. Time limits also apply to proceedings before the Crown Court.

NB: An offence 'triable either way' includes an offence which, although triable only on indictment in the case of an adult, is in the case of a juvenile person under 18 years of age triable summarily or on indictment under s 24 of the Magistrates' Courts Act 1980 (grave crimes procedure) (*R v Stratford Youth Court, ex p S* (1998) 162 JP 552).

J[1.52]

The court may extend the custody time limits on receipt of an application either orally or in writing but the court must not grant an extension *unless* satisfied that the need for it is justified by virtue of one of three criteria:

(a)   illness or absence of the accused, a necessary witness, a judge or magistrate; or

(b)   a postponement occasioned by the ordering by the court of separate trials in the case of two or more accused or two or more offences; or

(c)   some other good and sufficient cause.

The procedure for an application to extend time limits may be informal but the prosecution must still satisfy the court and the defendant be given an opportunity to test the application (*Wildman v DPP* [2001] EWHC 14 (Admin), (2001) 165 JP 453).

The unavailability of a suitable judge or a suitable courtroom within the maximum period specified in the CTL regulations may, in special cases and on appropriate facts, amount to good and sufficient cause for granting an extension of custody time limits. However, the CPS must provide evidence to support an extension. The court was reliant on information provided by HMCTS staff. That was wholly inadequate. The case was not given that intense level of scrutiny required. If the court had been provided with the correct information he would not have extended the CTL. The President of the Queen's Bench Division then proceeded to lay down guidance on the approach the Crown Court should take in a routine case where an extension to the CTL is sought because of a lack of resources: *R (on the application of McAuley (Clarke)) v Coventry Magistrates' Court and CPS* [2012] EWHC 680 (Admin), [2012] 3 All ER 519, [2012] 1 WLR 2766.

A successful application to vacate the trial by the defence is relevant to a reconsideration of a refusal to extend custody limits (*R (on the application of DPP) v Crown Court at Blackfriars* [2001] EWHC 56 (Admin), [2001] All ER (D) 205).

However, custody time limits were not extended when the defence requested an adjournment to consider disclosure which was two months late as the fault was that of the prosecution (*R (on the application of Holland) v Leeds Crown Court* [2002] EWHC 1862 (Admin), [2003] Crim LR 272).

J[1.53]

The court must also be satisfied the prosecution has acted with all due diligence as well as expedition. See *R v Central Criminal Court, ex p Johnson* [1999] 2 Cr App Rep 51. The fact that a trial could not proceed because of the illness of a victim is irrelevant if the prosecution have failed otherwise to act with due diligence (*R v Central Criminal Court, ex p Bennett* (1999) Times, 25 January). This approach was rejected by the High Court in *R v Leeds Crown Court, ex p Bagoutie* (1999) Times, 31 May as leading to absurd results so that it does not matter that the prosecution has not acted with all due diligence if there is good and sufficient cause in the eyes of the court. However, in complex matters where the defendant is asking for extensive disclosure the prosecution could expect reasonable notice of such enquiries to enable it to comply (*R (on the application of Smith) v Crown Court at Woolwich* [2002] EWHC 995 (Admin), [2002] All ER (D) 05 (May)).

J[1.54]

Where a custody time limit has expired the accused must be released on bail with or without conditions. However, a new charge will attract its own custody time limit (*R v Crown Court at Leeds, ex p Wardle* [2001] UKHL 12, [2002] 1 AC 754).

Conditional bail

Bail granted by the police

Police street bail

J[1.55]

Section 30A of PACE (inserted by the CJA 2003) gave the police power to release on bail an arrested person at 'any time before he arrives at a police station'. From April 1, 2007 the Police and Justice Act 2006 amended PACE to allow conditions to be imposed by a constable where they are necessary:

(a)   to secure that person's surrender to custody;
(b)   to secure that person does not commit an offence;
(c)   to secure that person does not interfere with witnesses or otherwise obstruct the course of justice;
(d)   for the person's protection/welfare.

Those conditions, however, cannot include:

(a)   a recognisance;
(b)   a security;
(c)   a surety;
(d)   residence at a bail hostel.

A bail notice given to the arrested person must specify:

(i)   the requirements imposed by the condition;
(ii)   the process for applying to vary those conditions.
(iii)

Application to vary can be made either to the police or to a magistrates' court. A magistrates' court may consider an application to vary police street bail conditions where:

(a)   the street conditions have previously been varied by the police,
(b)   a request for variation by the police has been made and refused, or
(c)   a request was made and more than 48 hours has elapsed and the application has neither been withdrawn nor granted (PACE, s 30CB as inserted by Police and Justice Act 2006, s 6 and Sch 10).

A constable may arrest without warrant a person released on conditional bail granted on the street if he has reasonable grounds for suspecting the person has broken any of the conditions imposed by the police. A person arrested for breach of street bail conditions must be taken to a police station as soon as is practicable after the arrest.

Police bail before charge

J[1.56]

Any grant of bail before charge may now have attached to it the full range of conditions similar to those outlined at J[1.55]. Applications to vary these conditions are dealt with under s 47(1E) of PACE and in accordance with r 19.6 of the Criminal Procedure Rules 2012. For variation of court bail see J[1.81A].

Police bail after charge

J[1.57]–[1.60]

A custody sergeant at the police station may grant an accused conditional bail and may do so for the same reasons as a bench of magistrates who may decide that the defendant cannot be released on unconditional bail. It is only if conditional bail would be inadequate that custody should be contemplated.

J[1.61]

Conditions are only to be attached to bail where it appears to the bench necessary to do so for the purpose of preventing the accused:

(a)   failing to surrender to custody; or
(b)   committing an offence while on bail; or
(c)   interfering with witnesses or obstructing the course of justice; or
(d)   from being harmed, ie for his own protection or in the case of a juvenile for his welfare.

J[1.62]

Conditions may also be imposed to enable a pre-sentence report to be prepared, or requiring a defendant to attend an interview with a legal representative before the next court hearing. The court must give its reasons for imposing conditions on the bail.

In the case of a person accused of *murder* see para (9) of J[1.32]–J[1.38] above. The court granting bail **shall**, unless it considers that satisfactory reports on the accused's mental condition have already been obtained, impose conditions: (a) a requirement that the accused shall undergo examination by two medical practitioners for the purpose of enabling such reports to be prepared; and (b) a requirement that he shall for that purpose attend such institution or place as the court directs and comply with any such directions which may be given to him for that purpose by either of those practitioners. One of the practitioners must be approved for the purposes of s 12 of the Mental Health Act 1983 (Bail Act 1976, ss 3(6A), (6B)).

When notified that arrangements for assessment are available in a given area, a person over 18 who has tested positive for a specified Class A drug and who the court is satisfied that his offending was motivated by drug misuse or that misuse contributed to the offending a court **must** impose a condition to undergo assessment and follow up if the defendant consents (Bail Act 1976, s 3(6D)). If the offender does not consent see J[1.32]–J[1.38].

J[1.63]

Commonly imposed conditions are:

- residence (absconding);
- curfew (fresh offences);
- reporting to a police station (absconding);
- non-association with specified people (interference with the course of justice);
- a security or surety (absconding).

Other conditions may be imposed provided they are reasonable and are enforceable, including a 'doorstep' condition for those on a curfew condition (*R v Chorley Justices* [2002] EWHC 2162 (Admin), 166 JP 764, sub nom R (DPP) v Chorley Justices [2002] 43 LS Gaz R 34).

See r 19.11 of the CPR 2012. The defence should give notice of any proposed address at which he/she would reside if granted bail to enable the court to assess the suitability of the address proposed.

J[1.64]

It must be emphasised that conditions are not to be imposed as a matter of course; they can only be imposed to prevent one of the occurrences mentioned above. If a condition is imposed it must relate to the mischief which is feared (a *guide* is given by the words in brackets above). Conditions must not be imposed which have no relevance to the reason given by the court, eg a surety because the bench fears fresh offences.

J[1.65]

Conditions may also be imposed to require defendants to comply with hostel rules where residing at a bail or probation hostel on remand or for assessment. Electronic monitoring of defendants on bail to enforce a curfew is also permitted. Electronic monitoring of children over the age of 12 is also permitted subject to the same restrictions imposed on the use of secure accommodation: s 3AA of the Bail Act 1976 (see J[1.6])*.

*When LASPOA 2012, s 151(1) is brought into force, the criteria for remanding children on bail with an electronic monitoring condition will be modified.

J[1.66]

Sureties. With one exception, mentioned below, no one has to deposit money or valuables to secure a person's release in remand proceedings. However, a third party may agree to stand as surety for an accused. A surety is a person who agrees to forfeit a sum of money fixed by the court (called a recognisance and pronounced 'reconnaissance') if the accused fails to surrender to custody. A surety's obligations are to ensure that the accused surrenders to custody; he is not there to ensure that the accused complies with the conditions of his bail. The court should specify that the person standing surety is to secure the accused's attendance at the next hearing or for each occasion to which the case may, from time to time, be adjourned.

J[1.67]

In deciding whether to accept a person as a surety, the court should in particular have regard to:

(a)   the surety's financial resources;
(b)   his character and any previous convictions of his;
(c)   his proximity (whether in point of kinship, place or otherwise) to the person for whom he is to be surety.

J[1.68]

Forfeiting the recognisance of a surety. If the accused fails to answer to his bail, the surety should be informed by the court that it is considering forfeiting his recognisance. Standing surety is a solemn obligation. The court will start from the basis that the whole amount is to be forfeited. The culpability of the surety will be investigated to see what steps he took to ensure the defendant's attendance. However, a surety should not forfeit his recognisance if he is not to blame for the defendant's failure to surrender when required to do so. When forfeiting a recognisance the court must take into account the surety's ability to pay.

J[1.69]

Depositing a security. An exception to the rule that an accused does not have to deposit money or valuables is where the court believes a security is necessary to ensure the defendant surrenders to custody. The usual security is money, but it could be a valuable item such as motor car, provided it is readily convertible into money.

In the case of a security the law presumes that the sum deposited by way of security should be forfeited and it is for the person who deposited the security – on receipt of a court notice – to show cause why the sum should not remain forfeited.

J[1.70]–[1.75]

The effectiveness of conditions. The usefulness of some conditions is questionable. A condition of reporting to the police at anything longer than 24-hour intervals is generally of little value and such a condition should be not imposed to make the accused more readily available for questioning. Nor should a condition be imposed for its nuisance value to the accused. A condition of depositing a passport is of little value, especially where the accused can travel within the EU without a passport.

Appeal by the prosecution

J[1.76]

The Bail (Amendment) Act 1993 (as amended) gives the Crown Prosecution

Service the right to appeal to a Crown Court Judge where a court grants bail to a person who is charged with or convicted of an offence punishable by imprisonment. Notice must be served within two hours of the decision and the hearing (see *R (Jeffrey) v Warwick Crown Court* (2003)). Such an appeal must be commenced within 48 hours of the date of the decision. See *R v Crown Court at Middlesex Guildhall, ex p Okoli* (2001) 165 JP 144, [2000] Crim LR 921.

Where bail is refused

J[1.77]

Making a further application. At the first hearing after that at which the court decided not to grant the defendant bail (which normally would have been the first time the case was remanded) he is entitled to apply for bail as of right. At any subsequent hearings the court need not hear any arguments as to fact or law which it has heard previously: see *R (on the application of B) v Brent Youth Court* [2010] All ER (D) 76 (Jul).

J[1.78]

The court must, however, always consider the matter of bail on each occasion on which the case is remanded. As the liberty of the accused is at stake, it is suggested that any doubt whether to allow a fresh application should be resolved in the accused's favour.

J[1.79]

Appeals. The defendant may appeal to the Crown Court against the imposition of bail conditions relating to residence (other than to a bail hostel), sureties and securities, curfew and contact with other persons. Such an application may only be made following the determination of an application to vary the bail conditions made in the magistrates' court. There is no concurrent power to appeal to the High Court.

Application to a Crown Court Judge in chambers. Where the magistrates have heard a full application and refused bail, their legal adviser will supply the accused with a certificate to that effect. He then has a right to make a bail application to a Crown Court Judge in chambers.

Bail in cases of murder, manslaughter and rape

J[1.80]

See J[1.38] and J[1.62].

Reconsideration of bail

J[1.81]

Where a court or a constable has granted bail for an indictable or either way offence the prosecution may apply to have that decision reconsidered by the court who may:

- vary the conditions of bail;
- impose conditions on unconditional bail;
- withhold bail.

This may only be done on the basis of fresh information not previously available to the court or constable who granted bail.

Application to vary bail conditions imposed by the court

J[1.81A]

Advance notice (24 hours minimum) must be given by the defence of an application to vary conditions of bail, including a change of address. A new rule 19.11 has been added to the Criminal Procedure Rules 2012 whereby the defence must give notice of the address at which the defendant would reside if the court granted or varied bail, to enable the court to assess the suitability of the address proposed.

Prosecution for failing to surrender to custody

J[1.82]

The law is that the accused is released on bail with a duty to turn up at court on the appointed day at the appointed time. If he fails to do so the first consequence is that a warrant may be issued for his arrest. Second, he may be prosecuted for the criminal offence of failing to surrender to custody. See [1.85] below.

J[1.83]

Where bail has been granted by a police officer for an accused to surrender either to a police station or a magistrates' court, any failure to surrender to custody should be initiated by charging the accused or laying an information. On the other hand, an accused who fails to answer to bail granted by the magistrates themselves should be brought before the court following his arrest. The court will then initiate proceedings following an express invitation by the prosecutor. The prosecutor will conduct the proceedings and, where the matter is contested, call the evidence. Any trial should normally take place immediately. In the meantime the defendant can expect to have bail revoked. In cases which cannot or are unlikely to result in custodial sentences a trial in the absence of the defendant may be a pragmatic solution. The bail offence should be dealt with immediately in normal circumstances (Revised Practice Direction (2004)).

J[1.84]

The offence is triable only summarily where bail was granted by magistrates and proceedings are begun on the invitation of the prosecution. The accused must be asked whether he pleads guilty or not guilty. Where a prosecution is contemplated the legal adviser should be consulted to ensure the correct procedure is followed.

J[1.85]–[1.90]

Defence. It is a defence to such a charge if he proves (that it is more probable than not) that he had a reasonable excuse for not answering his bail, or that having a reasonable excuse for failing to surrender to custody at the appointed time and place, he surrendered to custody at the appointed place as soon after the appointed time as was reasonably practicable. It is not a defence that the accused was not given a copy of the decision to grant him bail.

'Surrender to custody' means 'at the appointed time and place' and the mere fact that the defendant is eg half an hour late cannot afford him a defence (*R v Scott (Casim)* [2007] EWCA Crim 2757, 172 JP 149).

J[1.91]

Penalty. A maximum penalty of 3 months' imprisonment* and a fine on level 5 in the magistrates' court or the accused may be committed for sentence to the Crown Court**, where the maximum penalty is 12 months' imprisonment and an unlimited fine. In *R v Clarke* [2000] 1 Cr App Rep (S) 224, CA the Court of Appeal upheld a prison sentence for the offence. Any such sentence will normally be consecutive to the sentence for the substantive offence (*R v White* (2002) Times, 9 December).

*Section 34 of the Police and Justice Act 2006, when brought into force, makes it possible for a 'custodial sentence' to continue to be available for magistrates' courts dealing with those who fail to surrender to bail if and when s 181 of the Criminal Justice Act 2003 is brought into force. This has been achieved by amending the definition of 'sentence of imprisonment' in s 195 of the Criminal Justice Act 2003. The legislation provides that the definition does not include a sentence of imprisonment passed in respect of a summary conviction under s 6(1) or (2) of the Bail Act 1976. There is no provision in the Criminal Justice Act 2003 to amend or remove the power of the magistrates' court to commit for sentence under s 6(6)(a) or (b) of the Bail Act 1976.

**Custody plus and intermittent custody orders provided for by the CJA 2003, ss 181–188 and Schs 10 and 11 will be repealed at a future date by LASPOA 2012, s 89.

J[1.92]

Failing to comply with a condition. Failing to comply with a condition of bail is not an offence (see *R v Ashley* [2003] EWCA Crim 2571, [2003] All ER (D) 106 (Aug)). It does mean, however, that a police officer can arrest the accused forthwith and bring him before the court. His failure to comply with the condition may in itself constitute an exception to the general 'right to bail'. If a defendant is arrested in breach of a bail condition the court should ask if he admits or denies the breach. If a denial is recorded the magistrates should hear evidence or a statement of the arresting officer's 'reasonable grounds' for arrest.

In determining whether the accused has broken a condition of his bail, the court is entitled to apply the civil standard of proof i.e. a balance of probabilities. The court is entitled to receive written hearsay evidence eg the statement of the arresting officer; the court's duty is to then weigh the evidence having regard to the hearsay nature of the evidence and the fact that the evidence cannot be tested by cross-examination: see *R (on the application of Thomas) v Greenwich Magistrates' Court* [2009] EWHC 1180 (Admin), 173 JP 345).

If the court is of the opinion that the defendant was in breach of his bail conditions he may be further remanded either in custody or on bail. If there is no breach of condition there is an entitlement to bail on the same conditions. Only after a finding of breach does the consideration of the reasons for breach become relevant (*R (Vickers) v West London Magistrates Court* [2003] EWHC 1809 (Admin), [2003] All ER (D) 211 (Jul)).

When LASPOA 2012, s 90 is brought into force a new sub-s (5A) will be added to s 7 of the Bail Act 1976, and sub-s (6) will be amended as follows:

(5A) A justice of the peace may not remand a person in, or commit a person to, custody under subsection (5) if—

(a)   the person has attained the age of eighteen,

(b)   the person was released on bail in non-extradition proceedings,

(c)   the person has not been convicted of an offence in those proceedings, and

(d)   it appears to the justice of the peace that there is no real prospect that the person will be sentenced to a custodial sentence in the proceedings.

(6) Where the person so brought before the justice [a person brought before a justice under subsection (4) or (4B)] is a child or young person and the justice does not grant him bail, subsection (5) above shall have effect subject to the provisions of section 23 of the Children and Young Persons Act 1969 (remands to the care of local authorities) [section 91 of the Legal Aid, Sentencing and Punishment of Offenders Act 2012 (remands of children otherwise than on bail)].

Such hearing must be within 24 hours of arrest although there is power for the case to be put back in the list during that time period (*R (Hussain) v Derby Magistrates' Court* [2001] EWHC 507 (Admin), [2001] 1 WLR 2454). In *R (on the application of Culley) v Dorchester Crown Court* [2007] EWHC 109 (Admin), 172 JP 373, it was decided that:

(1)   Following the arrest of a person for breach of a bail condition, under s 7(4) Bail Act 1976 that person must be brought before a magistrates' court as soon as practicable and in any case within 24 hours of the arrest.

(2)   After the arrest of that person the court is required to complete the investigation and make a decision on whether there has been a breach of bail and, if there is a breach to remand in custody or to re-admit that person to bail.

(3)   Once 24 hours has elapsed after the arrest of that person, a magistrates' court no longer has jurisdiction under s 7(5) to deal with the breach of bail.

Bail pending appeal

J[1.93]

The policy of the Court of Appeal has for long been against the granting of bail pending the hearing of an appeal against a custodial sentence, unless there are exceptional circumstances. The appellant's remedy is to apply for an expedited appeal. It is generally felt to be unsatisfactory that a person sentenced to custody is released in the hope of a successful appeal and is subsequently required to return to prison to serve his sentence. Therefore, only exceptional circumstances will lead to the granting of bail (*R v Watton* (1978) 68 Cr App Rep 293, [1979] Crim LR 246, CA). The court considering the application is not concerned with whether it would have imposed the same sentence, but only whether the sentence was reasonable. Where the sentence is clearly appropriate for the offence, then personal matters which are the basis for an appeal for clemency should not influence the court considering the bail application.

Disqualification of justices to be removed

J[1.94]

When in the course of any bail application, a magistrate had been told of the accused's previous convictions, that magistrate could not hear the trial of the case if the accused subsequently pleaded not guilty (there was no such restriction if he pleaded guilty). The restriction which is to be found in s 42 of the Magistrates' Courts Act 1980 will be removed by virtue of Sch 37, Part 4 of the Criminal Justice Act 2003. The change reflects the law relating to the admissibility of bad character evidence in criminal proceedings which is to be found in Part II, Chapter I of the Criminal Justice Act 2003 (to date the provision has yet to be brought into force – editor).

J[2]

Summary of procedure at a remand hearing

J[2.1]

The procedure at a remand hearing can be summarised as follows:

(1)　Prosecution (or defence) applies for an adjournment. Bench decides whether to grant the application (length of adjournment may vary depending whether accused will be remanded in custody or on bail).

(2)　As the presumption is that an accused will be remanded on bail, the prosecution must put forward any exceptions to the right to bail. It is not necessary for evidence to be called and strict proof given.

(3)　Where the accused has had a previous application for bail refused, the court must consider whether he may put forward further arguments in support of bail.

(4)　The accused then makes his application for bail.

(5)　The bench consider whether there are any exceptions to the right to bail, that is:

　　(a)　can the accused be released on unconditional bail?
　　(b)　if not, would conditional bail suffice?
　　(c)　is there an exception to the right to bail?

(6)　The bench announces its decision:

　　(a)　if the remand is in custody:

　　　　(i)　the chairman will specify the exception to the right to bail which applies together with the reasons for applying that exception where appropriate;

　　　　(ii)　the accused is given a record of the decision and a certificate of refusal of bail after a full hearing;

　　　　(iii)　the court may inquire whether the accused will consent to further applications being heard in his absence or having heard representations from the parties, fix a date up to 28 days ahead, when it expects the next stage in the proceedings to take place.

　　(b)　If the remand is on conditional bail, the chairman will announce the conditions and the purpose of those conditions. If sureties are required they may be taken in court or the accused remanded in custody until a security is deposited or a surety is taken.

J[3]

Decision to refuse bail
(See the exceptions (1)(a)–(c), at J[1.32])

J[3.1]

You are refused bail in this case because we find that there are substantial grounds for believing that if released on bail you would:

[fail to surrender to custody]

[commit an offence while on bail]

[interfere with witnesses or otherwise obstruct the course of justice]

and in reaching our decision we have had regard to:

[the nature and seriousness of the offence [and the probable method of dealing with you for it]]

[your character, antecedents, associations and community ties]

[your record as respects the fulfillment of your obligations under previous grants of bail in criminal proceedings]

[the strength of the evidence of your having committed the offence]

You will therefore be remanded in custody to appear at this court on [*date*] at [*time*].

J[4]

Decision to grant bail
with conditions

J[4.1]

The court grants bail in this case. You will be released with a duty to surrender to the custody of this court on [*date*] at [*time*]. The bail will be subject to the following conditions:

You are:

　　[to reside at [*address*] in the meantime]

　　[to remain indoors at that address between the hours of . . . p.m. and . . . a.m.]

　　[to report at police station between the hours of and on [*specify days*]]

　　[not to associate with the following persons]

　　[to provide a security or surety[ies] in the sum of [*each*]]

The court considers it is necessary to impose the condition[s] to prevent you:

　　[failing to surrender to custody]

　　[committing an offence while on bail]

　　[interfering with witnesses or otherwise obstructing the course of justice]

Justices in the Crown Court

K[1]

Justices in the Crown Court

K[1.1]

The Crown Court is part of the Supreme Court of Judicature and exercises both civil and criminal jurisdiction. There are three kinds of professional Judges: High Court Judges, circuit Judges and recorders. The most serious cases are dealt with by a High Court Judge sitting alone but when circuit Judges and recorders deal with appeals they may sit with between one and four justices according to the type of case involved.

K[1.2]

The following Judges should be addressed in court as 'My Lord' (or 'My Lady' as the case may be):

- any circuit Judge or recorder when he is sitting as a High Court Judge;
- any Judge in the Central Criminal Court;
- any circuit Judge holding office as honorary Recorder of Liverpool or Manchester.

K[1.3]

Subject to the above rule, the following Judges should be addressed in court as 'Your Honour':

- a circuit Judge;
- a retired circuit Judge sitting as a deputy;
- a recorder;
- a deputy circuit Judge.

K[1.4]

When justices sit with a circuit Judge or recorder, the justices are as much a part of the court as is the professional Judge and the decision of the court is the decision of the majority of those on the bench. Only if there is an equality of votes does the Judge or recorder have a second or casting vote. The Judge or recorder must preside and his rulings on legal matters will bind the justices.

K[1.5]

The rules which prescribe the number of justices who must sit in the

Crown Court and their qualifications are complicated and liable to be changed by the Lord Chief Justice or the Lord Chancellor and such changes may affect all Crown Court centres or only one. Part 63 of the Criminal Procedure Rules 2012 makes clear that any appeal to the Crown Court can be heard with only one magistrate as well as a Crown Court Judge, instead of the usual two magistrates, if to wait for a second magistrate would cause unreasonable delay. Where no magistrate is available and where the parties agree the Judge has a discretion to continue the case without justices.

K[1.6]

Justices may deal with cases at the Crown Court even though the case arose in a part of the country for which they do not act as justices; for example, a justice for one county may sit at the Crown Court to hear an appeal from the decision of a court in a neighbouring county. Note, in the magistrates' court the justices now have jurisdiction to try any summary or either way offence committed in any part of England and Wales (s 2 Magistrates' Courts Act 1980 as amended by s 44 Courts Act 2003).

Where justices sit in the Crown Court to hear an appeal that sitting or sittings count as part of the annual returns made to the Lord Chancellor via the relevant local advisory committee.

K[1.7]

On appeal if the prisoner is found guilty in the Crown Court then the bench decides what sentence to impose (technically all persons before the Crown Court are prisoners; those who have been bailed must surrender to custody at the beginning of the hearing and thus become prisoners).

K[1.8]

There is no jury present when the Crown Court hears an appeal against conviction and/or sentence (see s 108 MCA 1980), or when the court hears an appeal from the decision of a Betting and Gaming Licensing Committee.

Under the Gambling Act 2005 appeals from decisions of the relevant local authority will lie to the local magistrates' court (ss 202–206). The same legislation makes no provision for appeals from magistrates' courts to the Crown Court.

Under the Licensing Act 2003 the only statutory provision for an appeal from a decision of the magistrates' court to the Crown Court is in relation to a closure order (s 166).

K[2]

Procedure

K[2.1]

The clerk of the court in the Crown Court wears a gown but does not perform the same functions as a legal adviser in a magistrates' court. He does not act as legal adviser to the court, although in practice he may from time to time draw the Judge's attention to some legal or procedural matter.

K[2.2]

The proceedings begin with the arraignment of the prisoner if he is to stand trial or in other cases with the announcement of the case by the clerk of the court. When the prisoner is arraigned he is addressed in rather more formal terms than he would be when charged before a magistrates' court, but the arraignment is simply the charging of the prisoner and asking for his plea. The charge is called an indictment and if there are several offences alleged then each is called a count, so that one indictment may contain several counts.

K[2.3]

If there is a guilty plea no jury is required. If any of the counts is denied and not withdrawn by the prosecution a jury is summoned. Justices no longer sit on trials following a not guilty plea but the following description is given for information. Each member of the jury takes the juror's oath separately because the prisoner may object to an individual sitting as a juror. The prisoner may object to a juror if he gives a reason for his objection. The bench will decide whether the reason is sufficient for dismissing the juror. The jury is then charged with the duty of deciding on the evidence the question of the prisoner's guilt or innocence. After this the trial proceeds in the same way as the hearing of a criminal charge in the magistrates' court until counsel have made their final speeches (the prosecution has a closing speech immediately before that of the defence) when the judge will sum up the evidence for the jury and instruct them, if necessary, on any legal points involved in the case. The clerk then gives the jury to the charge of the jury bailiff who not only ensures that they have no communication with anyone but also acts as their messenger to the court, so that, for example, he will warn the court that the jury has completed its deliberations and wishes to return, or that the jury wishes to have further guidance from the Judge.

K[2.4]

Frequently while a jury is 'out' on one case the court will occupy its time by dealing with another, perhaps a guilty plea or prisoner committed for sentence.

K[2.5]

When the jury returns the foreman will be questioned by the clerk of the court and will be asked for its verdict on each count separately. When this has been done the jury may be discharged and it remains for the Judge to decide the appropriate sentence if there has been a verdict of guilty to any count.

K[3]
Sentencing

K[3.1]

On an appeal against conviction and/or sentence from a magistrates' court (see s 108 MCA 1980) where the appeal is unsuccessful the sentence may be increased as well as reduced. The Crown Court may also award costs which the justices did not award (*Johnson v RSPCA* (2000) 164 JP 345, [2000] 20 LS Gaz R 42).

K[3.2]

The maximum sentences which may be imposed at the Crown Court are generally greater than those which may be imposed in a magistrates' court. They are noted in the appropriate sections of this book. Until the amendments envisaged by the CJA 2003 are brought into force imprisonment may not be imposed on persons under 21 years.

K[3.3]

In certain circumstances (eg for breach of community penalty) a 'nominal sentence' of imprisonment for one day may be imposed.

K[4]

Expenses

K[4.1]

Justices who attend the Crown Court are entitled to be paid travelling, subsistence and loss of earnings allowances at the same rates applicable in the case of attending the magistrates' court. These rates are changed from time to time and can be obtained from the court's administration.

K[5]

Disqualification

K[5.1]

A justice must not sit at the Crown Court on an appeal from the decision of a magistrates' court of which he was a member. Normally arrangements will already have been made between the Crown Court staff and magistrates' courts office which will ensure that a justice is not called to the Crown Court who is disqualified, but in any case of doubt the justice should inform the Judge with whom he is sitting before the case begins.

The role of the justices' clerk

L[1]

The justices' clerk

L[1.1]

Some justices' clerks continue to hold independent public office. They may not be dismissed without the approval of the Lord Chancellor, who must in turn consider any representations made to him by the magistrates for the local justice area concerned. Although more recently some justices' clerks are appointed on a fixed-term contract they are still the holder of an independent public office.

L[1.2]

The justices' clerk must be distinguished from those of his assistants ('legal advisers') who on his behalf give advice to justices in court when the justices' clerk is not personally in attendance. Both however are obliged to act compatibly with the ECHR.

Functions of the justices' clerk

L[1.3]

Some of the functions of the justices' clerk will be seen from the following extract from the Courts Act 2003, which is not an exhaustive statement:

> 'The functions of a justices' clerk include giving advice to any or all of the justices to whom he is clerk about matters of law (including procedure or practice) on questions arising in connection with the discharge of their functions, including questions arising when the clerk is not personally attending on them . . . The powers of a justices' clerk include, at any time when he thinks he should do so, bringing to the attention of any or all of the justices of the peace to whom he is clerk any point of law (including procedure or practice) that is or may be involved in any question so arising.'

L[1.4]

It should be noted that the term 'justices' clerk' is used in the Act where it is also defined so as to exclude a member of his staff.

The Courts Service and Structure

L[1.5]

The office of justices' chief executive was abolished by the Courts Act 2003. The Courts Act 2003 unified the court structure by abolishing magistrates' courts committees and bringing magistrates' courts within the Courts Service ('Her Majesty's Courts Service'). The Head of the Courts Service responsible for administration locally is the cluster manager but the head of the Service for the relevant region is the Delivery Director. The Delivery Director line manages both the cluster manager and the justices' clerk, although the judicial independence of the magistracy and justices' clerks (including legal advisers, whose advice in individual cases the justices' clerk is responsible for) is preserved by s 29 of the Courts Act 2003.

Advice in court

L[1.6]

Although the extract from the Courts Act 2003 above refers solely to the justices' clerk himself, it is recognised that in practice he may delegate his advisory functions to legal advisers who are either professionally qualified as barristers or solicitors or are qualified under the Justices' Clerks (Qualification of Assistants) Rules 1979 as amended. This is recognised by a Practice Direction on the role of the clerk from the Lord Chief Justice reissued in July 2002 which states:

'V. 55

1)   A justices' clerk is responsible for:
   a.   The legal advice tended to the justices within the area;
   b.   The performance of any other functions set out below by any member of his/her staff acting as legal adviser;
   c.   Ensuring that competent advice is available to justices when the justices' clerk is not personally present in court;
   d.   The effective delivery of case management and the reduction of unnecessary delay.

2)   Where a person other than the justices' clerk (a 'legal adviser'), who is authorised to do so, performs any other functions referred to in this direction he/she will have the same responsibilities as the justices' clerk. The legal adviser may consult the justices' clerk or other person authorised by the justices' clerk for that purpose before tendering advice to the bench. If the justices' clerk or that person gives any advice directly to the bench, he/she should give the parties or their advocates an opportunity of repeating any relevant submissions prior to the advice being given.

3)   It shall be the responsibility of the legal adviser to provide the justices with any advice they require to properly perform their

functions whether or not the justices have requested that advice, on:

i)   questions of law (including ECHR jurisprudence and those matters set out in section 2 (1) of the Human Rights Act 1998)

ii)   questions of mixed law and fact;

iii)   matters of practice and procedure;

iv)   the range of penalties available;

v)   any relevant decisions of the superior courts or other guidelines;

vi)   other issues relevant to the matter before the court;

vii)   the appropriate decision-making structure to be applied in any given case. In addition to advising the justices it shall be the legal adviser's responsibility to assist the court, where appropriate, as to the formulation of reasons and the recording of those reasons.

4)   A justices' clerk or legal adviser must not play any part in making findings of fact that may assist the bench by reminding them of the evidence, using any notes of the proceedings for this purpose.

5)   A justices' clerk or legal adviser may ask questions of witnesses and the parties in order to clarify the evidence and any issues in the case.

6)   A legal adviser has a duty to ensure that every case is conducted fairly.

7)   When advising the justices the justices' clerk or legal adviser whether or not previously in court, should:

i)   ensure that s/he is aware that of the relevant facts;

ii)   provide the parties with the information necessary to enable the parties to make any representations they wish as to the advice before it is given.

8)   At any time justices are entitled to receive advice to assist them in discharging their responsibilities. If they are in any doubt as to the evidence which has been given, they should seek the aid of their legal adviser, referring to his/her notes as appropriate. This should ordinarily be done in open court. Where the justices request their legal adviser to join them in the retiring room this request should be made in the presence of the parties in court. Any legal advice given to the justices other than in open court should be clearly stated to be provisional and the adviser should subsequently repeat the substance of the advice in open court and give the parties an opportunity to make any representations they wish on

the provisional advice. The legal adviser should then state in open court whether the provisional advice is confirmed or if it is varied the nature of the variation.

9)   The performance of a legal adviser may be appraised by a person authorised . . . to do so. For that purpose the appraiser may be present in the justices' retiring room. The content of the appraisal is confidential, but the fact that an appraisal has taken place and the presence of the appraiser in the retiring room, should be briefly explained in open court.

10)   The legal adviser is under a duty to assist unrepresented parties to present their case, but must do so without appearing to become an advocate for the party concerned.

11)   The role of legal advisers in fine default proceedings or any other proceedings for the enforcement of financial orders, obligations or penalties is to assist the court. They must not act in an adversarial or partisan manner. With the agreement of the justices a legal adviser may ask questions of the defaulter to elicit information which the justices will require to make an adjudication, for example to facilitate his or her explanation for the default. A legal adviser may also advise the justices in the normal way as to the options open to them in dealing with the case. It would be inappropriate for the legal adviser to set out to establish wilful refusal or neglect or any other type of culpable behaviour, to offer an opinion on the facts, or to urge particular course of action upon the justices. The duty of impartiality is the paramount consideration for the legal adviser at all times, and this takes precedence over any role he or she may have as a collecting officer. The appointment of other staff to "prosecute" the case for the collecting officer is not essential to ensure compliance with the law, including the Human Rights Act 1998 . . . '

Family proceedings: Note, the Practice Direction of 1981 was revoked and the above direction was issued with the concurrence of the President of the Family Division. However, the above Practice Direction is entitled (' . . . crime: consolidated'). Although it applies with modification to family proceedings courts, the role of the justices' clerk and legal adviser in family proceedings is somewhat modified to reflect the procedures and responsibilities under eg the Children Act 1989 and the Family Proceedings (Children Act) Rules 1991.

L[1.7]

In court the legal adviser's duties are both advisory and executive. He may, if the justices so desire, perform those many tasks which ensure the smooth progress of the court's business. For example, he may decide the order in which cases are called, identify, caution and charge defendants, take their pleas and put to them other offences for the court to take into consideration. He may deal with the swearing of witnesses, he may deal with such matters as the explanation of a sentence such as a supervision requirement and confirm the defendant's consent to the requirement. He is empowered to take recognisances which have been fixed by the court, dealing with the arrangements for paying monetary penalties and the questioning of witnesses or defendants on the justices' behalf, including the conduct of a means inquiry. When the justices' clerk (or one of his legal advisers) performs these or any other similar tasks, he carries out those functions on behalf of the justices. There are at least three good reasons why he should carry out most, if not all of these executive functions: his legal knowledge, experience and professional ethics will usually mean that he can perform these functions more effectively than a justice can; there will be more uniformity of procedure if these functions are left to the legal adviser; the less the chairman has to worry about procedural tasks, the more of his attention he can give to listening and decision making.

L[1.8]

The extent to which the legal adviser exercises these tasks, however, varies from court to court and even in the same place it may change according to which chairman is sitting or whether the justices' clerk himself or one of his staff is in court. Whatever the legal adviser does he should be careful to avoid giving to the general public the impression that he and not the chairman is in charge of the court's affairs. The conduct of the court is always the responsibility of the chairman in consultation with his colleagues on the bench; but a wise chairman will usually leave the general conduct of business in court to the legal adviser.

L[1.9]

The Lord Chief Justice has warned that justices who fail to take the clerk's advice on a legal point may be ordered to pay the costs of any resulting appeal. This warning arose in a case where justices insisted on finding 'special reasons' in spite of advice given to them in court by the clerk and later in writing.

L[1.10]–[1.15]

If the justices retire the legal adviser should not retire with them as a matter of course: either the chairman should specifically and audibly invite him to join the justices or the legal adviser should remain in court and be seen to have been sent for. **NB:** There is not the same prohibition on the legal adviser retiring immediately to join the justices in family proceedings eg in order to assist in the drawing up of the justices' reasons.

L[1.16]

If the justices retire the legal adviser may join them. All too often justices are themselves unaware that a point has arisen in their discussion upon which they need advice, and unless the legal adviser is with them to hear their discussion he too will be unaware that they need advice. Moreover, if he is present during their discussion the legal adviser may be able to help by reminding them of parts of the evidence they may have overlooked, or by explaining the legal significance of particular evidence, or by correcting errors of recollection. In the event that the justices are later asked to state a case the clerk will find it a considerable advantage to have listened to the justices' discussion in the retiring room. Once the legal adviser is satisfied that he can be of no further assistance to the justices he should return to his place in court.

L[1.17]

If the justices do not send for the clerk when they retire, he is entitled to go to advise them if he considers it necessary to do so, but will inform the parties as to what he is going to say to the justices, giving them an opportunity of making representations before that [provisional] advice is given. See *Clark v Kelly* [2003] UKPC D1, [2004] 1 AC 681 on the legality of the justices' clerk's advice and its compatibility with Article 6 of the ECHR.

Delegation

L[1.18]

Apart from his duty to provide justices with advice when they sit in court, the justices' clerk may perform those judicial functions of a single justice which are prescribed by the Justices' Clerks Rules 1999. Amongst the more important judicial functions which a justices' clerk can perform are: the issue of a summons, a witness summons, a distress warrant or a warrant for arrest following a defendant's failure to appear at court so long as no objection is raised on behalf of the accused. The justices' clerk may adjourn a case and grant bail to an accused in his absence with the consent of the prosecution and in the same terms as previously imposed.

L[1.19]

The justices' clerk may take a plea, fix a trial date and commit a criminal case to the Crown Court for trial pursuant to MCA 1980, s 6(2) where the defendant is on bail (the latter function will lapse when the allocation procedures under the CJA 2003 are brought into force). He may authorise a legal adviser to exercise these functions and under the Children Act 1989 to conduct directions appointments and appoint guardians ad litem. Delegation should be by specific authorisation and in writing.

Delegation in relation to the grant of legal representation in criminal proceedings is currently governed by the Access to Justice Act 1999 and regulations made thereunder. The Criminal Defence Service Act 2006, from a date to be appointed, envisages that responsibility for the grant of representation will ultimately shift to the Legal Services Commission. However, in the first instance it is anticipated that magistrates' courts will retain the power to grant or refuse representation. The Act and regulations envisage that those functions are administrative in nature and will be delegated to court staff via the Area Director..

L[1.20]

The justices' clerk and those of his assistants with delegated powers have case management powers which can be exercised as if by a single justice. Often referred to as 'Narey Courts' the justices' clerk may sit alone in an early first hearing court where simple cases can be listed and a guilty plea is anticipated. Where the case is more complex or a not guilty plea is anticipated the case can be listed for an early administrative hearing where the justices' clerk can deal with trial listing, conditional bail variation (with the consent of the prosecution and the defence) and warrants of arrest in the event of a non-appearance by the accused.

Applications to a justice

M[1]

Applications to a justice

M[1.1]

It would probably surprise most newly appointed magistrates to learn that a single justice may issue a document such as a warrant to enter premises either at a court house or at home. Fortunately it would be exceptional if any one magistrate found himself called upon to perform anything more than a small number of such duties away from the courthouse. This section does not catalogue the entire 'out of hours' magisterial functions but gives general advice and deals with some of the more common 'doorstep' applications.

M[1.2]

It sometimes happens that the press will telephone a magistrate seeking an opinion or comment, especially if he is senior court chairman or of a branch representative of the Magistrates' Association. It is unwise to deal with such a request immediately. In most cases the magistrate will refuse to make any initial response. Normally it would be appropriate to refer the inquiry to the justices' clerk or to the chairman of the bench. As a magistrate be very careful (having declined to make any comment, or words to that effect) that you are not drawn into a conversation, isolated parts of which may make tomorrow's headlines. Words spoken conversationally can take on a whole new meaning when reduced to journalistic print. There will be times however when it may be proper to make some statement to the press. In such cases ask the caller to ring again in 30 minutes and use that time to discuss the matter with the justices' clerk, the chairman of the bench or a senior colleague; this will help you to collect your own thoughts on the matter and then it might be helpful to prepare and retain some written note.

M[1.3]

You should invariably refuse to enter into any discussion of a case with any person who has been involved in a decision of the court. A persistent telephone caller can be warned that he is liable to prosecution for making annoying telephone calls. A persistent member of the public should be advised to put his complaint in a letter addressed to the justices' clerk or Area Director. If a magistrate should receive any letters he/she should hand them to the justices' clerk and not reply personally.

Children

M[1.4]

(Emergency procedures under the Children Act 1989 are referred to in Section D.)

Warrants

M[1.5]

A warrant is a document signed by a magistrate which authorises the person named in the warrant to carry out the action specified.

M[1.6]

Signing a warrant is an extremely serious matter and a magistrate would be well advised always to refer the applicant to the courthouse where the application can be made in the presence of a legal adviser. If that is not possible, the justices' clerk or a legal adviser should be telephoned for advice. The following notes are intended to give a broad description of the procedure. **They should not be taken to encourage the hearing of an application in the absence of a legal adviser.**

M[1.7]

Some benches go as far as appointing an out-of-hours panel of volunteer magistrates who are given special training. Even so, in such cases a legal adviser is always contacted first about the proposed application.

M[1.8]

For the purposes of this section warrants fall into three categories: warrants to enter premises (and, usually, search for goods which may then be seized); warrants to arrest an individual; and applications under the Proceeds of Crime Act 2002.

M[1.9]

An application under s 42 or Sch 5 of the Terrorism Act 2000 to search premises may be made to a justice of the peace or a district Judge. Applications for warrants of further detention under Sch 8 may only be made to a designated district Judge authorised by the Lord Chancellor.

M[2]

Warrants to enter premises

1 The applicant

M[2.1]

Usually such applications are made by a police officer. If not, the magistrate should check whether any authority is needed by the applicant, eg in the case of an official from a supplier of Gas or Electricity (see **M[2.31]**). As a sensible precaution, a police officer should be asked to produce his warrant card, and anyone else evidence of his identity, and where appropriate, his authority to bring proceedings.

2 Authority for issuing a warrant

M[2.2]

A warrant of entry may only be issued where a statute gives authority to do so. When considering an application the magistrate should ask the applicant under what Act and section he is applying for a warrant. The warrant and supporting paperwork should indicate the Act and section. Note that the Justices' Clerks' Society has produced a checklist (dated October 2011) and any magistrate who may be asked to deal with search warrant applications should be afforded access to that checklist.

M[2.3]

Applications by the police generally fall into one of two categories:

M[2.4]

Search for unlawful articles. These are powers of search for goods which generally it is an offence knowingly to possess, eg warrants to enter and search for:

- stolen goods – Theft Act 1968, s 26;
- drugs – Misuse of Drugs Act 1971, s 23;
- obscene articles – Obscene Publications Act 1959, s 3;
- firearm or ammunition – Firearms Act 1968, s 46.

Under the MDA 1971, s 23(4), a forcible search may be justified where the suspect refuses to submit to a request to spit out drugs which he was concealing in his mouth: see *James v DPP* [2012] EWHC 1317 (Admin), 176 JP 346, 176 CL&J 291.

M[2.5]

Search for evidence. Until the Police and Criminal Evidence Act 1984, there was no power to issue a warrant to search for *evidence*, eg of a murder, unless the object of the search was also an 'unlawful article' so that a warrant could be issued under the powers described above. The Police and

Criminal Evidence Act 1984, s 8 (as amended by the Serious Organised Crime and Police Act 2005) now provides a general power to search for evidence of an offence. However since the Police and Criminal Evidence Act 1984 also gives the police considerable powers of search without a warrant in connection with the arrest of a defendant, an application for a warrant to search for evidence will very often entail the power to enter the premises of a possibly innocent third party to look for evidence implicating the accused.

Issuing a warrant to search for evidence of an indictable offence (Police and Criminal Evidence Act 1984, s 8)

M[2.6]

The application must be made by the police and the magistrate must have reasonable grounds for believing:

(a)   that an indictable offence has been committed; and
(b)   that there is material on premises specified in the application which is likely to be of substantial value (whether by itself or together with other material) to the investigation of the offence; and
(c)   that the material is likely to be relevant evidence; and
(d)   that it does not consist of or include items subject to legal privilege, excluded material or special procedure material; and
(e)   that any of the following applies:
    (i)   that it is not practicable to communicate with any person entitled to grant entry to the premises;
    (ii)   that it is practicable to communicate with a person entitled to grant access to the premises but it is not practicable to communicate with any person entitled to grant access to the evidence;
    (iii)   that entry to the premises will not be granted unless a warrant is produced;
    (iv)   that the purpose of a search may be frustrated or seriously prejudiced unless a constable arriving at the premises can secure immediate entry to them.

In *R (on the application of Wood) v North Avon Magistrates' Court* [2009] EWHC 3614 (Admin), 174 JP 157 the High Court suggested that, save in exceptional circumstances, the officer applying for the warrant and giving evidence on oath must be an officer directly involved in the investigation.

M[2.7]

Reasonable grounds for believing. The magistrate himself must have reasonable grounds for believing etc and his judgment will be based on the information supplied by the officer. It is advisable for a short note to be kept by the magistrate of the reasons for granting or refusing a warrant (which can be attached to the application). In the Code of Practice issued for guidance to the police, the officer must take reasonable steps to check that the information is accurate, recent and has not been provided maliciously or irresponsibly. An application may not be made on the basis of information from an anonymous source unless corroboration is sought. The identity of an informant need not be disclosed but the officer should be prepared to deal with any questions from the magistrate about the accuracy of previous information provided by that source or other related matters. 'Belief' is something more than suspicion and implies an acceptance that something is true even though formal, admissible evidence may be lacking. It may be helpful to consider the reference to this matter made when considering the offence of handling stolen goods at A[49].

There was nothing in the 1984 Act which required the court to give reasons why it was satisfied that there were reasonable grounds for believing the matters set out in s 8(1)(a)–(e) was satisfied. In some cases it might be unnecessary to do so, such as where the written information was compelling as to the grounds for a belief and clearly addressed the specific matters in s 8(1)(a)–(d): *Glenn & Co (Essex) Ltd v Her Majesty's Commissioners for Revenues and Customs and East Berkshire Magistrates' Court* [2011] EWHC 2998 (Admin), [2012] 1 Cr App Rep 291, 176 JP 65.

Reasonable suspicion. Some legislation requires only 'reasonable suspicion' as opposed to 'reasonable grounds for belief'. In *R (on the application of Eastenders Barking Ltd) v South Western Magistrates' Court* 22 March 2011, QBD, it was held that the grant of a search warrant under s 46 of the Firearms Act 1968 required only reasonable suspicion that an offence had or might have been committed under the Act as opposed to the higher threshold of reasonable belief (see *R v Central Criminal Court, ex p Bright* [2001] 2 All ER 244, [2001]1 WLR 662, DC; *R v Windsor* [2011] EWCA Crim 143, [2011] 2 Cr App Rep 71, 175 CL&J 110.

The test for establishing reasonable suspicion was a two-fold test which comprised a subjective and objective element The issue was whether (a) the Judge or magistrate was satisfied that there were reasonable grounds for suspecting an offence had been committed under the Act; and (b) if he/she was, whether there was material before him/her on which he/she was entitled to be satisfied.

In the present case there were reasonable grounds to satisfy the objective test because intelligence existed which was reliable. The source of the evidence had been given to the Judge. The fact that more information could have been elicited did not mean there was insufficient evidence to give rise to reasonable suspicion, the threshold of which was relatively low.

M[2.8]

Indictable offence means an offence which, if committed by an adult, is triable on indictment, whether it is exclusively so or triable either way. The definition also includes a 'relevant offence' as defined in s 28D(4) of the Immigration Act 1971: s 8(5) PACE 1984.

M[2.9]

Relevant evidence means anything that would be admissible in evidence at a trial for the offence. The application (information) and the warrant should identify, so far as is practicable, the articles or persons to be sought:

see s 15(6)(b) of PACE and *Power-Hynes and Yuri Suzuki-Lahye v Norwich Magistrates' Court* [2009] EWHC 1512 (Admin), (2009) 173 JP 573.

M[2.10]

Premises. The premises referred to above are:

- one or more sets of premises specified in the application (a *'specific premises warrant'*); or
- any premises occupied or controlled by a person specified in the application, including such sets of premises as are so specified (an *'all premises warrant'*).

If the application is for an *'all premises warrant'*, the magistrate must also be satisfied:

- that because of the particulars of the offence referred to in the application, there are reasonable grounds for believing that it is necessary to search premises occupied or controlled by the person in question which are not specified in the application in order to find the material referred to in the application; and
- that it is not reasonably practicable to specify in the application all the premises which he occupies or controls and which might need to be searched.

The warrant may authorise entry to and search of premises on more than one occasion if, on the application, the magistrate is satisfied that it is necessary to authorise multiple entries in order to achieve for which he issues the warrant.

A copy of the search warrant issued under PACE, s 8 had, on its face, to record the address being searched so that when the occupier was served with a copy he would know for certain that the warrant as issued did indeed cover his premises: *Bhatti v Croydon Magistrates' Court* [2010] EWHC 522 (Admin).

M[2.11]–[2.15]

Legal privilege means in essence communications between a legal adviser and his client or communications between them and a third party in contemplation of legal proceedings. The legal adviser can supply a full definition.

M[2.16]

Excluded and special procedure material. This includes material held in confidence such as personal or business records, human tissues or fluids taken for the purpose of diagnosis or treatment and journalistic material. A magistrate cannot issue a warrant in respect of excluded or special procedure material; application can only be made, where applicable, to a circuit Judge: see *R (on the application of Bates) v Chief Constable of the Avon and Somerset Police and Bristol Magistrates' Court* [2009] EWHC 942 (Admin), 173 JP 313.

M[2.17]

May issue. Even where all the criteria have been fulfilled, the magistrate still has a discretion.

3 Procedure (for search warrants issued to the police for evidence under the Police and Criminal Evidence Act 1984, s 8 and under other statutes)

M[2.18]

(1) The application may be made by a constable but it must have been authorised by an inspector or more senior officer, or in a case of urgency, the senior officer on duty. Where application is made by a member of the Serious and Organised Crime Agency authorisation by a Grade 3 Officer or above is sufficient. Where the officer is not known to the magistrate, a warrant card may be produced to establish identity.

M[2.19]

(2) Except in a case of emergency, if there is reason to believe that a search might have an adverse effect on relations between the police and the community, the local Police Community Liaison Officer should have been consulted.

M[2.20]

(3) The application must be supported by an information in writing stating:

(a)   the ground on which he makes the application;
(b)   the enactment under which the warrant would be issued; and
(c)   if the application is for a warrant authorising entry and search on more than one occasion, the ground on which he applies for such a warrant, and whether he seeks a warrant authorising an unlimited number of entries, or (if not) the maximum number of entries desired;
(d)   to identify, so far as is practicable, the articles or persons to be sought; and
(e)   to specify the matters set out in **M[2.20A]** below.

M[2.20A]

The matters which must be specified as in (d) above are:

(a)   if the application relates to one or more sets of premises specified in the application, each set of premises which it is desired to search and enter;
(b)   if the application relates to any premises occupied or controlled by a person specified in the application:
     (i)   as many sets of premises which it is desired to enter and search as it is reasonable practicable to specify;
     (ii)   the person who is in occupation or control of those premises and any others which it is desired to enter and search;
     (iii)   why it is necessary to search more premises than those specified under (i) above; and

    (iv)   why it is not reasonably practicable to specify all the premises which it is desired to enter and search.

In *Redknapp v Comr of the City of London Police Department* [2008] EWHC 1177 (Admin) it was stressed that all the necessary material to justify the grant of a search warrant should be contained in the information provided in the relevant pro forma. If the magistrate, on an application under s 8 requires any further information in order to satisfy himself that the warrant was justified, a note should be made of the additional information so that there was a proper record of the full basis upon which the warrant has been granted.

M[2.21]

(4) The constable must answer on oath any questions which the magistrate may ask him. Apart from questions designed to ensure that the grounds for the application have been made out, eg under the Theft Act 1968, s 26, the magistrate might usefully inquire whether the officer has had the same application previously refused by another magistrate. The police cannot 'shop around' for a magistrate willing to sign the warrant. A second application can only be made where it is based on additional grounds. Finally, there is a discretion whether to issue a warrant.

M[2.22]

(5) The police will usually have prepared a warrant and two copies beforehand. If he is prepared to issue the warrant, the magistrate should read it carefully and check that it covers the matters referred to in (3) above.

M[2.23]

(6) The justices' clerk should retain the information and the police must forward to him, after three months at the latest, the warrant either unexecuted or endorsed as to whether the articles or persons sought were found; and whether any articles were seized, other than the articles which were sought.

M[2.24]

(7) A note of reasons for grant or refusal should be retained

4 Procedure for warrants issued to persons other than police officers

M[2.25]

The provisions outlined above might usefully be taken into account where relevant. For non-police warrants the information is laid on oath. The applicant will usually produce a prepared information and swear to it in the following words: 'I swear by Almighty God that this is my information and that the contents thereof are true to the best of my knowledge and belief.' If he prefers it, he may substitute for the words, 'I swear by Almighty God . . . ' the words, 'I solemnly and sincerely declare and affirm . . . '. If the wording on the information is not sufficient a further written statement should be appended to the information.

M[2.26]

As a matter of practice the informant signs the information and the magistrate should retain this and forward it to the justices' clerk.

Search warrants under section 161A Customs and Excise Management Act 1979

M[2.27]–[2.30]

The Justices' Clerks' Society was contacted by HM Revenue and Customs with regard to the above. There is a concern that the police are applying for search warrants when it should be an officer of HM Revenue and Customs.

The section states:

> 161A Power to search premises: search warrant

(1)   If a justice of the peace is satisfied by information upon oath given by an officer that there are reasonable grounds to suspect that anything liable to forfeiture under the customs and excise Acts is kept or concealed in any building or place, he may by warrant under his hand authorise any officer, and any person accompanying an officer, to enter and search the building or place named in the warrant.

(2)   An officer or other person so authorised has power—

      (a)   to enter the building or place at any time, whether by day or night, on any day, and search for, seize, and detain or remove any such thing, and

      (b)   so far as is necessary for the purpose of such entry, search, seizure, detention or removal, to break open any door, window or container and force and remove any other impediment or obstruction.

(3)   Where there are reasonable grounds to suspect that any still, vessel, utensil, spirits or materials for the manufacture of spirits is or are unlawfully kept or deposited in any building or place, subsections (1) and (2) above apply in relation to any constable as they would apply in relation to an officer.

(4)   The powers conferred by a warrant under this section are exercisable until the end of the period of one month beginning with the day on which the warrant is issued.

(5)   A person other than a constable shall not exercise the power of entry conferred by this section by night unless accompanied by a constable

Section 161A(1) allows an 'Officer' to make the application. 'Officer" is defined in s 1(1) of the Act as 'a person commissioned by the Commissioners' for Revenue and Customs. Section 8(2) qualifies this to allow other persons to act as and be given the powers of 'officers' when 'engaged by the orders or with the concurrence of the Commissioners'. Section 161A(3) gives powers to a police constable to make the application for a search warrant under this section but only where there are reasonable grounds to suspect that any 'still, vessel, utensil, spirits or materials for the manufacture of spirits is or are unlawfully kept or deposited in any building or place'.

There is a concern that the police are applying for search warrants where articles not listed in s 161A(3) are being searched for. The JCS believes the legislation is clear that the power is only available to the police where the conditions of sub-section (3) are satisfied; ie that an alcohol still or vessel etc is being searched for (dated 10 February 2012).

Warrants of entry for gas and electricity suppliers

M[2.31]

The provisions are complex and are summarised below. It is good practice for all such applications to be considered at a courthouse in the presence of a legal adviser from whom advice may be obtained. Those subject to the application should receive notification of the date and venue of the application.

M[2.32]

Applications may be made, for example, for entry to read a meter or to cut off the supply following non-payment of a bill. An electricity supplier may cut off the supply where the customer has not paid within 20 working days of a demand in writing and after two working days' notice of the supplier's intention to do so. However this power is not available where there is a genuine dispute about the amount owed. (Note – this procedure only applies to a bill for electricity supplied and would not include monies owed on an article supplied by way of a credit sale such as a cooker. Nor is it relevant that there is a genuine dispute about the quality of service since the customer may use a separate procedure to obtain compensation.) The relevant periods where a gas supply is concerned are 28 days after the demand in writing and seven days' notice of intent to cut off the supply.

M[2.33]

Right of entry. An officer of the supplier after one working day's notice (electricity) 24 hours' notice (gas) may at all reasonable times, on production of some duly authenticated document showing his authority, enter the premises for the purpose of cutting off the supply. No notice is required for entry to read a meter except where a warrant is to be applied for.

M[2.34]

Warrant of entry. No right of entry may be exercised except with the consent of the occupier of the premises or under the authority of a justice's warrant (except in cases of emergency).

M[2.35]

Requirements. There must be a sworn information in writing and the applicant must satisfy the justice:

(a)   that admission to the premises is reasonably required for the specified purpose;

(b)   the applicant has a right of entry to the premises;

(c)   the requirements of any relevant enactment have been complied with; and in particular

(d)   the relevant notices have been given, including notice of the hearing.

M[2.36]

The justice might also ensure that:

(e)   there is no genuine dispute about the amount owed; and

(f)   the amount owed is in respect of the supply of gas or electricity.

M[2.37]

Code of practice. Gas and electricity suppliers operate a Code of Practice (of which the clerk of the justices may be able to supply a copy) under which it is undertaken to provide assistance to domestic customers to meet their bills and the suppliers may refrain from cutting off the supply from those who are particularly vulnerable during the winter months; nevertheless where default has occurred, the suppliers may resort to the procedure outlined above.

M[2.38]

Duty to repair damage etc. Where a right of entry has been exercised the supplier must ensure that the premises concerned are left no less secure by reason of the entry and must make good or pay compensation for any damage caused in entering the premises or making them secure.

5 The warrant

M[2.39]

If the magistrate is satisfied with the application he will sign the warrant (which will normally have been prepared in advance by the applicant). This is handed back to the applicant and is his authority to enter and search etc. A magistrate who has issued a search warrant should say nothing to anyone about it, not even to a member of his own family. This is so that no suspicion falls on him in the event that it may appear that the occupier of the premises was expecting a search.

6 Who may sign

M[2.40]–[2.45]

Any magistrate may sign a search warrant provided he is not on the Supplemental List (ie retired from active work on the bench).

M[3]
Warrants of arrest

M[3.1]

Magistrates will frequently have encountered these during sittings at court, eg for failing to answer bail. The procedure is very similar to that for issuing warrants of entry. However, it is virtually inconceivable that it should be necessary to approach a magistrate at home. The Police and Criminal Evidence Act 1984 provides wide powers of arrest without warrant even for minor offences where there is doubt about the identity of the arrested person or an arrest is necessary to prevent harm to him or the public. Accordingly, a magistrate would be unwise to issue such a warrant unless he has the advice of his justices' clerk or a legal adviser. Such applications should, as a matter of practice, be heard at the courthouse.

Proceeds of Crime Act 2002

M[3.2]

Minimum amount. Section 294 of the 2002 Act allows a customs officer or constable to seize and apply for forfeiture of cash which is not less than £1,000 and is obtained through or intended to be used in unlawful conduct (see the Proceeds of Crime Act 2002 (Recovery of Cash in Summary Proceedings: Minimum amount) Order 2006, SI 2006/1699).

Search power. The police or customs may search a person or premises for tainted cash. An authorisation may be given by a single justice ex parte. A search warrant under this provision does not authorise entry to premises.

Detention of seized cash. Application may be made to any magistrate in England and Wales who may extend the officers right to detain cash for 48 hours, for up to three months. In calculating the 48 hours for which seized cash may initially be held, Saturdays, Sundays, Christmas Day, Good Friday and bank holidays should be ignored. The applicant must serve notice on anyone from whom the cash was seized, sent to or by. Service of the notice need not be proved.

Grounds for detention order. A magistrate may make the order for six months detention if he is satisfied that there are reasonable grounds for the officer's suspicion and the continued detention is justified for the purposes of investigation of its origins or use. Further extensions which may be for a total period of two years, must be made by a full court. Application for the release of detained money may also be made.

Forfeiture. The police or customs may apply for detained cash to be forfeited and a magistrates' court can make an order if it is satisfied that the cash is recoverable property or intended for use in unlawful conduct: s 298(2). A costs order may be made under s 64(1) of the Magistrates' Courts Act 1980. This includes the situation where the complaint is not proceeded with by virtue of s 52 of the Courts Act 1971 (see *Chief Constable of Cleveland Police v Vaughan* [2009] EWHC 2831 (Admin)). As to the principles see **F[1.16]**. In *R (on the application of Stone) v Camberwell Magistrates' Court* [2010] EWHC 2333 (Admin), the High Court declined to consider whether there was jurisdiction to award costs in forfeiture proceedings pursuant to either s 52 (3) of the Courts Act 1971 or s 64 of the Magistrates' Courts Act 1980 describing the legal position as 'difficult'.

Legal Notes

Cash. Means notes and coins, postal orders, cheques or traveller's cheques, bankers drafts and bearer bonds and shares.

Minimum amount. Cash is only subject to the act if it is a minimum sum of £1,000, singly or as part of a larger sum. The amount may be estimated to preserve evidence.

Notice of forfeiture proceedings. In *R (on the application of Harrison) v Birmingham Magistrates' Court* [2011] EWCA Civ 332, [2011] 14 LS Gaz R 21, a forfeiture order made in respect of cash confiscated by the police when searching the house of a person arrested on suspicion of fraud was quashed where her unchallenged evidence was that she had not received a notice of the forfeiture hearing. The appellant had appealed to the Crown Court against the forfeiture order which held that by virtue of s 299(2) it had no jurisdiction to hear the appeal out of time. The Court invited the Lord Chief Justice to consider an amendment to the Magistrates' Courts (Detention and Forfeiture of Cash) Rules 2002 to permit a person to show that, notwithstanding ostensible service, the purported recipient had not in fact received notice.

The guidance handed down was that pending any amendment to the 2002 Rules, magistrates should be particularly prudent about continuing with an application for a forfeiture order in the absence of a person with a claim to the money. If criminal proceedings were still ongoing, it might be worthwhile to give notice of the hearing to the solicitors dealing with the criminal case; albeit, those solicitors had not been instructed in the civil proceedings for forfeiture.

Following that judgment, the Magistrates' Courts (Detention and Forfeiture of Cash) (Amendment) Rules 2012, SI 2012/1275 have been made.

These Rules amend the 2002 Rules to allow for effective service of documents to be assumed unless the contrary is shown. The amended rules came into force on 2 July 2012.

Unlawful conduct. Includes conduct which is unlawful under the criminal law in the UK and conduct which occurs outside the UK if it would have been unlawful in the UK.

In *Angus v United Kingdom Border Agency* [2011] EWHC 461 (Admin), the appellant had been stopped at a British airport and £40,000 was found to be in her handbag, some of it wrapped in casino wrappings. She claimed that the monies represented repayment of a loan to her uncle. She later revised her story and said that the sums represented the repayment of loans made by her mother to two other individuals, repaid through their winnings obtained at casinos. An application for forfeiture was made pursuant to s 298 of the Proceeds of Crime Act 2002. The magistrates' court and on appeal, the Crown Court, found that the cash seized may well have been the proceeds of money laundering and that there was an irresistible inference that it was obtained through unlawful conduct. The appellant challenged the Crown Court's decision by way of case stated.

The Administrative Court held that irrespective of whether the litigation was High Court civil recovery proceedings or magistrates' court or Crown Court forfeiture proceedings, the test was the same. Applying the provisions of s 242(2)(b) of the PCA 2002, although it was not necessary to allege the commission of any specific offence, the matters that were alleged to constitute the particular kind or kinds of unlawful conduct by or in return for which the property was obtained had to be set out: *Director of Assets Recovery Agency v Green* [2005] EWHC 3168 (Admin), (2006) Times, 27 February considered. Accordingly, the answer to the question posed was that, in a case of cash forfeiture, a customs officer did have to show that the property seized was obtained through conduct of one of a number of kinds each of which would have been unlawful conduct.

In *Christopher Hendrik Weise v UK Border Agency* (2012) 29th June, CA, a forfeiture order made under the Proceeds of Crime Act 2002, s 298 was revoked as the Judge had not given adequate reasons for concluding that forfeited money which had been carried by a South African businessman in hand luggage and in the hold of an aeroplane constituted the proceeds of money laundering. Further, in *Begum v West Midlands Police* [2012] EWHC 2304 (Admin), it was held that a magistrates' court had erred in ordering the forfeiture of cash under s 298(2) by an offender who had failed to declare the extent of her savings in order to obtain benefits, since the undeclared cash had not been intended for use in unlawful conduct.

Legal aid. A criminal legal representation order is not available. Civil legal aid may apply subject to means.

Recoverable property. The police are not required to show that the apparent criminality of a company rendered the whole of its business unlawful. The police as claimant only had to show that there were 'reasonable grounds to suspect' that the property [cash] was in the company's hands because illegal labour had made a contribution to its acquisition *R (on the application of the Chief Constable of Greater Manchester Police v City of Salford Magistrates' Court and Sarfar and Sons (Knitwear Ltd)* [2008] EWHC 1651 (Admin), 172 JP 497.

Right of Appeal. May be made against the decision of a magistrates' court ordering forfeiture of cash by either party whether the application is dismissed or approved. In this case an appeal lies to the Crown Court: s 299.

M[4]

Miscellaneous

Recognisance

M[4.1]

A recognisance of a surety for bail should not be taken unless the proposed surety produces a certificate stating the amount and conditions of bail. The surety should be questioned so as to satisfy the magistrate that he has, or can easily obtain, the sum mentioned in the certificate. If the certificate states that a specific person is to be surety, evidence of identity should be required. The clerk or an officer in charge of a police station may take a recognisance and, in any case of doubt, the surety should be referred to one of these persons.

Certificate of good repute

M[4.2]

A magistrate should not sign a certificate of good reputation or good character. If approached to do so he should refer the applicant to a legal adviser.

Passports and driving licences

M[4.3]

A magistrate should neither endorse an application for a passport, nor sign the photograph therewith unless he knows the applicant sufficiently well to meet the criteria on the form. Similar considerations apply to applications for a photocard licence.

Removal to suitable premises of persons in need of care and attention (National Assistance Act 1948, s 47 and National Assistance (Amendment) Act 1951, s 1)

M[4.4]

The following provisions are for the purposes of securing the necessary care and attention for persons who:

(a)   are suffering from grave chronic disease or, being aged, infirm or physically incapacitated, are living in insanitary conditions; and

(b)   are unable to devote to themselves, and are not receiving from other persons, proper care and attention.

M[4.5]

Where the proper officer (formerly the medical officer of health) certifies in writing to the local authority that he is satisfied after thorough inquiry and consideration that in the interests of any such person residing in the local authority's area or for preventing injury to the health of, or serious nuisance to other persons, it is necessary to remove him from his residence, the local authority may apply to a court for an order of removal.

M[4.6]

If the proper officer and another registered medical practitioner certify that in their opinion it is necessary in the interests of that person to remove him without delay, the local authority or the proper officer where duly authorised may make an application to a single justice having jurisdiction for the place where the person resides. The justice being satisfied on oral evidence under oath of the allegations in the certificate and that it is expedient so to do, may order his removal to a hospital where one is available or to some other place in, or within convenient distance of, the local authority area. If the justice thinks it necessary, the order can be made without notifying or hearing the person concerned.

M[4.7]

Duration of the order. The order may be for a period of up to three weeks. After it has expired the local authority would have to make a full application to a court.

M[4.8]

It should be noted, however, that as an emergency ex parte application can also be made to a magistrate sitting in a courthouse; accordingly, applications should normally be considered there except where circumstances dictate otherwise.

Statutory declarations

M[4.9]

It is necessary to make sure that the clause at the end of the form is properly completed and dated. It is not necessary to read the document, nor need the magistrate be concerned to establish in his own mind the truth of the contents of it. His signature on the document simply attests that he was present and heard the maker of the document declare that the contents are true.

M[4.10]–[4.15]

The words for a statutory declaration are:

> 'I, AB, do solemnly and sincerely declare and affirm that the contents of this declaration are true to the best of my knowledge and belief, and I make this solemn declaration conscientiously believing the same to be true and by virtue of the provisions of the Statutory Declarations Act 1835.'

M[4.16]

A Holy Book is not required for a statutory declaration.

M[4.17]

Any magistrate, including those on the Supplemental List, may sign a statutory declaration.

Warrants to search for and remove mental patients

(Mental Health Act 1983, s 135)

M[4.18]

A justice to whom it appears that there is reasonable cause to suspect that a person believed to be suffering from mental disorder:

(a)   has been, or is being, ill-treated, neglected or kept otherwise than under proper control in any place within the jurisdiction of the justice; or

(b)   being unable to care for himself, is living alone in any such place;

may issue a warrant authorising his removal to a place of safety with a view to making an application under the Mental Health Act 1983 or other arrangements for his treatment or care.

M[4.19]

Application is by way of an information laid on oath by a social worker specially approved by the local authority for the purposes of the Mental Health Act 1983. The patient need not be named in the information.

M[4.20]

Warrant authorises a constable to enter (if need be by force) any premises specified in the warrant and if thought fit to remove him to a place of safety.

M[4.21]

Place of safety means residential accommodation provided by a local authority or a hospital, police station, mental nursing home, or residential home for mentally disturbed persons or any other suitable place where the occupier is willing to receive the patient.

M[4.22]

Duration. The detention in a place of safety may not be for more than 72 hours.

Administration of oaths etc in certain probate business

M[4.23]

Justices of the peace are empowered by the Courts and Legal Services Act 1990, s 56 to administer oaths and take affidavits in non-contentious probate matters. The Judicial Studies Board has issued the following guidance for the assistance of magistrates' courts:

'(a) The oaths envisaged in this Act are those which are non-contentious and of a probate nature, ie, civil proceedings, and should not therefore be of great urgency requiring their administration out of court hours. Each court should therefore publish set hours during which these oaths will be administered.

(b) Justices should be discouraged from administering these oaths outside court hours and away from supervision by suitably qualified court staff.

(c) Justices should not administer oaths for documents which are to be used in court proceedings [including civil proceedings], and court staff should look at document headings with great care, to ensure that there is no court name or reference number thereon which might indicate a current court action.

(d) The wording of the oath to be taken is different from a court witness oath and is 'I swear by Almighty God that the contents of this my [affidavit] [and the exhibits annexed thereto] are true'.

(e) Be prepared for the oath to be sworn by members of all religions in the appropriate form – another reason why 'out of hours oaths' should be discouraged.

(f) An interpreter may be needed and he should be sworn first, taking the appropriate oath.

(g) A deponent may wish to affirm, in which case he will do so in the appropriate form – again a reason for oaths to be administered in the court setting, as justices will not necessarily know the correct wording.

(h) Every alteration to the document has to be initialled by the administering justice.

(i) Any exhibit has to be dated and signed and must clearly indicate that it is the exhibit annexed to the affidavit produced and sworn by the deponent on that same occasion.

(j) The jurat or attestation shall state the date and place the oath or affidavit is taken or made [Courts and Legal Services Act 1990, s 56(2)].

(k) No justice shall exercise the powers conferred in any proceedings in which he is interested [Courts and Legal Services Act 1990, s 56(3)].

(l) In the event of any person being sufficiently handicapped to make it impossible for him or her to attend court to swear a document, arrangement could be made by the clerk to the justices for a justice and member of the court staff to attend upon that person at their home, or a mutually convenient place. This should not occur frequently, but should be provided for by courts.'

Index

A

Abandonment
child A19.18–A19.20
Abatement notice A74.9, A84.8
appeal against A84.9
consent of Secretary of State not
required A84.2, A84.8
contravention/failure to comply A84.10
Abatement order A84.22
Abduction
child or young person D16
Absconding *see* Failure to
surrender to custody
Absolute discharge B31
availability B5.24, E4.3
juveniles E4.3
sexual activity with a
child A52.15
sexual assault A53.16
Abuse of position
fraud by *see* Fraud
Abuse of process I1B.11–I1B.12
long delay I1B.12
maintenance orders D7.47
plea before venue and mode of
trial proceedings I4.8
youth courts E3.25
Access to child *see* Contact order
Accident
failing to report after accident C31.3, C32

Accident – *cont.*
failing to stop and give details
after C31
personal injury, involv-
ing C31.16
Action plan order B7A
Actual bodily harm
alternative verdict A8.25
assault occasioning A8
defences A8.17–A8.25
definition A8.9
exclusion order A8.33
grievous bodily harm distinguished A8.9, A70.6
husband and wife cases *see*
Domestic violence
inference of A8.9
intent A8.7–A8.8
licensed premises, assault on,
exclusion order A8.33
mode of trial A8.3–A8.4
provocation A8.17
psychological damage A8.9
racial, religious, disability or
sexual orientation aggravation A8.10–A8.16
reduction of charge A8.25
self-defence A8.18–A8.20
sentencing A8.31–A8.34
unconsciousness, assault causing A8.9
Adoption D18
adoption orders D18.8

Adoption – *cont.*
adoption orders – *cont.*
applicants D18.9–D18.12
application to
court D18.13–D18.14
consent D18.15
dispensing with con-
sent D18.16
residence of child with applicants D18.12
advertising
judicial guidance D18.5A
permission to adver-
tise D18.5A
CAFCASS, role
of D18.26–D18.32
Children and Family Court
Reporter (CFR) D18.29
consensual placement D18.2
contact post-adoption D18.16
disclosure of informa-
tion D18.39–D18.41
disclosure sys-
tem D18.42–D18.44
effects D18.36–D18.38
Family Procedure (Adoption)
Rules
2005 D18.21–D18.25
general prin-
ciples D18.17–D18.19
hearing
privacy D1.9
reporting restrictions D1.16
'no order' principle D18.18
parental consent D18.2, D18.6,
D18.15
dispensing with D18.16
partner, by D18.10
placement orders D18.3
applications D18.5
applications to make or revoke D18.7
consequences D18.4

Adoption – *cont.*
placement orders – *cont.*
revocation D18.7
specified proceedings D18.7
procedural require-
ments D18.20–D18.38
reporting offi-
cer D18.26–D18.27
reporting restrictions D1.16
Special Guardianship Orders
(SGOs) D18.33–D18.38
step parent, by D18.10
welfare checklist D18.19,
D18.35
Advertisement
application for personal licence/
premises licence F1.2
permission to advertise for
adoption D18.5A
Affray A2
intent A2.9
intoxication A2.10
person of reasonable firmness A2.6
sentencing A2.15
threats A2.5
using or threatening vio-
lence A2.4
violence, meaning A2.7–A2.8
Age of criminal responsibility E3.2
Aggravated vehicle-taking A66
**Aggressive commercial prac-
tice** A75
Aid and abet
dangerous driving C16.6
Air guns A11.3, A71, A76.7
age limit A71.5
Brococks A76.7
clubs and shooting galleries A71.6
forfeiture A33.13
possession A71.2

Air guns – *cont.*
 preventing person under 18
 having weapon with
 him A71A
 private premises A71.5
 public place A33, A71.4
 trespassing in a building or on
 land A77.9
Air weapon
 definition A33.7, A71.3
 high powered A76.7
 trespassing in a building or on
 land A77.9
Alcohol
 blood or urine, in
 analyst's certificate C22.19
 breath test *see* Breath test
 in charge of vehicle when
 'unfit through drink or
 drugs' C21
 drinking after driving C22.30
 driving when 'unfit through
 drink or drugs' C20
 excess alcohol offences C22
 fail to provide specimen for
 analysis C23
 laced drink defence C22.24
 offences C20, C21, C22, C23
 sentencing of high risk offenders C22.45–C22.46
 special rea-
 sons C22.24–C22.25,
 C22.50
 children, persistently selling
 alcohol to, closure no-
 tice F2.7
 driving when 'unfit through
 drink or drugs' C20
 excess alcohol
 disqualification reduced for
 attendance on
 course C22.56–C22.61

Alcohol – *cont.*
 excess alcohol – *cont.*
 drive/attempt to drive or in
 charge C22
 sentencing C22.32–C22.61,
 C22.65
 sentencing of high risk offenders C22.45–C22.46
 football-related offences A35
 fraudulently evade duty A4
 sale offences A3
 allowing sale to children A3.3
 sale to children A3.2
 sale to person who is
 drunk A3.1
 sentencing A3.5
 sporting events, football-related
 offences A35
Aliens
 deportation B23.4
Ammunition
 carrying a firearm in a public
 place A33.10
 excessive A76.4
 forfeiture A76.23, A86.32
 meaning A76.8
 police permits A76.10
 purchasing or possessing
 without certificate A76
 seizure A86.31
 shooting galleries A71.6
Amphetamine A22.5
Animal cruelty A5.1
 definition of animal A5.2
 deprivation of ownership A5.4
 destruction of animal A5.4
 disqualification A5.4
 docking of tails A5.2
 mutilation A5.2
 number of different animals on
 same occasion A5.2

Animal cruelty – *cont.*
person responsible for an animal A5.2
previous convictions A5.4
protected animal A5.2
sentencing A5.3–A5.4
time limits for prosecution A5.2
unnecessary suffering A5.2
Animal rights protestors
harassment A41.5
Animals
cruelty *see* Animal cruelty
definition A5.2
deprivation of ownership A5.4
destruction ordered by court A5.4
disqualification from keeping A5.4
docking of tails A5.2
dogs *see* Dogs
game, meaning A86.6, A86.17
litter and A83.31
meaning C31.6, C32.5
mutilation A5.2
person responsible A5.2
poaching *see* Poaching
road traffic offences C31.6, C32.5
wild *see* Wild creatures
Anti-social behaviour order (ASBO) B8
age limits B8.2
as ancillary order B8.8, A82.12
application B8.4
breach B8.13–B8.16
collateral attack on validity of order or its terms B8.13
commission of criminal offence B8.13
conditional discharge following B8.16

Anti-social behaviour order (ASBO) – *cont.*
breach – *cont.*
lesser degree of harm caused or intended B8.16
maximum penalty B8.14
no harm caused or intended B8.16
reasonable excuse B8.13
sentencing of young offenders B8.15A
serious harm caused or intended B8.16
SGC guideline B8.14
civil applications B8.1
commencement B8.13
criminal proceedings B8.8–B8.11
curfew condition B8.5
discharge B8.12
evidence of anti-social behaviour B8.5
extension B8.12
harassment, alarm or distress B8.5
hearsay evidence, reliance upon B8.4A
hooded tops B8.8
individual support order with B8.9
interim orders B8.7, B8.8
judicial guidance B8.5
kerb crawling A82.12
limitations B8.1–B8.13
maximum/minimum period B8.3
mentally disordered offenders B8.5
motoring offences B8.8
offensive weapons, prohibition on carrying B8.5
parenting order with B8.9

**Anti-social behaviour
order (ASBO)** – *cont.*
period of order B8.3, B8.9
press reporting E2.4
previous convictions B8.15
prohibition on association B8.5
proportionality B8.5
reporting restrictions E2.4
representation orders I7.1A
soliciting women for prostitution A82.12
special measures A52.10
statutory defence B8.6
terms B8.5
variation or discharge B8.12
youth court, in B8.4, E2.4
Antique firearms A76.17
Appropriation *see* Theft
Arrest warrant *see* Warrant
Arson A18
maximum penalty A18.2
venue for trial A18.2
Article with blade *see* Bladed
article/offensive weapon
Articles for fraud *see* Fraud
Assault
actual bodily harm *see* Actual
bodily harm
attempt A15.6
battery and A15.5, A15.6
common A15
accidental jostling A15.9
aggravation of offence A15.7
assault, mean-
ing A15.5–A15.6
attempt A15.6
certificate of dismissal A15.31
consent A15.11
defences A15.8–A15.32
disability of victim A15.7
execution of legal pro-
cess A15.20

Assault – *cont.*
common – *cont.*
horseplay A15.17
hostile intent A15.10
intent A15.4
justification A15.21
lawful sport A15.16, A15.18
misadventure A15.8
police constable/person assisting A9.9
provocation A15.32
racially or religiously
aggravated, mean-
ing A15.7
reasonable chastise-
ment A15.16
recklessness A15.4, A15.5
sado-masochistic activi-
ties A15.11
self-defence, onus of
proof A15.19
sentencing A15.33
sexual orientation of victim A15.7
triviality A15.21
two offences tried to-
gether A15.3
consent A15.11
constable in the execution of his
duty, on A9
alternative verdict A9.9
burden of proof A9.7
licensed premises A9.11
plain clothes officers carrying
out drugs search A9.8
reduction of charge A9.9
search of defendant A9.8
sentencing A9.10–A9.11
court security officer in the
execution of his duty,
on A9
sentencing A9.10–A9.11
definition A15.5–A15.6

Assault – *cont.*
exclusion order *see* Exclusion
order
indecent *see* Sexual assault
with intent to resist arrest A7
on licensed premises, exclusion
order *see* Licensed premises
motor vehicle, involving C5.5
person assisting constable,
on A9
racially or religiously aggravated
common assault A15
meaning A15.7
occasioning actual bodily
harm A8
sentencing A15.33
triable either way A15.3
two offences tried to-
gether A15.3
see also Actual bodily harm
reasonable chastisement A15.16
recklessness A8.7, A15.4,
A15.5, A70.5
sentencing
assault on constable or court
security officer in the
execution of his
duty A9.10–A9.11
assault with intent to resist
arrest A7.4
common assault A15.33
racially or religiously
aggravated
crimes A15.33
sexual *see* Sexual assault
unconsciousness, causing A8.9
Asylum seekers
assisting entry A81
bail applications A81.17
false documents A81.5
refugee status A81.5
see also Immigration offences

Attachment of earnings order
costs and compensation B33.29
enforcement B33.29
fines, enforcement B33.29,
B33.67, B33.76, B33.96
maintenance order, enforcement D7.2, D7.20–D7.21
see also Deductions from
benefits order; Deductions
from earnings order
Attempt
assault A15.6
imprisonment for B37.38
theft A57.19
Attendance centre
youth rehabilitation order requirement B50.10
Attendance centre orders B9
accessibility of centre B9.6
action plan order and B9.7
age limits B9.2
aims B9.16
ancillary orders B9.9
announcement B9.10, B9.17
availability B9.5
community sentences and B9.8
fine defaulters B33.76, B33.98
jurisdiction B9.1
juveniles B9.7
maximum period B9.3
minimum period B9.4
see also Community orders

B

Bad character
defendant I6.14
witness I6.15
Badger traps
destruction A18.19

Bail

adjournment of hearing,
where J1.1, J1.18

after conviction, length of J1.19

appeals against J1.76

appeals against conditions J1.79

asylum seekers facing criminal
charges A81.17

before conviction, length
of J1.18

breach of B16.20

committal or send to
Crown Court J1.20

conditional bail J1.4,
J1.55–J1.70

appeals J1.79

application to vary bail conditions J1.81A

common conditions J1.63

decision to grant J4

drug assessment and follow
up J1.62

effectiveness of condi-
tions J1.70

electronic monitoring J1.65

failure to comply with condition J1.92

hostel rules, compliance
with J1.65

police bail J1.55–J1.60

pre-sentence report J1.62

recognisance J1.66–J1.68,
M4.1

Crown Court, transfer to B16.7

Crown Prosecution Service,
appeal by J1.76

depositing a security J1.69

disqualification of justices removed J1.94

ECHR, challenges under J1.2

electronic monitoring J1.65

exceptions to right to
bail J1.26–J1.40

Bail – *cont.*

exceptions to right to bail –
cont.

custody time lim-
its J1.51–J1.54

failure to surrender to custody J1.47, J1.82–J1.91

further offences on bail J1.48

imprisonable offences J1.32,
J1.39

interference with the course of
justice J1.49

non-imprisonable of-
fences J1.40

police objections J1.46–J1.49

failure to answer I7.8

failure to comply with condition J1.92

failure to surrender to custody A10, B16.20, J1.47

defence J1.85

penalty J1.91

prosecution for J1.82–J1.91

sentencing A10.3

further offences on bail J1.2,
J1.39, J1.48

Human Rights Act and J1.2

imprisonable offences

indictable J1.32

summary only J1.39

Intensive Supervision and
Surveillance Programmes
(ISSPs) E4.8

juveniles J1.6, J1.32

length of remand on

after conviction J1.19

before conviction J1.18

life sentence, offences carrying J1.31

manslaughter cases J1.32

murder cases J1.62

juveniles J1.32

non-imprisonable offences J1.40

Bail – *cont.*
  opposed bail, grant of J1.25
  pending appeal J1.93
  police bail
    after charge J1.57–J1.60
    before charge J1.56
    street bail J1.55
  police objections J1.46–J1.49
  presumption of liberty J1.24
  procedure at remand hearing J2
  rape cases J1.32
  recognisance J1.66–J1.68, M4.1
  reconsideration J1.81
  refusal J1.77–J1.79
    appeals J1.79
    application to Crown Court
      judge in chambers J1.79
    decision to refuse bail J3
    further application af-
      ter J1.77–J1.78
  remand on B16.1, J1
    absence of accused,
      in J1.21–J1.23
    children and young per-
      sons E3.4
    committal or send to
      Crown Court J1.20
    decision whether to remand in
      custody or on
      bail J1.24–J1.39
    length of remand J1.18, J1.19
    video remands J1.22A
    where required J1.7–J1.10
  remission to another court
    on B1.2
  residence conditions, ap-
    peals J1.79
  security, depositing J1.69
  sexual offences J1.32
  street bail J1.55
  sureties J1.66–J1.68
    forfeiting of recogni-
      sance J1.68

Bail – *cont.*
  sureties – *cont.*
    recognisance J1.66–J1.68,
      M4.1
  unconditional bail J1.3
  young offenders J1.6, J1.31
Banned commercial practices A75
Banning order *see* Football
  banning order
Battery
  assault and A15.5, A15.6
  of a child A15.16
  meaning A15.5
Bench Training and
  Development Committees
  (BTDCs) D1.5, E2.1
Betting G1
Bicycle
  taking without consent A65
Binding over B10
  ancillary orders B10.4
  announcement B10.5
  antecedents B10.21
  breach of order B10.17
  burden of proof B10.21
  to come up for judg-
    ment B10.21
  consent B10.6
  Consolidated Criminal Practice
    Direction B10.1,
    B10.20–B10.21
  costs B10.4
  disorderly behaviour A20.20
  evidence B10.21
  intentional harassment A21.18
  to keep the peace B10.21
  kerb crawling A82.16
  maximum period B10.2
  minimum period B10.3
  misbehaviour in court I2.1
  parent or guard-
    ian B10.18–B10.19, B10.21

Binding over – *cont.*
parent or guardian – *cont.*
youth court, in E4.5
recognisance B10.21
complainant, by B10.8
forfeiture B10.17
refusal to enter into B10.6,
B10.21
witness, by B10.8
security for good behav-
iour B10.21
soliciting women for prostitution A82.16
sureties B10.6
threatening behaviour A21.18
written order B10.21
Bladed article/offensive weapon
aggravated burglary A12.2,
A13.2
ASBOs B8.5
butterfly knife A11.14
crossbows A11.3
curved blades A11.3
disguised knives A11.5
flick knives A11.4, A11.5
folding pocket knife A11.9
knuckle dusters A11.5
martial arts' weapons A11.4,
A11.12
pool cue A11.5
possession A11
burden of proof A11.9,
A11.13
'carrying' A11.6
defences to bladed ar-
ticle A11.11–A11.12
fear of attack A11.13
forgetfulness as to possession A11.7, A11.12,
A11.14
'have with him' A11.6
ignorance as to nature of
weapon A11.14

Bladed article/offensive weapon –
cont.
possession – *cont.*
intention A11.5
knowledge of posses-
sion A11.7
meaning A11.5
national costume A11.12
offensive weapon A11.5
public place A11.1, A11.8
reasonable excuse A11.7,
A11.13–A11.14
religious reasons A11.12
school premises A11.1,
A11.10
search of pupils A11.10
self-protection A11.13
sentencing A11.15
unintended possession, forgetfulness A11.7, A11.12
see also Air guns; Firearms
samurai swords A11.3
stealth knife A11.4
stun guns A11.4
Blood
alcohol in *see* Alcohol
Blood tests *see* Scientific tests
Borrowing
theft and A57.33
Brakes
braking distances C3
defective C9
sentencing C9.16–C9.20
shortest stopping distances C4
Breath test C22.10–C22.18
analysis C22.16
eructation (belching) during C22.25
failure to co-operate with
roadside breath test C24
legal advice C24.8
motorist in hospital C24.6

Breath test – *cont.*
failure to co-operate with roadside breath test – *cont.*
reasonable ex-
cuse C24.7–C24.8
failure to provide specimen for
analysis C23
legal advice C23.6A
reasonable excuse C23.4
warning as to conse-
quences C23.5
modification of device C22.16
motorist in hospital C24.6
negative, power of arrest
and C22.10
when required C22.10,
C24.3–C24.4
Bribery A89
Brococks A76.7
see also Air guns
Brothel-keeping A44
Bullying A19.16
Burglary
aggravated A12.2, A13.2
building, meaning A13.7
caravan, of A13.7
in a dwelling *see* Domestic
burglary
entering A12.7, A13.6
going equipped for theft A58
inhabited vehicle or ves-
sel A13.7
mode of trial A13.2–A13.5
non-domestic A13
rape and A12.3, A13.3
sentencing
domestic burglary A12.20
non-domestic bur-
glary A13.19
stealing, meaning A13.16
threatening violence A13.4
trespass A13.7, A13.17

Burglary in a dwelling *see*
Domestic burglary
Butterfly knife A11.14

C

Camera
concealed A20.9
see also Photograph
**Cannabis and cannabis
resin** A22.5
cultivation A27
meaning A25.11
possession
common law defence of necessity A25.8A
medical condition A25.8A
Car *see* Motor vehicle
Caravan
burglary in A12.15, A13.7
threatening behaviour in A21.9
Care order D6.23
age limit D6.25
applications D6.3–D6.22
appeal against refusal D1.19,
D6.49
grounds D6.4–D6.6
notifying the extended family D6.3
care plan D6.24
contact arrangements D6.24
directions appointments D6.2
discharge D6.47–D6.48
duration D6.31
effect D6.23
evidence D6.5, D6.24
interim orders D5.27,
D6.35–D6.37, D9.18
exclusion require-
ment D6.38–D6.46
interim care plan D6.35

Care order – *cont.*
  interim orders – *cont.*
    period of D6.36, D6.37
    local authority investiga-
      tion D5.27, D6.23, D6.35
    nature of D6.23
    non-school attendance
      and D17.6
    parent joined as party D6.3
    presumption of reasonable con-
      tact D6.24
    residential assessment D6.35
    termination of contact without
      court order D6.24
    variation D6.47–D6.48
Careless driving C25.16–C25.17
  causing death by careless or
    inconsiderate driving C16A
  dangerous driving and C25.16
  definition C25.5
  drive without due care and at-
    tention C25
    death C25.11
    emergencies C25.7
    emergency vehicles C25.18
    mechanical defect C25.8
    sentencing C25.20–C25.21
    warning of proceed-
      ings C25.10
  endorsement code C6.2
  reasonable consideration,
    driving without C46
  reduced disqualification for
    attendance on
    course C22.56–C22.61
  see also Dangerous driving;
    Driving

Cattle *see* Animals; Livestock
**Causing death by careless or
  inconsiderate driv-
  ing** C16A.10
CCTV evidence I6.9
Certificate of good repute M4.2
Change of plea I6.20, I6.26
Chastisement
  reasonable A15.16
Child
  abandoning A19.18–A19.20
  abduction D16
  access to *see* Contact order
  accommodation D6.1
  adoption *see* Adoption
  age, determination of E1.2
  alcohol, persistently selling to
    children, closure no-
    tice F2.7
  assessment order D9.4–D9.10
  battery of A15.16
  binding over parent or guard-
    ian B10.18–B10.19,
    B10.21, E4.5
  bullying A19.16
  care order *see* Care order
  care proceedings *see* Public law
    proceedings
  chastisement by parents A15.16
  child safety order D17A.1
  committal for trial E3.18
    procedure E3.20–E3.25
  contact order *see* Contact order
  cruelty *see* Cruelty to a child
  definition A19.6, E1.1
  education supervision or-
    der D17.6

Child – *cont.*

electronic monitoring J1.65

emergency protection order *see* Emergency protection order

evidence *see* Evidence

exposing to cruelty A19.21

family assistance order D5.28

Family Proceedings Court *see* Family Proceedings Court

financial provision *see* Maintenance orders

fines B33.5–B33.6

parental responsibility for payment B33.7–B33.10

guardian, appointment of D3.24

Guidelines for Judges Meeting Children subject to Family Proceedings D2.7

homicide by E3.18

ill-treating, meaning A19.16

indecency with *see* Sexual activity with a child

indecent photographs *see* Child prostitution and pornography; Indecent photographs of children

live video link

evidence via E3.22

vulnerable accused J1.22B

local authority care D6.1

local court, remission to E3.23

maintenance *see* Maintenance orders

neglect

meaning A19.17

presumption of guilt A19.23

oath E3.22

orders with respect to upbringing D4

parentage, proof of D3.9–D3.21

DNA genetic fingerprinting D3.20

scientific tests D3.16–D3.20

Child – *cont.*

parental responsibility *see* Parental responsibility

pornography *see* Child prostitution and pornography; Indecent photographs of children

private law proceedings D4.1

First Hearing Dispute Resolution Appointment (FHDRA) D4.1

Practice Direction: Revised Programme D4.1

prohibited steps order D4.5

persons who may apply for D5.1, D5.2

prostitution *see* Child prostitution and pornography

protection *see* Child protection

public law proceedings D6

see also Public law proceedings

punishment A15.16, A19.5

reasonable chastisement A15.16

recovery order D10

remand of E3.3, E3.4–E3.17A

reporting restrictions I1B.7, E2.4–E2.5

residence order *see* Residence order

school attendance proceedings D17

seat belts C48.9–C48.16

section 8 orders *see* Section 8 orders

sexual activity with *see* Sexual activity with a child

sexual offences by E3.18

specific issue order D4.7

persons who may apply for D5.1, D5.2

Child – *cont.*
supervision order *see*
Supervision order
taking out of UK D16
truancy proceedings D17
upbringing, orders respecting D4
warrant to search for or remove D9.32
welfare *see* Welfare of the child
youth court, trial in E2
Child assessment order D9.4–D9.10
Child Maintenance Enforcement Commission (CMEC) D3.19, D7.1, D7.47
Child prostitution and pornography A14
payment, meaning A14.5
pornography, meaning A14.3
possession of extreme pornographic images A14.1A
prostitute, meaning A14.4
sentencing A14.6
treatment of child prostitutes A82.9
see also Indecent photographs of children
Child protection D9
child assessment order D9.4–D9.10
child's guardian *see* Child's guardian
emergency protection order *see* Emergency protection order
interim residence order D4.6
local authority duties D9.2–D9.3
non molestation order *see* Non molestation order
police powers D9.1
recovery order D10

Child protection – *cont.*
residence order D4.6
see also Cruelty to a child
Child safety order D17A.1
Child Support Agency *see* Child Maintenance Enforcement Commission
Children and Family Court Advisory and Support Service (CAFCASS) officer D4.2, D5.28
adoption and placement role D18.26–D18.32
Children and Family Court Reporter (CFR) D18.29
Child's guardian
appointment in public law proceedings D6.17–D6.19
duties D6.19
parental responsibility D3.24
Civil proceedings
power to re-open B7.5
Closure notice
persistently selling alcohol to children F2.7
Closure orders
appeal A26.16
crack houses A26.12, A84.37
drug production or supply A26.12
duration F2.3, F2.7
grounds F2.2
on-licensed premises, disorderly and noisy F2
persistent disorder or nuisance A84.37
police powers F2
pornography offences B53
prostitution offences B53
Clubs
gun clubs A71.6

Cocaine A22.4

Codeine A22.5

Commercial practices

  aggressive practice A75

  banned commercial practices A75

  contrary to professional diligence A75

  definition A75.6

  misleading A75

  misleading omission A75

  sentencing A75.7–A75.10

  unfair or prohibited A75

Committal proceedings I5

  adjournment I5.4

  bail in case of J1.20

  custody, accused kept in J1.20

  found on enclosed premises A79.8

  hearing I5.4

  publicity I5.5–I5.6

  reporting restrictions I5.5–I5.6

  summary offences I5.7–I5.8

Common assault *see* Assault

Commonwealth citizens

  deportation and B23.3, B23.4

Communications network offences A16

  actus reus A16.2

  attitude of recipient A16.3

  ECHR compatibility A16.6

  freedom of express and A16.6

  intention A16.5

  sentencing A16.7

Community orders B3

  activity requirement B17.4

  age of offender B4.1

  alcohol treatment requirement B17.15

  amending terms to impose more onerous requirements A17.3

Community orders – *cont.*

  availability B5.31–B5.32, B17.1–B17.2

  breach A17

    amending terms to impose more onerous requirements A17.3

    approach to breach proceedings A17.3

    burden of proof A17.2

    failed to keep in touch A17.2

    reasonable excuse A17.2

    revocation and re-sentence A17.3

    sentencing A17.3, B37.47–B37.50

    standard of proof A17.2

  breach of a requirement B17.17

  curfew requirement B17.1, B17.7

  drug rehabilitation requirement B17.12

    periodic review B17.14

    provision for review by court B17.13

  electronic monitoring B17.1, B17.2, B17.7

  exclusion requirement B17.1, B17.8

  failed to keep in touch A17.2

  foreign travel prohibition requirement B17.9

  mental health treatment requirement B17.10

    treatment at place other than that specified in order B17.11

  permissible requirements B17.3–B17.18

  power to impose B17.1

  pre-sentence reports B3.5, B5.50

  previous convictions, taking into account B3.3

Community orders – *cont.*
proceedings for breach or revocation, costs in B20.23
programme requirement B17.5
prohibited activity requirement B17.6
refusal to consent to conditions in B2.16, B5.35
requirements imposed B17.3–B17.18
residence requirement B17.9
restrictions on imposing B3.2–B3.4
revocation B17.18
revocation and re-sentence A17.3
sentencing B17.2
setting date for completion of requirements B3.6, B17.1
SGC guidelines B17.2
specific sentencing reports B3.6
supervision requirement B17.16
suspended sentence compared B37.47
unpaid work requirement B17.3
Community punishment order
short or fast-delivery reports I6.36
see also Community orders
Community rehabilitation order
Intensive Supervision and Surveillance Programmes (ISSPs) E4.8
see also Community orders
Community sentences
see Community orders
Compensation order B18
amount B18.6
appeal B18.17
attachment order B33.29
availability of sentence B5.25
breach of contact order D5.26
criminal damage B18.3

Compensation order – *cont.*
deductions order B33.29
defendant's lack of means B34.10
deferment of sentence, in case of B21.10, B21.16
deprivation order and B18.15–18.B16
disposal of forfeited goods B18.16
discharge B18.18
dog worrying livestock A73.7
enforcement B33.29
exceptions B18.4
fixing the amount B18.6
football banning order B41.36
forgery A78.17
funeral expenses B18.2
juveniles E4.4
making B18.7–B18.10
making good deficiency B18.16
order B18
personal injury B18.2, B18.19–B18.23
proof of loss B18.5
reduction B18.18
review B18.17
social security benefit, false statement/representation to obtain A54.6
surcharge B18.1
theft, for A57.39, B18.3
victims of uninsured motorists, for C33.18–C33.22
youth offender panels B42.12
Computer
storing indecent images on A43.3
Computer program
article possessed for fraud A38.3
erasure of, as criminal damage A18.22

Concealed camera A20.9
Conditional discharge B31
  availability B5.24, E4.3
  Consolidated Criminal Practice
    Direction B10.20–B10.21
  deferment of sentence
    and B21.19
  juveniles E4.3
  security for good behav-
    iour B10.21
  sexual activity with a
    child A52.15
  sexual assault A53.16
Confiscation orders B19
  drug-trafficking offences A26.20
Constable *see* Police constable
Contact order D4.4
  breach of enforcement or-
    der D5.25
  contact activities D5.18
  contact activity condi-
    tions D5.18, D5.20, D5.21
  contact activity direc-
    tions D5.18, D5.19, D5.21
  domestic violence and D4.4,
    D6.4A
  effect D4.4
  enforcement or-
    ders D5.24–D5.25
  financial compensation or-
    ders D5.26
  interim order D6.37
  monitoring contact D5.22
  persons who may apply
    for D5.1
  public law proceedings,
    in D6.24
  split hearings D4.4
  warning notices D5.23
Contempt of court I3
  appeal I3.16
  disorderly defendants I3.10
  insult I3.1, I3.5

Contempt of court – *cont.*
  interruptions I3.1
  misbehaviour in court I2, I3.1
  non molestation or-
    der D8.19–D8.20, D8.22
  officer of the court I3.6
  overwhelming disorder in
    court I3.8
  photographs in court I1B.9, I3.4
    mobile phone, by I3.15
  procedure I3.7
  reporting restrictions I1B.7
  sketches in court I1B.9
  tape recorders, use of I1B.10
  witnesses, by I3.9
Contingent destruction order
  dangerous dogs A72.15
Contribution orders I7.2A
Convention on Human Rights *see*
    European Convention on
    Human Rights
Conveyance, taking without con-
    sent A65
  see also Motor vehicle; Vehicle
Costs B20
  advice of justices' clerk, failure
    to take I6.28, L1.9
  attachment order B33.29
  binding over order B10.4
  civil proceedings,
    in B20.24–B20.31
    litigants in person B20.1
    proceedings begun by way of
      application B20.31
    public funding B20.25
  criminal proceed-
    ings B20.1A–B20.22
    costs unnecessarily or
      improperly in-
      curred B20.19–B20.20A
    defence costs B20.16–B20.18
    enforcement B33.29

Costs – *cont.*
  criminal proceedings – *cont.*
    miscellaneous provi-
      sions B20.21–B20.23
    prosecution
      costs B20.2A–B20.15
    surcharge B20.1A
  Crown Court, award in K3.1
  deductions order B33.29
  defence costs B20.16–B20.18
    publicly aided defen-
      dant B20.17
    reducing amount of defen-
      dant's order B20.18
  interpreters B20.22
  juveniles E4.4
  legal representatives,
    against B20.20
  liquor licensing appeals F1.16
  litigants in person B20.1
  maintenance orders, complaints
    concerning B20.24
  medical reports B20.21
  possessing a controlled drug
    with intent to sup-
    ply A26.17
  prosecution
    costs B20.2A–B20.15
    central funds B20.3
    community orders,
      proceedings for breach or
      revocation B20.23
    health and safety at
      work A80.21
    juveniles B20.10
    monetary penalty not
      exceeding £5 B20.9
    ordering accused to
      pay B20.8
    private prosecu-
      tors B20.4–B20.6
    proportionate to maximum
      penalty B20.8

Costs – *cont.*
  prosecution costs – *cont.*
    reducing amount of prosecu-
      tor's order B20.7
  statutory nuisance, complaint by
    person aggrieved A84.31
  third parties, costs
    against B20.20A
  unnecessarily or improperly in-
    curred B20.19–B20.20A
  wasted costs order A84.31,
    B20.19, I6.12
Council tax H1
  recovery and enforcement H2
    committal proceedings H6
    court hearing H3
    evidential requirements H4
    liability order H5
    suspended commitments H7
Counterfeit money
  import or export A4.2
Coursing with hounds A86.25
Court room procedure
  abuse of process I1B.11–I1B.12
  appeals I6.45–I6.48
    against conviction and or sen-
      tence I6.46
    Crown Court, to I6.46
    High Court, to I6.47
    judicial review applica-
      tion I6.48
    by way of case stated I6.47
  committal for sentence
    plea before venue and mode
      of trial proceedings I4.5
    reasons for decisions B16.1
  contempt *see* Contempt of court
  human rights *see*
      European Convention on
      Human Rights; Human
      Rights Act
  indictable offences only I4.8
  legal advice *see* Legal adviser

Court room procedure – *cont.*
misbehaviour in court I2, I3.1
open court requirement I1B
abuse of process I1B.11–I1B.12
exceptions I1B.2
non-disclosure of evidence I1B.6
power to clear court I1B.3
reporting of court proceedings I1B.7–I1B.9
stay of proceedings I1B.11–I1B.12
plea before venue and mode of trial proceedings I4
allocation guidance I4.1
allocation guidelines I4.5–I4.8
committal for sentence I4.5
criminal damage offences I4.6
current procedures I4.1A
either way offences I4.1
indictable offences only I4.8
linked cases I4.7
matters to which court is to have regard I4.2
reasons for decisions I1A.1–I1A.5
committal for sentence B16.1
Family Proceedings Court D1.18
young offender institution B26.34
representation orders *see* Representation orders
stay of proceedings I1B.11–I1B.12
youth court E3.25
summary proceedings *see* Summary proceedings
transfer for trial at Crown Court I5
Court security officer
assaulting A9

Court security officer – *cont.*
definition A9.4
identifiability A9.6
obstructing or resisting in execution of duty A47
Courts Service L1.5
structure L1.5
Cows *see* Animals; Livestock
Crack houses
closure orders A26.12, A84.37
Criminal damage A18
arson A18
assessing value of damage A18.6–A18.8
badger traps, destruction of A18.19
belonging to another person, meaning A18.23–A18.24
compensation B18.3
computer program, erasure of A18.22
damage, meaning A18.22
destroy or damage A18.20
detention and training order B2.6
endangerment of life A18.2
graffiti as A18.22
intention A18.25
Iraq War protesters A18.19
maximum penalty A18.2–A18.5
mode of trial I4.6
multiple offences A18.9
plea before venue I4.6
possessing anything with intent to destroy or damage property A18B
property, definition A18.21
racially or religiously aggravated A18.16–A18.18
reasonable force to prevent commission of crime A18.19
recklessness A18.31

Criminal damage – *cont.*
  reparation orders B38.8
  sentencing A18.3, A18.32, B2.6
  temporary functional derangement A18.22
  threatening to destroy or damage property A18A
  trust property A18.24
  venue for trial A18.2–A18.5
  wheel clamp, removal of A18.19
  without lawful excuse A18.19
  see also Damage to property
Criminal Defence Service I7
  see also Representation orders
Criminal Injuries Compensation Authority
  compensation for personal injuries, guidelines B18.19–B18.32
Crossbows A11.3
Crown Court
  appeal to
    disqualification of justices K5
    increase of sentence K3.1
  arraignment of prisoner K2.2
  clerk of the court K2.1
  committal proceedings I5
    bail in case of J1.20
    custody, accused kept in J1.20
    publicity I5.5–I5.6
    reporting restrictions I5.5–I5.6
    summary offences I5.7–I5.8
  committal for sentence B11–B16, I4.5
    ancillary orders B16.4
    bail, on B16.1, B16.7
    custody, in B16.1
    dangerous offenders B16.5
    limitations B16.1–B16.3
    reasons for decisions B16.1

Crown Court – *cont.*
  committal for sentence – *cont.*
    violent or sexual offence B16.3
  committal for trial I5
  costs, award of K3.1
  disqualification from driving C5.40
  juries K2.3–K2.5
  justices K1
    circuit Judges K1.1, K1.4
    disqualification K5
    expenses K4
    forms of address K1.2–K1.3
    High Court judges K1.1
    Judge sitting alone K1.1
    numbers sitting K1.5
    qualifications K1.5
    recorders K1.1, K1.4
    sentencing K3
  press reports I1B.7
  procedure K2
  publicity I5.5–I5.6
  sentencing B11–B16, K3
    increase of sentence on appeal K3.1
    maximum sentences K3.2
    young offenders, of B26.33, K3.2
  summary offences, transfer for trial I5.7–I5.8
  transfer for sentence B11–B16
  transfer for trial at I5
    summary offences I5.7–I5.8
  young offenders B26.33
Cruelty to animals *see* Animal cruelty
Cruelty to a child A19
  abandoning A19.18–A19.20
  age of offender A19.4
  bullying A19.16
  definitions A19.6–A19.22

Cruelty to a child – *cont.*
  exemptions A19.5
  exposing in a manner likely to
      cause unnecessary suffering
      or injury to
      health A19.21–A19.22
  frightening A19.16
  ill-treating A19.16
  neglect A19.17, A19.23
  presumption of guilt A19.23
  punishment of child A19.5
  sentencing A19.32–A19.34
  wilfully, meaning A19.8
  young person, meaning A19.7
  see also Child protection
Crystal meth A22.4
Curfew
  ASBO requirement B8.5
  community order require-
      ment B17.1, B17.7
  YRO requirement B50.12
Curfew order
  electronic monitoring E3.4, J1.6
  specific sentence report B3.6
  see also Community orders
Custodial sentences B2
  aggravating or mitigating fac-
      tors B2.10
  availability of B5.33–B5.35
  consecutive sen-
      tences B37.22–B37.32
  custody plus B2.1, B5.33,
      B26.1, J1.91
  early release B37.53
    further of-
        fences B37.54–B37.55
  enforcement of
      fine B33.41–B33.51,
      B33.70
  immediate sentence for shortest
      time B2.17
  imprisonment *see* Imprisonment

Custodial sentences – *cont.*
  intermittent custody B2.1,
      B5.33, B26.0, B26.1, J1.91
  legal representation
    defendant's right to B2.8,
        B37.19
      contribution to legal
          costs B2.8
      young offenders B2.8,
          B26.21
    right to B2.8, B36.2
  length B2.18–B2.20,
      B37.35–B37.39
  mentally disordered defen-
      dant B2.23–B2.24, B37.18
  pre-sentence reports *see* Pre-
      sentence reports
  previous convictions, taking into
      account B2.10
  proportionality B5.49
  restrictions on imposing B2.9
  seriousness of offence B5.3
    determining B5.7–B5.16
    "first time offender" B5.7
    "range" B5.7
    sexual assault A53.16
    "starting point" B5.7
  see also Imprisonment;
      Sentencing; Young offender
      institution
Custody *see* Custodial sentences;
    Remand in custody
Custody plus B2.1, B5.33, B26.1,
    J1.91
Customs and excise duty *see*
    Revenue and Customs

D

Damage to property
  arson A18

Damage to property – *cont.*
  criminal damage A18
  possessing anything with intent
    to destroy or damage prop-
    erty A18B
  threatening to destroy or
    damage property A18A
  see also Criminal damage
Dangerous dogs A72
  age of owner A72.2
  change of ownership A72.25
  contingent destruction or-
    der A72.15
  control or destruction or-
    der A72.10,
    A72.21–A72.38
    additional powers A72.16
    appeal A72.19, A72.38
    disqualification and A72.17
    fighting dogs A72.20
    procedure at hearing A72.31
  dangerously out of control,
    meaning A72.3
  disqualification from keep-
    ing A72.17–A72.18,
    A72.20, A72.34–A72.35
    contravention A72.18,
    A72.37
  escape from enclosed
    area A72.4
  fighting dogs A72.20
  Japanese Tosas A72.20
  offence committed by omis-
    sion A72.4
  owner A72.2
  parked car, in A72.7
  physical control of dog A72.4
  pit bull terriers A72.20
  public place A72.5–A72.7
  sentencing A72.8–A72.19
Dangerous driving C16
  aggravated vehicle taking, af-
    ter A66

Dangerous driving – *cont.*
  aid and abet C16.6
  careless or inconsiderate driving
    and C25.16
  causing death by C9.5
  causing serious injury by C16C
  definitions A66.8,
    C16.3–C16.16
  disqualification C16.20
  endorsement of licence C16.20
  forfeiture of vehicle B34.17
  objective test C16.8
  sentencing C16.17–C16.30
  see also Careless driving;
    Driving
Dangerous drugs *see* Drugs
Dangerous offenders
  committal to Crown Court for
    sentence B16.5
  extended sentences B16.5
Declarations *see* Statutory
  declarations
Deductions from benefits order
  fines, payment of B33.28,
    B33.80
Deductions from earnings order
  costs and compensation, en-
    forcement B33.29
  fines, payment of B33.28
  see also Attachment of earnings
    order
Defective tyres C53
Defence of property
  reasonable force A8.18–A8.20
Deferment of sentence B21
  ancillary orders B21.5
  announcement B21.6–B21.7
  compensation provi-
    sions B21.10, B21.16
  conditional discharge B21.19
  consent B21.1
  failure to comply with require-
    ments B21.20

Deferment of sentence – *cont.*
limitations B21.1–B21.4
maximum period B21.17
offence during B21.21
reasons for B21.10
requirements as to conduct B21.4
sentence after period of deferral B21.2
undertaking to comply with requirements B21.1
victim of offence, concern of B21.16
when appropriate B21.10
Deportation B23
age of seventeen B23.5
aliens B23.4
citizens who cannot be deported B23.3
Commonwealth citizens B23.3, B23.4
criteria for making recommendation A81.71, B23.8–B23.16
EC/EU Nationals B23.4, B23.17–B23.25
effect of recommendation B23.31
Home Secretary's considerations B23.9–B23.16
persons who may be deported B23.4
recommendation B23.2
Deprivation order B34
availability of sentence B5.25
compensation order and B18.15–18.B16
conversion proceedings B34.5
effect of order B34.5
motor vehicles B34.17
personal loss or injury B34.10–B34.16
see also Forfeiture

Detention
for one day at court or police station B24, B33.53
young offender institution *see* Young offender institution
Detention of seized cash M3.2
grounds for detention order M3.2
Detention and training order B2.6, B25
availability of B5.33
breach of supervision B25.10
consecutive orders B25.8
Intensive Supervision and Surveillance Programmes (ISSPs) E4.8
length B2.20, B25.6–B25.8
time spent on bail subject to curfew condition/ electronic monitoring condition B2.20
time spent on remand B2.20
Dexedrine A22.5
Dihydroetrophine A22.4
Disability
aggravation relating to A8.10, A15.7, B5.2B
Discharge *see* Absolute discharge; Conditional discharge
Disorder *see* Violent disorder
Disorderly behaviour A20
arrest powers A20.18
binding over A20.20
the charge A20.4
concealed camera A20.9
defences A20.17
dwelling-house, in A20.16
football match, at *see* Football banning order; Football-related offences
harassment, alarm or distress A20

Disorderly behaviour – *cont.*
harassment, alarm or distress –
cont.
intent to cause A21
intent A20.10
intoxication A20.16
misbehaviour in court I2
racially or religiously aggravated A20, A21
meaning A20.6–A20.7
sentencing A20.19, A21.17
visible representation A20.11
within hearing or sight of
another person A20.8
Disqualification
animals, from keeping A5.4
dog, from keep-
ing A72.17–A72.18,
A72.20, A72.34–A72.35
contravention A72.18,
A72.37
driving, from *see* Driving; Road
traffic offences
Distance
speed and distance chart C2
Distress warrant
fine, enforcement of B33.54,
B33.76
maintenance order, enforcement
by means of D7.20
DNA genetic fingerprinting
proof of parentage D3.20
Dogs
dangerous *see* Dangerous dogs
disqualification from keeping A72.17–A72.18,
A72.34–A72.35
contravention A72.18,
A72.37
fighting dogs A72.20
hunting with A86.8, A86.25
threat to harm A41.7
worrying livestock A73

Dogs – *cont.*
see also Animals
Domestic burglary A12
aggravated burglary, meaning A12.2
building, mean-
ing A12.10–A12.15
caravan, of A12.15
Crown Court, committal
to A12.4, A12.18
entering, meaning A12.7
grievous bodily harm
and A12.3, A13.3
inhabited vehicle or ves-
sel A12.15
mode of trial A12.2–A12.6
rape and A12.3
sentencing A12.20
stealing, meaning A12.16
third conviction A12.4, A12.18
third offence becoming
indictable only A12.4
trespass A12.10, A12.17
violence, threatening or using A12.5
Domestic court *see* Family
proceedings court
Domestic football banning order
see Football banning order
Domestic violence
assault on constable in
execution of his duty
and A9.8
contact order and D4.4, D6.4A
definition D4.4
Practice Direction D4.4
residence order and D4.4,
D6.4A
sentencing A8.34
special measures, witnesses
under 18 years A52.10
split hearings D4.4

Domestic violence – *cont.*
  see also Child protection;
    Husband and wife; Non
    molestation order
**Domestic violence protection
  notice (DVPN)** B54
  representation orders I7.1A
**Domestic violence protection
  order (DVPO)** B55
  representation orders I7.1A
Drawings of court
  restrictions I1B.9
Drinking banning order B32A
  age limit B32A.1
  appeal B32A.6
  attendance at approved
    course B32A.2
  breach proceedings B32A.5
  criminal or disorderly behaviour
    requirement B32A.1
  discharge B32A.3
  duration B32A.2
  interim order B32A.4
  prohibitions B32A.2
  rules of court B32A.1
  terms B32A.2
  variation B32A.3
  see also Exclusion order
Driving
  alcohol over prescribed limit *see*
    Alcohol
  careless *see* Careless driving
  causing death by
    careless or inconsiderate driv-
      ing C16A
    unlicensed, disqualified or
      uninsured drivers C16B
  causing serious injury by
    dangerous driving C16C
  dangerous *see* Dangerous
    driving

Driving – *cont.*
  disqualification
    amount owing under Child
      Support Act,
      where D7.47
    kerb crawling C5.45
    litter A83.34
    pursuing game without a li-
      cence A86.32A
    road traffic offences *see* Road
      traffic offences
    unlawful tipping C5.45
    vehicle taking without con-
      sent A65.20
  disqualified, whilst, sentenc-
    ing C19.8–C19.17
  disqualified, whilst C5.38, C19
    causing death C16B
  drugs, while unfit through C20
  due care or attention, without
    see Careless driving
  excess alcohol, drive/attempt to
    drive or in charge C22
    emergency, in C22.50
    high risk offend-
      ers C22.45–C22.46
  inconsiderate *see* Inconsiderate
    driving
  learner drivers, provisions as
    to C18.3–C18.5
  meaning C18.8
  probationary period,
    endorsement dur-
      ing C5.46–C5.48
  reasonable consideration, with-
    out C46
  stationary vehicle C18.8
  towed vehicle C18.9
  'unfit through drink or drugs'
    alternative charge C20.18
    alternative verdict C20.18

Driving – *cont.*
  'unfit through drink or drugs' –
    cont.
    in charge of vehicle
      when C21
    drink, meaning C20.17
    drive/attempt drive C20
    emergency, in C22.25
    sentencing C20.19–C20.20
    unfit, meaning C20.9
  without appropriate licence C18
Driving licence
  appropriate, driving with-
    out C18
  codes C6
  disqualification *see* Driving;
    Road traffic offences
  driving whilst disqualified C19
  endorsement *see* Road traffic
    offences
  failure to produce C17
    defences C17.19–C17.20
    sentencing C17.21–C17.22
  large goods vehicle li-
    cence C18.24–C18.32
  offences C18
    driving whilst disquali-
      fied C19
  photocard licences C18.4
  signing application M4.3
  provisional
    failure to display 'L'
      plates C18.3
    offences C18.3–C18.5
    supervision C18.3, C18.5
  unlicensed drivers causing death
    by driving C16B
Driving test
  disqualification until
    passes C5.37–C5.38

Drug assessment
  failure to attend initial/remain
    for initial assessment A23
  follow-up assessment A23.2
Drug treatment and testing order
  refusal to consent B5.5, B5.35
  see also Community orders
Drugs
  cannabis *see* Cannabis and
    cannabis resin
  in charge of vehicle when 'unfit
    through drink or
    drugs' C21
  driving or attempting to drive
    when C20
  Class A A22.4, A23
    fail/refuse to provide
      sample A24
  Class B A22.5
  Class C A22.6
  closure orders A26.12
  cocaine A22.4
  controlled drug
    classes A22.4–A22.6
    definition A22.1
    fraudulent evasion of
      prohibition by bringing
      into/taking out of
      UK A27B
    possession *see* Possession of a
      controlled drug
    Revenue and Customs of-
      fences A4.2
    sentencing A25.16
    supply *see* Supplying or
      offering to supply a
      controlled drug
  crack houses, closure or-
    ders A26.12, A84.37
  drug-trafficking
    confiscation order A26.20

Drugs – *cont.*
  drug-trafficking – *cont.*
    minimum sentence A25.3
  ecstasy A22.4
  failure to attend initial/remain
    for initial drug assess-
    ment A23
  forfeiture A25.18, B5.52,
    B34.19, I6.33
  heroin A22.4
  LSD A22.4
  meaning C20.17
  misuse A22
  morphine A22.4, A22.5
  permitting premises to be
    used A27A
  possession *see* Possession of a
    controlled drug
  sample, failure to give A24
  'unfit through drink or
    drugs' C20, C21
Drunkenness A28
  affray and A2.10
  arrest without warrant A28.4
  disorderly behaviour A20.16
  driving when 'unfit through
    drink or drugs' C20
  drunk and disorderly A28
    arrest without warrant A28.4
    meaning A28.5
  evidence A28.4
  football-related offences A35
  'found' drunk, meaning A28.3
  glue sniffing A28.4
  highways A28
  lawfulness of arrest A28.3
  licensed premises A28
  meaning A28.7
  motoring, in relation to
    driving when 'unfit through
      drink or drugs' C20

Drunkenness – *cont.*
  motoring, in relation to – *cont.*
    excess alcohol offences C22
    failure to provide specimen
      for analysis C23
    high risk offend-
      ers C22.45–C22.46
    'unfit through drink and
      drugs', in charge of
      vehicle when C21
    see also Alcohol; Breath test
  public place A28
    meaning A28.6
  public service vehicle carrying
    passengers to sporting
    event A35
  sentencing A28.8–A28.9
  sexual assault A53.4, A53.6
  sporting events A35
  symptoms A28.4
  violent disorder A67.8
Due care and attention *see*
  Careless driving
Dumping
  litter A83
    consent of owner A83.25
    public open place, mean-
      ing A83.21
    sentencing A83.31–A83.34
    time limit for proceed-
      ings A83.23
  motor vehicles A83
    burden of proof A83.5
    part of A83.3
    sentencing A83.7–A83.9,
      A83.16–A83.17
Dwelling house
  burglary *see* Domestic burglary
  found on enclosed premises A79
  police cell not A21.9

Dwelling house – *cont.*
threatening behaviour in A21.9

E

Early cover payment scheme I7.5A
Early release B16.20,
B37.53–B37.55
further offences B16.20,
B37.54–B37.55
young offender institution B26.37–B26.46
Ecstasy A22.4
Education supervision order D17.6
see also School attendance and
truancy proceedings
Electricity
abstracting/use without authority A1
Electricity meters
"black boxes" A39.3
Electricity suppliers
warrant of entry M2.31–M2.38
Electronic communications
see Communications network
offences
Electronic monitoring
community orders B17.1,
B17.2, B17.7
conditional bail J1.65
curfew order E3.4, J1.6
juveniles E3.4, J1.6
youth rehabilitation order B50.3, B50.5, B50.22
Email *see* Communications
network offences
Emergency protection order D9.16–D9.34
discharge D9.34
duration D9.33

Emergency protection order –
cont.
effect D9.16, D9.21–D9.22
exclusion requirement D9.23–D9.34
grounds D9.10, D9.17
hearsay evidence D9.18
Public Law Outline D6.2A
residential assessment orders D9.18
undertaking D9.31
warrant of entry D9.32
Enclosed premises
found on A79
Endorsement of driving licence *see*
Road traffic offences
Engagement and Support Order A82.2
Entry
warrant of *see* Warrant
European Community
deportation of citizens of B23.4,
B23.17–B23.25
**European Convention on Human
Rights (ECHR)**
absolute rights I1.5, I1.6
arrest warrants H7.3
bail and J1.2
breach I1.5–I1.8
burden of proof
evidential I1.8
firearm, carrying in a public
place A33.5
firearms certificates A76.16
health and safety at
work A80.19
legal I1.8
possession of a controlled
drug A25.10
possession of a controlled
drug with intent to
supply to another A26.4B

European Convention on Human Rights (ECHR) – *cont.*
burden of proof – *cont.*
shotgun certificate exemption A88.7
vehicle-taking (aggravated) A66.10
witness intimidation A69.7
communications network offences A16.6
conventions rights, whether engaged I1.5
court room procedure I1
declaration of incompatibility I1.2
fair and public hearing I1B.1, I1B.2
freedom of expression A16.6, A21.5A, I1B.7
harassment A41.11
Human Rights Act and I1
justices' clerk and L1.2
legal adviser and L1.2
limited rights I1.5, I1.6
presumption of innocence I1.8
private and family life I1B.7
procedural steps I1.5–I1.8
qualified rights I1.5, I1.6
remands in custody and on bail J1.2
remedial order I1.2
reporting restrictions I1B.7
restraining orders A41.13
self-incrimination, privilege against C8.22
sentence, giving reasons for B5.53
silence C8.22
threatening behaviour A21.5A
European Court of Human Rights and the Commission
decision and opinions I1.3

Evidence
CCTV I6.9
children and young persons, by
age of child A52.7
assessment of capability A52.7
Bench Checklist for Young Witness cases I6.13A
care order D6.5
clearing the court A52.11, A53.13, I1B.3–I1B.5
competence to civil standard A52.7
corroboration not required A52.6, A52.13
cross-examination A52.8
live video link E3.22, J1.22B
reporting restrictions E2.4–E2.5, I1B.7
sexual offences, as to A52.6–A52.9, I1B.7
special measures direction A52.10
unsworn A52.6, E3.22
unwilling child D2.6
video recordings of evidence A52.7, A52.8, A52.9, A52.10
welfare of the child D2.6
wishes and feelings of the child D2.6
youth court I1B.7
council tax recovery and enforcement H4
expert evidence in family proceedings D6.2A
hearsay *see* Hearsay evidence
inference drawn from failure to give I6.22
live video link *see* Live video link
open court, in, non-disclosure I1B.6

Evidence – *cont.*
restitution orders B39.6
warrant to search for *see* Search warrant
Excessive noise *see* Noise
Excise licence
dishonoured cheque, payment by C47.16
fraudulently using C47.32–C47.36
keeping of unlicensed vehicle C47.3–C47.17
liability for back duty C47.19–47.31
Statutory Off Road Notification (SORN) C47.17
using vehicle without C47
Exclusion order B32
actual bodily harm, in case of A8.33
football banning order *see* Football banning order
interim care order, in case of D6.38–D6.46
licensed premises B32.1–B32.2
assault A8.33
assaulting a constable A9.11
expelling persons from B32.2
wounding/grievous bodily harm A70.21
period B32.1
see also Community orders; Drinking banning order
Expenses
justices attending Crown Court K4
Exposure A30
Extended sentences for certain violent or sexual offences B16.5

F

Failing to report after accident C31.3, C32
reasonably practicable C32.18
Failing to stop and give details after accident C31
Failure to surrender to custody J1.47
defence J1.85
penalty J1.91
prosecution for J1.82–J1.91
see also Bail
False accounting A31
False identity documents A32
False representation
fraud by *see* Fraud
Family assistance order D5.28
Family Proceedings Court
appeals D1.19, D6.49
case managers, allocation and continuity of D1
child made a party to proceedings D20
child protection *see* Child protection
evidence D1.17
expert evidence D6.2A
family proceedings panel D1.5–D1.6
financial provision D7
see also Maintenance order
hearsay evidence D1.17
jurisdiction D1.4
litigation friends D19.3
maintenance order *see* Maintenance orders
non molestation order *see* Non molestation order
panel D1.5–D1.6

Family Proceedings Court – *cont.*
party lacking capacity to
conduct proceedings D19
persons present during hearing D1.8
privacy rules D1.7–D1.16
reasons for decisions D1.18
reporting restric-
tions D1.10–D1.16, I1B.2
rules of court D1.4
section 8 orders *see* Section 8
orders
transfer of proceedings D5.9
**Fast-delivery or short re-
ports** I6.36
Father
acquisition of parental responsibility D3.8–D3.21
putative D3.9–D3.21
DNA genetic fingerprint-
ing D3.20
scientific tests D3.16–D3.20
Fighting dogs A72.20
Financial compensation order
breach of contact order D5.26
Financial provision *see*
Maintenance orders
Financial reporting order A4.18
Fines B33
announcement and time to
pay B33.26
assessment, sentencing process B33A
attachment order B33.29,
B33.67, B33.76, B33.96
availability of sentence B5.25
Central Criminal Court,
imposed
by B33.84–B33.85A
collection order B33.26,
B33.38, B33.39
discharge by court B33.62
contempt of court I3.4

Fines – *cont.*
Crown Courts, imposed
by B33.84–B33.85A
deductions from benefits order B33.28, B33.80
deductions from earnings order B33.28
default of payment B33.27
culpable neglect B33.70,
B33.78
existing defaulters B33.28
wilful refusal B33.70, B33.78
default sentence calculation,
interest included B33.85A
determining amount of any
fine B33.16–B33.25
ancillary orders, order of priority B33.16
assessment of financial circumstances B33.19
compensation or-
der and B33.16
expenses out of the ordi-
nary B33.20
financial circumstances of offender B33.16
fine bands B33.16
guilty plea, reduction
for B33.25
high income offenders B33.23
household having more than
one source of in-
come B33.22
low income/state ben-
efits B33.18A
multiple offences B33.16
offence committed for
"commercial" pur-
poses B33.24
offences outside SGC guidelines B33.16
potential earning capac-
ity B33.23

Fines – *cont.*
determining amount of any fine
– *cont.*
range of fine band B33.16
relevant weekly in-
come B33.17–B33.18
savings B33.21
seriousness of offence B33.16
starting point of fine
band B33.16
unusually low outgo-
ings B33.20
enforcement B33.38
attachment order B33.29,
B33.67, B33.76, B33.96
attendance centre or-
der B33.76, B33.98
clamping of offend-
er's car B33.38
committal to
prison B33.41–B33.51
county court, in B33.31
deductions from benefits order B33.28, B33.80
deductions from earnings order B33.28
defendant already in prison,
when B33.82
detention for one day or overnight B24, B33.53
distress warrant B33.54,
B33.76
fines payment work B33.83
High Court, in B33.31
immediate committal to
prison B33.70
immediate enforce-
ment B33.39–B33.61
imprisonment,
by B33.41–B33.51,
B33.70
means enquiry, fixing B33.61

Fines – *cont.*
enforcement – *cont.*
part payments B33.38,
B33.47
procedure B33.38
recognisance by par-
ent B33.96–B33.97
referral by fines officer, as
result of B33.62–B33.83
search B33.33, B33.40
supervision order B33.35,
B33.55
suspended committal or-
der B33.52
suspended committal to
prison B33.78
transfer for enforcement
without reference back to
court B33.38
transfer to High Court or
county court B33.81
young offend-
ers B33.96–B33.99
existing defaulters B33.28
fines payment work B33.83
guilty plea, reduction of amount
of fine for B33.25
health and safety prosecutions A80.22
imprisonment, enforcement
by B33.41–B33.51, B33.70
imprisonment combined with
immediate imprison-
ment B33.37
suspended imprison-
ment B33.36
imprisonment for default of payment B33.27
levels B33.3
limitations B33.1–B33.18
limited com-
panies B33.30–B33.31
maximum fine B33.2

Fines – *cont.*
  parental responsibility for pay-
    ment B33.7–B33.10,
    B33.95, E4.7
  part payments B33.38, B33.47
  partnership firm B33.33
  remission of whole or
    part B33.63, B33.85
  reserve payment order B33.28,
    B33.38
  road traffic offences, for
    maximum C1.1
  standard scale C1.1
  searching for money to
    pay B33.33, B33.40
  sentencing process B33A
  standard scale B33.3–B33.4,
    B33.41
    road traffic offences C1.1
  supervision order B33.35,
    B33.55, B33.96
  surcharge B18.1
  victims surcharge B33.4
  suspended committal or-
    der B33.52, B33.78
  suspended imprisonment
    and B33.36, B37.51
  time to pay B33.26
  victims surcharge B33.4
  young offenders B33.5–B33.6,
    E4.3, E4.7
    aged 10 to 17 B33.93–B33.95
    aged 18 to 21 B33.86–B33.92
    parental responsibility for
      payment B33.7–B33.10,
      B33.95, E4.7
    recognisance by par-
      ent B33.96–B33.97
Fines payment work B33.83
Firearms A11.3
  acquiring A76.3

Firearms – *cont.*
  aggravated burglary A12.2,
    A13.2
  air guns *see* Air guns
  air weapon *see* Air weapon
  ammunition *see* Ammunition
  antique firearms A76.17
  carrying in a public place A33
    ammunition A33.10
    forfeiture A33.13
    sentencing A33.11–A33.13
  certificate A76.5
    cancellation A76.24, A77.18
    exemptions A76.10
    purchasing etc without A76
  clubs A71.6
  control by more than one per-
    son A76.3
  forfeiture A33.13, A76.23,
    A77.17, A86.32, A88.10,
    B34.19, I6.33
  gun clubs A71.6
  imitation
    carrying in a public
      place A33
    forfeiture A33.13
    readily convertible into fire-
      arm A33.8, A76.6,
      A77.8
    trespassing in a building or on
      land and A77
  lethal weapon, meaning A33.8
  meaning A33.8, A76.6–A76.7,
    A77.8
  minding a weapon E3.18,
    E3.18A
  police permit A76.10
  possession A76.3
  proprietary control A76.3
  purchasing etc without certifi-
    cate A76

Firearms – *cont.*
purchasing etc without certificate – *cont.*
forfeiture A76.23
sentencing A76.18–A76.24
sentencing
carrying in a public place A33.11–A33.13
purchasing etc without certificate, sentencing A76.18–A76.24
trespassing in a building or on land A77.10–A77.18
shooting galleries A71.6
shotguns *see* Shotguns
starting pistols A33.9, A76.7, A77.8
stun guns A11.4
trespassing in a building or on land A77
cancellation of certificate A77.18
forfeiture A77.17
reasonable excuse A77.7
sentencing A77.10–A77.18
using someone to mind a weapon E3.18, E3.18A
visitor's permit A76.10, A88.6
wrongly possessing A76.3
First Hearing Dispute Resolution Appointment (FHDRA) D4.1
Fixed penalty offences
school attendance D17.4
see also Road traffic offences
Flick knife A11.4, A11.5
Foetus
threats to kill A59.4
Football banning order A34.17, B41
appeals B41.32, B41.35
application to terminate B41.24–B41.32

Football banning order – *cont.*
civil applications B41.33–B41.34
compensation B41.36
criterion B41.18
declaration of relevance B41.8, B41.18
disobedience B41.18
duration B41.21
effect A34.17, B41.22
enhanced obligations B41.22A
exemption B41.23
journey to or from match B41.7
length of order B41.37
offences committed abroad B41.17
police notice B41.34
procedure B41.19–B1.20
prohibited activity requirement B41.18
regulated football match, meaning B41.2
relevant offence B41.4–B41.5
relevant period B41.6
remanding offender B41.19, B41.34
representation orders I7.1A
Football-related offences A34
alcohol, control of A35
designated sporting event A35.5
exceptions A35.7
period of the event A35.6
prohibited articles A35.8–A35.9
public service vehicle A35.4
being or taking part at match A34.8
designated sports ground, meaning A35.10
football banning order *see* Football banning order

Football-related offences – *cont.*
football ground of-
fences A34.15–A34.17
indecent chanting A34.11
prohibited articles A35.8–A35.9
racialist chanting A34.11
regulated football match A34.6
sentencing A34.15–A34.17
throwing an object A34.10
Foreign travel prohibition
community order require-
ment B17.9
**Foreign travel restriction or-
der B52**
Forfeiture B34
ammunition A76.23, A86.32
compensation order and B18.16
costs order M3.2
deprivation order B34
compensation or-
der and B18.16
detained cash M3.2
drugs A25.18, B5.52, B34.19,
I6.33
firearms A33.13, A76.23,
A77.17, A88.10, B34.19,
I6.33
indecent photographs of children A43.11
motor vehicle B34.17
noise, equipment related
to A84.35
personal loss or in-
jury B34.10–B34.16
poaching, equipment
for A86.32
proceeds of crime M3.2
sentencing B5.52, B34.7, I6.33
subject of offence, of B34
consideration by magis-
trates I6.33
drugs A25.18, B5.52, I6.33

Forfeiture – *cont.*
subject of offence, of – *cont.*
equipment for poach-
ing A86.32
firearms A33.13, A76.23,
A77.17, A88.10, I6.33
noise, equipment related
to A84.35
youth offender panels B42.4
see also Deprivation order
Forgery A78
compensation A78.17
definitions A78.5–A78.9
intention A78.8
mode of trial A78.4
prejudice A78.9
sentencing A78.10–A78.17
Found on enclosed premises A79
Fraud
abuse of position A36.3, A36.9
mode of trial A36.5
relevant financial posi-
tion A36.9
dishonesty A36.7
failing to disclose information A36.2, A36.8
legal duty A36.8
mode of trial A36.5
false representation A36.1,
A36.6
meaning A36.7
mode of trial A36.5
fraudulently evade duty on alco-
hol/tobacco A4
fraudulently receiving programmes F3
gain and loss A36.7
income tax evasion A42
intent to defraud A4.5
making, adapting, supplying or
offering to supply ar-
ticles for A39
"black boxes" A39.3

Fraud – *cont.*
  making, adapting, supplying or
    offering to supply ar-
    ticles for – *cont.*
  mode of trial A39.2
  obtaining services dishon-
    estly A37
    mode of trial A37.2
  possession of articles for A38
  computer programs A38.3
    mode of trial A38.2
  tax credit fraud A55
  vehicle licence/registration
    fraud A64

G

Gambling Commission G1.2
Game *see* Poaching
Gaming licence G1
**Gammahydroxy-butyrate
  (GHB)** A22.6
Gas suppliers
  warrant of entry M2.31–M2.38
Genetic fingerprinting
  proof of parentage D3.20
Glue sniffing
  symptoms A28.4
Going equipped for theft *see* Theft
Goods vehicle
  brakes, defective C9
  dangerous condition/body-
    work C10
  definition C10.2
  large, driving without
    appropriate li-
    cence C18.24–C18.32
  no test certificate C51
  overloading/exceeding axle
    weight C38

Graffiti
  criminal damage, as A18.22
  reparation orders B38.8
Grievous bodily harm A70
  actual bodily harm distin-
    guished A8.9, A70.6
  alternative verdict A70.19
  burglary and A12.3, A13.3
  intent A70.5
  on licensed premises, exclusion
    order A70.21
  meaning A70.6
  provocation A70.7
  racially or religiously aggra-
    vated A70
  reduction of charge A70.19
  sentencing A70.7, A70.20
  sexual disease, infection through
    consensual sex A70.5
Guardian
  appointment D3.24
  binding over B10.18–B10.19,
    B10.21, E4.5
  parental responsibility,
    acquisition of D3.24
Guardian ad litem *see*
  Child's guardian
Guardianship order B35
  ancillary orders B35.6
  availability of B5.34
  effect B35.17
  medical evidence B35.8
  medical reports B35.2, B35.8,
    B35.9
  minimum age B35.3
  period of order B35.7
Guilty plea I6.24
  adjournment proceedings I6.18
  application to change I6.26
  application to withdraw I6.27
  avoiding misunderstand-
    ing I6.25

Guilty plea – *cont.*
complex cases I6.25
Crown Court procedure K2.3
fine, reduction of
amount B33.25
late B2.20
mitigating factor, as B5.46,
B5.65, I6.20
overwhelming prosecution
case B5.46
plea at first available opportunity B5.46
revised SGC definitive guidance B5.46
nature I6.24
Newton hearing I4.1, I6.24
post, by I6.40–I6.43
Gun clubs A71.6
Guns *see* Firearms

H

Handling stolen goods A40
consideration paid A40.11
dishonestly assisting retention of
stolen goods A40.5
failure to reveal stolen
goods A40.5
goods, meaning A40.7
handling, meaning A40.4
knowledge or be-
lief A40.8–A40.11
sentencing A40.12
Harassment A41
alternative verdict A41.6
animal rights protestors A41.5
behaviour likely to cause B8.5
course of conduct A41.5, A41.7
defences A41.10
disorderly behaviour A20.3A
ECHR and A41.11

Harassment – *cont.*
intent to cause A21
number of incidents A41.7
person in his home A41.5
presumed knowledge A41.8
racially or religiously aggravated A21, A41
restraining order *see* Restraining
order
sentencing A41.11A–A41.13
telephone calls A41.7
two or more complain-
ants A41.7
Hares
pursuing and killing A86.25
Health and safety at work A80
costs A80.21
defences A80.19
fines A80.22
mode of trial A80.5–A80.6
offences by bodies corpo-
rate A80.9
prosecution by inspec-
tors A80.10
remedial action, power to order A80.16
sentencing A80.20–A80.22
worker's contribution to accident A80.23
Hearsay evidence
adjournment applications I6.16
ASBOs B8.4A
Civil Procedure Rules I6.16
emergency protection or-
der D9.18
Family Proceed-
ings Court D1.17
Helmet
failure wear on motor
cycle C35
Heroin A22.4
Highway
drunkenness on A28

Highway – *cont.*
meaning A85.4
obstructing A85, C36
Homicide
bail J1.32, J1.62
juveniles J1.32
child or young person, by E3.18
Hooded tops
ASBOs and B8.8
Hospital
noise or disturbance on NHS
premises A74.1
Hospital order B36
application for dis-
charge B36.8–B36.9
availability of B5.34
effect B36.6–B36.21
insanity plea B36.2
interim order B36.22
legal representation B36.2
medical reports B36.3–B36.5
public policy consider-
ations B36.8
remand for report B36.21
renewal B36.7
restriction
clause B36.10–B36.16,
B36.18
Hounds
coursing with A86.25
hunting with A86.8
Hours of darkness
meaning C34.16
Human Rights Act
court room procedure I1
European Convention on
Human Rights and I1
family life, protection from state
intervention D6.1
remands in custody and on
bail J1.2
remedial order I1.2

Human Rights Convention *see*
European Convention on
Human Rights
Hunting with hounds A86.8
see also Poaching
Husband and wife
consensual activity be-
tween A15.16
financial provision *see*
Maintenance orders
violence *see* Domestic violence;
Non molestation order

I

Identity documents
false A32
Illegal entry A81
see also Immigration offences
Imitation firearms
carrying in a public place A33
forfeiture A33.13
readily convertible into firearm A33.8, A76.6, A77.8
trespassing in a building or on
land and A77
Immigration offences A81
arrest without warrant A81.7
asylum seekers *see* Asylum
seekers
bail applications A81.17
extended time limits for prosecution A81.6
facilitating entry A81.8
illegal entrants A81.8
immigration officer, definition A81.8
imprisonment for A81.16
knowingly remaining beyond
time limit A81.5
mode of trial A81.4

Immigration offences – *cont.*
possession of false documents A81.3, A81.5
search warrants A81.7
sentencing A81.9–A81.17
Immigration officer A81.8
Imprisonment B2.2, B37
age limit B37.3
ancillary orders B37.52
associated offence B37.7
attempted crimes, for B37.38
availability of B5.33
consecutive sentences B37.22–B37.32
criteria B37.4
early release B16.20, B37.53–37.55
young offender institution B26.37–B26.46
female defendants with children B37.6
fine combined with B33.36–B33.37
fine enforced by B33.41–B33.51, B33.70
fines, default of payment B33.27
immediate sentence for shortest time B2.17
immigration offences A81.16
intermittent custody B2.1, B5.33, B26.0, B26.1, J1.91
legal representation
contribution to legal costs B2.8
defendant's right to B2.8, B37.19
young offenders B2.8, B26.21
length of sentence B2.18–B2.20

Imprisonment – *cont.*
length of sentence – *cont.*
time on remand B2.20
time spent on bail subject to curfew condition/electronic monitoring condition B2.20
limitations B37.1–B37.19
maintenance order, enforcing D7.24–D7.46
mentally disturbed offenders B37.18
multiple offences B37.33–B37.34
nominal sentence K3.3
one day, for K3.3
period of imprisonment B2.2
determination B37.35–B37.39
persons with no previous convictions B37.6
pre-sentence reports *see* Pre-sentence reports
reasons for decision B16.1, B37.20
sentence, presence of accused, required B2.7
seriousness of offence B37.6
suspended sentences *see* Suspended sentences
young offender *see* Young offender
see also Custodial sentences; Sentencing
Income tax evasion A42
Inconsiderate driving C25.16
causing death by C16A
driving without reasonable consideration C46

Inconsiderate driving – *cont.*
meaning C25.5
Indecency with a child *see* Sexual
activity with a child
Indecent assault *see* Sexual assault
Indecent chanting
at football match A34.11
**Indecent photographs of chil-
dren** A43
defences A43.8
distribution A43.6
downloading indecent im-
ages A43.3
evidence A43.5
forfeiture A43.11
knowledge A43.7
meaning of "photograph" A43.3
mode of trial A43.2
notification require-
ments A43.12
pseudo-photographs A43.3,
A43.4
sentencing A43.9
see also Child prostitution and
pornography; Sexual
activity with a child
**Independent Barring
Board** A53.15
**Independent Safeguarding Author-
ity** A53.15
Individual support order B8.9
Insanity plea B36.2
Insulting words or behaviour *see*
Disorderly behaviour
Insurance
causing death by driving,
uninsured drivers C16B
failure to produce certificate C17
defences C17.19–C17.20
sentencing C17.21–C17.22
seven-day rule C17.19
no insurance C33

Insurance – *cont.*
no insurance – *cont.*
burden of proof C33.6
employed drivers C33.17
insurance certificate C33.7
Motor Insurers' Bu-
reau C33.18–C33.22
proof of insurance C33.7
security in respect of third
party risks C33.4
time limit C33.5
**Intensive Supervision and
Surveillance Programmes
(ISSPs)** E4.8
Intermittent custody B2.1, B5.33,
B26.0, B26.1, J1.91
Internet
downloading indecent im-
ages A43.3
Interpreters
costs B20.22
Intimidation of witness A69
Intoxication *see* Drunkenness
Iraq War protesters
criminal damage A18.19

J

Japanese Tosas A72.20
Judicial review
application I6.48
liquor licensing policy F1.7
Juries K2.3–K2.5
Justices' chief executive
abolition L1.5
Justices' clerk
advice in court L1.6–L1.17
see also Legal adviser
case management powers L1.20
costs, assessment of B20.6
delegation L1.18–L1.20

Justices' clerk – *cont.*
dismissal L1.1
functions L1.3–L1.4
grant of legal representation L1.19
judicial functions L1.18
legal adviser distinguished L1.2
Narey Courts L1.20
role L1
Juvenile
definition E1.1
see also Child; Young offender;
Young person
Juvenile court *see* Youth court

K

**Keeping a brothel used for prosti-
tution** A44
Kerb crawling A82
ASBO A82.12
binding-over orders A82.16
disqualification C5.45
Engagement and Support Order A82.2
Knives
article with blade or point in
public place *see* Bladed
article/offensive weapon
butterfly knife A11.14
disguised A11.5
flick knife A11.4, A11.5
folding pocket knife A11.9
stealth knife A11.4
Knuckle dusters A11.5

L

Larceny *see* Theft
Large goods vehicle
driving without appropriate licence C18.24–C18.32
Lavatory *see* Public lavatory
Legal adviser K2.1, L1.5,
L1.6–L1.17
certificates of good repute M4.2
failure to take advice L1.9,
I6.28
justices' clerk distinguished L1.2
responsibilities L1.6, I6.28
retiring with justices L1.16,
I6.28
role I6.28
see also Justices' clerk
Legal aid
adjournment applications I6.10
changes I7.1
representation orders I7.2
seizure of proceeds of
crime M3.2
Legal Aid Agency I7.1
Legal privilege M2.11
Legal representation
contribution to costs B2.8
costs against B20.20
Criminal Defence Service I7
defendant's rights B2.8, B37.19
grant in criminal proceedings L1.19
hospital order B36.2
legal aid I7.2
young offenders B2.8, B26.21,
I7
see also Representation orders

Legal Services Commission I7
  abolition I7.1
  grant of representation L1.19
  legal aid I7.2
Lending
  theft and A57.33
Licences *see* Driving licence; Excise
    licence; Liquor licensing; TV
    licence payment evasion
Licensed premises
  closure notice for persistently
    selling alcohol to chil-
    dren F2.7
  closure orders F2
  drunkenness on A28
  exclusion order B32.1–B32.2
    assault A8.33
    assaulting a constable A9.11
    expelling persons B32.2
    wounding/grievous bodily
      harm A70.21
  see also Liquor licensing
Lights
  defective C34
    exempted vehicles C34.17
    hours of darkness, mean-
      ing C34.16
Limited companies
  fines B33.30–B33.31
Liquor licensing
  appeals under Licensing Act
    2003 F1, F1.6–F1.7
  costs F1.16
  decision F1.15
  hearing F1.10–F1.11
  judicial review F1.7
  notices F1.8
  order of
    speeches F1.13–F1.14
  period of notice F1.9
  procedure F1.12
  right to appeal F1.6

Liquor licensing – *cont.*
  determination of application or
    licence F1.5
  licensable activities F1.3–F1.4
  see also Licensed premises;
    Personal licence; Premises
    licence
Litigants in person
  costs, recovery of B20.1
Litigation friends D19.3
Litter A83
  car dumping A83
  consent of owner A83.25
  defence A83.24
  public open place, mean-
    ing A83.21
  sentencing A83.31–A83.34
  time limit for proceed-
    ings A83.23
Live video link
  children and young per-
    sons E3.22, J1.22B
  vulnerable accused J1.22B
  vulnerable and intimidated wit-
    nesses I6.13A
  witnesses in criminal proceed-
    ings J1.22C
Livestock
  worrying by dogs A73
Local authority
  accommodation of
    children/young persons in
      remand E3.3
  care or supervision order,
    investigation before mak-
      ing D5.27, D6.23, D6.35
  child in care D6.1
    powers as to D5.3
  child protection du-
    ties D9.2–D9.3
  liquor licensing *see* Liquor
    licensing

Local authority – *cont.*
motor vehicle 'Certificate of Ownership' C17.18
proceedings by, statutory nuisance A84.7–A84.18
public law proceedings D5.3, D6.1, D6.23
Loudspeaker in a street
day time charge A74.6–A74.9
excessive noise A74
night time charge A74.2–A74.5
see also Noise
LSD A22.4
Lucofen A22.6

M

McKenzie Friends D1.8
Magistrates
administration of oaths etc in certain probate business M4.23
applications to M1–M4
certificate of good repute M4.2
judicial business at home M1.1
out-of-hours panels M1.7
passport applications, endorsing M4.3
photocard licence applications, signing M4.3
proceeds of crime, seizure and forfeiture M3.2
recognisance M4.1
removal to suitable premises of persons in need of care and attention M4.4–M4.8
sentencing by *see* Sentencing

Magistrates – *cont.*
statutory declarations M4.9–M4.17
warrant *see* Warrant
Magistrates' court
committal to Crown Court for sentence B11–B16, B26.33
family proceedings jurisdiction D1.1–D1.4
justices' clerk *see* Justices' clerk
legal adviser I6.28, K2.1
transfer of criminal proceedings B1A
youth court, remission to B1.3, B1.4
see also Court room procedure
Magistrates' Courts Committee
abolition L1.5
Maintenance orders D7
agreed orders D7.9–D7.16
enforcement D7.19–D7.47
abuse of process D7.47
attachment of earnings order D7.2, D7.20–D7.21
distress warrant D7.20
imprisonment D7.24–D7.46
liability order D7.47
maintenance assessment D7.47
suspended committal to prison D7.34–D7.37
time limit D7.47
lump sum payments D7.3
method of payment D7.2–D7.3
variation D7.17–D7.18
Making off without payment A45
dishonesty A45.4, A45.5
with intent to avoid payment of amount due A45.7

Making off without payment – *cont.*
payment on the spot A45.6
sentencing A45.8
Malicious wounding *see* Wounding
Mandrax A22.6
Married couple *see* Husband and
wife
Martial arts' weapons A11.4,
A11.12
MDMA A22.4
Mechanically propelled vehicle
definition A66.5
Medical reports
costs B20.21
custodial sentence B37.18
guardianship order B35.2,
B35.8, B35.9
hospital order B36.3–B36.5
mentally disordered offenders B2.23, B26.20, B36.3,
B37.18, I6.37
Mental patient
warrant to search for and remove M4.18–M4.22
Mentally disordered offenders
ASBOs B8.5
custodial sentence B2.24,
B37.18
guardianship order *see*
Guardianship order
hospital order *see* Hospital
order
insanity plea B36.2
medical reports B2.23, B26.20,
B36.3, B37.18, I6.37
pre-sentence reports B2.23,
B26.20, B37.18
sentencing B2.23–B2.24, B35,
B37.18, I6.37
young offender B26.20

Methadrine A22.5
Methylamphetamine (crystal
meth) A22.4
Misbehaviour in court I2, I3.1
Miscarriage
threats to cause A59.4
Misleading commercial prac-
tice A75
Misleading omission in
commercial practice A75
Mistake
as to age, sexual activity with a
child A52.5
getting property by A57.25
Mobile phone
taking photographs in
court I3.15
Molestation *see* Non molestation
order
Morphine A22.4
derivatives A22.5
Motor cycle
driving without appropriate licence C18
not wearing helmet C35
Motor Insurers' Bureau
compensation
scheme C33.18–C33.22
Motor vehicle
aggravated vehicle-taking A66
assault involving,
disqualification for C5.5
bodywork in dangerous condition C10
brakes, defective C9
braking distances C3
dangerous condition, using
in C10
defective lights C34
defective steering C50

Motor vehicle – *cont.*
defective tyres C53
definition A63.5, A65.6, A83.4,
  C9.7
dumping A83
burden of proof A83.5
part of motor vehicle A83.3
sentencing A83.7–A83.9,
  A83.16–A83.17
excise licence *see* Excise licence
forfeiture B34.17
Go-Ped C9.7
goods vehicle *see* Goods vehicle
insurance *see* Insurance
intended for use on road, meaning C9.7
interference A63
kerb crawling A82, C5.45
licence/registration fraud A64
lights, defective C34
no insurance C33
no test certificate C51
obstructing the highway C36,
  A85
opening door C37
overloading/exceeding axle
  weight C38
part of, dumping A83.3
road traffic offences *see* Road
  traffic offences
seat belt offences C48
shortest stopping distances C4
soliciting woman from A29.1,
  A82
speed assessment equipment
  detection devices, breach of
  requirement C38A
speed and distance chart C2
speeding *see* Speeding
steering, defective C50
stopping distances C4
taking without consent A65

Motor vehicle – *cont.*
taking without consent – *cont.*
aggravated A66
reduction of charge from
  theft A57.34, A65.10
sentencing A65.18
successful defence A65.16
time limits A65.11
test certificate *see* Test certificate
theft of
disqualification for A57.40
going equipped for A58,
  C5.5, C5.33
reduction of charge
  from A65.10
tyres, defective C53
use
causing to be used, mean-
  ing C9.5
with defective brakes C9
meaning C9.4
no test certificate C51
offences C51, C53
permitting, meaning C9.6
Motoring offences *see* Road traffic
  offences
Motorway
speeding on C49.20–C49.22
Murder cases
bail J1.32, J1.62
juveniles J1.32
see also Homicide
Mutilation of animals A5.2

N

Narey Courts L1.20
National Court Team (NCT)
hardship applica-
  tion I7.10–I7.11

National Health Service Premises
noise or disturbance on A74.1
Necessity, common law defence of
child abduction D16.5
possession of cannabis A25.8A
Neglect of child
meaning A19.17
presumption of guilt A19.23
Newton hearing A26.4, I4.1,
I6.24
No case to answer I6.21
Noise
abatement notice A74.9, A84.8
appeal against A84.9
closure of premises A84.7
defence A84.34
excessive noise A74
forfeiture of equipment A84.35
National Health Service Premises A74.1
nuisance A74.9, A84.2,
A84.33–A84.36
on-licensed premises F2
day time charge A74.6–A74.9
licence condition F1.15
night time
charge A74.2–A74.5
operating a loudspeaker in a
street A74
reasonable excuse A84.34
statutory nuisance A74.9,
A84.2, A84.33–A84.36
vibration A84.4
see also Nuisance
Non-attendance at school A49
Non-domestic burglary see
Burglary
Non molestation order D8
breach A46, D8.19–D8.20
duplicity A46.3

Non molestation order – *cont.*
civil contempt D8.19–D8.20,
D8.22
content D8.5
criteria for grant D8.3
duration D8.4
enforcement D8.10–D8.18
ex parte application D8.7
occupation order D8.23–D8.25
persons who may apply D8.2
power of arrest D8.9, D8.10,
D8.23
reasonable excuse de-
fence D8.19
sanction for
breach D8.19–D8.20
service D8.8
undertakings D8.21–D8.22
variation D8.6
see also Domestic violence
Not guilty plea I6.19–I6.23
amendment of charge or information I6.23
application to change to I6.26
change of I6.20
no case to answer I6.21
post, by I6.44
silence, inferences from I6.22
trial in absence I6.19
Nuisance A84
abatement notice A74.9, A84.8
statutory see Statutory nuisance

O

Oath
administration in certain
probate business M4.23
witness refusing to take I3.9

Oath – *cont.*
  youth court E3.22
  see also Statutory declarations
**Obstructing a court officer in
  execution of his duty** A47
Obstructing the highway A85,
  C36
**Obstructing or resisting a
  constable in execution of his
  duty** A47
**Obtaining services dishon-
  estly** A37
Occupation order D8.23–D8.25
  see also Non molestation order
Offensive conduct *see* Disorderly
  behaviour
Offensive weapon *see* Bladed
  article/offensive weapon
Open court
  requirements as to I1B
  see also Reporting restrictions
Operating licence G1.3
Opium A22.4
**Overloading/exceeding axle
  weight** C38

P

Parent
  binding over B10.18–B10.19,
    B10.21, E4.5
  fines of child, responsibility
    for B33.7–B33.10, B33.95,
    E4.7
  recognisance by B10.18–B10.19,
    B33.96–B33.97
Parentage
  proof of D3.9–D3.21
    DNA genetic fingerprint-
      ing D3.20
    scientific tests D3.16–D3.20

Parental responsibility D3
  acquisition by fa-
    ther D3.8–D3.21
  acquisition by guardian D3.24
  definition D3.6
  fines, for B33.7–B33.10,
    B33.95, E4.7
  persons having D3.3–D3.7
  step-parents D3.8
Parenting order B37A, E4.6
  announcement B37A.4
  appeals B37A.8
  ASBO with B8.9
  attendance at residential
    course B37A.5
  breach B37A.8, E4.6
  consent B37A.3
  counselling or guidance sessions
    requirement B37A.5
  limitations B37A.1
  period of order B37A.5
  reasons for, giving B37A.2
  referral order with B37A.1,
    B42.4
  representation orders I7.1A
  requirements B37A.5, B37A.7
  school attendance and D17.5
  variation B37A.8
  youth offender panels B37A.1,
    B42.4
Parking
  lights C34
  obstruction C36
Partnership
  fines, enforcement of B33.33
  theft of partnership prop-
    erty A57.36
Passenger
  seat belt offences C48
Passport
  applications, signing M4.3
  possession of false passport A81

Passport – *cont.*
possession of false passport – *cont.*
see also Immigration offences
Paternity dispute D3.9–D3.21
DNA genetic fingerprinting D3.20
evidence of a conviction D3.21
finding of adultery in previous matrimonial proceedings D3.21
scientific tests D3.16–D3.20
Pedal cycles
taking without consent A65
Pedestrian crossing
pelican/zebra crossing contravention C39
stopping on C40
Penalty points C5.10–C5.38, C8.20
fixed penalties C8
mitigating grounds C5.24–C5.31
period of disqualification C5.22–C5.23
points to be taken into account C5.20–C5.21
totting ban C5.20
see also Road traffic offences
Personal injury
compensation B18.2, B18.19–B18.23
Personal licence F1.1, F3
advertising of applications F1.2
appeals under Licensing Act 2003 F1
duration F1.2
forfeiture or suspension B47
fraudulently receiving programmes F3
grant F1.2, F1.5
see also Liquor licensing

Persons in need of care and attention
removal to suitable premises M4.4–M4.8
Photograph
indecent *see* Indecent photographs
prohibition on taking in court I1B.9, I3.4
mobile phone, by I3.15
see also Camera
Pit bull terriers A72.20
Plea *see* Guilty plea; Not guilty plea
Poaching A86
cancellation of game licence A86.7
claim of right A86.3
day-time offence A86.1–A86.8A
forfeiture of equipment A86.32
game, meaning A86.6, A86.17
hunting with hounds A86.8
night-time offences A86.9–A86.22A
pursuing game without licence A86.23–A86.32A
seizure of equipment A86.31
sentencing A86.31–A86.32A
three or more together A86.22
trespassing A86.4
Pointed article *see* Bladed article/offensive weapon; Knives
Police
bail, objections to J1.46–J1.49
child protection powers D9.1
closure orders F2
constable *see* Police constable
forfeiture of articles to B34.5
property in possession of *see* Property in possession of police
sex offenders' notifications to A52.15, A53.16

Police bail
after charge J1.57–J1.60
before charge J1.56
street bail J1.55
Police constable
assault in the execution of his
duty A9
alternative verdict A9.9
burden of proof A9.7
going beyond his duty A9.5
licensed premises, on,
exclusion order A9.11
plain clothes officers carrying
out drugs search A9.8
reasonable expectation of
breach of the peace A9.5
reduction of charge A9.9
search of defendant A9.8
sentencing A9.10–A9.11
assault on person assisting A9
obstructing a person assisting A47
obstructing or resisting in the
execution of his duty A47
burden of proof A47.13
private premises A47.12
rank A47.10
special constable A47.10
unlawful arrest A47.11
threatening behaviour to-
wards A21.10
Police station
detention for one day or
overnight at B24, B33.53
Pornography
closure orders B53
meaning A14.3
see also Child prostitution and
pornography

Possession of articles for
fraud A38
Possession of a controlled
drug A25
burden of proof A25.9–A25.10
ECHR and A25.10
cannabis A25.11
defences A25.8
burden of
proof A25.9–A25.10
common law defence of necessity A25.8A
medical condition A25.8A
establishing possession A25.7
expert examination A25.6
forfeiture A25.18, B5.52, I6.33
with intent to supply to another A26
aggravation of of-
fence A26.4A
appeal A26.16
closure orders A26.12
costs A26.17
crack houses A26.12
defences A26.4B
drug-trafficking A26.20
ECHR and A26.4B
intention A26.4
involuntary keeper of
drugs A26.4
sentencing A26.5–A26.20
maximum penalty A25.1
quantity A25.5
sentencing A25.16–A25.18
see also Drugs
Pre-sentence reports I6.34–I6.35,
I6.39
adjournment to obtain I6.34
community orders B3.5, B5.50

Pre-sentence reports – *cont.*
conditional bail and J1.62
custodial sentences B2.9, B2.10,
B2.20, B2.21–B2.22,
B37.16–B37.18
failure to obtain B26.19,
B37.17
imprisonment B37.16–B37.18
mentally disordered offenders B2.23, B26.20, B37.18
purpose I6.35
young offenders institu-
tion B26.17–B26.19
youth court I6.39
youth rehabilitation order B50.2
Preludin A22.5
Premises closure orders *see*
Closure orders
Premises licence F1.1
advertising of applications F1.2
appeals under Licensing Act
2003 F1
closure due to noise A84.7
fraudulently receiving programmes F3
gambling G1.3
licensable activities F1.3–F1.4
see also Liquor licensing
Press restrictions *see* Reporting
restrictions
Previous convictions
sentencing, effect on A5.4, B5.3,
B5.40, B8.15, I6.32
Prison *see* Imprisonment
Probate business
administration of oath M4.23
Proceeds of crime
appeal right M3.2
confiscation A26.20, B19,
B33.37
detention of seized cash M3.2
forfeiture M3.2

Proceeds of crime – *cont.*
grounds for detention or-
der M3.2
legal aid M3.2
notice of forfeiture proceedings M3.2
recoverable property M3.2
search power M3.2
unlawful conduct M3.2
Professional diligence
commercial practices contrary
to A75
**Prohibited commercial prac-
tices** A75
Prohibited steps order D4.5
persons who may apply
for D5.1, D5.2
Prohibition order A84.22
Property
belonging to another person,
meaning A18.23–A18.24
defence of, reasonable
force A8.18–A8.20
definition A18.21
deprivation order B34
destroying or damaging *see*
Damage to property
forfeiture *see* Forfeiture
mistake, getting by A57.25
possession of police in *see*
Property in possession of
police
roadside *see* Roadside property
stolen *see* Stolen goods
trust property A18.24
theft A57.23
wild creatures as A18.21
Property in possession of police
application for order for delivery A87
case unsuitable for
magistrates'
courts A87.17–A87.18

Property in possession of police – *cont.*
application for order for delivery – *cont.*
costs A87.20
Criminal Damage Act 1971 A87.19
delivery A87.10
hearing A87.6
powers of magistrates A87.7–A87.9
when applicable A87.3
conversion proceedings B34.5
Prostitution
child prostitution and pornography A14
closure orders B53
Engagement and Support Order A82.2
exploitation A29
keeping a brothel used for A44
kerb crawling A82, C5.45
meaning of 'prostitute' A14.4
paying for services of prostitute subjected to force A29.2
soliciting women for A29.1, A82
treatment of child prostitute A82.9
Protection order *see* Emergency protection order
Protective order
breach A46
see also Non molestation order; Restraining order
Provisional driving licence
learner plates, display C18.3
supervision C18.3, C18.5
Provocation
actual bodily harm A8.17
assault A15.32
grievous bodily harm A70.7

Psychological damage
actual bodily harm A8.9
Public electronic communications
see Communications network offences
Public lavatory
sexual activity in A51
Public law proceedings D6
access to child in care D6.24
allocation D1.4
binding over parent or guardian B10.18–B10.29
care order *see* Care order
case management conference D6.2B
case management, continuity of D6.2C
child's guardian, appointment of D6.17–D6.19
contact order D6.24
directions appointments D6.2
disclosure of documents D6.2
domestic violence and D6.4A
expert evidence D6.2A
final hearing D6.2B
guardianship order *see* Guardianship order
interim orders D6.35–D6.37
exclusion requirement D6.38–D6.46
issue and the first appointment (FA) D6.2B
issues resolution hearing (IRH) D6.2B
judicial continuity D6.2C
local authority powers D5.3, D6.1, D6.23
notifying the extended family D6.3
orders of the court D6.23–D6.34
Public Law Outline D6.2B

Public law proceedings – *cont.*
  supervision order *see*
    Supervision order
Public order
  harassment *see* Harassment
  offences against
    affray A2
    disorderly behaviour A20
    threatening behaviour A21
    violent disorder A67
Public place
  bladed article/offensive weapon,
    possession of A11
  highway A11.8
  premises A11.8
  school premises A11.10
  car park of dealership C25.4
  causeway linking island to main-
    land A33.3
  dangerous dogs A72.5–A72.7
  definition A33.3
  drunkenness A28
  firearms
    air guns A33, A71.4
    carrying A33
  kerb crawling A82
  litter in A83.21
  school premises A11.10
  sexual activity in a public lava-
    tory A51
  soliciting women for prostitu-
    tion A29.1, A82
  telephone kiosk A83.21
Public service vehicles
  carrying passengers to sporting
    event, control of alcohol
    on A35
  meaning A35.4

R

Racialist chanting
  at football match A34.11
**Racially or religiously aggravated
  crimes**
  assault
    common assault A15
    meaning A15.7
    occasioning actual bodily
      harm A8
    sentencing A15.33
    triable either way A15.3
    two offences tried to-
      gether A15.3
  criminal dam-
    age A18.16–A18.18
  disorderly behaviour A20, A21
  'foreigners' as racial
    group A18.17, A20.6,
    A21.10
  grievous bodily harm and
    malicious wounding A70
  harassment A41
  intent to cause A21
  meaning of 'racial or religious
    aggravation' A15.7,
    A18.17–A18.18,
    A20.6–A20.7
  sentencing A15.33, A20.19,
    A21.17, B5.2B
  threatening behaviour A21
  words used A18.17, A20.6,
    A21.10
  victim's perception of A8.16,
    A15.7, A18.18, A20.7
Railway fare evasion A48
Rape
  bail in cases of J1.32
  burglary and A12.3, A13.3

Rape – *cont.*
reporting restrictions I1B.7
Reasonable chastisement A15.16
Reasons for decisions I1A.1–I1A.5
committal for sentence B16.1
Family Proceedings Court D1.18
reparation order B38.16
young offender institution B26.34
Receiving *see* Stolen goods
Recklessness
assault A8.7, A15.4, A15.5, A70.5
criminal damage A18.31
driving, reckless *see* Dangerous driving
meaning A18.31
wounding A70.5
Recognisance M4.1
binding over, in case of B10.21
complainant, by B10.8
forfeiture B10.6
parent or guardian, by B10.18–B10.19
refusal to enter into B10.6, B10.21
witness, by B10.8
conditional bail and J1.66–J1.68
forfeiture B10.6, J1.68
parent or guardian, by binding over, in case of B10.18–B10.19
fine, to ensure payment of B10.18–B10.19, B33.96–B33.97
Recovery order D10
Referral order B48–B49
ancillary orders B48.6
appropriate officer B48.7
attendance of parent or guardian B48.7

Referral order – *cont.*
compulsory referral conditions B48.7
connected offence B48.7
discharge B48.9
extension B48.9
parenting order with B37A.1, B42.4
previous conviction B48.7
prohibited orders B48.8
revocation B48.9
variation B48.9
Refugees *see* Asylum seekers
Registration cards
possession of false A81
see also Immigration offences
Religiously aggravated crimes *see* Racially or religiously aggravated crimes
Remand on bail *see* Bail
Remand in custody J1.1, J1.5
absence of accused, in J1.21–J1.23
accused's own protection, for J1.32
adjournment of hearing, where J1.1
children E3.3, E3.4–E3.17A
committal or send to Crown Court J1.20
decision whether to remand in custody or on bail J1.24–J1.39
ECHR and J1.2
exceptions to right to bail J1.26–J1.40
Human Rights Act and J1.2
length
after conviction J1.19
before conviction J1.16–J1.18
deduction from sentence B37.39
time limits J1.51–J1.54

Remand in custody – *cont.*
pending appeal J1.93
procedure at remand hearing J2
required, where J1.7–J1.10
time limits J1.51–J1.54
application to extend J1.52
expiry J1.54
young persons E3.3,
E3.4–E3.17A
accused's own protection,
for J1.32
conditions E3.9
prison E3.16–E3.17
remand with a security requirement E3.16–E3.17
secure accommoda-
tion E3.5–E3.17
Remedial order I1.2
Remifentanil A22.4
**Remission on bail or in cus-
tody** B1.2
**Removal to suitable premises of
persons in need of care and
attention** M4.4–M4.8
Reparation order B38
breach B38.17–B38.18
direct or indirect reparation B38.8
limitations B38.1–B38.2
maximum periods B38.3–B38.4
reasons, giving B38.16
reparation in kind B38.9
reports B38.5, B38.8
Reporting restrictions I1B.7–I1B.9
address of service police officer I1B.7
adoption proceedings D1.16
anonymity of witness I1.7
children and young persons,
evidence by E2.4–E2.5,
I1B.7
committal proceedings I5.5–I5.6

Reporting restrictions – *cont.*
Family Proceed-
ings Court D1.10–D1.16,
I1B.2
identification of witnesses I1B.7
live, text-based communications I1B.8
matters exempted from
disclosure in court I1B.7
photographs and sketches of
court I1B.9
postponing publication of
reports of court proceed-
ings I1B.7
rape and sexual offences I1B.7
sexual activity with a
child A52.12
Twitter I1B.8
youth court E2.4–E2.5, I1B.2
Representation orders I7.1A–I7.8
appeals I7.9–I7.11
application in prescribed
form I7.3
availability I7.1A
backdated I7.3
co-defendants I7.5
contribution orders I7.2A
early cover payment
scheme I7.5A
extradition hearings I7.4
financial eligibility I7.2, I7.2A
hardship application to
National Court
Team I7.10–I7.11
indictable offences I7.4
interests of justice test I7.6–I7.8
appeals I7.9
more than one advocate I7.4
Queen's Counsel I7.4
review of means I7.10
scope I7.4
transfer I7.5B
triable either way offences I7.4

Representation orders – *cont.*
 withdrawal I7.2A
 written reasons for refusal I7.9
 see also Legal representation
Reserve payment order B33.28,
 B33.38
Residence order D4.6
 child in care of local authority D5.3
 domestic violence and D4.4,
 D6.4A
 effect D5.2
 interim order D4.6
 persons who may apply
 for D5.1
 split hearings D4.4
Residential assessment
 care order D6.35
 emergency protection or-
 der D9.18
Resist arrest
 assault with intent to A7
Resisting a constable
 execution of duty, in A47
Restitution order B39
 evidence B39.6
 innocent purchasers B39.4
Restraining order A41.13
 on acquittal A41.13
 breach A46
 on conviction A41.13
 ECHR and A41.13
 human rights issues A41.13
 terms of order A46.3
 variation A46.5
 see also Harassment
Restriction clause
 included in hospital or-
 der B36.10–B36.16

Restriction order *see* Football
 banning order
Revenue and Customs
 alcohol/tobacco, fraudulently
 evade duty A4
 income tax evasion A42
 search warrants M2.27
 VAT evasion A62
Review of decisions
 civil proceedings B7.5
 criminal proceedings B7.1–B7.4
Risk of sexual harm order
 sexual activity with a
 child A52.16
 sexual assault A53.17
Road fund licence *see* Excise
 licence
Road traffic offences
 alcohol, in connection with *see*
 Alcohol; Drunkenness
 ASBOs B8.8
 brakes, as to C9
 careless driving *see* Careless
 driving
 causing death by driving
 careless or inconsiderate driving C16A
 unlicensed, disqualified or
 uninsured drivers C16B
 causing serious injury by
 dangerous driving C16C
 dangerous condition/bodywork,
 using in C10
 dangerous driving *see*
 Dangerous driving
 defective brakes C9
 defective lights C34
 defective steering C50
 defective tyres C53

Road traffic offences – *cont.*
driving licence *see* Driving
licence
driving when 'unfit through
drink or drugs' C20
see also Drunkenness
driving whilst disqualified C19
drugs, in connection with *see*
Drugs
due care and attention, driving
without *see* Careless driving
endorsement and disqualification B5.52, C5
amount owing under Child
Support Act,
where D7.47
appeal against C5.36
assault involving motor vehicle C5.5
commencement of disqualification C5.8
compulsory endorse-
ment C5.1, C5.32
Crown Court, disqualification
by C5.40
dangerous driving C16.20
defective brakes C9.16A
disability C5.49
discretionary C5.20, C5.38
discretionary disqualification C5.20, C5.38
disqualification for any offence C5.45
disqualification for life C5.9
disqualification pending sentence C5.39
driving licence codes C6.1
driving off road unlaw-
fully C5.45
driving test, order to
take C5.37–C5.38
driving whilst disquali-
fied C19

Road traffic offences – *cont.*
endorsement and disqualification
– *cont.*
endorsement code C6.2
foreign licence C5.1
immediate effect C5.35
interim disqualification C5.39
juveniles E4.4
length of disqualifica-
tion C5.6–C5.8,
C5.22–C5.23
mandatory disqualifica-
tion C5.4, C5.10, C5.33,
C5.37
mitigating
grounds C5.24–C5.31
new drivers, effect of
endorsement
on C5.46–C5.48
offences for which im-
posed C6.2
penalty points sys-
tem C5.10–C5.38
period of disqualifica-
tion C5.6–C5.8,
C5.22–C5.23
reduced for attendance on
course C22.56–C22.61
sentence code C7
special reasons C5.2–C5.3,
C5.33, C5.34, C9.16A,
C9.17, C22.24–C22.25,
C22.50
theft of vehicle and A57.40
exceeding axle weight C38
excess alcohol, drive/attempt to
drive or in charge C22
excise licence
fraudulently us-
ing C47.32–C47.36
keeping of unlicensed ve-
hicle C47.3–C47.17

Road traffic offences – *cont.*
excise licence – *cont.*
liability for back
duty C47.19–47.31
no excise licence C47
failing to produce docu-
ments C17.21–17.22
failing to report after accident C31.3, C32
failing to stop and give details
after accident C31
failure to produce test certificate C17
fines
maximum C1.1
standard scale C1.1
fixed penalties C8
conditional of-
fer C8.21–C8.22
endorsable of-
fences C8.6–C8.8
enforcement of pay-
ment C8.19
graduated C8.8
instituting proceedings C8.16
non-endorsable offences C8.5
not paid, where C8.17–C8.18
offering C8.4–C8.8
payment C8.9–C8.10, C8.19
penalty points C8.20
index C1
insurance *see* Insurance
large goods vehicles, driving
without appropriate li-
cence C18.24–C18.32
lights, defective C34
mitigating grounds C5.2–C5.3,
C5.24–C5.31
motor cycle offences
driving without licence C18
not wearing helmet C35

Road traffic offences – *cont.*
name and address, duty to
give C31
no test certificate C51
non-endorsable C8.5
obstruction A85, C36
opening door C37
overloading/exceeding axle
weight C38
pedestrian crossing *see*
Pedestrian crossing
penalties C1
penalty points sys-
tem C5.10–C5.38
fixed penalties C8.20
graduated fixed penalty points
scheme C8.8
provisional licences, as to C18
reasonable consideration,
driving without C46
recklessness *see* Dangerous
driving
seat belt offences C48
sentence code C7
sentencing *see* Sentencing
speed and distance chart C2
speeding *see* Speeding
steering, defective C50
test certificate
failure to produce C17
no test certificate C51
traffic sign, failure to comply
with C52
tyres, defective C53
Roadside property
damage to
failure to report C31.3, C32
failure to stop and give details
after C31
meaning C31.7, C32.16

S

Sado-masochistic activities
consent A15.11
Safety at work *see* Health and
safety at work
Samurai swords A11.3
Sawn-off shotgun
possession A76.18
see also Shotguns
**School attendance and truancy
proceedings** D17
fixed penalty notice D17.4
parenting order D17.5
school attendance order D17.4
see also Education supervision
order
School non-attendance A49
unavoidable cause A49.3
School premises
bladed article/offensive weapon,
possession of A11.10
searches A11.10
meaning A11.10
Scientific tests
proof of parent-
age D3.16–D3.20
Search
bladed article/offensive weapon
on school premises A11.10
fines, enforcement of B33.33,
B33.40
Search warrant
checklist M2.2
child, search for or re-
move D9.32
forcible search M2.4
HM Revenue and Customs officers M2.27
immigration offences A81.7
mental patients, search for and
remove M4.18–M4.22

Search warrant – *cont.*
non-police war-
rants M2.25–M2.26
proceeds of crime M3.2
search for evidence M2.5
search for evidence of indictable
offence
application proce-
dure M2.18–M2.24
customs and excise of-
fences M2.27
discretion to issue M2.17
excluded and special
procedure mat-
erial M2.16
issue of warrant M2.6–M2.17
legal privilege M2.11
meaning of 'indictable offence' M2.8
premises M2.10
reasonable grounds for believing M2.7
reasonable suspicion M2.7
relevant evidence M2.9
search for unlawful ar-
ticles M2.4
signing M2.40
see also Warrant
Seat belt offences C48
Section 8 orders D4.3–D4.9,
D5.1–D5.16
availability D4.8
delay and court timetable D5.6
duration D5.8
investigation by local authority D5.27
persons who may apply for D5
split hearings D4.4
supplementary provisions D5.16
transfer of proceedings D5.9
Security
deposit of, as condition of
bail J1.69

Security for good behaviour
conditional discharge B10.21
Self-defence
assault
occasioning actual bodily
harm A8.18–A8.20
onus of proof A8.18, A15.19
attempt to retreat or call off
fight A8.18
bladed article/offensive weapon,
possession of A11.13
reasonable force A8.18–A8.20
threats to kill A59.3
two-fold test A8.20
use of violence against an
innocent third party A8.20
Self-incrimination
privilege against C8.22
Sentencing
actual bodily
harm A8.31–A8.34
affray A2.15
age of offender as mitigating
factor B5.38, B5.39
aggravating factors B2.10
list B5.2A
race, religion, disability,
sexual orientation or
transgender iden-
tity B5.2B
alcohol sale offences A3.5
alcohol/tobacco, fraudulently
evade duty A4.16–A4.18
ancillary orders I6.33
animal cruelty A5.3–A5.4
announcement of sen-
tence B5.63–B6.65, I6.31
ASBO B8
assault
common assault A15.33
constable or court security
officers in the execution
of duty, on A9.10–A9.11

Sentencing – *cont.*
assault – *cont.*
with intent to resist ar-
rest A7.4
racially or religiously aggravated A15.33
associated offence B5.9
attendance centre orders B9
availability of sen-
tences B5.21–B5.35
bail, failure to surrender A10.3
binding over B10
bladed article/offensive weapon,
possession A11.15
burglary
domestic A12.20
non-domestic A13.19
child prostitution and pornography A14.6
treatment of child prostitutes A82.9
children, cruelty
to A19.32–A19.34
choice of sentence B5.50–B5.52
commercial practices, unfair or
prohibited A75.7–A75.10
committal to Crown Court
for B11–B16
communications network offences A16.7
community
orders *see* Community
orders
community rehabilitation
order *see* Community
rehabilitation order
compensation order B18
concurrent sentences, totality
principle and B5.49
consecutive sentences
imprisonment B37.22–B37.32
totality principle and B5.49

Sentencing – *cont.*
consideration of sentences B5.36–B5.48
considerations to be taken into account B5.3–B5.6, B37.22–B37.63
costs B20
criminal damage A18.3, A18.32, B2.6
Crown Court K3
committal to, for sentencing B11–B16
increase of sentence on appeal K3.1
justices K3
maximum sentences K3.2
young offenders, of B26.33, K3.2
cruelty to a child A19.32–A19.34
custodial sentences *see* Custodial sentences
dangerous dogs A72.8–A72.19
dangerous offenders B16.5
decision B3.7, B4.1, B4.2, B4.3, B4.4
power to review B7
deferment of sentence *see* Deferment of sentence
deportation B23
deprivation order B34.7
detention and training order *see* Detention and training order
discharge *see* Absolute discharge; Conditional discharge
disorderly behaviour A20.19
domestic burglary A12.20
domestic violence A8.34
drug assessment, failure to attend initial/remain for initial assessment A23.3

Sentencing – *cont.*
drugs, controlled A25.16
Class A, fail/refuse to provide sample A24.2
cultivation of cannabis A27.3–A27.4
fraudulent evasion of prohibition by bringing into/taking out of UK A27B.4
permitting premises to be used A27A.4
possessing with intent to supply to another A26.5–A26.20
possession A25.16–A25.18
supplying or offering to supply a controlled drug A26.5–A26.20
trafficking A25.3, A26.20
drunk and disorderly in a public place A28.8–A28.9
early release *see* Early release
electricity abstraction/use without authority A1.4
Engagement and Support Order A82.2
exploitation of prostitution A29.4
exposure A30.3
extended sentences for certain violent or sexual offences B16.5
false accounting A31
false identity documents A32.3
female defendants with children B37.6
financial reporting order A4.18
fines *see* Fines
firearms
carrying in a public place A33.11–A33.13

Sentencing – *cont.*
firearms – *cont.*
purchasing etc without certificate A76.18–A76.24
trespassing in a building or on land A77.10–A77.18
football ground offences A34.15–A34.17
forfeiture, consideration of B5.52, B34.7, I6.33
forgery A78.10–A78.17
found on enclosed premises A79.6–A79.9
grievous bodily harm A70.7, A70.20
guardianship order B35
handling stolen goods A40.12
harassment A41.11A–A41.13
health and safety at work A80.20–A80.22
hospital order B36
immigration offences A81.9–A81.17
imprisonment B2.2, B37
inarticulate unrepresented defendant, mitigation and B5.48
indecent photographs of children A43.9
intimidation of witness A69.11
justices in the Crown Court K3
keeping a brothel used for prostitution A44.4
littering A83.31–A83.34
loss of employment etc, mitigating effects of B5.47
Magistrates' Courts Sentencing Guidance - Definitive Guideline B5.2
making off without payment A45.8
medical reports, consideration of I6.37

Sentencing – *cont.*
mentally disordered offenders B35, B2.23–B2.24, B37.18, I6.37
mitigation B5.37–B5.48
custodial sentences B2.10
guilty plea B5.37, B5.46, B5.65, I6.20
health and safety offences A80.20
list of mitigating factors B5.2A
loss of employment etc B5.47
offender mitigation B5.2A
older offenders B5.39
previous convictions B5.40
seriousness of offence and B5.6, B5.17–B5.20
unrepresented defendant B5.48
youth of offender B5.38
more than one charge B6
motor vehicle
dumping A83.7–A83.9, A83.16–A83.17
interference A63.6
taking without consent A65.18–A65.20
vehicle licence/registration fraud A64.5
multiplicity of charges B6
no previous convictions B37.6
non-domestic burglary A13.19
objectives of sentencing B5.4–B5.6
obstructing or resisting a constable in the execution of his duty A47.15
older offenders B5.39
options available B5.21–B5.35
poaching A86.31–A86.32A
powers
decision, to review B7

Sentencing – *cont.*
powers – *cont.*
tables B4.1–B4.3
pre-sentence reports *see* Pre-
sentence reports
previous convictions, effect
of B5.3, B5.40, B8.15,
I6.32
probation officer,
recommendation by B5.50
process of B5
prohibited commercial practices A75.7–A75.10
pronouncement of sen-
tence B5.63–B6.65, I6.31
proportionality B5.49, B8.5
prostitution
child prostitution and pornography A14.6
exploitation A29.4
keeping a brothel used
for A44.4
treatment of child prostitute A82.9
protection of public B5.4,
B26.16
protective order, breach A46.4
purposes of sentenc-
ing B5.4–B5.6
pursuing game without a licence A86.31–A86.32A
racially or religiously aggravated
assault A15.33
railway fare evasion A48.9
reasons for, giving B5.53,
B5.61, B37.20
young offenders, in case
of B16.1, B26.34
remission to another court B1
reparation order B38
reports, consideration
of I6.32–I6.39
rescission, powers as to B7

Sentencing – *cont.*
restitution order B39
restriction
clauses B36.10–B36.16
review decisions, power to B7
road traffic offences C1
careless driv-
ing C25.20–C25.21
dangerous condition/body-
work C10.7–C10.9
dangerous driv-
ing C16.17–C16.30
death by inconsiderate
driving, causing C16A.10
defective brakes C9.16–C9.20
disqualification pend-
ing C5.39
driving licence of-
fences C17.21–C17.22,
C18.21–C18.24
driving when 'unfit through
drink or
drugs' C20.19–C20.20
driving whilst disquali-
fied C19.8–C19.17
excess alcohol, drive/attempt
to drive or in
charge C22.32–22.61,
C22.65
failing to produce docu-
ments C17.21–17.22
failing to stop/report accident C31.17–C31.19
failure to co-operate with
roadside breath
test C24.9
failure to provide specimen
for analysis C23.7–C23.9
insurance certificate, failure to
produce C17.21–C17.22
lights, defec-
tive C34.21–C34.22
motor cyclist not wearing helmet C35.7–C35.8

Sentencing – *cont.*
road traffic offences – *cont.*
no excise licence C47.18
no insurance C33.23–C33.31
no test certificate C51
obstruction C36.10–C36.16
opening door C37.7–C37.9
overloading/exceeding axle
weight C38.20–C38.21
pelican/zebra crossing contravention C39.20–C39.21
penalty points sys-
tem C5.10–C5.38
reasonable consideration,
driving with-
out C46.19–C46.23
seat belt offences C48.19
speeding C49.36–C49.37
steering, defective C50.4
stopping on pedestrian crossing C40.10–C40.17
traffic signs, failing to comply
with C52.17–C52.18
tyres, defective C53.7–C53.8
'unfit through drink or drugs',
in charge
when C20.19–C20.20
unlicensed, disqualified or
uninsured drivers, causing
death by driving C16B.6
robbery offences E3.18
school non-attendance A49.4
seriousness of offence B5.3,
B5.6
associated offence B5.9
determining B5.7–B5.16
mitigation and B5.6,
B5.17–B5.20
sex offenders register, failure to
comply with notification
requirements A50.4
sexual activity in a public lavatory A51

Sentencing – *cont.*
sexual assault A52.14–A52.16,
A53.15–A53.17
child under
13 A52.14–A52.16
notification require-
ments A52.15
sexual offences, extended sentences B16.5
short or fast-delivery reports I6.36
social security benefit, false
statement/representation to
obtain A54.6
specific sentence reports B3.6
statement accompany-
ing B5.53–B5.54
victim personal state-
ment B5.55
structure, Magistrates' Courts
Sentencing Guidance -
Definitive Guideline B5.2
supervision order *see*
Supervision order
suspended sentence *see*
Suspended sentence
taxi-touting A56.3
theft A57.37–A57.40
going equipped for A58.8
threatening behaviour A21.16
threats to kill A59.5
totality principle B5.49
trade mark, unauthorised use of
etc A60.5
transfer of criminal proceedings B1A
TV licence payment eva-
sion A61.15
unfair commercial prac-
tices A75.7–A75.10
unrepresented defendant,
mitigation and B5.48
variation B7

Sentencing – *cont.*
vehicle interference A63.6
vehicle licence/registration
    fraud A64.5
vehicle taking
    aggravated A66.16–A66.17
    without con-
        sent A65.18–A65.20
victim personal statement B5.55
violent disorder A67.10
violent offences, extended sen-
    tences B16.5
voyeurism A68.5
witness intimidation A69.11
wounding A70.20
young offenders B1.3–B1.5,
    B4.1, B4.2, B4.3, B4.4
    Crown Court, in K3.2
    detention and training or-
        der B2.6
    remission to another
        court B1.3–B1.5
    supervision order *see*
        Supervision order
    young offender institution,
        committal to B2.3–B2.5,
        B26
youth of offender as
    mitigating factor B5.38
youth court B1.3–B1.5, B4.1,
    B4.2, B4.3, B4.4, E4.5–E4.7
Services
obtaining dishonestly A37
Sex offenders register
failure to comply with
    notification require-
    ments A50
Sexual activity with a child A52,
    A53.9
absolute discharge A52.15
age of child A52.5, A52.6,
    A52.7
anonymity of victim A52.12

Sexual activity with a child – *cont.*
child witnesses A52.8
clearing the court A52.11
conditional discharge A52.15
consent A52.4
corroboration not re-
    quired A52.6, A52.13
evidence of chil-
    dren A52.6–A52.9
age of child A52.7
child witnesses A52.8
clearing the court A52.11
cross-examination A52.8
video recordings A52.8,
    A52.9, A52.10
mistake as to age A52.5
notification requirements
    following convic-
    tion A52.15, A53.16
privacy A52.11
reporting restrictions A52.12
risk of sexual harm or-
    der A52.16
sentencing A52.14–A52.16
sexual activity A52.3
sexual offences prevention or-
    der A52.16, A53.17
special measures direc-
    tion A52.10
video recordings of evi-
    dence A52.8, A52.9,
    A52.10
see also Child prostitution and
    pornography; Indecent
    photographs of children
**Sexual activity in a public lava-
    tory** A51
Sexual assault A53
absolute discharge A53.16
anonymity of vic-
    tim A53.11–A53.13
clearing the court A53.13
conditional discharge A53.16

Sexual assault – *cont.*
consent A53.6
mental disorder A53.8
persons under 16 A53.7
reasonable belief A53.6
corroboration not re-
quired A53.14
custodial sentence A53.16
defences A53.6
intention A53.4, A53.6
juvenile offenders A53.16
meaning A53.4
notifications to police following
conviction A53.16
reporting restrictions I1B.7
risk of sexual harm or-
der A53.17
sentencing A52.14–A52.16,
A53.15–A53.17
touch A53.4, A53.5
voluntary intoxication A53.4,
A53.6
young offender A53.16
see also Sexual offences
prevention order
Sexual disease
infection through consensual
sex A70.5
Sexual offences prevention order
notification require-
ments A52.15
representation orders I7.1A
sexual activity with a
child A52.16
sexual assault A53.17
standard of proof A53.17
Sexual orientation, presumed
aggravation of offence A8.10,
A15.7, B5.2B

Sheep *see* Animals; Livestock
Shooting galleries A71.6
Short or fast-delivery reports I6.36
Shotguns A11.3
carrying in a public place A33
certificate A88.5
cancellation A76.24, A77.18,
A88.11
exemptions A88.6
forfeiture A33.13, A88.10,
I6.33
meaning A33.6, A88.4
purchasing etc without certificate A88
sawn-off shotgun A76.18
smooth bore A76.7
trespassing in a building or on
land A77.9
visitor's permit A76.10, A88.6
see also Firearms
Silence
inferences from I6.22
not guilty plea and I6.22
right to remain silent C8.22
Sketches of court
restrictions I1B.9
Social security benefit
false statement/representation to
obtain A54
causes or allows A54.5
sentencing A54.6
time limits A54.4
**Soliciting women for prostitu-
tion** A29.1, A82
Engagement and Support Order A82.2
Solicitor
right to consult B36.2

SORN (Statutory Off Road Notification) C47.17

Special constable
assault during execution of duty A9

Special Guardianship Orders (SGOs) D18.33–D18.35
effects D18.36–D18.38

Special measures direction
anti-social behaviour order proceedings A52.10
types of special measures I6.13A
vulnerable and intimidated witnesses I6.13A
witnesses under 18 years A52.10

Specific issue order D4.7
persons who may apply for D5.1, D5.2

Specific sentence report B3.6

Speed assessment equipment detection devices
breach of requirement as to C38A

Speeding C49
evidence C49.4–C49.9
limit prescribed for class of vehicle C49.31
motorways, on C49.20–C49.22
restricted roads, on C49.16–C49.19
sentencing C49.36–C49.37
speed and distance chart C2
speed limit signs C49.10
temporary or experimental limits C49.32–C49.35
unrestricted road, in C49.23–C49.25
warning of prosecution C49.3

Split hearings
section 8 orders D4.4

Sporting activities
assault and A15.16, A15.18

Sporting events
alcohol, control of A35
see also Football-related offences

Spouse see Husband and wife

Starting pistols A33.9, A76.7, A77.8

Statutory declarations M4.9–M4.17
signing M4.17
see also Oath

Statutory nuisance A84
abatement notice A74.9, A84.8
appeal against A84.9
contravention/failure to comply A84.10
abatement order A84.22
appeal A84.18
complaint by person aggrieved A84.19–A84.32
costs A84.31
defence A84.16–A84.17, A84.25
exceptions A84.5
local authority, court direction to A84.32
proceedings by A84.7–A84.18
magistrate's order A84.22
noise A74.1, A74.9, A84.2, A84.33–A84.36
see also Noise
prejudicial to health, meaning A84.3
prohibition order A84.22
reasonable excuse A84.17

Statutory Off Road Notification (SORN) C47.17

Stay of proceedings
abuse of process I1B.11–I1B.12
youth court E3.25

Stealing
meaning A12.16, A13.16,
A57.3
see also Burglary; Theft
Stealth knife A11.4
Steering
defective C50
Step-parent
adoption by D18.10
parental responsibility,
acquisition of D3.8
Stolen goods
consideration paid in respect
of A40.11
handling *see* Handling stolen
goods
police in possession of *see*
Property in possession of
police
restitution order B39
Stun guns A11.4
Summary proceedings
absence of accused, in 16.19
adjournment applications 16.5
application to change guilty
plea 16.26
application to withdraw guilty
plea 16.28
bad character 16.14, 16.15
CCTV evidence 16.9
checklist 16.6–16.18
disclosure of unused mat-
erial 16.12
first hearing 16.8
first/subsequent hearing 16.12
guilty plea entered 16.18
hearsay evidence 16.16
legal aid 16.10
not guilty plea 16.19, 16.26
plea 16.9
power to make, vary or
discharge pre-trial rul-
ings 16.13A

Summary proceedings – *cont.*
adjournment applications –
cont.
pre-trial issues 16.13
prosecution evidence (initial
disclosure) 16.11
special measures for
vulnerable and
intimidated wit-
nesses 16.13A
trial 16.17
amendment of charge or information 16.23
appeals
against conviction and or sentence 16.46
Crown Court, to 16.46
High Court, to 16.47
judicial review, application
for 16.48
by way of case stated 16.47
consideration of
guilt 16.30–16.31
Criminal Procedure Rules
(CPR) 16.1
adjournment applica-
tions 16.5–16.18
duty of the court 16.3
duty of the parties 16.4
notification of intention to
call defence wit-
nesses 16.2
overriding objective of
Part I 16.2
setting the timetable 16.3
guilty plea 16.24
application to change 16.26
application to withdraw 16.27
avoiding misunderstand-
ing 16.25
complex cases 16.25
mitigating factor, as 16.20
nature 16.24

Summary proceedings – *cont.*
guilty plea – *cont.*
Newton hearing I6.24
post, by I6.40–I6.43
judicial review, application
for I6.48
legal advice I6.28
no case to answer I6.21
not guilty plea I6.19–I6.23
amendment of charge or information I6.23
application to change to I6.26
change of I6.20
no case to answer I6.21
post, by I6.44
silence, inferences from I6.22
trial in absence I6.19
reports I6.32–I6.39
medical reports I6.37
pre-sentence re-
ports I6.34–I6.35
short or fast-delivery reports I6.36
timetable I6.3, I6.19
trial in absence I6.19
Supervision order
breach B25.10
detention in young offender
institution B2.4
criminal proceedings
fines, payment of B33.35,
B33.55, B33.96
Intensive Supervision and
Surveillance Programmes
(ISSPs) E4.8
public law proceedings D6.6,
D6.32
age limit D6.25
appeal against refusal of order D1.19, D6.49
applications D6.3–D6.22
compliance with requirements
of order D6.33, D6.34

Supervision order – *cont.*
public law proceedings – *cont.*
directions for treat-
ment D6.33
discharge of or-
der D6.47–D6.48
duration D6.32
education supervision or-
der D17.6
effect of order D6.32
interim order D6.35–D6.37,
D9.18
local authority investigation D5.27
renewal D6.32
variation of or-
der D6.47–D6.48
see also Community orders;
Public law proceedings
**Supplying or offering to supply a
controlled drug A26**
aggravation of offence 26.4A
defences A26.4B
ECHR and A26.4B
intent to supply 26.4
sentencing A26.5–A26.20
Surcharge
compensation order B18.1
criminal proceedings B20.1A
fines B18.1
victims surcharge B33.4
Surety M4.1
conditional bail
and J1.66–J1.68
see also Recognisance
Suspended sentences B2.2, B33.52,
B37.21, B37.40–B37.51
breach B37.47
sentencing B37.47–B37.50
community orders com-
pared B37.47
community requirement B37.46

Suspended sentences – *cont.*
fine payable in addition
to B33.36, B37.51
guidance B37.50
maintenance order, enforcing D7.34–D7.37
unpaid work require-
ment B37.46
young offender
institution B26.32

T

Taking without consent *see* Motor
vehicle
Tape recorders
use in court I1B.10
Tax credit fraud A55
**Taxi-touting/soliciting for
hire** A56
Telephone kiosk
as public place A83.21
Television
fraudulently receiving programmes F3
licence payment evasion A61
Temporary event notice
closure due to noise A84.7
Tent
threatening behaviour in A21.9
Test certificate
failure to produce C17
no test certificate C51
renewal C51.17
Theft A57
acquiring in good faith A57.16
appropriates A57.8–A57.16
attempting the impos-
sible A57.19
being entrusted with property A57.24

Theft – *cont.*
belonging to an-
other A57.22–A57.31
borrowing or lending A57.33
breach of trust A57
burglary *see* Burglary
compensation A57.39, B18.3
completion of offence A57.10
definition A57.3
dishonestly A57.5–A57.7
dwelling, from A57
going equipped for A58
disqualification C5.5
motor vehicles A58.1, C5.5,
C5.33
sentencing A58.8
intention of permanently depriving A57.32–A57.36
land, of A57.18
lending or borrowing A57.33
mistake, getting property
by A57.25
motor vehicle, of
disqualification A57.40
going equipped for A58.1,
C5.5, C5.33
reduction of charge A57.34,
A65.10
partnership property A57.36
person, from A57
proof of stealing one ar-
ticle enough A57.35
property A57.17–A57.21
repentance A57.10
sentencing A57.37–A57.40
shop, from A57
things growing wild A57.20
trust property A57.23
wild creatures A57.21
Threatening behaviour A21
binding over A21.18
dwelling-house, in A21.9

Threatening behaviour – *cont.*
ECHR and A21.5A
freedom of expression A21.5A
intent A21.7
police officers, towards A21.10
private premises A21.9
public place A21.9
racially or religiously aggravated A21.10
sentencing A21.16
threatening, abusive, insulting
words/behaviour A21.5
violence A21.6
see also Disorderly behaviour
**Threatening to destroy or damage
property** A18A
Threats
affray A2.5
burglary A13.4
witness intimidation A69
Threats to kill A59
foetus A59.4
lawful excuse A59.3
sentencing A59.5
Tobacco
fraudulently evade duty A4
**Trade mark, unauthorised use of
etc** A60
burden of proof A60.3
defences A60.3
reasonable belief A60.3
sentencing A60.5
validity of registration A60.3
Traffic signs
failure to comply with C52
Trafficking
drugs *see* Drugs
Trailer
dangerous condition/bodywork,
using in C10
defective brakes C9
defective tyres C53

Trailer – *cont.*
definition C9.9
interference A63.2
opening door C37
speed assessment equipment
detection devices C38A
**Transfer of criminal proceed-
ings** B1A
Transgender identity
aggravation of offence related
to B5.2B
Trespass
accidental A12.17, A13.17
aggravated A18.19
burglary A13.7, A13.17
Domestic burglary A12.10,
A12.17
firearm in a building or on land,
with A77
poaching A86.4
pursuit of game, in *see* Poaching
Truancy
proceedings as to D17
see also Education supervision
order
Trust property
criminal damage A18.24
theft A57.23
TV licence payment evasion A61
Twitter
use in open court I1B.8
Tyres
defective C53

U

Unconditional bail J1.3
Unfair commercial practices A75
**Unlicensed, disqualified or
uninsured drivers**
causing death by driving C16B

Unpaid work
community orders B17.3
suspended sentences B37.46
youth rehabilitation order B50.8
Urine
alcohol in *see* Alcohol

V

VAT evasion A62
Vehicle
inhabited, burglary in A12.15,
A13.7
interference A63
licence/registration fraud A64
taking
aggravated A66
without consent A65
threatening behaviour in A21.9
see also Motor vehicle
Vessel
inhabited, burglary in A12.15,
A13.7
threatening behaviour in A21.9
Vibration
as noise A84.4
Victim personal statement B5.55
Victims surcharge B33.4
Video link *see* Live video link
Video recordings
evidence of children by A52.7,
A52.8
adult magistrates'
courts A52.9
special measures direc-
tion A52.10
Video remands J1.22A
Villescon A22.6
Violence
arson A18.2
burglary A13.4

Violence – *cont.*
domestic *see* Child protection;
Domestic violence; Non
molestation order
endangerment of life A18.2
extended sentences B16.5
harassment A41
meaning A2.7–A2.8, A67.5
putting people in fear A41
threatened A21.6
see also Actual bodily harm;
Affray; Assault; Disorder;
Disorderly behaviour;
Grievous bodily harm;
Harassment; Threatening
behaviour; Violent disorder
Violent disorder A67
intent A67.7
intoxication A67.8
person of reasonable firmness A67.6
sentencing A67.10
three or more persons A67.4
violence, meaning A67.5
Violent offender order
appeals B51.7
application B51.3
breach B51.8
conditions B51.4
discharge B51.5
interim orders B51.6
notice provisions B51.7
notification requirements B51.4
prohibitions B51.4
qualifying offender B51.2
renewal B51.5
restrictions B51.4
variation B51.5
Violent offender order (VOO) B51
Voluntary restitution
electricity abstraction/use
without authority A1.4

Voyeurism A68

W

Warrant
arrest, of M3
bailed person failing to surrender J1.82
council tax recovery and enforcement H7.3
ECHR and H7.3
immigration offences A81.7
entry, of M2
applicant M2.1
authority to issue M2.2–M2.5
gas and electricity suppliers M2.31–M2.38
immigration offences A81.7
search for evidence/unlawful articles *see* Search warrant
meaning M1.5
out-of-hours panels M1.7
search warrant *see* Search warrant
signing M1.6, M2.39, M2.40
Terrorism Act 2000, applications under M1.9
Wasted costs order A84.31, B20.19, I6.12
Weapon
offensive *see* Bladed article/offensive weapon
using someone to mind a weapon E3.18, E3.18A
Welfare of the child D2
children's evidence D2.6
confidentiality D4.2
delay and D2.3
financial provision D7.5

Welfare of the child – *cont.*
Guidelines for Judges Meeting Children subject to Family Proceedings D2.7
maintenance order D7.5
national protocol D2.3, D6.2
'no order' principle D4.4, D5.7, D6.22, D18.18
presumption of no order D2.5
principle D2.1
reports D4.2
standard direction forms D2.3
welfare checklist D1.18, D2.4, D18.19, D18.35
welfare principle D2.1
wishes and feelings of child D2.6
Wheel clamping
fine defaulters B33.38
removal of clamp A18.19
Wife *see* Domestic violence; Husband and wife
Wild creatures
appropriating A57.21
as property A18.21
theft A57.21
Witness
anonymity I1.7
child or young person *see* Evidence
contempt of court by I3.9
intimidation A69
live video link in criminal proceedings I6.13A, J1.22C
notification of intention to call defence witnesses I6.2
preventing publication of matter leading to identification of I1B.7
recognisance by B10.8
refusal to take oath or answer question I3.9

Witness – *cont.*
  special measures *see* Special
    measures direction
Work permit
  possession of false A81
  see also Immigration offences
Wounding A70
  intent A70.5
  on licensed premises, exclusion
    order A70.21
  racially or religiously aggra-
    vated A70
  recklessness A70.5
  sentencing A70.20

Y

Young offender
  adult court, remittal to B1.5
  age, determining E1.2
  aged between 18 and 21
    attendance centre, committal
      to B9, B33.98
    Crown Court, sentencing
      in B16.1
    detention *see* Young offender
      institution
    imprisonable offence, mean-
      ing B26.3
    imprisonment E3.16–E3.17
    legal representation B2.8,
      B26.21, I7
    local court, remission to B1.4,
      E3.23
    remand in cus-
      tody E3.4–E3.17, J1.32
    remand with a security re-
      quirement E3.16
    representation orders I7
    sentencing B2.3–B2.5, B4.1,
      B4.2, B4.3, B4.4, B16.1

Young offender – *cont.*
  aged between 18 and 21 – *cont.*
    young offender institution,
      detention in *see* Young
      offender institution
  aged under 15 *see* Child
  ASBO *see* Anti-social behaviour
    order
  attendance centre orders B9
  bail
    murder charge J1.32
    remand on J1.6
  committal for sentence B16.1,
    E3.18B
  committal for trial E3.18
    procedure E3.20–E3.25
  criminal proceedings
    attendance centre orders B9
    committal for trial E3.18
    detention *see* Young offender
      institution
    fines B33.5–B33.6,
      B33.86–B33.99, E4.7
    guardianship order B35
    hospital order B36
    legal representation B2.8
    local court, remission to B1.4,
      E3.23
    oath E3.22
    remand E3.16–E3.17
    remission to adult
      court E3.24
    secure accommoda-
      tion E3.5–E3.17
    sentencing B4.1, B4.2, B4.3,
      B4.4
    sexual offences E3.18
    supervision order *see*
      Supervision order
    time limits E3.25
    young offender institution,
      detention in *see* Young
      offender institution

Young offender – *cont.*
curfew order, electronic monitoring E3.4, J1.6
detention and training order B25, B2.6
  availability B5.33
  breach of supervision B25.10
  consecutive orders B25.8
  length B2.20, B25.6–B25.8
  time spent on bail subject to curfew condition and electronic monitoring condition and B2.20
  time spent on remand and B2.20
education supervision order D17.6
electronic monitoring E3.4, J1.6
fines B33.5–B33.6, E4.7
  aged 10 to 17 B33.93–B33.95
  aged 18 to 21 B33.86–B33.92
  parental responsibility for payment B33.7–B33.10, B33.95, E4.7
homicide E3.18
incapable of following proceedings, abuse of process E3.25
Intensive Supervision and Surveillance Programmes (ISSPs) E4.8
legal representation B2.8, B26.21, I7
  see also Representation orders
males aged 15 and 16 years, remand with security requirement E3.17
mental illness, powers of court in case of B36
murder charge, bail and J1.32
pre-sentence reports B26.17–B26.19
referral order *see* Referral order

Young offender – *cont.*
rehabilitation order *see* Youth rehabilitation order
remand on bail J1.6
remand in custody *see* Remand in custody
remission to adult court E3.24
secure accommodation, remand in E3.5–E3.17
sentencing B1.3–B1.5, B4.1, B4.2, B4.3, B4.4
  Crown Court, in K3.2
  detention and training order B2.6
  remission to another court B1.3–B1.5
  supervision order *see* Supervision order
  young offender institution, committal to B2.3–B2.5, B26
  youth of offender as mitigating factor B5.38
sexual assault A53.16
sexual offences E3.18
supervision order *see* Supervision order
trial, committal for E3.18
using someone to mind a weapon E3.18, E3.18A
youth court *see* Youth court
youth rehabilitation order *see* Youth rehabilitation order
see also Young person
Young offender institution
age limits B2.3, B2.4, B26.4, B26.22
ancillary orders B26.36
announcement of sentence B26.35
associated offence B26.8
consecutive terms B26.31

Young offender institution – *cont.*
criteria for imposing sentence B26.5–B26.6
Crown Court, committal to B26.33
detention in B2.3–B2.5, B5.33, B26
replacement by imprisonment B2.3, B5.33
early release B26.37–B26.46
further offences B26.46
supervision following B26.38
imprisonable offence, meaning B26.3
legal representation B2.8, B26.21
length of sentence B2.5, B26.23–B26.32
maximum length of sentence B26.23
mentally disturbed offenders B26.20
minimum length of sentence B26.25
offences for which appropriate B26.7–B26.10
offenders under 18 B26.22
passing sentence B2.5, B26.23–B26.34
period of detention B2.5
pre-sentence reports B26.17–B26.18
failure to obtain B26.19
protection of public B26.16
reasons for decisions B26.34
seriousness of offence B26.7
sexual offences B26.10
suspended sentence B26.32
violent offence B26.9
Young person
abduction D16
adoption of *see* Adoption
age, determination of E1.2

Young person – *cont.*
air guns A71A
binding over parent or guardian B10.18–B10.19, B10.21, E4.5
child safety order D17A.1
cruelty to *see* Cruelty to a child
definition E3.3, A19.7
evidence by *see* Evidence
guardianship order B35
Guidelines for Judges Meeting Children subject to Family Proceedings D2.7
hospital order B36
juveniles, definition E1.1
meaning E1.1
parenting order B37A
public law proceedings *see* Public law proceedings
remand of E3.3
reporting restrictions I1B.7
school attendance order D17
truancy proceedings D17
warrant to search for or remove D9.32
see also Young offender
Youth court E2
abuse of process, youth incapable of following proceedings E3.25
adoption proceedings D18
age of criminal responsibility E3.2
age at date of sentence E3.17A
allocation and sending of juveniles to Crown Court for trial E3.18A
anti-social behaviour order B8.4, E2.4
attendance of parent E3.3
bail J1.6
murder charge J1.32

Youth court – *cont.*
binding over parent or guardian E4.5
committal for sentence E3.18B
committal for trial E3.18
procedure E3.20–E3.25
composition E2.1–E2.2
criminal proceedings E3
delay E3.25
detention and training order B2.6
education supervision order D17.6
fines B33.5–B33.6, B33.86–B33.99, E4.7
hearing, persons present at E2.3
hospital order, powers to make B36
Intensive Support and Surveillance Programmes (ISSPs) E4.8
interim orders D6.35–D6.37
hospital order B36.22
local court, remission to B1.4, E3.23
magistrates' court, remitting from B1.3, B1.4, E3.23
murder charge J1.32
oath E3.22
parenting order E4.6
persons present during hearing E2.3
pre-sentence reports I6.39
procedure E3.20–E3.25
public law proceedings *see* Public law proceedings
remand on bail E3.4
remand in custody *see* Remand in custody
remission to another court B1.4
adult court B1.5, E3.24
local court E3.23
reparation order B38

Youth court – *cont.*
reporting restrictions I1B.2, E2.4–E2.5
representation orders *see* Representation orders
school attendance and truancy proceedings D17
sentencing B1.3–B1.5, B4.1, B4.2, B4.3, B4.4, E4.5–E4.7
committal for sentence E3.18B–E3.19
sexual offences E3.18
stay of proceedings E3.25
supervision order *see* Supervision order
time limits E3.25
truancy proceedings D17
Youth offender panels B42.11
compensation orders B42.12
discretionary referral B42.2
non-recordable offences and B42.12
problems B42.12
referral order B42
ancillary orders B37A.1, B42.4
breach B42.5, B42.13
compulsory referral B42.1, B42.2
extension B42.5
length B42.3
parenting order and B37A.1, B42.4
revocation B42.5
Youth rehabilitation order (YRO) B7A, B50
amendment B50.26
application to revoke B50.25
breach B50.23
commission of further offence B50.24
length of order B50.2
pre-sentence reports B50.2

Youth rehabilitation order (YRO)
– *cont.*
requirements B50.2, B50.3,
  B50.4
activity B50.6
attendance centre B50.10
breach B50.23
curfew B50.12
drug treatment/drug test-
  ing B50.19
education B50.21
electronic monitoring B50.3,
  B50.5, B50.22
exclusion B50.13
fostering B50.3, B50.16
intensive supervision and surveillance B50.3, B50.5
intoxicating substance treatment B50.20
local authority resi-
  dence B50.3, B50.15
mental health treat-
  ment B50.17–B50.18

Youth rehabilitation order (YRO)
– *cont.*
requirements – *cont.*
  programme B50.9
  prohibited activity B50.11
  residence B50.14
  supervision B50.5, B50.7
  unpaid work B50.8
responsible officer B50.2
revocation B50.25
serious enough offences B50.2
statutory considerations B50.1

Z

Zebra crossing
  contravention C39
  stopping on C40
Zolpidem A22.6